Programming and Discrete Mathematics

Set text for course XX10190

Selected by J.H. Davenport, G.K. Sankaran and A. Spence
With thanks to Prof. I. G. Graham, who taught on this course 2009-12

Containing material from:

MATLAB® Programming with Applications for Engineers
(International Edition 1e) by Stephen J. Chapman – BAE SYSTEMS, Australia
ISBN-10: 0-495-66808-7
ISBN-13: 978-0-495-66808-4

and

Discrete Mathematics with Applications
(Fourth Edition) by Susanna S. Epp – DePaul University
ISBN-10: 0-495-82616-2
ISBN-13: 978-0-495-82616-3

and

**Updates to Essentials of MATLAB® Programming
and Additional Definitions**
Provided by the course lecturers

UNIVERSITY OF
BATH

CUSTOM
CENGAGE Learning

Australia • Brazil • Japan • Korea • Mexico • Singapore • Spain • United Kingdom • United States

CUSTOM
CENGAGE Learning·

**Programming and Discrete Mathematics,
Second Custom Edition**
University of Bath

Publishing Director: Linden Harris

Custom Editor: Isabel Florence

Production Controller: Eyvett Davis

Production Editor: Alison Cooke

For product information and technology assistance,
contact **emea.info@cengage.com**.

For permission to use material from this text or product,
and for permission queries,
email **emea.permissions@cengage.com**.

British Library Cataloguing-in-Publication Data
A catalogue record for this book is available from the British Library.

ISBN: 978-1-4080-7591-3

Cengage Learning EMEA
Cheriton House, North Way, Andover, Hampshire, SP10 5BE, United Kingdom

Cengage Learning products are represented in Canada by Nelson Education Ltd.

For your lifelong learning solutions, visit
www.cengage.co.uk

Purchase your next print book, e-book or e-chapter at
www.cengagebrain.com

Printed in the United Kingdom by TJ International
1 2 3 4 5 6 7 8 9 10 – 14 13 12

Foreword by the compilers

Note to the reader. In order to preserve the integrity of cross-references within each book (Chapman or Epp) that we have used in compiling this volume, we have kept all page numbers etc. unaltered within each book. Hence you will find that there are two pages numbered 96, for example, one in Chapman (where Exercise 2.16 of Chapman starts) and one in Epp (the first page of Chapter 3). Similarly there are two tables of contents: one for Chapman (a few pages further on from here) and one for Epp (shortly after the last page, numbered 531, of Chapman), and two indices.

Chapman: We have included all Chapters, 1, 2, 4, 5.1–5.3, 6, 7.1–7.5, 8.1–8.2, 9, 10.1–10.2, Appendix A, Appendix B and Appendix C.1 and C.2.

Epp: We have included Chapters 3 up to and excluding p.119, and all of chapters 4, 5, 8, 10 and 11. The chapters which have chosen from Epp are the ones most relevant to the course XX10190. Copies of the full Epp book will be available for reference in the Bath University Library.

Note to the student. You will be allowed to take your copy of the book (but nothing else) into some examinations and tests. However, we must remind you of the University regulations prohibiting the use of unfair means in any examination or test. Examples of how we consider these regulations to apply are given below. Please note however that it is the University authorities who make decisions about the propriety of conduct in examinations.

Fair. Use of emphasis, whether by underlining or highlighting. Adding your own cross- references, such as "see also page 200". Adding any explicit corrections, in the unlikely event that we announce any.

Unfair: Adding extra text to the book. Any form of insert or stuck-in page or other subversion of the description of Fair Use above, e.g. underlining that spells something out in binary/ASCII (see Chapman, p. 499).

J.H Davenport, G.K. Sankaran and A. Spence
XX10190-lecturers@bath.ac.uk

Acknowledgements

The content of this text has been adapted from the following product(s):

MATLAB Programming with Applications for Engineers, 1e
Chapman (9780495668084)

Discrete Mathematics with Applications, 4e
Epp (9780495826163)

Full copyright details and acknowledgements will appear in the aforementioned publications.

MATLAB®
Programming
with Applications
for Engineers

First Edition

Page:
- **181** – ndiv, nmod
- **246** – Induction
- **268** – Strong induction
- **273** – Binary proof
- **672** – Adjacency matrix
- **741** – Elips
- **727** – Orders of growth
- **751** – Horner's
- **755** – Binary
- ~~705~~ **775** – Megesort

Stephen J. Chapman

BAE Systems Australia

CENGAGE
Learning·

Australia • Brazil • Japan • Korea • Mexico • Singapore • Spain • United Kingdom • United States

Contents

Chapter 2 MATLAB Basics 25

Chapter 9   Cell Arrays, Structures, and Importing Data   375

Chapter 10   Handle Graphics and Animation   411

Preface

MATLAB® (short for MATrix LABoratory) is a special-purpose computer program optimized to perform engineering and scientific calculations. It started life as a program designed to perform matrix mathematics, but over the years it has grown into a flexible computing system capable of solving essentially any technical problem.

The MATLAB program implements the MATLAB language and provides a very extensive library of pre-defined functions to make technical programming tasks easier and more efficient. This extremely wide variety of functions makes it much easier to solve technical problems in MATLAB than in other languages such as Java, Fortran, or C++. This book introduces the MATLAB language, and shows how to use it to solve typical technical problems.

This book seeks to simultaneously teach MATLAB as a technical programming language and also to introduce the student to many of the practical functions that make solving problems in MATLAB so much easier than in other languages. The book provides a complete introduction to the fundamentals of good procedural programming, developing good design habits that will serve a student well in any other language that he or she may pick up later. There is a very strong emphasis on proper program design and structure. A standard program design process is introduced at the beginning of Chapter 4 and then followed regularly throughout the remainder of the text.

In addition, the book uses the programming topics and examples as a jumping off point for exploring the rich set of highly optimized application functions that are built directly into MATLAB. For example, in Chapter 4 we present a programming example that finds the roots of a quadratic equation. This serves as a jumping off point for exploring the MATLAB function `roots`, which can efficiently find the roots of polynomials of any order. In Chapter 5, we present a programming example that calculates the mean and standard deviation of a data set. This serves as a jumping off point for exploring the MATLAB functions `mean`, `median`, and `std`. There is also a programming example showing how to do a least-squares fit to a straight-line. This serves as a jumping off point for exploring MATLAB curve fitting functions such as `polyfit`, `polyval`, `spline`, and `ppval`. There are similar ties to MATLAB applications in many other chapters as well. In all cases, there are end of chapter exercises to reinforce the applications lessons learned in that chapter.

In addition, Chapter 11 is devoted totally to practical MATLAB applications, including solving systems of simultaneous equations, numerical differentiation, numerical integration (quadrature), and solving ordinary differential equations.

This book makes no pretense at being a complete description of all of MATLAB's hundreds of functions. Instead, it teaches the student how to use MATLAB as a language to solve problems, and how to locate any desired function with MATLAB's extensive on-line help facilities. It highlights quite a few of the key engineering applications, but there are far more good ones built into the language than can be covered in any course of reasonable length. With the skills developed here, students will be able to continue discovering features on their own.

The Advantages of MATLAB for Problem Solving

MATLAB has many advantages compared to conventional computer languages for technical problem solving. Among them are:

1. **Ease of Use.** MATLAB is very easy to use. The program can be used as a scratch pad to evaluate expressions typed at the command line, or it can be used to execute large pre-written programs. Programs may be easily written and modified with the built-in integrated development environment, and debugged with the MATLAB debugger. Because the language is so easy to use, it is ideal for educational use, and for the rapid prototyping of new programs.

   Many program development tools are provided to make the program easy to use. They include an integrated editor / debugger, on-line documentation and manuals, a workspace browser, and extensive demos.

2. **Platform Independence.** MATLAB is supported on many different computer systems, providing a large measure of platform independence. At the time of this writing, the language is supported on Windows XP/Vista/7, Linux, Unix, and the Macintosh. Programs written on any platform will run on all of the other platforms, and data files written on any platform may be read transparently on any other platform. As a result, programs written in MATLAB can migrate to new platforms when the needs of the user change.

3. **Pre-defined Functions.** MATLAB comes complete with an extensive library of pre-defined functions that provide tested and pre-packaged solutions to many basic technical tasks. For example, suppose that you are writing a program that must calculate the statistics associated with an input data set. In most languages, you would need to write your own sub-routines or functions to implement calculations such as the arithmetic mean, standard deviation, median, etc. These and hundreds of other functions are built right into the MATLAB language, making your job much easier.

The built-in functions can solve an astonishing range of problems, such as solving systems of simultaneous equations, sorting, plotting, finding roots of equations, numerical integration, curve fitting, solving ordinary and partial differential equations, and much, much more.

In addition to the large library of functions built into the basic MATLAB language, there are many special-purpose toolboxes available to help solve complex problems in specific areas. For example, a user can buy standard toolboxes to solve problems in Signal Processing, Control Systems, Communications, Image Processing, and Neural Networks, among many others.

4. **Device-Independent Plotting.** Unlike other computer languages, MATLAB has many integral plotting and imaging commands. The plots and images can be displayed on any graphical output device supported by the computer on which MATLAB is running. This capability makes MATLAB an outstanding tool for visualizing technical data. Plotting is introduced in Chapter 2, and covered extensively in Chapters 3 and 8. Advanced features such as animations and movies are covered in Chapter 10.

5. **Graphical User Interface.** MATLAB includes tools that allow a program to interactively construct a Graphical User Interface (GUI) for his or her program. With this capability, the programmer can design sophisticated data analysis programs that can be operated by relatively-inexperienced users.

Features of this Book

Many features of this book are designed to emphasize the proper way to write reliable MATLAB programs. These features should serve a student well as he or she is first learning MATLAB, and should also be useful to the practitioner on the job. They include:

1. **Emphasis on Top-Down Design Methodology.** The book introduces a top-down design methodology in Chapter 4, and then uses it consistently throughout the rest of the book. This methodology encourages a student

to think about the proper design of a program *before* beginning to code. It emphasizes the importance of clearly defining the problem to be solved and the required inputs and outputs before any other work is begun. Once the problem is properly defined, it teaches the student to employ stepwise refinement to break the task down into successively smaller sub-tasks, and to implement the subtasks as separate subroutines or functions. Finally, it teaches the importance of testing at all stages of the process, both unit testing of the component routines and exhaustive testing of the final product.

The formal design process taught by the book may be summarized as follows:

1. *Clearly state the problem that you are trying to solve.*

2. *Define the inputs required by the program and the outputs to be produced by the program.*

3. *Describe the algorithm that you intend to implement in the program.* This step involves top-down design and stepwise decomposition, using pseudocode or flow charts.

4. *Turn the algorithm into MATLAB statements.*

5. *Test the MATLAB program.* This step includes unit testing of specific functions, and also exhaustive testing of the final program with many different data sets.

2. **Emphasis on Functions.** The book emphasizes the use of functions to logically decompose tasks into smaller subtasks. It teaches the advantages of functions for data hiding. It also emphasizes the importance of unit testing functions before they are combined into the final program. In addition, the book teaches about the common mistakes made with functions, and how to avoid them.

3. **Emphasis on MATLAB Tools.** The book teaches the proper use of MATLAB's built-in tools to make programming and debugging easier. The tools covered include the Editor / Debugger, Workspace Browser, Help Browser, and GUI design tools.

4. **Emphasis on MATLAB applications.** The book teaches how to harness the power of MATLAB's rich set of functions to solve a wide variety of practical engineering problems. This introduction to MATLAB functions is spread throughout the book, and is generally tied to the topics and examples being discussed in a particular chapter.

5. **Good Programming Practice Boxes.** These boxes highlight good programming practices when they are introduced for the convenience of the student. In addition, the good programming practices introduced in a chapter are summarized at the end of the chapter. An example Good Programming Practice Box is shown below.

> ✳ **Good Programming Practice:**
>
> Always indent the body of an `if` construct by 2 or more spaces to improve the readability of the code.

6. **Programming Pitfalls Boxes**

   These boxes highlight common errors so that they can be avoided. An example Programming Pitfalls Box is shown below.

> 💣 **Programming Pitfalls:**
>
> Make sure that your variable names are unique in the first 63 characters. Otherwise, MATLAB will not be able to tell the difference between them.

Pedagogical Features

This book includes several features designed to aid student comprehension. A total of 13 quizzes appear scattered throughout the chapters, with answers to all questions included in Appendix D. These quizzes can serve as a useful self-test of comprehension. In addition, there are approximately 215 end-of-chapter exercises. Answers to all exercises are included in the Instructor's Manual. Good programming practices are highlighted in all chapters with special Good Programming Practice boxes, and common errors are highlighted in Programming Pitfalls boxes. End of chapter materials include Summaries of Good Programming Practice and Summaries of MATLAB Commands and Functions.

The book is accompanied by an Instructor's Manual, containing the solutions to all end-of-chapter exercises. The IM, PowerPoint slides of all figures and tables in the book, and the source code for all examples in the book are available from the companion Web site at www.cengage.com/international, and the source code for all solutions in the Instructor's Manual is available separately to instructors.

To access additional course materials [including CourseMate], please visit www.cengagebrain.com. At the cengagebrain.com home page, search for the ISBN of your title (from the back cover of your book) using the search box at the top of the page. This will take you to the product page where these resources can be found.

A Thank You to the Reviewers

I would like to offer a special thank you to the book's reviewers. Their invaluable suggestions have made this a significantly better book, and they certainly deserve thanks for the time they devoted to reviewing drafts of the text. The reviewers who were willing to be named are:

Steven A. Peralta, University of New Mexico
Jeffrey Ringenberg, University of Michigan
Lizzie Santiago, West Virginia University
John R. White, University of Massachusetts, Lowell

A Final Note to the User

No matter how hard I try to proofread a document like this book, it is inevitable that some typographical errors will slip through and appear in print. If you should spot any such errors, please drop me a note via the publisher, and I will do my best to get them eliminated from subsequent printings and editions. Thank you very much for your help in this matter.

STEPHEN J. CHAPMAN
Melbourne, Australia

Introduction to MATLAB

MATLAB (short for MATrix LABoratory) is a special-purpose computer program optimized to perform engineering and scientific calculations. It started life as a program designed to perform matrix mathematics, but over the years, it has grown into a flexible computing system capable of solving essentially any technical problem.

The MATLAB program implements the MATLAB programming language and provides an extensive library of predefined functions to make technical programming tasks easier and more efficient. This book introduces the MATLAB language as it is implemented in MATLAB Version 7.9 and shows how to use it to solve typical technical problems.

MATLAB is a huge program, with an incredibly rich variety of functions. Even the basic version of MATLAB without any toolkits is much richer than other technical programming languages. There are more than 1000 functions in the basic MATLAB product alone, and the toolkits extend this capability with many more functions in various specialties. Furthermore, these functions often solve very complex problems (solving differential equations, inverting matrices, and so forth) in a *single step*, saving large amounts of time. Doing the same thing in another computer language usually involves writing complex programs yourself or buying a third-party software package (such as IMSL or the NAG software libraries) that contains the functions.

The built-in MATLAB functions are almost always better than anything that an individual engineer could write on his or her own, because many people have worked on them and they have been tested against many different data sets. These functions are also robust, producing sensible results for wide ranges of input data and gracefully handling error conditions.

This book makes no attempt to introduce the user to all of MATLAB's functions. Instead, it teaches a user the basics of how to write, debug, and optimize good MATLAB programs and provides a subset of the most important functions used to solve common scientific and engineering problems. Just as importantly, it teaches the scientist or engineer how to use MATLAB's own tools to locate the right function for a specific purpose from the enormous amount of choices available. In addition, it teaches how to use MATLAB to solve many practical engineering problems, such as vector and matrix algebra, curve fitting, differential equations, and data plotting.

The MATLAB program is a combination of a procedural programming language, an integrated development environment (IDE) including an editor and debugger, and an extremely rich set of functions that can perform many types of technical calculations.

The MATLAB language is a procedural programming language, meaning that the engineer writes *procedures*, which are effectively mathematical recipes for solving a problem. This makes MATLAB very similar to other procedural languages such as C, Basic, Fortran, and Pascal. However, the extremely rich list of predefined functions and plotting tools makes it superior to these other languages for many engineering analysis applications.

1.1 The Advantages of MATLAB

MATLAB has many advantages compared to conventional computer languages for technical problem solving. Among them are:

1. **Ease of Use**

   MATLAB is an interpreted language, like many versions of Basic, and like Basic, it is very easy to use. The program can be used as a scratch pad to evaluate expressions typed at the command line, or it can be used to execute large prewritten programs. Programs may be easily written and modified with the built-in integrated development environment and can be debugged with the MATLAB debugger. Because the language is so easy to use, it is ideal for the rapid prototyping of new programs.

   Many program development tools are provided to make the program easy to use. They include an integrated editor/debugger, on-line documentation and manuals, a workspace browser, and extensive demos.

2. **Platform Independence**

   MATLAB is supported on many different computer systems, providing a large measure of platform independence. At the time of this writing, the language is supported on Windows XP/Vista/7, Linux, Unix, and the Macintosh. Programs written on any platform will run on all of the other platforms, and data files written on any platform may be read transparently on any other platform. As a result, programs written in MATLAB can migrate to new platforms when the needs of the user change.

3. **Predefined Functions**
   MATLAB comes complete with an extensive library of predefined functions that provide tested and prepackaged solutions to many basic technical tasks. For example, suppose that you are writing a program that must calculate the statistics associated with an input data set. In most languages, you would need to write your own subroutines or functions to implement calculations such as the arithmetic mean, standard deviation, median, and so forth. These and hundreds of other functions are built into the MATLAB language, making your job much easier.

   In addition to the large library of functions built into the basic MATLAB language, there are many special-purpose toolboxes available to help solve complex problems in specific areas. For example, a user can buy standard toolboxes to solve problems in signal processing, control systems, communications, image processing, and neural networks, among many others. There is also an extensive collection of free user-contributed MATLAB programs that are shared through the MATLAB website.

4. **Device-Independent Plotting**
   Unlike most other computer languages, MATLAB has many integral plotting and imaging commands. The plots and images can be displayed on any graphical output device supported by the computer on which MATLAB is running. This capability makes MATLAB an outstanding tool for visualizing technical data.

5. **Graphical User Interface**
   MATLAB includes tools that allow a engineer to interactively construct a graphical user interface (GUI) for his or her program. With this capability, the engineer can design sophisticated data-analysis programs that can be operated by relatively inexperienced users.

6. **MATLAB Compiler**
   MATLAB's flexibility and platform independence are achieved by compiling MATLAB programs into a device-independent p-code and then interpreting the p-code instructions at run-time. This approach is similar to that used by Microsoft's Visual Basic language or by Java. Unfortunately, the resulting programs can sometimes execute slowly because the MATLAB code is interpreted rather than compiled. Recent versions of MATLAB have partially overcome this problem by introducing just-in-time (JIT) compiler technology. The JIT compiler compiles portions of the MATLAB code as it is executed to increase overall speed.

   A separate MATLAB compiler is also available. This compiler can compile a MATLAB program into a stand-alone executable that can run on a computer without a MATLAB license. This is a great way to convert a prototype MATLAB program into an executable suitable for sale and distribution to users.

1.2 Disadvantages of MATLAB

MATLAB has two principal disadvantages. The first is that it is an interpreted language and therefore can execute more slowly than compiled languages. This problem can be mitigated by properly structuring the MATLAB program to maximize the performance of vectorized code and by using the JIT compiler.

The second disadvantage is cost: a full copy of MATLAB is five to ten times more expensive than a conventional C or Fortran compiler. This relatively high cost is more than offset by the reduced time required for an engineer or scientist to create a working program, so MATLAB is cost-effective for businesses. However, it is too expensive for most individuals to consider purchasing. Fortunately, there is also an inexpensive Student Edition of MATLAB, which is a great tool for students wishing to learn the language. The Student Edition of MATLAB is essentially identical to the full edition.

1.3 The MATLAB Environment

The fundamental unit of data in any MATLAB program is the **array**. An array is a collection of data values organized into rows and columns and known by a single name. Individual data values within an array can be accessed by including the name of the array followed by subscripts in parentheses that identify the row and column of the particular value. Even scalars are treated as arrays by MATLAB—they are simply arrays with only one row and one column. We will learn how to create and manipulate MATLAB arrays in Section 1.4.

When MATLAB executes, it can display several types of windows that accept commands or display information. The three most important types of windows are Command Windows, where commands may be entered; Figure Windows, which display plots and graphs; and Edit Windows, which permit a user to create and modify MATLAB programs. We will see examples of all three types of windows in this section.

In addition, MATLAB can display other windows that provide help and that allow the user to examine the values of variables defined in memory. We will examine some of these additional windows here; we will examine the others when we discuss how to debug MATLAB programs.

1.3.1 The MATLAB Desktop

When you start MATLAB Version 7.9, a special window called the MATLAB desktop appears. The desktop is a window that contains other windows showing MATLAB data, along with toolbars and a "Start" button similar to that used by Windows XP or Windows 7. By default, most MATLAB tools are "docked" to the desktop, so that they appear inside the desktop window. However, the user can choose to "undock" any or all tools, making them appear in windows separate from the desktop.

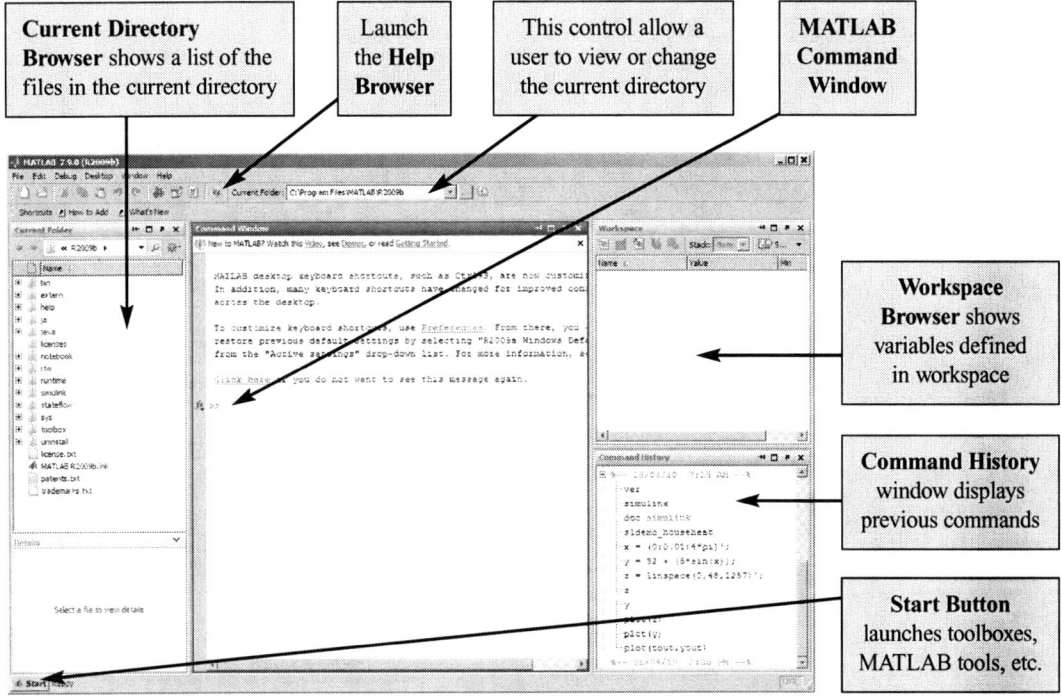

Figure 1.1   The default MATLAB desktop. The exact appearance of the desktop may differ slightly on different types of computers.

The default configuration of the MATLAB desktop is shown in Figure 1.1. It integrates many tools for managing files, variables, and applications within the MATLAB environment.

The major tools within or accessible from the MATLAB desktop are the following:

- The Command Window
- The Command History Window
- The Start Button
- The Documents Window, including the Editor/Debugger and Array Editor
- Figure Windows
- Workspace Browser
- The Help Browser
- The Path Browser

The functions of these tools are summarized in Table 1-1. They are discussed in later sections of this chapter.

Table I-I   Tools and Windows Included in the MATLAB Desktop

Tool	Description
Command Window	A window where the user can type commands and see immediate results
Command History Window	A window that displays recently used commands
Start Button	The starting point for accessing MATLAB tools and resources
Document Window	A window the displays MATLAB files, and allows the user to edit or debug them
Figure Window	A window that displays a MATLAB plot
Workspace Browser	A window that displays the names and values of variable stored in the MATLAB workspace
Help Browser	A tool to get help for MATLAB functions
Path Browser	A tool to display the MATLAB search path

1.3.2   The Command Window

The right-hand side of the default MATLAB desktop contains the **Command Window**. A user can enter interactive commands at the command prompt (») in the Command Window, and the commands will be executed on the spot.

As an example of a simple interactive calculation, suppose that you want to calculate the area of a circle with a radius of 2.5 m. This can be done in the MATLAB Command Window by typing:

```
» area = pi * 2.5^2
area =
    19.6350
```

MATLAB calculates the answer as soon as the Enter key is pressed and stores the answer in a variable (really a 1×1 array) called `area`. The contents of the variable are displayed in the Command Window as shown in Figure 1.2, and the variable can be used in further calculations. (Note that π is predefined in MATLAB, so we can just use `pi` without first declaring it to be 3.141592 . . . .)

If a statement is too long to type on a single line, it may be continued on successive lines by typing an **ellipsis** (. . .) at the end of the first line and then continuing on the next line. For example, the following two statements are identical:

```
x1 = 1 + 1/2 + 1/3 + 1/4 + 1/5 + 1/6
```

and

```
x1 = 1 + 1/2 + 1/3 + 1/4 + ...
    + 1/5 + 1/6
```

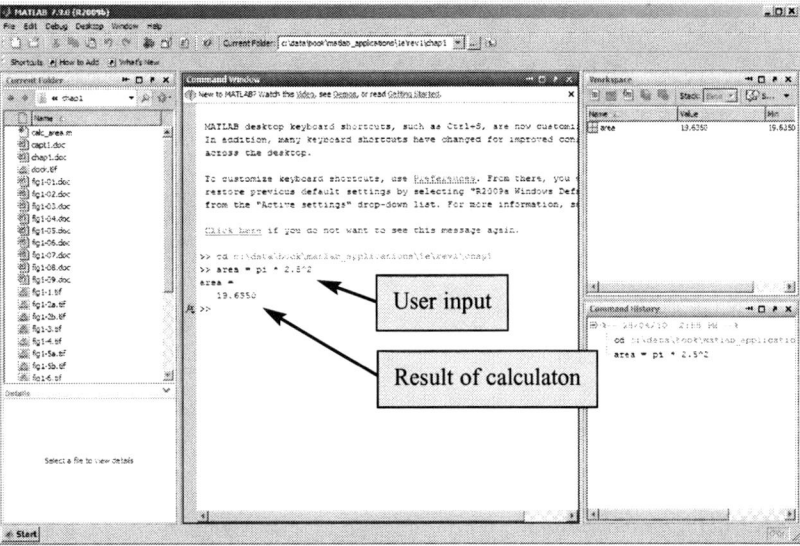

Figure 1.2   The Command Window appears in the center of the desktop. Users enter commands and see responses here.

As an alternative to typing commands directly in the Command Window, a series of commands can be placed into a file, and the entire file can be executed by typing its name in the Command Window. Such files are called **script files**. Script files (and functions, which we will see later) are also known as **M-files**, because they have a file extension of ".m".

1.3.3   The Command History Window

The Command History Window displays a list of the commands that a user has entered in the Command Window. The list of previous commands can extend back to previous executions of the program. Commands remain in the list until they are deleted. To reexecute any command, simply double-click it with the left mouse button. To delete one or more commands from the Command History Window, select the commands and right-click them with the mouse. A popup menu will be displayed that allows the user to delete the items (see Figure 1.3).

1.3.4   The Start Button

The Start Button (see Figure 1.4) allows a user to access MATLAB tools, desktop tools, help files, and so forth. It works just like the Start button on a Windows desktop. To start a particular tool, just click on the Start button and select the tool from the appropriate submenu.

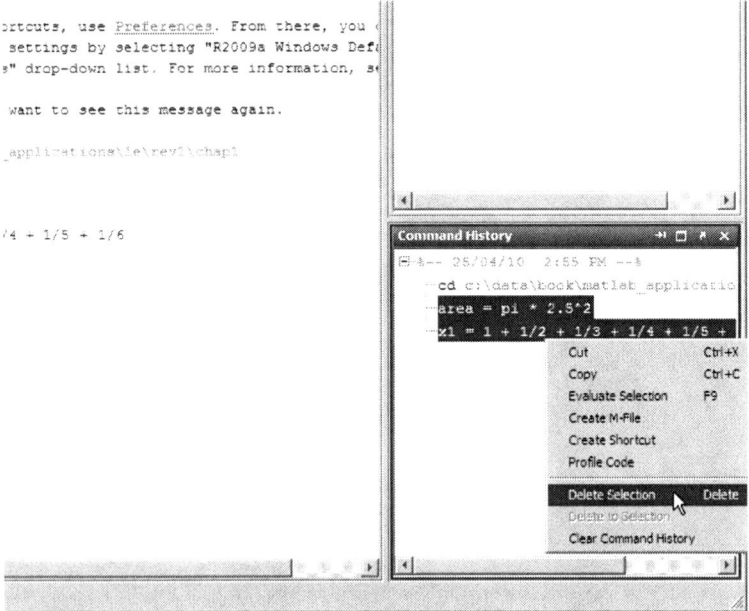

Figure 1.3 The Command History Window, showing two commands being deleted.

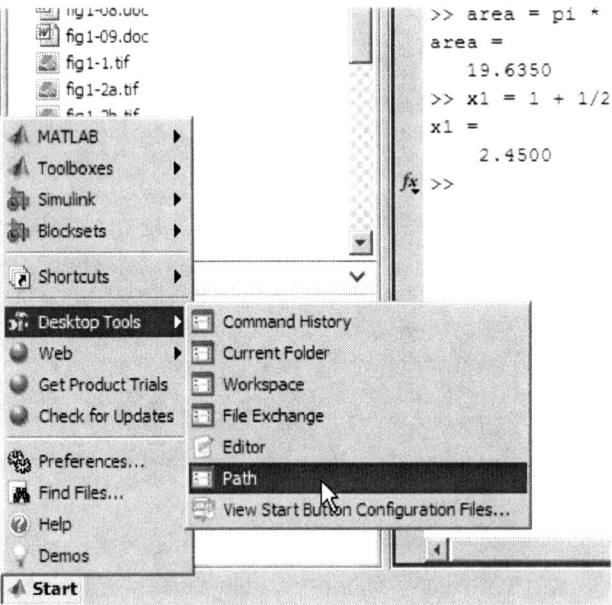

Figure 1.4 The Start button, which allows a user to select from a wide variety of MATLAB and desktop tools.

1.3.5   The Edit/Debug Window

An **Edit Window** is used to create new M-files or to modify existing ones. An Edit Window is created automatically when you create a new M-file or open an existing one. You can create a new M-file with the "File/New/M-file" selection from the desktop menu or by clicking the ⬜ toolbar icon. You can open an existing M-file file with the "File/Open" selection from the desktop menu or by clicking the 📂 toolbar icon.

An Edit Window displaying a simple M-file called `calc_area.m` is shown in Figure 1.5. This file calculates the area of a circle given its radius and displays the result. By default, the Edit Window is an independent window not docked to the desktop, as shown in Figure 1.5*(a)*. The Edit Window also can be docked to the MATLAB desktop. In that case, it appears within a container called the Documents Window, as shown in Figure 1.5*(b)*. We will learn how to dock and undock a window later in this chapter.

The Edit Window is essentially a programming text editor with the MATLAB languages features highlighted in different colors. Comments in an M-file file appear in green, variables and numbers appear in black, complete character strings appear in magenta, incomplete character strings appear in red, and language keywords appear in blue.

After an M-file is saved, it may be executed by typing its name in the Command Window. For the M-file in Figure 1.5, the results are as follows:

```
» calc_area
The area of the circle is 19.635
```

The Edit Window also doubles as a debugger, as we shall see in Chapter 2.

1.3.6   Figure Windows

A **Figure Window** is used to display MATLAB graphics. A figure can be a two- or three-dimensional plot of data, an image, or a graphical user interface (GUI). A simple script file that calculates and plots the function $\sin x$ is shown here.

```
% sin_x.m: This M-file calculates and plots the
% function sin(x) for 0 <= x <= 6.
x = 0:0.1:6
y = sin(x);
plot(x,y);
```

If this file is saved under the name `sin_x.m`, then a user can execute the file by typing "`sin_x`" in the Command Window. When this script file is executed, MATLAB opens a figure window and plots the function $\sin x$ in it. The resulting plot is shown in Figure 1.6.

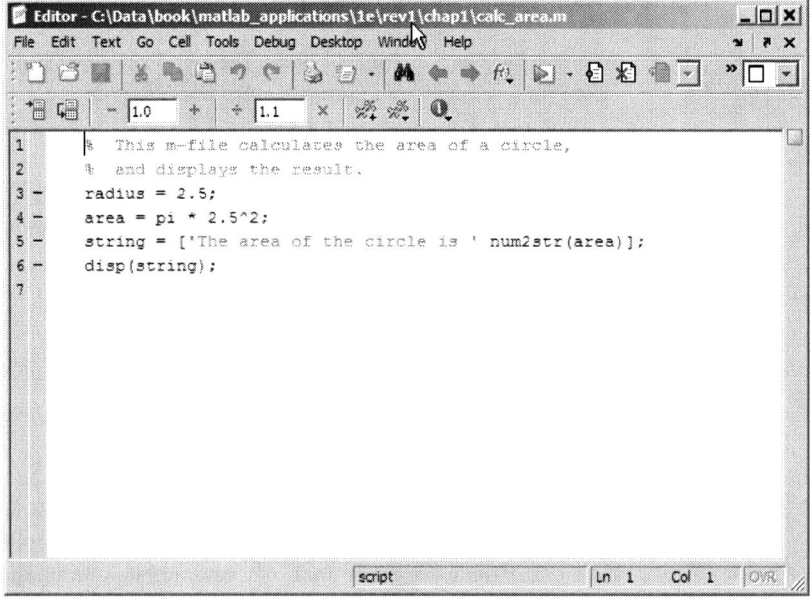

(a)

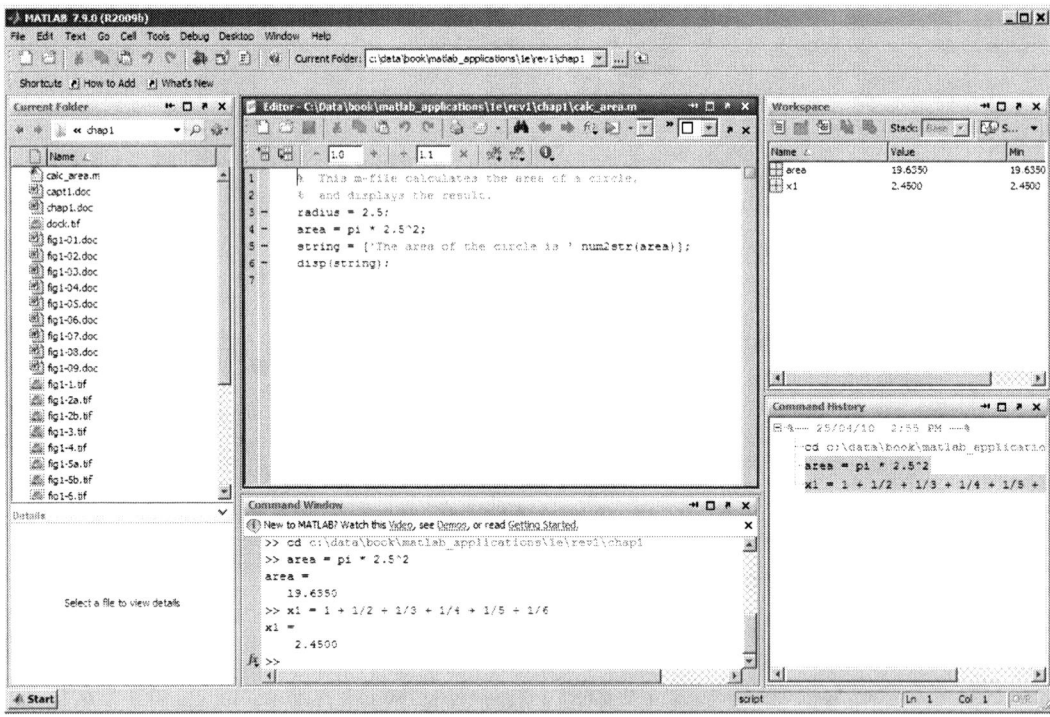

(b)

Figure 1.5 *(a)* The MATLAB Editor, displayed as an independent window. *(b)* The MATLAB Editor, docked to the MATLAB desktop.

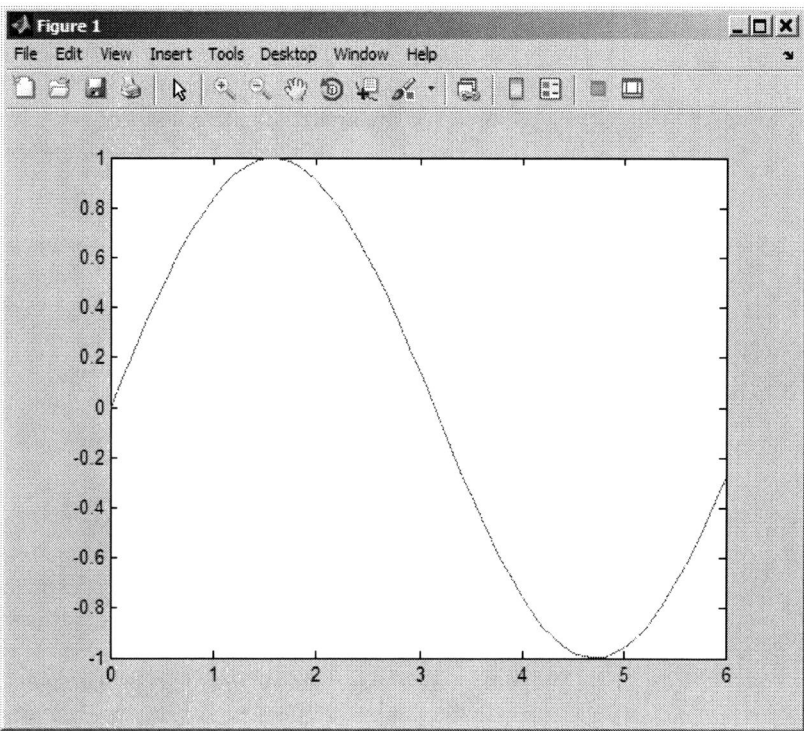

Figure 1.6 MATLAB plot of sin x versus x.

1.3.7 Docking and Undocking Windows

MATLAB windows such as the Command Window, the Edit Window, and Figure Windows can either be *docked* to the desktop or *undocked*. When a window is docked, it appears as a pane within the MATLAB desktop. When it is undocked, it appears as an independent window on the computer screen separate from the desktop. When a window is docked to the desktop, the upper right-hand corner contains a small button with an arrow pointing up and to the right (⬈). If this button is clicked, the window will become an independent window. When the window is an independent window, the upper-right corner contains a small button with an arrow pointing down and to the right (⬊). If this button is clicked, the window will be redocked with the desktop. Figure 1.5 shows the Edit Window in both its docked and undocked state. Note the undock and dock arrows in the upper-right corner.

1.3.8 The MATLAB Workspace

A statement such as

```
z = 10
```

creates a variable named z, stores the value 10 in it, and saves it in a part of computer memory known as the **workspace**. A workspace is the collection of all the variables and arrays that can be used by MATLAB when a particular command, M-file, or function is executing. All commands executed in the Command Window (and all script files executed from the Command Window) share a common workspace, so they can all share variables. As we will see later, MATLAB functions differ from script files in that each function has its own separate workspace.

A list of the variables and arrays in the current workspace can be generated with the `whos` command. For example, after M-files `calc_area` and `sin_x` are executed, the workspace contains the following variables:

```
» whos
  Name      Size      Bytes    Class       Attributes
  area      1x1           8    double
  radius    1x1           8    double
  string    1x32         64    char
  x         1x61        488    double
  y         1x61        488    double
```

Script file `calc_area` created variables `area`, `radius`, and `string`, while script file `sin_x` created variables `x` and `y`. Note that all of the variables are in the same workspace, so if two script files are executed in succession, the second script file can use variables created by the first script file.

The contents of any variable or array may be determined by typing the appropriate name in the Command Window. For example, the contents of `string` can be found as follows:

```
» string
string =
The area of the circle is 19.635
```

A variable can be deleted from the workspace with the `clear` command. The `clear` command takes the form

```
clear var1 var2 ...
```

where `var1` and `var2` are the names of the variables to be deleted. The command `clear variables` or simply `clear` deletes all variables from the current workspace.

1.3.9 The Workspace Browser

The contents of the current workspace also can be examined with a GUI-based Workspace Browser. The Workspace Browser appears by default in the upper-left corner of the desktop. It provides a graphic display of the same information as the `whos` command, and it also shows the actual contents of each array if the information is short enough to fit within the display area. The Workspace Browser is dynamically updated whenever the contents of the workspace change.

Array Editor allows the user to edit any variable or array selected in the Workspace Browser.

Workspace Browser shows a list of the variables defined in the workspace

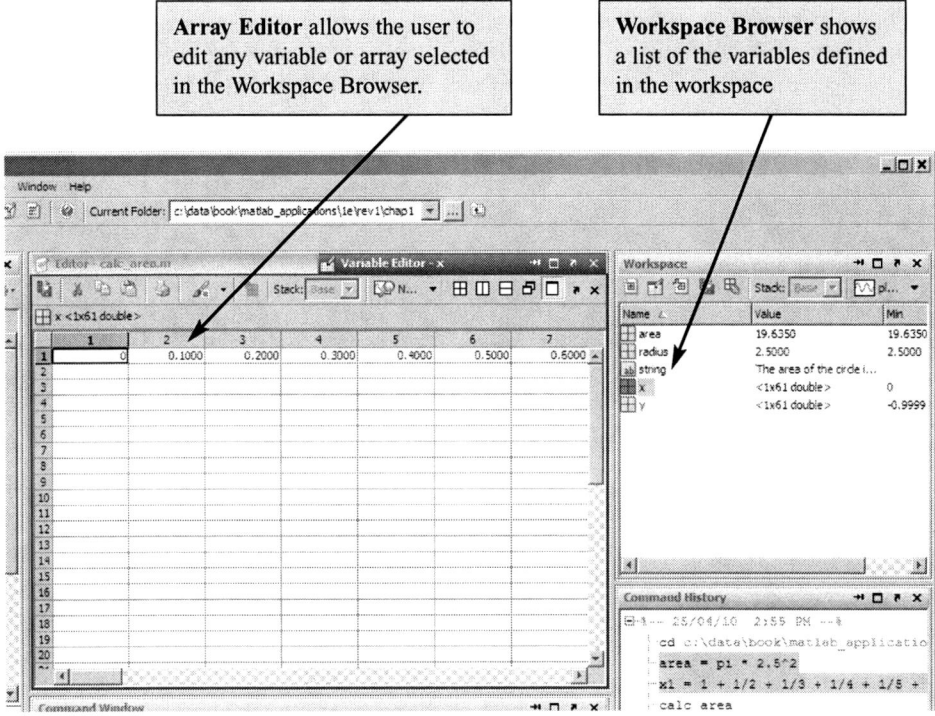

Figure 1.7 The Workspace Browser and the Array Editor. The Array Editor is invoked by double-clicking a variable in the Workspace Browser. It allows a user to change the values contained in a variable or array.

A typical Workspace Browser window is shown in Figure 1.7. As you can see, it displays the same information as the whos command. Double-clicking on any variable in the window will bring up the Array Editor, which allows the user to modify the information stored in the variable.

One or more variables may be deleted from the workspace by selecting them in the Workspace Browser with the mouse and pressing the delete key, or by right-clicking with the mouse and selecting the delete option.

1.3.10   Getting Help

There are three ways to get help in MATLAB. The preferred method is to use the Help Browser. The Help Browser can be started by selecting the ⟨?⟩ icon from the desktop toolbar or by typing helpdesk or helpwin in the Command Window. A user can get help by browsing the MATLAB documentation, or he or she can search for the details of a particular command. The Help Browser is shown in Figure 1.8.

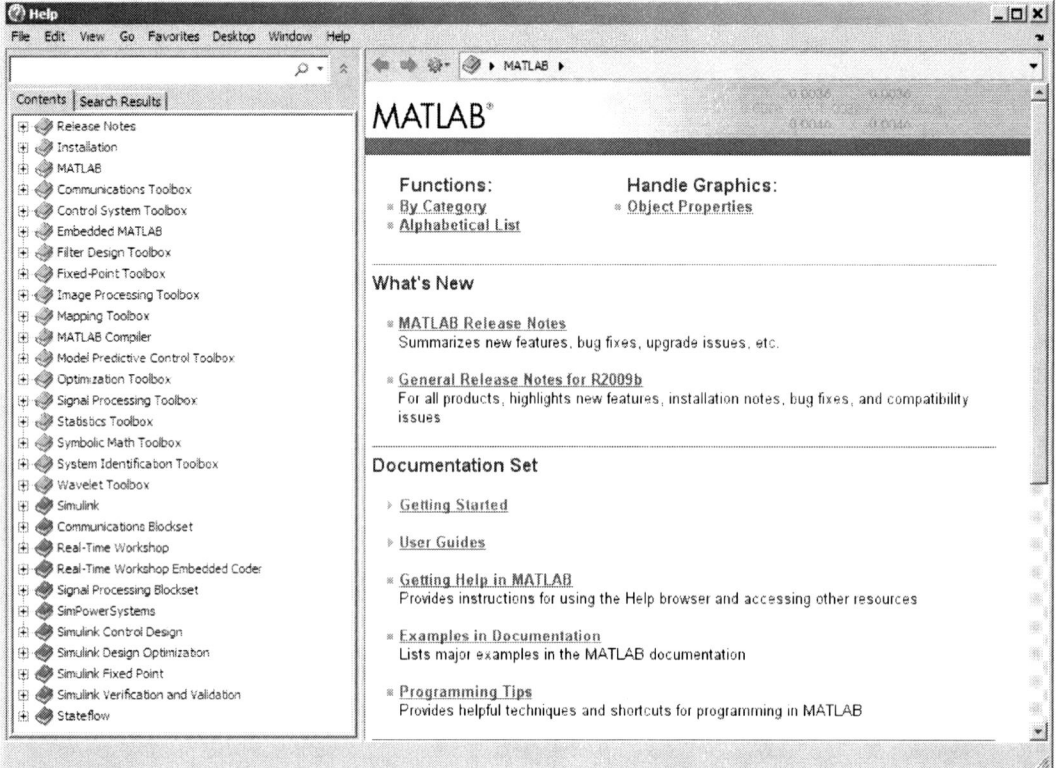

Figure 1.8 The Help Browser.

There are also two command-line–oriented ways to get help. The first way is to type help or help followed by a function name in the Command Window. If you just type help, MATLAB will display a list of possible help topics in the Command Window. If a specific function or a toolbox name is included, help will be provided for that particular function or toolbox.

The second way to get help is the lookfor command. The lookfor command differs from the help command in that the help command searches for an exact function name match, whereas the lookfor command searches the quick summary information in each function for a match. This makes lookfor slower than help, but it improves the chances of getting back useful information. For example, suppose that you were looking for a function to take the inverse of a matrix. Since MATLAB does not have a function named inverse, the command "help inverse" will produce nothing. On the other hand, the command "lookfor inverse" will produce the following results:

```
» lookfor inverse
INVHILB    Inverse Hilbert matrix.
ACOS       Inverse cosine.
ACOSH      Inverse hyperbolic cosine.
ACOT       Inverse cotangent.
ACOTH      Inverse hyperbolic cotangent.
ACSC       Inverse cosecant.
ACSCH      Inverse hyperbolic cosecant.
ASEC       Inverse secant.
ASECH      Inverse hyperbolic secant.
ASIN       Inverse sine.
ASINH      Inverse hyperbolic sine.
ATAN       Inverse tangent.
ATAN2      Four quadrant inverse tangent.
ATANH      Inverse hyperbolic tangent.
ERFINV     Inverse error function.
INV        Matrix inverse.
PINV       Pseudoinverse.
IFFT       Inverse discrete Fourier transform.
IFFT2      Two-dimensional inverse discrete Fourier transform.
IFFTN      N-dimensional inverse discrete Fourier transform.
IPERMUTE   Inverse permute array dimensions.
```

From this list, we can see that the function of interest is named `inv`.

1.3.11   A Few Important Commands

If you are new to MATLAB, a few demonstrations may help to give you a feel for its capabilities. To run MATLAB's built-in demonstrations, type `demo` in the Command Window, or select "demos" from the Start button.

The contents of the Command Window can be cleared at any time using the `clc` command, and the contents of the current figure window can be cleared at any time using the `clf` command. The variables in the workspace can be cleared with the `clear` command. As we have seen, the contents of the workspace persist between the executions of separate commands and M-files, so it is possible for the results of one problem to have an effect on the next one that you may attempt to solve. To avoid this possibility, it is a good idea to issue the `clear` command at the start of each new independent calculation.

Another important command is the **abort** command. If an M-file appears to be running for too long, it may contain an infinite loop, and it will never terminate. In this case, the user can regain control by typing control-c (abbreviated ^c) in the Command Window. This command is entered by holding down the control key while typing a "c". When MATLAB detects a ^c, it interrupts the running program and returns a command prompt.

It is also possible to scroll through recent commands typed in the Command Window using the up-arrow (↑) and down-arrow (↓) keys. Each time a user presses the up-arrow key, the next previous command is displayed on the command line ready for execution. Each time a user presses the down-arrow key, the next following command is displayed on the command line ready for execution. This feature allows a user to quickly modify and reuse recent commands without having to retype them from scratch.

There is also an auto-complete feature in MATLAB. If a user starts to type a command and then presses the Tab key, a popup list of recently typed commands and MATLAB functions that match the string will be displayed (see Figure 1.9). The user can complete the command by selecting one of the items from the list.

The exclamation point (!) is another important special character. Its purpose is to send a command to the computer's operating system. Any characters after the exclamation point will be sent to the operating system and executed as though they had been typed at the operating system's command prompt.

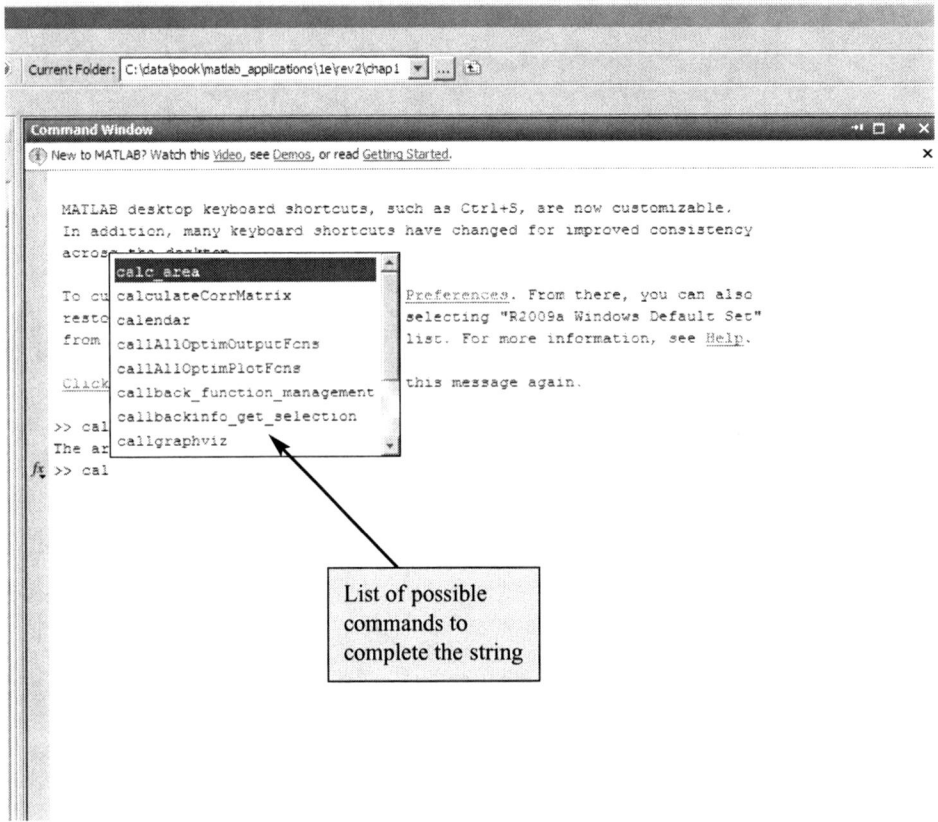

Figure 1.9 If a user types a partial command and then hits the Tab key, MATLAB will pop up a window of suggested commands or functions that match the string.

This feature lets you embed operating system commands directly into MATLAB programs.

Finally, it is possible to keep track of everything done during a MATLAB session with the **diary** command. The form of this command is

```
diary filename
```

After this command is typed, a copy of all input and most output typed in the Command Window is echoed in the diary file. This is a great tool for recreating events when something goes wrong during a MATLAB session. The command "diary off" suspends input into the diary file, and the command "diary on" resumes input again.

1.3.12   The MATLAB Search Path

MATLAB has a search path that it uses to find M-files. MATLAB's M-files are organized in directories on your file system. Many of these directories of M-files are provided along with MATLAB, and users may add others. If a user enters a name at the MATLAB prompt, the MATLAB interpreter attempts to find the name as follows:

1. It looks for the name as a variable. If it is a variable, MATLAB displays the current contents of the variable.
2. It checks to see if the name is an M-file in the current directory. If it is, MATLAB executes that function or command.
3. It checks to see if the name is an M-file in any directory in the search path. If it is, MATLAB executes that function or command.

Note that MATLAB checks for variable names first, so *if you define a variable with the same name as a MATLAB function or command, that function or command becomes inaccessible.* This is a common mistake made by novice users.

◆ Programming Pitfalls

Never use a variable with the same name as a MATLAB function or command. If you do so, that function or command will become inaccessible.

Also, if there is more than one function or command with the same name, the *first* one found on the search path will be executed, and all of the others will be inaccessible. This is a common problem for novice users, since they sometimes create M-files files with the same names as standard MATLAB functions, making them inaccessible.

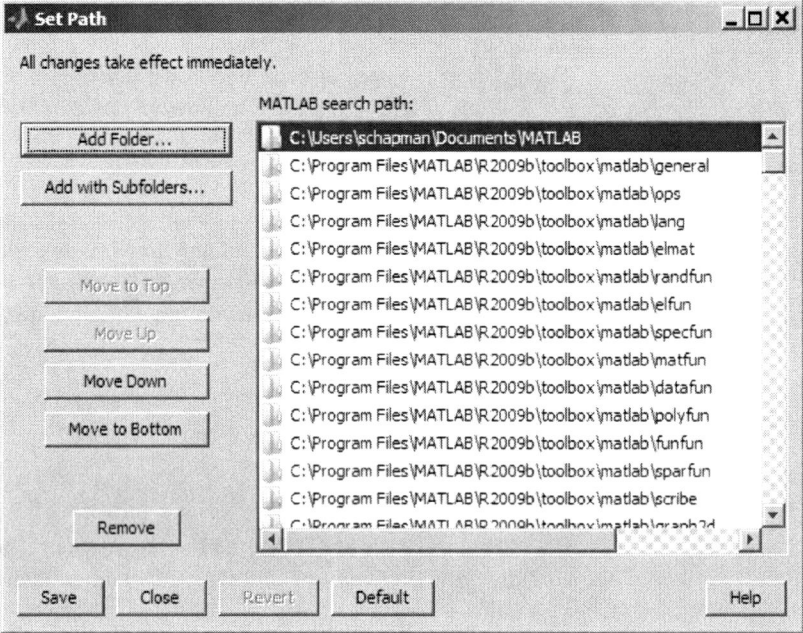

Figure 1.10 The Path Tool.

◉ Programming Pitfalls

Never create an M-file with the same name as a MATLAB function or command.

MATLAB includes a special command (which) to help you find out just which version of a file is being executed and where it is located. This can be useful in finding filename conflicts. The format of this command is which functionname, where functionname is the name of the function that you are trying to locate. For example, the cross-product function cross.m can be located as follows:

```
» which cross
C:\Program
Files\MATLAB\R2009b\toolbox\matlab\specfun\cross.m
```

The MATLAB search path can be examined and modified at any time by selecting "Desktop Tools/Path" from the Start button or by typing editpath in the Command Window. The Path Tool is shown in Figure 1.10. It allows a user to add, delete, or change the order of directories in the path.

Other path-related functions include

- `addpath`   Adds directory to MATLAB search path.
- `path`   Displays MATLAB search path.
- `savepath`   Saves the current MATLAB path to disk.
- `rmpath`   Removes directory from MATLAB search path.

1.4   Using MATLAB as a Calculator

In its simplest form, MATLAB can be used as a calculator to perform mathematical calculations. The calculations to be performed are typed directly into the Command Window, using the symbols +, −, *, /, and ^ for addition, subtraction, multiplication, division, and exponentiation, respectively. After an expression is typed, the results of the expression will be automatically calculated and displayed. If an equal sign is used in the expression, then the result of the calculation is saved in the variable name to the left of the equal sign.

For example, suppose that we would like to calculate the volume of a cylinder of radius r and length l. The area of the circle at the base of the cylinder is given by the equation

$$A = \pi r^2 \tag{1.1}$$

and the total volume of the cylinder will be

$$V = Al \tag{1.2}$$

If the radius of the cylinder is 0.1 m and the length is 0.5 m, then the volume of the cylinder can be found using the MATLAB statements (user inputs are shown in bold face):

```
» A = pi * 0.1^2
A =
    0.0314
» V = A * 0.5
V =
    0.0157
```

Note that `pi` is predefined to be the value 3.141592 . . . .

When the first expression is typed, the area at the base of the cylinder is calculated, stored in variable A, and displayed to the user. When the second expression is typed, the volume of the cylinder is calculated, stored in variable V, and displayed to the user. Note that the value stored in A was saved by MATLAB and reused when we calculated V.

If an expression *without an equal sign* is typed into the Command Window, MATLAB will evaluate it, store the result in a special variable called `ans`, and display the result.

```
» 200 / 7
ans =
    28.5714
```

The value in ans can be used in later calculations, but be careful! Every time a new expression without an equal sign is evaluated, the value saved in ans will be overwritten.

```
» » ans * 6
ans =
   171.4286
```

The value stored in ans is now 171.4286, not 28.5714.

If you want to save a calculated value and reuse it later, be sure to assign it to a specific name instead of using the default name ans.

⬤ Programming Pitfalls

If you want to reuse the result of a calculation in MATLAB, be sure to include a variable name to store the result. Otherwise, the result will be overwritten the next time that you perform a calculation.

Quiz 1.1

This quiz provides a quick check to see if you have understood the concepts introduced in Chapter 1. If you have trouble with the quiz, reread the sections, ask your instructor, or discuss the material with a fellow student. The answers to this quiz are found in the back of the book.

1. What is the purpose of the MATLAB Command Window? The Edit Window? The Figure Window?

2. List the different ways that you get help in MATLAB.

3. What is a workspace? How can you determine what is stored in a MATLAB workspace?

4. How can you clear the contents of a workspace?

5. The distance traveled by a ball falling in the air is given by the equation

$$x = x_0 + v_0 t + \frac{1}{2} a t^2$$

Use MATLAB to calculate the position of the ball at time $t = 5$ s if $x_0 = 10$ m, $v_0 = 15$ m/s, and $a = -9.81$ m/sec^2.

6. Suppose that $x = 3$ and $y = 4$. Use MATLAB to evaluate the following expression:

$$\frac{x^2 y^3}{(x - y)^2}$$

The following questions are intended to help you become familiar with MATLAB tools.

7. Execute the M-files `calc_area.m` and `sin_x.m` in the Command Window (these M-files are available from the book's website). Then use the Workspace Browser to determine what variables are defined in the current workspace.

8. Use the Array Editor to examine and modify the contents of variable `x` in the workspace. The type the command `plot(x,y)` in the Command Window. What happens to the data displayed in the Figure Window?

1.5   Summary

In this chapter, we learned about the MATLAB integrated development environment (IDE). We learned about basic types of MATLAB windows, the workspace, and how to get on-line help.

The MATLAB desktop appears when the program is started. It integrates many of the MATLAB tools in single location. These tools include the Command Window, the Command History Window, the Start button, the Workspace Browser, the Array Editor, and the Current Directory viewer. The Command Window is the most important of the windows. It is the one in which all commands are typed and results are displayed.

The Edit/Debug window is used to create or modify M-files. It displays the contents of the M-file with the contents of the file color-coded according to function: comments, keywords, strings, and so forth. This window can be docked to the desktop, but by default it is independent.

The Figure Window is used to display graphics.

A MATLAB user can get help by using either the Help Browser or the command-line help functions `help` and `lookfor`. The Help Browser allows full access to the entire MATLAB documentation set. The command-line function `help` displays help about a specific function in the Command Window. Unfortunately, you must know the name of the function in order to get help about it. The function `lookfor` searches for a given string in the first comment line of every MATLAB function and displays any matches.

When a user types a command in the Command Window, MATLAB searches for that command in the directories specified in the MATLAB path. It will execute the *first* M-file in the path that matches the command, and any further

M-files with the same name will never be found. The Path Tool can be used to add, delete, or modify directories in the MATLAB path.

1.5.1 MATLAB Summary

The following summary lists all of the MATLAB special symbols described in this chapter, along with a brief description of each one.

Special Symbols

+	Addition
−	Subtraction
*	Multiplication
/	Division
^	Exponentiation

1.6 Exercises

1.1 The following MATLAB statements plot the function $y(x) = 2e^{-0.2x}$ for the range $0 \le x \le 10$:

```
x = 0:0.1:10;
y = 2 * exp(-0.2 * x);
plot(x,y);
```

Use the MATLAB Edit Window to create a new empty M-file, type these statements into the file, and save the file with the name test1.m. Then, execute the program by typing the name test1 in the Command Window. What result do you get?

1.2 Get help on the MATLAB function exp using *(a)* The "help exp" command typed in the Command Window and *(b)* the Help Browser.

1.3 Use the lookfor command to determine how to take the base-10 logarithm of a number in MATLAB.

1.4 Suppose that $u = 1$ and $v = 3$. Evaluate the following expressions using MATLAB:

(a) $\dfrac{4u}{3v}$

(b) $\dfrac{2v^{-2}}{(u + v)^2}$

(c) $\dfrac{v^3}{v^3 - u^3}$

(d) $\dfrac{4}{3}\pi v^2$

1.5 Suppose that $x = 2$ and $y = -1$. Evaluate the following expressions using MATLAB:

(a) $\sqrt[4]{2x^3}$

(b) $\sqrt[4]{2y^3}$

Note that MATLAB evaluates expressions with complex or imaginary answers transparently.

1.6 Type the following MATLAB statements into the Command Window:

```
4 * 5
a = ans * pi
b = ans / pi
ans
```

What are the results in a, b, and ans? What is the final value saved in ans? Why was that value retained during the subsequent calculations?

1.7 Use the MATLAB Help Browser to find the command required to show MATLAB's current directory. What is the current directory when MATLAB starts up?

1.8 Use the MATLAB Help Browser to find out how to create a new directory from within MATLAB. Then, create a new directory called `mynewdir` under the current directory. Add the new directory to the top of MATLAB's path.

1.9 Change the current directory to `mynewdir`. Then open an Edit Window and add the following lines:

```
% Create an input array from -2*pi to 2*pi
t = -2*pi:pi/10:2*pi;

% Calculate |sin(t)|
x = abs(sin(t));

% Plot result
plot(t,x);
```

Save the file with the name `test2.m`, and execute it by typing `test2` in the Command Window. What happens?

1.10 Close the Figure Window, and change back to the original directory that MATLAB started up in. Next type "`test2`" in the Command Window. What happens, and why?

CHAPTER 2

MATLAB Basics

In this chapter, we will introduce some basic elements of the MATLAB language. By the end of the chapter, you will be able to write simple but functional MATLAB programs.

2.1 Variables and Arrays

The fundamental unit of data in any MATLAB program is the **array**. An array is a collection of data values organized into rows and columns and known by a single name (see Figure 2.1). Individual data values within an array are accessed by including the name of the array followed by subscripts in parentheses that identify the row and column of the particular value. Even scalars are treated as arrays by MATLAB—they are simply arrays with only one row and one column.

Arrays can be classified as either **vectors** or **matrices**. The term "vector" is usually used to describe an array with only one dimension, while the term "matrix" is usually used to describe an array with two or more dimensions. In this text, we will use the term "vector" when discussing one-dimensional arrays, and the term "matrix" when discussing arrays with two or more dimensions. If a particular discussion applies to both types of arrays, we will use the generic term "array."

The **size** of an array is specified by the number of rows and the number of columns in the array, with the number of rows mentioned first. The total number of elements in the array will be the product of the number of rows and the number of columns. For example, the sizes of the following arrays are

Array	Size
$a = \begin{bmatrix} 1 & 2 \\ 3 & 4 \\ 5 & 6 \end{bmatrix}$	This is a 3 × 2 matrix, containing 6 elements.
$b = \begin{bmatrix} 1 & 2 & 3 & 4 \end{bmatrix}$	This is a 1 × 4 array containing 4 elements, known as a **row vector**.
$c = \begin{bmatrix} 1 \\ 2 \\ 3 \end{bmatrix}$	This is a 3 × 1 array containing 3 elements, known as a **column vector**.

Individual elements in an array are addressed by the array name followed by the row and column of the particular element. If the array is a row or column vector, only one subscript is required. For example, in the preceding arrays, a(2,1) is 3 and c(2) is 2.

A MATLAB **variable** is a region of memory containing an array, which is known by a user-specified name. The contents of the array may be used or modified at any time by including its name in an appropriate MATLAB command.

MATLAB variable names must begin with a letter, followed by any combination of letters, numbers, and the underscore (_) character. Only the first 63

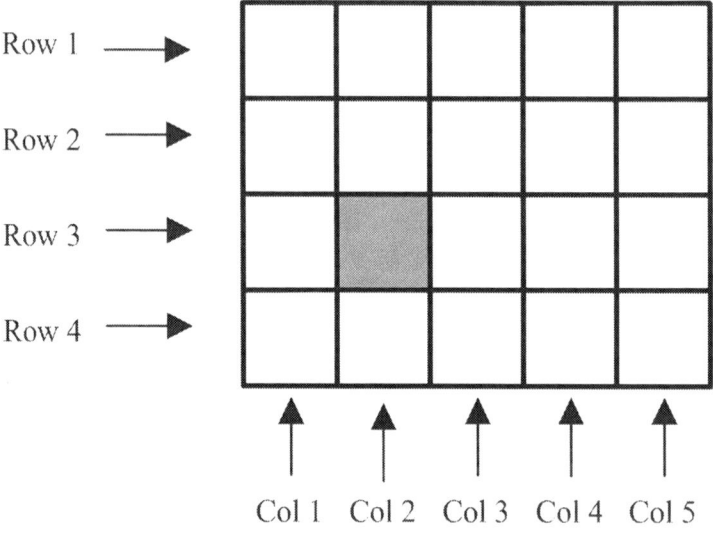

array arr

Figure 2.1 An array is a collection of data values organized into rows and columns.

characters are significant; if more than 63 are used, the remaining characters will be ignored. If two variables are declared with names that differ only in the 64th character, MATLAB will treat them as the same variable. MATLAB will issue a warning if it has to truncate a long variable name to 63 characters.

Programming Pitfalls

Make sure that your variable names are unique in the first 63 characters. Otherwise, MATLAB will not be able to tell the difference between them.

When writing a program, it is important to pick meaningful names for the variables. Meaningful names make a program *much* easier to read and to maintain. Names such as day, month, and year are quite clear even to a person seeing a program for the first time. Since spaces cannot be used in MATLAB variable names, underscore characters can be substituted to create meaningful names. For example, *exchange rate* might become exchange_rate.

Good Programming Practice

Always give your variables descriptive and easy-to-remember names. For example, a currency exchange rate could be given the name exchange_rate. This practice will make your programs clearer and easier to understand.

It is also important to include a **data dictionary** in the header of any program that you write. A data dictionary lists the definition of each variable used in a program. The definition should include both a description of the contents of the item and the units in which it is measured. A data dictionary may seem unnecessary when the program is being written, but it is invaluable when you or another person have to go back and modify the program at a later time.

Good Programming Practice

Create a data dictionary for each program to make program maintenance easier.

The MATLAB language is case-sensitive, which means that uppercase and lowercase letters are not the same. Thus the variables name, NAME, and Name are all different in MATLAB. You must be careful to use the same capitalization every time that variable name is used. While it is not required, it is customary to use all lowercase letters for ordinary variable names.

> ✳ **Good Programming Practice**
>
> Be sure to capitalize a variable exactly the same way each time that it is used. It is good practice to use only lowercase letters in variable names.

The most common types of MATLAB variables are `double` and `char`. Variables of type `double` consist of scalars or arrays of 64-bit double-precision floating-point numbers. They can hold real, imaginary, or complex values. The real and imaginary components of each variable can be positive or negative numbers in the range 10^{-308} to 10^{308}, with 15 to 16 significant decimal digits of accuracy. The `double` data type is the principal numerical data type in MATLAB.

A variable of type `double` is automatically created whenever a numerical value is assigned to a variable name. The numerical values assigned to `double` variables can be real, imaginary, or complex. A real value is just a number. For example, the following statement assigns the real value 10.5 to the `double` variable `var`:

```
var = 10.5
```

An imaginary number is defined by appending the letter `i` or `j` to a number.[1] For example, `10i` and `−4j` are both imaginary values. The following statement assigns the imaginary value $4i$ to the `double` variable `var`:

```
var = 4i
```

A complex value has both a real and an imaginary component. It is created by adding a real and an imaginary number together. For example, the following statement assigns the complex value $10 + 10i$ to variable `var`:

```
var = 10 + 10i
```

Variables of type `char` consist of scalars or arrays of 16-bit values, each representing a single character. Arrays of this type are used to hold character strings. They are automatically created whenever a single character or a character string is assigned to a variable name. For example, the following statement creates a variable of type `char` whose name is `comment` and stores the specified string in it. After the statement is executed, `comment` will be a 1×26 character array.

```
comment = 'This is a character string'
```

In a language such as C, the type of every variable must be explicitly declared in a program before it is used. These languages are said to be **strongly typed**. In contrast, MATLAB is a **weakly typed** language. Variables may be created at any

---

[1] An imaginary number is a number multiplied by $\sqrt{-1}$. The letter i is the symbol for $\sqrt{-1}$ used by most mathematicians and scientists. The letter j is the symbol for $\sqrt{-1}$ used by electrical engineers, because the letter i is usually reserved for currents in that discipline.

time by simply assigning values to them, and the type of data assigned to the variable determines the type of variable that is created.

2.2   Creating and Initializing Variables in MATLAB

MATLAB variables are automatically created when they are initialized. There are three common ways to initialize a variable in MATLAB:

1. Assign data to the variable in an assignment statement.
2. Input data into the variable from the keyboard.
3. Read data from a file.

The first two ways are discussed here, and the third approach is discussed in Section 2.6.

2.2.1   Initializing Variables in Assignment Statements

The simplest way to initialize a variable is to assign it one or more values in an **assignment statement**. An assignment statement has the general form

```
var = expression;
```

where `var` is the name of a variable and *expression* is a scalar constant, an array, or a combination of constants, other variables, and mathematical operations ($+$, $-$, etc.). The value of the expression is calculated using the normal rules of mathematics, and the resulting values are stored in named variables. The semicolon at the end of the statement is optional. If the semicolon is absent, the value assigned to `var` will be echoed in the Command Window. If it is present, nothing will be displayed in the Command Window even though the assignment has occurred.

Simple examples of initializing variables with assignment statements include

```
var = 40i;
var2 = var/5;
array = [1 2 3 4];
x = 1; y = 2;
```

The first example creates a scalar variable of type `double` and stores the imaginary number $40i$ in it. The second example creates a scalar variable and stores the result of the expression `var/5` in it. The third example creates a variable and stores a four-element row vector in it. The fourth example shows that multiple assignment statements can be placed on a single line, provided that they are separated by semicolons or commas. Note that if any of the variables had already existed when the statements were executed, their old contents would have been lost.

The third example shows that variables also can be initialized with arrays of data. Such arrays are constructed using brackets [ ] and semicolons. All of the elements of an array are listed in **row order**. In other words, the values in each row are listed from left to right, with the topmost row first and the bottommost row last. Individual values within a row are separated by blank spaces or commas, and the rows themselves are separated by semicolons or new lines. The following expressions are all legal arrays that can be used to initialize a variable:

`[3.4]`	This expression creates a 1 × 1 array (a scalar) containing the value 3.4. The brackets are not required in this case.
`[1.0 2.0 3.0]`	This expression creates a 1 × 3 array containing the row vector [1 2 3].
`[1.0; 2.0; 3.0]`	This expression creates a 3 × 1 array containing the column vector $\begin{bmatrix} 1 \\ 2 \\ 3 \end{bmatrix}$.
`[1, 2, 3; 4, 5, 6]`	This expression creates a 2 × 3 array containing the matrix $\begin{bmatrix} 1 & 2 & 3 \\ 4 & 5 & 6 \end{bmatrix}$.
`[1, 2, 3` `4, 5, 6]`	This expression creates a 2 × 3 array containing the matrix $\begin{bmatrix} 1 & 2 & 3 \\ 4 & 5 & 6 \end{bmatrix}$. The end of the first line terminates the first row.
`[]`	This expression creates an **empty array**, which contains no rows and no columns. (Note that this is not the same as an array containing zeros.)

The number of elements in every row of an array must be the same, and the number of elements in every column must be the same. An expression such as

```
[1 2 3; 4 5];
```

is illegal because row 1 has three elements while row 2 has only two elements.

● Programming Pitfalls

The number of elements in every row of an array must be the same, and the number of elements in every column must be the same. Attempts to define an array with different numbers of elements in its rows or different numbers of elements in its columns will produce an error when the statement is executed.

The expressions used to initialize arrays can include algebraic operations and all or portions of previously defined arrays. For example, the assignment statements

```
a = [0 1+7];
b = [a(2) 7 a];
```

will define an array a = [0 8] and an array b = [8 7 0 8].

Also, not all of the elements in an array must be defined when it is created. If a specific array element is defined and one or more of the elements that precede it are not, the earlier elements automatically will be created and initialized to zero. For example, if c is not previously defined, the statement

```
c(2,3) = 5;
```

will produce the matrix $c = \begin{bmatrix} 0 & 0 & 0 \\ 0 & 0 & 5 \end{bmatrix}$. Similarly, an array can be extended by specifying a value for an element beyond the currently defined size. For example, suppose that array $d = [1 \quad 2]$. Then the statement

```
d(4) = 4;
```

will produce the array $d = [1 \quad 2 \quad 0 \quad 4]$.

The semicolon at the end of each assignment statement shown previously has a special purpose: it *suppresses the automatic echoing of values* that normally occurs whenever an expression is evaluated in an assignment statement. If an assignment statement is typed without the semicolon, the result of the statement is automatically displayed in the Command Window:

```
» e = [1, 2, 3; 4, 5, 6]
e =
    1    2    3
    4    5    6
```

If a semicolon is added at the end of the statement, the echoing disappears. Echoing is an excellent way to quickly check your work, but it seriously slows down the execution of MATLAB programs. For that reason, we normally suppress echoing at all times by ending each line with a semicolon.

However, echoing the results of calculations makes a great quick-and-dirty debugging tool. If you are not certain what the results of a specific assignment statement are, just leave off the semicolon from that statement, and the results will be displayed in the Command Window as the statement is executed.

✳ Good Programming Practice

Use a semicolon at the end of all MATLAB assignment statements to suppress echoing of assigned values in the Command Window. This greatly speeds program execution.

✳ Good Programming Practice

If you need to examine the results of a statement during program debugging, you may remove the semicolon from that statement only so that its results are echoed in the Command Window.

2.2.2   Initializing with Shortcut Expressions

It is easy to create small arrays by explicitly listing each term in the array, but what happens when the array contains hundreds or even thousands of elements? It is just not practical to write out each element in the array separately!

MATLAB provides a special shortcut notation for these circumstances using the **colon operator**. The colon operator specifies a whole series of values by specifying the first value in the series, the stepping increment, and the last value in the series. The general form of a colon operator is

```
first:incr:last
```

where `first` is the first value in the series, `incr` is the stepping increment, and `last` is the last value in the series. If the increment is one, it may be omitted. This expression will generate an array containing the values `first`, `first+incr, first+2*incr, first+3*incr`, and so forth as long as the values are less than or equal to `last`. The list stops when the next value in the series is greater than the value of `last`.

For example, the expression 1:2:10 is a shortcut for a 1×5 row vector containing the values 1, 3, 5, 7, and 9. The next value in the series would be 11, which is greater than 10, so the series terminates at 9.

```
» x = 1:2:10
x =
     1   3   5   7   9
```

With colon notation, an array can be initialized to have the hundred values $\frac{\pi}{100}$, $\frac{2\pi}{100}$, $\frac{3\pi}{100}$, ..., π as follows:

```
angles = (0.01:0.01:1.00) * pi;
```

Shortcut expressions can be combined with the **transpose operator** (') to initialize column vectors and more complex matrices. The transpose operator swaps the row and columns of any array that it is applied to. Thus the expression

```
f = [1:4]';
```

generates a four-element row vector [1   2   3   4] and then transposes it into the four-element column vector $f = \begin{bmatrix} 1 \\ 2 \\ 3 \\ 4 \end{bmatrix}$. Similarly, the expressions

```
g = 1:4;
h = [g' g'];
```

will produce the matrix $h = \begin{bmatrix} 1 & 1 \\ 2 & 2 \\ 3 & 3 \\ 4 & 4 \end{bmatrix}$.

2.2.3   Initializing with Built-In Functions

Arrays also can be initialized using built-in MATLAB functions. For example, the function `zeros` can be used to create an all-zero array of any desired size. There are several forms of the `zeros` function. If the function has a single scalar argument, it will produce a square array using the single argument as both the number of rows and the number of columns. If the function has two scalar arguments, the first argument will be the number of rows, and the second argument will be the number of columns. Since the `size` function returns two values containing the number of rows and columns in an array, it can be combined with the `zeros` function to generate an array of zeros that is the same size as another array. Some examples using the `zeros` function follow:

```
a = zeros(2);
b = zeros(2,3);
c = [1 2; 3 4];
d = zeros(size(c));
```

These statements generate the following arrays:

$$a = \begin{bmatrix} 0 & 0 \\ 0 & 0 \end{bmatrix} \qquad b = \begin{bmatrix} 0 & 0 & 0 \\ 0 & 0 & 0 \end{bmatrix}$$

$$c = \begin{bmatrix} 1 & 2 \\ 3 & 4 \end{bmatrix} \qquad c = \begin{bmatrix} 0 & 0 \\ 0 & 0 \end{bmatrix}$$

Similarly, the `ones` function can be used to generate arrays containing all ones, and the `eye` function can be used to generate arrays containing **identity matrices**, in which all on-diagonal elements are one, while all off-diagonal elements are zero. Table 2-1 contains list of common MATLAB functions useful for initializing variables.

2.2.4   Initializing Variables with Keyboard Input

It is also possible to prompt a user and initialize a variable with data that the user types directly at the keyboard. This option allows a script file to prompt a user for input data values while it is executing. The `input` function displays a prompt string in the Command Window and then waits for the user to type in a response. For example, consider the following statement:

```
my_val = input('Enter an input value:');
```

Table 2-1   MATLAB Functions Useful for Initializing Variables

Function	Purpose
zeros(n)	Generates an n × n matrix of zeros.
zeros(m,n)	Generates an m × n matrix of zeros.
zeros(size(arr))	Generates a matrix of zeros of the same size as arr.
ones(n)	Generates an n × n matrix of ones.
ones(m,n)	Generates an m × n matrix of ones.
ones(size(arr))	Generates a matrix of ones of the same size as arr.
eye(n)	Generates an n × n identity matrix.
eye(m,n)	Generates an m × n identity matrix.
length(arr)	Returns the length of a vector, or the longest dimension of a 2-D array.
size(arr)	Returns two values specifying the number of rows and columns in arr.

When this statement is executed, MATLAB prints out the string `'Enter an input value:'` and then waits for the user to respond. If the user enters a single number, it just may be typed in. If the user enters an array, it must be enclosed in brackets. In either case, whatever is typed will be stored in the variable `my_val` when the return key is entered. If only the return key is entered, an empty matrix will be created and stored in the variable.

If the `input` function includes the character `'s'` as a second argument, the input data is returned to the user as a character string. Thus, the statement

```
» in1 = input('Enter data: ');
Enter data: 1.23
```

stores the value 1.23 into `in1`, whereas the statement

```
» in2 = input('Enter data: ','s');
Enter data: 1.23
```

stores the character string `'1.23'` into `in2`.

Quiz 2.1

This quiz provides a quick check to see if you have understood the concepts introduced in Sections 2.1 and 2.2. If you have trouble with the quiz, reread the sections, ask your instructor, or discuss the material with a fellow student. The answers to this quiz are found in the back of the book.

1. What is the difference between an array, a matrix, and a vector?

2. Answer the following questions for the array shown here.

$$c = \begin{bmatrix} 1.1 & -3.2 & 3.4 & 0.6 \\ 0.6 & 1.1 & -0.6 & 3.1 \\ 1.3 & 0.6 & 5.5 & 0.0 \end{bmatrix}$$

(a) What is the size of c?

(b) What is the value of c(2,3)?

(c) List the subscripts of all elements containing the value 0.6.

3. Determine the size of the following arrays. Check your answers by entering the arrays into MATLAB and using the whos command or the Workspace Browser. Note that the later arrays may depend on the definitions of arrays defined earlier in this exercise.

(a) u = [10 20*i 10+20];
(b) v = [-1; 20; 3];
(c) w = [1 0 -9; 2 -2 0; 1 2 3];
(d) x = [u' v];
(e) y(3,3) = -7;
(f) z = [zeros(4,1) ones(4,1) zeros(1,4)'];
(g) v(4) = x(2,1);

4. What is the value of w(2,1) in the w array calculated in part *(c)*?

5. What is the value of x(2,1) in the x array calculated in part *(d)*?

6. What is the value of y(2,1) in the y array calculated in part *(e)*?

7. What is the value of v(3) after statement *(g)* is executed?

2.3   Multidimensional Arrays

As we have seen, MATLAB arrays can have one or more dimensions. One-dimensional arrays can be visualized as a series of values laid out in a row or column, with a single subscript used to select the individual array elements (Figure 2.2*(a)*). Such arrays are useful to describe data that is a function of one independent variable, such as a series of temperature measurements made at fixed intervals of time.

Some types of data are functions of more than one independent variable. For example, we might wish to measure the temperature at five different locations at four different times. In this case, our 20 measurements could logically be grouped into five different columns of four measurements each, with a separate column for each location (Figure 2.2*(b)*). In this case, we will use two subscripts to access a given element in the array: the first one to select the row and the second one to select the column. Such arrays are called **two-dimensional arrays**. The number of elements in a two-dimensional array will be the product of the number of rows and the number of columns in the array.

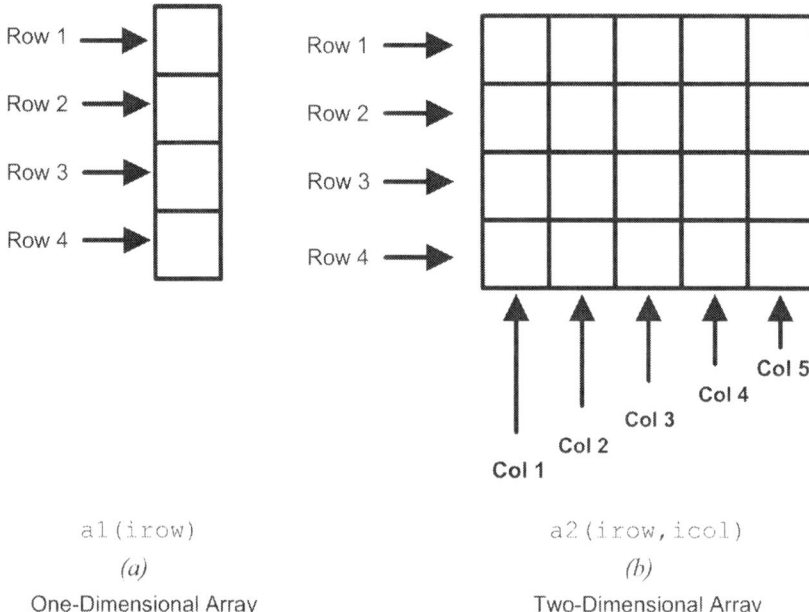

Row 1
Row 2
Row 3
Row 4

Row 1
Row 2
Row 3
Row 4

Col 5
Col 4
Col 3
Col 2
Col 1

a1(irow)

(a)

One-Dimensional Array

a2(irow,icol)

(b)

Two-Dimensional Array

Figure 2.2 Representations of one- and two-dimensional arrays.

MATLAB allows us to create arrays with as many dimensions as necessary for any given problem. These arrays have one subscript for each dimension, and an individual element is selected by specifying a value for each subscript. The total number of elements in the array will be the product of the maximum value of each subscript. For example, the following two statements create a $2 \times 3 \times 2$ array c:

```
» c(:,:,1)=[1 2 3; 4 5 6];
» c(:,:,2)=[7 8 9; 10 11 12];
» whos c

Name    Size    Bytes    Class    Attributes

c       2x3x2     96     double
```

This array contains 12 elements ($2 \times 3 \times 2$). It contents can be displayed just like any other array.

```
» c
c(:,:,1) =
        1    2    3
        4    5    6
c(:,:,2) =
        7    8    9
       10   11   12
```

2.3.1   Storing Multidimensional Arrays in Memory

A two-dimensional array with m rows and n columns will contain m × n elements, and these elements will occupy m × n successive locations in the computer's memory. How are the elements of the array arranged in the computer's memory? MATLAB always allocates array elements in **column major order**. That is, MATLAB allocates the first column in memory, then the second, then the third, and so forth, until all of the columns have been allocated. Figure 2.3 illustrates this memory allocation scheme for a 4 × 3 array a. As we can see, element a(1,2) is really the fifth element allocated in memory. The order in which elements are allocated in memory will become important when we discuss single-subscript addressing in the following section, and low-level I/O functions in Appendix B.

2.3.2   Accessing Multidimensional Arrays with One Dimension

One of MATLAB's peculiarities is that it will permit a user to treat a multidimensional array as though it were a one-dimensional array whose length is equal to the number of elements in the multidimensional array. If a multidimensional array is addressed with a single dimension, the elements will be accessed in the order in which they were allocated in memory.

For example, suppose that we declare the 4 × 3 element array a as follows:

```
» a = [1 2 3; 4 5 6; 7 8 9; 10 11 12]
a =
     1     2     3
     4     5     6
     7     8     9
    10    11    12
```

Then the value of a(5) will be 2, which is the value of element a(1,2), because a(1,2) was allocated fifth in memory.

Under normal circumstances, you should never use this feature of MATLAB. Addressing multidimensional arrays with a single subscript is a recipe for confusion.

✳ Good Programming Practice

Always use the proper number of dimensions when addressing a multidimensional array.

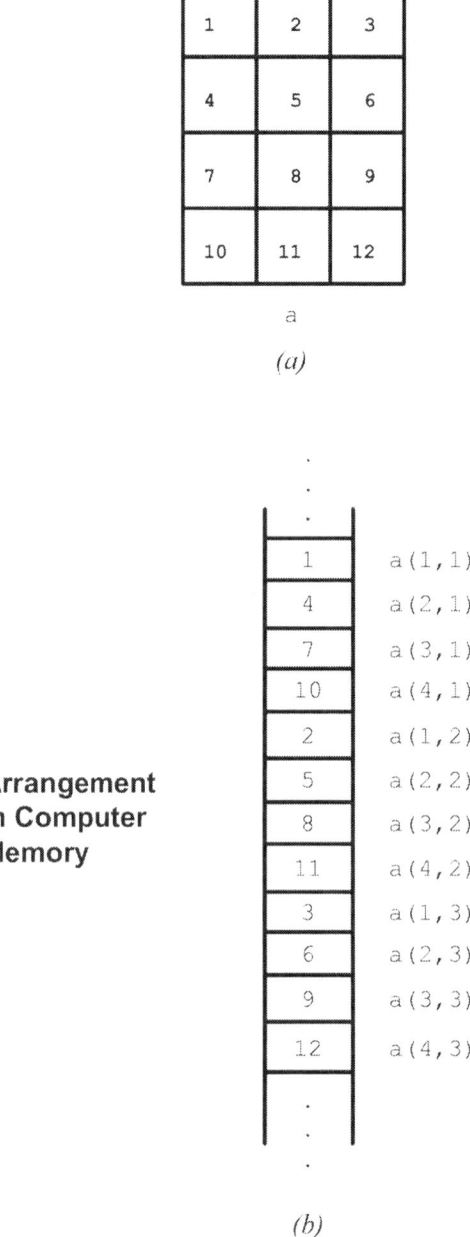

Arrangement in Computer Memory

Figure 2.3 *(a)* Data values for array a. *(b)* Layout of values in memory for array a.

2.4 Subarrays

It is possible to select and use subsets of MATLAB arrays as though they were separate arrays. To select a portion of an array, just include a list of all of the elements to be selected in the parentheses after the array name. For example, suppose array `arr1` is defined as follows:

```
arr1 = [1.1  -2.2  3.3  -4.4  5.5];
```

Then `arr1(3)` is just 3, `arr1([1  4])` is the array `[1.1  -4.4]`, and `arr1(1:2:5)` is the array `[1.1 3.3 5.5]`.

For a two-dimensional array, a colon can be used in a subscript to select all of the values of that subscript. For example, suppose

```
arr2 = [1 2 3; -2 -3 -4; 3 4 5];
```

This statement would create an array `arr2` containing the values $\begin{bmatrix} 1 & 2 & 3 \\ -2 & -3 & -4 \\ 3 & 4 & 5 \end{bmatrix}$.

With this definition, the subarray `arr2(1,:)` would be `[1  2  3]`, and the subarray `arr2(:,1:2:3)` would be $\begin{bmatrix} 1 & 3 \\ -2 & -4 \\ 3 & 5 \end{bmatrix}$.

2.4.1 The end Function

MATLAB includes a special function named end that is very useful for creating array subscripts. When used in an array subscript, end *returns the highest value taken on by that subscript.* For example, suppose that array `arr3` is defined as follows:

```
arr3 = [1 2 3 4 5 6 7 8];
```

Then `arr3(5:end)` would be the array `[5  6  7  8]`, and `array(end)` would be the value 8.

The value returned by end is always the *highest value* of a given subscript. If end appears in different subscripts, it can return *different* values within the same expression. For example, suppose that the 3 × 4 array `arr4` is defined as follows:

```
arr4 = [1 2 3 4; 5 6 7 8; 9 10 11 12];
```

Then the expression `arr4(2:end,2:end)` would return the array $\begin{bmatrix} 6 & 7 & 8 \\ 10 & 11 & 12 \end{bmatrix}$.

Note that the first end returned the value 3, while the second end returned the value 4!

2.4.2 Using Subarrays on the Left-Hand Side of an Assignment Statement

It is also possible to use subarrays on the left-hand side of an assignment statement to update only some of the values in an array, as long as the **shape** (the number of rows and columns) of the values being assigned matches the shape of the subarray. If the shapes do not match, an error will occur. For example, suppose that the 3×4 array arr4 is defined as follows:

```
» arr4 = [1 2 3 4; 5 6 7 8; 9 10 11 12]
arr4 =
        1     2     3     4
        5     6     7     8
        9    10    11    12
```

Then the following assignment statement is legal, since the expressions on both sides of the equal sign have the same shape (2×2):

```
» arr4(1:2,[1 4]) = [20 21; 22 23]
arr4 =
       20     2     3    21
       22     6     7    23
        9    10    11    12
```

Note that the array elements (1,1), (1,4), (2,1), and (2,4) were updated. In contrast, the following expression is illegal, because the two sides do not have the same shape.

```
» arr5(1:2,1:2) = [3 4]
??? In an assignment A(matrix,matrix) = B, the
number of rows in B and the number of elements in
the A row index matrix must be the same.
```

◆ Programming Pitfalls

For assignment statements involving subarrays, the *shapes of the subarrays on either side of the equal sign must match.* MATLAB will produce an error if they do not match.

There is a major difference in MATLAB between assigning values to a subarray and assigning values to an array. If values are assigned to a subarray, *only those values are updated, while all other values in the array remain unchanged.* On the other hand, if values are assigned to an array, *the entire contents of the array are deleted and replaced by the new values.* For example, suppose that the 3 × 4 array `arr4` is defined as follows:

```
» arr4 = [1 2 3 4; 5 6 7 8; 9 10 11 12]
arr4 =
      1     2     3     4
      5     6     7     8
      9    10    11    12
```

Then the following assignment statement replaces the *specified elements* of `arr4`:

```
» arr4(1:2,[1 4]) = [20 21; 22 23]
arr4 =
     20     2     3    21
     22     6     7    23
      9    10    11    12
```

In contrast, the following assignment statement replaces the *entire contents* of `arr4` with a 2 × 2 array:

```
» arr4 = [20 21; 22 23]
arr4 =
     20    21
     22    23
```

✳ Good Programming Practice

Be sure to distinguish between assigning values to a subarray and assigning values to an array. MATLAB behaves differently in these two cases.

2.4.3 Assigning a Scalar to a Subarray

A scalar value on the right-hand side of an assignment statement always matches the shape specified on the left-hand side. The scalar value is copied into every element specified on the left-hand side of the statement. For example, assume that the 3 × 4 array `arr4` is defined as follows:

```
arr4 = [1  2  3  4;  5  6  7  8;  9  10  11  12];
```

Then the following expression assigns the value one to four elements of the array.

```
» arr4(1:2,1:2) = 1
arr4 =
      1     1     3     4
      1     1     7     8
      9    10    11    12
```

2.5 Special Values

MATLAB includes a number of predefined special values. These predefined values may be used at any time in MATLAB without initializing them first. A list of the most common predefined values is given in Table 2-2.

These predefined values are stored in ordinary variables, so they can be over-written or modified by a user. If a new value is assigned to one of the predefined variables, that new value will replace the default one in all later calculations. For example, consider the following statements that calculate the circumference of a 10 cm circle:

```
circ1 = 2 * pi * 10
pi = 3;
circ2 = 2 * pi * 10
```

In the first statement, pi has its default value of 3.14159..., so circ1 is 62.8319, which is the correct circumference. The second statement redefines pi to be 3, so in the third statement circ2 is 60. Changing a predefined value in the program has created an incorrect answer and has also introduced a subtle and hard-to-find bug. Imagine trying to locate the source of such a hidden error in a 10,000 line program!

Table 2-2 Predefined Special Values

Function	Purpose
pi	Contains π to 15 significant digits.
i, j	Contain the value i ($\sqrt{-1}$).
Inf	This symbol represents machine infinity. It is usually generated as a result of a division by 0.
NaN	This symbol stands for not-a-number. It is the result of an undefined mathematical operation, such as the division of zero by zero.
clock	This special variable contains the current date and time in the form of a six-element row vector containing the year, month, day, hour, minute, and second.
date	Contains the current data in a character string format, such as 24-Nov-1998.
eps	This variable name is short for "epsilon." It is the smallest difference between two numbers that can be represented on the computer.
ans	A special variable used to store the result of an expression if that result is not explicitly assigned to some other variable.

💣 Programming Pitfalls

Never redefine the meaning of a predefined variable in MATLAB. It is a recipe for disaster, producing subtle and hard-to-find bugs.

Quiz 2.2

This quiz provides a quick check to see if you have understood the concepts introduced in Sections 2.3 through 2.5. If you have trouble with the quiz, reread the sections, ask your instructor, or discuss the material with a fellow student. The answers to this quiz are found in the back of the book.

1. Assume that array c is defined as shown, and determine the contents of the following sub-arrays:

$$c = \begin{bmatrix} 1.1 & -3.2 & 3.4 & 0.6 \\ 0.6 & 1.1 & -0.6 & 3.1 \\ 1.3 & 0.6 & 5.5 & 0.0 \end{bmatrix}$$

   (a) c(2,:)
   (b) c(:,end)
   (c) c(1:2,2:end)
   (d) c(6)
   (e) c(4:end)
   (f) c(1:2,2:4)
   (g) c([1 3],2)
   (h) c([2 2],[3 3])

2. Determine the contents of array a after the following statements are executed.

   (a) a = [1 2 3; 4 5 6; 7 8 9];
       a([3 1],:) = a([1 3],:);
   (b) a = [1 2 3; 4 5 6; 7 8 9];
       a([1 3],:) = a([2 2],:);
   (c) a = [1 2 3; 4 5 6; 7 8 9];
       a = a([2 2],:);

3. Determine the contents of array a after the following statements are executed.

   (a) a = eye(3,3);
       b = [1 2 3];
       a(2,:) = b;

(b) a = eye(3,3);
    b = [4 5 6];
    a(:,3) = b';

(c) a = eye(3,3);
    b = [7 8 9];
    a(3,:) = b([3 1 2]);

2.6 Displaying Output Data

There are several ways to display output data in MATLAB. This simplest way is one we have already seen—just leave the semicolon off of the end of a statement and it will be echoed to the Command Window. We will now explore a few other ways to display data.

2.6.1 Changing the Default Format

When data is echoed in the Command Window, integer values are always displayed as integers, character values are displayed as strings, and other values are printed using a **default format**. The default format for MATLAB shows four digits after the decimal point, and it may be displayed in scientific notation with an exponent if the number is too large or too small. For example, the statements

```
x = 100.11
y = 1001.1
z = 0.00010011
```

produce the following output

```
x =
    100.1100
y =
    1.0011e+003
z =
    1.0011e-004
```

This default format can be changed in one of two ways: from the main MATLAB Window menu, or using the **format** command. You can change the format by selecting the "File/Preferences" menu option (see Figure 2.4). This option will pop up the Preferences Window, and the format can be selected from the Command Window item in the preferences list.

Alternatively, a user can use the `format` command to change the preferences. The format command changes the default format according to the values given in Table 2-3. The default format can be modified to display more significant digits of data, force the display to be in scientific notation, to display data to two decimal digits, or to eliminate extra line feeds to get more data visible in the Command Window at a single time. Experiment with the commands in Table 2-3 for yourself.

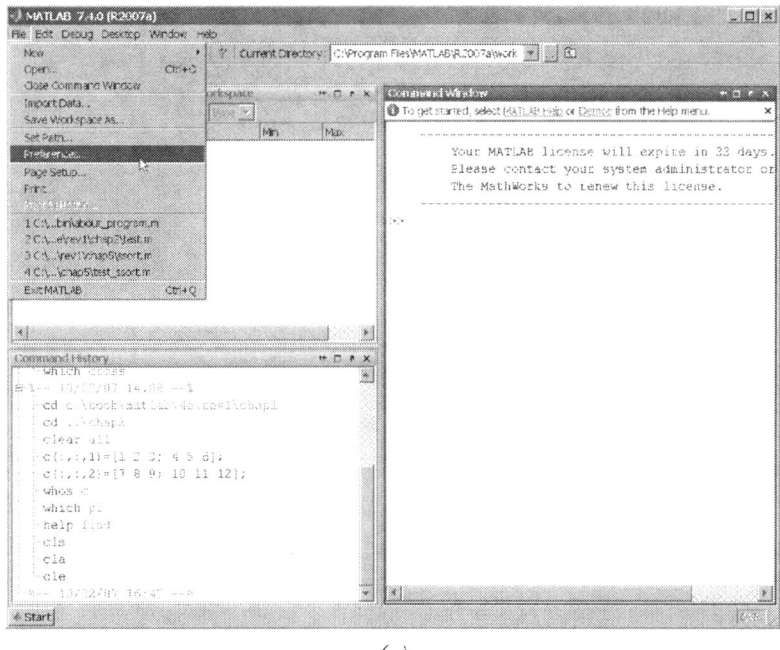

(a)

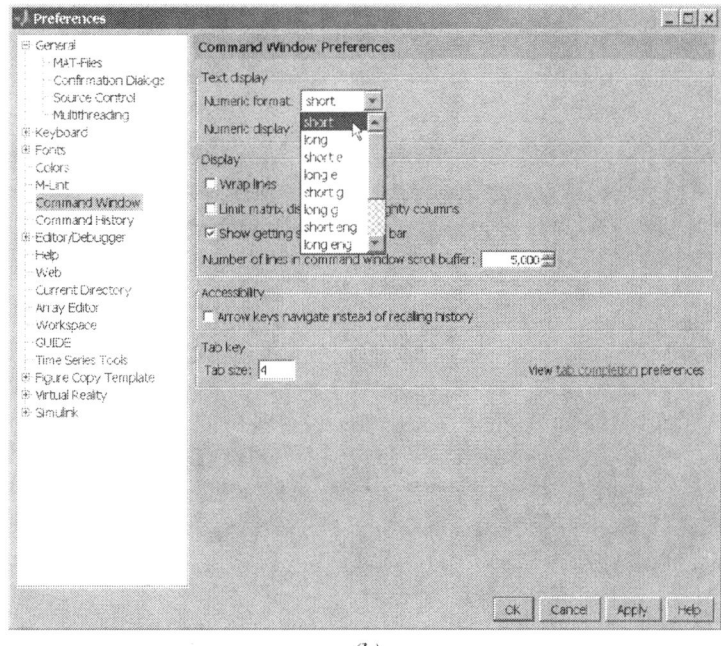

(b)

Figure 2.4 *(a)* Selecting preferences on the MATLAB menu. *(b)* Selecting the desired numeric format within the Command Window preferences.

Table 2-3 Output Display Formats

Format Command	Results	Example[1]
format short	4 digits after decimal (default format)	12.3457
format long	14 digits after decimal	12.34567890123457
format short e	5 digits plus exponent	1.2346e+001
format short g	5 total digits with or without exponent	12.346
format long e	15 digits plus exponent	1.234567890123457e+001
format long g	15 total digits with or without exponent	12.3456789012346
format bank	"dollars and cents" format	12.35
format hex	hexadecimal display of bits	4028b0fcd32f707a
format rat	approximate ratio of small integers	1000/81
format compact	suppress extra line feeds	
format loose	restore extra line feeds	
format +	only signs are printed	+

[1] The data value used for the example is 12.345678901234567 in all cases.

Which of these ways to change the data format is better? If you are working directly at the computer, it is probably easier to use the menu item. On the other hand, if you are writing programs, it is probably better to use the format command, because it can be embedded directly into a program.

2.6.2 The disp function

Another way to display data is with the disp function. The disp function accepts an array argument and displays the value of the array in the Command Window. If the array is of type char, the character string contained in the array is printed out.

This function is often combined with the functions num2str (convert a number to a string) and int2str (round a number to the nearest integer and convert it to a string) to create messages to be displayed in the Command Window. For example, the following MATLAB statements will display "The value of pi = 3.1416" in the Command Window. The first statement creates a string array containing the message, and the second statement displays the message.

```
str = ['The value of pi = ' num2str(pi)];
disp (str);
```

2.6.3 Formatted Output with the fprintf function

An even more flexible way to display data is with the fprintf function. The fprintf function displays one or more values together with related text and

Table 2-4   Common Special Characters in `fprintf` Format Strings

Format String	Results
`%d`	Display value as an integer.
`%e`	Display value in exponential format.
`%f`	Display value in floating-point format.
`%g`	Display value in either floating-point or exponential format, whichever is shorter.
`\n`	Skip to a new line.

lets the engineer control the way in which the displayed value appears. The general form of this function when it is used to print to the Command Window is

```
fprintf(format,data)
```

where `format` is a string describing the way the `data` is to be printed and data is one or more scalars or arrays to be printed. The `format` is a character string containing text to be printed along with special characters describing the format of the data. For example, the function

```
fprintf('The value of pi is %f \n',pi)
```

will print out `'The value of pi is 3.141593'` followed by a line feed. The characters `%f` are called **conversion characters**; they indicate that the a value in the data list should be printed out in floating-point format at that location in the format string. The characters `\n` are **escape characters**; they indicate that a line feed should be issued so that the following text starts on a new line. There are many types of conversion characters and escape characters that may be used in an `fprintf` function. A few of them are listed in Table 2-4, and a complete list can be found in Appendix B.

It is also possible to specify the width of the field in which a number will be displayed and the number of decimal places to display. This is done by specifying the the width and precision after the `%` sign and before the `f`. For example, the function

```
fprintf('The value of pi is %6.2f \n',pi)
```

will print out `'The value of pi is 3.14'` followed by a line feed. The conversion characters `%6.2f` indicate that the first data item in the function should be printed out in floating-point format in a field six characters wide, including two digits after the decimal point.

The `fprintf` function has one very significant limitation: *it displays only the real portion of a complex value*. This limitation can lead to misleading results when calculations produce complex answers. In those cases, it is better to use the `disp` function to display answers.

For example, the following statements calculate a complex value x and display it using both `fprintf` and `disp`:

```
x = 2 * ( 1 - 2*i )^3;
str = ['disp: x = ' num2str(x)];
```

```
disp(str);
fprintf('fprintf: x = %8.4f\n',x);
```

The results printed out by these statements are

```
disp: x = -22+4i
fprintf: x = -22.0000
```

Note that the `fprintf` function ignored the imaginary part of the answer.

💣 Programming Pitfalls

The `fprintf` function displays only the *real* part of a complex number, which can produce misleading answers when working with complex values.

2.7 Data Files

There are many ways to load and save data files in MATLAB, most of which are addressed in Appendix B. For the moment, we will consider only the **load** and **save** commands, which are the simplest ones to use.

The **save** command saves data from the current MATLAB workspace into a disk file. The most common form of this command is

```
save filename var1 var2 var3
```

where `filename` is the name of the file where the variables are saved and `var1`, `var2`, etc. are the variables to be saved in the file. By default, the file name will be given the extension "mat", and such data files are called MAT-files. If no variables are specified, then the entire contents of the workspace are saved.

MATLAB saves MAT-files in a special compact format that preserves many details, including the name and type of each variable, the size of each array, and all data values. A MAT-file created on any platform (PC, Mac, Unix, or Linux) can be read on any other platform, so using MAT-files is a good way to exchange data between computers if both computers run MATLAB. Unfortunately, the MAT-file is in a format that cannot be read by other programs. If data must be shared with other programs, the `-ascii` option should be specified, and the data values will be written to the file as ASCII character strings separated by spaces. However, the special information such as variable names and types is lost when the data is saved in ASCII format, and the resulting data file will be much larger.

For example, suppose the array x is defined as

```
x=[1.23 3.14 6.28; -5.1 7.00 0];
```

Then the command "save x.dat x -ascii" will produce a file named x.dat containing the following data:

```
1.2300000e+000    3.1400000e+000    6.2800000e+000
-5.1000000e+000   7.0000000e+000    0.0000000e+000
```

This data is in a format that can be read by spreadsheets or by programs written in other computer languages, so it makes it easy to share data between MATLAB programs and other applications.

✷ Good Programming Practice

If data must be exchanged between MATLAB and other programs, save the MATLAB data in ASCII format. If the data will be used only in MATLAB, save the data in MAT-file format.

MATLAB doesn't care what file extension is used for ASCII files. However, it is better for the user if a consistent naming convention is used, and an extension of "dat" is a common choice for ASCII files.

✷ Good Programming Practice

Save ASCII data files with a "dat" file extension to distinguish them from MAT-files, which have a "mat" file extension.

The **load** command is the opposite of the save command. It loads data from a disk file into the current MATLAB workspace. The most common form of this command is

```
load filename
```

where filename is the name of the file to be loaded. If the file is a MAT-file, then all of the variables in the file will be restored with the names and types the same as before. If a list of variables is included in the command, only those variables will be restored. If the given filename has no extent, or if the file extent is .mat, the load command will treat the file as a MAT-file.

MATLAB can load data created by other programs in comma- or space-separated ASCII format. If the given filename has any file extension other than .mat, the load command will treat the file as an ASCII file. The contents of an ASCII file will be converted into a MATLAB array having the same name as the file (without the file extension) that the data was loaded from. For example, suppose that an ASCII data file named x.dat contains the following data:

```
1.23    3.14    6.28
-5.1    7.00    0
```

Then the command "load x.dat" will create a 2 × 3 array named x in the current workspace, containing these data values.

The load statement can be forced to treat a file as a MAT-file by specifying the –mat option. For example, the statement

```
load -mat x.dat
```

would treat file x.dat as a MAT-file even though its file extent is not .mat. Similarly, the load statement can be forced to treat a file as an ASCII file by specifying the –ascii option. These options allow the user to load a file properly even if its file extent doesn't match the MATLAB conventions.

Quiz 2.3

This quiz provides a quick check to see if you have understood the concepts introduced in Sections 2.6 and 2.7. If you have trouble with the quiz, reread the sections, ask your instructor, or discuss the material with a fellow student. The answers to this quiz are found in the back of the book.

1. How would you tell MATLAB to display all real values in exponential format with 15 significant digits?

2. What do the following sets of statements do? What is the output from them?

   (a)
   ```
   radius = input('Enter circle radius:\n');
   area = pi * radius^2;
   str = ['The area is ' num2str(area)];
   disp(str);
   ```

   (b)
   ```
   value = int2str(pi);
   disp(['The value is ' value '!']);
   ```

3. What do the following sets of statements do? What is the output from them?

   ```
   value 5 123.4567e2;
   fprintf('value 5 %e\n',value);
   fprintf('value 5 %f\n',value);
   fprintf('value 5 %g\n',value);
   fprintf('value 5 %12.4f\n',value);
   ```

2.8   Scalar and Array Operations

Calculations are specified in MATLAB with an assignment statement, whose general form is

```
variable_name = expression;
```

The assignment statement calculates the value of the expression to the right of the equal sign and *assigns* that value to the variable named on the left of the equal sign. Note that the equal sign does not mean equality in the usual sense of the word. Instead, it means: *store the value of* expression *into location* variable_name. For this reason, the equal sign is called the **assignment operator**. A statement such as

```
ii = ii + 1;
```

is complete nonsense in ordinary algebra, but makes perfect sense in MATLAB. It means take the current value stored in variable ii, add one to it, and store the result back into variable ii.

2.8.1   Scalar Operations

The expression to the right of the assignment operator can be any valid combination of scalars, arrays, parentheses, and arithmetic operators. The standard arithmetic operations between two scalars are given in Table 2-5.

Parentheses may be used to group terms whenever desired. When parentheses are used, the expressions inside the parentheses are evaluated before the expressions outside the parentheses. For example, the expression 2 ^ ((8+2)/5) is evaluated as

```
2 ^ ((8+2)/5)  = 2 ^ (10/5)
               = 2 ^ 2
               = 4
```

2.8.2   Array and Matrix Operations

MATLAB supports two types of operations between arrays, known as *array operations* and *matrix operations*. **Array operations** are operations performed between arrays on an **element-by-element basis**. That is, the operation is performed on corresponding elements in the two arrays. For example, if $a = \begin{bmatrix} 1 & 2 \\ 3 & 4 \end{bmatrix}$ and $b = \begin{bmatrix} -1 & 3 \\ -2 & 1 \end{bmatrix}$, then $a + b = \begin{bmatrix} 0 & 5 \\ 1 & 5 \end{bmatrix}$. Note that for these operations to work, *the number of rows and columns in both arrays must be the same.* If not, MATLAB will generate an error message.

Table 2-5   Arithmetic Operations between Two Scalars

Operation	Algebraic Form	MATLAB Form
Addition	$a + b$	a + b
Subtraction	$a - b$	a - b
Multiplication	$a \times b$	a * b
Division	$\frac{a}{b}$	a / b
Exponentiation	a^b	a ^ b

Array operations may also occur between an array and a scalar. If the operation is performed between an array and a scalar, the value of the scalar is applied to every element of the array. For example, if $a = \begin{bmatrix} 1 & 2 \\ 3 & 4 \end{bmatrix}$, then $a + 4 = \begin{bmatrix} 5 & 6 \\ 7 & 8 \end{bmatrix}$.

In contrast, **matrix operations** follow the normal rules of linear algebra, such as matrix multiplication. In linear algebra, the product $c = a \times b$ is defined by the equation

$$c(i, j) = \sum_{k=1}^{n} a(i, k)\, b(k, j)$$

For example, if $a = \begin{bmatrix} 1 & 2 \\ 3 & 4 \end{bmatrix}$ and $b = \begin{bmatrix} -1 & 3 \\ -2 & 1 \end{bmatrix}$, then $a \times b = \begin{bmatrix} -5 & 5 \\ -11 & 13 \end{bmatrix}$.

Note that for matrix multiplication to work, *the number of columns in matrix* a *must be equal to the number of rows in matrix* b.

MATLAB uses a special symbol to distinguish array operations from matrix operations. In the cases where array operations and matrix operations have a different definition, MATLAB uses a period before the symbol to indicate an array operation (for example, .*). A list of common array and matrix operations is given in Table 2-6.

Table 2-6   Common Array and Matrix Operations

Operation	MATLAB Form	Comments
Array Addition	a + b	Array addition and matrix addition are identical.
Array Subtraction	a - b	Array subtraction and matrix subtraction are identical.
Array Multiplication	a .* b	Element-by-element multiplication of a and b. Both arrays must be the same shape, or one of them must be a scalar.
Matrix Multiplication	a * b	Matrix multiplication of a and b. The number of columns in a must equal the number of rows in b.
Array Right Division	a ./ b	Element-by-element division of a and b: a(i,j) / b(i,j). Both arrays must be the same shape, or one of them must be a scalar.
Array Left Division	a .\ b	Element-by-element division of a and b, but with b in the numerator: b(i,j) / a(i,j). Both arrays must be the same shape, or one of them must be a scalar.
Matrix Right Division	a / b	Matrix division defined by a * inv(b), where inv(b) is the inverse of matrix b.
Matrix Left Division	a \ b	Matrix division defined by inv(a) * b, where inv(a) is the inverse of matrix a.
Array Exponentiation	a .^ b	Element-by-element exponentiation of a and b: a(i,j) ^ b(i,j). Both arrays must be the same shape, or one of them must be a scalar.

Beginning users often confuse array operations and matrix operations. In some cases, substituting one for the other will produce an illegal operation, and MATLAB will report an error. In other cases, both operations are legal, and MATLAB will perform the wrong operation and come up with a wrong answer. The most common problem happens when working with square matrices. Both array multiplication and matrix multiplication are legal for two square matrices of the same size, but the resulting answers are totally different. Be careful to specify exactly what you want!

☀ Programming Pitfalls

Be careful to distinguish between array operations and matrix operations in your MATLAB code. It is especially common to confuse array multiplication with matrix multiplication.

▶

Example 2.1—Array and Matrix Operations

Assume that a, b, c, and d are defined as follows:

$$a = \begin{bmatrix} 1 & 0 \\ 2 & 1 \end{bmatrix} \qquad b = \begin{bmatrix} -1 & 2 \\ 0 & 1 \end{bmatrix}$$

$$c = \begin{bmatrix} 3 \\ 2 \end{bmatrix} \qquad d = 5$$

What is the result of each of the following expressions?

(a) a + b   *(e)* a + c
(b) a .* b   *(f)* a + d
(c) a * b   *(g)* a .* d
(d) a * c   *(h)* a * d

SOLUTION

(a) This is array or matrix addition: $a + b = \begin{bmatrix} 0 & 2 \\ 2 & 2 \end{bmatrix}$

(b) This is element-by-element array multiplication: $a * c = \begin{bmatrix} -1 & 0 \\ 0 & 1 \end{bmatrix}$

(c) This is matrix multiplication: $a * c = \begin{bmatrix} -1 & 2 \\ -2 & 5 \end{bmatrix}$

(d) This is matrix multiplication: $a * c = \begin{bmatrix} 3 \\ 8 \end{bmatrix}$

(e) This operation is illegal, since a and c have different numbers of columns.

(f) This is addition of an array to a scalar: $a + d = \begin{bmatrix} 6 & 5 \\ 7 & 6 \end{bmatrix}$

(g) This is array multiplication: $a \ .* \ d = \begin{bmatrix} 5 & 0 \\ 10 & 5 \end{bmatrix}$

(h) This is matrix multiplication: $a \ * \ d = \begin{bmatrix} 5 & 0 \\ 10 & 5 \end{bmatrix}$ ◀

The matrix left-division operation has a special significance that we must understand. A 3 × 3 set of simultaneous linear equations takes the form

$$a_{11}x_1 + a_{12}x_2 + a_{13}x_3 = b_1$$
$$a_{21}x_1 + a_{22}x_2 + a_{23}x_3 = b_2$$
$$a_{31}x_1 + a_{32}x_2 + a_{33}x_3 = b_3 \tag{2.1}$$

which can be expressed as

$$\mathbf{Ax = b} \tag{2.2}$$

where $\mathbf{A} = \begin{bmatrix} a_{11} & a_{12} & a_{13} \\ a_{21} & a_{22} & a_{23} \\ a_{31} & a_{32} & a_{33} \end{bmatrix}$, $\mathbf{b} = \begin{bmatrix} b_1 \\ b_2 \\ b_3 \end{bmatrix}$, and $\mathbf{x} = \begin{bmatrix} x_1 \\ x_2 \\ x_3 \end{bmatrix}$.

Equation (2.2) can be solved for x using linear algebra. The result is

$$\mathbf{x = A^{-1}b} \tag{2.3}$$

Since the left-division operator A\b is defined to be `inv(A) * b`, the left-division operator solves a system of simultaneous equations in a single statement!

☀ Good Programming Practice

Use the left-division operator to solve systems of simultaneous equations.

2.9 Hierarchy of Operations

Often, many arithmetic operations are combined into a single expression. For example, consider the equation for the distance traveled by an object starting from rest and subjected to a constant acceleration:

```
distance = 0.5 * accel * time ^ 2
```

Table 2-7   Hierarchy of Arithmetic Operations

Precedence	Operation
1	The contents of all parentheses are evaluated, starting from the innermost parentheses and working outward.
2	All exponentials are evaluated, working from left to right.
3	All multiplications and divisions are evaluated, working from left to right.
4	All additions and subtractions are evaluated, working from left to right.

There are two multiplications and an exponentiation in this expression. In such an expression, it is important to know the order in which the operations are evaluated. If exponentiation is evaluated before multiplication, this expression is equivalent to

```
distance = 0.5 * accel * (time ^ 2)
```

But if multiplication is evaluated before exponentiation, this expression is equivalent to

```
distance = (0.5 * accel * time) ^ 2
```

These two equations have different results, and we must be able to unambiguously distinguish between them.

To make the evaluation of expressions unambiguous, MATLAB has established a series of rules governing the hierarchy or order in which operations are evaluated within an expression. The rules generally follow the normal rules of algebra. The order in which the arithmetic operations are evaluated is given in Table 2-7.

▶
━━━

Example 2.2—Order of Operations

Variables a, b, c, and d have been initialized to the following values:
```
a = 3; b = 2; c = 5; d = 3;
```
Evaluate the following MATLAB assignment statements:

```
(a) output = a*b+c*d;
(b) output = a*(b+c)*d;
(c) output = (a*b)+(c*d);
(d) output = a^b^d;
(e) output = a^(b^d);
```

SOLUTION

    (a) Expression to evaluate:
        Fill in numbers:
        First, evaluate multiplications
        and divisions from left to right:

        Now evaluate additions:

```
output = a*b+c*d;
output = 3*2+5*3;

output = 6 +5*3;
output = 6 + 15;
output = 21
```

(b) Expression to evaluate: `output = a*(b+c)*d;`
Fill in numbers: `output = 3*(2+5)*3;`
First, evaluate parentheses: `output = 3*7*3;`
Now, evaluate multiplications
and divisions from left to right: `output = 21*3;`
     `output = 63;`

(c) Expression to evaluate: `output = (a*b)+(c*d);`
Fill in numbers: `output = (3*2)+(5*3);`
First, evaluate parentheses: `output = 6 + 15;`
Now evaluate additions: `output = 21`

(d) Expression to evaluate: `output = a^b^d;`
Fill in numbers: `output = 3^2^3;`
Evaluate exponentials from
left to right: `output = 9^3;`
     `output = 729;`

(e) Expression to evaluate: `output = a^(b^d);`
Fill in numbers: `output = 3^(2^3);`
First, evaluate parentheses: `output = 3^8;`
Now, evaluate exponential: `output = 6561;` ◄

As we saw in the preceding example, the order in which operations are performed has a major effect on the final result of an algebraic expression.

It is important that every expression in a program be made as clear as possible. Any program of value must not only be written but also be maintained and modified when necessary. You should always ask yourself: "Will I easily understand this expression if I come back to it in six months? Can another engineer look at my code and easily understand what I am doing?" If there is any doubt in your mind, use extra parentheses in the expression to make it as clear as possible.

✳ Good Programming Practice

Use parentheses as necessary to make your equations clear and easy to understand.

If parentheses are used within an expression, then the parentheses must be balanced. That is, there must be an equal number of open parentheses and close parentheses within the expression. It is an error to have more of one type than the other. Errors of this sort are usually typographical, and they are caught by the MATLAB interpreter when the command is executed. For example, the expression

```
(2 + 4) / 2)
```

produces an error when the expression is executed.

Quiz 2.4

This quiz provides a quick check to see if you have understood the concepts introduced in Sections 2.8 and 2.9. If you have trouble with the quiz, reread the sections, ask your instructor, or discuss the material with a fellow student. The answers to this quiz are found in the back of the book.

1. Assume that a, b, c, and d are defined as follows, and calculate the results of the following operations if they are legal. If an operation is illegal, explain why it is illegal.

$$a = \begin{bmatrix} 2 & 1 \\ -1 & 2 \end{bmatrix} \qquad\qquad b = \begin{bmatrix} 0 & -1 \\ 3 & 1 \end{bmatrix}$$

$$c = \begin{bmatrix} 1 \\ 2 \end{bmatrix} \qquad\qquad d = -3$$

(a) `result = a .* c;`
(b) `result = a * [c c];`
(c) `result = a .* [c c];`
(d) `result = a + b * c;`
(e) `result = a + b .* c;`

2. Solve for x in the equation $Ax = B$,

where $A = \begin{bmatrix} 1 & 2 & 1 \\ 2 & 3 & 2 \\ -1 & 0 & 1 \end{bmatrix}$ and $B = \begin{bmatrix} 1 \\ 1 \\ 0 \end{bmatrix}$.

2.10   Built-In MATLAB Functions

In mathematics, a **function** is an expression that accepts one or more input values and calculates a single result from them. Scientific and technical calculations usually require functions that are more complex than the simple addition, subtraction, multiplication, division, and exponentiation operations that we have discussed so far. Some of these functions are very common and are used in many different technical disciplines. Others are rarer and specific to a single problem or a small number of problems. Examples of very common functions are the trigonometric functions, logarithms, and square roots. Examples of rarer functions include the hyperbolic functions, Bessel functions, and so forth. One of MATLAB's greatest strengths is that it comes with an incredible variety of built-in functions ready for use.

2.10.1   Optional Results

Unlike mathematical functions, MATLAB functions can return *more than one result* to the calling program. The function max is an example of such a function. This function normally returns the maximum value of an input vector, but it can also return a second argument containing the location in the input vector where the maximum value was found. For example, the statement

```
maxval = max ([1 -5 6 -3])
```

returns the result maxval = 6. However, if two variables are provided to store results in, the function returns *both* the maximum value *and* the location of the maximum value.

```
[maxval, index] = max ([1 -5 6 -3])
```

produces the results maxval = 6 and index = 3.

2.10.2   Using MATLAB Functions with Array Inputs

Many MATLAB functions are defined for one or more scalar inputs and produce a scalar output. For example, the statement y = sin(x) calculates the sine of x and stores the result in y. If these functions receive an array of input values, then they will calculate an array of output values on an element-by-element basis. For example, if x = [0 pi/2 pi 3*pi/2 2*pi], then the statement

```
y = sin(x)
```

will produce the result y = [0 1 0 -1 0].

2.10.3   Common MATLAB Functions

A few of the most common and useful MATLAB functions are shown in Table 2-8. These functions will be used in many examples and homework problems. If you need to locate a specific function not on this list, you can search for the function alphabetically or by subject using the MATLAB Help Browser.

Note that unlike most computer languages, many MATLAB functions work correctly for both real and complex inputs. MATLAB functions automatically calculate the correct answer, even if the result is imaginary or complex. For example, the function sqrt(-2) will produce a runtime error in languages such as C++, Java, or Fortran. In contrast, MATLAB correctly calculates the imaginary answer:

```
» sqrt(-2)
ans =
     0 + 1.4142i
```

Table 2-8   Common MATLAB Functions

Function	Description
Mathematical functions	
abs(x)	Calculates $|x|$.
acos(x)	Calculates $\cos^{-1}x$.
angle(x)	Returns the phase angle of the complex value x, in radians.
asin(x)	Calculates $\sin^{-1}x$.
atan(x)	Calculates $\tan^{-1}x$.
atan2(y,x)	Calculates $\tan^{-1}\frac{y}{x}$ over all four quadrants of the circle (results in *radians* in the range $-\pi \leq \tan^{-1}\frac{y}{x} \leq \pi$).
cos(x)	Calculates $\cos x$, with x in radians.
exp(x)	Calculates e^x.
log(x)	Calculates the natural logarithm $\log_e x$.
[value,index] = max(x)	Returns the maximum value in vector x, and optionally the location of that value.
[value,index] = min(x)	Returns the minimum value in vector x, and optionally the location of that value.
mod(x,y)	Remainder or modulo function.
sin(x)	Calculates $\sin x$, with x in radians.
sqrt(x)	Calculates the square root of x.
tan(x)	Calculates $\tan x$, with x in radians.
Rounding functions	
ceil(x)	Rounds x to the nearest integer towards positive infinity: ceil(3.1) = 4 and ceil(-3.1) = -3.
fix(x)	Rounds x to the nearest integer towards zero: fix(3.1) = 3 and fix(-3.1) = -3.
floor(x)	Rounds x to the nearest integer towards minus infinity: floor(3.1) = 3 and floor(-3.1) = -4.
round(x)	Rounds x to the nearest integer.
String conversion functions	
char(x)	Converts a matrix of numbers into a character string. For ASCII characters, the matrix should contain numbers ≤ 127.
double(x)	Converts a character string into a matrix of numbers.
int2str(x)	Converts x into an integer character string.
num2str(x)	Converts x into a character string.
str2num(s)	Converts character string s into a numeric array.

2.11   Introduction to Plotting

MATLAB's extensive, device-independent plotting capabilities are among its most powerful features. They make it very easy to plot any data at any time. To plot a data set, just create two vectors containing the x and y values to be plotted and use the `plot` function.

For example, suppose that we wish to plot the function $y = x^2 - 10x + 15$ for values of x between 0 and 10. It takes only three statements to create this plot. The first statement creates a vector of x values between 0 and 10 using the colon operator. The second statement calculates the y values from the equation (note that we are using array operators here so that this equation is applied to each x value on an element-by-element basis). Finally, the third statement creates the plot.

```
x = 0:1:10;
y = x.^2 - 10.*x + 15;
plot(x,y);
```

When the `plot` function is executed, MATLAB opens a Figure Window and displays the plot in that window. The plot produced by these statements is shown in Figure 2.5.

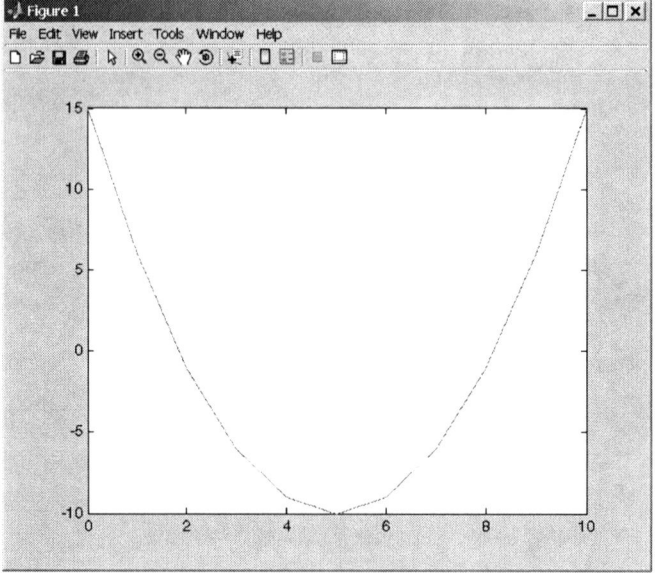

Figure 2.5   Plot of $y = x^2 - 10x + 15$ from 0 to 10.

2.11.1   Using Simple *xy* Plots

As we saw in the previous section, plotting is *very* easy in MATLAB. Any pair of vectors can be plotted versus each other as long as both vectors have the same length. However, the result is not a finished product, since there are no titles, axis labels, or grid lines on the plot.

Titles and axis labels can be added to a plot with the `title`, `xlabel`, and `ylabel` functions. Each function is called with a string containing the title or label to be applied to the plot. Grid lines can be added or removed from the plot with the `grid` command: `grid on` turns on grid lines, and `grid off` turns off grid lines. For example, the following statements generate a plot of the function $y = x^2 - 10x + 15$ with titles, labels, and gridlines. The resulting plot is shown in Figure 2.6.

```
x = 0:1:10;
y = x.^2 - 10.*x + 15;
plot(x,y);
title ('Plot of y = x.^2 - 10.*x + 15');
xlabel ('x');
ylabel ('y');
grid on;
```

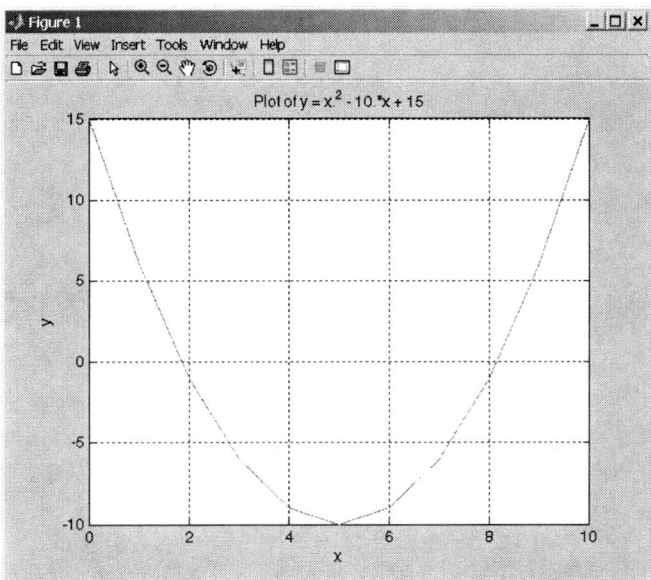

Figure 2.6   Plot of $y = x^2 - 10x + 15$ with a title, axis labels, and gridlines.

2.11.2   Printing a Plot

Once created, a plot may be printed on a printer with the `print` command or by clicking on the "print" icon in the Figure Window or by selecting the "File/Print" menu option in the Figure Window.

The `print` command is especially useful because it can be included in a MATLAB program, allowing the program to automatically print graphical images. The form of the `print` command is

```
print <options> <filename>
```

If no filename is included, this command prints a copy of the current figure on the system printer. If a filename is specified, the command prints a copy of the current figure to the specified file.

2.11.3   Exporting a Plot as a Graphical Image

A plot also can be saved as a graphical image using the "File/Save As" menu option on the Figure Window. In this case, the user selects the filename and the type of image to create from a standard dialog box (see Figure 2.7). MATLAB supports many image types, but perhaps the most common are the JPEG (`*.jpg`) and Portable Network Graphics (`*.png`) formats. JPEG files are commonly used in many web applications, but JPEG uses a "lossy" compression algorithm, which means that the compressed images are lower in quality than the original image. In contrast, the PNG format is lossless—the quality of a compressed image is the same as the quality of the original image. However, PNG files are usually larger than the corresponding JPEG files.

Graphical images saved in JPEG, PNG, or other formats can be imported into Word or other programs for use in reports or other documents.

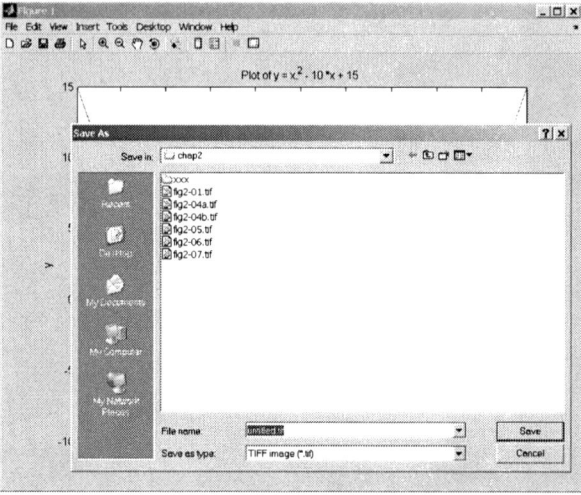

Figure 2.7   Exporting a plot as an image file using the "File/Save As" menu item.

Table 2-9 `print` **Options to Create Graphics Files**

Option	Description
-deps	Creates a monochrome encapsulated postscript image.
-depsc	Creates a color encapsulated postscript image.
-djpeg	Creates a JPEG image.
-dpng	Creates a Portable Network Graphic color image.
-dtiff	Creates a compressed TIFF image.

Images can be saved within an executing MATLAB program using the `print` command with appropriate options and a file name.

```
print <options> <filename>
```

There are many different options that specify the format of the output sent to a file. Two important options are −djpeg and −dpng, which produce JPEG and PNG images, respectively. For example, the following command will create a PNG image of the current figure and store it in a file called my_image.png:

```
print -dpng my_image.png
```

Other options allow image files to be created in other formats. Some of the most important image file formats are given in Table 2-9.

2.11.4 Saving a Plot in a Figure File

A MATLAB figure also can be saved as a MATLAB figure file (*.fig) using the "File/Save As" menu option on the Figure Window and selecting the "MATLAB Figure (*.fig)" format. A figure file is a special format that contains all of the information in the original figure. A figure file can be loaded back into MATLAB and modified at a later time using the "File/Open" menu option, if desired. Unlike the other formats, this one can be reused by MATLAB after it has been saved. However, it cannot be imported into word processors. As a result, many users save figures both as figure files (for reuse) and as JPEG or PNG files (for reports).

2.11.5 Multiple Plots

It is possible to plot multiple functions on the same graph by simply including more than one set of *(x,y)* values in the `plot` function. For example, suppose that we wanted to plot the function $f(x) = \sin 2x$ and its derivative on the same plot. The derivative of $f(x) = \sin 2x$ is

$$f'(x) = \frac{d}{dx}\sin 2x = 2 \cos 2x \tag{2.4}$$

To plot both functions on the same axes, we must generate a set of *x* values and the corresponding *y* values for each function. Then to plot the functions, we would simply list both sets of *(x, y)* values in the plot function as follows.

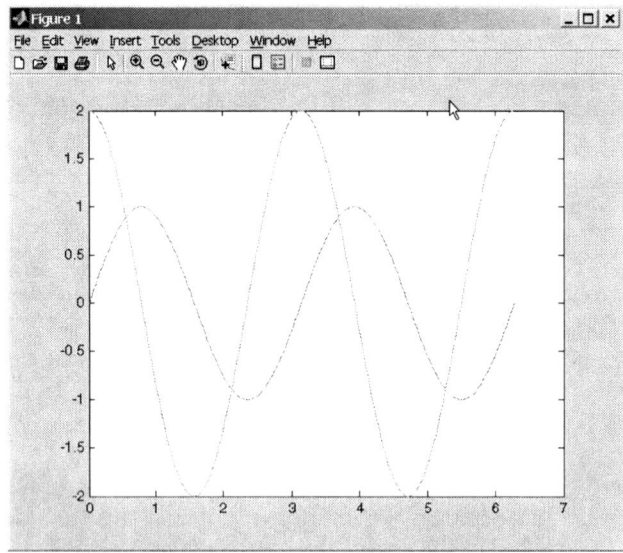

Figure 2.8 Plot of $f(x) = \sin 2x$ and $f'(x) = 2\cos 2x$ on the same axes.

```
x = 0:pi/100:2*pi;
y1 = sin(2*x);
y2 = 2*cos(2*x);
plot(x,y1,x,y2);
```

The resulting plot is shown in Figure 2.8.

2.11.6 Line Color, Line Style, Marker Style, and Legends

MATLAB allows an engineer to select the color of a line to be plotted, the style of the line to be plotted, and the type of marker to be used for data points on the line. These traits may be selected using an attribute character string after the x and y vectors in the plot function.

The attribute character string can have up to three characters, with the first character specifying the color of the line, the second character specifying the style of the marker, and the last character specifying the style of the line. The characters for various colors, markers, and line styles are shown in Table 2-10.

The attribute characters may be mixed in any combination, and more than one attribute string may be specified if more than one pair of *(x, y)* vectors is included in a single `plot` function call. For example, the following statements will plot the function $y = x^2 - 10x + 15$ with a dashed red line and will include the actual data points as blue circles (see Figure 2.9).

```
x = 0:1:10;
y = x.^2 - 10.*x + 15;
plot(x,y,'r--',x,y,'bo');
```

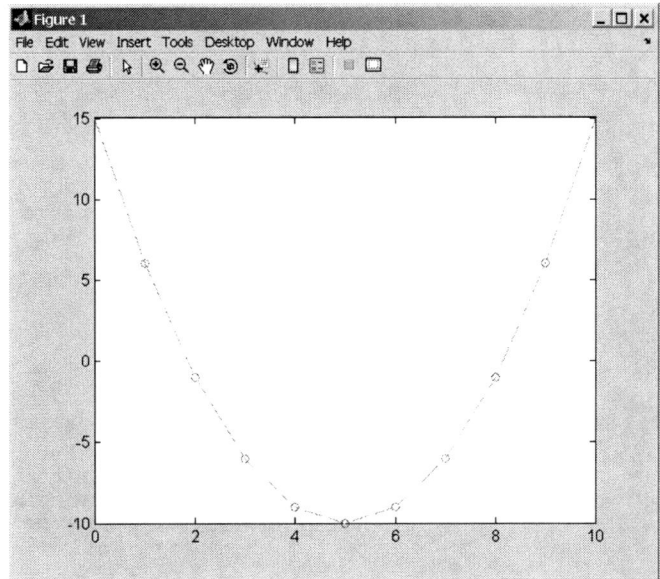

Figure 2.9   Plot of the function $y = x^2 - 10x + 15$ with a dashed red line, showing the actual data points as blue circles.

Table 2-10   Table of Plot Colors, Marker Styles, and Line Styles

Color		Marker Style		Line Style	
y	yellow	.	point	–	solid
m	magenta	o	circle	:	dotted
c	cyan	x	x-mark	–.	dash-dot
r	red	+	plus	–	dashed
g	green	*	star	<none>	no lines
b	blue	s	square		
w	white	d	diamond		
k	black	v	triangle (down)		
		^	triangle (up)		
		<	triangle (left)		
		>	triangle (right)		
		p	pentagram		
		h	hexagram		
		<none>	no marker		

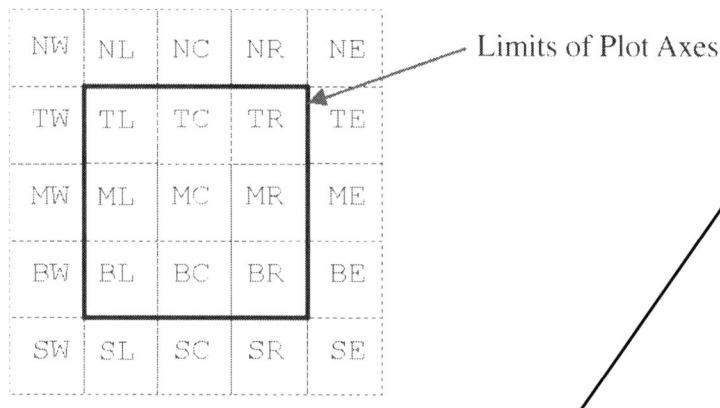

Figure 2.10 Possible locations for a plot legend.

Table 2-11   Values of pos in the legend Command

Value	Legend Location
'NW'	Above and to the left
'NL'	Above top-left corner
'NC'	Above center of top edge
'NR'	Above top-right corner
'NE'	Above and to right
'TW'	At top and to left
'TL'	Top-left corner
'TC'	At top center
'TR'	Top-right corner
'TE'	At top and to right
'MW'	At middle and to left
'ML'	Middle-left edge
'MC'	Middle and center
'MR'	Middle-right edge
'ME'	At middle and to right
'BW'	At bottom and to left
'BL'	Bottom-left corner
'BC'	At bottom center
'BR'	Bottom-right corner
'BE'	At bottom and to right
'SW'	Below and to left
'SL'	Below bottom-left corner
'SC'	Below center of bottom edge
'SR'	Below bottom-right corner
'SE'	Below and to right

Legends may be created with the `legend` function. The basic form of this function is

```
legend('string1','string2', . . ., pos)
```

where `string1`, `string2`, etc. are the labels associated with the lines plotted and `pos` is an string specifying where to place the legend. The possible values for `pos` are given in Table 2-11, and are shown graphically in Figure 2.10.[2]

The command `legend off` will remove an existing legend.

An example of a complete plot is shown in Figure 2.11, and the statements to produce that plot are shown below. They plot the function $f(x) = \sin 2x$ and its derivative $f'(x) = 2 \cos 2x$ on the same axes using two `plot` commands with a solid black line for $f(x)$ and a dashed red line for its derivative. The plot includes a title, axis labels, a legend in the top-left corner of the plot, and grid lines.

```
x = 0:pi/100:2*pi;
y1 = sin(2*x);
y2 = 2*cos(2*x);
plot(x,y1,'k-',x,y2,'b--');
title ('Plot of f(x) = sin(2x) and its derivative');
xlabel ('x');
ylabel ('y');
legend ('f(x)','d/dx f(x)','tl')
grid on;
```

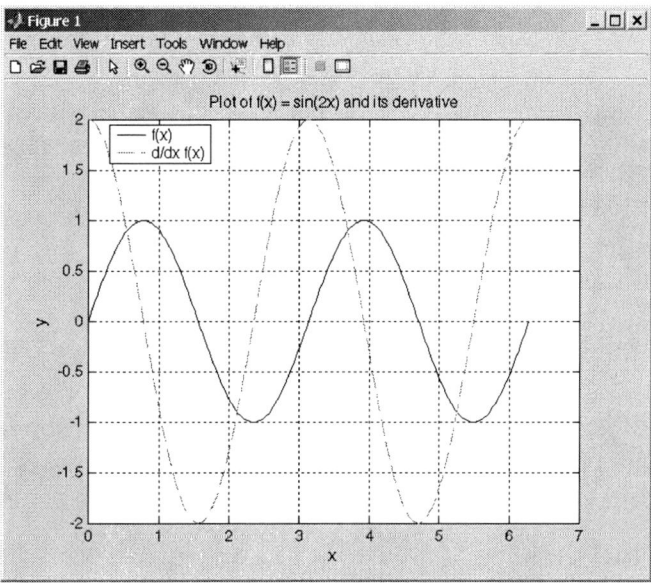

Figure 2.11 A complete plot with title, axis labels, legend, grid, and multiple line styles.

---

[2]Before MATLAB 7.0, the `pos` parameter took a number in the range 0 to 4 to specify the location of a legend. This usage is now obsolete, but it is still supported for backwards compatibility.

2.12   Examples

The following examples illustrate problem-solving with MATLAB.

▶
━━

Example 2.3—Temperature Conversion

Design a MATLAB program that reads an input temperature in degrees Fahrenheit, converts it to an absolute temperature in kelvin, and writes out the result.

SOLUTION   The relationship between temperature in degrees Fahrenheit (°F) and temperature in kelvin (K) can be found in any physics textbook. It is

$$T_K = \left[\frac{5}{9}(T_F - 32.0)\right] = 273.15 \tag{2.5}$$

The physics books also give us sample values on both temperature scales, which we can use to check the operation of our program. Two such values are

The boiling point of water	212° F	373.15 K
The sublimation point of dry ice	−110° F	194.26 K

Our program must perform the following steps:

1. Prompt the user to enter an input temperature in °F.
2. Read the input temperature.
3. Calculate the temperature in kelvin from Equation (2.5).
4. Write out the result, and stop.

We will use function input to get the temperature in degrees Fahrenheit and function fprintf to print the answer. The resulting program is shown here.

```
% Script file: temp_conversion
%
% Purpose:
%   To convert an input temperature from degrees Fahrenheit to
%   an output temperature in kelvin.
%
% Record of revisions:
%   Date            Engineer        Description of change
%   ====            ========        =====================
%   01/03/10    S. J. Chapman    Original code
%
% Define variables:
%   temp_f   -- Temperature in degrees Fahrenheit
%   temp_k   -- Temperature in kelvin

% Prompt the user for the input temperature.
temp_f = input('Enter the temperature in degrees Fahrenheit:');
```

```
% Convert to kelvin.
temp_k = (5/9) * (temp_f - 32) + 273.15;

% Write out the result.
fprintf('%6.2f degrees Fahrenheit = %6.2f kelvin.\n', ... temp_f,temp_k);
```

To test the completed program, we will run it with the known input values given previously. Note that user inputs appear in boldface.

```
» temp_conversion
Enter the temperature in degrees Fahrenheit: 212
212.00 degrees Fahrenheit = 373.15 kelvin.
» temp_conversion
Enter the temperature in degrees Fahrenheit: -110
-110.00 degrees Fahrenheit = 194.26 kelvin.
```

The results of the program match the values from the physics book.   ◄

In the foregoing program, we echoed the input values and printed the output values together with their units. The results of this program make sense only if the units (degrees Fahrenheit and kelvin) are included together with their values. As a general rule, the units associated with any input value should always be printed along with the prompt that requests the value, and the units associated with any output value should always be printed along with that value.

☀ Good Programming Practice

Always include the appropriate units with any values that you read or write in a program.

The foregoing program exhibits many of the good programming practices that we have described in this chapter. It includes a data dictionary defining the meanings of all of the variables in the program. It also uses descriptive variable names, and appropriate units are attached to all printed values.

►
Example 2.4—Electrical Engineering: Maximum Power Transfer to a Load

Figure 2.12 shows a voltage source $V = 120$ V with an internal resistance R_S of 50 Ω supplying a load of resistance R_L. Find the value of load resistance R_L that will result in the maximum possible power being supplied by the source to the load. How much power will be supplied in this case? Also, plot the power supplied to the load as a function of the load resistance R_L.

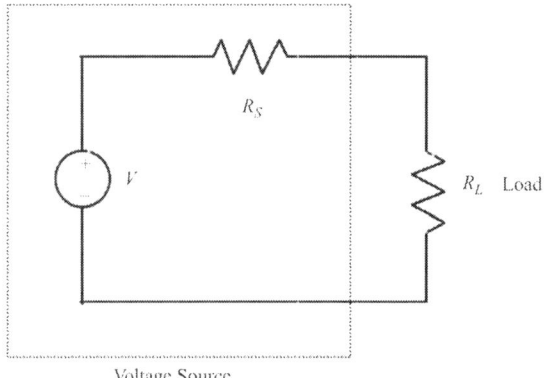

Voltage Source

Figure 2.12 A voltage source with a voltage V and an internal resistance R_S supplying a load of resistance R_L.

SOLUTION   In this program, we need to vary the load resistance R_L and compute the power supplied to the load at each value of R_L. The power supplied to the load resistance is given by the equation

$$P_L = I^2 R_L \qquad (2.6)$$

where I is the current supplied to the load. The current supplied to the load can be calculated by Ohm's law:

$$I = \frac{V}{R_{\text{TOT}}} = \frac{V}{R_S + R_L} \qquad (2.7)$$

The program must perform the following steps:

1. Create an array of possible values for the load resistance R_L. The array will vary R_L from 1 Ω to 100 Ω in 1 Ω steps.
2. Calculate the current for each value of R_L.
3. Calculate the power supplied to the load for each value of R_L.
4. Plot the power supplied to the load for each value of R_L, and determine the value of load resistance resulting in the maximum power.

The final MATLAB program is

```
% Script file: calc_power.m
%
% Purpose:
%   To calculate and plot the power supplied to a load
%   as a function of the load resistance.
%
% Record of revisions:
%     Date              Engineer           Description of change
%     ====              ========           =================
%   01/03/10         S. J. Chapman         Original code
%
```

```
% Define variables:
%   amps   -- Current flow to load (amps)
%   pl     -- Power supplied to load (watts)
%   rl     -- Resistance of the load (ohms)
%   rs     -- Internal resistance of the power source (ohms)
%   volts -- Voltage of the power source (volts)

% Set the values of source voltage and internal resistance
volts = 120;
rs = 50;

% Create an array of load resistances
rl = 1:1:100;

% Calculate the current flow for each resistance
amps = volts ./ ( rs + rl );

% Calculate the power supplied to the load
pl = (amps .^ 2) .* rl;

% Plot the power versus load resistance
plot(rl,pl);
title('Plot of power versus load resistance');
xlabel('Load resistance (ohms)');
ylabel('Power (watts)');
grid on;
```

When this program is executed, the resulting plot is shown in Figure 2.13. From this plot, we can see that the maximum power is supplied to the load when the load's resistance is 50 Ω. The power supplied to the load at this resistance is 72 watts.

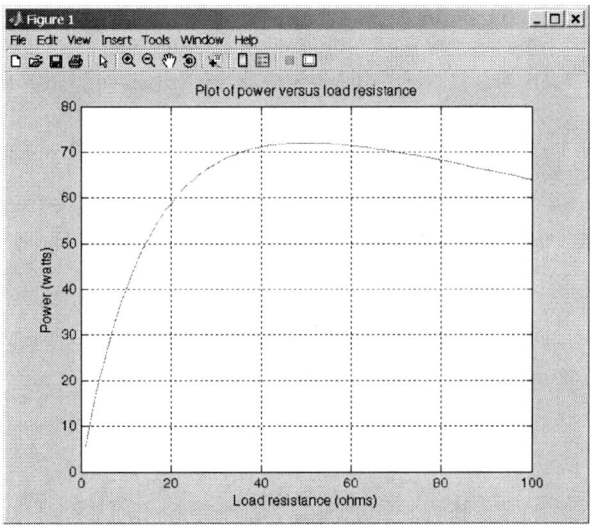

Figure 2.13   Plot of power supplied to load versus load resistance.

Note the use of the array operators . *, . ^, and . / in the previous program. These operators cause the arrays amps and pl to be calculated on an element-by-element basis.

▶

Example 2.5—Carbon 14 Dating

A radioactive isotope of an element is a form of the element which is not stable. Instead, it spontaneously decays into another element over a period of time. Radioactive decay is an exponential process. If Q_0 is the initial quantity of a radioactive substance at time $t = 0$, the amount of that substance that will be present at any time t in the future is given by

$$Q(t) = Q_0 e^{-\lambda t} \tag{2.8}$$

where λ is the radioactive decay constant.

Because radioactive decay occurs at a known rate, it can be used as a clock to measure the time since the decay started. If we know the initial amount of the radioactive material Q_0 present in a sample and the amount of the material Q left at the current time, we can solve for t in Equation (2.8) to determine how long the decay has been going on. The resulting equation is

$$t_{decay} = -\frac{1}{\lambda} \log_e \frac{Q}{Q_0} \tag{2.9}$$

Equation (2.9) has practical applications in many areas of science. For example, archaeologists use a radioactive clock based on carbon 14 to determine the time that has passed since a once living thing died. Carbon 14 is continually taken into the body while a plant or animal is living, so the amount of it present in the body at the time of death is assumed to be known. The decay constant λ of carbon 14 is well known to be 0.00012097/year, so if the amount of carbon 14 remaining now can be accurately measured, Equation (2.9) can be used to determine how long ago the living thing died. The amount of carbon 14 remaining as a function of time is shown in Figure 2.14.

Write a program that reads the percentage of carbon 14 remaining in a sample, calculates the age of the sample from it, and prints out the result with proper units.

SOLUTION   Our program must perform the following steps:

1. Prompt the user to enter the percentage of carbon 14 remaining in the sample.

2. Read in the percentage.

3. Convert the percentage into the fraction $\frac{Q}{Q_0}$.

4. Calculate the age of the sample in years using Equation (2.9).

5. Write out the result, and stop.

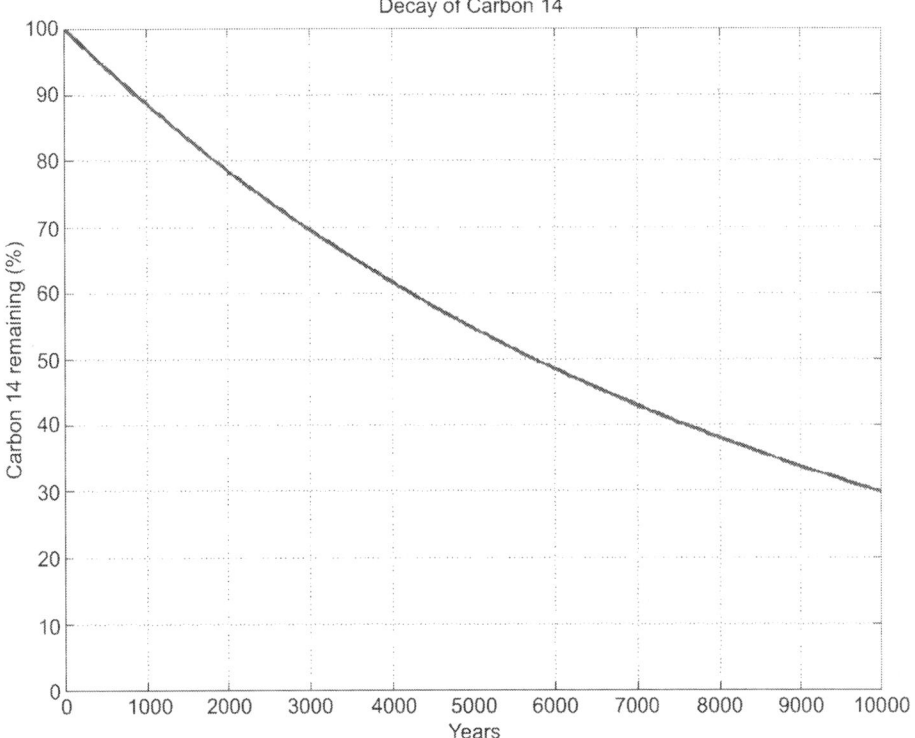

Figure 2.14 The radioactive decay of carbon 14 as a function of time. Notice that 50 percent of the original carbon 14 is left after about 5730 years have elapsed.

The resulting code is as follows:

```
% Script file: c14_date.m
%
% Purpose:
%   To calculate the age of an organic sample from the percentage
%   of the original carbon 14 remaining in the sample.
%
% Record of revisions:
%     Date              Engineer              Description of change
%     ====              ========              =====================
%   01/05/10          S. J. Chapman           Original code
%
% Define variables:
%   age         -- The age of the sample in years
%   lambda      -- The radioactive decay constant for carbon-14,
%                  in units of 1/years.
```

```
%  percent  --  The percentage of carbon 14 remaining
%               at the time of the measurement
%  ratio    --  The ratio of the carbon 14 remaining at
%               the time of the measurement to the
%               original amount of carbon 14.

% Set decay constant for carbon-14
lambda = 0.00012097;

% Prompt the user for the percentage of C-14 remaining.
percent = input('Enter the percentage of carbon 14 remaining:\n');

% Perform calculations
ratio = percent / 100;                   % Convert to fractional ratio
age = (-1.0 / lambda) * log(ratio); % Get age in years

% Tell the user about the age of the sample.
string = ['The age of the sample is' num2str(age) ' years.'];
disp(string);
```

To test the completed program, we will calculate the time it takes for half of the carbon 14 to disappear. This time is known as the *half-life* of carbon 14.

```
» c14_date
Enter the percentage of carbon 14 remaining:
50
The age of the sample is 5729.9097 years.
```

The *CRC Handbook of Chemistry and Physics* states that the half-life of carbon 14 is 5730 years, so output of the program agrees with the reference book.

◀

2.13   MATLAB Applications: Vector Mathematics

A **vector** is a mathematical quantity that has both a magnitude and a direction. This stands in contrast to a **scalar**, which is a quantity that has a magnitude only. We see examples of by vectors and scalars all the time in everyday life. The velocity of a car is an example of a vector (it has both a speed and a direction), while the temperature in a room is a scalar (it has a magnitude only). Many physical phenomena are represented by vectors, such as force, velocity, and displacement.

In a two-dimensional Cartesian coordinate system, there are two axes, usually labeled x and y. The location of any point on the plane can be represented by a displacement along the x axis and a displacement along the y axis (see Figure 2.15*(a)*). In this coordinate system, the line from one point P_1 to another point P_2 is a vector consisting of the difference between the x-positions of the two points and the difference between the y-positions of the two points.

$$\mathbf{v} = (\Delta x, \Delta y) \tag{2.10}$$

or

$$\mathbf{v} = \Delta x\,\hat{\mathbf{i}} + \Delta y\,\hat{\mathbf{j}} \tag{2.11}$$

where $\hat{\mathbf{i}}$ and $\hat{\mathbf{j}}$ are the unit vectors in the x and y directions. The magnitude of the vector $\mathbf{v}$ can be calculated from the Pythagorean theorem.

$$v = \sqrt{(\Delta x)^2 + (\Delta y)^2} \tag{2.12}$$

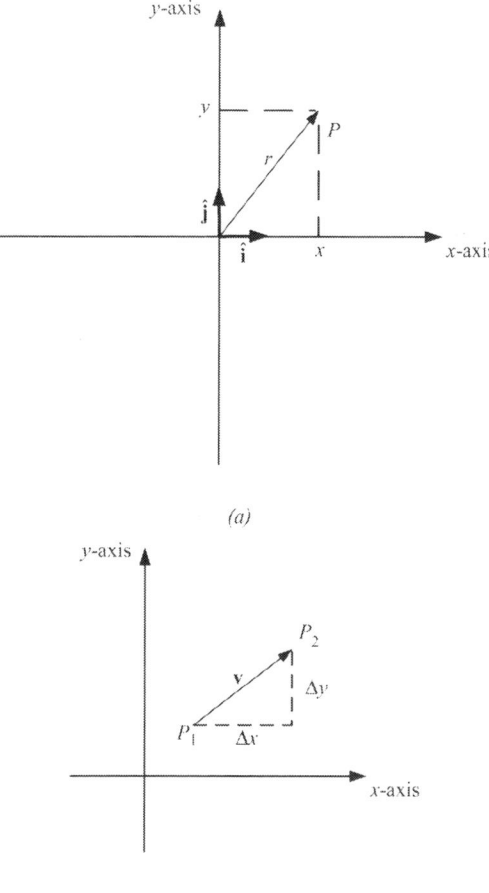

(a)

(b)

Figure 2.15 *(a)* Any point in a two-dimensional Cartesian coordinate system can be represented by a displacement along the x axis and a displacement along the y axis. *(b)* A vector $\mathbf{v}$ represents the difference in location between two points in the plane, so it is characterised by a Δx along the x axis and a Δy along the y axis.

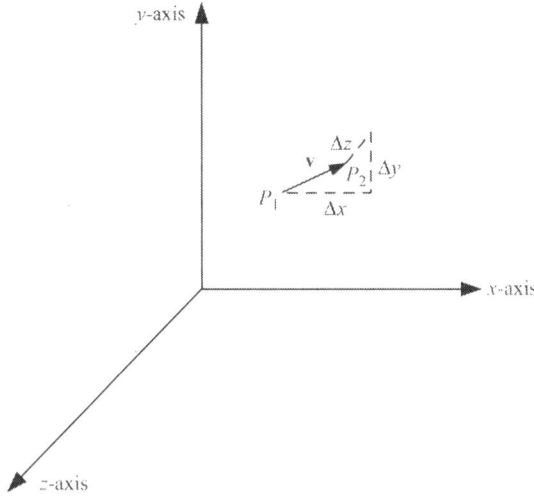

Figure 2.16 A three-dimensional vector $\mathbf{v}$ represents the difference in location between two points in the three-dimensional space, so it is characterised by a Δx along the x axis, a Δy along the y axis, and a Δz along the z axis.

In a three-dimensional coordinate system, there are three axes, usually labeled x, y, and z. The location of any point on the plane can be represented by a displacement along the x axis, a displacement along the y axis, and a displacement along the z axis. In this coordinate system, the line from one point P_1 to another point P_2 is a vector consisting of the difference between the x-positions of the two points, the difference between the y-positions of the two points, and the difference between the z-positions of the two points.

$$\mathbf{v} = (\Delta x, \Delta y, \Delta z) \tag{2.13}$$

or

$$\mathbf{v} = \Delta x\,\hat{\mathbf{i}} + \Delta y\,\hat{\mathbf{j}} + \Delta z\,\hat{\mathbf{k}} \tag{2.14}$$

where $\hat{\mathbf{i}}$, $\hat{\mathbf{j}}$, and $\hat{\mathbf{k}}$ are the unit vectors in the x, y, and z directions (see Figure 2.16). The magnitude of the vector $\mathbf{v}$ can be calculated from a generalization of the Pythagorean theorem.

$$v = \sqrt{(\Delta x)^2 + (\Delta y)^2 + (\Delta z)^2} \tag{2.15}$$

2.13.1 Vector Addition and Subtraction

To add two vectors, simply add the components of the vectors separately. To subtract two vectors, simply subtract the components of the vectors separately. For example, if vector $\mathbf{v}_1 = 3\,\hat{\mathbf{i}} + 4\,\hat{\mathbf{j}} + 5\,\hat{\mathbf{k}}$ and $\mathbf{v}_2 = -4\,\hat{\mathbf{i}} + 3\,\hat{\mathbf{j}} + 2\,\hat{\mathbf{k}}$, then the sum of the vectors $\mathbf{v}_1 + \mathbf{v}_2 = \hat{\mathbf{i}} + 7\,\hat{\mathbf{j}} + 7\,\hat{\mathbf{k}}$, and the difference of the vectors $\mathbf{v}_1 - \mathbf{v}_2 = 7\,\hat{\mathbf{i}} + \hat{\mathbf{j}} + 3\,\hat{\mathbf{k}}$.

2.13.2   Vector Multiplication

Vectors can be multiplied in two different ways, known as the **dot product** and the **cross product**.

The dot product is indicated by a dot ($\cdot$) between two vectors. The dot product of two vectors is a scalar value that is calculated by multiplying the corresponding x, y, and z components together and summing the products. If $\mathbf{v}_1 = x_1\,\hat{\mathbf{i}} + y_1\,\hat{\mathbf{j}} + z_1\,\hat{\mathbf{k}}$ and $\mathbf{v}_2 = x_2\,\hat{\mathbf{i}} + y_2\,\hat{\mathbf{j}} + z_2\,\hat{\mathbf{k}}$, then the dot product is

$$\mathbf{v}_1 \cdot \mathbf{v}_2 = x_1 x_2 + y_1 y_2 + z_1 z_2 \tag{2.16}$$

This operation is performed in MATLAB by the function dot, as shown here.

```
» a = [1 3 -5];
» b = [-2 1 -1];
» dot(a,b)
ans =
      6
```

The cross product is indicated by a cross ($\times$) between two vectors. The cross product of two vectors is a vector value that is calculated from the definition given in Equation (2.17). If $\mathbf{v}_1 = x_1\,\hat{\mathbf{i}} + y_1\,\hat{\mathbf{j}} + z_1\,\hat{\mathbf{k}}$ and $\mathbf{v}_2 = x_2\,\hat{\mathbf{i}} + y_2\,\hat{\mathbf{j}} + z_2\,\hat{\mathbf{k}}$, then the cross product is

$$\mathbf{v}_1 \times \mathbf{v}_2 = (y_1 z_2 - y_2 z_1)\,\hat{\mathbf{i}} + (z_1 x_2 - z_2 x_1)\,\hat{\mathbf{j}} + (x_1 y_2 - x_2 y_1)\hat{\mathbf{k}} \tag{2.17}$$

This operation is performed in MATLAB by the function cross, as shown here.

```
» a = [1 3 -5];
» b = [-2 1 -1];
» cross(a,b)
ans =
      2   11   7
```

All of these vector operations occur regularly in engineering problems, as we will see in the following examples.

▶

Example 2.6—Net Force and Acceleration on an Object

According to Newton's law, the net force on an object is equal to its mass times it acceleration.

$$\mathbf{F}_{\text{net}} = m\mathbf{a} \tag{2.18}$$

Suppose that a 2.0 kg ball has been released in the air and that the ball is subject to an applied force $\mathbf{F}_{\text{app}} = 10\,\hat{\mathbf{i}} + 20\,\hat{\mathbf{j}} + 5\,\hat{\mathbf{k}}$ N and also to the force of gravity.

(a) What is the net force on this ball?

(b) What is the magnitude of the net force on this ball?

(c) What is the instantaneous acceleration of the ball?

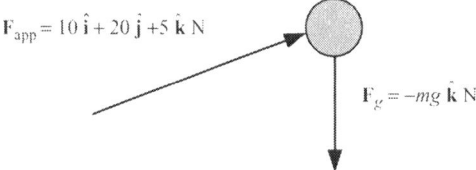

$F_{app} = 10\,\hat{i} + 20\,\hat{j} + 5\,\hat{k}$ N

$F_g = -mg\,\hat{k}$ N

Figure 2.17 The forces on a ball.

SOLUTION   The net force will be the vector sum of the applied force and the force due to gravity. (see Figure 2.17).

$$\mathbf{F}_{net} = \mathbf{F}_{app} + \mathbf{F}_{g} \tag{2.19}$$

The force due to gravity is straight down, and the magnitude of the acceleration due to gravity is 9.81 m/s^2, so

$$\mathbf{F}_{g} = -mg\,\hat{\mathbf{k}} = -(2.0\ \text{kg})(9.81\ \text{m/s}^2)\,\hat{\mathbf{k}} = -19.62\,\hat{\mathbf{k}}\ \text{N} \tag{2.20}$$

The final acceleration can be found by solving Newton's law for acceleration.

$$\mathbf{a} = \frac{\mathbf{F}_{net}}{m} \tag{2.21}$$

A MATLAB script that calculates the net force on the ball, the magnitude of that force, and the net acceleration of the ball is as follows:

```
% Constants
g = [0 0 -9.81];    % Acceleration due to gravity (m/s^2)
m = 2.0;            % Mass (kg)

% Get the forces applied to the ball
fapp = [10 20 5];
fg = m .* g;

% Calculate the net force on the ball
fnet = fapp + fg;

% Tell the user
disp(['The net force on the ball is ' num2str(fnet) ' N.']);

% Get the magnitude of the net force
fnet_mag = sqrt(fnet(1)^2 + fnet(2)^2 + fnet(3)^2);
disp(['The magnitude of the net force is ' num2str(fnet_mag) ' N.']);

% Get the acceleration
a = fnet ./ m;
disp(['The acceleration of the ball is ' num2str(a) ' m/s^2.']);
```

When this script is executed, the results are

```
» force_on_ball
The net force on the ball is 10              20          -14.62 N.
The magnitude of the net force is 26.716 N.
The acceleration of the ball is 5            10          -7.31 m/s^2.
```

Simple hand calculations show that these results are correct.   ◀

Example 2.7—Work Done Moving an Object

The work done by a force moving an object through a given displacement is given by the equation

$$W = \mathbf{F} \cdot \mathbf{d} \tag{2.22}$$

where $\mathbf{F}$ is the vector force on the object and $\mathbf{d}$ is the vector displacement through which the object moves. If the force is given in newtons and the displacement is in meters, then the resulting work is in joules. Calculate the work done on the object shown in Figure 2.18 when the force $\mathbf{F} = 10\,\hat{\mathbf{i}} - 4\,\hat{\mathbf{j}}$ N is applied though displacement $\mathbf{d} = 5\,\hat{\mathbf{i}}$ m.

SOLUTION   The work done will be given by Equation (2.22)

$$W = \mathbf{F} \cdot \mathbf{d} = (10\,\hat{\mathbf{i}} - 4\,\hat{\mathbf{j}}) \cdot (5\,\hat{\mathbf{i}}) = 50 \text{ J} \tag{2.23}$$

This can be calculated in MATLAB as follows:

```
» F = [10 -4];
» d = [5 0];
» W = dot(F,d)
W =
      50
```

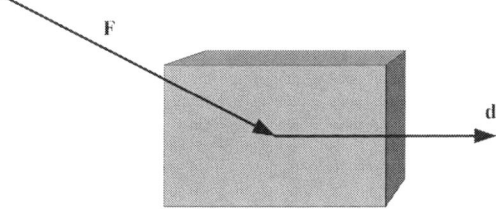

Figure 2.18   Application of a force on an object through a displacement.

Example 2.8—Torque on a Motor Shaft

Torque is the "twisting force" that makes the shafts of rotating objects turn. For example, pulling the handle of a wrench connected to a nut or bolt produces a torque (a "twisting force") that loosens or tightens the nut or bolt. Torque in the rotational world is the analog of force in linear space.

The torque applied to a bolt or to a machine shaft is a function of the force applied, the *moment arm* (which is the distance from the rotating point to the location where the force is applied), and the sine of the angle between the two of them (see Figure 2.19). The greater the force applied, the greater the "twisting action" that results. The greater the moment arm, the greater the "twisting action" that results. We are all familiar with this concept from tightening and loosening nuts—a bigger wrench requires less force to get the nuts to the desired tightness.

This relationship can be expressed in an equation as follows

$$\tau = rF \sin \theta \tag{2.24}$$

where r is the radius of the moment arm, F is the magnitude of the force, and θ is the angle between r and F. In vector terms, this relationship is

$$\tau = \mathbf{r} \times \mathbf{F} \tag{2.25}$$

where $\mathbf{r}$ is the vector radius of the moment arm and $\mathbf{F}$ is the vector force. The vector direction of the resulting torque is given by the right-hand rule: if the thumb of the right hand points in the direction of the first term in a cross product ($\mathbf{r}$) and the pointer finger points in the direction of the second term ($\mathbf{F}$), the third finger will point in the direction of the resulting cross product (see Figure 2.20).

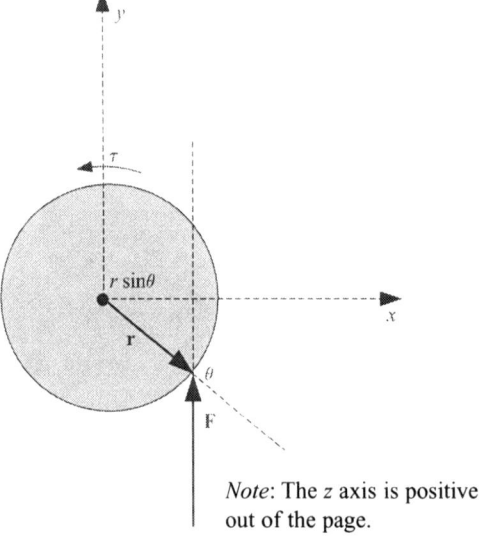

Note: The z axis is positive out of the page.

Figure 2.19 The torque on an object is a product of the force applied to the object and the perpendicular distance between the line of the force and the point of rotation.

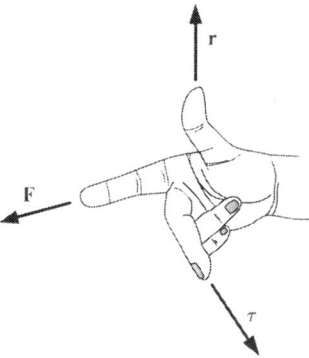

Figure 2.20   The right-hand rule: if the thumb of the right hand points in the direction of the first term in a cross product (**r**) and the pointer finger points in the direction of the second term (**F**), the third finger will point in the direction of the resulting cross product.

Calculate the torque applied to the object shown in Figure 2.19 if the moment arm $\mathbf{r} = 0.866, \hat{\mathbf{i}} - 0.5 \hat{\mathbf{j}}$ m, and $\mathbf{F} = 5 \hat{\mathbf{j}}$ N.

SOLUTION   The torque on the object is given by Equation (2.25)

$$\tau = \mathbf{r} \times \mathbf{F} \qquad (2.26)$$

This value can be calculated in MATLAB as follows:

```
» r = [0.866 -0.5 0];
» F = [0 5 0];
» tau = cross(r,F)
tau =
          0          0    4.3300
```

The torque is 4.33 N-m, oriented in the z direction, which is out of the page.   ◀

2.14   MATLAB Applications: Matrix Operations and Simultaneous Equations

The matrix operations in MATLAB provide a very powerful way to represent and solve systems of simultaneous equations. A set of simultaneous equations usually consists of *m* equations in *n* unknowns, and these equations are solved simultaneously to find the values of the unknown values. We all learned how to do this by substitution and similar methods in secondary school.

A system of simultaneous equations is usually expressed as a series of separate equations, for example

$$
\begin{aligned}
2x_1 + 5x_2 &= 11 \\
3x_1 - 2x_2 &= -12
\end{aligned}
\tag{2.27}
$$

However, it is possible to represent these equations as a single matrix equation and then use the rules of matrix algebra to manipulate them and solve for the unknowns. The set of equations shown previously can be represented in matrix form as

$$
\begin{bmatrix} 2 & 5 \\ 3 & -2 \end{bmatrix} \begin{bmatrix} x_1 \\ x_2 \end{bmatrix} = \begin{bmatrix} 11 \\ -12 \end{bmatrix}
\tag{2.28}
$$

which in turn can be represented in matrix notation as

$$
\mathbf{Ax} = \mathbf{b}
\tag{2.29}
$$

where the matrices and vectors $\mathbf{A}$, $\mathbf{x}$, and $\mathbf{b}$ are defined as follows:

$$
\mathbf{A} = \begin{bmatrix} 2 & 5 \\ 3 & -2 \end{bmatrix} \quad \mathbf{x} = \begin{bmatrix} x_1 \\ x_2 \end{bmatrix} \quad \mathbf{b} = \begin{bmatrix} 11 \\ -12 \end{bmatrix}
$$

In general, a set of m equations in n unknowns can be expressed in the form of Equation (2.29), where $\mathbf{A}$ has m rows and n columns and $\mathbf{x}$ and $\mathbf{b}$ are column vectors with m values.

2.14.1 The Matrix Inverse

In ordinary algebra, the solution of an equation of the form $ax = b$ is found by multiplying both sides of the equation by the reciprocal or multiplicative inverse of a:

$$
a^{-1}(ax) = a^{-1}(b)
\tag{2.30}
$$

or

$$
\frac{1}{a}(ax) = \frac{1}{a}(b)
\tag{2.31}
$$

$$
x = \frac{b}{a}
\tag{2.32}
$$

as long as $a \neq 0$.

This same idea can be extended to matrix algebra. The solution of Equation (2.29) is found by multiplying both sides of the equation by the inverse of $\mathbf{A}$:

$$
\mathbf{A}^{-1}\mathbf{Ax} = \mathbf{A}^{-1}\mathbf{b}
\tag{2.33}
$$

where $\mathbf{A}^{-1}$ is the *inverse* of matrix $\mathbf{A}$. The inverse of a matrix is a matrix with the property that

$$
\mathbf{A}^{-1}\mathbf{A} = \mathbf{A}\mathbf{A}^{-1} = \mathbf{I}
\tag{2.34}
$$

where **I** is the identity matrix, which is a matrix whose diagonal values are all 1 and whose off-diagonal values are all zero. The identity matrix has the special property that any matrix multiplied by **I** is just the original matrix.

$$\mathbf{IA} = \mathbf{AI} = \mathbf{A} \tag{2.35}$$

This is similar in concept to the multiplicative inverse of a scalar, where $\left(\dfrac{1}{a}\right)(a) = (a)\left(\dfrac{1}{a}\right) = 1$ and any value multiplied by 1 is just the original value. Applying Equation (2.34) to Equation (2.33) produces the final solution to the system of equations

$$\mathbf{x} = \mathbf{A}^{-1}\mathbf{b} \tag{2.36}$$

The inverse of a matrix **A** is defined if and only if the **A** is square and non-singular. A matrix is *singular* if the determinant $|\mathbf{A}|$ is zero. If $|\mathbf{A}|$ is zero, then there is no unique solution to the system of equations defined by Equation (2.29). The inverse of a matrix is computed by the MATLAB function `inv(A)`, and the determinant of a matrix is computed by the MATLAB function `det(A)`. If the inverse is calculated for a singular matrix, MATLAB will issue a warning and return floating-point infinity as the answer.

A set of equations whose inverse is nearly singular is called **ill-conditioned**. For such equations, the accuracy of the answers will depend on the number of significant digits used in the calculation. If there is not enough precision to calculate an answer accurately, MATLAB will issue a warning to the user.

▶

Example 2.9—Solving Systems of Simultaneous Equations

Solve the system of simultaneous equations given by Equations (2.27) using the matrix inverse.

$$\begin{aligned} 2x_1 + 5x_2 &= 11 \\ 3x_1 - 2x_2 &= -12 \end{aligned} \tag{2.27}$$

SOLUTION   For this system of equations,

$$\mathbf{A} = \begin{bmatrix} 2 & 5 \\ 3 & -2 \end{bmatrix} \quad \mathbf{b} = \begin{bmatrix} 11 \\ -12 \end{bmatrix}$$

The solution can be calculated in MATLAB as follows:

```
» A = [2 5; 3 -2];
» b = [11; -12];
» x = inv(A) * b
x =
    -2.0000
     3.0000
```

Note that from Table 2-6, A \ b is defined to be `inv(A) * b`, so this answer can also be calculated as

```
» x = A \ b
x =
    -2
     3
```

◄

2.15 Debugging MATLAB Programs

There is an old saying that the only sure things in life are death and taxes. We can add one more certainty to that list: if you write a program of any significant size, it won't work the first time you try it! Errors in programs are known as **bugs**, and the process of locating and eliminating them is known as **debugging**. Given that we have written a program and it is not working, how do we debug it?

Three types of errors are found in MATLAB programs. The first type of error is a **syntax error**. Syntax errors are errors in the MATLAB statement itself, such as spelling errors or punctuation errors. These errors are detected by the MATLAB compiler the first time an M-file is executed. For example, the statement

```
x = (y + 3) / 2);
```

contains a syntax error because it has unbalanced parentheses. If this statement appears in an M-file named `test.m`, the following message appears when `test` is executed:

```
» test
??? x = (y + 3) / 2)
                    |
Missing operator, comma, or semi-colon.

Error in ==> d:\book\matlab\chap1\test.m
On line 2 ==>
```

The second type of error is the **run-time error**. A run-time error occurs when an illegal mathematical operation is attempted during program execution (e.g., attempting to divide by 0). These errors cause the program to return `Inf` or `NaN`, which is then used in further calculations. The results of a program that contains calculations using `Inf` or `NaN` are usually invalid.

The third type of error is a **logical error**. Logical errors occur when the program compiles and runs successfully but produces the wrong answer.

The most common mistakes made during programming are *typographical errors*. Some typographical errors create invalid MATLAB statements. These errors produce syntax errors that are caught by the compiler. Other typographical errors occur in variable names. For example, the letters in some variable names might have been transposed, or an incorrect letter might be typed. The result will be a new variable, and MATLAB simply creates the new variable the first time it is referenced. MATLAB cannot detect this type of error. Typographical errors can also produce logical errors. For example, if variables `vel1` and `vel2` are both used for velocities in the program, one of them might be inadvertently used instead of the other one at some point. You must check for that sort of error by manually inspecting the code.

Sometimes a program will start to execute, but run-time errors or logical errors occur during execution. In this case, there is either something wrong with the input data or something wrong with the logical structure of the program. The first step in locating this sort of bug should be to *check the input data to the program.* Either remove semicolons from input statements or add extra output statements to verify that the input values are what you expect them to be.

If the variable names seem to be correct and the input data is correct, you are probably dealing with a logical error. You should check each of your assignment statements.

1. If an assignment statement is very long, break it into several smaller assignment statements. Smaller statements are easier to verify.
2. Check the placement of parentheses in your assignment statements. It is a very common error to have the operations in an assignment statement evaluated in the wrong order. If you have any doubts as to the order in which the variables are being evaluated, add extra sets of parentheses to make your intentions clear.
3. Make sure that you have initialized all of your variables properly.
4. Be sure that any functions you use are in the correct units. For example, the input to trigonometric functions must be in units of radians, not degrees.

If you are still getting the wrong answer, add output statements at various points in your program to see the results of intermediate calculations. If you can locate the point where the calculations go bad, then you know just where to look for the problem, which is 95 percent of the battle.

If you still cannot find the problem after taking all of these steps, explain what you are doing to another student or to your instructor and let that person look at the code. It is very common for people to see just what they expect to see when they look at their own code. Another person can often quickly spot an error that you have overlooked time after time.

☀ Good Programming Practice

To reduce your debugging effort, make sure that during your program design you should

1. Initialize all variables.
2. Use parentheses to make the functions of assignment statements clear.

MATLAB includes a special debugging tool called a *symbolic debugger*, which is embedded into the Edit/Debug Window. A symbolic debugger is a tool that allows you to walk through the execution of your program one statement at a time and to examine the values of any variables at each step along the way. Symbolic debuggers allow you to see all of the intermediate results without having to insert a lot of output statements into your code. We will learn how to use MATLAB's symbolic debugger in Chapter 4.

2.16   Summary

In this chapter, we have presented many of the fundamental concepts required to write functional MATLAB programs. We learned about the basic types of MATLAB windows, the workspace, and how to get on-line help.

We introduced two data types: `double` and `char`. We also introduced assignment statements, arithmetic calculations, intrinsic functions, input/output statements, and data files.

The order in which MATLAB expressions are evaluated follows a fixed hierarchy with operations at a higher level evaluated before operations at lower levels. The hierarchy of operations is summarized in Table 2-12.

The MATLAB language includes an extremely large number of built-in functions to help us solve problems. This list of functions is *much* richer than the list of functions found in other languages such as Fortran or C, and it includes device-independent plotting capabilities. A few of the common intrinsic functions are summarized in Table 2-8, and many others will be introduced throughout the remainder of the book. A complete list of all MATLAB functions is available through the on-line Help Desk.

2.16.1   Summary of Good Programming Practice

Every MATLAB program should be designed so that another person who is familiar with MATLAB can easily understand it. This is very important, since a good program may be used for a long period of time. Over that time, conditions

Table 2-12   Hierarchy of Operations

Precedence	Operation
1	The contents of all parentheses are evaluated, starting from the innermost parentheses and working outward.
2	All exponentials are evaluated, working from left to right.
3	All multiplications and divisions are evaluated, working from left to right.
4	All additions and subtractions are evaluated, working from left to right.

will change, and the program will need to be modified to reflect the changes. The program modifications may be done by someone other than the original engineer. The engineer making the modifications must understand the original program well before attempting to change it.

It is much harder to design clear, understandable, and maintainable programs than it is to simply write programs. To do so, an engineer must develop the discipline to properly document his or her work. In addition, the engineer must be careful to avoid known pitfalls along the path to good programs. The following guidelines will help you to develop good programs:

1. Use meaningful variable names whenever possible. Use names that can be understood at a glance, like `day`, `month`, and `year`.
2. Create a data dictionary for each program to make program maintenance easier.
3. Use only lowercase letters in variable names, so that there won't be errors due to capitalization differences in different occurrences of a variable name.
4. Use a semicolon at the end of all MATLAB assignment statements to suppress echoing of assigned values in the Command Window. If you need to examine the results of a statement during program debugging, you may remove the semicolon from that statement only.
5. If data must be exchanged between MATLAB and other programs, save the MATLAB data in ASCII format. If the data will only be used in MATLAB, save the data in MAT-file format.
6. Save ASCII data files with a "dat" file extent to distinguish them from MAT-files, which have a "mat" file extent.
7. Use parentheses as necessary to make your equations clear and easy to understand.
8. Always include the appropriate units with any values that you read or write in a program.

2.16.2   MATLAB Summary

The following summary lists all of the MATLAB special symbols, commands, and functions described in this chapter, along with a brief description of each one.

Special Symbols	
[ ]	Array constructor.
( )	Forms subscripts.
' '	Marks the limits of a character string.
,	1. Separates subscripts or matrix elements.
	2. Separates assignment statements on a line.

,	Separates subscripts or matrix elements.
;	1. Suppresses echoing in Command Window.
	2. Separates matrix rows.
	3. Separates assignment statements on a line.
%	Marks the beginning of a comment.
:	Colon operator, used to create shorthand lists.
+	Array and matrix addition.
−	Array and matrix subtraction.
.*	Array multiplication.
⋆	Matrix multiplication.
./	Array right division.
.\	Array left division.
/	Matrix right division.
\	Matrix left division.
.^	Array exponentiation.
'	Transpose operator.

Commands and Functions

...	Continues a MATLAB statement on the following line.
abs(x)	Calculates the absolute value of x.
ans	Default variable used to store the result of expressions not assigned to another variable.
acos(x)	Calculates the inverse cosine of x. The resulting angle is in radians between 0 and π.
asin(x)	Calculates the inverse sine of x. The resulting angle is in radians between $-\pi/2$ and $\pi/2$.
atan(x)	Calculates the inverse tangent of x. The resulting angle is in radians between $-\pi/2$ and $\pi/2$.
atan2(y,x)	Calculates the inverse tangent of y/x, valid over the entire circle. The resulting angle is in radians between $-\pi$ and π.
ceil(x)	Rounds x to the nearest integer towards positive infinity: floor(3.1) = 4 and floor(-3.1) = -3.
char	Converts a matrix of numbers into a character string. For ASCII characters, the matrix should contain numbers ≤ 127.
clock	Current time.
cos(x)	Calculates cosine of x, where x is in radians.
cross	Calculates the cross product of two vectors.
date	Current date.

disp	Displays data in Command Window.
doc	Open HTML Help Desk directly at a particular function description.
dot	Calculates the dot product of two vectors.
double	Converts a character string into a matrix of numbers.
eps	Represents machine precision.
exp(x)	Calculates e^x.
eye(m,n)	Generates an identity matrix.
fix(x)	Rounds x to the nearest integer towards zero: fix(3.1) = 3 and fix(-3.1) = -3.
floor(x)	Rounds x to the nearest integer towards minus infinity: floor(3.1) = 3 and floor(-3.1) = -4.
format +	Print + and − signs only.
format bank	Print in "dollars and cents" format.
format compact	Suppress extra linefeeds in output.
format hex	Print hexadecimal display of bits.
format long	Print with 14 digits after the decimal.
format long e	Print with 15 digits plus exponent.
format long g	Print with 15 digits with or without exponent.
format loose	Print with extra linefeeds in output.
format rat	Print as an approximate ratio of small integers.
format short	Print with 4 digits after the decimal.
format short e	Print with 5 digits plus exponent.
format short g	Print with 5 digits with or without exponent.
fprintf	Print formatted information.
grid	Add or remove a grid from a plot.
i	$\sqrt{-1}$.
Inf	Represents machine infinity (∞).
input	Writes a prompt and reads a value from the keyboard.
int2str	Converts x into an integer character string
j	$\sqrt{-1}$.
legend	Adds a legend to a plot.
length(arr)	Returns the length of a vector or the longest dimension of a two-dimensional array.
load	Load data from a file.
log(x)	Calculates the natural logarithm of x.
loglog	Generates a log-log plot.
lookfor	Looks for a matching term in the one-line MATLAB function descriptions.
max(x)	Returns the maximum value in vector x, and optionally the location of that value.

(continued)

min(x)	Returns the minimum value in vector x, and optionally the location of that value.
mod(m,n)	Remainder or modulo function.
NaN	Represents not-a-number.
num2str(x)	Converts x into a character string.
ones(m,n)	Generates an array of ones.
pi	Represents the number π.
plot	Generates a linear xy plot.
print	Prints a Figure Window.
round(x)	Rounds x to the nearest integer.
save	Saves data from workspace into a file.
semilogx	Generates a log-linear plot.
semilogy	Generates a linear-log plot.
sin(x)	Calculates sine of x, where x is in radians.
size	Get number of rows and columns in an array.
sqrt	Calculates the square root of a number.
str2num	Converts a character string into a number.
tan(x)	Calculates tangent of x, where x is in radians.
title	Adds a title to a plot.
zeros	Generates an array of zeros.

2.17 Exercises

2.1 **Position and Velocity of a Ball** If a stationary ball is released at a height h_0 above the surface of the Earth with a vertical velocity v_0, the position and velocity of the ball as a function of time will be given by the equations

$$h(t) = \frac{1}{2} gt^2 + v_0 t + h_0 \qquad (2.37)$$

$$v(t) = gt + v_0 \qquad (2.38)$$

where g is the acceleration due to gravity (-9.81 m/s^2), h is the height above the surface of the Earth (assuming no air friction), and v is the vertical component of velocity. Write a MATLAB program that prompts a user for the initial height of the ball in meters and the velocity of the ball in meters per second and plots the height and velocity as a function of time. Be sure to include proper labels in your plots.

2.2 The distance between two points (x_1, y_1) and (x_2, y_2) on a Cartesian coordinate plane is given by the equation

$$d = \sqrt{(x_1 - x_2)^2 + (y_1 - y_2)^2} \qquad (2.39)$$

(See Figure 2.21.) Write a program to calculate the distance between any two points (x_1, y_1) and (x_2, y_2) specified by the user. Use good programming practices in your program. Use the program to calculate the distance between the points $(-3, 2)$ and $(3, -6)$.

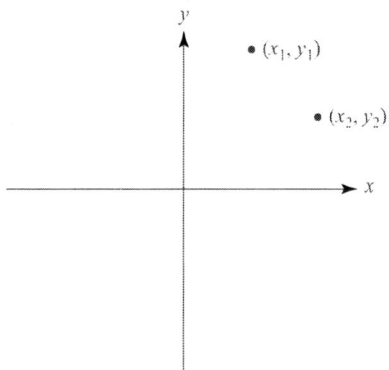

Figure 2.21   Distance between two points on a Cartesian plane.

2.3   A two-dimensional vector in a Cartesian plane can be represented in either rectangular coordinates *(x, y)* or the polar coordinates *(r, θ)*, as shown in Figure 2.22. The relationships among these two sets of coordinates are given by the following equations:

$$x = r \cos \theta \qquad (2.40)$$

$$y = r \sin \theta \qquad (2.41)$$

$$r = \sqrt{x^2 + y^2} \qquad (2.42)$$

$$\theta = \tan^{-1} \frac{y}{x} \qquad (2.43)$$

Use the MATLAB help system to look up function `atan2`, and use that function in answering the following questions.

(a) Write a program that accepts a two-dimensional vector in rectangular coordinates and calculates the vector in polar coordinates, with the angle θ expressed in degrees.

(b) Write a program that accepts a two-dimensional vector in polar coordinates (with the angle in degrees) and calculates the vector in rectangular coordinates.

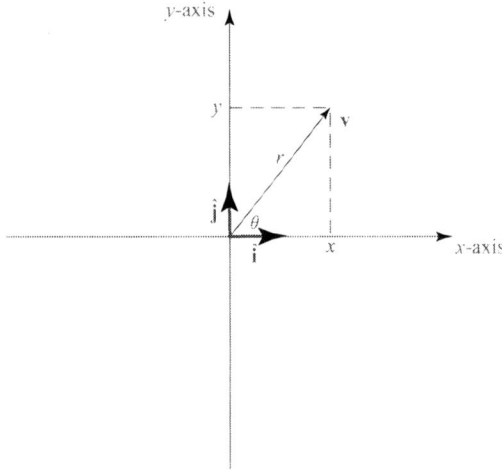

Figure 2.22   A vector **v** can be represented in either rectangular coordinates (x,y) or polar coordinates (r, θ).

2.4   The distance between two points (x_1, y_1, z_1) and (x_2, y_2, z_2) in a three-dimensional Cartesian coordinate system is given by the equation

$$d = \sqrt{(x_1 - x_2)^2 + (y_1 - y_2)^2 + (z_1 - z_2)^2} \qquad (2.44)$$

Write a program to calculate the distance between any two points (x_1, y_1, z_1) and (x_2, y_2, z_2) specified by the user. Use good programming practices in your program. Use the program to calculate the distance between the points $(-3, 2, 5)$ and $(3, -6, -5)$.

2.5   A three-dimensional vector can be represented in either rectangular coordinates *(x, y, z)* or the spherical coordinates *(r, θ, φ)*, as shown in Figure 2.23.[3] The relationships among these two sets of coordinates are given by the following equations:

$$x = r \cos \phi \cos \theta \qquad (2.45)$$

$$y = r \cos \phi \sin \theta \qquad (2.46)$$

$$z = r \sin \phi \qquad (2.47)$$

$$r = \sqrt{x^2 + y^2 + z^2} \qquad (2.48)$$

$$\theta = \tan^{-1} \frac{y}{x} \qquad (2.49)$$

---

[3]These definitions of the angles in spherical coordinates are non-standard according to international usage, but match the definitions employed by the MATLAB program.

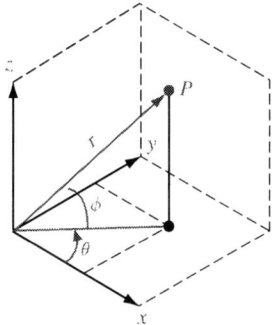

Figure 2.23   A three-dimensional vector **v** can be represented in either rectangular coordinates (x,y,z) or spherical coordinates (r, θ, ϕ).

$$\phi = \tan^{-1} \frac{z}{\sqrt{x^2 + y^2}} \tag{2.50}$$

Use the MATLAB help system to look up function `atan2`, and use that function in answering the following questions.

(a) Write a program that accepts a three-dimensional vector in rectangular coordinates and calculates the vector in spherical coordinates, with the angles θ and ϕ expressed in degrees.

(b) Write a program that accepts a three-dimensional vector in spherical coordinates (with the angles θ and ϕ in degrees) and calculates the vector in rectangular coordinates.

2.6   MATLAB includes two functions `cart2sph` and `sph2cart` to convert back and forth between Cartesian and spherical coordinates. Look these functions up in the MATLAB help system and rewrite the programs in Exercise 2.5 using these functions. How do the answers compare between the programs written using Equations (2.45) through (2.50) and the programs written using the built-in MATLAB functions?

2.7   **Calculating the Angle between Two Vectors** It can be shown that the dot product of two vectors is equal to the magnitude of each vector times the cosine of the angle between them.

$$\mathbf{u} \cdot \mathbf{v} = |\mathbf{u}||\mathbf{v}| \cos \theta \tag{2.51}$$

Note that this expression works for both two-dimensional and three-dimensional vectors. Use Equation (2.51) to write a program that calculates the angle between two user-supplied two-dimensional vectors.

2.8   Use Equation (2.51) to write a program that calculates the angle between two user-supplied three-dimensional vectors.

2.9 Plot the functions $f_1(x) = \sin x$ and $f_2(x) = \cos 2x$ for $-2\pi \le x \le 2\pi$ on the same axes, using a solid blue line for $f_1(x)$ and a dashed red line for $f_2(x)$. Then calculate and plot the function $f_3(x) = f_1(x) - f_2(x)$ on the same axes using a dotted black line. Be sure to include a title, axis labels, a legend, and a grid on the plot.

2.10 Plot the function $f(x) = 2e^{-2x} + 0.5e^{-0.1x}$ for $0 \le x \le 20$ on a linear set of axes. Now plot the function $f(x) = 2e^{-2x} + 0.5e^{-0.1x}$ for $0 \le x \le 20$ with a logarithmic y axis. Include a grid, title and axis labels on each plot. How do the two plots compare?

2.11 In the linear world, the relationship between the net force on an object and the acceleration of the object is given by Newton's law

$$\mathbf{F} = m\mathbf{a} \tag{2.52}$$

where $\mathbf{F}$ is the net vector force on the object, m is the mass of the object, and $\mathbf{a}$ is the acceleration of the object. If acceleration is in meters per second^2 and mass is in kilograms, then the force is in newtons.

In the rotational world, the relationship between the net torque on an object and the angular acceleration of the object is given by

$$\boldsymbol{\tau} = I\boldsymbol{\alpha} \tag{2.53}$$

where $\boldsymbol{\tau}$ is the net torque on the object, I is the moment of inertia of the object, and $\boldsymbol{\alpha}$ is the angular acceleration of the object. If angular acceleration is in radians per second squared and the moment of inertia is in kilograms-meters squared, then the torque is in newton-meters.

Suppose that torque of 20 N-m is applied to the shaft of a motor having a moment of inertia of 15 kg-m^2. What is the angular acceleration of the shaft?

2.12 **Decibels** Engineers often measure the ratio of two power measurements in *decibels*, or dB. The equation for the ratio of two power measurements in decibels is

$$dB = 10 \log_{10} \frac{P_2}{P_1} \tag{2.54}$$

where P_2 is the power level being measured and P_1 is some reference power level.

(a) Assume that the reference power level P_1 is 1 milliwatt, and write a program that accepts an input power P_2 and converts it into dB with respect to the 1 mW reference level. (Engineers have a special unit for dB power levels with respect to a 1 mW reference: dBm.) Use good programming practices in your program.

(b) Write a program that creates a plot of power in watts versus power in dBm with respect to a 1 mW reference level. Create both a linear *xy* plot and a log-linear *xy* plot.

2.13   **Power in a Resistor** Figure 2.24 shows a resistor with a voltage drop across it and a current flowing through it. The voltage across a resistor is related to the current flowing through it by Ohm's law

$$V = IR \qquad (2.55)$$

and the power consumed in the resistor is given by the equation

$$P = IV \qquad (2.56)$$

Write a program that creates a plot of the power consumed by a 1000 Ω resistor as the voltage across it is varied from 1 V to 200 V. Create two plots: one showing power in watts and one showing power in dBW (dB power levels with respect to a 1 W reference).

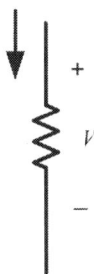

Figure 2.24   Voltage and current in a resistor.

2.14   **Hyperbolic Cosine** The hyperbolic cosine function is defined by the equation

$$\cosh x = \frac{e^x + e^{-x}}{2} \qquad (2.57)$$

Write a program to calculate the hyperbolic cosine of a user-supplied value x. Use the program to calculate the hyperbolic cosine of 3.0. Compare the answer that your program produces to the answer produced by the MATLAB intrinsic function `cosh(x)`. Also, use MATLAB to plot the function `cosh(x)`. What is the smallest value that this function can have? At what value of x does it occur?

2.15   **Energy Stored in a Spring** The force required to compress a linear spring is given by the equation

$$F = kx \qquad (2.58)$$

where F is the force in newtons and k is the spring constant in newtons per meter. The potential energy stored in the compressed spring is given by the equation

$$E = \frac{1}{2} kx^2 \qquad (2.59)$$

where E is the energy in joules. The following information is available for four springs:

	Spring 1	Spring 2	Spring 3	Spring 4
Force (N)	20	30	25	20
Spring constant k (N/m)	200	250	300	400

Determine the compression of each spring, and the potential energy stored in each spring. Which spring has the most energy stored in it?

2.16 **Radio Receiver** A simplified version of the front end of an AM radio receiver is shown in Figure 2.25. This receiver consists of an *RLC* tuned circuit containing a resistor, capacitor, and an inductor connected in series. The *RLC* circuit is connected to an external antenna and ground as shown in the picture.

The tuned circuit allows the radio to select a specific station out of all the stations transmitting on the AM band. At the resonant frequency of the circuit, essentially all of the signal V_0 appearing at the antenna appears across the resistor, which represents the rest of the radio. In other words, the radio receives its strongest signal at the resonant frequency. The resonant frequency of the LC circuit is given by the equation

$$ f_0 = \frac{1}{2\pi\sqrt{LC}} \tag{2.60} $$

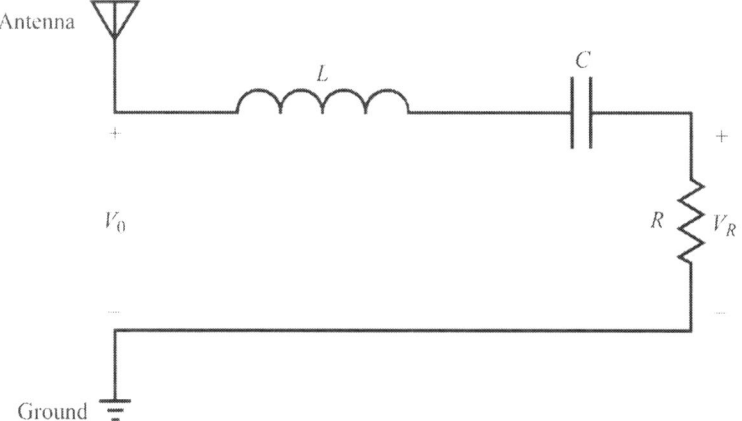

Figure 2.25 A simplified version of the front end of an AM radio receiver.

where L is inductance in henrys (H) and C is capacitance in farads (F). Write a program that calculates the resonant frequency of this radio set given specific values of L and C. Test your program by calculating the frequency of the radio when $L = 0.25$ mH and $C = 0.10$ nF.

2.17   **Radio Receiver** The average (rms) voltage across the resistive load in Figure 2.25 varies as a function of frequency according to Equation (2.61).

$$V_R = \frac{R}{\sqrt{R^2 + \left(\omega L - \dfrac{1}{\omega C}\right)^2}} V_0 \tag{2.61}$$

where $\omega = 2\pi f$ and f is the frequency in hertz. Assume that $L = 0.25$ mH, $C = 0.10$ nF, $R = 50\ \Omega$, and $V_0 = 10$ mV.

(a) Plot the rms voltage on the resistive load as a function of frequency. At what frequency does the voltage on the resitive load peak? What is the voltage on the load at this frequency? This frequency is called the resonant frequency f_0 of the circuit.

(b) If the frequency is changed to 10 percent greater than the resonant frequency, what is the voltage on the load? How selective is this radio receiver?

(c) At what frequencies will the voltage on the load drop to half of the voltage at the resonant frequency?

2.18   Suppose two signals were received at the antenna of the radio receiver described in the previous problem. One signal has a strength of 1 V at a frequency of 1000 kHz, and the other signal has a strength of 1 V at 950 kHz. Calculate the voltage V_R that will be received for each of these signals. How much power will the first signal supply to the resistive load R? How much power will the second signal supply to the resistive load R? Express the ratio of the power supplied by signal 1 to the power supplied by signal 2 in decibels (see Exercise 2.12 for the definition of a decibel). How much is the second signal enhanced or suppressed compared to the first signal? (*Note:* The power supplied to the resistive load can be calculated from the equation $P = V_R^2/R$.)

2.19   Find the solution to the following sets of simultaneous linear equations:

(a)
$$\begin{aligned} 2x_1 + 2x_2 + 3x_2 &= 1 \\ 4x_1 + 5x_2 + 6x_2 &= 2 \\ 7x_1 + 8x_2 + 9x_2 &= 3 \end{aligned}$$

(b)
$$\begin{aligned} x_1 + 2x_2 + 3x_2 &= 1 \\ 4x_1 + 5x_2 + 6x_2 &= 2 \\ 7x_1 + 8x_2 + 9x_2 &= 3 \end{aligned}$$

$$\begin{bmatrix} -2 & 5 & 1 & 3 & 4 & -1 & 2 & -1 & -5 & -2 \\ 6 & 4 & -1 & 6 & -4 & -5 & 3 & -1 & 4 & 2 \\ -6 & -5 & -2 & -2 & -3 & 6 & 4 & 2 & -6 & 4 \\ 2 & 4 & 4 & 4 & 5 & -4 & 0 & 0 & -4 & 6 \\ -4 & -1 & 3 & -3 & -4 & -4 & -4 & 4 & 3 & -3 \\ 4 & 3 & 5 & 1 & 1 & 1 & 0 & 3 & 3 & 6 \\ 1 & 2 & -2 & 0 & 3 & -5 & 5 & 0 & 1 & -4 \\ -3 & -4 & 2 & -1 & -2 & 5 & -1 & -1 & -4 & 1 \\ 5 & 5 & -2 & -5 & 1 & 4 & -1 & 0 & -2 & -3 \\ -5 & -2 & -5 & 2 & 1 & -3 & 4 & -1 & -4 & 4 \end{bmatrix} \mathbf{x} = \begin{bmatrix} -5 \\ -6 \\ -7 \\ 0 \\ 5 \\ -8 \\ 1 \\ -4 \\ -7 \\ 6 \end{bmatrix}$$

(c)

2.20 **Aircraft Turning Radius** An object moving in a circular path at a constant tangential velocity v is shown in Figure 2.26. The radial acceleration required for the object to move in the circular path is given by the Equation (2.62):

$$a = \frac{v^2}{r} \qquad (2.62)$$

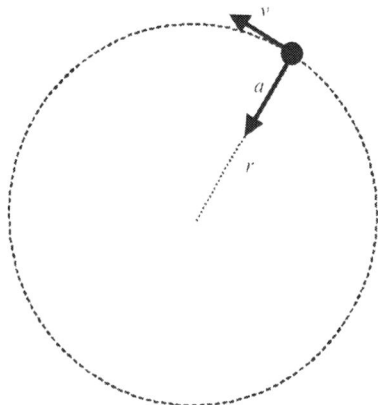

Figure 2.26 An object moving in uniform circular motion due to the centripetal acceleration a.

where a is the centripetal acceleration of the object in m/s², v is the tangential velocity of the object in m/s, and r is the turning radius in meters. Suppose that the object is an aircraft, and answer the following questions about it.

(a) Suppose that the aircraft is moving at Mach 0.85, or 85 percent of the speed of sound. If the centripetal acceleration is 2 g, what is the turning radius of the aircraft? (*Note:* For this problem, you may assume that Mach 1 is equal to 340 m/s and that 1 g = 9.81 m/s².)

(b) Suppose that the speed of the aircraft increases to Mach 1.5. What is the turning radius of the aircraft now?

(c) Plot the turning radius as a function of aircraft speed for speeds between Mach 0.5 and Mach 2.0, assuming that the acceleration remains 2 g.

(d) Suppose that the maximum acceleration that the pilot can stand is 7 g. What is the minimum possible turning radius of the aircraft at Mach 1.5?

(e) Plot the turning radius as a function of centripetal acceleration for accelerations between 2 g and 8 g, assuming a constant speed of Mach 0.85.

2.21 Answer the following questions for the following array.

$$
array1 = \begin{bmatrix} 0.0 & 0.5 & 2.1 & -3.5 & 6.0 \\ 0.0 & -1.1 & -6.6 & 2.8 & 3.4 \\ 2.1 & 0.1 & 0.3 & -0.4 & 1.3 \\ 1.1 & 5.1 & 0.0 & 1.1 & -2.0 \end{bmatrix}
$$

(a) What is the size of `array1`?

(b) What is the value of `array1(1,4)`?

(c) What is the size and value of `array1(:,1:2:5)`?

(d) What is the size and value of `array1([1 3],end)`?

2.22 Are the following MATLAB variable names legal or illegal? Why?

(a) `dog1`

(b) `1dog`

(c) `Do_you_know_the_way_to_san_jose`

(d) `_help`

(e) `What's_up?`

2.23 Determine the size and contents of the following arrays. Note that the later arrays may depend on the definitions of arrays defined earlier in this exercise.

(a) `a = 2:3:8;`

(b) `b = [a' a' a'];`

(c) `c = b(1:2:3,1:2:3);`

(d) `d = a + b(2,:);`

(e) `w = [zeros(1,3) ones(3,1)' 3:5'];`

(f) `b([1 3],2) = b([3 1],2);`

(g) `e = 1:-1:5;`

2.24 Assume that array `array1` is defined as shown, and determine the contents of the following sub-arrays.

$$
array1 = \begin{bmatrix} 1.1 & 0.0 & -2.1 & -3.5 & 6.0 \\ 0.0 & -3.0 & -5.6 & 2.8 & 4.3 \\ 2.1 & 0.3 & 0.1 & -0.4 & 1.3 \\ -1.4 & 5.1 & 0.0 & 1.1 & -3.0 \end{bmatrix}
$$

(a) `array1(3,:)`
(b) `array1(:,3)`
(c) `array1(1:2:3,[3 3 4])`
(d) `array1([1 1],:)`

2.25 Assume that `value` has been initialized to 10π, and determine what is printed out by each of the following statements.

```
disp (['value = ' num2str(value)]);
disp (['value = ' int2str(value)]);
fprintf('value = %e\n',value);
fprintf('value = %f\n',value);
fprintf('value = %g\n',value);
fprintf('value = %12.4f\n',value);
```

2.26 Assume that a, b, c, and d are defined as follows, and calculate the results of the following operations if they are legal. If an operation is illegal, explain why it is illegal.

$$a = \begin{bmatrix} 2 & 1 \\ -1 & 4 \end{bmatrix} \quad b = \begin{bmatrix} -1 & 3 \\ 0 & 2 \end{bmatrix}$$

$$c = \begin{bmatrix} 2 \\ 1 \end{bmatrix} \qquad d = \text{eye}(2)$$

(a) `result = a + b;`
(b) `result = a * d;`
(c) `result = a .* d;`
(d) `result = a * c;`
(e) `result = a .* c;`
(f) `result = a \ b;`
(g) `result = a .\ b;`
(h) `result = a .^ b;`

2.27 Evaluate each of the following expressions.

(a) `11 / 5 + 6`
(b) `(11 / 5) + 6`
(c) `11 / (5 + 6)`
(d) `3 ^ 2 ^ 3`
(e) `3 ^ (2 ^ 3)`
(f) `(3 ^ 2) ^ 3`
(g) `round(-11/5) + 6`
(h) `ceil(-11/5) + 6`
(i) `floor(-11/5) + 6`

2.28 Use MATLAB to evaluate each of the following expressions.

(a) $(3 - 4i)(-4 + 3i)$

(b) $\cos^{-1}(1.2)$

2.29 Evaluate the following expressions in MATLAB, where $t = 2$ s, $i = \sqrt{-1}$, and $\omega = 120\pi$ rad/s. How do the answers compare?

(a) $e^{-2t} \cos(\omega t)$

(b) $e^{-2t}[\cos(\omega t) + i \sin(\omega t)]$

(c) $e^{[-2t + i\omega t]}$

2.30 Solve the following system of simultaneous equations for x:

$$
\begin{array}{r}
-2.0\,x_1 + 5.0\,x_2 + 1.0\,x_3 + 3.0\,x_4 + 4.0\,x_5 - 1.0\,x_6 = 0.0 \\
2.0\,x_1 - 1.0\,x_2 - 5.0\,x_3 - 2.0\,x_4 + 6.0\,x_5 + 4.0\,x_6 = 1.0 \\
-1.0\,x_1 + 6.0\,x_2 - 4.0\,x_3 - 5.0\,x_4 + 3.0\,x_5 - 1.0\,x_6 = -6.0 \\
4.0\,x_1 + 3.0\,x_2 - 6.0\,x_3 - 5.0\,x_4 - 2.0\,x_5 - 2.0\,x_6 = 10.0 \\
-3.0\,x_1 + 6.0\,x_2 + 4.0\,x_3 + 2.0\,x_4 - 6.0\,x_5 + 4.0\,x_6 = -6.0 \\
2.0\,x_1 + 4.0\,x_2 + 4.0\,x_3 + 4.0\,x_4 + 5.0\,x_5 - 4.0\,x_6 = -2.0
\end{array}
$$

CHAPTER 4

Branching Statements
and Program Design

In Chapter 2, we developed several complete working MATLAB programs. However, all of the programs were very simple, consisting of a series of MATLAB statements that were executed one after another in a fixed order. Such programs are called *sequential* programs. They read input data, process it to produce a desired answer, print out the answer, and quit. There is no way to repeat sections of the program more than once, and there is no way to selectively execute only certain portions of the program depending on values of the input data.

In the next two chapters, we will introduce a number of MATLAB statements that allow us to control the order in which statements are executed in a program. There are two broad categories of control statements: **branches**, which select specific sections of the code to execute, and **loops**, which cause specific sections of the code to be repeated. Branches are discussed in this chapter, and loops are discussed in Chapter 5.

With the introduction of branches and loops, our programs are going to become more complex, and it will become easier to make mistakes. To help avoid programming errors, we will introduce a formal program design procedure based on the technique known as top-down design. We will also introduce a common algorithm development tool known as pseudocode.

We will also study the MATLAB logical data type before discussing branches, because branches are controlled by logical values and expressions.

This chapter includes an example in which we calculate the roots of the quadratic equation, so it concludes with an applications section showing how to use built-in MATLAB functions to calculate the roots of any polynomial.

4.1 Introduction to Top-Down Design Techniques

Suppose that you are an engineer working in industry and that you need to write a program to solve a problem. How do you begin?

When given a new problem, there is a natural tendency to sit down at a keyboard and start programming without "wasting" a lot of time thinking about the problem first. It is often possible to get away with this "on-the-fly" approach to programming for very small problems, such as many of the examples in this book. In the real world, however, problems are larger, and an engineer attempting this approach will become hopelessly bogged down. For larger problems, it pays to completely think out the problem and decide on the approach you are going to take to it before writing a single line of code.

We will introduce a formal program design process in this section, and then we will apply that process to every major application developed in the remainder of the book. For some of the simple examples that we will be doing, the design process will seem like overkill. However, as the problems that we solve get larger and larger, the process becomes more and more essential to successful programming.

When I was an undergraduate, one of my professors was fond of saying, "Programming is easy. It's knowing what to program that's hard." His point was forcefully driven home to me after I left university and began working in industry on larger-scale software projects. I found that the most difficult part of my job was to *understand the problem* I was trying to solve. Once I really understood the problem, it became easy to break the problem apart into smaller, more easily manageable pieces with well-defined functions and then to tackle those pieces one at a time.

Top-down design is the process of starting with a large task and breaking it down into smaller, more easily understandable pieces (sub-tasks), which perform a portion of the desired task. Each sub-task may in turn be subdivided into smaller sub-tasks if necessary. Once the program is divided into small pieces, each piece can be coded and tested independently. We do not attempt to combine the sub-tasks into a complete task until each of the sub-tasks has been verified to work properly by itself.

The concept of top-down design is the basis of our formal program design process. We will now introduce the details of the process, the steps of which are illustrated in Figure 4.1.

1. **Clearly state the problem that you are trying to solve.**
   Programs are usually written to fill some perceived need, but that need may not be articulated clearly by the person requesting the program. For example, a user may ask for a program to solve a system of simultaneous linear equations. This request is not clear enough to allow an engineer to design a program to meet the need; he or she must first know much more about the problem to be solved. Is the system of equations to be solved real or complex? What is the maximum number of equations and

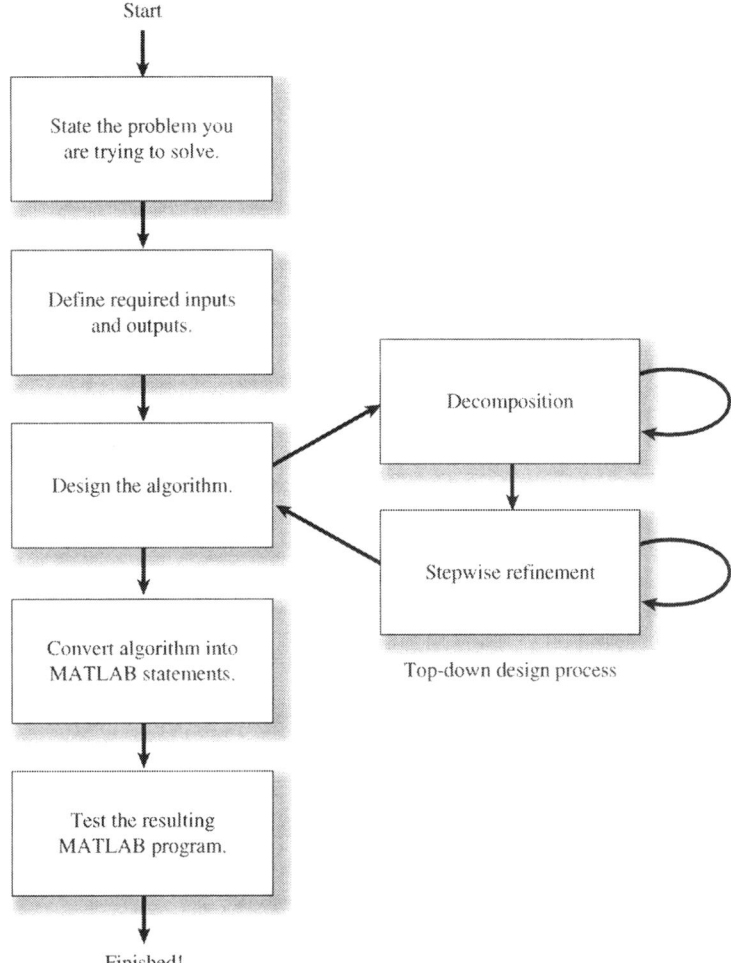

Figure 4.1   The program design process used in this book.

unknowns that the program must handle? Are there any symmetries in the equations that might be exploited to make the task easier? The program designer will have to talk with the user requesting the program, and the two of them will have to come up with a clear statement of exactly what they are trying to accomplish. A clear statement of the problem will prevent misunderstandings, and it will also help the program designer to properly organize his or her thoughts. In the example we were describing, a proper statement of the problem might have been: Design and write a program to solve a system of simultaneous linear equations having real coefficients and with up to 20 equations in 20 unknowns.

2. **Define the inputs required by the program and the outputs to be produced by the program.**

   The inputs to the program and the outputs produced by the program must be specified so that the new program will properly fit into the overall processing scheme. In the preceding example, the coefficients of the equations to be solved are probably in some preexisting order, and our new program must be able to read them in that order. Similarly, it must produce the answers required by the programs that may follow it in the overall processing scheme and write out those answers in the format needed by the programs following it.

3. **Design the algorithm that you intend to implement in the program.**

   An **algorithm** is a step-by-step procedure for finding the solution to a problem. It is at this stage in the process that top-down design techniques come into play. The designer looks for logical divisions within the problem and divides it up into sub-tasks along those lines. This process is called *decomposition*. If the sub-tasks are themselves large, the designer can break them up into even smaller sub-sub-tasks. This process continues until the problem has been divided into many small pieces, each of which does a simple, clearly understandable job.

   After the problem has been decomposed into small pieces, each piece is further refined through a process called *stepwise refinement*. In stepwise refinement, a designer starts with a general description of what the piece of code should do and then defines the functions of the piece in greater and greater detail until they are specific enough to be turned into MATLAB statements. Stepwise refinement is usually done with **pseudocode**, which is described in the following section.

   It is often helpful to solve a simple example of the problem by hand during the algorithm development process. If the designer understands the steps that he or she went through in solving the problem by hand, he or she will be better able to apply decomposition and stepwise refinement to the problem.

4. **Turn the algorithm into MATLAB statements.**

   If the decomposition and refinement process was carried out properly, this step will be very simple. All the engineer will have to do is to replace pseudocode with the corresponding MATLAB statements on a one-for-one basis.

5. **Test the resulting MATLAB program.**

   This step is the real killer. The components of the program must first be tested individually, if possible, and then the program as a whole must be tested. When testing a program, we must verify that it works correctly for *all legal input data sets*. It is very common for a program to be written, tested with some standard data set, and released for use, only to find that it produces the wrong answers (or crashes) with a different input data set.

If the algorithm implemented in a program includes different branches, we must test all of the possible branches to confirm that the program operates correctly under every possible circumstance. This exhaustive testing can be almost impossible in really large programs, so bugs can be discovered after the program has been in regular use for years.

Because the programs in this book are fairly small, we will not go through the sort of extensive testing we have described. However, we will follow the basic principles in testing all of our programs.

✳ Good Programming Practice

Follow the steps of the program design process to produce reliable, understandable MATLAB programs.

In a large programming project, the time actually spent programming is surprisingly small. In his book *The Mythical Man-Month*,[1] Frederick P. Brooks, Jr. suggests that in a typical large software project, one-third of the time is spent planning what to do (steps 1 through 3), one-sixth of the time is spent actually writing the program (step 4), and fully one-half of the time is spent in testing and debugging the program! Clearly, anything that we can do to reduce the testing and debugging time will be helpful. We can best reduce the testing and debugging time by doing a very careful job during the planning phase and by using good programming practices. Good programming practices will reduce the number of bugs in the program and will make the ones that do creep in easier to find.

4.2   Use of Pseudocode

As a part of the design process, it is necessary to describe the algorithm that you intend to implement. The description of the algorithm should be in a standard form that is easy for both you and other people to understand, and the description should aid you in turning your concept into MATLAB code. The standard forms that we use to describe algorithms are called **constructs** (or sometimes structures), and an algorithm described using these constructs is called a structured algorithm. When the algorithm is implemented in a MATLAB program, the resulting program is called a **structured program**.

The constructs used to build algorithms can be described in a special way called pseudocode. **Pseudocode** is a hybrid mixture of MATLAB and English. It is structured like MATLAB, with a separate line for each distinct idea or segment of code, but the descriptions on each line are in English. Each line of the

---

[1] *The Mythical Man-Month, Anniversary Edition*, by Frederick P. Brooks Jr., Addison-Wesley, 1995.

pseudocode should describe its idea in plain, easily understandable English. Pseudocode is useful for developing algorithms, since it is flexible and easy to modify. It is especially useful since pseudocode can be written and modified with the same editor or word processor used to write the MATLAB program—no special graphical capabilities are required.

For example, the pseudocode for the algorithm in Example 2-3 is

```
Prompt user to enter temperature in degrees Fahrenheit
Read temperature in degrees Fahrenheit (temp_f)
temp_k in kelvins ← (5/9) * (temp_f - 32) + 273.15
Write temperature in kelvins
```

Notice that a left arrow (←) is used instead of an equal sign (=) to indicate that a value is stored in a variable, since this avoids any confusion between assignment and equality. Pseudocode is intended to aid you in organizing your thoughts before converting them into MATLAB code.

4.3   Relational and Logic Operators

Relational and logic operators are operators that produce a `true` (the value 1) or `false` (the value 0) result. These operators are important, because they control which code gets executed in some MATLAB branching structures.

Relational operators are operators that compare two numbers and produce a `true` or `false` result. For example, `a > b` is a relational operator that compares the numbers in variables a and b. If the value in a is greater than the value in b, this operator returns a `true` result. Otherwise, the operator returns a `false` result.

Logic operators are operators that compare one or two logical values and produce a `true` or `false` result. For example, `&&` is a logical AND operator. The operator `a && b` compares the logical values stored in variables a and b. If both a and b are true (nonzero), the operator returns a `true` result. Otherwise, the operator returns a `false` result.

4.3.1   Relational Operators

Relational operators are operators with two numerical or string operands that return `true` (1) or `false` (0), depending on the relationship between the two operands. The general form of a relational operator is

$$a_1 \text{ op } a_2$$

where a_1 and a_2 are arithmetic expressions, variables, or strings and op is one of the relational operators in Table 4-1.

Table 4-1   Relational Operators.

Operator	Operation
==	Equal to
~=	Not equal to
>	Greater than
>=	Greater than or equal to
<	Less than
<=	Less than or equal to

If the relationship between a_1 and a_2 expressed by the operator is true, the operation returns a `true` value; otherwise, the operation returns `false`.

Some relational operations and their results are given here.

Operation	Result
3 < 4	true (1)
3 <= 4	true (1)
3 == 4	false (0)
3 > 4	false (0)
4 <= 4	true (1)
'A' < 'B'	true (1)

The last relational operation is true because characters are evaluated in alphabetical order.

Relational operators may be used to compare a scalar value with an array. For example, if a $= \begin{bmatrix} 1 & 0 \\ -2 & 1 \end{bmatrix}$ and b = 0, the expression a > b will yield the array $\begin{bmatrix} 1 & 0 \\ 0 & 1 \end{bmatrix}$. Relational operators also may be used to compare two arrays, as long as both arrays have the same size. For example, if a $= \begin{bmatrix} 1 & 0 \\ -2 & 1 \end{bmatrix}$ and b $= \begin{bmatrix} 0 & 2 \\ -2 & -1 \end{bmatrix}$, the expression a >= b will yield the array $\begin{bmatrix} 1 & 0 \\ 1 & 1 \end{bmatrix}$. If the arrays have different sizes, a runtime error will result.

Note that since strings are really arrays of characters, *relational operators can compare two strings only if they are of equal lengths.* If they are of unequal lengths, the comparison operation will produce an error. We will learn of a more general way to compare strings in Appendix C.

The equivalence relational operator is written with two equal signs, while the assignment operator is written with a single equal sign. These are very different operators, and beginning engineers often confuse them. The == symbol is a *comparison* operation that returns a logical (0 or 1) result, whereas the = symbol *assigns* the value of the expression to the right of the equal sign to the variable on the left of the equal sign. It is a common mistake for beginning engineers to use a single equal sign when trying to do a comparison.

Programming Pitfalls

Be careful not to confuse the equivalence relational operator (==) with the assignment operator (=).

In the hierarchy of operations, relational operators are evaluated after all arithmetic operators have been evaluated. Therefore, the following two expressions are equivalent (both are true).

```
7 + 3   <   2 + 11
(7 + 3) < (2 + 11)
```

4.3.2 A Caution About the == and ~= Operators

The equivalence operator (==) returns a `true` value (1) when the two values being compared are equal and a `false` (0) when the two values being compared are different. Similarly, the non-equivalence operator (~=) returns a `false` (0) when the two values being compared are equal and a `true` (1) when the two values being compared are different. These operators are generally safe to use for comparing strings, but they can sometimes produce surprising results when two numeric values are compared. Due to **roundoff errors** during computer calculations, two theoretically equal numbers can differ slightly, causing an equality or inequality test to fail.

For example, consider the following two numbers, both of which should be equal to 0.0.

```
a = 0;
b = sin(pi);
```

Since these numbers are theoretically the same, the relational operation a == b *should* produce a 1. In fact, the results of this MATLAB calculation are

```
» a = 0;
» b = sin(pi);
» a == b
ans =
    0
```

MATLAB reports that a and b are different because a slight roundoff error in the calculation of `sin(pi)` makes the result be 1.2246×10^{-16} instead of exactly zero. The two theoretically equal values differ slightly due to roundoff error!

Instead of comparing two numbers for *exact* equality, you should set up your tests to determine whether the two numbers *nearly* equal to each other within some accuracy take into account the roundoff error expected for the numbers being compared. The test

```
» abs(a - b) < 1.0E-14
ans =
      1
```

produces the correct answer, despite the roundoff error in calculating b.

❋ Good Programming Practice

Be cautious about testing for equality with numeric values, since roundoff errors may cause two variables that should be equal to fail a test for equality. Instead, test to see if the variables are *nearly* equal within the roundoff error to be expected on the computer you are working with.

4.3.3 Logic Operators

Logic operators are operators with one or two logical operands that yield a logical result. There are five binary logic operators: AND (& and &&), inclusive OR (| and ||), and exclusive OR (xor) and one unary logic operator: NOT (~). The general form of a binary logic operation is

$$l_1 \text{ op } l_2$$

The general form of a unary logic operation is

$$\text{op } l_1$$

where l_1 and l_2 are expressions or variables, and op is one of the logic operators shown in Table 4-2.

Table 4-2   Logic Operators

Operator	Operation
&	Logical AND
&&	Logical AND with shortcut evaluation
|	Logical Inclusive OR
||	Logical Inclusive OR with shortcut evaluation
xor	Logical Exclusive OR
~	Logical NOT

Table 4-3   Truth Tables For Logic Operators

Inputs		and		or		xor	not
l_1	l_2	l_1 & l_2	l_1 && l_2	l_1 | l_2	l_1 || l_2	$\text{xor}(l_1, l_2)$	$\sim l_1$
0	0	0	0	0	0	0	1
0	1	0	0	1	1	1	1
1	0	0	0	1	1	1	0
1	1	1	1	1	1	0	0

If the relationship between l_1 and l_2 expressed by the operator is true, the operation returns a true (1); otherwise, the operation returns a false (0). Note that logic operators treat any nonzero value as true and any zero value as false.

The results of the operators are summarized in **truth tables**, which show the result of each operation for all possible combinations of l_1 and l_2. Table 4-3 shows the truth tables for all logic operators.

Logical ANDs

The result of an AND operator is true (1) if and only if both input operands are true. If either or both operands are false, the result is false (0), as shown in Table 4-3.

Note that there are two logical AND operators: && and &. Why are there two AND operators, and what is the difference between them? The basic difference between && and & is that && supports *short-circuit evaluations* (or *partial evaluations*), while & doesn't. That is, && will evaluate expression l_1 and immediately return a false (0) value if l_1 is false. If l_1 is false, the operator never evaluates l_2, because the result of the operator will be false regardless of the value of l_2. In contrast, the & operator always evaluates both l_1 and l_2 before returning an answer.

A second difference between && and & is that && works only between scalar values, whereas & works with either scalar or array values, as long as the sizes of the arrays are compatible.

When should you use && and when should you use & in a program? Most of the time, it doesn't matter which AND operation is used. If you are comparing scalars and it is not necessary to always evaluate l_2, use the && operator. The partial evaluation will make the operation faster in the cases where the first operand is `false`.

Sometimes it is important to use shortcut expressions. For example, suppose that we wanted to test for the situation where the ratio of two variables a and b is greater than 10. The code to perform this test is

```
x = a / b > 10.0
```

This code normally works fine, but what about the case where b is zero? In that case, we would be dividing by zero, which produces an `Inf` instead of a number. The test could be modified to avoid this problem as follows:

```
x = (b ~= 0) && (a/b > 10.0)
```

This expression uses partial evaluation, so if b = 0, the expression `a/b > 10.0` will never be evaluated, and no `Inf` will occur.

☀ Good Programming Practice

Use the `&` AND operator if it is necessary to ensure that both operands are evaluated in an expression, or if the comparison is between arrays. Otherwise, use the `&&` AND operator, since the partial evaluation will make the operation faster in the cases where the first operand is `false`.

Logical Inclusive ORs

The result of an inclusive OR operator is true (1) if either or both of the input operands are true. If both operands are false, the result is false (0), as shown in Table 4-3.

Note that there are two inclusive OR operators: `||` and `|`. Why are there two inclusive OR operators, and what is the difference between them? The basic difference between `||` and `|` is that `||` supports partial evaluations, while `|` doesn't. That is, `||` will evaluate expression l_1 and immediately return a true value if l_1 is true. If l_1 is true, the operator never evaluates l_2, because the result of the operator will be true regardless of the value of l_2. In contrast, the `|` operator always evaluates both l_1 and l_2 before returning an answer.

A second difference between `||` and `|` is that `||` works only between scalar values, while `|` works with either scalar or array values, as long as the sizes of the arrays are compatible.

When should you use `||` and when should you use `|` in a program? Most of the time, it doesn't matter which OR operation is used. If you are comparing scalars and it is not necessary to always evaluate l_2, use the `||` operator. The partial evaluation will make the operation faster in the cases where the first operand is true.

☀ Good Programming Practice

Use the `|` inclusive OR operator if it is necessary to ensure that both operands are evaluated in an expression, or if the comparison is between arrays. Otherwise, use the `||` operator, since the partial evaluation will make the operation faster in the cases where the first operand is `true`.

Logical Exclusive OR

The result of an exclusive OR operator is true if and only if one operand is true and the other one is false. If both operands are true or both operands are false, the result is false, as shown in Table 4-3. Note that both operands always must be evaluated in order to calculate the result of an exclusive OR.

The logical exclusive OR operation is implemented as a function. For example,

```
a = 10;
b = 0;
x = xor(a, b);
```

The value in a is nonzero, so it is treated as true. The value in b is zero, so it is treated as false. Since one value is true and the other is false, the result of the xor operation will be true, and it returns a value of 1.

Logical NOT

The NOT operator (~) is a unary operator, having only one operand. The result of a NOT operator is true (1) if its operand is zero and false (0) if its operand is nonzero, as shown in Table 4-3.

Hierarchy of Operations

In the hierarchy of operations, logic operators are evaluated *after all arithmetic operations and all relational operators have been evaluated.* The order in which the operators in an expression are evaluated is

1. All arithmetic operators are evaluated first in the order previously described.
2. All relational operators (==, ~=, >, >=, <, <=) are evaluated, working from left to right.
3. All ~ operators are evaluated.
4. All & and && operators are evaluated, working from left to right.
5. All |, ||, and xor operators are evaluated, working from left to right.

As with arithmetic operations, parentheses can be used to change the default order of evaluation. Examples of some logic operators and their results are given in Example 4.1.

▶

Example 4.1

Assume that the following variables are initialized with the values shown and calculate the result of the specified expressions:

```
value1 = 1
value2 = 0
value3 = 2
value4 = -10
value5 = 0
value6 = [1 2; 0 1]
```

SOLUTION

Expression	Result	Comment
(a) `~value1`	false (0)	
(b) `~value3`	false (0)	The number 2 is treated as true, and the NOT operations is applied.
(c) `value1	value2`	true (1)	
(d) `value1 & value2`	false (0)	
(e) `value4 & value5`	false (0)	-10 is treated as true and 0 is treated as false when the AND operation is applied.
(f) `~(value4 & value5)`	true (1)	-10 is treated as true and 0 is treated as false when the AND operation is applied, and then the NOT operation reverses the result.
(g) `value1 + value4`	-9	
(h) `value1 + (~value4)`	1	The number `value4` is nonzero and so is considered true. When the NOT operation is performed, the result is false (0). Then `value1` is added to the 0, the final result is $1 + 0 = 1$.
(i) `value3 && value6`	Illegal	The && operator must be used with scalar operands.
(j) `value3 & value6`	$\begin{bmatrix} 1 & 1 \\ 0 & 1 \end{bmatrix}$	AND between a scalar and an array operand. The nonzero values of array `value6` are treated as true.

◄

The ~ operator is evaluated before other logic operators. Therefore, the parentheses in part *(f)* of the preceding example were required. If they had been absent, the expression in part *(f)* would have been evaluated in the order `(~value4) & value5`.

4.3.4 Logical Functions

MATLAB includes a number of logical functions that return `true` whenever the condition they test for is true and `false` whenever the condition they test for is false. These functions can be used with relational and logic operators to control the operation of branches and loops.

A few of the more important logical functions are given in Table 4-4.

Table 4-4 Selected MATLAB Logical Functions.

Function	Purpose
false	Returns a `false` (0) value.
ischar(a)	Returns `true` if a is a character array and `false` otherwise.
isempty(a)	Returns `true` if a is an empty array and `false` otherwise.
isinf(a)	Returns `true` if the value of a is infinite (`Inf`) and `false` otherwise.
isnan(a)	Returns `true` if the value of a is NaN (not a number) and `false` otherwise.
isnumeric(a)	Returns `true` if a is a numeric array and `false` otherwise.
logical	Converts numerical values to logical values; if a value is nonzero, it is converted to `true`. If it is zero, it is converted to `false`.
true	Returns a `true` (1) value.

Quiz 4.1

This quiz provides a quick check to see if you have understood the concepts introduced in Section 4.3. If you have trouble with the quiz, reread the sections, ask your instructor, or discuss the material with a fellow student. The answers to this quiz are found in the back of the book.

Assume that a, b, c, and d are as defined, and evaluate the following expressions.

$$a = 20; \quad b = -2;$$
$$c = 0; \quad d = 1;$$

1. a > b
2. b > d
3. a > b && c > d
4. a == b
5. a && b > c
6. ~~b

Assume that a, b, c, and d are as defined, and evaluate the following expressions:

$$a = 2; \qquad b = \begin{bmatrix} 1 & -2 \\ 0 & 10 \end{bmatrix};$$
$$c = \begin{bmatrix} 0 & 1 \\ 2 & 0 \end{bmatrix}; \qquad d = \begin{bmatrix} -2 & 1 & 2 \\ 0 & 1 & 0 \end{bmatrix};$$

7. ~(a > b)

8. a > c && b > c

9. c <= d

10. logical(d)

11. a * b > c

12. a * (b > c)

Assume that a, b, c, and d are as defined. Explain the order in which each of the following expressions are evaluated, and specify the results in each case:

$$a = 2; \qquad b = 3;$$
$$c = 10; \qquad d = 0;$$

13. a*b^2 > a*c

14. d || b > a

15. (d | b) > a

Assume that a, b, c, and d are as defined, and evaluate the following expressions.

$$a = 20; \quad b = -2;$$
$$c = 0; \quad d = \text{'Test'};$$

16. isinf(a/b)

17. isinf(a/c)

18. a > b && ischar(d)

19. isempty(c)

20. (~a) & b

21. (~a) + b

4.4 Branches

Branches are MATLAB statements that permit us to select and execute specific sections of code (called *blocks*) while skipping other sections of code. They are variations of the if construct, the switch construct, and the try/catch construct.

4.4.1   The `if` Construct

The `if` construct has the form

```
if control_expr_1
    Statement 1
    Statement 2                    Block 1
    ...
elseif control_expr_2
    Statement 1
    Statement 2                    Block 2
    ...
else
    Statement 1
    Statement 2                    Block 3
    ...
end
```

where the control expressions are logical expressions that control the operation of the `if` construct. If *control_expr_1* is true (nonzero), the program executes the statements in Block 1 and skips to the first executable statement following the `end`. Otherwise, the program checks for the status of *control_expr_2*. If *control_expr_2* is true (nonzero), the program executes the statements in Block 2 and skips to the first executable statement following the `end`. If all control expressions are zero, the program executes the statements in the block associated with the `else` clause.

There can be any number of `elseif` clauses (0 or more) in an `if` construct, but there can be at most one `else` clause. The control expression in each clause will be tested only if the control expressions in every clause above it are false (0). Once one of the expressions proves to be true and the corresponding code block is executed, the program skips to the first executable statement following the `end`. If all control expressions are false, the program executes the statements in the block associated with the `else` clause. If there is no `else` clause, execution continues after the `end` statement without executing any part of the `if` construct.

Note that the MATLAB keyword `end` in this construct is *completely different* from the MATLAB function `end` that we used in Chapter 2 to return the highest value of a given subscript. MATLAB tells the difference between these two uses of `end` from the context in which the word appears within an M-file.

In most circumstances, *the control expressions will be some combination of relational and logic operators.* As we learned earlier in this chapter, relational and logic operators produce a true (1) when the corresponding condition is true and a false (0) when the corresponding condition is false. When an operator is true, its result is nonzero, and the corresponding block of code will be executed.

As an example of an `if` construct, consider the solution of a quadratic equation of the form

$$ax^2 + bx + c = 0 \tag{4.1}$$

The solution to this equation is

$$x = \frac{-b \pm \sqrt{b^2 - 4ac}}{2a} \tag{4.2}$$

The term $b^2 - 4ac$ is known as the *discriminant* of the equation. If $b^2 - 4ac > 0$, there are two distinct real roots to the quadratic equation. If $b^2 - 4ac = 0$, there is a single repeated root to the equation, and if $b^2 - 4ac < 0$, there are two complex roots to the quadratic equation.

Suppose that we wanted to examine the discriminant of a quadratic equation and to tell a user whether the equation has two complex roots, two identical real roots, or two distinct real roots. In pseudocode, this construct would take the form

```
if (b^2 - 4*a*c) < 0
   Write msg that equation has two complex roots.
elseif (b**2 - 4*a*c) == 0
   Write msg that equation has two identical real roots.
else
   Write msg that equation has two distinct real roots.
end
```

The MATLAB statements to do this are

```
if (b^2 - 4*a*c) < 0
   disp('This equation has two complex roots.');
elseif (b^2 - 4*a*c) == 0
   disp('This equation has two identical real roots.');
else
   disp('This equation has two distinct real roots.');
end
```

For readability, the blocks of code within an `if` construct are usually indented by three or four spaces, but this is not actually required.

✳ Good Programming Practice

Always indent the body of an `if` construct by three or more spaces to improve the readability of the code. Note that indentation is automatic if you use the MATLAB editor to write your programs.

It is possible to write a complete `if` construct on a single line by separating the parts of the construct by commas or semicolons. Thus, the following two constructs are identical:

```
if x < 0
   y = abs(x);
end
```

and

```
if x < 0; y = abs(x); end
```

However, this should be done only for very simple constructs.

4.4.2 Examples Using `if` Constructs

We will now look at two examples that illustrate the use of `if` constructs.

▶
━━━

Example 4.2—The Quadratic Equation

Write a program to solve for the roots of a quadratic equation, regardless of type.

SOLUTION   We will follow the design steps outlined earlier in the chapter.

1. **State the problem.**
   The problem statement for this example is very simple. We want to write a program that will solve for the roots of a quadratic equation, whether they are distinct real roots, repeated real roots, or complex roots.

2. **Define the inputs and outputs.**
   The inputs required by this program are the coefficients a, b, and c of the quadratic equation

   $$ax^2 + bx + c = 0 \qquad (4.1)$$

   The output from the program will be the roots of the quadratic equation, whether they are distinct real roots, repeated real roots, or complex roots.

3. **Design the algorithm.**
   This task can be broken down into three major sections, whose functions are input, processing, and output:

   ```
   Read the input data
   Calculate the roots
   Write out the roots
   ```

   We will now break each of these major sections into smaller, more detailed pieces. There are three possible ways to calculate the roots, depending on the value of the discriminant, so it is logical to implement this algorithm with a three-branched `if` construct. The resulting pseudocode is

```
Prompt the user for the coefficients a, b, and c.
Read a, b, and c
discriminant ← b^2 - 4 * a * c
if discriminant > 0
    x1 ← ( -b + sqrt(discriminant) ) / ( 2 * a )
    x2 ← ( -b - sqrt(discriminant) ) / ( 2 * a )
    Write msg that equation has two distinct real roots.
    Write out the two roots.
```

```
       elseif discriminant == 0
          x1 ← -b / ( 2 * a )
          Write msg that equation has two identical real roots.
          Write out the repeated root.
       else
          real_part ← -b / ( 2 * a )
          imag_part ← sqrt ( abs ( discriminant ) ) / ( 2 * a )
          Write msg that equation has two complex roots.
          Write out the two roots.
       end
```

4. **Turn the algorithm into MATLAB statements.**
   The final MATLAB code is shown here.

```
%  Script file: calc_roots.m
%
%  Purpose:
%     This program solves for the roots of a quadratic equation
%     of the form a*x**2 + b*x + c = 0. It calculates the answers
%     regardless of the type of roots that the equation possesses.
%
%  Record of revisions:
%      Date           Programmer          Description of change
%      ====           ==========          =====================
%      01/02/10       S. J. Chapman       Original code
%
%  Define variables:
%      a              -- Coefficient of x^2 term of equation
%      b              -- Coefficient of x term of equation
%      c              -- Constant term of equation
%      discriminant   -- Discriminant of the equation
%      imag_part      -- Imag part of equation (for complex roots)
%      real_part      -- Real part of equation (for complex roots)
%      x1             -- First solution of equation (for real roots)
%      x2             -- Second solution of equation (for real roots)

%  Prompt the user for the coefficients of the equation
disp ('This program solves for the roots of a quadratic ');
disp ('equation of the form A*X^2 + B*X + C = 0. ');
a = input ('Enter the coefficient A: ');
b = input ('Enter the coefficient B: ');
c = input ('Enter the coefficient C: ');

% Calculate discriminant
discriminant = b^2 − 4 * a * c;
```

```
% Solve for the roots, depending on the value of the discriminant
if discriminant > 0 % there are two real roots, so...
    x1 = ( -b + sqrt(discriminant) ) / ( 2 * a );
    x2 = ( -b - sqrt(discriminant) ) / ( 2 * a );
    disp ('This equation has two real roots:');
    fprintf ('x1 = %f\n', x1);
    fprintf ('x2 = %f\n', x2);

elseif discriminant == 0 % there is one repeated root, so...
    x1 = ( -b ) / ( 2 * a );
    disp ('This equation has two identical real roots:');
    fprintf ('x1 = x2 = %f\n', x1);

else % there are complex roots, so ...
    real_part = ( -b ) / ( 2 * a );
    imag_part = sqrt ( abs ( discriminant ) ) / ( 2 * a );
    disp ('This equation has complex roots:');
    fprintf('x1 = %f +i %f\n', real_part, imag_part );
    fprintf('x1 = %f -i %f\n', real_part, imag_part );

end
```

5. **Test the program.**

   Next, we must test the program using real input data. Since there are three possible paths through the program, we must test all three paths before we can be certain that the program is working properly. From Equation (4.1), it is possible to verify the solutions to the equations given here.

$$x^2 + 5x + 6 = 0 \qquad x = -2 \text{ and } x = -3$$
$$x^2 + 4x + 4 = 0 \qquad x = -2$$
$$x^2 + 2x + 5 = 0 \qquad x = -1 \pm i2$$

   If this program is executed three times with the preceding coefficients, the results are as shown here (user inputs are shown in boldface):

```
» calc_roots
This program solves for the roots of a quadratic
equation of the form A*X^2 + B*X + C = 0.
Enter the coefficient A: 1
Enter the coefficient B: 5
Enter the coefficient C: 6
This equation has two real roots:
x1 = -2.000000
x2 = -3.000000
» calc_roots
This program solves for the roots of a quadratic
equation of the form A*X^2 + B*X + C = 0.
```

```
Enter the coefficient A: 1
Enter the coefficient B: 4
Enter the coefficient C: 4
This equation has two identical real roots:
x1 = x2 = -2.000000
» calc_roots
This program solves for the roots of a quadratic
equation of the form A*X^2 + B*X + C = 0.
Enter the coefficient A: 1
Enter the coefficient B: 2
Enter the coefficient C: 5
This equation has complex roots:
x1 = -1.000000 +i 2.000000
x1 = -1.000000 -i 2.000000
```

The program gives the correct answers for our test data in all three possible cases.

◀

▶

Example 4.3—Evaluating a Function of Two Variables

Write a MATLAB program to evaluate a function $f(x,y)$ for any two user-specified values x and y. The function $f(x,y)$ is defined as follows.

$$f(x,y) = \begin{cases} x + y & x \geq 0 \text{ and } y \geq 0 \\ x + y^2 & x \geq 0 \text{ and } y < 0 \\ x^2 + y & x < 0 \text{ and } y \geq 0 \\ x^2 + y^2 & x < 0 \text{ and } y < 0 \end{cases}$$

SOLUTION   The function $f(x,y)$ is evaluated differently depending on the signs of the two independent variables x and y. To determine the proper equation to apply, it will be necessary to check for the signs of the x and y values supplied by the user.

1. **State the problem.**
   This problem statement is very simple: Evaluate the function $f(x,y)$ for any user-supplied values of x and y.

2. **Define the inputs and outputs.**
   The inputs required by this program are the values of the independent variables x and y. The output from the program will be the value of the function $f(x,y)$.

3. **Design the algorithm.**
   This task can be broken down into three major sections, whose functions are input, processing, and output:

   ```
   Read the input values x and y
   Calculate f(x,y)
   Write out f(x,y)
   ```

   We will now break each of the above major sections into smaller, more detailed pieces. There are four possible ways to calculate the function $f(x,y)$, depending on the values of x and y, so it is logical to implement this algorithm with a four-branched IF statement. The resulting pseudocode is

   ```
   Prompt the user for the values x and y.
   Read x and y
   if x ≥ 0 and y ≥ 0
        fun ← x + y
   elseif x ≥ 0 and y < 0
        fun ← x + y^2
   elseif x < 0 and y ≥ 0
        fun ← x^2 + y
   else
        fun ← x^2 + y^2
   end
   Write out f(x,y)
   ```

4. **Turn the algorithm into MATLAB statements.**
   The final MATLAB code is shown here.

```
%  Script file: funxy.m
%
%
%  Purpose:
%     This program solves the function f(x,y) for a
%     user-specified x and y, where f(x,y) is defined as:
%
%
%                    ⎡ x + y              x >= 0 and y >= 0
%                    ⎢ x + y^2            x >= 0 and y < 0
%        f(x,y)  =   ⎢ x^2 + y            x < 0  and y >= 0
%                    ⎢ x^2 + y^2          x < 0  and y < 0
%                    ⎣
%
%
%  Record of revisions:
%       Date          Programmer          Description of change
%       ====          ==========          =====================
%     01/03/10       S. J. Chapman        Original code
%
```

```
% Define variables:
%    x      -- First independent variable
%    y      -- Second independent variable
%    fun    -- Resulting function

% Prompt the user for the values x and y
x = input ('Enter the x coefficient: ');
y = input ('Enter the y coefficient: ');

% Calculate the function f(x,y) based upon
% the signs of x and y.
if x >= 0 && y >= 0
    fun = x + y;
elseif x >= 0 && y < 0
    fun = x + y^2;
elseif x < 0 && y >= 0
    fun = x^2 + y;
else % x < 0 and y < 0, so
    fun = x^2 + y^2;
end

% Write the value of the function.
disp (['The value of the function is ' num2str(fun)]);
```

5. **Test the program.**

   Next, we must test the program using real input data. Since there are four possible paths through the program, we must test all four paths before we can be certain that the program is working properly. To test all four possible paths, we will execute the program with the four sets of input values $(x,y) = (2,3)$, $(2,-3)$, $(-2,3)$, and $(-2,-3)$. Calculating by hand, we see that

   $$f(2, 3) = 2 + 3 = 5$$
   $$f(2, -3) = 2 + (-3)^2 = 11$$
   $$f(-2, 3) = (-2)^2 + 3 = 7$$
   $$f(-2,-3) = (-2)^2 + (-3)^2 = 13$$

   If this program is compiled and then run four times with the preceding values, the results are

   ```
   » funxy
   Enter the x coefficient: 2
   Enter the y coefficient: 3
   The value of the function is 5
   » funxy
   Enter the x coefficient: 2
   Enter the y coefficient: -3
   The value of the function is 11
   ```

```
» funxy
Enter the x coefficient: -2
Enter the y coefficient: 3
The value of the function is 7
» funxy
Enter the x coefficient: -2
Enter the y coefficient: -3
The value of the function is 13
```

The program gives the correct answers for our test values in all four possible cases.

◀

4.4.3 Notes Concerning the Use of `if` Constructs

The `if` construct is very flexible. It must have one `if` statement and one `end` statement. In between, it can have any number of `elseif` clauses and also may have one `else` clause. With this combination of features, it is possible to implement any desired branching construct.

In addition, `if` constructs may be **nested**. Two `if` constructs are said to be nested if one of them lies entirely within a single code block of the other one. The following two `if` constructs are properly nested.

```
if x > 0
    ...
    if y < 0
        ...
    end
    ...
end
```

The MATLAB interpreter always associates a given `end` statement with the most recent `if` statement, so the first `end` above closes the `if y < 0` statement, while the second `end` closes the `if x > 0` statement. This works well for a properly written program but can cause the interpreter to produce confusing error messages in cases where the programmer makes a coding error. For example, suppose that we have a large program containing a construct like the one shown here.

```
    ...
if (test1)
    ...
    if (test2)
        ...
```

```
            if (test3)
               ...
            end
            ...
        end
        ...
    end
```

This program contains three nested `if` constructs that may span hundreds of lines of code. Now suppose that the first `end` statement is accidentally deleted during an editing session. When that happens, the MATLAB interpreter will automatically associate the second `end` with the innermost `if (test3)` construct and the third `end` with the middle `if (test2)`. When the interpreter reaches the end of the file, it will notice that the first `if (test1)` construct was never ended, and it will generate an error message saying that there is a missing end. Unfortunately, it can't tell *where* the problem occurred, so we will have to go back and manually search the entire program to locate the problem.

It is sometimes possible to implement an algorithm using either multiple `elseif` clauses or nested `if` statements. In that case, the program designer may choose whichever style he or she prefers.

▶

Example 4.4—Assigning Letter Grades

Suppose that we are writing a program which reads in a numerical grade and assigns a letter grade to it according to the following table:

```
95 < grade             A
86 < grade ≤ 95        B
76 < grade ≤ 86        C
66 < grade ≤ 76        D
 0 < grade ≤ 66        F
```

Write an `if` construct that will assign the grades as described previously using *(a)* multiple `elseif` clauses and *(b)* nested `if` constructs.

SOLUTION

(a) One possible structure using `elseif` clauses is

```
if grade > 95.0
   disp('The grade is A.');
elseif grade > 86.0
   disp('The grade is B.');
elseif grade > 76.0
   disp('The grade is C.');
```

```
      elseif grade > 66.0
         disp('The grade is D.');
      else
         disp('The grade is F.');
      end
```

(b) One possible structure using nested `if` constructs is

```
if grade > 95.0
   disp('The grade is A.');
else
   if grade > 86.0
      disp('The grade is B.');
   else
      if grade > 76.0
         disp('The grade is C.');
      else
         if grade > 66.0
            disp('The grade is D.');
         else
            disp('The grade is F.');
         end
      end
   end
end
```

◀

It should be clear from the preceding example that if there are a lot of mutually exclusive options, a single `if` construct with multiple `elseif` clauses will be simpler than a nested `if` construct.

✳ Good Programming Practice

For branches in which there are many mutually exclusive options, use a single `if` construct with multiple `elseif` clauses in preference to nested `if` constructs.

4.4.4 The switch Construct

The `switch` construct is another form of branching construct. It permits an engineer to select a particular code block to execute based on the value of a single integer, character, or logical expression. The general form of a `switch` construct is

```
switch (switch_expr)
case case_expr_1
    Statement 1      ⎫
    Statement 2      ⎬  Block 1
    ...              ⎭
case case_expr_2
    Statement 1      ⎫
    Statement 2      ⎬  Block 2
    ...              ⎭
...
otherwise
    Statement 1      ⎫
    Statement 2      ⎬  Block n
    ...              ⎭
end
```

If the value of *switch_expr* is equal to *case_expr_1*, the first code block will be executed and the program will jump to the first statement following the end of the switch construct. Similarly, if the value of *switch_expr* is equal to *case_expr_2*, the second code block will be executed and the program will jump to the first statement following the end of the switch construct. The same idea applies for any other cases in the construct. The otherwise code block is optional. If it is present, it will be executed whenever the value of *switch_expr* is outside the range of all of the case selectors. If it is not present and the value of *switch_expr* is outside the range of all of the case selectors, none of the code blocks will be executed. The pseudocode for the case construct looks just like its MATLAB implementation.

If many values of the *switch_expr* should cause the same code to execute, all of those values may be included in a single block by enclosing them in brackets, as shown at the end of this paragraph. If the switch expression matches any of the case expressions in the list, the block will be executed.

```
switch (switch_expr)
case {case_expr_1, case_expr_2, case_expr_3}
    Statement 1      ⎫
    Statement 2      ⎬  Block 1
    ...              ⎭
otherwise
    Statement 1      ⎫
    Statement 2      ⎬  Block n
    ...              ⎭
end
```

The *switch_expr* and each *case_expr* may be either numerical or string values.

Note that at most one code block can be executed. After a code block is executed, execution skips to the first executable statement after the end statement. Thus, if the switch expression matches more than one case expression, *only the first one of them will be executed.*

Let's look at a simple example of a switch construct. The following statements determine whether an integer between 1 and 10 is even or odd and print out an appropriate message. It illustrates the use of a list of values as case selectors as well as the use of the otherwise block.

```
switch (value)
case {1,3,5,7,9}
    disp('The value is odd.');
case {2,4,6,8,10}
    disp('The value is even.');
otherwise
    disp('The value is out of range.');
end
```

4.4.5 The try/catch Construct

The try/catch construct is a special form of branching construct designed to trap errors. Ordinarily, when a MATLAB program encounters an error while running, the program aborts. The try/catch construct modifies this default behavior. If an error occurs in a statement in the try block of this construct, then instead of aborting, the code in the catch block is executed and the program keeps running. This allows an engineer to handle errors within the program without causing the program to stop.

The general form of a try/catch construct is

```
try
    Statement 1
    Statement 2          ⎫
    ...                  ⎬  Try Block
                         ⎭
catch
    Statement 1
    Statement 2          ⎫
    ...                  ⎬  Catch Block
                         ⎭
end
```

When a try/catch construct is reached, the statements in the try block of a will be executed. If no error occurs, the statements in the catch block will be skipped, and execution will continue at the first statement following the end of the construct. On the other hand, if an error *does* occur in the try block, the program will stop executing the statements in the try block and will immediately execute the statements in the catch block.

An example program containing a try/catch construct follows. This program creates an array and asks the user to specify an element of the array to display.

The user will supply a subscript number, and the program will display the corresponding array element. The statements in the `try` block always will be executed in this program, while the statements in the `catch` block will be executed only if an error occurs in the `try` block.

```
% Initialize array
a = [ 1 -3 2 5];
try
   % Try to display an element
   index = input('Enter subscript of element to display: ');
   disp( ['a(' int2str(index) ') = ' num2str(a(index))] );
catch
   % If we get here an error occurred
   disp( ['Illegal subscript: ' int2str(index)] );
end
```

When this program is executed, the results are:

```
» try_catch
Enter subscript of element to display: 3
a(3) = 2
» try_catch
Enter subscript of element to display: 8
Illegal subscript: 8
```

Quiz 4.2

This quiz provides a quick check to see if you have understood the concepts introduced in Section 4.4. If you have trouble with the quiz, reread the section, ask your instructor, or discuss the material with a fellow student. The answers to this quiz are found in the back of the book.

Write MATLAB statements that perform the functions described here.

1. If x is greater than or equal to zero, assign the square root of x to variable `sqrt_x` and print out the result. Otherwise, print out an error message about the argument of the square root function and set `sqrt_x` to zero.

2. A variable `fun` is calculated as `numerator / denominator`. If the absolute value of `denominator` is less than 1.0E-300, write "Divide by 0 error." Otherwise, calculate and print out `fun`.

3. The cost per mile for a rented vehicle is $1.00 for the first 100 miles, $0.80 for the next 200 miles, and $0.70 for all miles in excess of 300 miles. Write MATLAB statements that determine the total cost and the average cost per mile for a given number of miles (stored in variable `distance`).

Examine the following MATLAB statements. Are they correct or incorrect? If they are correct, what do they output? If they are incorrect, what is wrong with them?

4.
```
if volts > 125
    disp('WARNING: High voltage on line.');
if volts < 105
    disp('WARNING: Low voltage on line.');
else
    disp('Line voltage is within tolerances.');
end
```

5.
```
color = 'yellow';
switch ( color )
case 'red',
    disp('Stop now!');
case 'yellow',
    disp('Prepare to stop.');
case 'green',
    disp('Proceed through intersection.');
otherwise,
    disp('Illegal color encountered.');
end
```

6.
```
if temperature > 37
    disp('Human body temperature exceeded.');
elseif temperature > 100
    disp('Boiling point of water exceeded.');
end
```

▶

Example 4.5—Electrical Engineering: Frequency Response of a Low-Pass Filter:

A simple low-pass filter circuit is shown in Figure 4.2. This circuit consists of a resistor and capacitor in series, and the ratio of the output voltage V_o to the input voltage V_i is given by the equation

$$\frac{V_o}{V_i} = \frac{1}{1 + j2\pi fRC} \tag{4.3}$$

where V_i is a sinusoidal input voltage of frequency f, R is the resistance in ohms, C is the capacitance in farads, and j is $\sqrt{-1}$ (electrical engineers use j instead of i for $\sqrt{-1}$, because the letter i is traditionally reserved for the current in a circuit).

Assume that the resistance $R = 16$ kΩ and capacitance $C = 1$ μF, and plot the amplitude and frequency response of this filter for the frequency range $0 <= f <= 1000$ Hz.

SOLUTION The amplitude response of a filter is the ratio of the amplitude of the output voltage to the amplitude of the input voltage, and the phase response of the filter is the difference between the phase of the output voltage and the phase of

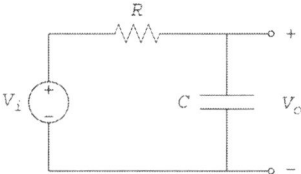

Figure 4.2 A simple low-pass filter circuit.

the input voltage. The simplest way to calculate the amplitude and phase response of the filter is to evaluate Equation (4.3) at many different frequencies. The plot of the magnitude of Equation (4.3) versus frequency is the amplitude response of the filter, and the plot of the angle of Equation (4.3) versus frequency is the phase response of the filter.

Because the frequency and amplitude response of a filter can vary over a wide range, it is customary to plot both of these values on logarithmic scales. On the other hand, the phase varies over a very limited range, so it is customary to plot the phase of the filter on a linear scale. Therefore, we will use a `loglog` plot for the amplitude response and a `semilogx` plot for the phase response of the filter. We will display both responses as two subplots within a figure.

We will also use stream modifiers to make the title and axis labels appear in boldface, as that improves the appearance of the plots.

The MATLAB code required to create and plot the responses is shown here.

```
%  Script file: plot_filter.m
%
%  Purpose:
%    This program plots the amplitude and phase responses
%    of a low-pass RC filter.
%
%  Record of revisions:
%      Date            Programmer          Description of change
%      ====            ==========          =====================
%    01/05/10     S. J. Chapman       Original code
%
% Define variables:
%    amp          -- Amplitude response
%    C            -- Capacitiance (farads)
%    f            -- Frequency of input signal (Hz)
%    phase        -- Phase response
%    R            -- Resistance (ohms)
%    res          -- Vo/Vi

% Initialize R & C
R = 16000;                        % 16 k ohms
C = 1.0E-6;                       % 1 uF
```

```
% Create array of input frequencies
f = 1:2:1000;

% Calculate response
res = 1 ./ ( 1 + j*2*pi*f*R*C );

% Calculate amplitude response
amp = abs(res);

% Calculate phase response
phase = angle(res);

% Create plots
subplot(2,1,1);
loglog( f, amp );
title('\bfAmplitude Response');
xlabel('\bfFrequency (Hz)');
ylabel('\bfOutput/Input Ratio');
grid on;

subplot(2,1,2);
semilogx( f, phase );
title('\bfPhase Response');
xlabel('\bfFrequency (Hz)');
ylabel('\bfOutput-Input Phase (rad)');
grid on;
```

The resulting amplitude and phase responses are shown in Figure 4.3. Note that this circuit is called a low-pass filter because low frequencies are passed through with little attenuation, while high frequencies are strongly attenuated.

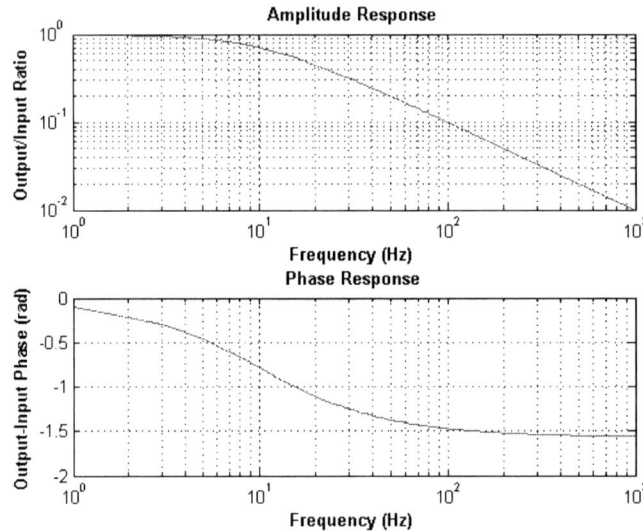

Figure 4.3 The amplitude and phase response of the low-pass filter circuit.

▶

Example 4.6—Thermodynamics: The Ideal Gas Law

An ideal gas is one in which all collisions between molecules are perfectly elastic. It is possible to think of the molecules in an ideal gas as perfectly hard billiard balls that collide and bounce off of each other without losing kinetic energy.

Such a gas can be characterized by three quantities: absolute pressure (P), volume (V), and absolute temperature (T). The relationship among these quantities in an ideal gas is known as the ideal gas law:

$$PV = nRT \qquad (4.4)$$

where P is the pressure of the gas in kilopascals (kPa), V is the volume of the gas in liters (L), n is the number of molecules of the gas in units of moles (mol), R is the universal gas constant (8.314 L·kPa/mol·K), and T is the absolute temperature in kelvins (K). (*Note*: 1 mol = 6.02×10^{23} molecules.)

Assume that a sample of an ideal gas contains 1 mole of molecules at a temperature of 273 K and answer the following questions.

(a) How does the volume of this gas vary as its pressure varies from 1 to 1000 kPa? Plot pressure versus volume for this gas on an appropriate set of axes. Use a solid red line, with a width of 2 pixels.

(b) Suppose that the temperature of the gas is increased to 373 K. How does the volume of this gas vary with pressure now? Plot pressure versus volume for this gas on the same set of axes as part *(a)*. Use a dashed blue line, with a width of 2 pixels.

Include a boldface title and *x*- and *y*-axis labels on the plot, as well as legends for each line.

SOLUTION   The values that we wish to plot both vary by a factor of 1000, so an ordinary linear plot will not produce a particularly useful result. Therefore, we will plot the data on a log-log scale.

Note that we must plot two curves on the same set of axes, so we must issue the commands hold on after the first one is plotted and hold off after the plot is complete. It will also be necessary to specify the color, style, and width of each line and to specify that labels be in boldface.

A program that calculates the volume of the gas as a function of pressure and creates the appropriate plot is shown at the end of this paragraph. The special features controlling the style of the plot are shown in boldface.

```
%   Script file: ideal_gas.m
%
%   Purpose:
%     This program plots the pressure versus volume of an
%     ideal gas.
%
```

```
%  Record of revisions:
%      Date           Programmer       Description of change
%      ====           ==========       =====================
%    01/16/10    S. J. Chapman       Original code
%
% Define variables:
%    n            -- Number of atoms (mol)
%    P            -- Pressure (kPa)
%    R            -- Ideal gas constant (L kPa/mol K)
%    T            -- Temperature (K)
%    V            -- volume (L)

% Initialize nRT
n = 1;                     % Moles of atoms
R = 8.314;                 % Ideal gas constant
T = 273;                   % Temperature (K)

% Create array of input pressures. Note that this
% array must be quite dense to catch the major
% changes in volume at low pressures.
P = 1:0.1:1000;

% Calculate volumes
V = (n * R * T) ./ P;
% Create first plot
figure(1);
loglog( P, V, 'r-', 'LineWidth', 2);
title('\bfVolume vs Pressure in an Ideal Gas');
xlabel('\bfPressure (kPa)');
ylabel('\bfVolume (L)');
grid on;
hold on;

% Now increase temperature
T = 373;                     % Temperature (K)

% Calculate volumes
V = (n * R * T) ./ P;

% Add second line to plot
figure(1);
loglog( P, V, 'b--', 'LineWidth', 2 );
hold off;

% Add legend
legend('T = 273 K','T = 373 k');
```

The resulting volume versus pressure plot shown in Figure 4.4.

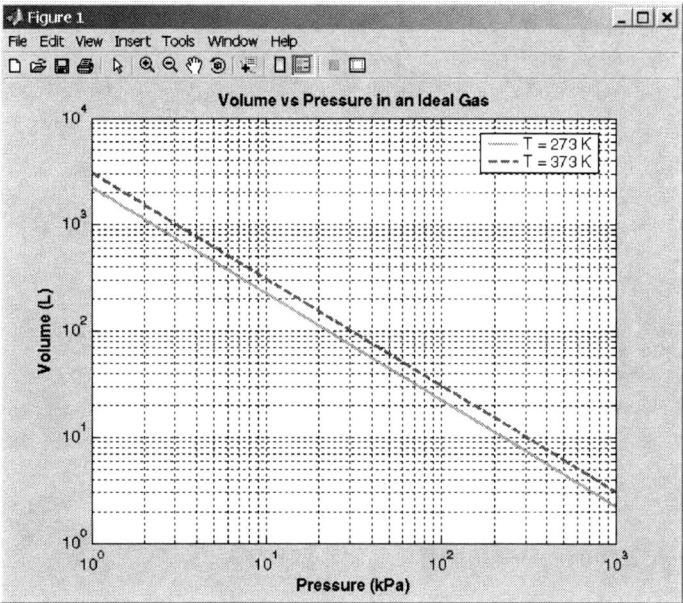

Figure 4.4   Pressure versus volume for an ideal gas.

4.5   More on Debugging MATLAB Programs

It is much easier to make a mistake when writing a program containing branches and loops than it is when writing simple sequential programs. Even after we have gone through the full design process, a program of any size is almost guaranteed not to be completely correct the first time it is used. Suppose that we have built the program and tested it, only to find that the output values are in error. How do we go about finding the bugs and fixing them?

Once programs start to include loops and branches, the best way to locate an error is to use the symbolic debugger supplied with MATLAB. This debugger is integrated with the MATLAB editor.

To use the debugger, first open the file that you would like to debug using the "File/Open" menu selection in the MATLAB Command Window. When the file is opened, it is loaded into the editor and the syntax is automatically color coded. Comments in the file appear in green, variables and numbers appear in black, character strings appear in red, and language keywords appear in blue. Figure 4.5 shows an example Edit/Debug window containing the file `calc_roots.m`.

Let's say that we would like to determine what happens when the program is executed. To do this, we can set one or more **breakpoints** by right-clicking the

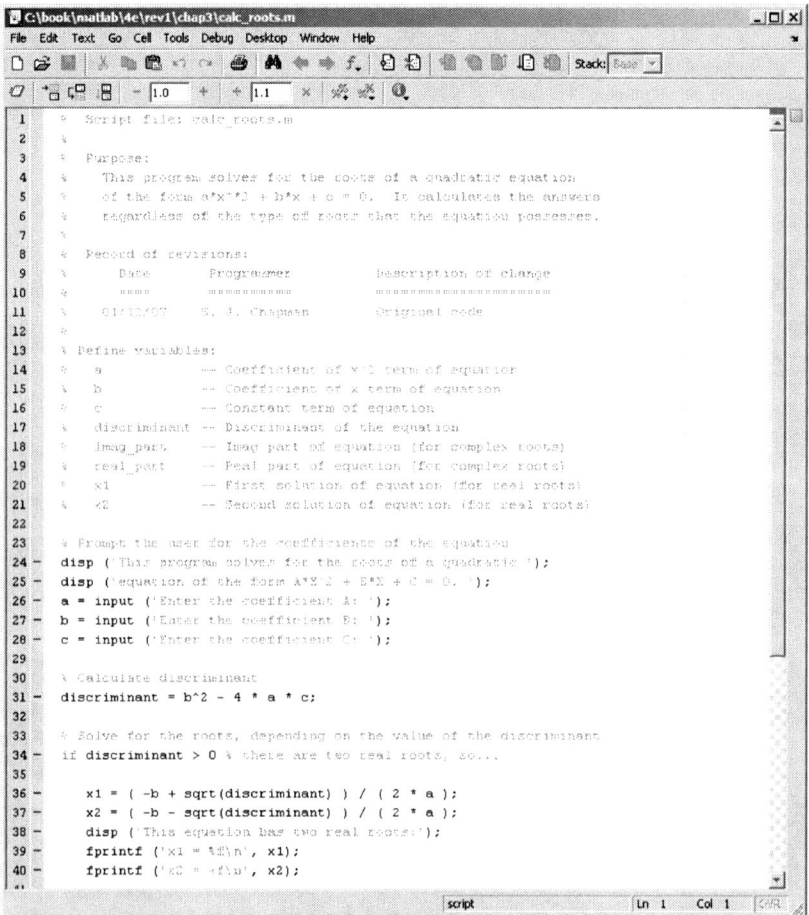

Figure 4.5 An Edit/Debug window with a MATLAB program loaded.

mouse on the lines of interest and choosing the "Set/Clear Breakpoint" option. When a breakpoint is set, a red dot appears to the left of that line containing the breakpoint, as shown in Figure 4.6.

Once the breakpoints have been set, execute the program as usual by typing calc_roots in the Command Window. The program will run until it reaches the first breakpoint and stop there. A green arrow will appear by the current line during the debugging process, as shown in Figure 4.7. When the breakpoint is reached, the programmer can examine and/or modify any variable in the workspace by typing its name in the Command Window. When the programmer is satisfied with the program at that point, he or she can either step through the program a line at a time by repeatedly pressing F10, or else run to the next breakpoint by pressing F5. It is always possible to examine the values of any variable at any point in the program.

Figure 4.6   The window after a breakpoint has been set. Note the red dot to the left of the line with the breakpoint.

When a bug is found, the programmer can use the Editor to correct the MATLAB program and save the modified version to disk. Note that all break-points may be lost when the program is saved to disk, so they may have to be set again before debugging can continue. This process is repeated until the program appears to be bug-free.

Two other very important features of the debugger are found in the "Debug" menu (see Figure 4.8). The first feature is "Set/Modify Conditional Breakpoint." A **conditional breakpoint** is a breakpoint where the code stops only if some con-dition is true. For example, a conditional breakpoint can be used to stop execu-tion inside a `for` loop on its 200th execution. This can be important if a bug appears only after a loop has been executed many times. The condition that causes the breakpoint to stop execution can be modified, and the breakpoint can be enabled or disabled during debugging.

The second feature is "Stop if Errors/Warnings." If an error is occurring in a program that causes it to crash or generate warning messages, the program developer

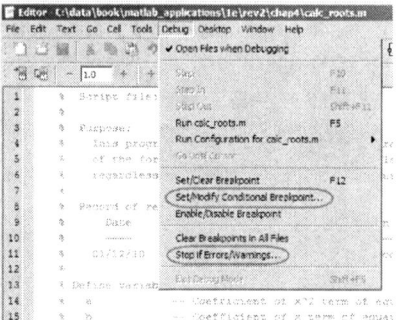

Figure 4.7 A green arrow will appear by the current line during the debugging process.

Figure 4.8 Options on the Debug menu.

can turn this item on and execute the program. It will run to the point of the error and stop there, allowing the developer to examine the values of variables and find out exactly what is causing the problem.

A final critical feature is a tool called M-Lint. M-Lint examines a MATLAB file and looks for potential problems. If it finds a problem, it shades that part of the code in the Editor (see Figure 4.9). If the developer places the mouse cursor over the shaded area, a popup will appear describing the problem so that it can be fixed. It is also possible to display a complete list of all problems in a MATLAB file using the "Tools > M-Lint > Show M-Lint Report" menu option.

M-Lint is a *great* tool for locating errors, poor usage, or obsolete features in MATLAB code, including such things as variables that are defined but never used. You should always run M-Lint over your programs when they are finished as a final check that everything has been done properly.

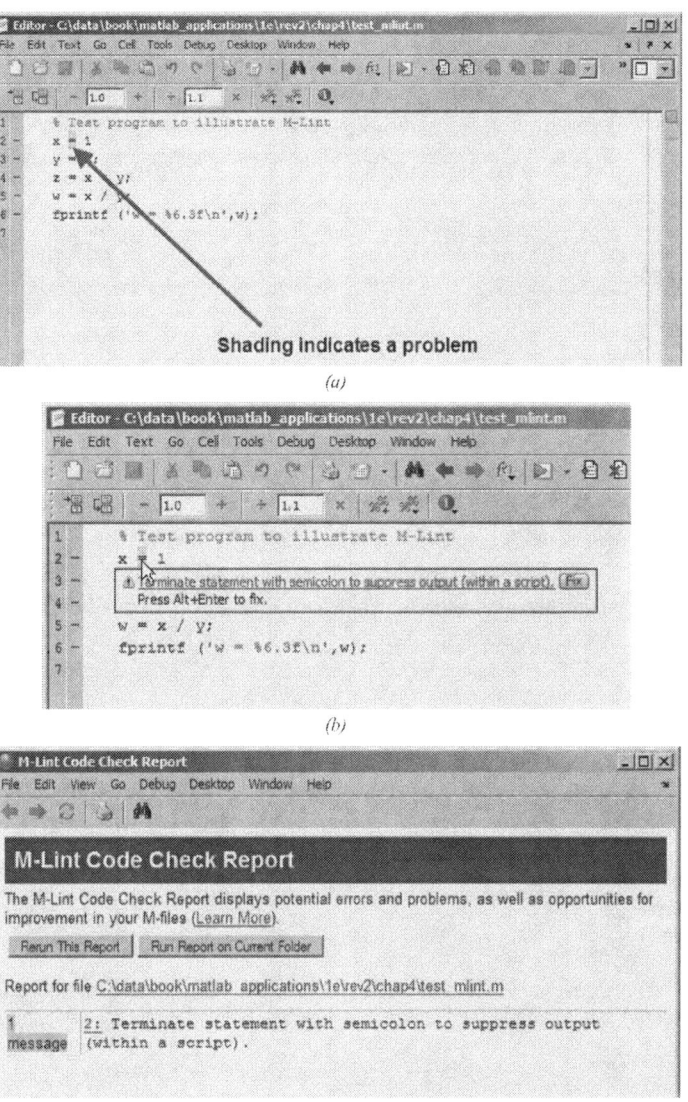

Figure 4.9   Using M-Lint: *(a)* A shaded area in the Editor indicates a problem. *(b)* Placing the mouse over the shaded area produces a popup describing the problem. *(c)* A full report also can be generated using the "Tools > M-Lint > Show M-Lint Report" menu option.

4.6 MATLAB Applications: Roots of Polynomials

The sample programs that we develop in this textbook are often special cases of a more general problem that is solved by one or more built-in MATLAB functions. The standard MATLAB functions are usually more general and more robust than anything that we could write in reasonable time on our own, because the Mathworks has had many people working on their algorithms for many years and they have "ironed out" all the bugs and issues. It is important to know of the existence of these functions and how to use them in any practical problems that we wish to solve in advanced science or engineering classes or in the real world after graduation.

A good example of this is in functions for finding the roots of polynomials. In Example 4.2, we developed a program that solved for the roots of the quadratic equation (a second-order polynomial). We designed the program, wrote the MATLAB code, and then tested it with examples of each possible type of output (the possible results of the discriminant).

The program in Example 4.2 was restricted to finding the roots of a second-order (quadratic) polynomial. A general polynomial is an equation of the form:

$$a_n x^n + a_{n-1} x^{n-1} + \ldots + a_1 x + a_0 = 0 \tag{4.5}$$

where n can be any positive integer. When $n = 2$, the polynomial is a second-order (quadratic) equation. When $n = 3$, the polynomial is a third-order (cubic) equation, and so forth.

In general, a polynomial equation of nth order has n roots, each of which may be real, repeated, or imaginary. There is no simple closed-form solution for the roots of arbitrary polynomials of any order, so solving for roots can be quite a difficult problem. Solving for roots is also critically important in many areas of engineering, since the roots of certain polynomials correspond to the vibrational modes of structures and similar real-world problems. In many engineering applications, writing the equations that represent the operation of an electrical or mechanical system is comparatively easy, but actually finding the behavior of the system requires us to solve for the roots of these systems of linear equations.[2]

Naturally, MATLAB comes with a built-in function to solve this problem. This function is called roots. It solves for the roots of any polynomial, and it does so in a very robust fashion. If you can represent the behavior of the system you are studying as a polynomial, MATLAB provides an easy way to solve for its roots.

The function roots has the form

$$r = roots(p)$$

where p is an array containing the coefficients of the polynomial whose roots are being sought

$$p = [a_n \quad a_{n-1} \quad \ldots \quad a_1 \quad a_2]$$

---

[2]These roots are called the *eigenvalues* of the system. If you haven't heard of this term yet, you will!

The resulting roots appear as a column vector in r.

The sample equations that we used to verify Example 4.2 are given here.

$$x^2 + 5x + 6 = 0 \qquad x = -2 \text{ and } x = -3$$
$$x^2 + 4x + 4 = 0 \qquad x = -2$$
$$x^2 + 2x + 5 = 0 \qquad x = -1 \pm i2$$

We can solve for the roots of these sample equations using the function `roots`:

```
» p = [1 5 6];
» r = roots(p)
r =
    -3.0000
    -2.0000
» p = [1 4 4];
» r = roots(p)
r =
    -2
    -2
» p = [1 2 5];
» r = roots(p)
r =
    -1.0000 + 2.0000i
    -1.0000 - 2.0000i
```

These are the same answers as we got before by hand calculation and by the program `calc_roots`.

MATLAB also includes a function `poly` that builds the coefficients of a polynomial from a list of roots. The function `poly` has the form

```
p = roots(r)
```

where r is an column vector of roots and p is an array containing the coefficients of the polynomial. This is the inverse function of `roots`: `roots` finds the roots of a given polynomial, and `poly` finds the polynomial that produces the given roots.

For example,

```
» r = [-2; -2];
» p = poly(r)
p =
    1    4    4
```

▶
═══

Example 4.7—Finding the Roots of a Polynomial

Find the roots of the fourth-order polynomial

$$y(x) = x^4 + 2x^3 + x^2 - 8x - 20 = 0 \tag{4.6}$$

Plot the function to show that the real roots of the polynomial are actually points where the function crosses the *x*-axis.

SOLUTION   The roots of this function can be found as follows:

```
» p = [1 2 1 -8 -20];
» r = roots(p)
r =
    2.0000
   -1.0000 + 2.0000i
   -1.0000 - 2.0000i
   -2.0000
```

The real roots of this polynomial are at -2 and 2. This function can be plotted using the following script:

```
x = [-3:0.05:3];
y = x.^4 + 2*x.^3 + x.^2 - 8*x -20];
plot(x,y)
grid on;
xlabel('\bf\itx');
ylabel('\bf\ity');
```

The resulting plot is shown in Figure 4.10. Note that the roots occur at -2 and 2, as calculated.

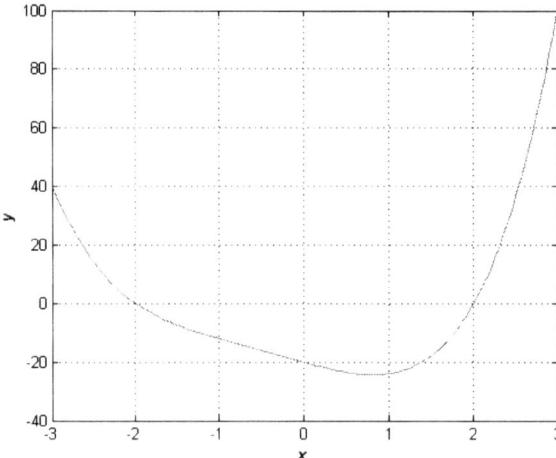

Figure 4.10   A plot of the function $y = x^4 + 2x^3 + x^2 - 8x - 20$. Note that the roots occur at -2 and 2, as calculated.

4.7   Summary

In Chapter 4, we have presented the basic types of MATLAB branches and the relational and logic operations used to control them. The principal type of branch is the `if` construct. This construct is very flexible. It can have as many `elseif` clauses as needed to construct any desired test. Furthermore, `if` constructs can be nested to produce more complex tests. A second type of branch is the `switch` construct. It may be used to select among mutually exclusive alternatives specified by a control expression. A third type of branch is the `try/catch` construct. It is used to trap errors that might occur during execution.

The MATLAB symbolic debugger and related tools such as M-Lint make debugging MATLAB code much easier. You should invest some time to become familiar with these tools.

Use the MATLAB function `roots` to find the roots of a polynomial. It works well for polynomials of any order.

4.7.1   Summary of Good Programming Practice

The following guidelines should be adhered to when programming with branch or loop constructs. If you follow them consistently, your code will contain fewer bugs, will be easier to debug, and will be more understandable to others who may need to work with it in the future.

1. Follow the steps of the program design process to produce reliable, understandable MATLAB programs.
2. Be cautious about testing for equality with numeric values, since roundoff errors may cause two variables that should be equal to fail a test for equality. Instead, test to see if the variables are *nearly* equal within the roundoff error to be expected on the computer you are working with.
3. Use the `&` AND operator if it is necessary to ensure that both operands are evaluated in an expression or if the comparison is between arrays. Otherwise, use the `&&` AND operator, since the partial evaluation will make the operation faster in the cases where the first operand is `false`.
4. Use the `|` inclusive OR operator if it is necessary to ensure that both operands are evaluated in an expression or if the comparison is between arrays. Otherwise, use the `||` operator, since the partial evaluation will make the operation faster in the cases where the first operand is `true`.
5. Always indent code blocks in `if`, `switch`, and `try/catch` constructs to make them more readable.
6. For branches in which there are many mutually exclusive options, use a single `if` construct with multiple `elseif` clauses in preference to nested `if` constructs.

4.7.2   MATLAB Summary

The following summary lists all of the MATLAB commands and functions described in this chapter, along with a brief description of each one.

Commands and Functions

if construct	Selects a block of statements to execute if a specified condition is satisfied.
ischar(a)	Returns a 1 if a is a character array and a 0 otherwise.
isempty(a)	Returns a 1 if a is an empty array and a 0 otherwise.
isinf(a)	Returns a 1 if the value of a is infinite (Inf) and a 0 otherwise.
isnan(a)	Returns a 1 if the value of a is NaN (not a number) and a 0 otherwise.
isnumeric(a)	Returns a 1 if the a is a numeric array and a 0 otherwise.
logical	Converts numeric data to logical data, with nonzero values becoming true and zero values becoming false.
poly	Converts a list of roots of a polynomial into the polynomial coefficients.
root	Calculates the roots of a polynomial expressed as a series of coefficients.
switch construct	Selects a block of statements to execute from a set of mutually exclusive choices based on the result of a single expression.
try/catch construct	A special construct used to trap errors. If an error occurs during the execution of the code in the try block, execution will stop, and the code in the catch block will be executed instead.

4.8   Exercises

4.1 **van der Waals Equation** The ideal gas law describes the temperature, pressure, and volume of an ideal gas. It is

$$PV = nRT \tag{4.4}$$

where P is the pressure of the gas in kilopascals (kPa), V is the volume of the gas in liters (L), n is the number of molecules of the gas in units of moles (mol), R is the universal gas constant (8.314 L·kPa/mol·K), and T is the absolute temperature in kelvins (K). (*Note*: 1 mol = 6.02×10^{23} molecules.)

Real gasses are not ideal because the molecules of the gas are not perfectly elastic—they tend to cling together a bit. The relationship between the temperature, pressure, and volume of a real gas can be represented by a modification of the ideal gas law called *van der Waals Equation*. It is

$$\left(P + \frac{n^2 a}{V^2}\right)(V - nb) = nRT \tag{4.7}$$

where P is the pressure of the gas in kilopascals (kPa), V is the volume of the gas in liters (L), a is a measure of attraction between the particles, n is the number of molecules of the gas in units of moles (mol), b is the volume of one mole of the particles, R is the universal gas constant (8.314 L·kPa/mol·K), and T is the absolute temperature in kelvins (K).

This equation can be solved for P to give pressure as a function of temperature and volume.

$$P = \frac{nRT}{V - nb} - \frac{n^2 a}{V^2} \qquad (4.8)$$

For carbon dioxide, the value of $a = 0.396$ kPa · L and the value of $b = 0.0427$ L/mol. Assume that a sample of carbon dioxide gas contains 1 mole of molecules at a temperature of 0°C (273 K) and occupies 30 L of volume. Answer the following questions.

(a) What is the pressure of the gas according to the ideal gas law?
(b) What is the pressure of the gas according to the van der Waals equation?
(c) Plot the pressure versus volume at this temperature according to the ideal gas law and according to the van der Waals equation on the same axes. Is the pressure of a real gas higher or lower than the pressure of an ideal gas under the same temperature conditions?

4.2 Suppose that a polynomial equation has the following six roots: -6, -2, $1 + i\sqrt{2}$, $1 - i\sqrt{2}$, 2, and 6. Find the coefficients of the polynomial.

4.3 Find the roots of the polynomial equation

$$y(x) = x^6 - x^5 - 6x^4 + 14x^3 - 12x^2$$

Plot the resulting function, and compare the observed roots to the calculated roots. Also, plot the location of the roots on a complex plane.

4.4 **Antenna Gain Pattern** The gain G of a certain microwave dish antenna can be expressed as a function of angle by the equation

$$G(\theta) = |\text{sinc } 4\theta| \text{ for } -\frac{\pi}{2} \le \theta \le \frac{\pi}{2} \qquad (4.9)$$

where θ is measured in radians from the boresite of the dish, and sinc $x = \sin x / x$. Plot this gain function on a polar plot, with the title "**Antenna Gain vs θ**" in boldface.

4.5 The author of this book now lives in Australia. In 2009, individual citizens and residents of Australia paid the following income taxes:

Taxable Income (in A$)	Tax on This Income
$0–$6,000	None
$6,001–$34,000	15¢ for each $1 over $6,000
$34,001–$80,000	$4,200 plus 30¢ for each $1 over $34,000
$80,001–$180,000	$18,000 plus 40¢ for each $1 over $80,000
Over $180,000	$58,000 plus 45¢ for each $1 over $180,000

In addition, a flat 1.5% Medicare levy is charged on all income. Write a program to calculate how much income tax a person will owe based on this information. The program should accept a total income figure from the user, and calculate the income tax, Medicare levy, and total tax payable by the individual.

4.6 In 2002, individual citizens and residents of Australia paid the following income taxes:

Taxable Income (in A$)	Tax on This Income
$0–$6,000	None
$6,001–$20,000	17¢ for each $1 over $6,000
$20,001–$50,000	$2,380 plus 30¢ for each $1 over $20,000
$50,001–$60,000	$11,380 plus 42¢ for each $1 over $50,000
Over $60,000	$15,580 plus 47¢ for each $1 over $60,000

In addition, a flat 1.5% Medicare levy was charged on all income. Write a program to calculate how much *less* income tax a person paid on a given amount of income in 2009 than he or she would have paid in 2002.

4.7 **Refraction** When a ray of light passes from a region with an index of refraction n_1 into a region with a different index of refraction n_2, the light ray is bent (see Figure 4.11). The angle at which the light is bent is given by *Snell's law*:

$$n_1 \sin \theta_1 = n_2 \sin \theta_2 \tag{4.10}$$

where θ_1 is the angle of incidence of the light in the first region and θ_2 is the angle of incidence of the light in the second region. Using Snell's law, it is possible to predict the angle of incidence of a light ray in Region 2 if the angle of incidence θ_1 in Region 1 and the indices of refraction n_1 and n_2 are known. The equation to perform this calculation is

$$\theta_2 = \sin^{-1}\left(\frac{n_2}{n_1} \sin \theta_1\right) \tag{4.11}$$

Write a program to calculate the angle of incidence (in degrees) of a light ray in Region 2 given the angle of incidence θ_1 in Region 1 and the indices of refraction n_1 and n_2. (*Note:* If $n_1 > n_2$, then for some angles θ_1, Equation 4.11 will have no real solution, because the absolute value of the quantity $\left(\frac{n_2}{n_1} \sin \theta_1\right)$ will be greater than 1.0. When this occurs, all light is reflected back into Region 1, and no light passes into Region 2 at all. Your program must be able to recognize and properly handle this condition.)

The program should also create a plot showing the incident ray, the boundary between the two regions, and the refracted ray on the other side of the boundary.

Test your program by running it for the following two cases: *(a)* $n_1 = 1.0$, $n_2 = 1.7$, and $\theta_1 = 45°$ and *(b)* $n_1 = 1.7$, $n_2 = 1.0$, and $\theta_1 = 45°$.

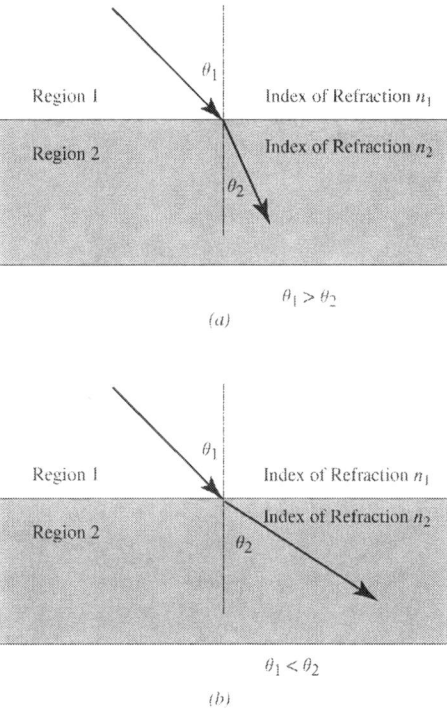

Figure 4.11   A ray of light bends as it passes from one medium into another one. *(a)* If the ray of light passes from a region with a low index of refraction into a region with a higher index of refraction, the ray of light bends more towards the vertical. *(b)* If the ray of light passes from a region with a high index of refraction into a region with a lower index of refraction, the ray of light bends away from the vertical.

4.8   High-Pass Filter Figure 4.12 shows a simple high-pass filter consisting of a resistor and a capacitor. The ratio of the output voltage V_o to the input voltage V_i is given by the equation

$$\frac{V_o}{V_i} = \frac{j2\pi fRC}{1 + j2\pi fRC} \tag{4.12}$$

Assume that $R = 16$ kΩ and $C = 1$ μF. Calculate and plot the amplitude and phase response of this filter as a function of frequency.

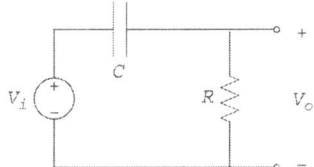

Figure 4.12   A simple high-pass filter circuit.

4.9 **Ideal Gas Law** A tank holds an amount gas pressurized at 200 kPa in the winter when the temperature of the tank is 0°C. What would the pressure in the tank be if it holds the same amount of gas when the temperature is 100°C? Create a plot showing the expected pressure as the temperature in the tank increases from 0°C to 200°C.

4.10 **Ideal Gas Law** The ideal gas law was defined in Example 4.6. Assume that the volume of 1 mole of this gas is 10 L, and plot the pressure of the gas as a function of temperature as the temperature is changed from 250 to 400 kelvins. What sort of plot (linear, semilogx, etc.) is most appropriate for this data?

4.11 Suppose that a student has the option of enrolling for a single elective during a term. The student must select a course from a limited list of options: "English," "History," "Astronomy," or "Literature." Construct a fragment of MATLAB code that will prompt the student for his or her choice, read in the choice, and use the answer as the case expression for a `switch` construct. Be sure to include a default case to handle invalid inputs.

4.12 Write a program that allows a user to enter a string containing a day of the week ('Sunday', 'Monday', 'Tuesday', etc.) and uses a `switch` construct to convert the day to its corresponding number, where Sunday is considered the first day of the week and Saturday is considered the last day of the week. Print out the resulting day number. Also, be sure to handle the case of an illegal day name! (*Note:* Be sure to use the `'s'` option on function `input` so that the input is treated as a string.)

4.13 Write a MATLAB program to evaluate the function

$$y(x) = \ln \frac{1}{1 - x}$$

for any user-specified value of x, where x is a number < 1.0 (note that ln is the natural logarithm, the logarithm to the base e). Use an `if` structure to verify that the value passed to the program is legal. If the value of x is legal, calculate $y(x)$. If not, write a suitable error message and quit.

4.14 In Example 4.3, we wrote a program to evaluate the function $f(x,y)$ for any two user-specified values x and y, where the function $f(x,y)$ was defined as follows.

$$f(x,y) = \begin{cases} x + y & x \geq 0 \text{ and } y \geq 0 \\ x + y^2 & x \geq 0 \text{ and } y < 0 \\ x^2 + y & x < 0 \text{ and } y \geq 0 \\ x^2 + y^2 & x < 0 \text{ and } y < 0 \end{cases}$$

The problem was solved by using a single `if` construct with four code blocks to calculate $f(x,y)$ for all possible combinations of x and y. Rewrite the program `funxy` to use nested `if` constructs, where the outer constructs evaluates the value of x and the inner constructs evaluate the value of y.

4.15 The cost of sending a package by an express delivery service is $15.00 for the first two pounds, and $5.00 for each pound or fraction thereof over two pounds. If the package weighs more than 70 pounds, a $15.00 excess weight surcharge is added to the cost. No package weighing more than 100 pounds will be accepted. Write a program that accepts the weight of a package in pounds and computes the cost of mailing the package. Be sure to handle the case of overweight packages.

4.16 The following statements are intended to alert a user to dangerously high oral thermometer readings (values are in degrees Fahrenheit). Are they correct or incorrect? If they are incorrect, explain why and correct them.

```
if temp < 97.5
    disp('Temperature below normal');
elseif temp > 97.5
    disp('Temperature normal');
elseif temp > 99.5
    disp('Temperature slightly high');
elseif temp > 103.0
    disp('Temperature dangerously high');
end
```

4.17 The tangent function is defined as $\tan \theta = \sin \theta / \cos \theta$. This expression can be evaluated to solve for the tangent as long as the magnitude of $\cos \theta$ is not too near to 0. (If $\cos \theta$ is 0, evaluating the equation for $\tan \theta$ will produce the nonnumerical value Inf.) Assume that θ is given in *degrees*, and write the MATLAB statements to evaluate $\tan \theta$ as long as the magnitude of $\cos \theta$ is greater than or equal to 10^{-20}. If the magnitude of $\cos \theta$ is less than 10^{-20}, write out an error message instead.

4.18 Evaluate the following MATLAB expressions.

(a) `5 >= 5.5`
(b) `20 > 20`
(c) `xor( 17 - pi < 15, pi < 3 )`
(d) `true > false`
(e) `~~(35 / 17) == (35 / 17)`
(f) `(7 <= 8) == (3 / 2 == 1)`
(g) `17.5 && (3.3 > 2.)`

Loops and Vectorization

Loops are MATLAB constructs that permit us to execute a sequence of statements more than once. There are two basic forms of loop constructs: `while` **loops** and `for` **loops**. The major difference between these two types of loops is in how the repetition is controlled. The code in a `while` loop is repeated an indefinite number of times until some user-specified condition is satisfied. By contrast, the code in a `for` loop is repeated a specified number of times, and the number of repetitions is known before the loops starts.

Vectorization is an alternative and faster way to perform the same function as many MATLAB `for` loops. After introducing loops, this chapter will show how to replace many loops with vectorized code for increased speed.

MATLAB programs that use loops often process very large amounts of data, and the programs need an efficient way to read that data in for processing. This chapter introduces the `textread` function to make it simple to read large datasets in from disk files.

This chapter includes examples in which we derive programs that calculate statistical values and perform least-squares fits, and it concludes with applications sections showing how to use built-in MATLAB functions to perform these calculations.

5.1 The `while` Loop

A `while` **loop** is a block of statements that are repeated indefinitely as long as some condition is satisfied. The general form of a `while` loop is

```
while expression
    ...
    ...                    } Code block
    ...
end
```

The controlling expression produces a logical value. If the *expression* is `true`, the code block will be executed and control will return to the `while` statement. If the *expression* is still `true`, the statements will be executed again. This process will be repeated until the *expression* becomes `false`. When control returns to the `while` statement and the expression is `false`, the program will execute the first statement after the `end`.

The pseudocode corresponding to a `while` loop is

```
while expr
    . . .
    . . .
    . . .
end
```

We will now show an example statistical analysis program that is implemented using a `while` loop.

Example 5.1—Statistical Analysis

It is very common in science and engineering to work with large sets of numbers, each of which is a measurement of some particular property that we are interested in. A simple example would be the grades on the first test in this course. Each grade would be a measurement of how much a particular student has learned in the course to date.

Much of the time, we are not interested in looking closely at every single measurement that we make. Instead, we want to summarize the results of a set of measurements with a few numbers that tell us a lot about the overall data set. Two such numbers are the *average* (or *arithmetic mean*) and the *standard deviation* of the set of measurements. The average or arithmetic mean of a set of numbers is defined as

$$\bar{x} = \frac{1}{N}\sum_{i=1}^{N} x_i \tag{5.1}$$

where x_i is sample i out of N samples. If all of the input values are available in an array, the average of a set of number may be calculated by MATLAB function `mean`. The standard deviation of a set of numbers is defined as

$$s = \sqrt{\frac{N\sum_{i=1}^{N} x_i^2 - \left(\sum_{i=1}^{N} x_i\right)^2}{N(N-1)}} \tag{5.2}$$

Standard deviation is a measure of the amount of scatter on the measurements; the greater the standard deviation, the more scattered the points in the data set are.

Implement an algorithm that reads in a set of measurements and calculates the mean and the standard deviation of the input data set.

SOLUTION   This program must be able to read in an arbitrary number of measurements and then calculate the mean and standard deviation of those measurements. We will use a while loop to accumulate the input measurements before performing the calculations.

When all of the measurements have been read, we must have some way of telling the program that there is no more data to enter. For now, we will assume that all the input measurements are either positive or zero, and we will use a negative input value as a *flag* to indicate that there is no more data to read. If a negative value is entered, the program will stop reading input values and will calculate the mean and standard deviation of the data set.

1. **State the problem.**

   Since we assume that the input numbers must be positive or zero, a proper statement of this problem would be: *calculate the average and the standard deviation of a set of measurements, assuming that all of the measurements are either positive or zero, and assuming that we do not know in advance how many measurements are included in the data set. A negative input value will mark the end of the set of measurements.*

2. **Define the inputs and outputs.**

   The inputs required by this program are an unknown number of positive or zero numbers. The outputs from this program are a printout of the mean and the standard deviation of the input data set. In addition, we will print out the number of data points input to the program, since this is a useful check that the input data was read correctly.

3. **Design the algorithm.**

   This program can be broken down into three major steps:

   ```
   Accumulate the input data
   Calculate the mean and standard deviation
   Write out the mean, standard deviation, and
     number of points
   ```

   The first major step of the program is to accumulate the input data. To do this, we will have to prompt the user to enter the desired numbers. When the numbers are entered, we will have to keep track of the number of values entered, plus the sum and the sum of the squares of those values. The pseudocode for these steps is

   ```
   Initialize n, sum_x, and sum_x2 to 0
   Prompt user for first number
   Read in first x
   while x >= 0
       n ← n + 1
       sum_x ← sum_x + x
       sum_x2 ← sum_x2 + x^2
       Prompt user for next number
       Read in next x
   end
   ```

Note that we have to read in the first value before the `while` loop starts so that the `while` loop can have a value to test the first time it executes.

Next, we must calculate the mean and standard deviation. The pseudocode for this step is just the MATLAB versions of Equations (5.1) and (5.2).

```
x_bar ← sum_x / n
std_dev ← sqrt((n*sum_x2 - sum_x^2) / (n*(n-1)))
```

Finally, we must write out the results.

```
Write out the mean value x_bar
Write out the standard deviation std_dev
Write out the number of input data points n
```

4. **Turn the algorithm into MATLAB statements.**
   The final MATLAB program is shown here.

```
%  Script file: stats_1.m
%
%  Purpose:
%   To calculate mean and the standard deviation of
%   an input data set containing an arbitrary number
%   of input values.
%
%  Record of revisions:
%     Date            Engineer          Description of change
%     ====            ========          ====================
%     01/24/10      S. J. Chapman       Original code
%
%  Define variables:
%   n         -- The number of input samples
%   std_dev   -- The standard deviation of the input samples
%   sum_x     -- The sum of the input values
%   sum_x2    -- The sum of the squares of the input values
%   x         -- An input data value
%   xbar      -- The average of the input samples

% Initialize sums.
n = 0; sum_x = 0; sum_x2 = 0;

% Read in first value
x = input('Enter first value: ');

% While Loop to read input values.
while x >= 0

   % Accumulate sums.
   n       = n + 1;
   sum_x   = sum_x + x;
   sum_x2  = sum_x2 + x^2;
```

```
    % Read in next value
    x = input('Enter next value: ');

end

% Calculate the mean and standard deviation
x_bar = sum_x / n;
std_dev = sqrt( (n * sum_x2 - sum_x^2) / (n * (n-1)) );

% Tell user.
fprintf('The mean of this data set is: %f\n', x_bar);
fprintf('The standard deviation is:    %f\n', std_dev);
fprintf('The number of data points is: %f\n', n);
```

5. **Test the program.**

   To test this program, we will calculate the answers by hand for a simple data set and then compare the answers to the results of the program. If we used three input values: 3, 4, and 5, the mean and standard deviation would be

   $$\bar{x} = \frac{1}{N} \sum_{i=1}^{N} x_i = \frac{1}{3}(12) = 4$$

   $$s = \sqrt{\frac{N \sum_{i=1}^{N} x_i^2 - \left(\sum_{i=1}^{N} x_i\right)^2}{N(N-1)}} = 1$$

When these values are fed into the program, the results are

```
» stats_1
Enter first value: 3
Enter next value: 4
Enter next value: 5
Enter next value: -1
The mean of this data set is: 4.000000
The standard deviation is:    1.000000
The number of data points is: 3.000000
```

The program gives the correct answers for our test data set.   ◄

In the preceding example, we failed to follow the design process completely. This failure has left the program with a fatal flaw! Did you spot it?

We have failed because *we did not completely test the program for all possible types of inputs*. Look at the example once again. If we enter either no numbers or only one number, then we will be dividing by zero in the preceding equations! The division-by-zero error will cause divide-by-zero warnings to be printed, and the output values will be NaN. We need to modify the program to detect this problem, tell the user what the problem is, and stop gracefully.

A modified version of the program called `stats_2` is shown at the end of this paragraph. Here, we check to see if there are enough input values before performing the calculations. If not, the program will print out an intelligent error message and quit. Test the modified program for yourself.

```
% Script file: stats_2.m
%
% Purpose:
%   To calculate mean and the standard deviation of
%   an input data set containing an arbitrary number
%   of input values.
%
% Record of revisions:
%      Date          Engineer         Description of change
%      ====          ========         =====================
%    01/24/10    S. J. Chapman     Original code
% 1. 01/24/10    S. J. Chapman     Correct divide-by-0 error if
%                                  0 or 1 input values given.
%
% Define variables:
%   n          -- The number of input samples
%   std_dev    -- The standard deviation of the input samples
%   sum_x      -- The sum of the input values
%   sum_x2     -- The sum of the squares of the input values
%   x          -- An input data value
%   xbar       -- The average of the input samples

% Initialize sums.
n = 0; sum_x = 0; sum_x2 = 0;

% Read in first value
x = input('Enter first value: ');

% While Loop to read input values.
while x >= 0

    % Accumulate sums.
    n       = n + 1;
    sum_x   = sum_x + x;
    sum_x2  = sum_x2 + x^2;

    % Read in next value
    x = input('Enter next value: ');

end

% Check to see if we have enough input data.
if n < 2   % Insufficient information

    disp('At least 2 values must be entered!');
```

```
else  % There is enough information, so
      % calculate the mean and standard deviation

      x_bar = sum_x / n;
      std_dev = sqrt( (n * sum_x2 - sum_x^2) / (n * (n-1)) );

      % Tell user.
      fprintf('The mean of this data set is:    %f\n', x_bar);
      fprintf('The standard deviation is:       %f\n', std_dev);
      fprintf('The number of data points is:    %f\n', n);

end
```

Note that the average and standard deviation could have been calculated with the built-in MATLAB functions mean and std if all of the input values are saved in a vector and that vector is passed to these functions. You will be asked to create a version of the program that uses the standard MATLAB functions in an exercise at the end of this chapter.

5.2   The for Loop

The for **loop** is a loop that executes a block of statements a specified number of times. The for loop has the form

```
for index = expr
   . . .
   . . .        } Body
   . . .
end
```

where index is the loop variable (also known as the **loop index**) and expr is the loop control expression, whose result is an array. The columns in the array produced by expr are stored one at a time in the variable index, and then the loop body is executed, so that the loop is executed once for each column in the array produced by expr. The expression usually takes the form of a vector in shortcut notation first:incr:last.

The statements between the for statement and the end statement are known as the *body* of the loop. They are executed repeatedly during each pass of the for loop. The for loop construct functions as follows:

1. At the beginning of the loop, MATLAB generates an array by evaluating the control expression.
2. The first time through the loop, the program assigns the first column of the array to the loop variable index, and the program executes the statements within the body of the loop.
3. After the statements in the body of the loop have been executed, the program assigns the next column of the array to the loop variable index, and the program executes the statements within the body of the loop again.

4. Step 3 is repeated over and over as long as there are additional columns in the array.

Let's look at a number of specific examples to make the operation of the for loop clearer. First, consider the following example:

```
for ii = 1:10
    Statement 1
    ...
    Statement n
end
```

In this loop, the control index is the variable ii.[1] In this case, the control expression generates a 1×10 array, so statements 1 through n will be executed 10 times. The loop index ii will be 1 the first time, 2 the second time, and so on. The loop index will be 10 on the last pass through the statements. When control is returned to the for statement after the tenth pass, there are no more columns in the control expression, so execution transfers to the first statement after the end statement. Note that the loop index ii is still set to 10 after the loop finishes executing.

Second, consider the following example:

```
for ii = 1:2:10
    Statement 1
    ...
    Statement n
end
```

In this case, the control expression generates a 1×5 array, so statements 1 through n will be executed five times. The loop index ii will be 1 the first time, 3 the second time, and so on. The loop index will be 9 on the fifth and last pass through the statements. When control is returned to the for statement after the fifth pass, there are no more columns in the control expression, so execution transfers to the first statement after the end statement. Note that the loop index ii is still set to 9 after the loop finishes executing.

Third, consider the following example:

```
for ii = [5 9 7]
    Statement 1
    ...
    Statement n
end
```

---

[1] By habit, programmers working in most programming languages use simple variable names like i and j as loop indices. However, MATLAB predefines the variables i and j to be the value $\sqrt{-1}$. Because of this definition, the examples in the book use ii and jj as example loop indices.

Here, the control expression is an explicitly written 1×3 array, so statements 1 through *n* will be executed three times with the loop index set to 5 the first time, 9 the second time, and 7 the final time. The loop index `ii` is still set to 7 after the loop finishes executing.

Finally, consider the example:

```
for ii = [1 2 3;4 5 6]
    Statement 1
    . . .
    Statement n
end
```

In this case, the control expression is a 2×3 array, so statements 1 through *n* will be executed three times. The loop index `ii` will be the column vector $\begin{bmatrix} 1 \\ 4 \end{bmatrix}$ the first time, $\begin{bmatrix} 2 \\ 5 \end{bmatrix}$ the second time, and $\begin{bmatrix} 3 \\ 6 \end{bmatrix}$ the third time. The loop index `ii` is still set to $\begin{bmatrix} 3 \\ 6 \end{bmatrix}$ after the loop finishes executing. This example illustrates the fact that a loop index can be a vector.

The pseudocode corresponding to a `for` loop looks like the loop itself:

```
for index = expression
    Statement 1
    . . .
    Statement n
end
```

▶

Example 5.2—The Factorial Function

To illustrate the operation of a `for` loop, we will use a `for` loop to calculate the factorial function. The factorial function is defined as

$$n! = \begin{cases} 1 & n = 0 \\ n \times (n-1) \times (n-2) \times \cdots \times 2 \times 1 & n > 0 \end{cases}$$

The MATLAB code to calculate *N* factorial for positive value of *N* would be

```
n_factorial = 1
for ii = 1:n
    n_factorial = n_factorial * ii;
end
```

Suppose that we wish to calculate the value of 5! If n is 5, the `for` loop control expression would be the row vector `[1 2 3 4 5]`. This loop will be executed five times, with the variable `ii` taking on values of 1, 2, 3, 4, and 5 in the successive loops. The resulting value of `n_factorial` will be $1 \times 2 \times 3 \times 4 \times 5 = 120$.

◀

▶
━━

Example 5.3—Calculating the Day of Year

The *day of year* is the number of days (including the current day) which have elapsed since the beginning of a given year. It is a number in the range 1 to 365 for ordinary years and 1 to 366 for leap years. Write a MATLAB program that accepts a day, month, and year and calculates the day of year corresponding to that date.

SOLUTION   To determine the day of year, this program will need to sum up the number of days in each month preceding the current month, plus the number of elapsed days in the current month. A `for` loop will be used to perform this sum. Since the number of days in each month varies, it is necessary to determine the correct number of days to add for each month. A `switch` construct will be used to determine the proper number of days to add for each month.

During a leap year, an extra day must be added to the day of year for any month after February. This extra day accounts for the presence of February 29 in the leap year. Therefore, to perform the day of year calculation correctly, we must determine which years are leap years. In the Gregorian calendar, leap years are determined by the following rules:

1. Years evenly divisible by 400 are leap years.
2. Years evenly divisible by 100 but *not* by 400 are not leap years.
3. All years divisible by 4 but *not* by 100 are leap years.
4. All other years are not leap years.

We will use the `mod` (for modulus) function to determine whether or not a year is evenly divisible by a given number. The `mod` function returns the remainder after the division of two numbers. For example, the remainder of 9/4 is 1, since 4 goes into 9 twice with a remainder of 1. If the result of the function `mod(year,4)` is zero, then we know that the year was evenly divisible by 4. Similarly, if the result of the function `mod(year,400)` is zero, then we know that the year was evenly divisible by 400.

A program to calculate the day of year is shown here. Note that the program sums up the number of days in each month before the current month and that it uses a `switch` construct to determine the number of days in each month.

```
%  Script file: doy.m
%
%  Purpose:
%    This program calculates the day of year corresponding
%    to a specified date. It illustrates the use switch and
%    for constructs.
%
%  Record of revisions:
%      Date          Engineer              Description of change
%      ====          ========              =====================
%    01/27/10     S. J. Chapman            Original code
```

```
%
%   Define variables:
%      day              -- Day (dd)
%      day_of_year      -- Day of year
%      ii               -- Loop index
%      leap_day         -- Extra day for leap year
%      month            -- Month (mm)
%      year             -- Year (yyyy)

% Get day, month, and year to convert
disp('This program calculates the day of year given the ');
disp(' specified date.');
month = input('Enter specified month (1-12): ');
day   = input('Enter specified day(1-31):    ');
year  = input('Enter specified year(yyyy):   ');

% Check for leap year, and add extra day if necessary
if mod(year,400) == 0
   leap_day = 1;     % Years divisible by 400 are leap years
elseif mod(year,100) == 0
   leap_day = 0;     % Other centuries are not leap years
elseif mod(year,4) == 0
   leap_day = 1;     % Otherwise every 4th year is a leap year
else
   leap_day = 0;     % Other years are not leap years
end

% Calculate day of year by adding current day to the
% days in previous months.
day_of_year = day;
for ii = 1:month-1

   % Add days in months from January to last month
   switch (ii)
   case {1,3,5,7,8,10,12},
      day_of_year = day_of_year + 31;
   case {4,6,9,11},
      day_of_year = day_of_year + 30;
   case 2,
      day_of_year = day_of_year + 28 + leap_day;
   end

end

% Tell user
fprintf('The date %2d/%2d/%4d is day of year %d.\n', ...
        month, day, year, day_of_year);
```

We will use the following known results to test the program:

1. Year 1999 is not a leap year. January 1 must be day of year 1, and December 31 must be day of year 365.
2. Year 2000 is a leap year. January 1 must be day of year 1, and December 31 must be day of year 366.
3. Year 2001 is not a leap year. March 1 must be day of year 60, since January has 31 days, February has 28 days, and this is the first day of March.

If this program is executed five times with the specified dates, the results are

```
» doy
This program calculates the day of year given the
specified date.
Enter specified month (1-12): 1
Enter specified day(1-31):    1
Enter specified year(yyyy):   1999
The date 1/ 1/1999 is day of year 1.
» doy
This program calculates the day of year given the
specified date.
Enter specified month (1-12): 12
Enter specified day(1-31):    31
Enter specified year(yyyy):   1999
The date 12/31/1999 is day of year 365.
» doy
This program calculates the day of year given the
specified date.
Enter specified month (1-12): 1
Enter specified day(1-31):    1
Enter specified year(yyyy):   2000
The date 1/ 1/2000 is day of year 1.
» doy
This program calculates the day of year given the
specified date.
Enter specified month (1-12): 12
Enter specified day(1-31):    31
Enter specified year(yyyy):   2000
The date 12/31/2000 is day of year 366.
» doy
This program calculates the day of year given the
specified date.
Enter specified month (1-12): 3
Enter specified day(1-31):    1
Enter specified year(yyyy):   2001
The date 3/ 1/2001 is day of year 60.
```

The program gives the correct answers for our test dates in all five test cases.   ◄

▶

Example 5.4—Statistical Analysis

Implement an algorithm that reads in a set of measurements and calculates the mean and the standard deviation of the input data set, when any value in the data set can be positive, negative, or zero.

SOLUTION   This program must be able to read in an arbitrary number of measurements and then calculate the mean and standard deviation of those measurements. Each measurement can be positive, negative, or zero.

Since we cannot use a data value as a flag this time, we will ask the user for the number of input values and then use a for loop to read in those values. The modified program that permits the use of any input value is shown next. Verify its operation for yourself by finding the mean and standard deviation of the following five input values: 3, −1, 0, 1, and −2.

```
%   Script file: stats_3.m
%
%   Purpose:
%     To calculate mean and the standard deviation of
%     an input data set, where each input value can be
%     positive, negative, or zero.
%
%   Record of revisions:
%       Date            Engineer            Description of change
%       ====            ========            =====================
%     01/27/10     S. J. Chapman          Original code
%
%   Define variables:
%     ii         -- Loop index
%     n          -- The number of input samples
%     std_dev  -- The standard deviation of the input samples
%     sum_x    -- The sum of the input values
%     sum_x2   -- The sum of the squares of the input values
%     x          -- An input data value
%     xbar       -- The average of the input samples

% Initialize sums.
sum_x = 0;  sum_x2 = 0;

% Get the number of points to input.
n = input('Enter number of points: ');

% Check to see if we have enough input data.
if n < 2   % Insufficient data

   disp ('At least 2 values must be entered.');
```

```
else % we will have enough data, so let's get it.

   % Loop to read input values.
   for ii = 1:n

      % Read in next value
      x = input('Enter value: ');

      % Accumulate sums.
      sum_x  = sum_x + x;
      sum_x2 = sum_x2 + x^2;

end

   % Now calculate statistics.
   x_bar = sum_x / n;
   std_dev = sqrt( (n * sum_x2 - sum_x^2) / (n * (n-1)) );

   % Tell user.
   fprintf('The mean of this data set is:  %f\n', x_bar);
   fprintf('The standard deviation is:     %f\n', std_dev);
   fprintf('The number of data points is:  %f\n', n);

end
```

◀

5.2.1   Details of Operation

Now that we have seen examples of a `for` loop in operation, we will examine some important details required to use `for` loops properly.

1. **Indent the bodies of loops.** It is not necessary to indent the body of a `for` loop, as we have shown previously. MATLAB will recognize the loop even if every statement in it starts in column 1. However, the code is much more readable if the body of the `for` loop is indented, so you should always indent the bodies of loops.

✳ Good Programming Practice

Always indent the body of a `for` loop by two or more spaces to improve the readability of the code.

2. **Don't modify the loop index within the body of a loop.** The loop index of a for loop *should not be modified anywhere within the body of the loop*. The index variable is often used as a counter within the loop, and modifying its value can cause strange and hard-to-find errors. The example that follows is intended to initialize the elements of an array, but the statement "ii = 5" has been accidentally inserted into the body of the loop. As a result, only a(5) is initialized, and it gets the values that should have gone into a(1), a(2), and so fourth.

```
for ii = 1:10
    ...
    ii = 5;      % Error!
    ...
    a(ii) = <calculation>
end
```

✳ Good Programming Practice

Never modify the value of a loop index within the body of the loop.

3. **Preallocating arrays.** We learned in Chapter 2 that it is possible to extend an existing array simply by assigning a value to a higher array element. For example, the statement

```
arr = 1:4;
```

defines a four-element array containing the values [1 2 3 4]. If the statement

```
arr(8) = 6;
```

is executed, the array will be automatically extended to eight elements and will contain the values [1 2 3 4 0 0 0 6]. Unfortunately, each time an array is extended, MATLAB has to *(1)* create a new array, *(2)* copy the contents of the old array to the new longer array, *(3)* add the new value to the array, and then *(4)* delete the old array. This process is very time-consuming for long arrays.

When a for loop stores values in a previously undefined array, the loop forces MATLAB to go through this process each time the loop is executed. On the other hand, if the array is **preallocated** to its maximum size before the loop starts executing, no copying is required, and the code executes much faster. The code fragment that follows shows how to pre-allocate an array before the starting the loop.

```
square = zeros(1,100);
for ii = 1:100
    square(ii) = ii^2;
end
```

> ✳ **Good Programming Practice**
>
> Always preallocate all arrays used in a loop before executing the loop. This practice greatly increases the execution speed of the loop.

5.2.2 Vectorization: A Faster Alternative to Loops

Many loops are used to apply the same calculations over and over to the elements of an array. For example, the following code fragment calculates the squares, square roots, and cube roots of all integers between 1 and 100 using a `for` loop.

```
for ii = 1:100
    square(ii) = ii^2;
    square_root(ii) = ii^(1/2);
    cube_root(ii) = ii^(1/3);
end
```

Here, the loop is executed 100 times, and one value of each output array is calculated during each cycle of the loop.

MATLAB offers a faster alternative for calculations of this sort: **vectorization**. Instead of executing each statement 100 times, MATLAB can do the calculation for all the elements in an array in a *single* statement. Because of the way MATLAB is designed, this single statement can be much faster than the loop and can perform exactly the same calculation.

For example, the following code fragment uses vectors to perform the same calculation as the loop shown previously. We first calculate a vector of the indices into the arrays and then perform each calculation only once, doing all 100 elements in the single statement.

```
ii = 1:100;
square = ii.^2;
square_root = ii.^(1/2);
cube_root = ii.^(1/3);
```

Even though these two calculations produce the same answers, they are *not* equivalent. The version with the `for` loop can be *more than 15 times slower* than the vectorized version! This happens because the statements in the `for` loop must be interpreted[2] and executed a line at a time by MATLAB during each pass of the loop. In effect, MATLAB must interpret and execute 300 separate lines of code. In contrast, MATLAB has to interpret and execute only four lines in the vectorized case. Since MATLAB is designed to implement vectorized statements in a very efficient fashion, it is much faster in that mode.

---

[2]But see the next item about the MATLAB Just-in-Time compiler.

In MATLAB, the process of replacing loops by vectorized statements is known as vectorization. Vectorization can yield dramatic improvements in performance for many MATLAB programs.

✳ Good Programming Practice

If it is possible to implement a calculation either with a for loop or by using vectors, implement the calculation with vectors. Your program will run much faster.

5.2.3 The MATLAB Just-in-Time (JIT) Compiler

A Just-in-Time (JIT) compiler was added to MATLAB 6.5 and later versions. The JIT compiler examines MATLAB code before it is executed and, where possible, compiles the code before executing it. Since the MATLAB code is compiled instead of being interpreted, it runs almost as fast as vectorized code. The JIT compiler can often dramatically speed up the execution of for loops.

The JIT compiler is a very nice tool when it works, since it speeds up the loops without any action by the engineer. However, the JIT compiler has some limitations that prevent it from speeding up all loops. The JIT compiler's limitations vary with MATLAB version, with fewer limitations being present in later versions of the program.[3]

✳ Good Programming Practice

Do not rely on the JIT compiler to speed up your code. It has limitations that vary with the version of MATLAB you are using, and an engineer typically can do a better job with manual vectorization.

▶

Example 5.5—Comparing Loops and Vectors

To compare the execution speeds of loops and vectors, perform and time the following four sets of calculations.

1. Calculate the squares of every integer from 1 to 10,000 in a for loop without first initializing the array of squares.
2. Calculate the squares of every integer from 1 to 10,000 in a for loop, using the zeros function to preallocate the array of squares first and

---

[3]As of April 2010, the Mathworks refuses to release a list of situations in which the JIT compiler works and situations in which it doesn't work, saying that it is complicated and that it varies between different versions of MATLAB. They suggest that you write your loops and then time them to see if they are fast or slow! The good news is that the JIT compiler works properly in more and more situations with each new release, but you never know...

calculating the square of the number in-line. (This will allow the JIT compiler to function.)

3. Calculate the squares of every integer from 1 to 10,000 with vectors.

SOLUTION This program must calculate the squares of the integers from 1 to 10,000 in each of the four ways described previously, timing the executions in each case. The timing can be accomplished using the MATLAB functions `tic` and `toc`. The function `tic` resets the built-in elapsed time counter, and the function `toc` returns the elapsed time in seconds since the last call to the function `tic`.

Since the real-time clocks in many computers have a fairly coarse granularity, it may be necessary to execute each set of instructions multiple times to get a valid average time.

A MATLAB program to compare the speeds of the three approaches is shown here.

```
%  Script file: timings.m
%
%  Purpose:
%    This program calculates the time required to
%    calculate the squares of all integers from 1 to
%    10,000 in four different ways:
%    1. Using a for loop with an uninitialized output
%       array.
%    2. Using a for loop with a pre-allocated output
%       array and the JIT compiler.
%    3. Using vectors.
%
%  Record of revisions:
%      Date           Engineer          Description of change
%      ====           ========          =====================
%    01/29/10     S. J. Chapman         Original code
%
%  Define variables:
%    ii, jj      -- Loop index
%    average1    -- Average time for calculation 1
%    average2    -- Average time for calculation 2
%    average3    -- Average time for calculation 3
%    maxcount    -- Number of times to loop calculation
%    square      -- Array of squares

%  Perform calculation with an uninitialized array
%  "square". This calculation is done only ten times
%  because it is so slow.
maxcount = 10;                  % Number of repetitions
tic;                            % Start timer
```

```
for jj = 1:maxcount
    clear square            % Clear output array
    for ii = 1:10000
        square(ii) = ii^2;   % Calculate square
    end
end
average1 = (toc)/maxcount;   % Calculate average time

%  Perform calculation with a pre-allocated array
%  "square". This calculation is averaged over 1000
%  loops.
maxcount = 1000;             % Number of repetitions
tic;                        % Start timer
for jj = 1:maxcount
    clear square            % Clear output array
    square = zeros(1,10000); % Pre-initialize array
    for ii = 1:10000
        square(ii) = ii^2;   % Calculate square
    end
end
average2 = (toc)/maxcount;   % Calculate average time

%  Perform calculation with vectors. This calculation
%  averaged over 1000 executions.
maxcount = 1000;             % Number of repetitions
tic;                        % Start timer
for jj = 1:maxcount
    clear square            % Clear output array
    ii = 1:10000;           % Set up vector
    square = ii.^2;         % Calculate square
end
average3 = (toc)/maxcount;   % Calculate average time

% Display results
fprintf('Loop / uninitialized array   = %8.5f\n', average1);
fprintf('Loop / initialized array / JIT = %8.5f\n', average2);
fprintf('Vectorized                   = %8.5f\n', average3);
```

When this program is executed using MATLAB 7.9 on a 1.8 GHz Core 2 Duo computer, the results are

```
» timings
Loop / uninitialized array     = 0.12534
Loop / initialized array / JIT = 0.00014
Vectorized                     = 0.00008
```

The loop with the uninitialized array was very slow compared with the loop executed with the JIT compiler or the vectorized loop. The vectorized loop was the fastest way to perform the calculation, but if the JIT compiler works for your loop, you get most of the acceleration without having to do anything! As you can see, designing loops to allow the JIT compiler to function or replacing the loops with vectorized calculations can make an incredible difference in the speed of your MATLAB code.

◀

The M-Lint code-checking tool can help you identify problems with uninitialized arrays that can slow the execution of a MATLAB program. For example, if we run M-Lint on program `timings.m`, the code checker will identify the uninitialized array and write out a warning message (see Figure 5.1).

5.2.4   The `break` and `continue` Statements

There are two additional statements that can be used to control the operation of `while` loops and `for` loops: the `break` and `continue` statements. The `break` statement terminates the execution of a loop and passes control to the next statement after the end of the loop, and the `continue` statement terminates the current pass through the loop and returns control to the top of the loop.

If a `break` statement is executed in the body of a loop, the execution of the body will stop, and control will be transferred to the first executable statement after the loop. An example of the `break` statement in a `for` loop is shown here.

```
for ii = 1:5
   if ii == 3;
      break;
   end
   fprintf('ii = %d\n',ii);
end
disp(['End of loop!']);
```

When this program is executed, the output is

```
» test_break
ii = 1
ii = 2
End of loop!
```

Note that the `break` statement was executed on the iteration when `ii` was 3, and control was transferred to the first executable statement after the loop without executing the `fprintf` statement.

If a `continue` statement is executed in the body of a loop, the execution of the current pass through the loop will stop, and control will return to the top of the loop. The controlling variable in the `for` loop will take on its next value, and

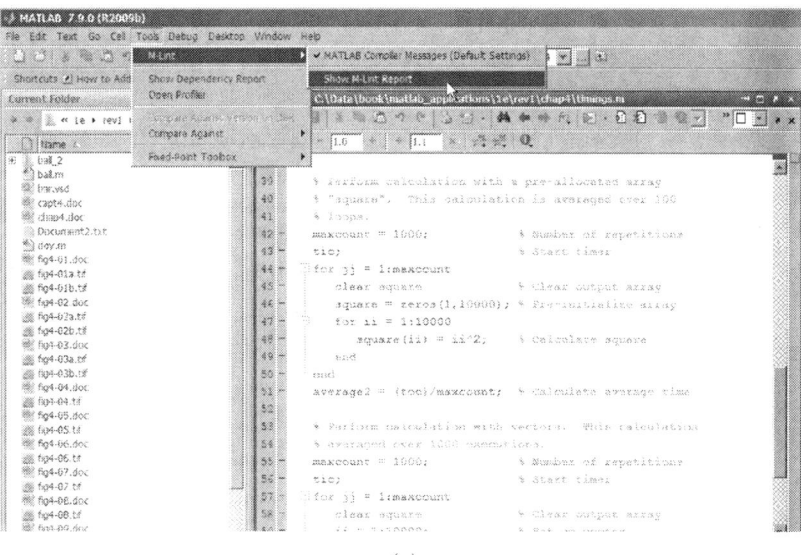

(a)

(b)

Figure 5.1 The M-Lint code checker can identify some problems that will slow down the execution of MATLAB loops.

the loop will be executed again. An example of the `continue` statement in a `for` loop is shown here.

```
for ii = 1:5
   if ii == 3;
      continue;
   end
   fprintf('ii = %d\n',ii);
end
disp(['End of loop!']);
```

When this program is executed, the output is

```
» test_continue
ii = 1
ii = 2
ii = 4
ii = 5
End of loop!
```

Note that the `continue` statement was executed on the iteration when `ii` was 3, and control was transferred to the top of the loop without executing the `fprintf` statement.

The `break` and `continue` statements work with both `while` loops and `for` loops.

5.2.5   Nesting Loops

It is possible for one loop to be completely inside another loop. If one loop is completely inside another one, the two loops are called **nested loops**. The following example shows two nested `for` loops used to calculate and write out the product of two integers.

```
for ii = 1:3
   for jj = 1:3
      product = ii * jj;
      fprintf('%d * %d = %d\n',ii,jj,product);
   end
end
```

In this example, the outer `for` loop will assign a value of 1 to index variable `ii`, and then the inner `for` loop will be executed. The inner `for` loop will be executed three times with index variable `jj` having values 1, 2, and 3. When the entire inner `for` loop has been completed, the outer `for` loop will assign a value of 2 to index variable `ii`, and the inner `for` loop will be executed again. This process repeats until the outer `for` loop has executed three times, and the resulting output is

```
1 * 1 = 1
1 * 2 = 2
1 * 3 = 3
```

```
2 * 1 = 2
2 * 2 = 4
2 * 3 = 6
3 * 1 = 3
3 * 2 = 6
3 * 3 = 9
```

Note that the inner for loop executes completely before the index variable of the outer for loop is incremented.

When MATLAB encounters an end *statement, it associates that statement with the innermost currently open construct.* Therefore, the first end statement in the preceding output closes the "for jj = 1:3" loop, and the second end statement closes the "for ii = 1:3" loop. This fact can produce hard-to-find errors if an end statement is accidentally deleted somewhere within a nested loop construct.

If for *loops are nested, they should have independent loop index variables.* If they have the same index variable, the inner loop will change the value of the loop index that the outer loop just set.

If a break or continue statement appears inside a set of nested loops, that statement refers to the *innermost* of the loops containing it. For example, consider the following program:

```
for ii = 1:3
    for jj = 1:3
        if jj == 3;
            break;
        end
        product = ii * jj;
        fprintf('%d * %d = %d\n',ii,jj,product);
    end
    fprintf('End of inner loop\n');
end
fprintf('End of outer loop\n');
```

If the inner loop counter jj is equal to 3, the break statement will be executed. This will cause the program to exit the innermost loop. The program will print out "End of inner loop," the index of the outer loop will be increased by 1, and execution of the innermost loop will start over. The resulting output values are

```
1 * 1 = 1
1 * 2 = 2
End of inner loop
2 * 1 = 2
2 * 2 = 4
End of inner loop
3 * 1 = 3
3 * 2 = 6
End of inner loop
End of outer loop
```

5.3   Logical Arrays and Vectorization

We learned about logical data in Chapter 4. Logical data can have one of two possible values: true (1) or false (0). Scalars and arrays of logical data are created as the output of relational and logic operators.

For example, consider the following statements:

```
a = [1 2 3; 4 5 6; 7 8 9];
b = a > 5;
```

These statements produced two arrays, a and b. Array a is a double array containing the values $\begin{bmatrix} 1 & 2 & 3 \\ 4 & 5 & 6 \\ 7 & 8 & 9 \end{bmatrix}$, whereas array b is a logical array containing the values $\begin{bmatrix} 0 & 0 & 0 \\ 0 & 0 & 1 \\ 1 & 1 & 1 \end{bmatrix}$. When the whos command is executed, the results are as shown here.

```
» whos
  Name                Size            Bytes   Class
  a                   3x3                72   double  array
  b                   3x3                 9   logical  array
Grand total is 18 elements using 81 bytes
```

Logical arrays have a very important special property—*they can serve as a mask for arithmetic operations*. A mask is an array that selects the elements of another array for use in an operation. The specified operation will be applied to the selected elements and *not* to the remaining elements.

For example, suppose that arrays a and b are as defined previously. Then the statement a(b) = sqrt(a(b)) will take the square root of all elements for which the logical array b is true and leave all the other elements in the array unchanged.

```
» a(b) = sqrt(a(b))
a =
      1.0000      2.0000      3.0000
      4.0000      5.0000      2.4495
      2.6458      2.8284      3.0000
```

This is a very fast and very clever way of performing an operation on a subset of an array without needing loops and branches.

The following two code fragments both take the square root of all elements in array a whose value is greater than 5, but the vectorized approach is more compact, more elegant, and faster than the loop approach.

```
for ii = 1:size(a,1)
    for jj = 1:size(a,2)
        if a(ii,jj) > 5
            a(ii,jj) = sqrt(a(ii,jj));
        end
    end
end

b = a > 5;
a(b) = sqrt(a(b));
```

5.3.1 Creating the Equivalent of if/else Constructs with Logical Arrays

Logical arrays also can be used to implement the equivalent of an if/else construct inside a set of for loops. As we saw in the preceding section, it is possible to apply an operation to selected elements of an array using a logical array as a mask. It is also possible to apply a different set of operations to the *unselected* elements of the array by simply adding the not operator (~) to the logical mask. For example, suppose that we wanted to take the square root of any elements in a two-dimensional array whose value is greater than 5 and to square the remaining elements in the array. The code for this operation using loops and branches is

```
for ii = 1:size(a,1)
    for jj = 1:size(a,2)
        if a(ii,jj) > 5
            a(ii,jj) = sqrt(a(ii,jj));
        else
            a(ii,jj) = a(ii,jj)^2;
        end
    end
end
```

The vectorized code for this operation is

```
b = a > 5;
a(b) = sqrt(a(b));
a(~b) = a(~b).^2;
```

The vectorized code is significantly faster than the loops-and-branches version.

Quiz 5.1

This quiz provides a quick check to see if you have understood the concepts introduced in Sections 5.1 through 5.3. If you have trouble with the quiz, reread the section, ask your instructor, or discuss the material with a fellow student. The answers to this quiz are found in the back of the book.

Examine the following `for` loops and determine how many times each loop will be executed.

1. `for index = 7:10`
2. `for jj = 7:-1:10`
3. `for index = 1:10:10`
4. `for ii = -10:3:-7`
5. `for kk = [0 5 ; 3 3]`

Examine the following loops and determine the value in `ires` at the end of each of the loops.

6.
```
ires = 0;
for index = 1:10
    ires = ires + 1;
end
```

7.
```
ires = 0;
for index = 1:10
    ires = ires + index;
end
```

8.
```
ires = 0;
for index1 = 1:10
    for index2 = index1:10
        if index2 == 6
            break;
        end
        ires = ires + 1;
    end
end
```

9.
```
ires = 0;
for index1 = 1:10
    for index2 = index1:10
        if index2 == 6
            continue;
        end
        ires = ires + 1;
    end
end
```

10. Write the MATLAB statements to calculate the values of the function

$$f(t) = \begin{cases} \sin t & \text{for all } t \text{ where } \sin t > 0 \\ 0 & \text{elsewhere} \end{cases}$$

for $-6\pi \leq t \leq 6\pi$ at intervals of $\pi/10$. Do this twice, once using loops and branches, and once using vectorized code.

CHAPTER 6

Basic User-Defined Functions

In Chapter 4, we learned the importance of good program design. The basic technique that we employed is **top-down design**. In top-down design, the engineer starts with a statement of the problem to be solved and the required inputs and outputs. Next, he or she describes the algorithm to be implemented by the program in broad outline and applies *decomposition* to break the algorithm down into logical subdivisions called sub-tasks. Then, the engineer breaks down each sub-task until he or she winds up with many small pieces, each of which does a simple, clearly understandable job. Finally, the individual pieces are turned into MATLAB code.

Although we have followed this design process in our examples, the results have been somewhat restricted, because we have had to combine the final MATLAB code generated for each sub-task into a single large program. There has been no way to code, verify, and test each sub-task independently before all the sub-tasks are combined into the final program.

Fortunately, MATLAB has a special mechanism designed to make sub-tasks easy to develop and debug independently before building the final program. It is possible to code each sub-task as a separate **function**, and each function can be tested and debugged independently of all of the other sub-tasks in the program.

Well-designed functions enormously reduce the effort required on a large programming project. Their benefits include

1. **Independent testing of sub-tasks**. Each sub-task can be written as an independent unit. The sub-task can be tested separately to ensure that it performs properly by itself before it is integrated into the larger program. This step is known as **unit testing**. It eliminates a major source of problems before the final program is even built.

2. **Reusable code.** In many cases, the same basic sub-task is needed in many parts of a program. For example, it may be necessary to sort a list of values into ascending order many different times within a program, or even in other programs. It is possible to design, code, test, and debug a *single* function to do the sorting and then to reuse that function whenever sorting is required. This reusable code has two major advantages: it reduces the total programming effort required, and it simplifies debugging, since the sorting function needs to be debugged only once.

3. **Isolation from unintended side effects.** Functions receive input data from the program that invokes them through a list of variables called an **input argument list** and returns results to the program through an **output argument list**. Each function has its own workspace with its own variables, which is independent of all other functions and of the calling program. *The only variables in the calling program that can be seen by the function are those in the input argument list, and the only variables in the function that can be seen by the calling program are those in the output argument list.* This is essential, since accidental programming mistakes within a function can only affect the variables within the function in which the mistake occurred.

Once a large program is written and released, it has to be *maintained*. Program maintenance involves fixing bugs and modifying the program to handle new and unforeseen circumstances. The engineer who modifies a program during maintenance is often not the person who originally wrote it. In poorly written programs, it is common for the engineer modifying the program to make a change in one region of the code and to have that change cause unintended side effects in a totally different part of the program. This happens because variable names are reused in different portions of the program. When the engineer changes the values left behind in some of the variables, those values are accidentally picked up and used in other portions of the code.

The use of well-designed functions minimizes this problem by **data hiding**. The variables in the main program are not visible to the function (except for those in the input argument list), and the variables in the main program cannot be accidentally modified by anything occurring in the function. Therefore, mistakes or changes in the function's variables cannot accidentally cause unintended side effects in the other parts of the program.

✷ Good Programming Practice

Break large program tasks into functions whenever practical to achieve the important benefits of independent component testing, reusability, and isolation from undesired side effects.

6.1   Introduction to MATLAB Functions

All of the M-files that we have seen so far have been **script files**. Script files are just collections of MATLAB statements that are stored in a file. When a script file is executed, the result is the same as it would be if all of the commands had been typed directly into the Command Window. Script files share the Command Window's workspace, so any variables that were defined before the script file starts are visible to the script file, and any variables created by the script file remain in the workspace after the script file finishes executing. A script file has no input arguments and returns no results, but script files can communicate with other script files through the data left behind in the workspace.

In contrast, a **MATLAB function** is a special type of M-file that runs in its own independent workspace. It receives input data through an **input argument list** and returns results to the caller through an **output argument list**. The general form of a MATLAB function is

```
function [outarg1, outarg2, ...] = fname(inarg1, inarg2, ...)
% H1 comment line
% Other comment lines
...
(Executable code)
...
(return)
(end)
```

The `function` statement marks the beginning of the function. It specifies the name of the function and the input and output argument lists. The input argument list appears in parentheses after the function name, and the output argument list appears in brackets to the left of the equal sign. (If there is only one output argument, the brackets can be dropped.)

Each ordinary MATLAB function should be placed in a file with the same name (including capitalization) as the function along with the file extention ".m". For example, if a function is named `My_fun`, that function should be placed in a file named `My_fun.m`.

The input argument list is a list of names representing values that will be passed from the caller to the function. These names are called **dummy arguments**. They are just placeholders for actual values that are passed from the caller when the function is invoked. Similarly, the output argument list contains a list of dummy arguments that are placeholders for the values returned to the caller when the function finishes executing.

A function is invoked by naming it in an expression together with a list of **actual arguments**. A function can be invoked by typing its name directly in the Command Window or by including it in a script file or another function.

The name in the calling program must *exactly match* the function name (including capitalization).[1] When the function is invoked, the value of the first actual argument is used in place of the first dummy argument, and so forth for each other actual argument/dummy argument pair.

Execution begins at the top of the function and ends when a `return` statement, an `end` statement, or the end of the function is reached. Because execution stops at the end of a function anyway, the `return` statement is not actually required in most functions and is rarely used. Each item in the output argument list must appear on the left side of a least one assignment statement in the function. When the function returns, the values stored in the output argument list are returned to the caller and may be used in further calculations.

The use of an `end` statement to terminate a function is a new feature of MATLAB 7.0. In earlier versions of MATLAB, the `end` statement was used only to terminate structures such as `if`, `for`, `while`, and the like. It is optional in MATLAB 7 unless a file includes nested functions, which are a special feature not covered in this book. We will not use the `end` statement to terminate a function unless it is actually needed, so you will not see it used in this book.

The initial comment lines in a function serve a special purpose. The first comment line after the function statement is called the **H1 comment line**. It should always contain a one-line summary of the purpose of the function. The special significance of this line is that it is searched and displayed by the `look-for` command. The remaining comment lines from the H1 line until the first blank line or the first executable statement are displayed by the `help` command. They should contain a brief summary of how to use the function.

A simple example of a user-defined function is shown next. The function `dist2` calculates the distance between points (x_1, y_1) and (x_2, y_2) in a Cartesian coordinate system.

```
function distance = dist2 (x1, y1, x2, y2)
%DIST2 Calculate the distance between two points
% Function DIST2 calculates the distance between
% two points (x1,y1) and (x2,y2) in a Cartesian
% coordinate system.
%
% Calling sequence:
%    distance = dist2(x1, y1, x2, y2)

% Define variables:
%    x1           -- x-position of point 1
```

---

[1] For example, suppose that a function has been declared with the name My_Fun, and placed in file My_Fun.m. Then this function should be called with the name My_Fun, not my_fun or MY_FUN. If the capitalization fails to match, this will produce an error on Linux, Unix, and Macintosh computers, and a warning on Windows-based computers.

```
%    y1         -- y-position of point 1
%    x2         -- x-position of point 2
%    y2         -- y-position of point 2
%    distance -- Distance between points

%    Record of revisions:
%      Date              Engineer              Description of change
%      ====              ========              =====================
%    02/01/10        S. J. Chapman          Original code

% Calculate distance.
distance = sqrt((x2-x1).^2 + (y2-y1).^2);
```

This function has four input arguments and one output argument. A simple script file using this function is shown here.

```
% Script file: test_dist2.m
%
% Purpose:
%   This program tests function dist2.
%
% Record of revisions:
%      Date              Engineer              Description of change
%      ====              ========              =====================
%    02/01/10        S. J. Chapman          Original code
%
% Define variables:
%    ax         -- x-position of point a
%    ay         -- y-position of point a
%    bx         -- x-position of point b
%    by         -- y-position of point b
%    result    -- Distance between the points

% Get input data.
disp('Calculate the distance between two points:');
ax = input('Enter x value of point a: ');
ay = input('Enter y value of point a: ');
bx = input('Enter x value of point b: ');
by = input('Enter y value of point b: ');

% Evaluate function
result = dist2 (ax, ay, bx, by);

% Write out result.
fprintf('The distance between points a and b is %f\n',result);
```

When this script file is executed, the results are

```
» test_dist2
Calculate the distance between two points:
Enter x value of point a: 1
Enter y value of point a: 1
Enter x value of point b: 4
Enter y value of point b: 5
The distance between points a and b is 5.000000
```

These results are correct, as we can verify from simple hand calculations.

The function dist2 also supports the MATLAB help subsystem. If we type "help dist2", the results are

```
» help dist2
DIST2 Calculate the distance between two points
   Function DIST2 calculates the distance between
   two points (x1,y1) and (x2,y2) in a Cartesian
   coordinate system.

   Calling sequence:
      res = dist2(x1, y1, x2, y2)
```

Similarly, "lookfor distance" produces the result

```
» lookfor distance
DIST2 Calculate the distance between two points
MAHAL Mahalanobis distance.
DIST Distances between vectors.
NBDIST Neighborhood matrix using vector distance.
NBGRID Neighborhood matrix using grid distance.
NBMAN Neighborhood matrix using Manhattan-distance.
```

To observe the behavior of the MATLAB workspace before, during, and after the function is executed, we will load the function dist2 and the script file test_dist2 into the MATLAB debugger and set breakpoints before, during, and after the function call (see Figure 6.1). When the program stops at the breakpoint *before* the function call, the workspace is as shown in Figure 6.2*(a)*. Note that variables ax, ay, bx, and by are defined in the workspace with the values that we have entered. When the program stops at the breakpoint *within* the function call, the function's workspace is active. This is as shown in Figure 6.2*(b)*. Note that variables x1, x2, y1, y2, and distance are defined in the function's workspace, and the variables defined in the calling M-file are not present. When the program stops in the calling program at the breakpoint *after* the function call, the workspace is as shown in Figure 6.2*(c)*. Now the original variables are back, with the variable result added to contain the value returned by the function. These figures show that the workspace of the function is different from the workspace of the calling M-file.

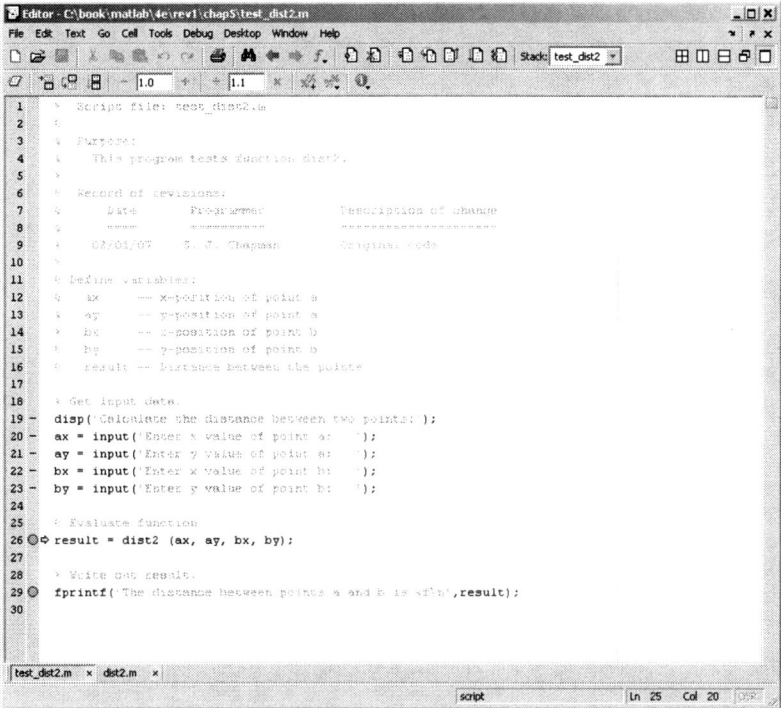

Figure 6.1 M-file `test_dist2` and the function `dist2` are loaded into the debugger with breakpoints set before, during, and after the function call.

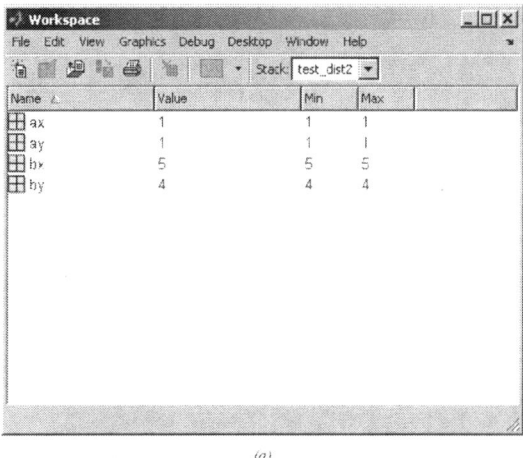

(a)

Figure 6.2 (a) The workspace before the function call. (b) The workspace during the function call. (c) The workspace after the function call.

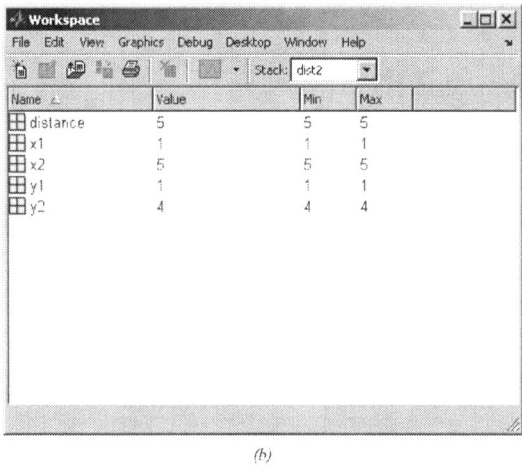

(b)

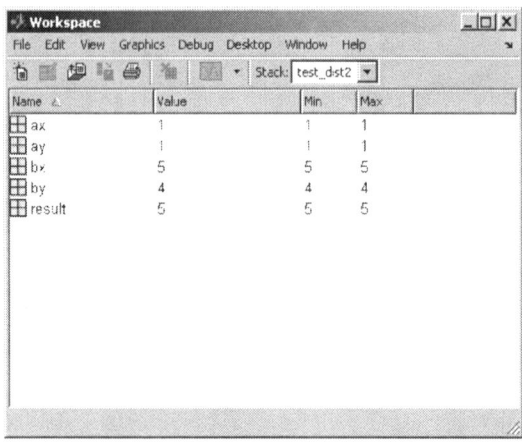

(c)

Figure 6.2   *(Continued)*

6.2   Variable Passing in MATLAB: The Pass-by-Value Scheme

MATLAB programs communicate with their functions using a **pass-by-value** scheme. When a function call occurs, MATLAB makes a *copy* of the actual arguments and passes them to the function. This copying is significant, because it means that even if the function modifies the input arguments, it won't affect the original data in the caller. This feature helps to prevent unintended side effects, in which an error in the function might unintentionally modify variables in the calling program.

This behavior is illustrated in the function shown that follows. This function has two input arguments: a and b. During its calculations, it modifies both input arguments.

```
function out = sample(a, b)
fprintf('In      sample: a = %f, b = %f %f\n',a,b);
a = b(1) + 2*a;
b = a .* b;
out = a + b(1);
fprintf('In      sample: a = %f, b = %f %f\n',a,b);
```

A simple test program to call this function is shown here.

```
a = 2; b = [6 4];
fprintf('Before sample: a = %f, b = %f %f\n',a,b);
out = sample(a,b);
fprintf('After  sample: a = %f, b = %f %f\n',a,b);
fprintf('After  sample: out = %f\n',out);
```

When this program is executed, the results are

```
» test_sample
Before sample: a = 2.000000, b = 6.000000 4.000000
In      sample: a = 2.000000, b = 6.000000 4.000000
In      sample: a = 10.000000, b = 60.000000 40.000000
After  sample: a = 2.000000, b = 6.000000 4.000000
After  sample: out = 70.000000
```

Note that a and b were both changed inside the function sample, but those changes had *no effect on the values in the calling program.*

Users of the C language will be familiar with the pass-by-value scheme, since C uses it for scalar values passed to functions. However C does *not* use the pass-by-value scheme when passing arrays, so an unintended modification to a dummy array in a C function can cause side effects in the calling program. MATLAB improves on this by using the pass-by-value scheme for both scalars and arrays.[2]

▶

Example 6.1—Rectangular-to-Polar Conversion

The location of a point in a Cartesian plane can be expressed in either the rectangular coordinates (x,y) or the polar coordinates (r,θ), as shown in Figure 6.3. The relationships among these two sets of coordinates are given by the following equations:

$$x = r \cos \theta \tag{6.1}$$

$$y = r \sin \theta \tag{6.2}$$

$$r = \sqrt{x^2 + y^2} \tag{6.3}$$

$$\theta = \tan^{-1} \frac{y}{x} \tag{6.4}$$

---

[2]The implementation of argument passing in MATLAB is actually more sophisticated than this discussion indicates. As pointed out in the main body of the text, the copying associated with pass-by-value takes up a lot of time, but it provides protection against unintended side effects. MATLAB actually uses the best of both approaches: it analyzes each argument of each function and determines whether or not the function modifies that argument. If the function modifies the argument, MATLAB makes a copy of it. If it does not modify the argument, MATLAB simply points to the existing value in the calling program. This practice increases speed while still providing protection against side effects!

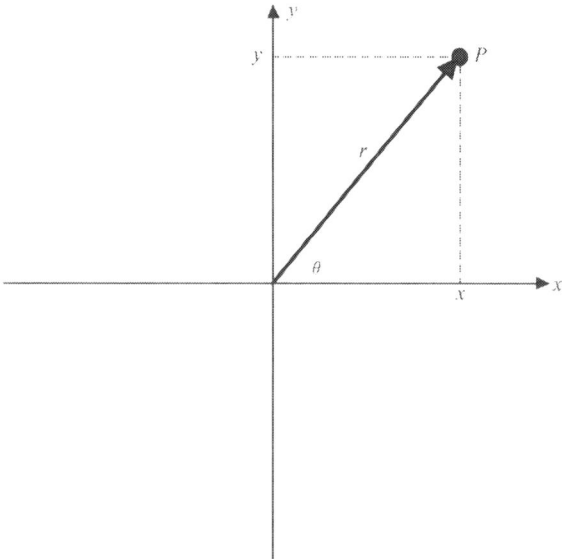

Figure 6.3 A point P in a Cartesian plane can be located by either the rectangular coordinates (x,y) or the polar coordinates (r,θ).

Write two functions `rect2polar` and `polar2rect` that convert coordinates from rectangular to polar form, and vice versa, where the angle θ is expressed in degrees.

SOLUTION We will apply our standard problem-solving approach to creating these functions. Note that MATLAB's trigonometric functions work in radians, so we must convert from degrees to radians, and vice versa, when solving this problem. The basic relationship between degrees and radians is

$$180° = \pi \text{ radians} \tag{6.5}$$

1. **State the problem.**
   A succinct statement of the problem is

   > Write a function that converts a location on a Cartesian plane expressed in rectangular coordinates into the corresponding polar coordinates, where the angle θ is expressed in degrees. Also, write a function that converts a location on a Cartesian plane expressed in polar coordinates with the angle θ expressed in degrees into the corresponding rectangular coordinates.

2. **Define the inputs and outputs.**
   The inputs to function `rect2polar` are the rectangular *(x,y)* location of a point. The outputs of the function are the polar *(r,θ)* location of the point.

The inputs to the function `polar2rect` are the polar (r, θ) location of a point. The outputs of the function are the rectangular (x,y) location of the point.

3. **Describe the algorithm.**

   These functions are very simple, so we can directly write the final pseudocode for them. The pseudocode for function `polar2rect` is

   ```
   x ← r * cos(theta * pi/180)
   y ← r * sin(theta * pi/180)
   ```

   The pseudocode for function `rect2polar` will use the function `atan2`, because that function works over all four quadrants of the Cartesian plane. (Look that function up in the MATLAB Help Browser!)

   ```
   r ← sqrt(x.^2 + y.^2)
   theta ← 180/pi * atan2(y,x)
   ```

4. **Turn the algorithm into MATLAB statements.**

   The MATLAB code for the selection `polar2rect` function is shown here.

```
function [x, y] = polar2rect(r,theta)
%POLAR2RECT Convert rectangular to polar coordinates
% Function POLAR2RECT accepts the polar coordinates
% (r,theta), where theta is expressed in degrees,
% and converts them into the rectangular coordinates
% (x,y).
%
% Calling sequence:
%    [x, y] = polar2rect(r,theta)

% Define variables:
%    r          -- Length of polar vector
%    theta      -- Angle of vector in degrees
%    x          -- x-position of point
%    y          -- y-position of point

% Record of revisions:
%       Date            Engineer            Description of change
%       ====            ========            =====================
%    02/01/10      S. J. Chapman       Original code

x = r * cos(theta * pi/180);
y = r * sin(theta * pi/180);
```

The MATLAB code for the selection `rect2polar` function is shown here.

```
function [r, theta] = rect2polar(x,y)
%RECT2POLAR Convert rectangular to polar coordinates
% Function RECT2POLAR accepts the rectangular coordinates
% (x,y) and converts them into the polar coordinates
% (r,theta), where theta is expressed in degrees.
%
% Calling sequence:
%   [r, theta] = rect2polar(x,y)

% Define variables:
%   r        -- Length of polar vector
%   theta    -- Angle of vector in degrees
%   x        -- x-position of point
%   y        -- y-position of point

% Record of revisions:
%     Date           Engineer          Description of change
%     ====           ========          =====================
%   02/01/10      S. J. Chapman       Original code

r = sqrt(x.^2 + y.^2);
theta = 180/pi * atan2(y,x);
```

Note that these functions both include help information, so they will work properly with MATLAB's help subsystem and with the `lookfor` command.

5. **Test the program.**

To test these functions, we will execute them directly in the MATLAB Command Window. We will test the functions using the 3-4-5 triangle, which is familiar to most people from secondary school. The smaller angle within a 3-4-5 triangle is approximately 36.87°. We will also test the function in all four quadrants of the Cartesian plane to ensure that the conversions are correct everywhere.

```
» [r, theta] = rect2polar(4,3)
r =
     5
theta =
    36.8699
» [r, theta] = rect2polar(-4,3)
r =
     5
theta =
   143.1301
» [r, theta] = rect2polar(-4,-3)
r =
     5
theta =
  -143.1301
```

```
» [r, theta] = rect2polar(4,-3)
r =
      5
theta =
  -36.8699
» [x, y] = polar2rect(5,36.8699)
x =
      4.0000
y =
      3.0000
» [x, y] = polar2rect(5,143.1301)
x =
     -4.0000
y =
      3.0000
» [x, y] = polar2rect(5,-143.1301)
x =
     -4.0000
y =
     -3.0000
» [x, y] = polar2rect(5,-36.8699)
x =
      4.0000
y =
     -3.0000
»
```

These functions appear to be working correctly in all quadrants of the Cartesian plane. ◄

►

Example 6.2—Sorting Data

In many scientific and engineering applications, it is necessary to take a random input data set and to sort it so that the numbers in the data set are either all in *ascending order* (lowest-to-highest) or all in *descending order* (highest-to-lowest). For example, suppose that you were a zoologist studying a large population of animals and that you wanted to identify the largest 5 percent of the animals in the population. The most straightforward way to approach this problem would be to sort the sizes of all of the animals in the population into ascending order, and take the top 5 percent of the values.

Sorting data into ascending or descending order seems to be an easy job. After all, we do it all the time. It is simple matter for us to sort the data (10, 3, 6, 4, 9) into the order (3, 4, 6, 9, 10). How do we do it? We first scan the input data list (10, 3, 6, 4, 9) to find the smallest value in the list (3), and then scan the remaining input data (10, 6, 4, 9) to find the next smallest value (4), and so forth until the complete list has been sorted.

In fact, sorting can be a very difficult job. As the number of values to be sorted increases, the time required to perform the simple sort just described increases rapidly, since we must scan the input data set once for each value sorted. For very large data sets, this technique takes too long to be practical. Even worse, how would we sort the data if there were too many numbers to fit into the main memory of the computer? The development of efficient sorting techniques for large data sets is an active area of research and is the subject of whole courses all by itself.

In this example, we will confine ourselves to the simplest possible algorithm to illustrate the concept of sorting. This simplest algorithm is called the **selection sort**. It is just a computer implementation of the mental math described previously. The basic algorithm for the selection sort is

1. Scan the list of numbers to be sorted to locate the smallest value in the list. Place that value at the front of the list by swapping it with the value currently at the front of the list. If the value at the front of the list is already the smallest value, then do nothing.
2. Scan the list of numbers from position 2 to the end to locate the next smallest value in the list. Place that value in position 2 of the list by swapping it with the value currently at that position. If the value in position 2 is already the next smallest value, then do nothing.
3. Scan the list of numbers from position 3 to the end to locate the third smallest value in the list. Place that value in position 3 of the list by swapping it with the value currently at that position. If the value in position 3 is already the third smallest value, then do nothing.
4. Repeat this process until the next-to-last position in the list is reached. After the next-to-last position in the list has been processed, the sort is complete.

Note that if we are sorting N values, this sorting algorithm requires $N - 1$ scans through the data to accomplish the sort.

This process is illustrated in Figure 6.4. Since there are five values in the data set to be sorted, we will make four scans through the data. During the first pass through the entire data set, the minimum value is 3, so the 3 is swapped with the 10 which was in position 1. Pass 2 searches for the minimum value in positions 2 through 5. That minimum is 4, so the 4 is swapped with the 10 in position 2. Pass 3 searches for the minimum value in positions 3 through 5. That minimum is 6, which is already in position 3, so no swapping is required. Finally, pass 4 searches for the minimum value in positions 4 through 5. That minimum is 9, so the 9 is swapped with the 10 in position 4, and the sort is completed.

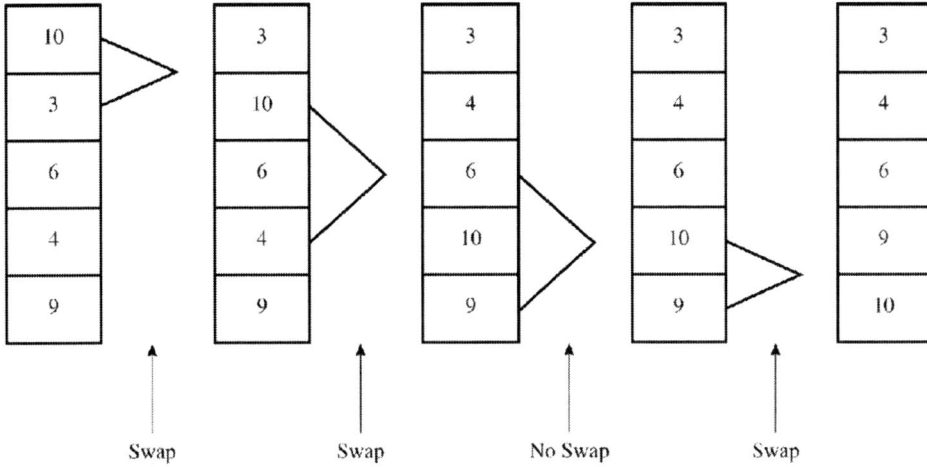

Figure 6.4 An example problem demonstrating the selection sort algorithm.

💣 Programming Pitfalls

The selection sort algorithm is the easiest sorting algorithm to understand, but it is computationally inefficient. *It should never be applied to sort large data sets* (say, sets with more than 1000 elements). Over the years, computer scientists have developed much more efficient sorting algorithms. The `sort` and `sortrows` functions built into MATLAB are extremely efficient and should be used for all real work.

We will now develop a program to read in a data set from the Command Window, sort it into ascending order, and display the sorted data set. The sorting will be done by a separate user-defined function.

SOLUTION   This program must be able to ask the user for the input data, sort the data, and write out the sorted data. The design process for this problem is given here.

1. **State the problem.**
   We have not yet specified the type of data to be sorted. If the data is numeric, the problem may be stated as follows:

   Develop a program to read an arbitrary number of numeric input values from the Command Window, sort the data into ascending order using a separate sorting function, and write the sorted data to the Command Window.

2. **Define the inputs and outputs.**

The inputs to this program are the numeric values typed in the Command Window by the user. The outputs from this program are the sorted data values written to the Command Window.

3. **Describe the algorithm.**

This program can be broken down into three major steps:

```
Read the input data into an array
Sort the data in ascending order
Write the sorted data
```

The first major step is to read in the data. We must prompt the user for the number of input data values and then read in the data. Since we will know how many input values there are to read, a for loop is appropriate for reading in the data. The detailed pseudocode is shown here.

```
Prompt user for the number of data values
Read the number of data values
Preallocate an input array
for ii = 1:number of values
    Prompt for next value
    Read value
end
```

Next we have to sort the data in a separate function. We will need to make nvals-1 passes through the data, finding the smallest remaining value each time. We will use a pointer to locate the smallest value in each pass. Once the smallest value is found, it will be swapped to the top of the list of it is not already there. The detailed pseudocode is shown here.

```
for ii = 1:nvals-1

    % Find the minimum value in a(ii) through a(nvals)
    iptr ← ii
    for jj == ii+1 to nvals
        if a(jj) < a(iptr)
            iptr ← jj
        end
    end

    % iptr now points to the min value, so swap a(iptr)
    % with a(ii) if iptr ~= ii.
    if i ~= iptr
        temp ← a(i)
        a(i) ← a(iptr)
        a(iptr) ← temp
    end
end
```

The final step is writing out the sorted values. No refinement of the pseudocode is required for that step. The final pseudocode is the combination of the reading, sorting, and writing steps.

4. **Turn the algorithm into MATLAB statements.**

The MATLAB code for the selection sort function is shown here.

```matlab
function out = ssort(a)
%SSORT Selection sort data in ascending order
% Function SSORT sorts a numeric data set into
% ascending order. Note that the selection sort
% is relatively inefficient. DO NOT USE THIS
% FUNCTION FOR LARGE DATA SETS. Use MATLAB's
% "sort" function instead.

% Define variables:
%   a        -- Input array to sort
%   ii       -- Index variable
%   iptr     -- Pointer to min value
%   jj       -- Index variable
%   nvals    -- Number of values in "a"
%   out      -- Sorted output array
%   temp     -- Temp variable for swapping

% Record of revisions:
%     Date          Engineer           Description of change
%     ====          ========           =====================
%   02/02/10     S. J. Chapman         Original code

% Get the length of the array to sort
nvals = length(a);

% Sort the input array
for ii = 1:nvals-1

   % Find the minimum value in a(ii) through a(n)
   iptr = ii;
   for jj = ii+1:nvals
      if a(jj) > a(iptr)
         iptr = jj;
      end
   end

   % iptr now points to the minimum value, so swap a(iptr)
   % with a(ii) if ii ~= iptr.
   if ii ~= iptr
      temp     = a(ii);
      a(ii)    = a(iptr);
      a(iptr)  = temp;
   end
end
end
```

```
% Pass data back to caller
out = a;
```

The program to invoke the selection sort function is shown here.

```
% Script file: test_ssort.m
%
% Purpose:
%   To read in an input data set, sort it into ascending
%   order using the selection sort algorithm, and to
%   write the sorted data to the Command Window. This
%   program calls function "ssort" to do the actual
%   sorting.
%
% Record of revisions:
%     Date          Engineer          Description of change
%     ====          ========          =====================
%   02/02/10      S. J. Chapman       Original code
%
% Define variables:
%   array    -- Input data array
%   ii       -- Index variable
%   nvals    -- Number of input values
%   sorted   -- Sorted data array

% Prompt for the number of values in the data set
nvals = input('Enter number of values to sort: ');

% Preallocate array
array = zeros(1,nvals);

% Get input values
for ii = 1:nvals

   % Prompt for next value
   string = ['Enter value ' int2str(ii) ': '];
   array(ii) = input(string);

end

% Now sort the data
sorted = ssort(array);

% Display the sorted result.
fprintf('\nSorted data:\n');
for ii = 1:nvals
   fprintf('  %8.4f\n',sorted(ii));
end
```

5. **Test the program.**

To test this program, we will create an input data set and run the program with it. The data set should contain a mixture of positive and negative numbers as well as at least one duplicated value to see if the program works properly under those conditions.

```
» test_ssort
Enter number of values to sort: 6
Enter value 1:   -5
Enter value 2:   4
Enter value 3:   -2
Enter value 4:   3
Enter value 5:   -2
Enter value 6:   0

Sorted data:
  -5.0000
  -2.0000
  -2.0000
   0.0000
   3.0000
   4.0000
```

The program gives the correct answers for our test data set. Note that it works for both positive and negative numbers as well as for repeated numbers. ◀

6.3   Optional Arguments

Many MATLAB functions support optional input arguments and output arguments. For example, we have seen calls to the `plot` function with as few as two or as many as seven input arguments. On the other hand, the function `max` supports either one or two output arguments. If there is only one output argument, `max` returns the maximum value of an array. If there are two output arguments, `max` returns both the maximum value and the location of the maximum value in an array. How do MATLAB functions know how many input and output arguments are present, and how do they adjust their behavior accordingly?

There are eight special functions that can be used by MATLAB functions to get information about their optional arguments and to report errors in those arguments. Six of these functions are introduced here, and the remaining two will be introduced in Chapter 9 after we learn about the cell array data type. The functions introduced now are

- `nargin`—This function returns the number of actual input arguments that were used to call the function.
- `nargout`—This function returns the number of actual output arguments that were used to call the function.

- `nargchk`—This function returns a standard error message if a function is called with too few or too many arguments.
- `error`—Display error message and abort the function producing the error. This function is used if the argument errors are fatal.
- `warning`—Display warning message and continue function execution. This function is used if the argument errors are not fatal, and execution can continue.
- `inputname`—This function returns the actual name of the variable that corresponds to a particular argument number.

When the functions `nargin` and `nargout` are called within a user-defined function, they return the number of actual input arguments and the number of actual output arguments that were used to when the user-defined function was called.

The function `nargchk` generates a string containing a standard error message if a function is called with too few or too many arguments. The syntax of this function is

```
message = nargchk(min_args,max_args,num_args);
```

where `min_args` is the minimum number of arguments, `max_args` is the maximum number of arguments, and `num_args` is the actual number of arguments. If the number of arguments is outside the acceptable limits, a standard error message is produced. If the number of arguments is within acceptable limits, an empty string is returned.

The function `error` is a standard way to display an error message and abort the user-defined function causing the error. The syntax of this function is `error('msg')`, where `msg` is a character string containing an error message. When `error` is executed, it halts the current function and returns to the keyboard, displaying the error message in the Command Window. If the message string is empty, `error` does nothing and execution continues. This function works well with `nargchk`, which produces a message string when an error occurs and an empty string when there is no error.

The function `warning` is a standard way to display a warning message that includes the function and line number where the problem occurred but lets execution continue. The syntax of this function is `warning('msg')`, where `msg` is a character string containing a warning message. When `warning` is executed, it displays the warning message in the Command Window and lists the function name and line number where the warning came from. If the message string is empty, `warning` does nothing. In either case, execution of the function continues.

The function `inputname` returns the name of the actual argument used when a function is called. The syntax of this function is

```
name = inputname(argno);
```

where `argno` is the number of the argument. If argument is a variable, its name is returned. If the argument is an expression, this function will return an empty string. For example, consider the function

```
function myfun(x,y,z)
name = inputname(2);
disp(['The second argument is named ' name]);
```

When this function is called, the results are

» **myfun(dog,cat)**
```
The second argument is named cat
```
» **myfun(1,2+cat)**
```
The second argument is named
```

The function inputname is useful for displaying argument names in warning and error messages.

►

Example 6.3—Using Optional Arguments

We will illustrate the use of optional arguments by creating a function that accepts an *(x,y)* value in rectangular coordinates and produces the equivalent polar representation consisting of a magnitude and an angle in degrees. The function will be designed to support two input arguments, *x* and *y*. However, if only one argument is supplied, the function will assume that the *y* value is zero and proceed with the calculation. The function will normally return both the magnitude and the angle in degrees, but if only one output argument is present, it will return only the magnitude. This function is shown below.

```
function [mag, angle] = polar_value(x,y)
%POLAR_VALUE Converts (x,y) to (r,theta)
% Function POLAR_VALUE converts an input (x,y)
% value into (r,theta), with theta in degrees.
% It illustrates the use of optional arguments.

% Define variables:
%   angle     -- Angle in degrees
%   msg       -- Error message
%   mag       -- Magnitude
%   x         -- Input x value
%   y         -- Input y value (optional)

% Record of revisions:
%    Date            Engineer            Description of change
%    ====            ========            =====================
%   02/03/10    S. J. Chapman       Original code

% Check for a legal number of input arguments.
msg = nargchk(1,2,nargin);
error(msg);

% If the y argument is missing, set it to 0.
if nargin < 2
   y = 0;
end
```

```
% Check for (0,0) input arguments, and print out
% a warning message.
if x == 0 & y == 0
   msg = 'Both x any y are zero: angle is meaningless!';
   warning(msg);
end

% Now calculate the magnitude.
mag = sqrt(x.^2 + y.^2);

% If the second output argument is present, calculate
% angle in degrees.
if nargout == 2
   angle = atan2(y,x) * 180/pi;
end
```

We will test this function by calling it repeatedly from the Command Window. First, we will try to call the function with too few or too many arguments.

```
» [mag angle] = polar_value
??? Error using ==> polar_value
Not enough input arguments.

» [mag angle] = polar_value(1,-1,1)
??? Error using ==> polar_value
Too many input arguments.
```

The function provides proper error messages in both cases. Next, we will try to call the function with one or two input arguments.

```
» [mag angle] = polar_value(1)
mag =
       1
angle =
       0
» [mag angle] = polar_value(1,-1)
mag =
           1.4142
angle =
     -45
```

The function provides the correct answer in both cases. Next, we will try to call the function with one or two output arguments.

```
» mag = polar_value(1,-1)
mag =
       1.4142
» [mag angle] = polar_value(1,-1)
mag =
       1.4142
angle =
     -45
```

The function provides the correct answer in both cases. Finally, we will try to call the function with both x and y equal to zero.

```
» [mag angle] = polar_value(0,0)
```

```
Warning: Both x any y are zero: angle is meaningless!
> In d:\book\matlab\chap6\polar_value.m at line 32
mag =
      0
angle =
      0
```

In this case, the function displays the warning message, but execution continues. ◀

Note that a MATLAB function may be declared to have more output arguments than are actually used, and this is *not* an error. The function does not actually have to check nargout to determine whether an output argument is present. For example, consider the following function:

```
function [z1, z2] = junk(x,y)
z1 = x + y;
z2 = x - y;
end % function junk
```

This function can be called successfully with one or two output arguments.

```
» a = junk(2,1)
a =
      3
» [a b] = junk(2,1)
a =
      3
b =
      1
```

The reason for checking nargout in a function is to prevent useless work. If a result is going to be thrown away anyway, why bother to calculate it in the first place? An engineer can speed up the operation of a program by not bothering with useless calculations.

Quiz 6.1

This quiz provides a quick check to see if you have understood the concepts introduced in Sections 6.1 through 6.3. If you have trouble with the quiz, reread the section, ask your instructor, or discuss the material with a fellow student. The answers to this quiz are found in the back of the book.

1. What are the differences between a script file and a function?

2. How does the `help` command work with user-defined functions?

3. What is the significance of the H1 comment line in a function?

4. What is the pass-by-value scheme? How does it contribute to good program design?

5. How can a MATLAB function be designed to have optional arguments?

For questions 6 and 7, determine whether the function calls are correct or not. If they are in error, specify what is wrong with them.

6.
```
out = test1(6);
function res = test1(x,y)
res = sqrt(x.^2 + y.^2);
```

7.
```
out = test2(12);
function res = test2(x,y)
error(nargchk(1,2,nargin));
if nargin == 2
   res = sqrt(x.^2 + y.^2);
else
   res = x;
end
```

6.4   Sharing Data Using Global Memory

We have seen that programs exchange data with the functions they call through a argument lists. When a function is called, each actual argument is copied and the copy is used by the function.

In addition to the argument list, MATLAB functions can exchange data with each other and with the base workspace through global memory. **Global memory** is a special type of memory that can be accessed from any workspace. If a variable is declared to be global in a function, it will be placed in the global memory instead of the local workspace. If the same variable is declared to be global in another function, that variable will refer to the *same memory location* as the variable in the first function. Each script file or function that declares the global variable will have access to the same data values, so *global memory provides a way to share data between functions.*

A global variable is declared with the **global** statement. The form of a global statement is

```
global var1 var2 var3 ...
```

where *var1*, *var2*, *var3*, and so forth are the variables to be placed in global memory. By convention, global variables are declared in all capital letters, but this is not actually a requirement.

✳ Good Programming Practice

Declare global variables in all capital letters to make them easy to distinguish from local variables.

Each global variable must be declared to be global before it is used for the first time in a function—it is an error to declare a variable to be global after it already has been created in the local workspace.[3] To avoid this error, it is customary to declare global variables immediately after the initial comments and before the first executable statement in a function.

✳ Good Programming Practice

Declare global variables immediately after the initial comments and before the first executable statement in each function that uses them.

Global variables are especially useful for sharing very large volumes of data among many functions, because the entire data set does not have to be copied each time that a function is called. The downside of using global memory to exchange data among functions is that the functions will work only for that specific data set. A function that exchanges data through input arguments can be reused by simply calling it with different arguments, but a function that exchanges data through global memory must actually be modified to allow it to work with a different data set.

Global variables are also useful for sharing hidden data among a group of related functions while keeping it invisible to the invoking program unit.

✳ Good Programming Practice

You may use global memory to pass large amounts of data among functions within a program.

---

[3]If a variable is declared `global` after it has already been defined in a function, MATLAB will issue a warning message and then change the local value to match the global value. You should never rely on this capability, though, because future versions of MATLAB may not allow it.

▶

Example 6.4—Random Number Generator

It is impossible to make perfect measurements in the real world. There will always be some *measurement noise* associated with each measurement. This fact is an important consideration in the design of systems to control the operation of such real-world devices as airplanes, refineries, and nuclear reactors. A good engineering design must take these measurement errors into account, so that the noise in the measurements will not lead to unstable behavior (no plane crashes, refinery explosions, or meltdowns!).

Most engineering designs are tested by running *simulations* of the operation of the system before it is ever built. These simulations involve creating mathematical models of the behavior of the system and feeding the models a realistic string of input data. If the models respond correctly to the simulated input data, we can have reasonable confidence that the real-world system will respond correctly to the real-world input data.

The simulated input data supplied to the models must be corrupted by a simulated measurement noise, which is just a string of random numbers added to the ideal input data. The simulated noise is usually produced by a *random number generator.*

A random number generator is a function that will return a different and apparently random number each time it is called. Since the numbers are in fact generated by a deterministic algorithm, they only appear to be random.[4] However, if the algorithm used to generate them is complex enough, the numbers will be random enough to use in the simulation.

One simple random-number generator algorithm is described below.[5] It relies on the unpredictability of the modulo function when applied to large numbers. Recall from Chapter 4 that the modulus function mod returns the remainder after the division of two numbers. Consider the following equation:

$$n_{i+1} = \bmod(8121 \, n_i + 28{,}411, \, 134{,}456) \tag{6.6}$$

Assume that n_i is a non-negative integer. Then because of the modulo function, n_{i+1} will be a number between 0 and 134,455 inclusive. Next, n_{i+1} can be fed into the equation to produce a number n_{i+2} that is also between 0 and 134,455. This process can be repeated forever to produce a series of numbers in the range [0,134455]. If we didn't know the numbers 8121, 28,411, and 134,456 in advance, it would be impossible to guess the order in which the values of n would be produced. Furthermore, it turns out that there is an equal (or uniform) probability that any given number will appear in the sequence. Because of these properties, Equation (6.6) can serve as the basis for a simple random number generator with a uniform distribution.

---

[4]For this reason, some people refer to these functions as *pseudorandom number generators.*
[5]This algorithm is adapted from the discussion found in Chapter 7 of *Numerical Recipes: The Art of Scientific Programming*, by Press, Flannery, Teukolsky, and Vetterling, Cambridge University Press, 1986.

We will now use Equation (6.6) to design a random number generator whose output is a real number in the range [0.0, 1.0).[6]

SOLUTION   We will write a function that generates one random number in the range $0 \le ran < 1.0$ each time it is called. The random number will be based on the equation

$$ran_i = \frac{n_i}{134456} \tag{6.7}$$

where n_i is a number in the range 0 to 134,455 produced by Equation (6.6).

The particular sequence produced by Equations (6.6) and (6.7) will depend on the initial value of n_0 (called the *seed*) of the sequence. We must provide a way for the user to specify n_0 so that the sequence may be varied from run to run.

1. **State the problem**.
   Write a function random0 that will generate and return an array ran containing one or more numbers with a uniform probability distribution in the range $0 \le$ ran < 1.0, based on the sequence specified by Equations (6.6) and (6.7). The function should have one or two input arguments (m and n) specifying the size of the array to return. If there is one argument, the function should generate a square array of size m $\times$ m. If there are two arguments, the function should generate an array of size m $\times$ n. The initial value of the seed n_0 will be specified by a call to a function called seed.

2. **Define the inputs and outputs**.
   There are two functions in this problem: seed and random0. The input to function seed is an integer to serve as the starting point of the sequence. There is no output from this function. The input to function random0 is one or two integers specifying the size of the array of random numbers to be generated. If only argument m is supplied, the function should generate a square array of size m $\times$ m. If both arguments m and n are supplied, the function should generate an array of size m $\times$ n. The output from the function is the array of random values in the range [0.0, 1.0).

3. **Describe the algorithm**.
   The pseudocode for function random0 is

   ```
   function ran = random0 ( m, n )
   Check for valid arguments
   Set n ← m if not supplied
   Create output array with "zeros" function
   ```

---

[6]The notation [0.0,1.0) implies that the range of the random numbers is between 0.0 and 1.0, including the number 0.0, but excluding the number 1.0.

```
for ii = 1:number of rows
    for jj = 1:number of columns
        ISEED ← mod (8121 * ISEED + 28411, 134456 )
        ran(ii,jj) ← ISEED / 134456
    end
end
```

where the value of ISEED is placed in global memory so that it is saved between calls to the function. The pseudocode for function seed is trivial:

```
function seed (new_seed)
new_seed ← round(new_seed)
ISEED ← abs(new_seed)
```

The round function is used in case the user fails to supply an integer, and the absolute value function is used in case the user supplies a negative seed. The user will not have to know in advance that only positive integers are legal seeds.

The variable ISEED will be placed in global memory so that it may be accessed by both functions.

4. **Turn the algorithm into MATLAB statements.**
Function random0 is shown here.

```
function ran = random0(m,n)
%RANDOM0 Generate uniform random numbers in [0,1)
% Function RANDOM0 generates an array of uniform
% random numbers in the range [0,1). The usage
% is:
%
% random0(m)    -- Generate an m x m array
% random0(m,n)  -- Generate an m x n array

% Define variables:
%   ii    -- Index variable
%   ISEED  -- Random number seed (global)
%   jj    -- Index variable
%   m     -- Number of columns
%   msg   -- Error message
%   n     -- Number of rows
%   ran   -- Output array
%
% Record of revisions:
%     Date          Engineer         Description of change
%     ====          ========         =====================
%   02/04/10     S. J. Chapman       Original code

% Declare global values
global ISEED            % Seed for random number generator
```

```
% Check for a legal number of input arguments.
msg = nargchk(1,2,nargin);
error(msg);

% If the n argument is missing, set it to m.
if nargin < 2
   n = m;
end

% Initialize the output array
ran = zeros(m,n);

% Now calculate random values
for ii = 1:m
   for jj = 1:n
      ISEED = mod(8121*ISEED + 28411, 134456 );
      ran(ii,jj) = ISEED / 134456;
   end
end
```

The function seed is shown here.

```
function seed(new_seed)
%SEED Set new seed for function random0
% Function SEED sets a new seed for function
% random0. The new seed should be a positive
% integer.

% Define variables:
% ISEED      -- Random number seed (global)
% new_seed   -- New seed

% Record of revisions:
%    Date          Engineer         Description of change
%    ====          ========         =====================
%   02/04/10    S. J. Chapman       Original code
%
% Declare globl values
global ISEED            % Seed for random number generator

% Check for a legal number of input arguments.
msg = nargchk(1,1,nargin);
error(msg);

% Save seed
new_seed = round(new_seed);
ISEED = abs(new_seed);
```

5. **Test the resulting MATLAB programs.**
If the numbers generated by these functions are truly uniformly distributed random numbers in the range $0 \leq \text{ran} < 1.0$, the average of many numbers should be close to 0.5 and the standard deviation of the numbers should be close to $\dfrac{1}{\sqrt{12}}$.

Furthermore, if the range between 0 and 1 is divided into a number of equal-sized bins, the number of random values falling in each bin should be about the same. A **histogram** is a plot of the number of values falling in each bin. The MATLAB function `hist` will create and plot a histogram from an input data set, so we will use it to verify the distribution of random number generated by `random0` (Figure 6.5).

To test the results of these functions, we will perform the following tests:

1. Call `seed` with `new_seed` set to 1024.
2. Call `random0(4)` to see that the results appear random.
3. Call `random0(4)` to verify that the results differ from call to call.
4. Call `seed` again with `new_seed` set to 1024.
5. Call `random0(4)` to see that the results are the same as in item (2). This verifies that the seed is properly being reset.
6. Call `random0(2,3)` to verify that both input arguments are being used correctly.
7. Call `random0(1,100000)` and calculate the average and standard deviation of the resulting data set using MATLAB functions `mean` and `std`. Compare the results to 0.5 and $\dfrac{1}{\sqrt{12}}$.
8. Create a histogram of the data from (7) to see if approximately equal numbers of values fall in each bin.

We will perform these tests interactively, checking the results as we go.

```
» seed(1024)
» random0(4)
ans =
    0.0598    1.0000    0.0905    0.2060
    0.2620    0.6432    0.6325    0.8392
    0.6278    0.5463    0.7551    0.4554
    0.3177    0.9105    0.1289    0.6230
» random0(4)
ans =
    0.2266    0.3858    0.5876    0.7880
    0.8415    0.9287    0.9855    0.1314
    0.0982    0.6585    0.0543    0.4256
    0.2387    0.7153    0.2606    0.8922
```

```
» seed(1024)
» random0(4)
ans =
       0.0598        1.0000        0.0905        0.2060
       0.2620        0.6432        0.6325        0.8392
       0.6278        0.5463        0.7551        0.4554
       0.3177        0.9105        0.1289        0.6230
» random0(2,3)
ans =
       0.2266        0.3858        0.5876
       0.7880        0.8415        0.9287
» arr = random0(1,100000);
» mean(arr)
ans =
       0.5001
» std(arr)
ans =
       0.2887
» hist(arr,10)
» title('\bfHistogram of the Output of random0');
» xlabel('Bin');
» ylabel('Count');
```

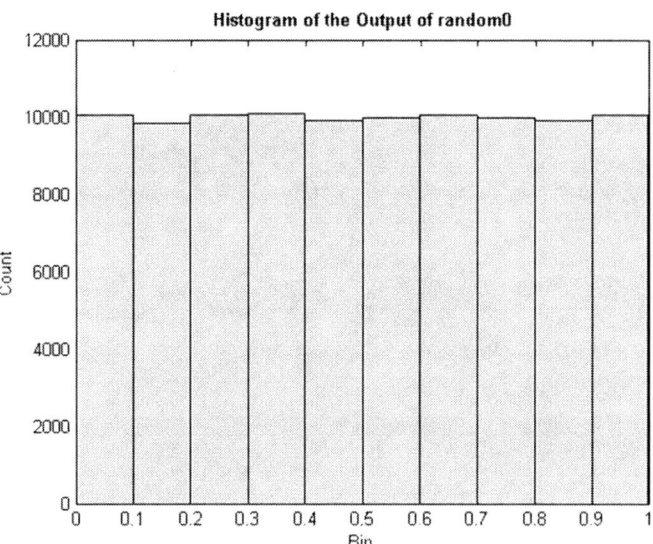

Figure 6.5 Histogram of the output of function random0.

The results of these tests look reasonable, so the function appears to be working. The average of the data set was 0.5001, which is quite close to the theoretical value of 0.5000, and the standard deviation of the data set was 0.2887, which is equal to the theoretical value of 0.2887 to the accuracy displayed. The histogram is shown in Figure 6.5, and the distribution of the random values is roughly even across all of the bins.   ◀

6.5   Preserving Data between Calls to a Function

When a function finishes executing, the special workspace created for that function is destroyed, so the contents of all local variables within the function will disappear. The next time the function is called, a new workspace will be created, and all of the local variables will be returned to their default values. This behavior is usually desirable, since it ensures that MATLAB functions behave in a repeatable fashion every time they are called.

However, it is sometimes useful to preserve some local information within a function between calls to the function. For example, we might wish to create a counter to count the number of times that the function has been called. If such a counter were destroyed every time the function exited, the count would never exceed 1!

MATLAB includes a special mechanism to allow local variables to be preserved between calls to a function. **Persistent memory** is a special type of memory that can be accessed only from within the function but is preserved unchanged between calls to the function.

A persistent variable is declared with the **persistent statement**. The form of a global statement is

```
persistent var1 var2 var3 ...
```

where *var1*, *var2*, *var3*, and so forth are the variables to be placed in persistent memory.

☀ Good Programming Practice

Use persistent memory to preserve the values of local variables within a function between calls to the function.

▶

Example 6.5—Running Averages

It is sometimes desirable to calculate running statistics on a data set on the fly as the values are being entered. The built-in MATLAB functions mean and std could perform this function, but we would have to pass the entire data set to them for recalculation after each new data value is entered. A better result can be achieved by writing a special function that keeps track of the appropriate running sums between calls and only needs the latest value to calculate the current average and standard deviation.

The average or arithmetic mean of a set of numbers is defined as

$$\bar{x} = \frac{1}{N} \sum_{i=1}^{N} x_i \tag{6.8}$$

where x_i is sample i out of N samples. The standard deviation of a set of numbers is defined as

$$s = \sqrt{\frac{N \sum_{i=1}^{N} x_i^2 - \left(\sum_{i=1}^{N} x_i \right)^2}{N(N-1)}} \tag{6.9}$$

Standard deviation is a measure of the amount of scatter on the measurements; the greater the standard deviation, the more scattered the points in the data set are. If we can keep track of the number of values N, the sum of the values Σx, and the sum of the squares of the values Σx^2, then we can calculate the average and standard deviation at any time from Equations (6.8) and (6.9).

Write a function to calculate the running average and standard deviation of a data set as it is being entered.

SOLUTION   This function must be able to accept input values one at a time and keep running sums of N, Σx, and Σx^2, which will be used to calculate the current average and standard deviation. It must store the running sums in global memory so that they are preserved between calls. Finally, there must be a mechanism to reset the running sums.

1. **State the problem.**
   Create a function to calculate the running average and standard deviation of a data set as new values are entered. The function must also include a feature to reset the running sums when desired.

2. **Define the inputs and outputs.**
   There are two types of inputs required by this function:

   1. The character string `'reset'` to reset running sums to zero.
   2. The numeric values from the input data set, presenting one value per function call.

   The outputs from this function are the mean and standard deviation of the data supplied to the function so far.

3. **Design the algorithm.**
   This function can be broken down into four major steps:

   ```
   Check for a legal number of arguments
   Check for a 'reset', and reset sums if present
   ```

Otherwise, add current value to running sums
Calculate and return running average and std dev
    if enough data is available. Return zeros if
    not enough data is available.

The detailed pseudocode for these steps is

```
Check for a legal number of arguments
if x == 'reset'
    n ← 0
    sum_x ← 0
    sum_x2 ← 0
else
    n ← n + 1
    sum_x ← sum_x + x
    sum_x2 ← sum_x2 + x^2
end

% Calculate ave and sd
if n == 0
    ave ← 0
    std ← 0
elseif n == 1
    ave ← sum_x
    std ← 0
else
    ave ← sum_x / n
    std ← sqrt((n*sum_x2 - sum_x^2) / (n*(n-1)))
end
```

4. **Turn the algorithm into MATLAB statements.**
   The final MATLAB function is shown here.

```
function [ave, std] = runstats(x)
%RUNSTATS Generate running ave / std deviation
% Function RUNSTATS generates a running average
% and standard deviation of a data set. The
% values x must be passed to this function one
% at a time. A call to RUNSTATS with the argument
% 'reset' will reset the running sums.

% Define variables:
%    ave      -- Running average
%    msg      -- Error message
%    n        -- Number of data values
%    std      -- Running standard deviation
```

```
%    sum_x      -- Running sum of data values
%    sum_x2     -- Running sum of data values squared
%    x          -- Input value
%
% Record of revisions:
%    Date            Engineer          Description of change
%    ====            ========          =====================
%    02/05/10    S. J. Chapman         Original code

% Declare persistent values
persistent n                % Number of input values
persistent sum_x            % Running sum of values
persistent sum_x2           % Running sum of values squared

% Check for a legal number of input arguments.
msg = nargchk(1,1,nargin);
error(msg);

% If the argument is 'reset', reset the running sums.
if x == 'reset'
   n = 0;
   sum_x = 0;
   sum_x2 = 0;
else
   n = n + 1;
   sum_x = sum_x + x;
   sum_x2 = sum_x2 + x^2;
end

% Calculate ave and sd
if n == 0
   ave = 0;
   std = 0;
elseif n == 1
   ave = sum_x;
   std = 0;
else
   ave = sum_x / n;
   std = sqrt((n*sum_x2 - sum_x^2) / (n*(n-1)));
end
```

5. **Test the program.**

   To test this function, we must create a script file that resets `runstats`, reads input values, calls `runstats`, and displays the running statistics. An appropriate script file is shown here.

```
% Script file: test_runstats.m
%
% Purpose:
%   To read in an input data set and calculate the
%   running statistics on the data set as the values
%   are read in. The running stats will be written
%   to the Command Window.
%
% Record of revisions:
%      Date            Engineer           Description of change
%      ====            ========           =====================
%   02/05/10     S. J. Chapman            Original code
%
% Define variables:
%   array    -- Input data array
%   ave      -- Running average
%   std      -- Running standard deviation
%   ii       -- Index variable
%   nvals    -- Number of input values
%   std      -- Running standard deviation

% First reset running sums
[ave std] = runstats('reset');

% Prompt for the number of values in the data set
nvals = input('Enter number of values in data set: ');

% Get input values
for ii = 1:nvals

   % Prompt for next value
   string = ['Enter value ' int2str(ii) ': '];
   x = input(string);

   % Get running statistics
   [ave std] = runstats(x);

   % Display running statistics
   fprintf('Average = %8.4f; Std dev = %8.4f\n',ave, std);
end
```

To test this function, we will calculate running statistics by hand for a set of 5 numbers, and compare the hand calculations to the results from the program. If a data set is created with the following 5 input values

3., 2., 3., 4., 2.8

the running statistics calculated by hand would be

Value	n	Σx	Σx^2	Average	Std_dev
3.0	1	3.0	9.0	3.00	0.000
2.0	2	5.0	13.0	2.50	0.707
3.0	3	8.0	22.0	2.67	0.577
4.0	4	12.0	38.0	3.00	0.816
2.8	5	14.8	45.84	2.96	0.713

The output of the test program for the same data set is

```
» test_runstats
Enter number of values in data set: 5
Enter value 1:  3
Average =   3.0000; Std dev =   0.0000
Enter value 2:  2
Average =   2.5000; Std dev =   0.7071
Enter value 3:  3
Average =   2.6667; Std dev =   0.5774
Enter value 4:  4
Average =   3.0000; Std dev =   0.8165
Enter value 5:  2.8
Average =   2.9600; Std dev =   0.7127
```

The results check to the accuracy shown in the hand calculations. ◄

6.6 MATLAB Applications: Sorting Functions

MATLAB includes two built-in sorting functions that are extremely efficient and should be used instead of the simple sort function we created in Example 6.2. These functions are enormously faster than the sort we created in Example 6.2, and the speed difference increases rapidly as the size of the data set to sort increases.

Function `sort` sorts a data set into ascending or descending order. If the data is a column or row vector, the entire data set is sorted. If the data is a two-dimensional matrix, the columns of the matrix are sorted separately.

The most common forms of the `sort` function are

```
res = sort(a);            % Sort in ascending order
res = sort(a,'ascend');   % Sort in ascending order
res = sort(a,'descend');  % Sort in descending order
```

If a is a vector, the data set is sorted in the specified order. For example,

```
» a= [1 4 5 2 8];
» sort(a)
ans =
        1    2    4    5    8
» sort(a,'ascend')
ans =
        1    2    4    5    8
» sort(a,'descend')
ans =
        8    5    4    2    1
```

If b is a matrix, the data set is sorted independently by column. For example,

```
» b = [1 5 2; 9 7 3; 8 4 6]
b =
        1    5    2
        9    7    3
        8    4    6
» sort(b)
ans =
        1    4    2
        8    5    3
        9    7    6
```

The function sortrows sorts a matrix of data into ascending or descending order *according to one or more specified columns.*

The most common forms of the sortrows function are

```
res = sortrows(a);         % Ascending sort of col 1
res = sortrows(a,n);       % Ascending sort of col n
res = sortrows(a,-n);      % Descending order of col n
```

It is also possible to sort by more than one column. For example, the statement

```
res = sortrows(a,[m n]);
```

would sort the rows by column m, and if two or more rows have the same value in column m, it would further sort those rows by column n.

For example, suppose b is a matrix, as defined below. Then sortrows(b) will sort the rows in ascending order of column 1, and `sortrows(b,[2  3])` will sort the row in ascending order of columns 2 and 3.

```
» b = [1 7 2; 9 7 3; 8 4 6]
b =
         1       7       2
         9       7       3
         8       4       6
» sortrows(b)
ans =
         1       7       2
         8       4       6
         9       7       3
» sortrows(b,[2  3])
ans =
         8       4       6
         1       7       2
         9       7       3
```

6.7   MATLAB Applications: Random Number Functions

MATLAB includes two standard functions that generate random values from different distributions. They are

- `rand` – Generates random values from a uniform distribution on the range [0,1)
- `randn` – Generates random values from a normal distribution

Both of them are much faster and much more "random" than the simple function that we have created. If you really need random numbers in your programs, use one of these functions.

In a uniform distribution, every number in the range [0,1) has an equal probability of appearing. In contrast, the normal distribution is a classic "bell-shaped curve" with the most likely number being 0.0 and a standard deviation of 1.0.

Functions `rand` and `randn` have the following calling sequences:

- `rand()`—Generates a single random value.
- `rand(n)`—Generates an $n \times n$ array of random values.
- `rand(m,n)`—Generates an $m \times n$ array of random values.

6.8 Summary

In Chapter 6, we presented an introduction to user-defined functions. Functions are special types of M-files that receive data through input arguments and return results through output arguments. Each function has its own independent workspace. Each function should appear in a separate file with the same name as the function, *including capitalization.*

Functions are called by naming them in the Command Window or another M-file. The names used should match the function name exactly, including capitalization. Arguments are passed to functions using a pass-by-value scheme, meaning that MATLAB copies each argument and passes the copy to the function. This copying is important, because the function can freely modify its input arguments without affecting the actual arguments in the calling program.

MATLAB functions can support varying numbers of input and output arguments. Function `nargin` reports the number of actual input arguments used in a function call, and function `nargout` reports the number of actual output arguments used in a function call.

Data also can be shared between MATLAB functions by placing the data in global memory. Global variables are declared using the `global` statement. Global variables may be shared by all functions that declare them. By convention, global variable names are written in all capital letters.

Internal data within a function can be preserved between calls to that function by placing the data in persistent memory. Persistent variables are declared using the `persistent` statement.

6.8.1 Summary of Good Programming Practice

The following guidelines should be adhered to when working with MATLAB functions.

1. Break large program tasks into smaller, more understandable functions whenever possible.
2. Declare global variables in all capital letters to make them easy to distinguish from local variables.
3. Declare global variables immediately after the initial comments and before the first executable statement in each function that uses them.
4. You may use global memory to pass large amounts of data among functions within a program.
5. Use persistent memory to preserve the values of local variables within a function between calls to the function.

6.8.2 MATLAB Summary

The following summary lists all of the MATLAB commands and functions described in this chapter, along with a brief description of each one.

Commands and Functions

error	Displays error message and aborts the function producing the error. This function is used if the argument errors are fatal.
global	Declares global variables.
nargchk	Returns a standard error message if a function is called with too few or too many arguments.
nargin	Returns the number of actual input arguments that were used to call the function.
nargout	Returns the number of actual output arguments that were used to call the function.
persistent	Declares persistent variables.
rand	Generates random values from a uniform distribution.
randn	Generates random values from a normal distribution.
return	Stop executing a function and return to caller.
sort	Sort data in ascending or descending order.
sortrows	Sort rows of a matrix in ascending or descending order based on a specified column.
warning	Displays a warning message and continues function execution. This function is used if the argument errors are not fatal, and execution can continue.

6.9   Exercises

6.1 Write a function `f_to_c` that accepts a temperature in degrees Fahrenheit and returns the temperature in degrees Celsius. The equation is

$$T_C = \frac{5}{9}(T_F - 32.0) \tag{6.10}$$

6.2 Write a function `c_to_f` that accepts a temperature in degrees Celsius and returns the temperature in degrees Fahrenheit. The equation is

$$T_F = \frac{9}{5}(T_C + 32) \tag{6.11}$$

Demonstrate that this function is the inverse of the one in Exercise 6.1. In other words, demonstrate that the expression `c_to_f(f_to_c(temp))` is just the original temperature `temp`.

6.3 The area of a triangle whose three vertices are points (x_1, y_1), (x_2, y_2), and (x_3, y_3) (see Figure 6.6) can be found from the equation

$$A = \frac{1}{2}\begin{vmatrix} x_1 & x_2 & x_3 \\ y_1 & y_2 & y_3 \\ 1 & 1 & 1 \end{vmatrix} \tag{6.12}$$

where $|\ |$ is the determinant operation. The area returned will be positive if the points are taken in counterclockwise order and negative if the points

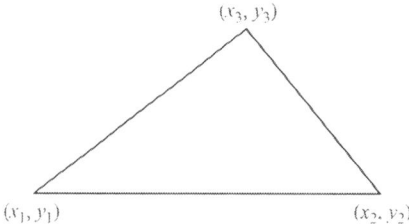

Figure 6.6   A triangle bounded by points (x_1, y_1), (x_2, y_2), and (x_3, y_3).

are taken in clockwise order. This determinant can be evaluated by hand to produce the following equation

$$A = \frac{1}{2}\left[x_1(y_2 - y_3) - x_2(y_1 - y_3) + x_3(y_1 - y_2)\right] \qquad (6.13)$$

Write a function `area2d` that calculates the area of a triangle, given the three bounding points (x_1, y_1), (x_2, y_2), and (x_3, y_3) using Equation (6.13). Then test your function by calculating the area of a triangle bounded by the points (0,0), (10,0), and (15,5).

6.4   The area inside any polygon can be broken down into a series of triangles, as shown in Figure 6.7. If there are n sides to the polygon, it can be divided into $n - 2$ triangles. Create a function that calculates the perimeter of the polygon and the area enclosed by the polygon. Use the function `area2d` from Exercise 6.3 to calculate the area of the polygon. Write a program that accepts an ordered list of points bounding a polygon and calls your function to return the perimeter and area of the polygon. Then test your function by calculating the perimeter and area of a polygon bounded by the points (0,0), (10,0), (8,8), (2,10), and (−4,5).

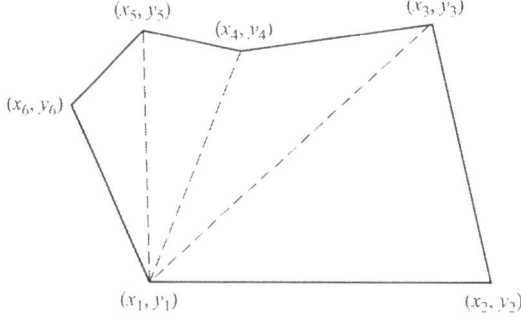

Figure 6.7   An arbitrary polygon can be divided into a series of triangles. If there are n sides to the polygon, it can be divided into $n - 2$ triangles.

6.5   **Inductance of a Transmission Line** The inductance per meter of a single-phase, two-wire transmission line is given by the equation

$$L = + \frac{\mu_0}{\pi} \left[\frac{1}{4} + \ln \left(\frac{D}{r} \right) \right] \tag{6.14}$$

where L is the inductance in henrys per meter of line, $\mu_0 = 4\pi \times 10^{-7}$ H/m is the permeability of free space, D is the distance between the two conductors, and r is the radius of each conductor. Write a function that calculates the total inductance of a transmission line as a function of its length in kilometers, the spacing between the two conductors, and the diameter of each conductor. Use this function to calculate the inductance of a 100 km transmission line with conductors of radius $r = 2$ cm and distance $D = 1.5$ m.

6.6   Based on Equation (6.14), would the inductance of a transmission line increase or decrease if the diameter of its conductors increase? How much would the inductance of the line change if the diameter of each conductor is doubled?

6.7   **Capacitance of a Transmission Line** The capacitance per meter of a single-phase, two-wire transmission line is given by the equation

$$C = \frac{\pi\varepsilon}{\ln \left(\dfrac{D - r}{r} \right)} \tag{6.15}$$

where C is the capacitance in farads per meter of line, $\varepsilon_0 = 4\pi \times 10^{-7}$ F/m is the permittivity of free space, D is the distance between the two conductors, and r is the radius of each conductor. Write a function that calculates the total capacitance of a transmission line as a function of its length in kilometers, the spacing between the two conductors, and the diameter of each conductor. Use this function to calculate the capacitance of a 100 km transmission line with conductors of radius $r = 2$ cm and distance $D = 1.5$ m.

6.8   What is the difference between a script file and a function?

6.9   When a function is called, how is data passed from the caller to the function, and how are the results of the function returned to the caller?

6.10   What are the advantages and disadvantages of the pass-by-value scheme used in MATLAB?

6.11   Modify the selection sort function developed in this chapter so that it accepts a second optional argument, which may be either 'up' or 'down'. If the argument is 'up', sort the data in ascending order. If the argument is 'down', sort the data in descending order. If the argument is missing, the default case is to sort the data in ascending order. (Be sure to handle the case of invalid arguments, and be sure to include the proper help information in your function.)

6.12 The inputs to MATLAB functions sin, cos, and tan are in radians, and the output of functions asin, acos, atan, and atan2 are in radians. Create a new set of functions sind, cosd, and so forth, whose inputs and outputs are in degrees. Be sure to test your functions.

6.13 **Road Traffic Density** The function random0 produces a number with a *uniform* probability distribution in the range [0.0, 1.0). This function is suitable for simulating random events if each outcome has an equal probability of occurring. However, in many events, the probability of occurrence is *not* equal for every event, and a uniform probability distribution is not suitable for simulating such events.

For example, when traffic engineers studied the number of cars passing a given location in a time interval of length t, they discovered that the probability of k cars passing during the interval is given by the equation

$$P(k,t) = e^{-\lambda t}\frac{(\lambda t)^k}{k!}\text{for } t \geq 0, \lambda > 0, \text{ and } k = 0, 1, 2, \ldots \tag{6.16}$$

This probability distribution is known as the *Poisson distribution*; it occurs in many applications in science and engineering. For example, the number of calls k to a telephone switchboard in time interval t, the number of bacteria k in a specified volume t of liquid, and the number of failures k of a complicated system in time interval t all have Poisson distributions.

Write a function to evaluate the Poisson distribution for any k, t, and λ. Test your function by calculating the probability of 0, 1, 2, ..., 5 cars passing a particular point on a highway in 1 minute, given that λ is 1.6 per minute for that highway. Plot the Poisson distribution for $t = 1$ and $\lambda = 1.6$.

6.14 Write three MATLAB functions to calculate the hyperbolic sine, cosine, and tangent functions:

$$\sinh(x) = \frac{e^x - e^{-x}}{2} \quad \cosh(x) = \frac{e^x + e^{-x}}{2} \quad \tanh(x) = \frac{e^x - e^{-x}}{e^x + e^{-x}}$$

Use your functions to plot the shapes of the hyperbolic sine, cosine, and tangent functions.

6.15 Write a MATLAB function to perform a running average filter on a data set, as described in Exercise 6.13. Test your function using the same data set used in Exercise 6.13.

6.16 Write a MATLAB function to perform a median filter on a data set, as described in Exercise 6.14. Test your function using the same data set used in Exercise 6.14.

6.17 What happens to the inductance and capacitance of a transmission line as the distance between the two conductors increases?

6.18 Use function random0 to generate a set of 100,000 random values. Sort this data set twice: once with the sort function of Example 6.2 and once with MATLAB's built-in sort function. Use tic and toc to time the two sort functions. How do the sort times compare? (*Note:* Be sure to copy the original array and present the same data to each sort function. To have a fair comparison, all functions must get the same input data set.)

6.19 Try the sort functions in Exercise 6.18 for array sizes of 10,000, 100,000, 1,000,000, and 10,000,000. How does the sorting time increase with data set size for the sort function of Example 6.2? How does the sorting time increase with data set size for the built-in `sort` function? Which function is more efficient?

6.20 Modify the function `random0` so that it can accept 0, 1, or 2 calling arguments. If it has no calling arguments, it should return a single random value. If it has one or two calling arguments, it should behave as it currently does.

6.21 As the function `random0` is currently written, it will fail if the function seed is not called first. Modify the function `random0` so that it will function properly with some default seed even if the function `seed` is never called.

6.22 **Dice Simulation** It is often useful to be able to simulate the throw of a fair die. Write a MATLAB function `dice` that simulates the throw of a fair die by returning some random integer between 1 and 6 every time it is called. (*Hint:* Call `random0` to generate a random number. Divide the possible values out of `random0` into six equal intervals, and return the number of the interval that a given random value falls into.)

6.23 **Linear Least-Squares Fit** Develop a function that will calculate slope *m* and intercept *b* of the least-squares line that best fits an input data set. The input data points *(x,y)* will be passed to the function in two input arrays, x and y. (The equations describing the slope and intercept of the least-squares line were given in Example 5.6 in the previous chapter.) Test your function using a test program and the following 20-point input data set:

Sample Data to Test Least-Squares Fit Routine

No.	x	y	No.	x	y
1	−4.91	−8.18	11	−0.94	0.21
2	−3.84	−7.49	12	0.59	1.73
3	−2.41	−7.11	13	0.69	3.96
4	−2.62	−6.15	14	3.04	4.26
5	−3.78	−6.62	15	1.01	6.75
6	−0.52	−3.30	16	3.60	6.67
7	−1.83	−2.05	17	4.53	7.70
8	−2.01	−2.83	18	6.13	7.31
9	0.28	−1.16	19	4.43	9.05
10	1.08	0.52	20	4.12	10.95

Also, compare the results of your function with the results from the built-in function `polyfit`.

6.24 Create a plot of the residuals between the raw data in the previous exercise and the fitted line. Does a straight line look like a good fit to this data set? Also, calculate the residual between the original data and the fitted line.

6.25 Use the function random0 to generate a set of three arrays of random numbers. The three arrays should be 100, 1000, and 2000 elements long. Then use functions tic and toc to determine the time it takes function ssort to sort each array. How does the elapsed time to sort increase as a function of the number of elements being sorted? (*Hint:* On a fast computer, you will need to sort each array many times and calculate the average sorting time in order to overcome the quantization error of the system clock.)

6.26 **Sort with Carry** It is often useful to sort an array arr1 into ascending order, while simultaneously carrying along a second array arr2. In such a sort, each time an element of array arr1 is exchanged with another element of arr1, the corresponding elements of array arr2 are also swapped. When the sort is over, the elements of array arr1 are in ascending order, and the elements of array arr2 that were associated with particular elements of array arr1 are still associated with them. For example, suppose we have the following two arrays:

Element	arr1	arr2
1.	6.	1.
2.	1.	0.
3.	2.	10.

After sorting array arr1 while carrying along array arr2, the contents of the two arrays will be

Element	arr1	arr2
1.	1.	0.
2.	2.	10.
3.	6.	1.

Write a function to sort one real array into ascending order while carrying along a second one. Test the function with the following two nine-element arrays:

```
a = [ 1,  11,  -6,  17,  -23,  0,  5,  1,  -1];
b = [ 31,  101,  36,  -17,  0,  10,  -8,  -1,  -1];
```

6.27 The sort-with-carry function of Exercise 6.26 is a special case of the built-in function sortrows, where the number of columns is two. Create a single matrix c with two columns consisting of the data in vectors a and b in the previous exercise, and sort the data using sortrows. How does the sorted data compare to the results of Exercise 6.26?

6.28   Correlation Coefficient of Least-Squares Fit Develop a function that
will calculate both the slope m and intercept b of the least-squares line that
best fits an input data set and the correlation coefficient of the fit. The
input data points (x,y) will be passed to the function in two input arrays, x
and y. The equations describing the slope and intercept of the least-
squares line are given in Example 5.1, and the equation for the correlation
coefficient is

$$r = \frac{n(\Sigma xy) - (\Sigma x)(\Sigma y)}{\sqrt{[(n\Sigma x^2) - (\Sigma x)^2][(n\Sigma y^2) - (\Sigma y)^2]}} \tag{6.16}$$

where

Σx is the sum of the x values
Σy is the sum of the y values
Σx^2 is the sum of the squares of the x values
Σy^2 is the sum of the squares of the y values

Σxy is the sum of the products of the corresponding x and y values
n is the number of points included in the fit

Test your function using a test driver program and the 20-point input data
set given in Exercise 6.23.

6.29   Figure 6.8 shows two ships steaming on the ocean. Ship 1 is at position
(x_1, y_1) and steaming on heading θ_1. Ship 2 is at position (x_2, y_2) and
steaming on heading θ_2. Suppose that ship 1 makes radar contact with
an object at range r_1 and bearing ϕ_1. Write a MATLAB function that will
calculate the range r_2 and bearing ϕ_2 at which ship 2 should see the
object.

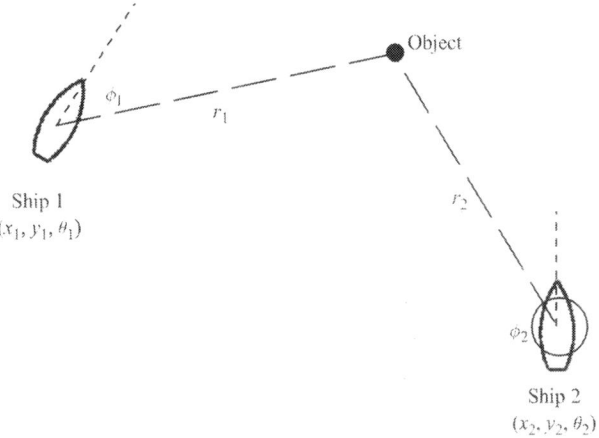

Figure 6.8   Two ships at positions (x_1, y_1) and (x_2, y_2), respectively. Ship 1 is traveling at heading θ_1,
and ship 2 is traveling at heading θ_2.

6.30 **Gaussian (Normal) Distribution** The function random0 returns a uniformly distributed random variable in the range [0,1), which means that there is an equal probability that any given number in the range will occur on a given call to the function. Another type of random distribution is the Gaussian distribution, in which the random value takes on the classic bell-shaped curve shown in Figure 6.9. A Gaussian distribution with an average of 0.0 and a standard deviation of 1.0 is called a *standardized normal distribution*, and the probability that any given value will occur in the standardized normal distribution is given by the equation

$$p(x) = \frac{1}{\sqrt{2\pi}} e^{-x^2/2} \tag{6.17}$$

It is possible to generate a random variable with a standardized normal distribution starting from a random variable with a uniform distribution in the range [−1,1) as follows

1. Select two uniform random variables x_1 and x_2 from the range [−1,1) such that $x_1^2 + x_2^2 < 1$. To do this, generate two uniform random variables in the range [−1,1), and see if the sum of their squares happens to be less than 1. If so, use them. If not, try again.

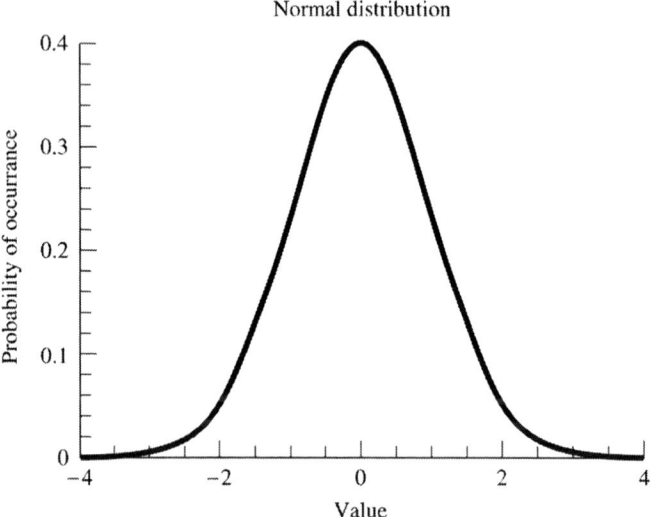

Figure 6.9 A normal probability distribution.

2. Then each of the values y_1 and y_2 in the equations below will be a normally distributed random variable.

$$y_1 = \sqrt{\frac{-2 \ln r}{r}} \, x_1 \tag{6.18}$$

$$y_2 = \sqrt{\frac{-2 \ln r}{r}} \, x_2 \tag{6.19}$$

where

$$p(x) = \frac{1}{\sqrt{2\pi}} e^{-x^2/2} \tag{6.20}$$

Write a function that returns a normally distributed random value each time it is called. Test your function by getting 1000 random values, calculating the standard deviation and plotting a histogram of the distribution. How close to 1.0 was the standard deviation?

6.31 Compare the performance of `sortrows` with the sort-with-carry function created in Exercise 6.26. To do this, create two copies of a 10,000 × 2 element array containing random values, and sort column 1 of each array while carrying along column 2 using both functions. Determine the execution times of each sort function using `tic` and `toc`. How does the speed of your function compare with the speed of the standard function `sortrows`?

6.32 Gravitational Force The gravitational force F between two bodies of masses m_1 and m_2 is given by the equation

$$F = \frac{Gm_1m_2}{r^2} \tag{6.21}$$

where G is the gravitation constant (6.672×10^{-11} N m^2 / kg^2), m_1 and m_2 are the masses of the bodies in kilograms, and r is the distance between the two bodies. Write a function to calculate the gravitational force between two bodies given their masses and the distance between them. Test your function by determining the force on an 800 kg satellite in orbit 38,000 km above the Earth. (The mass of the Earth is 6.98×10^{24} kg.)

6.33 Rayleigh Distribution The Rayleigh distribution is another random number distribution that appears in many practical problems. A Rayleigh-distributed random value can be created by taking the square root of the sum of the squares of two normally distributed random values. In other words, to generate a Rayleigh-distributed random value r, get two normally distributed random values (n_1 and n_2), and perform the following calculation:

$$r = \sqrt{n_1^2 + n_2^2} \tag{6.22}$$

(a) Create a function rayleigh(n,m) that returns an n × m array of Rayleigh-distributed random numbers. If only one argument is supplied [rayleigh(n)], the function should return an n × n array of Rayleigh-distributed random numbers. Be sure to design your function with input argument checking and with proper documentation for the MATLAB help system.

(b) Test your function by creating an array of 20,000 Rayleigh-distributed random values and plotting a histogram of the distribution. What does the distribution look like?

(c) Determine the mean and standard deviation of the Rayleigh distribution.

CHAPTER 7

Advanced Features of User-Defined Functions

In Chapter 6, we introduced the basic features of user-defined functions. This chapter continues the discussion with a selection of more advanced features.

7.1 Function Functions

"**Function function**" is the rather awkward name that MATLAB gives to a function whose input arguments include the names of other functions. The functions that are passed to the "function function" are normally used during that function's execution.

For example, MATLAB contains a function function called `fzero`. This function locates a zero of the function that is passed to it. For example, the statement `fzero('cos',[0 pi])` locates a zero of the function `cos` between 0 and π, and `fzero('exp(x)-2',[0 1])` locates a zero of the function `'exp(x)-2'` between 0 and 1. When these statements are executed, the result is:

```
» fzero('cos',[0 pi])
ans =
    1.5708
» fzero('exp(x)-2',[0 1])
ans =
    0.6931
```

The keys to the operation of function functions are two special MATLAB functions: `eval` and `feval`. Function `eval` *evaluates a character string* as though it had been typed in the Command Window, whereas function `feval` *evaluates a named function* at a specific input value.

The function `eval` evaluates a character string as though it has been typed in the Command Window. This function gives MATLAB functions a chance to construct executable statements during execution. The form of the `eval` function is

```
eval(string)
```

For example, the statement x = `eval('sin(pi/4)')` produces the result

```
» x = eval('sin(pi/4)')
x =
    0.7071
```

An example in which a character string is constructed and evaluated using the `eval` function is shown here.

```
x = 1;
str = ['exp(' num2str(x) ') -1'];
res = eval(str);
```

In this case, `str` contains the character string `'exp(1)  -1'`, which `eval` evaluates to get the result 1.7183.

Function `feval` evaluates a *named function* defined by an M-file at a specified input value. The general form of the `feval` function is

```
feval(fun,value)
```

For example, the statement x = `feval('sin',pi/4)` produces the result

```
» x = feval('sin',pi/4)
x =
    0.7071
```

Some of the more common MATLAB function functions are listed in Table 7-1. Type `help fun_name` to learn how to use each of these functions.

Table 7-1   Common MATLAB Function Functions

Function Name	Description
fminbnd	Minimizes a function of one variable.
fzero	Finds a zero of a function of one variable.
quad	Numerically integrates a function.
ezplot	Easy to use function plotter.
fplot	Plots a function by name.

▶

Example 7.1—Creating a Function Function

Create a function function that will plot any MATLAB function of a single variable between specified starting and ending values.

SOLUTION   This function has two input arguments: the first one containing the name of the function to plot and the second one containing a two-element vector with the range of values to plot.

1. **State the problem.**
   Create a function to plot any MATLAB function of a single variable between two user-specified limits.

2. **Define the inputs and outputs.**
   There are two inputs required by this function:

   ■ A character string containing the name of a function.
   ■ A two-element vector containing the first and last values to plot.

   The output from this function is a plot of the function specified in the first input argument.

3. **Design the algorithm.**
   This function can be broken down into four major steps:

   ```
   Check for a legal number of arguments
   Check that the second argument has two elements
   Calculate the value of the function between the
        start and stop points
   Plot and label the function
   ```

   The detailed pseudocode for the evaluation and plotting steps is

   ```
   n_steps ← 100
   step_size ← (xlim(2) - xlim(1)) / n_steps
   x ← xlim(1):step_size:xlim(2)
   y ← feval(fun,x)
   plot(x,y)
   title(['\bfPlot of function ' fun '(x)'])
   xlabel('\bfx')
   ylabel(['\bf' fun '(x)'])
   ```

4. **Turn the algorithm into MATLAB statements.**
   The final MATLAB function is shown here.

```
function quickplot(fun,xlim)
%QUICKPLOT Generate quick plot of a function
% Function QUICKPLOT generates a quick plot
% of a function contained in a external M-file,
% between user-specified x limits.
```

```
% Define variables:
%    fun        -- Name of function to plot in a char string
%    msg        -- Error message
%    n_steps    -- Number of steps to plot
%    step_size  -- Step size
%    x          -- X-values to plot
%    y          -- Y-values to plot
%    xlim       -- Plot x limits
%
% Record of revisions:
%     Date           Engineer            Description of change
%     ====           ========            =====================
%    02/10/10     S. J. Chapman          Original code

% Check for a legal number of input arguments.
msg = nargchk(2,2,nargin);
error(msg);

% Check the second argument to see if it has two
% elements. Note that this double test allows the
% argument to be either a row or a column vector.
if ( size(xlim,1) == 1 && size(xlim,2) == 2 ) | ...
   ( size(xlim,1) == 2 && size(xlim,2) == 1 )

   % Ok--continue processing.
   n_steps = 100;
   step_size = (xlim(2) - xlim(1)) / n_steps;
   x = xlim(1):step_size:xlim(2);
   y = feval(fun,x);
   plot(x,y);
   title(['\bfPlot of function ' fun '(x)']);
   xlabel('\bfx');
   ylabel(['\bf' fun '(x)']);

else
   % Else wrong number of elements in xlim.
   error('Incorrect number of elements in xlim.');
end
```

5. **Test the program.**
   To test this function, we must call it with correct and incorrect input arguments, verifying that it handles both correct inputs and errors properly. The results are shown here.

   ```
   » quickplot('sin')
   ??? Error using ==> quickplot
   Not enough input arguments.
   ```

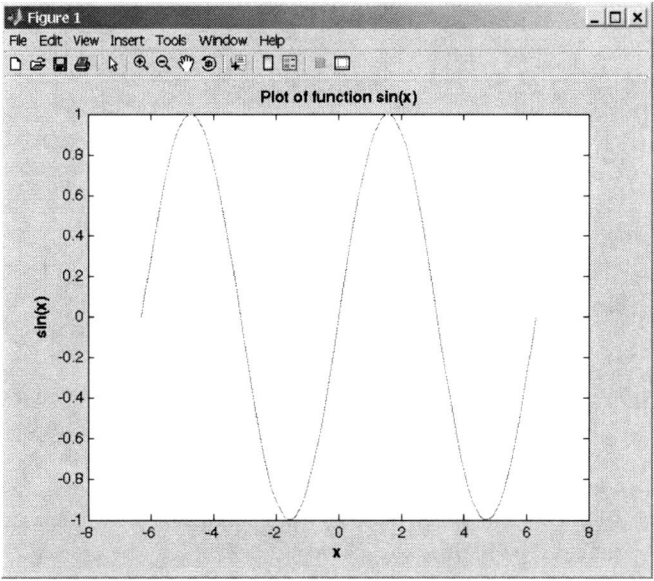

Figure 7.1   Plot of sin x versus x generated by function `quickplot`.

```
» quickplot('sin',[-2*pi 2*pi],3)
??? Error using ==> quickplot
Too many input arguments.

» quickplot('sin',-2*pi)
??? Error using ==> quickplot
Incorrect number of elements in xlim.

» quickplot('sin',[-2*pi 2*pi])
```

The last call was correct, and it produced the plot shown in Figure 7.1. ◀

7.2   Subfunctions and Private Functions

MATLAB includes several special types of functions that behave differently from the ordinary functions we have used so far. Ordinary functions can be called by any other function, as long as they are in the same directory or in any directory on the MATLAB path.

The **scope** of a function is defined as the locations within MATLAB from which the function can be accessed. The scope of an ordinary MATLAB function is the current working directory. If the function lies in a directory on the MATLAB path, then the scope extends to all MATLAB functions in a program, because they all check the path when trying to find a function with a given name.

In contrast, the scope of the other function types that we will discuss in the rest of this chapter is more limited in one way or another.

7.2.1 Subfunctions

It is possible to place more than one function in a single file. If more than one function is present in a file, the top function is a normal or **primary function**, while the ones below it are **subfunctions**. The primary function should have the same name as the file it appears in. Subfunctions look just like ordinary functions, but they are accessible only to the other functions within the same file. In other words, the scope of a subfunction is the other functions within the same file (see Figure 7.2).

Subfunctions are often used to implement "utility" calculations for a main function. For example, the file mystats.m shown at the end of this paragraph contains a primary function mystats and two subfunctions mean and median. Function mystats is a normal MATLAB function, so it can be called by any other MATLAB function in the same directory. If this file is in a directory included in the MATLAB search path, it can be called by any other MATLAB function, even if the other function is not in the same directory. By contrast, the scope of functions mean and median is restricted to other functions within the same file. Function mystats can call them, and they can call each other, but a function outside of the file cannot. They are "utility" functions that perform a part the job of the main function mystats.

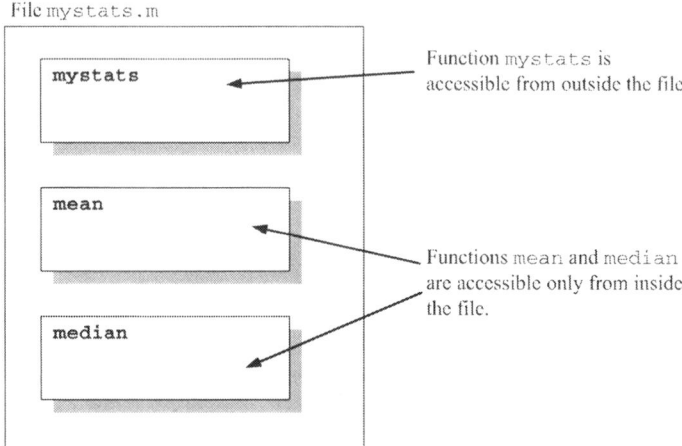

Figure 7.2 The first function in a file is called the primary function. It should have the same name as the file it appears in, and it is accessible from outside the file. The remaining functions in the file are subfunctions; they are accessible only from within the file.

```
function [avg, med] = mystats(u)
%MYSTATS Find mean and median with internal functions.
% Function MYSTATS calculates the average and median
% of a data set using subfunctions.

n = length(u);
avg = mean(u,n);
med = median(u,n);

function a = mean(v,n)
% Subfunction to calculate average.
a = sum(v)/n;

function m = median(v,n)
% Subfunction to calculate median.
w = sort(v);
if rem(n,2) == 1
    m = w((n+1)/2);
else
    m = (w(n/2)+w(n/2+1))/2;
end
```

7.2.2 Private Functions

Private functions are functions that reside in subdirectories with the special name `private`. They are visible only to other functions in the `private` directory or to functions in the parent directory. In other words, the scope of these functions is restricted to the private directory and to the parent directory that contains it.

For example, assume the directory `testing` is on the MATLAB search path. A subdirectory of `testing` called `private` can contain functions that only the functions in `testing` can call. Because private functions are invisible outside of the parent directory, they can use the same names as functions in other directories. This is useful if you want to create your own version of a particular function while retaining the original in another directory. Because MATLAB looks for private functions before standard M-file functions, it will find a private function named `test.m` before a nonprivate function named `test.m`.

You can create your own private directories by simply creating a subdirectory called `private` under the directory containing your functions. Do not place these private directories on your search path.

When a function is called from within an M-file, MATLAB first checks the file to see if the function is a subfunction defined in the same file. If not, it checks for a private function with that name. If it is not a private function, MATLAB checks the current directory for the function name. If it is not in the current directory, MATLAB checks the standard search path for the function.

If you have special-purpose MATLAB functions that should be used only by other functions and never be called directly by the user, consider hiding them as subfunctions or private functions. Hiding the functions will prevent their accidental use and will also prevent conflicts with other public functions of the same name.

7.2.3 Order of Function Evaluation

In a large program, there could possibly be multiple functions (subfunctions, private functions, nested functions, and public functions) with the same name. When a function with a given name is called, how do we know which copy of the function will be executed?

The answer this question is that MATLAB locates functions in a specific order as follows:

1. MATLAB checks to see if there is a subfunction with the specified name. If so, it is executed.
2. MATLAB checks for a private function with the specified name. If so, it is executed.
3. MATLAB checks for a function with the specified name in the current directory. If so, it is executed.
4. MATLAB checks for a function with the specified name on the MATLAB path. MATLAB will stop searching and execute the first function with the right name found on the path.

7.3 Function Handles

A **function handle** is a MATLAB data type that holds information to be used in referencing a function. When you create a function handle, MATLAB captures all of the information about the function that it needs to execute it later on. Once the handle is created, it can be used to execute the function at any time.

As is shown in Chapter 11, function handles are key to the operation of some important tools, such as differential equation solvers.

7.3.1 Creating and Using Function Handles

A function handle can be created either of two possible ways: the @ operator or the str2func function. To create a function handle with the @ operator, just place it in front of the function name. To create a function handle with the str2func function, call the function with the function name in a string. For example, suppose that function my_func is defined as follows:

```
function res = my_func(x)
res = x.^2 - 2*x + 1;
```

Then either of the following lines will create a function handle for function
my_func:

```
hndl = @my_func
hndl = str2func('my_func');
```

Once a function handle has been created, the function can be executed by
naming the function handle followed by any calling parameters. The result will be
exactly the same as if the function itself were named.

```
» hndl = @my_func
hndl =
    @my_func
» hndl(4)
ans =
      9
» my_func(4)
ans =
      9
```

If a function has no calling parameters, the function handle must be followed by
empty parentheses when it is used to call the function:

```
» h1 = @randn;
» h1()
ans =
    -0.4326
```

After a function handle is created, it appears in the current workspace with the
data type "function handle":

```
» whos
  Name    Size    Bytes Class        Attributes
  ans     1x1         8 double
  h1      1x1        16 function_handle
  hndl    1x1        16 function_handle
```

A function handle can also be executed using the feval function. This
provides a convenient way to execute function handles within a MATLAB
program.

```
» feval(hndl,4)
ans =
      9
```

It is possible to recover the function name from a function handle using the
func2str function.

```
» func2str(hndl)
ans =
my_func
```

This feature is very useful when we want to create descriptive messages, error messages, or labels inside a function that accepts and evaluates function handles. For example, the function below accepts a function handle in the first argument and plots the function at the points specified in the second argument. It also prints out a title containing the name of the function being plotted.

```
function plotfunc(fun,points)
%PLOTFUNC Plots a function between the specified points.
% Function PLOTFUNC accepts a function handle, and
% plots the function at the points specified.

% Define variables:
%    fun       -- Function handle
%    msg       -- Error message
%
% Record of revisions:
%     Date           Engineer           Description of change
%     ====           ========           =====================
%    03/05/10     S. J. Chapman         Original code

% Check for a legal number of input arguments.
msg = nargchk(2,2,nargin);
error(msg);

% Get function name
fname = func2str(fun);

% Plot the data and label the plot
plot(points,fun(points));
title(['\bfPlot of ' fname '(x) vs x']);
xlabel('\bfx');
ylabel(['\bf' fname '(x)']);
grid on;
```

For example, this function can be used to plot the function $\sin x$ from -2π to 2π with the following statement:

```
plotfunc(@sin,[-2*pi:pi/10:2*pi])
```

The resulting function is shown in Figure 7.3.

Note that the function functions such as `feval` and `fzero` accept function handles as well as function names in their calling arguments. For example, the following two statements are equivalent and produce the same answer:

```
» res = feval('sin',3*pi/2)
res =
    -1
» res = feval(@sin,3*pi/2)
res =
    -1
```

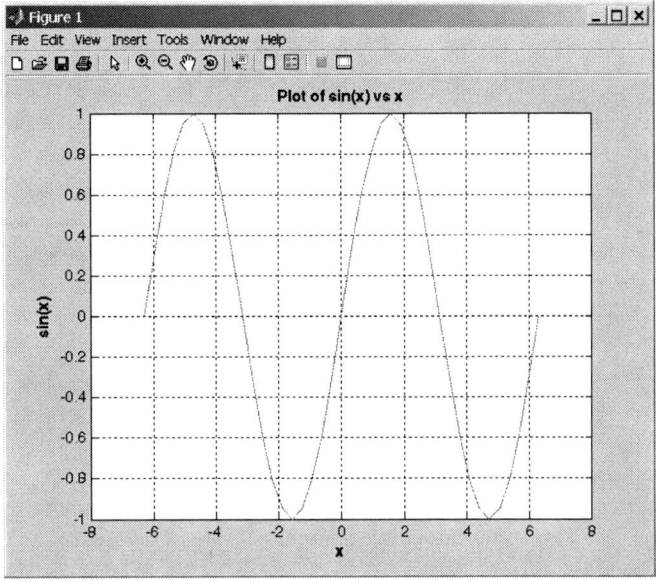

Figure 7.3   Plot of function $\sin x$ from -2π to 2π, created using function `plotfunc`.

Table 7-2   MATLAB Functions that Manipulate Function Handles

Function	Description
@	Creates a function handle.
feval	Evaluates a function using a function handle.
func2str	Recovers the function name associated with a given function handle.
functions	Recovers miscellaneous information from a function handle. The data is returned in a structure.
str2func	Creates a function handle from a specified string.

Some common MATLAB functions used with function handles are summarized in Table 7-2.

7.4   Anonymous Functions

An anonymous function is a function "without a name."[1] It is a function that is declared in a single MATLAB statement that returns a function handle, which can then be used to execute the function. The form of an anonymous function is

```
fhandle = @ (arglist) expr
```

---

[1]This is the meaning of the word "anonymous"!

where `fhandle` is a function handle used to reference the function, `arglist` is a list of calling variables, and `expr` is an expression involving the argument list that evaluates the function. For example, we can create a function to evaluate the expression $f(x) = x^2 - 2x - 2$ as follows:

```
myfunc = @ (x) x.^2 - 2*x - 2
```

The function then can be invoked using the function handle. For example, we can evaluate $f(2)$ as follows:

```
» myfunc(2)
ans =
    -2
```

Anonymous functions provide a quick way to write short functions that then can be used in function functions. For example, we can find a root of the function $f(x) = x^2 - 2x - 2$ by passing the anonymous function to `fzero` as follows:

```
» root = fzero(myfunc,[0 4])
root =
    2.7321
```

7.5 Recursive Functions

A function is said to be **recursive** if it the function calls itself. The factorial function is a good example of a recursive function. In Chapter 5, we defined the factorial function as

$$n! = \begin{cases} 1 & n = 0 \\ n \times (n-1) \times (n-2) \times \ldots \times 2 \times 1 & n > 0 \end{cases} \qquad (7.1)$$

This definition can also be written as

$$n! = \begin{cases} 1 & n = 0 \\ (n-1)! & n > 0 \end{cases} \qquad (7.2)$$

where the value of the factorial function $n!$ is defined using the factorial function itself. MATLAB functions are designed to be recursive, so Equation (7.2) can be implemented directly in MATLAB.

▶

Example 7.2—The Factorial Function

To illustrate the operation of a recursive function, we will implement the factorial function using the definition in Equation (7.2). The MATLAB code to calculate n factorial for positive value of n would be

```
function result = fact(n)
%FACT Calculate the factorial function
% Function FACT calcualates the factorial function
% by recursively calling itself.
```

```
% Define variables:
%   n              -- Non-negative integer input
%
% Record of revisions:
%     Date            Engineer          Description of change
%     ====            ========          =====================
%     07/07/10      S. J. Chapman       Original code

% Check for a legal number of input arguments.
msg = nargchk(1,1,nargin);
error(msg);

% Calculate function
if n == 0
   result = 1;
else
   result = n * fact(n-1);
end
```

When this program is executed, the results are as expected.

```
» fact(5)
ans =
    120
» fact(0)
ans =
      1
```

Complex Numbers and Three-Dimensional Plots

In this chapter, we will learn how to work with complex numbers and about the types of three-dimensional plots available in MATLAB.

8.1 Complex Data

Complex numbers are numbers with both a real and an imaginary component. Complex numbers occur in many problems in science and engineering. For example, complex numbers are used in electrical engineering to represent alternating current voltages, currents, and impedances. The differential equations that describe the behavior of most electrical and mechanical systems also give rise to complex numbers. Because they are so ubiquitous, it is impossible to work as an engineer without a good understanding of the use and manipulation of complex numbers.

A complex number has the general form

$$c = a + bi \tag{8.1}$$

where c is a complex number, a and b are both real numbers, and i is $\sqrt{-1}$. The number a is called the *real part* and b is called the *imaginary part* of the complex number c. Since a complex number has two components, it can be plotted as a point on a plane (see Figure 8.1). The horizontal axis of the plane is the real axis, and the vertical axis of the plane is the imaginary axis, so that any complex number $a + bi$ can be represented as a single point a units along the real axis and b units along the

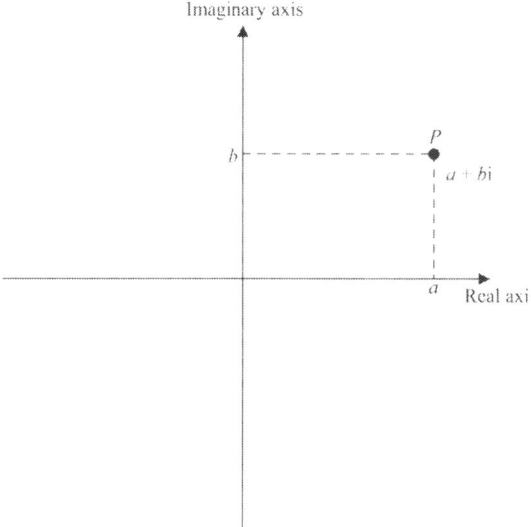

Figure 8.1 Representing a complex number in rectangular coordinates.

imaginary axis. A complex number represented this way is said to be in *rectangular coordinates*, since the real and imaginary axes define the sides of a rectangle.

A complex number also can be represented as a vector of length z and angle θ pointing from the origin of the plane to the point P (see Figure 8.2). A complex number represented this way is said to be in *polar coordinates*.

$$c = a + bi = z\angle\theta \tag{8.2}$$

The relationships among the rectangular and polar coordinate terms a, b, z, and θ are

$$a = z\cos\theta \tag{8.3}$$
$$b = z\sin\theta \tag{8.4}$$
$$z = \sqrt{a^2 + b^2} \tag{8.5}$$
$$\theta = \tan^{-1}\frac{b}{a} \tag{8.6}$$

MATLAB uses rectangular coordinates to represent complex numbers. Each complex number consists of a pair of real numbers (a,b). The first number (a) is the real part of the complex number, and the second number (b) is the imaginary part of the complex number.

If complex numbers c_1 and c_2 are defined as $c_1 = a_1 + b_1 i$ and $c_2 = a_2 + b_2 i$, then the addition, subtraction, multiplication, and division of c_1 and c_2 are defined as follows.

$$c_1 + c_2 = (a_1 + a_2) + (b_1 + b_2)i \tag{8.7}$$
$$c_1 - c_2 = (a_1 - a_2) + (b_1 - b_2)i \tag{8.8}$$

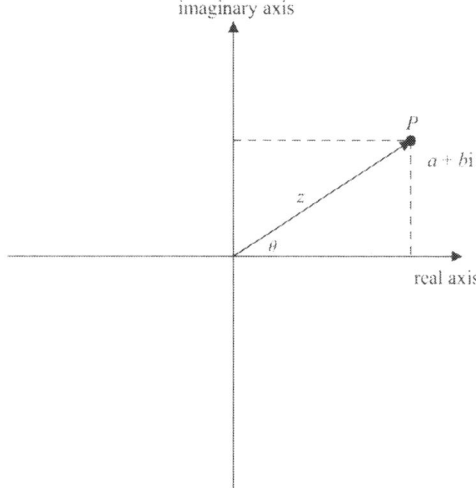

Figure 8.2   Representing a complex number in polar coordinates.

$$c_1 \times c_2 = (a_1a_2 - b_1b_2) + (a_1b_2 - b_1a_2)i \qquad (8.9)$$

$$\frac{c_1}{c_2} = \frac{a_1a_2 + b_1b_2}{a_2^2 + b_2^2} + \frac{b_1a_2 - a_1b_2}{a_2^2 + b_2^2}i \qquad (8.10)$$

When two complex numbers appear in a binary operation, MATLAB performs the required additions, subtractions, multiplications, or divisions between the two complex numbers, using versions of the these formulas.

8.1.1   Complex Variables

A complex variable is created automatically when a complex value is assigned to a variable name. This easiest way to create a complex value is to use the intrinsic values i or j, both of which are predefined to be $\sqrt{-1}$. For example, the following statement stores the complex value $4 + i3$ into variable c1.

```
» c1 = 4 + i*3
c1 =
    4.0000 + 3.0000i
```

Alternatively, the imaginary part can be specified by simply appending an i or j to the end of a number:

```
» c1 = 4 + 3i
c1 =
    4.0000 + 3.0000i
```

The function isreal can be used to determine whether a given array is real or complex. If any element of an array has an imaginary component, then the array is complex and isreal(array) returns a 0.

8.1.2 Using Complex Numbers with Relational Operators

It is possible to compare two complex numbers with the $==$ relational operator to see if they are equal to each other, and to compare them with the $\sim=$ operator to see if they are not equal to each other. Both of these operators produce the expected results. For example, if $c_1 = 4 + i3$ and $c_2 = 4 - i3$, then the relational operation $c_1 == c_2$ produces a 0 and the relational operation $c_1 \sim= c_2$ produces a 1.

However, *comparisons with the* $>$, $<$, $>=$, *or* $<=$ *operators do not produce the expected results.* When complex numbers are compared with these relational operators, only the *real parts* of the numbers are compared. For example, if $c_1 = 4 + i3$ and $c_2 = 3 + i8$, then the relational operation $c_1 > c_2$ produces a true (1) even though the magnitude of c_1 is really smaller than the magnitude of c_2.

If you ever need to compare two complex numbers with these operators, you will probably be more interested in the total magnitude of the number than in the magnitude of only its real part. The magnitude of a complex number can be calculated with the abs intrinsic function (see following text), or directly from Equation (8.5).

$$|c| = \sqrt{a^2 + b^2} \tag{8.5}$$

If we compare the *magnitudes* of c_1 and c_2 presented previously, the results are more reasonable: abs (c_1) > abs (c_2) produces a 0, since the magnitude of c_2 is greater than the magnitude of c_1.

☀ Programming Pitfalls

Be careful when using the relational operators with complex numbers. The relational operators $>$, $>=$, $<$, and $<=$ compare only the *real parts* of complex numbers, not their magnitudes. If you need these relational operators with a complex number, it will probably be more sensible to compare the total magnitudes rather than only the real components.

8.1.3 Complex Functions

MATLAB includes many functions that support complex calculations. These functions fall into three general categories.

1. **Type conversion functions** These functions convert data from the complex data type to the real (double) data type. Function real converts the *real part* of a complex number into the double data type and throws away the imaginary part of the complex number. Function imag converts the *imaginary part* of a complex number into a real number.

Table 8-1   Some Functions that Support Complex Numbers

Function	Description
`conj(c)`	Computes the complex conjugate of a number c. If $c = a + bi$, then `conj(c)` = a - bi.
`real(c)`	Returns the real portion of the complex number c.
`imag(c)`	Returns the imaginary portion of the complex number c.
`isreal(c)`	Returns true (1) if no element of array c has an imaginary component. Therefore, `~isreal(c)` returns true (1) if an array is complex.
`abs(c)`	Returns the magnitude of the complex number c.
`angle(c)`	Returns the angle of the complex number c in radians, computed from the expression `atan2(imag(c), real(c))`.

2. **Absolute value and angle functions** These functions convert a complex number to its polar representation. Function `abs(c)` calculates the absolute value of a complex number using the equation

$$abs(c) = \sqrt{a^2 + b^2}$$

where $c = a + bi$. Function `angle(c)` calculates the angle of a complex number using the equation

$$angle(c) = atan2 (imag(c), real(c))$$

producing an answer in the range $-\pi \le \theta \le \pi$.

3. **Mathematical functions** Most elementary mathematical functions are defined for complex values. These functions include exponential functions, logarithms, trigonometric functions, and square roots. The functions `sin`, `cos`, `log`, `sqrt`, and so forth will work as well with complex data as they will with real data.

Some of the intrinsic functions that support complex numbers are listed in Table 8-1.

▶

Example 8.1—The Quadratic Equation (Revisited)

The availability of complex numbers often simplifies the calculations required to solve problems. For example, when we solved the quadratic equation in Example 4.2, it was necessary to take three separate branches through the program, depending on the sign of the discriminant. With complex numbers available, the square root of a negative number presents no difficulties, so we can greatly simplify these calculations.

Write a general program to solve for the roots of a quadratic equation, regardless of type. Use complex variables so that no branches will be required based on the value of the discriminant.

SOLUTION

1. **State the problem.**
   Write a program that will solve for the roots of a quadratic equation, whether they are distinct real roots, repeated real roots, or complex roots, without requiring tests on the value of the discriminant.

2. **Define the inputs and outputs.**
   The inputs required by this program are the coefficients a, b, and c of the quadratic equation

$$ax^2 + bx + c = 0 \tag{4.1}$$

   The output from the program will be the roots of the quadratic equation, whether they are real, repeated, or complex.

3. **Describe the algorithm.**
   This task can be broken down into three major sections, whose functions are input, processing, and output:

```
Read the input data
Calculate the roots
Write out the roots
```

   We will now break each of these major sections into smaller, more detailed pieces. In this algorithm, the value of the discriminant is unimportant in determining how to proceed. The resulting pseudocode is

```
Prompt the user for the coefficients a, b, and c.
Read a, b, and c
discriminant ← b^2 - 4 * a * c
x1 ← ( -b + sqrt(discriminant) ) / ( 2 * a )
x2 ← ( -b - sqrt(discriminant) ) / ( 2 * a )
Print 'The roots of this equation are: '
Print 'x1 = ', real(x1), ' +i ', imag(x1)
Print 'x2 = ', real(x2), ' +i ', imag(x2)
```

4. **Turn the algorithm into MATLAB statements.**
   The final MATLAB code is shown here.

```
% Script file: calc_roots2.m
%
% Purpose:
%   This program solves for the roots of a quadratic equation
%   of the form a*x**2 + b*x + c = 0. It calculates the answers
%   regardless of the type of roots that the equation possesses.
%
```

```
% Record of revisions:
%       Date            Engineer            Description of change
%       ====            ========            =====================
%    02/24/10      S. J. Chapman        Original code
%
% Define variables:
%    a               -- Coefficient of x^2 term of equation
%    b               -- Coefficient of x term of equation
%    c               -- Constant term of equation
%    discriminant    -- Discriminant of the equation
%    x1              -- First solution of equation
%    x2              -- Second solution of equation

% Prompt the user for the coefficients of the equation
disp ('This program solves for the roots of a quadratic ');
disp ('equation of the form A*X^2 + B*X + C = 0. ');
a = input ('Enter the coefficient A: ');
b = input ('Enter the coefficient B: ');
c = input ('Enter the coefficient C: ');

% Calculate discriminant
discriminant = b^2 - 4 * a * c;

% Solve for the roots
x1 = ( -b + sqrt(discriminant) ) / ( 2 * a );
x2 = ( -b - sqrt(discriminant) ) / ( 2 * a );

% Display results
disp ('The roots of this equation are:');
fprintf ('x1 = (%f) +i (%f)\n', real(x1), imag(x1));
fprintf ('x2 = (%f) +i (%f)\n', real(x2), imag(x2));
```

5. **Test the program.**

   Next, we must test the program using real input data. We will test cases in which the discriminant is greater than, less than, and equal to 0 to be certain that the program is working properly under all circumstances. From Equation (4.1), it is possible to verify the solutions to the following equations:

   $$x^2 + 5x + 6 = 0 \qquad x = -2, \text{ and } x = -3$$
   $$x^2 + 4x + 4 = 0 \qquad x = -2$$
   $$x^2 + 2x + 5 = 0 \qquad x = -1 \pm 2i$$

   When these coefficients are fed into the program, the results are

   » **calc_roots2**
   This program solves for the roots of a quadratic equation of the form A*X^2 + B*X + C = 0.

```
Enter the coefficient A: 1
Enter the coefficient B: 5
Enter the coefficient C: 6
The roots of this equation are:
x1 = (-2.000000) +i (0.000000)
x2 = (-3.000000) +i (0.000000)
» calc_roots2
This program solves for the roots of a quadratic
equation of the form A*X^2 + B*X + C = 0.
Enter the coefficient A: 1
Enter the coefficient B: 4
Enter the coefficient C: 4
The roots of this equation are:
x1 = (-2.000000) +i (0.000000)
x2 = (-2.000000) +i (0.000000)
» calc_roots2
This program solves for the roots of a quadratic
equation of the form A*X^2 + B*X + C = 0.
Enter the coefficient A: 1
Enter the coefficient B: 2
Enter the coefficient C: 5
The roots of this equation are:
x1 = (-1.000000) +i (2.000000)
x2 = (-1.000000) +i (-2.000000)
```

The program gives the correct answers for our test data in all three possible cases. Note how much simpler this program is compared to the quadratic root solver found in Example 4.2. The complex data type has greatly simplified our program.

◄

►

Example 8.2—Series RC Circuit

Figure 8.3 shows a resistor and a capacitor connected in series and driven by a 100 V ac power source. The output voltage of this circuit can be found from the *voltage divider rule*:

$$\mathbf{V}_{out} = \frac{Z_2}{Z_1 + Z_2} \mathbf{V}_{in} \tag{8.11}$$

where $\mathbf{V}_{in}$ is the input voltage, $Z_1 = Z_R$ is the impedance of the resistor, and $Z_2 = Z_C$ is the impedance of the capacitor. If the input voltage is $\mathbf{V}_{in} = 100\angle 0° \text{ V}$, the impedance of the resistor $Z_R = 100 \ \Omega$ and the impedance of the capacitor $Z_C = -j100 \ \Omega$, what is the output voltage of this circuit?

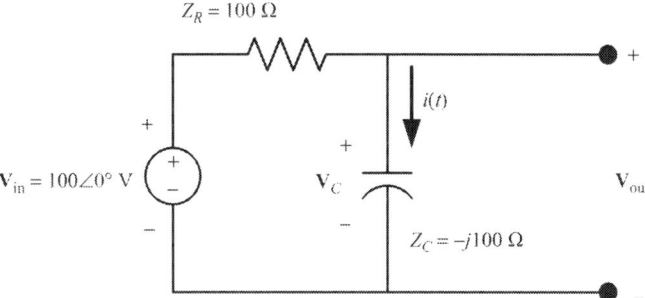

Figure 8.3   An ac voltage divider circuit.

SOLUTION   We will need to calculate the output voltage of this circuit in polar coordinates in order to get the magnitude output voltage. The output voltage in rectangular coordinates can be calculated from Equation (8.11), and then the magnitude of the output voltage can be found from Equation (8.5). The code to perform these calculations is given here.

```
% Script file: voltage_divider.m
%
% Purpose:
%   This program calculate the output voltage across an
%   AC voltage divider circuit.
%
% Record of revisions:
%     Date            Engineer           Description of change
%     ====            ========           =====================
%   02/28/10      S. J. Chapman       Original code
%
% Define variables:
%   vin           -- Input voltage
%   vout          -- Output voltage across z2
%   z1            -- Impedance of first element
%   z2            -- Impedance of second element

% Prompt the user for the coefficients of the equation
disp ('This program calculates the output voltage across a
voltage divider. ');
vin = input ('Enter input voltage: ');
z1  = input ('Enter z1: ');
z2  = input ('Enter z2: ');

% Calculate the output voltage
vout = z2 / (z1 + z2) * vin;
```

```
% Display results
disp ('The output voltage is:');
fprintf ('vout = %f at an angle of %f degrees\n', abs(vout),
angle(vout)*180/pi);
```

When this program is executed, the results are

```
» This program calculates the output voltage across a voltage
divider.
Enter input voltage: 100
Enter z1: 100
Enter z2: -100j
The output voltage is:
vout = 70.710678 at an angle of -45.000000 degrees
```

The program uses complex numbers to calculate the output voltage from this circuit. ◀

8.1.4 Plotting Complex Data

Complex data has both real and imaginary components, and plotting complex data with MATLAB is a bit different than plotting real data. For example, consider the function

$$y(t) = e^{-0.2t}(\cos t + i \sin t) \tag{8.12}$$

If this function is plotted with the conventional `plot` function, only the real data will be plotted—the imaginary part will be ignored. The following statements produce the plot shown in Figure 8.4, together with a warning message that the imaginary part of the data is being ignored.

```
t = 0:pi/20:4*pi;
y = exp(-0.2*t).*(cos(t)+i*sin(t));
plot(t,y,'LineWidth',2);
title('\bfPlot of Complex Function vs Time');
xlabel('\bf\itt');
ylabel('\bf\ity(t)');
```

If both the real and imaginary parts of the function are of interest, then the user has several choices. Both parts can be plotted as a function of time on the same axes using the statements that follows (see Figure 8.5).

```
t = 0:pi/20:4*pi;
y = exp(-0.2*t).*(cos(t)+i*sin(t));
plot(t,real(y),'b-','LineWidth',2);
```

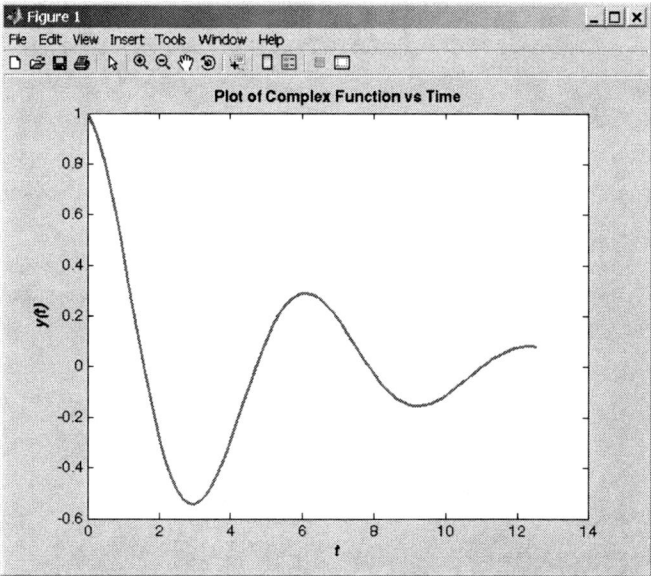

Figure 8.4   Plot of $y(t) = e^{-0.2t}(\cos t + i \sin t)$ using the command `plot(t,y)`.

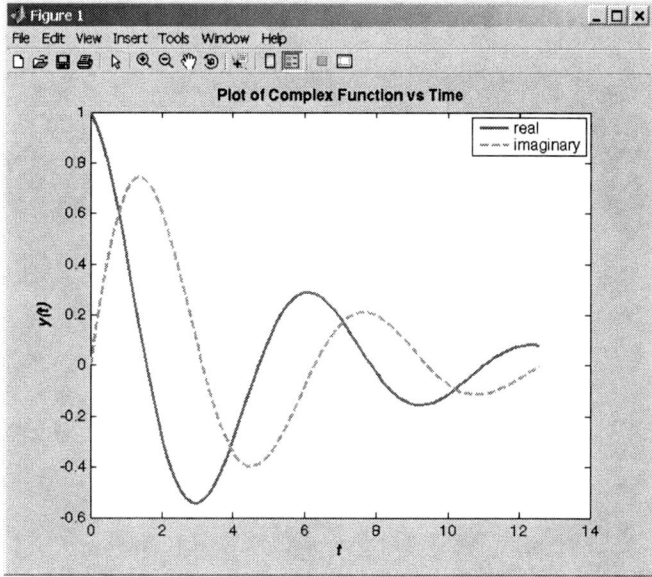

Figure 8.5   Plot of real and imaginary parts of $y(t)$ versus time.

```
hold on;
plot(t,imag(y),'r--','LineWidth',2);
title('\bfPlot of Complex Function vs Time');
xlabel('\bf\itt');
ylabel('\bf\ity(t)');
legend ('real','imaginary');
hold off;
```

Alternatively, the real part of the function can be plotted versus the imaginary part. If a *single* complex argument is supplied to the plot function, it automatically generates a plot of the real part versus the imaginary part. The statements to generate this plot are shown next, and the result is shown in Figure 8.6.

```
t = 0:pi/20:4*pi;
y = exp(-0.2*t).*(cos(t)+i*sin(t));
plot(y,'b-','LineWidth',2);
title('\bfPlot of Complex Function');
xlabel('\bfReal Part');
ylabel('\bfImaginary Part');
```

Finally, the function can be plotted as a polar plot showing magnitude versus angle. The statements to generate this plot are shown next, and the result is shown in Figure 8.7.

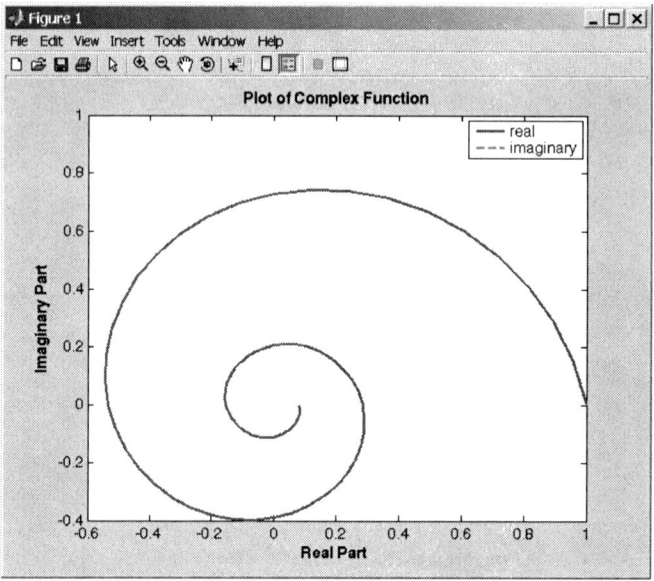

Figure 8.6 Plot of real versus imaginary parts of $y(t)$.

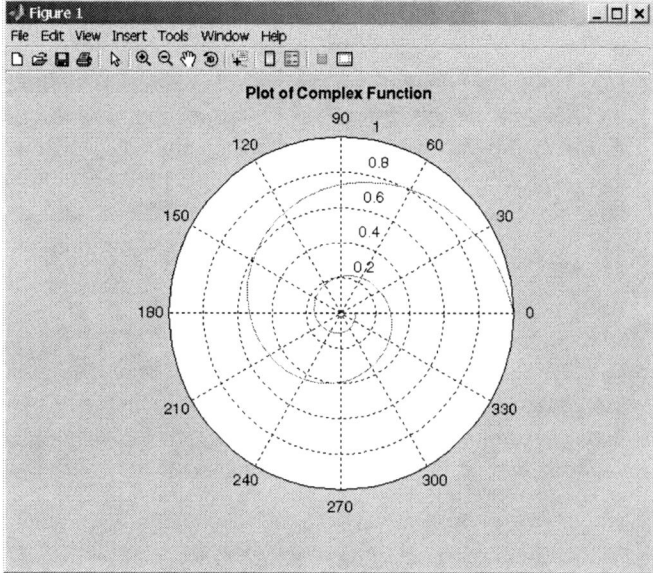

Figure 8.7 Polar plot of magnitude of $y(t)$ versus angle.

```
t = 0:pi/20:4*pi;
y = exp(-0.2*t).*(cos(t)+i*sin(t));
polar(angle(y),abs(y));
title('\bfPlot of Complex Function');
```

Quiz 8.1

This quiz provides a quick check to see if you have understood the concepts introduced in Sections 8.1 through 8.2. If you have trouble with the quiz, reread the section, ask your instructor, or discuss the material with a fellow student. The answers to this quiz are found in the back of the book.

1. What is the value of `result` in the following statements?
   (a)
   ```
   x = 12 + i*5;
   y = 5 - i*13;
   result = x > y;
   ```
   (b)
   ```
   x = 12 + i*5;
   y = 5 - i*13;
   result = abs(x) > abs(y);
   ```
   (c)
   ```
   x = 12 + i*5;
   y = 5 - i*13;
   result = real(x) - imag(y);
   ```
2. If `array` is a complex array, what does the function `plot(array)` do?

Multidimensional Arrays

MATLAB also supports arrays with more than two dimensions. These **multidimensional arrays** are useful for displaying data that intrinsically has more than two dimensions or for displaying multiple versions of two-dimensional data sets. For example, measurements of pressure and velocity throughout a three-dimensional volume are very important in such areas as aerodynamics and fluid dynamics. These areas naturally use multidimensional arrays.

Multidimensional arrays are a natural extension of two-dimensional arrays. Each additional dimension is represented by one additional subscript used to address the data.

It is easy to create a multidimensional array. They can be created either by assigning values directly in assignment statements or by using the same functions that are used to create one- and two-dimensional arrays. For example, suppose that you have a two-dimensional array created by the assignment statement

```
» a = [ 1 2 3 4; 5 6 7 8]
a =
     1      2      3      4
     5      6      7      8
```

This is a 2 × 4 array with each element addressed by two subscripts. The array can be extended to be a three-dimensional 2 × 4 × 3 array with the following assignment statements.

```
» a(:,:,2) = [ 9 10 11 12; 13 14 15 16];
» a(:,:,3) = [ 17 18 19 20; 21 22 23 24]
a(:,:,1) =
     1      2      3      4
     5      6      7      8
a(:,:,2) =
     9     10     11     12
    13     14     15     16
a(:,:,3) =
    17     18     19     20
    21     22     23     24
```

Individual elements in this multidimensional array can be addressed by the array name followed by three subscripts, and subsets of the data can be created using the colon operators. For example, the value of a(2,2,2) is

```
» a(2,2,2)
ans =
    14
```

and the vector a(1,1,:) is

```
» a(1,1,:)
ans(:,:,1) =
      1
ans(:,:,2) =
      9
ans(:,:,3) =
     17
```

Multidimensional arrays also can be created using the same functions as other arrays, for example:

```
» b = ones(4,4,2)
b(:,:,1) =
      1      1      1      1
      1      1      1      1
      1      1      1      1
      1      1      1      1
b(:,:,2) =
      1      1      1      1
      1      1      1      1
      1      1      1      1
      1      1      1      1
» c = randn(2,2,3)
c(:,:,1) =
    -0.4326      0.1253
    -1.6656      0.2877
c(:,:,2) =
    -1.1465      1.1892
     1.1909     -0.0376
c(:,:,3) =
     0.3273     -0.1867
     0.1746      0.7258
```

The number of dimensions in a multidimensional array can be found using the ndims function, and the size of the array can be found using the size function.

```
» ndims(c)
ans =
        3
» size(c)
ans =
        2      2      3
```

If you are writing applications that need multidimensional arrays, see the MATLAB Users Guide for more details on the behavior of various MATLAB functions with multidimensional arrays.

CHAPTER 9

Cell Arrays, Structures, and Importing Data

This chapter deals with three very useful features of MATLAB: cell arrays, structures, and importing data. These somewhat disparate topics are clumped together in this chapter, because the ability to import data from other programs such as Microsoft Excel is dependent on knowledge of cell arrays and structures.

Cell arrays are a very flexible type of array that can hold any sort of data. Each element of a cell array can hold any type of MATLAB data, and different elements within the same array can hold different types of data. They are used extensively in MATLAB graphical user interface (GUI) functions.

Structures are a special type of array with named subcomponents. Each structure can have any number of subcomponents—each with its own name and data type. Structures are the basis of MATLAB objects.

MATLAB includes a GUI-based tool called `uiimport`, which allows users to import data into MATLAB from files created by many other programs in a wide variety of formats. We will learn how to use this tool to import data from an outside program into a structure.

9.1 Cell Arrays

A **cell array** is a special MATLAB array whose elements are *cells*, which are containers that can hold other MATLAB arrays. For example, one cell of a cell array might contain an array of real numbers, another an array of strings, and yet another a vector of complex numbers (see Figure 9.1).

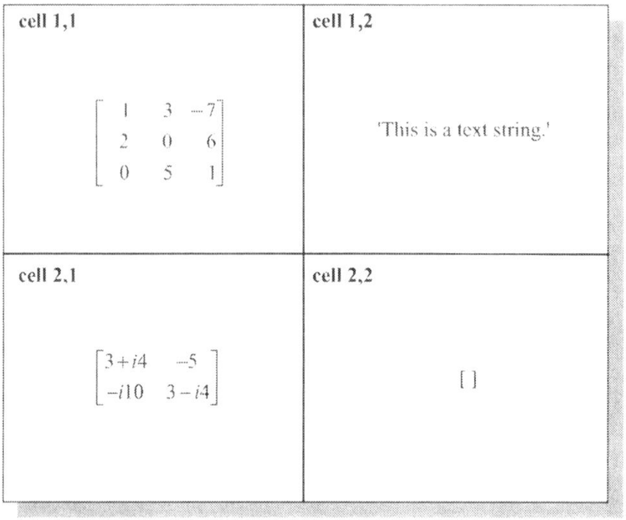

Figure 9.1 The individual elements of a cell array may point to real arrays, complex arrays, strings, other cell arrays, or even empty arrays.

In programming terms, each element of a cell array is a *pointer* to another data structure, and those data structures can be of different types. Figure 9.2 illustrates this concept. Cell arrays are great ways to collect information about a problem, since all of the information can be kept together and accessed by a single name.

Cell arrays use braces {} instead of parentheses ( ) for selecting and displaying the contents of cells. This difference is due to the fact that *cell arrays contain data structures instead of data.* Suppose that the cell array a is defined as shown in Figure 9.2. Then the contents of element a(1,1) is a data structure containing a 3 × 3 array of numeric data, and a reference to a(1,1) displays the *contents* of the cell, which is the data structure.

```
» a(1,1)
ans =
     [3x3 double]
```

By contrast, a reference to a{1,1} displays *the contents of the data item contained in the cell.*

```
» a{1,1}
ans =
     1     3    -7
     2     0     6
     0     5     1
```

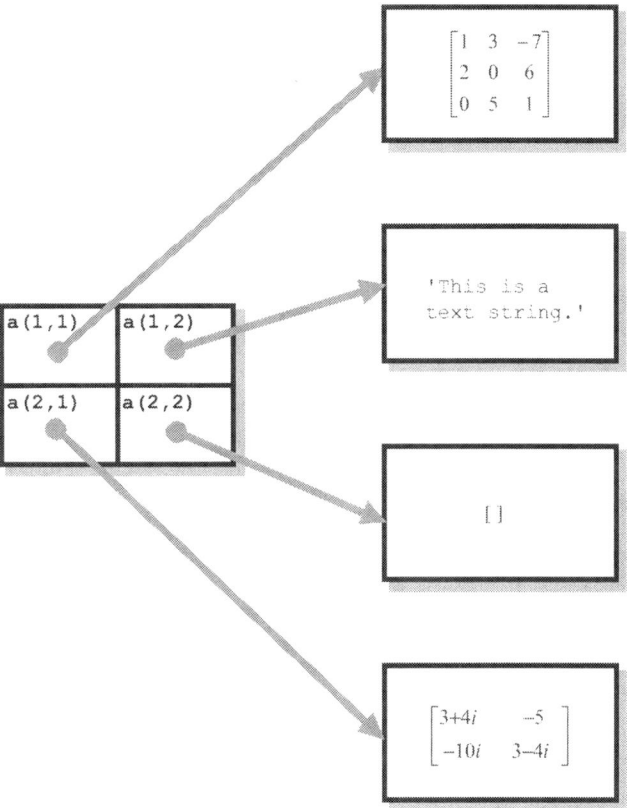

Figure 9.2   Each element of a cell array holds a *pointer* to another data structure, and different cells in the same cell array can point to different types of data structures.

In summary, the notation a(1,1) refers to the contents of cell a(1,1) (which is a data structure), while the notation a{1,1} refers to the contents of the data structure within the cell.

💣 Programming Pitfalls

Be careful not to confuse ( ) with { } when addressing cell arrays. They are very different operations!

9.1.1   Creating Cell Arrays

Cell arrays can be created in two ways:

1. By using assignment statements.
2. By preallocating a cell array using the cell function.

The simplest way to create a cell array is to directly assign data to individual cells one cell at a time. However, preallocating cell arrays is more efficient, so you should preallocate really large cell arrays.

Allocating Cell Arrays Using Assignment Statements

You can assign values to cell arrays one cell at a time using assignment statements. There are two ways to assign data to cells, known as **content indexing** and **cell indexing**.

Content indexing involves placing braces "{}" around the cell subscripts, together with cell contents in ordinary notation. For example, the following statement creates the 2 × 2 cell array in Figure 9.2:

```
a{1,1} = [1 3 -7; 2 0 6; 0 5 1];
a{1,2} = 'This is a text string.';
a{2,1} = [3+4*i -5; -10*i 3 - 4*i];
a{2,2} = [];
```

This type of indexing defines the *contents of the data structure contained in a cell.*

Cell indexing involves placing braces "{}" around the data to be stored in a cell, together with cell subscripts in ordinary subscript notation. For example, the following statements create the 2 × 2 cell array in Figure 9.2:

```
a(1,1) = {[1 3 -7; 2 0 6; 0 5 1]};
a(1,2) = {'This is a text string.'};
a(2,1) = {[3+4*i -5; -10*i 3 - 4*i]};
a(2,2) = {[]};
```

This type of indexing *creates a data structure containing the specified data and then assigns that data structure to a cell.*

These two forms of indexing are completely equivalent, and they may be freely mixed in any program.

💣 Programming Pitfalls

Do not attempt to create a cell array with the same name as an existing numeric array. If you do this, MATLAB will assume that you are trying to assign cell contents to an ordinary array, and it will generate an error message. Be sure to clear the numeric array before trying to create a cell array with the same name.

Preallocating Cell Arrays with the `cell` Function

The `cell` function allows you to preallocate empty cell arrays of the specified size. For example, the following statement creates an empty 2 × 2 cell array.

```
a = cell(2,2);
```

Once a cell array is created, you can use assignment statements to fill values in the cells.

9.1.2 Using Braces { } as Cell Constructors

It is possible to define many cells at once by placing all of the cell contents between a single set of braces. Individual cells on a row are separated by commas, and rows are separated by semicolons. For example, the following statement creates a 2 × 3 cell array:

```
b = {[1 2], 17, [2;4]; 3-4*i, 'Hello', eye(3)}
```

9.1.3 Viewing the Contents of Cell Arrays

MATLAB displays the data structures in each element of a cell array in a condensed form that limits each data structure to a single line. If the entire data structure can be displayed on the single line, it is. Otherwise, a summary is displayed. For example, cell arrays a and b would be displayed as:

```
» a
a =
    [3x3 double]    [1x22 char]
    [2x2 double]           []
» b
b =
          [1x2 double] [    17] [2x1 double]
    [3.0000- 4.0000i] 'Hello' [3x3 double]
```

Note that MATLAB *is displaying the data structures*, complete with brackets or apostrophes, not the entire contents of the data structures.

If you would like to see the full contents of a cell array, use the celldisp function. This function displays *the contents of the data structures in each cell*.

```
» celldisp(a)
a{1,1} =
       1    3   -7
       2    0    6
       0    5    1
a{2,1} =
     3.0000 + 4.0000i   -5.0000
          0 -10.0000i    3.0000 - 4.0000i
a{1,2} =
This is a text string.
a{2,2} =
     []
```

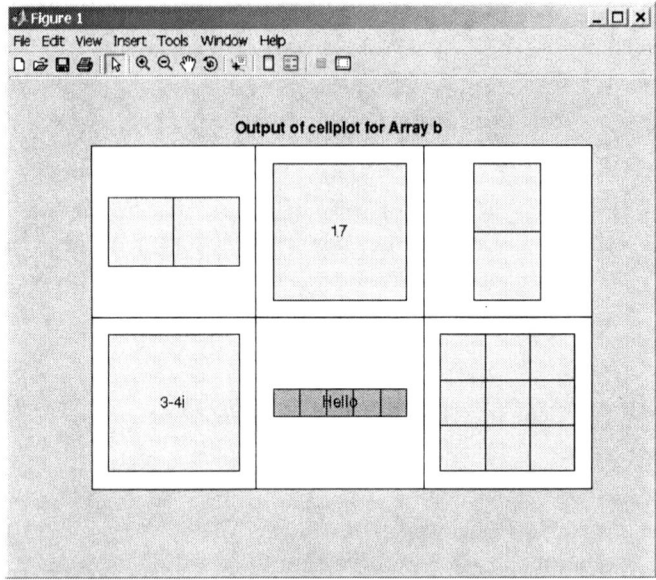

Figure 9.3   The structure of cell array b is displayed as a nested series of boxes by the function `cellplot`.

For a high-level graphical display of the structure of a cell array, use the function `cellplot`. For example, the function `cellplot(b)` produces the plot shown in Figure 9.3.

9.1.4   Extending Cell Arrays

If a value is assigned to a cell array element that does not currently exist, the element will be created automatically, and any additional cells necessary to preserve the shape of the array also will be created automatically. For example, suppose that array a has been defined to be a 2 × 2 cell array, as shown in Figure 9.1. If the following statement is executed

```
a{3,3} = 5
```

the cell array will be automatically extended to 3 × 3, as shown in Figure 9.4.

Preallocating cell arrays with the `cell` function is much more efficient than extending them one element at a time using assignment statements. When a new element is added to an existing array as we did here, MATLAB must create a new array large enough to include this new element, copy the old data into the new array, add the new value to the array, and then delete the old array. This is a very time-consuming process. Instead, you should always allocate the cell array to be the largest size that you can and then add values to it one element at a time. If you do that, only the new element needs to be added—the rest of the array can remain undisturbed.

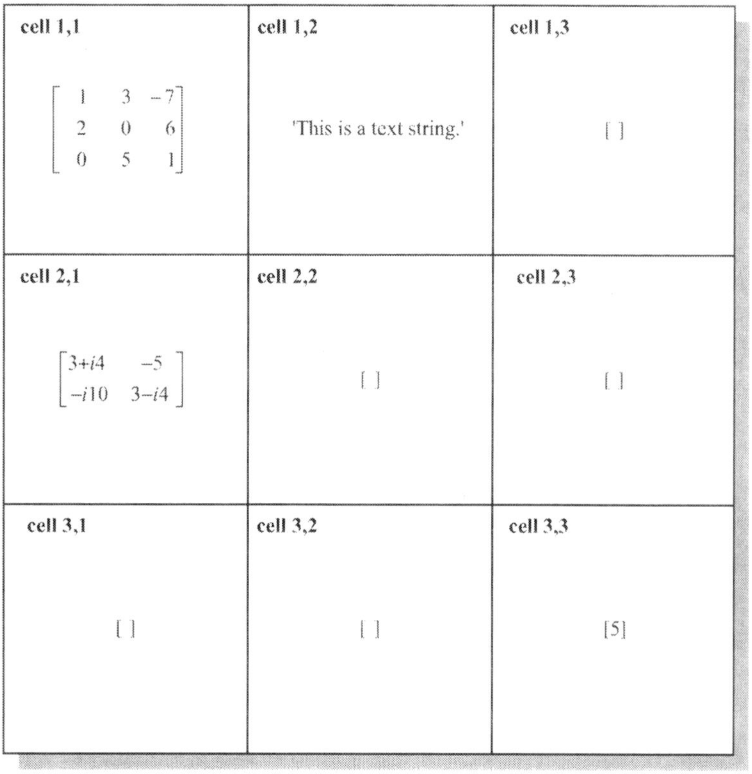

cell 1,1	cell 1,2	cell 1,3
$\begin{bmatrix} 1 & 3 & -7 \\ 2 & 0 & 6 \\ 0 & 5 & 1 \end{bmatrix}$	'This is a text string.'	[ ]
cell 2,1	cell 2,2	cell 2,3
$\begin{bmatrix} 3+i4 & -5 \\ -i10 & 3-i4 \end{bmatrix}$	[ ]	[ ]
cell 3,1	cell 3,2	cell 3,3
[ ]	[ ]	[5]

Figure 9.4   The result of assigning a value to a{3,3}. Note that four other empty cells were created to preserve the shape of the cell array.

The following program illustrates the advantages of preallocation. It creates a cell array containing 50,000 strings added one at a time, with and without preallocation.

```
% Script file: test_preallocate.m
%
% Purpose:
%   This program tests the creation of cell arrays with and
%   without preallocation.
%
% Record of revisions:
%    Date          Engineer        Description of change
%    ====          ========        =====================
%   03/04/10     S. J. Chapman     Original code
%
```

```
% Define variables:
%    a              -- Cell array
%    maxvals        -- Maximum values in cell array

% Create array without preallocation
clear all
maxvals = 50000;
tic
for ii = 1:maxvals
   a{ii} = ['Element ' int2str(ii)];
end
disp(['Elapsed time without preallocation = ' num2str(toc)]);

% Create array with preallocation
clear all
maxvals = 50000;
tic
a = cell(1,maxvals);
for ii = 1:maxvals
   a{ii} = ['Element ' int2str(ii)];
end
disp( ['Elapsed time with preallocation = ' num2str(toc)] );
```

When this program is executed using MATLAB 7.9 on a 1.8 GHz Pentium Core 2 Duo computer, the results are as shown here. The advantages of preallocation are obvious.

```
» test_preallocate
Elapsed time without preallocation = 8.4114
Elapsed time with preallocation    = 3.3583
```

✳ Good Programming Practice

Always preallocate all cell arrays before assigning values to the elements of the array. This practice greatly increases the execution speed of a program.

9.1.5 Deleting Cells in Arrays

To delete an entire cell array, use the clear command. Subsets of cells may be deleted by assigning an empty array to them. For example, assume that a is the 3 × 3 cell array defined previously.

```
» a
a =
    [3x3 double]    [1x22 char]    []
    [2x2 double]                []    []
              []                  []   [5]
```

It is possible to delete the entire third row with the statement

```
» a(3,:) = []
a =
    [3x3 double]    [1x22 char]    []
    [2x2 double]                []    []
```

9.1.6   Using Data in Cell Arrays

The data stored inside the data structures within a cell array may be used at any time with either content indexing or cell indexing. For example, suppose that a cell array c is defined as

```
c = {[1 2;3 4], 'dogs'; 'cats', i}
```

The contents of the array stored in cell c(1,1) can be accessed as follows.

```
» c{1,1}
ans =
        1    2
        3    4
```

and the contents of the array in cell c(2,1) can be accessed as follows.

```
» c{2,1}
ans =
        cats
```

Subsets of a cell's contents can be obtained by concatenating the two sets of subscripts. For example, suppose that we would like to get the element (1,2) from the array stored in cell c(1,1) of cell array c. To do this, we would use the expression c{1,1}(1,2), which says: select element (1,2) from the contents of the data structure contained in cell c(1,1).

```
» c{1,1}(1,2)
ans =
        2
```

9.1.7   Cell Arrays of Strings

It is often convenient to store groups of strings in a cell array instead of storing them in rows of a standard character array, because each string in a cell array can have a different length, whereas every row of a standard character array must have an identical length. This fact means that *strings in cell arrays do not have to be padded with blanks*.

Cell arrays of strings can be created in one of two ways. Either the individual strings can be inserted into the array with brackets, or else the function cellstr can be used to convert a two-dimensional string array into a cell array of strings.

The following example creates a cell array of strings by inserting the strings into the cell array one at a time and displays the resulting cell array. Note that the individual strings can be of different lengths.

```
» cellstring{1} = 'Stephen J. Chapman';
» cellstring{2} = 'Male';
» cellstring{3} = 'SSN 999-99-9999';
» cellstring
   'Stephen J. Chapman'  'Male'  'SSN 999-99-9999'
```

The function `cellstr` creates a cell array of strings from a two-dimensional string array. Consider the character array:

```
» data = ['Line 1 ';'Additional Line']
data =
Line 1
Additional Line
```

This 2 × 15 character array can be converted into an cell array of strings with the function `cellstr` as follows:

```
» c = cellstr(data)
c =
   'Line 1'
   'Additional Line'
```

and it can be converted back to a standard character array using the function `char`

```
» newdata = char(c)
newdata =
Line 1
Additional Line
```

9.1.8   The Significance of Cell Arrays

Cell arrays are extremely flexible, since any amount of any type of data can be stored in each cell. As a result, cell arrays are used in many internal MATLAB data structures. We must understand them in order to use many features of Handle Graphics and the graphical user interfaces.[1]

In addition, the flexibility of cell arrays makes them regular features of functions with variable numbers of input arguments and output arguments. A special input argument, `varargin`, is available within user-defined MATLAB functions to support variable numbers of input arguments. This argument appears as the last item in an input argument list, and it returns a cell array, so *a single*

---

[1]Graphical user interfaces are beyond the scope of this book.

dummy input argument can support any number of actual arguments. Each actual argument becomes one element of the cell array returned by `varargin`. If it is used, `varargin` must be the *last* input argument in a function, following all of the required input arguments.

For example, suppose that we are writing a function that may have any number of input arguments. This function could be implemented as shown.

```
function test1(varargin)
disp(['There are ' int2str(nargin) ' arguments.']);
disp('The input arguments are:');
disp(varargin);

end % function test1
```

When this function is executed with varying numbers of arguments, the results are

```
» test1
There are 0 arguments.
The input arguments are:
» test1(6)
There are 1 arguments.
The input arguments are:
    [6]
» test1(1,'test 1',[1 2;3 4])
There are 3 arguments.
The input arguments are:
    [1]     'test 1'    [2x2 double]
```

As you can see, the arguments become a cell array within the function.

A sample function making use of variable numbers of arguments is shown at the end of this paragraph. The function `plotline` accepts an arbitrary number of 1×2 row vectors, with each vector containing the (x,y) position of one point to plot. The function plots a line connecting all of the (x,y) values together. Note that this function also accepts an optional line specification string and passes that specification on to the `plot` function.

```
function plotline(varargin)
%PLOTLINE Plot points specified by [x,y] pairs.
% Function PLOTLINE accepts an arbitrary number of
% [x,y] points and plots a line connecting them.
% In addition, it can accept a line specification
% string, and pass that string on to function plot.

% Define variables:
%   ii        -- Index variable
%   jj        -- Index variable
%   linespec  -- String defining plot characteristics
%   msg       -- Error message
```

```
%     varargin   -- Cell array containing input arguments
%     x          -- x values to plot
%     y          -- y values to plot

% Record of revisions:
%     Date            Engineer          Description of change
%     ====            ========          =====================
%     03/18/10    S. J. Chapman         Original code

% Check for a legal number of input arguments.
% We need at least 2 points to plot a line...
msg = nargchk(2,Inf,nargin);
error(msg);

% Initialize values
jj = 0;
linespec = '';

% Get the x and y values, making sure to save the line
% specification string, if one exists.
for ii = 1:nargin

    % Is this argument an [x,y] pair or the line
    % specification?
    if ischar(varargin{ii})

        % Save line specification
        linespec = varargin{ii};

    else

        % This is an [x,y] pair. Recover the values.
        jj = jj + 1;
        x(jj) = varargin{ii}(1);
        y(jj) = varargin{ii}(2);

    end
end

% Plot function.
if isempty(linespec)
    plot(x,y);
else
    plot(x,y,linespec);
end
```

When this function is called with the arguments shown at the end of this paragraph, the resulting plot is shown in Figure 9.5. Try the function with different numbers of arguments and see for yourself how it behaves.

```
plotline([0 0],[1 1],[2 4],[3 9],'k--');
```

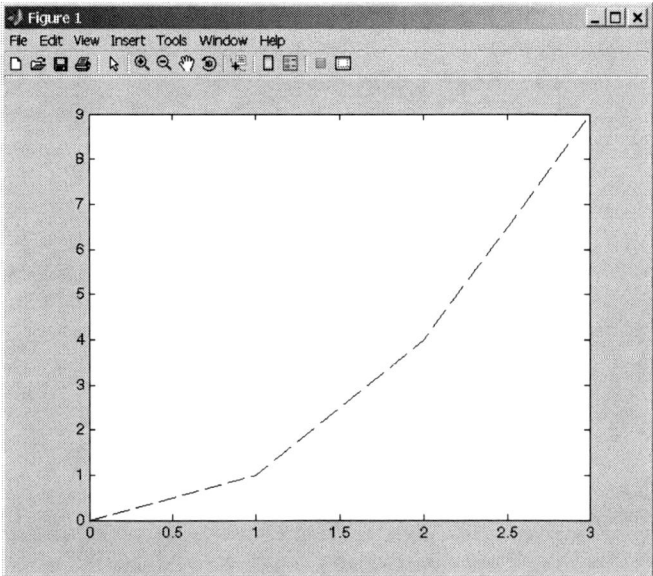

Figure 9.5 The plot produced by the function `plotline`.

There is also a special output argument, `varargout`, to support variable numbers of output arguments. This argument appears as the last item in an output argument list, and it returns a cell array, so *a single dummy output argument can support any number of actual arguments.* Each actual argument becomes one element of the cell array stored in `varargout`.

If it is used, `varargout` must be the *last* output argument in a function, following all of the required input arguments. The number of values to be stored in `varargout` can be determined from the function `nargout`, which specifies the number of actual output arguments for any given function call.

A sample function `test2` is shown further along in this paragraph. This function detects the number of output arguments expected by the calling program, using the function `nargout`. It returns the number of random values in the first output argument and then fills the remaining output arguments with random numbers taken from a Gaussian distribution. Note that the function uses `varargout` to hold the random numbers, so that there can be an arbitrary number of output values.

```
function [nvals,varargout] = test2(mult)
% nvals is the number of random values returned
% varargout contains the random values returned
nvals = nargout - 1;
for ii = 1:nargout-1
   varargout{ii} = randn * mult;
end
```

When this function is executed, the results are as shown here.

```
» test2(4)
ans =
     -1
» [a b c d] = test2(4)
a =
     3
b =
     -1.7303
c =
     -6.6623
d =
     0.5013
```

✳ Good Programming Practice

Use cell array arguments varargin and varargout to create functions that support varying numbers of input and output arguments.

9.1.9 Summary of cell Functions

The common MATLAB cell functions are summarized in Table 9-1.

Table 9-1   Common MATLAB Cell Functions

Function	Description
cell	Predefines a cell array structure.
celldisp	Displays contents of a cell array.
cellplot	Plots structure of a cell array.
cellstr	Converts a two-dimensional character array to a cell array of strings.
char	Converts a cell array of strings into a two-dimensional character array.

9.2 Structure Arrays

An *array* is a data type in which there is a name for the whole data structure, but individual elements within the array are known only by number. Thus, the fifth element in the array named arr would be accessed as arr(5). All of the individual elements in an array must be of the *same* type.

A *cell array* is a data type in which there is a name for the whole data structure, but individual elements within the array are known only by number. However, the individual elements in the cell array may be of *different* types.

In contrast, a **structure** is a data type in which each individual element has a name. The individual elements of a structure are known as **fields**, and each field in a structure may have a different type. The individual fields are addressed by combining the name of the structure with the name of the field, separated by a period.

Figure 9.6 shows a sample structure named `student`. This structure has five fields, called `name`, `addr1`, `city`, `state`, and `zip`. The field called "name" would be addressed as `student.name`.

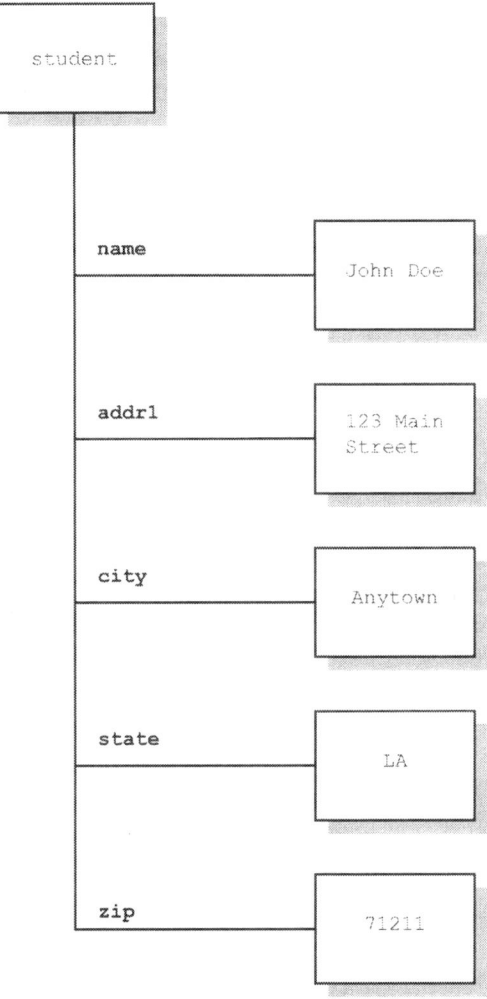

Figure 9.6 A sample structure. Each element within the structure is called a field, and each field is addressed by name.

A **structure array** is an array of structures. Each structure in the array will have identically the same fields, but the data stored in each field can differ. For example, a class could be described by an array of the structure `student`. The first student's name would be addressed as `student(1).name`, the second student's city would be addressed as `student(2).city`, and so forth.

9.2.1 Creating Structure Arrays

Structure arrays can be created in two ways:

1. A field at a time, using assignment statements.
2. All at once, using the `struct` function.

Building a Structure with Assignment Statements

You can build a structure a field at a time using assignment statements. Each time data is assigned to a field, that field is automatically created. For example, the structure shown in Figure 9.6 can be created with the following statements:

```
» student.name = 'John Doe';
» student.addr1 = '123 Main Street';
» student.city = 'Anytown';
» student.state = 'LA';
» student.zip = '71211'
student =
      name:  'John Doe'
     addr1:  '123 Main Street'
      city:  'Anytown'
     state:  'LA'
       zip:  '71211'
```

A second student can be added to the structure by adding a subscript to the structure name (*before* the period).

```
» student(2).name = 'Jane Q. Public'
student =
1x2 struct array with fields:
     name
     addr1
     city
     state
     zip
```

`student` is now a 1 × 2 array. Note that when a structure array has more than one element, only the field names are listed, not their contents. The contents of each element can be listed by typing the element separately in the Command Window.

```
» student(1)
ans =
      name: 'John Doe'
     addr1: '123 Main Street'
      city: 'Anytown'
     state: 'LA'
       zip: '71211'
» student(2)
ans =
      name: 'Jane Q. Public'
     addr1: []
      city: []
     state: []
       zip: []
```

Note that *all of the fields of a structure are created for each array element when-ever that element is defined*, even if they are not initialized. The uninitialized fields will contain empty arrays, which can be initialized with assignment state-ments at a later time.

The field names used in a structure can be recovered at any time using the fieldnames function. This function returns a list of the field names in a cell array of strings and is very useful for working with structure arrays within a program.

Creating Structures with the struct Function

The struct function allows you to preallocate a structure or an array of struc-tures. The basic form of this function is

```
str_array = struct('field1',val1,'field2',val2, ...)
```

where the arguments are field names and their initial values. With this syntax, the function struct initializes every field to the specified value.

To preallocate an entire array with the struct function, simply assign the output of the struct function to the *last value* in the array. All of the values before that will be created automatically at the same time. For example, the state-ments shown at the end of this paragraph create an array containing 1000 struc-tures of type student.

```
student(1000) = struct('name',[],'addr1',[], ...
                       'city',[],'state',[],'zip',[])
student =
1x1000 struct array with fields:
    name
    addr1
    city
    state
    zip
```

All of the elements of the structure are preallocated, which will speed up any program using the structure.

There is another version of the `struct` function that will preallocate an array and at the same time assign initial values to all of its fields. You will be asked to do this in an end-of-chapter exercise.

9.2.2 Adding Fields to Structures

If a new field name is defined for any element in a structure array, the field is automatically added to all of the elements in the array. For example, suppose that we add some exam scores to Jane Public's record:

```
» student(2).exams = [90 82 88]
student =
1x2 struct array with fields:
    name
    addr1
    city
    state
    zip
    exams
```

There is now a field called exams in every record of the array, as shown next. This field will be initialized for `student(2)` and will be an empty array for all other students until appropriate assignment statements are issued.

```
» student(1)
ans =
    name: 'John Doe'
    addr1: '123 Main Street'
    city: 'Anytown'
    state: 'LA'
    zip: '71211'
    exams: []
» student(2)
ans =
    name: 'Jane Q. Public'
    addr1: []
    city: []
    state: []
    zip: []
    exams: [90 82 88]
```

9.2.3 Removing Fields from Structures

A field may be removed from a structure array using the `rmfield` function. The form of this function is

```
struct2 = rmfield(str_array,'field')
```

where `str_array` is a structure array, `'field'` is the field to remove, and `struct2` is the name of a new structure with that field removed. For example, we can remove the field `'zip'` from structure array `student` with the following statement:

```
» stu2 = rmfield(student,'zip')
stu2 =
1x2 struct array with fields:
    name
    addr1
    city
    state
    exams
```

9.2.4   Using Data in Structure Arrays

Now let's assume that the structure array `student` has been extended to include three students, and all data has been filled in, as shown in Figure 9.7. How do we use the data in this structure array?

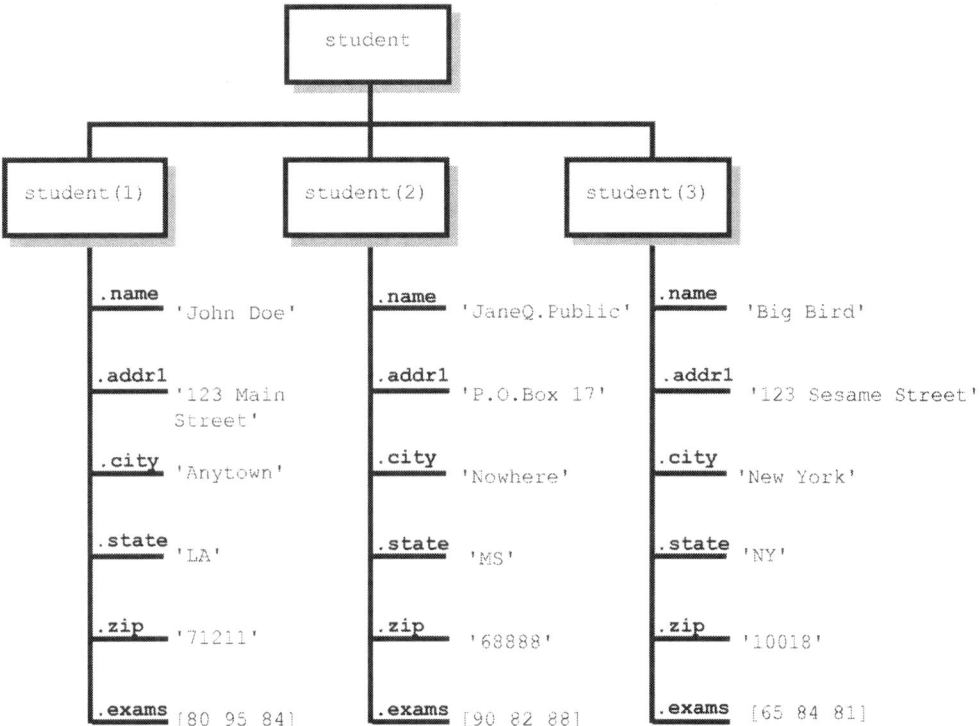

Figure 9.7   The student array with three elements and all fields filled in.

To access the information in any field of any array element, just name the array element followed by a period and the field name:

```
» student(2).addr1
ans =
P. O. Box 17
» student(3).exams
ans =
      65  84  81
```

To access an individual item within a field, add a subscript after the field name. For example, the second exam of the third student is

```
» student(3).exams(2)
ans =
      84
```

The fields in a structure array can be used as arguments in any function that supports that type of data. For example, to calculate `student(2)`'s exam average, we could use the function

```
» mean(student(2).exams)
ans =
    86.6667
```

To extract the values from a given field across multiple array elements, simply place the structure and field name inside a set of brackets. For example, we can get access to an array of zip codes with the expression `[student.zip]`:

```
» [student.zip]
ans =
        71211      68888      10018
```

Similarly, we can get the average of *all* exams from *all* students with the function `mean([student.exams])`.

```
» mean([student.exams])
ans =
    83.2222
        71211      68888      10018
```

9.2.5 The `getfield` and `setfield` Functions

Two MATLAB functions are available to make structure arrays easier to use in programs. The function `getfield` gets the current value stored in a field, and the function `setfield` inserts a new value into a field. The structure of function `getfield` is

```
f = getfield(array,{array_index},'field',{field_index})
```

where the `field_index` is optional and `array_index` is optional for a 1×1 structure array. The function call corresponds to the statement

```
f = array(array_index).field(field_index);
```

but it can be used even if the engineer doesn't know the names of the fields in the structure array at the time the program is written.

For example, suppose that we needed to write a function to read and manipulate the data in an unknown structure array. This function could determine the field names in the structure using a call to `fieldnames` and then could read the data using the function `getfield`. To read the zip code of the second student, the function would be

```
» zip = getfield(student,{2},'zip')
zip =
      68888
```

Similarly, a program could modify values in the structure using the function `setfield`. The structure of the function `setfield` is

```
f = setfield(array,{array_index},'field',{field_index},value)
```

where `f` is the output structure array, the `field_index` is optional, and `array_index` is optional for a 1×1 structure array. The function call corresponds to the statement

```
array(array_index).field(field_index) = value;
```

9.2.6   Dynamic Field Names

Beginning with MATLAB 7, there is an alternative way to access the elements of a structure: **dynamic field names**. A dynamic field name is a string enclosed in parentheses at a location where a field name is expected. For example, the name of student 1 can be retrieved with either static or dynamic field names as shown here.

```
» student(1).name        % Static field name
ans =
John Doe
» student(1).('name')    % Dynamic field name
ans =
John Doe
```

Dynamic field names perform the same function as static field names, but *dynamic field names can be changed during program execution*. This allows a user to access different information in the same function within a program.

For example, the following function accepts a structure array and a field name and calculates the average of the values in the specified field for all elements in the structure array. It returns that average (and optionally the number of values averaged) to the calling program.

```
function [ave, nvals] = calc_average(structure,field)
%CALC_AVERAGE Calculate the average of values in a field.
% Function CALC_AVERAGE calculates the average value
% of the elements in a particular field of a structure
% array. It returns the average value and (optionally)
% the number of items averaged.

% Define variables:
%    arr         -- Array of values to average
%    ave         -- Average of arr
%    ii          -- Index variable
%
% Record of revisions:
%    Date            Engineer            Description of change
%    ====            ========            =====================
%    03/04/10     S. J. Chapman          Original code
%
% Check for a legal number of input arguments.
msg = nargchk(2,2,nargin);
error(msg);

% Create an array of values from the field
arr = [];
for ii = 1:length(structure)
   arr = [arr structure(ii).(field)];
end

% Calculate average
ave = mean(arr);

% Return number of values averaged
if nargout == 2
   nvals = length(arr);
end
```

A program can average the values in different fields by simply calling this function multiple times with different structure names and different field names. For example, we can calculate the average values in fields exams and zip as follows.

```
» [ave,nvals] = calc_average(student,'exams')
ave =
    83.2222
nvals =
        9
» ave = calc_average(student,'zip')
ave =
50039
```

9.2.7 Using the `size` Function with Structure Arrays

When the `size` function is used with a structure array, it returns the size of the structure array itself. When the `size` function is used with a *field* from a particular element in a structure array, it returns the size of that field instead of the size of the whole array. For example,

```
» size(student)
ans =
     1     3
» size(student(1).name)
ans =
     1     8
```

9.2.8 Nesting Structure Arrays

Each field of a structure array can be of any data type, including a cell array or a structure array. For example, the following statements define a new structure array as a field under array `student` to carry information about each class that the student in enrolled in.

```
student(1).class(1).name = 'COSC 2021'
student(1).class(2).name = 'PHYS 1001'
student(1).class(1).instructor = 'Mr. Jones'
student(1).class(2).instructor = 'Mrs. Smith'
```

After these statements are issued, `student(1)` contains the following data. Note the technique used to access the data in the nested structures.

```
» student(1)
ans =
      name: 'John Doe'
     addr1: '123 Main Street'
      city: 'Anytown'
     state: 'LA'
       zip: '71211'
     exams: [80 95 84]
     class: [1x2 struct]
» student(1).class
ans =
1x2 struct array with fields:
    name
    instructor
» student(1).class(1)
ans =
          name: 'COSC 2021'
    instructor: 'Mr. Jones'
```

```
» student(1).class(2)
ans =
        name: 'PHYS 1001'
  instructor: 'Mrs. Smith'
» student(1).class(2).name
ans =
PHYS 1001
```

9.2.9 Summary of structure Functions

The common MATLAB structure functions are summarized in Table 9-2.

Table 9-2   Common MATLAB Structure Functions

fieldnames	Returns a list of field names in a cell array of strings.
getfield	Gets current value from a field.
rmfield	Removes a field from a structure array.
setfield	Sets new value into a field.
struct	Predefines a structure array.

QUIZ 9.1

This quiz provides a quick check to see if you have understood the concepts introduced in Sections 9.1 through 9.2. If you have trouble with the quiz, reread the section, ask your instructor, or discuss the material with a fellow student. The answers to this quiz are found in the back of the book.

1. What is a cell array? How does it differ from an ordinary array?

2. What is the difference between content indexing and cell indexing?

3. What is a structure? How does it differ from ordinary arrays and cell arrays?

4. What is the purpose of varargin? How does it work?

5. Given the definition of array a shown here, what will be produced by each of the following sets of statements? (*Note:* Some of these statements may be illegal. If a statement is illegal, explain why.)

```
a{1,1} = [1 2 3; 4 5 6; 7 8 9];
a(1,2) = {'Comment line'};
a{2,1} = j;
a{2,2} = a{1,1} - a{1,1}(2,2);
```

(a) a(1,1)

(b) a{1,1}

(c) 2*a(1,1)

(d) 2*a{1,1}

(e) `a{2,2}`

(f) `a(2,3) = {[-17; 17]}`

(g) `a{2,2}(2,2)`

6. Given the definition of structure array b shown here, what will be produced by each of the following sets of statements? (*Note:* Some of these statements may be illegal. If a statement is illegal, explain why.)

```
b(1).a = -2*eye(3);
b(1).b = 'Element 1';
b(1).c = [1 2 3];
b(2).a = [b(1).c' [-1; -2; -3] b(1).c'];
b(2).b = 'Element 2';
b(2).c = [1 0 -1];
```

(a) `b(1).a - b(2).a`

(b) `strncmp(b(1).b,b(2).b,6)`

(c) `mean(b(1).c)`

(d) `mean(b.c)`

(e) `b`

(f) `b(1).('b')`

(g) `b(1)`

▶

Example 9.1—Polar Vectors

As we discussed in Chapter 2, a vector is a mathematical quantity that has both a magnitude and a direction. It can be represented as a displacement along the x and y axes in rectangular coordinates, or by a distance r at an angle θ in polar coordinates (see Figure 9.8). The relationships amongst x, y, r, and θ are given by the following equations:

$$x = r \cos \theta \tag{9.1}$$
$$y = r \sin \theta \tag{9.2}$$
$$r = \sqrt{x^2 + y^2} \tag{9.3}$$
$$\theta = \tan^{-1} \frac{y}{x} \tag{9.4}$$

A vector in rectangular format can be represented as a structure having the fields x and y; for example,

```
rect.x = 3;
rect.y = 4;
```

and a vector in polar format can be represented as a structure having the fields r and theta (where theta is in degrees); for example,

```
polar.r = 5;
polar.theta = 36.8699;
```

Write a pair of functions that convert a vector in rectangular format to a vector in polar format, and vice versa.

SOLUTION   We will create two functions: `to_rect` and `to_polar`.

The function `to_rect` must accept a vector in polar format and convert it into rectangular format using Equations (9.1) and (9.2). This function will identify a vector in polar format, because it will be stored in a structure having fields `r` and `theta`. If the input parameter is not a structure having fields `r` and `theta`, the function should generate an error message and quit. The output from the function will be a structure having fields x and y.

Function `to_polar` must accept a vector in rectangular format and convert it into rectangular format using Equations (9.3) and (9.4). This function will identify a vector in rectangular format, because it will be stored in a structure having fields x and y. If the input parameter is not a structure having fields x and y, the function should generate an error message and quit. The output from the function will be a structure having fields `r` and `theta`.

The calculation for `r` can use Equation (9.3) directly, but the calculation for `theta` needs to use the MATLAB function `atan2(y,x)`, because Equation (9.3) produces output only over the range $-\dfrac{\pi}{2} < \theta < \dfrac{\pi}{2}$, while the function `atan2` is valid in all four quadrants of the circle. Consult the MATLAB Help System for details of the operation of function `atan2`.

1. **State the problem.**

   Assume that a polar vector is stored in a structure having fields `r` and `theta` (where `theta` is in degrees), and a rectangular vector is stored in a structure having fields x and y. Write a function `to_rect` to convert a polar vector to rectangular format and a function `to_polar` to convert a rectangular vector into polar format.

2. **Define the inputs and outputs.**

   The input to function `to_rect` is a vector in polar format stored in a structure with elements `r` and `theta`, and the output is a vector in rectangular format stored in a structure with elements x and y.

   The input to function `to_polar` is a vector in rectangular format stored in a structure with elements x and y, and the output is a vector in rectangular format stored in a structure with elements `r` and `theta`.

3. **Design the algorithm.**

   The pseudocode for function `to_rect` is

   ```
   Check to see that elements r and theta exist
   out.x ← in.r * cos(in.theta * pi/180)
   out.y ← in.r * sin(in.theta * pi/180)
   ```

   (Note that we have to convert the angle in degrees into an angle in radians before applying the sine and cosine functions.)

The pseudcode for function `to_polar` is

```
Check to see that elements r and theta exist
out.r ← sqrt(in.x.^2 + in.y.^2)
out.theta ← atan2(in.y,in.x) * 180 pi
```

(Note that we have to convert the angle in radians into an angle in degrees before saving it in `theta`.)

4. **Turn the algorithm into MATLAB statements.**
   The final MATLAB functions are shown here.

```
function out = to_rect(in)
%TO_RECT Convert a vector from polar to rect
% Function TO_RECT converts a vector from polar
% coordinates to rectangular coordiantes.
%
% Calling sequence:
%   out = to_rect(in)

% Define variables:
%   in    -- Structure containing fields r and theta (in degrees)
%   out   -- Structure containing fields x and y

% Record of revisions:
%     Date          Engineer          Description of change
%     ====          ========          =====================
%   09/01/10     S. J. Chapman         Original code

% Check for valid input
if ~isfield(in,'r') || ~isfield(in,'theta')
   error('Input argument does not contain fields "r" and "theta"');
else

   % Calculate output.
   out.x = in.r * cos(in.theta * pi/180);
   out.y = in.r * sin(in.theta * pi/180);
end

function out = to_rect(in)
%TO_POLAR Convert a vector from rect to polar
% Function TO_POLAR converts a vector from rect
% coordinates to polar coordiantes.
%
% Calling sequence:
%     out = to_rect(in)
```

```
% Define variables:
% in    -- Structure containing fields x and y
% out   -- Structure containing fields r and theta (in degrees)

% Record of revisions:
%      Date            Engineer           Description of change
%      ====            ========           =====================
%    09/01/10     S. J. Chapman           Original code

% Check for valid input
if ~isfield(in,'x') || ~isfield(in,'y')
   error('Input argument does not contain fields "x" and "y"');
else

   % Calculate output.
   out.r     = sqrt(in.x .^2 + in.y .^2);
   out.theta = atan2(in.y,in.x) * 180/pi;
end
```

5. **Test the program.**

   To test this program, we will use the example of a 3-4-5 right triangle. If the rectangular vector is $(x,y) = (3,4)$, then the polar form of the vector is

   $$r = \sqrt{3^2 + 4^2} = 5$$

   $$\theta = \tan^{-1}\frac{4}{3} = 53.13°$$

   When this program is executed, the results are

   ```
   » v.x = 3;
   » v.y = 4;
   » out1 = to_polar(v)
   out1 =
            r: 5
        theta: 53.1301
   » out2 = to_rect(out1)
   out2 =
        x: 3
        y: 4
   ```

   Going to polar coordinates and then back to rectangular coordinates produced the same results that we started with.

   ◄

9.3   **Importing Data into MATLAB**

Function `uiimport` is a GUI-based way to import data from a file or from the clipboard. This command takes the forms

```
uiimport
structure = uiimport;
```

In the first case, the imported data is inserted directly into the current MATLAB workspace. In the second case, the data is converted into a structure and saved in variable `structure`.

When the command `uiimport` is typed, the Import Wizard is displayed in a window (see Figure 9.8 for the Windows 7 version of this window). The user

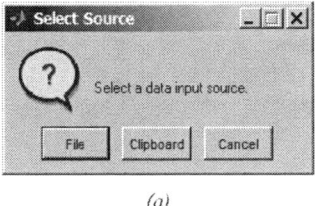

(a)

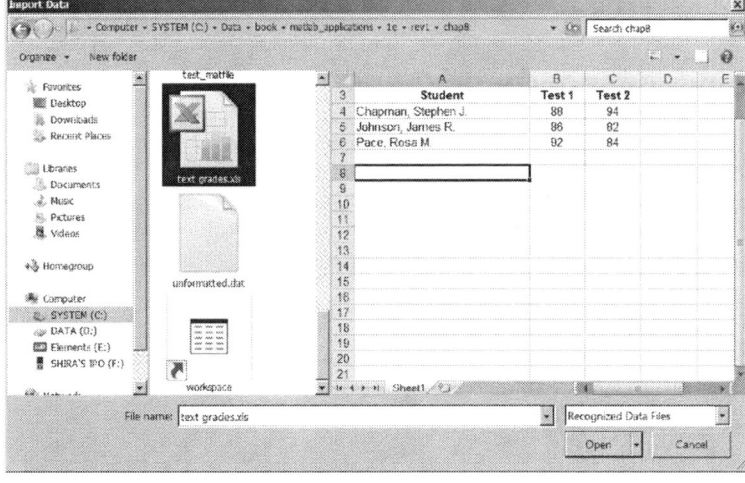

(b)

Figure 9.8   Using `uiimport`: *(a)* The Import Wizard first prompts the user to select a data source. *(b)* The Import Wizard after a file is selected but not yet loaded. *(c)* After a data file has been selected, one or more data arrays are created, and their contents can be examined. *(d)* Next, the user can select which of the data arrays will be imported into MATLAB.

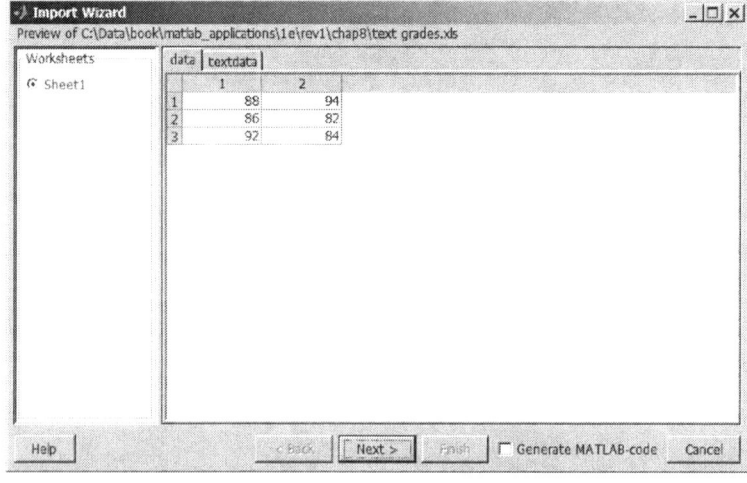

(c)

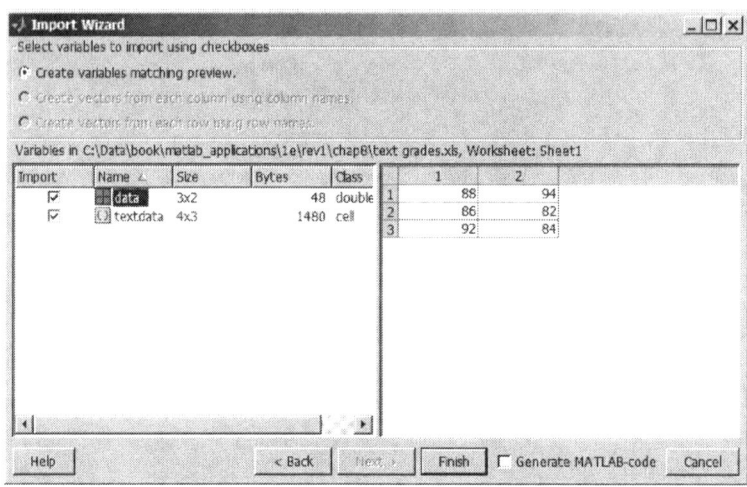

(d)

Figure 9.8 Continued

can then select the file that he or she would like to import from and the specific data within that file. Many different formats are supported—a partial list is given in Table 9-3. In addition, data can be imported from almost *any* application by saving the data on the clipboard. This flexibility can be very useful when you are trying to get data into MATLAB for analysis.

Table 9-3   Selected File Formats Supported by `uiimport`

File Extents	Meaning
`*.gif`	Image files
`*.jpg`	Image files
`*.jpeg`	Image files
`*.ico`	Image files
`*.png`	Image files
`*.pcx`	Image files
`*.tif`	Image files
`*.tiff`	Image files
`*.bmp`	Image files
`*.cur`	Cursor format
`*.hdf`	Hierarchical Data Format file
`*.au`	Sound files
`*.snd`	Sound files
`*.wav`	Sound files
`*.avi`	Movie file
`*.csv`	Spreadsheet files
`*.xls`	Spreadsheet files
`*.wk1`	Spreadsheet files
`*.txt`	Text files
`*.dat`	Text files
`*.dlm`	Text files
`*.tab`	Text files

9.4   Summary

Cell arrays are arrays whose elements are *cells*, containers that can hold other MATLAB arrays. Any sort of data may be stored in a cell, including structure arrays and other cell arrays. They provide a very flexible way to store data and are used in many internal MATLAB graphical user interface functions.

Structure arrays are a data type in which each individual element is given a name. The individual elements of a structure are known as fields, and each field in a structure may have a different type. The individual fields are addressed by combining the name of the structure with the name of the field, separated by a period. Structure arrays are useful for grouping together all of the data related to a particular person or thing into a single location.

MATLAB includes a GUI-based tool called `uiimport`, which allows users to import data into MATLAB from files created by many other programs in a wide variety of formats.

9.4.1 Summary of Good Programming Practice

The following guidelines should be adhered to:

1. Always preallocate all cell arrays before assigning values to the elements of the array. This practice greatly increases the execution speed of a program.
2. Use cell array arguments `varargin` and `varargout` to create functions that support varying numbers of input and output arguments.

9.4.2 MATLAB Summary

The following summary lists all of the MATLAB commands and functions described in this chapter, along with a brief description of each one.

Commands and Functions

`cell`	Predefines a cell array structure.
`celldisp`	Displays contents of a cell array.
`cellplot`	Plots structure of a cell array.
`cellstr`	Converts a two-dimensional character array to a cell array of strings.
`fieldnames`	Returns a list of field names in a cell array of strings.
`figure`	Creates a new figure and makes figure current.
`getfield`	Gets current value from a field.
`rmfield`	Removes a field from a structure array.
`setfield`	Sets new value into a field.
`uiimport`	Imports data to MATLAB from a file created by an external program.

9.5 Exercises

9.1 Write a MATLAB function that will accept a cell array of strings and sort them into ascending order according to the lexicographic order of the ASCII character set. (*Hint:* Look up the function `strcmp` in the MATLAB Help System.)

9.2 Write a MATLAB function that will accept a cell array of strings and sort them into ascending order according to *alphabetical order*. (This implies that you must treat 'A' and 'a' as the same letter.) (*Hint:* Look up the function `strcmpi` in the MATLAB Help System.)

9.3 Create a function that accepts any number of numeric input arguments and sums up all of the individual elements in the arguments. Test your function by passing it the four arguments a $= 10$, b $= \begin{bmatrix} 4 \\ -2 \\ 2 \end{bmatrix}$, c $= \begin{bmatrix} 1 & 0 & 3 \\ -5 & 1 & 2 \\ 1 & 2 & 0 \end{bmatrix}$, and d $= [1 \quad 5 \quad -2]$.

9.4 Modify the function of the previous exercise so that it can accept either ordinary numeric arrays or cell arrays containing numeric values. Test your function by passing it the two arguments a and b, where a $= \begin{bmatrix} 1 & 4 \\ -2 & 3 \end{bmatrix}$, b$\{1\} = [1 \quad 5 \quad 2]$, and b$\{2\} = \begin{bmatrix} 1 & -2 \\ 2 & 1 \end{bmatrix}$.

9.5 Create a structure array containing all of the information needed to plot a data set. At a minimum, the structure array should have the following fields:

- x_data   *x*-data (one or more data sets in separate cells)
- y_data   *y*-data (one or more data sets in separate cells)
- type   linear, semilogx, etc.
- plot_title   plot title
- x_label   *x*-axis label
- y_label   *y*-axis label
- x_range   *x*-axis range to plot
- y_range   *y*-axis range to plot

You may add additional fields that would enhance your control of the final plot.

After this structure array is created, create a MATLAB function that accepts an array of this structure and produces one plot for each structure in the array. The function should apply intelligent defaults if some data fields are missing. For example, if the plot_title field is an empty matrix, the function should not place a title on the graph. Think carefully about the proper defaults before starting to write your function!

To test your function, create a structure array containing the data for three plots of three different types, and pass that structure array to your function. The function should correctly plot all three data sets in three different figure windows.

9.6 Define a structure point containing two fields, x and y. The x field will contain the *x*-position of the point, and the y field will contain the *y*-position of the point. Then write a function dist3 that accepts two points and returns the distance between the two points on the Cartesian plane. Be sure to check the number of input arguments in your function.

9.7 Write a function that will accept a structure as an argument and will return two cell arrays containing the names of the fields of that structure, along with the data types of each field. Be sure to check that the input argument is a structure and will generate an error message if it is not.

9.8 Write a function that will accept a structure array of `student` as defined in this chapter, and calculate the final average of each one assuming that all exams have equal weighting. Add a new field to each array to contain the final average for that student, and return the updated structure to the calling program. Also, calculate and return the final class average.

9.9 Write a function that will accept two arguments: the first a structure array and the second a field name stored in a string. Check to make sure that these input arguments are valid. If they are not valid, print out an error message. If they are valid and the designated field is a string, concatenate all of the strings in the specified field of each element in the array, and return the resulting string to the calling program.

9.10 **Calculating Directory Sizes** Function `dir` returns the contents of a specified directory. The `dir` command returns a structure array with four fields, as shown here.

```
» d = dir('chap7')
d =
36x1 struct array with fields:
    name
    date
    bytes
    isdir
```

The field `name` contains the names of each file, `date` contains the last modification date for the file, `bytes` contains the size of the file in bytes, and `isdir` is 0 for conventional files and 1 for directories. Write a function that accepts a directory name and path and returns the total size of all files in the directory, in bytes.

9.11 **Recursion** A function is said to be *recursive* if the function calls itself. Modify the function created in Exercise 9.10 so that it calls itself when it finds a subdirectory and sums up the size of all files in the current directory plus all subdirectories.

9.12 **Vector Addition** Write a function that will accept two vectors defined in either rectangular or polar coordinates (as defined in Example 9.1), add them, and save the result in rectangular coordinates.

9.13 **Vector Subtraction** Write a function that will accept two vectors defined in either rectangular or polar coordinates (as defined in Example 9.1), subtract them, and save the result in rectangular coordinates.

9.14 **Vector Multiplication** If two vectors are defined in polar coordinates so that $\mathbf{v}_1 = r_1 \angle \theta_1$ and $\mathbf{v}_2 = r_2 \angle \theta_2$, the product of the two vectors is $\mathbf{v}_1 \mathbf{v}_2 = r_1 r_2 \angle \theta_1 + \theta_2$. Write a function that will accept two vectors defined in either rectangular or polar coordinates (as defined in Example 9.1), perform the multiplication, and save the result in polar coordinates.

9.15   **Vector Division** If two vectors are defined in polar coordinates so that $\mathbf{v}_1 = r_1 \angle \theta_1$ and $\mathbf{v}_2 = r_2 \angle \theta_2$, then $\dfrac{\mathbf{v}_1}{\mathbf{v}_2} = \dfrac{r_1}{r_2} \angle \theta_1 - \theta_2$. Write a function that will accept two vectors defined in either rectangular or polar coordinates (as defined in Example 9.1), perform the division, and save the result in polar coordinates.

9.16   **Distance Between Two Points** If $\mathbf{v}_1$ is the distance from the origin to point P_1 and $\mathbf{v}_2$ is the distance from the origin to point P_2, the distance between the two points will be $|\mathbf{v}_1 - \mathbf{v}_2|$. Write a function that will accept two vectors defined in either rectangular or polar coordinates (as defined in Example 9.1) and will return the distance between the two.

CHAPTER 10

Handle Graphics and Animation

In this chapter, we will learn about a low-level way to manipulate MATLAB plots (called handle graphics), and about how to created animations and movies in MATLAB.

10.1 Handle Graphics

Handle graphics is the name of a set of low-level graphics functions that control the characteristics of graphics objects generated by MATLAB. These functions are normally hidden inside M-files, but they are very important to program developers, since they allow them to have fine control of the appearance of the plots and graphs they generate. For example, it is possible to use handle graphics to turn on a grid on the *x*-axis only or to choose a line color such as orange, which is not supported by the standard `LineSpec` option of the `plot` command.

This section introduces the structure of the MATLAB graphics system and explains how to control the properties of graphical objects to create a desired display.

10.1.1 The MATLAB Graphics System

The MATLAB graphics system is based on a hierarchical system of **graphics objects**, each of which is known by a unique number called a **handle**. Each graphics object has special data called **properties** associated with it, and modifying those properties will modify the behavior of the object. For example, a **line** is one type of graphics object. The properties associated with a line object include *x*-data, *y*-data, color, line style, line width, marker type, and so forth. Modifying any of these properties will change the way the line is displayed in a Figure Window.

Every component of a MATLAB graph is a graphical object. For example, each line, axis, and text string is a separate object with its own unique identifying number (handle) and characteristics. All graphical objects are arranged in a hierarchy with **parent objects** and **child objects**, as shown in Figure 10.1. When a child object is created, it inherits many of its properties from its parent.

The highest-level graphics object in MATLAB is the **root**, which can be thought of as the entire computer screen. The handle of the root object is always 0. It is created automatically when MATLAB starts up, and it is always present until the program is shut down. The properties associated with the root object are the defaults that apply to all MATLAB windows.

Under the root, there can be one or more Figure Windows or just **figures**. Each figure is a separate window on the computer screen that can display graphical data, and each figure has its own properties. The properties associated with a figure include color, color map, paper size, paper orientation, pointer type, and so forth.

Each figure can contain seven types of objects: uimenus, uicontextmenus, uicontrols, uitoolbars, uipanels, uibuttongroups, and axes. Uimenus, uicontextmenus, uicontrols, uitoolbars,

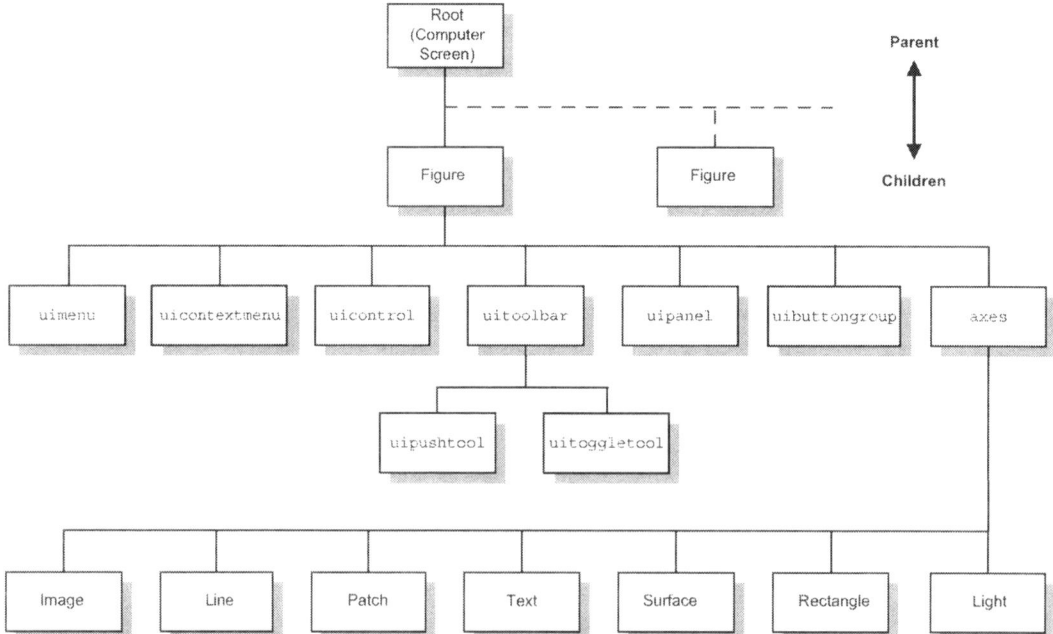

Figure 10.1 The hierarchy of handle graphics objects.

uipanels, and uibuttongroups are special graphics objects used to create graphical user interfaces—they are not discussed in this book. Axes are regions within a figure where data is actually plotted. There can be more than one set of axes in a single figure.

Each set of axes can contain as many lines, text strings, patches, and so forth as necessary to create the plot of interest.

10.1.2 Object Handles

Each graphics object has a unique name called a **handle**. The handle is a unique integer or real number that is used by MATLAB to identify the object. A handle is automatically returned by any function that creates a graphics object. For example, the function call

```
» hndl = figure;
```

creates a new figure and returns the handle of that figure in variable hndl. Another example is the plot function. The statement

```
» hndl = plot(x,y);
```

plots a line on the current axes (first creating a figure and axes, if they do not exist) and returns the handle of the variable hndl.

The handle of the root object is always 0, and the handle of each figure is normally a small positive integer, such as 1, 2, 3, ... The handles of all other graphics objects are arbitrary floating-point numbers.

There are MATLAB functions available to get the handles of figures, axes, and other objects. For example, the function gcf returns the handle of the currently selected figure, gca returns the handle of the currently selected axes within the currently selected figure, and gco returns the handle of the currently selected object. These functions are discussed in more detail later.

By convention, handles are usually stored in variables that begin with the letter h. This practice helps us to recognize handles in MATLAB programs.

10.1.3 Examining and Changing Object Properties

Object properties are special values associated with an object that control some aspect of how that object behaves. Each property has a **property name** and an associated value. The property names are strings that are typically displayed in mixed case with the first letter of each word capitalized, but MATLAB recognizes a property name regardless of the case in which it is written.

When an object is created, all of its properties are automatically initialized to default values. These default values can be overridden at creation time by including 'PropertyName', value pairs in the object creation function.[1] For example,

---

[1]Examples of object creation functions include figure, which creates a new figure; axes, which creates a new set of axes within a figure; and line, which creates a line within a set of axes. Highlevel functions such as plot are also object creation functions.

we saw in Chapter 3 that the width of a line could be modified in the `plot` command as follows.

```
plot(x,y,'LineWidth',2);
```

This function overrides the default `LineWidth` property with the value 2 at the time the line object is created.

The properties of any object can be examined at any time using the `get` function and can be modified using the `set` function. These functions are especially useful for programmers, because they can be directly inserted into MATLAB programs to modify a figure based on a user's input.

The most common forms of `get` function are

```
value = get(handle,'PropertyName');
value = get(handle);
```

where `value` is the value contained in the specified property of the object whose handle is supplied. If only the handle is included in the function call, the function returns a structure array in which the field names are all of the properties of the object, and the field values are the property values.

The most common form of the `set` function is

```
set(handle,'PropertyName1',value1,...);
```

where there can be any number of `'PropertyName'`,`value` pairs in a single function.

For example, suppose that we plotted the function $y(x) = x^2$ from 0 to 2 with the following statements:

```
x = 0:0.1:2;
y = x.^2;
hndl = plot(x,y);
```

The resulting plot is shown in Figure 10.2(a). The handle of the plotted line is stored in `hndl`, and we can use it to examine or modify the properties of the line. The function `get(hndl)` will return all of the properties of this line in a structure, with each property name being an element of the structure.

```
» result = get(hndl)
result =
                Color: [0 0 1]
            EraseMode: 'normal'
            LineStyle: '-'
            LineWidth: 0.5000
               Marker: 'none'
           MarkerSize: 6
      MarkerEdgeColor: 'auto'
      MarkerFaceColor: 'none'
                XData: [1x21 double]
                YData: [1x21 double]
```

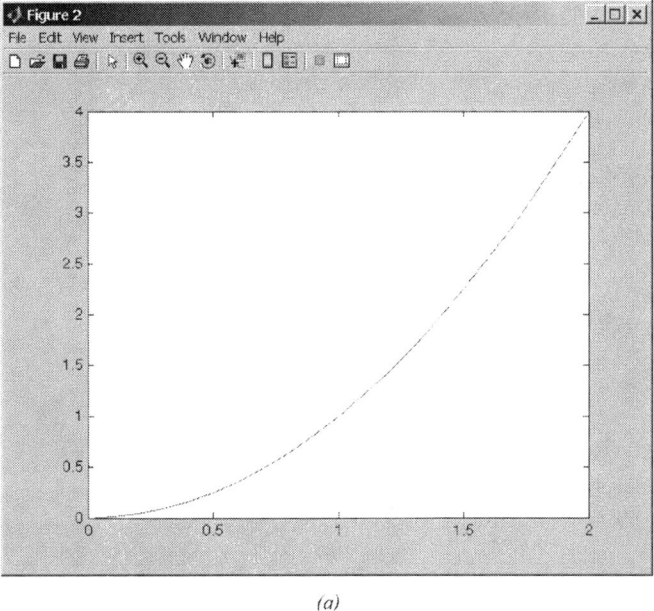

(a)

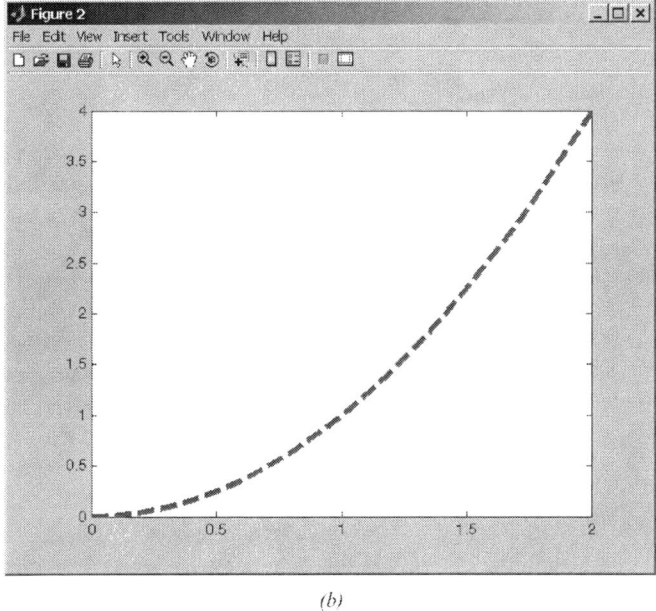

(b)

Figure 10.2 *(a)* Plot of the function $y = x^2$ using the default linewidth. *(b)* Plot of the function after modifying the LineWidth and LineStyle properties.

```
            ZData: [1x0 double]
     BeingDeleted: 'off'
    ButtonDownFcn: []
         Children: [0x1 double]
         Clipping: 'on'
        CreateFcn: []
        DeleteFcn: []
       BusyAction: 'queue'
 HandleVisibility: 'on'
          HitTest: 'on'
    Interruptible: 'on'
         Selected: 'off'
 SelectionHighlight: 'on'
              Tag: ''
             Type: 'line'
    UIContextMenu: []
         UserData: []
          Visible: 'on'
           Parent: 303.0004
      DisplayName: ''
        XDataMode: 'manual'
      XDataSource: ''
      YDataSource: ''
      ZDataSource: ''
```

Note that the current line width is 0.5 pixels and the current line style is a solid line. We can change the line width and the line style with the commands

```
» set(hndl,'LineWidth',4,'LineStyle','--')
```

The plot after this command is issued is shown in Figure 10.2(*b*).

For the end user, however, it is often easier to change the properties of a MATLAB object interactively. The Property Editor is a GUI-based tool designed for this purpose. The Property Editor is started by first selecting the Edit button (▷) on the figure toolbar and then clicking on the object that you want to modify with the mouse. Alternatively, the property editor can be started from the command line.

```
propedit(HandleList);
propedit;
```

For example, the following statements will create a plot containing the line $y = x^2$ over the range 0 to 2 and will open the Property Editor to allow the user to interactively change the properties of the line.

```
figure(2);
x = 0:0.1:2;
y = x.^2;
hndl = plot(x,y);
propedit(hndl);
```

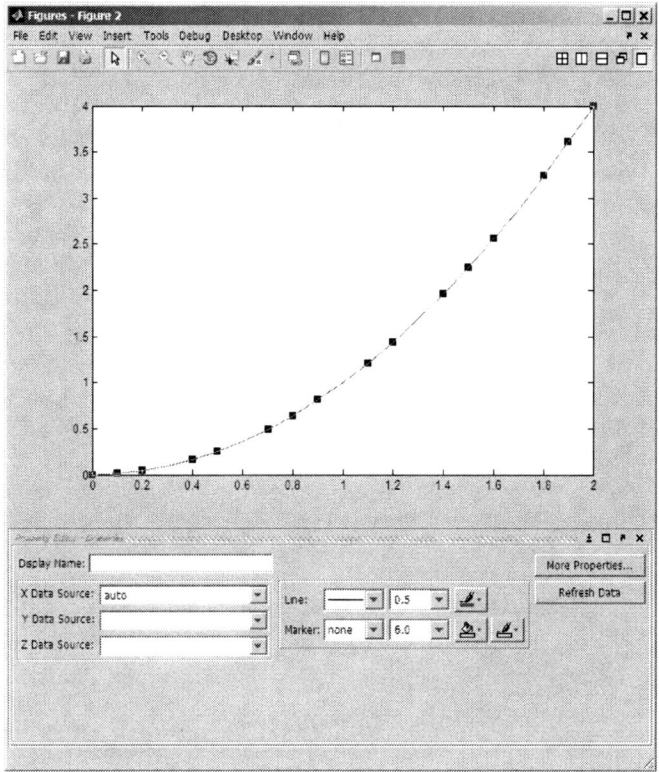

Figure 10.3 The Property Editor when editing a line object. Changes in style are immediately displayed on the figure as the object is edited.

The Property Editor invoked by these statements is shown in Figure 10.3. The Property Editor contains a series of panes that vary depending on the type of object being modified.

▶

Example 10.1—Using Low-Level Graphics Commands

The function sinc(x) is defined by the equation

$$\operatorname{sinc} x = \begin{cases} \dfrac{\sin x}{x} & x \neq 0 \\ 1 & x = 0 \end{cases} \tag{10.1}$$

Plot this function from $x = -3\pi$ to $x = 3\pi$. Use handle graphics functions to customize the plot as follows:

1. Make the figure background pink.
2. Use y-axis grid lines only (no x-axis grid lines).
3. Plot the function as a 2-point-wide solid orange line.

SOLUTION   To create this graph, we need to plot the function sinc x from $x = -3\pi$ to $x = 3\pi$ using the plot function. The plot function will return a handle for the line that we can save and use later.

After plotting the line, we need to modify the color of the *figure* object, the grid status of the *axes* object, and the color and width of the *line* object. These modifications require us to have access to the handles of the figure, axes, and line objects. The handle of the figure object is returned by the gcf function, the handle of the axes object is returned by the gca function, and the handle of the line object is returned by the plot function that created it.

The low-level graphics properties that need to be modified can be found by referring to the on-line MATLAB Help browser documentation under the topic "Handle Graphics." They are the 'Color' property of the current figure, the 'YGrid' property of the current axes, and the 'LineWidth' and 'Color' properties of the line.

1. **State the problem.**
   Plot the function sinc x from $x = -3\pi$ to $x = 3\pi$ using a figure with a pink background, y-axis grid lines only, and a 2-point-wide solid orange line.

2. **Define the inputs and outputs.**
   There are no inputs to this program, and the only output is the specified figure.

3. **Describe the algorithm.**
   This program can be broken down into three major steps:

   ```
   Calculate sinc(x)
   Plot sinc(x)
   Modify the required graphics object properties
   ```

   The first major step is to calculate sinc x from $x = -3\pi$ to $x = 3\pi$. This can be done with vectorized statements, but the vectorized statements will produce a NaN at $x = 0$, since the division of 0/0 is undefined. We must replace the NaN with a 1.0 before plotting the function. The detailed pseudocode for this step is

   ```
   % Calculate sinc(x)
   x = -3*pi:pi/10:3*pi
   y = sin(x) ./ x

   % Find the zero value and fix it up. The zero is
   % located in the middle of the x array.
   index = fix(length(y)/2) + 1
   y(index) = 1
   ```

   Next, we must plot the function, saving the handle of the resulting line for further modifications. The detailed pseudocode for this step is

   ```
   hndl = plot(x,y);
   ```

Now we must use handle graphics commands to modify the figure background, *y*-axis grid, and line width and color. Remember that the figure handle can be recovered with the function gcf, and the axis handle can be recovered with the function gca. The color pink can be created with the RGB vector [1 0.8 0.8], and the color orange can be created with the RGB vector [1 0.5 0]. The detailed pseudocode for this step is

```
set(gcf,'Color',[1 0.8 0.8])
set(gca,'YGrid','on')
set(hndl,'Color',[1 0.5 0],'LineWidth',2)
```

4. **Turn the algorithm into MATLAB statements.**
   The final MATLAB program is shown here.

```
% Script file: plotsinc.m
%
% Purpose:
%   This program illustrates the use of handle graphics
%   commands by creating a plot of sinc(x) from -3*pi to
%   3*pi, and modifying the characteristics of the figure,
%   axes, and line using the "set" function.
%
% Record of revisions:
%     Date          Programmer          Description of change
%     ====          ==========          =====================
%   04/02/10      S. J. Chapman         Original code
%
% Define variables:
%   hndl           -- Handle of line
%   x              -- Independent variable
%   y              -- sinc(x)

% Calculate sinc(x)
x = -3*pi:pi/10:3*pi;
y = sin(x) ./ x;

% Find the zero value and fix it up. The zero is
% located in the middle of the x array.
index = fix(length(y)/2) + 1;
y(index) = 1;

% Plot the function.
hndl = plot(x,y);

% Now modify the figure to create a pink background,
% modify the axis to turn on y-axis grid lines, and
% modify the line to be a 2-point wide orange line.
set(gcf,'Color',[1 0.8 0.8]);
set(gca,'YGrid','on');
set(hndl,'Color',[1 0.5 0],'LineWidth',2);
```

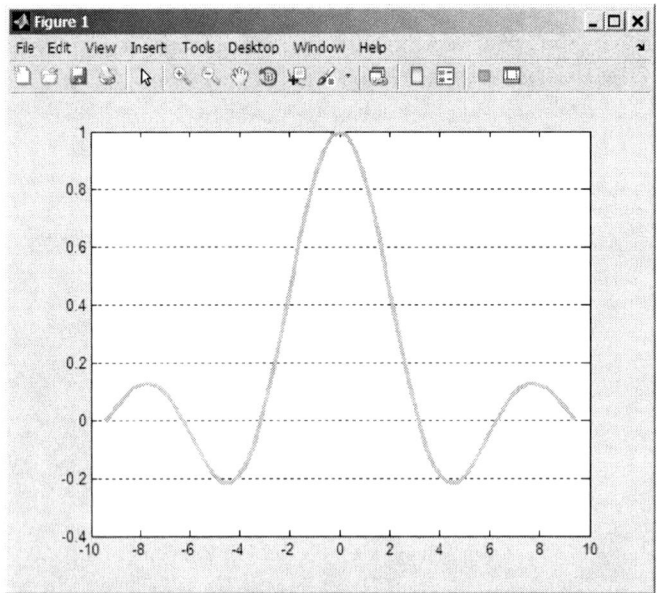

Figure 10.4 Plot of sinc *x* versus *x*.

5. **Test the program.**
   Testing this program is very simple—we just execute it and examine the
   resulting plot. The plot created is shown in Figure 10.4, and it does have
   the characteristics that we wanted.
   ◄

10.1.4   Using `set` to List Possible Property Values

The `set` function can be used to provide lists of possible property values. If a
`set` function call contains a property name but not a corresponding value, `set`
returns a list of all of the legal choices for that property. For example, the command `set(hndl,'LineStyle')` will return a list of all legal line styles with
the default choice in brackets:

```
» set(hndl,'LineStyle')
ans =
    '-'
    '--'
    ':'
    '-.'
    'none'
```

This function shows that the legal line styles are `'-'`, `'--'`, `':'`, `'-.'`, and
`'none'`, with the first choice as the default.

If the property does not have a fixed set of values, MATLAB returns an empty cell array:

```
» set(hndl,'LineWidth')
ans =
     {}
```

The function set(hndl) will return all of the possible choices for all of the properties of an object.

```
» xxx = set(hndl)
xxx =
                  Color: {}
              EraseMode: {4x1 cell}
              LineStyle: {5x1 cell}
              LineWidth: {}
                 Marker: {14x1 cell}
             MarkerSize: {}
        MarkerEdgeColor: {2x1 cell}
        MarkerFaceColor: {2x1 cell}
                  XData: {}
                  YData: {}
                  ZData: {}
          ButtonDownFcn: {}
               Children: {}
               Clipping: {2x1 cell}
              CreateFcn: {}
              DeleteFcn: {}
              BusyAction: {2x1 cell}
       HandleVisibility: {3x1 cell}
                HitTest: {2x1 cell}
          Interruptible: {2x1 cell}
               Selected: {2x1 cell}
     SelectionHighlight: {2x1 cell}
                    Tag: {}
          UIContextMenu: {}
               UserData: {}
                Visible: {2x1 cell}
                 Parent: {}
            DisplayName: {}
              XDataMode: {2x1 cell}
            XDataSource: {}
            YDataSource: {}
            ZDataSource: {}
```

Any of the items in this list can be expanded to see the available list of options.

```
» xxx.EraseMode
ans =
    'normal'
    'background'
    'xor'
    'none'
```

10.1.5 Finding Objects

Each new graphics object that is created has its own handle, and that handle is returned by the creating function. If you intend to modify the properties of an object that you create, it is a good idea to save the handle for later use with get and set.

✳ Good Programming Practice

If you intend to modify the properties of an object that you create, save the handle of that object for later use with get and set.

However, sometimes we might not have access to the handle. Suppose that we lost a handle for some reason. How can we examine and modify the graphics objects?

MATLAB provides four special functions to help find the handles of objects.

- gcf   Returns the handle of the current *figure.*
- gca   Returns the handle of the current *axes* in the current *figure.*
- gco   Returns the handle of the current *object.*
- findobj   Finds a graphics object with a specified property value.

The function gcf returns the handle of the current figure. If no figure exists, gcf *will create one* and return its handle. The function gca returns the handle of the current axes within the current figure. If no figure exists or if the current figure exists but contains no axes, gca *will create a set of axes* and return its handle. The function gco has the form

```
h_obj = gco;
h_obj = gco(h_fig);
```

where h_obj is the handle of the object and h_fig is the handle of a figure. The first form of this function returns the handle of the *current object in the current figure,* while the second form of the function returns the handle of the *current object in a specified figure.*

The current object is defined as the last object clicked on with the mouse. This object can be any graphics object except the root. There will not be a current object in a figure until a mouse click has occurred within that figure. Before the first mouse click, function gco will return an empty array [ ]. Unlike gcf and gca, gco does not create an object if it does not exist.

Once the handle of an object is known, we can determine the type of the object by examining its 'Type' property. The 'Type' property will be a character string, such as 'figure', 'line', 'text', and so forth.

```
h_obj = gco;
type = get(h_obj,'Type')
```

The easiest way to find an arbitrary MATLAB object is with the findobj function. The basic form of this function is

```
hndls = findobj('PropertyName1',value1,...)
```

This command starts at the root object and searches the entire tree for all objects that have the specified values for the specified properties. Note that multiple property/value pairs may be specified, and findobj returns only the handles of objects that match *all* of them.

For example, suppose that we have created Figures 1 and 3. Then the function findobj('Type','figure') will return the results:

```
» h_fig = findobj('Type','figure')
h_fig =
        3
        1
```

This form of the findobj function is very useful, but it can be slow, since it must search through the entire object tree to locate any matches. If you must use an object multiple times, make only one call to findobj and save the handle for re-use.

Restricting the number of objects that must be searched can increase the execution speed of this function. This can be done with the following form of the function:

```
hndls = findobj(Srchhndls,'PropertyName1', value1,...)
```

Here, only the handles listed in array Srchhndls and their children will be searched to find the object. For example, suppose that you wanted to find all of the dashed lines in Figure 1. The command to do this would be:

```
hndls = findobj(1,'Type','line','LineStyle','--');
```

✳ Good Programming Practice

If possible, restrict the scope of your searches with findobj to make them faster.

10.1.6 Selecting Objects with the Mouse

Function gco returns the handle of the current object, which is the last object clicked on by the mouse. Each object has a **selection region** associated with it, and any mouse click within that selection region is assumed to be a click on that object. This is important for thin objects such as lines or points—the selection region allows the user to be slightly sloppy in mouse position and still select the line. The width of and shape of the selection region varies for different types of objects. For instance, the selection region for a line is 5 pixels on either side of the line, while the selection region for a surface, patch, or text object is the smallest rectangle that can contain the object.

The selection region for an axes object is the area of the axes plus the area of the titles and labels. However, lines or other objects inside the axes have a higher priority, so to select the axes, you must click on a point within the axes that is not near lines or text. Clicking on a figure outside of the axes region will select the figure itself.

What happens if a user clicks on a point that has two or more objects, such as the intersection of two lines? The answer depends on the **stacking order** of the objects. The stacking order is the order in which MATLAB selects objects. This order is specified by the order of the handles listed in the 'Children' property of a figure. If a click is in the selection region of two or more objects, the one with the highest position in the 'Children' list will be selected.

MATLAB includes a function called waitforbuttonpress that is sometimes used when selecting graphics objects. The form of this function is

```
k = waitforbuttonpress
```

When this function is executed, it halts the program until either a key is pressed or a mouse button is clicked. The function returns 0 if it detects a mouse button click or 1 if it detects a key press.

The function can be used to pause a program until a mouse click occurs. After the mouse click occurs, the program can recover the handle of the selected object using the gco function.

▶

Example 10.2—Selecting Graphics Objects

The program that follows explores the properties of graphics objects and incidentally shows how to select objects using waitforbuttonpress and gco. The program allows objects to be selected repeatedly until a key press occurs.

```
% Script file: select_object.m
%
% Purpose:
%   This program illustrates the use of waitforbuttonpress
%   and gco to select graphics objects. It creates a plot
%   of sin(x) and cos(x), and then allows a user to select
%   any object and examine its properties. The program
%   terminates when a key press occurs.
```

```
%
% Record of revisions:
%      Date         Programmer          Description of change
%      ====         ==========          =====================
%    04/02/10     S. J. Chapman        Original code
%
% Define variables:
%    details       -- Object details
%    h1            -- handle of sine line
%    h2            -- handle of cosine line
%    handle        -- handle of current object
%    k             -- Result of waitforbuttonpress
%    type          -- Object type
%    x             -- Independent variable
%    y1            -- sin(x)
%    y2            -- cos(x)
%    yn            -- Yes/No

% Calculate sin(x) and cos(x)
x = -3*pi:pi/10:3*pi;
y1 = sin(x);
y2 = cos(x);

% Plot the functions.
h1 = plot(x,y1);
set(h1,'LineWidth',2);
hold on;
h2 = plot(x,y2);
set(h2,'LineWidth',2,'LineStyle',':','Color','r');
title('\bfPlot of sin \itx \rm\bf and cos \itx');
xlabel('\bf\itx');
ylabel('\bfsin \itx \rm\bf and cos \itx');
legend('sine','cosine');
hold off;

% Now set up a loop and wait for a mouse click.
k = waitforbuttonpress;

while k == 0

   % Get the handle of the object
   handle = gco;

   % Get the type of this object.
   type = get(handle,'Type');

   % Display object type
   disp (['Object type = ' type '.']);
```

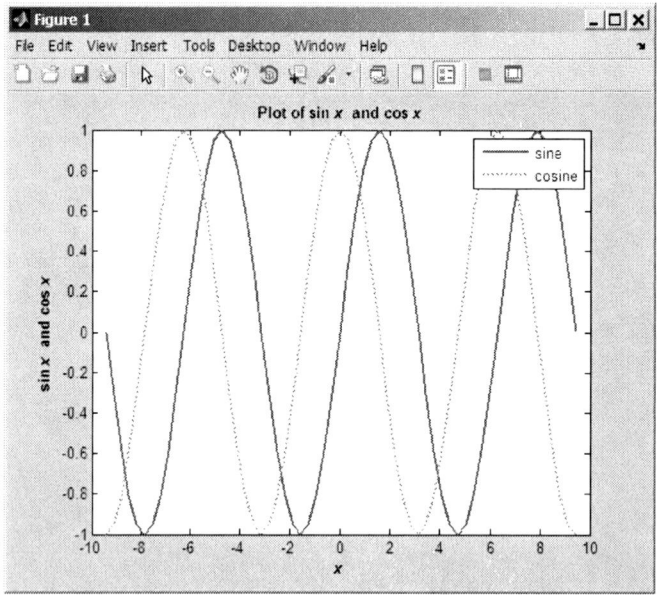

Figure 10.5 Plot of sin *x* and cos *x*.

```
% Do we display the details?
yn = input('Do you want to display details? (y/n) ','s');

if yn == 'y'
   details = get(handle);
   disp(details);
end

% Check for another mouse click
k = waitforbuttonpress;
end
```

When this program is executed, it produces the plot shown in Figure 10.5. Experiment by clicking on various objects on the plot and seeing the resulting characteristics. ◄

10.2 Position and Units

Many MATLAB objects have a `'position'` property, which specifies the size and position of the object on the computer screen. This property differs slightly for different kinds of objects, as described in the following text.

10.2.1   Positions of `figure` Objects

The `'position'` property for a figure specifies the location of that figure on the computer screen using a four-element row vector. The values in this vector are `[left bottom width height]`, where `left` is the leftmost edge of the figure, `bottom` is the bottom edge of the figure, `width` is the width of the figure, and `height` is the height of the figure. These position values are in the units specified in the `'Units'` property for the object. For example, the position and units associated with a the current figure can be found as follows:

```
» get(gcf,'Position')
ans =
    176   204   672   504
» get(gcf,'Units')
ans =
    pixels
```

This information specifies that the lower-left corner of the figure window is 176 pixels to the right and 204 pixels above the lower-left corner of the screen, and the figure is 672 pixels wide by 504 pixels high. This is the drawable region of the figure, excluding borders, scrollbars, menus, and the figure title area.

The `'units'` property of a figure defaults to pixels, but it can be inches, centimeters, points, characters, or normalized coordinates. Pixels are screen pixels, which are the smallest rectangular shape that can be drawn on a computer screen. Typical computer screens are at least 640 pixels wide × 480 pixels high, and screens can have more than 1000 pixels in each direction. Since the number of pixels varies from computer screen to computer screen, the size of an object specified in pixels will also vary.

Normalized coordinates are coordinates in the range 0 to 1, where the lower-left corner of the screen is at (0,0) and the upper-right corner of the screen is at (1,1). If an object position is specified in normalized coordinates, it will appear in the same relative position on the screen, regardless of screen resolution. For example, the following statements create a figure and place it into the upper-left quadrant of the screen on any computer, regardless of screen size.[2]

```
h1 = figure(1)
set(h1,'units','normalized','position',[0 .5 .5 .45])
```

✳ **Good Programming Practice**

If you would like to place a window in a specific location, it is easier to place the window at the desired location using normalized coordinates, and the results will be the same, regardless of the computer's screen resolution.

---

[2]The normalized height of this figure is reduced to 0.45 to allow room for the Figure title and menu bar, both of which are above the drawing area.

10.2.2   Positions of `axes` Objects

The position of `axes` objects is also specified by a 4-element vector, but the object position is specified relative to the lower-left corner of the *figure* instead of the position of the screen. In general, the `'Position'` property of a child object is relative to the position of its parent.

By default, the positions of axes objects are specified in *normalized* units within a figure, with (0,0) representing the lower-left corner of the figure and (1,1) representing the upper-right corner of the figure.

10.2.3   Positions of `text` Objects

Unlike other objects, `text` objects have a position property containing only two or three elements. These elements correspond to the x, y, and z values of the text object *within* an `axes` object. Note that these values are in the units being displayed on the axes themselves.

The position of the text object with respect to the specified point is controlled by the object's `HorizontalAlignment` and `VerticalAlignment` properties. The `HorizontalAlignment` can be {Left}, Center, or Right, and the `VerticalAlignment` can be Top, Cap, {Middle}, Baseline, or Bottom.

The size of `text` objects is determined by the font size and the number of characters being displayed, so there are no height and width values associated with them.

▶
━━

Example 10.3—Positioning Objects within a Figure

As we mentioned earlier, axes positions are defined relative to the lower-left corner of the frame they are contained in; whereas, text object positions are defined within axes in the data units being displayed on the axes.

To illustrate the positioning of graphics objects within a figure, we will write a program that creates two overlapping sets of axes within a single figure. The first set of axes will display $\sin x$ versus x and will have a text comment attached to the display line. The second set of axes will display $\cos x$ versus x and will have a text comment in the lower-left corner.

A program to create the figure is shown next. Note that we are using the `figure` function to create an empty figure and then two `axes` functions to create the two sets of axes within the figure. The position of the `axes` functions is specified in normalized units within the figure. The first set of axes, which starts at (0.05,0.05), is in the lower-left corner of the figure, and the second set of axes, which starts at (0.45,0.45), is in the upper-right corner of the figure. Each set of axes has the appropriate function plotted on it.

The first `text` object is attached to the first set of axes at position $(-\pi, 0)$, which is a point on the curve. The `'HorizontalAlignment'`, `'right'` property is selected, so the *attachment point* $(-\pi, 0)$ is on the *right-hand side* of the text string. As a result, the text appears to the *left* of the of the attachment point in the final figure. (This can be confusing for new programmers!)

The second `text` object is attached to the second set of axes at position (−7.5, −0.9), which is near the lower-left corner of the axes. This string uses the default horizontal alignment, which is `'left'`, so the attachment point (−7.5, −0.9) is on the *left-hand side* of the text string. As a result, the text appears to the right of the attachment point in the final figure.

```
% Script file: position_object.m
%
% Purpose:
%   This program illustrates the positioning of graphics
%   graphics objects. It creates a figure, and then places
%   two overlapping sets of axes on the figure. The first
%   set of axes is placed in the lower left hand corner of
%   the figure, and contains a plot of sin(x). The second
%   set of axes is placed in the upper right hand corner of
%   the figure, and contains a plot of cos(x). Then two
%   text strings are added to the axes, illustrating the
%   positioning of text within axes.
%
% Record of revisions:
%     Date          Programmer        Description of change
%     ====          ==========        =====================
%   04/02/10     S. J. Chapman        Original code
%
% Define variables:
%   h1               -- Handle of sine line
%   h2               -- Handle of cosine line
%   ha1              -- Handle of first axes
%   ha2              -- Handle of second axes
%   x                -- Independent variable
%   y1               -- sin(x)
%   y2               -- cos(x)
% Calculate sin(x) and cos(x)
x = -2*pi:pi/10:2*pi;
y1 = sin(x);
y2 = cos(x);

% Create a new figure
figure;

% Create the first set of axes and plot sin(x).
% Note that the position of the axes is expressed
% in normalized units.
ha1 = axes('Position',[.05 .05 .5 .5]);
h1 = plot(x,y1);
```

```
set(h1,'LineWidth',2);
title('\bfPlot of sin \itx');
xlabel('\bf\itx');
ylabel('\bfsin \itx');
axis([-8 8 -1 1]);

% Create the second set of axes and plot cos(x).
% Note that the position of the axes is expressed
% in normalized units.
ha2 = axes('Position',[.45 .45 .5 .5]);
h2 = plot(x,y1);
set(h2,'LineWidth',2,'Color','r','LineStyle','--');
title('\bfPlot of cos \itx');
xlabel('\bf\itx');
ylabel('\bfsin \itx');
axis([-8 8 -1 1]);

% Create a text string attached to the line on the first
% set of axes.
axes(ha1);
text(-pi,0.0,'sin(x)\rightarrow','HorizontalAlignment','right');

% Create a text string in the lower left hand corner
% of the second set of axes.
axes(ha2);
text(-7.5,-0.9,'Test string 2');
```

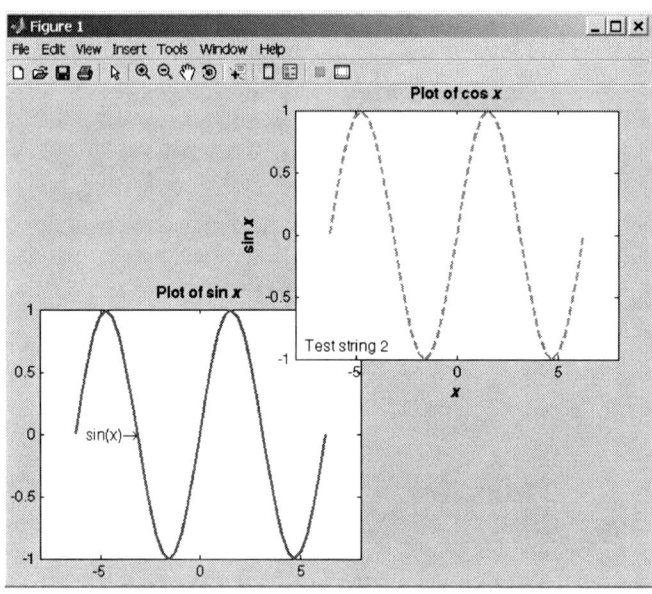

Figure 10.6 The output of program position_object.

ASCII
Character Set

MATLAB strings use the ASCII character set that consists of the 127 characters shown in the table that follows. The results of MATLAB string comparison operations depend on the *relative lexicographic positions* of the characters being compared. For example, the character 'a' in the ASCII character set is a position 97 in the table, while the character 'A' is at position 65. Therefore, the relational operator 'a' > 'A' will return a 1 (true), since 97 > 65.

Each MATLAB character is stored in a 16-bit field, which means that in the future, MATLAB can support the entire Unicode character set.

The table shown below shows the ASCII character set with the first two digits of the character number defined by the row and the third digit defined by the column. Thus, the letter 'R' is on row 8 and column 2, so it is character 82 in the ASCII character set.

	0	1	2	3	4	5	6	7	8	9
0	nul	soh	stx	etx	eot	enq	ack	bel	bs	ht
1	nl	vt	ff	cr	so	si	dle	dc1	dc2	dc3
2	dc4	nak	syn	etb	can	em	sub	esc	fs	gs
3	rs	us	sp	!	"	#	$	%	&	'
4	(	)	*	+	,	-	.	/	0	1
5	2	3	4	5	6	7	8	9	:	;
6	<	=	>	?	@	A	B	C	D	E
7	F	G	H	I	J	K	L	M	N	O
8	P	Q	R	S	T	U	V	W	X	Y
9	Z	[	\	]	^	_	`	a	b	c
10	d	e	f	g	h	I	j	k	l	m
11	n	o	p	q	r	s	t	u	v	w
12	x	y	z	{	|	}	~	del		

Additional MATLAB Input/Output Functions

In Chapter 2, we learned how to load and save MATLAB data using the `load` and `save` commands and how to write out formatted data using the `fprintf` function. In Chapter 5, we also learned about the `textread` function, and in Chapter 9, we learned about function `uiimport`. This appendix includes additional details about MATLAB's input/output capabilities.

B.1 MATLAB File Processing

To use files within a MATLAB program, we need some way to select the desired file and to read from or write to it. MATLAB has a series of C-like functions to read and write files, whether they are on disk, magnetic tape, or some other device attached to the computer. These functions open, read, write, and close files using a **file id** (sometimes known as **fid**). The file id is a number assigned to a file when it is opened and is used for all reading, writing, and control operations on that file. The file id is a positive integer. Two file id's are always open—file id 1 is the standard output device (`stdout`) and file id 2 is the standard error (`stderr`) device for the computer on which MATLAB is executing. Additional file id's are assigned as files are opened and released as files are closed.

Several MATLAB functions can be used to control disk file input and output. The file I/O functions are summarized in Table B-1. The file opening, closing, reading, and writing functions are described next. For details of the positioning and status functions, see the MATLAB documentation.

Table B-1 MATLAB Input/Output Functions

Category	Function	Description
File Opening and Closing	fopen	Open file.
	fclose	Close file.
Binary I/O	fread	Read binary data from file.
	fwrite	Write binary data to file.
Formatted I/O	fscanf	Read formatted data from file.
	fprintf	Write formatted data to file.
	fgetl	Read line from file, discard newline character.
	fgets	Read line from file, keep newline character.
File Positioning, Status, and Miscellaneous	delete	Delete file.
	exist	Check for the existence of a file.
	ferror	Inquire file I/O error status.
	feof	Test for end-of-file.
	fseek	Set file position.
	ftell	Check file position.
	frewind	Rewind file.
Temporary Files	tempdir	Get temporary directory name.
	tempname	Get temporary file name.

File id's are assigned to disk files or devices using the fopen statement and detached from them using the fclose statement. Once a file is attached to a file id using the fopen statement, we can read and write to that file using MATLAB file input and output statements. When we are through with the file, the fclose statement closes the file and makes the file id invalid. The frewind and fseek statements may be used to change the current reading or writing position in a file while it is open.

Data can be written to and read from files in two possible ways: as binary data or as formatted character data. Binary data consists of the actual bit patterns that are used to store the data in computer memory. Reading and writing binary data is very efficient, but a user cannot directly examine the data stored in the file. Data in formatted files is translated into characters that can be read directly by a user. However, formatted I/O operations are slower and less efficient than binary I/O operations. Both types of I/O operations are discussed later in this appendix.

B.2   File Opening and Closing

The file opening and closing functions, `fopen` and `fclose`, are described in the following subsections.

B.2.1   The `fopen` Function

The `fopen` function opens a file and returns a file id number for use with the file. The basic forms of this statement are

```
fid = fopen(filename,permission)
[fid, message] = fopen(filename,permission)
[fid, message] = fopen(filename,permission,format)
```

where *filename* is a string specifying the name of the file to open, *permission* is a character string specifying the mode in which the file is opened, and *format* is an optional string specifying the numeric format of the data in the file. If the open is successful, `fid` will contain a positive integer after this statement is executed, and `message` will be an empty string. If the open fails, `fid` will contain a −1 after this statement is executed, and `message` will be a string explaining the error. If a file is opened for reading and it is not in the current directory, MATLAB will search for it along the MATLAB search path.

The possible permission strings are shown in Table B-2.

Table B-2   `fopen` File Permissions

File Permission	Meaning
`'r'`	Open an existing file for reading only (default).
`'r+'`	Open an existing file for reading and writing.
`'w'`	Delete the contents of an existing file (or create a new file) and open it for writing only.
`'w+'`	Delete the contents of an existing file (or create a new file) and open it for reading and writing.
`'a'`	Open an existing file (or create a new file) and open it for writing only, appending to the end of the file.
`'a+'`	Open an existing file (or create a new file) and open it for reading and writing, appending to the end of the file.
`'W'`	Write without automatic flushing (special command for tape drives).
`'A'`	Append without automatic flushing (special command for tape drives).

On some platforms such as PCs, it is important to distinguish between text files and binary files. If a file is to be opened in text mode, then a t should be added to the permissions string (for example, 'rt' or 'rt+'). If a file is to be opened in binary mode, a b may be added to the permissions string (for example, 'rb'), but this is not actually required since files are opened in binary mode by default. This distinction between text and binary files does not exist on Unix or Linux computers, so the t or b is never needed on those systems.

The *format* string in the fopen function specifies the numeric format of the data stored in the file. This string is needed only when transferring files between computers with incompatible numeric data formats, so it is rarely used. A few of the possible numeric formats are shown in Table B-3; see the MATLAB Language Reference Manual for a complete list of possible numeric formats.

Table B-3   fopen Format Strings

File Permission	Meaning
'native' or 'n'	Numeric format for the machine MATLAB is executing on (default).
'ieee-le' or 'l'	IEEE floating point with little-endian byte ordering.
'ieee-be' or 'b'	IEEE floating point with big-endian byte ordering.
'ieee-le.l64' or 'a'	IEEE floating point with little-endian byte ordering and 64-bit long data type.
'ieee-le.b64' or 's'	IEEE floating point with big-endian byte ordering and 64-bit long data type.

There are also two forms of this function that provide information rather than open files. The function

```
fids = fopen('all')
```

returns a row vector containing a list of all file id's for currently open files (except for stdout and stderr). The number of elements in this vector is equal to the number of open files. The function

```
[filename, permission, format] = fopen(fid)
```

returns the file name, permission string, and numeric format for an open file specified by the file id.

Some examples of correct `fopen` functions are shown as follows.

Case 1: Opening a Binary File for Input
The function below opens a file named `example.dat` for binary input only.

```
fid = fopen('example.dat','r')
```

The permission string is `'r'`, indicating that the file is to be opened for reading only. The string could have been `'rb'`, but this is not required because binary access is the default case.

Case 2: Opening a File for Text Output
The functions that follow open a file named `outdat` for text output only.

```
fid = fopen('outdat','wt')
```

or

```
fid = fopen('outdat','at')
```

The `'wt'` permissions string specifies that the file is a new text file; if it already exists, the old file will be deleted and a new empty file will be opened for writing. This is the proper form of the `fopen` function for an *output file* if we want to replace preexisting data.

The `'at'` permissions string specifies that we want to append to an existing text file. If it already exists, it will be opened and new data will be appended to the currently existing information. This is the proper form of the `fopen` function for an *output file* if we don't want to replace pre-existing data.

Case 3: Opening a Binary File for Read/Write Access
This function opens a file named `junk` for binary input and output:

```
fid = fopen('junk','r+')
```

This function also opens the file for binary input and output:

```
fid = fopen('junk','w+')
```

The difference between the first and the second statements is that the first statement requires the file to exist before it is opened; whereas, the second statement will delete any preexisting file.

B.2.2   The `fclose` Function

The `fclose` function closes a file. Its form is

```
status = fclose(fid)
status = fclose('all')
```

where `fid` is a file id and `status` is the result of the operation. If the operation is successful, `status` will be 0, and if it is unsuccessful, `status` will be −1.

The form `status = fclose('all')` closes all open files except for stdout (fid = 1) and stderr (fid = 2). It returns a status of 0 if all files close successfully and −1 otherwise.

B.3 Binary I/O Functions

The binary I/O functions, `fwrite` and `fread`, are described in the following subsections.

B.3.1 The `fwrite` Function

The `fwrite` function writes binary data in a user-specified format to a file. Its form is

```
count = fwrite(fid,array,precision)
count = fwrite(fid,array,precision,skip)
```

where `fid` is the file id of a file opened with the `fopen` function, `array` is the array of values to write out, and `count` is the number of values written to the file.

MATLAB writes out data in *column order*, which means that the entire first column is written out, followed by the entire second column, and so forth. For example, if `array` $= \begin{bmatrix} 1 & 2 \\ 3 & 4 \\ 5 & 6 \end{bmatrix}$, the data will be written out in the order 1, 3, 5, 2, 4, 6.

The optional *precision* string specifies the format in which the data will be output. MATLAB supports both platform-independent precision strings, which are the same for all computers that MATLAB runs on, and platform-dependent precision strings, which vary among different types of computers. *You should use only the platform-independent strings*, and those are the only forms presented in this book.

For convenience, MATLAB accepts some C and Fortran data type equivalents for the MATLAB precision strings. If you are a C or Fortran programmer, you may find it more convenient to use the names of the data types in the language that you are most familiar with.

The possible platform-independent precisions are presented in Table B-4. All of these precisions work in units of bytes, except for `'bitN'` or `'ubitN'`, which work in units of bits.

The optional argument *skip* specifies the number of bytes to skip in the output file before each write. This option is useful for placing values at certain points in fixed-length records. Note that if *precision* is a bit format like `'bitN'` or `'ubitN'`, skip is specified in bits instead of bytes.

Table B-4   Selected MATLAB Precision Strings

MATLAB Precision String	C / Fortran Equivalent	Meaning
'char'	'char*1'	8-bit characters
'schar'	'signed char'	8-bit signed character
'uchar'	'unsigned char'	8-bit unsigned character
'int8'	'integer*1'	8-bit integer
'int16'	'integer*2'	16-bit integer
'int32'	'integer*4'	32-bit integer
'int64'	'integer*8'	64-bit integer
'uint8'	'integer*1'	8-bit unsigned integer
'uint16'	'integer*2'	16-bit unsigned integer
'uint32'	'integer*4'	32-bit unsigned integer
'uint64'	'integer*8'	64-bit unsigned integer
'float32'	'real*4'	32-bit floating point
'float64'	'real*8'	64-bit floating point
'bitN'		N-bit signed integer, $1 \leq N \leq 64$
'ubitN'		N-bit unsigned integer, $1 \leq N \leq 64$

B.3.2   The fread Function

The fread function reads binary data in a user-specified format from a file and returns the data in a (possibly different) user-specified format. Its form is

```
[array,count] = fread(fid,size,precision)
[array,count] = fread(fid,size,precision,skip)
```

where fid is the file id of a file opened with the fopen function, size is the number of values to read, array is the array to contain the data, and count is the number of values read from the file.

The optional argument *size* specifies the amount of data to be read from the file. There are three versions of this argument:

1. n—Read exactly n values. After this statement, array will be a column vector containing n values read from the file.
2. Inf—Read until the end of the file. After this statement, array will be a column vector containing all of the data until the end of the file.
3. [n m]—Read exactly n × m values, and format the data as an n × m array.

If fread reaches the end of the file and the input stream does not contain enough bits to write out a complete array element of the specified precision, fread pads the last byte or element with zero bits until the full value is obtained. If an error occurs, reading is done up to the last full value.

The *precision* argument specifies both the format of the data on the disk and the format of the data array to be returned to the calling program. The general form of the precision string is

'*disk_precision* => *array_precision*'

where both disk_precision and array_precision are one of the precision strings found in Table B-4. The array_precision value can be defaulted. If it is missing, the data is returned in a double array. There is also a shortcut form of this expression if the disk precision and the array precision are the same:

'**disk_precision*'.

A few examples of precision strings are shown here.

'single'	Read data in single precision format from disk, and return it in a double array.
'single=>single'	Read data in single precision format from disk, and return it in a single array.
'*single'	Read data in single precision format from disk, and return it in a single array (a shorthand version of the previous string).
'double=>real*4'	Read data in double precision format from disk, and return it in a single array.

Example B.1—Writing and Reading Binary Data

The example script file shown here creates an array containing 10,000 random values, opens a user-specified file for writing only, writes the array to disk in 64-bit floating-point format, and closes the file. It then opens the file for reading and reads the data back into a 100 × 100 array. It illustrates the use of binary I/O operations.

```
% Script file: binary_io.m
%
% Purpose:
%   To illustrate the use of binary i/o functions.
%
% Record of revisions:
%     Date            Programmer          Description of change
%     ====            ==========          =====================
%   04/21/10       S. J. Chapman       Original code
%
% Define variables:
%   count       -- Number of values read / written
%   fid         -- File id
```

```
%     filename  -- File name
%     in_array  -- Input array
%     msg       -- Open error message
%     out_array -- Output array
%     status    -- Operation status

% Prompt for file name
filename = input('Enter file name: ','s');

% Generate the data array
out_array = randn(1,10000);

% Open the output file for writing.
[fid,msg] = fopen(filename,'w');

% Was the open successful?
if fid > 0

   % Write the output data.
   count = fwrite(fid,out_array,'float64');

   % Tell user
   disp([int2str(count) ' values written...']);

   % Close the file
   status = fclose(fid);

else

   % Output file open failed. Display message.
   disp(msg);

end

% Now try to recover the data. Open the
% file for reading.
[fid,msg] = fopen(filename,'r');

% Was the open successful?
if fid > 0

   % Write the output data.
   [in_array, count] = fread(fid,[100 100],'float64');

   % Tell user
   disp([int2str(count) ' values read...']);

   % Close the file
   status = fclose(fid);

else

   % Input file open failed. Display message.
   disp(msg);

end
```

When this program is executed, the result are

```
» binary_io
Enter file name: testfile
10000 values written...
10000 values read...
```

An 80,000-byte file named testfile was created in the current directory. This file is 80,000 bytes long, because it contains 10,000 64-bit values and each value occupies 8 bytes.

◀

B.4 Formatted I/O Functions

The formatted I/O functions are described next.

B.4.1 The fprintf Function

The fprintf function writes formatted data in a user-specified format to a file. Its form is

```
count = fprintf(fid,format,val1,val2,...)
fprint(format,val1,val2,...)
```

where fid is the file id of a file to which the data will be written and format is the format string controlling the appearance of the data. If fid is missing, the data is written to the standard output device (the Command Window). This is the form of fprintf that we have been using since Chapter 2.

The format string specifies the alignment, significant digits, field width, and other aspects of output format. It can contain ordinary alphanumeric characters along with special sequences of characters that specify the exact format in which the output data will be displayed. The structure of a typical format is shown in Figure B.1. A single % character always marks the beginning of a format—if an

The Components of a Format Specifier

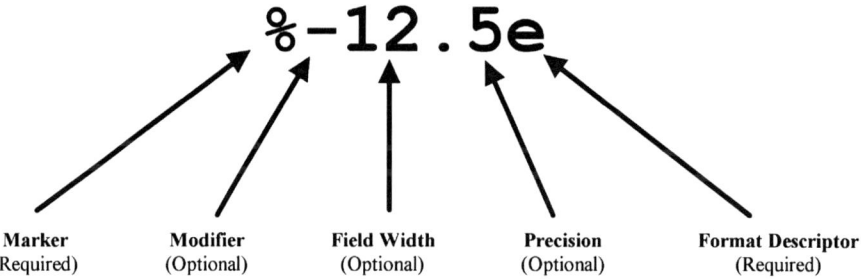

| Marker | Modifier | Field Width | Precision | Format Descriptor |
| (Required) | (Optional) | (Optional) | (Optional) | (Required) |

Figure B.1 The structure of a typical formal specifier.

ordinary % sign is to be printed out, it must appear in the format string as %%. After the % character, the format can have a flag, a field width and precision specifier, and a conversion specifier. The % character and the conversion specifier are always required in any format, while the field and field width and precision specifier are optional.

The possible conversion specifiers are listed in Table B-5, and the possible flags are listed in Table B-6. If a field width and precision are specified in a format, the number before the decimal point is the field width, which is the number of characters used to display the number. The number after the decimal point is the precision, which is the minimum number of significant digits to display after the decimal point.

Table B-5   Format Conversion Specifiers for `fprintf`

Specifier	Description
%c	Single character
%d	Decimal notation (signed)
%e	Exponential notation (using a lowercase e as in 3.1416e+00)
%E	Exponential notation (using an uppercase E as in 3.1416E+00)
%f	Fixed-point notation
%g	The more compact of %e or %f (insignificant zeros do not print)
%G	Same as %g, but using an uppercase E
%o	Octal notation (unsigned)
%s	String of characters
%u	Decimal notation (unsigned)
%x	Hexadecimal notation (using lowercase letters a–f)
%X	Hexadecimal notation (using uppercase letters A–F)

Table B-6   Format Flags

Flag	Description
Minus sign (−)	Left-justifies the converted argument in its field (*Example*: %−5.2d). If this flag is not present, the argument is right-justified.
+	Always print a + or − sign (Example: %+5.2d).
0	Pad argument with leading zeros instead of blanks (Example: %05.2d).

In addition to ordinary characters and formats, certain special escape characters can be used in a format string. These special characters are listed in Table B-7.

Table B-7   Escape Characters in Format Strings

Escape Sequences	Description
\n	New line
\t	Horizontal tab
\b	Backspace
\r	Carriage return
\f	Form feed
\\	Print an ordinary backslash (\) symbol
\'' or ''	Print an apostrophe or single quote
%%	Print an ordinary percent (%) symbol

B.4.2   Understanding Format Conversion Specifiers

The best way to understand the wide variety of format conversion specifiers is by example, so we will now present several examples along with their results.

Case 1: Displaying Decimal Data

Decimal (integer) data is displayed with the %d format conversion specifier. The d may be preceded by a flag and a field width and precision specifier, if desired. If used, the precision specifier set a minimum number of digits to display. If there are not enough digits, leading zeros will be added to the number.

Function	Result	Comment
fprintf('%d\n',123)	----|----| 123	Display the number using as many characters as required. For the number 123, three characters are required.
fprintf('%6d\n',123)	----|----| 123	Display the number in a 6-character-wide field. By default the number is *right justified* in the field.
fprintf('%6.4d\n',123)	----|----| 0123	Display the number in a 6-character-wide field using a minimum of 4 characters. By default the number is *right justified* in the field.
fprintf('%-6.4d\n',123)	----|----| 0123	Display the number in a 6-character-wide field using a minimum of 4 characters. The number is *left justified* in the field.
fprintf('%16.4d\n',123)	----|----| +0123	Display the number in a 6-character-wide field using a minimum of 4 characters plus a sign character. By default the number is *right justified* in the field.

If a nondecimal number is displayed with the `%d` conversion specifier, the specifier will be ignored, and the number will be displayed in exponential format. For example,

```
fprintf('%6d\n',123.4)
```

produces the result `1.234000e+002`.

Case 2: Displaying Floating-Point Data
Floating-point data can be displayed with the `%e`, `%f`, or `%g` format conversion specifiers. They may be preceded by a flag and a field width and precision specifier, if desired. If the specified field width is too small to display the number, it is ignored. Otherwise, the specified field width is used.

Function	Result	Comment
`fprintf('%f\n',123.4)`	`----|----|` `123.400000`	Display the number using as many characters as required. The default case for `%f` is to display 6 digits after the decimal place.
`fprintf('%8.2f\n',123.4)`	`----|----|` `  123.40`	Display the number in an 8-character-wide field, with two places after the decimal point. The number is *right justified* in the field.
`fprintf('%4.2f\n',123.4)`	`----|----|` `123.40`	Display the number in a 6-character-wide field. The width specification was ignored because it was too small to display the number.
`fprintf('%10.2e\n',123.4)`	`----|----|` `  1.23e+002`	Display the number in exponential format in a 10-character-wide field using 2 decimal places. By default the number is *right justified* in the field.
`fprintf('%10.2E\n',123.4)`	`----|----|` `  1.23E+002`	The same but with a capital E for the exponent.

Case 3: Displaying Character Data
Character data may be displayed with the `%c` or `%s` format conversion specifiers. They may be preceded by field width specifier, if desired. If the specified field with is too small to display the number, it is ignored. Otherwise, the specified field width is used.

Function	Result	Comment
fprintf('%c\n','s')	----|----| s	Displays a single character.
fprintf('%s\n','string')	----|----| string	Display the character string.
fprintf('%8s\n','string')	----|----| string	Display the character string in an 8-character-wide field. By default the string is *right justified* in the field.
fprintf('%-8s\n','string')	----|----| string	Display the character string in an 8-character-wide field. The string is *left justified* in the field.

B.4.3   The fscanf Function

The fscanf function reads formatted data in a user-specified format from a file. Its form is

```
array = fscanf(fid,format)
[array, count] = fscanf(fid,format,size)
```

where fid is the file id of a file from which the data will be read, format is the format string controlling how the data is read, and array is the array that receives the data. The output argument count returns the number of values read from the file.

The optional argument *size* specifies the amount of data to be read from the file. There are three versions of this argument.

1. n—Read exactly n values. After this statement, array will be a column vector containing n values read from the file.
2. Inf—Read until the end of the file. After this statement, array will be a column vector containing all of the data until the end of the file.
3. [n m]—Read exactly n $\times$ m values, and format the data as an n $\times$ m array.

The format string specifies the format of the data to be read. It can contain ordinary characters along with format conversion specifiers. The fscanf function compares the data in the file with the format conversion specifiers in the format string. As long as the two match, fscanf converts the value and stores it in the output array. This process continues until the end of the file or until the amount of data in *size* has been read, whichever comes first.

If the data in the file does not match the format conversion specifiers, the operation of fscanf stops immediately.

The format conversion specifiers for fscanf are basically the same as those for fprintf. The most common specifiers are shown in Table B-8.

Table B-8   Format Conversion Specifiers for `fscanf`

Specifier	Description
%c	Read a single character. This specifier reads any character including blanks, new lines, and so forth.
%Nc	Read N characters.
%d	Read a decimal number (ignores blanks).
%e %f %g	Read a floating-point number (ignores blanks).
%i	Read a signed integer (ignores blanks).
%s	Read a string of characters. The string is terminated by blanks or other special characters such as new lines.

To illustrate the use of `fscanf`, we will attempt to read a file called `x.dat` containing the following values on two lines:

```
10.00   20.00
30.00   40.00
```

1. If the file is read with the statement

```
[z, count] = fscanf(fid,'%f');
```

variable z will be the column vector $\begin{bmatrix} 10 \\ 20 \\ 30 \\ 40 \end{bmatrix}$ and count will be 4.

2. If the file is read with the statement

```
[z, count] = fscanf(fid,'%f',[2 2]);
```

variable z will be the array $\begin{bmatrix} 10 & 30 \\ 20 & 40 \end{bmatrix}$ and `count` will be 4.

3. Next, let's try to read this file as decimal values. If the file is read with the statement

```
[z, count] = fscanf(fid,'%d',Inf);
```

variable z will be the single value 10 and `count` will be 1. This happens because the decimal point in the 10.00 does not match the format conversion specifier and `fscanf` stops at the first mismatch.

4. If the file is read with the statement

```
[z, count] = fscanf(fid,'%d.%d',[1 Inf]);
```

variable z will be the row vector [10 0 20 0 30 0 40 0] and `count` will be 8. This happens because the decimal point is now matched in the format conversion specifier and the numbers on either side of the decimal point are interpreted as separate integers!

5. Now let's try to read the file as individual characters. If the file is read with the statement

```
[z, count] = fscanf(fid,'%c');
```

variable z will be a row vector containing every character in the file, including all spaces and newline characters! Variable count will be equal to the number of characters in the file.

6. Finally, let's try to read the file as a character string. If the file is read with the statement

```
[z, count] = fscanf(fid,'%s');
```

variable z will be a row vector containing the 20 characters 10.0020.0030.0040.00, and count will be 4. This happens because the string specifier ignores white space, and the function found four separate strings in the file.

B.4.4   The fgetl Function

The fgetl function reads the next line *excluding the end-of-line characters* from a file as a character string. It form is

```
line = fgetl(fid)
```

where fid is the file id of a file from which the data will be read and line is the character array that receives the data. If fgetl encounters the end of a file, the value of line is set to −1.

B.4.5   The fgets Function

The fgets function reads the next line *including the end-of-line characters* from a file as a character string. It form is

```
line = fgets(fid)
```

where fid is the file id of a file from which the data will be read and line is the character array that receives the data. If fgets encounters the end of a file, the value of line is set to −1.

B.5   The textscan Function

The textscan function reads ASCII files that are formatted into columns of data, where each column can be of a different type, and stores the contents into the columns of a cell array. This function is *very* useful for importing tables of data printed out by other applications. It is new in MATLAB 7.0. It is basically similar to textread, except that it is faster and more flexible.

The form of the `textscan` function is

```
a = textscan(fid, 'format')
a = textscan(fid, 'format', N)
a = textscan(fid, 'format', param, value,...)
a = textscan(fid, 'format', N, param, value,...)
```

where `fid` is the file id of a file that has already been opened with `fopen`, `format` is a string containing a description of the type of data in each column, and n is the number of times to use the format specifier. (If n is -1 or is missing, the function reads to the end of the file.) The format string contains the same types of format descriptors as function `fprintf`. Note that there is only one output argument with all of the values returned in a cell array. The cell array will contain a number of elements equal to the number of format descriptors to read.

For example, suppose that file `test_input1.dat` contains the following data:

```
James    Jones    O+   3.51   22   Yes
Sally    Smith    A+   3.28   23   No
Hans     Carter   B-   2.84   19   Yes
Sam      Spade    A+   3.12   21   Yes
```

This data could be read into a cell array with the following function:

```
fid = fopen('test_input1.dat','rt');
a = textscan(fid,'%s %s %s %f %d %s',-1);
fclose(fid);
```

When this command is executed, the results are

```
» fid = fopen('test_input1.dat','rt');
» a = textscan(fid,'%s %s %s %f %d %s',-1)
a =
    {4×1 cell} {4×1 cell} {4×1 cell} [4×1 double] [4×1
int32] {4×1 cell}
» a{1}
ans =
    'James'
    'Sally'
    'Hans'
    'Sam'
» a{2}
ans =
    'Jones'
    'Smith'
    'Carter'
    'Spade'
```

```
» a{3}
ans =
     'O+'
     'A+'
     'B-'
     'A+'
» a{4}
ans =
     3.5100
     3.2800
     2.8400
     3.1200
» fclose(fid);
```

This function can also skip selected columns by adding an asterisk to the corresponding format descriptor (for example, `%*s`). For example, the following statements read only the first name, last name, and `gpa` from the file:

```
fid = fopen('test_input1.dat','rt');
a = textscan(fid,'%s %s %*s %f %*d %*s',-1);
fclose(fid);
```

Function `textscan` is similar to function `textread`, but it is more flexible and faster. The advantages of `textscan` include

- The `textscan` function offers better performance than `textread`, making it a better choice when reading large files.
- With `textscan`, you can start reading at any point in the file. When the file is opened with `fopen`, you can move to any position in the file with `fseek` and begin the `textscan` at that point. The `textread` function requires that you start reading from the beginning of the file.
- Subsequent `textscan` operations start reading the file at a point where the last `textscan` left off. The `textread` function always begins at the start of the file, regardless of any prior `textread` operations.
- Function `textscan` returns a single cell array regardless of how many fields you read. With `textscan`, you don't need to match the number of output arguments with the number of fields being read, as you would with `textread`.
- Function `textscan` offers more choices in how the data being read is converted.

The function `textscan` has a number of additional options that increase its flexibility. Consult the MATLAB on-line documentation for details of these options.

Working with Character Strings

This appendix describes MATLAB strings and the functions available for working with strings. This material is very useful for anyone who might need to manipulate character data in MATLAB, but because it is not essential for basic engineering applications, it is relegated to an appendix.

C.1 String Functions

A MATLAB string is an array of type char. Each character is stored in two bytes of memory. A character variable is automatically created when a string is assigned to it. For example, the statement

```
str = 'This is a test';
```

creates a 14-element character array. The output of **whos** for this array is

```
» whos str
Name    Size        Bytes   Class    Attributes
str     1x14          28     char
```

A special function ischar can be used to check for character arrays. If a given variable is of type character, then ischar returns a true (1) value. If it is not, ischar returns a false (0) value.

The following subsections describe MATLAB functions useful for manipulating character strings.

C.1.1   String Conversion Functions

Variables may be converted from the `char` data type to the `double` data type using the `double` function. Thus, the statement `double(str)` yields the following result:

```
» x = double(str)
x =
Columns 1 through 12
  84 104 105 115 32 105 115 32 97 32 116 101
Columns 13 through 14
115 116
```

Variables also can be converted from the `double` data type to the `char` data type using the `char` function. If x is the 14-element array created previously, the statement `char(x)` yields the following result:

```
» z = char(x)
z =
This is a test
```

C.1.2   Creating Two-Dimensional Character Arrays

It is possible to create two-dimensional character arrays, but *each row of such an array must have exactly the same length.* If one of the rows is shorter than the other rows, the character array is invalid and will produce an error. For example, the following statement is illegal because the two rows being defined have different lengths.

```
name = ['Stephen J. Chapman';'Senior Engineer'];
```

The easiest way to produce two-dimensional character arrays is with the `char` function. This function will automatically pad all strings to the length of the largest input string.

```
» name = char('Stephen J. Chapman','Senior Engineer')
name =
Stephen J. Chapman
Senior Engineer
```

Two-dimensional character arrays also can be created with the function `strvcat`, which is described subsequently.

✳ Good Programming Practice

Use the `char` function to create two-dimensional character arrays without worrying about padding each row to the same length.

It is possible to remove any extra trailing blanks from a string when it is extracted from an array using the deblank function. For example, the following statements remove the second line from array name and compare the results with and without blank trimming.

```
» line2 = name(2,:)
line2 =
Senior Engineer
» line2_trim = deblank(name(2,:))
line2_trim =
Senior Engineer
» size(line2)
ans =
      1    18
» size(line2_trim)
ans =
      1    15
```

C.1.3 Concatenating Strings

Function strcat concatenates two or more strings horizontally, ignoring any trailing blanks but preserving blanks within the strings. This function produces the result shown here.

```
» result = strcat('String 1 ','String 2')
result =
String 1String 2
```

The result is 'String 1String 2'. Note that the trailing blanks in the first string were ignored.

The function strvcat concatenates two or more strings vertically, automatically padding the strings to make a valid two-dimensional array. This function produces the result shown here.

```
» result = strvcat('Long String 1 ','String 2')
result =
Long String 1
String 2
```

C.1.4 Comparing Strings

Strings and substrings can be compared in several ways:

- Two strings, or parts of two strings, can be compared for equality.
- Two individual characters can be compared for equality.
- Strings can be examined to determine whether each character is a letter or whitespace.

Comparing Strings for Equality

You can use four MATLAB functions to compare two strings as a whole for equality. They are

- `strcmp` determines whether two strings are identical.
- `strcmpi` determines whether two strings are identical ignoring case.
- `strncmp` determines whether the first `n` characters of two strings are identical.
- `strncmpi` determines whether the first `n` characters of two strings are identical ignoring case.

Function `strcmp` compares two strings, including any leading and trailing blanks, and returns a true (1) if the strings are identical.[1] Otherwise, it returns a false (0). Function `strcmpi` is the same as `strcmp`, except that it ignores the case of letters (i.e., it treats `'a'` as equal to `'A'`).

Function `strncmp` compares the first `n` characters of two strings, including any leading blanks, and returns a true (1) if the characters are identical. Otherwise, it returns a false (0). Function `strncmpi` is the same as `strncmp`, except that it ignores the case of letters.

To understand these functions, consider the three strings:

```
str1 = 'hello';
str2 = 'Hello';
str3 = 'help';
```

Strings `str1` and `str2` are not identical, but they differ only in the case of one letter. Therefore, `strcmp` returns false (0), while `strcmpi` returns true (1).

```
» c = strcmp(str1,str2)
c =
     0
» c = strcmpi(str1,str2)
c =
     1
```

Strings `str1` and `str3` are also not identical, and both `strcmp` and `strcmpi` will return a false (0). However, the first three characters of `str1` and `str3` *are* identical, so invoking `strncmp` with any value up to 3 returns a true (1):

```
» c = strncmp(str1,str3,2)
c =
     1
```

Comparing Individual Characters for Equality and Inequality

You can use MATLAB relational operators on character arrays to test for equality *one character at a time*, as long as the arrays you are comparing have equal dimensions, or one is a scalar. For example, you can use the equality operator (==) to determine which characters in two strings match.

---

[1]**Caution:** The behavior of this function is different from that of the `strcmp` in C. Users already familiar with C can be tripped up by this difference.

```
» a = 'fate';
» b = 'cake';
» result = a == b
result =
0  1  0  1
```

All of the relational operators (>, >=, <, <=, ==, ~=) compare the ASCII values of corresponding characters.

Unlike C, MATLAB does not have an intrinsic function to define a "greater than" or "less than" relationship between two strings taken as a whole. We will create such a function in an example at the end of this section.

Categorizing Characters within a String

There are three functions for categorizing characters on a character-by-character basis inside a string:

- `isletter` determines whether a character is a letter.
- `isspace` determines whether a character is whitespace (blank, tab, or new line).
- `isstrprop('str', 'category')` is a more general function. It determines whether a character falls into a user-specified category, such as alphabetic, alphanumeric, uppercase, lowercase, numeric, control, and so forth.

To understand these functions, let's create a string named `mystring`:

```
mystring = 'Room 23a';
```

We will use this string to test the categorizing functions.

The function `isletter` examines each character in the string, producing a `logical` output vector of the same length as `mystring` that contains a true (1) in each location corresponding to a character and a false (0) in the other locations. For example,

```
» a = isletter(mystring)
a =
1  1  1  1  0  0  0  1
```

The first four and the last elements in a are true (1), because the corresponding characters of `mystring` are letters.

The function `isspace` also examines each character in the string, producing a `logical` output vector of the same length as `mystring` that contains a true (1) in each location corresponding to whitespace and a false (0) in the other locations. "Whitespace" is any character that separates tokens in MATLAB: a space, a tab, a linefeed, carriage return, and so forth. For example,

```
» a = isspace(mystring)
a =
0  0  0  0  1  0  0  0
```

The fifth element in a is true (1), because the corresponding character of `mystring` is a space.

The function `isstrprop` is new in MATLAB 7. It is a more flexible replacement for `isletter`, `isspace`, and several other functions. This function has two arguments: `'str'` and `'category'`. The first argument is the string to characterize, and the second argument is the type of category to check for. Some possible categories are given in Table C-1.

This function examines each character in the string, producing a `logical` output vector of the same length as the input string that contains a true (1) in each location that matches the category and a false (0) in the other locations. For example, the following function checks to see which characters in `mystring` are numbers:

```
» a = isstrprop(mystring,'digit')
a =
0 0 0 0 0 1 1 0
```

Also, the following function checks to see which characters in `mystring` are lower case letters:

```
» a = isstrprop(mystring,'lower')
a =
0 1 1 1 0 0 0 1
```

Table C-1   Selected Categories for Function `isstrprop`

Category	Description
`'alpha'`	Return true (1) for each character of the string that is alphabetic, and false (0) otherwise.
`'alphanum'`	Return true (1) for each character of the string that is alphanumeric, and false (0) otherwise. [**Note:** This category replaces the function `isletter`.]
`'cntrl'`	Return true (1) for each character of the string that is a control character, and false (0) otherwise.
`'digit'`	Return true (1) for each character of the string that is a number, and false (0) otherwise.
`'lower'`	Return true (1) for each character of the string that is a lowercase letter, and false (0) otherwise.
`'wspace'`	Return true (1) for each character of the string that is whitespace, and false (0) otherwise. [**Note:** This category replaces the function `isspace`.]
`'upper'`	Return true (1) for each character of the string that is an uppercase letter, and false (0) otherwise.
`'xdigit'`	Return true (1) for each character of the string that is a hexadecimal digit, and false (0) otherwise.

✳ Good Programming Practice

Use function `isstrprop` to determine the characteristics of each character in a string array. This function replaces the older functions `isletter` and `isspace`, which may be deleted in a future version of MATLAB.

C.1.5   Searching and Replacing Characters within a String

MATLAB provides several functions for searching and replacing characters in a string. Consider a string named `test`:

```
test = 'This is a test!';
```

The function `findstr` returns the starting position of all occurrences of the shorter of two strings within a longer string. For example, to find all occurrences of the string `'is'` inside `test`,

```
» position = findstr(test,'is')
position =
        3       6
```

The string `'is'` occurs twice within `test`, starting at positions 3 and 6.

The function `strmatch` is another matching function. This one looks at the beginning characters of the *rows* of a two-dimensional character array and returns a list of those rows that start with the specified character sequence. The form of this function is

```
result = strmatch(str,array);
```

For example, suppose that we create a two-dimensional character array with the function `strvcat`:

```
array = strvcat('maxarray','min value','max value');
```

Then the following statement will return the row numbers of all rows beginning with the letters `'max'`:

```
» result = strmatch('max',array)
result =
        1
        3
```

The function `strrep` performs the standard search-and-replace operation. It finds all occurrences of one string within another one and replaces them with a third string. The form of this function is

```
result = strrep(str,srch,repl)
```

where `str` is the string being checked, `srch` is the character string to search for, and `repl` is the replacement character string. For example,

```
» test = 'This is a test!'
» result = strrep(test,'test','pest')
result =
This is a pest!
```

The `strtok` function returns the characters before the first occurrence of a delimiting character in an input string. The default delimiting characters compose the set of whitespace characters. The form of `strtok` is

```
[token,remainder] = strtok(string,delim)
```

where `string` is the input character string, `delim` is the (optional) set of delimiting characters, `token` is the first set of characters delimited by a character in `delim`, and `remainder` is the rest of the line. For example,

```
» [token,remainder] = strtok('This is a test!')
token =
This
remainder =
is a test!
```

You can use the `strtok` function to parse a sentence into words; for example,

```
function all_words = words(input_string)
remainder = input_string;
all_words = '';
while (any(remainder))
   [chopped,remainder] = strtok(remainder);
   all_words = strvcat(all_words,chopped);
end
```

C.1.6 Uppercase and Lowercase Conversion

The functions `upper` and `lower` convert all of the alphabetic characters within a string to uppercase and lowercase, respectively. For example,

```
» result = upper('This is test 1!')
result =
THIS IS TEST 1!
» result = lower('This is test 2!')
result =
this is test 2!
```

Note that the alphabetic characters were converted to the proper case, whereas the numbers and punctuation were unaffected.

C.1.7   Trimming Whitespace from Strings

There are two functions that trim leading and/or trailing whitespace from a string. Whitespace characters consists of the spaces, newlines, carriage returns, tabs, vertical tabs, and formfeeds.

The function `deblank` removes any extra *trailing* whitespace from a string, and the function `strtrim` removes any extra *leading and trailing* whitespace from a string.

For example, the following statements create a 21-character string with leading and trailing whitespace. Function `deblank` trims the trailing whitespace characters in the string only, and function `strtrim` trims both the leading and the trailing whitespace characters.

```
» test_string = ' This is a test. '
test_string =
   This is a test.
» length(test_string)
ans =
    21
» test_string_trim1= deblank(test_string)
test_string_trim1 =
   This is a test.
» length(test_string_trim1)
ans =
    18
» test_string_trim2 = strtrim(test_string)
test_string_trim2 =
This is a test.
» length(test_string_trim2)
ans =
    15
```

C.1.8   Numeric-to-String Conversions

MATLAB contains several functions to convert numeric values into character strings. We have already seen two such functions, `num2str` and `int2str`. Consider a scalar x:

```
x = 5317.1;
```

By default, MATLAB stores the number x as a 1×1 `double` array containing the value 5317.1. The `int2str` (integer to string) function rounds the value passed to it and displays the rounded number as a character string. For example, the function would convert the number 5317.1 into a 1 × 4 char array containing the string '5317':

```
» x = 5317.1;
» y = int2str(x);
» whos
  Name    Size           Bytes    Class        Attributes

   x       1x1               8    double
   y       1x4               8    char
```

The function num2str converts a double value into a string without rounding. It also provides more control of the output string format than int2str. An optional second argument sets the number of digits in the output string or specifies an actual format to use. The format specifications in the second argument are similar to those used by fprintf. For example,

```
» p = num2str(pi)
p =
3.1416
» p = num2str(pi,7)
p =
3.141593
» p = num2str(pi,'%10.5e')
p =
3.14159e+000
```

Both int2str and num2str are handy for labeling plots. For example, the following lines use num2str to prepare automated labels for the *x*-axis of a plot:

```
function plotlabel(x,y)
plot(x,y)
str1 = num2str(min(x));
str2 = num2str(max(x));
out = ['Value of f from ' str1 ' to ' str2];
xlabel(out);
```

There are also conversion functions designed to change numeric values into strings representing a decimal value in another base, such as a binary or hexadecimal representation. For example, the dec2hex function converts a decimal value into the corresponding hexadecimal string:

```
dec_num = 4035;
hex_num = dec2hex(dec_num)
hex_num =
FC3
```

Other functions of this type include hex2num, hex2dec, bin2dec, dec2bin, base2dec, and dec2base. MATLAB includes on-line help for all of these functions.

The MATLAB function mat2str converts an array to a string that MATLAB can evaluate. This string is useful input for a function such as eval, which evaluates input strings just as if they were typed at the MATLAB command line. For example, if we define array a as

```
» a = [1 2 3; 4 5 6]
a =
       1       2       3
       4       5       6
```

the function mat2str will return a string containing the result

```
» b = mat2str(a)
b =
[1 2 3; 4 5 6]
```

Finally, MATLAB includes a special function sprintf that is identical to function fprintf, except that the output goes into a character string instead of the Command Window. This function provides complete control over the formatting of the character string. For example,

```
» str = sprintf('The value of pi = %8.6f.',pi)
str =
The value of pi = 3.141593.
```

This function is extremely useful in creating complex titles and labels for plots.

C.1.9   String-to-Numeric Conversions

MATLAB also contains several functions to change character strings into numeric values. The most important of these functions are eval, str2double, and sscanf.

The function eval evaluates a string containing a MATLAB expression and returns the result. The expression can contain any combination of MATLAB functions, variables, constants, and operations. For example, the string a containing the characters '2 * 3.141592' can be converted to numeric form using the following statements:

```
» a = '2 * 3.141592';
» b = eval(a)
b =
    6.2832
» whos
  Name      Size          Bytes    Class       Attributes

  a         1x12             24    char
  b         1x1               8    double
```

The function str2double converts character strings into an equivalent double value.[2] For example, the string a containing the characters

---

[2]MATLAB also contains a function str2num that can convert a string into a number. For a variety of reasons mentioned in the MATLAB documentation, function str2double is better than function str2num. You should recognize function str2num when you see it, but always use function str2double in any new code that you write.

'3.141592' can be converted to numeric form by the following statements:

```
» a = '3.141592';
» b = str2double(a)
b =
    3.1416
```

Strings also can be converted to numeric form using the function sscanf. This function converts a string into a number according to a format conversion character. The simplest form of this function is

```
value = sscanf(string,format)
```

where string is the string to scan and format specifies the type of conversion to occur. The two most common conversion specifiers for sscanf are '%d' for decimals and '%g' for floating-point numbers.

The following examples illustrate the use of sscanf:

```
» a = '3.141592';
» value1 = sscanf(a,'%g')
value1 =
       3.1416
» value2 = sscanf(a,'%d')
value2 =
       3
```

C.1.10   Summary

The common MATLAB string functions are summarized in Table C-2.

Table C-2   Common MATLAB String Functions

Category	Function	Description
General	char	(1) Converts numbers to the corresponding character values. (2) Creates a two-dimensional character array from a series of strings.
	double	Converts characters to the corresponding numeric codes.
	blanks	Creates a string of blanks.
	deblank	Removes trailing whitespace from a string.
	strtrim	Removes leading and trailing whitespace from a string.

(*continued*)

Table C-3   (continued)

Category	Function	Description
String tests	ischar	Returns true (1) for a character array.
	isletter	Returns true (1) for letters of the alphabet.
	isspace	Returns true (1) for whitespace.
	isstrprop	Returns true (1) for characters matching the specified property.
String operations	strcat	Concatenates strings.
	strvcat	Concatenates strings vertically.
	strcmp	Returns true (1) if two strings are identical.
	strcmpi	Returns true (1) if two strings are identical, ignoring case.
	strncmp	Returns true (1) if first n characters of two strings are identical.
	strncmpi	Returns true (1) if first n characters of two strings are identical, ignoring case.
	findstr	Finds one string within another one.
	strjust	Justify string.
	strmatch	Finds matches for string.
	strrep	Replaces one string with another.
	strtok	Finds token in string.
	upper	Converts string to uppercase.
	lower	Converts string to lowercase.
Number-to-string conversion	int2str	Converts integer to string.
	num2str	Converts number to string.
	mat2str	Converts matrix to string.
	sprintf	Writes formatted data to string.
String-to-number conversion	eval	Evaluates the result of a MATLAB expression.
	str2double	Converts string to a double value.
	str2num	Converts string to number.
	sscanf	Reads formatted data from string.
Base number conversion	hex2num	Converts IEEE hexadecimal string to double.
	hex2dec	Converts hexadecimal string to decimal integer.
	dec2hex	Converts decimal to hexadecimal string.
	bin2dec	Converts binary string to decimal integer.
	dec2bin	Converts decimal integer to binary string.
	base2dec	Converts base B string to decimal integer.
	dec2base	Converts decimal integer to base B string.

Index

Note: **Boldface** numbers indicate illustrations or tables.

DISCRETE MATHEMATICS
WITH APPLICATIONS

FOURTH EDITION

SUSANNA S. EPP
DePaul University

BROOKS/COLE
CENGAGE Learning

Australia · Brazil · Japan · Korea · Mexico · Singapore · Spain · United Kingdom · United States

CONTENTS

CHAPTER 3

THE LOGIC OF QUANTIFIED STATEMENTS

In Chapter 2 we discussed the logical analysis of compound statements—those made of simple statements joined by the connectives $\sim$, $\wedge$, $\vee$, $\rightarrow$, and $\leftrightarrow$. Such analysis casts light on many aspects of human reasoning, but it cannot be used to determine validity in the majority of everyday and mathematical situations. For example, the argument

> All men are mortal.
>
> Socrates is a man.
>
> $\therefore$ Socrates is mortal.

is intuitively perceived as correct. Yet its validity cannot be derived using the methods outlined in Section 2.3. To determine validity in examples like this, it is necessary to separate the statements into parts in much the same way that you separate declarative sentences into subjects and predicates. And you must analyze and understand the special role played by words that denote quantities such as "all" or "some." The symbolic analysis of predicates and quantified statements is called the **predicate calculus.** The symbolic analysis of ordinary compound statements (as outlined in Sections 2.1–2.3) is called the **statement calculus** (or the **propositional calculus**).

3.1 Predicates and Quantified Statements I

. . . it was not till within the last few years that it has been realized how fundamental any and some are to the very nature of mathematics. — A. N. Whitehead (1861–1947)

As noted in Section 2.1, the sentence "He is a college student" is not a statement because it may be either true or false depending on the value of the pronoun *he.* Similarly, the sentence "$x + y$ is greater than 0" is not a statement because its truth value depends on the values of the variables x and y.

In grammar, the word *predicate* refers to the part of a sentence that gives information about the subject. In the sentence "James is a student at Bedford College," the word *James* is the subject and the phrase *is a student at Bedford College* is the predicate. The predicate is the part of the sentence from which the subject has been removed.

In logic, predicates can be obtained by removing some or all of the nouns from a statement. For instance, let P stand for "is a student at Bedford College" and let Q stand for "is a student at." Then both P and Q are *predicate symbols.* The sentences "x is a student at Bedford College" and "x is a student at y" are symbolized as $P(x)$ and as $Q(x, y)$ respectively, where x and y are *predicate variables* that take values in appropriate sets. When concrete values are substituted in place of predicate variables, a statement results. For simplicity, we define a *predicate* to be a predicate symbol together with suitable predicate variables. In some other treatments of logic, such objects are referred to as **propositional functions** or **open sentences.**

> **• Definition**
>
> A **predicate** is a sentence that contains a finite number of variables and becomes a statement when specific values are substituted for the variables. The **domain** of a predicate variable is the set of all values that may be substituted in place of the variable.

Example 3.1.1 Finding Truth Values of a Predicate

Let $P(x)$ be the predicate "$x^2 > x$" with domain the set **R** of all real numbers. Write $P(2)$, $P(\frac{1}{2})$, and $P(-\frac{1}{2})$, and indicate which of these statements are true and which are false.

Solution

$$P(2): \quad 2^2 > 2, \quad \text{or} \quad 4 > 2. \quad \text{True.}$$

$$P\left(\tfrac{1}{2}\right): \quad \left(\tfrac{1}{2}\right)^2 > \tfrac{1}{2}, \quad \text{or} \quad \tfrac{1}{4} > \tfrac{1}{2}. \quad \text{False.}$$

$$P\left(-\tfrac{1}{2}\right): \quad \left(-\tfrac{1}{2}\right)^2 > -\tfrac{1}{2}, \quad \text{or} \quad \tfrac{1}{4} > -\tfrac{1}{2}. \quad \text{True.} \quad ■$$

When an element in the domain of the variable of a one-variable predicate is substituted for the variable, the resulting statement is either true or false. The set of all such elements that make the predicate true is called the *truth set* of the predicate.

> **• Definition**
>
> If $P(x)$ is a predicate and x has domain D, the **truth set** of $P(x)$ is the set of all elements of D that make $P(x)$ true when they are substituted for x. The truth set of $P(x)$ is denoted
>
> $$\{x \in D \mid P(x)\}.$$

Note Recall that we read these symbols as "the set of all x in D such that $P(x)$."

Example 3.1.2 Finding the Truth Set of a Predicate

Let $Q(n)$ be the predicate "n is a factor of 8." Find the truth set of $Q(n)$ if

a. the domain of n is the set $\mathbf{Z}^+$ of all positive integers

b. the domain of n is the set **Z** of all integers.

Solution

a. The truth set is $\{1, 2, 4, 8\}$ because these are exactly the positive integers that divide 8 evenly.

b. The truth set is $\{1, 2, 4, 8, -1, -2, -4, -8\}$ because the negative integers $-1, -2, -4,$ and -8 also divide into 8 without leaving a remainder. ■

The Universal Quantifier: ∀

One sure way to change predicates into statements is to assign specific values to all their variables. For example, if x represents the number 35, the sentence "x is (evenly) divisible by 5" is a true statement since $35 = 5 \cdot 7$. Another way to obtain statements from predicates is to add **quantifiers.** Quantifiers are words that refer to quantities such as "some" or "all" and tell for how many elements a given predicate is true. The formal concept of quantifier was introduced into symbolic logic in the late nineteenth century by

Charles Sanders Peirce (1839–1914)

Culver Pictures

Note Think "for all" when you see the symbol ∀.

Friedrich Schiller, Universität Jena

Gottlob Frege (1848–1925)

the American philosopher, logician, and engineer Charles Sanders Peirce and, independently, by the German logician Gottlob Frege.

The symbol ∀ denotes "for all" and is called the **universal quantifier.** For example, another way to express the sentence "All human beings are mortal" is to write

$$∀ \text{ human beings } x, x \text{ is mortal.}$$

When the symbol x is introduced into the phrase "∀ human beings x," you are supposed to think of x as an individual, but generic, object—with all the properties shared by every human being but no other properties. Thus you should say "x is mortal" rather than "x are mortal." In other words, use the singular "is" rather than the plural verb "are" when describing the property satisfied by x. If you let H be the set of all human beings, then you can symbolize the statement more formally by writing

$$∀x ∈ H, x \text{ is mortal,}$$

which is read as "For all x in the set of all human beings, x is mortal."

The domain of the predicate variable is generally indicated between the ∀ symbol and the variable name (as in ∀ human beings x) or immediately following the variable name (as in $∀x ∈ H$). Some other expressions that can be used instead of *for all* are *for every, for arbitrary, for any, for each,* and *given any.* In a sentence such as "∀ real numbers x and $y, x + y = y + x$," the ∀ symbol is understood to refer to both x and y.*

Sentences that are quantified universally are defined as statements by giving them the truth values specified in the following definition:

> **• Definition**
>
> Let $Q(x)$ be a predicate and D the domain of x. A **universal statement** is a statement of the form "$∀x ∈ D, Q(x)$." It is defined to be true if, and only if, $Q(x)$ is true for every x in D. It is defined to be false if, and only if, $Q(x)$ is false for at least one x in D. A value for x for which $Q(x)$ is false is called a **counterexample** to the universal statement.

Example 3.1.3 Truth and Falsity of Universal Statements

a. Let $D = \{1, 2, 3, 4, 5\}$, and consider the statement

$$∀x ∈ D, x^2 ≥ x.$$

Show that this statement is true.

b. Consider the statement

$$∀x ∈ \mathbf{R}, x^2 ≥ x.$$

Find a counterexample to show that this statement is false.

Solution

a. Check that "$x^2 ≥ x$" is true for each individual x in D.

$$1^2 ≥ 1, \qquad 2^2 ≥ 2, \qquad 3^2 ≥ 3, \qquad 4^2 ≥ 4, \qquad 5^2 ≥ 5.$$

Hence "$∀x ∈ D, x^2 ≥ x$" is true.

---

*More formal versions of symbolic logic would require writing a separate ∀ for each variable: "$∀x ∈ \mathbf{R}(∀y ∈ \mathbf{R}(x + y = y + x))$."

b. *Counterexample:* Take $x = \frac{1}{2}$. Then x is in **R** (since $\frac{1}{2}$ is a real number) and

$$\left(\frac{1}{2}\right)^2 = \frac{1}{4} \not\geq \frac{1}{2}.$$

Hence "$\forall x \in \mathbf{R}, x^2 \geq x$" is false. ∎

The technique used to show the truth of the universal statement in Example 3.1.3(a) is called the **method of exhaustion.** It consists of showing the truth of the predicate separately for each individual element of the domain. (The idea is to exhaust the possibilities before you exhaust yourself!) This method can, in theory, be used whenever the domain of the predicate variable is finite. In recent years the prevalence of digital computers has greatly increased the convenience of using the method of exhaustion. Computer expert systems, or knowledge-based systems, use this method to arrive at answers to many of the questions posed to them. Because most mathematical sets are infinite, however, the method of exhaustion can rarely be used to derive general mathematical results.

The Existential Quantifier: ∃

The symbol ∃ denotes "there exists" and is called the **existential quantifier.** For example, the sentence "There is a student in Math 140" can be written as

∃ a person p such that p is a student in Math 140,

or, more formally,

Note Think "there
exists" when you see the
symbol ∃.

$\exists p \in P$ such that p is a student in Math 140,

where P is the set of all people. The domain of the predicate variable is generally indicated either between the ∃ symbol and the variable name or immediately following the variable name. The words *such that* are inserted just before the predicate. Some other expressions that can be used in place of *there exists* are *there is a, we can find a, there is at least one, for some,* and *for at least one.* In a sentence such as "∃ integers m and n such that $m + n = m \cdot n$," the ∃ symbol is understood to refer to both m and n.*

Sentences that are quantified existentially are defined as statements by giving them the truth values specified in the following definition.

> **• Definition**
>
> Let $Q(x)$ be a predicate and D the domain of x. An **existential statement** is a statement of the form "$\exists x \in D$ such that $Q(x)$." It is defined to be true if, and only if, $Q(x)$ is true for at least one x in D. It is false if, and only if, $Q(x)$ is false for all x in D.

Example 3.1.4 Truth and Falsity of Existential Statements

a. Consider the statement

$$\exists m \in \mathbf{Z}^+ \text{ such that } m^2 = m.$$

Show that this statement is true.

---

*In more formal versions of symbolic logic, the words *such that* are not written out (although they are understood) and a separate ∃ symbol is used for each variable: "$\exists m \in \mathbf{Z}(\exists n \in \mathbf{Z}(m + n = m \cdot n))$."

b. Let $E = \{5, 6, 7, 8\}$ and consider the statement

$$\exists m \in E \text{ such that } m^2 = m.$$

Show that this statement is false.

Solution

a. Observe that $1^2 = 1$. Thus "$m^2 = m$" is true for at least one integer m. Hence "$\exists m \in \mathbf{Z}$ such that $m^2 = m$" is true.

b. Note that $m^2 = m$ is not true for any integers m from 5 through 8:

$$5^2 = 25 \neq 5, \qquad 6^2 = 36 \neq 6, \qquad 7^2 = 49 \neq 7, \qquad 8^2 = 64 \neq 8.$$

Thus "$\exists m \in E$ such that $m^2 = m$" is false. ▧

Formal Versus Informal Language

It is important to be able to translate from formal to informal language when trying to make sense of mathematical concepts that are new to you. It is equally important to be able to translate from informal to formal language when thinking out a complicated problem.

Example 3.1.5 Translating from Formal to Informal Language

Rewrite the following formal statements in a variety of equivalent but more informal ways. Do not use the symbol ∀ or ∃.

a. $\forall x \in \mathbf{R}, x^2 \geq 0$.

b. $\forall x \in \mathbf{R}, x^2 \neq -1$.

c. $\exists m \in \mathbf{Z}^+$ such that $m^2 = m$.

Solution

Note The singular noun is used to refer to the domain when the ∀ symbol is translated as *every, any,* or *each.*

a. All real numbers have nonnegative squares.
   Or: Every real number has a nonnegative square.
   Or: Any real number has a nonnegative square.
   Or: The square of each real number is nonnegative.

b. All real numbers have squares that are not equal to -1.
   Or: No real numbers have squares equal to -1.
   (The words *none are* or *no . . . are* are equivalent to the words *all are not.*)

Note In ordinary English, the statement in part (c) might be taken to be true only if there are at least two positive integers equal to their own squares. In mathematics, we understand the last two statements in part (c) to mean the same thing.

c. There is a positive integer whose square is equal to itself.
   Or: We can find at least one positive integer equal to its own square.
   Or: Some positive integer equals its own square.
   Or: Some positive integers equal their own squares. ▧

Another way to restate universal and existential statements informally is to place the quantification at the end of the sentence. For instance, instead of saying "For any real number x, x^2 is nonnegative," you could say "x^2 is nonnegative for any real number x." In such a case the quantifier is said to "trail" the rest of the sentence.

Example 3.1.6 Trailing Quantifiers

Rewrite the following statements so that the quantifier trails the rest of the sentence.

a. For any integer n, $2n$ is even.

b. There exists at least one real number x such that $x^2 \le 0$.

Solution

a. $2n$ is even for any integer n.

b. $x^2 \le 0$ for some real number x.
   Or: $x^2 \le 0$ for at least one real number x. ▪

Example 3.1.7 Translating from Informal to Formal Language

Rewrite each of the following statements formally. Use quantifiers and variables.

a. All triangles have three sides.

b. No dogs have wings.

c. Some programs are structured.

Solution

a. ∀ triangles t, t has three sides.
   Or: $\forall t \in T$, t has three sides (where T is the set of all triangles).

b. ∀ dogs d, d does not have wings.
   Or: $\forall d \in D$, d does not have wings (where D is the set of all dogs).

c. ∃ a program p such that p is structured.
   Or: $\exists p \in P$ such that p is structured (where P is the set of all programs). ▪

Universal Conditional Statements

A reasonable argument can be made that the most important form of statement in mathematics is the **universal conditional statement:**

$$\forall x, \text{ if } P(x) \text{ then } Q(x).$$

Familiarity with statements of this form is essential if you are to learn to speak mathematics.

Example 3.1.8 Writing Universal Conditional Statements Informally

Rewrite the following statement informally, without quantifiers or variables.

$$\forall x \in \mathbf{R}, \text{ if } x > 2 \text{ then } x^2 > 4.$$

Solution   If a real number is greater than 2 then its square is greater than 4.
Or: Whenever a real number is greater than 2, its square is greater than 4.
Or: The square of any real number greater than 2 is greater than 4.
Or: The squares of all real numbers greater than 2 are greater than 4. ▪

Example 3.1.9 Writing Universal Conditional Statements Formally

Rewrite each of the following statements in the form

$$\forall \underline{\hspace{1cm}}, \text{ if } \underline{\hspace{1cm}} \text{ then } \underline{\hspace{1cm}}.$$

a. If a real number is an integer, then it is a rational number.

    b. All bytes have eight bits.

    c. No fire trucks are green.

Solution

    a. ∀ real numbers x, if x is an integer, then x is a rational number.
      Or: $\forall x \in \mathbf{R}$, if $x \in \mathbf{Z}$ then $x \in \mathbf{Q}$.

    b. $\forall x$, if x is a byte, then x has eight bits.

    c. $\forall x$, if x is a fire truck, then x is not green.

    It is common, as in (b) and (c) above, to omit explicit identification of the domain of predicate variables in universal conditional statements. ■

Careful thought about the meaning of universal conditional statements leads to another level of understanding for why the truth table for an if-then statement must be defined as it is. Consider again the statement

$$\forall \text{ real numbers } x, \text{ if } x > 2 \text{ then } x^2 > 4.$$

Your experience and intuition tell you that this statement is true. But that means that

$$\text{If } x > 2 \text{ then } x^2 > 4$$

must be true for every single real number x. Consequently, it must be true even for values of x that make its hypothesis "$x > 2$" false. In particular, both statements

$$\text{If } 1 > 2 \text{ then } 1^2 > 4 \quad \text{and} \quad \text{If } -3 > 2 \text{ then } (-3)^2 > 4$$

must be true. In both cases the hypothesis is false, but in the first case the conclusion "$1^2 > 4$" is false, and in the second case the conclusion "$(-3)^2 > 4$" is true. Hence, regardless of whether its conclusion is true or false, an if-then statement with a false hypothesis must be true.

    Note also that the definition of valid argument is a universal conditional statement:

      ∀ combinations of truth values for the component statements,
      if the premises are all true then the conclusion is also true.

Equivalent Forms of Universal and Existential Statements

Observe that the two statements "∀ real numbers x, if x is an integer then x is rational" and "∀ integers x, x is rational" mean the same thing. Both have informal translations "All integers are rational." In fact, a statement of the form

$$\forall x \in U, \text{ if } P(x) \text{ then } Q(x)$$

can always be rewritten in the form

$$\forall x \in D, Q(x)$$

by narrowing U to be the domain D consisting of all values of the variable x that make $P(x)$ true. Conversely, a statement of the form

$$\forall x \in D, Q(x)$$

can be rewritten as

$$\forall x, \text{ if } x \text{ is in } D \text{ then } Q(x).$$

Example 3.1.10 Equivalent Forms for Universal Statements

Rewrite the following statement in the two forms "$\forall x$, if _____ then _____" and "$\forall$ _____ x, _____": All squares are rectangles.

Solution
$\forall x$, if x is a square then x is a rectangle.

$\forall$ squares x, x is a rectangle. ▨

Similarly, a statement of the form "$\exists x$ such that $p(x)$ and $Q(x)$" can be rewritten as "$\exists x \varepsilon D$ such that $Q(x)$," where D is the set of all x for which $P(x)$ is true.

Example 3.1.11 Equivalent Forms for Existential Statements

A **prime number** is an integer greater than 1 whose only positive integer factors are itself and 1. Consider the statement "There is an integer that is both prime and even." Let Prime(n) be "n is prime" and Even(n) be "n is even." Use the notation Prime(n) and Even(n) to rewrite this statement in the following two forms:

a. $\exists n$ such that _____ $\wedge$ _____.

b. $\exists$ _____ n such that _____.

Solution

a. $\exists n$ such that Prime(n) $\wedge$ Even(n).

b. Two answers: $\exists$ a prime number n such that Even(n).
$\exists$ an even number n such that Prime(n). ▨

Implicit Quantification

Consider the statement

If a number is an integer, then it is a rational number.

As shown earlier, this statement is equivalent to a universal statement. However, it does not contain the telltale word *all* or *every* or *any* or *each*. The only clue to indicate its universal quantification comes from the presence of the indefinite article a. This is an example of *implicit* universal quantification.

Existential quantification can also be implicit. For instance, the statement "The number 24 can be written as a sum of two even integers" can be expressed formally as "$\exists$ even integers m and n such that $24 = m + n$."

Mathematical writing contains many examples of implicitly quantified statements. Some occur, as in the first example above, through the presence of the word *a* or *an*. Others occur in cases where the general context of a sentence supplies part of its meaning. For example, in an algebra course in which the letter x is always used to indicate a real number, the predicate

If $x > 2$ then $x^2 > 4$

is interpreted to mean the same as the statement

$\forall$ real numbers x, if $x > 2$ then $x^2 > 4$.

Mathematicians often use a double arrow to indicate implicit quantification symbolically. For instance, they might express the above statement as

$$x > 2 \quad \Rightarrow \quad x^2 > 4.$$

> **• Notation**
>
> Let $P(x)$ and $Q(x)$ be predicates and suppose the common domain of x is D.
>
> - The notation $P(x) \Rightarrow Q(x)$ means that every element in the truth set of $P(x)$ is in the truth set of $Q(x)$, or, equivalently, $\forall x, P(x) \rightarrow Q(x)$.
> - The notation $P(x) \Leftrightarrow Q(x)$ means that $P(x)$ and $Q(x)$ have identical truth sets, or, equivalently, $\forall x, P(x) \leftrightarrow Q(x)$.

Example 3.1.12 Using $\Rightarrow$ and $\Leftrightarrow$

Let

$$Q(n) \text{ be } \text{``}n \text{ is a factor of 8,''}$$
$$R(n) \text{ be } \text{``}n \text{ is a factor of 4,''}$$
$$S(n) \text{ be } \text{``}n < 5 \text{ and } n \neq 3,\text{''}$$

and suppose the domain of n is $\mathbf{Z}^+$, the set of positive integers. Use the $\Rightarrow$ and $\Leftrightarrow$ symbols to indicate true relationships among $Q(n)$, $R(n)$, and $S(n)$.

Solution

1. As noted in Example 3.1.2, the truth set of $Q(n)$ is $\{1, 2, 4, 8\}$ when the domain of n is $\mathbf{Z}^+$. By similar reasoning the truth set of $R(n)$ is $\{1, 2, 4\}$. Thus it is true that every element in the truth set of $R(n)$ is in the truth set of $Q(n)$, or, equivalently, $\forall n$ in $\mathbf{Z}^+$, $R(n) \rightarrow Q(n)$. So $R(n) \Rightarrow Q(n)$, or, equivalently

$$n \text{ is a factor of 4} \quad \Rightarrow \quad n \text{ is a factor of 8.}$$

2. The truth set of $S(n)$ is $\{1, 2, 4\}$, which is identical to the truth set of $R(n)$, or, equivalently, $\forall n$ in $\mathbf{Z}^+$, $R(n) \leftrightarrow S(n)$. So $R(n) \Leftrightarrow S(n)$, or, equivalently,

$$n \text{ is a factor of 4} \quad \Leftrightarrow \quad n < 5 \text{ and } n \neq 3.$$

Moreover, since every element in the truth set of $S(n)$ is in the truth set of $Q(n)$, or, equivalently, $\forall n$ in $\mathbf{Z}^+$, $S(n) \rightarrow Q(n)$, then $S(n) \Rightarrow Q(n)$, or, equivalently,

$$n < 5 \text{ and } n \neq 3 \quad \Rightarrow \quad n \text{ is a factor of 8.} \quad \blacksquare$$

Some questions of quantification can be quite subtle. For instance, a mathematics text might contain the following:

a. $(x + 1)^2 = x^2 + 2x + 1$.   b. Solve $3x - 4 = 5$.

Although neither (a) nor (b) contains explicit quantification, the reader is supposed to understand that the x in (a) is universally quantified whereas the x in (b) is existentially quantified. When the quantification is made explicit, (a) and (b) become

a. $\forall$ real numbers x, $(x + 1)^2 = x^2 + 2x + 1$.

b. Show (by finding a value) that $\exists$ a real number x such that $3x - 4 = 5$.

The quantification of a statement—whether universal or existential—crucially determines both how the statement can be applied and what method must be used to establish its truth. Thus it is important to be alert to the presence of hidden quantifiers when you read mathematics so that you will interpret statements in a logically correct way.

Tarski's World

Tarski's World is a computer program developed by information scientists Jon Barwise and John Etchemendy to help teach the principles of logic. It is described in their book *The Language of First-Order Logic*, which is accompanied by a CD-Rom containing the program Tarski's World, named after the great logician Alfred Tarski.

Example 3.1.13 Investigating Tarski's World

*Alfred Tarski
(1902–1983)*

The program for Tarski's World provides pictures of blocks of various sizes, shapes, and colors, which are located on a grid. Shown in Figure 3.1.1 is a picture of an arrangement of objects in a two-dimensional Tarski world. The configuration can be described using logical operators and—for the two-dimensional version—notation such as Triangle(x), meaning "x is a triangle," Blue(y), meaning "y is blue," and RightOf(x, y), meaning "x is to the right of y (but possibly in a different row)." Individual objects can be given names such as a, b, or c.

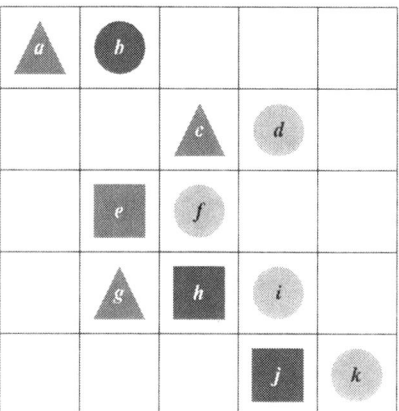

Figure 3.1.1

Determine the truth or falsity of each of the following statements. The domain for all variables is the set of objects in the Tarski world shown above.

a. $\forall t$, Triangle(t) $\rightarrow$ Blue(t).

b. $\forall x$, Blue(x) $\rightarrow$ Triangle(x).

c. $\exists y$ such that Square(y) $\wedge$ RightOf(d, y).

d. $\exists z$ such that Square(z) $\wedge$ Gray(z).

Solution

    a. This statement is true: All the triangles are blue.

    b. This statement is false. As a counterexample, note that e is blue and it is not a triangle.

    c. This statement is true because e and h are both square and d is to their right.

    d. This statement is false: All the squares are either blue or black.

Test Yourself

Answers to Test Yourself questions are located at the end of each section.

1. If $P(x)$ is a predicate with domain D, the truth set of $P(x)$ is denoted ____. We read these symbols out loud as ____.

2. Some ways to express the symbol $\forall$ in words are ____.

3. Some ways to express the symbol $\exists$ in words are ____.

4. A statement of the form $\forall x \in D$, $Q(x)$ is true if, and only if, $Q(x)$ is ____ for ____.

5. A statement of the form $\exists x \in D$ such that $Q(x)$ is true if, and only if, $Q(x)$ is ____ for ____.

Exercise Set 3.1*

1. A menagerie consists of seven brown dogs, two black dogs, six gray cats, ten black cats, five blue birds, six yellow birds, and one black bird. Determine which of the following statements are true and which are false.
   a. There is an animal in the menagerie that is red.
   b. Every animal in the menagerie is a bird or a mammal.
   c. Every animal in the menagerie is brown or gray or black.
   d. There is an animal in the menagerie that is neither a cat nor a dog.
   e. No animal in the menagerie is blue.
   f. There are in the menagerie a dog, a cat, and a bird that all have the same color.

2. Indicate which of the following statements are true and which are false. Justify your answers as best as you can.
   a. Every integer is a real number.
   b. 0 is a positive real number.
   c. For all real numbers r, $-r$ is a negative real number.
   d. Every real number is an integer.

3. Let $P(x)$ be the predicate "$x > 1/x$."
   a. Write $P(2)$, $P(\frac{1}{2})$, $P(-1)$, $P(-\frac{1}{2})$, and $P(-8)$, and indicate which of these statements are true and which are false.
   b. Find the truth set of $P(x)$ if the domain of x is $\mathbf{R}$, the set of all real numbers.
   c. If the domain is the set $\mathbf{R}^+$ of all positive real numbers, what is the truth set of $P(x)$?

4. Let $Q(n)$ be the predicate "$n^2 \leq 30$."
   a. Write $Q(2)$, $Q(-2)$, $Q(7)$, and $Q(-7)$, and indicate which of these statements are true and which are false.
   b. Find the truth set of $Q(n)$ if the domain of n is $\mathbf{Z}$, the set of all integers.
   c. If the domain is the set $\mathbf{Z}^+$ of all positive integers, what is the truth set of $Q(n)$?

5. Let $Q(x, y)$ be the predicate "If $x < y$ then $x^2 < y^2$" with domain for both x and y being the set $\mathbf{R}$ of real numbers.
   a. Explain why $Q(x, y)$ is false if $x = -2$ and $y = 1$.
   b. Give values different from those in part (a) for which $Q(x, y)$ is false.
   c. Explain why $Q(x, y)$ is true if $x = 3$ and $y = 8$.
   d. Give values different from those in part (c) for which $Q(x, y)$ is true.

6. Let $R(m, n)$ be the predicate "If m is a factor of n^2 then m is a factor of n," with domain for both m and n being the set $\mathbf{Z}$ of integers.
   a. Explain why $R(m, n)$ is false if $m = 25$ and $n = 10$.
   b. Give values different from those in part (a) for which $R(m, n)$ is false.
   c. Explain why $R(m, n)$ is true if $m = 5$ and $n = 10$.
   d. Give values different from those in part (c) for which $R(m, n)$ is true.

7. Find the truth set of each predicate.
   a. predicate: $6/d$ is an integer, domain: $\mathbf{Z}$
   b. predicate: $6/d$ is an integer, domain: $\mathbf{Z}^+$
   c. predicate: $1 \leq x^2 \leq 4$, domain: $\mathbf{R}$
   d. predicate: $1 \leq x^2 \leq 4$, domain: $\mathbf{Z}$

8. Let $B(x)$ be "$-10 < x < 10$." Find the truth set of $B(x)$ for each of the following domains.
   a. $\mathbf{Z}$ b. $\mathbf{Z}^+$ c. The set of all even integers

Find counterexamples to show that the statements in 9–12 are false.

9. $\forall x \in \mathbf{R}, x > 1/x$.

10. $\forall a \in \mathbf{Z}, (a - 1)/a$ is not an integer.

11. $\forall$ positive integers m and n, $m \cdot n \geq m + n$.

12. $\forall$ real numbers x and y, $\sqrt{x + y} = \sqrt{x} + \sqrt{y}$.

13. Consider the following statement:

$$\forall \text{ basketball players } x, x \text{ is tall.}$$

   Which of the following are equivalent ways of expressing this statement?
   a. Every basketball player is tall.
   b. Among all the basketball players, some are tall.
   c. Some of all the tall people are basketball players.
   d. Anyone who is tall is a basketball player.
   e. All people who are basketball players are tall.
   f. Anyone who is a basketball player is a tall person.

---

*For exercises with blue numbers or letters, solutions are given in Appendix B. The symbol H indicates that only a hint or a partial solution is given. The symbol $*$ signals that an exercise is more challenging than usual.

14. Consider the following statement:

$$\exists x \in \mathbf{R} \text{ such that } x^2 = 2.$$

Which of the following are equivalent ways of expressing this statement?
a. The square of each real number is 2.
b. Some real numbers have square 2.
c. The number x has square 2, for some real number x.
d. If x is a real number, then $x^2 = 2$.
e. Some real number has square 2.
f. There is at least one real number whose square is 2.

H 15. Rewrite the following statements informally in at least two different ways without using variables or quantifiers.
a. $\forall$ rectangles x, x is a quadrilateral.
b. $\exists$ a set A such that A has 16 subsets.

16. Rewrite each of the following statements in the form "$\forall$ _____ x, _____."
a. All dinosaurs are extinct.
b. Every real number is positive, negative, or zero.
c. No irrational numbers are integers.
d. No logicians are lazy.
e. The number 2,147,581,953 is not equal to the square of any integer.
f. The number -1 is not equal to the square of any real number.

17. Rewrite each of the following in the form "$\exists$ _____ x such that _____."
a. Some exercises have answers.
b. Some real numbers are rational.

18. Let D be the set of all students at your school, and let $M(s)$ be "s is a math major," let $C(s)$ be "s is a computer science student," and let $E(s)$ be "s is an engineering student." Express each of the following statements using quantifiers, variables, and the predicates $M(s)$, $C(s)$, and $E(s)$.
a. There is an engineering student who is a math major.
b. Every computer science student is an engineering student.
c. No computer science students are engineering students.
d. Some computer science students are also math majors.
e. Some computer science students are engineering students and some are not.

19. Consider the following statement:

$$\forall \text{ integers } n, \text{ if } n^2 \text{ is even then } n \text{ is even.}$$

Which of the following are equivalent ways of expressing this statement?
a. All integers have even squares and are even.
b. Given any integer whose square is even, that integer is itself even.
c. For all integers, there are some whose square is even.
d. Any integer with an even square is even.
e. If the square of an integer is even, then that integer is even.
f. All even integers have even squares.

H 20. Rewrite the following statement informally in at least two different ways without using variables or the symbol $\forall$ or the words "for all."

$$\forall \text{ real numbers } x, \text{ if } x \text{ is positive, then} \\ \text{the square root of } x \text{ is positive.}$$

21. Rewrite the following statements so that the quantifier trails the rest of the sentence.
a. For any graph G, the total degree of G is even.
b. For any isosceles triangle T, the base angles of T are equal.
c. There exists a prime number p such that p is even.
d. There exists a continuous function f such that f is not differentiable.

22. Rewrite each of the following statements in the form "$\forall$ _____ x, if _____ then _____."
a. All Java programs have at least 5 lines.
b. Any valid argument with true premises has a true conclusion.

23. Rewrite each of the following statements in the two forms "$\forall x$, if _____ then _____" and "$\forall$ _____ x, _____" (without an if-then).
a. All equilateral triangles are isosceles.
b. Every computer science student needs to take data structures.

24. Rewrite the following statements in the two forms "$\exists$ _____ x such that _____" and "$\exists x$ such that _____ and _____."
a. Some hatters are mad.   b. Some questions are easy.

25. The statement "The square of any rational number is rational" can be rewritten formally as "For all rational numbers x, x^2 is rational" or as "For all x, if x is rational then x^2 is rational." Rewrite each of the following statements in the two forms "$\forall$ _____ x, _____" and "$\forall x$, if _____, then _____" or in the two forms "$\forall$ _____ x and y, _____" and "$\forall x$ and y, if _____, then _____."
a. The reciprocal of any nonzero fraction is a fraction.
b. The derivative of any polynomial function is a polynomial function.
c. The sum of the angles of any triangle is 180°.
d. The negative of any irrational number is irrational.
e. The sum of any two even integers is even.
f. The product of any two fractions is a fraction.

26. Consider the statement "All integers are rational numbers but some rational numbers are not integers."
a. Write this statement in the form "$\forall x$, if _____ then _____, but $\exists$ _____ x such that _____."
b. Let Ratl(x) be "x is a rational number" and Int(x) be "x is an integer." Write the given statement formally using only the symbols Ratl(x), Int(x), $\forall$, $\exists$, $\wedge$, $\vee$, $\sim$, and $\rightarrow$.

27. Refer to the picture of Tarski's world given in Example 3.1.13. Let Above(x, y) mean that x is above y (but possibly in a different column). Determine the truth or falsity

of each of the following statements. Give reasons for your answers.

a. $\forall u$, Circle(u) → Gray(u).

b. $\forall u$, Gray(u) → Circle(u).

c. $\exists y$ such that Square(y) ∧ Above(y, d).

d. $\exists z$ such that Triangle(z) ∧ Above(f, z).

In 28–30, rewrite each statement without using quantifiers or variables. Indicate which are true and which are false, and justify your answers as best as you can.

28. Let the domain of x be the set D of objects discussed in mathematics courses, and let Real(x) be "x is a real number," Pos(x) be "x is a positive real number," Neg(x) be "x is a negative real number," and Int(x) be "x is an integer."
    a. Pos(0)
    b. $\forall x$, Real(x) ∧ Neg(x) → Pos($-x$).
    c. $\forall x$, Int(x) → Real(x).
    d. $\exists x$ such that Real(x) ∧ ∼Int(x).

29. Let the domain of x be the set of geometric figures in the plane, and let Square(x) be "x is a square" and Rect(x) be "x is a rectangle."
    a. $\exists x$ such that Rect(x) ∧ Square(x).
    b. $\exists x$ such that Rect(x) ∧ ∼Square(x).
    c. $\forall x$, Square(x) → Rect(x).

30. Let the domain of x be the set **Z** of integers, and let Odd(x) be "x is odd," Prime(x) be "x is prime," and Square(x) be

"x is a perfect square." (An integer n is said to be a **perfect square** if, and only if, it equals the square of some integer. For example, 25 is a perfect square because $25 = 5^2$.)

a. $\exists x$ such that Prime(x) ∧ ∼Odd(x).

b. $\forall x$, Prime(x) → ∼Square(x).

c. $\exists x$ such that Odd(x) ∧ Square(x).

H 31. In any mathematics or computer science text other than this book, find an example of a statement that is universal but is implicitly quantified. Copy the statement as it appears and rewrite it making the quantification explicit. Give a complete citation for your example, including title, author, publisher, year, and page number.

32. Let **R** be the domain of the predicate variable x. Which of the following are true and which are false? Give counter examples for the statements that are false.
    a. $x > 2 \Rightarrow x > 1$
    b. $x > 2 \Rightarrow x^2 > 4$
    c. $x^2 > 4 \Rightarrow x > 2$
    d. $x^2 > 4 \Leftrightarrow |x| > 2$

33. Let **R** be the domain of the predicate variables a, b, c, and d. Which of the following are true and which are false? Give counterexamples for the statements that are false.
    a. $a > 0$ and $b > 0 \Rightarrow ab > 0$
    b. $a < 0$ and $b < 0 \Rightarrow ab < 0$
    c. $ab = 0 \Rightarrow a = 0$ or $b = 0$
    d. $a < b$ and $c < d \Rightarrow ac < bd$

Answers for Test Yourself

1. $\{x \in D \mid P(x)\}$; the set of all x in D such that $P(x)$ 2. *Possible answers:* for all, for every, for any, for each, for arbitrary, given any   3. *Possible answers:* there exists, there exist, there exists at least one, for some, for at least one, we can find a   4. true; every x in D (*Alternative answers:* all x in D; each x in D)   5. true; at least one x in D (*Alternative answer:* some x in D)

3.2 Predicates and Quantified Statements II

TOUCHSTONE: *Stand you both forth now: stroke your chins, and swear by your beards that I am a knave.*

CELIA: *By our beards—if we had them—thou art.*

TOUCHSTONE: *By my knavery—if I had it—then I were; but if you swear by that that is not, you are not forsworn.* — William Shakespeare, *As You Like It*

This section continues the discussion of predicates and quantified statements begun in Section 3.1. It contains the rules for negating quantified statements; an exploration of the relation among $\forall$, $\exists$, ∧, and ∨; an introduction to the concept of vacuous truth of universal statements; examples of variants of universal conditional statements; and an extension of the meaning of *necessary, sufficient,* and *only if* to quantified statements.

Negations of Quantified Statements

Consider the statement "All mathematicians wear glasses." Many people would say that its negation is "No mathematicians wear glasses," but if even one mathematician does not wear glasses, then the sweeping statement that *all* mathematicians wear glasses is false. So a correct negation is "There is at least one mathematician who does not wear glasses."

The general form of the negation of a universal statement follows immediately from the definitions of negation and of the truth values for universal and existential statements.

Theorem 3.2.1 Negation of a Universal Statement

The negation of a statement of the form

$$\forall x \text{ in } D, \ Q(x)$$

is logically equivalent to a statement of the form

$$\exists x \text{ in } D \text{ such that } \sim Q(x).$$

Symbolically, $\sim(\forall x \in D, \ Q(x)) \equiv \exists x \in D \text{ such that } \sim Q(x).$

Thus

> **The negation of a universal statement ("all are") is logically equivalent to an existential statement ("some are not" or "there is at least one that is not").**

Note that when we speak of **logical equivalence for quantified statements,** we mean that the statements always have identical truth values no matter what predicates are substituted for the predicate symbols and no matter what sets are used for the domains of the predicate variables.

Now consider the statement "Some snowflakes are the same." What is its negation? For this statement to be false means that not a single snowflake is the same as any other. In other words, "No snowflakes are the same," or "All snowflakes are different."

The general form for the negation of an existential statement follows immediately from the definitions of negation and of the truth values for existential and universal statements.

Theorem 3.2.2 Negation of an Existential Statement

The negation of a statement of the form

$$\exists x \text{ in } D \text{ such that } Q(x)$$

is logically equivalent to a statement of the form

$$\forall x \text{ in } D, \sim Q(x).$$

Symbolically, $\sim(\exists x \in D \text{ such that } Q(x)) \equiv \forall x \in D, \sim Q(x).$

Thus

> **The negation of an existential statement ("some are") is logically equivalent to a universal statement ("none are" or "all are not").**

Example 3.2.1 Negating Quantified Statements

Write formal negations for the following statements:

a. ∀ primes p, p is odd.

b. ∃ a triangle T such that the sum of the angles of T equals 200°.

Solution

a. By applying the rule for the negation of a ∀ statement, you can see that the answer is

∃ a prime p such that p is not odd.

b. By applying the rule for the negation of a ∃ statement, you can see that the answer is

∀ triangles T, the sum of the angles of T does not equal 200°.   ■

You need to exercise special care to avoid mistakes when writing negations of statements that are given informally. One way to avoid error is to rewrite the statement formally and take the negation using the formal rule.

Example 3.2.2 More Negations

Rewrite the following statement formally. Then write formal and informal negations.

No politicians are honest.

Solution

Formal version: ∀ politicians x, x is not honest.

Formal negation: ∃ a politician x such that x is honest.

Informal negation: Some politicians are honest.   ■

Another way to avoid error when taking negations of statements that are given in informal language is to ask yourself, "What *exactly* would it mean for the given statement to be false? What statement, if true, would be equivalent to saying that the given statement is false?"

Example 3.2.3 Still More Negations

Write informal negations for the following statements:

a. All computer programs are finite.

b. Some computer hackers are over 40.

c. The number 1,357 is divisible by some integer between 1 and 37.

Solution

a. What exactly would it mean for this statement to be false? The statement asserts that all computer programs satisfy a certain property. So for it to be false, there would have to be at least one computer program that does not satisfy the property. Thus the answer is

There is a computer program that is not finite.

Or: Some computer programs are infinite.

b. This statement is equivalent to saying that there is at least one computer hacker with a certain property. So for it to be false, not a single computer hacker can have that property. Thus the negation is

No computer hackers are over 40.

Or: All computer hackers are 40 or under.

Note   Which is true: the statement in part (c) or its negation? Is 1,357 divisible by some integer between 1 and 37? Or is 1,357 not divisible by any integer between 1 and 37?

Caution!   Just inserting the word *not* to negate a quantified statement can result in a statement that is ambiguous.

c. This statement has a trailing quantifier. Written formally it becomes:

$$\exists \text{ an integer } n \text{ between 1 and 37 such that 1,357 is divisible by } n.$$

Its negation is therefore

$$\forall \text{ integers } n \text{ between 1 and 37; 1,357 is not divisible by } n.$$

An informal version of the negation is

The number 1,357 is not divisible by any integer between 1 and 37.   ∎

Informal negations of many universal statements can be constructed simply by inserting the word *not* or the words *do not* at an appropriate place. However, the resulting statements may be ambiguous. For example, a possible negation of "All mathematicians wear glasses" is "All mathematicians do not wear glasses." The problem is that this sentence has two meanings. With the proper verbal stress on the word *not*, it could be interpreted as the logical negation. (What! You say that all mathematicians wear glasses? Nonsense! All mathematicians do *not* wear glasses.) On the other hand, stated in a flat tone of voice (try it!), it would mean that all mathematicians are nonwearers of glasses; that is, not a single mathematician wears glasses. This is a much stronger statement than the logical negation: It implies the negation but is not equivalent to it.

Negations of Universal Conditional Statements

Negations of universal conditional statements are of special importance in mathematics. The form of such negations can be derived from facts that have already been established.
    By definition of the negation of a *for all* statement,

$$\sim(\forall x, P(x) \to Q(x)) \equiv \exists x \text{ such that } \sim(P(x) \to Q(x)).   \quad 3.2.1$$

But the negation of an if-then statement is logically equivalent to an *and* statement. More precisely,

$$\sim(P(x) \to Q(x)) \equiv P(x) \land \sim Q(x).   \quad 3.2.2$$

Substituting (3.2.2) into (3.2.1) gives

$$\sim(\forall x, P(x) \to Q(x)) \equiv \exists x \text{ such that } (P(x) \land \sim Q(x)).$$

Written less symbolically, this becomes

Negation of a Universal Conditional Statement

$$\sim(\forall x, \text{ if } P(x) \text{ then } Q(x)) \equiv \exists x \text{ such that } P(x) \text{ and } \sim Q(x).$$

Example 3.2.4 Negating Universal Conditional Statements

Write a formal negation for statement (a) and an informal negation for statement (b).

a. ∀ people p, if p is blond then p has blue eyes.

b. If a computer program has more than 100,000 lines, then it contains a bug.

Solution

a. ∃ a person p such that p is blond and p does not have blue eyes.

b. There is at least one computer program that has more than 100,000 lines and does not contain a bug.   ∎

The Relation among ∀, ∃, ∧, and ∨

The negation of a *for all* statement is a *there exists* statement, and the negation of a *there exists* statement is a *for all* statement. These facts are analogous to De Morgan's laws, which state that the negation of an *and* statement is an *or* statement and that the negation of an *or* statement is an *and* statement. This similarity is not accidental. In a sense, universal statements are generalizations of *and* statements, and existential statements are generalizations of *or* statements.

If $Q(x)$ is a predicate and the domain D of x is the set $\{x_1, x_2, \ldots, x_n\}$, then the statements

$$\forall x \in D, Q(x)$$

and

$$Q(x_1) \wedge Q(x_2) \wedge \cdots \wedge Q(x_n)$$

are logically equivalent. For example, let $Q(x)$ be "$x \cdot x = x$" and suppose $D = \{0, 1\}$. Then

$$\forall x \in D, Q(x)$$

can be rewritten as

$$\forall \text{ binary digits } x, x \cdot x = x.$$

This is equivalent to

$$0 \cdot 0 = 0 \quad \text{and} \quad 1 \cdot 1 = 1,$$

which can be rewritten in symbols as

$$Q(0) \wedge Q(1).$$

Similarly, if $Q(x)$ is a predicate and $D = \{x_1, x_2, \ldots, x_n\}$, then the statements

$$\exists x \in D \text{ such that } Q(x)$$

and

$$Q(x_1) \vee Q(x_2) \vee \cdots \vee Q(x_n)$$

are logically equivalent. For example, let $Q(x)$ be "$x + x = x$" and suppose $D = \{0, 1\}$. Then

$$\exists x \in D \text{ such that } Q(x)$$

can be rewritten as

$$\exists \text{ a binary digit } x \text{ such that } x + x = x.$$

This is equivalent to

$$0 + 0 = 0 \quad \text{or} \quad 1 + 1 = 1,$$

which can be rewritten in symbols as

$$Q(0) \vee Q(1).$$

Vacuous Truth of Universal Statements

Suppose a bowl sits on a table and next to the bowl is a pile of five blue and five gray balls, any of which may be placed in the bowl. If three blue balls and one gray ball are placed in the bowl, as shown in Figure 3.2.1(a), the statement "All the balls in the bowl are blue" would be false (since one of the balls in the bowl is gray).

Now suppose that no balls at all are placed in the bowl, as shown in Figure 3.2.1(b). Consider the statement

All the balls in the bowl are blue.

Is this statement true or false? The statement is false if, and only if, its negation is true. And its negation is

There exists a ball in the bowl that is not blue.

But the only way this negation can be true is for there actually to be a nonblue ball in the bowl. And there is not! Hence the negation is false, and so the statement is true "by default."

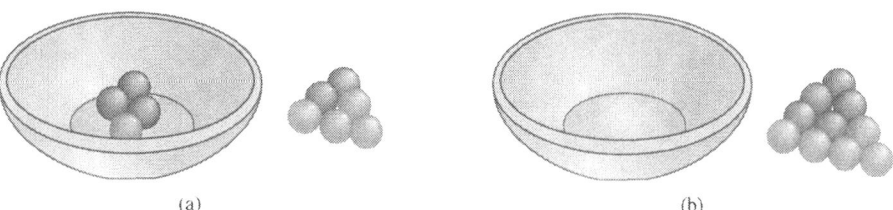

(a)   (b)

Figure 3.2.1

In general, a statement of the form

$$\forall x \text{ in } D, \text{ if } P(x) \text{ then } Q(x)$$

is called **vacuously true** or **true by default** if, and only if, $P(x)$ is false for every x in D.

By the way, in ordinary language the words *in general* mean that something is usually, but not always, the case. (In general, I take the bus home, but today I walked.) In mathematics, the words *in general* are used quite differently. When they occur just after discussion of a particular example (as in the preceding paragraph), they are a signal that what is to follow is a generalization of some aspect of the example that always holds true.

Variants of Universal Conditional Statements

Recall from Section 2.2 that a conditional statement has a contrapositive, a converse, and an inverse. The definitions of these terms can be extended to universal conditional statements.

• Definition

Consider a statement of the form: $\forall x \in D$, if $P(x)$ then $Q(x)$.

1. Its **contrapositive** is the statement: $\forall x \in D$, if $\sim Q(x)$ then $\sim P(x)$.

2. Its **converse** is the statement: $\forall x \in D$, if $Q(x)$ then $P(x)$.

3. Its **inverse** is the statement: $\forall x \in D$, if $\sim P(x)$ then $\sim Q(x)$.

Example 3.2.5 Contrapositive, Converse, and Inverse of a Universal Conditional Statement

Write a formal and an informal contrapositive, converse, and inverse for the following statement:

> If a real number is greater than 2, then its square is greater than 4.

Solution   The formal version of this statement is $\forall x \in \mathbf{R}$, if $x > 2$ then $x^2 > 4$.

Contrapositive: $\forall x \in \mathbf{R}$, if $x^2 \leq 4$ then $x \leq 2$.
Or: If the square of a real number is less than or equal to 4, then the number is less than or equal to 2.

Converse: $\forall x \in \mathbf{R}$, if $x^2 > 4$ then $x > 2$.
Or: If the square of a real number is greater than 4, then the number is greater than 2.

Inverse: $\forall x \in \mathbf{R}$, if $x \leq 2$ then $x^2 \leq 4$.
Or: If a real number is less than or equal to 2, then the square of the number is less than or equal to 4.

Note that in solving this example, we have used the equivalence of "$x \not> a$" and "$x \leq a$" for all real numbers x and a. (See page 33.) ∎

In Section 2.2 we showed that a conditional statement is logically equivalent to its contrapositive and that it is not logically equivalent to either its converse or its inverse. The following discussion shows that these facts generalize to the case of universal conditional statements and their contrapositives, converses, and inverses.

Let $P(x)$ and $Q(x)$ be any predicates, let D be the domain of x, and consider the statement

$$\forall x \in D, \text{ if } P(x) \text{ then } Q(x)$$

and its contrapositive

$$\forall x \in D, \text{ if } \sim Q(x) \text{ then } \sim P(x).$$

Any particular x in D that makes "if $P(x)$ then $Q(x)$" true also makes "if $\sim Q(x)$ then $\sim P(x)$" true (by the logical equivalence between $p \to q$ and $\sim q \to \sim p$). It follows that the sentence "If $P(x)$ then $Q(x)$" is true for all x in D if, and only if, the sentence "If $\sim Q(x)$ then $\sim P(x)$" is true for all x in D.

Thus we write the following and say that a universal conditional statement is logically equivalent to its contrapositive:

$$\forall x \in D, \text{ if } P(x) \text{ then } Q(x) \equiv \forall x \in D, \text{ if } \sim Q(x) \text{ then } \sim P(x)$$

In Example 3.2.5 we noted that the statement

$$\forall x \in \mathbf{R}, \text{ if } x > 2 \text{ then } x^2 > 4$$

has the converse

$$\forall x \in \mathbf{R}, \text{ if } x^2 > 4 \text{ then } x > 2.$$

Observe that the statement is true whereas its converse is false (since, for instance, $(-3)^2 = 9 > 4$ but $-3 \not> 2$). This shows that a universal conditional statement may have a different truth value from its converse. Hence a universal conditional statement is not logically equivalent to its converse. This is written in symbols as follows:

$$\forall x \in D, \text{ if } P(x) \text{ then } Q(x) \not\equiv \forall x \in D, \text{ if } Q(x) \text{ then } P(x).$$

In the exercises at the end of this section, you are asked to show similarly that a universal conditional statement is not logically equivalent to its inverse.

$$\forall x \in D, \text{ if } P(x) \text{ then } Q(x) \not\equiv \forall x \in D, \text{ if } \sim P(x) \text{ then } \sim Q(x).$$

Necessary and Sufficient Conditions, Only If

The definitions of *necessary*, *sufficient*, and *only if* can also be extended to apply to universal conditional statements.

• Definition

- "$\forall x, r(x)$ is a **sufficient condition** for $s(x)$" means "$\forall x,$ if $r(x)$ then $s(x)$."
- "$\forall x, r(x)$ is a **necessary condition** for $s(x)$" means "$\forall x,$ if $\sim r(x)$ then $\sim s(x)$" or, equivalently, "$\forall x,$ if $s(x)$ then $r(x)$."
- "$\forall x, r(x)$ **only if** $s(x)$" means "$\forall x,$ if $\sim s(x)$ then $\sim r(x)$" or, equivalently, "$\forall x,$ if $r(x)$ then $s(x)$."

Example 3.2.6 Necessary and Sufficient Conditions

Rewrite the following statements as quantified conditional statements. Do not use the word *necessary* or *sufficient*.

a. Squareness is a sufficient condition for rectangularity.

b. Being at least 35 years old is a necessary condition for being President of the United States.

Solution

a. A formal version of the statement is

$\forall x$, if x is a square, then x is a rectangle.

Or, in informal language:

If a figure is a square, then it is a rectangle.

b. Using formal language, you could write the answer as

$\forall$ people x, if x is younger than 35, then x cannot be President of the United States.

Or, by the equivalence between a statement and its contrapositive:

$\forall$ people x, if x is President of the United States, then x is at least 35 years old. ■

Example 3.2.7 Only If

Rewrite the following as a universal conditional statement:

A product of two numbers is 0 only if one of the numbers is 0.

Solution   Using informal language, you could write the answer as

If neither of two numbers is 0, then the product of the numbers is not 0.

Or, by the equivalence between a statement and its contrapositive,

If a product of two numbers is 0, then one of the numbers is 0. ■

Test Yourself

1. A negation for "All R have property S" is "There is ____ R that ____."

2. A negation for "Some R have property S" is "____."

3. A negation for "For all x, if x has property P then x has property Q" is "____."

4. The converse of "For all x, if x has property P then x has property Q" is "____."

5. The contrapositive of "For all x, if x has property P then x has property Q" is "____."

6. The inverse of "For all x, if x has property P then x has property Q" is "____."

Exercise Set 3.2

1. Which of the following is a negation for "All discrete mathematics students are athletic"? More than one answer may be correct.

a. There is a discrete mathematics student who is nonathletic.

b. All discrete mathematics students are nonathletic.

c. There is an athletic person who is a discrete mathematics student.

d. No discrete mathematics students are athletic.

e. Some discrete mathematics students are nonathletic.

f. No athletic people are discrete mathematics students.

2. Which of the following is a negation for "All dogs are loyal"? More than one answer may be correct.
   a. All dogs are disloyal.   b. No dogs are loyal.
   c. Some dogs are disloyal.   d. Some dogs are loyal.
   e. There is a disloyal animal that is not a dog.
   f. There is a dog that is disloyal.
   g. No animals that are not dogs are loyal.
   h. Some animals that are not dogs are loyal.

3. Write a formal negation for each of the following statements:
   a. ∀ fish x, x has gills.
   b. ∀ computers c, c has a CPU.
   c. ∃ a movie m such that m is over 6 hours long.
   d. ∃ a band b such that b has won at least 10 Grammy awards.

4. Write an informal negation for each of the following statements. Be careful to avoid negations that are ambiguous.
   a. All dogs are friendly.
   b. All people are happy.
   c. Some suspicions were substantiated.
   d. Some estimates are accurate.

5. Write a negation for each of the following statements.
   a. Any valid argument has a true conclusion.
   b. Every real number is positive, negative, or zero.

6. Write a negation for each of the following statements.
   a. Sets A and B do not have any points in common.
   b. Towns P and Q are not connected by any road on the map.

7. Informal language is actually more complex than formal language. For instance, the sentence "There are no orders from store A for item B" contains the words *there are*. Is the statement existential? Write an informal negation for the statement, and then write the statement formally using quantifiers and variables.

8. Consider the statement "There are no simple solutions to life's problems." Write an informal negation for the statement, and then write the statement formally using quantifiers and variables.

Write a negation for each statement in 9 and 10.

9. ∀ real numbers x, if $x > 3$ then $x^2 > 9$.

10. ∀ computer programs P, if P compiles without error messages, then P is correct.

In each of 11–14 determine whether the proposed negation is correct. If it is not, write a correct negation.

11.   *Statement:* The sum of any two irrational numbers is irrational.
       Proposed negation: The sum of any two irrational numbers is rational.

12.   *Statement:* The product of any irrational number and any rational number is irrational.

Proposed negation: The product of any irrational number and any rational number is rational.

13.   *Statement:* For all integers n, if n^2 is even then n is even.
       Proposed negation: For all integers n, if n^2 is even then n is not even.

14.   *Statement:* For all real numbers x_1 and x_2, if $x_1^2 = x_2^2$ then $x_1 = x_2$.
       Proposed negation: For all real numbers x_1 and x_2, if $x_1^2 = x_2^2$ then $x_1 \neq x_2$.

15. Let $D = \{-48, -14, -8, 0, 1, 3, 16, 23, 26, 32, 36\}$. Determine which of the following statements are true and which are false. Provide counterexamples for those statements that are false.
   a. $\forall x \in D$, if x is odd then $x > 0$.
   b. $\forall x \in D$, if x is less than 0 then x is even.
   c. $\forall x \in D$, if x is even then $x \leq 0$.
   d. $\forall x \in D$, if the ones digit of x is 2, then the tens digit is 3 or 4.
   e. $\forall x \in D$, if the ones digit of x is 6, then the tens digit is 1 or 2.

In 16–23, write a negation for each statement.

16. ∀ real numbers x, if $x^2 \geq 1$ then $x > 0$.

17. ∀ integers d, if $6/d$ is an integer then $d = 3$.

18. $\forall x \in \mathbf{R}$, if $x(x+1) > 0$ then $x > 0$ or $x < -1$.

19. $\forall n \in \mathbf{Z}$, if n is prime then n is odd or $n = 2$.

20. ∀ integers a, b and c, if $a - b$ is even and $b - c$ is even, then $a - c$ is even.

21. ∀ integers n, if n is divisible by 6, then n is divisible by 2 and n is divisible by 3.

22. If the square of an integer is odd, then the integer is odd.

23. If a function is differentiable then it is continuous.

24. Rewrite the statements in each pair in if-then form and indicate the logical relationship between them.
   a. All the children in Tom's family are female.
      All the females in Tom's family are children.
   b. All the integers greater than 5 that end in 1, 3, 7, or 9 are prime.
      All the integers greater than 5 that are prime end in 1, 3, 7, or 9.

25. Each of the following statements is true. In each case write the converse of the statement, and give a counterexample showing that the converse is false.
   a. If n is any prime number that is greater than 2, then $n + 1$ is even.
   b. If m is any odd integer, then $2m$ is even.
   c. If two circles intersect in exactly two points, then they do not have a common center.

In 26–33, for each statement in the referenced exercise write the converse, inverse, and contrapositive. Indicate as best as you can which among the statement, its converse, its inverse, and its contrapositive are true and which are false. Give a counterexample for each that is false.

26. Exercise 16   27. Exercise 17

28. Exercise 18   29. Exercise 19

30. Exercise 20   31. Exercise 21

32. Exercise 22   33. Exercise 23

34. Write the contrapositive for each of the following statements.
    a. If n is prime, then n is not divisible by any prime number between 1 and $\sqrt{n}$ inclusive. (Assume that n is a fixed integer that is greater than 1.)
    b. If A and B do not have any elements in common, then they are disjoint. (Assume that A and B are fixed sets.)

35. Give an example to show that a universal conditional statement is not logically equivalent to its inverse.

✳ 36. If $P(x)$ is a predicate and the domain of x is the set of all real numbers, let R be "$\forall x \in \mathbf{Z}, P(x)$," let S be "$\forall x \in \mathbf{Q}, P(x)$," and let T be the "$\forall x \in \mathbf{R}, P(x)$."
    a. Find a definition for $P(x)$ (but do not use "$x \in \mathbf{Z}$") so that R is true and both S and T are false.
    b. Find a definition for $P(x)$ (but do not use "$x \in \mathbf{Q}$") so that both R and S are true and T is false.

37. Consider the following sequence of digits: 0204. A person claims that all the 1's in the sequence are to the left of all the 0's in the sequence. Is this true? Justify your answer. (*Hint:* Write the claim formally and write a formal negation for it. Is the negation true or false?)

38. True or false? All occurrences of the letter u in *Discrete Mathematics* are lowercase. Justify your answer.

Rewrite each statement of 39–42 in if-then form.

39. Earning a grade of C− in this course is a sufficient condition for it to count toward graduation.

40. Being divisible by 8 is a sufficient condition for being divisible by 4.

41. Being on time each day is a necessary condition for keeping this job.

42. Passing a comprehensive exam is a necessary condition for obtaining a master's degree.

Use the facts that the negation of a ∀ statement is a ∃ statement and that the negation of an if-then statement is an *and* statement to rewrite each of the statements 43–46 without using the word *necessary* or *sufficient*.

43. Being divisible by 8 is not a necessary condition for being divisible by 4.

44. Having a large income is not a necessary condition for a person to be happy.

45. Having a large income is not a sufficient condition for a person to be happy.

46. Being a polynomial is not a sufficient condition for a function to have a real root.

47. The computer scientists Richard Conway and David Gries once wrote:

    The absence of error messages during translation of a computer program is only a necessary and not a sufficient condition for reasonable [program] correctness.

    Rewrite this statement without using the words *necessary* or *sufficient*.

48. A frequent-flyer club brochure states, "You may select among carriers only if they offer the same lowest fare." Assuming that "only if" has its formal, logical meaning, does this statement guarantee that if two carriers offer the same lowest fare, the customer will be free to choose between them? Explain.

Answers for Test Yourself

1. some (*Alternative answers:* at least one; an); does not have property S.   2. No R have property S.   3. There is an x such that x has property P and x does not have property Q.   4. For all x, if x has property Q then x has property P.   5. For all x, if x does not have property Q then x does not have property P.   6. For all x, if x does not have property P then x does not have property Q.

3.3 Statements with Multiple Quantifiers

It is not enough to have a good mind. The main thing is to use it well. — René Descartes

Imagine you are visiting a factory that manufactures computer microchips. The factory guide tells you,

There is a person supervising every detail of the production process.

Note that this statement contains informal versions of both the existential quantifier *there is* and the universal quantifier *every*. Which of the following best describes its meaning?

- There is one single person who supervises all the details of the production process.
- For any particular production detail, there is a person who supervises that detail, but there might be different supervisors for different details.

As it happens, either interpretation could be what the guide meant. (Reread the sentence to be sure you agree!) Taken by itself, his statement is genuinely ambiguous, although other things he may have said (the context for his statement) might have clarified it. In our ordinary lives, we deal with this kind of ambiguity all the time. Usually context helps resolve it, but sometimes we simply misunderstand each other.

In mathematics, formal logic, and computer science, by contrast, it is essential that we all interpret statements in exactly the same way. For instance, the initial stage of software development typically involves careful discussion between a programmer analyst and a client to turn vague descriptions of what the client wants into unambiguous program specifications that client and programmer can mutually agree on.

Because many important technical statements contain both ∃ and ∀, a convention has developed for interpreting them uniformly. When a statement contains more than one quantifier, we imagine the actions suggested by the quantifiers as being performed in the order in which the quantifiers occur. For instance, consider a statement of the form

$$\forall x \text{ in set } D, \exists y \text{ in set } E \text{ such that } x \text{ and } y \text{ satisfy property } P(x, y).$$

To show that such a statement is true, you must be able to meet the following challenge:

- Imagine that someone is allowed to choose any element whatsoever from the set D, and imagine that the person gives you that element. Call it x.
- The challenge for you is to find an element y in E so that the person's x and your y, taken together, satisfy property $P(x, y)$.

Note that ***because you do not have to specify the y until after the other person has specified the x, you are allowed to find a different value of y for each different x you are given.***

Example 3.3.1 Truth of a ∀∃ Statement in a Tarski World

Consider the Tarski world shown in Figure 3.3.1.

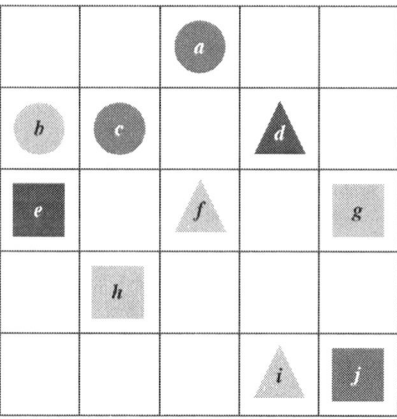

Figure 3.3.1

Show that the following statement is true in this world:

For all triangles x, there is a square y such that x and y have the same color.

Solution   The statement says that no matter which triangle someone gives you, you will be able to find a square of the same color. There are only three triangles, d, f, and i. The following table shows that for each of these triangles a square of the same color can be found.

Given $x =$	choose $y =$	and check that y is the same color as x.
d	e	yes ✓
f or i	h or g	yes ✓

Now consider a statement containing both ∀ and ∃, where the ∃ comes before the ∀:

∃ an x in D such that ∀y in E, x and y satisfy property $P(x, y)$.

To show that a statement of this form is true:

You must find one single element (call it x) in D with the following property:

- After you have found your x, someone is allowed to choose any element whatsoever from E. The person challenges you by giving you that element. Call it y.
- Your job is to show that your x together with the person's y satisfy property $P(x, y)$.

Note that your x has to work for *any* y the person gives you; **you are not allowed to change your x once you have specified it initially.**

Example 3.3.2 Truth of a ∃∀ Statement in a Tarski World

Consider again the Tarski world in Figure 3.3.1. Show that the following statement is true: There is a triangle x such that for all circles y, x is to the right of y.

Solution   The statement says that you can find a triangle that is to the right of all the circles. Actually, either d or i would work for all of the three circles, a, b, and c, as you can see in the following table.

Choose $x =$	Then, given $y =$	check that x is to the right of y.
d or i	a	yes ✓
	b	yes ✓
	c	yes ✓

Here is a summary of the convention for interpreting statements with two different quantifiers:

Interpreting Statements with Two Different Quantifiers

If you want to establish the truth of a statement of the form

∀x in D, ∃y in E such that $P(x, y)$

your challenge is to allow someone else to pick whatever element x in D they wish and then you must find an element y in E that "works" for that particular x.

If you want to establish the truth of a statement of the form

∃x in D such that ∀y in E, $P(x, y)$

your job is to find one particular x in D that will "work" no matter what y in E anyone might choose to challenge you with.

CHAPTER 4

ELEMENTARY NUMBER THEORY AND METHODS OF PROOF

The underlying content of this chapter is likely to be familiar to you. It consists of properties of integers (whole numbers), rational numbers (integer fractions), and real numbers. The underlying theme of this chapter is the question of how to determine the truth or falsity of a mathematical statement.

Here is an example involving a concept used frequently in computer science. Given any real number x, the *floor* of x, or greatest integer in x, denoted $\lfloor x \rfloor$, is the largest integer that is less than or equal to x. On the number line, $\lfloor x \rfloor$ is the integer immediately to the left of x (or equal to x if x is, itself, an integer). Thus $\lfloor 2.3 \rfloor = 2$, $\lfloor 12.99999 \rfloor = 12$, and $\lfloor -1.5 \rfloor = -2$. Consider the following two questions:

1. For any real number x, is $\lfloor x - 1 \rfloor = \lfloor x \rfloor - 1$?

2. For any real numbers x and y, is $\lfloor x - y \rfloor = \lfloor x \rfloor - \lfloor y \rfloor$?

Take a few minutes to try to answer these questions for yourself.

It turns out that the answer to (1) is yes, whereas the answer to (2) is no. Are these the answers you got? If not, don't worry. In Section 4.5 you will learn the techniques you need to answer these questions and more. If you did get the correct answers, congratulations! You have excellent mathematical intuition. Now ask yourself, "How sure am I of my answers? Were they plausible guesses or absolute certainties? Was there any difference in certainty between my answers to (1) and (2)? Would I have been willing to bet a large sum of money on the correctness of my answers?"

One of the best ways to think of a mathematical proof is as a carefully reasoned argument to convince a skeptical listener (often yourself) that a given statement is true. Imagine the listener challenging your reasoning every step of the way, constantly asking, "Why is that so?" If you can counter every possible challenge, then your proof as a whole will be correct.

As an example, imagine proving to someone not very familiar with mathematical notation that if x is a number with $5x + 3 = 33$, then $x = 6$. You could argue as follows:

If $5x + 3 = 33$, then $5x + 3$ minus 3 will equal $33 - 3$ since subtracting the same number from two equal quantities gives equal results. But $5x + 3$ minus 3 equals $5x$ because adding 3 to $5x$ and then subtracting 3 just leaves $5x$. Also, $33 - 3 = 30$. Hence $5x = 30$. This means that x is a number which when multiplied by 5 equals 30. But the only number with this property is 6. Therefore, if $5x + 3 = 33$ then $x = 6$.

Of course there are other ways to phrase this proof, depending on the level of mathematical sophistication of the intended reader. In practice, mathematicians often omit reasons for certain steps of an argument when they are confident that the reader can easily supply them. When you are first learning to write proofs, however, it is better to err on the side of supplying too many reasons rather than too few. All too frequently, when even the best mathematicians carefully examine some "details" in their arguments, they discover that those details are actually false. One of the most important reason's for requiring proof in mathematics is that writing a proof forces us to become aware of weaknesses in our arguments and in the unconscious assumptions we have made.

Sometimes correctness of a mathematical argument can be a matter of life or death. Suppose, for example, that a mathematician is part of a team charged with designing a new type of airplane engine, and suppose that the mathematician is given the job of determining whether the thrust delivered by various engine types is adequate. If you knew that the mathematician was only fairly sure, but not positive, of the correctness of his analysis, you would probably not want to ride in the resulting aircraft.

At a certain point in Lewis Carroll's *Alice in Wonderland* (see exercise 28 in Section 2.2), the March Hare tells Alice to "say what you mean." In other words, she should be precise in her use of language: If she means a thing, then that is exactly what she should say. In this chapter, perhaps more than in any other mathematics course you have ever taken, you will find it necessary to say what you mean. Precision of thought and language is essential to achieve the mathematical certainty that is needed if you are to have complete confidence in your solutions to mathematical problems.

4.1 Direct Proof and Counterexample I: Introduction

Mathematics, as a science, commenced when first someone, probably a Greek, proved propositions about "any" things or about "some" things without specification of definite particular things. — Alfred North Whitehead, 1861–1947

Both discovery and proof are integral parts of problem solving. When you think you have discovered that a certain statement is true, try to figure out why it is true. If you succeed, you will know that your discovery is genuine. Even if you fail, the process of trying will give you insight into the nature of the problem and may lead to the discovery that the statement is false. For complex problems, the interplay between discovery and proof is not reserved to the end of the problem-solving process but, rather, is an important part of each step.

Assumptions

- In this text we assume a familiarity with the laws of basic algebra, which are listed in Appendix A.
- We also use the three properties of equality: For all objects A, B, and C,
  (1) $A = A$, (2) if $A = B$ then $B = A$, and (3) if $A = B$ and $B = C$, then $A = C$.
- In addition, we assume that there is no integer between 0 and 1 and that the set of all integers is closed under addition, subtraction, and multiplication. This means that sums, differences, and products of integers are integers.
- Of course, most quotients of integers are not integers. For example, $3 \div 2$, which equals $3/2$, is not an integer, and $3 \div 0$ is not even a number.

The mathematical content of this section primarily concerns even and odd integers and prime and composite numbers.

Definitions

In order to evaluate the truth or falsity of a statement, you must understand what the statement is about. In other words, you must know the meanings of all terms that occur in the statement. Mathematicians define terms very carefully and precisely and consider it important to learn definitions virtually word for word.

> **• Definitions**
>
> An integer n is **even** if, and only if, n equals twice some integer. An integer n is **odd** if, and only if, n equals twice some integer plus 1.
>
> Symbolically, if n is an integer, then
>
> n is even $\Leftrightarrow$ ∃ an integer k such that $n = 2k$.
>
> n is odd $\Leftrightarrow$ ∃ an integer k such that $n = 2k + 1$.

It follows from the definition that if you are doing a problem in which you happen to know that a certain integer is even, you can deduce that it has the form $2 \cdot$ (some integer). Conversely, if you know in some situation that an integer equals $2 \cdot$ (some integer), then you can deduce that the integer is even.

Know a particular integer n is even.	$\xrightarrow{\text{deduce}}$	n has the form $2 \cdot$ (some integer).
Know n has the form $2 \cdot$ (some integer).	$\xrightarrow{\text{deduce}}$	n is even.

Example 4.1.1 Even and Odd Integers

Use the definitions of *even* and *odd* to justify your answers to the following questions.

a. Is 0 even?

b. Is -301 odd?

c. If a and b are integers, is $6a^2b$ even?

d. If a and b are integers, is $10a + 8b + 1$ odd?

e. Is every integer either even or odd?

Solution

a. Yes, $0 = 2 \cdot 0$.

b. Yes, $-301 = 2(-151) + 1$.

c. Yes, $6a^2b = 2(3a^2b)$, and since a and b are integers, so is $3a^2b$ (being a product of integers).

d. Yes, $10a + 8b + 1 = 2(5a + 4b) + 1$, and since a and b are integers, so is $5a + 4b$ (being a sum of products of integers).

e. The answer is yes, although the proof is not obvious. (Try giving a reason yourself.) We will show in Section 4.4 that this fact results from another fact known as the quotient-remainder theorem. ∎

The integer 6, which equals $2 \cdot 3$, is a product of two smaller positive integers. On the other hand, 7 cannot be written as a product of two smaller positive integers; its only positive factors are 1 and 7. A positive integer, such as 7, that cannot be written as a product of two smaller positive integers is called *prime*.

• Definition

An integer n is **prime** if, and only if, $n > 1$ and for all positive integers r and s, if $n = rs$, then either r or s equals n. An integer n is **composite** if, and only if, $n > 1$ and $n = rs$ for some integers r and s with $1 < r < n$ and $1 < s < n$.

In symbols: For all integers n with $n > 1$,

$$n \text{ is prime} \quad \Leftrightarrow \quad \forall \text{ positive integers } r \text{ and } s, \text{ if } n = rs$$
$$\text{then either } r = 1 \text{ and } s = n \text{ or } r = n \text{ and } s = 1.$$

$$n \text{ is composite} \quad \Leftrightarrow \quad \exists \text{ positive integers } r \text{ and } s \text{ such that } n = rs$$
$$\text{and } 1 < r < n \text{ and } 1 < s < n.$$

Example 4.1.2 Prime and Composite Numbers

    a. Is 1 prime?

    b. Is every integer greater than 1 either prime or composite?

    c. Write the first six prime numbers.

    d. Write the first six composite numbers.

Solution

Note The reason for not allowing 1 to be prime is discussed in Section 4.3.

    a. No. A prime number is required to be greater than 1.

    b. Yes. Let n be any integer that is greater than 1. Consider all pairs of positive integers r and s such that $n = rs$. There exist at least two such pairs, namely $r = n$ and $s = 1$ and $r = 1$ and $s = n$. Moreover, since $n = rs$, all such pairs satisfy the inequalities $1 \le r \le n$ and $1 \le s \le n$. If n is prime, then the two displayed pairs are the only ways to write n as rs. Otherwise, there exists a pair of positive integers r and s such that $n = rs$ and neither r nor s equals either 1 or n. Therefore, in this case $1 < r < n$ and $1 < s < n$, and hence n is composite.

    c. 2, 3, 5, 7, 11, 13

    d. 4, 6, 8, 9, 10, 12

Proving Existential Statements

According to the definition given in Section 3.1, a statement in the form

$$\exists x \in D \text{ such that } Q(x)$$

is true if, and only if,

$$Q(x) \text{ is true for at least one } x \text{ in } D.$$

One way to prove this is to find an x in D that makes $Q(x)$ true. Another way is to give a set of directions for finding such an x. Both of these methods are called **constructive proofs of existence**.

Example 4.1.3 Constructive Proofs of Existence

a. Prove the following: ∃ an even integer n that can be written in two ways as a sum of two prime numbers.

b. Suppose that r and s are integers. Prove the following: ∃ an integer k such that $22r + 18s = 2k$.

Solution

a. Let $n = 10$. Then $10 = 5 + 5 = 3 + 7$ and 3, 5, and 7 are all prime numbers.

b. Let $k = 11r + 9s$. Then k is an integer because it is a sum of products of integers; and by substitution, $2k = 2(11r + 9s)$, which equals $22r + 18s$ by the distributive law of algebra. ▪

A **nonconstructive proof of existence** involves showing either (a) that the existence of a value of x that makes $Q(x)$ true is guaranteed by an axiom or a previously proved theorem or (b) that the assumption that there is no such x leads to a contradiction. The disadvantage of a nonconstructive proof is that it may give virtually no clue about where or how x may be found. The widespread use of digital computers in recent years has led to some dissatisfaction with this aspect of nonconstructive proofs and to increased efforts to produce constructive proofs containing directions for computer calculation of the quantity in question.

Disproving Universal Statements by Counterexample

To disprove a statement means to show that it is false. Consider the question of disproving a statement of the form

$$\forall x \text{ in } D, \text{ if } P(x) \text{ then } Q(x).$$

Showing that this statement is false is equivalent to showing that its negation is true. The negation of the statement is existential:

$$\exists x \text{ in } D \text{ such that } P(x) \text{ and not } Q(x).$$

But to show that an existential statement is true, we generally give an example, and because the example is used to show that the original statement is false, we call it a *counterexample*. Thus the method of disproof by *counterexample* can be written as follows:

> **Disproof by Counterexample**
>
> To disprove a statement of the form "$\forall x \in D$, if $P(x)$ then $Q(x)$," find a value of x in D for which the hypothesis $P(x)$ is true and the conclusion $Q(x)$ is false. Such an x is called a **counterexample.**

Example 4.1.4 Disproof by Counterexample

Disprove the following statement by finding a counterexample:

$$\forall \text{ real numbers } a \text{ and } b, \text{ if } a^2 = b^2 \text{ then } a = b.$$

Solution   To disprove this statement, you need to find real numbers a and b such that the hypothesis $a^2 = b^2$ is true and the conclusion $a = b$ is false. The fact that both positive and negative integers have positive squares helps in the search. If you flip through some possibilities in your mind, you will quickly see that 1 and -1 will work (or 2 and -2, or 0.5 and -0.5, and so forth).

Statement: $\forall$ real numbers a and b, if $a^2 = b^2$, then $a = b$.

Counterexample: Let $a = 1$ and $b = -1$. Then $a^2 = 1^2 = 1$ and $b^2 = (-1)^2 = 1$, and so $a^2 = b^2$. But $a \neq b$ since $1 \neq -1$.

It is a sign of intelligence to make generalizations. Frequently, after observing a property to hold in a large number of cases, you may guess that it holds in all cases. You may, however, run into difficulty when you try to prove your guess. Perhaps you just have not figured out the key to the proof. But perhaps your guess is false. Consequently, when you are having serious difficulty proving a general statement, you should interrupt your efforts to look for a counterexample. Analyzing the kinds of problems you are encountering in your proof efforts may help in the search. It may even happen that if you find a counterexample and therefore prove the statement false, your understanding may be sufficiently clarified that you can formulate a more limited but true version of the statement. For instance, Example 4.1.4 shows that it is not always true that if the squares of two numbers are equal, then the numbers are equal. However, it is true that if the squares of two *positive* numbers are equal, then the numbers are equal.

Proving Universal Statements

The vast majority of mathematical statements to be proved are universal. In discussing how to prove such statements, it is helpful to imagine them in a standard form:

$$\forall x \in D, \text{if } P(x) \text{ then } Q(x).$$

Sections 1.1 and 3.1 give examples showing how to write any universal statement in this form. When D is finite or when only a finite number of elements satisfy $P(x)$, such a statement can be proved by the method of exhaustion.

Example 4.1.5 The Method of Exhaustion

Use the method of exhaustion to prove the following statement:

$\forall n \in \mathbf{Z}$, if n is even and $4 \leq n \leq 26$, then n can be written as a sum of two prime numbers.

Solution

$4 = 2 + 2$	$6 = 3 + 3$	$8 = 3 + 5$	$10 = 5 + 5$
$12 = 5 + 7$	$14 = 11 + 3$	$16 = 5 + 11$	$18 = 7 + 11$
$20 = 7 + 13$	$22 = 5 + 17$	$24 = 5 + 19$	$26 = 7 + 19$

In most cases in mathematics, however, the method of exhaustion cannot be used. For instance, can you prove by exhaustion that *every* even integer greater than 2 can be written as a sum of two prime numbers? No. To do that you would have to check every even integer, and because there are infinitely many such numbers, this is an impossible task.

Even when the domain is finite, it may be infeasible to use the method of exhaustion. Imagine, for example, trying to check by exhaustion that the multiplication circuitry of a particular computer gives the correct result for every pair of numbers in the computer's range. Since a typical computer would require thousands of years just to compute all possible products of all numbers in its range (not to mention the time it would take to check the accuracy of the answers), checking correctness by the method of exhaustion is obviously impractical.

The most powerful technique for proving a universal statement is one that works regardless of the size of the domain over which the statement is quantified. It is called the *method of generalizing from the generic particular*. Here is the idea underlying the method:

Method of Generalizing from the Generic Particular

To show that every element of a set satisfies a certain property, suppose x is a *particular* but *arbitrarily chosen* element of the set, and show that x satisfies the property.

Example 4.1.6 Generalizing from the Generic Particular

At some time you may have been shown a "mathematical trick" like the following. You ask a person to pick any number, add 5, multiply by 4, subtract 6, divide by 2, and subtract twice the original number. Then you astound the person by announcing that their final result was 7. How does this "trick" work? Let an empty box □ or the symbol x stand for the number the person picks. Here is what happens when the person follows your directions:

Step	Visual Result	Algebraic Result
Pick a number.	□	x
Add 5.	□ |||||	$x + 5$
Multiply by 4.	□ ||||| □ ||||| □ ||||| □ |||||	$(x + 5) \cdot 4 = 4x + 20$
Subtract 6.	□ || □ || □ ||||| □ |||||	$(4x + 20) - 6 = 4x + 14$
Divide by 2.	□ || □ |||||	$\dfrac{4x + 14}{2} = 2x + 7$
Subtract twice the original number.	|| |||||	$(2x + 7) - 2x = 7$

Thus no matter what number the person starts with, the result will always be 7. Note that the x in the analysis above is *particular* (because it represents a single quantity), but it is also *arbitrarily chosen* or *generic* (because any number whatsoever can be put in its place). This illustrates the process of drawing a general conclusion from a particular but generic object. ∎

The point of having x be arbitrarily chosen (or generic) is to make a proof that can be generalized to all elements of the domain. By choosing x arbitrarily, you are making no special assumptions about x that are not also true of all other elements of the domain. The word *generic* means "sharing all the common characteristics of a group or class." Thus everything you deduce about a generic element x of the domain is equally true of any other element of the domain.

When the method of generalizing from the generic particular is applied to a property of the form "If $P(x)$ then $Q(x)$," the result is the method of *direct proof*. Recall that the only way an if-then statement can be false is for the hypothesis to be true and the conclusion to be false. Thus, given the statement "If $P(x)$ then $Q(x)$," if you can show that the truth of $P(x)$ compels the truth of $Q(x)$, then you will have proved the statement. It follows by the method of generalizing from the generic particular that to show that "$\forall x$, if $P(x)$ then $Q(x)$," is true for *all* elements x in a set D, you suppose x is a particular but arbitrarily chosen element of D that makes $P(x)$ true, and then you show that x makes $Q(x)$ true.

Method of Direct Proof

1. Express the statement to be proved in the form "$\forall x \in D$, if $P(x)$ then $Q(x)$." (This step is often done mentally.)

2. Start the proof by supposing x is a particular but arbitrarily chosen element of D for which the hypothesis $P(x)$ is true. (This step is often abbreviated "Suppose $x \in D$ and $P(x)$.")

3. Show that the conclusion $Q(x)$ is true by using definitions, previously established results, and the rules for logical inference.

Example 4.1.7 A Direct Proof of a Theorem

Prove that the sum of any two even integers is even.

Caution! The word *two* in this statement does not necessarily refer to two distinct integers. If a choice of integers is made arbitrarily, the integers are very likely to be distinct, but they might be the same.

Solution   Whenever you are presented with a statement to be proved, it is a good idea to ask yourself whether you believe it to be true. In this case you might imagine some pairs of even integers, say $2 + 4, 6 + 10, 12 + 12, 28 + 54$, and mentally check that their sums are even. However, since you cannot possibly check all pairs of even numbers, you cannot know for sure that the statement is true in general by checking its truth in these particular instances. Many properties hold for a large number of examples and yet fail to be true in general.

To prove this statement in general, you need to show that no matter what even integers are given, their sum is even. But given any two even integers, it is possible to represent them as $2r$ and $2s$ for some integers r and s. And by the distributive law of algebra, $2r + 2s = 2(r + s)$, which is even. Thus the statement is true in general.

Suppose the statement to be proved were much more complicated than this. What is the method you could use to derive a proof?

Formal Restatement: $\forall$ integers m and n, if m and n are even then $m + n$ is even.

This statement is universally quantified over an infinite domain. Thus to prove it in general, you need to show that no matter what two integers you might be given, if both of them are even then their sum will also be even.

Next ask yourself, "Where am I starting from?" or "What am I supposing?" The answer to such a question gives you the starting point, or first sentence, of the proof.

Starting Point: Suppose m and n are particular but arbitrarily chosen integers that are even.

Or, in abbreviated form:

Suppose m and n are any even integers.

Then ask yourself, "What conclusion do I need to show in order to complete the proof?"

To Show: $m + n$ is even.

At this point you need to ask yourself, "How do I get from the starting point to the conclusion?" Since both involve the term *even integer,* you must use the definition of this term—and thus you must know what it means for an integer to be even. It follows from the definition that since m and n are even, each equals twice some integer. One of the basic laws of logic, called *existential instantiation*, says, in effect, that if you know something exists, you can give it a name. However, you cannot use the same name to refer to two different things, both of which are currently under discussion.

Existential Instantiation

If the existence of a certain kind of object is assumed or has been deduced then it can be given a name, as long as that name is not currently being used to denote something else.

Caution!   Because m and n are arbitrarily chosen, they could be any pair of even integers whatsoever. Once r is introduced to satisfy $m = 2r$, then r is not available to represent something else. If you had set $m = 2r$, and $n = 2r$, then m would equal n, which need not be the case.

Thus since m equals twice some integer, you can give that integer a name, and since n equals twice some integer, you can also give that integer a name:

$$m = 2r, \text{ for some integer } r \qquad \text{and} \qquad n = 2s, \text{ for some integer } s.$$

Now what you want to show is that $m + n$ is even. In other words, you want to show that $m + n$ equals $2 \cdot$ (some integer). Having just found alternative representations for m (as $2r$) and n (as $2s$), it seems reasonable to substitute these representations in place of m and n:

$$m + n = 2r + 2s.$$

Your goal is to show that $m + n$ is even. By definition of even, this means that $m + n$ can be written in the form

$$2 \cdot \text{(some integer)}.$$

This analysis narrows the gap between the starting point and what is to be shown to showing that

$$2r + 2s = 2 \cdot \text{(some integer)}.$$

Why is this true? First, because of the distributive law from algebra, which says that

$$2r + 2s = 2(r + s),$$

and, second, because the sum of any two integers is an integer, which implies that $r + s$ is an integer.

This discussion is summarized by rewriting the statement as a theorem and giving a formal proof of it. (In mathematics, the word *theorem* refers to a statement that is known to be true because it has been proved.) The formal proof, as well as many others in this text, includes explanatory notes to make its logical flow apparent. Such comments are purely a convenience for the reader and could be omitted entirely. For this reason they are italicized and enclosed in italic square brackets: *[ ]*.

Donald Knuth, one of the pioneers of the science of computing, has compared constructing a computer program from a set of specifications to writing a mathematical proof based on a set of axioms.* In keeping with this analogy, the bracketed comments can be thought of as similar to the explanatory documentation provided by a good programmer. Documentation is not necessary for a program to run, but it helps a human reader understand what is going on.

Theorem 4.1.1

The sum of any two even integers is even.

Proof:

Suppose m and n are *[particular but arbitrarily chosen]* even integers. *[We must show that $m + n$ is even.]* By definition of even, $m = 2r$ and $n = 2s$ for some integers r and s. Then

$$m + n = 2r + 2s \quad \text{by substitution}$$
$$= 2(r + s) \quad \text{by factoring out a 2.}$$

Note   Introducing t to equal $r + s$ is another use of existential instantiation.

Let $t = r + s$. Note that t is an integer because it is a sum of integers. Hence

$$m + n = 2t \quad \text{where } t \text{ is an integer.}$$

It follows by definition of even that $m + n$ is even. *[This is what we needed to show.]*[†]

Most theorems, like the one above, can be analyzed to a point where you realize that as soon as a certain thing is shown, the theorem will be proved. When that thing has been shown, it is natural to end the proof with the words "this is what we needed to show." The Latin words for this are *quod erat demonstrandum,* or Q.E.D. for short. Proofs in older mathematics books end with these initials.

Note that both the *if* and the *only if* parts of the definition of even were used in the proof of Theorem 4.1.1. Since m and n were known to be even, the *only if* ($\Rightarrow$) part of the definition was used to deduce that m and n had a certain general form. Then, after some algebraic substitution and manipulation, the *if* ($\Leftarrow$) part of the definition was used to deduce that $m + n$ was even.

Directions for Writing Proofs of Universal Statements

Think of a proof as a way to communicate a convincing argument for the truth of a mathematical statement. When you write a proof, imagine that you will be sending it to a capable classmate who has had to miss the last week or two of your course. Try to be clear and complete. Keep in mind that your classmate will see only what you actually write down, not any unexpressed thoughts behind it. Ideally, your proof will lead your classmate to understand *why* the given statement is true.

---

*Donald E. Knuth, *The Art of Computer Programming,* 2nd ed., Vol. I (Reading, MA: Addison-Wesley, 1973), p. ix.

[†]See page 134 for a discussion of the role of universal modus ponens in this proof.

Over the years, the following rules of style have become fairly standard for writing the final versions of proofs:

1. Copy the statement of the theorem to be proved on your paper.

2. Clearly mark the beginning of your proof with the word Proof.

3. Make your proof self-contained.

    This means that you should explain the meaning of each variable used in your proof in the body of the proof. Thus you will begin proofs by introducing the initial variables and stating what kind of objects they are. The first sentence of your proof would be something like "Suppose m and n are any even integers" or "Let x be a real number such that x is greater than 2." This is similar to declaring variables and their data types at the beginning of a computer program.

    At a later point in your proof, you may introduce a new variable to represent a quantity that is known at that point to exist. For example, if you have assumed that a particular integer n is even, then you know that n equals 2 times some integer, and you can give this integer a name so that you can work with it concretely later in the proof. Thus if you decide to call the integer, say, s, you would write, "Since n is even, $n = 2s$ for some integer s," or "since n is even, there exists an integer s such that $n = 2s$."

4. Write your proof in complete, gramatically correct sentences.

    This does not mean that you should avoid using symbols and shorthand abbreviations, just that you should incorporate them into sentences. For example, the proof of Theorem 4.1.1 contains the sentence

$$\text{Then } m + n = 2r + 2s$$
$$= 2(r + s).$$

    To read such text as a sentence, read the first equals sign as "equals" and each subsequent equals sign as "which equals."

5. Keep your reader informed about the status of each statement in your proof.

    Your reader should never be in doubt about whether something in your proof has been assumed or established or is still to be deduced. If something is assumed, preface it with a word like *Suppose* or *Assume*. If it is still to be shown, preface it with words like, *We must show that* or *In other words, we must show that*. This is especially important if you introduce a variable in rephrasing what you need to show. (See Common Mistakes on the next page.)

6. Give a reason for each assertion in your proof.

    Each assertion in a proof should come directly from the hypothesis of the theorem, or follow from the definition of one of the terms in the theorem, or be a result obtained earlier in the proof, or be a mathematical result that has previously been established or is agreed to be assumed. Indicate the reason for each step of your proof using phrases such as *by hypothesis, by definition of . . .*, and *by theorem . . . .*

7. Include the "little words and phrases" that make the logic of your arguments clear.

    When writing a mathematical argument, especially a proof, indicate how each sentence is related to the previous one. Does it follow from the previous sentence or from a combination of the previous sentence and earlier ones? If so, start the sentence by stating the reason why it follows or by writing *Then*, or *Thus*, or *So*, or *Hence*, or *Therefore*, or *Consequently*, or *It follows that*, and include the reason at the end of the sentence. For instance, in the proof of Theorem 4.1.1, once you know that m is even, you can write: "By definition of even, $m = 2r$ for some integer r," or you can write, "Then $m = 2r$ for some integer r by definition of even."

If a sentence expresses a new thought or fact that does not follow as an immediate consequence of the preceding statement but is needed for a later part of a proof, introduce it by writing *Observe that,* or *Note that,* or *But,* or *Now.*

Sometimes in a proof it is desirable to define a new variable in terms of previous variables. In such a case, introduce the new variable with the word *Let.* For instance, in the proof of Theorem 4.1.1, once it is known that $m + n = 2(r + s)$, where r and s are integers, a new variable t is introduced to represent $r + s$. The proof goes on to say, "Let $t = r + s$. Then t is an integer because it is a sum of two integers."

8. **Display equations and inequalities.**

The convention is to display equations and inequalities on separate lines to increase readability, both for other people and for ourselves so that we can more easily check our work for accuracy. We follow the convention in the text of this book, but in order to save space, we violate it in a few of the exercises and in many of the solutions contained in Appendix B. So you may need to copy out some parts of solutions on scratch paper to understand them fully. Please follow the convention in your own work. Leave plenty of empty space, and don't be stingy with paper!

Variations among Proofs

It is rare that two proofs of a given statement, written by two different people, are identical. Even when the basic mathematical steps are the same, the two people may use different notation or may give differing amounts of explanation for their steps, or may choose different words to link the steps together into paragraph form. An important question is how detailed to make the explanations for the steps of a proof. This must ultimately be worked out between the writer of a proof and the intended reader, whether they be student and teacher, teacher and student, student and fellow student, or mathematician and colleague. Your teacher may provide explicit guidelines for you to use in your course. Or you may follow the example of the proofs in this book (which are generally explained rather fully in order to be understood by students at various stages of mathematical development). Remember that the phrases written inside brackets *[ ]* are intended to elucidate the logical flow or underlying assumptions of the proof and need not be written down at all. It is entirely your decision whether to include such phrases in your own proofs.

Common Mistakes

The following are some of the most common mistakes people make when writing mathematical proofs.

1. **Arguing from examples.**

Looking at examples is one of the most helpful practices a problem solver can engage in and is encouraged by all good mathematics teachers. However, it is a mistake to think that a general statement can be proved by showing it to be true for some special cases. A property referred to in a universal statement may be true in many instances without being true in general.

Here is an example of this mistake. It is an incorrect "proof" of the fact that the sum of any two even integers is even. (Theorem 4.1.1).

This is true because if $m = 14$ and $n = 6$, which are both even,
then $m + n = 20$, which is also even.

Some people find this kind of argument convincing because it does, after all, consist of evidence in support of a true conclusion. But remember that when we discussed valid arguments, we pointed out that an argument may be invalid and yet have a true conclusion. In the same way, an argument from examples may be mistakenly used to "prove" a true statement. In the previous example, it is not sufficient to show that the conclusion "$m + n$ is even" is true for $m = 14$ and $n = 6$. You must give an argument to show that the conclusion is true for any even integers m and n.

2. **Using the same letter to mean two different things.**

Some beginning theorem provers give a new variable quantity the same letter name as a previously introduced variable. Consider the following "proof" fragment:

> Suppose m and n are any odd integers. Then by definition of odd,
> $m = 2k + 1$ and $n = 2k + 1$ for some integer k.

This is incorrect. Using the same symbol, k, in the expressions for both m and n implies that $m = 2k + 1 = n$. It follows that the rest of the proof applies only to integers m and n that equal each other. This is inconsistent with the supposition that m and n are arbitrarily chosen odd integers. For instance, the proof would not show that the sum of 3 and 5 is even.

3. **Jumping to a conclusion.**

To jump to a conclusion means to allege the truth of something without giving an adequate reason. Consider the following "proof" that the sum of any two even integers is even.

> Suppose m and n are any even integers. By definition of even, $m = 2r$ and $n = 2s$ for some integers r and s. Then $m + n = 2r + 2s$. So $m + n$ is even.

The problem with this "proof" is that the crucial calculation

$$2r + 2s = 2(r + s)$$

is missing. The author of the "proof" has jumped prematurely to a conclusion.

4. **Assuming what is to be proved.**

To assume what is to be proved is a variation of jumping to a conclusion. As an example, consider the following "proof" of the fact that the product of any two odd integers is odd:

> Suppose m and n are any odd integers. When any odd integers are multiplied, their product is odd. Hence mn is odd.

5. **Confusion between what is known and what is still to be shown.**

A more subtle way to engage in circular reasoning occurs when the conclusion to be shown is restated using a variable. Here is an example in a "proof" that the product of any two odd integers is odd:

> Suppose m and n are any odd integers. We must show that mn is odd. This means that there exists an integer s such that

$$mn = 2s + 1.$$

> Also by definition of odd, there exist integers a and b such that

$$m = 2a + 1 \text{ and } n = 2b + 1.$$

> Then

$$mn = (2a + 1)(2b + 1) = 2s + 1.$$

> So, since s is an integer, mn is odd by definition of odd.

In this example, when the author restated the conclusion to be shown (that mn is odd), the author wrote "there exists an integer s such that $mn = 2s + 1$." Later the author jumped to an unjustified conclusion by assuming the existence of this s when that had not, in fact, been established. This mistake might have been avoided if the author had written "This means that we must show that there exists an integer s such that

$$mn = 2s + 1.$$

An even better way to avoid this kind of error is not to introduce a variable into a proof unless it is either part of the hypothesis or deducible from it.

6. Use of *any* rather than *some*.

There are a few situations in which the words *any* and *some* can be used interchangeably. For instance, in starting a proof that the square of any odd integer is odd, one could correctly write "Suppose m is any odd integer" or "Suppose m is some odd integer." In most situations, however, the words *any* and *some* are not interchangeable. Here is the start of a "proof" that the square of any odd integer is odd, which uses *any* when the correct word is *some*:

Suppose m is a particular but arbitrarily chosen odd integer.
By definition of odd, $m = 2a + 1$ for any integer a.

In the second sentence it is incorrect to say that "$m = 2a + 1$ for any integer a" because a cannot be just "any" integer; in fact, solving $m = 2a + 1$ for a shows that the only possible value for a is $(m - 1)/2$. The correct way to finish the second sentence is, "$m = 2a + 1$ for some integer a" or "there exists an integer a such that $m = 2a + 1$."

7. Misuse of the word *if*.

Another common error is not serious in itself, but it reflects imprecise thinking that sometimes leads to problems later in a proof. This error involves using the word *if* when the word *because* is really meant. Consider the following proof fragment:

Suppose p is a prime number. If p is prime, then p cannot be written as a product of two smaller positive integers.

The use of the word *if* in the second sentence is inappropriate. It suggests that the primeness of p is in doubt. But p is known to be prime by the first sentence. It cannot be written as a product of two smaller positive integers *because* it is prime. Here is a correct version of the fragment:

Suppose p is a prime number. Because p is prime, p cannot be written as a product of two smaller positive integers.

Getting Proofs Started

Believe it or not, once you understand the idea of generalizing from the generic particular and the method of direct proof, you can write the beginnings of proofs even for theorems you do not understand. The reason is that the starting point and what is to be shown in a proof depend only on the linguistic form of the statement to be proved, not on the content of the statement.

Example 4.1.8 Identifying the "Starting Point" and the "Conclusion to Be Shown"

Note You are not expected to know anything about complete, bipartite graphs.

Write the first sentence of a proof (the "starting point") and the last sentence of a proof (the "conclusion to be shown") for the following statement:

Every complete, bipartite graph is connected.

Solution   It is helpful to rewrite the statement formally using a quantifier and a variable:

$$\overbrace{}^{\text{domain}} \qquad \overbrace{}^{\text{hypothesis}} \qquad \overbrace{}^{\text{conclusion}}$$

Formal Restatement: ∀ graphs G, if G is complete and bipartite, then G is connected.

The first sentence, or starting point, of a proof supposes the existence of an object (in this case G) in the domain (in this case the set of all graphs) that satisfies the hypothesis of the if-then part of the statement (in this case that G is complete and bipartite). The conclusion to be shown is just the conclusion of the if-then part of the statement (in this case that G is connected).

Starting Point: **Suppose** G is a *[particular but arbitrarily chosen]* graph such that G is complete and bipartite.

Conclusion to Be Shown: G is connected.

Thus the proof has the following shape:

Proof:

Suppose G is a *[particular but arbitrarily chosen]* graph such that G is complete and bipartite.

$\vdots$

Therefore, G is connected.   ∎

Showing That an Existential Statement Is False

Recall that the negation of an existential statement is universal. It follows that to prove an existential statement is false, you must prove a universal statement (its negation) is true.

Example 4.1.9 Disproving an Existential Statement

Show that the following statement is false:

There is a positive integer n such that $n^2 + 3n + 2$ is prime.

Solution   Proving that the given statement is false is equivalent to proving its negation is true. The negation is

For all positive integers n, $n^2 + 3n + 2$ is not prime.

Because the negation is universal, it is proved by generalizing from the generic particular.

Claim: The statement "There is a positive integer n such that $n^2 + 3n + 2$ is prime" is false.

Proof:

Suppose n is any *[particular but arbitrarily chosen]* positive integer. *[We will show that $n^2 + 3n + 2$ is not prime.]* We can factor $n^2 + 3n + 2$ to obtain $n^2 + 3n + 2 = (n + 1)(n + 2)$. We also note that $n + 1$ and $n + 2$ are integers (because they are sums of integers) and that both $n + 1 > 1$ and $n + 2 > 1$ (because $n \geq 1$). Thus $n^2 + 3n + 2$ is a product of two integers each greater than 1, and so $n^2 + 3n + 2$ is not prime.   ∎

Conjecture, Proof, and Disproof

More than 350 years ago, the French mathematician Pierre de Fermat claimed that it is impossible to find positive integers x, y, and z with $x^n + y^n = z^n$ if n is an integer that is at least 3. (For $n = 2$, the equation has many integer solutions, such as $3^2 + 4^2 = 5^2$ and $5^2 + 12^2 = 13^2$.) Fermat wrote his claim in the margin of a book, along with the comment "I have discovered a truly remarkable PROOF of this theorem which this margin

Pierre de Fermat
(1601–1665)

Andrew Wiles
(born 1953)

is too small to contain." No proof, however, was found among his papers, and over the years some of the greatest mathematical minds tried and failed to discover a proof or a counterexample, for what came to be known as Fermat's last theorem.

In 1986 Kenneth Ribet of the University of California at Berkeley showed that if a certain other statement, the Taniyama–Shimura conjecture, could be proved, then Fermat's theorem would follow. Andrew Wiles, an English mathematician and faculty member at Princeton University, had become intrigued by Fermat's claim while still a child and, as an adult, had come to work in the branch of mathematics to which the Taniyama–Shimura conjecture belonged. As soon as he heard of Ribet's result, Wiles immediately set to work to prove the conjecture. In June of 1993, after 7 years of concentrated effort, he presented a proof to worldwide acclaim.

During the summer of 1993, however, while every part of the proof was being carefully checked to prepare for formal publication, Wiles found that he could not justify one step and that that step might actually be wrong. He worked unceasingly for another year to resolve the problem, finally realizing that the gap in the proof was a genuine error but that an approach he had worked on years earlier and abandoned provided a way around the difficulty. By the end of 1994, the revised proof had been thoroughly checked and pronounced correct in every detail by experts in the field. It was published in the *Annals of Mathematics* in 1995. Several books and an excellent documentary television show have been produced that convey the drama and excitement of Wiles's discovery.*

One of the oldest problems in mathematics that remains unsolved is the Goldbach conjecture. In Example 4.1.5 it was shown that every even integer from 4 to 26 can be represented as a sum of two prime numbers. More than 250 years ago, Christian Goldbach (1690–1764) conjectured that every even integer greater than 2 can be so represented. Explicit computer-aided calculations have shown the conjecture to be true up to at least 10^{18}. But there is a huge chasm between 10^{18} and infinity. As pointed out by James Gleick of the *New York Times*, many other plausible conjectures in number theory have proved false. Leonhard Euler (1707–1783), for example, proposed in the eighteenth century that $a^4 + b^4 + c^4 = d^4$ had no nontrivial whole number solutions. In other words, no three perfect fourth powers add up to another perfect fourth power. For small numbers, Euler's conjecture looked good. But in 1987 a Harvard mathematician, Noam Elkies, proved it wrong. One counterexample, found by Roger Frye of Thinking Machines Corporation in a long computer search, is $95,800^4 + 217,519^4 + 414,560^4 = 422,481^4$.[†]

In May 2000, "to celebrate mathematics in the new millennium," the Clay Mathematics Institute of Cambridge, Massachusetts, announced that it would award prizes of $1 million each for the solutions to seven longstanding, classical mathematical questions. One of them, "P vs. NP," asks whether problems belonging to a certain class can be solved on a computer using more efficient methods than the very inefficient methods that are presently known to work for them. This question is discussed briefly at the end of Chapter 11.

Test Yourself

Answers to Test Yourself questions are located at the end of each section.

1. An integer is even if, and only if, _____.

2. An integer is odd if, and only if, _____.

3. An integer n is prime if, and only if, _____.

4. The most common way to disprove a universal statement is to find _____.

*"The Proof," produced in 1997, for the series *Nova* on the Public Broadcasting System; *Fermat's Enigma: The Epic Quest to Solve the World's Greatest Mathematical Problem,* by Simon Singh and John Lynch (New York: Bantam Books, 1998); *Fermat's Last Theorem: Unlocking the Secret of an Ancient Mathematical Problem* by Amir D. Aczel (New York: Delacorte Press, 1997).
†James Gleick, "Fermat's Last Theorem Still Has Zero Solutions," *New York Times,* 17 April 1988.

5. According to the method of generalizing from the generic particular, to show that every element of a set satisfies a certain property, suppose x is a _____, and show that _____.

6. To use the method of direct proof to prove a statement of the form, "For all x in a set D, if $P(x)$ then $Q(x)$," one supposes that _____ and one shows that _____.

Exercise Set 4.1*

In 1–3, use the definitions of even, odd, prime, and composite to justify each of your answers.

1. Assume that k is a particular integer.
   a. Is -17 an odd integer?   b. Is 0 an even integer?
   c. Is $2k - 1$ odd?

2. Assume that m and n are particular integers.
   a. Is $6m + 8n$ even?   b. Is $10mn + 7$ odd?
   c. If $m > n > 0$, is $m^2 - n^2$ composite?

3. Assume that r and s are particular integers.
   a. Is $4rs$ even?   b. Is $6r + 4s^2 + 3$ odd?
   c. If r and s are both positive, is $r^2 + 2rs + s^2$ composite?

Prove the statements in 4–10.

4. There are integers m and n such that $m > 1$ and $n > 1$ and $\frac{1}{m} + \frac{1}{n}$ is an integer.

5. There are distinct integers m and n such that $\frac{1}{m} + \frac{1}{n}$ is an integer.

6. There are real numbers a and b such that
$$\sqrt{a + b} = \sqrt{a} + \sqrt{b}.$$

7. There is an integer $n > 5$ such that $2^n - 1$ is prime.

8. There is a real number x such that $x > 1$ and $2^x > x^{10}$.

> **Definition:** An integer n is called a **perfect square** if, and only if, $n = k^2$ for some integer k.

9. There is a perfect square that can be written as a sum of two other perfect squares.

10. There is an integer n such that $2n^2 - 5n + 2$ is prime.

Disprove the statements in 11–13 by giving a counterexample.

11. For all real numbers a and b, if $a < b$ then $a^2 < b^2$.

12. For all integers n, if n is odd then $\frac{n-1}{2}$ is odd.

13. For all integers m and n, if $2m + n$ is odd then m and n are both odd.

In 14–16, determine whether the property is true for all integers, true for no integers, or true for some integers and false for other integers. Justify your answers.

14. $(a + b)^2 = a^2 + b^2$ H 15. $-a^n = (-a)^n$

16. The average of any two odd integers is odd.

Prove the statements in 17 and 18 by the method of exhaustion.

17. Every positive even integer less than 26 can be expressed as a sum of three or fewer perfect squares. (For instance, $10 = 1^2 + 3^2$ and $16 = 4^2$.)

18. For each integer n with $1 \leq n \leq 10$, $n^2 - n + 11$ is a prime number.

19. a. Rewrite the following theorem in three different ways: as $\forall$ _____, if _____ then _____, as $\forall$ _____, _____ (without using the words *if* or *then*), and as If _____, then _____ (without using an explicit universal quantifier).
    b. Fill in the blanks in the proof of the theorem.

    Theorem: The sum of any even integer and any odd integer is odd.

    Proof: Suppose m is any even integer and n is ___(a)___. By definition of even, $m = 2r$ for some ___(b)___, and by definition of odd, $n = 2s + 1$ for some integer s. By substitution and algebra,
$$m + n = \underline{\text{(c)}} = 2(r + s) + 1.$$
    Since r and s are both integers, so is their sum $r + s$. Hence $m + n$ has the form twice some integer plus one, and so ___(d)___ by definition of odd.

Each of the statements in 20–23 is true. For each, (a) rewrite the statement with the quantification implicit as If _____, then _____, and (b) write the first sentence of a proof (the "starting point") and the last sentence of a proof (the "conclusion to be shown"). Note that you do not need to understand the statements in order to be able to do these exercises.

20. For all integers m, if $m > 1$ then $0 < \frac{1}{m} < 1$.

21. For all real numbers x, if $x > 1$ then $x^2 > x$.

22. For all integers m and n, if $mn = 1$ then $m = n = 1$ or $m = n = -1$.

23. For all real numbers x, if $0 < x < 1$ then $x^2 < x$.

---

*For exercises with blue numbers, solutions are given in Appendix B. The symbol H indicates that only a hint or partial solution is given. The symbol $*$ signals that an exercise is more challenging than usual.

Prove the statements in 24–34. In each case use only the definitions of the terms and the Assumptions listed on page 146, not any previously established properties of odd and even integers. Follow the directions given in this section for writing proofs of universal statements.

24. The negative of any even integer is even.

25. The difference of any even integer minus any odd integer is odd.

H 26. The difference between any odd integer and any even integer is odd. (*Note:* The "proof" shown in exercise 39 contains an error. Can you spot it?)

27. The sum of any two odd integers is even.

28. For all integers n, if n is odd then n^2 is odd.

29. For all integers n, if n is odd then $3n + 5$ is even.

30. For all integers m, if m is even then $3m + 5$ is odd.

31. If k is any odd integer and m is any even integer, then, $k^2 + m^2$ is odd.

32. If a is any odd integer and b is any even integer, then, $2a + 3b$ is even.

33. If n is any even integer, then $(-1)^n = 1$.

34. If n is any odd integer, then $(-1)^n = -1$.

Prove that the statements in 35–37 are false.

35. There exists an integer $m \geq 3$ such that $m^2 - 1$ is prime.

36. There exists an integer n such that $6n^2 + 27$ is prime.

37. There exists an integer $k \geq 4$ such that $2k^2 - 5k + 2$ is prime.

Find the mistakes in the "proofs" shown in 38–42.

38. **Theorem:** For all integers k, if $k > 0$ then $k^2 + 2k + 1$ is composite.
   "**Proof:** For $k = 2$, $k^2 + 2k + 1 = 2^2 + 2 \cdot 2 + 1 = 9$. But $9 = 3 \cdot 3$, and so 9 is composite. Hence the theorem is true."

39. **Theorem:** The difference between any odd integer and any even integer is odd.
   "**Proof:** Suppose n is any odd integer, and m is any even integer. By definition of odd, $n = 2k + 1$ where k is an integer, and by definition of even, $m = 2k$ where k is an integer. Then

$$n - m = (2k + 1) - 2k = 1.$$

   But 1 is odd. Therefore, the difference between any odd integer and any even integer is odd."

40. **Theorem:** For all integers k, if $k > 0$ then $k^2 + 2k + 1$ is composite.
   "**Proof:** Suppose k is any integer such that $k > 0$. If $k^2 + 2k + 1$ is composite, then $k^2 + 2k + 1 = rs$ for some integers r and s such that

$$1 < r < (k^2 + 2k + 1)$$

and

$$1 < s < (k^2 + 2k + 1).$$

Since

$$k^2 + 2k + 1 = rs$$

and both r and s are strictly between 1 and $k^2 + 2k + 1$, then $k^2 + 2k + 1$ is not prime. Hence $k^2 + 2k + 1$ is composite as was to be shown."

41. **Theorem:** The product of an even integer and an odd integer is even.
   "**Proof:** Suppose m is an even integer and n is an odd integer. If $m \cdot n$ is even, then by definition of even there exists an integer r such that $m \cdot n = 2r$. Also since m is even, there exists an integer p such that $m = 2p$, and since n is odd there exists an integer q such that $n = 2q + 1$. Thus

$$mn = (2p)(2q + 1) = 2r,$$

where r is an integer. By definition of even, then, $m \cdot n$ is even, as was to be shown."

42. **Theorem:** The sum of any two even integers equals $4k$ for some integer k.
   "**Proof:** Suppose m and n are any two even integers. By definition of even, $m = 2k$ for some integer k and $n = 2k$ for some integer k. By substitution,

$$m + n = 2k + 2k = 4k.$$

This is what was to be shown."

In 43–60 determine whether the statement is true or false. Justify your answer with a proof or a counterexample, as appropriate. In each case use only the definitions of the terms and the Assumptions listed on page 146 not any previously established properties.

43. The product of any two odd integers is odd.

44. The negative of any odd integer is odd.

45. The difference of any two odd integers is odd.

46. The difference of any two odd integers is even.

47. If a sum of two integers is even, then one of the summands is even. (In the expression $a + b$, a and b are called **summands**.)

48. The difference of any two even integers is even.

49. The product of any even integer and any integer is even.

50. For all integers n and m, if $n - m$ is even then $n^3 - m^3$ is even.

51. For all integers n, if n is prime then $(-1)^n = -1$.

52. For all integers n, $n^2 - n + 11$ is a prime number.

53. For all integers m, if $m > 2$ then $m^2 - 4$ is composite.

54. For all integers n, $4(n^2 + n + 1) - 3n^2$ is a perfect square.

55. For all nonnegative real numbers a and b, $\sqrt{ab} = \sqrt{a}\sqrt{b}$. (Note that if x is a nonnegative real number, then there is a unique nonnegative real number y, denoted $\sqrt{x}$, such that $y^2 = x$.)

✦ ✱ 56. (Two integers are **consecutive** if, and only if, one is one more than the other.) Any product of four consecutive integers is one less than a perfect square.

57. If m and n are positive integers and mn is a perfect square, then m and n are perfect squares.

58. The difference of the squares of any two consecutive integers is odd.

59. Every positive integer can be expressed as a sum of three or fewer perfect squares.

60. For all nonnegative real numbers a and b,
$$\sqrt{a+b} = \sqrt{a} + \sqrt{b}.$$

61. Suppose that integers m and n are perfect squares. Then $m + n + 2\sqrt{mn}$ is also a perfect square. Why?

H ✱ 62. If p is a prime number, must $2^p - 1$ also be prime? Prove or give a counterexample.

✱ 63. If n is a nonnegative integer, must $2^{2^n} + 1$ be prime? Prove or give a counterexample.

Answers for Test Yourself

1. it equals twice some integer   2. it equals twice some integer plus 1   3. n is greater than 1 and if n equals the product of any two positive integers, then one of the integers equals 1 and the other equals n.   4. a counterexample   5. particular but arbitrarily chosen element of the set; x satisfies the given property   6. x is a particular but arbitrarily chosen element of the set D that makes the hypothesis $P(x)$ true; x makes the conclusion $Q(x)$ true.

4.2 Direct Proof and Counterexample II: Rational Numbers

Such, then, is the whole art of convincing. It is contained in two principles: to define all notations used, and to prove everything by replacing mentally the defined terms by their definitions. — Blaise Pascal, 1623–1662

Sums, differences, and products of integers are integers. But most quotients of integers are not integers. Quotients of integers are, however, important; they are known as *rational numbers.*

• **Definition**

A real number r is **rational** if, and only if, it can be expressed as a quotient of two integers with a nonzero denominator. A real number that is not rational is **irrational.** More formally, if r is a real number, then

$$r \text{ is rational} \iff \exists \text{ integers } a \text{ and } b \text{ such that } r = \frac{a}{b} \text{ and } b \neq 0.$$

The word *rational* contains the word *ratio,* which is another word for quotient. A rational number can be written as a ratio of integers.

Example 4.2.1 Determining Whether Numbers Are Rational or Irrational

a. Is 10/3 a rational number?

b. Is $-\frac{5}{39}$ a rational number?

c. Is 0.281 a rational number?

d. Is 7 a rational number?

e. Is 0 a rational number?

f. Is 2/0 a rational number?

g. Is 2/0 an irrational number?

h. Is 0.12121212... a rational number (where the digits 12 are assumed to repeat forever)?

i. If m and n are integers and neither m nor n is zero, is $(m + n)/mn$ a rational number?

Solution

a. Yes, 10/3 is a quotient of the integers 10 and 3 and hence is rational.

b. Yes, $-\frac{5}{39} = \frac{-5}{39}$, which is a quotient of the integers -5 and 39 and hence is rational.

c. Yes, $0.281 = 281/1000$. Note that the real numbers represented on a typical calculator display are all finite decimals. An explanation similar to the one in this example shows that any such number is rational. It follows that a calculator with such a display can represent only rational numbers.

d. Yes, $7 = 7/1$.

e. Yes, $0 = 0/1$.

f. No, 2/0 is not a number (division by 0 is not allowed).

g. No, because every irrational number is a number, and 2/0 is not a number. We discuss additional techniques for determining whether numbers are irrational in Sections 4.6, 4.7, and 9.4.

h. Yes. Let $x = 0.12121212\ldots$ Then $100x = 12.12121212\ldots$ Thus

$$100x - x = 12.12121212\ldots - 0.12121212\ldots = 12.$$

But also $100x - x = 99x$ by basic algebra

Hence $99x = 12,$

and so $x = \dfrac{12}{99}.$

Therefore, $0.12121212\ldots = 12/99$, which is a ratio of two nonzero integers and thus is a rational number.

    Note that you can use an argument similar to this one to show that any repeating decimal is a rational number. In Section 9.4 we show that any rational number can be written as a repeating or terminating decimal.

i. Yes, since m and n are integers, so are $m + n$ and mn (because sums and products of integers are integers). Also $mn \neq 0$ by the *zero product property*. One version of this property says the following:

Zero Product Property

If neither of two real numbers is zero, then their product is also not zero.

(See Theorem T11 in Appendix A and exercise 8 at the end of this section.) It follows that $(m + n)/mn$ is a quotient of two integers with a nonzero denominator and hence is a rational number. ∎

More on Generalizing from the Generic Particular

Some people like to think of the method of generalizing from the generic particular as a challenge process. If you claim a property holds for all elements in a domain, then someone can challenge your claim by picking any element in the domain whatsoever and asking you to prove that that element satisfies the property. To prove your claim, you must be able to meet all such challenges. That is, you must have a way to convince the challenger that the property is true for an *arbitrarily chosen* element in the domain.

For example, suppose "A" claims that every integer is a rational number. "B" challenges this claim by asking "A" to prove it for $n = 7$. "A" observes that

$$7 = \frac{7}{1} \qquad \text{which is a quotient of integers and hence rational.}$$

"B" accepts this explanation but challenges again with $n = -12$. "A" responds that

$$-12 = \frac{-12}{1} \qquad \text{which is a quotient of integers and hence rational.}$$

Next "B" tries to trip up "A" by challenging with $n = 0$, but "A" answers that

$$0 = \frac{0}{1} \qquad \text{which is a quotient of integers and hence rational.}$$

As you can see, "A" is able to respond effectively to all "B"s challenges because "A" has a general procedure for putting integers into the form of rational numbers: "A" just divides whatever integer "B" gives by 1. That is, no matter what integer n "B" gives "A", "A" writes

$$n = \frac{n}{1} \qquad \text{which is a quotient of integers and hence rational.}$$

This discussion proves the following theorem.

Theorem 4.2.1

Every integer is a rational number.

In exercise 11 at the end of this section you are asked to condense the above discussion into a formal proof.

Proving Properties of Rational Numbers

The next example shows how to use the method of generalizing from the generic particular to prove a property of rational numbers.

Example 4.2.2 A Sum of Rationals Is Rational

Prove that the sum of any two rational numbers is rational.

Solution   Begin by mentally or explicitly rewriting the statement to be proved in the form "∀ _____, if _____ then _____."

Formal Restatement: ∀ real numbers r and s, if r and s are rational then $r + s$ is rational.

Next ask yourself, "Where am I starting from?" or "What am I supposing?" The answer gives you the starting point, or first sentence, of the proof.

Starting Point: Suppose r and s are particular but arbitrarily chosen real numbers such that r and s are rational; or, more simply,

Suppose r and s are rational numbers.

Then ask yourself, "What must I show to complete the proof?"

To Show: $r + s$ is rational.

Finally ask, "How do I get from the starting point to the conclusion?" or "Why must $r + s$ be rational if both r and s are rational?" The answer depends in an essential way on the definition of rational.

Rational numbers are quotients of integers, so to say that r and s are rational means that

$$r = \frac{a}{b} \quad \text{and} \quad s = \frac{c}{d} \quad \text{for some integers } a, b, c, \text{ and } d \text{ where } b \neq 0 \text{ and } d \neq 0.$$

It follows by substitution that

$$r + s = \frac{a}{b} + \frac{c}{d}.$$

You need to show that $r + s$ is rational, which means that $r + s$ can be written as a single fraction or ratio of two integers with a nonzero denominator. But the right-hand side of equation (4.2.1) in

$$\frac{a}{b} + \frac{c}{d} = \frac{ad}{bd} + \frac{bc}{bd} \quad \text{rewriting the fraction with a common denominator}$$

$$= \frac{ad + bc}{bd} \quad \text{adding fractions with a common denominator.}$$

Is this fraction a ratio of integers? Yes. Because products and sums of integers are integers, $ad + bc$ and bd are both integers. Is the denominator $bd \neq 0$? Yes, by the zero product property (since $b \neq 0$ and $d \neq 0$). Thus $r + s$ is a rational number.

This discussion is summarized as follows:

Theorem 4.2.2

The sum of any two rational numbers is rational.

Proof:

Suppose r and s are rational numbers. *[We must show that $r + s$ is rational.]* Then, by definition of rational, $r = a/b$ and $s = c/d$ for some integers a, b, c, and d with $b \neq 0$ and $d \neq 0$. Thus

$$r + s = \frac{a}{b} + \frac{c}{d} \quad \text{by substitution}$$

$$= \frac{ad + bc}{bd} \quad \text{by basic algebra.}$$

Let $p = ad + bc$ and $q = bd$. Then p and q are integers because products and sums of integers are integers and because a, b, c, and d are all integers. Also $q \neq 0$ by the zero product property. Thus

$$r + s = \frac{p}{q} \text{ where } p \text{ and } q \text{ are integers and } q \neq 0.$$

Therefore, $r + s$ is rational by definition of a rational number. *[This is what was to be shown.]*

Deriving New Mathematics from Old

Section 4.1 focused on establishing truth and falsity of mathematical theorems using only the basic algebra normally taught in secondary school; the fact that the integers are closed under addition, subtraction, and multiplication; and the definitions of the terms in the theorems themselves. In the future, when we ask you to **prove something directly from the definitions,** we will mean that you should restrict yourself to this approach. However, once a collection of statements has been proved directly from the definitions, another method of proof becomes possible. The statements in the collection can be used to derive additional results.

Example 4.2.3 Deriving Additional Results about Even and Odd Integers

Suppose that you have already proved the following properties of even and odd integers:

1. The sum, product, and difference of any two even integers are even.

2. The sum and difference of any two odd integers are even.

3. The product of any two odd integers is odd.

4. The product of any even integer and any odd integer is even.

5. The sum of any odd integer and any even integer is odd.

6. The difference of any odd integer minus any even integer is odd.

7. The difference of any even integer minus any odd integer is odd.

Use the properties listed above to prove that if a is any even integer and b is any odd integer, then $\frac{a^2+b^2+1}{2}$ is an integer.

Solution   Suppose a is any even integer and b is any odd integer. By property 3, b^2 is odd, and by property 1, a^2 is even. Then by property 5, $a^2 + b^2$ is odd, and because 1 is also odd, the sum $(a^2 + b^2) + 1 = a^2 + b^2 + 1$ is even by property 2. Hence, by definition of even, there exists an integer k such that $a^2 + b^2 + 1 = 2k$. Dividing both sides by 2 gives $\frac{a^2+b^2+1}{2} = k$, which is an integer. Thus $\frac{a^2+b^2+1}{2}$ is an integer *[as was to be shown]*.

A **corollary** is a statement whose truth can be immediately deduced from a theorem that has already been proved.

Example 4.2.4 The Double of a Rational Number

Derive the following as a corollary of Theorem 4.2.2.

> **Corollary 4.2.3**
>
> **The double of a rational number is rational.**

Solution   The double of a number is just its sum with itself. But since the sum of any two rational numbers is rational (Theorem 4.2.2), the sum of a rational number with itself is rational. Hence the double of a rational number is rational. Here is a formal version of this argument:

Proof:

Suppose r is any rational number. Then $2r = r + r$ is a sum of two rational numbers. So, by Theorem 4.2.2, $2r$ is rational. ∎

Test Yourself

1. To show that a real number is rational, we must show that we can write it as _____.

2. An irrational number is a _____ that is _____.

3. Zero is a rational number because _____.

Exercise Set 4.2

The numbers in 1–7 are all rational. Write each number as a ratio of two integers.

1. $-\dfrac{35}{6}$

2. 4.6037

3. $\dfrac{4}{5} + \dfrac{2}{9}$

4. 0.37373737...

5. 0.56565656...

6. 320.5492492492...

7. 52.4672167216721...

8. The zero product property, says that if a product of two real numbers is 0, then one of the numbers must be 0.
   a. Write this property formally using quantifiers and variables.
   b. Write the contrapositive of your answer to part (a).
   c. Write an informal version (without quantifier symbols or variables) for your answer to part (b).

9. Assume that a and b are both integers and that $a \neq 0$ and $b \neq 0$. Explain why $(b - a)/(ab^2)$ must be a rational number.

10. Assume that m and n are both integers and that $n \neq 0$. Explain why $(5m + 12n)/(4n)$ must be a rational number.

11. Prove that every integer is a rational number.

12. Fill in the blanks in the following proof that the square of any rational number is rational:

    Proof: Suppose that r is __(a)__. By definition of rational, $r = a/b$ for some __(b)__ with $b \neq 0$. By substitution,
    $$r^2 = \underline{\text{(c)}} = a^2/b^2.$$
    Since a and b are both integers, so are the products a^2 and __(d)__. Also $b^2 \neq 0$ by the __(e)__. Hence r^2 is a ratio of two integers with a nonzero denominator, and so __(f)__ by definition of rational.

13. Consider the statement: The negative of any rational number is rational.
    a. Write the statement formally using a quantifier and a variable.
    b. Determine whether the statement is true or false and justify your answer.

14. Consider the statement: The cube of any rational number is a rational number.
    a. Write the statement formally using a quantifier and a variable.
    b. Determine whether the statement is true or false and justify your answer.

Determine which of the statements in 15–20 are true and which are false. Prove each true statement directly from the definitions, and give a counterexample for each false statement.

In case the statement is false, determine whether a small change would make it true. If so, make the change and prove the new statement. Follow the directions for writing proofs on page 154.

15. The product of any two rational numbers is a rational number.

H 16. The quotient of any two rational numbers is a rational number.

H 17. The difference of any two rational numbers is a rational number.

H 18. If r and s are any two rational numbers, then $\frac{r+s}{2}$ is rational.

H 19. For all real numbers a and b, if $a < b$ then $a < \frac{a+b}{2} < b$. (You may use the properties of inequalities in T17–T27 of Appendix A.)

20. Given any two rational numbers r and s with $r < s$, there is another rational number between r and s. (*Hint:* Use the results of exercises 18 and 19.)

Use the properties of even and odd integers that are listed in Example 4.2.3 to do exercises 21–23. Indicate which properties you use to justify your reasoning.

21. True or false? If m is any even integer and n is any odd integer, then $m^2 + 3n$ is odd. Explain.

22. True or false? If k is any even integer and m is any odd integer, then $(k + 2)^2 - (m - 1)^2$ is even. Explain.

23. True or false? If a is any odd integer, then $a^2 + a$ is even. Explain.

Derive the statements in 24–26 as corollaries of Theorems 4.2.1, 4.2.2, and the results of exercises 12, 13, 14, 15, and 17.

24. For any rational numbers r and s, $2r + 3s$ is rational.

25. For any rational number s, $5s^3 + 8s^2 - 7$ is rational.

26. If r is any rational number, then $3r^2 - 2r + 4$ is rational.

27. It is a fact that if n is any nonnegative integer, then

$$1 + \frac{1}{2} + \frac{1}{2^2} + \frac{1}{2^3} + \cdots + \frac{1}{2^n} = \frac{1 - (1/2^{n+1})}{1 - (1/2)}.$$

(A more general form of this statement is proved in Section 5.2). Is the right-hand side of this equation rational? If so, express it as a ratio of two integers.

28. Suppose $a, b, c,$ and d are integers and $a \neq c$. Suppose also that x is a real number that satisfies the equation

$$\frac{ax + b}{cx + d} = 1.$$

Must x be rational? If so, express x as a ratio of two integers.

∗ 29. Suppose $a, b,$ and c are integers and $x, y,$ and z are nonzero real numbers that satisfy the following equations:

$$\frac{xy}{x + y} = a \quad \text{and} \quad \frac{xz}{x + z} = b \quad \text{and} \quad \frac{yz}{y + z} = c.$$

Is x rational? If so, express it as a ratio of two integers.

30. Prove that if one solution for a quadratic equation of the form $x^2 + bx + c = 0$ is rational (where b and c are rational), then the other solution is also rational. (Use the fact that if the solutions of the equation are r and s, then $x^2 + bx + c = (x - r)(x - s)$.)

31. Prove that if a real number c satisfies a polynomial equation of the form

$$r_3x^3 + r_2x^2 + r_1x + r_0 = 0,$$

where $r_0, r_1, r_2,$ and r_3 are rational numbers, then c satisfies an equation of the form

$$n_3x^3 + n_2x^2 + n_1x + n_0 = 0,$$

where $n_0, n_1, n_2,$ and n_3 are integers.

> **Definition:** A number c is called a **root** of a polynomial $p(x)$ if, and only if, $p(c) = 0$.

∗ 32. Prove that for all real numbers c, if c is a root of a polynomial with rational coefficients, then c is a root of a polynomial with integer coefficients.

Use the properties of even and odd integers that are listed in Example 4.2.3 to do exercises 33 and 34.

33. When expressions of the form $(x - r)(x - s)$ are multiplied out, a quadratic polynomial is obtained. For instance, $(x - 2)(x - (-7)) = (x - 2)(x + 7) = x^2 + 5x - 14$.

H a. What can be said about the coefficients of the polynomial obtained by multiplying out $(x - r)(x - s)$ when both r and s are odd integers? when both r and s are even integers? when one of r and s is even and the other is odd?

b. It follows from part (a) that $x^2 - 1253x + 255$ cannot be written as a product of two polynomials with integer coefficients. Explain why this is so.

∗ 34. Observe that $(x - r)(x - s)(x - t)$
$$= x^3 - (r + s + t)x^2 + (rs + rt + st)x - rst.$$

a. Derive a result for cubic polynomials similar to the result in part (a) of exercise 33 for quadratic polynomials.

b. Can $x^3 + 7x^2 - 8x - 27$ be written as a product of three polynomials with integer coefficients? Explain.

In 35–39 find the mistakes in the "proofs" that the sum of any two rational numbers is a rational number.

35. "**Proof:** Any two rational numbers produce a rational number when added together. So if r and s are particular but arbitrarily chosen rational numbers, then $r + s$ is rational."

36. "**Proof:** Let rational numbers $r = \frac{1}{4}$ and $s = \frac{1}{2}$ be given. Then $r + s = \frac{1}{4} + \frac{1}{2} = \frac{3}{4}$, which is a rational number. This is what was to be shown."

37. "**Proof:** Suppose r and s are rational numbers. By definition of rational, $r = a/b$ for some integers a and b with $b \neq 0$, and $s = a/b$ for some integers a and b with $b \neq 0$. Then

$$r + s = \frac{a}{b} + \frac{a}{b} = \frac{2a}{b}.$$

Let $p = 2a$. Then p is an integer since it is a product of integers. Hence $r + s = p/b$, where p and b are integers and $b \neq 0$. Thus $r + s$ is a rational number by definition of rational. This is what was to be shown."

38. "**Proof:** Suppose r and s are rational numbers. Then $r = a/b$ and $s = c/d$ for some integers $a, b, c,$ and d with $b \neq 0$ and $d \neq 0$ (by definition of rational). Then

$$r + s = \frac{a}{b} + \frac{c}{d}.$$

But this is a sum of two fractions, which is a fraction. So $r + s$ is a rational number since a rational number is a fraction."

39. "**Proof:** Suppose r and s are rational numbers. If $r + s$ is rational, then by definition of rational $r + s = a/b$ for some integers a and b with $b \neq 0$. Also since r and s are rational, $r = i/j$ and $s = m/n$ for some integers $i, j, m,$ and n with $j \neq 0$ and $n \neq 0$. It follows that

$$r + s = \frac{i}{j} + \frac{m}{n} = \frac{a}{b},$$

which is a quotient of two integers with a nonzero denominator. Hence it is a rational number. This is what was to be shown."

Answers for Test Yourself

1. a ratio of integers with a nonzero denominator   2. real number; not rational   3. $0 = \dfrac{0}{1}$

4.3 Direct Proof and Counterexample III: Divisibility

The essential quality of a proof is to compel belief. — Pierre de Fermat

When you were first introduced to the concept of division in elementary school, you were probably taught that 12 divided by 3 is 4 because if you separate 12 objects into groups of 3, you get 4 groups with nothing left over.

| XXX | XXX | XXX | XXX |

You may also have been taught to describe this fact by saying that "12 is evenly divisible by 3" or "3 divides 12 evenly."

The notion of divisibility is the central concept of one of the most beautiful subjects in advanced mathematics: **number theory,** the study of properties of integers.

• Definition

If n and d are integers and $d \neq 0$ then

n is **divisible by** d if, and only if, n equals d times some integer.

Instead of "n is divisible by d," we can say that

n **is a multiple of** d, or
d **is a factor of** n, or
d **is a divisor of** n, or
d **divides** n.

The notation $\mathbf{d \mid n}$ is read "d divides n." Symbolically, if n and d are integers and $d \neq 0$:

$$d \mid n \quad \Leftrightarrow \quad \exists \text{ an integer } k \text{ such that } n = dk.$$

Example 4.3.1 Divisibility

  a. Is 21 divisible by 3? b. Does 5 divide 40? c. Does $7 \mid 42$?

  d. Is 32 a multiple of -16? e. Is 6 a factor of 54? f. Is 7 a factor of -7?

Solution

  a. Yes, $21 = 3 \cdot 7$. b. Yes, $40 = 5 \cdot 8$. c. Yes, $42 = 7 \cdot 6$.

  d. Yes, $32 = (-16) \cdot (-2)$. e. Yes, $54 = 6 \cdot 9$. f. Yes, $-7 = 7 \cdot (-1)$. ■

Example 4.3.2 Divisors of Zero

  If k is any nonzero integer, does k divide 0?

Solution Yes, because $0 = k \cdot 0$. ■

  Two useful properties of divisibility are (1) that if one positive integer divides a second positive integer, then the first is less than or equal to the second, and (2) that the only divisors of 1 are 1 and -1.

Theorem 4.3.1 A Positive Divisor of a Positive Integer

For all integers a and b, if a and b are positive and a divides b, then $a \le b$.

Proof:

Suppose a and b are positive integers and a divides b. *[We must show that $a \le b$.]* Then there exists an integer k so that $b = ak$. By property T25 of Appendix A, k must be positive because both a and b are positive. It follows that

$$1 \le k$$

because every positive integer is greater than or equal to 1. Multiplying both sides by a gives

$$a \le ka = b$$

because multiplying both sides of an inequality by a positive number preserves the inequality by property T20 of Appendix A. Thus $a \le b$ *[as was to be shown].*

 ■

Theorem 4.3.2 Divisors of 1

The only divisors of 1 are 1 and -1.

Proof:

Since $1 \cdot 1 = 1$ and $(-1)(-1) = 1$, both 1 and -1 are divisors of 1. Now suppose m is any integer that divides 1. Then there exists an integer n such that $1 = mn$. By Theorem T25 in Appendix A, either both m and n are positive or both m and n are negative. If both m and n are positive, then m is a positive integer divisor of 1. By Theorem 4.3.1, $m \le 1$, and, since the only positive integer that is less than or equal

---

continued on page 172

to 1 is 1 itself, it follows that $m = 1$. On the other hand, if both m and n are negative, then, by Theorem T12 in Appendix A, $(-m)(-n) = mn = 1$. In this case $-m$ is a positive integer divisor of 1, and so, by the same reasoning, $-m = 1$ and thus $m = -1$. Therefore there are only two possibilities: either $m = 1$ or $m = -1$. So the only divisors of 1 are 1 and -1.

Example 4.3.3 Divisibility of Algebraic Expressions

a. If a and b are integers, is $3a + 3b$ divisible by 3?

b. If k and m are integers, is $10km$ divisible by 5?

Solution

a. Yes. By the distributive law of algebra, $3a + 3b = 3(a + b)$ and $a + b$ is an integer because it is a sum of two integers.

b. Yes. By the associative law of algebra, $10km = 5 \cdot (2km)$ and $2km$ is an integer because it is a product of three integers. ■

When the definition of divides is rewritten formally using the existential quantifier, the result is

$$d \mid n \quad \Leftrightarrow \quad \exists \text{ an integer } k \text{ such that } n = dk.$$

Since the negation of an existential statement is universal, it follows that d does not divide n (denoted $d \nmid n$) if, and only if, $\forall$ integers k, $n \neq dk$, or, in other words, the quotient n/d is not an integer.

$$\text{For all integers } n \text{ and } d, \quad d \nmid n \quad \Leftrightarrow \quad \frac{n}{d} \text{ is not an integer.}$$

Example 4.3.4 Checking Nondivisibility

Does $4 \mid 15$?

Solution   No, $\frac{15}{4} = 3.75$, which is not an integer. ■

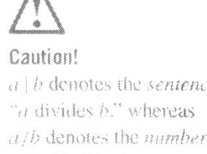

Caution!
$a \mid b$ denotes the *sentence*
"a divides b," whereas
a/b denotes the *number*
a divided by b.

Be careful to distinguish between the notation $a \mid b$ and the notation a/b. The notation $a \mid b$ stands for the sentence "a divides b," which means that there is an integer k such that $b = ak$. Dividing both sides by a gives $b/a = k$, an integer. Thus, when $a \neq 0$, $a \mid b$ if, and only if, b/a is an integer. On the other hand, the notation a/b stands for the number a/b which is the result of dividing a by b and which may or may not be an integer. In particular, be sure to avoid writing things like

$$4 \mid (3 + 5) = 4 \mid 8.$$

If read out loud, this becomes, "4 divides the quantity 3 plus 5 equals 4 divides 8," which is nonsense.

Example 4.3.5 Prime Numbers and Divisibility

An alternative way to define a prime number is to say that an integer $n > 1$ is prime if, and only if, its only positive integer divisors are 1 and itself. ■

Proving Properties of Divisibility

One of the most useful properties of divisibility is that it is transitive. If one number divides a second and the second number divides a third, then the first number divides the third.

Example 4.3.6 Transitivity of Divisibility

Prove that for all integers a, b, and c, if $a \mid b$ and $b \mid c$, then $a \mid c$.

Solution   Since the statement to be proved is already written formally, you can immediately pick out the starting point, or first sentence of the proof, and the conclusion that must be shown.

Starting Point: Suppose a, b, and c are particular but arbitrarily chosen integers such that $a \mid b$ and $b \mid c$.

To Show: $a \mid c$.

You need to show that $a \mid c$, or, in other words, that

$$c = a \cdot (\text{some integer}).$$

But since $a \mid b$,

$$b = ar \quad \text{for some integer } r. \tag{4.3.1}$$

And since $b \mid c$,

$$c = bs \quad \text{for some integer } s. \tag{4.3.2}$$

Equation 4.3.2 expresses c in terms of b, and equation 4.3.1 expresses b in terms of a. Thus if you substitute 4.3.1 into 4.3.2, you will have an equation that expresses c in terms of a.

$$\begin{aligned} c &= bs & \text{by equation 4.3.2} \\ &= (ar)s & \text{by equation 4.3.1.} \end{aligned}$$

But $(ar)s = a(rs)$ by the associative law for multiplication. Hence

$$c = a(rs).$$

Now you are almost finished. You have expressed c as $a \cdot (\text{something})$. It remains only to verify that that something is an integer. But of course it is, because it is a product of two integers.

This discussion is summarized as follows:

Theorem 4.3.3 Transitivity of Divisibility

For all integers a, b, and c, if a divides b and b divides c, then a divides c.

Proof:

Suppose a, b, and c are *[particular but arbitrarily chosen]* integers such that a divides b and b divides c. *[We must show that a divides c.]* By definition of divisibility,

$$b = ar \quad \text{and} \quad c = bs \quad \text{for some integers } r \text{ and } s.$$

continued on page 174

By substitution

$$c = bs$$
$$= (ar)s$$
$$= a(rs) \quad \text{by basic algebra.}$$

Let $k = rs$. Then k is an integer since it is a product of integers, and therefore

$$c = ak \quad \text{where } k \text{ is an integer.}$$

Thus a divides c by definition of divisibility. *[This is what was to be shown.]*

It would appear from the definition of prime that to show that an integer is prime you would need to show that it is not divisible by any integer greater than 1 and less than itself. In fact, you need only check whether it is divisible by a prime number less than or equal to itself. This follows from Theorems 4.3.1, 4.3.3, and the following theorem, which says that any integer greater than 1 is divisible by a prime number. The idea of the proof is quite simple. You start with a positive integer. If it is prime, you are done; if not, it is a product of two smaller positive factors. If one of these is prime, you are done; if not, you can pick one of the factors and write it as a product of still smaller positive factors. You can continue in this way, factoring the factors of the number you started with, until one of them turns out to be prime. This must happen eventually because all the factors can be chosen to be positive and each is smaller than the preceding one.

Theorem 4.3.4 Divisibility by a Prime

Any integer $n > 1$ is divisible by a prime number.

Proof:

Suppose n is a *[particular but arbitrarily chosen]* integer that is greater than 1. *[We must show that there is a prime number that divides n.]* If n is prime, then n is divisible by a prime number (namely itself), and we are done. If n is not prime, then, as discussed in Example 4.1.2b,

$$n = r_0 s_0 \quad \text{where } r_0 \text{ and } s_0 \text{ are integers and}$$
$$1 < r_0 < n \text{ and } 1 < s_0 < n.$$

It follows by definition of divisibility that $r_0 \mid n$.
    If r_0 is prime, then r_0 is a prime number that divides n, and we are done. If r_0 is not prime, then

$$r_0 = r_1 s_1 \quad \text{where } r_1 \text{ and } s_1 \text{ are integers and}$$
$$1 < r_1 < r_0 \text{ and } 1 < s_1 < r_0.$$

It follows by the definition of divisibility that $r_1 \mid r_0$. But we already know that $r_0 \mid n$. Consequently, by transitivity of divisibility, $r_1 \mid n$.
    If r_1 is prime, then r_1 is a prime number that divides n, and we are done. If r_1 is not prime, then

$$r_1 = r_2 s_2 \quad \text{where } r_2 \text{ and } s_2 \text{ are integers and}$$
$$1 < r_2 < r_1 \text{ and } 1 < s_2 < r_1.$$

It follows by definition of divisibility that $r_2 \mid r_1$. But we already know that $r_1 \mid n$. Consequently, by transitivity of divisibility, $r_2 \mid n$.

If r_2 is prime, then r_2 is a prime number that divides n, and we are done. If r_2 is not prime, then we may repeat the previous process by factoring r_2 as $r_3 s_3$.

We may continue in this way, factoring successive factors of n until we find a prime factor. We must succeed in a finite number of steps because each new factor is both less than the previous one (which is less than n) and greater than 1, and there are fewer than n integers strictly between 1 and n.* Thus we obtain a sequence

$$r_0, r_1, r_2, \ldots, r_k,$$

where $k \geq 0$, $1 < r_k < r_{k-1} < \cdots < r_2 < r_1 < r_0 < n$, and $r_i \mid n$ for each $i = 0, 1, 2, \ldots, k$. The condition for termination is that r_k should be prime. Hence r_k is a prime number that divides n. *[This is what we were to show.]*

Counterexamples and Divisibility

To show that a proposed divisibility property is not universally true, you need only find one pair of integers for which it is false.

Example 4.3.7 Checking a Proposed Divisibility Property

Is the following statement true or false? For all integers a and b, if $a \mid b$ and $b \mid a$ then $a = b$.

Solution   This statement is false. Can you think of a counterexample just by concentrating for a minute or so?

The following discussion describes a mental process that may take just a few seconds. It is helpful to be able to use it consciously, however, to solve more difficult problems.

To discover the truth or falsity of a statement such as the one given above, start off much as you would if you were trying to prove it.

Starting Point: Suppose a and b are integers such that $a \mid b$ and $b \mid a$.

Ask yourself, "*Must* it follow that $a = b$, or *could* it happen that $a \neq b$ for some a and b?" Focus on the supposition. What does it mean? By definition of divisibility, the conditions $a \mid b$ and $b \mid a$ mean that

$$b = ka \quad \text{and} \quad a = lb \quad \text{for some integers } k \text{ and } l.$$

Must it follow that $a = b$, or can you find integers a and b that satisfy these equations for which $a \neq b$? The equations imply that

$$b = ka = k(lb) = (kl)b.$$

Since $b \mid a$, $b \neq 0$, and so you can cancel b from the extreme left and right sides to obtain

$$1 = kl.$$

In other words, k and l are divisors of 1. But, by Theorem 4.3.2, the only divisors of 1 are 1 and -1. Thus k and l are both 1 or are both -1. If $k = l = 1$, then $b = a$. But

---

*Strictly speaking, this statement is justified by an axiom for the integers called the well-ordering principle, which is discussed in Section 5.4. Theorem 4.3.4 can also be proved using strong mathematical induction, as shown in Example 5.4.1.

if $k = l = -1$, then $b = -a$ and so $a \neq b$. This analysis suggests that you can find a counterexample by taking $b = -a$. Here is a formal answer:

Proposed Divisibility Property: For all integers a and b, if $a \mid b$ and $b \mid a$ then $a = b$.

Counterexample: Let $a = 2$ and $b = -2$. Then

$$a \mid b \text{ since } 2 \mid (-2) \text{ and } b \mid a \text{ since } (-2) \mid 2, \text{ but } a \neq b \text{ since } 2 \neq -2.$$

Therefore, the statement is false.

The search for a proof will frequently help you discover a counterexample (provided the statement you are trying to prove is, in fact, false). Conversely, in trying to find a counterexample for a statement, you may come to realize the reason why it is true (if it is, in fact, true). The important thing is to keep an open mind until you are convinced by the evidence of your own careful reasoning.

The Unique Factorization of Integers Theorem

The most comprehensive statement about divisibility of integers is contained in the *unique factorization of integers theorem*. Because of its importance, this theorem is also called the *fundamental theorem of arithmetic.* Although Euclid, who lived about 300 B.C., seems to have been acquainted with the theorem, it was first stated precisely by the great German mathematician Carl Friedrich Gauss (rhymes with *house*) in 1801.

The unique factorization of integers theorem says that any integer greater than 1 either is prime or can be written as a product of prime numbers in a way that is unique except, perhaps, for the order in which the primes are written. For example,

$$72 = 2 \cdot 2 \cdot 2 \cdot 3 \cdot 3 = 2 \cdot 3 \cdot 3 \cdot 2 \cdot 2 = 3 \cdot 2 \cdot 2 \cdot 3 \cdot 2$$

and so forth. The three 2's and two 3's may be written in any order, but any factorization of 72 as a product of primes must contain exactly three 2's and two 3's—no other collection of prime numbers besides three 2's and two 3's multiplies out to 72.

Note This theorem is the reason the number 1 is not allowed to be prime. If 1 were prime, then factorizations would not be unique. For example, $6 = 2 \cdot 3 = 1 \cdot 2 \cdot 3$, and so forth.

Theorem 4.3.5 Unique Factorization of Integers Theorem
(Fundamental Theorem of Arithmetic)

Given any integer $n > 1$, there exist a positive integer k, distinct prime numbers $p_1, p_2, \ldots, p_k$, and positive integers $e_1, e_2, \ldots, e_k$ such that

$$n = p_1^{e_1} p_2^{e_2} p_3^{e_3} \cdots p_k^{e_k},$$

and any other expression for n as a product of prime numbers is identical to this except, perhaps, for the order in which the factors are written.

The proof of the unique factorization of integers theorem is outlined in the exercises for Sections 5.4 and 8.4.

Because of the unique factorization theorem, any integer $n > 1$ can be put into a *standard factored form* in which the prime factors are written in ascending order from left to right.

> **• Definition**
>
> Given any integer $n > 1$, the **standard factored form** of n is an expression of the form
>
> $$n = p_1^{e_1} p_2^{e_2} p_3^{e_3} \cdots p_k^{e_k},$$
>
> where k is a positive integer; $p_1, p_2, \ldots, p_k$ are prime numbers; $e_1, e_2, \ldots, e_k$ are positive integers; and $p_1 < p_2 < \cdots < p_k$.

Example 4.3.8 Writing Integers in Standard Factored Form

Write 3,300 in standard factored form.

Solution   First find all the factors of 3,300. Then write them in ascending order:

$$3{,}300 = 100 \cdot 33 = 4 \cdot 25 \cdot 3 \cdot 11$$
$$= 2 \cdot 2 \cdot 5 \cdot 5 \cdot 3 \cdot 11 = 2^2 \cdot 3^1 \cdot 5^2 \cdot 11^1.$$

∎

Example 4.3.9 Using Unique Factorization to Solve a Problem

Suppose m is an integer such that

$$8 \cdot 7 \cdot 6 \cdot 5 \cdot 4 \cdot 3 \cdot 2 \cdot m = 17 \cdot 16 \cdot 15 \cdot 14 \cdot 13 \cdot 12 \cdot 11 \cdot 10.$$

Does $17 \mid m$?

Solution   Since 17 is one of the prime factors of the right-hand side of the equation, it is also a prime factor of the left-hand side (by the unique factorization of integers theorem). But 17 does not equal any prime factor of 8, 7, 6, 5, 4, 3, or 2 (because it is too large). Hence 17 must occur as one of the prime factors of m, and so $17 \mid m$.

∎

Test Yourself

1. To show that a nonzero integer d divides an integer n, we must show that _____.

2. To say that d divides n means the same as saying that _____ is divisible by _____.

3. If a and b are positive integers and $a \mid b$, then _____ is less than or equal to _____.

4. For all integers n and d, $d \nmid n$ if, and only if, _____.

5. If a and b are integers, the notation $a \mid b$ denotes _____ and the notation a/b denotes _____.

6. The transitivity of divisibility theorem says that for all integers a, b, and c, if _____ then _____.

7. The divisibility by a prime theorem says that every integer greater than 1 is _____.

8. The unique factorization of integers theorem says that any integer greater than 1 is either _____ or can be written as _____ in a way that is unique except possibly for the _____ in which the numbers are written.

Exercise Set 4.3

Give a reason for your answer in each of 1–13. Assume that all variables represent integers.

1. Is 52 divisible by 13?   2. Does $7 \mid 56$?

3. Does $5 \mid 0$?

4. Does 3 divide $(3k + 1)(3k + 2)(3k + 3)$?

5. Is $6m(2m + 10)$ divisible by 4?

6. Is 29 a multiple of 3?   7. Is -3 a factor of 66?

8. Is $6a(a + b)$ a multiple of $3a$?

9. Is 4 a factor of $2a \cdot 34b$?

10. Does $7 \mid 34$? 11. Does $13 \mid 73$?

12. If $n = 4k + 1$, does 8 divide $n^2 - 1$?

13. If $n = 4k + 3$, does 8 divide $n^2 - 1$?

14. Fill in the blanks in the following proof that for all integers a and b, if $a \mid b$ then $a \mid (-b)$.

    Proof: Suppose a and b are any integers such that __(a)__. By definition of divisibility, there exists an integer r such that __(b)__. By substitution,

    $$-b = -ar = a(-r).$$

    Let $t = $ __(c)__. Then t is an integer because $t = (-1) \cdot r$, and both -1 and r are integers. Thus, by substitution, $-b = at$, where t is an integer, and so by definition of divisibility, __(d)__, as was to be shown.

Prove statements 15 and 16 directly from the definition of divisibility.

15. For all integers a, b, and c, if $a \mid b$ and $a \mid c$ then $a \mid (b + c)$.

H 16. For all integers a, b, and c, if $a \mid b$ and $a \mid c$ then $a \mid (b - c)$.

17. Consider the following statement: The negative of any multiple of 3 is a multiple of 3.
    a. Write the statement formally using a quantifier and a variable.
    b. Determine whether the statement is true or false and justify your answer.

18. Show that the following statement is false: For all integers a and b, if $3 \mid (a + b)$ then $3 \mid (a - b)$.

For each statement in 19–31, determine whether the statement is true or false. Prove the statement directly from the definitions if it is true, and give a counterexample if it is false.

H 19. For all integers a, b, and c, if a divides b then a divides bc.

20. The sum of any three consecutive integers is divisible by 3. (Two integers are **consecutive** if, and only if, one is one more than the other.)

21. The product of any two even integers is a multiple of 4.

H 22. A necessary condition for an integer to be divisible by 6 is that it be divisible by 2.

23. A sufficient condition for an integer to be divisible by 8 is that it be divisible by 16.

24. For all integers a, b, and c, if $a \mid b$ and $a \mid c$ then $a \mid (2b - 3c)$.

25. For all integers a, b, and c, if a is a factor of c then ab is a factor of c.

H 26. For all integers a, b, and c, if $ab \mid c$ then $a \mid c$ and $b \mid c$.

H 27. For all integers a, b, and c, if $a \mid (b + c)$ then $a \mid b$ or $a \mid c$.

28. For all integers a and b, if $a \mid 10b$ then $a \mid 10$ or $a \mid b$.

29. For all integers a, b, and c, if $a \mid bc$ then $a \mid b$ or $a \mid c$.

30. For all integers a and n, if $a \mid n^2$ and $a \le n$ then $a \mid n$.

31. For all integers a and b, if $a \mid b$ then $a^2 \mid b^2$.

32. A fast-food chain has a contest in which a card with numbers on it is given to each customer who makes a purchase. If some of the numbers on the card add up to 100, then the customer wins $100. A certain customer receives a card containing the numbers

    $$72, 21, 15, 36, 69, 81, 9, 27, 42, \text{ and } 63.$$

    Will the customer win $100? Why or why not?

33. Is it possible to have a combination of nickels, dimes, and quarters that add up to $4.72? Explain.

34. Is it possible to have 50 coins, made up of pennies, dimes, and quarters, that add up to $3? Explain.

35. Two athletes run a circular track at a steady pace so that the first completes one round in 8 minutes and the second in 10 minutes. If they both start from the same spot at 4 P.M., when will be the first time they return to the start together?

36. It can be shown (see exercises 44–48) that an integer is divisible by 3 if, and only if, the sum of its digits is divisible by 3. An integer is divisible by 9 if, and only if, the sum of its digits is divisible by 9. An integer is divisible by 5 if, and only if, its right-most digit is a 5 or a 0. And an integer is divisible by 4 if, and only if, the number formed by its right-most two digits is divisible by 4. Check the following integers for divisibility by 3, 4, 5 and 9.
    a. 637,425,403,705,125 b. 12,858,306,120,312
    c. 517,924,440,926,512 d. 14,328,083,360,232

37. Use the unique factorization theorem to write the following integers in standard factored form.
    a. 1,176 b. 5,733 c. 3,675

38. Suppose that in standard factored form $a = p_1^{e_1} p_2^{e_2} \cdots p_k^{e_k}$, where k is a positive integer; $p_1, p_2, \ldots, p_k$ are prime numbers; and $e_1, e_2, \ldots, e_k$ are positive integers.
    a. What is the standard factored form for a^2?
    b. Find the least positive integer n such that $2^5 \cdot 3 \cdot 5^2 \cdot 7^3 \cdot n$ is a perfect square. Write the resulting product as a perfect square.
    c. Find the least positive integer m such that $2^2 \cdot 3^5 \cdot 7 \cdot 11 \cdot m$ is a perfect square. Write the resulting product as a perfect square.

39. Suppose that in standard factored form $a = p_1^{e_1} p_2^{e_2} \cdots p_k^{e_k}$, where k is a positive integer; $p_1, p_2, \ldots, p_k$ are prime numbers; and $e_1, e_2, \ldots, e_k$ are positive integers.
    a. What is the standard factored form for a^3?
    b. Find the least positive integer k such that $2^4 \cdot 3^5 \cdot 7 \cdot 11^2 \cdot k$ is a perfect cube (i.e., equals an integer to the third power). Write the resulting product as a perfect cube.

40. a. If a and b are integers and $12a = 25b$, does $12 \mid b$? does $25 \mid a$? Explain.

    b. If x and y are integers and $10x = 9y$, does $10 \mid y$? does $9 \mid x$? Explain.

H 41. How many zeros are at the end of $45^8 \cdot 88^5$? Explain how you can answer this question without actually computing the number. (*Hint:* $10 = 2 \cdot 5$.)

42. If n is an integer and $n > 1$, then $n!$ is the product of n and every other positive integer that is less than n. For example, $5! = 5 \cdot 4 \cdot 3 \cdot 2 \cdot 1$.

    a. Write 6! in standard factored form.

    b. Write 20! in standard factored form.

    c. Without computing the value of $(20!)^2$ determine how many zeros are at the end of this number when it is written in decimal form. Justify your answer.

∗ 43. In a certain town 2/3 of the adult men are married to 3/5 of the adult women. Assume that all marriages are monogamous (no one is married to more than one other person). Also assume that there are at least 100 adult men in the town. What is the least possible number of adult men in the town? of adult women in the town?

Definition: Given any nonnegative integer n, the **decimal representation** of n is an expression of the form

$$d_k d_{k-1} \cdots d_2 d_1 d_0,$$

where k is a nonnegative integer; $d_0, d_1, d_2, \ldots, d_k$ (called the **decimal digits** of n) are integers from 0 to 9 inclusive; $d_k \neq 0$ unless $n = 0$ and $k = 0$; and

$$n = d_k \cdot 10^k + d_{k-1} \cdot 10^{k-1} + \cdots + d_2 \cdot 10^2 + d_1 \cdot 10 + d_0.$$

(For example, $2,503 = 2 \cdot 10^3 + 5 \cdot 10^2 + 0 \cdot 10 + 3$.)

---

44. Prove that if n is any nonnegative integer whose decimal representation ends in 0, then $5 \mid n$. (*Hint:* If the decimal representation of a nonnegative integer n ends in d_0, then $n = 10m + d_0$ for some integer m.)

45. Prove that if n is any nonnegative integer whose decimal representation ends in 5, then $5 \mid n$.

46. Prove that if the decimal representation of a nonnegative integer n ends in $d_1 d_0$ and if $4 \mid (10d_1 + d_0)$, then $4 \mid n$. (*Hint:* If the decimal representation of a nonnegative integer n ends in $d_1 d_0$, then there is an integer s such that $n = 100s + 10d_1 + d_0$.)

H ∗ 47. Observe that

$$7524 = 7 \cdot 1000 + 5 \cdot 100 + 2 \cdot 10 + 4$$
$$= 7(999 + 1) + 5(99 + 1) + 2(9 + 1) + 4$$
$$= (7 \cdot 999 + 7) + (5 \cdot 99 + 5) + (2 \cdot 9 + 2) + 4$$
$$= (7 \cdot 999 + 5 \cdot 99 + 2 \cdot 9) + (7 + 5 + 2 + 4)$$
$$= (7 \cdot 111 \cdot 9 + 5 \cdot 11 \cdot 9 + 2 \cdot 9) + (7 + 5 + 2 + 4)$$
$$= (7 \cdot 111 + 5 \cdot 11 + 2) \cdot 9 + (7 + 5 + 2 + 4)$$
$$= \text{(an integer divisible by 9)}$$
$$+ \text{(the sum of the digits of 7524)}.$$

Since the sum of the digits of 7524 is divisible by 9, 7524 can be written as a sum of two integers each of which is divisible by 9. It follows from exercise 15 that 7524 is divisible by 9.

Generalize the argument given in this example to any nonnegative integer n. In other words, prove that for any nonnegative integer n, if the sum of the digits of n is divisible by 9, then n is divisible by 9.

∗ 48. Prove that for any nonnegative integer n, if the sum of the digits of n is divisible by 3, then n is divisible by 3.

∗ 49. Given a positive integer n written in decimal form, the alternating sum of the digits of n is obtained by starting with the right-most digit, subtracting the digit immediately to its left, adding the next digit to the left, subtracting the next digit, and so forth. For example, the alternating sum of the digits of 180,928 is $8 - 2 + 9 - 0 + 8 - 1 = 22$. Justify the fact that for any nonnegative integer n, if the alternating sum of the digits of n is divisible by 11, then n is divisible by 11.

Answers for Test Yourself

1. n equals d times some integer (Or: there is an integer r such that $n = dr$)   2. n; d 3. a; b 4. $\frac{n}{d}$ is not an integer   5. the sentence "a divides b"; the number obtained when a is divided by b 6. a divides b and b divides c; a divides c 7. divisible by some prime number   8. prime; a product of prime numbers; order

4.4 Direct Proof and Counterexample IV: Division into Cases and the Quotient-Remainder Theorem

Be especially critical of any statement following the word "obviously."
— Anna Pell Wheeler 1883–1966

When you divide 11 by 4, you get a quotient of 2 and a remainder of 3.

Another way to say this is that 11 equals 2 groups of 4 with 3 left over:

XXXX	XXXX	XXX
↑		↑
2 groups of 4		3 left over

Or,

$$11 = 2 \cdot 4 + 3.$$

↑   ↑
2 groups of 4   3 left over

Of course, the number left over (3) is less than the size of the groups (4) because if 4 or more were left over, another group of 4 could be separated off.

The quotient-remainder theorem says that when any integer n is divided by any positive integer d, the result is a quotient q and a nonnegative remainder r that is smaller than d.

Theorem 4.4.1 The Quotient-Remainder Theorem

Given any integer n and positive integer d, there exist unique integers q and r such that

$$n = dq + r \quad \text{and} \quad 0 \le r < d.$$

The proof that there exist integers q and r with the given properties is in Section 5.4; the proof that q and r are unique is outlined in exercise 18 in Section 4.7.

If n is positive, the quotient-remainder theorem can be illustrated on the number line as follows:

If n is negative, the picture changes. Since $n = dq + r$, where r is nonnegative, d must be multiplied by a negative integer q to go below n. Then the nonnegative integer r is added to come back up to n. This is illustrated as follows:

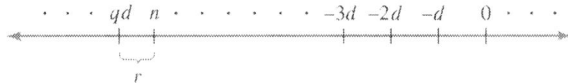

Example 4.4.1 The Quotient-Remainder Theorem

For each of the following values of n and d, find integers q and r such that $n = $.
and $0 \leq r < d$.

a. $n = 54$, $d = 4$ b. $n = -54$, $d = 4$ c. $n = 54$, $d = 70$

Solution

a. $54 = 4 \cdot 13 + 2$; hence $q = 13$ and $r = 2$.

b. $-54 = 4 \cdot (-14) + 2$; hence $q = -14$ and $r = 2$.

c. $54 = 70 \cdot 0 + 54$; hence $q = 0$ and $r = 54$.

div and mod

A number of computer languages have built-in functions that enable you to compute many values of q and r for the quotient-remainder theorem. These functions are called **div** and **mod** in Pascal, are called / and % in C and C++, are called / and % in Java, and are called / (or \\) and **mod** in .NET. The functions give the values that satisfy the quotient-remainder theorem when a *nonnegative* integer n is divided by a positive integer d and the result is assigned to an integer variable. However, they do not give the values that satisfy the quotient-remainder theorem when a negative integer n is divided by a positive integer d.

• **Definition**

Given an integer n and a positive integer d,

$$n \ \textbf{div} \ d = \text{the integer quotient obtained}$$
$$\text{when } n \text{ is divided by } d, \text{ and}$$

$$n \ \textbf{mod} \ d = \text{the nonnegative integer remainder obtained}$$
$$\text{when } n \text{ is divided by } d.$$

Symbolically, if n and d are integers and $d > 0$, then

$$n \ \textbf{div} \ d = q \quad \text{and} \quad n \ \textbf{mod} \ d = r \quad \Leftrightarrow \quad n = dq + r$$

where q and r are integers and $0 \leq r < d$.

Note that it follows from the quotient-remainder theorem that n *mod* d equals one of the integers from 0 through $d - 1$ (since the remainder of the division of n by d must be one of these integers). Note also that a necessary and sufficient condition for an integer n to be divisible by an integer d is that n *mod* $d = 0$. You are asked to prove this in the exercises at the end of this section.

You can also use a calculator to compute values of *div* and *mod*. For instance, to compute n *div* d for a nonnegative integer n and a positive integer d, you just divide n by d and ignore the part of the answer to the right of the decimal point. To find n *mod* d, you can use the fact that if $n = dq + r$, then $r = n - dq$. Thus $n = d \cdot (n \ div \ d) + n \ mod \ d$, and so

$$n \ mod \ d = n - d \cdot (n \ div \ d).$$

Hence, to find n *mod* d compute n *div* d, multiply by d, and subtract the result from n.

Example 4.4.2 Computing *div* and *mod*

Compute 32 *div* 9 and 32 *mod* 9 by hand and with a calculator.

Solution   Performing the division by hand gives the following results:

$$
\begin{array}{r}
3 \quad\longleftarrow\; 32\ div\ 9 \\
9\overline{)\ 32\quad} \\
27 \\
\hline
5 \quad\longleftarrow\; 32\ mod\ 9
\end{array}
$$

If you use a four-function calculator to divide 32 by 9, you obtain an expression like 3.555555556. Discarding the fractional part gives 32 *div* 9 = 3, and so

$$32\ mod\ 9 = 32 - 9 \cdot (32\ div\ 9) = 32 - 27 = 5.$$

A calculator with a built-in integer-part function iPart allows you to input a single expression for each computation:

$$32\ div\ 9 = \mathrm{iPart}(32/9)$$
$$\text{and}\quad 32\ mod\ 9 = 32 - 9 \cdot \mathrm{iPart}\,(32/9) = 5.$$

■

Example 4.4.3 Computing the Day of the Week

Suppose today is Tuesday, and neither this year nor next year is a leap year. What day of the week will it be 1 year from today?

Solution   There are 365 days in a year that is not a leap year, and each week has 7 days. Now

$$365\ div\ 7 = 52 \quad\text{and}\quad 365\ mod\ 7 = 1$$

because $365 = 52 \cdot 7 + 1$. Thus 52 weeks, or 364 days, from today will be a Tuesday, and so 365 days from today will be 1 day later, namely Wednesday.

More generally, if *DayT* is the day of the week today and *DayN* is the day of the week in N days, then

$$DayN = (DayT + N)\ mod\ 7, \qquad\qquad\qquad 4.4.1$$

where Sunday = 0, Monday = 1, . . . , Saturday = 6.

■

Example 4.4.4 Solving a Problem about *mod*

Suppose m is an integer. If $m\ mod\ 11 = 6$, what is $4m\ mod\ 11$?

Solution   Because $m\ mod\ 11 = 6$, the remainder obtained when m is divided by 11 is 6. This means that there is some integer q so that

$$m = 11q + 6.$$

Thus $$4m = 44q + 24 = 44q + 22 + 2 = 11(4q + 2) + 2.$$

Since $4q + 2$ is an integer (because products and sums of integers are integers) and since $2 < 11$, the remainder obtained when $4m$ is divided by 11 is 2. Therefore,

$$4m\ mod\ 11 = 2.$$

■

Representations of Integers

In Section 4.1 we defined an even integer to have the form twice some integer. At that time we could have defined an odd integer to be one that was not even. Instead, because it was more useful for proving theorems, we specified that an odd integer has the form twice some integer plus one. The quotient-remainder theorem brings these two ways of describing odd integers together by guaranteeing that any integer is either even or odd. To see why, let n be any integer, and consider what happens when n is divided by 2. By the quotient-remainder theorem (with $d = 2$), there exist unique integers q and r such that

$$n = 2q + r \quad \text{and} \quad 0 \le r < 2.$$

But the only integers that satisfy $0 \le r < 2$ are $r = 0$ and $r = 1$. It follows that given any integer n, there exists an integer q with

$$n = 2q + 0 \quad \text{or} \quad n = 2q + 1.$$

In the case that $n = 2q + 0 = 2q$, n is even. In the case that $n = 2q + 1$, n is odd. Hence n is either even or odd, and, because of the uniqueness of q and r, n cannot be both even and odd.

The *parity* of an integer refers to whether the integer is even or odd. For instance, 5 has odd parity and 28 has even parity. We call the fact that any integer is either even or odd the **parity property.**

Example 4.4.5 Consecutive Integers Have Opposite Parity

Prove that given any two consecutive integers, one is even and the other is odd.

Solution   Two integers are called *consecutive* if, and only if, one is one more than the other. So if one integer is m, the next consecutive integer is $m + 1$.

To prove the given statement, start by supposing that you have two particular but arbitrarily chosen consecutive integers. If the smaller is m, then the larger will be $m + 1$. How do you know for sure that one of these is even and the other is odd? You might imagine some examples: 4, 5; 12, 13; 1,073, 1,074. In the first two examples, the smaller of the two integers is even and the larger is odd; in the last example, it is the reverse. These observations suggest dividing the analysis into two cases.

Case 1: The smaller of the two integers is even.

Case 2: The smaller of the two integers is odd.

In the first case, when m is even, it appears that the next consecutive integer is odd. Is this always true? If an integer m is even, must $m + 1$ necessarily be odd? Of course the answer is yes. Because if m is even, then $m = 2k$ for some integer k, and so $m + 1 = 2k + 1$, which is odd.

In the second case, when m is odd, it appears that the next consecutive integer is even. Is this always true? If an integer m is odd, must $m + 1$ necessarily be even? Again, the answer is yes. For if m is odd, then $m = 2k + 1$ for some integer k, and so $m + 1 = (2k + 1) + 1 = 2k + 2 = 2(k + 1)$, which is even.

This discussion is summarized on the following page.

Theorem 4.4.2 The Parity Property

Any two consecutive integers have opposite parity.

Proof:

Suppose that two *[particular but arbitrarily chosen]* consecutive integers are given; call them m and $m + 1$. *[We must show that one of m and m + 1 is even and that the other is odd.]* By the parity property, either m is even or m is odd. *[We break the proof into two cases depending on whether m is even or odd.]*

Case 1 (*m is even*): In this case, $m = 2k$ for some integer k, and so $m + 1 = 2k + 1$, which is odd *[by definition of odd]*. Hence in this case, one of m and $m + 1$ is even and the other is odd.

Case 2 (*m is odd*): In this case, $m = 2k + 1$ for some integer k, and so $m + 1 = (2k + 1) + 1 = 2k + 2 = 2(k + 1)$. But $k + 1$ is an integer because it is a sum of two integers. Therefore, $m + 1$ equals twice some integer, and thus $m + 1$ is even. Hence in this case also, one of m and $m + 1$ is even and the other is odd.

It follows that regardless of which case actually occurs for the particular m and $m + 1$ that are chosen, one of m and $m + 1$ is even and the other is odd. *[This is what was to be shown.]*

The division into cases in a proof is like the transfer of control for an **if-then-else** statement in a computer program. If m is even, control transfers to case 1; if not, control transfers to case 2. For any given integer, only one of the cases will apply. You must consider both cases, however, to obtain a proof that is valid for an arbitrarily given integer whether even or not.

There are times when division into more than two cases is called for. Suppose that at some stage of developing a proof, you know that a statement of the form

$$A_1 \text{ or } A_2 \text{ or } A_3 \text{ or} \ldots \text{ or } A_n$$

is true, and suppose you want to deduce a conclusion C. By definition of *or*, you know that at least one of the statements A_i is true (although you may not know which). In this situation, you should use the method of division into cases. First assume A_1 is true and deduce C; next assume A_2 is true and deduce C; and so forth until you have assumed A_n is true and deduced C. At that point, you can conclude that regardless of which statement A_i happens to be true, the truth of C follows.

Method of Proof by Division into Cases

To prove a statement of the form "If A_1 or A_2 or $\ldots$ or A_n, then C," prove all of the following:

If A_1, then C,

If A_2, then C,

$$\vdots$$

If A_n, then C.

This process shows that C is true regardless of which of $A_1, A_2, \ldots, A_n$ happens to be the case.

Proof by division into cases is a generalization of the argument form shown in Example 2.3.7, whose validity you were asked to establish in exercise 21 of Section 2.3. This method of proof was combined with the quotient-remainder theorem for $d = 2$ to prove Theorem 4.4.2. Allowing d to take on additional values makes it possible to obtain a variety of other results. We begin by showing what happens when $a = 4$.

Example 4.4.6 Representations of Integers Modulo 4

Show that any integer can be written in one of the four forms

$$n = 4q \quad \text{or} \quad n = 4q + 1 \quad \text{or} \quad n = 4q + 2 \quad \text{or} \quad n = 4q + 3$$

for some integer q.

Solution   Given any integer n, apply the quotient-remainder theorem to n with $d = 4$. This implies that there exist an integer quotient q and a remainder r such that

$$n = 4q + r \quad \text{and} \quad 0 \le r < 4.$$

But the only nonnegative remainders r that are less than 4 are 0, 1, 2, and 3. Hence

$$n = 4q \quad \text{or} \quad n = 4q + 1 \quad \text{or} \quad n = 4q + 2 \quad \text{or} \quad n = 4q + 3$$

for some integer q.   ■

The next example illustrates how the alternative representations for integers modulo 4 can help establish a result in number theory. The solution is broken into two parts: a discussion and a formal proof. These correspond to the stages of actual proof development. Very few people, when asked to prove an unfamiliar theorem, immediately write down the kind of formal proof you find in a mathematics text. Most need to experiment with several possible approaches before they find one that works. A formal proof is much like the ending of a mystery story—the part in which the action of the story is systematically reviewed and all the loose ends are carefully tied together.

Example 4.4.7 The Square of an Odd Integer

Note Another way to state this fact is that if you square an odd integer and divide by 8, you will always get a remainder of 1. Try a few examples!

Prove: The square of any odd integer has the form $8m + 1$ for some integer m.

Solution   Begin by asking yourself, "Where am I starting from?" and "What do I need to show?" To help answer these questions, introduce variables to represent the quantities in the statement to be proved.

Formal Restatement: ∀ odd integers n, ∃ an integer m such that $n^2 = 8m + 1$.

From this, you can immediately identify the starting point and what is to be shown.

Starting Point: Suppose n is a particular but arbitrarily chosen odd integer.

To Show: ∃ an integer m such that $n^2 = 8m + 1$.

This looks tough. Why should there be an integer m with the property that $n^2 = 8m + 1$? That would say that $(n^2 - 1)/8$ is an integer, or that 8 divides $n^2 - 1$. Perhaps you could make use of the fact that $n^2 - 1 = (n - 1)(n + 1)$. Does 8 divide $(n - 1)(n + 1)$? Since n is odd, both $(n - 1)$ and $(n + 1)$ are even. That means that their product is divisible by 4. But that's not enough. You need to show that the product is divisible by 8. This seems to be a blind alley.

You could try another tack. Since n is odd, you could represent n as $2q + 1$ for some integer q. Then $n^2 = (2q + 1)^2 = 4q^2 + 4q + 1 = 4(q^2 + q) + 1$. It is clear from this analysis that n^2 can be written in the form $4m + 1$, but it may not be clear that it can be written as $8m + 1$. This also seems to be a blind alley.*

Yet another possibility is to use the result of Example 4.4.6. That example showed that any integer can be written in one of the four forms $4q, 4q + 1, 4q + 2$, or $4q + 3$. Two of these, $4q + 1$ and $4q + 3$, are odd. Thus any odd integer can be written in the form $4q + 1$ or $4q + 3$ for some integer q. You could try breaking into cases based on these two different forms.

It turns out that this last possibility works! In each of the two cases, the conclusion follows readily by direct calculation. The details are shown in the following formal proof:

Note Desperation can spur creativity. When you have tried all the obvious approaches without success and you really care about solving a problem, you reach into the odd corners of your memory for *anything* that may help.

Theorem 4.4.3

The square of any odd integer has the form $8m + 1$ for some integer m.

Proof:

Suppose n is a *[particular but arbitrarily chosen]* odd integer. By the quotient-remainder theorem, n can be written in one of the forms

$$4q \quad \text{or} \quad 4q + 1 \quad \text{or} \quad 4q + 2 \quad \text{or} \quad 4q + 3$$

for some integer q. In fact, since n is odd and $4q$ and $4q + 2$ are even, n must have one of the forms

$$4q + 1 \quad \text{or} \quad 4q + 3.$$

Case 1 ($n = 4q + 1$ for some integer q): [We must find an integer m such that $n^2 = 8m + 1$.] Since $n = 4q + 1$,

$$
\begin{aligned}
n^2 &= (4q + 1)^2 && \text{by substitution} \\
&= (4q + 1)(4q + 1) && \text{by definition of square} \\
&= 16q^2 + 8q + 1 \\
&= 8(2q^2 + q) + 1 && \text{by the laws of algebra.}
\end{aligned}
$$

Let $m = 2q^2 + q$. Then m is an integer since 2 and q are integers and sums and products of integers are integers. Thus, substituting,

$$n^2 = 8m + 1 \quad \text{where } m \text{ is an integer.}$$

Case 2 ($n = 4q + 3$ for some integer q): [We must find an integer m such that $n^2 = 8m + 1$.] Since $n = 4q + 3$,

$$
\begin{aligned}
n^2 &= (4q + 3)^2 && \text{by substitution} \\
&= (4q + 3)(4q + 3) && \text{by definition of square} \\
&= 16q^2 + 24q + 9 \\
&= 16q^2 + 24q + (8 + 1) \\
&= 8(2q^2 + 3q + 1) + 1 && \text{by the laws of algebra.}
\end{aligned}
$$

[The motivation for the choice of algebra steps was the desire to write the expression in the form $8 \cdot (some\ integer) + 1$.]

---

*See exercise 18 for a different perspective.

Let $m = 2q^2 + 3q + 1$. Then m is an integer since 1, 2, 3, and q are integers and sums and products of integers are integers. Thus, substituting,

$$n^2 = 8m + 1 \quad \text{where } m \text{ is an integer.}$$

Cases 1 and 2 show that given any odd integer, whether of the form $4q + 1$ or $4q + 3$, $n^2 = 8m + 1$ for some integer m. *[This is what we needed to show.]*

Note that the result of Theorem 4.4.3 can also be written, "For any odd integer n, $n^2 \bmod 8 = 1$."

In general, according to the quotient-remainder theorem, if an integer n is divided by an integer d, the possible remainders are $0, 1, 2, \ldots, (d-1)$. This implies that n can be written in one of the forms

$$dq, \; dq + 1, \; dq + 2, \, , \; \ldots, \; dq + (d-1) \qquad \text{for some integer } q.$$

Many properties of integers can be obtained by giving d a variety of different values and analyzing the cases that result.

Absolute Value and the Triangle Inequality

The triangle inequality is one of the most important results involving absolute value. It has applications in many areas of mathematics.

• Definition

For any real number x, the **absolute value of x**, denoted $|x|$, is defined as follows:

$$|x| = \begin{cases} x & \text{if } x \geq 0 \\ -x & \text{if } x < 0 \end{cases}.$$

The triangle inequality says that the absolute value of the sum of two numbers is less than or equal to the sum of their absolute values. We give a proof based on the following two facts, both of which are derived using division into cases. We state both as lemmas. A **lemma** is a statement that does not have much intrinsic interest but is helpful in deriving other results.

Lemma 4.4.4

For all real numbers r, $-|r| \leq r \leq |r|$.

Proof:

Suppose r is any real number. We divide into cases according to whether $r \geq 0$ or $r < 0$.
Case 1 ($r \geq 0$): In this case, by definition of absolute value, $|r| = r$. Also, since r is positive and $-|r|$ is negative, $-|r| < r$. Thus it is true that

$$-|r| \leq r \leq |r|.$$

continued on page 188

Case 2 (r < 0): In this case, by definition of absolute value, $|r| = -r$. Multiplying both sides by -1 gives that $-|r| = r$. Also, since r is negative and $|r|$ is positive, $r < |r|$. Thus it is also true in this case that

$$-|r| \le r \le |r|.$$

Hence, in either case,

$$-|r| \le r \le |r|$$

[as was to be shown].

Lemma 4.4.5

For all real numbers r, $|-r| = |r|$.

Proof:

Suppose r is any real number. By Theorem T23 in Appendix A, if $r > 0$, then $-r < 0$, and if $r < 0$, then $-r > 0$. Thus

$$|-r| = \begin{cases} -r & \text{if } -r > 0 \\ 0 & \text{if } -r = 0 \\ -(-r) & \text{if } -r < 0 \end{cases} \quad \text{by definition of absolute value}$$

$$= \begin{cases} -r & \text{if } -r > 0 \\ 0 & \text{if } -r = 0 \\ r & \text{if } -r < 0 \end{cases} \quad \begin{array}{l}\text{because } -(-r) = r \text{ by Theorem T4}\\ \text{in Appendix A}\end{array}$$

$$= \begin{cases} -r & \text{if } r < 0 \\ 0 & \text{if } -r = 0 \\ r & \text{if } r > 0 \end{cases} \quad \begin{array}{l}\text{because, by Theorem T24 in Appendix A, when}\\ -r > 0, \text{ then } r < 0, \text{ when } -r < 0, \text{ then } r > 0,\\ \text{and when } -r = 0, \text{ then } r = 0\end{array}$$

$$= \begin{cases} r & \text{if } r \ge 0 \\ -r & \text{if } r < 0 \end{cases} \quad \text{by reformatting the previous result}$$

$$= |r| \quad \text{by definition of absolute value.}$$

Lemmas 4.4.4 and 4.4.5 now provide a basis for proving the triangle inequlity.

Theorem 4.4.6 The Triangle Inequality

For all real numbers x and y, $|x + y| \le |x| + |y|$.

Proof:

Suppose x and y, are any real numbers.

Case 1 (x + y ≥ 0): In this case, $|x + y| = x + y$, and so, by Lemma 4.4.4,

$$x \le |x| \quad \text{and} \quad y \le |y|.$$

Hence, by Theorem T26 of Appendix A,

$$|x + y| = x + y \le |x| + |y|.$$

Case 2 (x + y < 0): In this case, $|x + y| = -(x + y) = (-x) + (-y)$, and so, by Lemmas 4.4.4 and 4.4.5,

$$-x \leq |-x| = |x| \quad \text{and} \quad -y \leq |-y| = |y|.$$

It follows, by Theorem T26 of Appendix A, that

$$|x + y| = (-x) + (-y) \leq |x| + |y|.$$

Hence in both cases $|x + y| \leq |x| + |y|$ *[as was to be shown]*.

Test Yourself

1. The quotient-remainder theorem says that for all integers n and d with $d \geq 0$, there exist _____ q and r such that _____ and _____.

2. If n and d are integers with $d > 0$, n *div* d is _____ and n *mod* d is _____.

3. The parity of an integer indicates whether the integer is _____.

4. According to the quotient-remainder theorem, if an integer n is divided by a positive integer d, the possible remainders are _____. This implies that n can be written in one of the forms _____ for some integer q.

5. To prove a statement of the form "If A_1 or A_2 or A_3, then C," prove _____ and _____ and _____.

6. The triangle inequality says that for all real numbers x and y, _____.

Exercise Set 4.4

For each of the values of n and d given in 1–6, find integers q and r such that $n = dq + r$ and $0 \leq r < d$.

1. $n = 70, d = 9$
2. $n = 62, d = 7$
3. $n = 36, d = 40$
4. $n = 3, d = 11$
5. $n = -45, d = 11$
6. $n = -27, d = 8$

Evaluate the expressions in 7–10.

7. a. 43 *div* 9   b. 43 *mod* 9
8. a. 30 *div* 2   b. 30 *mod* 2
9. a. 28 *div* 5   b. 28 *mod* 5
10. a. 50 *div* 7   b. 50 *mod* 7

11. Check the correctness of formula (4.4.1) given in Example 4.4.3 for the following values of *DayT* and N.
    a. *DayT* = 6 (Saturday) and $N = 15$
    b. *DayT* = 0 (Sunday) and $N = 7$
    c. *DayT* = 4 (Thursday) and $N = 12$

✳ 12. Justify formula (4.4.1) for general values of *DayT* and N.

13. On a Monday a friend says he will meet you again in 30 days. What day of the week will that be?

H 14. If today is Tuesday, what day of the week will it be 1,000 days from today?

15. January 1, 2000, was a Saturday, and 2000 was a leap year. What day of the week will January 1, 2050, be?

16. Suppose d is a positive integer and n is any integer. If $d \mid n$, what is the remainder obtained when the quotient-remainder theorem is applied to n with divisor d?

17. Prove that for all integers n, $n^2 - n + 3$ is odd.

18. The result of exercise 17 suggests that the second apparent blind alley in the discussion of Example 4.4.7 might not be a blind alley after all. Write a new proof of Theorem 4.4.3 based on this observation.

19. Prove that the product of any two consecutive integers is even.

20. Suppose a is an integer. If a *mod* $7 = 4$, what is $5a$ *mod* 7? In other words, if division of a by 7 gives a remainder of 4, what is the remainder when $5a$ is divided by 7?

21. Suppose b is an integer. If b *mod* $12 = 5$, what is $8b$ *mod* 12? In other words, if division of b by 12 gives a remainder of 5, what is the remainder when $8b$ is divided by 12?

22. Suppose c is an integer. If c *mod* $15 = 3$, what is $10c$ *mod* 15? In other words, if division of c by 15 gives a remainder of 3, what is the remainder when $10c$ is divided by 15?

23. Prove that for all integers n, if n *mod* $5 = 3$ then n^2 *mod* $5 = 4$.

24. Prove that for all integers m and n, if m *mod* $5 = 2$ and n *mod* $5 = 1$ then mn *mod* $5 = 2$.

25. Prove that for all integers a and b, if a *mod* $7 = 5$ and b *mod* $7 = 6$ then ab *mod* $7 = 2$.

H 26. Prove that a necessary and sufficient condition for a non-negative integer n to be divisible by a positive integer d is that n *mod* $d = 0$.

27. Show that any integer n can be written in one of the three forms

$$n = 3q \quad \text{or} \quad n = 3q + 1 \quad \text{or} \quad n = 3q + 2$$

for some integer q.

28. a. Use the quotient-remainder theorem with $d = 3$ to prove that the product of any three consecutive integers is divisible by 3.

b. Use the *mod* notation to rewrite the result of part (a).

H 29. a. Use the quotient-remainder theorem with $d = 3$ to prove that the square of any integer has the form $3k$ or $3k + 1$ for some integer k.

b. Use the *mod* notation to rewrite the result of part (a).

30. a. Use the quotient-remainder theorem with $d = 3$ to prove that the product of any two consecutive integers has the form $3k$ or $3k + 2$ for some integer k.

b. Use the *mod* notation to rewrite the result of part (a).

In 31–33, you may use the properties listed in Example 4.2.3.

31. a. Prove that for all integers m and n, $m + n$ and $m - n$ are either both odd or both even.

b. Find all solutions to the equation $m^2 - n^2 = 56$ for which both m and n are positive integers.

c. Find all solutions to the equation $m^2 - n^2 = 88$ for which both m and n are positive integers.

32. Given any integers a, b, and c, if $a - b$ is even and $b - c$ is even, what can you say about the parity of $2a - (b + c)$? Prove your answer.

33. Given any integers a, b, and c, if $a - b$ is odd and $b - c$ is even, what can you say about the parity of $a - c$? Prove your answer.

H 34. Given any integer n, if $n > 3$, could n, $n + 2$, and $n + 4$ all be prime? Prove or give a counterexample.

Prove each of the statements in 35–46.

35. The square of any integer has the form $4k$ or $4k + 1$ for some integer k.

H 36. The product of any four consecutive integers is divisible by 8.

37. The fourth power of any integer has the form $8m$ or $8m + 1$ for some integer m.

H 38. For any integer n, $n^2 + 5$ is not divisible by 4.

H 39. The sum of any four consecutive integers has the form $4k + 2$ for some integer k.

40. For all integers m, $m^2 = 5k$, or $m^2 = 5k + 1$, or $m^2 = 5k + 4$ for some integer k.

41. For any integer n, $n(n^2 - 1)(n + 2)$ is divisible by 4.

H 42. Every prime number except 2 and 3 has the form $6q + 1$ or $6q + 5$ for some integer q.

43. If n is an odd integer, then $n^4 \bmod 16 = 1$.

H 44. For all real numbers x and y, $|x| \cdot |y| = |xy|$.

45. For all real numbers r and c with $c \geq 0$, if $-c \leq r \leq c$, then $|r| \leq c$.

46. For all real numbers r and c with $c \geq 0$, if $|r| \leq c$, then $-c \leq r \leq c$.

47. A matrix **M** has 3 rows and 4 columns.

$$\begin{bmatrix} a_{11} & a_{12} & a_{13} & a_{14} \\ a_{21} & a_{22} & a_{23} & a_{24} \\ a_{31} & a_{32} & a_{33} & a_{34} \end{bmatrix}$$

The 12 entries in the matrix are to be stored in *row major* form in locations 7,609 to 7,620 in a computer's memory. This means that the entries in the first row (reading left to right) are stored first, then the entries in the second row, and finally the entries in the third row.

a. Which location will a_{22} be stored in?

b. Write a formula (in i and j) that gives the integer n so that a_{ij} is stored in location $7{,}609 + n$.

c. Find formulas (in n) for r and s so that a_{rs} is stored in location $7{,}609 + n$.

48. Let **M** be a matrix with m rows and n columns, and suppose that the entries of **M** are stored in a computer's memory in row major form (see exercise 47) in locations N, $N + 1$, $N + 2$, ..., $N + mn - 1$. Find formulas in k for r and s so that a_{rs} is stored in location $N + k$.

✱ 49. If m, n, and d are integers, $d > 0$, and $m \bmod d = n \bmod d$, does it necessarily follow that $m = n$? That $m - n$ is divisible by d? Prove your answers.

✱ 50. If m, n, and d are integers, $d > 0$, and $d \mid (m - n)$, what is the relation between $m \bmod d$ and $n \bmod d$? Prove your answer.

✱ 51. If m, n, a, b, and d are integers, $d > 0$, and $m \bmod d = a$ and $n \bmod d = b$, is $(m + n) \bmod d = a + b$? Is $(m + n) \bmod d = (a + b) \bmod d$? Prove your answers.

✱ 52. If m, n, a, b, and d are integers, $d > 0$, and $m \bmod d = a$ and $n \bmod d = b$, is $(mn) \bmod d = ab$? Is $(mn) \bmod d = ab \bmod d$? Prove your answers.

53. Prove that if m, d, and k are integers and $d > 0$, then $(m + dk) \bmod d = m \bmod d$.

Answers for Test Yourself

1. integers; $n = dq + r$; $0 \leq r < d$ 2. the quotient obtained when n is divided by d; the nonnegative remainder obtained when n is divided by d 3. odd or even   4. $0, 1, 2, \ldots, (d - 1)$; dq, $dq + 1$, $dq + 2$, ..., $dq + (d - 1)$ 5. If A_1, then C; If A_2, then C; If A_3, then C 6. $|x + y| \leq |x| + |y|$

4.5 *Direct Proof and Counterexample V: Floor and Ceiling*

Proof serves many purposes simultaneously. In being exposed to the scrutiny and judgment of a new audience, [a] proof is subject to a constant process of criticism and revalidation. Errors, ambiguities, and misunderstandings are cleared up by constant exposure. Proof is respectability. Proof is the seal of authority.

Proof, in its best instances, increases understanding by revealing the heart of the matter. Proof suggests new mathematics. The novice who studies proofs gets closer to the creation of new mathematics. Proof is mathematical power, the electric voltage of the subject which vitalizes the static assertions of the theorems.

Finally, proof is ritual, and a celebration of the power of pure reason.

— Philip J. Davis and Reuben Hersh, *The Mathematical Experience,* 1981

Imagine a real number sitting on a number line. The *floor* and *ceiling* of the number are the integers to the immediate left and to the immediate right of the number (unless the number is, itself, an integer, in which case its floor and ceiling both equal the number itself). Many computer languages have built-in functions that compute floor and ceiling automatically. These functions are very convenient to use when writing certain kinds of computer programs. In addition, the concepts of floor and ceiling are important in analyzing the efficiency of many computer algorithms.

> **• Definition**
>
> Given any real number x, the **floor of x,** denoted $\lfloor x \rfloor$, is defined as follows:
>
> $$\lfloor x \rfloor = \text{that unique integer } n \text{ such that } n \leq x < n+1.$$
>
> Symbolically, if x is a real number and n is an integer, then
>
> $$\lfloor x \rfloor = n \quad \Leftrightarrow \quad n \leq x < n+1.$$

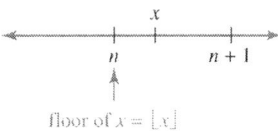

floor of $x = \lfloor x \rfloor$

> **• Definition**
>
> Given any real number x, the **ceiling of x,** denoted $\lceil x \rceil$, is defined as follows:
>
> $$\lceil x \rceil = \text{that unique integer } n \text{ such that } n-1 < x \leq n.$$
>
> Symbolically, if x is a real number and n is an integer, then
>
> $$\lceil x \rceil = n \quad \Leftrightarrow \quad n-1 < x \leq n.$$

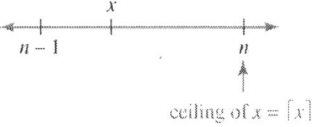

ceiling of $x = \lceil x \rceil$

Example 4.5.1 Computing Floors and Ceilings

Compute $\lfloor x \rfloor$ and $\lceil x \rceil$ for each of the following values of x:

a. $25/4$ b. 0.999 c. -2.01

Solution

a. $25/4 = 6.25$ and $6 < 6.25 < 7$; hence $\lfloor 25/4 \rfloor = 6$ and $\lceil 25/4 \rceil = 7$.

b. $0 < 0.999 < 1$; hence $\lfloor 0.999 \rfloor = 0$ and $\lceil 0.999 \rceil = 1$.

c. $-3 < -2.01 < -2$; hence $\lfloor -2.01 \rfloor = -3$ and $\lceil -2.01 \rceil = -2$.

Note that on some calculators $\lfloor x \rfloor$ is denoted INT (x). ■

Example 4.5.2 An Application

The 1,370 students at a college are given the opportunity to take buses to an out-of-town game. Each bus holds a maximum of 40 passengers.

a. For reasons of economy, the athletic director will send only full buses. What is the maximum number of buses the athletic director will send?

b. If the athletic director is willing to send one partially filled bus, how many buses will be needed to allow all the students to take the trip?

Solution

a. $\lfloor 1370/40 \rfloor = \lfloor 34.25 \rfloor = 34$ b. $\lceil 1370/40 \rceil = \lceil 34.25 \rceil = 35$ ■

Example 4.5.3 Some General Values of Floor

If k is an integer, what are $\lfloor k \rfloor$ and $\lfloor k + 1/2 \rfloor$? Why?

Solution   Suppose k is an integer. Then

$$\lfloor k \rfloor = k \text{ because } k \text{ is an integer and } k \leq k < k + 1,$$

and

$$\left\lfloor k + \frac{1}{2} \right\rfloor = k \text{ because } k \text{ is an integer and } k \leq k + \frac{1}{2} < k + 1. \quad ■$$

Example 4.5.4 Disproving an Alleged Property of Floor

Is the following statement true or false?

For all real numbers x and y, $\lfloor x + y \rfloor = \lfloor x \rfloor + \lfloor y \rfloor$.

Solution   The statement is false. As a counterexample, take $x = y = \frac{1}{2}$. Then

$$\lfloor x \rfloor + \lfloor y \rfloor = \left\lfloor \frac{1}{2} \right\rfloor + \left\lfloor \frac{1}{2} \right\rfloor = 0 + 0 = 0,$$

whereas

$$\lfloor x + y \rfloor = \left\lfloor \frac{1}{2} + \frac{1}{2} \right\rfloor = \lfloor 1 \rfloor = 1.$$

Hence $\lfloor x + y \rfloor \neq \lfloor x \rfloor + \lfloor y \rfloor$.

To arrive at this counterexample, you could have reasoned as follows: Suppose x and y are real numbers. Must it necessarily be the case that $\lfloor x + y \rfloor = \lfloor x \rfloor + \lfloor y \rfloor$, or could x and y be such that $\lfloor x + y \rfloor \neq \lfloor x \rfloor + \lfloor y \rfloor$? Imagine values that the various quantities could take. For instance, if both x and y are positive, then $\lfloor x \rfloor$ and $\lfloor y \rfloor$ are the integer parts of $\lfloor x \rfloor$ and $\lfloor y \rfloor$ respectively; just as

$$2\frac{3}{5} = 2 + \frac{3}{5}$$

integer part   fractional part

so is

$$x = \lfloor x \rfloor + \text{fractional part of } x$$

and

$$y = \lfloor y \rfloor + \text{fractional part of } y.$$

where the term *fractional part* is understood here to mean the part of the number to the right of the decimal point when the number is written in decimal notation. Thus if x and y are positive,

$$x + y = \lfloor x \rfloor + \lfloor y \rfloor + \textit{the sum of the fractional parts of } x \textit{ and } y.$$

But also

$$x + y = \lfloor x + y \rfloor + \textit{the fractional part of } (x + y).$$

These equations show that if there exist numbers x and y such that the sum of the fractional parts of x and y is at least 1, then a counterexample can be found. But there do exist such x and y; for instance, $x = \frac{1}{2}$ and $y = \frac{1}{2}$ as before. ◼

The analysis of Example 4.5.4 indicates that if x and y are positive and the sum of their fractional parts is less than 1, then $\lfloor x + y \rfloor = \lfloor x \rfloor + \lfloor y \rfloor$. In particular, if x is positive and m is a positive integer, then $\lfloor x + m \rfloor = \lfloor x \rfloor + \lfloor m \rfloor = \lfloor x \rfloor + m$. (The fractional part of m is 0; hence the sum of the fractional parts of x and m equals the fractional part of x, which is less than 1.) It turns out that you can use the definition of floor to show that this equation holds for all real numbers x and for all integers m.

Example 4.5.5 Proving a Property of Floor

Prove that for all real numbers x and for all integers m, $\lfloor x + m \rfloor = \lfloor x \rfloor + m$.

Solution   Begin by supposing that x is a particular but arbitrarily chosen real number and that m is a particular but arbitrarily chosen integer. You must show that $\lfloor x + m \rfloor = \lfloor x \rfloor + m$. Since this is an equation involving $\lfloor x \rfloor$ and $\lfloor x + m \rfloor$, it is reasonable to give one of these quantities a name: Let $n = \lfloor x \rfloor$. By definition of floor,

$$n \text{ is an integer} \quad \text{and} \quad n \leq x < n + 1.$$

This double inequality enables you to compute the value of $\lfloor x + m \rfloor$ in terms of n by adding m to all sides:

$$n + m \leq x + m < n + m + 1.$$

Thus the left-hand side of the equation to be shown is

$$\lfloor x + m \rfloor = n + m.$$

On the other hand, since $n = \lfloor x \rfloor$, the right-hand side of the equation to be shown is

$$\lfloor x \rfloor + m = n + m$$

also. Thus $\lfloor x + m \rfloor = \lfloor x \rfloor + m$. This discussion is summarized as follows:

Theorem 4.5.1

For all real numbers x and all integers m, $\lfloor x + m \rfloor = \lfloor x \rfloor + m$.

Proof:

Suppose a real number x and an integer m are given. *[We must show that $\lfloor x + m \rfloor = \lfloor x \rfloor + m$.]* Let $n = \lfloor x \rfloor$. By definition of floor, n is an integer and

$$n \leq x < n + 1.$$

Add m to all three parts to obtain

$$n + m \leq x + m < n + m + 1$$

[since adding a number to both sides of an inequality does not change the direction of the inequality].

  Now $n + m$ is an integer *[since n and m are integers and a sum of integers is an integer]*, and so, by definition of floor, the left-hand side of the equation to be shown is

$$\lfloor x + m \rfloor = n + m.$$

But $n = \lfloor x \rfloor$. Hence, by substitution,

$$n + m = \lfloor x \rfloor + m,$$

which is the right-hand side of the equation to be shown. Thus $\lfloor x + m \rfloor = \lfloor x \rfloor + m$ *[as was to be shown].*

The analysis of a number of computer algorithms, such as the binary search and merge sort algorithms, requires that you know the value of $\lfloor n/2 \rfloor$, where n is an integer. The formula for computing this value depends on whether n is even or odd.

Theorem 4.5.2 The Floor of $n/2$

For any integer n,

$$\left\lfloor \frac{n}{2} \right\rfloor = \begin{cases} \dfrac{n}{2} & \text{if } n \text{ is even} \\[2ex] \dfrac{n-1}{2} & \text{if } n \text{ is odd.} \end{cases}$$

Proof:

Suppose n is a *[particular but arbitrarily chosen]* integer. By the quotient-remainder theorem, either n is odd or n is even.

Case 1 (n is odd): In this case, $n = 2k + 1$ for some integer k. *[We must show that $\lfloor n/2 \rfloor = (n-1)/2$.]* But the left-hand side of the equation to be shown is

$$\left\lfloor \frac{n}{2} \right\rfloor = \left\lfloor \frac{2k+1}{2} \right\rfloor = \left\lfloor \frac{2k}{2} + \frac{1}{2} \right\rfloor = \left\lfloor k + \frac{1}{2} \right\rfloor = k$$

because k is an integer and $k \leq k + 1/2 < k + 1$. And the right-hand side of the equation to be shown is

$$\frac{n-1}{2} = \frac{(2k+1)-1}{2} = \frac{2k}{2} = k$$

also. So since both the left-hand and right-hand sides equal k, they are equal to each other. That is, $\left\lfloor \dfrac{n}{2} \right\rfloor = \dfrac{n-1}{2}$ *[as was to be shown]*.

Case 2 (n is even): In this case, $n = 2k$ for some integer k. *[We must show that $\lfloor n/2 \rfloor = n/2$.]* The rest of the proof of this case is left as an exercise.

Given any integer n and a positive integer d, the quotient-remainder theorem guarantees the existence of unique integers q and r such that

$$n = dq + r \quad \text{and} \quad 0 \leq r < d.$$

The following theorem states that the floor notation can be used to describe q and r as follows:

$$q = \left\lfloor \frac{n}{d} \right\rfloor \quad \text{and} \quad r = n - d \left\lfloor \frac{n}{d} \right\rfloor.$$

Thus if, on a calculator or in a computer language, floor is built in but *div* and *mod* are not, *div* and *mod* can be defined as follows: For a nonnegative integer n and a positive integer d,

$$n \ div \ d = \left\lfloor \frac{n}{d} \right\rfloor \quad \text{and} \quad n \ mod \ d = n - d \left\lfloor \frac{n}{d} \right\rfloor. \qquad 4.5.1$$

Note that d divides n if, and only if, $n \ mod \ d = 0$, or, in other words, $n = d \lfloor n/d \rfloor$. You are asked to prove this in exercise 13.

Theorem 4.5.3

If n is any integer and d is a positive integer, and if $q = \lfloor n/d \rfloor$ and $r = n - d\lfloor n/d \rfloor$, then

$$n = dq + r \quad \text{and} \quad 0 \le r < d.$$

Proof:

Suppose n is any integer, d is a positive integer, $q = \lfloor n/d \rfloor$, and $r = n - d\lfloor n/d \rfloor$. *[We must show that $n = dq + r$ and $0 \le r < d$.]* By substitution,

$$dq + r = d\left\lfloor \frac{n}{d} \right\rfloor + \left(n - d\left\lfloor \frac{n}{d} \right\rfloor \right) = n.$$

So it remains only to show that $0 \le r < d$. But $q = \lfloor n/d \rfloor$. Thus, by definition of floor,

$$q \le \frac{n}{d} < q + 1.$$

Then

$$dq \le n < dq + d \qquad \text{by multiplying all parts by } d$$

and so

$$0 \le n - dq < d \qquad \text{by subtracting } dq \text{ from all parts}$$

But

$$r = n - d\left\lfloor \frac{n}{d} \right\rfloor = n - dq.$$

Hence

$$0 \le r < d \qquad \text{by substitution.}$$

[This is what was to be shown.]

Example 4.5.6 Computing *div* and *mod*

Use the floor notation to compute 3850 *div* 17 and 3850 *mod* 17.

Solution By formula (4.5.1),

$$3850 \ div \ 17 = \lfloor 3850/17 \rfloor = \lfloor 226.4705882 \ldots \rfloor = 226$$
$$3850 \ mod \ 17 = 3850 - 17 \cdot \lfloor 3850/17 \rfloor$$
$$= 3850 - 17 \cdot 226$$
$$= 3850 - 3842 = 8. \qquad \blacksquare$$

Test Yourself

1. Given any real number x, the floor of x is the unique integer n such that _____.

2. Given any real number x, the ceiling of x is the unique integer n such that _____.

Exercise Set 4.5

Compute $\lfloor x \rfloor$ and $\lceil x \rceil$ for each of the values of x in 1–4.

1. 37.999

2. 17/4

3. −14.00001

4. −32/5

5. Use the floor notation to express 259 *div* 11 and 259 *mod* 11.

6. If k is an integer, what is $\lceil k \rceil$? Why?

7. If k is an integer, what is $\lceil k + \frac{1}{2} \rceil$? Why?

8. Seven pounds of raw material are needed to manufacture each unit of a certain product. Express the number of units that can be produced from n pounds of raw material using either the floor or the ceiling notation. Which notation is more appropriate?

9. Boxes, each capable of holding 36 units, are used to ship a product from the manufacturer to a wholesaler. Express the number of boxes that would be required to ship n units of the product using either the floor or the ceiling notation. Which notation is more appropriate?

10. If $0 =$ Sunday, $1 =$ Monday, $2 =$ Tuesday, $\ldots$, $6 =$ Saturday, then January 1 of year n occurs on the day of the week given by the following formula:

$$\left(n + \left\lfloor \frac{n-1}{4} \right\rfloor - \left\lfloor \frac{n-1}{100} \right\rfloor + \left\lfloor \frac{n-1}{400} \right\rfloor \right) mod\ 7.$$

   a. Use this formula to find January 1 of
     i. 2050   ii. 2100   iii. the year of your birth.
H b. Interpret the different components of this formula.

11. Suppose n and d are integers and $d \neq 0$. Prove each of the following.
   a. If $d \mid n$, then $n = \lfloor n/d \rfloor \cdot d$.
   b. If $n = \lfloor n/d \rfloor \cdot d$, then $d \mid n$.
   c. Use the floor notation to state a necessary and sufficient condition for an integer n to be divisible by an integer d.

12. Prove that if n is any even integer, then $\lfloor n/2 \rfloor = n/2$.

13. State a necessary and sufficient condition for the floor of a real number to equal that number.

Some of the statements in 14–22 are true and some are false. Prove each true statement and find a counterexample for each false statement, but do not use Theorem 4.5.1. in your proofs.

14. For all real numbers x and y, $\lfloor x - y \rfloor = \lfloor x \rfloor - \lfloor y \rfloor$.

15. For all real numbers x, $\lfloor x - 1 \rfloor = \lfloor x \rfloor - 1$.

16. For all real numbers x, $\lfloor x^2 \rfloor = \lfloor x \rfloor^2$.

H 17. For all integers n,

$$\lfloor n/3 \rfloor = \begin{cases} n/3 & \text{if } n \bmod 3 = 0 \\ (n-1)/3 & \text{if } n \bmod 3 = 1 \\ (n-2)/3 & \text{if } n \bmod 3 = 2 \end{cases}.$$

H 18. For all real numbers x and y, $\lceil x + y \rceil = \lceil x \rceil + \lceil y \rceil$.

H 19. For all real numbers x, $\lceil x - 1 \rceil = \lceil x \rceil - 1$.

20. For all real numbers x and y, $\lceil xy \rceil = \lceil x \rceil \cdot \lceil y \rceil$.

21. For all odd integers n, $\lceil n/2 \rceil = (n+1)/2$.

22. For all real numbers x and y, $\lceil xy \rceil = \lceil x \rceil \cdot \lfloor y \rfloor$.

Prove each of the statements in 23–29.

23. For any real number x, if x is not an integer, then $\lfloor x \rfloor + \lfloor -x \rfloor = -1$.

24. For any integer m and any real number x, if x is not an integer, then $\lfloor x \rfloor + \lfloor m - x \rfloor = m - 1$.

H 25. For all real numbers x, $\lfloor \lfloor x/2 \rfloor / 2 \rfloor = \lfloor x/4 \rfloor$.

26. For all real numbers x, if $x - \lfloor x \rfloor < 1/2$ then $\lfloor 2x \rfloor = 2\lfloor x \rfloor$.

27. For all real numbers x, if $x - \lfloor x \rfloor \geq 1/2$ then $\lfloor 2x \rfloor = 2\lfloor x \rfloor + 1$.

28. For any odd integer n,

$$\left\lceil \frac{n^2}{4} \right\rceil = \frac{n^2 + 3}{4}.$$

29. For any odd integer n,

$$\left\lfloor \frac{n^2}{4} \right\rfloor = \left(\frac{n-1}{2} \right) \left(\frac{n+1}{2} \right).$$

30. Find the mistake in the following "proof" that $\lfloor n/2 \rfloor = (n-1)/2$ if n is an odd integer.
"**Proof:** Suppose n is any odd integer. Then $n = 2k + 1$ for some integer k. Consequently,

$$\left\lfloor \frac{2k+1}{2} \right\rfloor = \frac{(2k+1) - 1}{2} = \frac{2k}{2} = k.$$

But $n = 2k + 1$. Solving for k gives $k = (n-1)/2$. Hence, by substitution, $\lfloor n/2 \rfloor = (n-1)/2$."

Answers for Test Yourself

1. $n \leq x < n + 1$ 2. $n - 1 < x \leq n$

4.6 Indirect Argument: Contradiction and Contraposition

Reductio ad absurdum is one of a mathematician's finest weapons. It is a far finer gambit than any chess gambit: a chess player may offer the sacrifice of a pawn or even a piece, but the mathematician offers the game. — G. H. Hardy, 1877–1947

In a direct proof you start with the hypothesis of a statement and make one deduction after another until you reach the conclusion. Indirect proofs are more roundabout. One kind of indirect proof, *argument by contradiction,* is based on the fact that either a statement is true or it is false but not both. So if you can show that the assumption that a given statement is not true leads logically to a contradiction, impossibility, or absurdity, then that assumption must be false: and, hence, the given statement must be true. This method of proof is also known as *reductio ad impossible* or *reductio ad absurdum* because it relies on reducing a given assumption to an impossibility or absurdity.

Argument by contradiction occurs in many different settings. For example, if a man accused of holding up a bank can prove that he was some place else at the time the crime was committed, he will certainly be acquitted. The logic of his defense is as follows:

Suppose I did commit the crime. Then at the time of the crime, I would have had to be at the scene of the crime. In fact, at the time of the crime I was in a meeting with 20 people far from the crime scene, as they will testify. This contradicts the assumption that I committed the crime since it is impossible to be in two places at one time. Hence that assumption is false.

Another example occurs in debate. One technique of debate is to say, "Suppose for a moment that what my opponent says is correct." Starting from this supposition, the debater then deduces one statement after another until finally arriving at a statement that is completely ridiculous and unacceptable to the audience. By this means the debater shows the opponent's statement to be false.

The point of departure for a proof by contradiction is the supposition that the statement to be proved is false. The goal is to reason to a contradiction. Thus proof by contradiction has the following outline:

Note Be very careful when writing the negation!

Method of Proof by Contradiction

1. Suppose the statement to be proved is false. That is, suppose that the negation of the statement is true.

2. Show that this supposition leads logically to a contradiction.

3. Conclude that the statement to be proved is true.

There are no clear-cut rules for when to try a direct proof and when to try a proof by contradiction, but there are some general guidelines. Proof by contradiction is indicated if you want to show that there is no object with a certain property, or if you want to show that a certain object does not have a certain property. The next two examples illustrate these situations.

Example 4.6.1 There Is No Greatest Integer

Use proof by contradiction to show that there is no greatest integer.

Solution   Most small children believe there is a greatest integer—they often call it a "zillion." But with age and experience, they change their belief. At some point they realize that if there were a greatest integer, they could add 1 to it to obtain an integer that was greater still. Since that is a contradiction, no greatest integer can exist. This line of reasoning is the heart of the formal proof.

For the proof, the "certain property" is the property of being the greatest integer. To prove that there is no object with this property, begin by supposing the negation: that there is an object with the property.

Starting Point: Suppose not. Suppose there is a greatest integer; call it N.

This means that $N \geq n$ for all integers n.

To Show: This supposition leads logically to a contradiction.

Theorem 4.6.1

There is no greatest integer.

Proof:

[We take the negation of the theorem and suppose it to be true.] Suppose not. That is, suppose there is a greatest integer N. *[We must deduce a contradiction.]* Then $N \geq n$ for every integer n. Let $M = N + 1$. Now M is an integer since it is a sum of integers. Also $M > N$ since $M = N + 1$. Thus M is an integer that is greater than N. So N is the greatest integer and N is not the greatest integer, which is a contradiction. *[This contradiction shows that the supposition is false and, hence, that the theorem is true.]*

After a contradiction has been reached, the logic of the argument is always the same: "This is a contradiction. Hence the supposition is false and the theorem is true." Because of this, most mathematics texts end proofs by contradiction at the point at which the contradiction has been obtained.

The contradiction in the next example is based on the fact that $1/2$ is not an integer.

Example 4.6.2 No Integer Can Be Both Even and Odd

The fact that no integer can be both even and odd follows from the uniqueness part of the quotient-remainder theorem. A full proof of this part of the theorem is outlined in exercise 18 of section 4.7. This example shows how to use proof by contradiction to prove one specific case.

Theorem 4.6.2

There is no integer that is both even and odd.

Proof:

[We take the negation of the theorem and suppose it to be true.] Suppose not. That is, suppose there is at least one integer n that is both even and odd. *[We must deduce a contradiction.]* By definition of even, $n = 2a$ for some integer a, and by definition of odd, $n = 2b + 1$ for some integer b. Consequently,

$$2a = 2b + 1 \qquad \text{by equating the two expressions for } n$$

continued on page 200

and so

$$2a - 2b = 1$$
$$2(a - b) = 1$$
$$a - b = 1/2 \quad \text{by algebra}$$

Now since a and b are integers, the difference $a - b$ must also be an integer. But $a - b = 1/2$, and $1/2$ is not an integer. Thus $a - b$ is an integer and $a - b$ is not an integer, which is a contradiction. *[This contradiction shows that the supposition is false and, hence, that the theorem is true.]*

The next example asks you to show that the sum of any rational number and any irrational number is irrational. One way to think of this is in terms of a certain object (the sum of a rational and an irrational) not having a certain property (the property of being rational). This suggests trying a proof by contradiction: suppose the object has the property and deduce a contradiction.

Example 4.6.3 The Sum of a Rational Number and an Irrational Number

Use proof by contradiction to show that the sum of any rational number and any irrational number is irrational.

Caution! The negation of "The sum of any irrational number and any rational number is irrational" is NOT "The sum of any irrational number and any rational number is rational."

Solution Begin by supposing the negation of what you are to prove. Be very careful when writing down what this means. If you take the negation incorrectly, the entire rest of the proof will be flawed. In this example, the statement to be proved can be written formally as

$\forall$ real numbers r and s, if r is rational and s is irrational, then $r + s$ is irrational.

From this you can see that the negation is

$\exists$ a rational number r and an irrational number s such that $r + s$ is rational.

It follows that the starting point and what is to be shown are as follows:

Starting Point: Suppose not. That is, suppose there is a rational number r and an irrational number s such that $r + s$ is rational.

To Show: This supposition leads to a contradiction.

To derive a contradiction, you need to understand what you are supposing: that there are numbers r and s such that r is rational, s is irrational, and $r + s$ is rational. By definition of rational and irrational, this means that s cannot be written as a quotient of any two integers but that r and $r + s$ can:

$$r = \frac{a}{b} \quad \text{for some integers } a \text{ and } b \text{ with } b \neq 0, \text{ and} \qquad 4.6.1$$

$$r + s = \frac{c}{d} \quad \text{for some integers } c \text{ and } d \text{ with } d \neq 0. \qquad 4.6.2$$

If you substitute (4.6.1) into (4.6.2), you obtain

$$\frac{a}{b} + s = \frac{c}{d}.$$

Subtracting a/b from both sides gives

$$s = \frac{c}{d} - \frac{a}{b}$$

$$= \frac{bc}{bd} - \frac{ad}{bd} \qquad \text{by rewriting } c/d \text{ and } a/b \text{ as equivalent fractions}$$

$$= \frac{bc - ad}{bd} \qquad \text{by the rule for subtracting fractions with the same denominator.}$$

But both $bc - ad$ and bd are integers because products and differences of integers are integers, and $bd \neq 0$ by the zero product property. Hence s can be expressed as a quotient of two integers with a nonzero denominator, and so s is rational, which contradicts the supposition that it is irrational.

   This discussion is summarized in a formal proof.

Theorem 4.6.3

The sum of any rational number and any irrational number is irrational.

Proof:

[We take the negation of the theorem and suppose it to be true.] Suppose not. That is, suppose there is a rational number r and an irrational number s such that $r + s$ is rational. *[We must deduce a contradiction.]* By definition of rational, $r = a/b$ and $r + s = c/d$ for some integers $a, b, c,$ and d with $b \neq 0$ and $d \neq 0$. By substitution,

$$\frac{a}{b} + s = \frac{c}{d},$$

and so

$$s = \frac{c}{d} - \frac{a}{b} \qquad \text{by subtracting } a/b \text{ from both sides}$$

$$= \frac{bc - ad}{bd} \qquad \text{by the laws of algebra.}$$

Now $bc - ad$ and bd are both integers *[since $a, b, c,$ and d are integers and since products and differences of integers are integers]*, and $bd \neq 0$ *[by the zero product property]*. Hence s is a quotient of the two integers $bc - ad$ and bd with $bd \neq 0$. Thus, by definition of rational, s is rational, which contradicts the supposition that s is irrational. *[Hence the supposition is false and the theorem is true.]*

Argument by Contraposition

A second form of indirect argument, *argument by contraposition,* is based on the logical equivalence between a statement and its contrapositive. To prove a statement by contraposition, you take the contrapositive of the statement, prove the contrapositive by a direct proof, and conclude that the original statement is true. The underlying reasoning is that since a conditional statement is logically equivalent to its contrapositive, if the contrapositive is true then the statement must also be true.

Method of Proof by Contraposition

1. Express the statement to be proved in the form

$$\forall x \text{ in } D, \text{ if } P(x) \text{ then } Q(x).$$

(This step may be done mentally.)

2. Rewrite this statement in the contrapositive form

$$\forall x \text{ in } D, \text{ if } Q(x) \text{ is false then } P(x) \text{ is false.}$$

(This step may also be done mentally.)

3. Prove the contrapositive by a direct proof.

a. Suppose x is a (particular but arbitrarily chosen) element of D such that $Q(x)$ is false.

b. Show that $P(x)$ is false.

Example 4.6.4 If the Square of an Integer Is Even, Then the Integer Is Even

Prove that for all integers n, if n^2 is even then n is even.

Solution First form the contrapositive of the statement to be proved.

Contrapositive: For all integers n, if n is not even then n^2 is not even.

By the quotient-remainder theorem with $d = 2$, any integer is even or odd, so any integer that is not even is odd. Also by Theorem 4.6.2, no integer can be both even and odd. So if an integer is odd, then it is not even. Thus the contrapositive can be restated as follows:

Contrapositive: For all integers n, if n is odd then n^2 is odd.

A straightforward computation is the heart of a direct proof for this statement, as shown below.

Proposition 4.6.4

For all integers n, if n^2 is even then n is even.

Proof (by contraposition):

Suppose n is any odd integer. *[We must show that n^2 is odd.]* By definition of odd, $n = 2k + 1$ for some integer k. By substitution and algebra,

$$n^2 = (2k + 1)^2 = 4k^2 + 4k + 1 = 2(2k^2 + 2k) + 1.$$

But $2k^2 + 2k$ is an integer because products and sums of integers are integers. So $n^2 = 2 \cdot (\text{an integer}) + 1$, and thus, by definition of odd, n^2 is odd *[as was to be shown]*.

We used the word *proposition* here rather than *theorem* because although the word *theorem* can refer to any statement that has been proved, mathematicians often restrict it to especially important statements that have many and varied consequences. Then they use the word **proposition** to refer to a statement that is somewhat less consequential but nonetheless worth writing down. We will use Proposition 4.6.4 in Section 4.7 to prove that $\sqrt{2}$ is irrational.   ◼

Relation between Proof by Contradiction and Proof by Contraposition

Observe that any proof by contraposition can be recast in the language of proof by contradiction. In a proof by contraposition, the statement

$$\forall x \text{ in } D, \text{ if } P(x) \text{ then } Q(x)$$

is proved by giving a direct proof of the equivalent statement

$$\forall x \text{ in } D, \text{ if } \sim Q(x) \text{ then } \sim P(x).$$

To do this, you suppose you are given an arbitrary element x of D such that $\sim Q(x)$. You then show that $\sim P(x)$. This is illustrated in Figure 4.6.1.

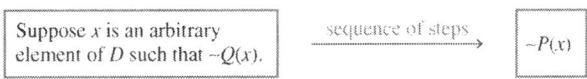

Figure 4.6.1 **Proof by Contraposition**

Exactly the same sequence of steps can be used as the heart of a proof by contradiction for the given statement. The only thing that changes is the context in which the steps are written down.

To rewrite the proof as a proof by contradiction, you suppose there is an x in D such that $P(x)$ and $\sim Q(x)$. You then follow the steps of the proof by contraposition to deduce the statement $\sim P(x)$. But $\sim P(x)$ is a contradiction to the supposition that $P(x)$ and $\sim Q(x)$. (Because to contradict a conjunction of two statements, it is only necessary to contradict one of them.) This process is illustrated in Figure 4.6.2.

Figure 4.6.2 **Proof by Contradiction**

As an example, here is a proof by contradiction of Proposition 4.6.4, namely that for any integer n, if n^2 is even then n is even.

Proposition 4.6.4

For all integers n, if n^2 is even then n is even.

Proof (by contradiction):

[We take the negation of the theorem and suppose it to be true.] Suppose not. That is, suppose there is an integer n such that n^2 is even and n is not even. *[We must deduce a contradiction.]* By the quotient-remainder theorem with $d = 2$, any integer

continued on page 204

is even or odd. Hence, since n is not even it is odd, and thus, by definition of odd, $n = 2k + 1$ for some integer k. By substitution and algebra:

$$n^2 = (2k + 1)^2 = 4k^2 + 4k + 1 = 2(2k^2 + 2k) + 1.$$

But $2k^2 + 2k$ is an integer because products and sums of integers are integers. So $n^2 = 2 \cdot (\text{an integer}) + 1$, and thus, by definition of odd, n^2 is odd. Therefore, n^2 is both even and odd. This contradicts Theorem 4.6.2, which states that no integer can be both even and odd. *[This contradiction shows that the supposition is false and, hence, that the proposition is true.]*

Note that when you use proof by contraposition, you know exactly what conclusion you need to show, namely the negation of the hypothesis; whereas in proof by contradiction, it may be difficult to know what contradiction to head for. On the other hand, when you use proof by contradiction, once you have deduced any contradiction whatsoever, you are done. The main advantage of contraposition over contradiction is that you avoid having to take (possibly incorrectly) the negation of a complicated statement. The disadvantage of contraposition as compared with contradiction is that you can use contraposition only for a specific class of statements—those that are universal and conditional. The previous discussion shows that any statement that can be proved by contraposition can be proved by contradiction. But the converse is not true. Statements such as "$\sqrt{2}$ is irrational" (discussed in the next section) can be proved by contradiction but not by contraposition.

Proof as a Problem-Solving Tool

Direct proof, disproof by counterexample, proof by contradiction, and proof by contraposition are all tools that may be used to help determine whether statements are true or false. Given a statement of the form

For all elements in a domain, if (hypothesis) then (conclusion),

imagine elements in the domain that satisfy the hypothesis. Ask yourself: Must they satisfy the conclusion? If you can see that the answer is "yes" in all cases, then the statement is true and your insight will form the basis for a direct proof. If after some thought it is not clear that the answer is "yes," ask yourself whether there are elements of the domain that satisfy the hypothesis and *not* the conclusion. If you are successful in finding some, then the statement is false and you have a counterexample. On the other hand, if you are not successful in finding such elements, perhaps none exist. Perhaps you can show that assuming the existence of elements in the domain that satisfy the hypothesis and not the conclusion leads logically to a contradiction. If so, then the given statement is true and you have the basis for a proof by contradiction. Alternatively, you could imagine elements of the domain for which the conclusion is false and ask whether such elements also fail to satisfy the hypothesis. If the answer in all cases is "yes," then you have a basis for a proof by contraposition.

Solving problems, especially difficult problems, is rarely a straightforward process. At any stage of following the guidelines above, you might want to try the method of a previous stage again. If, for example, you fail to find a counterexample for a certain statement, your experience in trying to find it might help you decide to reattempt a direct argument rather than trying an indirect one. Psychologists who have studied problem solving have found that the most successful problem solvers are those who are flexible and willing to use a variety of approaches without getting stuck in any one of them for very long. Mathematicians sometimes work for months (or longer) on difficult problems. Don't be discouraged if some problems in this book take you quite a while to solve.

Learning the skills of proof and disproof is much like learning other skills, such as those used in swimming, tennis, or playing a musical instrument. When you first start out, you may feel bewildered by all the rules, and you may not feel confident as you attempt new things. But with practice the rules become internalized and you can use them in conjunction with all your other powers—of balance, coordination, judgment, aesthetic sense—to concentrate on winning a meet, winning a match, or playing a concert successfully.

Now that you have worked through the first five sections of this chapter, return to the idea that, above all, a proof or disproof should be a convincing argument. You need to know how direct and indirect proofs and counterexamples are structured. But to use this knowledge effectively, you must use it in conjunction with your imaginative powers, your intuition, and especially your common sense.

Test Yourself

1. To prove a statement by contradiction, you suppose that _____ and you show that _____.

2. A proof by contraposition of a statement of the form "$\forall x \in D$, if $P(x)$ then $Q(x)$" is a direct proof of _____.

3. To prove a statement of the form "$\forall x \in D$, if $P(x)$ then $Q(x)$" by contraposition, you suppose that _____ and you show that _____.

Exercise Set 4.6

1. Fill in the blanks in the following proof by contradiction that there is no least positive real number.

   Proof: Suppose not. That is, suppose that there is a least positive real number x. *[We must deduce __(a)__]* Consider the number $x/2$. Since x is a positive real number, $x/2$ is also __(b)__. In addition, we can deduce that $x/2 < x$ by multiplying both sides of the inequality $1 < 2$ by __(c)__ and dividing __(d)__. Hence $x/2$ is a positive real number that is less than the least positive real number. This is a __(e)__ *[Thus the supposition is false, and so there is no least positive real number.]*

2. Is $\dfrac{1}{0}$ an irrational number? Explain.

3. Use proof by contradiction to show that for all integers n, $3n + 2$ is not divisible by 3.

4. Use proof by contradiction to show that for all integers m, $7m + 4$ is not divisible by 7.

Carefully formulate the negations of each of the statements in 5–7. Then prove each statement by contradiction.

5. There is no greatest even integer.

6. There is no greatest negative real number.

7. There is no least positive rational number.

8. Fill in the blanks for the following proof that the difference of any rational number and any irrational number is irrational.

   Proof: Suppose not. That is, suppose that there exist __(a)__ x and __(b)__ y such that $x - y$ is rational. By definition of rational, there exist integers a, b, c, and d with $b \neq 0$ and $d \neq 0$ so that $x = $ __(c)__ and $x - y = $ __(d)__. By substitution,

$$\frac{a}{b} - y = \frac{c}{d}$$

Adding y and subtracting $\dfrac{c}{d}$ on both sides gives

$$y = \text{(e)}$$
$$= \frac{ad}{bd} - \frac{bc}{bd}$$
$$= \frac{ad - bc}{bd} \qquad \text{by algebra.}$$

Now both $ad - bc$ and bd are integers because products and differences of __(f)__ are __(g)__. And $bd \neq 0$ by the __(h)__. Hence y is a ratio of integers with a nonzero denominator, and thus y is __(i)__ by definition of rational. We therefore have both that y is irrational and that y is rational, which is a contradiction. *[Thus the supposition is false and the statement to be proved is true.]*

9. a. When asked to prove that the difference of any irrational number and any rational number is irrational, a student began, "Suppose not. That is, suppose the difference of any irrational number and any rational number is rational." What is wrong with beginning the proof in this way? (*Hint*: Review the answer to exercise 11 in Section 3.2.)

   b. Prove that the difference of any irrational number and any rational number is irrational.

Prove each statement in 10–17 by contradiction.

10. The square root of any irrational number is irrational.

11. The product of any nonzero rational number and any irrational number is irrational.

12. If a and b are rational numbers, $b \neq 0$, and r is an irrational number, then $a + br$ is irrational.

H 13. For any integer n, $n^2 - 2$ is not divisible by 4.

H 14. For all prime numbers a, b, and c, $a^2 + b^2 \neq c^2$.

H 15. If a, b, and c are integers and $a^2 + b^2 = c^2$, then at least one of a and b is even.

✦ 16. For all odd integers a, b, and c, if z is a solution of $ax^2 + bx + c = 0$ then z is irrational. (In the proof, use the properties of even and odd integers that are listed in Example 4.2.3.)

17. For all integers a, if $a \bmod 6 = 3$, then $a \bmod 3 \neq 2$.

18. Fill in the blanks in the following proof by contraposition that for all integers n, if $5 \nmid n^2$ then $5 \nmid n$.

 Proof (by contraposition): *[The contrapositive is: For all integers n, if $5 \mid n$ then $5 \mid n^2$.]* Suppose n is any integer such that (a) . *[We must show that (b) .]* By definition of divisibility, $n =$ (c) for some integer k. By substitution, $n^2 =$ (d) $= 5(5k^2)$. But $5k^2$ is an integer because it is a product of integers. Hence $n^2 = 5 \cdot$ (an integer), and so (e) *[as was to be shown]*.

Prove the statements in 19 and 20 by contraposition.

19. If a product of two positive real numbers is greater than 100, then at least one of the numbers is greater than 10.

20. If a sum of two real numbers is less than 50, then at least one of the numbers is less than 25.

21. Consider the statement "For all integers n, if n^2 is odd then n is odd."
 a. Write what you would suppose and what you would need to show to prove this statement by contradiction.
 b. Write what you would suppose and what you would need to show to prove this statement by contraposition.

22. Consider the statement "For all real numbers r, if r^2 is irrational then r is irrational."
 a. Write what you would suppose and what you would need to show to prove this statement by contradiction.
 b. Write what you would suppose and what you would need to show to prove this statement by contraposition.

Prove each of the statements in 23–29 in two ways: (a) by contraposition and (b) by contradiction.

23. The negative of any irrational number is irrational.

24. The reciprocal of any irrational number is irrational. (The **reciprocal** of a nonzero real number x is $1/x$.)

H 25. For all integers n, if n^2 is odd then n is odd.

26. For all integers a, b, and c, if $a \nmid bc$ then $a \nmid b$. (Recall that the symbol $\nmid$ means "does not divide.")

H 27. For all integers m and n, if $m + n$ is even then m and n are both even or m and n are both odd.

28. For all integers m and n, if mn is even then m is even or n is even.

29. For all integers a, b, and c, if $a \mid b$ and $a \nmid c$, then $a \nmid (b + c)$. (*Hint:* To prove $p \rightarrow q \vee r$, it suffices to prove either $p \wedge {\sim}q \rightarrow r$ or $p \wedge {\sim}r \rightarrow q$. See exercise 14 in Section 2.2.)

30. The following "proof" that every integer is rational is incorrect. Find the mistake.

 "**Proof (by contradiction):** Suppose not. Suppose every integer is irrational. Then the integer 1 is irrational. But $1 = 1/1$, which is rational. This is a contradiction. *[Hence the supposition is false and the theorem is true.]*"

31. a. Prove by contraposition: For all positive integers n, r, and s, if $rs \leq n$, then $r \leq \sqrt{n}$ or $s \leq \sqrt{n}$.
 b. Prove: For all integers $n > 1$, if n is not prime, then there exists a prime number p such that $p \leq \sqrt{n}$ and n is divisible by p. (*Hints:* Use the result of part (a), Theorems 4.3.1, 4.3.3, and 4.3.4, and the transitive property of order.)
 c. State the contrapositive of the result of part (b).
 The results of exercise 31 provide a way to test whether an integer is prime.

> Test for Primality
>
> Given an integer $n > 1$, to test whether n is prime check to see if it is divisible by a prime number less than or equal to its square root. If it is not divisible by any of these numbers, then it is prime.

32. Use the test for primality to determine whether the following numbers are prime or not.
 a. 667   b. 557   c. 613   d. 527

33. The sieve of Eratosthenes, named after its inventor, the Greek scholar Eratosthenes (276–194 B.C.E.), provides a way to find all prime numbers less than or equal to some fixed number n. To construct it, write out all the integers from 2 to n. Cross out all multiples of 2 except 2 itself, then all multiples of 3 except 3 itself, then all multiples of 5 except 5 itself, and so forth. Continue crossing out the

multiples of each successive prime number up to $\sqrt{n}$. The numbers that are not crossed out are all the prime numbers from 2 to n. Here is a sieve of Eratosthenes that includes the numbers from 2 to 27. The multiples of 2 are crossed out with a /, the multiples of 3 with a \, and the multiples of 5 with a —.

2　3　A̸　5　6̸　7　8̸　9̸　1̸0̸　11　1̸2　13　1̸4
1̸5̸　1̸6̸　17　1̸8̸　19　2̸0̸　2̸1̸　2̸2̸　23　2̸4̸　2̸5̸　26　2̸7̸

Use the sieve of Eratosthenes to find all prime numbers less than 100.

34. Use the test for primality and the result of exercise 33 to determine whether the following numbers are prime.
a. 9,269　　h. 9,103　　c. 8,623　　d. 7,917

H ✱ 35. Use proof by contradiction to show that every integer greater than 11 is a sum of two composite numbers.

Answers for Test Yourself

1. the statement is false; this supposition leads to a contradiction　2. the contrapositive of the statement, namely, $\forall x \in D$, if $\sim Q(x)$ then $\sim P(x)$　3. x is any *[particular but arbitrarily chosen]* element of D for which $Q(x)$ is false; $P(x)$ is false

4.7 Indirect Argument: Two Classical Theorems

He is unworthy of the name of man who does not know that the diagonal of a square is incommensurable with its side.—Plato (ca. 428–347 B.C.E.)

This section contains proofs of two of the most famous theorems in mathematics: that $\sqrt{2}$ is irrational and that there are infinitely many prime numbers. Both proofs are examples of indirect arguments and were well known more than 2,000 years ago, but they remain exemplary models of mathematical argument to this day.

The Irrationality of $\sqrt{2}$

When mathematics flourished at the time of the ancient Greeks, mathematicians believed that given any two line segments, say A: —— and B: ————, a certain unit of length could be found so that segment A was exactly a units long and segment B was exactly b units long. (The segments were said to be *commensurable* with respect to this special unit of length.) Then the ratio of the lengths of A and B would be in the same proportion as the ratio of the integers a and b. Symbolically:

$$\frac{\text{length } A}{\text{length } B} = \frac{a}{b}.$$

Now it is easy to find a line segment of length $\sqrt{2}$; just take the diagonal of the unit square:

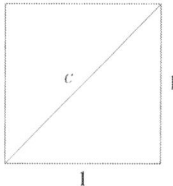

By the Pythagorean theorem, $c^2 = 1^2 + 1^2 = 2$, and so $c = \sqrt{2}$. If the belief of the ancient Greeks were correct, there would be integers a and b such that

$$\frac{\text{length (diagonal)}}{\text{length (side)}} = \frac{a}{b}.$$

And this would imply that

$$\frac{c}{1} = \frac{\sqrt{2}}{1} = \sqrt{2} = \frac{a}{b}.$$

But then $\sqrt{2}$ would be a ratio of two integers, or, in other words, $\sqrt{2}$ would be rational.

In the fourth or fifth century B.C.E., the followers of the Greek mathematician and philosopher Pythagoras discovered that $\sqrt{2}$ was not rational. This discovery was very upsetting to them, for it undermined their deep, quasi-religious belief in the power of whole numbers to describe phenomena.

The following proof of the irrationality of $\sqrt{2}$ was known to Aristotle and is similar to that in the tenth book of Euclid's *Elements of Geometry*. The Greek mathematician Euclid is best known as a geometer. In fact, knowledge of the geometry in the first six books of his *Elements* has been considered an essential part of a liberal education for more than 2,000 years. Books 7–10 of his *Elements*, however, contain much that we would now call number theory.

The proof begins by supposing the negation: $\sqrt{2}$ is rational. This means that there exist integers m and n such that $\sqrt{2} = m/n$. Now if m and n have any common factors, these may be factored out to obtain a new fraction, equal to m/n, in which the numerator and denominator have no common factors. (For example, $18/12 = (6 \cdot 3)/(6 \cdot 2) = 3/2$, which is a fraction whose numerator and denominator have no common factors.) Thus, without loss of generality, we may assume that m and n had no common factors in the first place. We will then derive the contradiction that m and n *do* have a common factor of 2. The argument makes use of Proposition 4.6.4. If the square of an integer is even, then that integer is even.

Euclid
(fl. 300 B.C.E.)

Note Strictly speaking, being able to assume that m and n have no common factors is a consequence of the "well-ordering principle for the integers," which is discussed in Section 5.4.

Theorem 4.7.1 Irrationality of $\sqrt{2}$

$\sqrt{2}$ is irrational.

Proof:

[We take the negation and suppose it to be true.] Suppose not. That is, suppose $\sqrt{2}$ is rational. Then there are integers m and n with no common factors such that

$$\sqrt{2} = \frac{m}{n} \qquad 4.7.1$$

[by dividing m and n by any common factors if necessary]. *[We must derive a contradiction.]* Squaring both sides of equation (4.7.1) gives

$$2 = \frac{m^2}{n^2}.$$

Or, equivalently,

$$m^2 = 2n^2. \qquad 4.7.2$$

Note that equation (4.7.2) implies that m^2 is even (by definition of even). It follows that m is even (by Proposition 4.6.4). We file this fact away for future reference and also deduce (by definition of even) that

$$m = 2k \quad \text{for some integer } k. \qquad 4.7.3$$

Substituting equation (4.7.3) into equation (4.7.2), we see that

$$m^2 = (2k)^2 = 4k^2 = 2n^2.$$

Dividing both sides of the right-most equation by 2 gives

$$n^2 = 2k^2.$$

Consequently, n^2 is even, and so n is even (by Proposition 4.6.4). But we also know that m is even. *[This is the fact we filed away.]* Hence both m and n have a common factor of 2. But this contradicts the supposition that m and n have no common factors. *[Hence the supposition is false and so the theorem is true.]*

Now that you have seen the proof that $\sqrt{2}$ is irrational, you can use the irrationality of $\sqrt{2}$ to derive the irrationality of certain other real numbers.

Example 4.7.1 Irrationality of $1 + 3\sqrt{2}$

Prove by contradiction that $1 + 3\sqrt{2}$ is irrational.

Solution   The essence of the argument is the observation that if $1 + 3\sqrt{2}$ could be written as a ratio of integers, then so could $\sqrt{2}$. But by Theorem 4.7.1, we know that to be impossible.

Proposition 4.7.2

$1 + 3\sqrt{2}$ is irrational.

Proof:

Suppose not. Suppose $1 + 3\sqrt{2}$ is rational. *[We must derive a contradiction.]* Then by definition of rational,

$$1 + 3\sqrt{2} = \frac{a}{b} \quad \text{for some integers } a \text{ and } b \text{ with } b \neq 0.$$

It follows that

$$3\sqrt{2} = \frac{a}{b} - 1 \qquad \text{by subtracting 1 from both sides}$$

$$= \frac{a}{b} - \frac{b}{b} \qquad \text{by substitution}$$

$$= \frac{a - b}{b} \qquad \text{by the rule for subtracting fractions with a common denominator.}$$

Hence

$$\sqrt{2} = \frac{a - b}{3b} \qquad \text{by dividing both sides by 3.}$$

But $a - b$ and $3b$ are integers (since a and b are integers and differences and products of integers are integers), and $3b \neq 0$ by the zero product property. Hence $\sqrt{2}$ is a quotient of the two integers $a - b$ and $3b$ with $3b \neq 0$, and so $\sqrt{2}$ is rational (by definition of rational.) This contradicts the fact that $\sqrt{2}$ is irrational. *[This contradiction shows that the supposition is false.]* Hence $1 + 3\sqrt{2}$ is irrational.

Are There Infinitely Many Prime Numbers?

You know that a prime number is a positive integer that cannot be factored as a product of two smaller positive integers. Is the set of all such numbers infinite, or is there a largest prime number? The answer was known to Euclid, and a proof that the set of all prime numbers is infinite appears in Book 9 of his *Elements of Geometry*.

Euclid's proof requires one additional fact we have not yet established: If a prime number divides an integer, then it does not divide the next successive integer.

Proposition 4.7.3

For any integer a and any prime number p, if $p \mid a$ then $p \nmid (a + 1)$.

Proof:

Suppose not. That is, suppose there exists an integer a and a prime number p such that $p \mid a$ and $p \mid (a + 1)$. Then, by definition of divisibility, there exist integers r and s such that $a = pr$ and $a + 1 = ps$. It follows that

$$1 = (a + 1) - a = ps - pr = p(s - r),$$

and so (since $s - r$ is an integer) $p \mid 1$. But, by Theorem 4.3.2, the only integer divisors of 1 are 1 and -1, and $p > 1$ because p is prime. Thus $p \le 1$ and $p > 1$, which is a contradiction. *[Hence the supposition is false, and the proposition is true.]*

The idea of Euclid's proof is this: Suppose the set of prime numbers were finite. Then you could take the product of all the prime numbers and add one. By Theorem 4.3.4 this number must be divisible by some prime number. But by Proposition 4.7.3, this number is not divisible by any of the prime numbers in the set. Hence there must be a prime number that is not in the set of all prime numbers, which is impossible.

The following formal proof fills in the details of this outline.

Theorem 4.7.4 Infinitude of the Primes

The set of prime numbers is infinite.

Proof (by contradiction):

Suppose not. That is, suppose the set of prime numbers is finite. *[We must deduce a contradiction.]* Then some prime number p is the largest of all the prime numbers, and hence we can list the prime numbers in ascending order:

$$2, \ 3, \ 5, \ 7, \ 11, \ldots, p.$$

Let N be the product of all the prime numbers plus 1:

$$N = (2 \cdot 3 \cdot 5 \cdot 7 \cdot 11 \cdots p) + 1$$

Then $N > 1$, and so, by Theorem 4.3.4, N is divisible by some prime number q. Because q is prime, q must equal one of the prime numbers 2, 3, 5, 7, 11, ..., p.

Thus, by definition of divisibility, q divides $2 \cdot 3 \cdot 5 \cdot 7 \cdot 11 \cdots p$, and so, by Proposition 4.7.3, q does not divide $(2 \cdot 3 \cdot 5 \cdot 7 \cdot 11 \cdots p) + 1$, which equals N. Hence N is divisible by q and N is not divisible by q, and we have reached a contradiction. *[Therefore, the supposition is false and the theorem is true.]*

The proof of Theorem 4.7.4 shows that if you form the product of all prime numbers up to a certain point and add one, the result, N, is divisible by a prime number not on the list. The proof does not show that N is, itself, prime. In the exercises at the end of this section you are asked to find an example of an integer N constructed in this way that is not prime.

When to Use Indirect Proof

The examples in this section and Section 4.6 have not provided a definitive answer to the question of when to prove a statement directly and when to prove it indirectly. Many theorems can be proved either way. Usually, however, when both types of proof are possible, indirect proof is clumsier than direct proof. In the absence of obvious clues suggesting indirect argument, try first to prove a statement directly. Then, if that does not succeed, look for a counterexample. If the search for a counterexample is unsuccessful, look for a proof by contradiction or contraposition.

Open Questions in Number Theory

In this section we proved that there are infinitely many prime numbers. There is no known formula for obtaining primes, but a few formulas have been found to be more successful at producing them than other formulas. One such is due to Marin Mersenne, a French monk who lived from 1588–1648. *Mersenne primes* have the form $2^p - 1$, where p is prime. Not all numbers of this form are prime, but because Mersenne primes are easier to test for primality than are other numbers, most of the largest known prime numbers are Mersenne primes.

An interesting question is whether there are infinitely many Mersenne primes. As of the date of publication of this book, the answer is not known, but new mathematical discoveries are being made every day and by the time you read this someone may have discovered the answer. Another formula that seems to produce a relatively large number of prime numbers is due to Fermat. *Fermat primes* are prime numbers of the form $2^{2^n} + 1$, where n is a positive integer. Are there infinitely many Fermat primes? Again, as of now, no one knows. Similarly unknown are whether there are infinitely many primes of the form $n^2 + 1$, where n is a positive integer, and whether there is always a prime number between integers n^2 and $(n + 1)^2$.

Ben Joseph Green
(born 1977)

Another famous open question involving primes is the *twin primes conjecture,* which states that there are infinitely many pairs of prime numbers of the form p and $p + 2$. As with other well-known problems in number theory, this conjecture has withstood computer testing up to extremely large numbers, and some progress has been made toward a proof. In 2004, Ben Green and Terence Tao showed that for any integer $m > 1$, there is a sequence of m equally spaced integers all of which are prime. In other words, there are positive integers n and k so that the following numbers are all prime:

$$n, n + k, \ n + 2k, \ n + 3k, \ \ldots, \ n + (m - 1)k.$$

Terence Chi-Shen Tao
(born 1975)

Related to the twin primes conjecture is a conjecture made by Sophie Germain, a French mathematician born in 1776, who made significant progress toward a proof of Fermat's Last Theorem. Germain conjectured that there are infinitely many prime number

*Marie-Sophie Germain
(1776–1831)*

pairs of the form p and $2p + 1$. Initial values of p with this property are 2, 3, 5, 11, 23, 29, 41, and 53, and computer testing has verified the conjecture for many additional values. In fact, as of the writing of this book, the largest prime p for which $2p + 1$ is also known to be prime is $183027 \cdot 2^{265440} - 1$. This is a number with 79911 decimal digits! But compared with infinity, any number, no matter how large, is less than a drop in the bucket.

In 1844, the Belgian mathematician Eugène Catalan conjectured that the only solutions to the equation $x^n - y^m = 1$, where x, y, n, and m are all integers greater than 1, is $3^2 - 2^3 = 1$. This conjecture also remains unresolved to this day.

In 1993, while trying to prove Fermat's last theorem, an amateur number theorist, Andrew Beal, became intrigued by the equation $x^m + y^n = z^k$, where no two of x, y, or z have any common factor other than ± 1. When diligent effort, first by hand and then by computer, failed to reveal any solutions, Beal conjectured that no solutions exist. His conjecture has become known as *Beal's conjecture*, and he has offered a prize of $100,000 to anyone who can either prove or disprove it.

These are just a few of a large number of open questions in number theory. Many people believe that mathematics is a fixed subject that changes very little from one century to the next. In fact, more mathematical questions are being raised and more results are being discovered now than ever before in history.

Test Yourself

1. The ancient Greeks discovered that in a right triangle where both legs have length 1, the ratio of the length of the hypotenuse to the length of one of the legs is not equal to a ratio of _____.

2. One way to prove that $\sqrt{2}$ is an irrational number is to assume that $\sqrt{2} = a/b$ for some integers a and b that have no common factor greater than 1, use the lemma that says

that if the square of an integer is even then _____, and eventually show that a and b _____.

3. One way to prove that there are infinitely many prime numbers is to assume that there is a largest prime number p, construct the number _____, and then show that this number has to be divisible by a prime number that is greater than

_____.

Exercise Set 4.7

1. A calculator display shows that $\sqrt{2} = 1.414213562$, and $1.414213562 = \dfrac{1414213562}{1000000000}$. This suggests that $\sqrt{2}$ is a rational number, which contradicts Theorem 4.7.1. Explain the discrepancy.

2. Example 4.2.1(h) illustrates a technique for showing that any repeating decimal number is rational. A calculator display shows the result of a certain calculation as 40.72727272727. Can you be sure that the result of the calculation is a rational number? Explain.

Determine which statements in 3–13 are true and which are false. Prove those that are true and disprove those that are false.

3. $6 - 7\sqrt{2}$ is irrational.

4. $3\sqrt{2} - 7$ is irrational.

5. $\sqrt{4}$ is irrational.

6. $\sqrt{2}/6$ is rational.

7. The sum of any two irrational numbers is irrational.

8. The difference of any two irrational numbers is irrational.

9. The positive square root of a positive irrational number is irrational.

10. If r is any rational number and s is any irrational number, then r/s is irrational.

11. The sum of any two positive irrational numbers is irrational.

12. The product of any two irrational numbers is irrational.

H 13. If an integer greater than 1 is a perfect square, then its cube root is irrational.

14. Give an example to show that if d is not prime and n^2 is divisible by d, then n need not be divisible by d.

15. a. Prove that for all integers a, if a^3 is even then a is even.
    b. Prove that $\sqrt[3]{2}$ is irrational.

16. a. Use proof by contradiction to show that for any integer n, it is impossible for n to equal both $3q_1 + r_1$ and $3q_2 + r_2$, where q_1, q_2, r_1, and r_2, are integers, $0 \leq r_1 < 3, 0 \leq r_2 < 3$, and $r_1 \neq r_2$.
    b. Use proof by contradiction, the quotient-remainder theorem, division into cases, and the result of part (a) to prove that for all integers n, if n^2 is divisible by 3 then n is divisible by 3.
    c. Prove that $\sqrt{3}$ is irrational.

17. Consider the following sentence: If x is rational then $\sqrt{x}$ is irrational. Is this sentence always true, sometimes true and sometimes false, or always false? Justify your answer.

H 18. The quotient-remainder theorem says not only that there exist quotients and remainders but also that the quotient and remainder of a division are unique. Prove the uniqueness. That is, prove that if a and d are integers with $d > 0$ and if $q_1, r_1, q_2,$ and r_2 are integers such that

$$a = dq_1 + r_1 \quad \text{where } 0 \le r_1 < d$$

and

$$a = dq_2 + r_2 \quad \text{where } 0 \le r_2 < d,$$

then

$$q_1 = q_2 \quad \text{and} \quad r_1 = r_2.$$

H 19. Prove that $\sqrt{5}$ is irrational.

H 20. Prove that for any integer a, $9 \nmid (a^2 - 3)$.

21. An alternative proof of the irrationality of $\sqrt{2}$ counts the number of 2's on the two sides of the equation $2n^2 = m^2$ and uses the unique factorization of integers theorem to deduce a contradiction. Write a proof that uses this approach.

22. Use the proof technique illustrated in exercise 21 to prove that if n is any positive integer that is not a perfect square, then $\sqrt{n}$ is irrational.

H 23. Prove that $\sqrt{2} + \sqrt{3}$ is irrational.

* 24. Prove that $\log_5(2)$ is irrational. (*Hint*: Use the unique factorisation of integers theorem.)

H 25. Let $N = 2 \cdot 3 \cdot 5 \cdot 7 + 1$. What remainder is obtained when N is divided by 2? 3? 5? 7? Is N prime? Justify your answer.

H 26. Suppose a is an integer and p is a prime number such that $p \mid a$ and $p \mid (a + 3)$. What can you deduce about p? Why?

27. Let $p_1, p_2, p_3, \ldots$ be a list of all prime numbers in ascending order. Here is a table of the first six:

p_1	p_2	p_3	p_4	p_5	p_6
2	3	5	7	11	13

H a. For each $i = 1, 2, 3, 4, 5, 6$, let $N_i = p_1 p_2 \cdots p_i + 1$. Calculate $N_1, N_2, N_3, N_4, N_5,$ and N_6.

b. For each $i = 1, 2, 3, 4, 5, 6$, find the smallest prime number q_i such that q_i divides N_i. (*Hint*: Use the test for primality from exercise 31 in Section 4.6 to determine your answers.)

For exercises 28 and 29, use the fact that for all integers n,

$$n! = n(n - 1) \ldots 3 \cdot 2 \cdot 1.$$

28. An alternative proof of the infinitude of the prime numbers begins as follows:

Proof: Suppose there are only finitely many prime numbers. Then one is the largest. Call it p. Let $M = p! + 1$. We will show that there is a prime number q such that $q > p$. Complete this proof.

H * 29. Prove that for all integers n, if $n > 2$ then there is a prime number p such that $n < p < n!$.

H * 30. Prove that if $p_1, p_2, \ldots,$ and p_n are distinct prime numbers with $p_1 = 2$ and $n > 1$, then $p_1 p_2 \cdots p_n + 1$ can be written in the form $4k + 3$ for some integer k.

H 31. a. Fermat's last theorem says that for all integers $n > 2$, the equation $x^n + y^n = z^n$ has no positive integer solution (solution for which x, y, and z are positive integers). Prove the following: If for all prime numbers $p > 2$, $x^p + y^p = z^p$ has no positive integer solution, then for any integer $n > 2$ that is not a power of 2, $x^n + y^n = z^n$ has no positive integer solution.

b. Fermat proved that there are no integers x, y, and z such that $x^4 + y^4 = z^4$. Use this result to remove the restriction in part (a) that n not be a power of 2. That is, prove that if n is a power of 2 and $n > 4$, then $x^n + y^n = z^n$ has no positive integer solution.

For exercises 32–35 note that to show there is a unique object with a certain property, show that (1) there is an object with the property and (2) if objects A and B have the property, then $A = B$.

32. Prove that there exists a unique prime number of the form $n^2 - 1$, where n is an integer that is greater than or equal to 2.

33. Prove that there exists a unique prime number of the form $n^2 + 2n - 3$, where n is a positive integer.

34. Prove that there is at most one real number a with the property that $a + r = r$ for all real numbers r. (Such a number is called an *additive identity*.)

35. Prove that there is at most one real number b with the property that $br = r$ for all real numbers r. (Such a number is called a *multiplicative identity*.)

Answers for Test Yourself

1. two integers   2. the integer is even; have a common factor greater than 1   3. $2 \cdot 3 \cdot 5 \cdot 7 \cdot 11 \cdots p + 1$; p

4.8 Application: Algorithms

Begin at the beginning . . . and go on till you come to the end: then stop.
— Lewis Carroll, *Alice's Adventures in Wonderland,* 1865

Lady Lovelace (1815–1852)

In this section we will show how the number theory facts developed in this chapter form the basis for some useful computer algorithms.

The word *algorithm* refers to a step-by-step method for performing some action. Some examples of algorithms in everyday life are food preparation recipes, directions for assembling equipment or hobby kits, sewing pattern instructions, and instructions for filling out income tax forms. Much of elementary school mathematics is devoted to learning algorithms for doing arithmetic such as multidigit addition and subtraction, multidigit (or long) multiplication, and long division.

The idea of a computer algorithm is credited to Ada Augusta, Countess of Lovelace. Trained as a mathematician, she became very interested in Charles Babbage's design for an "Analytical Engine," a machine similar in concept to a modern computer. Lady Lovelace extended Babbage's explorations of how such a machine would operate, recognizing that its importance lay "in the possibility of using a given sequence of instructions repeatedly, the number of times being either preassigned or dependent on the results of the computation." This is the essence of a modern computer algorithm.

An Algorithmic Language

The algorithmic language used in this book is a kind of pseudocode, combining elements of Pascal, C, Java, and VB.NET, and ordinary, but fairly precise, English. We will use some of the formal constructs of computer languages—such as assignment statements, loops, and so forth—but we will ignore the more technical details, such as the requirement for explicit end-of-statement delimiters, the range of integer values available on a particular installation, and so forth. The algorithms presented in this text are intended to be precise enough to be easily translated into virtually any high-level computer language.

In high-level computer languages, the term **variable** is used to refer to a specific storage location in a computer's memory. To say that the variable x has the value 3 means that the memory location corresponding to x contains the number 3. A given storage location can hold only one value at a time. So if a variable is given a new value during program execution, then the old value is erased. The **data type** of a variable indicates the set in which the variable takes its values, whether the set of integers, or real numbers, or character strings, or the set $\{0, 1\}$ (for a Boolean variable), and so forth.

An **assignment statement** gives a value to a variable. It has the form

$$x := e,$$

where x is a variable and e is an expression. This is read "x is assigned the value e" or "let x be e." When an assignment statement is executed, the expression e is evaluated (using the current values of all the variables in the expression), and then its value is placed in the memory location corresponding to x (replacing any previous contents of this location).

Ordinarily, algorithm statements are executed one after another in the order in which they are written. **Conditional statements** allow this natural order to be overridden by using the current values of program variables to determine which algorithm statement will be executed next. Conditional statements are denoted either

a. **if** *(condition)*   or   b. **if** *(condition)* **then** s_1

　　　then s_1

　　　else s_2

where *condition* is a predicate involving algorithm variables and where s_1 and s_2 are algorithm statements or groups of algorithm statements. We generally use indentation to indicate that statements belong together as a unit. When ambiguity is possible, however, we may explicitly bind a group of statements together into a unit by preceding the group with the word **do** and following it with the words **end do.**

Execution of an **if-then-else** statement occurs as follows:

1. The *condition* is evaluated by substituting the current values of all algorithm variables appearing in it and evaluating the truth or falsity of the resulting statement.

2. If *condition* is true, then s_1 is executed and execution moves to the next algorithm statement following the **if-then-else** statement.

3. If *condition* is false, then s_2 is executed and execution moves to the next algorithm statement following the **if-then-else** statement.

Execution of an **if-then** statement is similar to execution of an **if-then-else** statement, except that if *condition* is false, execution passes immediately to the next algorithm statement following the **if-then** statement.

Often *condition* is called a **guard** because it is stationed before s_1 and s_2 and restricts access to them.

Example 4.8.1 Execution of if-then-else and if-then Statements

Consider the following algorithm segments:

a. **if** $x > 2$ b. $y := 0$
    then $y := x + 1$ **if** $x > 2$ **then** $y := 2^x$
    else do $x := x - 1$
        $y := 3 \cdot x$ **end do**

What is the value of y after execution of these segments for the following values of x?

i. $x = 5$ ii. $x = 2$

Solution

a.   (i) Because the value of x is 5 before execution, the guard condition $x > 2$ is true at the time it is evaluated. Hence the statement following **then** is executed, and so the value of $x + 1 = 5 + 1$ is computed and placed in the storage location corresponding to y. So after execution, $y = 6$.

     (ii) Because the value of x is 2 before execution, the guard condition $x > 2$ is false at the time it is evaluated. Hence the statement following **else** is executed. The value of $x - 1 = 2 - 1$ is computed and placed in the storage location corresponding to x, and the value of $3 \cdot x = 3 \cdot 1$ is computed and placed in the storage location corresponding to y. So after execution, $y = 3$.

b.   (i) Since $x = 5$ initially, the condition $x > 2$ is true at the time it is evaluated. So the statement following **then** is executed, and y obtains the value $2^5 = 32$.

     (ii) Since $x = 2$ initially, the condition $x > 2$ is false at the time it is evaluated. Execution, therefore, moves to the next statement following the if-then statement, and the value of y does not change from its initial value of 0.   ■

Iterative statements are used when a sequence of algorithm statements is to be executed over and over again. We will use two types of iterative statements: **while** loops and **for-next** loops.

A **while** loop has the form

$$\textbf{while } (condition)$$

*[statements that make up
the body of the loop]*

end while

where *condition* is a predicate involving algorithm variables. The word **while** marks the beginning of the loop, and the words **end while** mark its end. Execution of a **while** loop occurs as follows:

1. The *condition* is evaluated by substituting the current values of all the algorithm variables and evaluating the truth or falsity of the resulting statement.

2. If *condition* is true, all the statements in the body of the loop are executed in order. Then execution moves back to the beginning of the loop and the process repeats.

3. If *condition* is false, execution passes to the next algorithm statement following the loop.

The loop is said to be **iterated** (IT-a-rate-ed) each time the statements in the body of the loop are executed. Each execution of the body of the loop is called an **iteration** (it-er-AY-shun) of the loop.

Example 4.8.2 Tracing Execution of a **while** Loop

Trace the execution of the following algorithm segment by finding the values of all the algorithm variables each time they are changed during execution:

$$i := 1, s := 0$$
$$\textbf{while } (i \leq 2)$$
$$s := s + i$$
$$i := i + 1$$
$$\textbf{end while}$$

Solution Since i is given an initial value of 1, the condition $i \leq 2$ is true when the **while** loop is entered. So the statements within the loop are executed in order:

$$s = 0 + 1 = 1 \quad \text{and} \quad i = 1 + 1 = 2.$$

Then execution passes back to the beginning of the loop.

The condition $i \leq 2$ is evaluated using the current value of i, which is 2. The condition is true, and so the statements within the loop are executed again:

$$s = 1 + 2 = 3 \quad \text{and} \quad i = 2 + 1 = 3.$$

Then execution passes back to the beginning of the loop.

The condition $i \leq 2$ is evaluated using the current value of i, which is 3. This time the condition is false, and so execution passes beyond the loop to the next statement of the algorithm.

This discussion can be summarized in a table, called a **trace table,** that shows the current values of algorithm variables at various points during execution. The trace table for a **while** loop generally gives all values immediately following each iteration of the loop. ("After the zeroth iteration" means the same as "before the first iteration.")

Trace Table

		Iteration Number		
		0	1	2
Variable Name	i	1	2	3
	s	0	1	3

The second form of iteration we will use is a **for-next** loop. A **for-next** loop has the following form:

> **for** *variable* := *initial expression* **to** *final expression*
>
> *[statements that make up*
> *the body of the loop]*
>
> **next** *(same) variable*

A **for-next** loop is executed as follows:

1. The **for-next** loop *variable* is set equal to the value of *initial expression*.

2. A check is made to determine whether the value of *variable* is less than or equal to the value of *final expression*.

3. If the value of *variable* is less than or equal to the value of *final expression*, then the statements in the body of the loop are executed in order, *variable* is increased by 1, and execution returns back to step 2.

4. If the value of *variable* is greater than the value of *final expression*, then execution passes to the next algorithm statement following the loop.

Example 4.8.3 Trace Table for a for-next Loop

Convert the **for-next** loop shown below into a **while** loop. Construct a trace table for the loop.

> **for** $i := 1$ **to** 4
> $x := i^2$
> **next** i

Solution The given **for-next** loop is equivalent to the following:

> $i := 1$
> **while** $(i \leq 4)$
> $x := i^2$
> $i := i + 1$
> **end while**

Its trace table is as follows:

Trace Table

		Iteration Number				
		0	1	2	3	4
Variable Name	x		1	4	9	16
	i	1	2	3	4	5

A Notation for Algorithms

We will express algorithms as subroutines that can be called upon by other algorithms as needed and used to transform a set of input variables with given values into a set of output variables with specific values. The output variables and their values are assumed to be returned to the calling algorithm. For example, the division algorithm specifies a procedure for taking any two positive integers as input and producing the quotient and remainder of the division of one number by the other as output. Whenever an algorithm requires such a computation, the algorithm can just "call" the division algorithm to do the job.

We generally include the following information when describing algorithms formally:

1. The name of the algorithm, together with a list of input and output variables.

2. A brief description of how the algorithm works.

3. The input variable names, labeled by data type (whether integer, real number, and so forth).

4. The statements that make up the body of the algorithm, possibly with explanatory comments.

5. The output variable names, labeled by data type.

al-Khowârizmî
(ca. 780–850)

You may wonder where the word *algorithm* came from. It evolved from the last part of the name of the Persian mathematician Abu Ja'far Mohammed ibn Mûsâ al-Khowârizmî. During Europe's Dark Ages, the Arabic world enjoyed a period of intense intellectual activity. One of the great mathematical works of that period was a book written by al-Khowârizmî that contained foundational ideas for the subject of algebra. The translation of this book into Latin in the thirteenth century had a profound influence on the development of mathematics during the European Renaissance.

The Division Algorithm

For an integer a and a positive integer d, the quotient-remainder theorem guarantees the existence of integers q and r such that

$$a = dq + r \quad \text{and} \quad 0 \leq r < d.$$

In this section, we give an algorithm to calculate q and r for given a and d where a is nonnegative. (The extension to negative a is left to the exercises at the end of this section.) The following example illustrates the idea behind the algorithm. Consider trying to find the quotient and the remainder of the division of 32 by 9, but suppose that you do not remember your multiplication table and have to figure out the answer from basic principles. The quotient represents that number of 9's that are contained in 32. The remainder is the number left over when all possible groups of 9 are subtracted. Thus you can calculate the quotient and remainder by repeatedly subtracting 9 from 32 until you obtain a number less than 9:

$$32 - 9 = 23 \geq 9, \text{ and}$$
$$32 - 9 - 9 = 14 \geq 9, \text{ and}$$
$$32 - 9 - 9 - 9 = 5 < 9.$$

This shows that 3 groups of 9 can be subtracted from 32 with 5 left over. Thus the quotient is 3 and the remainder is 5.

Algorithm 4.8.1 Division Algorithm

[Given a nonnegative integer a and a positive integer d, the aim of the algorithm is to find integers q and r that satisfy the conditions $a = dq + r$ and $0 \leq r < d$. This is done by subtracting d repeatedly from a until the result is less than d but is still nonnegative.

$$0 \leq a - d - d - d - \cdots - d = a - dq < d.$$

The total number of d's that are subtracted is the quotient q. The quantity $a - dq$ equals the remainder r.]

Input: *a [a nonnegative integer], d [a positive integer]*

Algorithm Body:

    $r := a, q := 0$

    [Repeatedly subtract d from r until a number less than d is obtained. Add 1 to q each time d is subtracted.]

    while $(r \geq d)$

        $r := r - d$

        $q := q + 1$

    end while

    *[After execution of the **while** loop, $a = dq + r$.]*

Output: *q, r [nonnegative integers]*

Note that the values of q and r obtained from the division algorithm are the same as those computed by the *div* and *mod* functions built into a number of computer languages. That is, if q and r are the quotient and remainder obtained from the division algorithm with input a and d, then the output variables q and r satisfy

$$q = a \ div \ d \quad \text{and} \quad r = a \ mod \ d.$$

The next example asks for a trace of the division algorithm.

Example 4.8.4 Tracing the Division Algorithm

Trace the action of Algorithm 4.8.1 on the input variables $a = 19$ and $d = 4$.

Solution   Make a trace table as shown below. The column under the kth iteration gives the states of the variables after the kth iteration of the loop.

		Iteration Number				
		0	1	2	3	4
	a	19				
Variable Name	d	4				
	r	19	15	11	7	3
	q	0	1	2	3	4

The Euclidean Algorithm

The greatest common divisor of two integers a and b is the largest integer that divides both a and b. For example, the greatest common divisor of 12 and 30 is 6. The Euclidean algorithm provides a very efficient way to compute the greatest common divisor of two integers.

• Definition

Let a and b be integers that are not both zero. The **greatest common divisor** of a and b, denoted **gcd(a, b)**, is that integer d with the following properties:

1. d is a common divisor of both a and b. In other words,

$$d \mid a \quad \text{and} \quad d \mid b.$$

2. For all integers c, if c is a common divisor of both a and b, then c is less than or equal to d. In other words,

$$\text{for all integers } c, \text{ if } c \mid a \text{ and } c \mid b, \text{ then } c \leq d.$$

Example 4.8.5 Calculating Some gcd's

a. Find gcd(72, 63).

b. Find gcd($10^{20}, 6^{30}$).

c. In the definition of greatest common divisor, gcd(0, 0) is not allowed. Why not? What would gcd(0, 0) equal if it were found in the same way as the greatest common divisors for other pairs of numbers?

Solution

a. $72 = 9 \cdot 8$ and $63 = 9 \cdot 7$. So $9 \mid 72$ and $9 \mid 63$, and no integer larger than 9 divides both 72 and 63. Hence gcd(72, 63) $= 9$.

b. By the laws of exponents, $10^{20} = 2^{20} \cdot 5^{20}$ and $6^{30} = 2^{30} \cdot 3^{30} = 2^{20} \cdot 2^{10} \cdot 3^{30}$. It follows that

$$2^{20} \mid 10^{20} \quad \text{and} \quad 2^{20} \mid 6^{30},$$

and by the unique factorization of integers theorem, no integer larger than 2^{20} divides both 10^{20} and 6^{30} (because no more than twenty 2's divide 10^{20}, no 3's divide 10^{20}, and no 5's divide 6^{30}). Hence gcd($10^{20}, 6^{30}$) $= 2^{20}$.

c. Suppose gcd(0, 0) were defined to be the largest common factor that divides 0 and 0. The problem is that *every* positive integer divides 0 and there is no largest integer. So there is no largest common divisor! ∎

Calculating gcd's using the approach illustrated in Example 4.8.5 works only when the numbers can be factored completely. By the unique factorization of integers theorem, all numbers can, in principle, be factored completely. But, in practice, even using the highest-speed computers, the process is unfeasibly long for very large integers. Over 2,000 years ago, Euclid devised a method for finding greatest common divisors that is easy to use and is much more efficient than either factoring the numbers or repeatedly testing both numbers for divisibility by successively larger integers.

The Euclidean algorithm is based on the following two facts, which are stated as lemmas.

Lemma 4.8.1

If r is a positive integer, then $\gcd(r, 0) = r$.

Proof:

Suppose r is a positive integer. *[We must show that the greatest common divisor of both r and 0 is r.]* Certainly, r is a common divisor of both r and 0 because r divides itself and also r divides 0 (since every positive integer divides 0). Also no integer larger than r can be a common divisor of r and 0 (since no integer larger than r can divide r). Hence r is the greatest common divisor of r and 0.

The proof of the second lemma is based on a clever pattern of argument that is used in many different areas of mathematics: To prove that $A = B$, prove that $A \leq B$ and that $B \leq A$.

Lemma 4.8.2

If a and b are any integers not both zero, and if q and r are any integers such that

$$a = bq + r,$$

then

$$\gcd(a, b) = \gcd(b, r).$$

Proof:

[The proof is divided into two sections: (1) proof that $\gcd(a, b) \leq \gcd(b, r)$, and (2) proof that $\gcd(b, r) \leq \gcd(a, b)$. Since each $\gcd$ is less than or equal to the other, the two must be equal.]

1. **gcd (a, b) ≤ gcd (b, r):**

   a. *[We will first show that any common divisor of a and b is also a common divisor of b and r.]*

      Let a and b be integers, not both zero, and let c be a common divisor of a and b. Then $c \mid a$ and $c \mid b$, and so, by definition of divisibility, $a = nc$ and $b = mc$, for some integers n and m. Now substitute into the equation

      $$a = bq + r$$

   to obtain

      $$nc = (mc)q + r.$$

   Then solve for r:

      $$r = nc - (mc)q = (n - mq)c.$$

   But $n - mq$ is an integer, and so, by definition of divisibility, $c \mid r$. Because we already know that $c \mid b$, we can conclude that c is a common divisor of b and r *[as was to be shown].*

continued on page 222

b. *[Next we show that* $\gcd(a, b) \leq \gcd(b, r)$.*]*

By part (a), every common divisor of a and b is a common divisor of b and r. It follows that the greatest common divisor of a and b is defined because a and b are not both zero, and it is a common divisor of b and r. But then $\gcd(a, b)$ (being one of the common divisors of b and r) is less than or equal to the greatest common divisor of b and r:

$$\gcd(a, b) \leq \gcd(b, r).$$

2. **gcd (b, r) ≤ gcd (a, b):**

The second part of the proof is very similar to the first part. It is left as an exercise.

The Euclidean algorithm can be described as follows:

1. Let A and B be integers with $A > B \geq 0$.

2. To find the greatest common divisor of A and B, first check whether $B = 0$. If it is, then $\gcd(A, B) = A$ by Lemma 4.8.1. If it isn't, then $B > 0$ and the quotient-remainder theorem can be used to divide A by B to obtain a quotient q and a remainder r:

$$A = Bq + r \quad \text{where } 0 \leq r < B.$$

By Lemma 4.8.2, $\gcd(A, B) = \gcd(B, r)$. Thus the problem of finding the greatest common divisor of A and B is reduced to the problem of finding the greatest common divisor of B and r.

What makes this piece of information useful is that B and r are smaller numbers than A and B. To see this, recall that we assumed

$$A > B \geq 0.$$

Also the r found by the quotient-remainder theorem satisfies

$$0 \leq r < B.$$

Putting these two inequalities together gives

$$0 \leq r < B < A.$$

So the larger number of the pair (B, r) is smaller than the larger number of the pair (A, B).

Note Strictly speaking, the fact that the repetitions eventually terminate is justified by the well-ordering principle for the integers, which is discussed in Section 5.4.

3. Now just repeat the process, starting again at (2), but use B instead of A and r instead of B. The repetitions are guaranteed to terminate eventually with $r = 0$ because each new remainder is less than the preceding one and all are nonnegative.

By the way, it is always the case that the number of steps required in the Euclidean algorithm is at most five times the number of digits in the smaller integer. This was proved by the French mathematician Gabriel Lamé (1795–1870).

The following example illustrates how to use the Euclidean algorithm.

Example 4.8.6 Hand-Calculation of gcd's Using the Euclidean Algorithm

Use the Euclidean algorithm to find gcd(330, 156).

Solution

1. Divide 330 by 156:

$$
\begin{array}{r}
2 \leftarrow \text{quotient} \\
156\overline{)330} \\
\underline{312} \\
18 \leftarrow \text{remainder}
\end{array}
$$

Thus $330 = 156 \cdot 2 + 18$ and hence $\gcd(330, 156) = \gcd(156, 18)$ by Lemma 4.8.2.

2. Divide 156 by 18:

$$
\begin{array}{r}
8 \leftarrow \text{quotient} \\
18\overline{)156} \\
\underline{144} \\
12 \leftarrow \text{remainder}
\end{array}
$$

Thus $156 = 18 \cdot 8 + 12$ and hence $\gcd(156, 18) = \gcd(18, 12)$ by Lemma 4.8.2.

3. Divide 18 by 12:

$$
\begin{array}{r}
1 \leftarrow \text{quotient} \\
12\overline{)18} \\
\underline{12} \\
6 \leftarrow \text{remainder}
\end{array}
$$

Thus $18 = 12 \cdot 1 + 6$ and hence $\gcd(18, 12) = \gcd(12, 6)$ by Lemma 4.8.2.

4. Divide 12 by 6:

$$
\begin{array}{r}
2 \leftarrow \text{quotient} \\
6\overline{)12} \\
\underline{12} \\
0 \leftarrow \text{remainder}
\end{array}
$$

Thus $12 = 6 \cdot 2 + 0$ and hence $\gcd(12, 6) = \gcd(6, 0)$ by Lemma 4.8.2.

Putting all the equations above together gives

$$
\begin{aligned}
\gcd(330, 156) &= \gcd(156, 18) \\
&= \gcd(18, 12) \\
&= \gcd(12, 6) \\
&= \gcd(6, 0) \\
&= 6 \qquad \text{by Lemma 4.8.1.}
\end{aligned}
$$

Therefore, $\gcd(330, 156) = 6$. ■

The following is a version of the Euclidean algorithm written using formal algorithm notation.

Algorithm 4.8.2 Euclidean Algorithm

[Given two integers A and B with $A > B \geq 0$, this algorithm computes $\gcd(A, B)$. It is based on two facts:

1. $\gcd(a, b) = \gcd(b, r)$ *if $a, b, q,$ and r are integers with $a = b \cdot q + r$ and $0 \leq r < b$.*

2. $\gcd(a, 0) = a.]$

Input: A, B *[integers with $A > B \geq 0$]*

Algorithm Body:

    $a := A, b := B, r := B$

    [If $b \neq 0$, compute a mod b, the remainder of the integer division of a by b, and set r equal to this value. Then repeat the process using b in place of a and r in place of b.]

    while $(b \neq 0)$

        $r := a \bmod b$

    [The value of a mod b can be obtained by calling the division algorithm.]

        $a := b$

        $b := r$

    end while

    *[After execution of the **while** loop, $\gcd(A, B) = a.]$*

    $\gcd := a$

Output: gcd *[a positive integer]*

Test Yourself

1. When an algorithm statement of the form $x := e$ is executed, _____.

2. Consider an algorithm statement of the following form.

    if (*condition*)

    then s_1

    else s_2

    When such a statement is executed, the truth or falsity of the *condition* is evaluated. If *condition* is true, _____. If *condition* is false, _____.

3. Consider an algorithm statement of the following form.

    while (*condition*)

    [statements that make up the body of the loop]

    end while

    When such a statement is executed, the truth or falsity of the *condition* is evaluated. If *condition* is true, _____. If *condition* is false, _____.

4. Consider an algorithm statement of the following form.

    for *variable* := *initial expression* **to** *final expression.*

    [statements that make up the body of the loop]

    next (*same*) *variable*

When such a statement is executed, *variable* is set equal to the value of the *initial expression*, and a check is made to determine whether the value of *variable* is less than or equal to the value of *final expression*. If so, _____. If not, _____.

5. Given a nonnegative integer a and a positive integer d the division algorithm computes _____.

6. Given integers a and b, not both zero, $\gcd(a, b)$ is the integer d that satisfies the following two conditions: _____ and _____.

7. If r is a positive integer, then $\gcd(r, 0) =$ _____.

8. If a and b are integers not both zero and if q and r are nonnegative integers such that $a = bq + r$ then $\gcd(a, b) =$ _____.

9. Given positive integers A and B with $A > B$, the Euclidean algorithm computes _____.

Exercise Set 4.8

Find the value of z when each of the algorithm segments in 1 and 2 is executed.

1. $i := 2$
   if $(i > 3$ or $i \leq 0)$
      then $z := 1$
      else $z := 0$

2. $i := 3$
   if $(i \leq 3$ or $i > 6)$
      then $z := 2$
      else $z := 0$

3. Consider the following algorithm segment:

   if $x \cdot y > 0$ then do $y := 3 \cdot x$
                    $x := x + 1$ end do
     $z := x \cdot y$

   Find the value of z if prior to execution x and y have the values given below.
   a. $x = 2, y = 3$ b. $x = 1, y = 1$

Find the values of a and e after execution of the loops in 4 and 5:

4. $a := 2$
   for $i := 1$ to 2
      $a := \dfrac{a}{2} + \dfrac{1}{a}$
   next i

5. $e := 0, f := 2$
   for $j := 1$ to 4
      $f := f \cdot j$
      $e := e + \dfrac{1}{f}$
   next j

Make a trace table to trace the action of Algorithm 4.8.1 for the input variables given in 6 and 7.

6. $a = 26, d = 7$ 7. $a = 59, d = 13$

8. The following algorithm segment makes change; given an amount of money A between 1¢ and 99¢, it determines a breakdown of A into quarters (q), dimes (d), nickels (n), and pennies (p).

   $$q := A \ div \ 25$$
   $$A := A \ mod \ 25$$
   $$d := A \ div \ 10$$
   $$A := A \ mod \ 10$$
   $$n := A \ div \ 5$$
   $$p := A \ mod \ 5$$

   a. Trace this algorithm segment for $A = 69$.
   b. Trace this algorithm segment for $A = 87$.

Find the greatest common divisor of each of the pairs of integers in 9–12. (Use any method you wish.)

9. 27 and 72   10. 5 and 9

11. 7 and 21   12. 48 and 54

Use the Euclidean algorithm to hand-calculate the greatest common divisors of each of the pairs of integers in 13–16.

13. 1,188 and 385   14. 509 and 1,177

15. 832 and 10,933   16. 4,131 and 2,431

Make a trace table to trace the action of Algorithm 4.8.2 for the input variables given in 17 and 18.

17. 1,001 and 871   18. 5,859 and 1,232

H 19. Prove that for all positive integers a and b, $a \mid b$ if, and only if, $\gcd(a, b) = a$. (Note that to prove "A if, and only if, B," you need to prove "if A then B" and "if B then A.")

20. a. Prove that if a and b are integers, not both zero, and $d = \gcd(a, b)$, then a/d and b/d are integers with no common divisor that is greater than one.
   b. Write an algorithm that accepts the numerator and denominator of a fraction as input and produces as output the numerator and denominator of that fraction written in lowest terms. (The algorithm may call upon the Euclidean algorithm as needed.)

21. Complete the proof of Lemma 4.8.2 by proving the following: If a and b are any integers with $b \neq 0$ and q and r are any integers such that

   $$a = bq + r.$$

   then $\gcd(b, r) \leq \gcd(a, b)$.

H 22. a. Prove: If a and d are positive integers and q and r are integers such that $a = dq + r$ and $0 < r < d$, then

   $$-a = d(-(q + 1)) + (d - r)$$

   and $0 < d - r < d$.

   b. Indicate how to modify Algorithm 4.8.1 to allow for the input a to be negative.

23. a. Prove that if a, d, q, and r are integers such that $a = dq + r$ and $0 \leq r < d$, then

   $$q = \lfloor a/d \rfloor \quad \text{and} \quad r = a - \lfloor a/d \rfloor \cdot d.$$

   b. In a computer language with a built-in-floor function, div and mod can be calculated as follows:

   $$a \ div \ d = \lfloor a/d \rfloor \quad \text{and} \quad a \ mod \ d = a - \lfloor a/d \rfloor \cdot d.$$

   Rewrite the steps of Algorithm 4.8.2 for a computer language with a built-in floor function but without div and mod.

24. An alternative to the Euclidean algorithm uses subtraction rather than division to compute greatest common divisors. (After all, division is repeated subtraction.) It is based on the following lemma:

   Lemma 4.8.3

   If $a \geq b > 0$, then $\gcd(a, b) = \gcd(b, a - b)$.

Algorithm 4.8.3 Computing gcd's by Subtraction

[Given two positive integers A and B, variables a and b are set equal to A and B. Then a repetitive process begins. If a $\neq$ 0, and b $\neq$ 0, then the larger of a and b is set equal to a − b (if a $\geq$ b) or to b − a (if a < b), and the smaller of a and b is left unchanged. This process is repeated over and over until eventually a or b becomes 0. By Lemma 4.8.3, after each repetition of the process,

$$gcd(A, B) = gcd(a, b).$$

After the last repetition,

$$gcd(A, B) = gcd(a, 0) \quad or \quad gcd(A, B) = gcd(0, b)$$

depending on whether a or b is nonzero. But by Lemma 4.8.1,

$$gcd(a, 0) = a \quad and \quad gcd(0, b) = b.$$

Hence, after the last repetition,

$$gcd(A, B) = a \ if \ a \neq 0 \quad or \quad gcd(A, B) = b \ if \ b \neq 0.]$$

Input: A, B *[positive integers]*
Algorithm Body:
  $a := A, b := B$
  while ($a \neq 0$ and $b \neq 0$)
    if $a \geq b$ **then** $a := a - b$
      else $b := b - a$
  end while
    if $a = 0$ **then** gcd $:= b$
    else gcd $:= a$
    *[After execution of the **if-then-else** statement,*
    gcd = gcd(A, B).]
Output: gcd *[a positive integer]*

a. Prove Lemma 4.8.3.
b. Trace the execution of Algorithm 4.8.3 for $A = 630$ and $B = 336$.
c. Trace the execution of Algorithm 4.8.3 for $A = 768$ and $B = 348$.

Exercises 25–29 refer to the following definition.

Definition: The **least common multiple** of two nonzero integers a and b, denoted **lcm(a, b)**, is the positive integer c such that
a. $a \mid c$ and $b \mid c$
b. for all positive integers m, if $a \mid m$ and $b \mid m$, then $c \leq m$.

25. Find
  a. lcm(12, 18)   b. lcm($2^2 \cdot 3 \cdot 5, 2^3 \cdot 3^2$)
  c. lcm(2800, 6125)

26. Prove that for all positive integers a and b, gcd$(a, b) =$ lcm(a, b) if, and only if, $a = b$.

27. Prove that for all positive integers a and b, $a \mid b$ if, and only if, lcm$(a, b) = b$.

28. Prove that for all integers a and b, gcd$(a, b) \mid$ lcm(a, b).

H 29. Prove that for all positive integers a and b,
  gcd$(a, b) \cdot$ lcm$(a, b) = ab$.

Answers for Test Yourself

1. the expression *e* is evaluated (using the current values of all the variables in the expression), and this value is placed in the memory location corresponding to *x* (replacing any previous contents of the location)   2. statement s_1 is executed; statement s_2 is executed   3. all statements in the body of the loop are executed in order and then execution moves back to the beginning of the loop and the process repeats; execution passes to the next algorithm statement following the loop   4. the statements in the body of the loop are executed in order, *variable* is increased by 1, and execution returns to the top of the loop; execution passes to the next algorithm statement following the loop   5. integers *q* and *r* with the property that $n = dq + r$ and $0 \leq r < d$ 6. *d* divides both *a* and *b*; if *c* is a common divisor of both *a* and *b*, then $c \leq d$ 7. *r*   8. gcd(b, r) 9. the greatest common divisor of *A* and *B* (*Or*: gcd(A,B))

CHAPTER 5

SEQUENCES, MATHEMATICAL INDUCTION, AND RECURSION

One of the most important tasks of mathematics is to discover and characterize regular patterns, such as those associated with processes that are repeated. The main mathematical structure used in the study of repeated processes is the *sequence,* and the main mathematical tool used to verify conjectures about sequences is *mathematical induction.* In this chapter we introduce the notation and terminology of sequences, show how to use both ordinary and strong mathematical induction to prove properties about them, illustrate the various ways recursively defined sequences arise, describe a method for obtaining an explicit formula for a recursively defined sequence, and explain how to verify the correctness of such a formula. We also discuss a principle—the well-ordering principle for the integers—that is logically equivalent to the two forms of mathematical induction, and we show how to adapt mathematical induction to prove the correctness of computer algorithms. In the final section we discuss more general recursive definitions, such as the one used for the careful formulation of the concept of Boolean expression, and the idea of recursive function.

5.1 Sequences

A mathematician, like a painter or poet, is a maker of patterns.
— G. H. Hardy, *A Mathematician's Apology,* 1940

Imagine that a person decides to count his ancestors. He has two parents, four grandparents, eight great-grandparents, and so forth, These numbers can be written in a row as

$$2, 4, 8, 16, 32, 64, 128, \ldots$$

The symbol "..." is called an *ellipsis.* It is shorthand for "and so forth."

To express the pattern of the numbers, suppose that each is labeled by an integer giving its position in the row.

Position in the row	1	2	3	4	5	6	7 ...
Number of ancestors	2	4	8	16	32	64	128 ...

The number corresponding to position 1 is 2, which equals 2^1. The number corresponding to position 2 is 4, which equals 2^2. For positions 3, 4, 5, 6, and 7, the corresponding

Note Strictly speaking, the true value of A_k is less than 2^k when k is large, because ancestors from one branch of the family tree may also appear on other branches of the tree.

numbers are 8, 16, 32, 64, and 128, which equal 2^3, 2^4, 2^5, 2^6, and 2^7, respectively. For a general value of k, let A_k be the number of ancestors in the kth generation back. The pattern of computed values strongly suggests the following for each k:

$$A_k = 2^k.$$

> **• Definition**
>
> A **sequence** is a function whose domain is either all the integers between two given integers or all the integers greater than or equal to a given integer.

We typically represent a sequence as a set of elements written in a row. In the sequence denoted

$$a_m, a_{m+1}, a_{m+2}, \ldots, a_n,$$

each individual element a_k (read "a sub k") is called a **term**. The k in a_k is called a **subscript** or **index,** m (which may be any integer) is the subscript of the **initial term,** and n (which must be greater than or equal to m) is the subscript of the **final term.** The notation

$$a_m, a_{m+1}, a_{m+2}, \ldots$$

denotes an **infinite sequence.** An **explicit formula** or **general formula** for a sequence is a rule that shows how the values of a_k depend on k.

The following example shows that it is possible for two different formulas to give sequences with the same terms.

Example 5.1.1 Finding Terms of Sequences Given by Explicit Formulas

Define sequences $a_1, a_2, a_3, \ldots$ and $b_2, b_3, b_4, \ldots$ by the following explicit formulas:

$$a_k = \frac{k}{k+1} \quad \text{for all integers } k \geq 1,$$

$$b_i = \frac{i-1}{i} \quad \text{for all integers } i \geq 2.$$

Compute the first five terms of both sequences.

Solution

$$a_1 = \frac{1}{1+1} = \frac{1}{2} \qquad b_2 = \frac{2-1}{2} = \frac{1}{2}$$

$$a_2 = \frac{2}{2+1} = \frac{2}{3} \qquad b_3 = \frac{3-1}{3} = \frac{2}{3}$$

$$a_3 = \frac{3}{3+1} = \frac{3}{4} \qquad b_4 = \frac{4-1}{4} = \frac{3}{4}$$

$$a_4 = \frac{4}{4+1} = \frac{4}{5} \qquad b_5 = \frac{5-1}{5} = \frac{4}{5}$$

$$a_5 = \frac{5}{5+1} = \frac{5}{6} \qquad b_6 = \frac{6-1}{6} = \frac{5}{6}$$

As you can see, the first terms of both sequences are $\frac{1}{2}, \frac{2}{3}, \frac{3}{4}, \frac{4}{5}, \frac{5}{6}$; in fact, it can be shown that all terms of both sequences are identical. ∎

The next example shows that an infinite sequence may have a finite number of values.

Example 5.1.2 An Alternating Sequence

Compute the first six terms of the sequence $c_0, c_1, c_2, \ldots$ defined as follows:

$$c_j = (-1)^j \quad \text{for all integers } j \geq 0.$$

Solution
$$c_0 = (-1)^0 = 1$$
$$c_1 = (-1)^1 = -1$$
$$c_2 = (-1)^2 = 1$$
$$c_3 = (-1)^3 = -1$$
$$c_4 = (-1)^4 = 1$$
$$c_5 = (-1)^5 = -1$$

Thus the first six terms are $1, -1, 1, -1, 1, -1$. By exercises 33 and 34 of Section 4.1, even powers of -1 equal 1 and odd powers of -1 equal -1. It follows that the sequence oscillates endlessly between 1 and -1. ∎

In Examples 5.1.1 and 5.1.2 the task was to compute the first few values of a sequence given by an explicit formula. The next example treats the question of how to find an explicit formula for a sequence with given initial terms. Any such formula is a guess, but it is very useful to be able to make such guesses.

Example 5.1.3 Finding an Explicit Formula to Fit Given Initial Terms

Find an explicit formula for a sequence that has the following initial terms:

$$1, \quad -\frac{1}{4}, \quad \frac{1}{9}, \quad -\frac{1}{16}, \quad \frac{1}{25}, \quad -\frac{1}{36}, \ldots$$

Solution   Denote the general term of the sequence by a_k and suppose the first term is a_1. Then observe that the denominator of each term is a perfect square. Thus the terms can be rewritten as

$$\frac{1}{1^2}, \quad \frac{(-1)}{2^2}, \quad \frac{1}{3^2}, \quad \frac{(-1)}{4^2}, \quad \frac{1}{5^2}, \quad \frac{(-1)}{6^2}.$$
$$\quad \updownarrow \qquad \updownarrow \qquad \updownarrow \qquad \updownarrow \qquad \updownarrow \qquad \updownarrow$$
$$\quad a_1 \qquad a_2 \qquad a_3 \qquad a_4 \qquad a_5 \qquad a_6$$

Note that the denominator of each term equals the square of the subscript of that term, and that the numerator equals ± 1. Hence

$$a_k = \frac{\pm 1}{k^2}.$$

Also the numerator oscillates back and forth between $+1$ and -1; it is $+1$ when k is odd and -1 when k is even. To achieve this oscillation, insert a factor of $(-1)^{k+1}$ (or $(-1)^{k-1}$) into the formula for a_k. *[For when k is odd, $k + 1$ is even and thus $(-1)^{k+1} = +1$; and when k is even, $k + 1$ is odd and thus $(-1)^{k+1} = -1$.]* Consequently, an explicit formula that gives the correct first six terms is

$$a_k = \frac{(-1)^{k+1}}{k^2} \quad \text{for all integers } k \geq 1.$$

Note that making the first term a_0 would have led to the alternative formula

$$a_k = \frac{(-1)^k}{(k+1)^2} \quad \text{for all integers } k \geq 0.$$

You should check that this formula also gives the correct first six terms. ■

Summation Notation

Consider again the example in which $A_k = 2^k$ represents the number of ancestors a person has in the kth generation back. What is the total number of ancestors for the past six generations? The answer is

$$A_1 + A_2 + A_3 + A_4 + A_5 + A_6 = 2^1 + 2^2 + 2^3 + 2^4 + 2^5 + 2^6 = 126.$$

It is convenient to use a shorthand notation to write such sums. In 1772 the French mathematician Joseph Louis Lagrange introduced the capital Greek letter sigma, Σ, to denote the word *sum* (or *summation*), and defined the summation notation as follows:

CORBIS

Joseph Louis Lagrange (1736–1813)

• Definition

If m and n are integers and $m \leq n$, the symbol $\displaystyle\sum_{k=m}^{n} a_k$, read the **summation from k equals m to n of a-sub-k**, is the sum of all the terms $a_m, a_{m+1}, a_{m+2}, \ldots, a_n$. We say that $a_m + a_{m+1} + a_{m+2} + \ldots + a_n$ is the **expanded form** of the sum, and we write

$$\sum_{k=m}^{n} a_k = a_m + a_{m+1} + a_{m+2} + \cdots + a_n.$$

We call k the **index** of the summation, m the **lower limit** of the summation, and n the **upper limit** of the summation.

Example 5.1.4 Computing Summations

Let $a_1 = -2, a_2 = -1, a_3 = 0, a_4 = 1$, and $a_5 = 2$. Compute the following:

a. $\displaystyle\sum_{k=1}^{5} a_k$ b. $\displaystyle\sum_{k=2}^{2} a_k$ c. $\displaystyle\sum_{k=1}^{2} a_{2k}$

Solution

a. $\displaystyle\sum_{k=1}^{5} a_k = a_1 + a_2 + a_3 + a_4 + a_5 = (-2) + (-1) + 0 + 1 + 2 = 0$

b. $\displaystyle\sum_{k=2}^{2} a_k = a_2 = -1$

c. $\displaystyle\sum_{k=1}^{2} a_{2k} = a_{2 \cdot 1} + a_{2 \cdot 2} = a_2 + a_4 = -1 + 1 = 0$ ■

Oftentimes, the terms of a summation are expressed using an explicit formula. For instance, it is common to see summations such as

$$\sum_{k=1}^{5} k^2 \quad \text{or} \quad \sum_{i=0}^{8} \frac{(-1)^i}{i+1}.$$

Example 5.1.5 When the Terms of a Summation Are Given by a Formula

Compute the following summation:

$$\sum_{k=1}^{5} k^2.$$

Solution
$$\sum_{k=1}^{5} k^2 = 1^2 + 2^2 + 3^2 + 4^2 + 5^2 = 55.$$
∎

When the upper limit of a summation is a variable, an ellipsis is used to write the summation in expanded form.

Example 5.1.6 Changing from Summation Notation to Expanded Form

Write the following summation in expanded form:

$$\sum_{i=0}^{n} \frac{(-1)^i}{i+1}.$$

Solution
$$\sum_{i=0}^{n} \frac{(-1)^i}{i+1} = \frac{(-1)^0}{0+1} + \frac{(-1)^1}{1+1} + \frac{(-1)^2}{2+1} + \frac{(-1)^3}{3+1} + \cdots + \frac{(-1)^n}{n+1}$$

$$= \frac{1}{1} + \frac{(-1)}{2} + \frac{1}{3} + \frac{(-1)}{4} + \cdots + \frac{(-1)^n}{n+1}$$

$$= 1 - \frac{1}{2} + \frac{1}{3} - \frac{1}{4} + \cdots + \frac{(-1)^n}{n+1}$$
∎

Example 5.1.7 Changing from Expanded Form to Summation Notation

Express the following using summation notation:

$$\frac{1}{n} + \frac{2}{n+1} + \frac{3}{n+2} + \cdots + \frac{n+1}{2n}.$$

Solution   The general term of this summation can be expressed as $\dfrac{k+1}{n+k}$ for integers k from 0 to n. Hence

$$\frac{1}{n} + \frac{2}{n+1} + \frac{3}{n+2} + \cdots + \frac{n+1}{2n} = \sum_{k=0}^{n} \frac{k+1}{n+k}.$$
∎

For small values of n, the expanded form of a sum may appear ambiguous. For instance, consider

$$1^2 + 2^2 + 3^2 + \cdots + n^2.$$

This expression is intended to represent the sum of squares of consecutive integers starting with 1^2 and ending with n^2. Thus, if $n = 1$ the sum is just 1^2, if $n = 2$ the sum is $1^2 + 2^2$, and if $n = 3$ the sum is $1^2 + 2^2 + 3^2$.

Example 5.1.8 Evaluating $a_1, a_2, a_3, \ldots, a_n$ for Small n

What is the value of the expression $\dfrac{1}{1 \cdot 2} + \dfrac{1}{2 \cdot 3} + \dfrac{1}{3 \cdot 4} + \cdots + \dfrac{1}{n \cdot (n+1)}$ when $n = 1$? $n = 2$? $n = 3$?

Caution! Do not write that for $n = 1$, the sum is

This is crossed out because it is incorrect

Solution

When $n = 1$, the expression equals $\dfrac{1}{1 \cdot 2} = \dfrac{1}{2}$.

When $n = 2$, it equals $\dfrac{1}{1 \cdot 2} + \dfrac{1}{2 \cdot 3} = \dfrac{1}{2} + \dfrac{1}{6} = \dfrac{2}{3}$.

When $n = 3$, it is $\dfrac{1}{1 \cdot 2} + \dfrac{1}{2 \cdot 3} + \dfrac{1}{3 \cdot 4} = \dfrac{1}{2} + \dfrac{1}{6} + \dfrac{1}{12} = \dfrac{3}{4}$.

A more mathematically precise definition of summation, called a *recursive definition*, is the following:* If m is any integer, then

$$\sum_{k=m}^{m} a_k = a_m \quad \text{and} \quad \sum_{k=m}^{n} a_k = \sum_{k=m}^{n-1} a_k + a_n \quad \text{for all integers } n > m.$$

When solving problems, it is often useful to rewrite a summation using the recursive form of the definition, either by separating off the final term of a summation or by adding a final term to a summation.

Example 5.1.9 Separating Off a Final Term and Adding On a Final Term

a. Rewrite $\displaystyle\sum_{i=1}^{n+1} \dfrac{1}{i^2}$ by separating off the final term.

b. Write $\displaystyle\sum_{k=0}^{n} 2^k + 2^{n+1}$ as a single summation.

Solution

a. $\displaystyle\sum_{i=1}^{n+1} \dfrac{1}{i^2} = \sum_{i=1}^{n} \dfrac{1}{i^2} + \dfrac{1}{(n+1)^2}$

b. $\displaystyle\sum_{k=0}^{n} 2^k + 2^{n+1} = \sum_{k=0}^{n+1} 2^k$

In certain sums each term is a difference of two quantities. When you write such sums in expanded form, you sometimes see that all the terms cancel except the first and the last. Successive cancellation of terms collapses the sum like a telescope.

Example 5.1.10 A Telescoping Sum

Some sums can be transformed into telescoping sums, which then can be rewritten as a simple expression. For instance, observe that

$$\frac{1}{k} - \frac{1}{k+1} = \frac{(k+1) - k}{k(k+1)} = \frac{1}{k(k+1)}.$$

Use this identity to find a simple expression for $\displaystyle\sum_{k=1}^{n} \frac{1}{k(k+1)}$.

*Other recursively defined sequences are discussed later in this section and, in greater detail, in Section 5.6.

Solution

$$\sum_{k=1}^{n} \frac{1}{k(k+1)} = \sum_{k=1}^{n} \left(\frac{1}{k} - \frac{1}{k+1} \right)$$

$$= \left(\frac{1}{1} - \frac{1}{2} \right) + \left(\frac{1}{2} - \frac{1}{3} \right) + \left(\frac{1}{3} - \frac{1}{4} \right) + \cdots + \left(\frac{1}{n-1} - \frac{1}{n} \right) + \left(\frac{1}{n} - \frac{1}{n+1} \right)$$

$$= 1 - \frac{1}{n+1}.$$

∎

Product Notation

The notation for the product of a sequence of numbers is analogous to the notation for their sum. The Greek capital letter pi, Π, denotes a product. For example,

$$\prod_{k=1}^{5} a_k = a_1 a_2 a_3 a_4 a_5.$$

> **• Definition**
>
> If m and n are integers and $m \leq n$, the symbol $\displaystyle\prod_{k=m}^{n} a_k$, read the **product from k equals m to n of a-sub-k**, is the product of all the terms a_m, a_{m+1}, a_{m+2}, $\ldots$, a_n.
> We write
> $$\prod_{k=m}^{n} a_k = a_m \cdot a_{m+1} \cdot a_{m+2} \cdots a_n.$$

A recursive definition for the product notation is the following: If m is any integer, then

$$\prod_{k=m}^{m} a_k = a_m \qquad \text{and} \qquad \prod_{k=m}^{n} a_k = \left(\prod_{k=m}^{n-1} a_k \right) \cdot a_n \quad \text{for all integers } n > m.$$

Example 5.1.11 Computing Products

Compute the following products:

a. $\displaystyle\prod_{k=1}^{5} k$

b. $\displaystyle\prod_{k=1}^{1} \frac{k}{k+1}$

Solution

a. $\displaystyle\prod_{k=1}^{5} k = 1 \cdot 2 \cdot 3 \cdot 4 \cdot 5 = 120$

b. $\displaystyle\prod_{k=1}^{1} \frac{k}{k+1} = \frac{1}{1+1} = \frac{1}{2}$ ∎

Properties of Summations and Products

The following theorem states general properties of summations and products. The proof of the theorem is discussed in Section 5.6.

Theorem 5.1.1

If $a_m, a_{m+1}, a_{m+2}, \ldots$ and $b_m, b_{m+1}, b_{m+2}, \ldots$ are sequences of real numbers and c is any real number, then the following equations hold for any integer $n \geq m$:

1. $\displaystyle\sum_{k=m}^{n} a_k + \sum_{k=m}^{n} b_k = \sum_{k=m}^{n}(a_k + b_k)$

2. $\displaystyle c \cdot \sum_{k=m}^{n} a_k = \sum_{k=m}^{n} c \cdot a_k$ generalized distributive law

3. $\displaystyle\left(\prod_{k=m}^{n} a_k\right) \cdot \left(\prod_{k=m}^{n} b_k\right) = \prod_{k=m}^{n}(a_k \cdot b_k).$

Example 5.1.12 Using Properties of Summation and Product

Let $a_k = k + 1$ and $b_k = k - 1$ for all integers k. Write each of the following expressions as a single summation or product:

a. $\displaystyle\sum_{k=m}^{n} a_k + 2 \cdot \sum_{k=m}^{n} b_k$ b. $\displaystyle\left(\prod_{k=m}^{n} a_k\right) \cdot \left(\prod_{k=m}^{n} b_k\right)$

Solution

a. $\displaystyle\sum_{k=m}^{n} a_k + 2 \cdot \sum_{k=m}^{n} b_k = \sum_{k=m}^{n}(k+1) + 2 \cdot \sum_{k=m}^{n}(k-1)$ by substitution

$\displaystyle = \sum_{k=m}^{n}(k+1) + \sum_{k=m}^{n} 2 \cdot (k-1)$ by Theorem 5.1.1 (2)

$\displaystyle = \sum_{k=m}^{n}((k+1) + 2 \cdot (k-1))$ by Theorem 5.1.1 (1)

$\displaystyle = \sum_{k=m}^{n}(3k-1)$ by algebraic simplification

b.

$\displaystyle\left(\prod_{k=m}^{n} a_k\right) \cdot \left(\prod_{k=m}^{n} b_k\right) = \left(\prod_{k=m}^{n}(k+1)\right) \cdot \left(\prod_{k=m}^{n}(k-1)\right)$ by substitution

$\displaystyle = \prod_{k=m}^{n}(k+1) \cdot (k-1)$ by Theorem 5.1.1 (3)

$\displaystyle = \prod_{k=m}^{n}(k^2 - 1)$ by algebraic simplification

Change of Variable

Observe that

$$\sum_{k=1}^{3} k^2 = 1^2 + 2^2 + 3^2$$

and also that

$$\sum_{i=1}^{3} i^2 = 1^2 + 2^2 + 3^2.$$

Hence
$$\sum_{k=1}^{3} k^2 = \sum_{i=1}^{3} i^2.$$

This equation illustrates the fact that the symbol used to represent the index of a summation can be replaced by any other symbol as long as the replacement is made in each location where the symbol occurs. As a consequence, the index of a summation is called a dummy variable. A **dummy variable** is a symbol that derives its entire meaning from its local context. Outside of that context (both before and after), the symbol may have another meaning entirely.

The appearance of a summation can be altered by more complicated changes of variable as well. For example, observe that

$$\sum_{j=2}^{4} (j-1)^2 = (2-1)^2 + (3-1)^2 + (4-1)^2$$
$$= 1^2 + 2^2 + 3^2$$
$$= \sum_{k=1}^{3} k^2.$$

A general procedure to transform the first summation into the second is illustrated in Example 5.1.13.

Example 5.1.13 Transforming a Sum by a Change of Variable

Transform the following summation by making the specified change of variable.

$$\text{summation: } \sum_{k=0}^{6} \frac{1}{k+1} \qquad \text{change of variable: } j = k+1$$

Solution First calculate the lower and upper limits of the new summation:

$$\text{When } k = 0, \quad j = k+1 = 0+1 = 1.$$
$$\text{When } k = 6, \quad j = k+1 = 6+1 = 7.$$

Thus the new sum goes from $j = 1$ to $j = 7$.

Next calculate the general term of the new summation. You will need to replace each occurrence of k by an expression in j:

$$\text{Since } j = k+1, \text{ then } k = j-1.$$
$$\text{Hence } \frac{1}{k+1} = \frac{1}{(j-1)+1} = \frac{1}{j}.$$

Finally, put the steps together to obtain

$$\sum_{k=0}^{6} \frac{1}{k+1} = \sum_{j=1}^{7} \frac{1}{j}.$$

5.1.1

Equation (5.1.1) can be given an additional twist by noting that because the j in the right-hand summation is a dummy variable, it may be replaced by any other variable name, as long as the substitution is made in every location where j occurs. In particular, it is legal to substitute k in place of j to obtain

$$\sum_{j=1}^{7} \frac{1}{j} = \sum_{k=1}^{7} \frac{1}{k}.$$

5.1.2

Putting equations (5.1.1) and (5.1.2) together gives

$$\sum_{k=0}^{6} \frac{1}{k+1} = \sum_{k=1}^{7} \frac{1}{k}.$$

Sometimes it is necessary to shift the limits of one summation in order to add it to another. An example is the algebraic proof of the binomial theorem, given in Section 9.7. A general procedure for making such a shift when the upper limit is part of the summand is illustrated in the next example.

Example 5.1.14 When the Upper Limit Appears in the Expression to Be Summed

a. Transform the following summation by making the specified change of variable.

$$summation: \sum_{k=1}^{n+1} \left(\frac{k}{n+k} \right) \qquad change\ of\ variable:\ j = k - 1$$

b. Transform the summation obtained in part (a) by changing all j's to k's.

Solution

a. When $k = 1$, then $j = k - 1 = 1 - 1 = 0$. (So the new lower limit is 0.) When $k = n + 1$, then $j = k - 1 = (n + 1) - 1 = n$. (So the new upper limit is n.)
   Since $j = k - 1$, then $k = j + 1$. Also note that n is a constant as far as the terms of the sum are concerned. It follows that

$$\frac{k}{n+k} = \frac{j+1}{n+(j+1)}$$

and so the general term of the new summation is

$$\frac{j+1}{n+(j+1)}.$$

Therefore,

$$\sum_{k=1}^{n+1} \frac{k}{n+k} = \sum_{j=0}^{n} \frac{j+1}{n+(j+1)}.$$

5.1.3

b. Changing all the j's to k's in the right-hand side of equation (5.1.3) gives

$$\sum_{j=0}^{n} \frac{j+1}{n+(j+1)} = \sum_{k=0}^{n} \frac{k+1}{n+(k+1)}.$$

5.1.4

Combining equations (5.1.3) and (5.1.4) results in

$$\sum_{k=1}^{n+1} \frac{k}{n+k} = \sum_{k=0}^{n} \frac{k+1}{n+(k+1)}.$$

Factorial and "n Choose r" Notation

The product of all consecutive integers up to a given integer occurs so often in mathematics that it is given a special notation—*factorial* notation.

> **• Definition**
>
> For each positive integer n, the quantity n **factorial** denoted $n!$, is defined to be the product of all the integers from 1 to n:
>
> $$n! = n \cdot (n-1) \cdots 3 \cdot 2 \cdot 1.$$
>
> **Zero factorial**, denoted $0!$, is defined to be 1:
>
> $$0! = 1.$$

The definition of zero factorial as 1 may seem odd, but, as you will see when you read Chapter 9, it is convenient for many mathematical formulas.

Example 5.1.15 The First Ten Factorials

$$0! = 1 \qquad\qquad 1! = 1$$
$$2! = 2 \cdot 1 = 2 \qquad\qquad 3! = 3 \cdot 2 \cdot 1 = 6$$
$$4! = 4 \cdot 3 \cdot 2 \cdot 1 = 24 \qquad\qquad 5! = 5 \cdot 4 \cdot 3 \cdot 2 \cdot 1 = 120$$
$$6! = 6 \cdot 5 \cdot 4 \cdot 3 \cdot 2 \cdot 1 = 720 \qquad 7! = 7 \cdot 6 \cdot 5 \cdot 4 \cdot 3 \cdot 2 \cdot 1 = 5{,}040$$
$$8! = 8 \cdot 7 \cdot 6 \cdot 5 \cdot 4 \cdot 3 \cdot 2 \cdot 1 \qquad 9! = 9 \cdot 8 \cdot 7 \cdot 6 \cdot 5 \cdot 4 \cdot 3 \cdot 2 \cdot 1$$
$$= 40{,}320 \qquad\qquad = 362{,}880$$

∎

As you can see from the example above, the values of $n!$ grow very rapidly. For instance, $40! \cong 8.16 \times 10^{47}$, which is a number that is too large to be computed exactly using the standard integer arithmetic of the machine-specific implementations of many computer languages. (The symbol $\cong$ means "is approximately equal to.")

A recursive definition for factorial is the following: Given any nonnegative integer n,

$$n! = \begin{cases} 1 & \text{if } n = 0 \\ n \cdot (n-1)! & \text{if } n \geq 1. \end{cases}$$

Caution! Note that $n \cdot (n-1)!$ is to be interpreted as $n \cdot [(n-1)!]$.

The next example illustrates the usefulness of the recursive definition for making computations.

Example 5.1.16 Computing with Factorials

Simplify the following expressions:

a. $\dfrac{8!}{7!}$ b. $\dfrac{5!}{2! \cdot 3!}$ c. $\dfrac{1}{2! \cdot 4!} + \dfrac{1}{3! \cdot 3!}$ d. $\dfrac{(n+1)!}{n!}$ e. $\dfrac{n!}{(n-3)!}$

Solution

a. $\dfrac{8!}{7!} = \dfrac{8 \cdot 7!}{7!} = 8$

b. $\dfrac{5!}{2! \cdot 3!} = \dfrac{5 \cdot 4 \cdot 3!}{2! \cdot 3!} = \dfrac{5 \cdot 4}{2 \cdot 1} = 10$

c.
$$\frac{1}{2!\cdot 4!} + \frac{1}{3!\cdot 3!} = \frac{1}{2!\cdot 4!}\cdot\frac{3}{3} + \frac{1}{3!\cdot 3!}\cdot\frac{4}{4}$$
by multiplying each numerator and denominator by just what is necessary to obtain a common denominator

$$= \frac{3}{3\cdot 2!\cdot 4!} + \frac{4}{3!\cdot 4\cdot 3!}$$
by rearranging factors

$$= \frac{3}{3!\cdot 4!} + \frac{4}{3!\cdot 4!}$$
because $3\cdot 2! = 3!$ and $4\cdot 3! = 4!$

$$= \frac{7}{3!\cdot 4!}$$
by the rule for adding fractions with a common denominator

$$= \frac{7}{144}$$

d. $\dfrac{(n+1)!}{n!} = \dfrac{(n+1)\cdot \cancel{n!}}{\cancel{n!}} = n+1$

e. $\dfrac{n!}{(n-3)!} = \dfrac{n\cdot(n-1)\cdot(n-2)\cdot\cancel{(n-3)!}}{\cancel{(n-3)!}} = n\cdot(n-1)\cdot(n-2)$

$$= n^3 - 3n^2 + 2n$$

An important use for the factorial notation is in calculating values of quantities, called *n choose r*, that occur in many branches of mathematics, especially those connected with the study of counting techniques and probability.

• Definition

Let n and r be integers with $0 \leq r \leq n$. The symbol

$$\binom{n}{r}$$

is read "**n choose r**" and represents the number of subsets of size r that can be chosen from a set with n elements.

Observe that the definition implies that $\binom{n}{r}$ will always be an integer because it is a number of subsets. In Section 9.5 we will explore many uses of n choose r for solving problems involving counting, and we will prove the following computational formula:

• Formula for Computing $\binom{n}{r}$

For all integers n and r with $0 \leq r \leq n$,

$$\binom{n}{r} = \frac{n!}{r!(n-r)!}.$$

In the meantime, we will provide a few experiences with using it. Because n choose r is always an integer, you can be sure that all the factors in the denominator of the formula will be canceled out by factors in the numerator. Many electronic calculators have keys for computing values of $\binom{n}{r}$. These are denoted in various ways such as nCr, $C(n,r)$, ^nC_r, and $C_{n,r}$. The letter C is used because the quantities $\binom{n}{r}$ are also called *combinations*. Sometimes they are referred to as *binomial coefficients* because of the connection with the binomial theorem discussed in Section 9.7.

Example 5.1.17 Computing $\binom{n}{r}$ by Hand

Use the formula for computing $\binom{n}{r}$ to evaluate the following expressions:

a. $\binom{8}{5}$ b. $\binom{4}{0}$ c. $\binom{n+1}{n}$

Solution

a. $\binom{8}{5} = \dfrac{8!}{5!(8-5)!}$

$= \dfrac{8 \cdot 7 \cdot \cancel{6} \cdot \cancel{5} \cdot \cancel{4} \cdot \cancel{3} \cdot \cancel{2} \cdot \cancel{1}}{(\cancel{5} \cdot \cancel{4} \cdot \cancel{3} \cdot \cancel{2} \cdot 1) \cdot (\cancel{3} \cdot \cancel{2} \cdot \cancel{1})}$

always cancel common factors
before multiplying

$= 56.$

b. $\binom{4}{4} = \dfrac{4!}{4!(4-4)!} = \dfrac{4!}{4!0!} = \dfrac{\cancel{4 \cdot 3 \cdot 2 \cdot 1}}{\cancel{(4 \cdot 3 \cdot 2 \cdot 1)}(1)} = 1$

The fact that $0! = 1$ makes this formula computable. It gives the correct value because a set of size 4 has exactly one subset of size 4, namely itself.

c. $\binom{n+1}{n} = \dfrac{(n+1)!}{n!((n+1)-n)!} = \dfrac{(n+1)!}{n!1!} = \dfrac{(n+1) \cdot \cancel{n!}}{\cancel{n!}} = n+1$ ■

Sequences in Computer Programming

An important data type in computer programming consists of finite sequences. In computer programming contexts, these are usually referred to as *one-dimensional arrays*. For example, consider a program that analyzes the wages paid to a sample of 50 workers. Such a program might compute the average wage and the difference between each individual wage and the average. This would require that each wage be stored in memory for retrieval later in the calculation. To avoid the use of entirely separate variable names for all of the 50 wages, each is written as a term of a one-dimensional array:

$$W[1], W[2], W[3], \ldots, W[50].$$

Note that the subscript labels are written inside square brackets. The reason is that until relatively recently, it was impossible to type actual dropped subscripts on most computer keyboards.

The main difficulty programmers have when using one-dimensional arrays is keeping the labels straight.

Example 5.1.18 Dummy Variable in a Loop

The index variable for a **for-next** loop is a dummy variable. For example, the following three algorithm segments all produce the same output:

1. **for** $i := 1$ **to** n	2. **for** $j := 0$ **to** $n-1$	3. **for** $k := 2$ **to** $n+1$
print $a[i]$	**print** $a[j+1]$	**print** $a[k-1]$
next i	**next** j	**next** k

■

The recursive definitions for summation, product, and factorial lead naturally to computational algorithms. For instance, here are two sets of pseudocode to find the sum of $a[1], a[2], \ldots, a[n]$. The one on the left exactly mimics the recursive definition by initializing the sum to equal $a[1]$; the one on the right initializes the sum to equal 0. In both cases the output is $\sum_{k=1}^{n} a[k]$.

$s := a[1]$	$s := 0$
for $k := 2$ **to** n	**for** $k := 1$ **to** n
$\quad s := s + a[k]$	$\quad s := s + a[k]$
next k	**next** k

Application: Algorithm to Convert from Base 10 to Base 2 Using Repeated Division by 2

Section 2.5 contains some examples of converting integers from decimal to binary notation. The method shown there, however, is only convenient to use with small numbers. A systematic algorithm to convert any nonnegative integer to binary notation uses repeated division by 2.

Suppose a is a nonnegative integer. Divide a by 2 using the quotient-remainder theorem to obtain a quotient $q[0]$ and a remainder $r[0]$. If the quotient is nonzero, divide by 2 again to obtain a quotient $q[1]$ and a remainder $r[1]$. Continue this process until a quotient of 0 is obtained. At each stage, the remainder must be less than the divisor, which is 2. Thus each remainder is either 0 or 1. The process is illustrated below for $a = 38$. (Read the divisions from the bottom up.)

The results of all these divisions can be written as a sequence of equations:

$$38 = 19 \cdot 2 + 0,$$
$$19 = 9 \cdot 2 + 1,$$
$$9 = 4 \cdot 2 + 1,$$
$$4 = 2 \cdot 2 + 0,$$
$$2 = 1 \cdot 2 + 0,$$
$$1 = 0 \cdot 2 + 1.$$

By repeated substitution, then,

$$
\begin{aligned}
38 &= 19 \cdot 2 + 0 \\
&= (9 \cdot 2 + 1) \cdot 2 + 0 = 9 \cdot 2^2 + 1 \cdot 2 + 0 \\
&= (4 \cdot 2 + 1) \cdot 2^2 + 1 \cdot 2 + 0 = 4 \cdot 2^3 + 1 \cdot 2^2 + 1 \cdot 2 + 0 \\
&= (2 \cdot 2 + 0) \cdot 2^3 + 1 \cdot 2^2 + 1 \cdot 2 + 0 \\
&= 2 \cdot 2^4 + 0 \cdot 2^3 + 1 \cdot 2^2 + 1 \cdot 2 + 0 \\
&= (1 \cdot 2 + 0) \cdot 2^4 + 0 \cdot 2^3 + 1 \cdot 2^2 + 1 \cdot 2 + 0 \\
&= 1 \cdot 2^5 + 0 \cdot 2^4 + 0 \cdot 2^3 + 1 \cdot 2^2 + 1 \cdot 2 + 0.
\end{aligned}
$$

Note that each coefficient of a power of 2 on the right-hand side of the previous page is one of the remainders obtained in the repeated division of 38 by 2. This is true for the left-most 1 as well, because $1 = 0 \cdot 2 + 1$. Thus

$$38_{10} = 100110_2 = (r[5]r[4]r[3]r[2]r[1]r[0])_2.$$

In general, if a nonnegative integer a is repeatedly divided by 2 until a quotient of zero is obtained and the remainders are found to be $r[0], r[1], \ldots, r[k]$, then by the quotient-remainder theorem each $r[i]$ equals 0 or 1, and by repeated substitution from the theorem,

$$a = 2^k \cdot r[k] + 2^{k-1} \cdot r[k-1] + \cdots + 2^2 \cdot r[2] + 2^1 \cdot r[1] + 2^0 \cdot r[0]. \qquad 5.1.5$$

Thus the binary representation for a can be read from equation (5.1.5):

$$a_{10} = (r[k]r[k-1] \cdots r[2]r[1]r[0])_2.$$

Example 5.1.19 Converting from Decimal to Binary Notation Using Repeated Division by 2

Use repeated division by 2 to write the number 29_{10} in binary notation.

Solution

				0	remainder $= r[4] = 1$
			2	1	remainder $= r[3] = 1$
		2	3		remainder $= r[2] = 1$
	2	7			remainder $= r[1] = 0$
2	14				remainder $= r[0] = 1$
2	29				

Hence $29_{10} = (r[4]r[3]r[2]r[1]r[0])_2 = 11101_2.$

The procedure we have described for converting from base 10 to base 2 is formalized in the following algorithm:

Algorithm 5.1.1 Decimal to Binary Conversion Using Repeated Division by 2

[In Algorithm 5.1.1 the input is a nonnegative integer a. The aim of the algorithm is to produce a sequence of binary digits $r[0], r[1], r[2], \ldots, r[k]$ so that the binary representation of a is

$$(r[k]r[k-1] \cdots r[2]r[1]r[0])_2.$$

That is,

$$a = 2^k \cdot r[k] + 2^{k-1} \cdot r[k-1] + \cdots + 2^2 \cdot r[2] + 2^1 \cdot r[1] + 2^0 \cdot r[0].]$$

continued on page 242

Input: a [a nonnegative integer]
Algorithm Body:

$q := a, i := 0$

[Repeatedly perform the integer division of q by 2 until q becomes 0. Store successive remainders in a one-dimensional array $r[0], r[1], r[2], \ldots, r[k]$. Even if the initial-value of q equals 0, the loop should execute one time (so that $r[0]$ is computed). Thus the guard condition for the **while** loop is $i = 0$ or $q \neq 0$.]

while ($i = 0$ or $q \neq 0$)

$r[i] := q \bmod 2$

$q := q \operatorname{div} 2$

[$r[i]$ and q can be obtained by calling the division algorithm.]

$i := i + 1$

end while

[After execution of this step, the values of $r[0], r[1], \ldots, r[i-1]$ are all 0's and 1's, and $a = (r[i-1]r[i-2]\cdots r[2]r[1]r[0])_2$.]

Output: $r[0], r[1], r[2], \ldots, r[i-1]$ [a sequence of integers]

Test Yourself

Answers to Test Yourself questions are located at the end of each section.

1. The notation $\displaystyle\sum_{k=m}^{n} a_k$ is read "_____."

2. The expanded form of $\displaystyle\sum_{k=m}^{n} a_k$ is _____.

3. The value of $a_1 + a_2 + a_3 + \cdots + a_n$ when $n = 2$ is "_____."

4. The notation $\displaystyle\prod_{k=m}^{n} a_k$ is read "_____."

5. If n is a positive integer, then $n! =$ _____.

6. $\displaystyle\sum_{k=m}^{n} a_k + c \sum_{k=m}^{n} b_k =$ _____.

7. $\displaystyle\left(\prod_{k=m}^{n} a_k\right)\left(\prod_{k=m}^{n} b_k\right) =$ _____.

Exercise Set 5.1*

Write the first four terms of the sequences defined by the formulas in 1–6.

1. $a_k = \dfrac{k}{10+k}$, for all integers $k \geq 1$.

2. $d_m = 1 + \left(\dfrac{1}{2}\right)^m$ for all integers $m \geq 0$.

3. $c_i = \dfrac{(-1)^i}{3^i}$, for all integers $i \geq 0$.

4. $b_j = \dfrac{5-j}{5+j}$, for all integers $j \geq 1$.

5. $e_n = \left\lfloor \dfrac{n}{2} \right\rfloor \cdot 2$, for all integers $n \geq 0$.

6. $f_n = \left\lfloor \dfrac{n}{4} \right\rfloor \cdot 4$, for all integers $n \geq 1$.

7. Let $a_k = 2k + 1$ and $b_k = (k-1)^3 + k + 2$ for all integers $k \geq 0$. Show that the first three terms of these sequences are identical but that their fourth terms differ.

Compute the first fifteen terms of each of the sequences in 8 and 9. and describe the general behavior of these sequences in words. (A definition of logarithm is given in Section 7.1.)

8. $g_n = \lfloor \log_2 n \rfloor$ for all integers $n \geq 1$.

9. $h_n = n\lfloor \log_2 n \rfloor$ for all integers $n \geq 1$.

*For exercises with blue numbers or letters, solutions are given in Appendix B. The symbol H indicates that only a hint or a partial solution is given. The symbol $*$ signals that an exercise is more challenging than usual.

Find explicit formulas for sequences of the form $a_1, a_2, a_3, \ldots$ with the initial terms given in 10–16.

10. $-1, 1, -1, 1, -1, 1$ 11. $0, 1, -2, 3, -4, 5$

12. $\dfrac{1}{4}, \dfrac{2}{9}, \dfrac{3}{16}, \dfrac{4}{25}, \dfrac{5}{36}, \dfrac{6}{49}$

13. $3, 6, 12, 24, 48, 96$

14. $\dfrac{1}{3}, \dfrac{4}{9}, \dfrac{9}{27}, \dfrac{16}{81}, \dfrac{25}{243}, \dfrac{36}{729}$

15. $0, -\dfrac{1}{2}, \dfrac{2}{3}, -\dfrac{3}{4}, \dfrac{4}{5}, -\dfrac{5}{6}, \dfrac{6}{7}$

16. $1 - \dfrac{1}{2}, \dfrac{1}{2} - \dfrac{1}{3}, \dfrac{1}{3} - \dfrac{1}{4}, \dfrac{1}{4} - \dfrac{1}{5}, \dfrac{1}{5} - \dfrac{1}{6}, \dfrac{1}{6} - \dfrac{1}{7}$

$*$ 17. Consider the sequence defined by $a_n = \dfrac{2n + (-1)^n - 1}{4}$ for all integers $n \geq 0$. Find an alternative explicit formula for a_n that uses the floor notation.

18. Let $a_0 = 2$, $a_1 = 3$, $a_2 = -2$, $a_3 = 1$, $a_4 = 0$, $a_5 = -1$, and $a_6 = -2$. Compute each of the summations and products below.

a. $\displaystyle\sum_{i=0}^{6} a_i$ b. $\displaystyle\sum_{i=0}^{0} a_i$ c. $\displaystyle\sum_{j=1}^{3} a_{2j}$ d. $\displaystyle\prod_{k=0}^{6} a_k$ e. $\displaystyle\prod_{k=2}^{2} a_k$

Compute the summations and products in 19–28.

19. $\displaystyle\sum_{k=1}^{5}(k+1)$ 20. $\displaystyle\prod_{k=2}^{4} k^2$ 21. $\displaystyle\sum_{m=0}^{3} \dfrac{1}{2^m}$

22. $\displaystyle\prod_{k=2}^{2}\left(1 - \dfrac{1}{k}\right)$ 23. $\displaystyle\sum_{i=1}^{1} i(i+1)$ 24. $\displaystyle\sum_{j=0}^{0}(j+1)\cdot 2^j$

25. $\displaystyle\prod_{j=0}^{4}(-1)^j$ 26. $\displaystyle\prod_{i=2}^{5} \dfrac{i(i+2)}{(i-1)\cdot(i+1)}$

27. $\displaystyle\sum_{n=1}^{10}\left(\dfrac{1}{n} - \dfrac{1}{n+1}\right)$ 28. $\displaystyle\sum_{k=-1}^{1}(k^2+3)$

Write the summations in 29–32 in expanded form.

29. $\displaystyle\sum_{i=1}^{n}(-2)^i$ 30. $\displaystyle\sum_{j=1}^{n} j(j+1)$ 31. $\displaystyle\sum_{k=0}^{n+1}\dfrac{1}{k!}$ 32. $\displaystyle\sum_{i=1}^{k+1} i(i!)$

Evaluate the summations and products in 33–36 for the indicated values of the variable.

33. $\dfrac{1}{1^2} + \dfrac{1}{2^2} + \dfrac{1}{3^2} + \ldots + \dfrac{1}{n^2}$; $n = 1$

34. $1(1!) + 2(2!) + 3(3!) + \ldots + m(m!)$; $m = 2$

35. $\left(\dfrac{1}{1+1}\right)\left(\dfrac{2}{2+1}\right)\left(\dfrac{3}{3+1}\right)\cdots\left(\dfrac{k}{k+1}\right)$; $k = 3$

36. $\left(\dfrac{1\cdot 2}{3\cdot 4}\right)\left(\dfrac{4\cdot 5}{6\cdot 7}\right)\left(\dfrac{6\cdot 7}{8\cdot 9}\right)\cdots\left(\dfrac{m\cdot(m+1)}{(m+2)\cdot(m+3)}\right)$; $m = 1$

Rewrite 37–39 by separating off the final term.

37. $\displaystyle\sum_{i=1}^{k+1} i(i!)$ 38. $\displaystyle\sum_{k=1}^{m+1} k^2$ 39. $\displaystyle\sum_{m=1}^{n+1} m(m+1)$

Write each of 40–42 as a single summation.

40. $\displaystyle\sum_{i=1}^{k} i^3 + (k+1)^3$ 41. $\displaystyle\sum_{k=1}^{m}\dfrac{k}{k+1} + \dfrac{m+1}{m+2}$

42. $\displaystyle\sum_{m=0}^{n}(m+1)2^m + (n+2)2^{n+1}$

Write each of 43–52 using summation or product notation.

43. $1^2 - 2^2 + 3^2 - 4^2 + 5^2 - 6^2 + 7^2$

44. $(1^3 - 1) - (2^3 - 1) + (3^3 - 1) - (4^3 - 1) + (5^3 - 1)$

45. $(2^2 - 1)\cdot(3^2 - 1)\cdot(4^2 - 1)$

46. $\dfrac{2}{3\cdot 4} - \dfrac{3}{4\cdot 5} + \dfrac{4}{5\cdot 6} - \dfrac{5}{6\cdot 7} + \dfrac{6}{7\cdot 8}$

47. $1 - r + r^2 - r^3 + r^4 - r^5$

48. $(1 - t)\cdot(1 - t^2)\cdot(1 - t^3)\cdot(1 - t^4)$

49. $1^3 + 2^3 + 3^3 + \cdots + n^3$

50. $\dfrac{1}{2!} + \dfrac{2}{3!} + \dfrac{3}{4!} + \cdots + \dfrac{n}{(n+1)!}$

51. $n + (n-1) + (n-2) + \cdots + 1$

52. $n + \dfrac{n-1}{2!} + \dfrac{n-2}{3!} + \dfrac{n-3}{4!} + \cdots + \dfrac{1}{n!}$

Transform each of 53 and 54 by making the change of variable $i = k + 1$.

53. $\displaystyle\sum_{k=0}^{5} k(k-1)$ 54. $\displaystyle\prod_{k=1}^{n}\dfrac{k}{k^2+4}$

Transform each of 55–58 by making the change of variable $j = i - 1$.

55. $\displaystyle\sum_{i=1}^{n+1}\dfrac{(i-1)^2}{i\cdot n}$ 56. $\displaystyle\sum_{i=3}^{n}\dfrac{i}{i+n-1}$

57. $\displaystyle\sum_{i=1}^{n-1}\dfrac{i}{(n-i)^2}$ 58. $\displaystyle\prod_{i=n}^{2n}\dfrac{n-i+1}{n+i}$

Write each of 59–61 as a single summation or product.

59. $3\cdot\displaystyle\sum_{k=1}^{n}(2k-3) + \sum_{k=1}^{n}(4 - 5k)$

60. $2\cdot\displaystyle\sum_{k=1}^{n}(3k^2 + 4) + 5\cdot\sum_{k=1}^{n}(2k^2 - 1)$

61. $\left(\displaystyle\prod_{k=1}^{n}\dfrac{k}{k+1}\right)\cdot\left(\prod_{k=1}^{n}\dfrac{k+1}{k+2}\right)$

Compute each of 62–76. Assume the values of the variables are restricted so that the expressions are defined.

62. $\dfrac{4!}{3!}$ 63. $\dfrac{6!}{8!}$ 64. $\dfrac{4!}{0!}$

65. $\dfrac{n!}{(n-1)!}$ 66. $\dfrac{(n-1)!}{(n+1)!}$ 67. $\dfrac{n!}{(n-2)!}$

68. $\dfrac{((n+1)!)^2}{(n!)^2}$ 69. $\dfrac{n!}{(n-k)!}$ 70. $\dfrac{n!}{(n-k+1)!}$

71. $\dbinom{5}{3}$ 72. $\dbinom{7}{4}$ 73. $\dbinom{3}{0}$

74. $\dbinom{5}{5}$ 75. $\dbinom{n}{n-1}$ 76. $\dbinom{n+1}{n-1}$

77. a. Prove that $n! + 2$ is divisible by 2, for all integers $n \geq 2$.
    b. Prove that $n! + k$ is divisible by k, for all integers $n \geq 2$ and $k = 2, 3, \ldots, n$.
  H c. Given any integer $m \geq 2$, is it possible to find a sequence of $m - 1$ consecutive positive integers none of which is prime? Explain your answer.

78. Prove that for all nonnegative integers n and r with
$$r + 1 \leq n, \quad \binom{n}{r+1} = \frac{n-r}{r+1}\binom{n}{r}.$$

79. Prove that if p is a prime number and r is an integer with $0 < r < p$, then $\dbinom{p}{r}$ is divisible by p.

80. Suppose $a[1], a[2], a[3], \ldots, a[m]$ is a one-dimensional array and consider the following algorithm segment:

   $sum := 0$
   for $k := 1$ **to** m
       $sum := sum + a[k]$
   next k

Fill in the blanks below so that each algorithm segment performs the same job as the one given previously.

a. $sum := 0$
   for $i := 0$ **to** _____
       $sum :=$ _____
   next i

b. $sum := 0$
   for $j := 2$ **to** _____
       $sum :=$ _____
   next j

Use repeated division by 2 to convert (by hand) the integers in 81–83 from base 10 to base 2.

81. 90   82. 98   83. 205

Make a trace table to trace the action of Algorithm 5.1.1 on the input in 84–86.

84. 23   85. 28   86. 44

87. Write an informal description of an algorithm (using repeated division by 16) to convert a nonnegative integer from decimal notation to hexadecimal notation (base 16).

Use the algorithm you developed for exercise 87 to convert the integers in 88–90 to hexadecimal notation.

88. 287   89. 693   90. 2,301

91. Write a formal version of the algorithm you developed for exercise 87.

Answers for Test Yourself

1. the summation from k equals m to n of a-sub-k 2. $a_m + a_{m+1} + a_{m+2} + \cdots + a_n$ 3. $a_1 + a_2$ 4. the product from k equals m to n of a-sub-k 5. $n \cdot (n-1) \cdots 3 \cdot 2 \cdot 1$ (Or: $n \cdot (n-1)!$)   6. $\displaystyle\sum_{k=m}^{n}(a_k + cb_k)$ 7. $\displaystyle\prod_{k=m}^{n} a_k b_k$

5.2 Mathematical Induction I

[Mathematical induction is] the standard proof technique in computer science.
— Anthony Ralston, 1984

Mathematical induction is one of the more recently developed techniques of proof in the history of mathematics. It is used to check conjectures about the outcomes of processes that occur repeatedly and according to definite patterns. We introduce the technique with an example.

Some people claim that the United States penny is such a small coin that it should be abolished. They point out that frequently a person who drops a penny on the ground does not even bother to pick it up. Other people argue that abolishing the penny would not give enough flexibility for pricing merchandise. What prices could still be paid with exact change if the penny were abolished and another coin worth 3¢ were introduced? The answer is that the only prices that could not be paid with exact change would be 1¢, 2¢, 4¢, and 7¢. In other words,

Any whole number of cents of at least 8¢ can be obtained using 3¢ and 5¢ coins.

More formally:

For all integers $n \geq 8$, n cents can be obtained using 3¢ and 5¢ coins.

Even more formally:

> For all integers $n \geq 8$, $P(n)$ is true, where $P(n)$ is the sentence "n cents can be obtained using 3¢ and 5¢ coins."

You could check that $P(n)$ is true for a few particular values of n, as is done in the table below.

Number of Cents	How to Obtain It
8¢	3¢ + 5¢
9¢	3¢ + 3¢ + 3¢
10¢	5¢ + 5¢
11¢	3¢ + 3¢ + 5¢
12¢	3¢ + 3¢ + 3¢ + 3¢
13¢	3¢ + 5¢ + 5¢
14¢	3¢ + 3¢ + 3¢ + 5¢
15¢	5¢ + 5¢ + 5¢
16¢	3¢ + 3¢ + 5¢ + 5¢
17¢	3¢ + 3¢ + 3¢ + 3¢ + 5¢

The cases shown in the table provide inductive evidence to support the claim that $P(n)$ is true for general n. Indeed, *$P(n)$ is true for all $n \geq 8$ if, and only if, it is possible to continue filling in the table for arbitrarily large values of n.*

The kth line of the table gives information about how to obtain k¢ using 3¢ and 5¢ coins. To continue the table to the next row, directions must be given for how to obtain $(k + 1)$¢ using 3¢ and 5¢ coins. The secret is to observe first that if k¢ can be obtained using at least one 5¢ coin, then $(k + 1)$¢ can be obtained by replacing the 5¢ coin by two 3¢ coins, as shown in Figure 5.2.1.

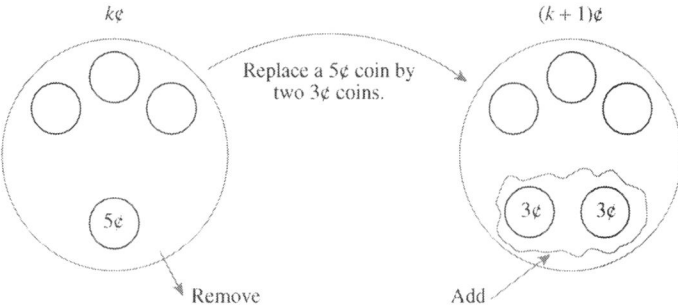

Figure 5.2.1

If, on the other hand, k¢ is obtained without using a 5¢ coin, then 3¢ coins are used exclusively. And since the total is at least 8¢, three or more 3¢ coins must be included. Three of the 3¢ coins can be replaced by two 5¢ coins to obtain a total of $(k + 1)$¢, as shown in Figure 5.2.2.

The structure of the argument above can be summarized as follows: To show that $P(n)$ is true for all integers $n \geq 8$, (1) show that $P(8)$ is true, and (2) show that the truth of $P(k + 1)$ follows necessarily from the truth of $P(k)$ for each $k \geq 8$.

Any argument of this form is an argument by *mathematical induction*. In general, mathematical induction is a method for proving that a property defined for integers n is true for all values of n that are greater than or equal to some initial integer.

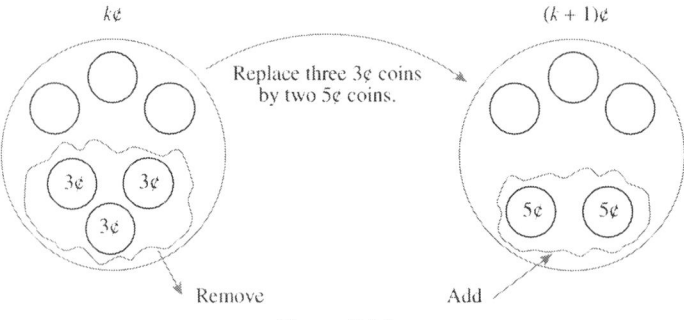

Figure 5.2.2

Principle of Mathematical Induction

Let $P(n)$ be a property that is defined for integers n, and let a be a fixed integer. Suppose the following two statements are true:

1. $P(a)$ is true.

2. For all integers $k \geq a$, if $P(k)$ is true then $P(k + 1)$ is true.

Then the statement

$$\text{for all integers } n \geq a, P(n)$$

is true.

The first known use of mathematical induction occurs in the work of the Italian scientist Francesco Maurolico in 1575. In the seventeenth century both Pierre de Fermat and Blaise Pascal used the technique, Fermat calling it the "method of infinite descent." In 1883 Augustus De Morgan (best known for De Morgan's laws) described the process carefully and gave it the name *mathematical induction*.

To visualize the idea of mathematical induction, imagine an infinite collection of dominoes positioned one behind the other in such a way that if any given domino falls backward, it makes the one behind it fall backward also. (See Figure 5.2.3) Then imagine that the first domino falls backward. What happens? ... They all fall down!

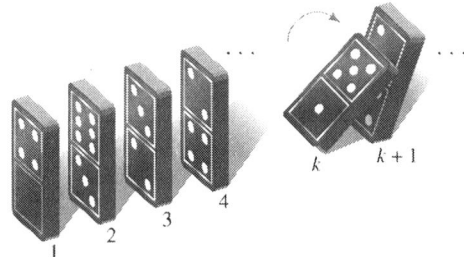

Figure 5.2.3 **If the kth domino falls backward, it pushes the $(k + 1)$st domino backward also.**

To see the connection between this image and the principle of mathematical induction, let $P(n)$ be the sentence "The nth domino falls backward." It is given that for each $k \geq 1$, if $P(k)$ is true (the kth domino falls backward), then $P(k + 1)$ is also true (the $(k + 1)$st domino falls backward). It is also given that $P(1)$ is true (the first domino falls backward). Thus by the principle of mathematical induction, $P(n)$ (the nth domino falls backward) is true for every integer $n \geq 1$.

The validity of proof by mathematical induction is generally taken as an
That is why it is referred to as the *principle* of mathematical induction rather than as a
theorem. It is equivalent to the following property of the integers, which is easy to accept
on intuitive grounds:

> Suppose S is any set of integers satisfying (1) $a \in S$, and (2) for all
> integers $k \geq a$, if $k \in S$ then $k + 1 \in S$. Then S must contain every integer
> greater than or equal to a.

To understand the equivalence of this formulation and the one given earlier, just let S be
the set of all integers for which $P(n)$ is true.

Proving a statement by mathematical induction is a two-step process. The first step is
called the *basis step,* and the second step is called the *inductive step.*

Method of Proof by Mathematical Induction

Consider a statement of the form, "For all integers $n \geq a$, a property $P(n)$ is true."
To prove such a statement, perform the following two steps:

Step 1 (basis step): Show that $P(a)$ is true.

Step 2 (inductive step): Show that for all integers $k \geq a$, if $P(k)$ is true then
$\quad\quad P(k + 1)$ is true. To perform this step,

> **suppose** that $P(k)$ is true, where k is any
> particular but arbitrarily chosen integer with $k \geq a$.
> *[This supposition is called the **inductive hypothesis.**]*

Then

> **show** that $P(k + 1)$ is true.

Here is a formal version of the proof about coins previously developed informally.

Proposition 5.2.1

For all integers $n \geq 8$, $n\text{¢}$ can be obtained using 3¢ and 5¢ coins.

Proof (by mathematical induction):

Let the property $P(n)$ be the sentence

$\quad\quad n\text{¢}$ can be obtained using 3¢ and 5¢ coins.　　← $P(n)$

Show that P(8) is true:
$P(8)$ is true because 8¢ can be obtained using one 3¢ coin and one 5¢ coin.

Show that for all integers $k \geq 8$, if P(k) is true then P(k+1) is also true:

[Suppose that P(k) is true for a particular but arbitrarily chosen integer $k \geq 8$. That is:]
Suppose that k is any integer with $k \geq 8$ such that

$\quad\quad k\text{¢}$ can be obtained using 3¢ and 5¢ coins.　　← $P(k)$
$\quad\quad\quad\quad\quad\quad\quad\quad\quad\quad\quad\quad\quad\quad\quad$ inductive hypothesis

[We must show that $P(k + 1)$ is true. That is:] We must show that

$\quad\quad (k + 1)\text{¢}$ can be obtained using 3¢ and 5¢ coins.　　← $P(k + 1)$

Case 1 (There is a 5¢ coin among those used to make up the k¢.): In this case
replace the 5¢ coin by two 3¢ coins; the result will be $(k + 1)$¢.

continued on page 248

Case 2 (*There is not a 5¢ coin among those used to make up the k¢.*): In this case, because $k \geq 8$, at least three 3¢ coins must have been used. So remove three 3¢ coins and replace them by two 5¢ coins; the result will be $(k + 1)¢$.

Thus in either case $(k + 1)¢$ can be obtained using 3¢ and 5¢ coins *[as was to be shown].*

[Since we have proved the basis step and the inductive step, we conclude that the proposition is true.]

The following example shows how to use mathematical induction to prove a formula for the sum of the first n integers.

Example 5.2.1 Sum of the First n Integers

Use mathematical induction to prove that

$$1 + 2 + \cdots + n = \frac{n(n + 1)}{2} \quad \text{for all integers } n \geq 1.$$

Solution To construct a proof by induction, you must first identify the property $P(n)$. In this case, $P(n)$ is the equation

$$1 + 2 + \cdots + n = \frac{n(n + 1)}{2}. \qquad \leftarrow \text{ the property } (P(n))$$

[To see that $P(n)$ is a sentence, note that its subject is "the sum of the integers from 1 to n" and its verb is "equals."]

In the basis step of the proof, you must show that the property is true for $n = 1$, or, in other words that $P(1)$ is true. Now $P(1)$ is obtained by substituting 1 in place of n in $P(n)$. The left-hand side of $P(1)$ is the sum of all the successive integers starting at 1 and ending at 1. This is just 1. Thus $P(1)$ is

Note To write $P(1)$, just copy $P(n)$ and replace each n by 1.

$$1 = \frac{1(1 + 1)}{2}. \qquad \leftarrow \text{ basis } (P(1))$$

Of course, this equation is true because the right-hand side is

$$\frac{1(1 + 1)}{2} = \frac{1 \cdot 2}{2} = 1,$$

which equals the left-hand side.

In the inductive step, you assume that $P(k)$ is true, for a particular but arbitrarily chosen integer k with $k \geq 1$. *[This assumption is the inductive hypothesis.]* You must then show that $P(k + 1)$ is true. What are $P(k)$ and $P(k + 1)$? $P(k)$ is obtained by substituting k for every n in $P(n)$. Thus $P(k)$ is

Note To write $P(k)$, just copy $P(n)$ and replace each n by k.

$$1 + 2 + \cdots + k = \frac{k(k + 1)}{2}. \qquad \leftarrow \text{ inductive hypothesis } (P(k))$$

Note To write
$P(k + 1)$, just copy $P(n)$
and replace each n by
$(k + 1)$.

Similarly, $P(k + 1)$ is obtained by substituting the quantity $(k + 1)$ for every n that appears in $P(n)$. Thus $P(k + 1)$ is

$$1 + 2 + \cdots + (k + 1) = \frac{(k + 1)((k + 1) + 1)}{2},$$

or, equivalently,

$$1 + 2 + \cdots + (k + 1) = \frac{(k + 1)(k + 2)}{2}. \qquad \leftarrow \text{to show } (P(k+1))$$

Now the inductive hypothesis is the supposition that $P(k)$ is true. How can this supposition be used to show that $P(k + 1)$ is true? $P(k + 1)$ is an equation, and the truth of an equation can be shown in a variety of ways. One of the most straightforward is to use the inductive hypothesis along with algebra and other known facts to transform separately the left-hand and right-hand sides until you see that they are the same. In this case, the left-hand side of $P(k + 1)$ is

$$1 + 2 + \cdots + (k + 1),$$

which equals

$$(1 + 2 + \cdots + k) + (k + 1) \qquad \text{The next-to-last term is } k \text{ because the terms are}$$

successive integers and the last term is $k + 1$.

But by substitution from the inductive hypothesis,

$$(1 + 2 + \cdots + k) + (k + 1)$$

$$= \frac{k(k + 1)}{2} + (k + 1) \qquad \text{since the inductive hypothesis says}$$
that $1 + 2 + \cdots + k = \frac{k(k+1)}{2}$

$$= \frac{k(k + 1)}{2} + \frac{2(k + 1)}{2} \qquad \text{by multiplying the numerator and}$$
denominator of the second term by 2
to obtain a common denominator

$$= \frac{k^2 + k}{2} + \frac{2k + 2}{2} \qquad \text{by multiplying out the two numerators}$$

$$= \frac{k^2 + 3k + 2}{2} \qquad \text{by adding fractions with the same}$$
denominator and combining like terms.

So the left-hand side of $P(k + 1)$ is $\dfrac{k^2 + 3k + 2}{2}$. Now the right-hand side of $P(k + 1)$ is

$$\frac{(k + 1)(k + 2)}{2} = \frac{k^2 + 3k + 2}{2} \qquad \text{by multiplying out the numerator.}$$

Thus the two sides of $P(k + 1)$ are equal to each other, and so the equation $P(k + 1)$ is true.

This discussion is summarized as follows:

Theorem 5.2.2 Sum of the First n Integers

For all integers $n \geq 1$,

$$1 + 2 + \cdots + n = \frac{n(n + 1)}{2}.$$

Proof (by mathematical induction):

Let the property $P(n)$ be the equation

$$1 + 2 + 3 + \cdots + n = \frac{n(n + 1)}{2}. \qquad \leftarrow P(n)$$

continued on page 250

Show that P(1) is true:

To establish $P(1)$, we must show that

$$1 = \frac{1(1+1)}{2} \qquad \leftarrow \quad P(1)$$

But the left-hand side of this equation is 1 and the right-hand side is

$$\frac{1(1+1)}{2} = \frac{2}{2} = 1$$

also. Hence $P(1)$ is true.

Show that for all integers k ≥ 1, if P(k) is true then P(k + 1) is also true:
[Suppose that P(k) is true for a particular but arbitrarily chosen integer k ≥ 1. That is:] Suppose that k is any integer with $k \geq 1$ such that

$$1 + 2 + 3 + \cdots + k = \frac{k(k+1)}{2} \qquad \begin{array}{l} \leftarrow P(k) \\ \text{inductive hypothesis} \end{array}$$

[We must show that P(k + 1) is true. That is:] We must show that

$$1 + 2 + 3 + \cdots + (k+1) = \frac{(k+1)[(k+1)+1]}{2},$$

or, equivalently, that

$$1 + 2 + 3 + \cdots + (k+1) = \frac{(k+1)(k+2)}{2}. \qquad \leftarrow P(k+1)$$

[We will show that the left-hand side and the right-hand side of P(k + 1) are equal to the same quantity and thus are equal to each other.]

The left-hand side of $P(k + 1)$ is

$$1 + 2 + 3 + \cdots + (k+1)$$

$$= 1 + 2 + 3 + \cdots + k + (k+1) \qquad \begin{array}{l} \text{by making the next-to-last} \\ \text{term explicit} \end{array}$$

$$= \frac{k(k+1)}{2} + (k+1) \qquad \begin{array}{l} \text{by substitution from the} \\ \text{inductive hypothesis} \end{array}$$

$$= \frac{k(k+1)}{2} + \frac{2(k+1)}{2}$$

$$= \frac{k^2 + k}{2} + \frac{2k+2}{2}$$

$$= \frac{k^2 + 3k + 1}{2} \qquad \text{by algebra.}$$

And the right-hand side of $P(k + 1)$ is

$$\frac{(k+1)(k+2)}{2} = \frac{k^2 + 3k + 1}{2}.$$

Thus the two sides of $P(k + 1)$ are equal to the same quantity and so they are equal to each other. Therefore the equation $P(k + 1)$ is true *[as was to be shown].*
[Since we have proved both the basis step and the inductive step, we conclude that the theorem is true.]

The story is told that one of the greatest mathematicians of all time, Carl Friedrich Gauss (1777–1855), was given the problem of adding the numbers from 1 to 100 by his teacher when he was a young child. The teacher had asked his students to compute the sum, supposedly to gain himself some time to grade papers. But after just a few moments, Gauss produced the correct answer. Needless to say, the teacher was dumbfounded. How could young Gauss have calculated the quantity so rapidly? In his later years, Gauss explained that he had imagined the numbers paired according to the following schema.

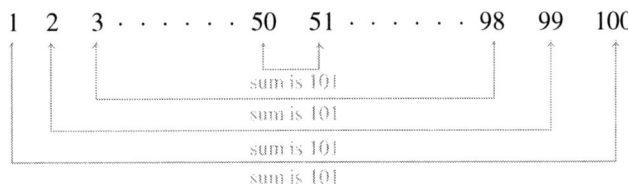

The sum of the numbers in each pair is 101, and there are 50 pairs in all; hence the total sum is $50 \cdot 101 = 5{,}050$.

> **• Definition Closed Form**
>
> If a sum with a variable number of terms is shown to be equal to a formula that does not contain either an ellipsis or a summation symbol, we say that it is written **in closed form**.

For example, writing $1 + 2 + 3 + \cdots + n = \dfrac{n(n+1)}{2}$ expresses the sum $1 + 2 + 3 + \cdots + n$ in closed form.

Example 5.2.2 Applying the Formula for the Sum of the First n Integers

a. Evaluate $2 + 4 + 6 + \cdots + 500$.

b. Evaluate $5 + 6 + 7 + 8 + \cdots + 50$.

c. For an integer $h \geq 2$, write $1 + 2 + 3 + \cdots + (h - 1)$ in closed form.

Solution

a. $2 + 4 + 6 + \cdots + 500 = 2 \cdot (1 + 2 + 3 + \cdots + 250)$

$$= 2 \cdot \left(\frac{250 \cdot 251}{2} \right) \qquad \text{by applying the formula for the sum of the first } n \text{ integers with } n = 250$$

$$= 62{,}750.$$

b. $5 + 6 + 7 + 8 + \cdots + 50 = (1 + 2 + 3 + \cdots + 50) - (1 + 2 + 3 + 4)$

$$= \frac{50 \cdot 51}{2} - 10 \qquad \text{by applying the formula for the sum of the first } n \text{ integers with } n = 50$$

$$= 1{,}265$$

c. $1 + 2 + 3 + \cdots + (h - 1) = \dfrac{(h - 1) \cdot [(h - 1) + 1]}{2} \qquad \text{by applying the formula for the sum of the first } n \text{ integers with } n = h - 1$

$$= \frac{(h - 1) \cdot h}{2} \qquad \text{since } (h - 1) + 1 = h.$$

The next example asks for a proof of another famous and important formula in mathematics—the formula for the sum of a geometric sequence. In a **geometric sequence,** each term is obtained from the preceding one by multiplying by a constant factor. If the first term is 1 and the constant factor is r, then the sequence is $1, r, r^2, r^3, \ldots, r^n, \ldots$. The sum of the first n terms of this sequence is given by the formula

$$\sum_{i=0}^{n} r^i = \frac{r^{n+1} - 1}{r - 1}$$

for all integers $n \geq 0$ and real numbers r not equal to 1. The expanded form of the formula is

$$r^0 + r^1 + r^2 + \cdots + r^n = \frac{r^{n+1} - 1}{r - 1},$$

and because $r^0 = 1$ and $r^1 = r$, the formula for $n \geq 1$ can be rewritten as

$$1 + r + r^2 + \cdots + r^n = \frac{r^{n+1} - 1}{r - 1}.$$

Example 5.2.3 Sum of a Geometric Sequence

Prove that $\sum_{i=0}^{n} r^i = \frac{r^{n+1} - 1}{r - 1}$, for all integers $n \geq 0$ and all real numbers r except 1.

Solution   In this example the property $P(n)$ is again an equation, although in this case it contains a real variable r:.

$$\sum_{i=0}^{n} r^i = \frac{r^{n+1} - 1}{r - 1}. \qquad \leftarrow \text{the property } (P(n))$$

Because r can be any real number other than 1, the proof begins by supposing that r is a particular but arbitrarily chosen real number not equal to 1. Then the proof continues by mathematical induction on n, starting with $n = 0$. In the basis step, you must show that $P(0)$ is true; that is, you show the property is true for $n = 0$. So you substitute 0 for each n in $P(n)$:

$$\sum_{i=0}^{0} r^i = \frac{r^{0+1} - 1}{r - 1}. \qquad \leftarrow \text{basis } (P(0))$$

In the inductive step, you suppose k is any integer with $k \geq 0$ for which $P(k)$ is true; that is, you suppose the property is true for $n = k$. So you substitute k for each n in $P(n)$:

$$\sum_{i=0}^{k} r^i = \frac{r^{k+1} - 1}{r - 1}. \qquad \leftarrow \text{inductive hypothesis } (P(k))$$

Then you show that $P(k + 1)$ is true; that is, you show the property is true for $n = k + 1$. So you substitute $k + 1$ for each n in $P(n)$:

$$\sum_{i=0}^{k+1} r^i = \frac{r^{(k+1)+1} - 1}{r - 1},$$

or, equivalently,

$$\boxed{\sum_{i=0}^{k+1} r^i = \frac{r^{k+2} - 1}{r - 1}.}$$ ← to show $(P(k + 1))$

In the inductive step for this proof we use another common technique for showing that an equation is true: We start with the left-hand side and transform it step-by-step into the right-hand side using the inductive hypothesis together with algebra and other known facts.

Theorem 5.2.3 Sum of a Geometric Sequence

For any real number r except 1, and any integer $n \geq 0$,

$$\sum_{i=0}^{n} r^i = \frac{r^{n+1} - 1}{r - 1}.$$

Proof (by mathematical induction):

Suppose r is a particular but arbitrarily chosen real number that is not equal to 1, and let the property $P(n)$ be the equation

$$\sum_{i=0}^{n} r^i = \frac{r^{i+1} - 1}{r - 1}   \quad \leftarrow P(n)$$

We must show that $P(n)$ is true for all integers $n \geq 0$. We do this by mathematical induction on n.

Show that P(0) is true:

To establish $P(0)$, we must show that

$$\sum_{i=0}^{0} r^i = \frac{r^{0+1} - 1}{r - 1}   \quad \leftarrow P(0)$$

The left-hand side of this equation is $r^0 = 1$ and the right-hand side is

$$\frac{r^{0+1} - 1}{r - 1} = \frac{r - 1}{r - 1} = 1$$

also because $r^1 = r$ and $r \neq 1$. Hence $P(0)$ is true.

Show that for all integers $k \geq 0$, if P(k) is true then P(k + 1) is also true:
[Suppose that P(k) is true for a particular but arbitrarily chosen integer $k \geq 0$. That is:]
Let k be any integer with $k \geq 0$, and suppose that

$$\sum_{i=0}^{k} r^i = \frac{r^{k+1} - 1}{r - 1}   \quad \begin{array}{l} \leftarrow P(k) \\ \text{inductive hypothesis} \end{array}$$

continued on page 254

[We must show that P(k + 1) is true. That is:] We must show that

$$\sum_{i=0}^{k+1} r^i = \frac{r^{(k+1)+1} - 1}{r - 1},$$

or, equivalently, that

$$\sum_{i=0}^{k+1} r^i = \frac{r^{k+2} - 1}{r - 1}. \qquad \leftarrow P(k+1)$$

[We will show that the left-hand side of P(k + 1) equals the right-hand side.]
The left-hand side of $P(k + 1)$ is

$$\sum_{i=0}^{k+1} r^i = \sum_{i=0}^{k} r^i + r^{k+1} \qquad \text{by writing the } (k+1)\text{st term separately from the first } k \text{ terms}$$

$$= \frac{r^{k+1} - 1}{r - 1} + r^{k+1} \qquad \text{by substitution from the inductive hypothesis}$$

$$= \frac{r^{k+1} - 1}{r - 1} + \frac{r^{k+1}(r - 1)}{r - 1} \qquad \text{by multiplying the numerator and denominator of the second term by } (r - 1) \text{ to obtain a common denominator}$$

$$= \frac{(r^{k+1} - 1) + r^{k+1}(r - 1)}{r - 1} \qquad \text{by adding fractions}$$

$$= \frac{r^{k+1} - 1 + r^{k+2} - r^{k+1}}{r - 1} \qquad \text{by multiplying out and using the fact that } r^{k-1} \cdot r = r^{k-1} \cdot r^1 = r^{k+2}$$

$$= \frac{r^{k+2} - 1}{r - 1} \qquad \text{by canceling the } r^{k+1}\text{'s.}$$

which is the right-hand side of $P(k + 1)$ *[as was to be shown.]*
[Since we have proved the basis step and the inductive step, we conclude that the theorem is true.]

Proving an Equality

The proofs of the basis and inductive steps in Examples 5.2.1 and 5.2.3 illustrate two different ways to show that an equation is true: (1) transforming the left-hand side and the right-hand side independently until they are seen to be equal, and (2) transforming one side of the equation until it is seen to be the same as the other side of the equation.

Sometimes people use a method that they believe proves equality but that is actually invalid. For example, to prove the basis step for Theorem 5.2.3, they perform the following steps:

Caution!   Don't do this!

$$\sum_{i=0}^{0} r^i = \frac{r^{0+1} - 1}{r - 1}$$

$$r^0 = \frac{r^1 - 1}{r - 1}$$

$$1 = \frac{r - 1}{r - 1}$$

$$1 = 1$$

The problem with this method is that starting from a statement and deducing a true conclusion does not prove that the statement is true. A true conclusion can also be deduced from a false statement. For instance, the steps below show how to deduce the true conclusion that $1 = 1$ from the false statement that $1 = 0$:

$$1 = 0 \qquad \text{false}$$
$$0 = 1$$
$$1 + 0 = 0 + 1$$
$$1 = 1 \qquad \leftarrow \text{true}$$

When using mathematical induction to prove formulas, be sure to use a method that avoids invalid reasoning, both for the basis step and for the inductive step.

Deducing Additional Formulas

The formula for the sum of a geometric sequence can be thought of as a family of different formulas in r, one for each real number r except 1.

Example 5.2.4 Applying the Formula for the Sum of a Geometric Sequence

In each of (a) and (b) below, assume that m is an integer that is greater than or equal to 3. Write each of the sums in closed form.

a. $1 + 3 + 3^2 + \cdots + 3^{m-2}$

b. $3^2 + 3^3 + 3^4 + \cdots + 3^m$

Solution

a. $1 + 3 + 3^2 + \cdots + 3^{m-2} = \dfrac{3^{(m-2)+1} - 1}{3 - 1}$
    by applying the formula for the sum of a geometric sequence with $r = 3$ and $n = m - 2$

$$= \dfrac{3^{m-1} - 1}{2}.$$

b. $3^2 + 3^3 + 3^4 + \cdots + 3^m = 3^2 \cdot (1 + 3 + 3^2 + \cdots + 3^{m-2})$ by factoring out 3^2

$$= 9 \cdot \left(\dfrac{3^{m-1} - 1}{2} \right) \qquad \text{by part (a).} \qquad \blacksquare$$

As with the formula for the sum of the first n integers, there is a way to think of the formula for the sum of the terms of a geometric sequence that makes it seem simple and intuitive. Let

$$S_n = 1 + r + r^2 + \cdots + r^n.$$

Then

$$r S_n = r + r^2 + r^3 + \cdots + r^{n+1},$$

and so

$$r S_n - S_n = (r + r^2 + r^3 + \cdots + r^{n+1}) - (1 + r + r^2 + \cdots + r^n)$$
$$= r^{n+1} - 1. \qquad\qquad 5.2.1$$

But

$$r S_n - S_n = (r - 1) S_n. \qquad\qquad 5.2.2$$

Equating the right-hand sides of equations (5.2.1) and (5.2.2) and dividing by $r - 1$ gives

$$S_n = \frac{r^{n+1} - 1}{r - 1}.$$

This derivation of the formula is attractive and is quite convincing. However, it is not as logically airtight as the proof by mathematical induction. To go from one step to another in the previous calculations, the argument is made that each term among those indicated by the ellipsis $(\ldots)$ has such-and-such an appearance and when these are canceled such-and-such occurs. But it is impossible actually to see each such term and each such calculation, and so the accuracy of these claims cannot be fully checked. With mathematical induction it is possible to focus exactly on what happens in the middle of the ellipsis and verify without doubt that the calculations are correct.

Test Yourself

1. Mathematical induction is a method for proving that a property defined for integers n is true for all values of n that are _____.

2. Let $P(n)$ be a property defined for integers n and consider constructing a proof by mathematical induction for the statement "$P(n)$ is true for all $n \geq a$."

(a) In the basis step one must show that _____.

(b) In the inductive step one supposes that _____ for some particular but arbitrarily chosen value of an integer $k \geq a$. This supposition is called the _____. One then has to show that _____.

Exercise Set 5.2

1. Use mathematical induction (and the proof of Proposition 5.2.1 as a model) to show that any amount of money of at least 14¢ can be made up using 3¢ and 8¢ coins.

2. Use mathematical induction to show that any postage of at least 12¢ can be obtained using 3¢ and 7¢ stamps.

3. For each positive integer n, let $P(n)$ be the formula

$$1^2 + 2^2 + \cdots + n^2 = \frac{n(n + 1)(2n + 1)}{6}.$$

a. Write $P(1)$. Is $P(1)$ true?
b. Write $P(k)$.
c. Write $P(k + 1)$.
d. In a proof by mathematical induction that the formula holds for all integers $n \geq 1$, what must be shown in the inductive step?

4. For each integer n with $n \geq 2$, let $P(n)$ be the formula

$$\sum_{i=1}^{n-1} i(i + 1) = \frac{n(n - 1)(n + 1)}{3}.$$

a. Write $P(2)$. Is $P(2)$ true?
b. Write $P(k)$.
c. Write $P(k + 1)$.
d. In a proof by mathematical induction that the formula holds for all integers $n \geq 2$, what must be shown in the inductive step?

5. Fill in the missing pieces in the following proof that

$$1 + 3 + 5 + \cdots + (2n - 1) = n^2$$

for all integers $n \geq 1$.

Proof: Let the property $P(n)$ be the equation

$$1 + 3 + 5 + \cdots + (2n - 1) = n^2. \quad \leftarrow P(n)$$

Show that $P(1)$ is true: To establish $P(1)$, we must show that when 1 is substituted in place of n, the left-hand side equals the right-hand side. But when $n = 1$, the left-hand side is the sum of all the odd integers from 1 to $2 \cdot 1 - 1$, which is the sum of the odd integers from 1 to 1, which is just 1. The right-hand side is (a)_____, which also equals 1. So $P(1)$ is true.

Show that for all integers $k \geq 1$, if $P(k)$ is true then $P(k + 1)$ is true: Let k be any integer with $k \geq 1$.

[Suppose $P(k)$ is true. That is:]

Suppose $1 + 3 + 5 + \cdots + (2k - 1) = $ (b)_____. $\leftarrow P(k)$
[This is the inductive hypothesis.]

[We must show that $P(k + 1)$ is true. That is:]

We must show that

(c)_____ = (d)_____. $\leftarrow P(k+1)$

But the left-hand side of $P(k + 1)$ is

$1 + 3 + 5 + \cdots + (2(k + 1) - 1)$

$\qquad = 1 + 3 + 5 + \cdots + (2k + 1) \qquad$ by algebra

$\qquad = [1 + 3 + 5 + \cdots + (2k - 1)] + (2k + 1)$
$\qquad\qquad$ the next-to-last term is $2k - 1$ because ___(e)___

$\qquad = k^2 + (2k + 1) \qquad$ by ___(f)___

$\qquad = (k + 1)^2 \qquad$ by algebra

which is the right-hand side of $P(k + 1)$ *[as was to be shown.]*

[Since we have proved the basis step and the inductive step, we conclude that the given statement is true.]

The previous proof was annotated to help make its logical flow more obvious. In standard mathematical writing, such annotation is omitted.

Prove each statement in 6–9 using mathematical induction. Do not derive them from Theorem 5.2.2 or Theorem 5.2.3.

6. For all integers $n \geq 1$, $2 + 4 + 6 + \cdots + 2n = n^2 + n$.

7. For all integers $n \geq 1$,

$$1 + 6 + 11 + 16 + \cdots + (5n - 4) = \frac{n(5n - 3)}{2}.$$

8. For all integers $n \geq 0$, $1 + 2 + 2^2 + \cdots + 2^n = 2^{n+1} - 1$.

9. For all integers $n \geq 3$,

$$4^3 + 4^4 + 4^5 + \cdots + 4^n = \frac{4(4^n - 16)}{3}.$$

Prove each of the statements in 10–17 by mathematical induction.

10. $1^2 + 2^2 + \cdots + n^2 = \dfrac{n(n + 1)(2n + 1)}{6}$, for all integers $n \geq 1$.

11. $1^3 + 2^3 + \cdots + n^3 = \left[\dfrac{n(n + 1)}{2}\right]^2$, for all integers $n \geq 1$.

12. $\dfrac{1}{1 \cdot 2} + \dfrac{1}{2 \cdot 3} + \cdots + \dfrac{1}{n(n + 1)} = \dfrac{n}{n + 1}$, for all integers $n \geq 1$.

13. $\displaystyle\sum_{i=1}^{n-1} i(i + 1) = \dfrac{n(n - 1)(n + 1)}{3}$, for all integers $n \geq 2$.

14. $\displaystyle\sum_{i=1}^{n+1} i \cdot 2^i = n \cdot 2^{n+2} + 2$, for all integers $n \geq 0$.

H 15. $\displaystyle\sum_{i=1}^{n} i(i!) = (n + 1)! - 1$, for all integers $n \geq 1$.

16. $\left(1 - \dfrac{1}{2^2}\right)\left(1 - \dfrac{1}{3^2}\right) \cdots \left(1 - \dfrac{1}{n^2}\right) = \dfrac{n + 1}{2n}$, for all integers $n \geq 2$.

17. $\displaystyle\prod_{i=0}^{n}\left(\dfrac{1}{2i + 1} \cdot \dfrac{1}{2i + 2}\right) = \dfrac{1}{(2n + 2)!}$, for all integers $n \geq 0$.

H * 18. If x is a real number not divisible by π, then for all integers $n \geq 1$,

$$\sin x + \sin 3x + \sin 5x + \cdots + \sin (2n - 1)x = \frac{1 - \cos 2nx}{2 \sin x}.$$

19. (For students who have studied calculus) Use mathematical induction, the product rule from calculus, and the facts that $\dfrac{d(x)}{dx} = 1$ and that $x^{k+1} = x \cdot x^k$ to prove that for all integers $n \geq 1$, $\dfrac{d(x^n)}{dx} = nx^{n-1}$.

Use the formula for the sum of the first n integers and/or the formula for the sum of a geometric sequence to evaluate the sums in 20–29 or to write them in closed form.

20. $4 + 8 + 12 + 16 + \cdots + 200$

21. $5 + 10 + 15 + 20 + \cdots + 300$

22. $3 + 4 + 5 + 6 + \cdots + 1000$

23. $7 + 8 + 9 + 10 + \cdots + 600$

24. $1 + 2 + 3 + \cdots + (k - 1)$, where k is an integer and $k \geq 2$.

25. a. $1 + 2 + 2^2 + \cdots + 2^{25}$
    b. $2 + 2^2 + 2^3 + \cdots + 2^{26}$

26. $3 + 3^2 + 3^3 + \cdots + 3^n$, where n is an integer with $n \geq 1$

27. $5^3 + 5^4 + 5^5 + \cdots + 5^k$, where k is any integer with $k \geq 3$.

28. $1 + \dfrac{1}{2} + \dfrac{1}{2^2} + \cdots + \dfrac{1}{2^n}$, where n is a positive integer

29. $1 - 2 + 2^2 - 2^3 + \cdots + (-1)^n 2^n$, where n is a positive integer

H 30. Find a formula in n, a, m, and d for the sum $(a + md) + (a + (m + 1)d) + (a + (m + 2)d) + \cdots + (a + (m + n)d)$, where m and n are integers, $n \geq 0$, and a and d are real numbers. Justify your answer.

31. Find a formula in a, r, m, and n for the sum

$$ar^m + ar^{m+1} + ar^{m+2} + \cdots + ar^{m+n}$$

where m and n are integers, $n \geq 0$, and a and r are real numbers. Justify your answer.

32. You have two parents, four grandparents, eight great-grandparents, and so forth.
    a. If all your ancestors were distinct, what would be the total number of your ancestors for the past 40 generations (counting your parents' generation as number one)? (*Hint:* Use the formula for the sum of a geometric sequence.)
    b. Assuming that each generation represents 25 years, how long is 40 generations?
    c. The total number of people who have ever lived is approximately 10 billion, which equals 10^{10} people. Compare this fact with the answer to part (a). What do you deduce?

Find the mistakes in the proof fragments in 33–35.

33. **Theorem:** For any integer $n \geq 1$,

$$1^2 + 2^2 + \cdots + n^2 = \frac{n(n+1)(2n+1)}{6}.$$

"**Proof (by mathematical induction):** Certainly the theorem is true for $n = 1$ because $1^2 = 1$ and

$$\frac{1(1+1)(2 \cdot 1 + 1)}{6} = 1.$$ So the basis step is true.

For the inductive step, suppose that for some integer $k \geq 1$,

$$k^2 = \frac{k(k+1)(2k+1)}{6}.$$ We must show that

$$(k+1)^2 = \frac{(k+1)((k+1)+1)(2(k+1)+1)}{6}."$$

H 34. **Theorem:** For any integer $n \geq 0$,

$$1 + 2 + 2^2 + \cdots + 2^n = 2^{n+1} - 1.$$

"**Proof (by mathematical induction):** Let the property $P(n)$ be $1 + 2 + 2^2 + \cdots + 2^n = 2^{n+1} - 1$.

Show that P(0) is true:

The left-hand side of $P(0)$ is $1 + 2 + 2^2 + \cdots + 2^0 = 1$ and the right-hand side is $2^{0+1} - 1 = 2 - 1 = 1$ also. So $P(0)$ is true."

H 35. **Theorem:** For any integer $n \geq 1$,

$$\sum_{i=1}^{n} i(i!) = (n+1)! - 1.$$

"**Proof (by mathematical induction): Let the property** $P(n)$ be $\sum_{i=1}^{n} i(i!) = (n+1)! - 1$.

Show that P(1) is true: When $n = 1$

$$\sum_{i=1}^{1} i(i!) = (1+1)! - 1$$

So $\qquad 1(1!) = 2! - 1$

and $\qquad 1 = 1$

Thus $P(1)$ is true."

* 36. Use Theorem 5.2.2 to prove that if m and n are any positive integers and m is odd, then $\sum_{k=0}^{m-1} (n+k)$ is divisible by m. Does the conclusion hold if m is even? Justify your answer.

H * 37. Use Theorem 5.2.2 and the result of exercise 10 to prove that if p is any prime number with $p \geq 5$, then the sum of squares of any p consecutive integers is divisible by p.

Answers for Test Yourself

1. greater than or equal to some initial value   2. (a) $P(a)$ is true   (b) $P(k)$ is true; inductive hypothesis; $P(k+1)$ is true

5.3 Mathematical Induction II

A good proof is one which makes us wiser. — I. Manin, A Course in Mathematical Logic, 1977

In natural science courses, deduction and induction are presented as alternative modes of thought—deduction being to infer a conclusion from general principles using the laws of logical reasoning, and induction being to enunciate a general principle after observing it to hold in a large number of specific instances. In this sense, then, *mathematical* induction is not inductive but deductive. Once proved by mathematical induction, a theorem is known just as certainly as if it were proved by any other mathematical method. Inductive reasoning, in the natural sciences sense, *is* used in mathematics, but only to make conjectures, not to prove them. For example, observe that

$$1 - \frac{1}{2} = \frac{1}{2}$$

$$\left(1 - \frac{1}{2}\right)\left(1 - \frac{1}{3}\right) = \frac{1}{3}$$

$$\left(1 - \frac{1}{2}\right)\left(1 - \frac{1}{3}\right)\left(1 - \frac{1}{4}\right) = \frac{1}{4}$$

This pattern seems so unlikely to occur by pure chance that it is reasonable to conjecture (though it is by no means certain) that the pattern holds true in general. In a case like this, a proof by mathematical induction (which you are asked to write in exercise 1 at the end of this section) gets to the essence of why the pattern holds in general. It reveals the mathematical mechanism that necessitates the truth of each successive case from the previous one. For instance, in this example observe that if

$$\left(1 - \frac{1}{2}\right)\left(1 - \frac{1}{3}\right)\cdots\left(1 - \frac{1}{k}\right) = \frac{1}{k},$$

then by substitution

$$\left(1 - \frac{1}{2}\right)\left(1 - \frac{1}{3}\right)\cdots\left(1 - \frac{1}{k}\right)\left(1 - \frac{1}{k+1}\right)$$

$$= \frac{1}{k}\left(1 - \frac{1}{k+1}\right) = \frac{1}{k}\left(\frac{k+1-1}{k+1}\right) = \frac{1}{k}\left(\frac{k}{k+1}\right) = \frac{1}{k+1}.$$

Thus mathematical induction makes knowledge of the general pattern a matter of mathematical certainty rather than vague conjecture.

In the remainder of this section we show how to use mathematical induction to prove additional kinds of statements such as divisibility properties of the integers and inequalities. The basic outlines of the proofs are the same in all cases, but the details of the basis and inductive steps differ from one to another.

Example 5.3.1 Proving a Divisibility Property

Use mathematical induction to prove that for all integers $n \geq 0$, $2^{2n} - 1$ is divisible by 3.

Solution　　As in the previous proofs by mathematical induction, you need to identify the property $P(n)$. In this example, $P(n)$ is the sentence

> $2^{2n} - 1$ is divisible by 3.　　← the property ($P(n)$)

By substitution, the statement for the basis step, $P(0)$, is

> $2^{2 \cdot 0} - 1$ is divisible by 3.　　← basis ($P(0)$)

The supposition for the inductive step, $P(k)$, is

> $2^{2k} - 1$ is divisible by 3,　　← inductive hypothesis ($P(k)$)

and the conclusion to be shown, $P(k+1)$, is

> $2^{2(k+1)} - 1$ is divisible by 3.　　← to show ($P(k+1)$)

Recall that an integer m is divisible by 3 if, and only if, $m = 3r$ for some integer r. Now the statement $P(0)$ is true because $2^{2 \cdot 0} - 1 = 2^0 - 1 = 1 - 1 = 0$, which is divisible by 3 because $0 = 3 \cdot 0$.

To prove the inductive step, you suppose that k is any integer greater than or equal to 0 such that $P(k)$ is true. This means that $2^{2k} - 1$ is divisible by 3. You must then prove the truth of $P(k+1)$. Or, in other words, you must show that $2^{2(k+1)} - 1$ is divisible by 3. But

$$2^{2(k+1)} - 1 = 2^{2k+2} - 1$$
$$= 2^{2k} \cdot 2^2 - 1 \qquad \text{by the laws of exponents}$$
$$= 2^{2k} \cdot 4 - 1.$$

The aim is to show that this quantity, $2^{2k} \cdot 4 - 1$, is divisible by 3. Why should that be so? By the inductive hypothesis, $2^{2k} - 1$ is divisible by 3, and $2^{2k} \cdot 4 - 1$ resembles $2^{2k} - 1$. Observe what happens, if you subtract $2^{2k} - 1$ from $2^{2k} \cdot 4 - 1$:

$$2^{2k} \cdot 4 - 1 - (2^{2k} - 1) = 2^{2k} \cdot 3.$$

divisible by 3? divisible by 3 divisible by 3

Adding $2^{2k} - 1$ to both sides gives

$$2^{2k} \cdot 4 - 1 = 2^{2k} \cdot 3 + 2^{2k} - 1.$$

divisible by 3? divisible by 3 divisible by 3

Both terms of the sum on the right-hand side of this equation are divisible by 3; hence the sum is divisible by 3. (See exercise 15 of Section 4.3.) Therefore, the left-hand side of the equation is also divisible by 3, which is what was to be shown.

This discussion is summarized as follows:

Proposition 5.3.1

For all integers $n \geq 0$, $2^{2n} - 1$ is divisible by 3.

Proof (by mathematical induction):

Let the property $P(n)$ be the sentence "$2^{2n} - 1$ is divisible by 3."

$$2^{2n} - 1 \text{ is divisible by 3.} \qquad \leftarrow P(n)$$

Show that $P(0)$ is true:
To establish $P(0)$, we must show that

$$2^{2 \cdot 0} - 1 \text{ is divisible by 3.} \qquad \leftarrow P(0)$$

But

$$2^{2 \cdot 0} - 1 = 2^0 - 1 = 1 - 1 = 0$$

and 0 is divisible by 3 because $0 = 3 \cdot 0$. Hence $P(0)$ is true.

Show that for all integers $k \geq 0$, if $P(k)$ is true then $P(k+1)$ is also true:
[Suppose that $P(k)$ is true for a particular but arbitrarily chosen integer $k \geq 0$. That is:]
Let k be any integer with $k \geq 0$, and suppose that

$$2^{2k} - 1 \text{ is divisible by 3.} \qquad \leftarrow P(k)$$

inductive hypothesis

By definition of divisibility, this means that

$$2^{2k} - 1 = 3r \quad \text{for some integer } r.$$

[We must show that $P(k+1)$ is true. That is:] We must show that

$$2^{2(k+1)} - 1 \text{ is divisible by 3.} \qquad \leftarrow P(k+1)$$

But

$$2^{2(k+1)} - 1 = 2^{2k+2} - 1$$

$$= 2^{2k} \cdot 2^2 - 1 \qquad \text{by the laws of exponents}$$

$$= 2^{2k} \cdot 4 - 1$$

$$= 2^{2k}(3+1) - 1$$

$$= 2^{2k} \cdot 3 + (2^{2k} - 1) \qquad \text{by the laws of algebra}$$

$$= 2^{2k} \cdot 3 + 3r \qquad \text{by inductive hypothesis}$$

$$= 3(2^{2k} + r) \qquad \text{by factoring out the 3.}$$

But $2^{2k} + r$ is an integer because it is a sum of products of integers, and so, by definition of divisibility, $2^{2(k+1)} - 1$ is divisible by 3 *[as was to be shown]*.
[Since we have proved the basis step and the inductive step, we conclude that the proposition is true.]

∎

The next example illustrates the use of mathematical induction to prove an inequality.

Example 5.3.2 Proving an Inequality

Use mathematical induction to prove that for all integers $n \geq 3$,

$$2n + 1 < 2^n.$$

Solution   In this example the property $P(n)$ is the inequality

$$2n + 1 < 2^n. \qquad \leftarrow \text{the property } (P(n))$$

By substitution, the statement for the basis step, $P(3)$, is

$$2 \cdot 3 + 1 < 2^3. \qquad \leftarrow \text{basis } (P(3))$$

The supposition for the inductive step, $P(k)$, is

$$2k + 1 < 2^k, \qquad \leftarrow \text{inductive hypothesis } (P(k))$$

and the conclusion to be shown is

$$2(k+1) + 1 < 2^{k+1}. \qquad \leftarrow \text{to show } (P(k+1))$$

To prove the basis step, observe that the statement $P(3)$ is true because $2 \cdot 3 + 1 = 7$, $2^3 = 8$, and $7 < 8$.

To prove the inductive step, suppose the inductive hypothesis, that $P(k)$ is true for an integer $k \geq 3$. This means that $2k + 1 < 2^k$ is assumed to be true for a particular but arbitrarily chosen integer $k \geq 3$. Then derive the truth of $P(k+1)$. Or, in other words, show that the inequality $2(k+1) + 1 < 2^{k+1}$ is true. But by multiplying out and regrouping,

$$2(k+1) + 1 = 2k + 3 = (2k+1) + 2, \qquad \text{5.3.1}$$

and by substitution from the inductive hypothesis,

$$(2k + 1) + 2 < 2^k + 2. \qquad\qquad 5.3.2$$

Hence

$$2(k + 1) + 1 < 2^k + 2 \qquad \text{The left-most part of equation (5.3.1) is less than the right-most part of inequality (5.3.2).}$$

Note Properties of order are listed in Appendix A.

If it can be shown that $2^k + 2$ is less than 2^{k+1}, then the desired inequality will have been proved. But since the quantity 2^k can be added to or subtracted from an inequality without changing its direction,

$$2^k + 2 < 2^{k+1} \quad\Leftrightarrow\quad 2 < 2^{k+1} - 2^k = 2^k(2 - 1) = 2^k.$$

And since multiplying or dividing an inequality by 2 does not change its direction,

$$2 < 2^k \quad\Leftrightarrow\quad 1 = \frac{2}{2} < \frac{2^k}{2} = 2^{k-1} \qquad \text{by the laws of exponents.}$$

This last inequality is clearly true for all $k \geq 2$. Hence it is true that $2(k + 1) + 1 < 2^{k+1}$.

This discussion is made more flowing (but less intuitive) in the following formal proof:

Proposition 5.3.2

For all integers $n \geq 3$, $2n + 1 < 2^n$.

Proof (by mathematical induction):

Let the property $P(n)$ be the inequality

$$2n + 1 < 2^n. \qquad \longleftarrow P(n)$$

Show that P(3) is true:
To establish $P(3)$, we must show that

$$2 \cdot 3 + 1 < 2^3. \qquad \longleftarrow P(3)$$

But

$$2 \cdot 3 + 1 = 7 \quad \text{and} \quad 2^3 = 8 \quad \text{and} \quad 7 < 8.$$

Hence $P(3)$ is true.

Show that for all integers $k \geq 3$, if P(k) is true then P(k + 1) is also true:
[Suppose that P(k) is true for a particular but arbitrarily chosen integer $k \geq 3$. That is:]
Suppose that k is any integer with $k \geq 3$ such that

$$2k + 1 < 2^k. \qquad \longleftarrow P(k)$$
$$\text{inductive hypothesis}$$

[We must show that $P(k + 1)$ is true. That is:] We must show that

$$2(k + 1) + 1 < 2^{(k+1)},$$

or, equivalently,

$$2k + 3 < 2^{(k+1)}. \qquad \longleftarrow P(k + 1)$$

But

$$2k + 3 = (2k + 1) + 2 \quad \text{by algebra}$$
$$< 2^k + 2^k \quad \begin{array}{l} \text{because } 2k + 1 < 2^k \text{ by the inductive hypothesis} \\ \text{and because } 2 < 2^k \text{ for all integers } k \geq 2 \end{array}$$
$$\therefore 2k + 3 < 2 \cdot 2^k = 2^{k+1} \quad \text{by the laws of exponents.}$$

[This is what we needed to show.]
[Since we have proved the basis step and the inductive step, we conclude that the proposition is true.]

■

The next example demonstrates how to use mathematical induction to show that the terms of a sequence satisfy a certain explicit formula.

Example 5.3.3 Proving a Property of a Sequence

Define a sequence $a_1, a_2, a_3, \ldots$ as follows.*

$$a_1 = 2$$
$$a_k = 5a_{k-1} \quad \text{for all integers } k \geq 2.$$

a. Write the first four terms of the sequence.

b. It is claimed that for each integer $n \geq 0$, the nth term of the sequence has the same value as that given by the formula $2 \cdot 5^{n-1}$. In other words, the claim is that the terms of the sequence satisfy the equation $a_n = 2 \cdot 5^{n-1}$. Prove that this is true.

Solution

a. $a_1 = 2$.
$a_2 = 5a_{2-1} = 5a_1 = 5 \cdot 2 = 10$
$a_3 = 5a_{3-1} = 5a_2 = 5 \cdot 10 = 50$
$a_4 = 5a_{4-1} = 5a_3 = 5 \cdot 50 = 250$.

b. To use mathematical induction to show that every term of the sequence satisfies the equation, begin by showing that the first term of the sequence satisfies the equation. Then suppose that an arbitrarily chosen term a_k satisfies the equation and prove that the next term a_{k+1} also satisfies the equation.

Proof:

Let $a_1, a_2, a_3, \ldots$ be the sequence defined by specifying that $a_1 = 2$ and $a_k = 5a_{k-1}$ for all integers $k \geq 2$, and let the property $P(n)$ be the equation

$$a_n = 2 \cdot 5^{n-1}. \qquad \leftarrow P(n)$$

We will use mathematical induction to prove that for all integers $n \geq 1$, $P(n)$ is true.

Show that P(1) is true:
To establish $P(1)$, we must show that

$$a_1 = 2 \cdot 5^{1-1}. \qquad \leftarrow P(1)$$

*This is another example of a recursive definition. The general subject of recursion is discussed in Section 5.6.

But the left-hand side of $P(1)$ is

$$a_1 = 2 \qquad \text{by definition of } a_1, a_2, a_3, \ldots,$$

and the right-hand side of $P(1)$ is

$$2 \cdot 5^{1-1} = 2 \cdot 5^0 = 2 \cdot 1 = 2.$$

Thus the two sides of $P(1)$ are equal to the same quantity, and hence $P(1)$ is true.

Show that for all integers $k \geq 1$, if $P(k)$ is true then $P(k+1)$ is also true:
[Suppose that $P(k)$ is true for a particular but arbitrarily chosen integer $k \geq 1$. That is:] Let k be any integer with $k \geq 0$, and suppose that

$$a_k = 2 \cdot 5^{k-1}. \qquad \leftarrow P(k)$$
$$\text{inductive hypothesis}$$

By definition of divisibility, this means that

$$a_k = 2 \cdot 5^{k-1}.$$

[We must show that $P(k+1)$ is true. That is:] We must show that

$$a_{k+1} = 2 \cdot 5^{(k+1)-1},$$

or, equivalently,

$$a_{k+1} = 2 \cdot 5^k. \qquad \leftarrow P(k+1)$$

But the left-hand side of $P(k+1)$ is

$$
\begin{aligned}
a_{k+1} &= 5 a_{(k+1)-1} & & \text{by definition of } a_1, a_2, a_3, \ldots \\
&= 5 a_k & & \text{since } (k+1) - 1 = k \\
&= 5 \cdot (2 \cdot 5^{k-1}) & & \text{by inductive hypothesis} \\
&= 2 \cdot (5 \cdot 5^{k-1}) & & \text{by regrouping} \\
&= 2 \cdot 5^k & & \text{by the laws of exponents}
\end{aligned}
$$

which is the right-hand side of the equation *[as was to be shown.]*

[Since we have proved the basis step and the inductive step, we conclude that the formula holds for all terms of the sequence.] ▪

A Problem with Trominoes

The word *polyomino*, a generalization of *domino*, was introduced by Solomon Golomb in 1954 when he was a 22-year-old student at Harvard. Subsequently, he and others proved many interesting properties about them, and they became the basis for the popular computer game Tetris. A particular type of polyomino, called a *tromino*, is made up of three attached squares, which can be of two types:

straight ▯▯▯ and L-shaped ⌐

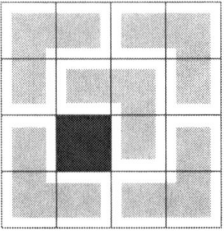

Call a checkerboard that is formed using m squares on a side an $m \times m$ ("m by m") checkerboard. Observe that if one square is removed from a 4×4 checkerboard, the remaining squares can be completely covered by L-shaped trominoes. For instance, a covering for one such board is illustrated in the figure to the left.

In his first article about polyominoes, Golomb included a proof of the following theorem. It is a beautiful example of an argument by mathematical induction.

Theorem Covering a Board with Trominoes

For any integer $n \geq 1$, if one square is removed from a $2^n \times 2^n$ checkerboard, the remaining squares can be completely covered by L-shaped trominoes.

The main insight leading to a proof of this theorem is the observation that because $2^{k+1} = 2 \cdot 2^k$, when a $2^{k+1} \times 2^{k+1}$ board is split in half both vertically and horizontally, each half side will have length 2^k and so each resulting quadrant will be a $2^k \times 2^k$ checkerboard.

Proof (by mathematical induction):

Let the property $P(n)$ be the sentence

> If any square is removed from a $2^n \times 2^n$ checkerboard,
> then the remaining squares can be completely covered.   ← *P(n)*
> by L-shaped trominoes

Show that P(1) is true:

A $2^1 \times 2^1$ checkerboard just consists of four squares. If one square is removed, the remaining squares form an L, which can be covered by a single L-shaped tromino, as illustrated in the figure to the left. Hence $P(1)$ is true.

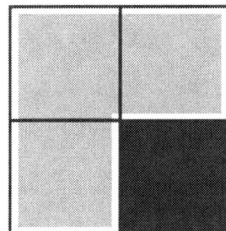

Show that for all integers $k \geq 1$, if $P(k)$ is true then $P(k+1)$ is also true:

[Suppose that $P(k)$ is true for a particular but arbitrarily chosen integer $k \geq 3$. That is:] Let k be any integer such that $k \geq 1$, and suppose that

> If any square is removed from a $2^k \times 2^k$ checkerboard,
> then the remaining squares can be completely covered   ← *P(k)*
> by L-shaped trominoes.

$P(k)$ is the inductive hypothesis.
  [We must show that $P(k+1)$ is true. That is:] We must show that

> If any square is removed from a $2^{k+1} \times 2^{k+1}$ checkerboard,
> then the remaining squares can be completely covered   ← *P(k + 1)*
> by L-shaped trominoes.

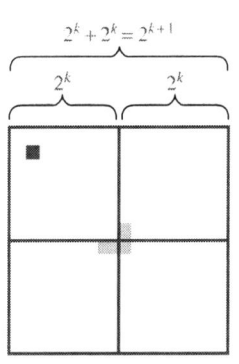

$$2^k + 2^k = 2^{k+1}$$

$$2^k \qquad 2^k$$

Consider a $2^{k+1} \times 2^{k+1}$ checkerboard with one square removed. Divide it into four equal quadrants: Each will consist of a $2^k \times 2^k$ checkerboard. In one of the quadrants, one square will have been removed, and so, by inductive hypothesis, all the remaining squares in this quadrant can be completely covered by L-shaped trominoes. The other three quadrants meet at the center of the checkerboard, and the center of the checkerboard serves as a corner of a square from each of those quadrants. An L-shaped tromino can, therefore, be placed on those three central squares. This situation is illustrated in the figure to the left. By inductive hypothesis, the remaining squares in each of the three quadrants can be completely covered by L-shaped trominoes. Thus every square in the $2^{k+1} \times 2^{k+1}$ checkerboard except the one that was removed can be completely covered by L-shaped trominoes *[as was to be shown]*.

Test Yourself

1. Mathematical induction differs from the kind of induction used in the natural sciences because it is actually a form of _____ reasoning.

2. Mathematical induction can be used to _____ conjectures that have been made using inductive reasoning.

Exercise Set 5.3

1. Based on the discussion of the product $\left(1 - \frac{1}{2}\right)\left(1 - \frac{1}{3}\right)$ $\left(1 - \frac{1}{4}\right) \cdots \left(1 - \frac{1}{n}\right)$ at the beginning of this section, conjecture a formula for general n. Prove your conjecture by mathematical induction.

2. Evaluate the sum $\displaystyle\sum_{k=1}^{n} \frac{k}{(k+1)!}$ for $n = 1, 2, 3, 4,$ and 5.

   Make a conjecture about a formula for this sum for general n, and prove your conjecture by mathematical induction.

3. Observe that

$$\frac{1}{1 \cdot 3} = \frac{1}{3}$$

$$\frac{1}{1 \cdot 3} + \frac{1}{3 \cdot 5} = \frac{2}{5}$$

$$\frac{1}{1 \cdot 3} + \frac{1}{3 \cdot 5} + \frac{1}{5 \cdot 7} = \frac{3}{7}$$

$$\frac{1}{1 \cdot 3} + \frac{1}{3 \cdot 5} + \frac{1}{5 \cdot 7} + \frac{1}{7 \cdot 9} = \frac{4}{9}$$

   Guess a general formula and prove it by mathematical induction.

H 4. Observe that

$$1 = 1,$$
$$1 - 4 = -(1 + 2),$$
$$1 - 4 + 9 = 1 + 2 + 3,$$
$$1 - 4 + 9 - 16 = -(1 + 2 + 3 + 4),$$
$$1 - 4 + 9 - 16 + 25 = 1 + 2 + 3 + 4 + 5.$$

   Guess a general formula and prove it by mathematical induction.

5. Experiment with computing values of the product $\left(1 + \frac{1}{1}\right)\left(1 + \frac{1}{2}\right)\left(1 + \frac{1}{3}\right) \cdots \left(1 + \frac{1}{n}\right)$ for small values of n to conjecture a formula for this product for general n. Prove your conjecture by mathematical induction.

6. For each positive integer n, let $P(n)$ be the property

$$5^n - 1 \text{ is divisible by } 4.$$

   a. Write $P(0)$. Is $P(0)$ true?
   b. Write $P(k)$.
   c. Write $P(k+1)$.
   d. In a proof by mathematical induction that this divisibility property holds for all integers $n \geq 0$, what must be shown in the inductive step?

7. For each positive integer n, let $P(n)$ be the property

$$2^n < (n+1)!.$$

   a. Write $P(2)$. Is $P(2)$ true?
   b. Write $P(k)$.
   c. Write $P(k+1)$.
   d. In a proof by mathematical induction that this inequality holds for all integers $n \geq 2$, what must be shown in the inductive step?

Prove each statement in 8–23 by mathematical induction.

8. $5^n - 1$ is divisible by 4, for each integer $n \geq 0$.

9. $7^n - 1$ is divisible by 6, for each integer $n \geq 0$.

10. $n^3 - 7n + 3$ is divisible by 3, for each integer $n \geq 0$.

11. $3^{2n} - 1$ is divisible by 8, for each integer $n \geq 0$.

12. For any integer $n \geq 0$, $7^n - 2^n$ is divisible by 5.

H 13. For any integer $n \geq 0$, $x^n - y^n$ is divisible by $x - y$, where x and y are any integers with $x \neq y$.

H 14. $n^3 - n$ is divisible by 6, for each integer $n \geq 0$.

15. $n(n^2 + 5)$ is divisible by 6, for each integer $n \geq 0$.

16. $2^n < (n+1)!$, for all integers $n \geq 2$.

17. $2^n < (n+2)!$, for all integers $n \geq 0$.

18. $5^n + 9 < 6^n$, for all integers $n \geq 2$.

19. $n^2 < 2^n$, for all integers $n \geq 5$.

20. $1 + 3n \leq 4^n$, for every integer $n \geq 0$.

21. $\sqrt{n} < \frac{1}{\sqrt{1}} + \frac{1}{\sqrt{2}} + \cdots + \frac{1}{\sqrt{n}}$, for all integers $n \geq 2$.

22. $1 + nx \leq (1 + x)^n$, for all real numbers $x > -1$ and integers $n \geq 2$.

23. a. $n^3 > 2n + 1$, for all integers $n \geq 2$.
    b. $n! > n^2$, for all integers $n \geq 4$.

24. A sequence $a_1, a_2, a_3, \ldots$ is defined by letting $a_1 = 3$ and $a_k = 7a_{k-1}$ for all integers $k \geq 2$. Show that $a_n = 3 \cdot 7^{n-1}$ for all integers $n \geq 1$.

25. A sequence $c_0, c_1, c_2, \ldots$ is defined by letting $c_0 = 3$ and $c_k = (c_{k-1})^2$ for all integers $k \geq 1$. Show that $c_n = 3^{2^n}$ for all integers $n \geq 0$.

26. A sequence $b_0, b_1, b_2, \ldots$ is defined by letting $b_0 = 5$ and $b_k = 4 + b_{k-1}$ for all integers $k \geq 1$. Show that $b_n > 4n$ for all integers $n \geq 0$.

27. A sequence $d_1, d_2, d_3, \ldots$ is defined by letting $d_1 = 2$ and $d_k = \dfrac{d_{k-1}}{k}$ for all integers $k \geq 2$. Show that for all integers $n \geq 1, d_n = \dfrac{2}{n!}$.

28. As each of a group of businesspeople arrives at a meeting, each shakes hands with all the other people present. Use mathematical induction to show that if n people come to the meeting then $[n(n-1)]/2$ handshakes occur.

29. Prove that for all integers $n \geq 1$,

$$\frac{1}{3} = \frac{1+3}{5+7} = \frac{1+3+5}{7+9+11} = \cdots$$
$$= \frac{1+3+\cdots+(2n-1)}{(2n+1)+\cdots+(4n-1)}.$$

In order for a proof by mathematical induction to be valid, the basis statement must be true for $n = a$ and the argument of the inductive step must be correct for every integer $k \geq a$. In 30 and 31 find the mistakes in the "proofs" by mathematical induction.

30. **"Theorem:"** For any integer $n \geq 1$, all the numbers in a set of n numbers are equal to each other.

   "Proof (by mathematical induction): It is obviously true that all the numbers in a set consisting of just one number are equal to each other, so the basis step is true. For the inductive step, let $A = \{a_1, a_2, \ldots, a_k, a_{k+1}\}$ be any set of $k + 1$ numbers. Form two subsets each of size k:

   $$B = \{a_1, a_2, a_3, \ldots, a_k\} \quad \text{and}$$
   $$C = \{a_1, a_3, a_4, \ldots, a_{k+1}\}.$$

   (B consists of all the numbers in A except a_{k+1}, and C consists of all the numbers in A except a_2.) By inductive hypothesis, all the numbers in B equal a_1 and all the numbers in C equal a_1 (since both sets have only k numbers). But every number in A is in B or C, so all the numbers in A equal a_1; hence all are equal to each other."

31. **"Theorem:"** For all integers $n \geq 1, 3^n - 2$ is even.

   "Proof (by mathematical induction): Suppose the theorem is true for an integer k, where $k \geq 1$. That is, suppose $3^k - 2$ is even. We must show that $3^{k+1} - 2$ is even. But

   $$3^{k+1} - 2 = 3^k \cdot 3 - 2 = 3^k(1+2) - 2$$
   $$= (3^k - 2) + 3^k \cdot 2.$$

   Now $3^k - 2$ is even by inductive hypothesis and $3^k \cdot 2$ is even by inspection. Hence the sum of the two quantities is even (by Theorem 4.1.1). It follows that $3^{k+1} - 2$ is even, which is what we needed to show."

32. Some 5×5 checkerboards with one square removed can be completely covered by L-shaped trominoes, whereas other 5×5 checkerboards cannot. Find examples of both kinds of checkerboards. Justify your answers.

33. Consider a 4×6 checkerboard. Draw a covering of the board by L-shaped trominoes.

34. a. Use mathematical induction to prove that any checkerboard with dimensions $2 \times 3n$ can be completely covered with L-shaped trominoes for any integer $n \geq 1$.
    b. Let n be any integer greater than or equal to 1. Use the result of part (a) to prove by mathematical induction that for all integers m, any checkerboard with dimensions $2m \times 3n$ can be completely covered with L-shaped trominoes.

35. Let m and n be any integers that are greater than or equal to 1.
    a. Prove that a necessary condition for an $m \times n$ checkerboard to be completely coverable by L-shaped trominoes is that mn be divisible by 3.
    b. Prove that having mn be divisible by 3 is not a sufficient condition for an $m \times n$ checkerboard to be completely coverable by L-shaped trominoes.

36. In a round-robin tournament each team plays every other team exactly once. If the teams are labeled $T_1, T_2, \ldots, T_n$, then the outcome of such a tournament can be represented by a drawing, called a *directed graph,* in which the teams are represented as dots and an arrow is drawn from one dot to another if, and only if, the team represented by the first dot beats the team represented by the second dot. For example, the directed graph below shows one outcome of a round-robin tournament involving five teams, A, B, C, D, and E.

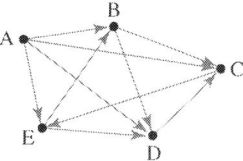

Use mathematical induction to show that in any round-robin tournament involving n teams, where $n \geq 2$, it is possible to label the teams $T_1, T_2, \ldots, T_n$ so that T_i beats T_{i+1} for all $i = 1, 2, \ldots, n - 1$. (For instance, one such labeling in the example above is $T_1 = A, T_2 = B, T_3 = C, T_4 = E, T_5 = D$.) (*Hint:* Given $k + 1$ teams, pick one— say T'—and apply the inductive hypothesis to the remaining teams to obtain an ordering $T_1, T_2, \ldots, T_k$. Consider three cases: T' beats T_1, T' loses to the first m teams (where $1 \leq m \leq k - 1$) and beats the $(m + 1)$st team, and T' loses to all the other teams.)

37. On the outside rim of a circular disk the integers from 1 through 30 are painted in random order. Show that no matter what this order is, there must be three successive integers whose sum is at least 45.

H 38. Suppose that n a's and n b's are distributed around the outside of a circle. Use mathematical induction to prove that for all integers $n \geq 1$, given any such arrangement, it is possible to find a starting point so that if one travels around the circle in a clockwise direction, the number of a's one has passed is never less than the number of b's one has passed. For example, in the diagram shown below, one could start at the a with an asterisk.

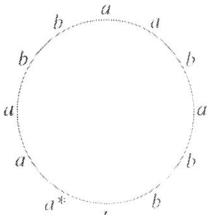

39. For a polygon to be **convex** means that given any two points on or inside the polygon, the line joining the points lies entirely inside the polygon. Use mathematical induction to prove that for all integers $n \geq 3$, the angles of any n-sided convex polygon add up to $180(n - 2)$ degrees.

40. a. Prove that in an 8×8 checkerboard with alternating black and white squares, if the squares in the top right and bottom left corners are removed the remaining board cannot be covered with dominoes. (*Hint*: Mathematical induction is not needed for this proof.)

H b. Use mathematical induction to prove that for all integers n, if a $2n \times 2n$ checkerboard with alternating black and white squares has one white square and one black square removed anywhere on the board, the remaining squares can be covered with dominoes.

Answers for Test Yourself

1. deductive   2. prove

5.4 Strong Mathematical Induction and the Well-Ordering Principle for the Integers

Mathematics takes us still further from what is human into the region of absolute necessity, to which not only the actual world, but every possible world, must conform.
— Bertrand Russell, 1902

Strong mathematical induction is similar to ordinary mathematical induction in that it is a technique for establishing the truth of a sequence of statements about integers. Also, a proof by strong mathematical induction consists of a basis step and an inductive step. However, the basis step may contain proofs for several initial values, and in the inductive step the truth of the predicate $P(n)$ is assumed not just for one value of n but for *all* values through k, and then the truth of $P(k + 1)$ is proved.

Principle of Strong Mathematical Induction

Let $P(n)$ be a property that is defined for integers n, and let a and b be fixed integers with $a \leq b$. Suppose the following two statements are true:

1. $P(a), P(a + 1), \ldots,$ and $P(b)$ are all true. (**basis step**)

2. For any integer $k \geq b$, if $P(i)$ is true for all integers i from a through k, then $P(k + 1)$ is true. (**inductive step**)

Then the statement

$$\text{for all integers } n \geq a, \; P(n)$$

is true. (The supposition that $P(i)$ is true for all integers i from a through k is called the **inductive hypothesis.** Another way to state the inductive hypothesis is to say that $P(a), P(a + 1), \ldots, P(k)$ are all true.)

Any statement that can be proved with ordinary mathematical induction can be proved with strong mathematical induction. The reason is that given any integer $k \geq b$, if the truth of $P(k)$ alone implies the truth of $P(k + 1)$, then certainly the truth of $P(a)$, $P(a + 1), \ldots$, and $P(k)$ implies the truth of $P(k + 1)$. It is also the case that any statement that can be proved with strong mathematical induction can be proved with ordinary mathematical induction. A proof is sketched in exercise 27 at the end of this section.

Strictly speaking, the principle of strong mathematical induction can be written without a basis step if the inductive step is changed to "$\forall k \geq a - 1$, if $P(i)$ is true for all integers i from a through k, then $P(k + 1)$ is true." The reason for this is that the statement "$P(i)$ is true for all integers i from a through k" is vacuously true for $k = a-1$. Hence, if the implication in the inductive step is true, then the conclusion $P(a)$ must also be true,* which proves the basis step. However, in many cases the proof of the implication for $k > b$ does not work for $a \leq k \leq b$. So it is a good idea to get into the habit of thinking separately about the cases where $a \leq k \leq b$ by explicitly including a basis step.

The principle of strong mathematical induction is known under a variety of different names including the *second principle of induction*, the *second principle of finite induction*, and the *principle of complete induction*.

Applying Strong Mathematical Induction

The divisibility-by-a-prime theorem states that any integer greater than 1 is divisible by a prime number. We prove this theorem using strong mathematical induction.

Example 5.4.1 Divisibility by a Prime

Prove Theorem 4.3.4: Any integer greater than 1 is divisible by a prime number.

Solution   The idea for the inductive step is this: If a given integer greater than 1 is not itself prime, then it is a product of two smaller positive integers, each of which is greater than 1. Since you are assuming that each of these smaller integers is divisible by a prime number, by transitivity of divisibility, those prime numbers also divide the integer you started with.

Proof (by strong mathematical induction):

Let the property $P(n)$ be the sentence

$$n \text{ is divisible by a prime number.} \qquad \leftarrow P(n)$$

Show that P(2) is true:
To establish $P(2)$, we must show that

$$2 \text{ is divisible by a prime number.} \qquad \leftarrow P(2)$$

But this is true because 2 is divisible by 2 and 2 is a prime number.

Show that for all integers $k \geq 2$, if $P(i)$ is true for all integers i from 2 through k, then $P(k + 1)$ is also true:

continued on page 270

---

*If you have proved that a certain if-then statement is true and if you also know that the hypothesis is true, then the conclusion must be true.

Let k be any integer with $k \geq 2$ and suppose that

i is divisible by a prime number for all integers
i from 2 through k.   ← inductive hypothesis

We must show that

$k + 1$ is divisible by a prime number.   ← $P(k + 1)$

Case 1 ($k + 1$ is prime): In this case $k + 1$ is divisible by a prime number, namely itself.

Case 2 ($k + 1$ is not prime): In this case $k + 1 = ab$ where a and b are integers with $1 < a < k + 1$ and $1 < b < k + 1$. Thus, in particular, $2 \leq a \leq k$, and so by inductive hypothesis, a is divisible by a prime number p. In addition because $k + 1 = ab$, we have that $k + 1$ is divisible by a. Hence, since $k + 1$ is divisible by a and a is divisible by p, by transitivity of divisibility, $k + 1$ is divisible by the prime number p.

Therefore, regardless of whether $k + 1$ is prime or not, it is divisible by a prime number *[as was to be shown]*.

[Since we have proved both the basis and the inductive step of the strong mathematical induction, we conclude that the given statement is true.]

Both ordinary and strong mathematical induction can be used to show that the terms of certain sequences satisfy certain properties. The next example shows how this is done using strong induction.

Example 5.4.2 Proving a Property of a Sequence with Strong Induction

Define a sequence $s_0, s_1, s_2, \ldots$ as follows:

$$s_0 = 0, \quad s_1 = 4, \quad s_k = 6a_{k-1} - 5a_{k-2} \quad \text{for all integers } k \geq 2.$$

a. Find the first four terms of this sequence.

b. It is claimed that for each integer $n \geq 0$, the nth term of the sequence has the same value as that given by the formula $5^n - 1$. In other words, the claim is that all the terms of the sequence satisfy the equation $s_n = 5^n - 1$. Prove that this is true.

Solution

a. $s_0 = 0, \qquad s_1 = 4, \qquad s_2 = 6s_1 - 5s_0 = 6 \cdot 4 - 5 \cdot 0 = 24,$
$s_3 = 6s_2 - 5s_1 = 6 \cdot 24 - 5 \cdot 4 = 144 - 20 = 124$

b. To use strong mathematical induction to show that every term of the sequence satisfies the equation, the basis step must show that the first two terms satisfy it. This is necessary because, according to the definition of the sequence, computing values of later terms requires knowing the values of the *two* previous terms. So if the basis step only shows that the first term satisfies the equation, it would not be possible to use the inductive step to deduce that the second term satisfies the equation. In the inductive step you suppose that for an arbitrarily chosen integer $k \geq 1$, all the terms of the sequence from s_0 through s_k satisfy the given equation and you then deduce that s_{k+1} must also satisfy the equation.

Proof:

Let $s_0, s_1, s_2, \ldots$ be the sequence defined by specifying that $s_0 = 0$, $s_1 = 4$, and $s_k = 6a_{k-1} - 5a_{k-2}$ for all integers $k \geq 2$, and let the property $P(n)$ be the formula

$$s_n = 5^n - 1 \qquad \leftarrow P(n)$$

We will use strong mathematical induction to prove that for all integers $n \geq 0$, $P(n)$ is true.

Show that P(0) and P(1) are true:
To establish $P(0)$ and $P(1)$, we must show that

$$s_0 = 5^0 - 1 \quad \text{and} \quad s_1 = 5^1 - 1. \qquad \leftarrow P(0) \quad \text{and} \quad P(1)$$

But, by definition of $s_0, s_1, s_2, \ldots$, we have that $s_0 = 0$ and $s_1 = 4$. Since $5^0 - 1 = 1 - 1 = 0$ and $5^1 - 1 = 5 - 1 = 4$, the values of s_0 and s_1 agree with the values given by the formula.

Show that for all integers $k \geq 1$, if $P(i)$ is true for all integers i from 0 through k, then $P(k + 1)$ is also true:
Let k be any integer with $k \geq 1$ and suppose that

$$s_i = 5^i - 1 \text{ for all integers } i \text{ with } 0 \leq i \leq k. \qquad \leftarrow \text{inductive hypothesis}$$

We must show that

$$s_{k+1} = 5^{k+1} - 1. \qquad \leftarrow P(k+1)$$

But since $k \geq 1$, we have that $k + 1 \geq 2$, and so

$$
\begin{aligned}
s_{k+1} &= 6s_k - 5s_{k-1} && \text{by definition of } s_0, s_1, s_2, \ldots \\
&= 6(5^k - 1) - 5(5^{k-1} - 1) && \text{by definition hypothesis} \\
&= 6 \cdot 5^k - 6 - 5^k + 5 && \text{by multiplying out and applying} \\
& && \text{a law of exponents} \\
&= (6 - 1)5^k - 1 && \text{by factoring out 6 and arithmetic} \\
&= 5 \cdot 5^k - 1 && \text{by arithmetic} \\
&= 5^{k+1} - 1 && \text{by applying a law of exponents,}
\end{aligned}
$$

[as was to be shown].

[Since we have proved both the basis and the inductive step of the strong mathematical induction, we conclude that the given statement is true.]

Another use of strong induction concerns the computation of products. A product of four numbers may be computed in a variety of different ways as indicated by the placement of parentheses. For instance,

> $((x_1 x_2)x_3)x_4$ means multiply x_1 and x_2, multiply the result by x_3, and then multiply that number by x_4.

And

> $(x_1 x_2)(x_3 x_4)$ means multiply x_1 and x_2, multiply x_3 and x_4, and then take the product of the two.

Note that in both examples above, although the factors are multiplied in a different order, the number of multiplications—three—is the same. Strong mathematical induction is used to prove a generalization of this fact.

Convention

Let us agree to say that a single number x_1 is a product with one factor and can be computed with zero multiplications.

Example 5.4.3 The Number of Multiplications Needed to Multiply n Numbers

Prove that for any integer $n \geq 1$, if $x_1, x_2, \ldots, x_n$ are n numbers, then no matter how the parentheses are inserted into their product, the number of multiplications used to compute the product is $n - 1$.

Solution   The truth of the basis step follows immediately from the convention about a product with one factor. The inductive step is based on the fact that when several numbers are multiplied together, each step of the process involves multiplying two individual quantities. For instance, the final step for computing $((x_1 x_2) x_3)(x_4 x_5)$ is to multiply $(x_1 x_2) x_3$ and $x_4 x_5$. In general, if $k + 1$ numbers are multiplied, the two quantities in the final step each consist of fewer than $k + 1$ factors. This is what makes it possible to use the inductive hypothesis.

Proof (by strong mathematical induction):

Let the property $P(n)$ be the sentence

> If $x_1, x_2, \ldots, x_n$ are n numbers, then
> no matter how parentheses are inserted into their
> product, the number of multiplications used to   ← $P(n)$
> compute the product is $n - 1$.

Show that $P(1)$ is true:
To establish $P(1)$, we must show that

> The number of multiplications needed to compute
> the product of x_1 is $1 - 1$.   ← $P(1)$

This is true because, by convention, x_1 is a product that can be computed with 0 multiplications, and $0 = 1 - 1$.

Show that for all integers $k \geq 1$, if $P(i)$ is true for all integers i from 1 through k, then $P(k + 1)$ is also true:
Let k by any integer with $k \geq 1$ and suppose that

> For all integers i from 1 through k, if $x_1, x_2, \ldots, x_i$
> are numbers, then no matter how parentheses
> are inserted into their product, the number   ← inductive hypothesis
> of multiplications used to compute the
> product is $i - 1$.

We must show that

> If $x_1, x_2, \ldots, x_{k+1}$ are $k + 1$ numbers, then no
> matter how parentheses are inserted into their
> product, the number of multiplications used to   ← $P(k + 1)$
> compute the product is $(k + 1) - 1 = k$.

Consider a product of $k + 1$ factors: $x_1, x_2 \ldots, x_{k+1}$. When parentheses are inserted in order to compute the product, some multiplication is the final one and each of

5.4 Strong Mathematical Induction and the Well-Ordering Principle for the Int...

274

the two factors making up the final multiplication is a product of fewer th...
factors. Let L be the product of the left-hand factors and R be the produ...
right-hand factors, and suppose that L is composed of l factors and R is composed
of r factors. Then $l + r = k + 1$, the total number of factors in the product, and

$$1 \le l \le k \quad \text{and} \quad 1 \le r \le k.$$

By inductive hypothesis, evaluating L takes $l - 1$ multiplications and evaluating R
takes $r - 1$ multiplications. Because one final multiplication is needed to evaluate
$L \cdot R$, the number of multiplications needed to evaluate the product of all $k + 1$ factors is

$$(l - 1) + (r - 1) + 1 = (l + r) - 1 = (k + 1) - 1 = k.$$

[This is what was to be shown.]
*[Since we have proved the basis step and the inductive step of the strong mathematical
induction, we conclude that the given statement is true.]*

Strong mathematical induction makes possible a proof of the fact used frequently in computer science that every positive integer n has a unique binary integer representation. The
proof looks complicated because of all the notation needed to write down the various
steps. But the idea of the proof is simple. It is that if smaller integers than n have unique
representations as sums of powers of 2, then the unique representation for n as a sum of
powers of 2 can be found by taking the representation for $n/2$ (or for $(n - 1)/2$ if n is
odd) and multiplying it by 2.

Theorem 5.4.1 Existence and Uniqueness of Binary Integer Representations

Given any positive integer n, n has a unique representation in the form

$$n = c_r \cdot 2^r + c_{r-1} \cdot 2^{r-1} + \cdots + c_2 \cdot 2^2 + c_1 \cdot 2 + c_0,$$

where r is a nonnegative integer, $c_r = 1$, and $c_j = 1$ or 0 for all $j = 0, 1, 2, \ldots, r - 1$.

Proof:

We give separate proofs by strong mathematical induction to show first the existence
and second the uniqueness of the binary representation.

Existence (proof by strong mathematical induction): Let the property $P(n)$ be the
equation

$$n = c_r \cdot 2^r + c_{r-1} \cdot 2^{r-1} + \cdots + c_2 \cdot 2^2 + c_1 \cdot 2 + c_0, \qquad \leftarrow P(n)$$

where r is a nonnegative integer, $c_r = 1$, and $c_j = 1$ or 0 for all $j = 0, 1, 2, \ldots, r - 1$.

Show that $P(1)$ is true:
Let $r = 0$ and $c_0 = 1$. Then $1 = c_r \cdot 2^r$, and so $n = 1$ can be written in the required
form.

***Show that for all integers $k \ge 1$, if $P(i)$ is true for all integers i from 1 through k,
then $P(k + 1)$ is also true:***

continued on page 274

Let k be an integer with $k \geq 1$. Suppose that for all integers i from 1 through k,

$$i = c_r \cdot 2^r + c_{r-1} \cdot 2^{r-1} + \cdots + c_2 \cdot 2^2 + c_1 \cdot 2 + c_0, \quad \leftarrow \text{inductive hypothesis}$$

where r is a nonnegative integer, $c_r = 1$, and $c_j = 1$ or 0 for all $j = 0, 1, 2, \ldots, r - 1$. We must show that $k + 1$ can be written as a sum of powers of 2 in the required form.

Case 1 ($k + 1$ is even): In this case $(k + 1)/2$ is an integer, and by inductive hypothesis, since $1 \leq (k + 1)/2 \leq k$, then,

$$\frac{k + 1}{2} = c_r \cdot 2^r + c_{r-1} \cdot 2^{r-1} + \cdots + c_2 \cdot 2^2 + c_1 \cdot 2 + c_0,$$

where r is a nonnegative integer, $c_r = 1$, and $c_j = 1$ or 0 for all $j = 0, 1, 2, \ldots, r - 1$. Multiplying both sides of the equation by 2 gives

$$k + 1 = c_r \cdot 2^{r+1} + c_{r-1} \cdot 2^r + \cdots + c_2 \cdot 2^3 + c_1 \cdot 2^2 + c_0 \cdot 2,$$

which is a sum of powers of 2 of the required form.

Case 2 ($k + 1$ is odd): In this case $k/2$ is an integer, and by inductive hypothesis, since $1 \leq k/2 \leq k$, then

$$\frac{k}{2} = c_r \cdot 2^r + c_{r-1} \cdot 2^{r-1} + \cdots + c_2 \cdot 2^2 + c_1 \cdot 2 + c_0,$$

where r is a nonnegative integer, $c_r = 1$, and $c_j = 1$ or 0 for all $j = 0, 1, 2, \ldots, r - 1$. Multiplying both sides of the equation by 2 and adding 1 gives

$$k + 1 = c_r \cdot 2^{r+1} + c_{r-1} \cdot 2^r + \cdots + c_2 \cdot 2^3 + c_1 \cdot 2^2 + c_0 \cdot 2 + 1,$$

which is also a sum of powers of 2 of the required form.

The preceding arguments show that regardless of whether $k + 1$ is even or odd, $k + 1$ has a representation of the required form. *[Or, in other words, $P(k + 1)$ is true as was to be shown.]*

[Since we have proved the basis step and the inductive step of the strong mathematical induction, the existence half of the theorem is true.]

Uniqueness: To prove uniqueness, suppose that there is an integer n with two different representations as a sum of nonnegative integer powers of 2. Equating the two representations and canceling all identical terms gives

$$2^r + c_{r-1} \cdot 2^{r-1} + \cdots + c_1 \cdot 2 + c_0 = 2^s + d_{s-1} \cdot 2^{s-1} + \cdots + d_1 \cdot 2 + d_0 \quad 5.4.1$$

where r and s are nonnegative integers, and each c_i and each d_i equal 0 or 1. Without loss of generality, we may assume that $r < s$. But by the formula for the sum of a geometric sequence (Theorem 5.2.3) and because $r < s$,

$$2^r + c_{r-1} \cdot 2^{r-1} + \cdots + c_1 \cdot 2 + c_0 \leq 2^r + 2^{r-1} + \cdots + 2 + 1 = 2^{r+1} - 1$$
$$< 2^s.$$

Thus

$$2^r + c_{r-1} \cdot 2^{r-1} + \cdots + c_1 \cdot 2 + c_0 < 2^s + d_{s-1} \cdot 2^{s-1} + \cdots + d_1 \cdot 2 + d_0,$$

which contradicts equation (5.4.1). Hence the supposition is false, so any integer n has only one representation as a sum of nonnegative integer powers of 2.

The Well-Ordering Principle for the Integers

The well-ordering principle for the integers looks very different from both the ordinary and the strong principles of mathematical induction, but it can be shown that all three principles are equivalent. That is, if any one of the three is true, then so are both of the others.

> **Well-Ordering Principle for the Integers**
>
> Let S be a set of integers containing one or more integers all of which are greater than some fixed integer. Then S has a least element.

Note that when the context makes the reference clear, we will write simply "the well-ordering principle" rather than "the well-ordering principle for the integers."

Example 5.4.4 Finding Least Elements

In each case, if the set has a least element, state what it is. If not, explain why the well-ordering principle is not violated.

a. The set of all positive real numbers.

b. The set of all nonnegative integers n such that $n^2 < n$.

c. The set of all nonnegative integers of the form $46 - 7k$, where k is an integer.

Solution

a. There is no least positive real number. For if x is any positive real number, then $x/2$ is a positive real number that is less than x. No violation of the well-ordering principle occurs because the well-ordering principle refers only to sets of integers, and this set is not a set of integers.

b. There is no *least* nonnegative integer n such that $n^2 < n$ because there is *no* nonnegative integer that satisfies this inequality. The well-ordering principle is not violated because the well-ordering principle refers only to sets that contain at least one element.

c. The following table shows values of $46 - 7k$ for various values of k.

k	0	1	2	3	4	5	6	7	$\cdots$	-1	-2	-3	$\cdots$
$46 - 7k$	46	39	32	25	18	11	4	-3	$\cdots$	53	60	67	$\cdots$

The table suggests, and you can easily confirm, that $46 - 7k < 0$ for $k \geq 7$ and that $46 - 7k \geq 46$ for $k \leq 0$. Therefore, from the other values in the table it is clear that 4 is the least nonnegative integer of the form $46 - 7k$. This corresponds to $k = 6$. ■

Another way to look at the analysis of Example 5.4.4(c) is to observe that subtracting six 7's from 46 leaves 4 left over and this is the least nonnegative integer obtained by repeated subtraction of 7's from 46. In other words, 6 is the quotient and 4 is the remainder for the division of 46 by 7. More generally, in the division of any integer n by any positive integer d, the remainder r is the least nonnegative integer of the form $n - dk$. This is the heart of the following proof of the existence part of the quotient-remainder theorem (the part that guarantees the existence of a quotient and a remainder of the division of an integer by a positive integer). For a proof of the uniqueness of the quotient and remainder, see exercise 18 of Section 4.6.

Quotient-Remainder Theorem (Existence Part)

Given any integer n and any positive integer d, there exist integers q and r such that

$$n = dq + r \quad \text{and} \quad 0 \le r < d.$$

Proof:

Let S be the set of all nonnegative integers of the form

$$n - dk,$$

where k is an integer. This set has at least one element. *[For if n is nonnegative, then*

$$n - 0 \cdot d = n \ge 0,$$

and so $n - 0 \cdot d$ is in S. And if n is negative, then

$$n - nd = n(1 - d) \ge 0,$$

$$\underset{<0}{\uparrow} \qquad \underset{<0 \ since \ d \ is \ a \ positive \ integer}{\frown}$$

and so $n - nd$ is in S.] It follows by the well-ordering principle for the integers that S contains a least element r. Then, for some specific integer $k = q$,

$$n - dq = r$$

[because every integer in S can be written in this form]. Adding dq to both sides gives

$$n = dq + r.$$

Furthermore, $r < d$. *[For suppose $r \ge d$. Then*

$$n - d(q + 1) = n - dq - d = r - d \ge 0,$$

and so $n - d(q + 1)$ would be a nonnegative integer in S that would be smaller than r. But r is the smallest integer in S. This contradiction shows that the supposition $r \ge d$ must be false.] The preceding arguments prove that there exist integers r and q for which

$$n = dq + r \quad \text{and} \quad 0 \le r < d.$$

[This is what was to be shown.]

Another consequence of the well-ordering principle is the fact that any strictly decreasing sequence of nonnegative integers is finite. That is, if $r_1, r_2, r_3, \ldots$ is a sequence of nonnegative integers satisfying

$$r_i > r_{i+1}$$

for all $i \ge 1$, then $r_1, r_2, r_3, \ldots$ is a finite sequence. *[For by the well-ordering principle such a sequence would have to have a least element r_k. It follows that r_k must be the final term of the sequence because if there were a term r_{k+1}, then since the sequence is strictly decreasing, $r_{k+1} < r_k$, which would be a contradiction.]* This fact is frequently used in computer science to prove that algorithms terminate after a finite number of steps.

Test Yourself

1. In a proof by strong mathematical induction the basis step may require checking a property $P(n)$ for more _____ value of n.

2. Suppose that in the basis step for a proof by strong mathematical induction the property $P(n)$ was checked for all integers n from a through b. Then in the inductive step one assumes that for any integer $k \geq b$, the property $P(n)$ is true for all values of i from _____ through _____ and one shows that _____ is true.

3. According to the well-ordering principle for the integers, if a set S of integers contains at least _____ and if there is some integer that is less than or equal to every _____, then _____.

Exercise Set 5.4

1. Suppose $a_1, a_2, a_3, \ldots$ is a sequence defined as follows:

$$a_1 = 1, \ a_2 = 3,$$
$$a_k = a_{k-2} + 2a_{k-1} \quad \text{for all integers } k \geq 3.$$

Prove that a_n is odd for all integers $n \geq 1$.

2. Suppose $b_1, b_2, b_3, \ldots$ is a sequence defined as follows:

$$b_1 = 4, \ b_2 = 12$$
$$b_k = b_{k-2} + b_{k-1} \quad \text{for all integers } k \geq 3.$$

Prove that b_n is divisible by 4 for all integers $n \geq 1$.

3. Suppose that $c_0, c_1, c_2, \ldots$ is a sequence defined as follows:

$$c_0 = 2, \ c_1 = 2, \ c_2 = 6,$$
$$c_k = 3c_{k-3} \quad \text{for all integers } k \geq 3.$$

Prove that c_n is even for all integers $n \geq 0$.

4. Suppose that $d_1, d_2, d_3, \ldots$ is a sequence defined as follows:

$$d_1 = \frac{9}{10}, \ d_2 = \frac{10}{11},$$
$$d_k = d_{k-1} \cdot d_{k-2} \quad \text{for all integers } k \geq 3.$$

Prove that $0 < d_n \leq 1$ for all integers $n \geq 1$.

5. Suppose that $e_0, e_1, e_2, \ldots$ is a sequence defined as follows:

$$e_0 = 12, \ e_1 = 29$$
$$e_k = 5e_{k-1} - 6e_{k-2} \quad \text{for all integers } k \geq 2.$$

Prove that $e_n = 5 \cdot 3^n + 7 \cdot 2^n$ for all integers $n \geq 0$.

6. Suppose that $f_0, f_1, f_2, \ldots$ is a sequence defined as follows:

$$f_0 = 5, \ f_1 = 16$$
$$f_k = 7f_{k-1} - 10f_{k-2} \quad \text{for all integers } k \geq 2.$$

Prove that $f_n = 3 \cdot 2^n + 2 \cdot 5^n$ for all integers $n \geq 0$.

7. Suppose that $g_1, g_2, g_3, \ldots$ is a sequence defined as follows:

$$g_1 = 3, \ g_2 = 5$$
$$g_k = 3g_{k-1} - 2g_{k-2} \quad \text{for all integers } k \geq 3.$$

Prove that $g_n = 2^n + 1$ for all integers $n \geq 1$.

8. Suppose that $h_0, h_1, h_2, \ldots$ is a sequence defined as follows:

$$h_0 = 1, \ h_1 = 2, \ h_2 = 3,$$
$$h_k = h_{k-1} + h_{k-2} + h_{k-3} \quad \text{for all integers } k \geq 3.$$

a. Prove that $h_n \leq 3^n$ for all integers $n \geq 0$.

b. Suppose that s is any real number such that $s^3 \geq s^2 + s + 1$. (This implies that $2 > s > 1.83$.) Prove that $h_n \leq s^n$ for all $n \geq 2$.

9. Define a sequence $a_1, a_2, a_3, \ldots$ as follows: $a_1 = 1, a_2 = 3$, and $a_k = a_{k-1} + a_{k-2}$ for all integers $k \geq 3$. (This sequence is known as the Lucas sequence.) Use strong mathematical induction to prove that $a_n \leq \left(\frac{7}{4}\right)^n$ for all integers $n \geq 1$.

H 10. The problem that was used to introduce ordinary mathematical induction in Section 5.2 can also be solved using strong mathematical induction. Let $P(n)$ be "any n¢ can be obtained using a combination of 3¢ and 5¢ coins." Use strong mathematical induction to prove that $P(n)$ is true for all integers $n \geq 8$.

11. You begin solving a jigsaw puzzle by finding two pieces that match and fitting them together. Each subsequent step of the solution consists of fitting together two blocks made up of one or more pieces that have previously been assembled. Use strong mathematical induction to prove that the number of steps required to put together all n pieces of a jigsaw puzzle is $n - 1$.

H 12. The sides of a circular track contain a sequence of cans of gasoline. The total amount in the cans is sufficient to enable a certain car to make one complete circuit of the track, and it could all fit into the car's gas tank at one time. Use mathematical induction to prove that it is possible to find an initial location for placing the car so that it will be able to traverse the entire track by using the various amounts of gasoline in the cans that it encounters along the way.

H 13. Use strong mathematical induction to prove the existence part of the unique factorization of integers (Theorem 4.3.5): Every integer greater than 1 is either a prime number or a product of prime numbers.

14. Any product of two or more integers is a result of successive multiplications of two integers at a time. For instance,

here are a few of the ways in which $a_1a_2a_3a_4$ might be computed: $(a_1a_2)(a_3a_4)$ or $((a_1a_2)a_3)a_4)$ or $a_1((a_2a_3)a_4)$. Use strong mathematical induction to prove that any product of two or more odd integers is odd.

15. Define the "sum" of one integer to be that integer, and use strong mathematical induction to prove that for all integers $n \geq 1$, any sum of n even integers is even.

H 16. Use strong mathematical induction to prove that for any integer $n \geq 2$, if n is even, then any sum of n odd integers is even, and if n is odd, then any sum of n odd integers is odd.

17. Compute $4^1, 4^2, 4^3, 4^4, 4^5, 4^6, 4^7$, and 4^8. Make a conjecture about the units digit of 4^n where n is a positive integer. Use strong mathematical induction to prove your conjecture.

18. Compute $9^0, 9^1, 9^2, 9^3, 9^4$, and 9^5. Make a conjecture about the units digit of 9^n where n is a positive integer. Use strong mathematical induction to prove your conjecture.

19. Find the mistake in the following "proof" that purports to show that every nonnegative integer power of every nonzero real number is 1.

"**Proof:** Let r be any nonzero real number and let the property $P(n)$ be the equation $r^n = 1$.

Show that P(0) is true: $P(0)$ is true because $r^0 = 1$ by definition of zeroth power.
Show that for all integers k ≥ 0, if P(i) is true for all integers i from 0 through k, then P(k + 1) is also true: Let k be any integer with $k \geq 0$ and suppose that $r^i = 1$ for all integers i from 0 through k. This is the inductive hypothesis. We must show that $r^{k+1} = 1$. Now

$$r^{k+1} = r^{k+k-(k-1)} \quad \text{because } k + k - (k - 1) \\ = k + k - k + 1 = k + 1$$
$$= \frac{r^k \cdot r^k}{r^{k-1}} \quad \text{by the laws of exponents}$$
$$= \frac{1 \cdot 1}{1} \quad \text{by inductive hypothesis}$$
$$= 1.$$

Thus $r^{k+1} = 1$ *[as was to be shown]*.

[Since we have proved the basis step and the inductive step of the strong mathematical induction, we conclude that the given statement is true.]"

20. Use the well-ordering principle for the integers to prove Theorem 4.3.4: Every integer greater than 1 is divisible by a prime number.

21. Use the well-ordering principle for the integers to prove the existence part of the unique factorization of integers theorem: Every integer greater than 1 is either prime or a product of prime numbers.

22. a. The Archimedean property for the rational numbers states that for all rational numbers r, there is an integer n such that $n > r$. Prove this property.
b. Prove that given any rational number r, the number $-r$ is also rational.
c. Use the results of parts (a) and (b) to prove that given any rational number r, there is an integer m such that $m < r$.

H 23. Use the results of exercise 22 and the well-ordering principle for the integers to show that given any rational number r, there is an integer m such that $m \leq r < m + 1$.

24. Use the well-ordering principle to prove that given any integer $n \geq 1$, there exists an odd integer m and a nonnegative integer k such that $n = 2^k \cdot m$.

25. Imagine a situation in which eight people, numbered consecutively 1–8, are arranged in a circle. Starting from person #1, every second person in the circle is eliminated. The elimination process continues until only one person remains. In the first round the people numbered 2, 4, 6, and 8 are eliminated, in the second round the people numbered 3 and 7 are eliminated, and in the third round person #5 is eliminated. So after the third round only person #1 remains, as shown below.

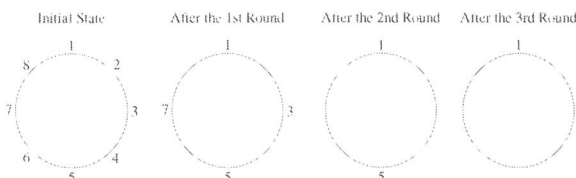

Initial State   After the 1st Round   After the 2nd Round   After the 3rd Round

a. Given a set of sixteen people arranged in a circle and numbered, consecutively 1–16, list the numbers of the people who are eliminated in each round if every second person is eliminated and the elimination process continues until only one person remains. Assume that the starting point is person #1.
b. Use mathematical induction to prove that for all integers $n \geq 1$, given any set of 2^n people arranged in a circle and numbered consecutively 1 through 2^n, if one starts from person #1 and goes repeatedly around the circle successively eliminating every second person, eventually only person #1 will remain.
c. Use the result of part (b) to prove that for any nonnegative integers n and m with $2^n \leq 2^n + m < 2^{n+1}$, if $r = 2^n + m$, then given any set of r people arranged in a circle and numbered consecutively 1 through r, if one starts from person #1 and goes repeatedly around the circle successively eliminating every second person, eventually only person #$(2m + 1)$ will remain.

26. Suppose $P(n)$ is a property such that
    1. $P(0)$, $P(1)$, $P(2)$ are all true,
    2. for all integers $k \geq 0$, if $P(k)$ is true, then $P(3k)$ is true. Must it follow that $P(n)$ is true for all integers $n \geq 0$? If yes, explain why; if no, give a counterexample.

27. Prove that if a statement can be proved by strong mathematical induction, then it can be proved by ordinary mathematical induction. To do this, let $P(n)$ be a property that is defined for integers n, and suppose the following two statements are true:
    1. $P(a)$, $P(a + 1)$, $P(a + 2)$, ..., $P(b)$.
    2. For any integer $k \geq b$, if $P(i)$ is true for all integers i from a through k, then $P(k + 1)$ is true.
    The principle of strong mathematical induction would allow us to conclude immediately that $P(n)$ is true for all integers $n \geq a$. Can we reach the same conclusion using the principle of ordinary mathematical induction? Yes! To see this, let $Q(n)$ be the property

    $$P(j) \text{ is true for all integers } j \text{ with } a \leq j \leq n.$$

    Then use ordinary mathematical induction to show that $Q(n)$ is true for all integers $n \geq b$. That is, prove
    1. $Q(b)$ is true.
    2. For any integer $k \geq b$, if $Q(k)$ is true then $Q(k + 1)$ is true.

28. Give examples to illustrate the proof of Theorem 5.4.1.

H 29. It is a fact that every integer $n \geq 1$ can be written in the form

$$c_r \cdot 3^r + c_{r-1} \cdot 3^{r-1} + \cdots + c_2 \cdot 3^2 + c_1 \cdot 3 + c_0,$$

where $c_r = 1$ or 2 and $c_i = 0, 1,$ or 2 for all integers $i = 0, 1, 2, \ldots, r - 1$. Sketch a proof of this fact.

H ✱ 30. Use mathematical induction to prove the existence part of the quotient-remainder theorem for integers $n \geq 0$.

H ✱ 31. Prove that if a statement can be proved by ordinary mathematical induction, then it can be proved by the well-ordering principle.

H 32. Use the principle of ordinary mathematical induction to prove the well-ordering principle for the integers.

Answers for Test Yourself

1. than one   2. a; k; $P(k + 1)$ 3. one integer; integer in S; S contains a least element

5.5 Application: Correctness of Algorithms

[P]rogramming reliably—must be an activity of an undeniably mathematical nature .... You see, mathematics is about thinking, and doing mathematics is always trying to think as well as possible. — Edsger W. Dijkstra (1981)

The University of Texas at Austin

Edsger W. Dijkstra (1930–2002)

What does it mean for a computer program to be correct? Each program is designed to do a specific task—calculate the mean or median of a set of numbers, compute the size of the paychecks for a company payroll, rearrange names in alphabetical order, and so forth. We will say that a program is correct if it produces the output specified in its accompanying documentation for each set of input data of the type specified in the documentation.*

Most computer programmers write their programs using a combination of logical analysis and trial and error. In order to get a program to run at all, the programmer must first fix all syntax errors (such as writing **ik** instead of **if,** failing to declare a variable, or using a restricted keyword for a variable name). When the syntax errors have been removed, however, the program may still contain logical errors that prevent it from producing correct output. Frequently, programs are tested using sets of sample data for which the correct output is known in advance. And often the sample data are deliberately chosen to test the correctness of the program under extreme circumstances. But for most programs the number of possible sets of input data is either infinite or unmanageably large, and so no amount of program testing can give perfect confidence that the program will be correct for all possible sets of legal input data.

*Consumers of computer programs want an even more stringent definition of correctness. If a user puts in data of the wrong type, the user wants a decent error message, not a system crash.

Robert W. Floyd
(1936–2002)

Since 1967, with the publication of a paper by Robert W. Floyd,[*] considerable effort has gone into developing methods for proving programs correct at the time they are composed. One of the pioneers in this effort, Edsger W. Dijkstra, asserted that "we now take the position that it is not only the programmer's task to produce a correct program but also to demonstrate its correctness in a convincing manner."[†] Another leader in the field, David Gries, went so far as to say that "a program and its proof should be developed hand-in-hand, with the *proof* usually leading the way."[**] If such methods can eventually be used to write large scientific and commercial programs, the benefits to society will be enormous.

As with most techniques that are still in the process of development, methods for proving program correctness are somewhat awkward and unwieldy. In this section we give an overview of the general format of correctness proofs and the details of one crucial technique, the *loop invariant procedure*. At this point, we switch from using the term *program,* which refers to a particular programming language, to the more general term *algorithm.*

Assertions

Consider an algorithm that is designed to produce a certain final state from a certain initial state. Both the initial and final states can be expressed as predicates involving the input and output variables. Often the predicate describing the initial state is called the **pre-condition for the algorithm,** and the predicate describing the final state is called the **post-condition for the algorithm.**

Example 5.5.1 Algorithm Pre-Conditions and Post-Conditions

Here are pre- and post-conditions for some typical algorithms.

a. Algorithm to compute a product of nonnegative integers

  Pre-condition: The input variables m and n are nonnegative integers.

  Post-condition: The output variable p equals mn.

b. Algorithm to find quotient and remainder of the division of one positive integer by another

  Pre-condition: The input variables a and b are positive integers.

  Post-condition: The output variables q and r are integers such that
  $a = bq + r$ and $0 \leq r < b$.

c. Algorithm to sort a one-dimensional array of real numbers

  Pre-condition: The input variable $A[1], A[2], \ldots, A[n]$ is a one-dimensional array of real numbers.

  Post-condition: The output variable $B[1], B[2], \ldots, B[n]$ is a one-dimensional array of real numbers with same elements as $A[1], A[2], \ldots,$ $A[n]$ but with the property that $B[i] \leq B[j]$ whenever $i \leq j$. ∎

---

[*]R. W. Floyd, "Assigning meanings to programs," *Proc. Symp. Appl. Math.,* Amer. Math. Soc. **19** (1967), 19–32.

[†]Edsger Dijkstra in O. J. Dahl, E. W. Dijkstra, and C. A. R. Hoare, *Structured Programming* (London: Academic Press, 1972), p. 5.

[**]David Gries, *The Science of Programming* (New York: Springer-Verlag, 1981), p. 164.

A proof of algorithm correctness consists of showing that if the pre-condition for the algorithm is true for a collection of values for the input variables and if the statements of the algorithms are executed, then the post-condition is also true.

The divide-and-conquer principle has been useful in many aspects of computer programming, and proving algorithm correctness is no exception. The steps of an algorithm are divided into sections with assertions about the current state of algorithm variables inserted at strategically chosen points:

[*Assertion* 1: *pre-condition for the algorithm*]

{Algorithm statements}

[*Assertion* 2]

{Algorithm statements}

$\vdots$

[*Assertion k* − 1]

{Algorithm statements}

[*Assertion k: post-condition for the algorithm*]

Successive pairs of assertions are then treated as pre- and post-conditions for the algorithm statements between them. For each $i = 1, 2, \ldots, k - 1$, one proves that if Assertion i is true and all the algorithm statements between Assertion i and Assertion $(i + 1)$ are executed, then Assertion $(i + 1)$ is true. Once all these individual proofs have been completed, one knows that Assertion k is true. And since Assertion 1 is the same as the pre-condition for the algorithm and Assertion k is the same as the post-condition for the algorithm, one concludes that the entire algorithm is correct with respect to its pre- and post-conditions.

Loop Invariants

The method of loop invariants is used to prove correctness of a loop with respect to certain pre- and post-conditions. It is based on the principle of mathematical induction. Suppose that an algorithm contains a **while** loop and that entry to this loop is restricted by a condition G, called the **guard.** Suppose also that assertions describing the current states of algorithm variables have been placed immediately preceding and immediately following the loop. The assertion just preceding the loop is called the **pre-condition for the loop** and the one just following is called the **post-condition for the loop.** The annotated loop has the following appearance:

[*Pre-condition for the loop*]

while (G)

[*Statements in the body of the loop.*
None contain branching statements
that lead outside the loop.]

end while

[*Post-condition for the loop*]

> **• Definition**
>
> A loop is defined as **correct with respect to its pre- and post-conditions** if, and only if, whenever the algorithm variables satisfy the pre-condition for the loop and the loop terminates after a finite number of steps, the algorithm variables satisfy the post-condition for the loop.

C. A. R. Hoare
(born 1934)

Courtesy of Tony Hoare

Establishing the correctness of a loop uses the concept of loop invariant. A **loop invariant** is a predicate with domain a set of integers, which satisfies the condition: For each iteration of the loop, if the predicate is true before the iteration, the it is true after the iteration. Furthermore, if the predicate satisfies the following two additional conditions, the loop will be correct with respect to it pre- and post-conditions:

1. It is true before the first iteration of the loop.

2. If the loop terminates after a finite number of iterations, the truth of the loop invariant ensures the truth of the post-condition of the loop.

The following theorem, called the *loop invariant theorem*, formalizes these ideas. It was first developed by C. A. R. Hoare in 1969.

Theorem 5.5.1 Loop Invariant Theorem

Let a **while** loop with guard G be given, together with pre- and post-conditions that are predicates in the algorithm variables. Also let a predicate $I(n)$, called the **loop invariant,** be given. If the following four properties are true, then the loop is correct with respect to its pre- and post-conditions.

I.   Basis Property: The pre-condition for the loop implies that $I(0)$ is true before the first iteration of the loop.

II. Inductive Property: For all integers $k \geq 0$, if the guard G and the loop invariant $I(k)$ are both true before an iteration of the loop, then $I(k+1)$ is true after iteration of the loop.

III. Eventual Falsity of Guard: After a finite number of iterations of the loop, the guard G becomes false.

IV. Correctness of the Post-Condition: If N is the least number of iterations after which G is false and $I(N)$ is true, then the values of the algorithm variables will be as specified in the post-condition of the loop.

Proof: The loop invariant theorem follows easily from the principle of mathematical induction. Assume that $I(n)$ is a predicate that satisfies properties I–IV of the loop invariant theorem. *[We will prove that the loop is correct with respect to its pre- and post-conditions.]* Properties I and II are the basis and inductive steps needed to prove the truth of the following statement:

For all integers $n \geq 0$, if the **while** loop
iterates n times, then $I(n)$ is true.   5.5.1

Thus, by the principle of mathematical induction, since both I and II are true, statement (5.5.1) is also true.

Property III says that the guard G eventually becomes false. At that point the loop will have been iterated some number, say N, of times. Since $I(n)$ is true after the nth iteration for every $n \geq 0$, then $I(n)$ is true after the Nth iteration. That is, after the Nth iteration the guard is false and $I(N)$ is true. But this is the hypothesis of property IV, which is an if-then statement. Since statement IV is true (by assumption) and its hypothesis is true (by the argument just given), it follows (by modus ponens) that its conclusion is also true. That is, the values of all algorithm variables after execution of the loop are as specified in the post-condition for the loop.

The loop invariant in the procedure for proving loop correctness may seem like a rabbit in a hat. Where does it come from? The fact is that developing a good loop invariant is a tricky process. Although learning how to do it is beyond the scope of this book, it is worth pursuing in a more advanced course. People who have become good at the process claim it has significantly altered their outlook on programming and has greatly improved their ability to write good code.

Another tricky aspect of handling correctness proofs arises from the fact that execution of an algorithm is a dynamic process—it takes place in time. As execution progresses, the values of variables keep changing, yet often their names stay the same. In the following discussion, when we need to make a distinction between the values of a variable just before execution of an algorithm statement and just after execution of the statement, we will attach the subscripts *old* and *new* to the variable name.

Example 5.5.2 Correctness of a Loop to Compute a Product

The following loop is designed to compute the product mx for a nonnegative integer m and a real number x, without using a built-in multiplication operation. Prior to the loop, variables i and *product* have been introduced and given initial values $i = 0$ and *product* $= 0$.

> *[Pre-condition: m is a nonnegative integer,*
> *x is a real number, i = 0, and product = 0.]*
>
> **while** $(i \neq m)$
>
> 1. *product* $:= product + x$
> 2. $i := i + 1$
>
> **end while**
>
> *[Post-condition: product = mx]*

Let the loop invariant be

$$\boxed{I(n): i = n \quad \text{and} \quad product = nx}$$

The guard condition G of the **while** loop is

$$\boxed{G: i \neq m}$$

Use the loop invariant theorem to prove that the **while** loop is correct with respect to the given pre- and post-conditions.

Solution

I. Basis Property: *[I(0) is true before the first iteration of the loop.]*

$I(0)$ is "$i = 0$ and *product* $= 0 \cdot x$", which is true before the first iteration of the loop because $0 \cdot x = 0$.

II. Inductive Property: *[If $G \wedge I(k)$ is true before a loop iteration (where $k \geq 0$), then $I(k + 1)$ is true after the loop iteration.]*

Suppose k is a nonnegative integer such that $G \wedge I(k)$ is true before an iteration of the loop. Then as execution reaches the top of the loop, $i \neq m$, *product* $= kx$, and $i = k$. Since $i \neq m$, the guard is passed and statement 1 is executed. Before execution of statement 1,

$$\text{product}_{\text{old}} = kx.$$

Thus execution of statement 1 has the following effect:

$$\text{product}_{\text{new}} = \text{product}_{\text{old}} + x = kx + x = (k+1)x.$$

Similarly, before statement 2 is executed,

$$i_{\text{old}} = k,$$

so after execution of statement 2,

$$i_{\text{new}} = i_{\text{old}} + 1 = k + 1.$$

Hence after the loop iteration, the statement $I(k+1)$, namely, $(i = k+1$ and $product = (k+1)x)$, is true. This is what we needed to show.

III. **Eventual Falsity of Guard:** *[After a finite number of iterations of the loop, G becomes false.]*

The guard G is the condition $i \neq m$, and m is a nonnegative integer. By I and II, it is known that

for all integers $n \geq 0$, if the loop is iterated
n times, then $i = n$ and $product = nx$.

So after m iterations of the loop, $i = m$. Thus G becomes false after m iterations of the loop.

IV. **Correctness of the Post-Condition:** *[If N is the least number of iterations after which G is false and I(N) is true, then the value of the algorithm variables will be as specified in the post-condition of the loop.]*

According to the post-condition, the value of *product* after execution of the loop should be mx. But if G becomes false after N iterations, $i = m$. And if $I(N)$ is true, $i = N$ and $product = Nx$. Since both conditions (G false and $I(N)$ true) are satisfied, $m = i = N$ and $product = mx$ as required. ▨

In the remainder of this section, we present proofs of the correctness of the crucial loops in the division algorithm and the Euclidean algorithm. (These algorithms were given in Section 4.8.)

Correctness of the Division Algorithm

The division algorithm is supposed to take a nonnegative integer a and a positive integer d and compute nonnegative integers q and r such that $a = dq + r$ and $0 \leq r < d$. Initially, the variables r and q are introduced and given the values $r = a$ and $q = 0$. The crucial loop, annotated with pre- and post-conditions, is the following:

*[Pre-condition: a is a nonnegative integer
and d is a positive integer, r = a, and q = 0.]*

    while $(r \geq d)$

        1. $r := r - d$
        2. $q := q + 1$

    end while

*[Post-condition: q and r are nonnegative integers
with the property that a = qd + r and 0 ≤ r < d.]*

Proof:

To prove the correctness of the loop, let the loop invariant be

$$I(n): r = a - nd \geq 0 \quad \text{and} \quad n = q.$$

The guard of the **while** loop is

$$G: r \geq d$$

I. **Basis property:** *[$I(0)$ is true before the first iteration of the loop.]*

   $I(0)$ is "$r = a - 0 \cdot d \geq 0$ and $q = 0$." But by the pre-condition, $r = a$, $a \geq 0$, and $q = 0$. So since $a = a - 0 \cdot d$, then $r = a - 0 \cdot d$ and $I(0)$ is true before the first iteration of the loop.

II. **Inductive Property:** *[If $G \wedge I(k)$ is true before an iteration of the loop (where $k \geq 0$), then $I(k+1)$ is true after iteration of the loop.]*

   Suppose k is a nonnegative integer such that $G \wedge I(k)$ is true before an iteration of the loop. Since G is true, $r \geq d$ and the loop is entered. Also since $I(k)$ is true, $r = a - kd \geq 0$ and $k = q$. Hence, before execution of statements 1 and 2,

$$r_{\text{old}} \geq d \quad \text{and} \quad r_{\text{old}} = a - kd \quad \text{and} \quad q_{\text{old}} = k.$$

When statements 1 and 2 are executed, then,

$$r_{\text{new}} = r_{\text{old}} - d = (a - kd) - d = a - (k+1)d \qquad 5.5.2$$

and

$$q_{\text{new}} = q_{\text{old}} + 1 = k + 1 \qquad 5.5.3$$

In addition, since $r_{\text{old}} \geq d$ before execution of statements 1 and 2, after execution of these statements,

$$r_{\text{new}} = r_{\text{old}} - d \geq d - d \geq 0. \qquad 5.5.4$$

Putting equations (5.5.2), (5.5.3), and (5.5.4) together shows that after iteration of the loop,

$$r_{\text{new}} \geq 0 \quad \text{and} \quad r_{\text{new}} = a - (k+1)d \quad \text{and} \quad q_{\text{new}} = k + 1.$$

Hence $I(k+1)$ is true.

III. **Eventual Falsity of the Guard:** *[After a finite number of iterations of the loop, G becomes false.]*

   The guard G is the condition $r \geq d$. Each iteration of the loop reduces the value of r by d and yet leaves r nonnegative. Thus the values of r form a decreasing sequence of nonnegative integers, and so (by the well-ordering principle) there must be a smallest such r, say r_{min}. Then $r_{\text{min}} < d$. *[If r_{min} were greater than d, the loop would iterate another time, and a new value of r equal to $r_{\text{min}} - d$ would be obtained. But this new value would be smaller than r_{min} which would contradict the fact that r_{min} is the smallest remainder obtained by repeated iteration of the loop.]* Hence as soon as the value $r = r_{\text{min}}$ is computed, the value of r becomes less than d, and so the guard G is false.

IV. **Correctness of the Post-Condition:** *[If N is the least number of iterations after which G is false and $I(N)$ is true, then the values of the algorithm variables will be as specified in the post-condition of the loop.]*

Suppose that for some nonnegative integer N, G is false and $I(N)$ is true. Then $r < d, r = a - Nd, r \geq 0$, and $q = N$. Since $q = N$, by substitution,

$$r = a - qd.$$

Or, adding qd to both sides,

$$a = qd + r.$$

Combining the two inequalities involving r gives

$$0 \leq r < d.$$

But these are the values of q and r specified in the post-condition, so the proof is complete. ■

Correctness of the Euclidean Theorem

The Euclidean algorithm is supposed to take integers A and B with $A > B \geq 0$ and compute their greatest common divisor. Just before the crucial loop, variables a, b, and r have been introduced with $a = A, b = B$, and $r = B$. The crucial loop, annotated with pre- and post-conditions, is the following:

[Pre-condition: A and B are integers
with $A > B \geq 0, a = A, b = B, r = B$.]

while $(b \neq 0)$
    1. $r := a \bmod b$
    2. $a := b$
    3. $b := r$
end while

[Post-condition: $a = \gcd(A, B)$]

Proof:

To prove the correctness of the loop, let the invariant be

$I(n)$: $\gcd(a, b) = \gcd(A, B)$ and $0 \leq b < a.$

The guard of the **while** loop is

G: $b \neq 0.$

I. Basis Property: *[$I(0)$ is true before the first iteration of the loop.]*
    $I(0)$ is

$$\gcd(A, B) = \gcd(a, b) \quad \text{and} \quad 0 \leq b < a.$$

According to the pre-condition,

$$a = A, \quad b = B, \quad r = B, \quad \text{and} \quad 0 \leq B < A.$$

Hence $\gcd(A, B) = \gcd(a, b)$. Since $0 \leq B < A$, $b = B$, and $a = A$ then $0 \leq b < a$. Hence $I(0)$ is true.

II. Inductive Property: *[If $G \wedge I(k)$ is true before an iteration of the loop (where $k \geq 0$), then $I(k + 1)$ is true after iteration of the loop.]*

Suppose k is a nonnegative integer such that $G \wedge I(k)$ is true before an iteration of the loop. *[We must show that $I(k+1)$ is true after iteration of the loop.]* Since G is true, $b_{old} \neq 0$ and the loop is entered. And since $I(k)$ is true, immediately before statement 1 is executed,

$$\gcd(a_{old}, b_{old}) = \gcd(A, B) \quad \text{and} \quad 0 \leq b_{old} < a_{old}. \qquad 5.5.5$$

After execution of statement 1,

$$r_{new} = a_{old} \bmod b_{old}.$$

Thus, by the quotient-remainder theorem,

$$a_{old} = b_{old} \cdot q + r_{new} \quad \text{for some integer } q$$

and r_{new} has the property that

$$0 \leq r_{new} < b_{old}. \qquad 5.5.6$$

By Lemma 4.8.2,

$$\gcd(a_{old}, b_{old}) = \gcd(b_{old}, r_{new}).$$

So by the equation of (5.5.5),

$$\gcd(b_{old}, r_{new}) = \gcd(A, B). \qquad 5.5.7$$

When statements 2 and 3 are executed,

$$a_{new} = b_{old} \quad \text{and} \quad b_{new} = r_{new}. \qquad 5.5.8$$

Substituting equations (5.5.8) into equation (5.5.7) yields

$$\gcd(a_{new}, b_{new}) = \gcd(A, B). \qquad 5.5.9$$

And substituting the values from the equations in (5.5.8) into inequality (5.5.6) gives

$$0 \leq b_{new} < a_{new}. \qquad 5.5.10$$

Hence after the iteration of the loop, by equation (5.5.9) and inequality (5.5.10),

$$\gcd(a, b) = \gcd(A, B) \quad \text{and} \quad 0 \leq b < a,$$

which is $I(k+1)$. *[This is what we needed to show.]*

III. **Eventual Falsity of the Guard:** *[After a finite number of iterations of the loop, G becomes false.]*

Each value of b obtained by repeated iteration of the loop is nonnegative and less than the previous value of b. Thus, by the well-ordering principle, there is a least value b_{min}. The fact is that $b_{min} = 0$. *[If b_{min} is not 0, then the guard is true, and so the loop is iterated another time. In this iteration a value of r is calculated that is less than the previous value of b, b_{min}. Then the value of b is changed to r, which is less than b_{min}. This contradicts the fact that b_{min} is the least value of b obtained by repeated iteration of the loop. Hence $b_{min} = 0$.]* Since $b_{min} = 0$, the guard is false immediately following the loop iteration in which b_{min} is calculated.

IV. **Correctness of the Post-Condition:** *[If N is the least number of iterations after which G is false and $I(N)$ is true, then the values of the algorithm variables will be as specified in the post-condition.]*

Suppose that for some nonnegative integer N, G is false and $I(N)$ is true. *[We must show the truth of the post-condition: $a = \gcd(A, B)$.]* Since G is false, $b = 0$, and since $I(N)$ is true,

$$\gcd(a, b) = \gcd(A, B). \qquad 5.5.11$$

Substituting $b = 0$ into equation (5.5.11) gives

$$\gcd(a, 0) = \gcd(A, B).$$

But by Lemma 4.8.1,

$$\gcd(a, 0) = a.$$

Hence $a = \gcd(A, B)$ *[as was to be shown].*

Test Yourself

1. A pre-condition for an algorithm is _____ and a post-condition for an algorithm is _____.

2. A loop is defined as correct with respect to its pre- and post-conditions if, and only if, whenever the algorithm variables satisfy the pre-condition for the loop and the loop terminates after a finite number of steps, then _____.

3. For each iteration of a loop, if a loop invariant is true before iteration of the loop, then _____.

4. Given a **while** loop with guard G and a predicate $I(n)$ if the following four properties are true, then the loop is correct with respect to its pre- and post-conditions:

   (a) The pre-condition for the loop implies that _____ before the first iteration of the loop;

   (b) For all integers $k \geq 0$, if the guard G and the predicate $I(k)$ are both true before an iteration of the loop, then _____;

   (c) After a finite number of iterations of the loop, _____;

   (d) If N is the least number of iterations after which G is false and $I(N)$ is true, then the values of the algorithm variables will be as specified _____.

Exercise Set 5.5

Exercises 1–5 contain a while loop and a predicate. In each case show that if the predicate is true before entry to the loop, then it is also true after exit from the loop.

1. loop: **while** $(m \geq 0 \text{ and } m \leq 100)$
   $$m := m + 1$$
   $$n := n - 1$$
   end while

   predicate: $m + n = 100$

2. loop: **while** $(m \geq 0 \text{ and } m \leq 100)$
   $$m := m + 4$$
   $$n := n - 2$$
   end while

   predicate: $m + n$ is odd

3. loop: **while** $(m \geq 0 \text{ and } m \leq 100)$
   $$m := 3 \cdot m$$
   $$n := 5 \cdot n$$
   end while

   predicate: $m^3 > n^2$

4. loop: **while** $(n \geq 3 \text{ and } n \leq 100)$
   $$n := n + 1$$
   end while

   predicate: $2n + 1 \leq 2^n$

5. loop: **while** $(n \geq 0 \text{ and } n \leq 100)$
   $$n := n + 1$$
   end while

   predicate: $2^n < (n + 2)!$

Exercises 6–9 each contain a while loop annotated with a pre- and a post-condition and also a loop invariant. In each case, use the loop invariant theorem to prove the correctness of the loop with respect to the pre- and post-conditions.

6. *[Pre-condition: m is a nonnegative integer, x is a real number, i = 0, and exp = 1.]*

   while $(i \neq m)$
   1. $exp := exp \cdot x$
   2. $i := i + 1$
   end while

   [Post-condition: $exp = x^m$]
   loop invariant: $I(n)$ is "$exp = x^n$ and $i = n$."

7. *[Pre-condition: largest = A[1] and i = 1]*

   while $(i \neq m)$
   1. $i := i + 1$
   2. **if** $A[i] >$ largest **then** largest $:= A[i]$
   end while

   [Post-condition: largest = maximum value of A[1], A[2], ..., A[m]]

loop invariant: $I(n)$ is "largest = maximum value of $A[1]$, $A[2], \ldots, A[n+1]$ and $i = n+1$."

8. [Pre-condition: sum $= A[1]$ and $i = 1$]

> **while** $(i \neq m)$
>> 1. $i := i + 1$
>> 2. sum: $=$ sum $+ A[i]$
>
> **end while**

[Post-condition: sum $= A[1] + A[2] + \cdots + A[m]$]

loop invariant: $I(n)$ is "$i = n+1$ and $sum = A[1] + A[2] + \cdots + A[n+1]$."

9. [Pre-condition: $a = A$ and A is a positive integer.]

> **while** $(a > 0)$
>> 1. $a := a - 2$
>
> **end while**

[Post-condition: $a = 0$ if A is even and $a = -1$ if A is odd.]
loop invariant: $I(n)$ is "Both a and A are even integers or both are odd integers and, in either case, $a \geq -1$."

✶ 10. Prove correctness of the **while** loop of Algorithm 4.8.3 (in exercise 24 of Exercise Set 4.8) with respect to the following pre- and post-conditions:

Pre-condition: A and B are positive integers, $a = A$, and $b = B$.

Post-condition: One of a or b is zero and the other is nonzero. Whichever is nonzero equals gcd(A, B).

Use the loop invariant

$I(n)$ "(1) a and b are nonnegative integers with gcd$(a, b) =$ gcd(A, B).
(2) at most one of a and b equals 0,
(3) $0 \leq a + b \leq A + B - n$."

11. The following **while** loop implements a way to multiply two numbers that was developed by the ancient Egyptians.

[Pre-condition: A and B are positive integers, $x = A$, $y = B$, and product $= 0$.]

> **while** $(y \neq 0)$
>> $r := y \bmod 2$
>>
>> **if** $r = 0$
>>> **then do** $x := 2 \cdot x$
>>>> $y := y \ div \ 2$
>>>
>>> **end do**
>>
>> **if** $r = 1$
>>> **then do** $product := product + x$
>>>> $y := y - 1$
>>>
>>> **end do**
>
> **end while**

[Post-condition: product $= A \cdot B$]

Prove the correctness of this loop with respect to its pre- and post-conditions by using the loop invariant

$$I(n): \quad "xy + product = A \cdot B."$$

✶ 12. The following sentence could be added to the loop invariant for the Euclidean algorithm:

> There exist integers u, v, s, and t such that
> $$a = uA + vB \quad \text{and} \quad b = sA + tB. \qquad 5.5.12$$

a. Show that this sentence is a loop invariant for

> **while** $(b \neq 0)$
>> $r := a \bmod b$
>> $a := b$
>> $b := r$
>
> **end while**

b. Show that if initially $a = A$ and $b = B$, then sentence (5.5.12) is true before the first iteration of the loop.
c. Explain how the correctness proof for the Euclidean algorithm together with the results of (a) and (b) above allow you to conclude that given any integers A and B with $A > B \geq 0$, there exist integers u and v so that gcd$(A, B) = uA + vB$.
d. By actually calculating u, v, s, and t at each stage of execution of the Euclidean algorithm, find integers u and v so that gcd$(330, 156) = 330u + 156v$.

Answers for Test Yourself

1. a predicate that describes the initial state of the input variables for the algorithm; a predicate that describes the final state of the output variables for the algorithm   2. the algorithm variables satisfy the post-condition for the loop   3. it is true after iteration of the loop   4. (a) $I(0)$ is true   (b) $I(k+1)$ is true after the iteration of the loop   (c) the guard G becomes false   (d) in the post-condition of the loop

5.6 Defining Sequences Recursively

So, Nat'ralists observe, a Flea/Hath smaller Fleas that on him prey,/And these have smaller Fleas to bite 'em,/And so proceed ad infinitum. — Jonathan Swift, 1733

A sequence can be defined in a variety of different ways. One informal way is to write the first few terms with the expectation that the general pattern will be obvious. We might say, for instance, "consider the sequence 3, 5, 7, ..." Unfortunately, misunderstandings can occur when this approach is used. The next term of the sequence could be 9 if we mean a sequence of odd integers, or it could be 11 if we mean the sequence of odd prime numbers.

The second way to define a sequence is to give an explicit formula for its nth term. For example, a sequence $a_0, a_1, a_2 \ldots$ can be specified by writing

$$a_n = \frac{(-1)^n}{n+1} \quad \text{for all integers } n \geq 0.$$

The advantage of defining a sequence by such an explicit formula is that each term of the sequence is uniquely determined and can be computed in a fixed, finite number of steps, by substitution.

The third way to define a sequence is to use recursion, as was done in Examples 5.3.3 and 5.4.2. This requires giving both an equation, called a *recurrence relation*, that defines each later term in the sequence by reference to earlier terms and also one or more initial values for the sequence.

Sometimes it is very difficult or impossible to find an explicit formula for a sequence, but it *is* possible to define the sequence using recursion. Note that defining sequences recursively is similar to proving theorems by mathematical induction. The recurrence relation is like the inductive step and the initial conditions are like the basis step. Indeed, the fact that sequences can be defined recursively is equivalent to the fact that mathematical induction works as a method of proof.

• Definition

A **recurrence relation** for a sequence $a_0, a_1, a_2, \ldots$ is a formula that relates each term a_k to certain of its predecessors $a_{k-1}, a_{k-2}, \ldots, a_{k-i}$, where i is an integer with $k - i \geq 0$. The **initial conditions** for such a recurrence relation specify the values of $a_0, a_1, a_2, \ldots, a_{i-1}$, if i is a fixed integer, or $a_0, a_1, \ldots, a_m$, where m is an integer with $m \geq 0$, if i depends on k.

Example 5.6.1 Computing Terms of a Recursively Defined Sequence

Define a sequence $c_0, c_1, c_2, \ldots$ recursively as follows: For all integers $k \geq 2$,

$$(1) \quad c_k = c_{k-1} + kc_{k-2} + 1 \quad \text{recurrence relation}$$
$$(2) \quad c_0 = 1 \quad \text{and} \quad c_1 = 2 \quad \text{initial conditions.}$$

Find $c_2, c_3,$ and c_4.

Solution

$$c_2 = c_1 + 2c_0 + 1 \quad \text{by substituting } k = 2 \text{ into (1)}$$
$$= 2 + 2 \cdot 1 + 1 \quad \text{since } c_1 = 2 \text{ and } c_0 = 1 \text{ by (2)}$$

$$(3) \quad \therefore c_2 \quad = 5$$
$$c_3 \quad = c_2 + 3c_1 + 1 \qquad \text{by substituting } k = 3 \text{ into (1)}$$
$$= 5 + 3 \cdot 2 + 1 \qquad \text{since } c_2 = 5 \text{ by (3) and } c_1 = 2 \text{ by (2)}$$

$$(4) \quad \therefore c_3 \quad = 12$$
$$c_4 \quad = c_3 + 4c_2 + 1 \qquad \text{by substituting } k = 4 \text{ into (1)}$$
$$= 12 + 4 \cdot 5 + 1 \qquad \text{since } c_3 = 12 \text{ by (4) and } c_2 = 5 \text{ by (3)}$$
$$(5) \quad \therefore c_4 \quad = 33$$

■

A given recurrence relation may be expressed in several different ways.

Example 5.6.2 Writing a Recurrence Relation in More Than One Way

Note Think of the recurrence relation as $s_{\Box} = 3s_{\Box-1} - 1$, where any positive integer expression may be placed in the box.

Let $s_0, s_1, s_2, \ldots$ be a sequence that satisfies the following recurrence relation:

$$\text{for all integers } k \geq 1, \quad s_k = 3s_{k-1} - 1.$$

Explain why the following statement is true:

$$\text{for all integers } k \geq 0, \quad s_{k+1} = 3s_k - 1.$$

Solution In informal language, the recurrence relation says that any term of the sequence equals 3 times the previous term minus 1. Now for any integer $k \geq 0$, the term previous to s_{k+1} is s_k. Thus for any integer $k \geq 0$, $s_{k+1} = 3s_k - 1$. ■

A sequence defined recursively need not start with a subscript of zero. Also, a given recurrence relation may be satisfied by many different sequences; the actual values of the sequence are determined by the initial conditions.

Example 5.6.3 Sequences That Satisfy the Same Recurrence Relation

Let $a_1, a_2, a_3, \ldots$ and $b_1, b_2, b_3, \ldots$ satisfy the recurrence relation that the kth term equals 3 times the $(k-1)$st term for all integers $k \geq 2$:

$$(1) \quad a_k = 3a_{k-1} \quad \text{and} \quad b_k = 3b_{k-1}.$$

But suppose that the initial conditions for the sequences are different:

$$(2) \quad a_1 = 2 \quad \text{and} \quad b_1 = 1.$$

Find (a) a_2, a_3, a_4 and (b) b_2, b_3, b_4.

Solution

a. $\quad a_2 = 3a_1 = 3 \cdot 2 = 6 \qquad\qquad$ b. $\quad b_2 = 3b_1 = 3 \cdot 1 = 3$
$\quad\quad a_3 = 3a_2 = 3 \cdot 6 = 18 \qquad\qquad\qquad\quad b_3 = 3b_2 = 3 \cdot 3 = 9$
$\quad\quad a_4 = 3a_3 = 3 \cdot 18 = 54 \qquad\qquad\qquad b_4 = 3b_3 = 3 \cdot 9 = 27$

Thus $\qquad\qquad a_1, a_2, a_3, \ldots$ begins $2, 6, 18, 54, \ldots$ and
$\qquad\qquad\qquad b_1, b_2, b_3, \ldots$ begins $1, 3, 9, 27, \ldots$.

■

Example 5.6.4 Showing That a Sequence Given by an Explicit Formula Satisfies a Certain Recurrence Relation

The sequence of **Catalan numbers**, named after the Belgian mathematician Eugène Catalan (1814–1894), arises in a remarkable variety of different contexts in discrete mathematics. It can be defined as follows: For each integer $n \geq 1$,

$$C_n = \frac{1}{n+1}\binom{2n}{n}.$$

a. Find $C_1, C_2,$ and C_3.

b. Show that this sequence satisfies the recurrence relation $C_k = \frac{4k-2}{k+1}C_{k-1}$ for all integers $k \geq 2$

Solution

Eugène Catalan
(1814–1894)

Academie Royale de Belgique

a. $C_1 = \frac{1}{2}\binom{2}{1} = \frac{1}{2}\cdot 2 = 1, \quad C_2 = \frac{1}{3}\binom{4}{2} = \frac{1}{3}\cdot 6 = 2, \quad C_3 = \frac{1}{4}\binom{6}{3} = \frac{1}{4}\cdot 20 = 5$

b. To obtain the kth and $(k-1)$st terms of the sequence, just substitute k and $k-1$ in place of n in the explicit formula for $C_1, C_2, C_3, \ldots$.

$$C_k = \frac{1}{k+1}\binom{2k}{k}$$

$$C_{k+1} = \frac{1}{(k-1)+1}\binom{2(k-1)}{k-1} = \frac{1}{k}\binom{2k-2}{k-1}.$$

Then start with the right-hand side of the recurrence relation and transform it into the left-hand side: For each integer $k \geq 2$,

$$\frac{4k-2}{k+1}C_{k-1} = \frac{4k-2}{k+1}\left[\frac{1}{k}\binom{2k-2}{k-1}\right] \qquad \text{by substituting}$$

$$= \frac{2(2k-1)}{k+1}\cdot\frac{1}{k}\cdot\frac{(2k-2)!}{(k-1)!(2k-2-(k-1))!} \qquad \text{by the formula for } n \text{ choose } r$$

$$= \frac{1}{k+1}\cdot(2(2k-1))\cdot\frac{(2k-2)!}{(k(k-1)!)(k-1)!} \qquad \text{by rearranging the factors}$$

$$= \frac{1}{k+1}\cdot(2(2k-1))\cdot\frac{1}{k!(k-1)!}\cdot(2k-2)!\cdot\frac{1}{2}\cdot\frac{1}{k}\cdot 2k. \qquad \text{because } \tfrac{1}{2}\cdot\tfrac{1}{k}\cdot 2k = 1$$

$$= \frac{1}{k+1}\cdot\frac{2}{2}\cdot\frac{1}{k!}\cdot\frac{1}{(k-1)!}\cdot\frac{1}{k}\cdot(2k)\cdot(2k-1)\cdot(2k-2)! \qquad \text{by rearranging the factors}$$

$$= \frac{1}{k+1}\cdot\frac{(2k)!}{k!k!} \qquad \text{because } k(k-1)! = k!, \; \tfrac{2}{2} = 1, \text{ and } 2k\cdot(2k-1)\cdot(2k-2)! = (2k)!$$

$$= \frac{1}{k+1}\binom{2k}{k} \qquad \text{by the formula for } n \text{ choose } r$$

$$= C_k \qquad \text{by definition of } C_1, C_2, C_3, \ldots$$

∎

Examples of Recursively Defined Sequences

Recursion is one of the central ideas of computer science. To solve a problem recursively means to find a way to break it down into smaller subproblems each having the same form as the original problem—and to do this in such a way that when the process is repeated many times, the last of the subproblems are small and easy to solve and the solutions of the subproblems can be woven together to form a solution to the original problem.

Probably the most difficult part of solving problems recursively is to figure out how knowing the solution to smaller subproblems of the same type as the original problem will give you a solution to the problem as a whole. You *suppose* you know the solutions to smaller subproblems and ask yourself how you would best make use of that knowledge to solve the larger problem. The supposition that the smaller subproblems have already been solved has been called the *recursive paradigm* or the *recursive leap of faith*. Once you take this leap, you are right in the middle of the most difficult part of the problem, but generally, the path to a solution from this point, though difficult, is short. The recursive leap of faith is similar to the inductive hypothesis in a proof by mathematical induction.

Example 5.6.5 The Tower of Hanoi

Courtesy of Francis Lucas

Édouard Lucas (1842–1891)

In 1883 a French mathematician, Édouard Lucas, invented a puzzle that he called The Tower of Hanoi (La Tour D'Hanoï). The puzzle consisted of eight disks of wood with holes in their centers, which were piled in order of decreasing size on one pole in a row of three. A facsimile of the cover of the box is shown in Figure 5.6.1. Those who played the game were supposed to move all the disks one by one from one pole to another, never placing a larger disk on top of a smaller one. The directions to the puzzle claimed it was based on an old Indian legend:

On the steps of the altar in the temple of Benares, for many, many years Brahmins have been moving a tower of 64 golden disks from one pole to another; one by one, never placing a larger on top of a smaller. When all the disks have been transferred the Tower and the Brahmins will fall, and it will be the end of the world.

Courtesy of Paul Stockmeyer

Figure 5.6.1

The puzzle offered a prize of ten thousand francs (about $34,000 US today) to anyone who could move a tower of 64 disks by hand while following the rules of the game. (See Figure 5.6.2 on the following page.) Assuming that you transferred the disks as efficiently as possible, how many moves would be required to win the prize?

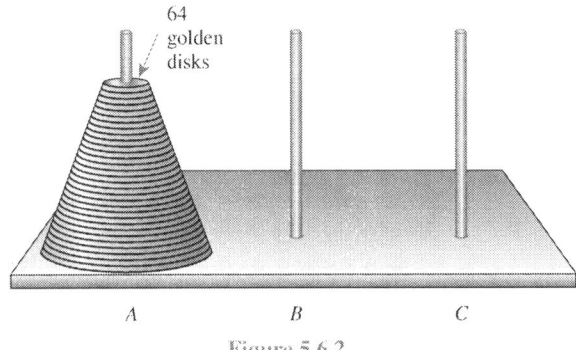

64
golden
disks

A   *B*   *C*

Figure 5.6.2

Solution   An elegant and efficient way to solve this problem is to think recursively. Suppose that you, somehow or other, have found the most efficient way possible to transfer a tower of $k - 1$ disks one by one from one pole to another, obeying the restriction that you never place a larger disk on top of a smaller one. What is the most efficient way to transfer a tower of k disks from one pole to another? The answer is sketched in Figure 5.6.3, where pole A is the initial pole and pole C is the target pole, and is described as follows:

Step 1 : Transfer the top $k - 1$ disks from pole A to pole B. If $k > 2$, execution of this step will require a number of moves of individual disks among the three poles. But the point of thinking recursively is not to get caught up in imagining the details of how those moves will occur.

Step 2 : Move the bottom disk from pole A to pole C.

Step 3 : Transfer the top $k - 1$ disks from pole B to pole C. (Again, if $k > 2$, execution of this step will require more than one move.)

To see that this sequence of moves is most efficient, observe that to move the bottom disk of a stack of k disks from one pole to another, you must first transfer the top $k - 1$ disks to a third pole to get them out of the way. Thus transferring the stack of k disks from pole A to pole C requires at least two transfers of the top $k - 1$ disks: one to transfer them off the bottom disk to free the bottom disk so that it can be moved and another to transfer them back on top of the bottom disk after the bottom disk has been moved to pole C. If the bottom disk were not moved directly from pole A to pole C but were moved to pole B first, at least two additional transfers of the top $k - 1$ disks would be necessary: one to move them from pole A to pole C so that the bottom disk could be moved from pole A to pole B and another to move them off pole C so that the bottom disk could be moved onto pole C. This would increase the total number of moves and result in a less efficient transfer.

Thus the minimum sequence of moves must include going from the initial position (a) to position (b) to position (c) to position (d). It follows that

Note   Defining the
sequence is a crucial step
in solving the problem.
The recurrence relation
and initial conditions are
specified in terms of the
sequence.

$$
\begin{bmatrix} \text{the minimum} \\ \text{number of moves} \\ \text{needed to transfer} \\ \text{a tower of } k \text{ disks} \\ \text{from pole } A \text{ to} \\ \text{pole } C \end{bmatrix} = \begin{bmatrix} \text{the minimum} \\ \text{number of} \\ \text{moves needed} \\ \text{to go from} \\ \text{position (a)} \\ \text{to position (b)} \end{bmatrix} + \begin{bmatrix} \text{The minimum} \\ \text{number of} \\ \text{moves needed} \\ \text{to go from} \\ \text{position (b)} \\ \text{to position (c)} \end{bmatrix} + \begin{bmatrix} \text{the minimum} \\ \text{number of} \\ \text{moves needed} \\ \text{to go from} \\ \text{position (c)} \\ \text{to position (d)} \end{bmatrix} \quad 5.6.1
$$

For each integer $n \geq 1$, let

$$
m_n = \begin{bmatrix} \text{the minimum number of moves needed to transfer} \\ \text{a tower of } n \text{ disks from one pole to another} \end{bmatrix}
$$

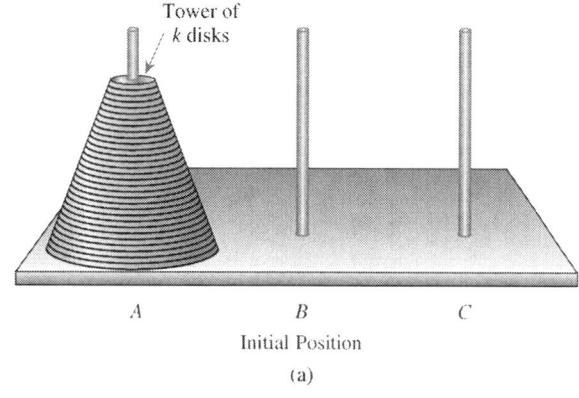

Initial Position

(a)

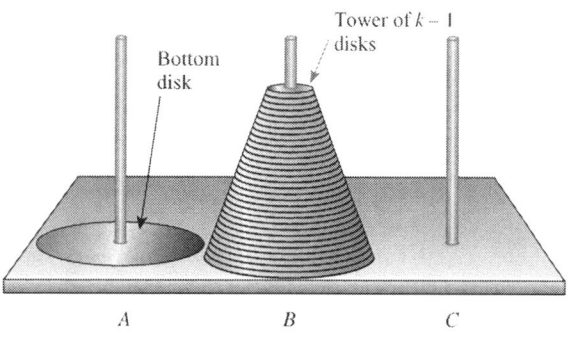

Position after Transferring $k - 1$ Disks from A to B

(b)

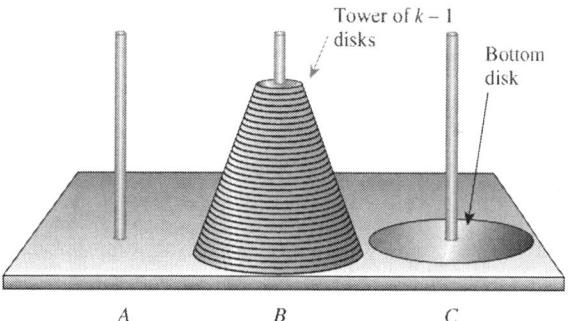

Position after Moving the Bottom Disk from A to C

(c)

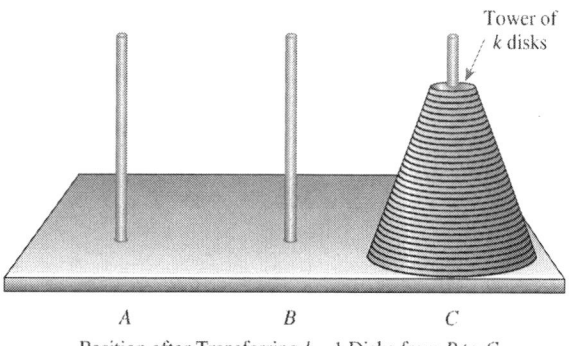

Position after Transferring $k - 1$ Disks from B to C

(d)

Figure 5.6.3 **Moves for the Tower of Hanoi**

Note that the numbers m_n are independent of the labeling of the poles; it takes the same minimum number of moves to transfer n disks from pole A to pole C as to transfer n disks from pole A to pole B, for example. Also the values of m_n are independent of the number of larger disks that may lie below the top n, provided these remain stationary while the top n are moved. Because the disks on the bottom are all larger than the ones on the top, the top disks can be moved from pole to pole as though the bottom disks were not present.

Going from position (a) to position (b) requires m_{k-1} moves, going from position (b) to position (c) requires just one move, and going from position (c) to position (d) requires m_{k-1} moves. By substitution into equation (5.6.1), therefore,

$$m_k = m_{k-1} + 1 + m_{k-1}$$
$$= 2m_{k-1} + 1 \qquad \text{for all integers } k \geq 2.$$

The initial condition, or base, of this recursion is found by using the definition of the sequence. Because just one move is needed to move one disk from one pole to another,

$$m_1 = \left[\begin{array}{c} \text{the minimum number of moves needed to move} \\ \text{a tower of one disk from one pole to another} \end{array} \right] = 1.$$

Hence the complete recursive specification of the sequence $m_1, m_2, m_3, \ldots$ is as follows: For all integers $k \geq 2$,

$$(1) \quad m_k = 2m_{k-1} + 1 \qquad \text{recurrence relation}$$

$$(2) \quad m_1 = 1 \qquad \text{initial conditions}$$

Here is a computation of the next five terms of the sequence:

$$(3) \quad m_2 = 2m_1 + 1 = 2 \cdot 1 + 1 = 3 \qquad \text{by (1) and (2)}$$
$$(4) \quad m_3 = 2m_2 + 1 = 2 \cdot 3 + 1 = 7 \qquad \text{by (1) and (3)}$$
$$(5) \quad m_4 = 2m_3 + 1 = 2 \cdot 7 + 1 = 15 \qquad \text{by (1) and (4)}$$
$$(6) \quad m_5 = 2m_4 + 1 = 2 \cdot 15 + 1 = 31 \qquad \text{by (1) and (5)}$$
$$(7) \quad m_6 = 2m_5 + 1 = 2 \cdot 31 + 1 = 63 \qquad \text{by (1) and (6)}$$

Going back to the legend, suppose the priests work rapidly and move one disk every second. Then the time from the beginning of creation to the end of the world would be m_{64} seconds. In the next section we derive an explicit formula for m_n. Meanwhile, we can compute m_{64} on a calculator or a computer by continuing the process started above (Try it!). The approximate result is

$$1.844674 \times 10^{19} \text{ seconds} \cong 5.84542 \times 10^{11} \text{ years}$$
$$\cong 584.5 \text{ billion years,}$$

which is obtained by the estimate of

$$60 \cdot 60 \cdot 24 \cdot (365.25) = 31,557,600$$

		minutes	hours	days	seconds
seconds per minute		per hour	per day	per year	per year

seconds in a year (figuring 365.25 days in a year to take leap years into account). Surprisingly, this figure is close to some scientific estimates of the life of the universe! ▩

Example 5.6.6 The Fibonacci Numbers

Fibonacci (Leonardo of Pisa)
(ca. 1175–1250)

One of the earliest examples of a recursively defined sequence arises in the writings of Leonardo of Pisa, commonly known as Fibonacci, who was the greatest European mathematician of the Middle Ages. In 1202 Fibonacci posed the following problem:

A single pair of rabbits (male and female) is born at the beginning of a year. Assume the following conditions:

1. Rabbit pairs are not fertile during their first month of life but thereafter give birth to one new male/female pair at the end of every month.

2. No rabbits die.

How many rabbits will there be at the end of the year?

Solution One way to solve this problem is to plunge right into the middle of it using recursion. Suppose you know how many rabbit pairs there were at the ends of previous months. How many will there be at the end of the current month?

The crucial observation is that the number of rabbit pairs born at the end of month k is the same as the number of pairs alive at the end of month $k - 2$. Why? Because it is exactly the rabbit pairs that were alive at the end of month $k - 2$ that were fertile during month k. The rabbits born at the end of month $k - 1$ were not.

$$\begin{array}{ccccc}
\text{month} & k-2 & & k-1 & k \\
\hline
\end{array}$$

Each pair alive here ↑   gives birth to a pair here ↑

Now the number of rabbit pairs alive at the end of month k equals the ones alive at the end of month $k - 1$ plus the pairs newly born at the end of the month. Thus

$$\begin{bmatrix} \text{the number} \\ \text{of rabbit} \\ \text{pairs alive} \\ \text{at the end} \\ \text{of month } k \end{bmatrix} = \begin{bmatrix} \text{the number} \\ \text{of rabbit} \\ \text{pairs alive} \\ \text{at the end} \\ \text{of month } k-1 \end{bmatrix} + \begin{bmatrix} \text{the number} \\ \text{of rabbit} \\ \text{pairs born} \\ \text{at the end} \\ \text{of month } k \end{bmatrix}$$

$$= \begin{bmatrix} \text{the number} \\ \text{of rabbit} \\ \text{pairs alive} \\ \text{at the end} \\ \text{of month } k-1 \end{bmatrix} + \begin{bmatrix} \text{the number} \\ \text{of rabbit} \\ \text{pairs alive} \\ \text{at the end} \\ \text{of month } k-2 \end{bmatrix} \qquad 5.6.2$$

Note It is essential to rephrase this observation in terms of a sequence.

For each integer $n \geq 1$, let

$$F_n = \begin{bmatrix} \text{the number of rabbit pairs} \\ \text{alive at the end of month } n \end{bmatrix}$$

and let

$$F_0 = \text{the initial number of rabbit pairs}$$
$$= 1.$$

Then by substitution into equation (5.6.2), for all integers $k \geq 2$,

$$F_k = F_{k-1} + F_{k-2}.$$

Now $F_0 = 1$, as already noted, and $F_1 = 1$ also, because the first pair of rabbits is not fertile until the second month. Hence the complete specification of the Fibonacci sequence is as follows: For all integers $k \geq 2$,

(1) $F_k = F_{k-1} + F_{k-2}$ recurrence relation

(2) $F_0 = 1, \quad F_1 = 1$ initial conditions.

To answer Fibonacci's question, compute F_2, F_3, and so forth through F_{12}:

(3) $F_2 = F_1 + F_0 = 1 + 1 \quad = 2$ by (1) and (2)

(4) $F_3 = F_2 + F_1 = 2 + 1 \quad = 3$ by (1), (2) and (3)

(5) $F_4 = F_3 + F_2 = 3 + 2 \quad = 5$ by (1), (3) and (4)

(6) $F_5 = F_4 + F_3 = 5 + 3 \quad = 8$ by (1), (4) and (5)

(7) $F_6 = F_5 + F_4 = 8 + 5 \quad = 13$ by (1), (5) and (6)

(8) $F_7 = F_6 + F_5 = 13 + 8 \quad = 21$ by (1), (6) and (7)

(9) $F_8 = F_7 + F_6 = 21 + 13 \ = 34$ by (1), (7) and (8)

(10) $F_9 = F_8 + F_7 = 34 + 21 \ = 55$ by (1), (8) and (9)

(11) $F_{10} = F_9 + F_8 = 55 + 34 \ = 89$ by (1), (9) and (10)

(12) $F_{11} = F_{10} + F_9 = 89 + 55 \ = 144$ by (1), (10) and (11)

(13) $F_{12} = F_{11} + F_{10} = 144 + 89 = 233$ by (1), (11) and (12)

At the end of the twelfth month there are 233 rabbit pairs, or 466 rabbits in all.   ■

Example 5.6.7 Compound Interest

On your twenty-first birthday you get a letter informing you that on the day you were born an eccentric rich aunt deposited $100,000 in a bank account earning 4% interest compounded annually and she now intends to turn the account over to you, provided you can figure out how much it is worth. What is the amount currently in the account?

Solution   To approach this problem recursively, observe that

$$
\begin{bmatrix} \text{the amount in} \\ \text{the account at} \\ \text{the end of any} \\ \text{particular year} \end{bmatrix} = \begin{bmatrix} \text{the amount in} \\ \text{the account at} \\ \text{the end of the} \\ \text{previous year} \end{bmatrix} + \begin{bmatrix} \text{the interest} \\ \text{earned on the} \\ \text{account during} \\ \text{the year} \end{bmatrix} .
$$

Now the interest earned during the year equals the interest rate, $4\% = 0.04$ times the amount in the account at the end of the previous year. Thus

$$
\begin{bmatrix} \text{the amount in} \\ \text{the account at} \\ \text{the end of any} \\ \text{particular year} \end{bmatrix} = \begin{bmatrix} \text{the amount in} \\ \text{the account at} \\ \text{the end of the} \\ \text{previous year} \end{bmatrix} + (0.04) \cdot \begin{bmatrix} \text{the amount in} \\ \text{the account at} \\ \text{the end of the} \\ \text{previous year} \end{bmatrix} . \quad 5.6.3
$$

For each positive integer n, let

Note   Again, a crucial step is to define the sequence explicitly.

$$
A_n = \begin{bmatrix} \text{the amount in the account} \\ \text{at the end of year } n \end{bmatrix}
$$

and let

$$
A_0 = \begin{bmatrix} \text{the initial amount} \\ \text{in the account} \end{bmatrix} = \$100,000.
$$

Then for any particular year k, substitution into equation (5.6.3) gives

$$A_k = A_{k-1} + (0.04) \cdot A_{k-1}$$
$$= (1 + 0.04) \cdot A_{k-1} = (1.04) \cdot A_{k-1} \qquad \text{by factoring out } A_{k-1}.$$

Consequently, the values of the sequence $A_0, A_1, A_2, \dots$ are completely specified as follows: for all integers $k \geq 1$,

$$(1) \quad A_k = (1.04) \cdot A_{k-1} \quad \text{recurrence relation}$$
$$(2) \quad A_0 = \$100,000 \quad \text{initial condition.}$$

The number 1.04 is called the *growth factor* of the sequence.

In the next section we derive an explicit formula for the value of the account in any year n. The value on your twenty-first birthday can also be computed by repeated substitution as follows:

$$(3) \quad A_1 \ = 1.04 \cdot A_0 \ = (1.04) \cdot \$100,000 \ = \$104,000 \qquad \text{by (1) and (2)}$$
$$(4) \quad A_2 \ = 1.04 \cdot A_1 \ = (1.04) \cdot \$104,000 \ = \$108,160 \qquad \text{by (1) and (3)}$$
$$(5) \quad A_3 \ = 1.04 \cdot A_2 \ = (1.04) \cdot \$108,160 \ = \$112,486.40 \quad \text{by (1) and (4)}$$

$$\vdots \qquad\qquad\qquad\qquad\qquad \vdots$$

$$(22) \quad A_{20} \ = 1.04 \cdot A_{19} \ \cong (1.04) \cdot \$210,684.92 \ \cong \$219,112.31 \quad \text{by (1) and (21)}$$
$$(23) \quad A_{21} \ = 1.04 \cdot A_{20} \ \cong (1.04) \cdot \$219,112.31 \ \cong \$227,876.81 \quad \text{by (1) and (22)}$$

The amount in the account is \$227,876.81 (to the nearest cent). Fill in the dots (to check the arithmetic) and collect your money! ∎

Example 5.6.8 Compound Interest with Compounding Several Times a Year

When an annual interest rate of i is compounded m times per year, the interest rate paid per period is i/m. For instance, if $3\% = 0.03$ annual interest is compounded quarterly, then the interest rate paid per quarter is $0.03/4 = 0.0075$.

For each integer $k \geq 1$, let $P_k =$ the amount on deposit at the end of the kth period, assuming no additional deposits or withdrawals. Then the interest earned during the kth period equals the amount on deposit at the end of the $(k - 1)$st period times the interest rate for the period:

$$\text{interest earned during } k\text{th period} = P_{k-1}\left(\frac{i}{m}\right).$$

The amount on deposit at the end of the kth period, P_k, equals the amount at the end of the $(k - 1)$st period, P_{k-1}, plus the interest earned during the kth period:

$$P_k = P_{k-1} + P_{k-1}\left(\frac{i}{m}\right) = P_{k-1}\left(1 + \frac{i}{m}\right). \qquad 5.6.4$$

Suppose \$10,000 is left on deposit at 3% compounded quarterly.

a. How much will the account be worth at the end of one year, assuming no additional deposits or withdrawals?

b. The **annual percentage rate** (**APR**) is the percentage increase in the value of the account over a one-year period. What is the APR for this account?

Solution

a. For each integer $n \geq 1$, let $P_n =$ the amount on deposit after n consecutive quarters, assuming no additional deposits or withdrawals, and let P_0 be the initial \$10,000. Then by equation (5.6.4) with $i = 0.03$ and $m = 4$, a recurrence relation for the sequence $P_0, P_1, P_2, \ldots$ is

(1) $\quad P_k = P_{k-1}(1 + 0.0075) = (1.0075) \cdot P_{k-1} \quad$ for all integers $k \geq 1$.

The amount on deposit at the end of one year (four quarters), P_4, can be found by successive substitution:

(2) $\quad P_0 = \$10,000$

(3) $\quad P_1 = 1.0075 \cdot P_0 = (1.0075) \cdot \$10,000.00 = \$10,075.00 \quad$ by (1) and (2)

(4) $\quad P_2 = 1.0075 \cdot P_1 = (1.0075) \cdot \$10,075.00 = \$10,150.56 \quad$ by (1) and (3)

(5) $\quad P_3 = 1.0075 \cdot P_2 \cong (1.0075) \cdot \$10,150.56 = \$10,226.69 \quad$ by (1) and (4)

(6) $\quad P_4 = 1.0075 \cdot P_3 \cong (1.0075) \cdot \$10,226.69 = \$10,303.39 \quad$ by (1) and (5)

Hence after one year there is \$10,303.39 (to the nearest cent) in the account.

b. The percentage increase in the value of the account, or APR, is

$$\frac{10303.39 - 10000}{10000} = 0.03034 = 3.034\%.$$

Recursive Definitions of Sum and Product

Addition and multiplication are called *binary* operations because only two numbers can be added or multiplied at a time. Careful definitions of sums and products of more than two numbers use recursion.

• Definition

Given numbers $a_1, a_2, \ldots, a_n$, where n is a positive integer, the **summation from $i = 1$ to n of the a_i**, denoted $\sum_{i=1}^{n} a_i$, is defined as follows:

$$\sum_{i=1}^{1} a_i = a_1 \quad \text{and} \quad \sum_{i=1}^{n} a_i = \left(\sum_{i=1}^{n-1} a_i \right) + a_n, \quad \text{if } n > 1.$$

The **product from $i = 1$ to n of the a_i**, denoted $\prod_{i=1}^{n} a_i$, is defined by

$$\prod_{i=1}^{1} a_i = a_1 \quad \text{and} \quad \prod_{i=1}^{n} a_i = \left(\prod_{i=1}^{n-1} a_i \right) \cdot a_n, \quad \text{if } n > 1.$$

The effect of these definitions is to specify an *order* in which sums and products of more than two numbers are computed. For example,

$$\sum_{i=1}^{4} a_i = \left(\sum_{i=1}^{3} a_i \right) + a_4 = \left(\left(\sum_{i=1}^{2} a_i \right) + a_3 \right) + a_4 = ((a_1 + a_2) + a_3) + a_4.$$

The recursive definitions are used with mathematical induction to establish various properties of general finite sums and products.

Example 5.6.9 A Sum of Sums

Prove that for any positive integer n, if $a_1, a_2, \ldots, a_n$ and $b_1, b_2, \ldots, b_n$ are real numbers, then

$$\sum_{i=1}^{n}(a_i + b_i) = \sum_{i=1}^{n} a_i + \sum_{i=1}^{n} b_i.$$

Solution   The proof is by mathematical induction. Let the property $P(n)$ be the equation

$$\sum_{i=1}^{n}(a_i + b_i) = \sum_{i=1}^{n} a_i + \sum_{i=1}^{n} b_i. \qquad \leftarrow P(n)$$

We must show that $P(n)$ is true for all integers $n \geq 0$. We do this by mathematical induction on n.

Show that $P(1)$ is true: To establish $P(1)$, we must show that

$$\sum_{i=1}^{1}(a_i + b_i) = \sum_{i=1}^{1} a_i + \sum_{i=1}^{1} b_i. \qquad \leftarrow P(1)$$

But

$$\sum_{i=1}^{1}(a_i + b_i) = a_1 + b_1 \qquad \text{by definition of } \Sigma$$

$$= \sum_{i=1}^{1} a_i + \sum_{i=1}^{1} b_i \qquad \text{also by definition of } \Sigma.$$

Hence $P(1)$ is true.

Show that for all integers $k \geq 1$, if $P(k)$ is true then $P(k+1)$ is also true:
Suppose $a_1, a_2, \ldots, a_k, a_{k+1}$ and $b_1, b_2, \ldots, b_k, b_{k+1}$ are real numbers and that for some $k \geq 1$

$$\sum_{i=1}^{k}(a_i + b_i) = \sum_{i=1}^{k} a_i + \sum_{i=1}^{k} b_i. \qquad \leftarrow P(k) \text{ inductive hypothesis}$$

We must show that

$$\sum_{i=1}^{k+1}(a_i + b_i) = \sum_{i=1}^{k+1} a_i + \sum_{i=1}^{k+1} b_i. \qquad \leftarrow P(k+1)$$

[We will show that the left-hand side of this equation equals the right-hand side.]

But the left-hand side of the equation is

$$\begin{aligned}
\sum_{i=1}^{k+1}(a_i + b_i) &= \sum_{i=1}^{k}(a_i + b_i) + (a_{k+1} + b_{k+1}) && \text{by definition of } \Sigma \\
&= \left(\sum_{i=1}^{k} a_i + \sum_{i=1}^{k} b_i\right) + (a_{k+1} + b_{k+1}) && \text{by inductive hypothesis} \\
&= \left(\sum_{i=1}^{k} a_i + a_{k+1}\right) + \left(\sum_{i=1}^{k} b_i + b_{k+1}\right) && \text{by the associative and commutative laws of algebra} \\
&= \sum_{i=1}^{k+1} a_i + \sum_{i=1}^{k+1} b_i && \text{by definition of } \Sigma
\end{aligned}$$

which equals the right-hand side of the equation. *[This is what was to be shown.]* ▪

Test Yourself

1. A recursive definition for a sequence consists of a _____ and _____.

2. A recurrence relation is an equation that defines each later term of a sequence by reference to _____ in the sequence.

3. Initial conditions for a recursive definition of a sequence consist of one or more of the _____ of the sequence.

4. To solve a problem recursively means to divide the problem into smaller subproblems of the same type as the initial problem, to suppose _____, and to figure out how to use the supposition to _____.

5. A crucial step for solving a problem recursively is to define a _____ in terms of which the recurrence relation and initial conditions can be specified.

Exercise Set 5.6

Find the first four terms of each of the recursively defined sequences in 1–8.

1. $a_k = 2a_{k-1} + k$, for all integers $k \geq 2$
   $a_1 = 1$

2. $b_k = b_{k-1} + 3k$, for all integers $k \geq 2$
   $b_1 = 1$

3. $c_k = k(c_{k-1})^2$, for all integers $k \geq 1$
   $c_0 = 1$

4. $v_k = v_{k-1} + v_{k-2} + 1$, for all integers $k \geq 3$
   $v_1 = 1, \ v_2 = 3$

5. $s_k = s_{k-1} + 2s_{k-2}$, for all integers $k \geq 2$
   $s_0 = 1, \ s_1 = 1$

6. $t_k = t_{k-1} + 2t_{k-2}$, for all integers $k \geq 2$
   $t_0 = -1, \ t_1 = 2$

7. $u_k = ku_{k-1} - u_{k-2}$, for all integers $k \geq 3$
   $u_1 = 1, \ u_2 = 1$

8. $d_k = k(d_{k-1})^2$, for all integers $k \geq 1$
   $d_0 = 3$

9. Let $a_0, a_1, a_2, \ldots$ be defined by the formula $a_n = 3n + 1$, for all integers $n \geq 0$. Show that this sequence satisfies the recurrence relation $a_k = a_{k-1} + 3$, for all integers $k \geq 1$.

10. Let $b_0, b_1, b_2, \ldots$ be defined by the formula $b_n = 4^n$, for all integers $n \geq 0$. Show that this sequence satisfies the recurrence relation $b_k = 4b_{k-1}$, for all integers $k \geq 1$.

11. Let $c_0, c_1, c_2, \ldots$ be defined by the formula $c_n = 2^n - 1$ for all integers $n \geq 0$. Show that this sequence satisfies the recurrence relation
    $$c_k = 2c_{k-1} + 1.$$

12. Let $s_0, s_1, s_2, \ldots$ be defined by the formula $s_n = \dfrac{(-1)^n}{n!}$ for all integers $n \geq 0$. Show that this sequence satisfies the recurrence relation
    $$s_k = \frac{-s_{k-1}}{k}.$$

13. Let $t_0, t_1, t_2, \ldots$ be defined by the formula $t_n = 2 + n$ for all integers $n \geq 0$. Show that this sequence satisfies the recurrence relation
    $$t_k = 2t_{k-1} - t_{k-2}.$$

14. Let $d_0, d_1, d_2, \ldots$ be defined by the formula $d_n = 3^n - 2^n$ for all integers $n \geq 0$. Show that this sequence satisfies the recurrence relation
    $$d_k = 5d_{k-1} - 6d_{k-2}.$$

H 15. For the sequence of Catalan numbers defined in Example 5.6.4, prove that for all integers $n \geq 1$,
    $$C_n = \frac{1}{4n+2} \binom{2n+2}{n+1}.$$

16. Use the recurrence relation and values for the Tower of Hanoi sequence $m_1, m_2, m_3, \ldots$ discussed in Example 5.6.5 to compute m_7 and m_8.

17. *Tower of Hanoi with Adjacency Requirement:* Suppose that in addition to the requirement that they never move a larger disk on top of a smaller one, the priests who move the disks of the Tower of Hanoi are also allowed only to move disks one by one from one pole to an *adjacent* pole. Assume poles A and C are at the two ends of the row and pole B is in the middle. Let

$$a_n = \begin{bmatrix} \text{the minimum number of moves} \\ \text{needed to transfer a tower of } n \\ \text{disks from pole } A \text{ to pole } C \end{bmatrix}.$$

a. Find a_1, a_2, and a_3. b. Find a_4.
c. Find a recurrence relation for $a_1, a_2, a_3, \ldots$.

18. *Tower of Hanoi with Adjacency Requirement:* Suppose the same situation as in exercise 17. Let

$$b_n = \begin{bmatrix} \text{the minimum number of moves} \\ \text{needed to transfer a tower of } n \\ \text{disks from pole } A \text{ to pole } B \end{bmatrix}.$$

a. Find b_1, b_2, and b_3. b. Find b_4.

c. Show that $b_k = a_{k-1} + 1 + b_{k-1}$ for all integers $k \geq 2$, where $a_1, a_2, a_3, \ldots$ is the sequence defined in exercise 17.

d. Show that $b_k \leq 3b_{k-1} + 1$ for all integers $k \geq 2$.

H ✳ e. Show that $b_k = 3b_{k-1} + 1$ for all integers $k \geq 2$.

19. *Four-Pole Tower of Hanoi*: Suppose that the Tower of Hanoi problem has four poles in a row instead of three. Disks can be transferred one by one from one pole to any other pole, but at no time may a larger disk be placed on top of a smaller disk. Let s_n be the minimum number of moves needed to transfer the entire tower of n disks from the left-most to the right-most pole.

a. Find s_1, s_2, and s_3.   b. Find s_4.

c. Show that $s_k \leq 2s_{k-2} + 3$ for all integers $k \geq 3$.

20. *Tower of Hanoi Poles in a Circle:* Suppose that instead of being lined up in a row, the three poles for the original Tower of Hanoi are placed in a circle. The monks move the disks one by one from one pole to another, but they may only move disks one over in a clockwise direction and they may never move a larger disk on top of a smaller one. Let c_n be the minimum number of moves needed to transfer a pile of n disks from one pole to the next adjacent pole in the clockwise direction.

a. Justify the inequality $c_k \leq 4c_{k-1} + 1$ for all integers $k \geq 2$.

b. The expression $4c_{k-1} + 1$ is not the minimum number of moves needed to transfer a pile of k disks from one pole to another. Explain, for example, why

$$c_3 \neq 4c_2 + 1.$$

21. *Double Tower of Hanoi*: In this variation of the Tower of Hanoi there are three poles in a row and $2n$ disks, two of each of n different sizes, where n is any positive integer. Initially one of the poles contains all the disks placed on top of each other in pairs of decreasing size. Disks are transferred one by one from one pole to another, but at no time may a larger disk be placed on top of a smaller disk. However, a disk may be placed on top of one of the same size. Let t_n be the minimum number of moves needed to transfer a tower of $2n$ disks from one pole to another.

a. Find t_1 and t_2.   b. Find t_3.

c. Find a recurrence relation for $t_1, t_2, t_3, \ldots$.

22. *Fibonacci Variation*: A single pair of rabbits (male and female) is born at the beginning of a year. Assume the following conditions (which are more realistic than Fibonacci's):

(1) Rabbit pairs are not fertile during their first month of life but thereafter give birth to four new male/female pairs at the end of every month.

(2) No rabbits die.

a. Let r_n = the number of pairs of rabbits alive at the end of month n, for each integer $n \geq 1$, and let $r_0 = 1$. Find a recurrence relation for $r_0, r_1, r_2, \ldots$.

b. Compute $r_0, r_1, r_2, r_3, r_4, r_5$, and r_6.

c. How many rabbits will there be at the end of the year?

23. *Fibonacci Variation*: A single pair of rabbits (male and female) is born at the beginning of a year. Assume the following conditions:

(1) Rabbit pairs are not fertile during their first *two* months of life, but thereafter give birth to three new male/female pairs at the end of every month.

(2) No rabbits die.

a. Let s_n = the number of pairs of rabbits alive at the end of month n, for each integer $n \geq 1$, and let $s_0 = 1$. Find a recurrence relation for $s_0, s_1, s_2, \ldots$.

b. Compute s_0, s_1, s_2, s_3, s_4, and s_5.

c. How many rabbits will there be at the end of the year?

In 24–34, $F_0, F_1, F_2, \ldots$ is the Fibonacci sequence.

24. Use the recurrence relation and values for $F_0, F_1, F_2, \ldots$ given in Example 5.6.6 to compute F_{13} and F_{14}.

25. The Fibonacci sequence satisfies the recurrence relation $F_k = F_{k-1} + F_{k-2}$, for all integers $k \geq 2$.

a. Explain why the following is true:

$$F_{k+1} = F_k + F_{k-1} \quad \text{for all integers } k \geq 1.$$

b. Write an equation expressing F_{k+2} in terms of F_{k+1} and F_k.

c. Write an equation expressing F_{k+3} in terms of F_{k+2} and F_{k+1}

26. Prove that $F_k = 3F_{k-3} + 2F_{k-4}$ for all integers $k \geq 4$.

27. Prove that $F_k^2 - F_{k-1}^2 = F_k F_{k-1} - F_{k+1} F_{k-1}$, for all integers $k \geq 1$.

28. Prove that $F_{k+1}^2 - F_k^2 = F_{k-1} F_{k+2}$, for all integers $k \geq 1$.

29. Prove that $F_{k+1}^2 - F_k^2 - F_{k-1}^2 = 2F_k F_{k-1}$, for all integers $k \geq 1$.

30. Use mathematical induction to prove that for all integers $n \geq 0$, $F_{n+2} F_n - F_{n+1}^2 = (-1)^n$.

✳ 31. Use strong mathematical induction to prove that $F_n < 2^n$ for all integers $n \geq 1$.

H ✳ 32. Let $F_0, F_1, F_2, \ldots$ be the Fibonacci sequence defined in Section 5.6. Prove that for all integers $n \geq 0$, $\gcd(F_{n+1}, F_n) = 1$.

33. It turns out that the Fibonacci sequence satisfies the following explicit formula: For all integers $F_n \geq 0$,

$$F_n = \frac{1}{\sqrt{5}} \left[\left(\frac{1 + \sqrt{5}}{2} \right)^{n+1} - \left(\frac{1 - \sqrt{5}}{2} \right)^{n+1} \right]$$

Verify that the sequence defined by this formula satisfies the recurrence relation $F_k = F_{k-1} + F_{k-2}$ for all integers $k \geq 2$.

H 34. (For students who have studied calculus) Find $\lim\limits_{n \to \infty} \left(\dfrac{F_{n+1}}{F_n} \right)$, assuming that the limit exists.

H ✳ 35. (For students who have studied calculus) Prove that
$$\lim_{n \to \infty} \left(\frac{F_{n+1}}{F_n} \right) \text{ exists.}$$

36. (For students who have studied calculus) Define $x_0, x_1, x_2, \ldots$ as follows:
$$x_k = \sqrt{2 + x_{k-1}} \qquad \text{for all integers } k \geq 1$$
$$x_0 = 0$$

Find $\lim_{n \to \infty} x_n$. (Assume that the limit exists.)

37. *Compound Interest*: Suppose a certain amount of money is deposited in an account paying 4% annual interest compounded quarterly. For each positive integer n, let R_n = the amount on deposit at the end of the nth quarter, assuming no additional deposits or withdrawals, and let R_0 be the initial amount deposited.
    a. Find a recurrence relation for $R_0, R_1, R_2, \ldots$.
    b. If $R_0 = \$5000$, find the amount of money on deposit at the end of one year.
    c. Find the APR for the account.

38. *Compound Interest*: Suppose a certain amount of money is deposited in an account paying 3% annual interest compounded monthly. For each positive integer n, let S_n = the amount on deposit at the end of the nth month, and let S_0 be the initial amount deposited.
    a. Find a recurrence relation for $S_0, S_1, S_2, \ldots$, assuming no additional deposits or withdrawals during the year.
    b. If $S_0 = \$10,000$, find the amount of money on deposit at the end of one year.
    c. Find the APR for the account.

39. With each step you take when climbing a staircase, you can move up either one stair or two stairs. As a result, you can climb the entire staircase taking one stair at a time, taking two at a time, or taking a combination of one- and two-stair increments. For each integer $n \geq 1$, if the staircase consists of n stairs, let c_n be the number of different ways to climb the staircase. Find a recurrence relation for $c_1, c_2, c_3, \ldots$.

40. A set of blocks contains blocks of heights 1, 2, and 4 centimeters. Imagine constructing towers by piling blocks of different heights directly on top of one another. (A tower of height 6 cm could be obtained using six 1-cm blocks, three 2-cm blocks one 2-cm block with one 4-cm block on top, one 4-cm block with one 2-cm block on top, and so forth.) Let t be the number of ways to construct a tower of height n cm using blocks from the set. (Assume an unlimited supply of blocks of each size.) Find a recurrence relation for $t_1, t_2, t_3, \ldots$.

41. Use the recursive definition of summation, together with mathematical induction, to prove the generalized distributive law that for all positive integers n, if $a_1, a_2, \ldots, a_n$ and c are real numbers, then
$$\sum_{i=1}^{n} ca_i = c \left(\sum_{i=1}^{n} a_i \right).$$

42. Use the recursive definition of product, together with mathematical induction, to prove that for all positive integers n, if $a_1, a_2, \ldots, a_n$ and $b_1, b_2, \ldots, b_n$ are real numbers, then
$$\prod_{i=1}^{n} (a_i b_i) = \left(\prod_{i=1}^{n} a_i \right) \left(\prod_{i=1}^{n} b_i \right).$$

43. Use the recursive definition of product, together with mathematical induction, to prove that for all positive integers n, if $a_1, a_2, \ldots, a_n$ and c are real numbers, then
$$\prod_{i=1}^{n} (ca_i) = c^n \left(\prod_{i=1}^{n} a_i \right).$$

H 44. The triangle inequality for absolute value states that for all real numbers a and b, $|a + b| \leq |a| + |b|$. Use the recursive definition of summation, the triangle inequality, the definition of absolute value, and mathematical induction to prove that for all positive integers n, if $a_1, a_2, \ldots, a_n$ are real numbers, then
$$\left| \sum_{i=1}^{n} a_i \right| \leq \sum_{i=1}^{n} |a_i|.$$

Answers for Test Yourself

1. recurrence relation; initial conditions   2. earlier terms   3. values of the first few terms   4. that the smaller subproblems have already been solved; solve the initial problem   5. sequence

5.7 Solving Recurrence Relations by Iteration

The keener one's sense of logical deduction, the less often one makes hard and fast inferences. — Bertrand Russell, 1872–1970

Suppose you have a sequence that satisfies a certain recurrence relation and initial conditions. It is often helpful to know an explicit formula for the sequence, especially if you need to compute terms with very large subscripts or if you need to examine general properties of the sequence. Such an explicit formula is called a **solution** to the recurrence relation. In this section, we discuss methods for solving recurrence relations. For example, in the text and exercises of this section, we will show that the Tower of Hanoi sequence of Example 5.6.5 satisfies the formula

$$m_n = 2^n - 1,$$

and that the compound interest sequence of Example 5.6.7 satisfies

$$A_n = (1.04)^n \cdot \$100,000.$$

The Method of Iteration

The most basic method for finding an explicit formula for a recursively defined sequence is **iteration**. Iteration works as follows: Given a sequence $a_0, a_1, a_2, \ldots$ defined by a recurrence relation and initial conditions, you start from the initial conditions and calculate successive terms of the sequence until you see a pattern developing. At that point you guess an explicit formula.

Example 5.7.1 Finding an Explicit Formula

Let $a_0, a_1, a_2, \ldots$ be the sequence defined recursively as follows: For all integers $k \geq 1$,

(1) $a_k = a_{k-1} + 2$ recurrence relation

(2) $a_0 = 1$ initial condition.

Use iteration to guess an explicit formula for the sequence.

Solution   Recall that to say

$$a_k = a_{k-1} + 2 \quad \text{for all integers } k \geq 1$$

means

$$a_\square = a_{\square-1} + 2 \qquad \text{no matter what positive integer is placed into the box } \square.$$

In particular,

$$a_1 = a_0 + 2,$$
$$a_2 = a_1 + 2,$$
$$a_3 = a_2 + 2,$$

and so forth. Now use the initial condition to begin a process of successive substitutions into these equations, not just of numbers (as was done in Section 5.6) but of *numerical expressions*.

The reason for using numerical expressions rather than numbers is that in these problems you are seeking a numerical pattern that underlies a general formula. The secret of success is to leave most of the arithmetic undone. However, you do need to eliminate parentheses as you go from one step to the next. Otherwise, you will soon end up with a bewilderingly large nest of parentheses. Also, it is nearly always helpful to use shorthand notations for regrouping additions, subtractions, and multiplications of numbers that repeat. Thus, for instance, you would write

$$5 \cdot 2 \qquad \text{instead of } 2 + 2 + 2 + 2 + 2$$

and

$$2^5 \qquad \text{instead of } 2 \cdot 2 \cdot 2 \cdot 2 \cdot 2.$$

Notice that you don't lose any information about the number patterns when you use these shorthand notations.

Here's how the process works for the given sequence:

$a_0 = 1$ — the initial condition

$a_1 = a_0 + 2 = 1 + 2$ — by substitution

$a_2 = a_1 + 2 = (1 + 2) + 2 \qquad = 1 + 2 + 2$ — eliminate parentheses

$a_3 = a_2 + 2 = (1 + 2 + 2) + 2 \qquad = 1 + 2 + 2 + 2$ — eliminate parentheses again; write $3 \cdot 2$ instead of $2 + 2 + 2$?

$a_4 = a_3 + 2 = (1 + 2 + 2 + 2) + 2 = 1 + 2 + 2 + 2 + 2$ — eliminate parentheses again; definitely write $4 \cdot 2$ instead of $2 + 2 + 2 + 2$—the length of the string of 2's is getting out of hand.

Tip Do no arithmetic *except*

* replace $n \cdot 1$ and $1 \cdot n$ by n
* reformat repeated numbers
* get rid of parentheses

Since it appears helpful to use the shorthand $k \cdot 2$ in place of $2 + 2 + \cdots + 2$ (k times), we do so, starting again from a_0.

$a_0 = 1 \qquad\qquad = 1 + 0 \cdot 2$ — the initial condition

$a_1 = a_0 + 2 = 1 + 2 \qquad = 1 + 1 \cdot 2$ — by substitution

$a_2 = a_1 + 2 = (1 + 2) + 2 \quad = 1 + 2 \cdot 2$

$a_3 = a_2 + 2 = (1 + 2 \cdot 2) + 2 = 1 + 3 \cdot 2$

$a_4 = a_3 + 2 = (1 + 3 \cdot 2) + 2 = 1 + 4 \cdot 2$ — At this point it certainly seems likely that the general pattern is $1 + n \cdot 2$; check whether the next calculation supports this.

$a_5 = a_4 + 2 = (1 + 4 \cdot 2) + 2 = 1 + 5 \cdot 2$ — It does! So go ahead and write an answer. It's only a guess, after all.

$\vdots$

Guess: $\quad a_n = 1 + n \cdot 2 = 1 + 2n$

The answer obtained for this problem is just a guess. To be sure of the correctness of this guess, you will need to check it by mathematical induction. Later in this section, we will show how to do this. ◼

A sequence like the one in Example 5.7.1, in which each term equals the previous term plus a fixed constant, is called an *arithmetic sequence*. In the exercises at the end of this section you are asked to show that the nth term of an arithmetic sequence always equals the initial value of the sequence plus n times the fixed constant.

> **• Definition**
>
> A sequence $a_0, a_1, a_2, \ldots$ is called an **arithmetic sequence** if, and only if, there is a constant d such that
>
> $$a_k = a_{k-1} + d \quad \text{for all integers } k \geq 1.$$
>
> It follows that,
>
> $$a_n = a_0 + dn \quad \text{for all integers } n \geq 0.$$

Example 5.7.2 An Arithmetic Sequence

Under the force of gravity, an object falling in a vacuum falls about 9.8 meters per second (m/sec) faster each second than it fell the second before. Thus, neglecting air resistance, a skydiver's speed upon leaving an airplane is approximately 9.8 m/sec one second after departure, $9.8 + 9.8 = 19.6$ m/sec two seconds after departure, and so forth. If air resistance is neglected, how fast would the skydiver be falling 60 seconds after leaving the airplane?

Solution Let s_n be the skydiver's speed in m/sec n seconds after exiting the airplane if there were no air resistance. Thus s_0 is the initial speed, and since the diver would travel 9.8 m/sec faster each second than the second before,

$$s_k = s_{k-1} + 9.8 \text{ m/sec} \quad \text{for all integers } k \geq 1.$$

It follows that $s_0, s_1, s_2, \ldots$ is an arithmetic sequence with a fixed constant of 9.8, and thus

$$s_n = s_0 + (9.8)n \quad \text{for each integer } n \geq 0.$$

Hence sixty seconds after exiting and neglecting air resistance, the skydiver would travel at a speed of

$$s_{60} = 0 + (9.8)(60) = 588 \text{ m/sec}.$$

Note that 588 m/sec is over half a kilometer per second or over a third of a mile per second, which is very fast for a human being to travel. Happily for the skydiver, taking air resistance into account cuts the speed considerably. ∎

In an arithmetic sequence, each term equals the previous term plus a fixed constant. In a geometric sequence, each term equals the previous term *times* a fixed constant. Geometric sequences arise in a large variety of applications, such as compound interest certain models of population growth, radioactive decay, and the number of operations needed to execute certain computer algorithms.

Example 5.7.3 The Explicit Formula for a Geometric Sequence

Let r be a fixed nonzero constant, and suppose a sequence $a_0, a_1, a_2, \ldots$ is defined recursively as follows:

$$a_k = r a_{k-1} \quad \text{for all integers } k \geq 1,$$
$$a_0 = a.$$

Use iteration to guess an explicit formula for this sequence.

Solution

$$a_0 = a$$

$$a_1 = ra_0 = ra$$

$$a_2 = ra_1 = r(ra) = r^2a$$

$$a_3 = ra_2 = r(r^2a) = r^3a$$

$$a_4 = ra_3 = r(r^3a) = r^4a$$

$$\vdots$$

Guess: $a_n = r^na = ar^n$ for any arbitrary integer $n \geq 0$

In the exercises at the end of this section, you are asked to prove that this formula is correct. ■

• Definition

A sequence $a_0, a_1, a_2, \ldots$ is called a **geometric sequence** if, and only if, there is a constant r such that

$$a_k = ra_{k-1} \quad \text{for all integers } k \geq 1.$$

It follows that,

$$a_n = a_0r^n \quad \text{for all integers } n \geq 0.$$

Example 5.7.4 A Geometric Sequence

As shown in Example 5.6.7, if a bank pays interest at a rate of 4% per year compounded annually and A_n denotes the amount in the account at the end of year n, then $A_k = (1.04)A_{k-1}$, for all integers $k \geq 1$, assuming no deposits or withdrawals during the year. Suppose the initial amount deposited is $100,000, and assume that no additional deposits or withdrawals are made.

a. How much will the account be worth at the end of 21 years?

b. In how many years will the account be worth $1,000,000?

Solution

a. $A_0, A_1, A_2, \ldots$ is a geometric sequence with initial value 100,000 and constant multiplier 1.04. Hence,

$$A_n = \$100{,}000 \cdot (1.04)^n \quad \text{for all integers } n \geq 0.$$

After 21 years, the amount in the account will be

$$A_{21} = \$100{,}000 \cdot (1.04)^{21} \cong \$227{,}876.81.$$

This is the same answer as that obtained in Example 5.6.7 but is computed much more easily (at least if a calculator with a powering key, such as $\boxed{\wedge}$ or $\boxed{x^y}$, is used).

b. Let t be the number of years needed for the account to grow to \$1,000,000. Then

$$\$1,000,000 = \$100,000 \cdot (1.04)^t.$$

Dividing both sides by 100,000 gives

$$10 = (1.04)^t,$$

and taking natural logarithms of both sides results in

$$\ln(10) = \ln(1.04)^t.$$

Note Properties of
logarithms are reviewed
in Section 7.2.

Then

$$\ln(10) \cong t \ \ln(1.04) \qquad \text{because } \log_b(x^a) = a \log_b(x) \\ \text{(see exercise 35 of Section 7.2)}$$

and so

$$t = \frac{\ln(10)}{\ln(1.04)} \cong 58.7$$

Hence the account will grow to \$1,000,000 in approximately 58.7 years. ∎

An important property of a geometric sequence with constant multiplier greater than 1 is that its terms increase very rapidly in size as the subscripts get larger and larger. For instance, the first ten terms of a geometric sequence with a constant multiplier of 10 are

$$1, \ 10, \ 10^2, \ 10^3, \ 10^4, \ 10^5, \ 10^6, \ 10^7, \ 10^8, \ 10^9.$$

Thus, by its tenth term, the sequence already has the value $10^9 = 1,000,000,000 = 1$ billion. The following box indicates some quantities that are approximately equal to certain powers of 10.

$10^7 \cong$ number of seconds in a year

$10^9 \cong$ number of bytes of memory in a personal computer

$10^{11} \cong$ number of neurons in a human brain

$10^{17} \cong$ age of the universe in seconds (according to one theory)

$10^{31} \cong$ number of seconds to process all possible positions of a checkers game if moves are processed at a rate of 1 per billionth of a second

$10^{81} \cong$ number of atoms in the universe

$10^{111} \cong$ number of seconds to process all possible positions of a chess game if moves are processed at a rate of 1 per billionth of a second

---

Using Formulas to Simplify Solutions Obtained by Iteration

Explicit formulas obtained by iteration can often be simplified by using formulas such as those developed in Section 5.2. For instance, according to the formula for the sum of a geometric sequence with initial term 1 (Theorem 5.2.3), for each real number r except $r = 1$,

$$1 + r + r^2 + \cdots + r^n = \frac{r^{n+1} - 1}{r - 1} \qquad \text{for all integers } n \geq 0.$$

And according to the formula for the sum of the first n integers (Theorem 5.2.2),

$$1 + 2 + 3 + \cdots + n = \frac{n(n + 1)}{2} \qquad \text{for all integers } n \geq 1.$$

Example 5.7.5 An Explicit Formula for the Tower of Hanoi Sequence

Recall that the Tower of Hanoi sequence $m_1, m_2, m_3, \ldots$ of Example 5.6.5 satisfies the recurrence relation

$$m_k = 2m_{k-1} + 1 \quad \text{for all integers } k \geq 2$$

and has the initial condition

$$m_1 = 1.$$

Use iteration to guess an explicit formula for this sequence, and make use of a formula from Section 5.2 to simplify the answer.

Solution   By iteration

$$m_1 = 1$$

$$m_2 = 2m_1 + 1 = 2 \cdot 1 + 1 \qquad\qquad = 2^1 + 1,$$

$$m_3 = 2m_2 + 1 = 2\,(2 + 1) + 1 \qquad\qquad = 2^2 + 2 + 1,$$

$$m_4 = 2m_3 + 1 = 2\,(2^2 + 2 + 1) + 1 \qquad = 2^3 + 2^2 + 2 + 1,$$

$$m_5 = 2m_4 + 1 = 2\,(2^3 + 2^2 + 2 + 1) + 1 = 2^4 + 2^3 + 2^2 + 2 + 1.$$

These calculations show that each term up to m_5 is a sum of successive powers of 2, starting with $2^0 = 1$ and going up to 2^k, where k is 1 less than the subscript of the term. The pattern would seem to continue to higher terms because each term is obtained from the preceding one by multiplying by 2 and adding 1; multiplying by 2 raises the exponent of each component of the sum by 1, and adding 1 adds back the 1 that was lost when the previous 1 was multiplied by 2. For instance, for $n = 6$,

$$m_6 = 2m_5 + 1 = 2(2^4 + 2^3 + 2^2 + 2 + 1) + 1 = 2^5 + 2^4 + 2^3 + 2^2 + 2 + 1.$$

Thus it seems that, in general,

$$m_n = 2^{n-1} + 2^{n-2} + \cdots + 2^2 + 2 + 1.$$

By the formula for the sum of a geometric sequence (Theorem 5.2.3),

$$2^{n-1} + 2^{n-2} + \cdots + 2^2 + 2 + 1 = \frac{2^n - 1}{2 - 1} = 2^n - 1.$$

Hence the explicit formula seems to be

$$m_n = 2^n - 1 \quad \text{for all integers } n \geq 1. \qquad\qquad \blacksquare$$

A common mistake people make when doing problems such as this is to misuse the laws of algebra. For instance, by the distributive law,

$$a \cdot (b + c) = a \cdot b + a \cdot c \quad \text{for all real numbers } a, \ b, \ \text{and } c.$$

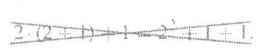
Thus, in particular, for $a = 2$, $b = 2$, and $c = 1$,

$$2 \cdot (2 + 1) = 2 \cdot 2 + 2 \cdot 1 = 2^2 + 2.$$

It follows that

$$2 \cdot (2 + 1) + 1 = (2^2 + 2) + 1 = 2^2 + 2 + 1.$$

Example 5.7.6 Using the Formula for the Sum of the First n Positive Integers

Let K_n be the picture obtained by drawing n dots (which we call *vertices*) and join-ing each pair of vertices by a line segment (which we call an *edge*). (In Chapter 10 we discuss these objects in a more general context.) Then K_1, K_2, K_3, and K_4 are as follows:

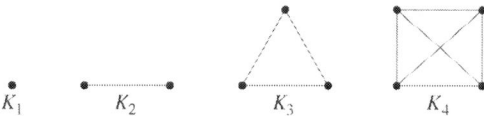

K_1 K_2 K_3 K_4

Observe that K_5 may be obtained from K_4 by adding one vertex and drawing edges between this new vertex and all the vertices of K_4 (the old vertices). The reason this procedure gives the correct result is that each pair of old vertices is already joined by an edge, and adding the new edges joins each pair of vertices consisting of an old one and the new one.

New vertex

K_5

Thus   the number of edges of $K_5 = 4 +$ the number of edges of K_4.

By the same reasoning, for all integers $k \geq 2$, the number of edges of K_k is $k - 1$ more than the number of edges of K_{k-1}. That is, if for each integer $n \geq 1$

$$s_n = \text{the number of edges of } K_n,$$

then $s_k = s_{k-1} + (k - 1)$ for all integers $k \geq 2$.

Note that s_1, is the number of edges in K_1, which is 0, and use iteration to find an explicit formula for s_1, s_2, s_3, ...

Solution Because

$$s_k = s_{k-1} + (k - 1) \quad \text{for } all \text{ integers } k \geq 2$$

and

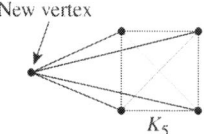

$$s_1 = 0$$

then, in particular,

$$s_2 = s_1 + 1 = 0 + 1,$$

$$s_3 = s_2 + 2 = (0 + 1) + 2 = 0 + 1 + 2,$$

$$s_4 = s_3 + 3 = (0 + 1 + 2) + 3 = 0 + 1 + 2 + 3,$$

$$s_5 = s_4 + 4 = (0 + 1 + 2 + 3) + 4 = 0 + 1 + 2 + 3 + 4,$$

$$\vdots$$

Guess: $s_n = 0 + 1 + 2 + \cdots + (n - 1).$

But by Theorem 5.2.2,

$$0 + 1 + 2 + 3 + \cdots + (n-1) = \frac{(n-1)n}{2} = \frac{n(n-1)}{2}.$$

Hence it appears that

$$s_n = \frac{n(n-1)}{2}.$$

■

Checking the Correctness of a Formula by Mathematical Induction

As you can see from some of the previous examples, the process of solving a recurrence relation by iteration can involve complicated calculations. It is all too easy to make a mistake and come up with the wrong formula. That is why it is important to confirm your calculations by checking the correctness of your formula. The most common way to do this is to use mathematical induction.

Example 5.7.7 Using Mathematical Induction to Verify the Correctness of a Solution to a Recurrence Relation

In Example 5.6.5 we obtained a formula for the Tower of Hanoi sequence. Use mathematical induction to show that this formula is correct.

Solution   What does it mean to show the correctness of a formula for a recursively defined sequence? Given a sequence of numbers that satisfies a certain recurrence relation and initial condition, your job is to show that each term of the sequence satisfies the proposed explicit formula. In this case, you need to prove the following statement:

> If $m_1, m_2, m_3, \ldots$ is the sequence defined by
>
> $m_k = 2m_{k-1} + 1$ for all integers $k \geq 2$, and
> $m_1 = 1$,
>
> then $m_n = 2^n - 1$ for all integers $n \geq 1$.

Proof of Correctness:

Let $m_1, m_2, m_3, \ldots$ be the sequence defined by specifying that $m_1 = 1$ and $m_k = 2m_{k+1} + 1$ for all integers $k \geq 2$, and let the property $P(n)$ be the equation

$$m_n = 2^n - 1 \qquad \leftarrow P(n)$$

We will use mathematical induction to prove that for all integers $n \geq 1$, $P(n)$ is true.

Show that P(1) is true:
To establish $P(1)$, we must show that

$$m_1 = 2^1 - 1. \qquad \leftarrow P(1)$$

But the left-hand side of $P(1)$ is

$$m_1 = 1 \qquad \text{by definition of } m_1, m_2, m_3, \ldots$$

and the right-hand side of $P(1)$ is

$$2^1 - 1 = 2 - 1 = 1.$$

Thus the two sides of $P(1)$ equal the same quantity, and hence $P(1)$ is true.

Show that for all integers $k \geq 1$, if $P(k)$ is true then $P(k+1)$ is also true:
[Suppose that $P(k)$ is true for a particular but arbitrarily chosen integer $k \geq 1$. That is:]
Suppose that k is any integer with $k \geq 1$ such that

$$m_k = 2^k - 1. \qquad \leftarrow P(k)$$
inductive hypothesis

[We must show that $P(k+1)$ is true. That is:] We must show that

$$m_{k+1} = 2^{k+1} - 1. \qquad \leftarrow P(k+1)$$

But the left-hand side of $P(k+1)$ is

$$
\begin{aligned}
m_{k+1} &= 2m_{(k+1)-1} + 1 \quad \text{by definition of } m_1, m_2, m_3, \dots \\
&= 2m_k + 1 \\
&= 2(2^k - 1) + 1 \quad \text{by substitution from the inductive hypothesis} \\
&= 2^{k+1} - 2 + 1 \quad \text{by the distributive law and the fact that } 2 \cdot 2^k = 2^{k+1} \\
&= 2^{k+1} - 1 \quad \text{by basic algebra}
\end{aligned}
$$

which equals the right-hand side of $P(k+1)$. *[Since the basis and inductive steps have been proved, it follows by mathematical induction that the given formula holds for all integers $n \geq 1$.]* ∎

Discovering That an Explicit Formula Is Incorrect

The following example shows how the process of trying to verify a formula by mathematical induction may reveal a mistake.

Example 5.7.8   Using Verification by Mathematical Induction to Find a Mistake

Let $c_0, c_1, c_2, \dots$ be the sequence defined as follows:

$$
\begin{aligned}
c_k &= 2c_{k-1} + k \qquad \text{for all integers } k \geq 1, \\
c_0 &= 1.
\end{aligned}
$$

Suppose your calculations suggest that $c_0, c_1, c_2, \dots$ satisfies the following explicit formula:

$$c_n = 2^n + n \qquad \text{for all integers } n \geq 0.$$

Is this formula correct?

Solution   Start to prove the statement by mathematical induction and see what develops. The proposed formula passes the basis step of the inductive proof with no trouble, for on the one hand, $c_0 = 1$ by definition and on the other hand, $2^0 + 0 = 1 + 0 = 1$ also.
In the inductive step, you suppose

$$c_k = 2^k + k \qquad \text{for some integer } k \geq 0 \qquad \text{This is the inductive hypothesis.}$$

and then you must show that

$$c_{k+1} = 2^{k+1} + (k+1).$$

To do this, you start with c_{k+1}, substitute from the recurrence relation, and then use the inductive hypothesis as follows:

$$c_{k+1} = 2c_k + (k + 1) \qquad \text{by the recurrence relation}$$
$$= 2(2^k + k) + (k + 1) \qquad \text{by substitution from the inductive hypothesis}$$
$$= 2^{(k+1)} + 3k + 1 \qquad \text{by basic algebra}$$

To finish the verification, therefore, you need to show that

$$2^{k+1} + 3k + 1 = 2^{k+1} + (k + 1).$$

Now this equation is equivalent to

$$2k = 0 \qquad \text{by subtracting } 2^{k-1} + k + 1 \text{ from both sides.}$$

which is equivalent to

$$k = 0 \qquad \text{by dividing both sides by 2.}$$

But this is false since k may be *any* nonnegative integer.
Observe that when $k = 0$, then $k + 1 = 1$, and

$$c_1 = 2 \cdot 1 + 1 = 3 \quad \text{and} \quad 2^1 + 1 = 3.$$

Thus the formula gives the correct value for c_1. However, when $k = 1$, then $k + 1 = 2$, and

$$c_2 = 2 \cdot 3 + 2 = 8 \quad \text{whereas} \quad 2^2 + 2 = 4 + 2 = 6.$$

So the formula does not give the correct value for c_2. Hence the sequence $c_0, c_1, c_2, \ldots$ does not satisfy the proposed formula. ∎

Once you have found a proposed formula to be false, you should look back at your calculations to see where you made a mistake, correct it, and try again.

Test Yourself

1. To use iteration to find an explicit formula for a recursively defined sequence, start with the _____ and use successive substitution into the _____ to look for a numerical pattern.

2. At every step of the iteration process, it is important to eliminate _____.

3. If a single number, say a, is added to itself k times in one of the steps of the iteration, replace the sum by the expression _____.

4. If a single number, say a, is multiplied by itself k times in one of the steps of the iteration, replace the product by the expression _____.

5. A general arithmetic sequence $a_0, a_1, a_2, \ldots$ with initial value a_0 and fixed constant d satisfies the recurrence relation _____ and has the explicit formula _____.

6. A general geometric sequence $a_0, a_1, a_2, \ldots$ with initial value a_0 and fixed constant r satisfies the recurrence relation _____ and has the explicit formula _____.

7. When an explicit formula for a recursively defined sequence has been obtained by iteration, its correctness can be checked by _____.

Exercise Set 5.7

1. The formula

$$1 + 2 + 3 + \cdots + n = \frac{n(n + 1)}{2}$$

is true for all integers $n \geq 1$. Use this fact to solve each of the following problems:

a. If k is an integer and $k \geq 2$, find a formula for the expression $1 + 2 + 3 + \cdots + (k - 1)$.

b. If n is an integer and $n \geq 1$, find a formula for the expression $3 + 2 + 4 + 6 + 8 + \cdots + 2n$.

c. If n is an integer and $n \geq 1$, find a formula for the expression $3 + 3 \cdot 2 + 3 \cdot 3 + \cdots + 3 \cdot n + n$.

2. The formula

$$1 + r + r^2 + \cdots + r^n = \frac{r^{n+1} - 1}{r - 1}$$

is true for all real numbers r except $r = 1$ and for all integers $n \geq 0$. Use this fact to solve each of the following problems:

a. If i is an integer and $i \geq 1$, find a formula for the expression $1 + 2 + 2^2 + \cdots + 2^{i-1}$.

b. If n is an integer and $n \geq 1$, find a formula for the expression $3^{n-1} + 3^{n-2} + \cdots + 3^2 + 3 + 1$.

c. If n is an integer and $n \geq 2$, find a formula for the expression $2^n + 2^{n-2} \cdot 3 + 2^{n-3} \cdot 3 + \cdots + 2^2 \cdot 3 + 2 \cdot 3 + 3$

d. If n is an integer and $n \geq 1$, find a formula for the expression

$$2^n - 2^{n-1} + 2^{n-2} - 2^{n-3} + \cdots + (-1)^{n-1} \cdot 2 + (-1)^n.$$

In each of 3–15 a sequence is defined recursively. Use iteration to guess an explicit formula for the sequence. Use the formulas from Section 5.2 to simplify your answers whenever possible.

3. $a_k = k a_{k-1}$, for all integers $k \geq 1$
   $a_0 = 1$

4. $b_k = 4b_{k-1} + 5$, for all integers $k \geq 1$
   $b_0 = 2$

5. $c_k = 3c_{k-1} + 1$, for all integers $k \geq 2$
   $c_1 = 1$

H 6. $d_k = 2d_{k-1} + 3$, for all integers $k \geq 2$
   $d_1 = 2$

7. $e_k = \dfrac{e_{k-1}}{1 + e_{k-1}}$, for all integers $k \geq 1$
   $e_0 = 1$

8. $f_k = f_{k-1} + 2 \cdot 3^k$
   $f_1 = 2$

H 9. $g_k = \dfrac{g_{k-1}}{g_{k-1} + 2}$, for all integers $k \geq 2$
   $g_1 = 1$

10. $h_k = 2^k - h_{k-1}$, for all integers $k \geq 1$
   $h_0 = 1$

11. $p_k = p_{k-1} + 2^k$, for all integers $k \geq 2$
   $p_1 = 1$

12. $s_k = s_{k-1} + 2k$, for all integers $k \geq 1$
   $s_0 = 3$

13. $t_k = t_{k-1} + 3k + 1$, for all integers $k \geq 1$
   $t_0 = 0$

✳ 14. $x_k = 3x_{k-1} + k$, for all integers $k \geq 2$
   $x_1 = 1$

15. $y_k = y_{k-1} + k^2$, for all integers $k \geq 2$
   $y_1 = 1$

16. Solve the recurrence relation obtained as the answer to exercise 17(c) of Section 5.6.

17. Solve the recurrence relation obtained as the answer to exercise 21(c) of Section 5.6.

18. Suppose d is a fixed constant and $a_0, a_1, a_2, \ldots$ is a sequence that satisfies the recurrence relation $a_k = a_{k-1} + d$, for all integers $k \geq 1$. Use mathematical induction to prove that $a_n = a_0 + nd$, for all integers $n \geq 0$.

19. A worker is promised a bonus if he can increase his productivity by 2 units a day every day for a period of 30 days. If on day 0 he produces 170 units, how many units must he produce on day 30 to qualify for the bonus?

20. A runner targets herself to improve her time on a certain course by 3 seconds a day. If on day 0 she runs the course in 3 minutes, how fast must she run it on day 14 to stay on target?

21. Suppose r is a fixed constant and $a_0, a_1, a_2 \ldots$ is a sequence that satisfies the recurrence relation $a_k = r a_{k-1}$, for all integers $k \geq 1$ and $a_0 = a$. Use mathematical induction to prove that $a_n = ar^n$, for all integers $n \geq 0$.

22. As shown in Example 5.6.8, if a bank pays interest at a rate of i compounded m times a year, then the amount of money P_k at the end of k time periods (where one time period $= 1/m$th of a year) satisfies the recurrence relation $P_k = [1 + (i/m)]P_{k-1}$ with initial condition $P_0 = $ the initial amount deposited. Find an explicit formula for P_n.

23. A certain computer algorithm executes twice as many operations when it is run with an input of size k as when it is run with an input of size $k - 1$ (where k is an integer that is greater than 1). When the algorithm is run with an input of size 1, it executes seven operations. How many operations does it execute when it is run with an input of size 25?

24. A chain letter works as follows: One person sends a copy of the letter to five friends, each of whom sends a copy to five friends, each of whom sends a copy to five friends, and so forth. How many people will have received copies of the letter after the twentieth repetition of this process, assuming no person receives more than one copy?

25. Suppose the population of a country increases at a steady rate of 3% per year. If the population is 50 million at a certain time, what will it be 25 years later?

26. A person saving for retirement makes an initial deposit of $1,000 to a bank account earning interest at a rate of 3% per year compounded monthly, and each month she adds an additional $200 to the account.

a. For each nonnegative integer n, let A_n be the amount in the account at the end of n months. Find a recurrence relation relating A_k to A_{k-1}.

H b. Use iteration to find an explicit formula for A_n.

c. Use mathematical induction to prove the correctness of the formula you obtained in part (b).

d. How much will the account be worth at the end of 20 years? At the end of 40 years?

H e. In how many years will the account be worth $10,000?

27. A person borrows $3,000 on a bank credit card at a nominal rate of 18% per year, which is actually charged at a rate of 1.5% per month.

  H a. What is the annual percentage rate (APR) for the card? (See Example 5.6.8 for a definition of APR.)

  b. Assume that the person does not place any additional charges on the card and pays the bank $150 each month to pay off the loan. Let B_n be the balance owed on the card after n months. Find an explicit formula for B_n.

  H c. How long will be required to pay off the debt?

  d. What is the total amount of money the person will have paid for the loan?

In 28–42 use mathematical induction to verify the correctness of the formula you obtained in the referenced exercise.

28. Exercise 3   29. Exercise 4   30. Exercise 5

31. Exercise 6   32. Exercise 7   33. Exercise 8

34. Exercise 9   *H* 35. Exercise 10   36. Exercise 11

H 37. Exercise 12   38. Exercise 13   39. Exercise 14

40. Exercise 15   41. Exercise 16   42. Exercise 17

In each of 43–49 a sequence is defined recursively. (a) Use iteration to guess an explicit formula for the sequence. (b) Use strong mathematical induction to verify that the formula of part (a) is correct.

43. $a_k = \dfrac{a_{k-1}}{2a_{k-1} - 1}$, for all integers $k \geq 1$
   $a_0 = 2$

44. $t_k = k - t_{k-1}$, for all integers $k \geq 1$,
   $t_0 = 0$.

45. $v_k = v_{\lfloor k/2 \rfloor} + v_{\lfloor (k+1)/2 \rfloor} + 2$, for all integers $k \geq 2$,
   $v_1 = 1$.

H 46. $s_k = 2s_{k-2}$, for all integers $k \geq 2$,
   $s_0 = 1, s_1 = 2$.

47. $b_k = \dfrac{2}{b_{k-1}}$, for all integers $k \geq 2$
   $b_1 = 1$

H 48. $w_k = w_{k-2} + k$, for all integers $k \geq 3$,
   $w_1 = 1, w_2 = 2$.

H 49. $u_k = u_{k-2} \cdot u_{k-1}$, for all integers $k \geq 2$,
   $u_0 = u_1 = 2$.

In 50 and 51 determine whether the given recursively defined sequence satisfies the explicit formula $a_n = (n - 1)^2$, for all integers $n \geq 1$.

50. $a_k = 2a_{k-1} + k - 1$, for all integers $k \geq 2$
   $a_1 = 0$

51. $a_k = (a_{k-1} + 1)^2$, for all integers $k \geq 2$
   $a_1 = 0$

52. A single line divides a plane into two regions. Two lines (by crossing) can divide a plane into four regions; three lines can divide it into seven regions (see the figure). Let P_n be the maximum number of regions into which n lines divide a plane, where n is a positive integer.

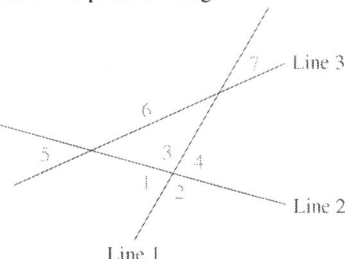

Line 3

Line 2

Line 1

  a. Derive a recurrence relation for P_k in terms of P_{k-1}, for all integers $k \geq 2$.

  b. Use iteration to guess an explicit formula for P_n.

H 53. Compute $\begin{bmatrix} 1 & 1 \\ 1 & 0 \end{bmatrix}^n$ for small values of n (up to about 5 or 6). Conjecture explicit formulas for the entries in this matrix, and prove your conjecture using mathematical induction.

54. In economics the behavior of an economy from one period to another is often modeled by recurrence relations. Let Y_k be the income in period k and C_k be the consumption in period k. In one economic model, income in any period is assumed to be the sum of consumption in that period plus investment and government expenditures (which are assumed to be constant from period to period), and consumption in each period is assumed to be a linear function of the income of the preceding period. That is,

$$Y_k = C_k + E \qquad \text{where } E \text{ is the sum of investment plus government expenditures}$$

$$C_k = c + mY_{k-1} \qquad \text{where } c \text{ and } m \text{ are constants.}$$

Substituting the second equation into the first gives $Y_k = E + c + mY_{k-1}$.

  a. Use iteration on the above recurrence relation to obtain

$$Y_n = (E + c)\left(\frac{m^n - 1}{m - 1}\right) + m^n Y_0$$

for all integers $n \geq 1$.

  b. (For students who have studied calculus) Show that if $0 < m < 1$, then $\displaystyle\lim_{n \to \infty} Y_n = \frac{E + c}{1 - m}$.

Answers for Test Yourself

1. initial conditions; recurrence relation   2. parentheses   3. $k \cdot a$ 4. a^k 5. $a_k = a_{k-1} + d$; $a_n = a_0 + dn$ 6. $a_k = ra_{k-1}$; $a_n = a_0 r^n$ 7. mathematical induction

5.8 Second-Order Linear Homogeneous Recurrence Relations with Constant Coefficients

Genius is 1% inspiration and 99% perspiration. — Thomas Alva Edison, 1932

In section 5.7 we discussed finding explicit formulas for recursively defined sequences using iteration. This is a basic technique that does not require any special tools beyond the ability to discern patterns. In many cases, however, a pattern is not readily discernible and other methods must be used. A variety of techniques are available for finding explicit formulas for special classes of recursively defined sequences. The method explained in this section is one that works for the Fibonacci and other similarly defined sequences.

> **• Definition**
>
> A **second-order linear homogeneous recurrence relation with constant coefficients** is a recurrence relation of the form
>
> $$a_k = Aa_{k-1} + Ba_{k-2} \quad \text{for all integers } k \geq \text{ some fixed integer,}$$
>
> where A and B are fixed real numbers with $B \neq 0$.

"Second-order" refers to the fact that the expression for a_k contains the two previous terms a_{k-1} and a_{k-2}, "linear" to the fact that a_{k-1} and a_{k-2} appear in separate terms and to the first power, "homogeneous" to the fact that the total degree of each term is the same (thus there is no constant term), and "constant coefficients" to the fact that A and B are fixed real numbers that do not depend on k.

Example 5.8.1 Second-Order Linear Homogeneous Recurrence Relations with Constant Coefficients

State whether each of the following is a second-order linear homogeneous recurrence relation with constant coefficients:

a. $a_k = 3a_{k-1} + 2a_{k-2}$

b. $b_k = b_{k-1} + b_{k-2} + b_{k-3}$

c. $c_k = \frac{1}{2}c_{k-1} - \frac{3}{7}c_{k-2}$

d. $d_k = d_{k-1}^2 + d_{k-1} \cdot d_{k-2}$

e. $e_k = 2e_{k-2}$

f. $f_k = 2f_{k-1} + 1$

g. $g_k = g_{k-1} + g_{k-2}$

h. $h_k = (-1)h_{k-1} + (k-1)h_{k-2}$

Solution

a. Yes; $A = 3$ and $B = 2$

b. No; not second-order

c. Yes; $A = \frac{1}{2}$ and $B = -\frac{3}{7}$

d. No; not linear

e. Yes; $A = 0$ and $B = 2$

f. No; not homogeneous

g. Yes; $A = 1$ and $B = 1$

h. No; nonconstant coefficients

The Distinct-Roots Case

Consider a second-order linear homogeneous recurrence relation with constant coefficients:

$$a_k = Aa_{k-1} + Ba_{k-2} \quad \text{for all integers } k \geq 2, \tag{5.8.1}$$

where A and B are fixed real numbers. Relation (5.8.1) is satisfied when all the $a_i = 0$, but it has nonzero solutions as well. *Suppose* that for some number t with $t \neq 0$, the sequence

$$1, t, t^2, t^3, \ldots, t^n, \ldots$$

satisfies relation (5.8.1). This means that each term of the sequence equals A times the previous term plus B times the term before that. So for all integers $k \geq 2$,

$$t^k = At^{k-1} + Bt^{k-2}.$$

In particular, when $k = 2$, the equation becomes

$$t^2 = At + B,$$

or, equivalently,

$$t^2 - At - B = 0. \tag{5.8.2}$$

This is a quadratic equation, and the values of t that make it true can be found either by factoring or by using the quadratic formula.

Now work backward. *Suppose t is any number that satisfies equation (5.8.2).* Does the sequence $1, t, t^2, t^3, \ldots, t^n, \ldots$ satisfy relation (5.8.1)? To answer this question, multiply equation (5.8.2) by t^{k-2} to obtain

$$t^{k-2} \cdot t^2 - t^{k-2} \cdot At - t^{k-2} \cdot B = 0.$$

This is equivalent to

$$t^k - At^{k-1} - Bt^{k-2} = 0$$

or

$$t^k = At^{k-1} + Bt^{k-2}.$$

Hence the answer is yes: $1, t, t^2, t^3, \ldots, t^n, \ldots$ satisfies relation (5.8.1).

This discussion proves the following lemma.

Lemma 5.8.1

Let A and B be real numbers. A recurrence relation of the form

$$a_k = Aa_{k-1} + Ba_{k-2} \quad \text{for all integers } k \geq 2 \tag{5.8.1}$$

is satisfied by the sequence

$$1, t, t^2, t^3, \ldots, t^n, \ldots,$$

where t is a nonzero real number, if, and only if, t satisfies the equation

$$t^2 - At - B = 0 \tag{5.8.2}$$

Equation (5.8.2) is called the *characteristic equation* of the recurrence relation.

> **• Definition**
>
> Given a second-order linear homogeneous recurrence relation with constant coefficients:
>
> $$a_k = Aa_{k-1} + Ba_{k-2} \quad \text{for all integers } k \geq 2, \tag{5.8.1}$$
>
> the **characteristic equation of the relation** is
>
> $$t^2 - At - B = 0. \tag{5.8.2}$$

Example 5.8.2 Using the Characteristic Equation to Find Solutions to a Recurrence Relation

Consider the recurrence relation that specifies that the kth term of a sequence equals the sum of the $(k - 1)$st term plus twice the $(k - 2)$nd term. That is,

$$a_k = a_{k-1} + 2a_{k-2} \quad \text{for all integers } k \geq 2. \tag{5.8.3}$$

Find all sequences that satisfy relation (5.8.3) and have the form

$$1, t, t^2, t^3, \ldots, t^n, \ldots,$$

where t is nonzero.

Solution By Lemma 5.8.1, relation (5.8.3) is satisfied by a sequence $1, t, t^2, t^3, \ldots, t^n, \ldots$ if, and only if, t satisfies the characteristic equation

$$t^2 - t - 2 = 0.$$

Since

$$t^2 - t - 2 = (t - 2)(t + 1),$$

the only possible values of t are 2 and -1. It follows that the sequences

$$1, 2, 2^2, 2^3, \ldots, 2^n, \ldots \quad \text{and} \quad 1, \ -1, \ (-1)^2, \ (-1)^3, \ \ldots, \ (-1)^n, \ldots.$$

are both solutions for relation (5.8.3) and there are no other solutions of this form. Note that these sequences can be rewritten more simply as

$$1, 2, 2^2, 2^3, \ldots, 2^n, \ldots \quad \text{and} \quad 1, \ -1, \ 1, -1, \ \ldots, \ (-1)^n, \ldots. \quad \blacksquare$$

The example above shows how to find two distinct sequences that satisfy a given second-order linear homogeneous recurrence relation with constant coefficients. It turns out that any linear combination of such sequences produces another sequence that also satisfies the relation.

> **Lemma 5.8.2**
>
> If $r_0, r_1, r_2, \ldots$ and $s_0, s_1, s_2, \ldots$ are sequences that satisfy the same second-order linear homogeneous recurrence relation with constant coefficients, and if C and D are *any* numbers, then the sequence $a_0, a_1, a_2, \ldots$ defined by the formula
>
> $$a_n = Cr_n + Ds_n \quad \text{for all integers } n \geq 0$$
>
> also satisfies the same recurrence relation.
>
> *continued on page 320*

Proof: Suppose $r_0, r_1, r_2, \ldots$ and $s_0, s_1, s_2, \ldots$ are sequences that satisfy the same second-order linear homogeneous recurrence relation with constant coefficients. In other words, suppose that for some real numbers A and B,

$$r_k = Ar_{k-1} + Br_{k-2} \quad \text{and} \quad s_k = As_{k-1} + Bs_{k-2} \qquad 5.8.4$$

for all integers $k \geq 2$. Suppose also that C and D are any numbers. Let $a_0, a_1, a_2, \ldots$ be the sequence defined by

$$a_n = Cr_n + Ds_n \quad \text{for all integers } n \geq 0. \qquad 5.8.5$$

[We must show that $a_0, a_1, a_2, \ldots$ satisfies the same recurrence relation as $r_0, r_1, r_2, \ldots$ and $s_0, s_1, s_2, \ldots.$ That is, we must show that $a_k = Aa_{k-1} + Ba_{k-2}$, for all integers] $k \geq 2$.

For all integers $k \geq 2$,

$$
\begin{aligned}
Aa_{k-1} + Ba_{k-2} &= A(Cr_{k-1} + Ds_{k-1}) + B(Cr_{k-2} + Ds_{k-2}) && \text{by substitution from (5.8.5)} \\
&= C(Ar_{k-1} + Br_{k-2}) + D(As_{k-1} + Bs_{k-2}) && \text{by basic algebra} \\
&= Cr_k + Ds_k && \text{by substitution from (5.8.4)} \\
&= a_k && \text{by substitution from (5.8.5)}
\end{aligned}
$$

Hence $a_0, a_1, a_2, \ldots$ satisfies the same recurrence relation as $r_0, r_1, r_2, \ldots$ and $s_0, s_1, s_2, \ldots$ *[as was to be shown].*

Given a second-order linear homogeneous recurrence relation with constant coefficients, if the characteristic equation has two distinct roots, then Lemmas 5.8.1 and 5.8.2 can be used together to find a particular sequence that satisfies both the recurrence relation and two specific initial conditions.

Example 5.8.3 Finding the Linear Combination That Satisfies the Initial Conditions

Find a sequence that satisfies the recurrence relation of Example 5.8.2,

$$a_k = a_{k-1} + 2a_{k-2} \quad \text{for all integers } k \geq 2, \qquad 5.8.3$$

and that also satisfies the initial conditions

$$a_0 = 1 \quad \text{and} \quad a_1 = 8.$$

Solution   Example 5.8.2, the sequences

$$1, 2, 2^2, 2^3, \ldots, 2^n, \ldots \quad \text{and} \quad 1, -1, 1, -1, \ldots, (-1)^n, \ldots$$

both satisfy relation (5.8.3) (though neither satisfies the given initial conditions). By Lemma 5.8.2, therefore, any sequence $a_0, a_1, a_2, \ldots$ that satisfies an explicit formula of the form

$$a_n = C \cdot 2^n + D(-1)^n \qquad 5.8.6$$

where C and D are numbers, also satisfies relation (5.8.3). You can find C and D so that $a_0, a_1, a_2, \ldots$ satisfies the specified initial conditions by substituting $n = 0$ and $n = 1$ into equation (5.8.6) and solving for C and D:

$$a_0 = 1 = C \cdot 2^0 + D(-1)^0,$$
$$a_1 = 8 = C \cdot 2^1 + D(-1)^1.$$

When you simplify, you obtain the system

$$1 = C + D$$
$$8 = 2C - D,$$

which can be solved in various ways. For instance, if you add the two equations, you get

$$9 = 3C,$$

and so

$$C = 3.$$

Then, by substituting into $1 = C + D$, you get

$$D = -2.$$

It follows that the sequence $a_0, a_1, a_2, \ldots$ given by

$$a_n = 3 \cdot 2^n + (-2)(-1)^n = 3 \cdot 2^n - 2(-1)^n,$$

for integers $n \geq 0$, satisfies both the recurrence relation and the given initial conditions.   ▨

The techniques of Examples 5.8.2 and 5.8.3 can be used to find an explicit formula for *any* sequence that satisfies a second-order linear homogeneous recurrence relation with constant coefficients for which the characteristic equation has distinct roots, provided that the first two terms of the sequence are known. This is made precise in the next theorem.

Theorem 5.8.3 Distinct-Roots Theorem

Suppose a sequence $a_0, a_1, a_2, \ldots$ satisfies a recurrence relation

$$a_k = Aa_{k-1} + Ba_{k-2} \qquad \text{5.8.1}$$

for some real numbers A and B with $B \neq 0$ and all integers $k \geq 2$. If the characteristic equation

$$t^2 - At - B = 0 \qquad \text{5.8.2}$$

has two distinct roots r and s, then $a_0, a_1, a_2, \ldots$ is given by the explicit formula

$$a_n = Cr^n + Ds^n,$$

where C and D are the numbers whose values are determined by the values a_0 and a_1.

Note: To say "C and D are determined by the values of a_0 and a_1" means that C and D are the solutions to the system of simultaneous equations

$$a_0 = Cr^0 + Ds^0 \quad \text{and} \quad a_1 = Cr^1 + Ds^1,$$

or, equivalently,

$$a_0 = C + D \quad \text{and} \quad a_1 = Cr + Ds.$$

In exercise 19 at the end of this section you are asked to verify that this system always has a solution when $r \neq s$.

Proof: Suppose that for some real numbers A and B, a sequence $a_0, a_1, a_2, \ldots$ satisfies the recurrence relation $a_k = Aa_{k-1} + Ba_{k-2}$, for all integers $k \geq 2$, and suppose the characteristic equation $t^2 - At - B = 0$ has two distinct roots r and s. We will show that

$$\text{for all integers } n \geq 0, \quad a_n = Cr^n + Ds^n,$$

where C and D are numbers such that

$$a_0 = Cr^0 + Ds^0 \quad \text{and} \quad a_1 = Cr^1 + Ds^1.$$

Let $P(n)$ be the equation

$$a_n = Cr^n + Ds^n. \qquad \longleftarrow P(n)$$

We use strong mathematical induction to prove that $P(n)$ is true for all integers $n \geq 0$. In the basis step, we prove that $P(0)$ and $P(1)$ are true. We do this because in the inductive step we need the equation to hold for $n = 0$ and $n = 1$ in order to prove that it holds for $n = 2$.

Show that $P(0)$ and $P(1)$ are true: The truth of $P(0)$ and $P(1)$ is automatic because C and D are exactly those numbers that make the following equations true:

$$a_0 = Cr^0 + Ds^0 \quad \text{and} \quad a_1 = Cr^1 + Ds^1.$$

Show that for all integers $k \geq 1$, if $P(i)$ is true for all integers i from 0 through k, then $P(k+1)$ is also true: Suppose that $k \geq 1$ and for all integers i from 0 through k,

$$a_i = Cr^i + Ds^i. \qquad \text{inductive hypothesis}$$

We must show that

$$a_{k+1} = Cr^{k+1} + Ds^{k+1}. \qquad \longleftarrow P(k+1)$$

Now by the inductive hypothesis,

$$a_k = Cr^k + Ds^k \quad \text{and} \quad a_{k-1} = Cr^{k-1} + Ds^{k-1},$$

so

$$
\begin{aligned}
a_{k+1} &= Aa_k + Ba_{k-1} && \text{by definition of } a_0, a_1, a_2, \ldots \\
&= A(Cr^k + Ds^k) + B(Cr^{k-1} + Ds^{k-1}) && \text{by inductive hypothesis} \\
&= C(Ar^k + Br^{k-1}) + D(As^k + Bs^{k-1}) && \text{by combining like terms} \\
&= Cr^{k+1} + Ds^{k+1} && \text{by Lemma 5.8.1.}
\end{aligned}
$$

This is what was to be shown.

[The reason the last equality follows from Lemma 5.8.1 is that since r and s satisfy the characteristic equation (5.8.2), the sequences $r^0, r^1, r^2, \ldots$ and $s^0, s^1, s^2, \ldots$ satisfy the recurrence relation (5.8.1).]

Remark The t of Lemma 5.8.1 and the C and D of Lemma 5.8.2 and Theorem 5.8.3 are referred to simply as numbers. This is to allow for the possibility of complex as well as real number values. If both roots of the characteristic equation of the recurrence relation are real numbers, then C and D will be real. But if the roots are nonreal complex numbers, then C and D will be nonreal complex numbers.

The next example shows how to use the distinct-roots theorem to find an explicit formula for the Fibonacci sequence.

Example 5.8.4 A Formula for the Fibonacci Sequence

The Fibonacci sequence $F_0, F_1, F_2, \ldots$ satisfies the recurrence relation

$$F_k = F_{k-1} + F_{k-2} \quad \text{for all integers } k \geq 2$$

with initial conditions

$$F_0 = F_1 = 1.$$

Find an explicit formula for this sequence.

Solution   The Fibonacci sequence satisfies part of the hypothesis of the distinct-roots theorem since the Fibonacci relation is a second-order linear homogeneous recurrence relation with constant coefficients ($A = 1$ and $B = 1$). Is the second part of the hypothesis also satisfied? Does the characteristic equation

$$t^2 - t - 1 = 0$$

have distinct roots? By the quadratic formula, the roots are

$$t = \frac{1 \pm \sqrt{1 - 4(-1)}}{2} = \begin{cases} \dfrac{1 + \sqrt{5}}{2} \\ \dfrac{1 - \sqrt{5}}{2} \end{cases}$$

and so the answer is yes. It follows from the distinct-roots theorem that the Fibonacci sequence is given by the explicit formula

$$F_n = C \left(\frac{1 + \sqrt{5}}{2} \right)^n + D \left(\frac{1 - \sqrt{5}}{2} \right)^n \qquad \text{for all integers } n \geq 0, \qquad \text{5.8.7}$$

where C and D are the numbers whose values are determined by the fact that $F_0 = F_1 = 1$. To find C and D, write

$$F_0 = 1 = C \left(\frac{1 + \sqrt{5}}{2} \right)^0 + D \left(\frac{1 - \sqrt{5}}{2} \right)^0 = C \cdot 1 + D \cdot 1 = C + D$$

and

$$F_1 = 1 = C \left(\frac{1 + \sqrt{5}}{2} \right)^1 + D \left(\frac{1 - \sqrt{5}}{2} \right)^1$$

$$= C \left(\frac{1 + \sqrt{5}}{2} \right) + D \left(\frac{1 - \sqrt{5}}{2} \right)$$

Thus the problem is to find numbers C and D such that

$$C + D = 1$$

and

$$C \left(\frac{1 + \sqrt{5}}{2} \right) + D \left(\frac{1 - \sqrt{5}}{2} \right) = 1.$$

This may look complicated, but in fact it is just a system of two equations in two unknowns. In exercise 7 at the end of this section, you are asked to show that

$$C = \frac{1 + \sqrt{5}}{2\sqrt{5}} \quad \text{and} \quad D = \frac{-(1 - \sqrt{5})}{2\sqrt{5}}.$$

Substituting these values for C and D into formula (5.8.7) gives

$$F_n = \left(\frac{1 + \sqrt{5}}{2\sqrt{5}}\right)\left(\frac{1 + \sqrt{5}}{2}\right)^n + \left(\frac{-(1 - \sqrt{5})}{2\sqrt{5}}\right)\left(\frac{1 - \sqrt{5}}{2}\right)^n,$$

Note The numbers
$(1 + \sqrt{5})/2$ and
$(1 - \sqrt{5})/2$ are related to
the golden ratio of Greek
mathematics. See exercise
24 at the end of this
section.

or, simplifying,

$$F_n = \frac{1}{\sqrt{5}}\left(\frac{1 + \sqrt{5}}{2}\right)^{n+1} - \frac{1}{\sqrt{5}}\left(\frac{1 - \sqrt{5}}{2}\right)^{n+1} \qquad 5.8.8$$

for all integers $n \geq 0$. Remarkably, even though the formula for F_n involves $\sqrt{5}$, all of the values of the Fibonacci sequence are integers. ∎

The Single-Root Case

Consider again the recurrence relation

$$a_k = Aa_{k-1} + Ba_{k-2} \quad \text{for all integers } k \geq 2, \qquad 5.8.1$$

where A and B are real numbers, but suppose now that the characteristic equation

$$t^2 - At - B = 0 \qquad 5.8.2$$

has a single real root r. By Lemma 5.8.1, one sequence that satisfies the recurrence relation is

$$1, r, r^2, r^3, \ldots, r^n, \ldots$$

But another sequence that also satisfies the relation is

$$0, r, 2r^2, 3r^3, \ldots, nr^n, \ldots$$

To see why this is so, observe that since r is the unique root of $t^2 - At - B = 0$, the left-hand side of the equation can be factored as $(t - r)^2$, and so

$$t^2 - At - B = (t - r)^2 = t^2 - 2rt + r^2. \qquad 5.8.9$$

Equating coefficients in equation (5.8.9) gives

$$A = 2r \quad \text{and} \quad B = -r^2. \qquad 5.8.10$$

Let $s_0, s_1, s_2, \ldots$ be the sequence defined by the formula

$$S_n = nr^n \quad \text{for all integers } n \geq 0.$$

Then

$$
\begin{aligned}
As_{k-1} + Bs_{k-2} &= A(k-1)r^{k-1} + B(k-2)r^{k-2} && \text{by definition} \\
&= 2r(k-1)r^{k-1} - r^2(k-2)r^{k-2} && \text{by substitution from 5.8.10} \\
&= 2(k-1)r^k - (k-2)r^k \\
&= (2k - 2 - k + 2)r^k \\
&= kr^k && \text{by basic algebra} \\
&= s_k && \text{by definition.}
\end{aligned}
$$

Thus $s_0, s_1, s_2, \ldots$ satisfies the recurrence relation. This argument proves the following lemma.

Lemma 5.8.4

Let A and B be real numbers and suppose the characteristic equation

$$t^2 - At - B = 0$$

has a single root r. Then the sequences $1, r^1, r^2, r^3, \ldots, r^n, \ldots$ and $0, r, 2r^2, 3r^3, \ldots, nr^n, \ldots$ both satisfy the recurrence relation

$$a_k = Aa_{k-1} + Ba_{k-2}$$

for all integers $k \geq 2$.

Lemmas 5.8.2 and 5.8.4 can be used to establish the *single-root theorem*, which tells how to find an explicit formula for any recursively defined sequence satisfying a second-order linear homogeneous recurrence relation with constant coefficients for which the characteristic equation has just one root. Taken together, the distinct-roots and single-root theorems cover all second-order linear homogeneous recurrence relations with constant coefficients. The proof of the single-root theorem is very similar to that of the distinct-roots theorem and is left as an exercise.

Theorem 5.8.5 Single-Root Theorem

Suppose a sequence $a_0, a_1, a_2, \ldots$ satisfies a recurrence relation

$$a_k = Aa_{k-1} + Ba_{k-2}$$

for some real numbers A and B with $B \neq 0$ and for all integers $k \geq 2$. If the characteristic equation $t^2 - At - B = 0$ has a single (real) root r, then $a_0, a_1, a_2, \ldots$ is given by the explicit formula

$$a_n = Cr^n + Dnr^n,$$

where C and D are the real numbers whose values are determined by the values of a_0 and any other known value of the sequence.

Example 5.8.5 Single-Root Case

Suppose a sequence $b_0, b_1, b_2, \ldots$ satisfies the recurrence relation

$$b_k = 4b_{k-1} - 4b_{k-2} \quad \text{for all integers } k \geq 2, \tag{5.8.11}$$

with initial conditions

$$b_0 = 1 \quad \text{and} \quad b_1 = 3.$$

Find an explicit formula for $b_0, b_1, b_2, \ldots$.

Solution   This sequence satisfies part of the hypothesis of the single-root theorem because it satisfies a second-order linear homogeneous recurrence relation with constant coefficients ($A = 4$ and $B = -4$). The single-root condition is also met because the characteristic equation

$$t^2 - 4t + 4 = 0$$

has the unique root $r = 2$ *[since $t^2 - 4t + 4 = (t - 2)^2$]*.

It follows from the single-root theorem that $b_0, b_1, b_2, \ldots$ is given by the explicit formula

$$b_n = C \cdot 2^n + Dn2^n \quad \text{for all integers } n \geq 0, \qquad \text{5.8.12}$$

where C and D are the real numbers whose values are determined by the fact that $b_0 = 1$ and $b_1 = 3$. To find C and D, write

$$b_0 = 1 = C \cdot 2^0 + D \cdot 0 \cdot 2^0 = C$$

and

$$b_1 = 3 = C \cdot 2^1 + D \cdot 1 \cdot 2^1 = 2C + 2D.$$

Hence the problem is to find numbers C and D such that

$$C = 1$$

and

$$2C + 2D = 3.$$

Substitute $C = 1$ into the second equation to obtain

$$2 + 2D = 3,$$

and so

$$D = \frac{1}{2}.$$

Now substitute $C = 1$ and $D = \frac{1}{2}$ into formula (5.8.12) to conclude that

$$b_n = 2^n + \frac{1}{2}n2^n = 2^n \left(1 + \frac{n}{2}\right) \quad \text{for all integers } n \geq 0. \qquad ■$$

Test Yourself

1. A second-order linear homogeneous recurrence relation with constant coefficients is a recurrence relation of the form _____ for all integers $k \geq$ _____, where _____.

2. Given a recurrence relation of the form $a_k = Aa_{k-1} + Ba_{k-2}$ for all integers $k \geq 2$, the characteristic equation of the relation is _____.

3. If a sequence $a_1, a_2, a_3, \ldots$ is defined by a second-order linear homogeneous recurrence relation with constant coeffi-

cients and the characteristic equation for the relation has two distinct roots r and s (which could be complex numbers), then the sequence is given by an explicit formula of the form _____.

4. If a sequence $a_1, a_2, a_3, \ldots$ is defined by a second-order linear homogeneous recurrence relation with constant coefficients and the characteristic equation for the relation has only a single root r, then the sequence is given by an explicit formula of the form _____.

Exercise Set 5.8

1. Which of the following are second-order linear homogeneous recurrence relations with constant coefficients?
   a. $a_k = 2a_{k-1} - 5a_{k-2}$ b. $b_k = kb_{k-1} + b_{k-2}$
   c. $c_k = 3c_{k-1} \cdot c_{k-2}^2$ d. $d_k = 3d_{k-1} + d_{k-2}$
   e. $r_k = r_{k-1} - r_{k-2} - 2$ f. $s_k = 10s_{k-2}$

2. Which of the following are second-order linear homogeneous recurrence relations with constant coefficients?
   a. $a_k = (k - 1)a_{k-1} + 2ka_{k-2}$
   b. $b_k = -b_{k-1} + 7b_{k-2}$
   c. $c_k = 3c_{k-1} + 1$
   d. $d_k = 3d_{k-1}^2 + d_{k-2}$
   e. $r_k = r_{k-1} - 6r_{k-3}$
   f. $s_k = s_{k-1} + 10s_{k-2}$

3. Let $a_0, a_1, a_2, \ldots$ be the sequence defined by the explicit formula

   $$a_n = C \cdot 2^n + D \quad \text{for all integers } n \geq 0,$$

   where C and D are real numbers.
   a. Find C and D so that $a_0 = 1$ and $a_1 = 3$. What is a_2 in this case?
   b. Find C and D so that $a_0 = 0$ and $a_1 = 2$. What is a_2 in this case?

4. Let $b_0, b_1, b_2, \ldots$ be the sequence defined by the explicit formula
$$b_n = C \cdot 3^n + D(-2)^n \quad \text{for all integers } n \geq 0,$$
where C and D are real numbers.

   a. Find C and D so that $b_0 = 0$ and $b_1 = 5$. What is b_2 in this case?

   b. Find C and D so that $b_0 = 3$ and $b_1 = 4$. What is b_2 in this case?

5. Let $a_0, a_1, a_2, \ldots$ be the sequence defined by the explicit formula
$$a_n = C \cdot 2^n + D \quad \text{for all integers } n \geq 0,$$
where C and D are real numbers. Show that for any choice of C and D,
$$a_k = 3a_{k-1} - 2a_{k-2} \quad \text{for all integers } k \geq 2.$$

6. Let $b_0, b_1, b_2, \ldots$ be the sequence defined by the explicit formula
$$b_n = C \cdot 3^n + D(-2)^n \quad \text{for all integers } n \geq 0,$$
where C and D are real numbers. Show that for any choice of C and D,
$$b_k = b_{k-1} + 6b_{k-2} \quad \text{for all integers } k \geq 2.$$

7. Solve the system of equations in Example 5.8.4 to obtain
$$C = \frac{1 + \sqrt{5}}{2\sqrt{5}} \quad \text{and} \quad D = \frac{-(1 - \sqrt{5})}{2\sqrt{5}}.$$

In each of 8–10: (a) suppose a sequence of the form $1, t, t^2, t^3, \ldots, t^n, \ldots$ where $t \neq 0$, satisfies the given recurrence relation (but not necessarily the initial conditions), and find all possible values of t; (b) suppose a sequence satisfies the given initial conditions as well as the recurrence relation, and find an explicit formula for the sequence.

8. $a_k = 2a_{k-1} + 3a_{k-2}$, for all integers $k \geq 2$
$a_0 = 1, a_1 = 2$

9. $b_k = 7b_{k-1} - 10b_{k-2}$, for all integers $k \geq 2$
$b_0 = 2, b_1 = 2$

10. $c_k = c_{k-1} + 6c_{k-2}$, for all integers $k \geq 2$
$c_0 = 0, c_1 = 3$

In each of 11–16 suppose a sequence satisfies the given recurrence relation and initial conditions. Find an explicit formula for the sequence.

11. $d_k = 4d_{k-2}$, for all integers $k \geq 2$
$d_0 = 1, d_1 = -1$

12. $e_k = 9e_{k-2}$, for all integers $k \geq 2$
$e_0 = 0, e_1 = 2$

13. $r_k = 2r_{k-1} - r_{k-2}$, for all integers $k \geq 2$
$r_0 = 1, r_1 = 4$

14. $s_k = -4s_{k-1} - 4s_{k-2}$, for all integers $k \geq 2$
$s_0 = 0, s_1 = -1$

15. $t_k = 6t_{k-1} - 9t_{k-2}$, for all integers $k \geq 2$
$t_0 = 1, t_1 = 3$

H 16. $s_k = 2s_{k-1} + 2s_{k-2}$, for all integers $k \geq 2$
$s_0 = 1, s_1 = 3$

17. Find an explicit formula for the sequence of exercise 39 in Section 5.6

18. Suppose that the sequences $s_0, s_1, s_2, \ldots$ and $t_0, t_1, t_2, \ldots$ both satisfy the same second-order linear homogeneous recurrence relation with constant coefficients:
$$s_k = 5s_{k-1} - 4s_{k-2} \quad \text{for all integers } k \geq 2,$$
$$t_k = 5t_{k-1} - 4t_{k-2} \quad \text{for all integers } k \geq 2.$$
Show that the sequence $2s_0 + 3t_0, 2s_1 + 3t_1, 2s_2 + 3t_2, \ldots$ also satisfies the same relation. In other words, show that
$$2s_k + 3t_k = 5(2s_{k-1} + 3t_{k-1}) - 4(2s_{k-2} + 3t_{k-2})$$
for all integers $k \geq 2$. Do *not* use Lemma 5.8.2.

19. Show that if r, s, a_0, and a_1 are numbers with $r \neq s$, then there exist unique numbers C and D so that
$$C + D = a_0$$
$$Cr + Ds = a_1.$$

20. Show that if r is a nonzero real number, k and m are distinct integers, and a_k and a_m are any real numbers, then there exist unique real numbers C and D so that
$$Cr^k + kDr^k = a_k$$
$$Cr^m + lDr^m = a_m.$$

H 21. Prove Theorem 5.8.5 for the case where the values of C and D are determined by a_0 and a_1.

Exercises 22 and 23 are intended for students who are familiar with complex numbers.

22. Find an explicit formula for a sequence $a_0, a_1, a_2, \ldots$ that satisfies
$$a_k = 2a_{k-1} - 2a_{k-2} \quad \text{for all integers } k \geq 2$$
with initial conditions $a_0 = 1$ and $a_1 = 2$.

23. Find an explicit formula for a sequence $b_0, b_1, b_2, \ldots$ that satisfies
$$b_k = 2b_{k-1} - 5b_{k-2} \quad \text{for all integers } k \geq 2$$
with initial conditions $b_0 = 1$ and $b_1 = 1$.

24. The numbers $\dfrac{1+\sqrt{5}}{2}$ and $\dfrac{1-\sqrt{5}}{2}$ that appear in the explicit formula for the Fibonacci sequence are related to a quantity called the *golden ratio* in Greek mathematics. Consider a rectangle of length ϕ units and height 1, where $\phi > 1$.

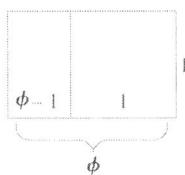

Divide the rectangle into a rectangle and a square as shown in the preceding diagram. The square is 1 unit on each side, and the rectangle has sides of lengths 1 and $\phi - 1$.

The ancient Greeks considered the outer rectangle to be perfectly proportioned (saying that the lengths of its sides were in a *golden ratio* to each other) if the ratio of the length to the width of the outer rectangle equaled the ratio of the length to the width of the inner rectangle. That is,

$$\frac{\phi}{1} = \frac{1}{\phi - 1}.$$

a. Show that ϕ satisfies the following quadratic equation: $t^2 - t - 1 = 0$.
b. Find the two solutions of $t^2 - t - 1 = 0$ and call them ϕ_1 and ϕ_2.
c. Express the explicit formula for the Fibonacci sequence in terms of ϕ_1 and ϕ_2.

Answers for Test Yourself

1. $a_k = Aa_{k-1} + Ba_{k-2}$; 2; A and B are fixed real numbers with $B \neq 0$ 2. $t^2 - At - B = 0$ 3. $a_n = Cr^n + Ds^n$, where C and D are real or complex numbers 4. $a_n = Cr^n + Dnr^n$, where C and D are real numbers

5.9 General Recursive Definitions and Structural Induction

GENTE: Oh, aren't you acquainted with recursive acronyms? I thought everybody knew about them. You see, "GOD" stands for "GOD Over Djinn"—which can be expanded as "GOD Over Djinn, Over Djinn"—and that can, in turn, be expanded to "GOD Over Djinn, Over Djinn, Over Djinn"—which can, in its turn, be further expanded.... You can go as far as you like.
ACHILLES: But I'll never finish!
GENIE: Of course not. You can never totally expand GOD.
—Douglas Hofstadter, *Gödel, Escher, Bach*, 1979

Sequences of numbers are not the only objects that can be defined recursively. In this section we discuss recursive definitions for sets and functions. We also introduce *structural induction*, which is a version of mathematical induction that is used to prove properties of recursively defined sets.

Recursively Defined Sets

To define a set of objects recursively, you identify a few core objects as belonging to the set and give rules showing how to build new set elements from old. More formally, a recursive definition for a set consists of the following three components:

    I. **BASE:** A statement that certain objects belong to the set.

    II. **RECURSION:** A collection of rules indicating how to form new set objects from those already known to be in the set.

    III. **RESTRICTION:** A statement that no objects belong to the set other than those coming from I and II.

Example 5.9.1 Recursive Definition of Boolean Expressions

Note   An example of "legal" expression is $p \wedge (q \vee \sim r)$, and an example of an "illegal" one is $\wedge \sim pqr \vee$.

The set of Boolean expressions was introduced in Section 2.4 as "legal" expressions involving letters from the alphabet such as $p, q,$ and r, and the symbols $\wedge$, $\vee$, and $\sim$. To make precise which expressions are legal, the set of Boolean expressions over a general alphabet is defined recursively.

I. BASE: Each symbol of the alphabet is a Boolean expression.

II. RECURSION: If P and Q are Boolean expressions, then so are

$$(a) \ (P \wedge Q) \ \text{ and (b) } \ (P \vee Q) \ \text{ and (c) } \ \sim P.$$

III. RESTRICTION: There are no Boolean expressions over the alphabet other than those obtained from I and II.

Derive the fact that the following is a Boolean expression over the English alphabet $\{a, b, c, \ldots, x, y, z\}$:

$$(\sim(p \wedge q) \vee (\sim r \wedge p)).$$

Solution   (1) By I, $p, q,$ and r are Boolean expressions.

(2) By (1) and II(a) and (c), $(p \wedge q)$ and $\sim r$ are Boolean expressions.

(3) By (2) and II(c) and (a), $\sim(p \wedge q)$ and $(\sim r \wedge p)$ are Boolean expressions.

(4) By (3) and II(b), $(\sim(p \wedge q) \vee (\sim r \wedge p))$ is a Boolean expression.   ■

• Definition

Let S be a finite set with at least one element. A **string over** S is a finite sequence of elements from S. The elements of S are called **characters** of the string, and the **length** of a string is the number of characters it contains. The **null string over** S is defined to be the "string" with no characters. It is usually denoted ϵ and is said to have length 0.

Example 5.9.2 The Set of Strings over an Alphabet

Consider the set S of all strings in a's and b's. S is defined recursively as follows:

I. BASE: ϵ is in S, where ϵ is the null string.

II. RECURSION: If $s \in S$, then

$$(a) \ sa \in S \ \text{ and (b) } \ sb \in S,$$

where sa and sb are the concatenations of s with a and b respectively.

III. RESTRICTION: Nothing is in S other than objects defined in I and II above. Derive the fact that $ab \in S$.

Solution   (1) By I, $\epsilon \in S$.

(2) By (1) and II(a), $\epsilon a \in S$. But ϵa is the concatenation of the null string and a, which equals a. So $a \in S$.

(3) By (2) and II(b), $ab \in S$.   ■

Example 5.9.3 Sets of Strings with Certain Properties

In *Gödel, Escher, Bach*, Douglas Hofstadter introduces the following recursively defined set of strings of M's, I's, and U's, which he calls the MIU-system.*

I. BASE: MI is in the MIU-system.

II. RECURSION:

    a. If xI is in the MIU-system, where x is a string, then xIU is in the MIU-system. (In other words, you can add a U to any string that ends in I. For example, since MI is in the system, so is MIU.)

    b. If Mx is in the MIU-system, where x is a string, then Mxx is in the MIU-system. (In other words, you can repeat all the characters in a string that follow an initial M. For example, if MUI is in the system, so is $MUIUI$.)

    c. If $xIIIy$ is in the MIU-system, where x and y are strings (possibly null), then xUy is also in the MIU-system. (In other words, you can replace III by U. For example, if $MIIII$ is in the system, so are MIU and MUI.)

    d. If $xUUy$ is in the MIU-system, where x and y are strings (possibly null), then xUy is also in the MIU-system. (In other words, you can replace UU by U. For example, if $MIIUU$ is in the system, so is $MIIU$.)

III. RESTRICTION: No strings other than those derived from I and II are in the MIU-system.

Derive the fact that $MUIU$ is in the MIU-system.

Solution   (1) By I, MI is in the MIU-system.

    (2) By (1) and II(b), MII is in the MIU-system.

    (3) By (2) and II(b), $MIIII$ is in the MIU-system.

    (4) By (3) and II(c), MUI is in the MIU-system.

    (5) By (4) and II(a), $MUIU$ is in the MIU-system.   ■

Example 5.9.4 Parenthesis Structures

Certain configurations of parentheses in algebraic expressions are "legal" *[such as(())() and()()()]*, whereas others are not *[such as)()))) and()))((( ]*. Here is a recursive definition to generate the set P of legal configurations of parentheses.

I. BASE: () is in P.

II. RECURSION:

    a. If E is in P, so is (E).

    b. If E and F are in P, so is EF.

III. RESTRICTION: No configurations of parentheses are in P other than those derived from I and II above.

Derive the fact that (())() is in P.

Solution   (1) By I, () is in P.

    (2) By (1) and II(a), (()) is in P.

    (3) By (2), (1), and II(b), (())() is in P.   ■

---

*Douglas Hofstadter, *Gödel, Escher, Bach* (New York: Basic Books), pp. 33–35.

Proving Properties about Recursively Defined Sets

When a set has been defined recursively, a version of mathematical induction, called **structural induction**, can be used to prove that every object in the set satisfies a given property.

> **Structural Introduction for Recursively Defined Sets**
>
> Let S be a set that has been defined recursively, and consider a property that objects in S may or may not satisfy. To prove that every object in S satisfies the property:
>
> 1. Show that each object in the BASE for S satisfies the property;
>
> 2. Show that for each rule in the RECURSION, if the rule is applied to objects in S that satisfy the property, then the objects defined by the rule also satisfy the property.
>
> Because no objects other than those obtained through the BASE and RECURSION conditions are contained in S, it must be the case that every object in S satisfies the property.

Example 5.9.5 A Property of the Set of Parenthesis Structures

Consider the set P of all grammatical configurations of parentheses defined in Example 5.9.4. Prove that every configuration in P contains an equal number of left and right parentheses.

Solution

Proof (by structural induction): Given any parenthesis configuration, let the property be the claim that it has an equal number of left and right parentheses.

Show that each object in the BASE for P satisfies the property: The only object in the base for P is (), which has one left parenthesis and one right parenthesis, so it has an equal number of left and right parentheses.

Show that for each rule in the RECURSION for P, if the rule is applied to an object in P that satisfies the property, then the object defined by the rule also satisfies the property: The recursion for P consists of two rules denoted II(a) and II(b).

Suppose E is a parenthesis configuration that has an equal number of left and right parentheses. When rule II(a) is applied to E, the result is (E), so both the number of left parentheses and the number of right parentheses are increased by one. Since these numbers were equal to start with, they remain equal when each is increased by one.

Suppose E and F are parenthesis configurations with equal numbers of left and right parentheses. Say E has m left and right parentheses, and F has n left and right parentheses. When rule II(b) is applied, the result is EF, which has an equal number, namely $m + n$, of left and right parentheses.

Thus when each rule in the RECURSION is applied to a configuration of parentheses in P with an equal number of left and right parentheses, the result is a configuration with an equal number of left and right parentheses.

Therefore, every structure in P has an equal number of left and right parentheses. ▪

Recursive Functions

A function is said to be **defined recursively** or to be a **recursive function** if its rule of definition refers to itself. Because of this self-reference, it is sometimes difficult to tell whether a given recursive function is well defined. Recursive functions are of great importance in the theory of computation in computer science.

Example 5.9.6 McCarthy's 91 Function

John McCarthy (born 1927)

The following function $M : \mathbf{Z}^+ \to \mathbf{Z}$ was defined by John McCarthy, a pioneer in the theory of computation and in the study of artificial intelligence:

$$M(n) = \begin{cases} n - 10 & \text{if } n > 100 \\ M(M(n + 11)) & \text{if } n \le 100 \end{cases}$$

for all positive integers n. Find $M(99)$.

Solution   By repeated use of the definition of M,

$$\begin{aligned}
M(99) &= M(M(110)) &&\text{since } 99 < 100 \\
&= M(100) &&\text{since } 110 > 100 \\
&= M(M(111)) &&\text{since } 100 \le 100 \\
&= M(101) &&\text{since } 111 > 100 \\
&= 91 &&\text{since } 101 > 100
\end{aligned}$$

The remarkable thing about this function is that it takes the value 91 for all positive integers less than or equal to 101. (You are asked to show this in exercise 20 at the end of this section.) Of course, for $n > 101$, $M(n)$ is well defined because it equals $n - 10$. ∎

Example 5.9.7 The Ackermann Function

Wilhelm Ackermann (1896–1962)

In the 1920s the German logician and mathematician Wilhelm Ackermann first defined a version of the function that now bears his name. This function is important in computer science because it helps answer the question of what can and what cannot be computed on a computer. It is defined on the set of all pairs of nonnegative integers as follows:

$$\begin{aligned}
A(0, n) &= n + 1 &&\text{for all nonnegative integers } n &&5.9.1 \\
A(m, 0) &= A(m - 1, 1) &&\text{for all positive integers } m &&5.9.2 \\
A(m, n) &= A(m - 1, A(m, n - 1)) &&\text{for all positive integers } m \text{ and } n &&5.9.3
\end{aligned}$$

Find $A(1, 2)$.

Solution

$$\begin{aligned}
A(1, 2) &= A(0, A(1, 1)) &&\text{by (5.9.3) with } m = 1 \text{ and } n = 2 \\
&= A(0, A(0, A(1, 0))) &&\text{by (5.9.3) with } m = 1 \text{ and } n = 1 \\
&= A(0, A(0, A(0, 1))) &&\text{by (5.9.2) with } m = 1 \\
&= A(0, A(0, 2)) &&\text{by (5.9.1) with } n = 1 \\
&= A(0, 3) &&\text{by (5.9.1) with } n = 2 \\
&= 4 &&\text{by (5.9.1) with } n = 3.
\end{aligned}$$

The special properties of the Ackermann function are a consequence of its phenomenal rate of growth. While the values of $A(0, 0) = 1$, $A(1, 1) = 3$, $A(2, 2) = 7$, and $A(3, 3) = 61$ are not especially impressive,

$$A(4, 4) \cong 2^{2^{2^{65536}}}$$

and the values of $A(n, n)$ continue to increase with extraordinary rapidity thereafter. ■

The argument is somewhat technical, but it is not difficult to show that the Ackermann function is well defined. The following is an example of a recursive "definition" that does not define a function.

Example 5.9.8   A Recursive "Function" That Is Not Well Defined

Consider the following attempt to define a recursive function G from $\mathbf{Z}^+$ to $\mathbf{Z}$. For all integers $n \geq 1$,

$$G(n) = \begin{cases} 1 & \text{if } n \text{ is 1} \\ 1 + G\left(\dfrac{n}{2}\right) & \text{if } n \text{ is even} \\ G(3n - 1) & \text{if } n \text{ is odd and } n > 1. \end{cases}$$

Is G well defined? Why?

Solution   Suppose G is a function. Then by definition of G,

$G(1) = 1$,
$G(2) = 1 + G(1) = 1 + 1 = 2$,
$G(3) = G(8) = 1 + G(4) = 1 + (1 + G(2)) = 1 + (1 + 2) = 4$,
$G(4) = 1 + G(2) = 1 + 2 = 3$.

However,
$$\begin{aligned} G(5) &= G(14) = 1 + G(7) = 1 + G(20) \\ &= 1 + (1 + G(10)) = 1 + (1 + (1 + G(5))) = 3 + G(5). \end{aligned}$$

Subtracting $G(5)$ from both sides gives $0 = 3$, which is false. Since the supposition that G is a function leads logically to a false statement, it follows that G is not a function. ■

A slight modification of the formula of Example 5.9.8 produces a "function" whose status of definition is unknown. Consider the following formula: For all integers $n \geq 1$,

$$T(n) = \begin{cases} 1 & \text{if } n \text{ is 1} \\ T\left(\dfrac{n}{2}\right) & \text{if } n \text{ is even} \\ T(3n + 1) & \text{if } n \text{ is odd.} \end{cases}$$

In the 1930s, a student, Luther Collatz, became interested in the behavior of a related function g, which is defined as follows: $g(n) = n/2$ if n is even, and $g(n) = 3n + 1$ if n is odd. Collatz conjectured that for any initial positive number n, computation of successive values of $g(n), g^2(n), g^3(n), \ldots$ would eventually produce the number 1. Determining whether this conjecture is true or false is called the **$3n + 1$ problem** (or the **$3x + 1$ problem**). If Collatz's conjecture is true, the formula for T defines a function; if the conjecture is false, T is not well defined. As of the publication of this book the answer is not known, although computer calculation has established that it holds for extremely large values of n.

Test Yourself

1. The BASE for a recursive definition of a set is _____.

2. The RECURSION for a recursive definition of a set is _____.

3. The RESTRICTION for a recursive definition of a set is _____.

4. One way to show that a given element is in a recursively defined set is to start with an element or elements in the _____ and apply the rules from the _____ until you obtain the given element.

5. Another way to show that a given element is in a recursively defined set is to use _____ to characterize all the elements of the set and then observe that the given element satisfies the characterization.

6. To prove that every element in a recursively defined set S satisfies a certain property, you show that _____ and that, for each rule in the RECURSION, if _____ then _____.

7. A function is said to be defined recursively if, and only if, _____.

Exercise Set 5.9

1. Consider the set of Boolean expressions defined in Example 5.9.1. Give derivations showing that each of the following is a Boolean expression over the English alphabet $\{a, b, c, \ldots, x, y, z\}$.
   a. $(\sim p \vee (q \wedge (r \vee \sim s)))$
   b. $((p \vee q) \vee \sim ((p \wedge \sim s) \wedge r))$

2. Let S be defined as in Example 5.9.2. Give derivations showing that each of the following is in S.
   a. *aab* b. *bb*

3. Consider the MIU-system discussed in Example 5.9.3. Give derivations showing that each of the following is in the MIU-system.
   a. $MIUI$
   b. $MUIIU$

4. The set of arithmetic expressions over the real numbers can be defined recursively as follows:
   I. BASE: Each real number r is an arithmetic expression.
   II. RECURSION: If u and v are arithmetic expressions, then the following are also arithmetic expressions:
   a. $(+u)$ b. $(-u)$
   c. $(u + v)$ d. $(u - v)$
   e. $(u \cdot v)$ f. $\left(\dfrac{u}{v}\right)$
   III. RESTRICTION: There are no arithmetic expressions over the real numbers other than those obtained from I and II.
   (Note that the *expression* $\left(\dfrac{u}{v}\right)$ is legal even though the value of v may be 0.) Give derivations showing that each of the following is an arithmetic expression.
   a. $((2 \cdot (0.3 – 4.2)) + (-7))$ b. $\left(\dfrac{(9 \cdot (6.1 + 2))}{((4 – 7) \cdot 6)}\right)$

5. Define a set S recursively as follows:
   I. BASE: $1 \in S$
   II. RECURSION: If $s \in S$, then
   a. $0s \in S$ b. $1s \in S$
   III. RESTRICTION: Nothing is in S other than objects defined in I and II above.
   Use structural induction to prove that every string in S ends in a 1.

6. Define a set S recursively as follows:
   I. BASE: $a \in S$
   II. RECURSION: If $s \in S$, then,
   a. $sa \in S$ b. $sb \in S$
   III. RESTRICTION: Nothing is in S other than objects defined in I and II above.
   Use structural induction to prove that every string in S begins with an a.

7. Define a set S recursively as follows:
   I. BASE: $\epsilon \in S$
   II. RECURSION: If $s \in S$, then
   a. $bs \in S$ b. $sb \in S$
   c. $saa \in S$ d. $aas \in S$
   III. RESTRICTION: Nothing is in S other than objects defined in I and II above.
   Use structural induction to prove that every string in S contains an even number of a's.

8. Define a set S recursively as follows:
   I. BASE: $0 \in S$
   II. RECURSION: If $s \in S$, then
      a. $s + 3 \in S$ b. $s - 3 \in S$
   III. RESTRICTION: Nothing is in S other than objects defined in I and II above.

   Use structural induction to prove that every integer in S is divisible by 3.

H 9. Define a set S recursively as follows:
   I. BASE: $1 \in S$, $3 \in S$, $5 \in S$, $7 \in S$, $9 \in S$
   II. RECURSION: If $s \in S$ and $t \in S$ then
      a. $st \in S$ b. $2s \in S$
      c. $4s \in S$ d. $6s \in S$
      e. $8s \in S$
   III. RESTRICTION: Nothing is in S other than objects defined in I and II above.

   Use structural induction to prove that every string in S represents an odd integer.

H 10. Define a set S recursively as follows:
   I. BASE: $0 \in S$, $5 \in S$
   II. RECURSION: If $s \in S$ and $t \in S$ then
      a. $s + t \in S$ b. $s - t \in S$
   III. RESTRICTION: Nothing is in S other than objects defined in I and II above.

   Use structural induction to prove that every integer in S is divisible by 5.

11. Define a set S recursively as follows:
   I. BASE: $1 \in S$, $2 \in S$, $3 \in S$, $4 \in S$, $5 \in S$, $6 \in S$, $7 \in S$, $8 \in S$, $9 \in S$
   II. RECURSION: If $s \in S$ and $t \in S$, then
      a. $s0 \in S$ b. $st \in S$
   III. RESTRICTION: Nothing is in S other than objects defined in I and II above.

   Use structural induction to prove that no string in S represents an integer with a leading zero.

H* 12. Is the string MU in the MIU-system? Use structural induction to prove your answer.

13. Consider the set P of parenthesis structures defined in Example 5.9.4. Give derivations showing that each of the following is in P.
   a. ()(())   b. (())(())

* 14. Determine whether either of the following parenthesis structures is in the set P defined in Example 5.9.4. Use structural induction to prove your answers.
   a. ()((b. (())())()

15. Give a recursive definition for the set of all strings of 0's and 1's that have the same number of 0's as 1's.

16. Give a recursive definition for the set of all strings of 0's and 1's for which all the 0's precede all the 1's.

17. Give a recursive definition for the set of all strings of a's and b's that contain an odd number of a's.

18. Give a recursive definition for the set of all strings of a's and b's that contain exactly one a.

19. Use the definition of McCarthy's 91 function in Example 5.9.6 to show the following:
   a. $M(86) = M(91)$ b. $M(91) = 91$

* 20. Prove that McCarthy's 91 function equals 91 for all positive integers less than or equal to 101.

21. Use the definition of the Ackermann function in Example 5.9.7 to compute the following:
   a. $A(1, 1)$ b. $A(2, 1)$

22. Use the definition of the Ackermann function to show the following:
   a. $A(1, n) = n + 2$, for all nonnegative integers n.
   b. $A(2, n) = 3 + 2n$, for all nonnegative integers n.
   c. $A(3, n) = 8 \cdot 2^n - 3$, for all nonnegative integers n.

23. Compute $T(2)$, $T(3)$, $T(4)$, $T(5)$, $T(6)$, and $T(7)$ for the "function" T defined after Example 5.9.8.

24. Student A tries to define a function $F : \mathbf{Z}^+ \to \mathbf{Z}$ by the rule

$$F(n) = \begin{cases} 1 & \text{if } n \text{ is 1} \\ F\left(\dfrac{n}{2}\right) & \text{if } n \text{ is even} \\ 1 + F(5n - 9) & \text{if } n \text{ is odd and } n > 1 \end{cases}$$

for all integers $n \geq 1$. Student B claims that F is not well defined. Justify student B's claim.

25. Student C tries to define a function $G : \mathbf{Z}^+ \to \mathbf{Z}$ by the rule

$$G(n) = \begin{cases} 1 & \text{if } n \text{ is 1} \\ G\left(\dfrac{n}{2}\right) & \text{if } n \text{ is even} \\ 2 + G(3n - 5) & \text{if } n \text{ is odd and } n > 1 \end{cases}$$

for all integers $n \geq 1$. Student D claims that G is not well defined. Justify student D's claim.

Answers for Test Yourself

1. a statement that certain objects belong to the set   2. a collection of rules indicating how to form new set objects from those already known to be in the set   3. a statement that no objects belong to the set other than those coming from either the BASE or the RECURSION   4. BASE; RECURSION   5. structural induction   6. each object in the BASE satisfies the property; the rule is applied to objects in the BASE; the objects defined by the rule also satisfy the property   7. its rule of definition refers to itself

CHAPTER 8

RELATIONS

In this chapter we discuss the mathematics of relations defined on sets, focusing on ways to represent relations and exploring various properties they may have. The concept of equivalence relation is introduced in Section 8.3 and applied in Section 8.4 to modular arithmetic and cryptography. Partial order relations are discussed in Section 8.5, and an application is given showing how to use these relations to help coordinate and guide the flow of individual tasks that must be performed to accomplish a complex, large-scale project.

8.1 Relations on Sets

Strange as it may sound, the power of mathematics rests on its evasion of all
unnecessary thought and on its wonderful saving of mental operations. — Ernst Mach,
1838–1916

A more formal way to refer to the kind of relation defined in Section 1.3 is to call it a **binary relation** because it is a subset of a Cartesian product of two sets. At the end of this section we define an *n-ary relation* to be a subset of a Cartesian product of *n* sets, where *n* is any integer greater than or equal to two. Such a relation is the fundamental structure used in relational databases. However, because we focus on binary relations in this text, when we use the term *relation* by itself, we will mean binary relation.

Example 8.1.1 The Less-than Relation for Real Numbers

Define a relation L from **R** to **R** as follows: For all real numbers x and y,

$$x \, L \, y \Leftrightarrow x < y.$$

a. Is $57 \, L \, 53$?   b. Is $(-17) \, L \, (-14)$?   c. Is $143 \, L \, 143$?   d. Is $(-35) \, L \, 1$?

e. Draw the graph of L as a subset of the Cartesian plane **R** × **R**

Solution

a. No, $57 > 53$ b. Yes, $-17 < -14$ c. No, $143 = 143$ d. Yes, $-35 < 1$

e. For each value of x, all the points (x, y) with $y > x$ are on the graph. So the graph consists of all the points above the line $x = y$.

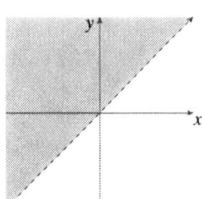

Example 8.1.2 The Congruence Modulo 2 Relation

Define a relation E from $\mathbf{Z}$ to $\mathbf{Z}$ as follows: For all $(m, n) \in \mathbf{Z} \times \mathbf{Z}$,

$$m \; E \; n \quad \Leftrightarrow \quad m - n \text{ is even.}$$

a. Is $4 \; E \; 0$? Is $2 \; E \; 6$? Is $3 \; E \; (-3)$? Is $5 \; E \; 2$?

b. List five integers that are related by E to 1.

c. Prove that if n is any odd integer, then $n \; E \; 1$.

Solution

a. Yes, $4 \; E \; 0$ because $4 - 0 = 4$ and 4 is even.
   Yes, $2 \; E \; 6$ because $2 - 6 = -4$ and -4 is even.
   Yes, $3 \; E \; (-3)$ because $3 - (-3) = 6$ and 6 is even.
   No, $5 \; \not{E} \; 2$ because $5 - 2 = 3$ and 3 is not even.

b. There are many such lists. One is

$$
\begin{array}{rl}
1 & \text{because } 1 - 1 = 0 \text{ is even,} \\
3 & \text{because } 3 - 1 = 2 \text{ is even,} \\
5 & \text{because } 5 - 1 = 4 \text{ is even,} \\
-1 & \text{because } -1 - 1 = -2 \text{ is even,} \\
-3 & \text{because } -3 - 1 = -4 \text{ is even.}
\end{array}
$$

c. **Proof:** Suppose n is any odd integer. Then $n = 2k + 1$ for some integer k. Now by definition of E, $n \; E \; 1$ if, and only if, $n - 1$ is even. But by substitution,

$$n - 1 = (2k + 1) - 1 = 2k,$$

and since k is an integer, $2k$ is even. Hence $n \; E \; 1$ *[as was to be shown]*.

It can be shown (see exercise 2 at the end of this section) that integers m and n are related by E if, and only if, $m \bmod 2 = n \bmod 2$ (that is, both are even or both are odd). When this occurs m and n are said to be **congruent modulo 2.** ■

Example 8.1.3 A Relation on a Power Set

Let $X = \{a, b, c\}$. Then $\mathscr{P}(X) = \{\emptyset, \{a\}, \{b\}, \{c\}, \{a, b\}, \{a, c\}, \{b, c\}, \{a, b, c\}\}$. Define a relation $\mathbf{S}$ from $\mathscr{P}(X)$ to $\mathbf{Z}$ as follows: For all sets A and B in $\mathscr{P}(X)$ (i.e., for all subsets A and B of X),

$$A \; \mathbf{S} \; B \quad \Leftrightarrow \quad A \text{ has at least as many elements as } B.$$

a. Is $\{a, b\} \; \mathbf{S} \; \{b, c\}$?   b. Is $\{a\} \; \mathbf{S} \; \emptyset$?   c. Is $\{b, c\} \; \mathbf{S} \; \{a, b, c\}$?   d. Is $\{c\} \; \mathbf{S} \; \{a\}$?

Solution

a. Yes, both sets have two elements.

b. Yes, $\{a\}$ has one element and $\emptyset$ has zero elements, and $1 \geq 0$.

c. No, $\{b, c\}$ has two elements and $\{a, b, c\}$ has three elements and $2 < 3$.

d. Yes, both sets have one element. ■

The Inverse of a Relation

If R is a relation from A to B, then a relation R^{-1} from B to A can be defined by interchanging the elements of all the ordered pairs of R.

> **• Definition**
>
> Let R be a relation from A to B. Define the inverse relation R^{-1} from B to A as follows:
>
> $$R^{-1} = \{(y, x) \in B \times A \mid (x, y) \in R\}.$$

This definition can be written operationally as follows:

> For all $x \in A$ and $y \in B$, $\quad (y, x) \in R^{-1} \quad \Leftrightarrow \quad (x, y) \in R.$

Example 8.1.4 The Inverse of a Finite Relation

Let $A = \{2, 3, 4\}$ and $B = \{2, 6, 8\}$ and let R be the "divides" relation from A to B: For all $(x, y) \in A \times B$,

$$x\ R\ y \quad \Leftrightarrow \quad x \mid y \qquad\qquad x \text{ divides } y.$$

a. State explicitly which ordered pairs are in R and R^{-1}, and draw arrow diagrams for R and R^{-1}.

b. Describe R^{-1} in words.

Solution

a. $R \quad = \{(2, 2), (2, 6), (2, 8), (3, 6), (4, 8)\}$
$R^{-1} = \{(2, 2), (6, 2), (8, 2), (6, 3), (8, 4)\}$

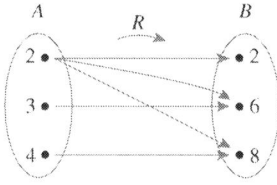

To draw the arrow diagram for R^{-1}, you can copy the arrow diagram for R but reverse the directions of the arrows.

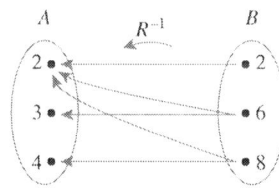

Or you can redraw the diagram so that B is on the left.

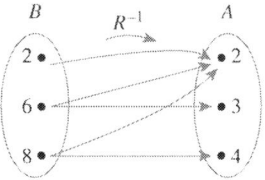

b. R^{-1} can be described in words as follows: For all $(y, x) \in B \times A$,

$$y \ R^{-1} \ x \quad \Leftrightarrow \quad y \text{ is a multiple of } x.$$

Example 8.1.5 The Inverse of an Infinite Relation

Define a relation R from $\mathbf{R}$ to $\mathbf{R}$ as follows: For all $(x, y) \in \mathbf{R} \times \mathbf{R}$,

$$x \ R \ y \quad \Leftrightarrow \quad y = 2|x|.$$

Draw the graphs of R and R^{-1} in the Cartesian plane. Is R^{-1} a function?

Solution   A point (v, u) is on the graph of R^{-1} if, and only if, (u, v) is on the graph of R. Note that if $x \geq 0$, then the graph of $y = 2|x| = 2x$ is a straight line with slope 2. And if $x < 0$, then the graph of $y = 2|x| = 2(-x) = -2x$ is a straight line with slope -2. Some sample values are tabulated and the graphs are shown below.

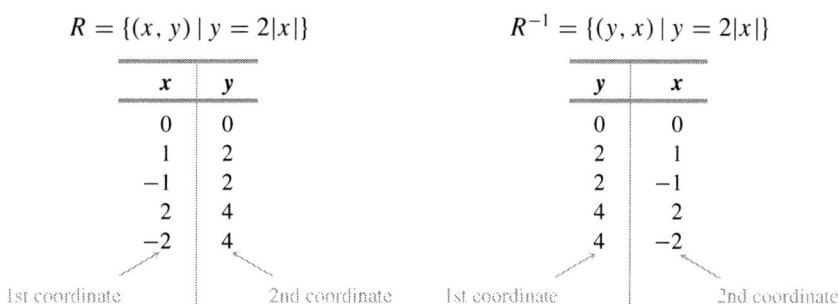

$R = \{(x, y) \mid y = 2|x|\}$

x	y
0	0
1	2
−1	2
2	4
−2	4

1st coordinate — 2nd coordinate

$R^{-1} = \{(y, x) \mid y = 2|x|\}$

y	x
0	0
2	1
2	−1
4	2
4	−2

1st coordinate — 2nd coordinate

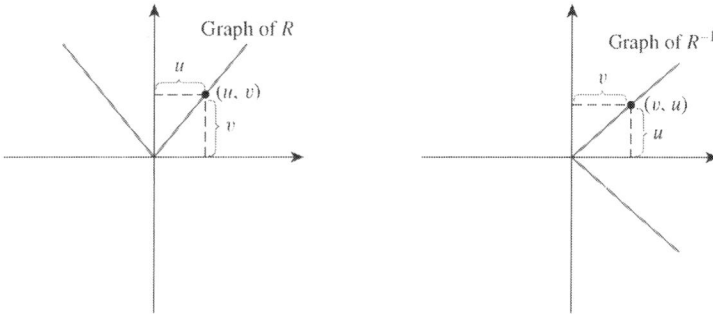

Graph of R

Graph of R^{-1}

R^{-1} is not a function because, for instance, both $(2, 1)$ and $(2, -1)$ are in R^{-1}.

Directed Graph of a Relation

In the remaining sections of this chapter, we discuss important properties of relations that are defined from a set to itself.

Note It is important to distinguish clearly between a relation and the set on which it is defined.

> • **Definition**
>
> A **relation on a set** A is a relation from A to A.

When a relation R is defined *on* a set A, the arrow diagram of the relation can be modified so that it becomes a **directed graph.** Instead of representing A as two separate sets of points, represent A only once, and draw an arrow from each point of A to each related point. As with an ordinary arrow diagram,

> For all points x and y in A,
>
> there is an arrow from x to y $\Leftrightarrow$ $x\ R\ y$ $\Leftrightarrow$ $(x, y) \in R$.

If a point is related to itself, a loop is drawn that extends out from the point and goes back to it.

Example 8.1.6 Directed Graph of a Relation

Let $A = \{3, 4, 5, 6, 7, 8\}$ and define a relation R on A as follows: For all $x, y \in A$,

$$x\ R\ y \quad \Leftrightarrow \quad 2 \mid (x - y).$$

Draw the directed graph of R.

Solution   Note that 3 R 3 because $3 - 3 = 0$ and $2 \mid 0$ since $0 = 2 \cdot 0$. Thus there is a loop from 3 to itself. Similarly, there is a loop from 4 to itself, from 5 to itself, and so forth, since the difference of each integer with itself is 0, and $2 \mid 0$.
   Note also that 3 R 5 because $3 - 5 = -2 = 2 \cdot (-1)$. And 5 R 3 because $5 - 3 = 2 = 2 \cdot 1$. Hence there is an arrow from 3 to 5 and also an arrow from 5 to 3. The other arrows in the directed graph, as shown below, are obtained by similar reasoning.

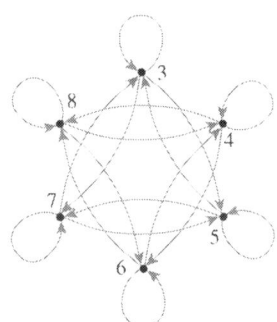

N-ary Relations and Relational Databases

N-ary relations form the mathematical foundation for relational database theory. A binary relation is a subset of a Cartesian product of two sets, similarly, an *n-ary* relation is a subset of a Cartesian product of *n* sets.

> ● **Definition**
>
> Given sets $A_1, A_2, \ldots, A_n$, an **n-ary relation** R on $A_1 \times A_2 \times \cdots \times A_n$ is a subset of $A_1 \times A_2 \times \cdots \times A_n$. The special cases of 2-ary, 3-ary, and 4-ary relations are called **binary, ternary,** and **quaternary relations,** respectively.

Example 8.1.7 A Simple Database

The following is a radically simplified version of a database that might be used in a hospital. Let A_1 be a set of positive integers, A_2 a set of alphabetic character strings, A_3 a set of numeric character strings, and A_4 a set of alphabetic character strings. Define a quaternary relation R on $A_1 \times A_2 \times A_3 \times A_4$ as follows:

$(a_1, a_2, a_3, a_4) \in R \quad \Leftrightarrow \quad$ a patient with patient ID number a_1, named a_2, was admitted on date a_3, with primary diagnosis a_4.

At a particular hospital, this relation might contain the following 4-tuples:

(011985, John Schmidt, 020710, asthma)

(574329, Tak Kurosawa, 0114910, pneumonia)

(466581, Mary Lazars, 0103910, appendicitis)

(008352, Joan Kaplan, 112409, gastritis)

(011985, John Schmidt, 021710, pneumonia)

(244388, Sarah Wu, 010310, broken leg)

(778400, Jamal Baskers, 122709, appendicitis)

In discussions of relational databases, the tuples are normally thought of as being written in tables. Each row of the table corresponds to one tuple, and the header for each column gives the descriptive attribute for the elements in the column.

Operations within a database allow the data to be manipulated in many different ways. For example, in the database language SQL, if the above database is denoted S, the result of the query

SELECT Patient_ID#, Name FROM S WHERE

Admission_Date = 010310

would be a list of the ID numbers and names of all patients admitted on 01-03-10:

466581   Mary Lazars,

244388   Sarah Wu.

This is obtained by taking the intersection of the set $A_1 \times A_2 \times \{010310\} \times A_4$ with the database and then projecting onto the first two coordinates. (See exercise 25 of Section 7.1.) Similarly, SELECT can be used to obtain a list of all admission dates of a given patient. For John Schmidt this list is

02-07-10   and

02-17-10

Individual entries in a database can be added, deleted, or updated, and most databases can sort data entries in various ways. In addition, entire databases can be merged, and the entries common to two databases can be moved to a new database. ∎

Test Yourself

Answers to Test Yourself questions are located at the end of each section.

1. If R is a relation from A to B, $x \in A$, and $y \in B$, the notation $x\, R\, y$ means that _____.

2. If R is a relation from A to B, $x \in A$, and $y \in B$, the notation $x\, \cancel{R}\, y$ means that _____.

3. If R is a relation from A to B, $x \in A$, and $y \in B$, then $(y, x) \in R^{-1}$ if, and only if, _____.

4. A relation on a set A is a relation from _____ to _____.

5. If R is a relation on a set A, the directed graph of R has an arrow from x to y if, and only if, _____.

Exercise Set 8.1*

1. As in Example 8.1.2, the **congruence modulo 2** relation E is defined from $\mathbf{Z}$ to $\mathbf{Z}$ as follows: For all integers m and n,

$$m\, E\, n \quad \Leftrightarrow \quad m - n \text{ is even.}$$

a. Is $0\, E\, 0$? Is $5\, E\, 2$? Is $(6, 6) \in E$? Is $(-1, 7) \in E$?
b. Prove that for any even integer n, $n\, E\, 0$.

H 2. Prove that for all integers m and n, $m - n$ is even if, and only if, both m and n are even or both m and n are odd.

3. The **congruence modulo 3** relation, T, is defined from $\mathbf{Z}$ to $\mathbf{Z}$ as follows: For all integers m and n,

$$m\, T\, n \quad \Leftrightarrow \quad 3 \mid (m - n).$$

a. Is $10\, T\, 1$? Is $1\, T\, 10$? Is $(2, 2) \in T$? Is $(8, 1) \in T$?
b. List five integers n such that $n\, T\, 0$.
c. List five integers n such that $n\, T\, 1$.
d. List five integers n such that $n\, T\, 2$.
H e. Make and prove a conjecture about which integers are related by T to 0, which integers are related by T to 1, and which integers are related by T to 2.

4. Define a relation P on $\mathbf{Z}$ as follows: For all $m, n \in \mathbf{Z}$,

$$m\, P\, n \quad \Leftrightarrow \quad m \text{ and } n \text{ have a common prime factor.}$$

a. Is $15\, P\, 25$?   b. $22\, P\, 27$?
c. Is $0\, P\, 5$?   d. Is $8\, P\, 8$?

5. Let $X = \{a, b, c\}$. Recall that $\mathscr{P}(X)$ is the power set of X. Define a relation $\mathbf{R}$ on $\mathscr{P}(X)$ as follows: For all $A, B \in \mathscr{P}(X)$,

$$A\, \mathbf{R}\, B \quad \Leftrightarrow \quad A \text{ has the same number of elements as } B.$$

a. Is $\{a, b\}\, \mathbf{R}\, \{b, c\}$?   b. Is $\{a\}\, \mathbf{R}\, \{a, b\}$?
c. Is $\{c\}\, \mathbf{R}\, \{b\}$?

6. Let $X = \{a, b, c\}$. Define a relation $\mathbf{J}$ on $\mathscr{P}(X)$ as follows: For all $A, B \in \mathscr{P}(X)$,

$$A\, \mathbf{J}\, B \quad \Leftrightarrow \quad A \cap B \neq \emptyset.$$

a. Is $\{a\}\, \mathbf{J}\, \{c\}$?   b. Is $\{a, b\}\, \mathbf{J}\, \{b, c\}$?
c. Is $\{a, b\}\, \mathbf{J}\, \{a, b, c\}$?

7. Define a relation R on $\mathbf{Z}$ as follows: For all integers m and n,

$$m\, R\, n \quad \Leftrightarrow \quad 5 \mid (m^2 - n^2).$$

a. Is $1\, R\, (-9)$?   b. Is $2\, R\, 13$?
c. Is $2\, R\, (-8)$?   d. Is $(-8)\, R\, 2$?

8. Let A be the set of all strings of a's and b's of length 4. Define a relation R on A as follows: For all $s, t \in A$,

$$s\, R\, t \quad \Leftrightarrow \quad s \text{ has the same first two characters as } t.$$

a. Is $abaa\, R\, abba$?   b. Is $aabb\, R\, bbaa$?
c. Is $aaaa\, R\, aaab$?   d. Is $baaa\, R\, abaa$?

9. Let A be the set of all strings of 0's, 1's, and 2's of length 4. Define a relation R on A as follows: For all $s, t \in A$,

$$s\, R\, t \quad \Leftrightarrow \quad \begin{array}{l} \text{the sum of the characters in } s \text{ equals} \\ \text{the sum of the characters in } t. \end{array}$$

a. Is $0121\, R\, 2200$?   b. Is $1011\, R\, 2101$?
c. Is $2212\, R\, 2121$?   d. Is $1220\, R\, 2111$?

10. Let $A = \{3, 4, 5\}$ and $B = \{4, 5, 6\}$ and let R be the "less than" relation. That is, for all $(x, y) \in A \times B$,

$$x\, R\, y \quad \Leftrightarrow \quad x < y.$$

State explicitly which ordered pairs are in R and R^{-1}.

11. Let $A = \{3, 4, 5\}$ and $B = \{4, 5, 6\}$ and let S be the "divides" relation. That is, for all $(x, y) \in A \times B$,

$$x\, S\, y \quad \Leftrightarrow \quad x \mid y.$$

State explicitly which ordered pairs are in S and S^{-1}.

12. a. Suppose a function $F\colon X \to Y$ is one-to-one but not onto. Is F^{-1} (the inverse relation for F) a function? Explain your answer.
b. Suppose a function $F\colon X \to Y$ is onto but not one-to-one. Is F^{-1} (the inverse relation for F) a function? Explain your answer.

---

*For exercises with blue numbers or letters, solutions are given in Appendix B. The symbol H indicates that only a hint or a partial solution is given. The symbol $*$ signals that an exercise is more challenging than usual.

Draw the directed graphs of the relations defined in 13–18.

13. Define a relation R on $A = \{0, 1, 2, 3\}$ by $R = \{(0, 0),$ $(1, 2), (2, 2)\}$.

14. Define a relation S on $B = \{a, b, c, d\}$ by $S = \{(a, b),$ $(a, c), (b, c), (d, d)\}$.

15. Let $A = \{2, 3, 4, 5, 6, 7, 8\}$ and define a relation R on A as follows: For all $x, y \in A$,

$$x \, R \, y \quad \Leftrightarrow \quad x \mid y.$$

H 16. Let $A = \{5, 6, 7, 8, 9, 10\}$ and define a relation S on A as follows: For all $x, y \in A$,

$$x \, S \, y \quad \Leftrightarrow \quad 2 \mid (x - y).$$

17. Let $A = \{2, 3, 4, 5, 6, 7, 8\}$ and define a relation T on A as follows: For all $x, y \in A$,

$$x \, T \, y \quad \Leftrightarrow \quad 3 \mid (x - y).$$

18. Let $A = \{0, 1, 2, 3, 4, 5, 6, 7, 8\}$ and define a relation V on A as follows: For all $x, y \in A$,

$$x \, V \, y \Leftrightarrow 5 \mid (x^2 - y^2).$$

Exercises 19–20 refer to unions and intersections of relations. Since relations are subsets of Cartesian products, their unions and intersections can be calculated as for any subsets. Given two relations R and S from A to B,

$R \cup S = \{(x, y) \in A \times B \mid (x, y) \in R \text{ or } (x, y) \in S\}$
$R \cap S = \{(x, y) \in A \times B \mid (x, y) \in R \text{ and } (x, y) \in S\}$.

19. Let $A = \{2, 4\}$ and $B = \{6, 8, 10\}$ and define relations R and S from A to B as follows: For all $(x, y) \in A \times B$,

$$x \, R \, y \quad \Leftrightarrow \quad x \mid y \quad \text{and}$$
$$x \, S \, y \quad \Leftrightarrow \quad y - 4 = x.$$

State explicitly which ordered pairs are in $A \times B$, R, S, $R \cup S$, and $R \cap S$.

20. Let $A = \{-1, 1, 2, 4\}$ and $B = \{1, 2\}$ and define relations R and S from A to B as follows: For all $(x, y) \in A \times B$,

$$x \, R \, y \quad \Leftrightarrow \quad |x| = |y| \quad \text{and}$$
$$x \, S \, y \quad \Leftrightarrow \quad x - y \text{ is even.}$$

State explicitly which ordered pairs are in $A \times B$, R, S, $R \cup S$, and $R \cap S$.

21. Define relations R and S on **R** as follows:

$$R = \{(x, y) \in \mathbf{R} \times \mathbf{R} \mid x < y\} \quad \text{and}$$
$$S = \{(x, y) \in \mathbf{R} \times \mathbf{R} \mid x = y\}.$$

That is, R is the "less than" relation and S is the "equals" relation on **R**. Graph R, S, $R \cup S$, and $R \cap S$ in the Cartesian plane.

22. Define relations R and S on **R** as follows:

$$R = \{(x, y) \in \mathbf{R} \times \mathbf{R} \mid y = |x|\} \quad \text{and}$$
$$S = \{(x, y) \in \mathbf{R} \times \mathbf{R} \mid y = 1\}.$$

Graph R, S, $R \cup S$, and $R \cap S$ in the Cartesian plane.

23. Define relations R and S on **R** as follows:

$$R = \{(x, y) \in \mathbf{R} \times \mathbf{R} \mid x^2 + y^2 = 4\} \quad \text{and}$$
$$S = \{(x, y) \in \mathbf{R} \times \mathbf{R} \mid x = y\}.$$

Graph R, S, $R \cup S$, and $R \cap S$ in the Cartesian plane.

24. In Example 8.1.7 the result of the query SELECT Patient_ID#, Name FROM S WHERE Primary_Diagnosis $= X$ is the projection onto the first two coordinates of the intersection of the set $A_1 \times A_2 \times A_3 \times \{X\}$ with the database.
   a. Find the result of the query SELECT Patient_ID#, Name FROM S WHERE Primary_Diagnosis $=$ pneumonia.
   b. Find the result of the query SELECT Patient_ID#, Name FROM S WHERE Primary_Diagnosis $=$ appendicitis.

Answers for Test Yourself

1. x is related to y by R 2. x is not related to y by R 3. $(x, y) \in R$ 4. A; A 5. x is related to y by R

8.2 Reflexivity, Symmetry, and Transitivity

Mathematics is the tool specially suited for dealing with abstract concepts of any kind and there is no limit to its power in this field. — P. A. M. Dirac, 1902–1984

Let $A = \{2, 3, 4, 6, 7, 9\}$ and define a relation R on A as follows: For all $x, y \in A$,

$$x \, R \, y \quad \Leftrightarrow \quad 3 \mid (x - y).$$

Note For reference:

$x\, R\, y \quad \Leftrightarrow \quad 3\,|\,(x-y).$

Then $2\, R\, 2$ because $2 - 2 = 0$, and $3\,|\,0$. Similarly, $3\, R\, 3$, $4\, R\, 4$, $6\, R\, 6$, $7\, R\, 7$, and $9\, R\, 9$. Also $6\, R\, 3$ because $6 - 3 = 3$, and $3\,|\,3$. And $3\, R\, 6$ because $3 - 6 = -(6 - 3) = -3$, and $3\,|\,(-3)$. Similarly, $3\, R\, 9$, $9\, R\, 3$, $6\, R\, 9$, $9\, R\, 6$, $4\, R\, 7$, and $7\, R\, 4$. Thus the directed graph for R has the appearance shown below.

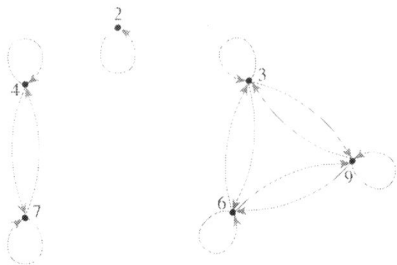

This graph has three important properties:

1. Each point of the graph has an arrow looping around from it back to itself.

2. In each case where there is an arrow going from one point to a second, there is an arrow going from the second point back to the first.

3. In each case where there is an arrow going from one point to a second and from the second point to a third, there is an arrow going from the first point to the third. That is, there are no "incomplete directed triangles" in the graph.

Properties (1), (2), and (3) correspond to properties of general relations called *reflexivity, symmetry,* and *transitivity.*

• Definition

Let R be a relation on a set A.

1. R is **reflexive** if, and only if, for all $x \in A$, $x\, R\, x$.

2. R is **symmetric** if, and only if, for all $x, y \in A$, **if** $x\, R\, y$ then $y\, R\, x$.

3. R is **transitive** if, and only if, for all $x, y, z \in A$, **if** $x\, R\, y$ and $y\, R\, z$ then $x\, R\, z$.

Caution! The definition of symmetric does not say that x is related to y by R; only that if it happens that x is related to y, then y must be related to x.

Because of the equivalence of the expressions $x\, R\, y$ and $(x, y) \in R$ for all x and y in A, the reflexive, symmetric, and transitive properties can also be written as follows:

---

1. R is reflexive $\quad \Leftrightarrow \quad$ for all x in A, $(x, x) \in R$.

2. R is symmetric $\quad \Leftrightarrow \quad$ for all x and y in A, **if** $(x, y) \in R$ then $(y, x) \in R$.

3. R is transitive $\quad \Leftrightarrow \quad$ for all x, y and z in A, **if** $(x, y) \in R$ and $(y, z) \in R$ then $(x, z) \in R$.

Caution! The "first," "second," and "third" elements in the informal versions need not all be distinct. This is a disadvantage of informality: It may mask nuances that a formal definition makes clear.

In informal terms, properties (1)–(3) say the following:

1. **Reflexive:** Each element is related to itself.

2. **Symmetric:** If any one element is related to any other element, then the second element is related to the first.

3. **Transitive:** If any one element is related to a second and that second element is related to a third, then the first element is related to the third.

Note that the definitions of reflexivity, symmetry, and transitivity are universal statements. This means that to prove a relation has one of the properties, you use either the method of exhaustion or the method of generalizing from the generic particular.

Now consider what it means for a relation *not* to have one of the properties defined previously. Recall that the negation of a universal statement is existential. Hence if R is a relation on a set A, then

1. R **is not reflexive** $\Leftrightarrow$ there is an element x in A such that $x \not{R} x$ [*that is, such that* $(x, x) \notin R$].

2. R **is not symmetric** $\Leftrightarrow$ there are elements x and y in A such that $x \, R \, y$ but $y \not{R} x$ [*that is, such that* $(x, y) \in R$ *but* $(y, x) \notin R$].

3. R **is not transitive** $\Leftrightarrow$ there are elements x, y and z in A such that $x \, R \, y$ and $y \, R \, z$ but $x \not{R} z$ [*that is, such that* $(x, y) \in R$ *and* $(y, z) \in R$ *but* $(x, z) \notin R$].

It follows that you can show that a relation does *not* have one of the properties by finding a counterexample.

Example 8.2.1 Properties of Relations on Finite Sets

Let $A = \{0, 1, 2, 3\}$ and define relations R, S, and T on A as follows:

$$R = \{(0, 0), (0, 1), (0, 3), (1, 0), (1, 1), (2, 2), (3, 0), (3, 3)\},$$
$$S = \{(0, 0), (0, 2), (0, 3), (2, 3)\},$$
$$T = \{(0, 1), (2, 3)\}.$$

a. Is R reflexive? symmetric? transitive?

b. Is S reflexive? symmetric? transitive?

c. Is T reflexive? symmetric? transitive?

Solution

a. The directed graph of R has the appearance shown below.

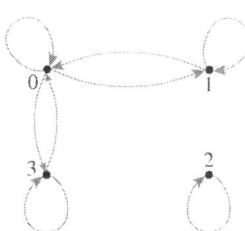

R is reflexive: There is a loop at each point of the directed graph. This means that each element of A is related to itself, so R is reflexive.

R is symmetric: In each case where there is an arrow going from one point of the graph to a second, there is an arrow going from the second point back to the first. This means that whenever one element of A is related by R to a second, then the second is related to the first. Hence R is symmetric.

R is not transitive: There is an arrow going from 1 to 0 and an arrow going from 0 to 3, but there is no arrow going from 1 to 3. This means that there are elements of A—0, 1, and 3—such that $1 \, R \, 0$ and $0 \, R \, 3$ but $1 \not{R} 3$. Hence R is not transitive.

b. The directed graph of S has the appearance shown below.

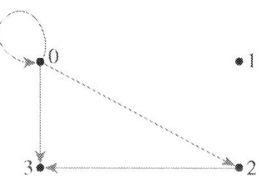

***S is not reflexive*:** There is no loop at 1, for example. Thus $(1, 1) \notin S$, and so S is not reflexive.

***S is not symmetric*:** There is an arrow from 0 to 2 but not from 2 to 0. Hence $(0, 2) \in S$ but $(2, 0) \notin S$, and so S is not symmetric.

***S is transitive*:** There are three cases for which there is an arrow going from one point of the graph to a second and from the second point to a third: Namely, there are arrows going from 0 to 2 and from 2 to 3; there are arrows going from 0 to 0 and from 0 to 2; and there are arrows going from 0 to 0 and from 0 to 3. In each case there is an arrow going from the first point to the third. (Note again that the "first," "second," and "third" points need not be distinct.) This means that whenever $(x, y) \in S$ and $(y, z) \in S$, then $(x, z) \in S$, for all $x, y, z \in \{0, 1, 2, 3\}$, and so S is transitive.

c. The directed graph of T has the appearance shown below.

***T is not reflexive*:** There is no loop at 0, for example. Thus $(0, 0) \notin T$, so T is not reflexive.

***T is not symmetric*:** There is an arrow from 0 to 1 but not from 1 to 0. Thus $(0, 1) \in T$ but $(1, 0) \notin T$, and so T is not symmetric.

Note T is transitive by default because it is *not* not transitive!

***T is transitive*:** The transitivity condition is vacuously true for T. To see this, observe that the transitivity condition says that

For all $x, y, z \in A$, if $(x, y) \in T$ and $(y, z) \in T$ then $(x, z) \in T$.

The only way for this to be false would be for there to exist elements of A that make the hypothesis true and the conclusion false. That is, there would have to be elements x, y, and z in A such that

$(x, y) \in T$ and $(y, z) \in T$ and $(x, z) \notin T$.

In other words, there would have to be two ordered pairs in T that have the potential to "link up" by having the *second* element of one pair be the *first* element of the other pair. But the only elements in T are $(0, 1)$ and $(2, 3)$, and these do not have the potential to link up. Hence the hypothesis is never true. It follows that it is impossible for T *not* to be transitive, and thus T is transitive.

When a relation R is defined on a finite set A, it is possible to write computer algorithms to check whether R is reflexive, symmetric, and transitive. One way to do this is to represent A as a one-dimensional array, $(a[1], a[2], \ldots, a[n])$ and use a modification of the algorithm of exercise 38 in Section 6.1 to check whether an ordered pair in $A \times A$ is in R. Checking whether R is reflexive can be done with a loop that examines each element $a[i]$ of A in turn. If, for some i, $(a[i], a[i]) \notin R$, then R is not reflexive. Otherwise, R is reflexive. Checking for symmetry can be done with a nested loop that examines each pair $(a[i], a[j])$ of $A \times A$ in turn. If, for some i and j, $(a[i], a[j]) \in R$ and $(a[j], a[i]) \notin R$, then R is not symmetric. Otherwise, R is symmetric. Checking whether R is transitive can be done with a triply nested loop that examines each triple $(a[i], a[j], a[k])$ of $A \times A \times A$ in turn. If, for some triple, $(a[i], a[j]) \in R$, $(a[j], a[k]) \in R$, and $(a[i], a[k]) \notin R$, then R is not transitive. Otherwise, R is transitive. In the exercises for this section, you are asked to formalize these algorithms.

Properties of Relations on Infinite Sets

Suppose a relation R is defined on an infinite set A. To prove the relation is reflexive, symmetric, or transitive, first write down what is to be proved. For instance, for symmetry you need to prove that

$$\forall x, y \in A, \text{ if } x \ R \ y \text{ then } y \ R \ x.$$

Then use the definitions of A and R to rewrite the statement for the particular case in question. For instance, for the "equality" relation on the set of real numbers, the rewritten statement is

$$\forall x, y \in \mathbf{R}, \text{ if } x = y \text{ then } y = x.$$

Sometimes the truth of the rewritten statement will be immediately obvious (as it is here). At other times you will need to prove it using the method of generalizing from the generic particular. We give examples of both cases in this section. We begin with the relation of equality, one of the simplest and yet most important relations.

Example 8.2.2 Properties of Equality

Define a relation R on $\mathbf{R}$ (the set of all real numbers) as follows: For all real numbers x and y.

$$\boxed{x \ R \ y \quad \Leftrightarrow \quad x = y.}$$

a. Is R reflexive?   b. Is R symmetric?   c, Is R transitive?

Solution

a. ***R is reflexive:*** R is reflexive if, and only if, the following statement is true:

$$\text{For all } x \in \mathbf{R}, \quad x \ R \ x.$$

Since $x \ R \ x$ just means that $x = x$, this is the same as saying

$$\text{For all } x \in \mathbf{R}, \quad x = x.$$

But this statement is certainly true; every real number is equal to itself.

b. ***R is symmetric:*** R is symmetric if, and only if, the following statement is true:

$$\text{For all } x, y \in \mathbf{R}, \quad \text{if } x \ R \ y \text{ then } y \ R \ x.$$

By definition of R, $x\ R\ y$ means that $x = y$ and $y\ R\ x$ means that $y = x$. Hence R is symmetric if, and only if,

$$\text{For all } x, y \in \mathbf{R}, \quad \text{if } x = y \text{ then } y = x.$$

But this statement is certainly true; if one number is equal to a second, then the second is equal to the first.

c. **R is transitive:** R is transitive if, and only if, the following statement is true:

$$\text{For all } x, y, z \in \mathbf{R}, \quad \text{if } x\ R\ y \text{ and } y\ R\ z \text{ then } x\ R\ z.$$

By definition of R, $x\ R\ y$ means that $x = y$, $y\ R\ z$ means that $y = z$, and $x\ R\ z$ means that $x = z$. Hence R is transitive if, and only if, the following statement is true:

$$\text{For all } x, y, z \in \mathbf{R}, \quad \text{if } x = y \text{ and } y = z \text{ then } x = z.$$

But this statement is certainly true: If one real number equals a second and the second equals a third, then the first equals the third. ■

Example 8.2.3 Properties of "Less Than"

Define a relation R on $\mathbf{R}$ (the set of all real numbers) as follows: For all $x, y \in R$,

$$\boxed{x\ R\ y \quad \Leftrightarrow \quad x < y.}$$

a. Is R reflexive?   b. Is R symmetric?   c. Is R transitive?

Solution

a. **R is not reflexive:** R is reflexive if, and only if, $\forall x \in \mathbf{R}, x\ R\ x$. By definition of R, this means that $\forall x \in \mathbf{R}, x < x$. But this is false: $\exists x \in \mathbf{R}$ such that $x \not< x$. As a counterexample, let $x = 0$ and note that $0 \not< 0$. Hence R is not reflexive.

b. **R is not symmetric:** R is symmetric if, and only if, $\forall x, y \in \mathbf{R}$, if $x\ R\ y$ then $y\ R\ x$. By definition of R, this means that $\forall x, y \in \mathbf{R}$, if $x < y$ then $y < x$. But this is false: $\exists x, y \in \mathbf{R}$ such that $x < y$ and $y \not< x$. As a counterexample, let $x = 0$ and $y = 1$ and note that $0 < 1$ but $1 \not< 0$. Hence R is not symmetric.

c. **R is transitive:** R is transitive if, and only if, for all $x, y, z \in \mathbf{R}$, if $x\ R\ y$ and $y\ R\ z$ then $x\ R\ z$. By definition of R, this means that for all $x, y, z \in \mathbf{R}$, if $x < y$ and $y < z$, then $x < z$. But this statement is true by the transitive law of order for real numbers (Appendix A, T18). Hence R is transitive. ■

Sometimes a property is "universally false" in the sense that it is false for *every* element of its domain. It follows immediately, of course, that the property is false for each particular element of the domain and hence counterexamples abound. In such a case, it may seem more natural to prove the universal falseness of the property rather than to give a single counterexample. In the example above, for instance, you might find it natural to answer (a) and (b) as follows:

Alternative Answer to (a): R is not reflexive because $x \not< x$ for all real numbers x (by the trichotomy law—Appendix A, T17).

Alternative Answer to (b): R is not symmetric because for all x and y in A, if $x < y$, then $y \not< x$ (by the trichotomy law).

Example 8.2.4 Properties of Congruence Modulo 3

Define a relation T on $\mathbf{Z}$ (the set of all integers) as follows: For all integers m and n,

$$m \; T \; n \quad \Leftrightarrow \quad 3 \mid (m - n).$$

This relation is called **congruence modulo 3.**

a. Is T reflexive?   b. Is T symmetric?   c. Is T transitive?

Solution

a. **T is reflexive:** To show that T is reflexive, it is necessary to show that

$$\text{For all } m \in \mathbf{Z}, \quad m \; T \; m.$$

By definition of T, this means that

$$\text{For all } m \in \mathbf{Z}, \quad 3 \mid (m - m).$$

Or, since $m - m = 0$,   For all $m \in \mathbf{Z}, \quad 3 \mid 0.$

But this is true: $3 \mid 0$ since $0 = 3 \cdot 0$. Hence T is reflexive. This reasoning is formalized in the following proof.

> **Proof of Reflexivity:** Suppose m is a particular but arbitrarily chosen integer. *[We must show that $m \; T \; m$.]* Now $m - m = 0$. But $3 \mid 0$ since $0 = 3 \cdot 0$. Hence $3 \mid (m - m)$. Thus, by definition of T, $m \; T \; m$ *[as was to be shown].*

b. **T is symmetric:** To show that T is symmetric, it is necessary to show that

$$\text{For all } m, n \in \mathbf{Z}, \quad \text{if } m \; T \; n \text{ then } n \; T \; m.$$

By definition of T this means that

$$\text{For all } m, n \in \mathbf{Z}, \quad \text{if } 3 \mid (m - n) \text{ then } 3 \mid (n - m).$$

Is this true? Suppose m and n are particular but arbitrarily chosen integers such that $3 \mid (m - n)$. Must it follow that $3 \mid (n - m)$? *[In other words, can we find an integer so that $n - m = 3 \cdot (that\ integer)?]* By definition of "divides," since

$$3 \mid (m - n),$$

then $m - n = 3k$ for some integer k.

The crucial observation is that $n - m = -(m - n)$. Hence, you can multiply both sides of this equation by -1 to obtain

$$-(m - n) = -3k,$$

which is equivalent to $n - m = 3(-k).$

[Thus we have found an integer, namely $-k$, so that $n - m = 3 \cdot (that\ integer).]
Since $-k$ is an integer, this equation shows that

$$3 \mid (n - m).$$

It follows that T is symmetric.
   The reasoning above is formalized in the following proof.

Proof of Symmetry: Suppose m and n are particular but arbitrarily chosen integers that satisfy the condition $m\ T\ n$. *[We must show that $n\ T\ m$.]* By definition of T, since $m\ T\ n$ then $3\,|\,(m-n)$. By definition of "divides," this means that $m-n=3k$, for some integer k. Multiplying both sides by -1 gives $n-m=3(-k)$. Since $-k$ is an integer, this equation shows that $3\,|\,(n-m)$. Hence, by definition of T, $n\ T\ m$ *[as was to be shown].*

c. **T is transitive:** To show that T is transitive, it is necessary to show that

$$\text{For all } m, n, p \in \mathbf{Z}, \quad \text{if } m\ T\ n \text{ and } n\ T\ p \text{ then } m\ T\ p.$$

By definition of T this means that

$$\text{For all } m, n \in \mathbf{Z}, \quad \text{if } 3\,|\,(m-n) \text{ and } 3\,|\,(n-p) \text{ then } 3\,|\,(m-p).$$

Is this true? Suppose $m, n,$ and p are particular but arbitrarily chosen integers such that $3\,|\,(m-n)$ and $3\,|\,(n-p)$. Must it follow that $3\,|\,(m-p)$? *[In other words, can we find an integer so that $m-p = 3 \cdot (\text{that integer})?]$* By definition of "divides," since

$$3\,|\,(m-n) \quad \text{and} \quad 3\,|\,(n-p),$$

then $$m-n = 3r \quad \text{for some integer } r,$$

and $$n-p = 3s \quad \text{for some integer } s.$$

The crucial observation is that $(m-n) + (n-p) = m-p$. Add these two equations together to obtain

$$(m-n) + (n-p) = 3r + 3s,$$

which is equivalent to $$m-p = 3(r+s).$$

[Thus we have found an integer so that $m-p = 3 \cdot (\text{that integer}).]$
Since r and s are integers, $r+s$ is an integer. So this equation shows that

$$3\,|\,(m-p).$$

It follows that T is transitive.
    The reasoning above is formalized in the following proof.

Proof of Transitivity: Suppose $m, n,$ and p are particular but arbitrarily chosen integers that satisfy the condition $m\ T\ n$ and $n\ T\ p$. *[We must show that $m\ T\ p$.]* By definition of T, since $m\ T\ n$ and $n\ T\ p$, then $3\,|\,(m-n)$ and $3\,|\,(n-p)$. By definition of "divides," this means that $m-n = 3r$ and $n-p = 3s$, for some integers r and s. Adding the two equations gives $(m-n) + (n-p) = 3r + 3s$, and simplifying gives that $m-p = 3(r+s)$. Since $r+s$ is an integer, this equation shows that $3\,|\,(m-p)$. Hence, by definition of T, $m\ T\ p$ *[as was to be shown].*

The Transitive Closure of a Relation

Generally speaking, a relation fails to be transitive because it fails to contain certain ordered pairs. For example, if $(1, 3)$ and $(3, 4)$ are in a relation R, then the pair $(1, 4)$ *must* be in R if R is to be transitive. To obtain a transitive relation from one that is not transitive, it is necessary to add ordered pairs. Roughly speaking, the relation obtained by adding the least number of ordered pairs to ensure transitivity is called the *transitive closure* of the relation. In a sense made precise by the formal definition, the transitive closure of a relation is the smallest transitive relation that contains the relation.

• Definition

Let A be a set and R a relation on A. The **transitive closure** of R is the relation R^t on A that satisfies the following three properties:

1. R^t is transitive.

2. $R \subseteq R^t$.

3. If S is any other transitive relation that contains R, then $R^t \subseteq S$.

Example 8.2.5 Transitive Closure of a Relation

Let $A = \{0, 1, 2, 3\}$ and consider the relation R defined on A as follows:

$$R = \{(0, 1), (1, 2), (2, 3)\}.$$

Find the transitive closure of R.

Solution   Every ordered pair in R is in R^t, so

$$\{(0, 1), (1, 2), (2, 3)\} \subseteq R^t.$$

Thus the directed graph of R contains the arrows shown below.

Since there are arrows going from 0 to 1 and from 1 to 2, R^t must have an arrow going from 0 to 2. Hence $(0, 2) \in R^t$. Then $(0, 2) \in R^t$ and $(2, 3) \in R^t$, so since R^t is transitive, $(0, 3) \in R^t$. Also, since $(1, 2) \in R^t$ and $(2, 3) \in R^t$, then $(1, 3) \in R^t$. Thus R^t contains at least the following ordered pairs:

$$\{(0, 1), (0, 2), (0, 3), (1, 2), (1, 3), (2, 3)\}.$$

But this relation *is* transitive; hence it equals R^t. Note that the directed graph of R^t is as shown below.

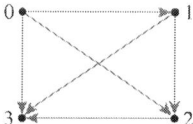

Test Yourself

1. For a relation R on a set A to be reflexive means that _____.

2. For a relation R on a set A to be symmetric means that _____.

3. For a relation R on a set A to be transitive means that _____.

4. To show that a relation R on an infinite set A is reflexive, you suppose that _____ and you show that _____.

5. To show that a relation R on an infinite set A is symmetric, you suppose that _____ and you show that _____.

6. To show that a relation R on an infinite set A is transitive, you suppose that _____ and you show that _____.

7. To show that a relation R on a set A is not reflexive, you _____.

8. To show that a relation R on a set A is not symmetric, you _____.

9. To show that a relation R on a set A is not transitive, you _____.

10. Given a relation R on a set A, the transitive closure of R is the relation R^t on A that satisfies the following three properties: _____, _____, and _____.

Exercise Set 8.2

In 1–8 a number of relations are defined on the set $A = \{0, 1, 2, 3\}$. For each relation:
a. Draw the directed graph.
b. Determine whether the relation is reflexive.
c. Determine whether the relation is symmetric.
d. Determine whether the relation is transitive.
Give a counterexample in each case in which the relation does not satisfy one of the properties.

1. $R_1 = \{(0, 0), (0, 1), (0, 3), (1, 1), (1, 0), (2, 3), (3, 3)\}$

2. $R_2 = \{(0, 0), (0, 1), (1, 1), (1, 2), (2, 2), (2, 3)\}$

3. $R_3 = \{(2, 3), (3, 2)\}$

4. $R_4 = \{(1, 2), (2, 1), (1, 3), (3, 1)\}$

5. $R_5 = \{(0, 0), (0, 1), (0, 2), (1, 2)\}$

6. $R_6 = \{(0, 1), (0, 2)\}$

7. $R_7 = \{(0, 3), (2, 3)\}$

8. $R_8 = \{(0, 0), (1, 1)\}$

In 9–33 determine whether the given relation is reflexive, symmetric, transitive, or none of these. Justify your answers.

9. R is the "greater than or equal to" relation on the set of real numbers: For all $x, y \in \mathbf{R}$, $x \, R \, y \Leftrightarrow x \geq y$.

10. C is the circle relation on the set of real numbers: For all $x, y \in \mathbf{R}$, $x \, C \, y \Leftrightarrow x^2 + y^2 = 1$.

11. D is the relation defined on $\mathbf{R}$ as follows: For all $x, y \in \mathbf{R}$, $x \, D \, y \Leftrightarrow xy \geq 0$.

12. E is the congruence modulo 2 relation on $\mathbf{Z}$: For all $m, n \in \mathbf{Z}$, $m \, E \, n \Leftrightarrow 2 \mid (m - n)$.

13. F is the congruence modulo 5 relation on $\mathbf{Z}$: For all $m, n \in \mathbf{Z}$, $m \, F \, n \Leftrightarrow 5 \mid (m - n)$.

14. A is the "absolute value" relation on $\mathbf{R}$: For all real numbers x and y, $x \, A \, y \Leftrightarrow |x| = |y|$.

15. D is the "divides" relation on $\mathbf{Z}^+$: For all positive integers m and n, $m \, D \, n \Leftrightarrow m \mid n$.

16. O is the relation defined on $\mathbf{Z}$ as follows: For all $m, n \in \mathbf{Z}$, $m \, O \, n \Leftrightarrow m - n$ is odd.

17. Recall that a prime number is an integer that is greater than 1 and has no positive integer divisors other than 1 and itself. (In particular, 1 is not prime.) A relation P is defined on $\mathbf{Z}$ as follows: For all $m, n \in \mathbf{Z}$, $m \, P \, n \Leftrightarrow \exists$ a prime number p such that $p \mid m$ and $p \mid n$.

H 18. Define a relation Q on $\mathbf{R}$ as follows: For all real numbers x and y, $x \, Q \, y \Leftrightarrow x - y$ is rational.

19. Define a relation I on $\mathbf{R}$ as follows: For all real numbers x and y, $x \, I \, y \Leftrightarrow x - y$ is irrational.

20. Let $X = \{a, b, c\}$ and $\mathscr{P}(X)$ be the power set of X (the set of all subsets of X). A relation $\mathbf{E}$ is defined on $\mathscr{P}(X)$ as follows: For all $A, B \in \mathscr{P}(X)$, $A \, \mathbf{E} \, B \Leftrightarrow$ the number of elements in A equals the number of elements in B.

21. Let $X = \{a, b, c\}$ and $\mathscr{P}(X)$ be the power set of X. A relation $\mathbf{L}$ is defined on $\mathscr{P}(X)$ as follows: For all $A, B \in \mathscr{P}(X)$, $A \, \mathbf{L} \, B \Leftrightarrow$ the number of elements in A is less than the number of elements in B.

22. Let $X = \{a, b, c\}$ and $\mathscr{P}(X)$ be the power set of X. A relation $\mathbf{N}$ is defined on $\mathscr{P}(X)$ as follows: For all $A, B \in \mathscr{P}(X)$, $A \, \mathbf{N} \, B \Leftrightarrow$ the number of elements in A is not equal to the number of elements in B.

23. Let X be a nonempty set and $\mathscr{P}(X)$ the power set of X. Define the "subset" relation $\mathbf{S}$ on $\mathscr{P}(X)$ as follows: For all $A, B \in \mathscr{P}(X)$, $A \, \mathbf{S} \, B \Leftrightarrow A \subseteq B$.

24. Let X be a nonempty set and $\mathscr{P}(X)$ the power set of X. Define the "not equal to" relation $\mathbf{U}$ on $\mathscr{P}(X)$ as follows: For all $A, B \in \mathscr{P}(X)$, $A \, \mathbf{U} \, B \Leftrightarrow A \neq B$.

25. Let A be the set of all strings of a's and b's of length 4. Define a relation R on A as follows: For all $s, t \in A$, $s \, R \, t \Leftrightarrow s$ has the same first two characters as t.

26. Let A be the set of all strings of 0's, 1's and 2's of length 4. Define a relation R on A as follows: For all $s, t \in A$, $s \, R \, t \Leftrightarrow$ the sum of the characters in s equals the sum of the characters in t.

27. Let A be the set of all English statements. A relation $\mathbf{I}$ is defined on A as follows: For all $p, q \in A$,

$$p \, \mathbf{I} \, q \Leftrightarrow p \rightarrow q \text{ is true.}$$

28. Let $A = \mathbf{R} \times \mathbf{R}$. A relation $\mathbf{F}$ is defined on A as follows: For all (x_1, y_1) and (x_2, y_2) in A,

$$(x_1, y_1) \, \mathbf{F} \, (x_2, y_2) \Leftrightarrow x_1 = x_2.$$

29. Let $A = \mathbf{R} \times \mathbf{R}$. A relation $\mathbf{S}$ is defined on A as follows: For all (x_1, y_1) and (x_2, y_2) in A,

$$(x_1, y_1) \, \mathbf{S} \, (x_2, y_2) \Leftrightarrow y_1 = y_2.$$

30. Let A be the "punctured plane"; that is, A is the set of all points in the Cartesian plane except the origin $(0, 0)$. A relation R is defined on A as follows: For all p_1 and p_2 in A, $p_1 \, R \, p_2 \Leftrightarrow p_1$ and p_2 lie on the same half line emanating from the origin.

31. Let A be the set of people living in the world today. A relation R is defined on A as follows: For all $p, q \in A$, $p \, R \, q \Leftrightarrow p$ lives within 100 miles of q.

32. Let A be the set of all lines in the plane. A relation R is defined on A as follows: For all l_1 and l_2 in A, $l_1 \, R \, l_2 \Leftrightarrow l_1$ is parallel to l_2. (Assume that a line is parallel to itself.)

33. Let A be the set of all lines in the plane. A relation R is defined on A as follows: For all l_1 and l_2 in A,
$$l_1 \, R \, l_2 \Leftrightarrow l_1 \text{ is perpendicular to } l_2.$$

In 34–36, assume that R is a relation on a set A. Prove or disprove each statement.

34. If R is reflexive, then R^{-1} is reflexive.

35. If R is symmetric, then R^{-1} is symmetric.

36. If R is transitive, then R^{-1} is transitive.

In 37–42, assume that R and S are relations on a set A. Prove or disprove each statement.

37. If R and S are reflexive, is $R \cap S$ reflexive? Why?

H 38. If R and S are symmetric, is $R \cap S$ symmetric? Why?

39. If R and S are transitive, is $R \cap S$ transitive? Why?

40. If R and S are reflexive, is $R \cup S$ reflexive? Why?

41. If R and S are symmetric, is $R \cup S$ symmetric? Why?

42. If R and S are transitive, is $R \cup S$ transitive? Why?

In 43–50 the following definitions are used: A relation on a set A is defined to be

irreflexive if, and only if, for all $x \in A$, $x \not\!R \, x$;

asymmetric if, and only if, for all $x, y \in A$, if $x \, R \, y$ then $y \not\!R \, x$;

intransitive if, and only if, for all $x, y, z \in A$, if $x \, R \, y$ and $y \, R \, z$ then $x \not\!R \, z$.

For each of the relations in the referenced exercise, determine whether the relation is irreflexive, asymmetric, intransitive, or none of these.

43. Exercise 1   44. Exercise 2

45. Exercise 3   46. Exercise 4

47. Exercise 5   48. Exercise 6

49. Exercise 7   50. Exercise 8

In 51–53, R, S, and T are relations defined on $A = \{0, 1, 2, 3\}$.

51. Let $R = \{(0, 1), (0, 2), (1, 1), (1, 3), (2, 2), (3, 0)\}$. Find R^t, the transitive closure of R.

52. Let $T = \{(0, 2), (1, 0), (2, 3), (3, 1)\}$. Find T^t, the transitive closure of T.

53. Let $S = \{(0, 0), (0, 3), (1, 0), (1, 2), (2, 0), (3, 2)\}$. Find S^t, the transitive closure of S.

54. Write a computer algorithm to test whether a relation R defined on a finite set A is reflexive, where $A = \{a[1], a[2], \ldots, a[n]\}$.

55. Write a computer algorithm to test whether a relation R defined on a finite set A is symmetric, where $A = \{a[1], a[2], \ldots, a[n]\}$.

56. Write a computer algorithm to test whether a relation R defined on a finite set A is transitive, where $A = \{a[1], a[2], \ldots, a[n]\}$.

Answers for Test Yourself

1. for all x in A, $x \, R \, x$ 2. for all x and y in A, if $x \, R \, y$ then $y \, R \, x$ 3. for all x, y, and z in A, if $x \, R \, y$ and $y \, R \, z$ then $x \, R \, z$ 4. x is any element of A; $x \, R \, x$ 5. x and y are any elements of A such that $x \, R \, y$; $y \, R \, x$ 6. x, y, and z are any elements of A such that $x \, R \, y$ and $y \, R \, z$; $x \, R \, z$ 7. show that there is an element x in A such that $x \not\!R \, x$ 8. show that there are elements x and y in A such that $x \, R \, y$ but $y \not\!R \, x$ 9. show that there are elements x, y, and z in A such that $x \, R \, y$ and $y \, R \, z$ but $x \not\!R \, z$ 10. R^t is transitive; $R \subseteq R^t$; if S is any other transitive relation that contains R, then $R^t \subseteq S$

8.3 Equivalence Relations

"You are sad" the Knight said in an anxious tone: "let me sing you a song to comfort you."

"Is it very long?" Alice asked, for she had heard a good deal of poetry that day.

"It's long," said the Knight, "but it's very, very beautiful. Everybody that hears me sing it—either it brings the tears into the eyes, or else—"

"Or else what?" said Alice, for the Knight had made a sudden pause.

"Or else it doesn't, you know. The name of the song is called 'Haddocks' Eyes.'"

"Oh, that's the name of the song, is it?" Alice said, trying to feel interested.

"No, you don't understand," the Knight said, looking a little vexed. "That's what the name is called. *The name really is 'The Aged Aged Man.' "*

"Then I ought to have said 'That's what the song is called'?" Alice corrected herself.

"No, you oughtn't: that's quite another thing! The song is called 'Ways and Means': but that's only what it's called, *you know!"*

"Well, what is *the song, then?" said Alice, who was by this time completely bewildered.*

"I was coming to that," the Knight said. "The song really is 'A-sitting on a Gate': and the tune's my own invention."

So saying, he stopped his horse and let the reins fall on its neck: then, slowly beating time with one hand, and with a faint smile lighting up his gentle foolish face, as if he enjoyed the music of his song, he began.

— Lewis Carroll, *Through the Looking Glass*, 1872

You know from your early study of fractions that each fraction has many equivalent forms. For example,

$$\frac{1}{2}, \frac{2}{4}, \frac{3}{6}, \frac{-1}{-2}, \frac{-3}{-6}, \frac{15}{30}, \ldots, \text{ and so on}$$

are all different ways to represent the same number. They may look different; they may be called different names; but they are all equal. The idea of grouping together things that "look different but are really the same" is the central idea of equivalence relations.

The Relation Induced by a Partition

A **partition** of a set A is a finite or infinite collection of nonempty, mutually disjoint subsets whose union is A. The diagram of Figure 8.3.1 illustrates a partition of a set A by subsets $A_1, A_2, \ldots, A_6$.

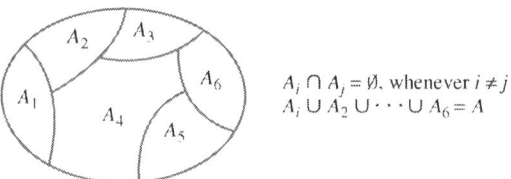

$A_i \cap A_j = \emptyset$, whenever $i \neq j$
$A_i \cup A_2 \cup \cdots \cup A_6 = A$

Figure 8.3.1 A Partition of a Set

• Definition

Given a partition of a set A, the **relation induced by the partition,** R, is defined on A as follows: For all $x, y \in A$,

$$x \mathrel{R} y \quad \Leftrightarrow \quad \text{there is a subset } A_i \text{ of the partition such that both } x \text{ and } y \text{ are in } A_i.$$

Example 8.3.1 Relation Induced by a Partition

Let $A = \{0, 1, 2, 3, 4\}$ and consider the following partition of A:

$$\{0, 3, 4\}, \{1\}, \{2\}.$$

Find the relation R induced by this partition.

Solution   Since {0, 3, 4} is a subset of the partition,

$$0 \; R \; 3 \quad \text{because both 0 and 3 are in } \{0, 3, 4\},$$
$$3 \; R \; 0 \quad \text{because both 3 and 0 are in } \{0, 3, 4\},$$
$$0 \; R \; 4 \quad \text{because both 0 and 4 are in } \{0, 3, 4\},$$
$$4 \; R \; 0 \quad \text{because both 4 and 0 are in } \{0, 3, 4\},$$
$$3 \; R \; 4 \quad \text{because both 3 and 4 are in } \{0, 3, 4\}, \quad \text{and}$$
$$4 \; R \; 3 \quad \text{because both 4 and 3 are in } \{0, 3, 4\}.$$

Note   These statements may seem strange, but, after all, they are not false!

Also,

$$0 \; R \; 0 \quad \text{because both 0 and 0 are in } \{0, 3, 4\}$$
$$3 \; R \; 3 \quad \text{because both 3 and 3 are in } \{0, 3, 4\}, \quad \text{and}$$
$$4 \; R \; 4 \quad \text{because both 4 and 4 are in } \{0, 3, 4\}.$$

Since {1} is a subset of the partition,

$$1 \; R \; 1 \quad \text{because both 1 and 1 are in } \{1\},$$

and since {2} is a subset of the partition,

$$2 \; R \; 2 \quad \text{because both 2 and 2 are in } \{2\}.$$

Hence

$$R = \{(0, 0), (0, 3), (0, 4), (1, 1), (2, 2), (3, 0), (3, 3), (3, 4), (4, 0), (4, 3), (4, 4)\}. \quad \blacksquare$$

The fact is that a relation induced by a partition of a set satisfies all three properties studied in Section 8.2: reflexivity, symmetry, and transitivity.

Theorem 8.3.1

Let A be a set with a partition and let R be the relation induced by the partition. Then R is reflexive, symmetric, and transitive.

Proof:

Suppose A is a set with a partition. In order to simplify notation, we assume that the partition consists of only a finite number of sets. The proof for an infinite partition is identical except for notation. Denote the partition subsets by

$$A_1, A_2, \ldots, A_n.$$

Then $A_i \cap A_j = \emptyset$ whenever $i \neq j$, and $A_1 \cup A_2 \cup \cdots \cup A_n = A$. The relation R induced by the partition is defined as follows: For all $x, y \in A$,

$$x \; R \; y \quad \Leftrightarrow \quad \text{there is a set } A_i \text{ of the partition such that } x \in A_i \text{ and } y \in A_i.$$

[Idea for the proof of reflexivity: For R to be reflexive means that each element of A is related by R to itself. But by definition of R, for an element x to be related to itself means that x is in the same subset of the partition as itself. Well, if x is in some subset of the partition, then it is certainly in the same subset as itself. But x is in some subset of the

continued on page 462

partition because the union of the subsets of the partition is all of A. This reasoning is formalized as follows.]

Proof that R is reflexive: Suppose $x \in A$. Since $A_1, A_2, \ldots, A_n$ is a partition of A, it follows that $x \in A_i$ for some i. But then the statement

there is a set A_i of the partition such that $x \in A_i$ and $x \in A_i$

is true. Thus, by definition of R, $x \ R \ x$.

Note The fact that $x \in A_i$ and $x \in A_i$ follows from the logical equivalence of the statement forms p and $p \wedge p$.

[Idea for the proof of symmetry: For R to be symmetric means that any time one element is related to a second, then the second is related to the first. Now for one element x to be related to a second element y means that x and y are in the same subset of the partition. But if this is the case, then y is in the same subset of the partition as x, so y is related to x by definition of R. This reasoning is formalized as follows.]

Proof that R is symmetric: Suppose x and y are elements of A such that $x \ R \ y$. Then

there is a subset A_i of the partition such that $x \in A_i$ and $y \in A_i$

by definition of R. It follows that the statement

there is a subset A_i of the partition such that $y \in A_i$ and $x \in A_i$

is also true. Hence, by definition of R, $y \ R \ x$.

Note The fact that $y \in A_i$ and $x \in A_i$ follows from the logical equivalence of the statement forms $p \wedge q$ and $q \wedge p$.

[Idea for the proof of transitivity: For R to be transitive means that any time one element of A is related by R to a second and that second is related to a third, then the first element is related to the third. But for one element to be related to another means that there is a subset of the partition that contains both. So suppose x, y, and z are elements such that x is in the same subset as y and y is in the same subset as z. Must x be in the same subset as z? Yes, because the subsets of the partition are mutually disjoint. Since the subset that contains x and y has an element in common with the subset that contains y and z (namely y), the two subsets are equal. But this means that x, y, and z are all in the same subset, and so in particular, x and z are in the same subset. Hence x is related by R to z. This reasoning is formalized as follows.]

Proof that R is transitive: Suppose x, y, and z are in A and $x \ R \ y$ and $y \ R \ z$. By definition of R, there are subsets A_i and A_j of the partition such that

$$x \text{ and } y \text{ are in } A_i \quad \text{and} \quad y \text{ and } z \text{ are in } A_j.$$

Suppose $A_i \neq A_j$. *[We will deduce a contradiction.]* Then $A_i \cap A_j = \emptyset$ since $\{A_1, A_2, A_3, \ldots, A_n\}$ is a partition of A. But y is in A_i and y is in A_j also. Hence $A_i \cap A_j \neq \emptyset$. *[This contradicts the fact that $A_i \cap A_j = \emptyset$.]* Thus $A_i = A_j$. It follows that x, y, and z are all in A_i, and so in particular,

$$x \text{ and } z \text{ are in } A_i.$$

Thus, by definition of R, $x \ R \ z$.

Definition of an Equivalence Relation

A relation on a set that satisfies the three properties of reflexivity, symmetry, and transitivity is called an *equivalence relation*.

• Definition

Let A be a set and R a relation on A. R is an **equivalence relation** if, and only if, R is reflexive, symmetric, and transitive.

Thus, according to Theorem 8.3.1, the relation induced by a partition is an equivalence relation. A variety of additional examples of equivalence relations are given below and in the exercises.

Example 8.3.2 An Equivalence Relation on a Set of Subsets

Let X be the set of all nonempty subsets of $\{1, 2, 3\}$. Then

$$X = \{\{1\}, \{2\}, \{3\}, \{1, 2\}, \{1, 3\}, \{2, 3\}, \{1, 2, 3\}\}$$

Define a relation **R** on X as follows: For all A and B in X,

$$A \textbf{ R } B \Leftrightarrow \text{the least element of } A \text{ equals the least element of } B.$$

Prove that **R** is an equivalence relation on X.

Solution

R *is reflexive:* Suppose A is a nonempty subset of $\{1, 2, 3\}$. *[We must show that A **R** A.]* It is true to say that the least element of A equals the least element of A. Thus, by definition of R, A **R** A.

R *is symmetric:* Suppose A and B are nonempty subsets of $\{1, 2, 3\}$ and A **R** B. *[We must show that B **R** A.]* Since A **R** B, the least element of A equals the least element of B. But this implies that the least element of B equals the least element of A, and so, by definition of **R**, B **R** A.

R *is transitive:* Suppose A, B, and C are nonempty subsets of $\{1, 2, 3\}$, A **R** B, and B R C. *[We must show that A **R** C.]* Since A **R** B, the least element of A equals the least element of B and since B **R** C, the least element of B equals the least element of C. Thus the least element of A equals the least element of C, and so, by definition of **R**, A **R** C. ∎

Example 8.3.3 Equivalence of Digital Logic Circuits Is an Equivalence Relation

Let S be the set of all digital logic circuits with a fixed number n of inputs. Define a relation **E** on S as follows: For all circuits C_1 and C_2 in S,

$$C_1 \textbf{ E } C_2 \quad \Leftrightarrow \quad C_1 \text{ has the same input/output table as } C_2.$$

If C_1 **E** C_2, then circuit C_1 is said to be *equivalent* to circuit C_2. Prove that **E** is an equivalence relation on S.

Solution

E *is reflexive:* Suppose C is a digital logic circuit in S. *[We must show that C **E** C.]* Certainly C has the same input/output table as itself. Thus, by definition of **E**, C **E** C *[as was to be shown]*.

E *is symmetric:* Suppose C_1 and C_2 are digital logic circuits in S such that C_1 **E** C_2. *[We must show that C_2 **E** C_1.]* By definition of **E**, since C_1 **E** C_2, then C_1 has the same input/output table as C_2. It follows that C_2 has the same input/output table as C_1. Hence, by definition of **E**, C_2 **E** C_1 *[as was to be shown]*.

E *is transitive*: Suppose $C_1, C_2,$ and C_3 are digital logic circuits in S such that C_1 **E** C_2 and C_2 **E** C_3. *[We must show that C_1 **E** C_3.]* By definition of **E**, since C_1 **E** C_2 and C_2 **E** C_3, then

$$C_1 \text{ has the same input/output table as } C_2$$

and $\qquad\qquad C_2$ has the same input/output table as C_3.

It follows that $\qquad\qquad C_1$ has the same input/output table as C_3.

Hence, by definition of **E**, C_1 **E** C_3 *[as was to be shown]*.

Since **E** is reflexive, symmetric, and transitive, **E** is an equivalence relation on S. ■

Certain implementations of computer languages do not place a limit on the allowable length of an identifier. This permits a programmer to be as precise as necessary in naming variables without having to worry about exceeding length limitations. However, compilers for such languages often ignore all but some specified number of initial characters: As far as the compiler is concerned, two identifiers are the same if they have the same initial characters, even though they may look different to a human reader of the program. For example, to a compiler that ignores all but the first eight characters of an identifier, the following identifiers would be the same:

NumberOfScrews   NumberOfBolts.

Obviously, in using such a language, the programmer has to be sure to avoid giving two distinct identifiers the same first eight characters. When a compiler lumps identifiers together in this way, it sets up an equivalence relation on the set of all possible identifiers in the language. Such a relation is described in the next example.

Example 8.3.4 A Relation on a Set of Identifiers

Let L be the set of all allowable identifiers in a certain computer language, and define a relation R on L as follows: For all strings s and t in L,

> $s \, R \, t \quad \Leftrightarrow \quad$ the first eight characters of s equal the first eight characters of t.

Prove that R is an equivalence relation on L.

Solution

***R is reflexive*:** Let $s \in L$. *[We must show that $s \, R \, s$.]* Clearly s has the same first eight characters as itself. Thus, by definition of R, $s \, R \, s$ *[as was to be shown]*.

***R is symmetric*:** Let s and t be in L and suppose that $s \, R \, t$. *[We must show that $t \, R \, s$.]* By definition of R, since $s \, R \, t$, the first eight characters of s equal the first eight characters of t. But then the first eight characters of t equal the first eight characters of s. And so, by definition of R, $t \, R \, s$ *[as was to be shown]*.

R is transitive: Let s, t, and u be in L and suppose that $s \; R \; t$ and $t \; R \; u$. *[We must show that $s \; R \; u$.]* By definition of R, since $s \; R \; t$ and $t \; R \; u$, the first eight characters of s equal the first eight characters of t, and the first eight characters of t equal the first eight characters of u. Hence the first eight characters of s equal the first eight characters of u. Thus, by definition of R, $s \; R \; u$ *[as was to be shown].*

Since R is reflexive, symmetric, and transitive, R is an equivalence relation on L. ■

Equivalence Classes of an Equivalence Relation

Suppose there is an equivalence relation on a certain set. If a is any particular element of the set, then one can ask, "What is the subset of all elements that are related to a?" This subset is called the *equivalence class* of a.

Note Be careful to distinguish among the following: a relation on a set, the (underlying) set itself, and the equivalence class for an element of the (underlying) set.

> **• Definition**
>
> Suppose A is a set and R is an equivalence relation on A. For each element a in A, the **equivalence class of a,** denoted **[a]** and called the **class of a** for short, is the set of all elements x in A such that x is related to a by R.
>
> In symbols:
>
> $$[a] = \{x \in A \mid x \; R \; a\}$$

When several equivalence relations on a set are under discussion, the notation $[a]_R$ is often used to denote the equivalence class of a under R.

The procedural version of this definition is

$$\text{for all } x \in A, \quad x \in [a] \quad \Leftrightarrow \quad x \; R \; a.$$

Example 8.3.5 Equivalence Classes of a Relation Given as a set of Ordered Pairs

Let $A = \{0, 1, 2, 3, 4\}$ and define a relation R on A as follows:

$$R = \{(0, 0), (0, 4), (1, 1), (1, 3), (2, 2), (3, 1), (3, 3), (4, 0), (4, 4)\}.$$

The directed graph for R is as shown below. As can be seen by inspection, R is an equivalence relation on A. Find the distinct equivalence classes of R.

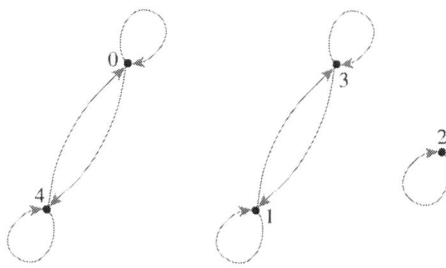

Solution First find the equivalence class of every element of A.

$$[0] = \{x \in A \mid x \ R \ 0\} = \{0, 4\}$$
$$[1] = \{x \in A \mid x \ R \ 1\} = \{1, 3\}$$
$$[2] = \{x \in A \mid x \ R \ 2\} = \{2\}$$
$$[3] = \{x \in A \mid x \ R \ 3\} = \{1, 3\}$$
$$[4] = \{x \in A \mid x \ R \ 4\} = \{0, 4\}$$

Note that $[0] = [4]$ and $[1] = [3]$. Thus the *distinct* equivalence classes of the relation are

$$\{0, 4\}, \{1, 3\}, \text{ and } \{2\}.$$

When a problem asks you to find the *distinct* equivalence classes of an equivalence relation, you will generally solve the problem in two steps. In the first step you either explicitly construct (as in Example 8.3.5) or imagine constructing (as in infinite cases) the equivalence class for every element of the domain A of the relation. Usually several of the classes will contain exactly the same elements, so in the second step you must take a careful look at the classes to determine which are the same. You then indicate the distinct equivalence classes by describing them without duplication.

Example 8.3.6 Equivalence Classes of a Relation on a Set of Subsets

In Example 8.3.2 it was shown that the relation **R** was an equivalence relation, where for nonempty subsets A and B of $\{1, 2, 3\}$ to be related by **R** means that they have the same least element. Describe the distinct equivalence classes of **R**.

Solution The equivalence class of $\{1\}$ is the set of all the nonempty subsets of $\{1, 2, 3\}$ whose least element is 1. Thus

$$[\{1\}] = \{\{1\}, \{1, 2\}, \{1, 3\}, \{1, 2, 3\}\}.$$

The equivalence class of $\{2\}$ is the set of all the nonempty subsets of $\{1, 2, 3\}$ whose least element is 2. Thus

$$[\{2\}] = \{\{2\}, \{2, 3\}\}.$$

The equivalence class of $\{3\}$ is the set of all the nonempty subsets of $\{1, 2, 3\}$ whose least element is 3. There is only one such set, namely $\{3\}$ itself. Thus

$$[\{3\}] = \{\{3\}\}.$$

Since all the nonempty subsets of $\{1, 2, 3\}$ are in one of the equivalence classes, this is a complete listing. Moreover, these classes are all distinct.

Example 8.3.7 Equivalence Classes of Identifiers

In Example 8.3.4 it was shown that the relation R of having the same first eight characters is an equivalence relation on the set L of allowable identifiers in a computer language. Describe the distinct equivalence classes of R.

Solution By definition of R, two strings in L are related by R if, and only if, they have the same first eight characters. Given any string s in L,

$$[s] = \{t \in L \mid t \ R \ s\}$$
$$= \{t \in L \mid \text{the first eight characters of } t \text{ equal the first eight characters of } s\}.$$

Thus the distinct equivalence classes of R are sets of strings such that (1) each class consists entirely of strings all of which have the same first eight characters, and (2) any two distinct classes contain strings that differ somewhere in their first eight characters.

Example 8.3.8 Equivalence Classes of the Identity Relation

Let A be any set and define a relation R on A as follows: For all x and y in A,

$$x \; R \; y \quad \Leftrightarrow \quad x = y.$$

Then R is an equivalence relation. *[To prove this, just generalize the argument used in Example 8.2.2.]* Describe the distinct equivalence classes of R.

Solution   Given any a in A, the class of a is

$$[a] = \{x \in A \mid x \; R \; a\}.$$

But by definition of R, $a \; R \; x$ if, and only if, $a = x$. So

$$[a] = \{x \in A \mid x = a\}$$
$$= \{a\} \qquad \text{since the only element of } A \text{ that equals } a \text{ is } a.$$

Hence, given any a in A,

$$[a] = \{a\},$$

and if $x \neq a$, then $\{x\} \neq \{a\}$. Consequently, all the classes of all the elements of A are distinct, and the distinct equivalence classes of R are all the single-element subsets of A.

In each of Examples 8.3.5, 8.3.6, 8.3.7 and 8.3.8, the set of distinct equivalence classes of the relation consists of mutually disjoint subsets whose union is the entire domain A of the relation. This means that the set of equivalence classes of the relation forms a partition of the domain A. In fact, it is always the case that the equivalence classes of an equivalence relation partition the domain of the relation into a union of mutually disjoint subsets. We establish the truth of this statement in stages, first proving two lemmas and then proving the main theorem.

The first lemma says that if two elements of A are related by an equivalence relation R, then their equivalence classes are the same.

Lemma 8.3.2

Suppose A is a set, R is an equivalence relation on A, and a and b are elements of A. If $a \; R \; b$, then $[a] = [b]$.

This lemma says that if a certain condition is satisfied, then $[a] = [b]$. Now $[a]$ and $[b]$ are *sets,* and two sets are equal if, and only if, each is a subset of the other. Hence the proof of the lemma consists of two parts: first, a proof that $[a] \subseteq [b]$ and second, a proof that $[b] \subseteq [a]$. To show each subset relation, it is necessary to show that every element in the left-hand set is an element of the right-hand set.

Proof of Lemma 8.3.2:

Let A be a set, let R be an equivalence relation on A, and suppose

a and b are elements of A such that $a\ R\ b$.

[We must show that $[a] = [b]$.]

Proof that $[a] \subseteq [b]$: Let $x \in [a]$. *[We must show that $x \in [b]$.]* Since

$$x \in [a]$$

then $\qquad\qquad\qquad\qquad\qquad x\ R\ a$

by definition of class. But $\qquad\qquad a\ R\ b$

by hypothesis. Thus, by transitivity of R,

$$x\ R\ b.$$

Hence $\qquad\qquad\qquad\qquad\qquad x \in [b]$

by definition of class. *[This is what was to be shown.]*

Proof that $[b] \subseteq [a]$: Let $x \in [b]$. *[We must show that $x \in [a]$.]* Since

$$x \in [b]$$

then $\qquad\qquad\qquad\qquad\qquad x\ R\ b$

by definition of class. Now $\qquad\qquad a\ R\ b$

by hypothesis. Thus, since R is symmetric,

$$b\ R\ a$$

also. Then, since R is transitive and $x\ R\ b$ and $b\ R\ a$,

$$x\ R\ a.$$

Hence, $\qquad\qquad\qquad\qquad\qquad x \in [a]$

by definition of class. *[This is what was to be shown.]*

Since $[a] \subseteq [b]$ and $[b] \subseteq [a]$, it follows that $[a] = [b]$ by definition of set equality.

The second lemma says that any two equivalence classes of an equivalence relation are either mutually disjoint or identical.

Lemma 8.3.3

If A is a set, R is an equivalence relation on A, and a and b are elements of A, then

$$\text{either} \quad [a] \cap [b] = \emptyset \quad \text{or} \quad [a] = [b].$$

The statement of Lemma 8.3.3 has the form

$$\text{if } p \text{ then } (q \text{ or } r),$$

Note You can always prove a statement of the form "if p then (q or r)" by proving one of the logically equivalent statements: "if (p and not q) then r" or "if (p and not r) then q."*

where p is the statement "A is a set, R is an equivalence relation on A, and a and b are elements of A," q is the statement "$[a] \cap [b] = \emptyset$," and r is the statement "$[a] = [b]$." To prove the lemma, we will prove the logically equivalent statement

$$\text{if } (p \text{ and not } q) \text{ then } r.$$

That is, we will prove the following:

> If A is a set, R is an equivalence relation on A, a and b are elements of A, and $[a] \cap [b] \neq \emptyset$, then $[a] = [b]$.

Proof of Lemma 8.3.3:

Suppose A is a set, R is an equivalence relation on A, a and b are elements of A, and

$$[a] \cap [b] \neq \emptyset.$$

[We must show that $[a] = [b]$.] Since $[a] \cap [b] \neq \emptyset$, there exists an element x in A such that $x \in [a] \cap [b]$. By definition of intersection,

$$x \in [a] \quad \text{and} \quad x \in [b]$$

and so
$$x \ R \ a \quad \text{and} \quad x \ R \ b$$

by definition of class. Since R is symmetric *[being an equivalence relation]* and $x \ R \ a$, then $a \ R \ x$. But R is also transitive *[since it is an equivalence relation]*, and so, since $a \ R \ x$ and $x \ R \ b$,

$$a \ R \ b.$$

Now a and b satisfy the hypothesis of Lemma 8.3.2. Hence, by that lemma,

$$[a] = [b].$$

[This is what was to be shown.]

Theorem 8.3.4 The Partition Induced by an Equivalence Relation

If A is a set and R is an equivalence relation on A, then the distinct equivalence classes of R form a partition of A; that is, the union of the equivalence classes is all of A, and the intersection of any two distinct classes is empty.

The proof of Theorem 8.3.4 is divided into two parts: first, a proof that A is the union of the equivalence classes of R and second, a proof that the intersection of any two distinct equivalence classes is empty. The proof of the first part follows from the fact that the relation is reflexive. The proof of the second part follows from Lemma 8.3.3.

Proof of Theorem 8.3.4:

Suppose A is a set and R is an equivalence relation on A. For notational simplicity, we assume that R has only a finite number of distinct equivalence classes, which we denote

$$A_1, A_2, \ldots, A_n,$$

continued on page 470

---

* See exercise 14 in Section 2.2.

where n is a positive integer. (When the number of classes is infinite, the proof is identical except for notation.)

Proof that $A = A_1 \cup A_2 \cup \cdots \cup A_n$: *[We must show that $A \subseteq A_1 \cup A_2 \cup \cdots \cup A_n$ and that $A_1 \cup A_2 \cup \cdots \cup A_n \subseteq A.$]*

To show that $A \subseteq A_1 \cup A_2 \cup \cdots \cup A_n$, suppose x is any element of A. *[We must show that $x \in A_1 \cup A_2 \cup \cdots \cup A_n$.]* By reflexivity of R, $x \mathbin{R} x$. But this implies that $x \in [x]$ by definition of class. Since x is in *some* equivalence class, it must be in one of the distinct equivalence classes $A_1, A_2, \ldots,$ or A_n. Thus $x \in A_i$ for some index i, and hence $x \in A_1 \cup A_2 \cup \cdots \cup A_n$ by definition of union *[as was to be shown]*.

To show that $A_1 \cup A_2 \cup \cdots \cup A_n \subseteq A$, suppose $x \in A_1 \cup A_2 \cup \cdots \cup A_n$. *[We must show that $x \in A$.]* Then $x \in A_i$ for some $i = 1, 2, \ldots, n$, by definition of union. But each A_i is an equivalence class of R. And equivalence classes are subsets of A. Hence $A_i \subseteq A$ and so $x \in A$ *[as was to be shown]*.

Since $A \subseteq A_1 \cup A_2 \cup \cdots \cup A_n$ and $A_1 \cup A_2 \cup \cdots \cup A_n \subseteq A$, then by definition of set equality, $A = A_1 \cup A_2 \cup \cdots \cup A_n$.

Proof that the distinct classes of R are mutually disjoint: Suppose that A_i and A_j are any two distinct equivalence classes of R. *[We must show that A_i and A_j are disjoint.]* Since A_i and A_j are distinct, then $A_i \neq A_j$. And since A_i and A_j are equivalence classes of R, there must exist elements a and b in A such that $A_i = [a]$ and $A_j = [b]$. By Lemma 8.3.3,

$$\text{either} \quad [a] \cap [b] = \emptyset \quad \text{or} \quad [a] = [b].$$

But $[a] \neq [b]$ because $A_i \neq A_j$. Hence $[a] \cap [b] = \emptyset$. Thus $A_i \cap A_j = \emptyset$, and so A_i and A_j are disjoint *[as was to be shown]*.

Example 8.3.9 Equivalence Classes of Digital Logic Circuits

In Example 8.3.3 it was shown that the relation of equivalence among circuits is an equivalence relation. Let S be the set of all digital logic circuits with exactly two inputs and one output. The binary relation **E** is defined on S as follows: For all C_1 and C_2 in S,

$$C_1 \mathbf{E} C_2 \quad \Leftrightarrow \quad C_1 \text{ has the same input/output table as } C_2.$$

Describe the equivalence classes of this relation. How many distinct equivalence classes are there? Find two different circuits that are in one of the classes.

Solution   Given a circuit C, the equivalence class of C is the set of all circuits with two input signals and one output signal that have the same input/output table as C. Now each input/output table has exactly four rows, corresponding to the four possible combinations of inputs: 11, 10, 01, and 00. A typical input/output table is the following:

Input		Output
P	**Q**	**R**
1	1	0
1	0	0
0	1	0
0	0	1

There are exactly as many such tables as there are binary strings of length 4. The reason is that distinct input/output tables can be formed by changing the pattern of the four 0's and 1's in the output column, and there are as many ways to do that as there are strings of four 0's and 1's. But the number of binary strings of length 4 is $2^4 = 16$. Hence there are 16 distinct input/output tables.

This implies that there are exactly 16 equivalence classes of circuits, one for each distinct input/output table. However, there are infinitely many circuits that give rise to each table. For instance, two circuits for the previous input/output table are shown below.

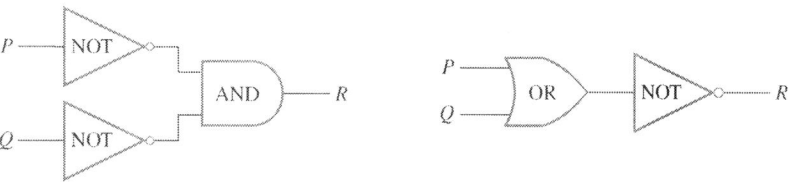

Congruence Modulo n

Example 8.2.4 showed that the relation of congruence modulo 3 is reflexive, symmetric, and transitive. Therefore, it is an equivalence relation.

Example 8.3.10 Equivalence Classes of Congruence Modulo 3

Let R be the relation of congruence modulo 3 on the set $\mathbf{Z}$ of all integers. That is, for all integers m and n,

$$m \, R \, n \quad \Leftrightarrow \quad 3 \mid (m - n) \quad \Leftrightarrow \quad m \equiv n \, (\text{mod } 3).$$

Describe the distinct equivalence classes of R.

Solution For each integer a,

$$[a] = \{x \in \mathbf{Z} \mid x \, R \, a\}$$
$$= \{x \in \mathbf{Z} \mid 3 \mid (x - a)\}$$
$$= \{x \in \mathbf{Z} \mid x - a = 3k, \text{ for some integer } k\}.$$

Therefore,

$$[a] = \{x \in \mathbf{Z} \mid x = 3k + a, \text{ for some integer } k\}.$$

In particular,

$$[0] = \{x \in \mathbf{Z} \mid x = 3k + 0, \text{ for some integer } k\}$$
$$= \{x \in \mathbf{Z} \mid x = 3k, \text{ for some integer } k\}$$
$$= \{\ldots - 9, -6, -3, 0, 3, 6, 9, \ldots\},$$
$$[1] = \{x \in \mathbf{Z} \mid x = 3k + 1, \text{ for some integer } k\}$$
$$= \{\ldots - 8, -5, -2, 1, 4, 7, 10, \ldots\},$$
$$[2] = \{x \in \mathbf{Z} \mid x = 3k + 2, \text{ for some integer } k\}$$
$$= \{\ldots - 7, -4, -1, 2, 5, 8, 11, \ldots\}.$$

Now since 3 R 0, then by Lemma 8.3.2,

$$[3] = [0].$$

More generally, by the same reasoning,

$$[0] = [3] = [-3] = [6] = [-6] = \ldots, \text{ and so on.}$$

Similarly,

$$[1] = [4] = [-2] = [7] = [-5] = \ldots, \text{ and so on.}$$

And

$$[2] = [5] = \lceil -1 \rceil = [8] = [-4] = \ldots, \text{ and so on.}$$

Notice that every integer is in class [0], [1], or [2]. Hence the distinct equivalence classes are

$$\{x \in \mathbf{Z} \mid x = 3k, \text{ for some integer } k\},$$
$$\{x \in \mathbf{Z} \mid x = 3k + 1, \text{ for some integer } k\}, \quad \text{and}$$
$$\{x \in \mathbf{Z} \mid x = 3k + 2, \text{ for some integer } k\}.$$

In words, the three classes of congruence modulo 3 are (1) the set of all integers that are divisible by 3, (2) the set of all integers that leave a remainder of 1 when divided by 3, and (3) the set of all integers that leave a remainder of 2 when divided by 3.   ■

Example 8.3.10 illustrates a very important property of equivalence classes, namely that an equivalence class may have many different names. In Example 8.3.10, for instance, the class of 0, [0], may also be *called* the class of 3, [3], or the class of −6, [−6]. But what the class *is* is the set

$$\{x \in \mathbf{Z} \mid x = 3k, \text{ for some integers } k\}.$$

(The quote at the beginning of this section refers in a humorous way to the philosophically interesting distinction between what things are *called* and what they *are*.)

> **• Definition**
>
> Suppose R is an equivalence relation on a set A and S is an equivalence class of R. A **representative** of the class S is any element a such that $[a] = S$.

In exercises 36–41 at the end of this section, you are asked to show in effect, that if a is any element of an equivalence class S, then $S = [a]$. Hence *any* element of an equivalence class is a representative of that class.

The following notation is used frequently when referring to congruence relations. It was introduced by Carl Friedrich Gauss in the first chapter of his book *Disquisitiones Arithmeticae*. This work, which was published when Gauss was only 24, laid the foundation for modern number theory.

Carl Friedrich Gauss
(1777–1855)

Bettmann/CORBIS

> **● Definition**
>
> Let m and n be integers and let d be a positive integer. We say that **m is congruent to n modulo d** and write
>
> $$m \equiv n \ (\textbf{mod } d)$$
>
> if, and only if, $\qquad\qquad\qquad\qquad d \mid (m - n).$
>
> Symbolically: $\qquad\qquad m \equiv n \ (\text{mod } d) \quad \Leftrightarrow \quad d \mid (m - n)$

Exercise 17(b) at the end of this section asks you to show that $m \equiv n \ (\text{mod } d)$ if, and only if, $m \ mod \ d = n \ mod \ d$, where m, n, and d are integers and d is positive.

Example 8.3.11 Evaluating Congruences

Determine which of the following congruences are true and which are false.

a. $12 \equiv 7 \ (\text{mod } 5)$ b. $6 \equiv -8 \ (\text{mod } 4)$ c. $3 \equiv 3 \ (\text{mod } 7)$

Solution

a. True. $12 - 7 = 5 = 5 \cdot 1$. Hence $5 \mid (12 - 7)$, and so $12 \equiv 7 \ (\text{mod } 5)$.

b. False. $6 - (-8) = 14$, and $4 \nmid 14$ because $14 \neq 4 \cdot k$ for any integer k. Consequently, $6 \not\equiv -8 \ (\text{mod } 4)$.

c. True. $3 - 3 = 0 = 7 \cdot 0$. Hence $7 \mid (3 - 3)$, and so $3 \equiv 3 \ (\text{mod } 7)$. ■

A Definition for Rational Numbers

For a moment, forget what you know about fractional arithmetic and look at the numbers

$$\frac{1}{3} \quad \text{and} \quad \frac{2}{6}$$

as *symbols*. Considered as symbolic expressions, these *appear* quite different. In fact, if they were written as ordered pairs

$$(1, 3) \quad \text{and} \quad (2, 6)$$

they would *be* different. The fact that we regard them as "the same" is a specific instance of our general agreement to regard any two numbers

$$\frac{a}{b} \quad \text{and} \quad \frac{c}{d}$$

as equal provided the *cross products* are equal: $ad = bc$. This can be formalized as follows, using the language of equivalence relations.

Example 8.3.12 Rational Numbers Are Really Equivalence Classes

Let A be the set of all ordered pairs of integers for which the second element of the pair is nonzero. Symbolically,

$$A = \mathbf{Z} \times (\mathbf{Z} - \{0\}).$$

Define a relation R on A as follows: For all $(a, b), (c, d) \in A$,

$$(a, b) \; R \; (c, d) \quad \Leftrightarrow \quad ad = bc.$$

The fact is that R is an equivalence relation.

a. Prove that R is transitive. (Proofs that R is reflexive and symmetric are left to exercise 42 at the end of the section.)

b. Describe the distinct equivalence classes of R.

Solution

a. *[We must show that for all $(a, b), (c, d), (e, f) \in A$, if $(a, b) \; R \; (c, d)$ and $(c, d) R \; (e, f)$, then $(a, b) \; R \; (e, f)$.]* Suppose $(a, b), (c, d)$, and (e, f) are particular but arbitrarily chosen elements of A such that $(a, b) \quad R \quad (c, d)$ and $(c, d) \quad R \quad (e, f)$. *[We must show that $(a, b) \; R \; (e, f)$.]* By definition of R,

$$(1) \; ad = bc \quad \text{and} \quad (2) \; cf = de.$$

Since the second elements of all ordered pairs in A are nonzero, $b \neq 0, d \neq 0$, and $f \neq 0$. Multiply both sides of equation (1) by f and both sides of equation (2) by b to obtain

$$(1') \; adf = bcf \quad \text{and} \quad (2') \; bcf = bde.$$

Thus

$$adf = bde$$

and, since $d \neq 0$, it follows from the cancellation law for multiplication (T7 in Appendix A) that

$$af = be.$$

It follows, by definition of R, that $(a, b) \; R \; (e, f)$ *[as was to be shown]*.

b. There is one equivalence class for each distinct rational number. Each equivalence class consists of all ordered pairs (a, b) that, if written as fractions a/b, would equal each other. The reason for this is that the condition for two rational numbers to be equal is the same as the condition for two ordered pairs to be related. For instance, the class of $(1, 2)$ is

$$[(1, 2)] = \{(1, 2), (-1, -2), (2, 4), (-2, -4), (3, 6), (-3, -6), \ldots\}$$

since $\dfrac{1}{2} = \dfrac{-1}{-2} = \dfrac{2}{4} = \dfrac{-2}{-4} = \dfrac{3}{6} = \dfrac{-3}{-6}$ and so forth.

It is possible to expand the result of Example 8.3.12 to define operations of addition and multiplication on the equivalence classes of R that satisfy all the same properties as the addition and multiplication of rational numbers. (See exercise 43.) It follows that the rational numbers can be defined as equivalence classes of ordered pairs of integers. Similarly (see exercise 44), it can be shown that all integers, negative and zero included, can be defined as equivalence classes of ordered pairs of positive integers. But in the late nineteenth century, F. L. G. Frege and Giuseppe Peano showed that the positive integers can be defined entirely in terms of sets. And just a little earlier, Richard Dedekind (1848–1916) showed that all real numbers can be defined as sets of rational numbers. All together, these results show that the real numbers can be defined using logic and set theory alone.

Test Yourself

1. For a relation on a set to be an equivalence relation, it must be _____.

2. The notation $m \equiv n \pmod{d}$ is read "_____" and means that _____.

3. Given an equivalence relation R on a set A and given an element a in A, the equivalence class of a is denoted _____ and is defined to be _____.

4. If A is a set, R is an equivalence relation on A, and a and b are elements of A, then either $[a] = [b]$ or _____.

5. If A is a set and R is an equivalence relation on A, then the distinct equivalence classes of R form _____.

6. Let $A = \mathbf{Z} \times (\mathbf{Z} - \{0\})$, and define a relation R on A by specifying that for all (a, b) and (c, d) in A, $(a, b)\, R\, (c, d)$ if, and only if, $ad = bc$. Then there is exactly one equivalence class of R for each _____.

Exercise Set 8.3

1. Suppose that $S = \{a, b, c, d, e\}$ and R is a relation on S such that $a\,R\,b$, $b\,R\,c$, and $d\,R\,e$. List all of the following that must be true if R is (a) reflexive (but not symmetric or transitive), (b) symmetric (but not reflexive or transitive), (c) transitive (but not reflexive or symmetric), and (d) an equivalence relation.

   $c\,R\,b \quad c\,R\,c \quad a\,R\,c \quad b\,R\,a \quad a\,R\,d \quad e\,R\,a \quad e\,R\,d \quad c\,R\,a$

2. Each of the following partitions of $\{0, 1, 2, 3, 4\}$ induces a relation R on $\{0, 1, 2, 3, 4\}$. In each case, find the ordered pairs in R.
   a. $\{0, 2\}, \{1\}, \{3, 4\}$ b. $\{0\}, \{1, 3, 4\}, \{2\}$
   c. $\{0\}, \{1, 2, 3, 4\}$

In each of 3–14, the relation R is an equivalence relation on the set A. Find the distinct equivalence classes of R.

3. $A = \{0, 1, 2, 3, 4\}$
   $R = \{(0, 0), (0, 4), (1, 1), (1, 3), (2, 2), (3, 1), (3, 3), (4, 0), (4, 4)\}$

4. $A = \{a, b, c, d\}$
   $R = \{(a, a), (b, b), (b, d), (c, c), (d, b), (d, d)\}$

5. $A = \{1, 2, 3, 4, \ldots, 20\}$. R is defined on A as follows:

   For all $x, y \in A$, $\quad x\,R\,y \quad \Leftrightarrow \quad 4 \mid (x - y)$.

6. $A = \{-4, -3, -2, -1, 0, 1, 2, 3, 4, 5\}$. R is defined on A as follows:

   For all $x, y \in A$, $\quad x\,R\,y \quad \Leftrightarrow \quad 3 \mid (x - y)$.

7. $A = \{(1, 3), (2, 4), (-4, -8), (3, 9), (1, 5), (3, 6)\}$. R is defined on A as follows: For all $(a, b), (c, d) \in A$,

   $(a, b)\, R\, (c, d) \quad \Leftrightarrow \quad ad = bc$.

8. $X = \{a, b, c\}$ and $A = \mathscr{P}(X)$. R is defined on A as follows: For all sets U and V in $\mathscr{P}(X)$,

   $$U\,R\,V \quad \Leftrightarrow \quad N(U) = N(V).$$

   (That is, the number of elements in U equals the number of elements in v.)

9. $X = \{-1, 0, 1\}$ and $A = \mathscr{P}(X)$. R is defined on $\mathscr{P}(X)$ as follows: For all sets s and T in $\mathscr{P}(X)$,

   $s\,R\,T \quad \Leftrightarrow \quad$ the sum of the elements in s equals the sum of the elements in T.

10. $A = \{-5, -4, -3, -2, -1, 0, 1, 2, 3, 4, 5\}$. R is defined on A as follows: For all $m, n \in \mathbf{Z}$,

    $m\,R\,n \quad \Leftrightarrow \quad 3 \mid (m^2 - n^2)$.

11. $A = \{-4, -3, -2, -1, 0, 1, 2, 3, 4\}$. R is defined on A as follows: For all $(m, n) \in A$,

    $m\,R\,n \Leftrightarrow 4 \mid (m^2 - n^2)$.

12. $A = \{-4, -3, -2, -1, 0, 1, 2, 3, 4\}$. R is defined on A as follows: For all $(m, n) \in A$,

    $m\,R\,n \Leftrightarrow 5 \mid (m^2 - n^2)$.

13. A is the set of all strings of length 4 in a's and b's. R is defined on A as follows: For all strings s and t in A,

    $s\,R\,t \quad \Leftrightarrow \quad s$ has the same first two characters as t.

14. A is the set of all strings of length 2 in 0's, 1's, and 2's. R is defined on A as follows: For all strings s and t in A,

    $s\,R\,t \quad \Leftrightarrow \quad$ the sum of the characters in s equals the sum of the characters in t.

15. Determine which of the following congruence relations are true and which are false.
    a. $17 \equiv 2 \pmod 5$ b. $4 \equiv -5 \pmod 7$
    c. $-2 \equiv -8 \pmod 3$ d. $-6 \equiv 22 \pmod 2$

16. a. Let R be the relation of congruence modulo 3. Which of the following equivalence classes are equal?

    $[7], [-4], [-6], [17], [4], [27], [19]$

    b. Let R be the relation of congruence modulo 7. Which of the following equivalence classes are equal?

    $[35], [3], [-7], [12], [0], [-2], [17]$

17. a. Prove that for all integers m and n, $m \equiv n \pmod 3$ if, and only if, $m \bmod 3 = n \bmod 3$.
    b. Prove that for all integers m and n and any positive integer d, $m \equiv n \pmod d$ if, and only if, $m \bmod d = n \bmod d$.

18. a. Give an example of two sets that are distinct but not disjoint.
    b. Find sets A_1 and A_2 and elements x, y and z such that x and y are in A_1 and y and z are in A_2 but x and z are not both in either of the sets A_1 or A_2.

In 19–31, (1) prove that the relation is an equivalence relation, and (2) describe the distinct equivalence classes of each relation.

19. A is the set of all students at your college.
    a. R is the relation defined on A as follows: For all x and y in A,

    $$x \, R \, y \quad \Leftrightarrow \quad x \text{ has the same major (or double major) as } y.$$

    (Assume "undeclared" is a major.)
    b. S is the relation defined on A as follows: For all $x, y \in A$,

    $$x \, S \, y \quad \Leftrightarrow \quad x \text{ is the same age as } y.$$

20. E is the relation defined on $\mathbf{Z}$ as follows:

    For all $m, n \in \mathbf{Z}, \quad m \, E \, n \quad \Leftrightarrow \quad 2 \,|\, (m - n)$.

21. F is the relation defined on $\mathbf{Z}$ as follows:

    For all $m, n \in \mathbf{Z}, \quad m \, F \, n \quad \Leftrightarrow \quad 4 \,|\, (m - n)$.

22. Let P be a set of parts shipped to a company from various suppliers. S is the relation defined on P as follows: For all $x, y \in P$,

    $$x \, S \, y \quad \Leftrightarrow \quad x \text{ has the same part number and is shipped from the same supplier as } y.$$

23. Let A be the set of all statement forms in three variables p, q, and r. $\mathbf{R}$ is the relation defined on A as follows: For all P and Q in A,

    $$\text{P} \, \mathbf{R} \, \text{Q} \quad \Leftrightarrow \quad \text{P and Q have the same truth table.}$$

24. Let A be the set of identifiers in a computer program. It is common for identifiers to be used for only a short part of the execution time of a program and not to be used again to execute other parts of the program. In such cases, arranging for identifiers to share memory locations makes efficient use of a computer's memory capacity. Define a relation R on A as follows: For all identifiers x and y,

    $$x \, R \, y \quad \Leftrightarrow \quad \text{the values of } x \text{ and } y \text{ are stored in the same memory location during execution of the program.}$$

25. A is the "absolute value" relation defined on $\mathbf{R}$ as follows:

    For all $x, y \in \mathbf{R}, \quad x \, A \, y \quad \Leftrightarrow \quad |x| = |y|$.

H 26. D is the relation defined on $\mathbf{Z}$ as follows: For all $m, n \in \mathbf{Z}$,

    $$m \, D \, n \quad \Leftrightarrow \quad 3 \,|\, (m^2 - n^2).$$

27. R is the relation defined on $\mathbf{Z}$ as follows: For all $(m, n) \in \mathbf{Z}$,

    $$m \, R \, n \quad \Leftrightarrow \quad 4 \,|\, (m^2 - n^2).$$

28. I is the relation defined on $\mathbf{R}$ as follows:

    For all $x, y \in \mathbf{R}, \quad x \, I \, y \quad \Leftrightarrow \quad x - y \text{ is an integer.}$

29. Define P on the set $\mathbf{R} \times \mathbf{R}$ of ordered pairs of real numbers as follows: For all $(w, x), (y, z) \in \mathbf{R} \times \mathbf{R}$,

    $$(w, x) \, P \, (y, z) \quad \Leftrightarrow \quad w = y.$$

30. Define Q on the set $\mathbf{R} \times \mathbf{R}$ as follows: For all $(w, x), (y, z) \in \mathbf{R} \times \mathbf{R}$,

    $$(w, x) \, Q \, (y, z) \quad \Leftrightarrow \quad x = z.$$

31. Let P be the set of all points in the Cartesian plane except the origin. R is the relation defined on P as follows: For all p_1 and p_2 in P,

    $$p_1 \, R \, p_2 \quad \Leftrightarrow \quad p_1 \text{ and } p_2 \text{ lie on the same half-line emanating from the origin.}$$

32. Let A be the set of all straight lines in the Cartesian plane. Define a relation $\|$ on A as follows:

    For all l_1 and l_2 in $A, \quad l_1 \, \| \, l_2 \quad \Leftrightarrow \quad l_1 \text{ is parallel to } l_2.$

    Then $\|$ is an equivalence relation on A. Describe the equivalence classes of this relation.

33. Let A be the set of points in the rectangle with x and y coordinates between 0 and 1. That is,

    $$A = \{(x, y) \in \mathbf{R} \times \mathbf{R} \,|\, 0 \le x \le 1 \quad \text{and} \quad 0 \le y \le 1\}.$$

    Define a relation R on A as follows: For all (x_1, y_1) and (x_2, y_2) in A,

    $(x_1, y_1) \, R \, (x_2, y_2) \Leftrightarrow$
    $\qquad (x_1, y_1) = (x_2, y_2); \quad$ or
    $\qquad x_1 = 0 \quad \text{and} \quad x_2 = 1 \quad \text{and} \quad y_1 = y_2; \quad$ or
    $\qquad x_1 = 1 \quad \text{and} \quad x_2 = 0 \quad \text{and} \quad y_1 = y_2; \quad$ or
    $\qquad y_1 = 0 \quad \text{and} \quad y_2 = 1 \quad \text{and} \quad x_1 = x_2; \quad$ or
    $\qquad y_1 = 1 \quad \text{and} \quad y_2 = 0 \quad \text{and} \quad x_1 = x_2.$

    In other words, all points along the top edge of the rectangle are related to the points along the bottom edge directly beneath them, and all points directly opposite each other along the left and right edges are related to each other. The points in the interior of the rectangle are not related to anything other than themselves. Then R is an equivalence relation on A. Imagine gluing together all the points that are in the same equivalence class. Describe the resulting figure.

34. The documentation for the computer language Java recommends that when an "equals method" is defined for an object, it be an equivalence relation. That is, if R is defined as follows:

$$x \ R \ y \quad \Leftrightarrow \quad x.equals(y) \quad \text{for all objects in the class,}$$

then R should be an equivalence relation. Suppose that in trying to optimize some of the mathematics of a graphics application, a programmer creates an object called a point, consisting of two coordinates in the plane. The programmer defines an equals method as follows: If p and q are any points, then

$$p.equals(q) \quad \Leftrightarrow \quad \text{the distance from } p \text{ to } q \text{ is} \\ \text{less than or equal to } c$$

where c is a small positive number that depends on the resolution of the computer display. Is the programmer's equals method an equivalence relation? Justify your answer.

35. Find an additional representative circuit for the input/output table of Example 8.3.9.

Let R be an equivalence relation on a set A. Prove each of the statements in 36–41 directly from the definitions of equivalence relation and equivalence class without using the results of Lemma 8.3.2, Lemma 8.3.3, or Theorem 8.3.4.

36. For all a in A, $a \in [a]$.

37. For all a and b in A, if $b \in [a]$ then $a \ R \ b$.

38. For all a, b and c in A, if $b \ R \ c$ and $c \in [a]$ then $b \in [a]$.

39. For all a and b in A, if $[a] = [b]$ then $a \ R \ b$.

40. For all a, b, and x in A, if $a \ R \ b$ and $x \in [a]$, then $x \in [b]$.

H 41. For all a and b in A, if $a \in [b]$ then $[a] = [b]$.

42. Let R be the relation defined in Example 8.3.12.
   a. Prove that R is reflexive.
   b. Prove that R is symmetric.
   c. List four distinct elements in $[(1, 3)]$.
   d. List four distinct elements in $[(2, 5)]$.

✳ 43. In Example 8.3.12, define operations of addition $(+)$ and multiplication $(\cdot)$ as follows: For all (a, b), $(c, d) \in A$,

$$[(a, b)] + [(c, d)] = [(ad + bc, bd)]$$
$$[(a, b)] \cdot [(c, d)] = [(ac, bd)].$$

   a. Prove that this addition is well defined. That is, show that if $[(a, b)] = [(a', b')]$ and $[(c, d)] = [(c', d')]$, then $[(ad + bc, bd)] = [(a'd' + b'c', b'd')]$.
   b. Prove that this multiplication is well defined. That is, show that if $[(a, b)] = [(a', b')]$ and $[(c, d)] = [(c', d')]$, then $[(ac, bd)] = [(a'c', b'd')]$.

c. Show that $[(0, 1)]$ is an identity element for addition. That is, show that for any $(a, b) \in A$,

$$[(a, b)] + [(0, 1)] = [(0, 1)] + [(a, b)] = [(a, b)].$$

   d. Find an identity element for multiplication. That is, find (i, j) in A so that for all (a, b) in A. $[(a, b)] \cdot [(i, j)] = [(i, j)] \cdot [(a, b)] = [(a, b)]$.
   e. For any $(a, b) \in A$, show that $[(-a, b)]$ is an inverse for $[(a, b)]$ for addition. That is, show that $[(-a, b)] + [(a, b)] = [(a, b)] + [(-a, b)] = [(0, 1)]$.
   f. Given any $(a, b) \in A$ with $a \neq 0$, find an inverse for $[(a, b)]$ for multiplication. That is, find (c, d) in A so that $[(a, b)] \cdot [(c, d)] = [(c, d)] \cdot [(a, b)] = [(i, j)]$, where $[(i, j)]$ is the identity element you found in part (d).

44. Let $A = \mathbf{Z}^+ \times \mathbf{Z}^+$. Define a relation R on A as follows: For all (a, b) and (c, d) in A,

$$(a, b) \ R \ (c, d) \quad \Leftrightarrow \quad a + d = c + b.$$

   a. Prove that R is reflexive.
   b. Prove that R is symmetric.
   H c. Prove that R is transitive.
   d. List five elements in $[(1, 1)]$.
   e. List five elements in $[(3, 1)]$.
   f. List five elements in $[(1, 2)]$.
   g. Describe the distinct equivalence classes of R.

45. The following argument claims to prove that the requirement that an equivalence relation be reflexive is redundant. In other words, it claims to show that if a relation is symmetric and transitive, then it is reflexive. Find the mistake in the argument.

   "**Proof:** Let R be a relation on a set A and suppose R is symmetric and transitive. For any two elements x and y in A, if $x \ R \ y$ then $y \ R \ x$ since R is symmetric. But then it follows by transitivity that $x \ R \ x$. Hence R is reflexive."

46. Let R be a relation on a set A and suppose R is symmetric and transitive. Prove the following: If for every x in A there is a y in A such that $x \ R \ y$, then R is an equivalence relation.

47. Refer to the quote at the beginning of this section to answer the following questions.
   a. What is the name of the Knight's song called?
   b. What is the name of the Knight's song?
   c. What is the Knight's song called?
   d. What *is* the Knight's song?
   e. What is your (full, legal) name?
   f. What are you called?
   g. What *are* you? (Do not answer this on paper; just think about it.)

Answers for Test Yourself

1. reflexive, symmetric, and transitive   2. m is congruent to n modulo d; d divides $m - n$ 3. $[a]$; the set of all x in A such that $x \ R \ a$
4. $[a] \cap [b] = \emptyset$ 5. a partition of A 6. rational number

8.4 Modular Arithmetic with Applications to Cryptography

The "real" mathematics of the "real" mathematicians, the mathematics of Fermat and Euler and Gauss and Abel and Riemann, is almost wholly "useless." ... It is not possible to justify the life of any genuine professional mathematician on the ground of the "utility" of his work. — G. H. Hardy, *A Mathematician's Apology,* 1941

Cryptography is the study of methods for sending secret messages. It involves **encryption,** in which a message, called **plaintext,** is converted into a form, called **ciphertext,** that may be sent over channels possibly open to view by outside parties. The receiver of the ciphertext uses **decryption** to convert the ciphertext back into plaintext.

In the past the primary use of cryptography was for government and military intelligence, and this use continues to be important. In fact, the National Security Agency, whose main business is cryptography, is the largest employer of mathematicians in the United States. With the rise of electronic communication systems, however, especially the Internet, an extremely important current use of cryptography is to make it possible to send private information, such as credit card numbers, banking data, medical records, and so forth, over electronic channels.

Many systems for sending secret messages require both the sender and the receiver to know both the encryption and the decryption procedures. For instance, an encryption system once used by Julius Caesar, and now called the **Caesar cipher**, encrypts messages by changing each letter of the alphabet to the one three places farther along, with X wrapping around to A, Y to B, and Z to C. In other words, say each letter of the alphabet is coded by its position relative to the others—so that $A = 01, B = 02, \ldots, Z = 26$. If the numerical version of the plaintext for a letter is denoted M and the numeric version of the ciphertext is denoted C, then

$$C = (M + 3) \bmod 26.$$

The receiver of such a message can easily decrypt it by using the formula

$$M = (C - 3) \bmod 26.$$

For reference, here are the letters of the alphabet, together with their numeric equivalents:

A	B	C	D	E	F	G	H	I	J	K	L	M
01	02	03	04	05	06	07	08	09	10	11	12	13
N	O	P	Q	R	S	T	U	V	W	X	Y	Z
14	15	16	17	18	19	20	21	22	23	24	25	26

Example 8.4.1 Encrypting and Decrypting with the Caesar Cipher

a. Use the Caesar cipher to encrypt the message HOW ARE YOU.

b. Use the Caesar cipher to decrypt the message L DP ILQH.

Solution

a. First translate the letters of HOW ARE YOU into their numeric equivalents:

08 15 23   01 18 05   25 15 21.

Next encrypt the message by adding 3 to each number. The result is

11 18 26   04 21 08   02 18 24.

Finally, substitute the letters that correspond to these numbers. The encrypted message becomes

KRZ   DUH   BRX.

b. First translate the letters of L DP ILQH into their numeric equivalents:

12   04 16   09 12 17 08.

Next decrypt the message by subtracting 3 from each number:

09   01 13   06 09 14 05.

Then translate back into letters to obtain the original message: I AM FINE. ▓

One problem with the Caesar cipher is that given a sufficient amount of ciphertext a person with knowledge of letter frequencies in the language can easily figure out the cipher. Partly for this reason, even Caesar himself did not make extensive use of it. Another problem with a system like the Caesar cipher is that knowledge of how to encrypt a message automatically gives knowledge of how to decrypt it. When a potential recipient of messages passes the encryption information to a potential sender of messages, the channel over which the information is passed may itself be insecure. Thus the information may leak out, enabling an outside party to decrypt messages intended to be kept secret.

With public-key cryptography, a potential recipient of encrypted messages openly distributes a public key containing the encryption information. However, knowledge of the public key provides virtually no clue about how messages are decrypted. Only the recipient has that knowledge. Regardless of how many people learn the encryption information, only the recipient should be able to decrypt messages that are sent.

The first public-key cryptography system was developed in 1976–1977 by three young mathematician/computer scientists working at M.I.T.: Ronald Rivest, Adi Shamir, and

From left to right: Ronald Rivest (born 1948), Adi Shamir (born 1952), and Leonard Adleman (born 1945)

Leonard Adleman. In their honor it is called the RSA cipher. In order for you to learn how it works, you need to know some additional properties of congruence modulo n.

Properties of Congruence Modulo n

The first theorem in this section brings together a variety of equivalent ways of expressing the same basic arithmetic fact. Sometimes one way is most convenient; sometimes another way is best. You need to be comfortable moving from one to another, depending on the nature of the problem you are trying to solve.

Theorem 8.4.1 Modular Equivalences

Let a, b, and n be any integers and suppose $n > 1$. The following statements are all equivalent:

1. $n \mid (a - b)$

2. $a \equiv b \,(\text{mod } n)$

3. $a = b + kn$ for some integer k

4. a and b have the same (nonnegative) remainder when divided by n

5. $a \bmod n = b \bmod n$

Proof:

We will show that $(1) \Rightarrow (2) \Rightarrow (3) \Rightarrow (4) \Rightarrow (5) \Rightarrow (1)$. It will follow by the transitivity of if-then that all five statements are equivalent.

So let a, b, and n be any integers with $n > 1$.

Proof that $(1) \Rightarrow (2)$**:** Suppose that $n \mid (a - b)$. By definition of congruence modulo n, we can immediately conclude that $a \equiv b \,(\text{mod } n)$.

Proof that $(2) \Rightarrow (3)$**:** Suppose that $a \equiv b \,(\text{mod } n)$. By definition of congruence modulo n, $n \mid (a - b)$. Thus, by definition of divisibility, $a - b = kn$, for some integer k. Adding b to both sides gives that $a = b + kn$.

Proof that $(3) \Rightarrow (4)$**:** Suppose that $a = b + kn$, for some integer k. Use the quotient-remainder theorem to divide a by n to obtain

$$a = qn + r \quad \text{where } q \text{ and } r \text{ are integers and } 0 \le r < n.$$

Substituting $b + kn$ for a in this equation gives that

$$b + kn = qn + r$$

and subtracting kn from both sides and factoring out n yields

$$b = (q - k)n + r.$$

But since $0 \le r < n$, the uniqueness property of the quotient-remainder theorem guarantees that r is also the remainder obtained when b is divided by n. Thus a and b have the same remainder when divided by n.

Proof that $(4) \Rightarrow (5)$**:** Suppose that a and b have the same remainder when divided by n. It follows immediately from the definition of the *mod* function that $a \bmod n = b \bmod n$.

***Proof that* (5)** $\Rightarrow$ **(1):** Suppose that $a \bmod n = b \bmod n$. By definition of the *mod* function, a and b have the same remainder when divided by n. Thus, by the quotient-remainder theorem, we can write

$$a = q_1 n + r \quad \text{and} \quad b = q_2 n + r \quad \text{where } q_1, q_2, \text{ and } r \text{ are integers and } 0 \le r < n.$$

It follows that

$$a - b = (q_1 n + r) - (q_2 n + r) = (q_1 - q_2)n.$$

Therefore, since $q_1 - q_2$ is an integer, $n \mid (a - b)$.

Another consequence of the quotient-remainder theorem is this: When an integer a is divided by a positive integer n, a unique quotient q and remainder r are obtained with the property that $a = nq + r$ and $0 \le r < n$. Because there are exactly n integers that satisfy the inequality $0 \le r < n$ (the numbers from 0 through $n - 1$), there are exactly n possible remainders that can occur. These are called the *least nonnegative residues modulo n* or simply the *residues modulo n*.

• Definition

Given integers a and n with $n > 1$, **the residue of a modulo n** is $a \bmod n$, the non-negative remainder obtained when a is divided by n. The numbers $0, 1, 2, \ldots, n - 1$ are called a **complete set of residues modulo n**. To **reduce a number modulo n** means to set it equal to its residue modulo n. If a modulus $n > 1$ is fixed throughout a discussion and an integer a is given, the words "modulo n" are often dropped and we simply speak of **the residue of a**.

The following theorem generalizes several examples from Section 8.3.

Theorem 8.4.2 Congruence Modulo n Is an Equivalence Relation

If n is any integer with $n > 1$, congruence modulo n is an equivalence relation on the set of all integers. The distinct equivalence classes of the relation are the sets $[0], [1], [2], \ldots, [n - 1]$, where for each $a = 0, 1, 2, \ldots, n - 1$,

$$[a] = \{m \in Z \mid m \equiv a \pmod{n}\},$$

or, equivalently,

$$[a] = \{m \in Z \mid m = a + kn \text{ for some integer } k\}.$$

Proof:

Suppose n is any integer with $n > 1$. We must show that congruence modulo n is reflexive, symmetric, and transitive.

***Proof of reflexivity*:** Suppose a is any integer. To show that $a \equiv a \pmod{n}$, we must show that $n \mid (a - a)$. But $a - a = 0$, and $n \mid 0$ because $0 = n \cdot 0$. Therefore $a \equiv a \pmod{n}$.

continued on page 482

Proof of symmetry: Suppose a and b are any integers such that $a \equiv b \pmod{n}$. We must show that $b \equiv a \pmod{n}$. But since $a \equiv b \pmod{n}$, then $n \mid (a - b)$. Thus, by definition of divisibility, $a - b = nk$, for some integer k. Multiply both sides of this equation by -1 to obtain

$$-(a - b) = -nk,$$

or, equivalently,

$$b - a = n(-k).$$

Thus, by definition of divisibility $n \mid (b - a)$, and so, by definition of congruence modulo n, $b \equiv a \pmod{n}$.

Proof of transitivity: This is left as exercise 5 at the end of the section.

Proof that the distinct equivalence classes are $[0], [1], [2], \ldots, [n - 1]$: This is left as exercise 6 at the end of the section.

Observe that there is a one-to-one correspondence between the distinct equivalence classes for congruence modulo n and the elements of a complete set of residues modulo n.

Modular Arithmetic

A fundamental fact about congruence modulo n is that if you first perform an addition, subtraction, or multiplication on integers and then reduce the result modulo n, you will obtain the same answer as if you had first reduced each of the numbers modulo n, performed the operation, and then reduced the result modulo n. For instance, instead of computing

$$(5 \cdot 8) = 40 \equiv 1 \pmod 3$$

you will obtain the same answer if you compute

$$(5 \bmod 3)(8 \bmod 3) = 2 \cdot 2 = 4 \equiv 1 \pmod 3.$$

The fact that this process works is a result of the following theorem.

Theorem 8.4.3 Modular Arithmetic

Let $a, b, c, d,$ and n be integers with $n > 1$, and suppose

$$a \equiv c \pmod n \text{ and } b \equiv d \pmod n.$$

Then

1. $(a + b) \equiv (c + d) \pmod n$

2. $(a - b) \equiv (c - d) \pmod n$

3. $ab \equiv cd \pmod n$

4. $a^m \equiv c^m \pmod n$ for all positive integers m.

Proof:

Because we will make greatest use of part 3 of this theorem, we prove it here and leave the proofs of the remaining parts of the theorem to exercises 9–11 at the end of the section.

Proof of Part 3: Suppose a, b, c, d, and n are integers with $n > 1$, and suppose $a \equiv b \pmod{n}$ and $c \equiv d \pmod{n}$. By Theorem 8.4.1, there exist integers s and t such that

$$a = c + sn \quad \text{and} \quad b = d + tn.$$

Then

$$\begin{aligned} ab &= (c + sn)(d + tn) & \text{by substitution} \\ &= cd + ctn + snd + sntn \\ &= cd + n(ct + sd + stn) & \text{by algebra.} \end{aligned}$$

Let $k = ct + sd + stn$. Then k is an integer and $ab = cd + nk$. Thus by Theorem 8.4.1, $ab \equiv cd \pmod{n}$.

Example 8.4.2 Getting Started with Modular Arithmetic

The most practical use of modular arithmetic is to reduce computations involving large integers to computations involving smaller ones. For instance, note that $55 \equiv 3 \pmod{4}$ because $55 - 3 = 52$, which is divisible by 4, and $26 \equiv 2 \pmod{4}$ because $26 - 2 = 24$, which is also divisible by 4. Verify the following statements.

a. $55 + 26 \equiv (3 + 2) \pmod{4}$ b. $55 - 26 \equiv (3 - 2) \pmod{4}$

c. $55 \cdot 26 \equiv (3 \cdot 2) \pmod{4}$ d. $55^2 \equiv 3^2 \pmod{4}$

Solution

a. Compute $55 + 26 = 81$ and $3 + 2 = 5$. By definition of congruence modulo n, to show that $81 \equiv 5 \pmod{4}$, you need to show that $4 \mid (81 - 5)$. But this is true because $81 - 5 = 76$, and $4 \mid 76$ since $76 = 4 \cdot 19$.

b. Compute $55 - 26 = 29$ and $3 - 2 = 1$. By definition of congruence modulo n, to show that $29 \equiv 1 \pmod{4}$, you need to show that $4 \mid (29 - 1)$. But this is true because $29 - 1 = 28$, and $4 \mid 28$ since $28 = 4 \cdot 7$.

c. Compute $55 \cdot 26 = 1430$ and $3 \cdot 2 = 6$. By definition of congruence modulo n, to show that $1430 \equiv 6 \pmod{4}$, you need to show that $4 \mid (1430 - 6)$. But this is true because $1430 - 6 = 1424$, and $4 \mid 1424$ since $1424 = 4 \cdot 356$.

d. Compute $55^2 = 3025$ and $3^2 = 9$. By definition of congruence modulo n, to show that $3025 \equiv 9 \pmod{4}$, you need to show that $4 \mid (3025 - 9)$. But this is true because $3025 - 9 = 3016$, and $4 \mid 3016$ since $3016 = 4 \cdot 754$. ■

In order to facilitate the computations performed in this section, it is convenient to express part 3 of Theorem 8.4.3 in a slightly differently form.

Corollary 8.4.4

Let a, b, and n be integers with $n > 1$. Then

$$ab \equiv [(a \bmod n)(b \bmod n)] \pmod{n},$$

or, equivalently,

$$ab \bmod n = [(a \bmod n)(b \bmod n)] \bmod n.$$

In particular, if m is a positive integer, then

$$a^m \equiv [(a \bmod n)^m] \pmod{n}.$$

Example 8.4.3 Computing a Product Modulo n

As in Example 8.4.2, note that $55 \equiv 3 \pmod 4$ and $26 \equiv 2 \pmod 4$. Because both 3 and 2 are less than 4, each of these numbers is a least nonnegative residue modulo 4. Therefore, $55 \bmod 4 = 3$ and $26 \bmod 4 = 2$. Use the notation of Corollary 8.4.4 to find the residue of $55 \cdot 26$ modulo 4.

Solution   Recall that to use a calculator to compute remainders, you can use the formula $n \bmod d = n - d \cdot \lfloor n/d \rfloor$. If you are using a hand calculator with an "integer part" feature and both n and d are positive, then $\lfloor n/d \rfloor$ is the integer part of the division of n by d. When you divide a positive integer n by a positive integer d with a more basic calculator, you can see $\lfloor n/d \rfloor$ on the calculator display by simply ignoring the digits that follow the decimal point.

By Corollary 8.4.4,

$$
\begin{aligned}
(55 \cdot 26) \bmod 4 &= \{(55 \bmod 4)(26 \bmod 4)\} \bmod 4 \\
&\equiv (3 \cdot 2) \bmod 4 \qquad \text{because } 55 \bmod 4 = 3 \text{ and } 26 \bmod 4 = 2 \\
&\equiv 6 \bmod 4 \\
&\equiv 2 \qquad \text{because } 4 \mid (6 - 2) \text{ and } 2 < 4.
\end{aligned}
$$

When modular arithmetic is performed with very large numbers, as is the case for RSA crytography, computations are facilitated by using two properties of exponents. The first is

$$ x^{2a} = (x^a)^2 \quad \text{for all real numbers } x \text{ and } a \text{ with } x \geq 0. \qquad 8.4.1 $$

Thus, for instance, if x is any positive real number, then

$$
\begin{aligned}
x^4 \bmod n &= (x^2)^2 \bmod n \qquad \text{because } (x^2)^2 = x^4 \\
&= (x^2 \bmod n)^2 \bmod n \qquad \text{by Corollary 8.4.4.}
\end{aligned}
$$

Hence you can reduce x^4 modulo n by reducing x^2 modulo n and then reducing the square of the result modulo n. Because all the residues are less than n, this process limits the size of the computations to numbers that are less than n^2, which makes them easier to work with, both for humans (when the numbers are relatively small) and for computers (when the numbers are very large).

A second useful property of exponents is

$$ x^{a+b} = x^a x^b \quad \text{for all real numbers } x, a, \text{ and } b \text{ with } x \geq 0. \qquad 8.4.2 $$

For instance, because $7 = 4 + 2 + 1$,

$$ x^7 = x^4 x^2 x^1 $$

Thus, by Corollary 8.4.4,

$$ x^7 \bmod n = \{(x^4 \bmod n)(x^2 \bmod n)(x^1 \bmod n)\} \bmod n. $$

We first show an example that illustrates the application of formula (8.4.1) and then an example that uses both (8.4.1) and (8.4.2).

Example 8.4.4 Computing $a^k \bmod n$ When k Is a Power of 2

Find $144^4 \bmod 713$.

Solution Use property (8.4.1) to write $144^4 = (144^2)^2$. Then

$$
\begin{aligned}
144^4 \bmod 713 &= (144^2)^2 \bmod 713 \\
&= (144^2 \bmod 713)^2 \bmod 713 \\
&= (20736 \bmod 713)^2 \bmod 713 \quad \text{because } 144^2 = 20736 \\
&= 59^2 \bmod 713 \quad \text{because } 20736 \bmod 713 = 59 \\
&= 3481 \bmod 713 \quad \text{because } 59^2 = 3481 \\
&= 629 \quad \text{because } 3481 \bmod 713 = 629. \quad \blacksquare
\end{aligned}
$$

Example 8.4.5 Computing $a^k \bmod n$ When k Is Not a Power of 2

Find $12^{43} \bmod 713$.

Solution First write the exponent as a sum of powers of 2:

$$43 = 2^5 + 2^3 + 2 + 1 = 32 + 8 + 2 + 1.$$

Next compute 12^{2^k} for $k = 1, 2, 3, 4, 5$.

$$
\begin{aligned}
12 \bmod 713 &= 12 \\
12^2 \bmod 713 &= 144 \\
12^4 \bmod 713 &= 144^2 \bmod 713 &= 59 \quad && \text{by Example 8.4.4} \\
12^8 \bmod 713 &= 59^2 \bmod 713 &= 629 \quad && \text{by Example 8.4.4} \\
12^{16} \bmod 713 &= 629^2 \bmod 713 &= 639 \quad && \text{by the method of Example 8.4.4} \\
12^{32} \bmod 713 &= 639^2 \bmod 713 &= 485 \quad && \text{by the method of Example 8.4.4}
\end{aligned}
$$

By property (8.4.2),

$$12^{43} = 12^{32+8+2+1} = 12^{32} \cdot 12^8 \cdot 12^2 \cdot 12^1.$$

Thus, by Corollary 8.4.4,

$12^{43} \bmod 713$

$$= \{(12^{32} \bmod 713) \cdot (12^8 \bmod 713) \cdot (12^2 \bmod 713) \cdot (12 \bmod 713)\} \bmod 713.$$

By substitution,

$$
\begin{aligned}
12^{43} \bmod 713 &= (485 \cdot 629 \cdot 144 \cdot 12) \bmod 713 \\
&= 527152320 \bmod 713 \\
&= 48. \quad \blacksquare
\end{aligned}
$$

It is important to understand how to do the computations in Example 8.4.5 by hand using only a simple electronic calculator, but if you are computing a lot of residues, especially ones involving large numbers, you may want to write a short computer or calculator program to do the computations for you.

Extending the Euclidean Algorithm

An extended version of the Euclidean algorithm can be used to find a concrete expression for the greatest common divisor of integers a and b.

● **Definition**

An integer d is said to be a **linear combination of integers** a and b if, and only if, there exist integers s and t such that $as + bt = d$.

Theorem 8.4.5 Writing a Greatest Common Divisor as a Linear Combination

For all integers a and b, not both zero, if $d = \gcd(a, b)$, then there exist integers s and t such that $as + bt = d$.

Proof:

Given integers a and b, not both zero, and given $d = \gcd(a, b)$, let

$$S = \{x \mid x \text{ is a positive integer and } x = as + bt \text{ for some integers } s \text{ and } t\}.$$

Note that S is a nonempty set because (1) if $a > 0$ then $1 \cdot a + 0 \cdot b \in S$, (2) if $a < 0$ then $(-1) \cdot a + 0 \cdot b \in S$, and (3) if $a = 0$, then by assumption $b \neq 0$, and hence $0 \cdot a + 1 \cdot b \in S$ or $0 \cdot a + (-1) \cdot b \in S$. Thus, because S is a nonempty subset of positive integers, by the well-ordering principle for the integers there is a least element c in S. By definition of S,

$$c = as + bt \quad \text{for some integers } s \text{ and } t. \tag{8.4.3}$$

We will show that (1) $c \geq d$, and (2) $c \leq d$, and we will therefore be able to conclude that $c = d = \gcd(a, b)$.

(1) *Proof that $c \geq d$:*
[In this part of the proof, we show that d is a divisor of c and thus that $d \leq c$.] Because $d = \gcd(a, b)$, by definition of greatest common divisor, $d \mid a$ and $d \mid b$. Hence $a = dx$ and $b = dy$ for some integers x and y. Then

$$
\begin{aligned}
c &= as + bt & \text{by (8.4.3)} \\
&= (dx)s + (dy)t & \text{by substitution} \\
&= d(xs + yt) & \text{by factoring out the } d.
\end{aligned}
$$

But $xs + yt$ is an integer because it is a sum of products of integers. Thus, by definition of divisibility, $d \mid c$. Both c and d are positive, and hence, by Theorem 4.3.1, $c \geq d$.

(2) *Proof that $c \leq d$:*
[In this part of the proof, we show that c is a divisor of both a and b and therefore that c is less than or equal to the greatest common divisor of a and b, which is d.] Apply the quotient-remainder theorem to the division of a by c to obtain

$$a = cq + r \quad \text{for some integers } q \text{ and } r \text{ with } 0 \leq r < c. \tag{8.4.4}$$

Thus for some integers q and r with $0 \leq r < c$,

$$r = a - cq$$

Now $c = as + bt$. Therefore, for some integers q and r with $0 \leq r < c$,

$$
\begin{aligned}
r &= a - (as + bt)q & \text{by substitution} \\
&= a(1 - sq) - btq.
\end{aligned}
$$

Thus r is a linear combination of a and b. If $r > 0$, then r would be in S, and so r would be a smaller element of S than c, which would contradict the fact that c is the least element of S. Hence $r = 0$. By substitution into (8.4.4),

$$a = cq$$

and therefore $c \mid a$.

An almost identical argument establishes that $c \mid b$ and is left as exercise 30 at the end of the section.

Because $c \mid a$ and $c \mid b$, c is a common divisor of a and b. Hence it is less than or equal to the greatest common divisor of a and b. In other words, $c \leq d$.

From (1) and (2), we conclude that $c = d$. It follows that d, the greatest common divisor of a and b, is equal to $as + bt$.

The following example shows a practical method for expressing the greatest common divisor of two integers as a linear combination of the two.

Example 8.4.6 Expressing a Greatest Common Divisor as a Linear Combination

In Example 4.8.6 we showed how to use the Euclidean algorithm to find that the greatest common divisor of 330 and 156 is 6. Use the results of those calculations to express gcd(330, 156) as a linear combination of 330 and 156.

Solution   The first four steps of the solution restate and extend results from Example 4.8.6, which were obtained by successive applications of the quotient-remainder theorem. The fifth step shows how to find the coefficients of the linear combination by substituting back through the results of the previous steps.

Step 1: $330 = 156 \cdot 2 + 18$, which implies that $18 = 330 - 156 \cdot 2$.

Step 2: $156 = 18 \cdot 8 + 12$, which implies that $12 = 156 - 18 \cdot 8$.

Step 3: $18 = 12 \cdot 1 + 6$, which implies that $6 = 18 - 12 \cdot 1$.

Step 4: $12 = 6 \cdot 2 + 0$, which implies that gcd(330, 156) = 6.

Step 5: By substituting back through steps 3 to 1:

$$
\begin{aligned}
6 &= 18 - 12 \cdot 1 & &\text{from step 3}\\
&= 18 - (156 - 8 \cdot 18) \cdot 1 & &\text{by substitution from step 2}\\
&= 9 \cdot 18 + (-1) \cdot 156 & &\text{by algebra}\\
&= 9 \cdot (330 - 156 \cdot 2) + (-1) \cdot 156 & &\text{by substitution from step 1}\\
&= 9 \cdot 330 + (-19) \cdot 156 & &\text{by algebra.}
\end{aligned}
$$

Thus gcd(330, 156) $= 9 \cdot 330 + (-19) \cdot 156$. (It is always a good idea to check the result of a calculation like this to be sure you did not make a mistake. In this case, you find that $9 \cdot 330 + (-19) \cdot 156$ does indeed equal 6.) ■

The Euclidean algorithm given in Section 4.8 can be adapted so as to compute the coefficients of the linear combination of the gcd at the same time as it computes the gcd itself. This extended Euclidean algorithm is described in the exercises at the end of the section.

Finding an Inverse Modulo n

Suppose you want to solve the following congruence for x:

$$2x \equiv 3 \,(\text{mod } 5)$$

Note that $3 \cdot 2 = 6 \equiv 1 \,(\text{mod } 5)$. So you can think of 3 as a kind of inverse for 2 modulo 5 and multiply both sides of the congruence to be solved by 3 to obtain

$$6x = 3 \cdot 2x \equiv 3 \cdot 3 \,(\text{mod } 5) \equiv 9 \,(\text{mod } 5) \equiv 4 \,(\text{mod } 5).$$

But $6 \equiv 1 \,(\text{mod } 5)$, and so by Theorem 8.4.3(3), $6x \equiv 1x \,(\text{mod } 5) \equiv x \,(\text{mod } 5)$. Thus, by the symmetric and transitive properties of modular congruence,

$$x \equiv 4 \,(\text{mod } 5),$$

and hence a solution is $x = 4$. (You can check that $2 \cdot 4 = 8 \equiv 3 \,(\text{mod } 5)$.)

Unfortunately, it is not always possible to find an "inverse" modulo an integer n. For instance, observe that

$$2 \cdot 1 \equiv 2 \,(\text{mod } 4)$$
$$2 \cdot 2 \equiv 0 \,(\text{mod } 4)$$
$$2 \cdot 3 \equiv 2 \,(\text{mod } 4).$$

By Theorem 8.4.3, these calculations suffice for us to conclude that the number 2 does not have an inverse modulo 4.

Describing the circumstances in which inverses exist in modular arithmetic requires the concept of relative primeness.

• **Definition**

Integers a and b are **relatively prime** if, and only if, $\gcd(a, b) = 1$. Integers $a_1, a_2, a_3, \ldots, a_n$ are **pairwise relatively prime** if, and only if, $\gcd(a_i, a_j) = 1$ for all integers i and j with $1 \le i, j \le n$, and $i \ne j$.

Given the definition of relatively prime integers, the following corollary is an immediate consequence of Theorem 8.4.5.

Corollary 8.4.6

If a and b are relatively prime integers, then there exist integers s and t such that $as + bt = 1$.

Example 8.4.7 Expressing 1 as a Linear Combination of Relatively Prime Integers

Show that 660 and 43 are relatively prime, and find a linear combination of 660 and 43 that equals 1.

Solution

Step 1: Divide 660 by 43 to obtain $660 = 43 \cdot 15 + 15$, which implies that $15 = 660 - 43 \cdot 15$.

Step 2: Divide 43 by 15 to obtain $43 = 15 \cdot 2 + 13$, which implies that $13 = 43 - 15 \cdot 2$.

Step 3: Divide 15 by 13 to obtain $15 = 13 \cdot 1 + 2$, which implies that $2 = 15 - 13$.

Step 4: Divide 13 by 2 to obtain $13 = 2 \cdot 6 + 1$, which implies that $1 = 13 - 2 \cdot 6$.

Step 5: Divide 2 by 1 to obtain $2 = 1 \cdot 2 + 0$, which implies that $\gcd(660, 43) = 1$ and so 660 and 43 are relatively prime.

Step 6: To express 1 as a linear combination of 660 and 43, substitute back through steps 4 to 1:

$$
\begin{aligned}
1 &= 13 - 2 \cdot 6 & &\text{from step 4} \\
  &= 13 - (15 - 13) \cdot 6 & &\text{by substitution from step 3} \\
  &= 7 \cdot 13 - 6 \cdot 15 & &\text{by algebra} \\
  &= 7 \cdot (43 - 15 \cdot 2) - 6 \cdot 15 & &\text{by substitution from step 2} \\
  &= 7 \cdot 43 - 20 \cdot 15 & &\text{by algebra} \\
  &= 7 \cdot 43 - 20 \cdot (660 - 43 \cdot 15) & &\text{by substitution from step 1} \\
  &= 307 \cdot 43 - 20 \cdot 660 & &\text{by algebra.}
\end{aligned}
$$

Thus $\gcd(660, 43) = 1 = 307 \cdot 43 - 20 \cdot 660$. (And a check by direct computation confirms that $307 \cdot 43 - 20 \cdot 660$ does indeed equal 1.)   ∎

A consequence of Corollary 8.4.6 is that under certain circumstances, it is possible to find an inverse for an integer modulo n.

Corollary 8.4.7 Existence of Inverses Modulo n

For all integers a and n, if $\gcd(a, n) = 1$, then there exists an integer s such that $as \equiv 1 \pmod{n}$. The integer s is called the **inverse of a modulo n.**

Proof:

Suppose a and n are integers and $\gcd(a, n) = 1$. By Corollary 8.4.6, there exist integers s and t such that

$$as + nt = 1.$$

Subtracting nt from both sides gives that

$$as = 1 - nt = 1 + (-t)n.$$

Thus, by definition of congruence modulo n,

$$as \equiv 1 \pmod{n}.$$

Example 8.4.8   Finding an Inverse Modulo n

a. Find an inverse for 43 modulo 660. That is, find an integer s such that $43s \equiv 1 \pmod{660}$.

b. Find a positive inverse for 3 modulo 40. That is, find a positive integer s such that $3s \equiv 1 \pmod{40}$.

Solution

a. By Example 8.4.7,

$$307 \cdot 43 - 20 \cdot 660 = 1.$$

Adding $20 \cdot 660$ to both sides gives that

$$307 \cdot 43 = 1 + 20 \cdot 660.$$

Thus, by definition of congruence modulo 660,

$$307 \cdot 43 \equiv 1 \pmod{660},$$

so 307 is an inverse for 43 modulo 660.

b. Use the technique of Example 8.4.7 to find a linear combination of 3 and 40 that equals 1.

Step 1: Divide 40 by 3 to obtain $40 = 3 \cdot 13 + 1$. This implies that $1 = 40 - 3 \cdot 13$.

Step 2: Divide 3 by 1 to obtain $3 = 3 \cdot 1 + 0$. This implies that $\gcd(3, 40) = 1$.

Step 3: Use the result of step 1 to write

$$3 \cdot (-13) = 1 + (-1)40.$$

This result implies that -13 is an inverse for 3 modulo 40. In symbols, $3 \cdot (-13) \equiv 1 \pmod{40}$. To find a positive inverse, compute $40 - 13$. The result is 27, and

$$27 \equiv -13 \pmod{40}$$

because $27 - (-13) = 40$. So, by Theorem 8.4.3(3),

$$3 \cdot 27 \equiv 3 \cdot (-13) \equiv 1 \pmod{40},$$

and thus by the transitive property of congruence modulo n, 27 is a positive integer that is an inverse for 3 modulo 40.

RSA Cryptography

At this point we have developed enough number theory to explain how to encrypt and decrypt messages using the RSA cipher. The effectiveness of the system is based on the fact that although modern computer algorithms make it quite easy to find two distinct large integers p and q—say on the order of several hundred digits each—that are virtually certain to be prime, even the fastest computers are not currently able to factor their product, an integer with approximately twice that many digits. In order to encrypt a message using the RSA cipher, a person needs to know the value of pq and of another integer e, both of which are made publicly available. But only a person who knows the individual values of p and q can decrypt an encrypted message.

We first give an example to show *how* the cipher works and then discuss some of the theory to explain *why* it works. The example is unrealistic in the sense that because p and q are so small, it would be easy to figure out what they are just by knowing their product. But working with small numbers conveys the idea of the system, while keeping the computations in a range that can be performed with a hand calculator.

Suppose Alice decides to set up an RSA cipher. She chooses two prime numbers, say $p = 5$ and $q = 11$, and computes $pq = 55$. She then chooses a positive integer e that is relatively prime to $(p - 1)(q - 1)$. In this case, $(p - 1)(q - 1) = 4 \cdot 10 = 40$, so she may take $e = 3$ because 3 is relatively prime to 40. (In practice, taking e to be small could compromise the secrecy of the cipher, so she would take a larger number than 3. However, the mathematics of the cipher works as well for 3 as for a larger number, and the smaller number makes for easier calculations.)

The two numbers $pq = 55$ and $e = 3$ are the **public key,** which she may distribute widely. Because the RSA cipher works only on numbers, Alice also informs people how she will interpret the numbers in the messages they send her. Let us suppose that she encodes letters of the alphabet the same way as was done for the Caesar cipher:

$$A = 1, B = 2, C = 3, \ldots, Z = 26.$$

Let us also assume that the messages Alice receives consist of blocks, each of which, for simplicity, is taken to be a single, numerically encoded letter of the alphabet.

Someone who wants to send Alice a message breaks the message into blocks, each consisting of a single letter, and finds the numeric equivalent for each block. The plaintext, M, in a block is converted into ciphertext, C, according to the following formula:

$$C = M^e \bmod pq. \tag{8.4.5}$$

Note that because both pq and e are public keys, anyone who is given the keys and knows modular arithmetic can encrypt a message to send to Alice.

Example 8.4.9 Encrypting a Message Using RSA Cryptography

Bob wants to send Alice the message HI. What is the ciphertext for his message?

Solution   Bob will send his message in two blocks, one for the H and another for the I. Because H is the eighth letter in the alphabet, it is encoded as 08, or 8. The corresponding ciphertext is computed using formula (8.4.5) as follows:

$$
\begin{aligned}
C &= 8^3 \bmod 55 \\
&= 512 \bmod 55 \\
&= 17.
\end{aligned}
$$

Because I is the ninth letter in the alphabet, it is encoded as 09, or 9. The corresponding ciphertext is

$$
\begin{aligned}
C &= 9^3 \bmod 55 \\
&= 729 \bmod 55 \\
&= 14.
\end{aligned}
$$

Accordingly, Bob sends Alice the message: 17 14.

To decrypt the message, Alice needs to compute the decryption key, a number d that is a positive inverse to e modulo $(p-1)(q-1)$. She obtains the plaintext M from the ciphertext C by the formula

$$M = C^d \bmod pq. \tag{8.4.6}$$

Note that because $M + kpq \equiv M \ (\text{mod } pq)$, M must be taken to be less than pq, as in the above example, in order for the decryption to be guaranteed to produce the original message. But because p and q are normally taken to be so large, this requirement does not cause problems. Long messages are broken into blocks of symbols to meet the restriction and several symbols are included in each block to prevent decryption based on knowledge of letter frequencies.

Example 8.4.10 Decrypting a Message Using RSA Cryptography

Imagine that Alice has hired you to help her decrypt messages and has shared with you the values of p and q. Decrypt the following ciphertext for her: 17 14.

Solution   Because $p = 5$ and $q = 11$, $(p - 1)(q - 1) = 40$, and so you first need to find the decryption key, which is a positive inverse for 3 modulo 40. Knowing that you would be needing this number, we computed it in Example 8.4.8(b) and found it to be 27. Thus you need to compute $M = 17^{27} mod\ 55$. To do so, note that $27 = 16 + 8 + 2 + 1 = 2^4 + 2^3 + 2 + 1$. Thus you will find the residues obtained when 17 is raised to successively higher powers of 2, up to $2^4 = 16$.

$$
\begin{aligned}
17\ mod\ 55 &= 17\ mod\ 55 &= 17 \\
17^2\ mod\ 55 &= 17^2\ mod\ 55 &= 14 \\
17^4\ mod\ 55 &= (17^2)^2\ mod\ 55 &= 14^2\ mod\ 55 &= 31 \\
17^8\ mod\ 55 &= (17^4)^2\ mod\ 55 &= 31^2\ mod\ 55 &= 26 \\
17^{16}\ mod\ 55 &= (17^8)^2\ mod\ 55 &= 26^2\ mod\ 55 &= 16
\end{aligned}
$$

Then you will use the fact that

$$17^{27} = 17^{16+8+2+1} = 17^{16} \cdot 17^8 \cdot 17^2 \cdot 17^1$$

to write

$$
\begin{aligned}
17^{27}\ mod\ 55 &= (17^{16} \cdot 17^8 \cdot 17^2 \cdot 17)\ mod\ 55 \\
&\equiv [(17^{16}\ mod\ 55)(17^8\ mod\ 55)(17^2\ mod\ 55)(17\ mod\ 55)]\ (mod\ 55) \\
&\qquad\qquad\qquad\qquad\qquad\qquad\qquad\qquad\qquad\qquad\quad \text{by Corollary 8.4.4} \\
&\equiv (16 \cdot 26 \cdot 14 \cdot 17)\ (mod\ 55) \\
&\equiv 99008\ (mod\ 55) \\
&\equiv 8\ (mod\ 55).
\end{aligned}
$$

Hence $17^{27}\ mod\ 55 = 8$, and thus the plaintext of the first part of Bob's message is 8, or 08. In the last step, you find the letter corresponding to 08, which is H. In exercises 14 and 15 at the end of this section, you are asked to show that when you decrypt 14, the result is 9, which corresponds to the letter I, so you can tell Alice that Bob's message is HI. ■

Euclid's Lemma

Another consequence of Theorem 8.4.5 is known as *Euclid's lemma*. It is the crucial fact behind the unique factorization theorem for the integers and is also of great importance in many other parts of number theory.

Theorem 8.4.8 Euclid's Lemma

For all integers a, b, and c, if $\gcd(a, c) = 1$ and $a \mid bc$, then $a \mid b$.

Proof:

Suppose a, b and c are integers, $\gcd(a, c) = 1$, and $a \mid bc$. *[We must show that $a \mid b$.]* By Theorem 8.4.5, there exist integers s and t so that

$$as + ct = 1.$$

Multiply both sides of this equation by b to obtain

$$bas + bct = b. \qquad\qquad 8.4.7$$

Since $a \mid bc$, by definition of divisibility there exists an integer k such that

$$bc = ak. \qquad\qquad 8.4.8$$

Substituting (8.4.8) into (8.4.7), rewriting, and factoring out an a gives that

$$b = bas + (ak)t = a(bs + kt).$$

Let $r = bs + kt$. Then r is an integer (because b, s, k, and t are all integers), and $b = ar$. Thus $a \mid b$ by definition of divisibility.

The unique factorization theorem for the integers states that any integer greater than 1 has a unique representation as a product of prime numbers, except possibly for the order in which the numbers are written. The hint for exercise 13 of Section 5.4 outlined a proof of the existence part of the proof, and the uniqueness of the representation follows quickly from Euclid's lemma. In exercise 41 at the end of this section, we outline a proof for you to complete.

Another application of Euclid's lemma is a cancellation theorem for congruence modulo n. This theorem allows us—under certain circumstances—to divide out a common factor in a congruence relation.

Theorem 8.4.9 Cancellation Theorem for Modular Congruence

For all integers a, b, c, and n with $n > 1$, if $\gcd(c, n) = 1$ and $ac \equiv bc \pmod{n}$, then $a \equiv b \pmod{n}$.

Proof:

Suppose a, b, c, and n are any integers, $\gcd(c, n) = 1$, and $ac \equiv bc \pmod{n}$. [*We must show that $a \equiv b \pmod{n}$.*] By definition of congruence modulo n,

$$n \mid (ac - bc).$$

and so, since

$$ac - bc = (a - b)c,$$
$$n \mid (a - b)c.$$

Because $\gcd(c, n) = 1$, we may apply Euclid's lemma to obtain

$$n \mid (a - b),$$

and so, by definition of congruence modulo n,

$$a \equiv b \pmod{n}.$$

An alternative proof for Theorem 8.4.9 uses Corollary 8.4.7. Because $\gcd(c, n) = 1$, the corollary guarantees an inverse for c modulo n. In the proof of Theorem 8.4.9, let d denote an inverse for c. Apply Theorem 8.4.3(3) repeatedly, first to multiply both sides of $ac \equiv bc \pmod{n}$ by d to obtain $(ac)d \equiv (bd)d \pmod{n}$, and then to use the fact that $cd \equiv 1 \pmod{n}$ to simplify the congruence and conclude that $a \equiv b \pmod{n}$.

Fermat's Little Theorem

Fermat's little theorem was given that name to distinguish it from Fermat's last theorem, which we discussed in Section 4.1. It provides the theoretical underpinning for RSA cryptography.

Theorem 8.4.10 Fermat's Little Theorem

If p is any prime number and a is any integer such that $p \nmid a$, then $a^{p-1} \equiv 1 \pmod{p}$.

Proof:

Suppose p is any prime number and a is any integer such that $p \nmid a$. Note that $a \neq 0$ because otherwise p would divide a. Consider the set of integers

$$S = \{a, 2a, 3a, \ldots, (p-1)a\}.$$

We claim that no two elements of S are congruent modulo p. For suppose $sa \equiv ra \pmod{p}$ for some integers s and r with $1 \leq r < s \leq p - 1$. Then, by definition of congruence modulo p,

$$p \mid (sa - ra), \quad \text{or, equivalently,} \quad p \mid (s - r)a.$$

Now $p \nmid a$ by hypothesis, and because p is prime, $\gcd(a, p) = 1$. Thus, by Euclid's lemma, $p \mid (s - r)$. But this is impossible because $0 < s - r < p$.

Consider the function F from S to the set $T = \{1, 2, 3, \ldots, (p-1)\}$ that sends each element of S to its residue modulo p. Then F is one-to-one because no two elements of S are congruent modulo p. In Section 9.4 we prove that if a function from one finite set to another is one-to-one, then it is also onto. Hence F is onto, and so the $p - 1$ residues of the $p - 1$ elements of S are exactly the numbers $1, 2, 3, \ldots, (p-1)$.

It follows by Theorem 8.4.3(3) that

$$a \cdot 2a \cdot 3a \cdots (p-1)a \equiv [1 \cdot 2 \cdot 3 \cdots (p-1)] \pmod{p},$$

or equivalently,

$$a^{p-1}(p-1)! \equiv (p-1)! \pmod{p}.$$

But because p is prime, p and $(p-1)!$ are relatively prime. Thus, by the cancellation theorem for modular congruence (Theorem 8.4.9),

$$a^{p-1} \equiv 1 \pmod{p}.$$

Why Does the RSA Cipher Work?

For the RSA cryptography method, the formula

$$M = C^d \bmod pq$$

is supposed to produce the original plaintext message, M, when the encrypted message is C. How can we be sure that it always does so? Recall that we require that $M < pq$, and we know that $C = M^e \bmod pq$. So, by substitution,

$$C^d \bmod pq = (M^e \bmod pq)^d \bmod pq.$$

By Theorem 8.4.3(4),

$$(M^e \bmod pq)^d \equiv M^{ed} \pmod{pq}.$$

Thus $C^d \bmod pq \equiv M^{ed} \pmod{pq}$, and so it suffices to show that

$$M \equiv M^{ed} \pmod{pq}.$$

Recall that d was chosen to be a positive inverse for e modulo $(p-1)(q-1)$, which exists because $\gcd(e, (p-1)(q-1)) = 1$. In other words,

$$ed \equiv 1 \pmod{(p-1)(q-1)},$$

or, equivalently,

$$ed = 1 + k(p-1)(q-1) \quad \text{for some positive integer } k.$$

Therefore,

$$M^{ed} = M^{1+k(p-1)(q-1)} = M(M^{p-1})^{k(q-1)} = M(M^{q-1})^{k(p-1)}$$

If $p \nmid M$, then by Fermat's little theorem, $M^{p-1} \equiv 1 \pmod{p}$, and so

$$M^{ed} = M(M^{p-1})^{k(q-1)} \equiv M(1)^{k(q-1)} \pmod{p} = M \pmod{p}.$$

Similarly, if $q \nmid M$, then by Fermat's little theorem, $M^{q-1} \equiv 1 \pmod{q}$, and so

$$M^{ed} = M(M^{q-1})^{k(p-1)} \equiv M(1)^{k(p-1)} = M \pmod{q}.$$

Thus, if M is relatively prime to pq,

$$M^{ed} \equiv M \pmod{p} \quad \text{and} \quad M^{ed} \equiv M \pmod{q}.$$

If M is not relatively prime to pq, then either $p \mid M$ or $q \mid M$. Without loss of generality, assume $p \mid M$. It follows that $M^{ed} \equiv 0 \equiv M \pmod{p}$. Moreover, because $M < pq$, $q \mid M$, and thus, as above, $M^{ed} \equiv M \pmod{q}$. Therefore, in this case also,

$$M^{ed} \equiv M \pmod{p} \quad \text{and} \quad M^{ed} \equiv M \pmod{q}.$$

By Theorem 8.4.1,

$$p \mid (M^{ed} - M) \quad \text{and} \quad q \mid (M^{ed} - M),$$

and, by definition of divisibility,

$$M^{ed} - M = pt \text{ for some integer } t.$$

By substitution, $$q \mid pt,$$

and since q and p are distinct prime numbers, Euclid's lemma applies to give

$$q \mid t.$$

Thus $$t = qu \text{ for some integer } u$$

by definition of divisibility. By substitution,

$$M - M^{ed} = pt = p(qu) = (pq)u,$$

where u is an integer, and so,

$$pq \mid (M - M^{ed})$$

by definition of divisibility. Thus

$$M - M^{ed} \equiv 0 \pmod{pq}$$

by definition of congruence, or, equivalently,

$$M \equiv M^{ed} \pmod{pq}.$$

Because $M < pq$, this last congruence implies that

$$M = M^{ed} \bmod pq,$$

and thus the RSA cipher gives the correct result.

Additional Remarks on Number Theory and Cryptography

The famous British mathematician G. H. Hardy (1877–1947) was fond of comparing the beauty of pure mathematics, especially number theory, to the beauty of art. Indeed, the theorems in this section have many beautiful and striking consequences beyond those we have had the space to describe, and the subject of number theory extends far beyond these theorems. Hardy also enjoyed describing pure mathematics as useless. Hence it is ironic that there are now whole books devoted to applications of number theory to computer science, RSA cryptography being just one such application. Furthermore, as the need for public-key cryptography has developed, techniques from other areas of mathematics, such as abstract algebra and algebraic geometry, have been used to develop additional cryptosystems.

Test Yourself

1. When letters of the alphabet are encrypted using the Caesar cipher, the encrypted version of a letter is _____.

2. If a, b, and n are integers with $n > 1$, all of the following are different ways to express the fact that $n \mid (a - b)$: _____, _____, _____, _____.

3. If a, b, c, d, m, and n are integers with $n > 1$ and if $a \equiv c \pmod{n}$ and $b \equiv d \pmod{n}$, then $a + b \equiv$ _____, $a - b \equiv$ _____, $ab \equiv$ _____, and $a^m \equiv$ _____.

4. If a, n, and k are positive integers with $n > 1$, an efficient way to compute $a^k \pmod{n}$ is to write k as a _____ and use the facts about computing products and powers modulo n.

5. To express a greatest common divisor of two integers as a linear combination of the integers, use the extended _____ algorithm.

6. To find an inverse for a positive integer a modulo an integer n with $n > 1$, you express the number 1 as _____.

7. To encrypt a message M using RSA cryptography with public key pq and e, you use the formula _____, and to decrypt a message C, you use the formula _____, where _____.

8. Euclid's lemma says that for all integers a, b, and c if $\gcd(a, c) = 1$ and $a \mid bc$, then _____.

9. Format's little theorem says that if p is any prime number and a is any integer such that $p \mid a$ then _____.

10. The crux of the proof that the RSA cipher works is that if (1) p and q are distinct large prime numbers, (2) $M < pq$, (3) M is relatively prime to pq, (4) e is relatively prime to $(p - 1)(q - 1)$, and (5) d is a positive inverse for e modulo $(p - 1)(q - 1)$, then $M =$ _____.

Exercise Set 8.4

1. a. Use the Caesar cipher to encrypt the message WHERE SHALL WE MEET.
   b. Use the Caesar cipher to decrypt the message LQ WKH FDIHWHULD.

2. a. Use the Caesar cipher to encrypt the message AN APPLE A DAY.

   b. Use the Caesar cipher to decrypt the message NHHSV WKH GRFWRU DZDB.

3. Let $a = 25, b = 19$, and $n = 3$.
   a. Verify that $3 \mid (25 - 19)$.
   b. Explain why $25 \equiv 19 \pmod{3}$.
   c. What value of k has the property that $25 = 19 + 3k$?

d. What is the (nonnegative) remainder obtained when 25 is divided by 3? When 19 is divided by 3?

e. Explain why 25 *mod* 3 = 19 *mod* 3.

4. Let $a = 68$, $b = 33$, and $n = 7$.
   a. Verify that $7 \mid (68 - 33)$.
   b. Explain why $68 \equiv 33 \pmod{7}$.
   c. What value of k has the property that $68 = 33 + 7k$?
   d. What is the (nonnegative) remainder obtained when 68 is divided by 7? When 33 is divided by 7?
   e. Explain why $68 \bmod 7 = 33 \bmod 7$.

5. Prove the transitivity of modular congruence. That is, prove that for all integers a, b, c, and n with $n > 1$, if $a \equiv b \pmod{n}$ and $b \equiv c \pmod{n}$ then $a \equiv c \pmod{n}$.

H 6. Prove that the distinct equivalence classes of the relation of congruence modulo n are the sets $[0], [1], [2], \ldots, [n-1]$, where for each $a = 0, 1, 2, \ldots, n-1$,

$$[a] = \{m \in Z \mid m \equiv a \pmod{n}\}.$$

7. Verify the following statements.
   a. $128 \equiv 2 \pmod{7}$ and $61 \equiv 5 \pmod{7}$
   b. $(128 + 61) \equiv (2 + 5) \pmod{7}$
   c. $(128 - 61) \equiv (2 - 5) \pmod{7}$
   d. $(128 \cdot 61) \equiv (2 \cdot 5) \pmod{7}$
   e. $128^2 \equiv 2^2 \pmod{7}$

8. Verify the following statements.
   a. $45 \equiv 3 \pmod{6}$ and $104 \equiv 2 \pmod{6}$
   b. $(45 + 104) \equiv (3 + 2) \pmod{6}$
   c. $(45 - 104) \equiv (3 - 2) \pmod{6}$
   d. $(45 \cdot 104) \equiv (3 \cdot 2) \pmod{6}$
   e. $45^2 \equiv 3^2 \pmod{6}$

In 9–11, prove each of the given statements, assuming that a, b, c, d, and n are integers with $n > 1$ and that $a \equiv c \pmod{n}$ and $b \equiv d \pmod{n}$.

9. a. $(a + b) \equiv (c + d) \pmod{n}$
   b. $(a - b) \equiv (c - d) \pmod{n}$

10. $a^2 \equiv c^2 \pmod{n}$

11. $a^m \equiv c^m \pmod{n}$ for all integers $m \geq 1$ (Use mathematical induction on m.)

12. a. Prove that for all integers $n \geq 0$, $10^n \equiv 1 \pmod{9}$.
    b. Use part (a) to prove that a positive integer is divisible by 9 if, and only if, the sum of its digits is divisible by 9.

13. a. Prove that for all integers $n \geq 1$, $10^n \equiv (-1)^n \pmod{11}$.
    b. Use part (a) to prove that a positive integer is divisible by 11 if, and only if, the alternating sum of its digits is divisible by 11. (For instance, the alternating sum of the digits of 82,379 is $8 - 2 + 3 - 7 + 9 = 11$ and $82,379 = 11 \cdot 7489$.)

14. Use the technique of Example 8.4.4 to find $14^2 \bmod 55$, $14^4 \bmod 55$, $14^8 \bmod 55$, and $14^{16} \bmod 55$.

15. Use the result of exercise 14 and the technique of Example 8.4.5 to find $14^{27} \bmod 55$.

In 16–18, use the techniques of Example 8.4.4 and Example 8.4.5 to find the given numbers.

16. $675^{307} \bmod 713$

17. $89^{307} \bmod 713$

18. $48^{307} \bmod 713$

In 19–24, use the RSA cipher from Examples 8.4.9 and 8.4.10. In 19–21, translate the message into its numeric equivalent and encrypt it. In 22–24, decrypt the ciphertext and translate the result into letters of the alphabet to discover the message.

19. HELLO   20. WELCOME   21. EXCELLENT

22. 13 20 20 09   23. 08 05 15   24. 51 14 49 15

H 25. Use Theorem 5.2.3 to prove that if a and n are positive integers and $a^n - 1$ is prime, then $a = 2$ and n is prime.

In 26 and 27, use the extended Euclidean algorithm to find the greatest common divisor of the given numbers and express it as a linear combination of the two numbers.

26. 6664 and 765   27. 4158 and 1568

Exercises 28 and 29 refer to the following formal version of the extended Euclidean algorithm.

Algorithm 8.4.1 Extended Euclidean Algorithm

[Given integers A and B with A > B > 0, this algorithm computes gcd(A, B) and finds integers s and t such that $sA + tB = $ gcd(A, B).]

Input: A, B *[integers with $A > B > 0$]*

Algorithm Body:

$a := A, b := B, s := 1, t := 0, u := 0, v := 1,$
[pre-condition: $a = sA + tB$ and $b = uA + vB$]

while $(b \neq 0)$

    [loop invariant: $a = sA + tB$ and $b = uA + vB$, gcd(a, b) = gcd(A, B)]

    $r := a \bmod b, q := a \text{ div } b$

    $a := b, b := r$

    $newu := s - uq, newv := t - vq$

    $s := u, t := v$

    $u := newu, v := newv$

end while

$gcd := a$

[post-condition: gcd(A, B) = a = sA + tB]

Output: gcd *[a positive integer], s, t [integers]*

In 28 and 29, for the given values of A and B, make a table showing the value of s, t, and $sA + tB$ before the start of the while loop and after each iteration of the loop.

28. $A = 330$, $B = 156$ 29. $A = 284$, $B = 168$

30. Finish the proof of Theorem 8.4.5 by proving that if a, b and c are as in the proof, then $c \mid b$.

31. a. Find an inverse for 210 modulo 13.
    b. Find a positive inverse for 210 modulo 13.
    c. Find a positive solution for the congruence $210x \equiv 8$ (mod 13).

32. a. Find an inverse for 41 modulo 660.
    b. Find the least positive solution for the following congruence: $41x \equiv 125$ (mod 660).

H 33. Use Theorem 8.4.5 to prove that for all integers a, b, and c, if $\gcd(a, b) = 1$ and $a \mid c$ and $b \mid c$, then $ab \mid c$.

34. Give a counterexample to show that the converse of exercise 33 is false.

35. Corollary 8.4.7 guarantees the existence of an inverse modulo n for an integer a when a and n are relatively prime. Use Euclid's lemma to prove that the inverse is unique modulo n. In other words, show that any two integers whose product with a is congruent to 1 modulo n are congruent to each other modulo n.

In 36, 37, 39, and 40, use the RSA cipher with public key $n = 713 = 23 \cdot 31$ and $e = 43$. In 36 and 37, encode the messages into their numeric equivalents and encrypt them. In 39 and 40, decrypt the given ciphertext and find the original messages.

36. HELP   37. COME

38. Find the least positive inverse for 43 modulo 660.

39. 675 089 089 048

40. 028 018 675 129

H 41. a. Use mathematical induction and Euclid's lemma to prove that for all positive integers s, if p and $q_1, q_2, \ldots, q_s$ are prime numbers and $p \mid q_1 q_2 \cdots q_s$, then $p = q_i$ for some i with $1 \le i \le s$.

b. The uniqueness part of the unique factorization theorem for the integers says that given any integer n, if

$$n = p_1 p_2 \cdots p_r = q_1 q_2 \cdots q_s$$

for some positive integers r and s and prime numbers $p_1 \le p_2 \le \cdots \le p_r$ and $q_1 \le q_2 \le \cdots \le q_s$, then $r = s$ and $p_i = q_i$ for all integers i with $1 \le i \le r$.

Use the result of part (a) to fill in the details of the following sketch of a proof: Suppose that n is an integer with two different prime factorizations: $n = p_1 p_2 \cdots p_t = q_1 q_2 \cdots q_u$. All the prime factors that appear on both sides can be cancelled (as many times as they appear on both sides) to arrive at the situation where $p_1 p_2 \cdots p_r = q_1 q_2 \cdots q_s$, $p_1 \le p_2 \le \cdots \le p_r$, $q_1 \le q_2 \le \cdots \le q_s$, and $p_i \ne q_j$ for any integers i and j. Then use part (a) to deduce a contradiction, and so the prime factorization of n is unique except, possibly, for the order in which the prime factors are written.

42. According to Fermat's little theorem, if p is a prime number and a and p are relatively prime, then $a^{p-1} \equiv 1$ (mod p). Verify that this theorem gives correct results for
    a. $a = 15$ and $p = 7$ b. $a = 8$ and $p = 11$

43. Fermat's little theorem can be used to show that a number is not prime by finding a number a relatively prime to p with the property that $a^{p-1} \not\equiv 1$ (mod p). However, it cannot be used to show that a number *is* prime. Find an example to illustrate this fact. That is, find integers a and p such that a and p are relatively prime and $a^{p-1} \equiv 1$ (mod p) but p is not prime.

Answers for Test Yourself

1. three places in the alphabet to the right of the letter, with X wrapped around to A, Y to B, and Z to C
2. $a \equiv b$ (mod n); $a = b + kn$ for some integer k; a and b have the same nonnegative remainder when divided by n; a mod $n = b$ mod n 3. $(c + d)$ (mod n); $(c - d)$ (mod n); (cd) (mod n); c^m (mod n)   4. sum of powers of 2   5. version of the Euclidean   6. a linear combination of a and n 7. $C = M^c$ mod pq; $M = C^d$ mod pq; d is a positive inverse for e modulo $(p - 1)(q - 1)$ 8. $a \mid b$
9. $a^{p-1} \equiv 1$ (mod p)   10. M^{ed} mod pq

8.5 Partial Order Relations

There is no branch of mathematics, however abstract, which may not some day be applied to phenomena of the real world. — Nicolai Ivanovitch Lobachevsky, 1792–1856

In order to obtain a degree in computer science at a certain university, a student must take a specified set of required courses, some of which must be completed before others can be started. Given the prerequistite structure of the program, one might ask what is the least number of school terms needed to fulfill the degree requirements, or what is the maximum number of courses that can be taken in the same term, or whether there is a sequence in which a part-time student can take the courses one per term. Later in this section, we will show how representing the prerequisite structure of the program as a partial order relation makes it relatively easy to answer such questions.

Antisymmetry

In Section 8.2 we defined three properties of relations: reflexivity, symmetry, and transitivity. A fourth property of relations is called *antisymmetry*. In terms of the arrow diagram of a relation, saying that a relation is antisymmetric is the same as saying that whenever there is an arrow going from one element to another *distinct* element, there is *not* an arrow going back from the second to the first.

• Definition

Let R be a relation on a set A. R is **antisymmetric** if, and only if,

for all a and b in A,   if $a\ R\ b$ and $b\ R\ a$ then $a = b$.

By taking the negation of the definition, you can see that a relation R is **not** **antisymmetric** if, and only if,

there are elements a and b in A such that $a\ R\ b$ and $b\ R\ a$ but $a \neq b$.

Example 8.5.1 Testing for Antisymmetry of Finite Relations

Let R_1 and R_2 be the relations on $\{0, 1, 2\}$ defined as follows: Draw the directed graphs for R_1 and R_2 and indicate which relations are antisymmetric.

a. $R_1 = \{(0, 2), (1, 2), (2, 0)\}$

b. $R_2 = \{(0, 0), (0, 1), (0, 2), (1, 1), (1, 2)\}$

Solution

a. R_1 is not antisymmetric.

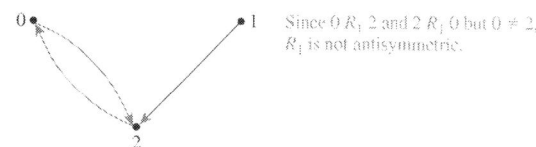

Since $0\ R_1\ 2$ and $2\ R_1\ 0$ but $0 \neq 2$, R_1 is not antisymmetric.

b. R_2 is antisymmetric.

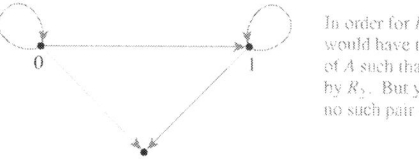

In order for R_2 not to be antisymmetric, there would have to exist a pair of distinct elements of A such that each is related to the other by R_2. But you can see by inspection that no such pair exists.

Example 8.5.2 Testing for Antisymmetry of "Divides" Relations

Let R_1 be the "divides" relation on the set of all positive integers, and let R_2 be the "divides" relation on the set of all integers.

For all $a, b \in Z^+$, $a\ R_1\ b$ $\Leftrightarrow$ $a \mid b$.
For all $a, b \in Z$, $a\ R_2\ b$ $\Leftrightarrow$ $a \mid b$.

a. Is R_1 antisymmetric? Prove or give a counterexample.

b. Is R_2 antisymmetric? Prove or give a counterexample.

Solution

a. R_1 is antisymmetric.

Proof:

Suppose a and b are positive integers such that $a \ R_1 \ b$ and $b \ R_1 \ a$. [*We must show that $a = b$.*] By definition of R_1, $a \mid b$ and $b \mid a$. Thus, by definition of divides, there are integers k_1 and k_2 with $b = k_1 a$ and $a = k_2 b$. It follows that

$$b = k_1 a = k_1(k_2 b) = (k_1 k_2)b.$$

Dividing both sides by b gives

$$k_1 k_2 = 1.$$

Now since a and b are both integers k_1 and k_2 are both positive integers also. But the only product of two positive integers that equals 1 is $1 \cdot 1$. Thus

$$k_1 = k_2 = 1$$

and so
$$a = k_2 b = 1 \cdot b = b.$$

[*This is what was to be shown.*]

b. R_2 is not antisymmetric.

Counterexample:

Let $a = 2$ and $b = -2$. Then $a \mid b$ [*since $-2 = (-1) \cdot 2$*] and $b \mid a$ [*since $2 = (-1)(-2)$*]. Hence $a \ R_2 \ b$ and $b \ R_2 \ a$ but $a \neq b$. ∎

Example 8.5.2 illustrates the fact that a relation may be antisymmetric on a subset of a set but not antisymmetric on the set itself.

Partial Order Relations

A relation that is reflexive, antisymmetric, and transitive is called a *partial order*.

• **Definition**

Let R be a relation defined on a set A. R is a **partial order relation** if, and only if, R is reflexive, antisymmetric, and transitive.

Two fundamental partial order relations are the "less than or equal to" relation on a set of real numbers and the "subset" relation on a set of sets. These can be thought of as models, or paradigms, for general partial order relations.

Example 8.5.3 The "Subset" Relation

Let $\mathcal{A}$ be any collection of sets and define the "subset" relation, $\subseteq$, on $\mathcal{A}$ as follows: For all $U, V \in \mathcal{A}$,

$$U \subseteq V \quad \Leftrightarrow \quad \text{for all } x, \text{ if } x \in U \text{ then } x \in V.$$

By an argument almost identical to that of the solution for exercise 23 of Section 8.2, $\subseteq$ is reflexive and transitive. Finish the proof that $\subseteq$ is a partial order relation by proving that $\subseteq$ is antisymmetric.

Solution   For $\subseteq$ to be antisymmetric means that for all sets U and V in $\mathscr{A}$ if $U \subseteq V$ and $V \subseteq U$ then $U = V$. But this is true by definition of equality of sets.   ■

Example 8.5.4 A "Divides" Relation on a Set of Positive Integers

Let $|$ be the "divides" relation on a set A of positive integers. That is, for all $a, b \in A$,

$$a \mid b \quad \Leftrightarrow \quad b = ka \text{ for some integer } k.$$

Prove that $|$ is a partial order relation on A.

Solution

$|$ *is reflexive*: *[We must show that for all $a \in A, a \mid a$.]* Suppose $a \in A$. Then $a = 1 \cdot a$, so $a \mid a$ by definition of divisibility.

$|$ *is antisymmetric*: *[We must show that for all $a, b \in A$, if $a \mid b$ and $b \mid a$ then $a = b$.]* The proof of this is virtually identical to that of Example 8.5.2(a).

$|$ *is transitive*: To show transitivity means to show that for all $a, b, c \in A$, if $a \mid b$ and $b \mid c$ then $a \mid c$. But this was proved as Theorem 4.3.3.

Since $|$ is reflexive, antisymmetric, and transitive, $|$ is a partial order relation on A.

■

Example 8.5.5 The "Less Than or Equal to" Relation

Let S be a set of real numbers and define the "less than or equal to" relation, $\leq$, on S as follows: For all real numbers x and y in S,

$$x \leq y \quad \Leftrightarrow \quad x < y \text{ or } x = y.$$

Show that $\leq$ is a partial order relation.

Solution

$\leq$ *is reflexive*: For $\leq$ to be reflexive means that $x \leq x$ for all real numbers x in S. But $x \leq x$ means that $x < x$ or $x = x$, and $x = x$ is always true.

$\leq$ *is antisymmetric*: For $\leq$ to be antisymmetric means that for all real numbers x and y in S, if $x \leq y$ and $y \leq x$ then $x = y$. This follows immediately from the definition of $\leq$ and the trichotomy property (see Appendix A, T17), which says that given any real numbers, x and y, exactly one of the following holds: $x < y$ or $x = y$ or $x > y$.

$\leq$ *is transitive*: For $\leq$ to be transitive means that for all real numbers x, y, and z in S if $x \leq y$ and $y \leq z$ then $x \leq z$. This follows from the definition of $\leq$ and the transitivity property of order (see Appendix A, T18), which says that given any real numbers x, y, and z, if $x < y$ and $y < z$ then $x < z$.

Because $\leq$ is reflexive, antisymmetric, and transitive, it is a partial order relation.   ■

Because of the special paradigmatic role played by the $\leq$ relation in the study of partial order relations, the symbol $\preceq$ is often used to refer to a general partial order relation, and the notation $x \preceq y$ is read "x is less than or equal to y" or "y is greater than or equal to x."

Lexicographic Order

To figure out which of two words comes first in an English dictionary, you compare their letters one by one from left to right. If all letters have been the same to a certain point and one word runs out of letters, that word comes first in the dictionary. For example, *play* comes before *playhouse*. If all letters up to a certain point are the same and the next letters differ, then the word whose next letter is located earlier in the alphabet comes first in the dictionary. For instance, *playhouse* comes before *playmate*.

More generally, if A is any set with a partial order relation, then a *dictionary* or *lexicographic* order can be defined on a set of strings over A as indicated in the following theorem.

Theorem 8.5.1

Let A be a set with a partial order relation R, and let S be a set of strings over A. Define a relation $\preceq$ on S as follows:

For any two strings in S, $a_1 a_2 \cdots a_m$ and $b_1 b_2 \cdots b_n$, where m and n are positive integers,

1. If $m \leq n$ and $a_i = b_i$ for all $i = 1, 2, \ldots, m$, then

$$a_1 a_2 \cdots a_m \preceq b_1 b_2 \cdots b_n.$$

2. If for some integer k with $k \leq m$, $k \leq n$, and $k \geq 1$, $a_i = b_i$ for all $i = 1, 2, \ldots, k-1$, and $a_k \neq b_k$, but $a_k \, R \, b_k$ then

$$a_1 a_2 \cdots a_m \preceq b_1 b_2 \cdots b_n.$$

3. If ε is the null string and s is any string in S, then $\epsilon \preceq s$.

If no strings are related other than by these three conditions, then $\preceq$ is a partial order relation.

The proof of Theorem 8.5.1 is technical but straightforward. It is left for the exercises.

The partial order relation of Theorem 8.5.1 is called the **lexicographic order for S** that corresponds to the partial order R on A.

Example 8.5.6 A Lexicographic Order

Let $A = \{x, y\}$ and let R be the following partial order relation on A:

$$R = \{(x, x), (x, y), (y, y)\}.$$

Let S be the set of all strings over A, and denote by $\preceq$ the lexicographic order for S that corresponds to R.

a. Is $x \preceq xx$? $x \preceq xy$? $xx \preceq xxx$? $yxy \preceq yxyxxx$?

b. Is $x \preceq y$? $xx \preceq xyx$? $xxxy \preceq xy$? $yxyxxyy \preceq yxyxy$?

c. Is $\epsilon \preceq x$? $\epsilon \preceq xy$? $\epsilon \preceq yyxy$?

Solution

a. Yes in all cases, by property (1) of the definition of $\preceq$.

b. Yes in all cases, by property (2) of the definition of $\preceq$.

c. Yes in all cases, by property (3) of the definition of $\preceq$.

Hasse Diagrams

Let $A = \{1, 2, 3, 9, 18\}$ and consider the "divides" relation on A: For all $a, b \in A$,

$$a \mid b \quad \Leftrightarrow \quad b = ka \text{ for some integer } k.$$

The directed graph of this relation has the following appearance:

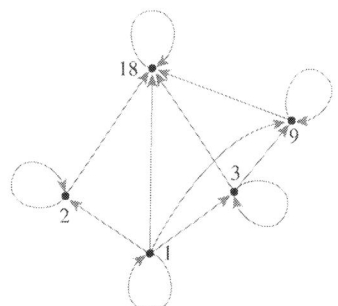

Note that there is a loop at every vertex, all other arrows point in the same direction (upward), and any time there is an arrow from one point to a second and from the second point to a third, there is an arrow from the first point to the third. Given any partial order relation defined on a finite set, it is possible to draw the directed graph in such a way that all of these properties are satisfied. This makes it possible to associate a somewhat simpler graph, called a **Hasse diagram** (after Helmut Hasse, a twentieth-century German number theorist), with a partial order relation defined on a finite set. To obtain a Hasse diagram, proceed as follows:

Start with a directed graph of the relation, placing vertices on the page so that all arrows point upward. Then eliminate

1. the loops at all the vertices,

2. all arrows whose existence is implied by the transitive property,

3. the direction indicators on the arrows.

For the relation given previously, the Hasse diagram is as follows:

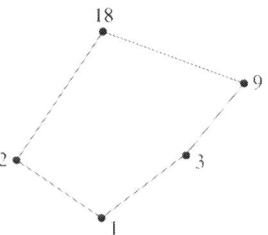

Example 8.5.7 Constructing a Hasse Diagram

Consider the "subset" relation, $\subseteq$, on the set $\mathcal{P}(\{a, b, c\})$. That is, for all sets U and V in $\mathcal{P}(\{a, b, c\})$,

$$U \subseteq V \quad \Leftrightarrow \quad \forall x, \text{ if } x \in U \text{ then } x \in V.$$

Construct the Hasse diagram for this relation.

Solution   Draw the directed graph of the relation in such a way that all arrows except loops point upward.

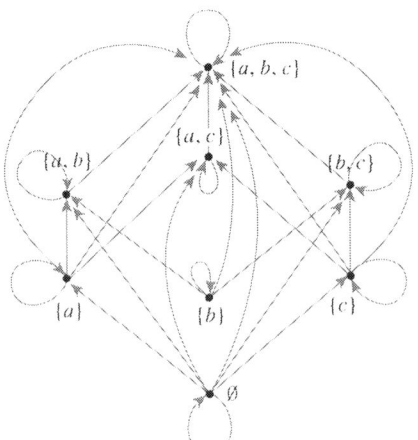

Then strip away all loops, unnecessary arrows, and direction indicators to obtain the Hasse diagram.

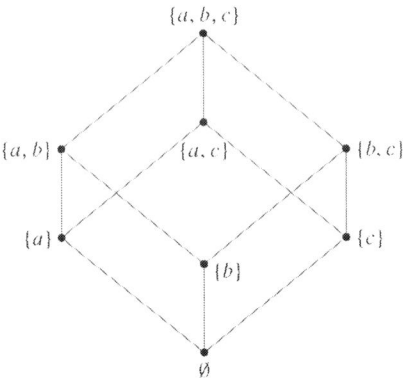

To recover the directed graph of a relation from the Hasse diagram, just reverse the instructions given previously, using the knowledge that the original directed graph was sketched so that all arrows pointed upward:

1. Reinsert the direction markers on the arrows making all arrows point upward.

2. Add loops at each vertex.

3. For each sequence of arrows from one point to a second and from that second point to a third, add an arrow from the first point to the third.

Example 8.5.8 Obtaining the Directed Graph of a Partial Order Relation from the Hasse Diagram of the Relation

A partial order relation R has the following Hasse diagram. Find the directed graph of R.

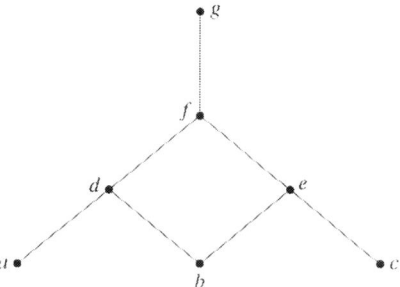

Solution

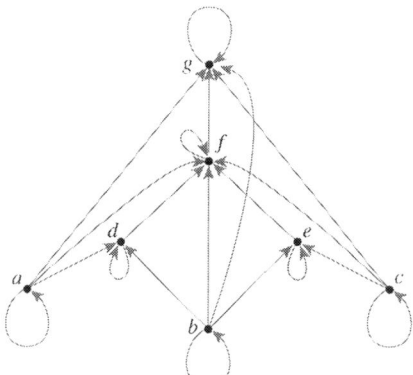

Partially and Totally Ordered Sets

Given any two real numbers x and y, either $x \leq y$ or $y \leq x$. In a situation like this, the elements x and y are said to be *comparable*. On the other hand, given two subsets A and B of $\{a, b, c\}$, it may be the case that neither $A \subseteq B$ nor $B \subseteq A$. For instance, let $A = \{a, b\}$ and $B = \{b, c\}$. Then $A \nsubseteq B$ and $B \nsubseteq A$. In such a case, A and B are said to be *noncomparable*.

> **• Definition**
>
> Suppose $\preceq$ is a partial order relation on a set A. Elements a and b of A are said to be **comparable** if, and only if, either $a \preceq b$ or $b \preceq a$. Otherwise, a and b are called **noncomparable.**

When all the elements of a partial order relation are comparable, the relation is called a *total order*.

• Definition

If R is a partial order relation on a set A, and for any two elements a and b in A either $a \, R \, b$ or $b \, R \, a$, then R is a **total order relation** on A.

Both the "less than or equal to" relation on sets of real numbers and the lexicographic order of the set of words in a dictionary are total order relations. Note that the Hasse diagram for a total order relation can be drawn as a single vertical "chain."

Many important partial order relations have elements that are not comparable and are, therefore, not total order relations. For instance, the subset relation on $\mathscr{P}(\{a, b, c\})$ is not a total order relation because, as shown previously, the subsets $\{a, b\}$ and $\{a, c\}$ of $\{a, b, c\}$ are not comparable. In addition, a "divides" relation is not a total order relation unless the elements are all powers of a single integer. (See exercise 21 at the end of this section.)

A set A is called a **partially ordered set** (or **poset**) with respect to a relation $\preceq$ if, and only if, $\preceq$ is a partial order relation on A. For instance, the set of real numbers is a partially ordered set with respect to the "less than or equal to" relation $\leq$, and a set of sets is partially ordered with respect to the "subset" relation $\subseteq$. It is entirely straightforward to show that *any subset of a partially ordered set is partially ordered.* (See exercise 35 at the end of this section.) This, of course, assumes the "same definition" for the relation on the subset as for the set as a whole. A set A is called a **totally ordered set** with respect to a relation $\preceq$ if, and only if, A is partially ordered with respect to $\preceq$ and $\preceq$ is a total order.

A set that is partially ordered but not totally ordered may have totally ordered subsets. Such subsets are called *chains*.

• Definition

Let A be a set that is partially ordered with respect to a relation $\preceq$. A subset B of A is called a **chain** if, and only if, the elements in each pair of elements in B is comparable. In other words, $a \preceq b$ or $b \preceq a$ for all a and b in B. The **length of a chain** is one less than the number of elements in the chain.

Observe that if B is a chain in A, then B is a totally ordered set with respect to the "restriction" of $\preceq$ to B.

Example 8.5.9 A Chain of Subsets

The set $\mathscr{P}(\{a, b, c\})$ is partially ordered with respect to the subset relation. Find a chain of length 3 in $\mathscr{P}(\{a, b, c\})$.

Solution   Since $\emptyset \subseteq \{a\} \subseteq \{a, b, \} \subseteq \{a, b, c\}$, the set

$$S = \{\emptyset, \{a\}, \{a, b\}, \{a, b, c\}\}$$

is a chain of length 3 in $\mathscr{P}(\{a, b, c\})$. ∎

In exercise 39 at the end of this section, you are asked to show that a set that is partially ordered with respect to a relation $\preceq$ is totally ordered with respect to $\preceq$ if, and only if, it is a chain.

A *maximal element* in a partially ordered set is an element that is greater than or equal to every element to *which it is comparable*. (There may be many elements to which it is *not* comparable.) A *greatest element* in a partially ordered set is an element that is greater than or equal to *every* element in the set (so it is comparable to every element in the set). Minimal and least elements are defined similarly.

• Definition

Let a set A be partially ordered with respect to a relation $\preceq$.

1. An element a in A is called a **maximal element of A** if, and only if, for all b in A, either $b \preceq a$ or b and a are not comparable.

2. An element a in A is called a **greatest element of A** if, and only if, for all b in A, $b \preceq a$.

3. An element a in A is called a **minimal element of A** if, and only if, for all b in A, either $a \preceq b$ or b and a are not comparable.

4. An element a in A is called a **least element of A** if, and only if, for all b in A, $a \preceq b$.

A greatest element is maximal, but a maximal element need not be a greatest element. However, every finite subset of a totally ordered set has both a least element and a greatest element. (See exercise 40 at the end of the section.) Similarly, a least element is minimal, but a minimal element need not be a least element. Furthermore, a set that is partially ordered with respect to a relation can have at most one greatest element and one least element (see exercise 42 at the end of the section), but it may have more than one maximal or minimal element. The next example illustrates some of these facts.

Example 8.5.10 Maximal, Minimal, Greatest, and Least Elements

Let $A = \{a, b, c, d, e, f, g, h, i\}$ have the partial ordering $\preceq$ defined by the following Hasse diagram. Find all maximal, minimal, greatest, and least elements of A.

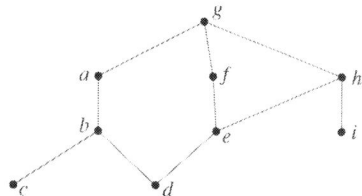

Solution   There is just one maximal element, g, which is also the greatest element. The minimal elements are c, d, and i, and there is no least element. ∎

Topological Sorting

Is it possible to input the sets of $\mathscr{P}(\{a, b, c\})$ into a computer in a way that is *compatible* with the subset relation $\subseteq$ in the sense that if set U is a subset of set V, then U is input before V? The answer, as it turns out, is yes. For instance, the following input order satisfies the given condition:

$$\varnothing, \{a\}, \{b\}, \{c\}, \{a, b\}, \{a, c\}, \{b, c\}, \{a, b, c\}.$$

Another input order that satisfies the condition is

$$\varnothing, \{a\}, \{b\}, \{a, b\}, \{c\}, \{b, c\}, \{a, c\}, \{a, b, c\}.$$

• Definition

Given partial order relations $\preceq$ and $\preceq'$ on a set A, $\preceq'$ is **compatible** with $\preceq$ if, and only if, for all a and b in A, if $a \preceq b$ then $a \preceq' b$.

Given an arbitrary partial order relation $\preceq$ on a set A, is there a total order $\preceq'$ on A that is compatible with $\preceq$? If the set on which the partial order is defined is finite, then the answer is yes. A total order that is compatible with a given order is called a *topological sorting*.

• Definition

Given partial order relations $\preceq$ and $\preceq'$ on a set A, $\preceq'$ is a **topological sorting** for $\preceq$ if, and only if, $\preceq'$ is a total order that is compatible with $\preceq$.

The construction of a topological sorting for a general finite partially ordered set is based on the fact that *any partially ordered set that is finite and nonempty has a minimal element.* (See exercise 41 at the end of the section.) To create a total order for a partially ordered set, simply pick any minimal element and make it number one. Then consider the set obtained when this element is removed. Since the new set is a subset of a partially ordered set, it is partially ordered. If it is empty, stop the process. If not, pick a minimal element from it and call that element number two. Then consider the set obtained when this element also is removed. If this set is empty, stop the process. If not, pick a minimal element and call it number three. Continue in this way until all the elements of the set have been used up.

Here is a somewhat more formal version of the algorithm:

Constructing a Topological Sorting

Let $\preceq$ be a partial order relation on a nonempty finite set A. To construct a topological sorting,

1. Pick any minimal element x in A. *[Such an element exists since A is nonempty.]*

2. Set $A' := A - \{x\}$.

3. Repeat steps a–c while $A' \neq \varnothing$.
   a. Pick any minimal element y in A'.
   b. Define $x \preceq' y$.
   c. Set $A' := A' - \{y\}$ and $x := y$.
   [Completion of steps 1–3 of this algorithm gives enough information to construct the Hasse diagram for the total ordering $\preceq'$. We have already shown how to use the Hasse diagram to obtain a complete directed graph for a relation.]

Example 8.5.11 A Topological Sorting

Consider the set $A = \{2, 3, 4, 6, 18, 24\}$ ordered by the "divides" relation $|$. The Hasse diagram of this relation is the following:

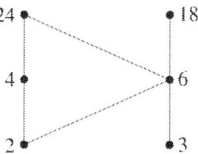

The ordinary "less than or equal to" relation $\leq$ on this set is a topological sorting for it since for positive integers a and b, if $a \mid b$ then $a \leq b$. Find another topological sorting for this set.

Solution   The set has two minimal elements: 2 and 3. Either one may be chosen; say you pick 3. The beginning of the total order is

$$\text{total order: } 3.$$

Set $A' = A - \{3\}$. You can indicate this by removing 3 from the Hasse diagram as shown below.

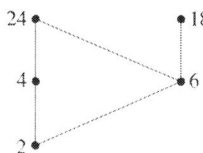

Next choose minimal element from $A' - \{3\}$. Only 2 is minimal, so you must pick it. The total order thus far is

$$\text{total order: } 3 \preceq 2.$$

Set $A' = (A - \{3\}) - \{2\} = A - \{3, 2\}$. You can indicate this by removing 2 from the Hasse diagram, as is shown below.

Choose a minimal element from $A' - \{3, 2\}$. Again you have two choices: 4 and 6. Say you pick 6. The total order for the elements chosen thus far is

$$\text{total order: } 3 \preceq 2 \preceq 6.$$

You continue in this way until every element of A has been picked. One possible sequence of choices gives

$$\text{total order: } 3 \preceq 2 \preceq 6 \preceq 18 \preceq 4 \preceq 24.$$

You can verify that this order is compatible with the "divides" partial order by checking that for each pair of elements a and b in A such that $a \mid b$, then $a \preceq b$. Note that it is *not* the case that if $a \preceq b$ then $a \mid b$. ▪

An Application

To return to the example that introduced this section, note that the following defines a partial order relation on the set of courses required for a university degree: For all required courses x and y,

$$x \preceq y \quad \Leftrightarrow \quad x = y \quad \text{or} \quad x \text{ is a prerequisite for } y$$

If the Hasse diagram for the relation is drawn, then the questions raised at the beginning of this section can be answered easily. For instance, consider the Hasse diagram for the requirements at a particular university, which is shown in Figure 8.5.1.

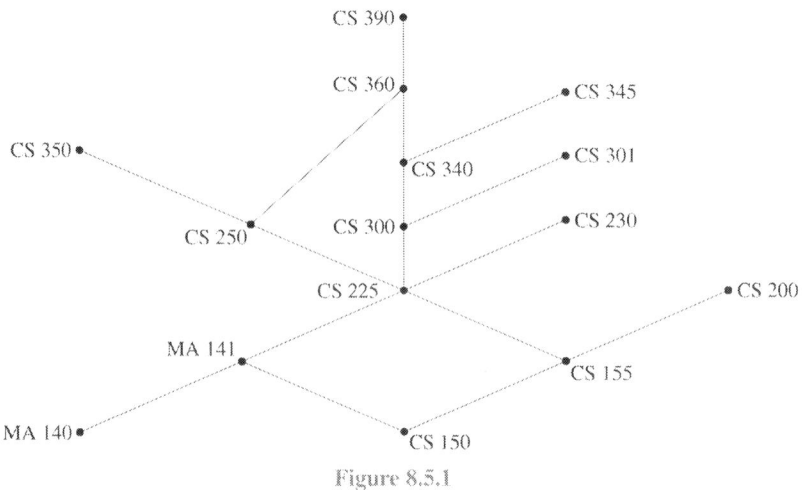

Figure 8.5.1

The minimum number of school terms needed to complete the requirements is the size of a longest chain, which is 7 (150, 155, 225, 300, 340, 360, 390, for example). The maximum number of courses that could be taken in the same term (assuming the university allows it) is the maximum number of noncomparable courses, which is 6 (350, 360, 345, 301, 230, 200, for example). A part-time student could take the courses in a sequence determined by constructing a topological sorting for the set. (One such sorting is 140, 150, 141, 155, 200, 225, 230, 300, 250, 301, 340, 345, 350, 360, 390. There are many others.)

PERT and CPM

Two important and widely used applications of partial order relations are **PERT** (Program Evaluation and Review Technique) and **CPM** (Critical Path Method). These techniques came into being in the 1950s as planners came to grips with the complexities of scheduling the individual activities needed to complete very large projects, and although they are very similar, their developments were independent. PERT was developed by the U.S. Navy to help organize the construction of the Polaris submarine, and CPM was developed by the E. I. Du Pont de Nemours company for scheduling chemical plant maintenance. Here is a somewhat simplified example of the way the techniques work.

Example 8.5.12 A Job Scheduling Problem

At an automobile assembly plant, the job of assembling an automobile can be broken down into these tasks:

1. Build frame.

2. Install engine, power train components, gas tank.

3. Install brakes, wheels, tires.

4. Install dashboard, floor, seats.

5. Install electrical lines.

6. Install gas lines.

7. Install brake lines.

8. Attach body panels to frame.

9. Paint body.

Certain of these tasks can be carried out at the same time, whereas some cannot be started until other tasks are finished. Table 8.5.1 summarizes the order in which tasks can be performed and the time required to perform each task.

Table 8.5.1

Task	Immediately Preceding Tasks	Time Needed to Perform Task
1		7 hours
2	1	6 hours
3	1	3 hours
4	2	6 hours
5	2, 3	3 hours
6	4	1 hour
7	2, 3	1 hour
8	4, 5	2 hours
9	6, 7, 8	5 hours

Let T be the set of all tasks, and consider the partial order relation $\preceq$ defined on T as follows: For all tasks x and y in T,

$$x \preceq y \quad \Leftrightarrow \quad x = y \text{ or } x \text{ precedes } y.$$

If the Hasse diagram of this relation is turned sideways (as is customary in PERT and CPM analysis), it has the appearance shown below.

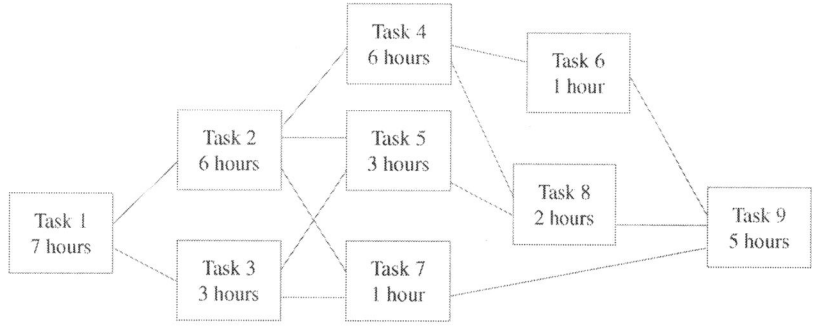

What is the minimum time required to assemble a car? You can determine this by working from left to right across the diagram, noting for each task (say, just above the box representing that task) the minimum time needed to complete that task starting from the beginning of the assembly process. For instance, you can put a 7 above the box for task 1 because task 1 requires 7 hours. Task 2 requires completion of task 1 (7 hours) plus 6 hours for itself, so the minimum time required to complete task 2, starting at the beginning of the assembly process, is $7 + 6 = 13$ hours. You can put a 13 above the box for task 2. Similarly, you can put a 10 above the box for task 3 because $7 + 3 = 10$. Now consider what number you should write above the box for task 5. The minimum times to complete tasks 2 and 3, starting from the beginning of the assembly process, are 13 and 10 hours respectively. Since *both* tasks must be completed before task 5 can be started, the minimum time to complete task 5, starting from the beginning, is the time needed for task 5 itself (3 hours) plus the *maximum* of the times to complete tasks 2 and 3 (13 hours), and this equals $3 + 13 = 16$ hours. Thus you should place the number 16 above the box for task 5. The same reasoning leads you to place a 14 above the box for task 7. Similarly, you can place a 19 above the box for task 4, a 20 above the box for task 6, a 21 above the box for task 8, and a 26 above the box for task 9, as shown below.

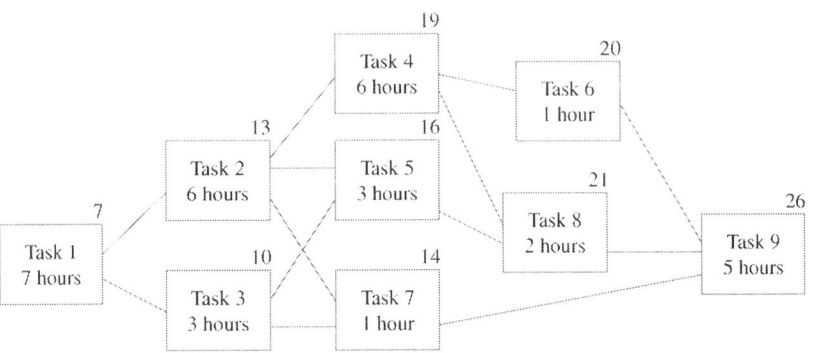

This analysis shows that at least 26 hours are required to complete task 9 starting from the beginning of the assembly process. When task 9 is finished, the assembly is complete, so 26 hours is the minimum time needed to accomplish the whole process.

Note that the minimum time required to complete tasks 1, 2, 4, 8, and 9 in sequence is exactly 26 hours. This means that a delay in performing any one of these tasks causes a delay in the total time required for assembly of the car. For this reason, the path through tasks 1, 2, 4, 8, and 9 is called a **critical path.** ▨

Test Yourself

1. For a relation R on a set A to be antisymmetric means that _____.

2. To show that a relation R on an infinite set A is antisymmetric, you suppose that _____ and you show that _____.

3. To show that a relation R on a set A is not antisymmetric, you _____.

4. To construct a Hasse diagram for a partial order relation, you start with a directed graph of the relation in which all arrows point upward and you eliminate _____, _____, and _____.

5. If A is a set that is partially ordered with respect to a relation $\preceq$ and if a and b are elements of A, we say that a and b are comparable if, and only if, _____ or _____.

6. A relation $\preceq$ on a set A is a total order if, and only if, _____.

7. If A is a set that is partially ordered with respect to a relation $\preceq$, and if B is a subset of A, then B is a chain if, and only if, for all a and b in B, _____.

8. Let A be a set that is partially ordered with respect to a relation $\preceq$, and let a be an element of A.

   (a) a is maximal if, and only if, _____.

   (b) a is a greatest element of A if, and only if, _____.

   (c) a is minimal if, and only if, _____.

   (d) a is a least element of A if, and only if, _____.

Exercise Set 8.5

1. Each of the following is a relation on $\{0, 1, 2, 3\}$. Draw directed graphs for each relation, and indicate which relations are antisymmetric.
   a. $R_1 = \{(0, 0), (0, 2), (1, 0), (1, 3), (2, 2), (3, 0), (3, 1)\}$
   b. $R_2 = \{(0, 1), (0, 2), (1, 1), (1, 2), (1, 3), (2, 2), (3, 2)\}$
   c. $R_3 = \{(0, 0), (0, 3), (1, 0), (1, 3), (2, 2), (3, 3), (3, 2)\}$
   d. $R_4 = \{(0, 0), (1, 0), (1, 2), (1, 3), (2, 0), (2, 1), (3, 2),$
   $(3, 0)\}$

2. Let P be the set of all people in the world and define a relation R on P as follows: For all $x, y \in P$,
   $$x\, R\, y \quad \Leftrightarrow \quad x \text{ is no older than } y.$$
   Is R antisymmetric? Prove or give a counterexample.

3. Let S be the set of all strings of a's and b's. Define a relation R on S as follows: For all $t \in S$,
   $$s\, R\, t \quad \Leftrightarrow \quad l(s) \le l(t),$$
   where $l(x)$ denotes the length of a string x. Is R antisymmetric? Prove or give a counterexample.

4. Define a relation R on the set $\mathbf{Z}$ of all integers as follows: For all $m, n \in \mathbf{Z}$,
   $$m\, R\, n \quad \Leftrightarrow \quad \text{every prime factor of } m$$
   $$\text{is a prime factor of } n.$$
   Is R a partial order relation? Prove or give a counterexample.

5. Let $\mathbf{R}$ be the set of all real numbers and define a relation R on $\mathbf{R} \times \mathbf{R}$ as follows: For all (a, b) and (c, d) in $\mathbf{R} \times \mathbf{R}$,
   $$(a, b)\, R\, (c, d) \quad \Leftrightarrow \quad \text{either } a < c \text{ or both } a = c$$
   $$\text{and } b \le d.$$
   Is R a partial order relation? Prove or give a counterexample.

6. Let P be the set of all people who have ever lived and define a relation R on P as follows: For all $r, s \in P$,
   $$r\, R\, s \quad \Leftrightarrow \quad r \text{ is an ancestor of } s \text{ or } r = s.$$
   Is R a partial order relation? Prove or give a counterexample.

7. Let R be the "less than" relation on the set $\mathbf{R}$ of all real numbers: For all $x, y \in \mathbf{R}$,
   $$x\, R\, y \quad \Leftrightarrow \quad x < y.$$
   Is R antisymmetric? Prove or give a counterexample.

9. Given a set A that is partially ordered with respect to a relation $\preceq$, the relation $\preceq'$ is a topological sorting for $\preceq$, if, and only if, $\preceq'$ is a _____ and for all a and b in A if $a \preceq b$ then _____.

10. PERT and CPM are used to produce efficient _____.

8. Define a relation R on the set $\mathbf{Z}$ of all integers as follows: For all $m, n \in \mathbf{Z}$,
   $$m\, R\, n \quad \Leftrightarrow \quad m + n \text{ is even.}$$
   Is R a partial order relation? Prove or give a counterexample.

9. Define a relation R on the set of all real numbers $\mathbf{R}$ as follows: For all $x, y \in \mathbf{R}$,
   $$x\, R\, y \quad \Leftrightarrow \quad x^2 \le y^2.$$
   Is R a partial order relation? Prove or give a counterexample.

10. Suppose R and S are antisymmetric relations on a set A. Must $R \cup S$ also be antisymmetric? Explain.

11. Let $A = \{a, b\}$, and suppose A has the partial order relation R where $R = \{(a, a), (a, b), (b, b)\}$. Let S be the set of all strings in a's and b's and let $\preceq$ be the corresponding lexicographic order on S. Indicate which of the following statements are true, and for each true statement cite as a reason part (1), (2), or (3) of the definition of lexicographic order given in Theorem 8.5.1.
    a. $aab \preceq aaba$
    b. $bbab \preceq bba$
    c. $\epsilon \preceq aba$
    d. $aba \preceq abb$
    e. $bbab \preceq bbaa$
    f. $ababa \preceq ababaa$
    g. $bbaba \preceq bbabb$

12. Prove Theorem 8.5.1.

13. Let $A = \{a, b\}$. Describe all partial order relations on A.

14. Let $A = \{a, b, c\}$.
    a. Describe all partial order relations on A for which a is a maximal element.
    b. Describe all partial order relations on A for which a is a minimal element.

H 15. Suppose a relation R on a set A is reflexive, symmetric, transitive, and antisymmetric. What can you conclude about R? Prove your answer.

16. Consider the "divides" relation on each of the following sets A. Draw the Hasse diagram for each relation.
    a. $A = \{1, 2, 4, 5, 10, 15, 20\}$
    b. $A = \{2, 3, 4, 6, 8, 9, 12, 18\}$

17. Consider the "subset" relation on $\mathscr{P}(S)$ for each of the following sets S. Draw the Hasse diagram for each relation.
    a. $S = \{0, 1\}$ b. $S = \{0, 1, 2\}$

18. Let $S = \{0, 1\}$ and consider the partial order relation R defined on $S \times S$ as follows: For all ordered pairs (a, b) and (c, d) in $S \times S$,

$(a, b)\, R\, (c, d) \quad \Leftrightarrow \quad$ either $a < c$ or both $a = c$ and $b \leq d$,

where $<$ denotes the usual "less than" and $\leq$ denotes the usual "less than or equal to" relation for real numbers. Draw the Hasse diagram for R.

19. Let $S = \{0, 1\}$ and consider the partial order relation R defined on $S \times S \times S$ as follows: For all ordered triples (a, b, c) and (d, e, f) in $S \times S \times S$,

$(a, b, c)\, R\, (d, e, f) \quad \Leftrightarrow \quad a \leq d, b \leq e,$ and $c \leq f,$

where $\leq$ denotes the usual "less than or equal to" relation for real numbers. Draw the Hasse diagram for R.

20. Let $S = \{0, 1\}$ and consider the partial order relation R defined on $S \times S$ as follows: For all ordered pairs (a, b) and (c, d) in $S \times S$,

$(a, b)\, R\, (c, d) \quad \Leftrightarrow \quad a \leq c$ and $b \leq d,$

where $\leq$ denotes the usual "less than or equal to" relation for real numbers. Draw the Hasse diagram for R.

21. Consider the "divides" relation defined on the set $A = \{1, 2, 2^2, 2^3, \ldots, 2^n\}$, where n is a nonnegative integer.

   a. Prove that this relation is a total order relation on A.
   b. Draw the Hasse diagram for this relation for $n = 4$.

In 22–29, find all greatest, least, maximal, and minimal elements for the relations in each of the referenced exercises.

22. Exercise 16(a)   23. Exercise 16(b)

24. Exercise 17(a)   25. Exercise 17(b)

26. Exercise 18   27. Exercise 19

28. Exercise 20   29. Exercise 21

30. Each of the following sets is partially ordered with respect to the "less than or equal to" relation, $\leq$, for real numbers. In each case, determine whether the set has a greatest or least element.
   a. $\mathbf{R}$ b. $\{x \in \mathbf{R} \mid 0 \leq x \leq 1\}$
   c. $\{x \in \mathbf{R} \mid 0 < x < 1\}$ d. $\{x \in \mathbf{Z} \mid 0 < x < 10\}$

31. Let $A = \{a, b, c, d\}$, and let R be the relation

$$R = \{(a, a), (b, b), (c, c), (d, d), (c, a), (a, d),$$
$$(c, d), (b, c), (b, d), (b, a)\}.$$

   Is R a total order on A? Justify your answer.

32. Let $A = \{a, b, c, d\}$, and let R be the relation

$$R = \{(a, a), (b, b), (c, c), (d, d), (c, b), (a, d),$$
$$(b, a), (b, d), (c, d), (c, a)\}.$$

   Is R a total order on A? Justify your answer.

33. Consider the set $A = \{12, 24, 48, 3, 9\}$ ordered by the "divides" relation. Is A totally ordered with respect to the relation? Justify your answer.

H 34. Suppose that R is a partial order relation on a set A and that B is a subset of A. The **restriction of R to B** is defined as follows:

   The restriction of R to B

$$= \{(x, y) \mid x \in B, y \in B, \text{ and } (x, y) \in R\}.$$

   In other words, two elements of B are related by the restriction of R to B if, and only if, they are related by R. Prove that the restriction of R to B is a partial order relation on B. (In less formal language, this says that a subset of a partially ordered set is partially ordered.)

35. The set $\mathscr{P}(\{w, x, y, z\})$ is partially ordered with respect to the "subset" relation $\subseteq$. Find a chain of length 4 in $\mathscr{P}(\{w, x, y, z\})$.

36. The set $A = \{2, 4, 3, 6, 12, 18, 24\}$ is partially ordered with respect to the "divides" relation. Find a chain of length 3 in A.

37. Find a chain of length 2 for the relation defined in exercise 19.

38. Prove that a partially ordered set is totally ordered if, and only if, it is a chain.

39. Suppose that A is a totally ordered set. Use mathematical induction to prove that for any integer $n \geq 1$, every subset of A with n elements has both a least element and a greatest element.

40. Prove that a nonempty finite partially ordered set has
   a. at least one minimal element,
   b. at least one maximal element.

41. Prove that a finite partially ordered set has
   a. at most one greatest element,
   b. at most one least element.

42. Draw a Hasse diagram for a partially ordered set that has two maximal elements and two minimal elements and is such that each element is comparable to exactly two other elements.

43. Draw a Hasse diagram for a partially ordered set that has three maximal elements and three minimal elements and is such that each element is either greater than or less than exactly two other elements.

44. Use the algorithm given in the text to find a topological sorting for the relation of exercise 16(a) that is different from the "less than or equal to" relation $\leq$.

45. Use the algorithm given in the text to find a topological sorting for the relation of exercise 16(b) that is different from the "less than or equal to" relation $\leq$.

46. Use the algorithm given in the text to find a topological sorting for the relation of exercise 19.

47. Use the algorithm given in the text to find a topological sorting for the relation of exercise 20.

48. Use the algorithm given in the text to find a topological sorting for the "subset" relation on $\mathscr{P}(\{a, b, c, d\})$.

49. Refer to the prerequisite structure shown in Figure 8.5.1.
    a. Find a list of six noncomparable courses that is different from the list given in the text.
    b. Find two topological sortings that are different from the one given in the text.

50. A set S of jobs can be ordered by writing $x \preceq y$ to mean that either $x = y$ or x must be done before y, for all x and y in S. The following is a Hasse diagram for this relation for a particular set S of jobs.

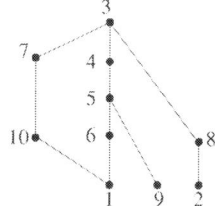

    a. If one person is to perform all the jobs, one after another, find an order in which the jobs can be done.

b. Suppose enough people are available to perform any number of jobs simultaneously.
    (i) If each job requires one day to perform, what is the least number of days needed to perform all ten jobs?
    (ii) What is the maximum number of jobs that can be performed at the same time?

51. Suppose the tasks described in Example 8.5.12 require the following performance times:

Task	Time Needed to Perform Task
1	9 hours
2	7 hours
3	4 hours
4	5 hours
5	7 hours
6	3 hours
7	2 hours
8	4 hours
9	6 hours

a. What is the minimum time required to assemble a car?
b. Find a critical path for the assembly process.

Answers for Test Yourself

1. for all a and b in A, if $a \, R \, b$ and $b \, R \, a$ then $a = b$ 2. a and b are any elements of A with $a \, R \, b$ and $b \, R \, a$; $a = b$ 3. show that there are elements a and b in A such that $a \, R \, b$ and $b \, R \, a$ and $a \neq b$ 4. all loops; all arrows whose existence is implied by the transitive property; the direction indicators on the arrows   5. $a \preceq b$; $b \preceq a$ 6. for any two elements a and b in A, either $a \preceq b$ or $b \preceq a$ 7. a and b are comparable   8. (a) for all b in A either $b \preceq a$ or b and a are not comparable   (b) for all b in A, $b \preceq a$ (c) for all b in A either $a \preceq b$ or b and a are not comparable   (d) for all b in A, $a \preceq' b$ 9. total order; $a \preceq' b$ 10. scheduling of tasks

CHAPTER 10

GRAPHS AND TREES

Graphs and trees have appeared previously in this book as convenient visualizations. For instance, a possibility tree shows all possible outcomes of a multistep operation with a finite number of outcomes for each step, the directed graph of a relation on a set shows which elements of the set are related to which a Hasse diagram illustrates the relations among elements in a partially ordered set, and a PERT diagram shows which tasks must precede which in executing a project.

In this chapter we present some of the mathematics of graphs and trees, discussing concepts such as the degree of a vertex, connectedness, Euler and Hamiltonian circuits, representation of graphs by matrices, isomorphisms of graphs, the relation between the number of vertices and the number of edges of a tree, properties of rooted trees spanning trees, and shortest paths in graphs. Applications include uses of graphs and trees in the study of artificial intelligence, chemistry, scheduling problems, and transportation systems.

10.1 Graphs: Definitions and Basic Properties

The whole of mathematics consists in the organization of a series of aids to the imagination in the process of reasoning. — Alfred North Whitehead, 1861–1947

Imagine an organization that wants to set up teams of three to work on some projects. In order to maximize the number of people on each team who had previous experience working together successfully, the director asked the members to provide names of their past partners. This information is displayed below both in a table and in a diagram.

Name	Past Partners
Ana	Dan, Flo
Bev	Cai, Flo, Hal
Cai	Bev, Flo
Dan	Ana, Ed
Ed	Dan, Hal
Flo	Cai, Bev, Ana
Gia	Hal
Hal	Gia, Ed, Bev, Ira
Ira	Hal

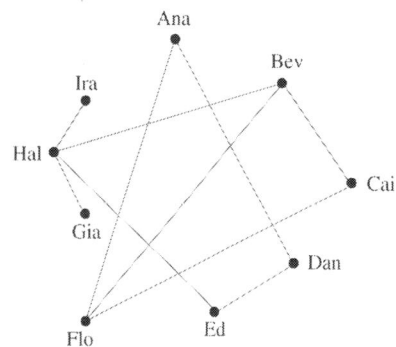

From the diagram, it is easy to see that Bev, Cai, and Flo are a group of three past partners, and so they should form one of these teams. The figure on the next page shows the result when these three names are removed from the diagram.

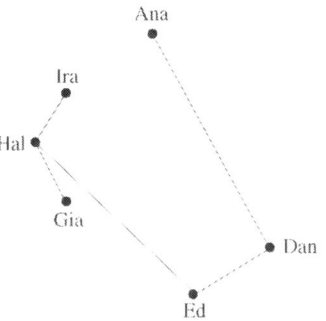

This drawing shows that placing Hal on the same team as Ed would leave Gia and Ira on a team containing no past partners. However, if Hal is placed on a team with Gia and Ira, then the remaining team would consist of Ana, Dan, and Ed, and both teams would contain at least one pair of past partners.

Drawings such as these are illustrations of a structure known as a *graph*. The dots are called *vertices* (plural of *vertex*) and the line segments joining vertices are called *edges*. As you can see from the first drawing, it is possible for two edges to cross at a point that is not a vertex. Note also that the type of graph described here is quite different from the "graph of an equation" or the "graph of a function."

In general, a graph consists of a set of vertices and a set of edges connecting various pairs of vertices. The edges may be straight or curved and should either connect one vertex to another or a vertex to itself, as shown below.

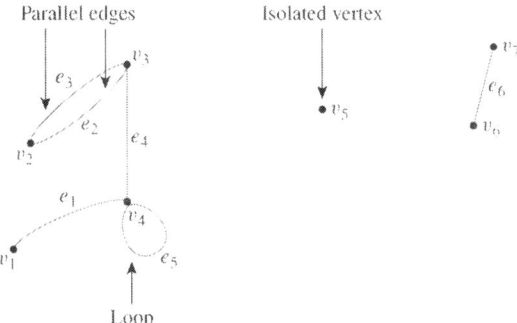

In this drawing, the vertices have been labeled with v's and the edges with e's. When an edge connects a vertex to itself (as e_5 does), it is called a *loop*. When two edges connect the same pair of vertices (as e_2 and e_3 do), they are said to be *parallel*. It is quite possible for a vertex to be unconnected by an edge to any other vertex in the graph (as v_5 is), and in that case the vertex is said to be *isolated*. The formal definition of a graph follows.

> **• Definition**
>
> A **graph** G consists of two finite sets: a nonempty set $V(G)$ of **vertices** and a set $E(G)$ of **edges,** where each edge is associated with a set consisting of either one or two vertices called its **endpoints.** The correspondence from edges to endpoints is called the **edge-endpoint function.**
>
> An edge with just one endpoint is called a **loop,** and two or more distinct edges with the same set of endpoints are said to be **parallel.** An edge is said to **connect** its endpoints; two vertices that are connected by an edge are called **adjacent;** and a vertex that is an endpoint of a loop is said to be **adjacent to itself.**
>
> An edge is said to be **incident on** each of its endpoints, and two edges incident on the same endpoint are called **adjacent.** A vertex on which no edges are incident is called **isolated.**

Graphs have pictorial representations in which the vertices are represented by dots and the edges by line segments. A given pictorial representation uniquely determines a graph.

Example 10.1.1 Terminology

Consider the following graph:

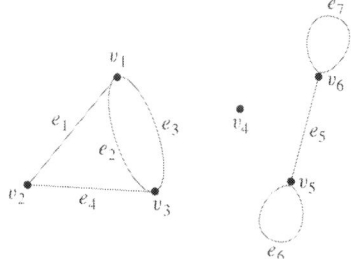

a. Write the vertex set and the edge set, and give a table showing the edge-endpoint function.

b. Find all edges that are incident on v_1, all vertices that are adjacent to v_1, all edges that are adjacent to e_1, all loops, all parallel edges, all vertices that are adjacent to themselves, and all isolated vertices.

Solution

a. vertex set $= \{v_1, v_2, v_3, v_4, v_5, v_6\}$
edge set $= \{e_1, e_2, e_3, e_4, e_5, e_6, e_7\}$
edge-endpoint function:

Edge	Endpoints
e_1	$\{v_1, v_2\}$
e_2	$\{v_1, v_3\}$
e_3	$\{v_1, v_3\}$
e_4	$\{v_2, v_3\}$
e_5	$\{v_5, v_6\}$
e_6	$\{v_5\}$
e_7	$\{v_6\}$

Note that the isolated vertex v_4 does not appear in this table. Although each edge must have either one or two endpoints, a vertex need not be an endpoint of an edge.

b. e_1, e_2, and e_3 are incident on v_1.
v_2 and v_3 are adjacent to v_1.
e_2, e_3, and e_4 are adjacent to e_1.
e_6 and e_7 are loops.
e_2 and e_3 are parallel.
v_5 and v_6 are adjacent to themselves.
v_4 is an isolated vertex.

As noted earlier, a given pictorial representation uniquely determines a graph. However, a given graph may have more than one pictorial representation. Such things as the lengths or curvatures of the edges and the relative position of the vertices on the page may vary from one pictorial representation to another.

Example 10.1.2 Drawing More Than One Picture for a Graph

Consider the graph specified as follows:

$$\text{vertex set} = \{v_1, v_2, v_3, v_4\}$$
$$\text{edge set} = \{e_1, e_2, e_3, e_4\}$$

edge-endpoint function:

Edge	Endpoints
e_1	$\{v_1, v_3\}$
e_2	$\{v_2, v_4\}$
e_3	$\{v_2, v_4\}$
e_4	$\{v_3\}$

Both drawings (a) and (b) shown below are pictorial representations of this graph.

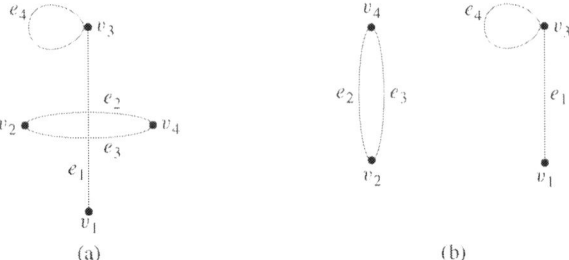

Example 10.1.3 Labeling Drawings to Show They Represent the Same Graph

Consider the two drawings shown in Figure 10.1.1. Label vertices and edges in such a way that both drawings represent the same graph.

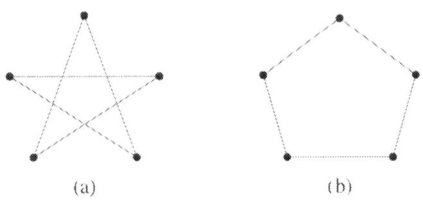

Figure 10.1.1

Solution   Imagine putting one end of a piece of string at the top vertex of Figure 10.1.1(a) (call this vertex v_1), then laying the string to the next adjacent vertex on the lower right (call this vertex v_2), then laying it to the next adjacent vertex on the upper left (v_3), and so forth, returning finally to the top vertex v_1. Call the first edge e_1, the second e_2, and so forth, as shown below.

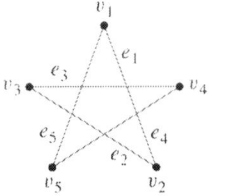

Now imagine picking up the piece of string, together with its labels, and repositioning it as follows:

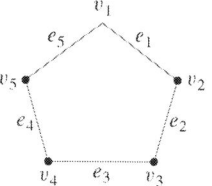

This is the same as Figure 10.1.1(b), so both drawings are representations of the graph with vertex set $\{v_1, v_2, v_3, v_4, v_5\}$, edge set $\{e_1, e_2, e_3, e_4, e_5\}$, and edge-endpoint function as follows:

Edge	Endpoints
e_1	$\{v_1, v_2\}$
e_2	$\{v_2, v_3\}$
e_3	$\{v_3, v_4\}$
e_4	$\{v_4, v_5\}$
e_5	$\{v_5, v_1\}$

In Chapter 8 we discussed the directed graph of a binary relation on a set. The general definition of directed graph is similar to the definition of graph, except that one associates an *ordered pair* of vertices with each edge instead of a *set* of vertices. Thus each edge of a directed graph can be drawn as an arrow going from the first vertex to the second vertex of the ordered pair.

> **• Definition**
>
> A **directed graph,** or **digraph,** consists of two finite sets: a nonempty set $V(G)$ of vertices and a set $D(G)$ of directed edges, where each is associated with an ordered pair of vertices called its **endpoints.** If edge e is associated with the pair (v, w) of vertices, then e is said to be the (**directed**) **edge** from v to w.

Note that each directed graph has an associated ordinary (undirected) graph, which is obtained by ignoring the directions of the edges.

Examples of Graphs

Graphs are a powerful problem-solving tool because they enable us to represent a complex situation with a single image that can be analyzed both visually and with the aid of a computer. A few examples follow, and others are included in the exercises.

Example 10.1.4 Using a Graph to Represent a Network

Telephone, electric power, gas pipeline, and air transport systems can all be represented by graphs, as can computer networks—from small local area networks to the global Internet system that connects millions of computers worldwide. Questions that arise in the design of such systems involve choosing connecting edges to minimize cost, optimize a certain type of service, and so forth. A typical network, called a hub and spoke model, is shown on the next page.

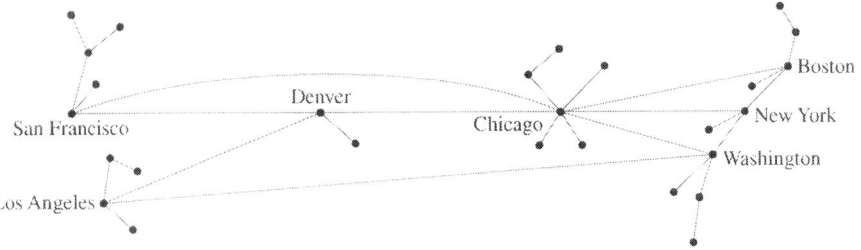

Example 10.1.5 Using a Graph to Represent the World Wide Web

The World Wide Web, or Web, is a system of interlinked documents, or webpages, contained on the Internet. Users employing Web browsers, such as Internet Explorer, Google Chrome, Apple Safari, and Opera, can move quickly from one webpage to another by clicking on hyperlinks, which use versions of software called hypertext transfer protocols (HTTPs). Individuals and individual companies create the pages, which they transmit to servers that contain software capable of delivering them to those who request them through a Web browser. Because the amount of information currently on the Web is so vast, search engines, such as Google, Yahoo, and Bing, have algorithms for finding information very efficiently.

The picture below shows a minute fraction of the hyperlink connections on the Internet that radiate in and out from the Wikipedia main page.

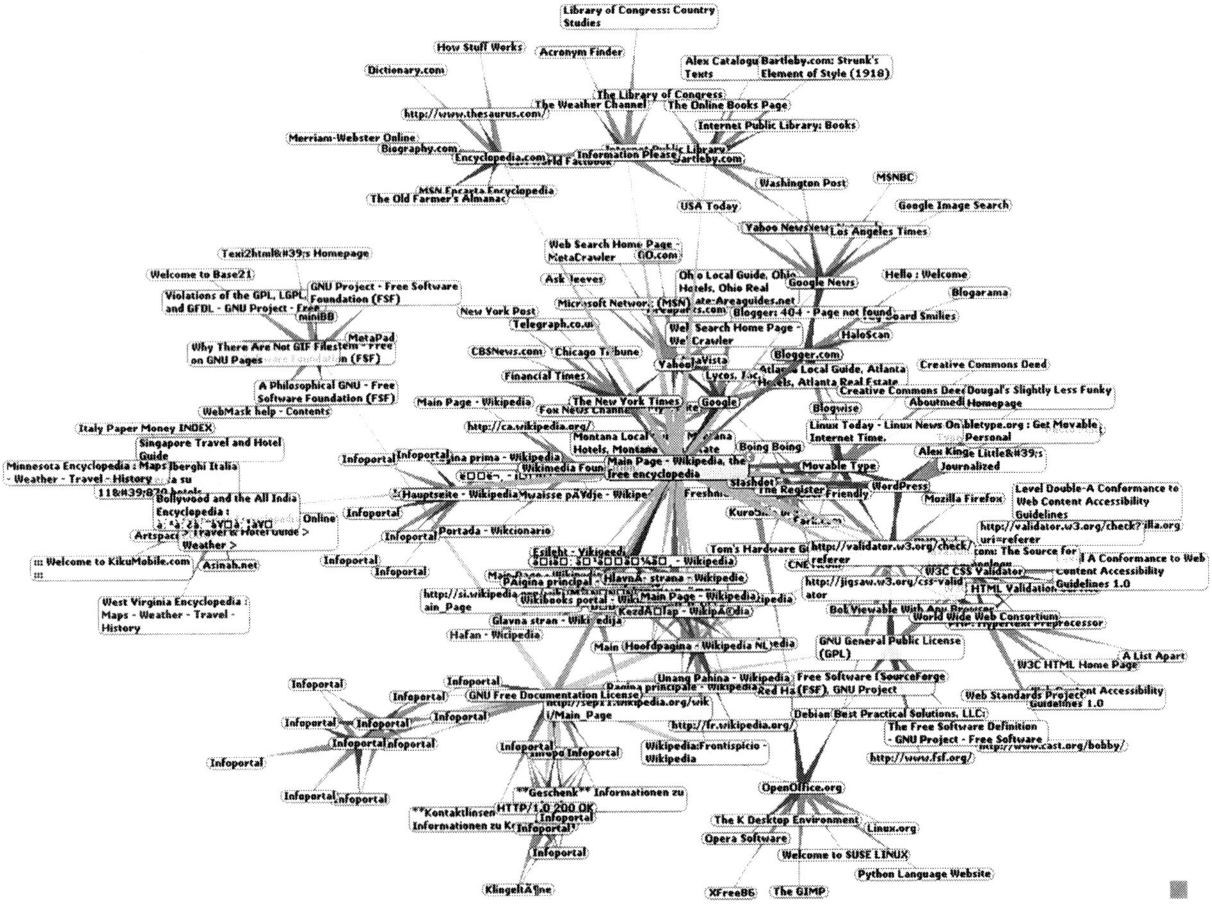

Example 10.1.6   Using a Graph to Represent Knowledge

In many applications of artifical intelligence, a knowledge base of information is collected and represented inside a computer. Because of the way the knowledge is represented and because of the properties that govern the artificial intelligence program, the computer is not limited to retrieving data in the same form as it was entered; it can also derive new facts from the knowledge base by using certain built-in rules of inference. For example, from the knowledge that the *Los Angeles Times* is a big-city daily and that a big-city daily contains national news, an artifical intelligence program could infer that the *Los Angeles Times* contains national news. The directed graph shown in Figure 10.1.2 is a pictorial representation for a simplified knowledge base about periodical publications.

According to this knowledge base, what paper finish does the *New York Times* use?

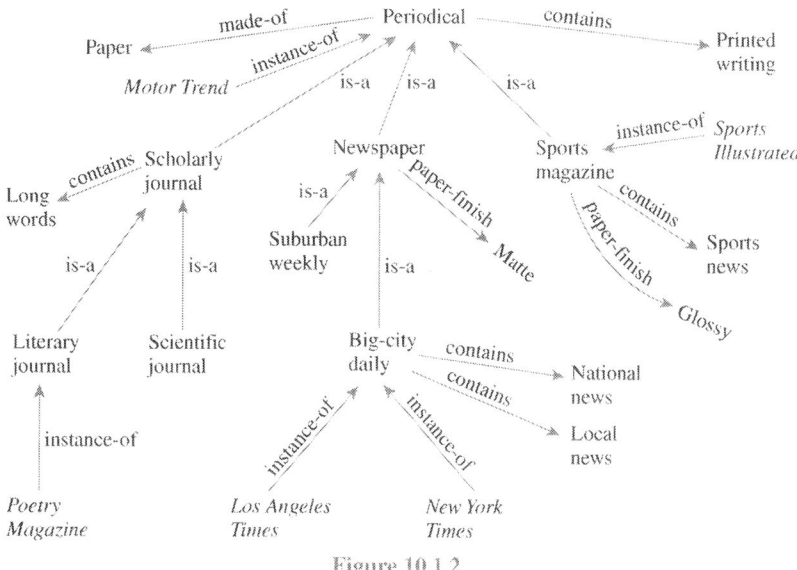

Figure 10.1.2

Solution   The arrow going from *New York Times* to big-city daily (labeled "instance-of") shows that the *New York Times* is a big-city daily. The arrow going from big-city daily to newspaper (labeled "is-a") shows that a big-city daily is a newspaper. The arrow going from newspaper to matte (labeled "paper-finish") indicates that the paper finish on a newspaper is matte. Hence it can be inferred that the paper finish on the *New York Times* is matte. ∎

Example 10.1.7   Using a Graph to Solve a Problem: Vegetarians and Cannibals

The following is a variation of a famous puzzle often used as an example in the study of artificial intelligence. It concerns an island on which all the people are of one of two types, either vegetarians or cannibals. Initially, two vegetarians and two cannibals are on the left bank of a river. With them is a boat that can hold a maximum of two people. The aim of the puzzle is to find a way to transport all the vegetarians and cannibals to the right bank of the river. What makes this difficult is that at no time can the number of cannibals on either bank outnumber the number of vegetarians. Otherwise, disaster befalls the vegetarians!

Solution   A systematic way to approach this problem is to introduce a notation that can indicate all possible arrangements of vegetarians, cannibals, and the boat on the banks of the river. For example, you could write (vvc/Bc) to indicate that there are two vegetarians and one cannibal on the left bank and one cannibal and the boat on the right bank. Then $(vvccB/)$ would indicate the initial position in which both vegetarians, both cannibals, and the boat are on the left bank of the river. The aim of the puzzle is to figure out a sequence of moves to reach the position $(/Bvvcc)$ in which both vegetarians, both cannibals, and the boat are on the right bank of the river.

Construct a graph whose vertices are the various arrangements that can be reached in a sequence of legal moves starting from the initial position. Connect vertex x to vertex y if it is possible to reach vertex y in one legal move from vertex x. For instance, from the initial position there are four legal moves: one vegetarian and one cannibal can take the boat to the right bank; two cannibals can take the boat to the right bank; one cannibal can take the boat to the right bank; or two vegetarians can take the boat to the right bank. You can show these by drawing edges connecting vertex $(vvccB/)$ to vertices (vc/Bvc), (vv/Bcc), $(vvcBc)$, and (cc/Bvv). (It might seem natural to draw directed edges rather than undirected edges from one vertex to another. The rationale for drawing undirected edges is that each legal move is reversible.) From the position (vc/Bvc), the only legal moves are to go back to $(vvccB/)$ or to go to $(vvcB/c)$. You can also show these by drawing in edges. Continue this process until finally you reach $(/Bvvcc)$. From Figure 10.1.3 it is apparent that one successful sequence of moves is $(vvccB/) \rightarrow (vc/Bvc) \rightarrow (vvcB/c) \rightarrow (c/Bvvc) \rightarrow (ccB/vv) \rightarrow (/Bvvcc)$.

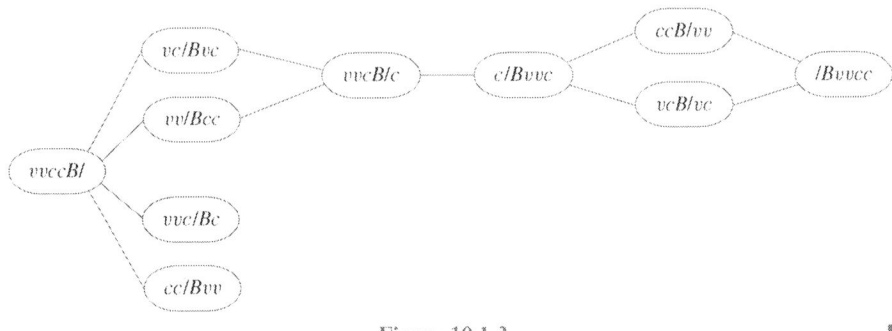

Figure 10.1.3

Special Graphs

One important class of graphs consists of those that do not have any loops or parallel edges. Such graphs are called *simple*. In a simple graph, no two edges share the same set of endpoints, so specifying two endpoints is sufficient to determine an edge.

> **• Definition and Notation**
>
> A **simple graph** is a graph that does not have any loops or parallel edges. In a simple graph, an edge with endpoints v and w is denoted $\{v, w\}$.

Example 10.1.8 A Simple Graph

Draw all simple graphs with the four vertices $\{u, v, w, x\}$ and two edges, one of which is $\{u, v\}$.

Solution   Each possible edge of a simple graph corresponds to a subset of two vertices. Given four vertices, there are $\binom{4}{2} = 6$ such subsets in all: $\{u, v\}, \{u, w\}, \{u, x\}, \{v, w\}, \{v, x\}$, and $\{w, x\}$. Now one edge of the graph is specified to be $\{u, v\}$, so any of the remaining five from this list can be chosen to be the second edge. The possibilities are shown on the next page.

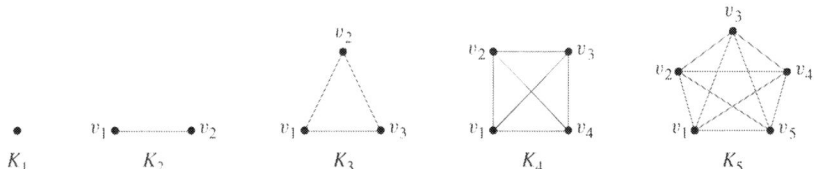

Another important class of graphs consists of those that are "complete" in the sense that all pairs of vertices are connected by edges.

> **• Definition**
>
> Let n be a positive integer. A **complete graph on n vertices,** denoted K_n, is a simple graph with n vertices and exactly one edge connecting each pair of distinct vertices.

Example 10.1.9 Complete Graphs on n Vertices: K_1, K_2, K_3, K_4, K_5

The complete graphs K_1, K_2, K_3, K_4, and K_5 can be drawn as follows:

$$K_1 \quad K_2 \quad K_3 \quad K_4 \quad K_5$$

In yet another class of graphs, the vertex set can be separated into two subsets: Each vertex in one of the subsets is connected by exactly one edge to each vertex in the other subset, but not to any vertices in its own subset. Such a graph is called *complete bipartite*.

> **• Definition**
>
> Let m and n be positive integers. A **complete bipartite graph on (m, n) vertices,** denoted $K_{m,n}$, is a simple graph with distinct vertices $v_1, v_2, \ldots, v_m$ and $w_1, w_2, \ldots, w_n$ that satisfies the following properties: For all $i, k = 1, 2, \ldots, m$ and for all $j, l = 1, 2, \ldots, n$,
>
> 1. There is an edge from each vertex v_i to each vertex w_j.
> 2. There is no edge from any vertex v_i to any other vertex v_k.
> 3. There is no edge from any vertex w_j to any other vertex w_l.

Example 10.1.10 Complete Bipartite Graphs: $K_{3,2}$ and $K_{3,3}$

The complete bipartite graphs $K_{3,2}$ and $K_{3,3}$ are illustrated below.

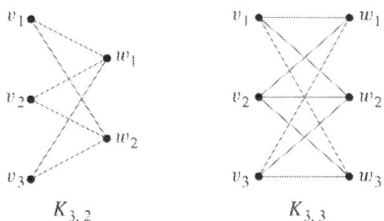

$$K_{3,2} \qquad K_{3,3}$$

> ● **Definition**
>
> A graph H is said to be a **subgraph** of a graph G if, and only if, every vertex in H is also a vertex in G, every edge in H is also an edge in G, and every edge in H has the same endpoints as it has in G.

Example 10.1.11 Subgraphs

List all subgraphs of the graph G with vertex set $\{v_1, v_2\}$ and edge set $\{e_1, e_2, e_3\}$, where the endpoints of e_1 are v_1 and v_2, the endpoints of e_2 are v_1 and v_2, and e_3 is a loop at v_1.

Solution G can be drawn as shown below.

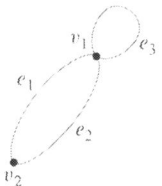

There are 11 subgraphs of G, which can be grouped according to those that do not have any edges, those that have one edge, those that have two edges, and those that have three edges. The 11 subgraphs are shown in Figure 10.1.4.

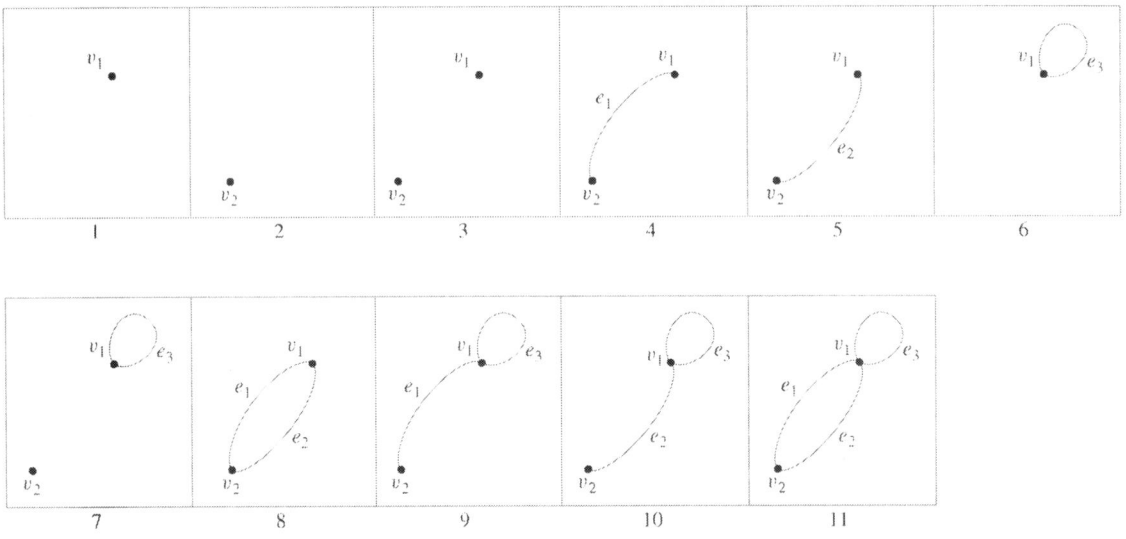

Figure 10.1.4

The Concept of Degree

The *degree of a vertex* is the number of end segments of edges that "stick out of" the vertex. We will show that the sum of the degrees of all the vertices in a graph is twice the number of edges of the graph.

> **● Definition**
>
> Let G be a graph and v a vertex of G. The **degree of v,** denoted **deg(v),** equals the number of edges that are incident on v, with an edge that is a loop counted twice. The **total degree of G** is the sum of the degrees of all the vertices of G.

Since an edge that is a loop is counted twice, the degree of a vertex can be obtained from the drawing of a graph by counting how many end segments of edges are incident on the vertex. This is illustrated below.

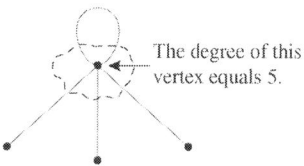

The degree of this vertex equals 5.

Example 10.1.12 Degree of a Vertex and Total Degree of a Graph

Find the degree of each vertex of the graph G shown below. Then find the total degree of G.

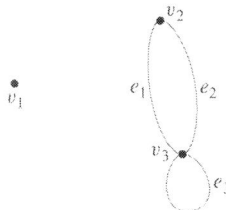

Solution $\deg(v_1) = 0$ since no edge is incident on v_1 (v_1 is isolated).

$\deg(v_2) = 2$ since both e_1 and e_2 are incident on v_2.

$\deg(v_3) = 4$ since e_1 and e_2 are incident on v_3 and the loop e_3 is also incident on v_3 (and contributes 2 to the degree of v_3).

total degree of $G = \deg(v_1) + \deg(v_2) + \deg(v_3) = 0 + 2 + 4 = 6$.   ■

Note that the total degree of the graph G of Example 10.1.12, which is 6, equals twice the number of edges of G, which is 3. Roughly speaking, this is true because each edge has two end segments, and each end segment is counted once toward the degree of some vertex. This result generalizes to any graph.

In fact, for any graph without loops, the general result can be explained as follows: Imagine a group of people at a party. Depending on how social they are, each person shakes hands with various other people. So each person participates in a certain number of handshakes—perhaps many, perhaps none—but because each handshake is experienced by two different people, if the numbers experienced by each person are added together, the sum will equal twice the total number of handshakes. This is such an attractive way of understanding the situation that the following theorem is often called the *handshake lemma* or the *handshake theorem*. As the proof demonstrates, the conclusion is true even if the graph contains loops.

> **Theorem 10.1.1 The Handshake Theorem**
>
> If G is any graph, then the sum of the degrees of all the vertices of G equals twice the number of edges of G. Specifically, if the vertices of G are $v_1, v_2, \ldots, v_n$, where n is a nonnegative integer, then
>
> $$\text{the total degree of } G = \deg(v_1) + \deg(v_2) + \cdots + \deg(v_n)$$
> $$= 2 \cdot (\text{the number of edges of } G).$$

Proof:

Let G be a particular but arbitrarily chosen graph, and suppose that G has n vertices $v_1, v_2, \ldots, v_n$ and m edges, where n is a positive integer and m is a nonnegative integer. We claim that each edge of G contributes 2 to the total degree of G. For suppose e is an arbitrarily chosen edge with endpoints v_i and v_j. This edge contributes 1 to the degree of v_i and 1 to the degree v_j. As shown below, this is true even if $i = j$, because an edge that is a loop is counted twice in computing the degree of the vertex on which it is incident.

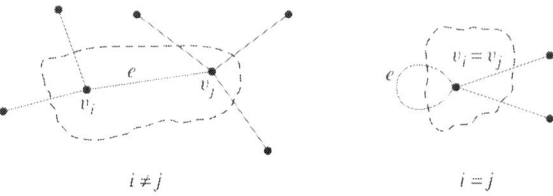

$$i \neq j \qquad\qquad\qquad i = j$$

Therefore, e contributes 2 to the total degree of G. Since e was arbitrarily chosen, this shows that *each* edge of G contributes 2 to the total degree of G. Thus

$$\text{the total degree of } G = 2 \cdot (\text{the number of edges of } G).$$

The following corollary is an immediate consequence of Theorem 10.1.1.

> **Corollary 10.1.2**
>
> The total degree of a graph is even.

Proof:

By Theorem 10.1.1 the total degree of G equals 2 times the number of edges, which is an integer, and so the total degree of G is even.

Example 10.1.13 Determining Whether Certain Graphs Exist

Draw a graph with the specified properties or show that no such graph exists.

a. A graph with four vertices of degrees 1, 1, 2, and 3

b. A graph with four vertices of degrees 1, 1, 3, and 3

c. A simple graph with four vertices of degrees 1, 1, 3, and 3

Solution

a. No such graph is possible. By Corollary 10.1.2, the total degree of a graph is even. But a graph with four vertices of degrees 1, 1, 2, and 3 would have a total degree of $1 + 1 + 2 + 3 = 7$, which is odd.

b. Let G be any of the graphs shown below.

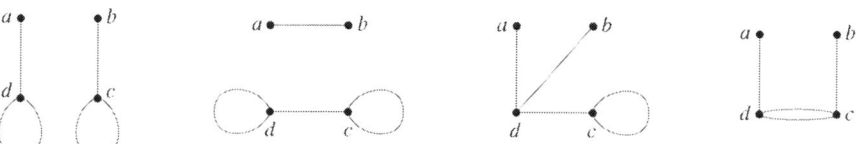

In each case, no matter how the edges are labeled, $\deg(a) = 1$, $\deg(b) = 1$, $\deg(c) = 3$, and $\deg(d) = 3$.

c. There is no simple graph with four vertices of degrees 1, 1, 3, and 3.

Proof (by contradiction):

Suppose there were a simple graph G with four vertices of degrees 1, 1, 3, and 3. Call a and b the vertices of degree 1, and call c and d the vertices of degree 3. Since $\deg(c) = 3$ and G does not have any loops or parallel edges (because it is simple), there must be edges that connect c to a, b, and d.

By the same reasoning, there must be edges connecting d to a, b, and c.

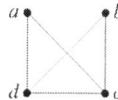

But then $\deg(a) \geq 2$ and $\deg(b) \geq 2$, which contradicts the supposition that these vertices have degree 1. Hence the supposition is false, and consequently there is no simple graph with four vertices of degrees 1, 1, 3, and 3. ▪

Example 10.1.14 Application to an Acquaintance Graph

Is it possible in a group of nine people for each to be friends with exactly five others?

Solution The answer is no. Imagine constructing an "acquaintance graph" in which each of the nine people represented by a vertex and two vertices are joined by an edge if, and only if, the people they represent are friends. Suppose each of the people were friends with exactly five others. Then the degree of each of the nine vertices of the graph would be five, and so the total degree of the graph would be 45. But this contradicts Corollary 10.1.2, which says that the total degree of a graph is even. This contradiction shows that the supposition is false, and hence it is impossible for each person in a group of nine people to be friends with exactly five others. ▪

The following proposition is easily deduced from Corollary 10.1.2 using properties of even and odd integers.

Proposition 10.1.3

In any graph there are an even number of vertices of odd degree.

Proof:

Suppose G is any graph, and suppose G has n vertices of odd degree and m vertices of even degree, where n is a positive integer and m is a nonnegative integer. *[We must show that n is even.]* Let E be the sum of the degrees of all the vertices of even degree, O the sum of the degrees of all the vertices of odd degree, and T the total degree of G. If $u_1, u_2, \ldots, u_m$ are the vertices of even degree and $v_1, v_2, \ldots, v_n$ are the vertices of odd degree, then

$$E = \deg(u_1) + \deg(u_2) + \cdots + \deg(u_m),$$
$$O = \deg(v_1) + \deg(v_2) + \cdots + \deg(v_n), \quad \text{and}$$
$$T = \deg(u_1) + \cdots + \deg(u_m) + \deg(v_1) + \cdots + \deg(v_n) = E + O.$$

Now T, the total degree of G, is an even integer by Corollary 10.1.2. Also E is even since either E is zero, which is even, or E is a sum of the numbers $\deg(u_i)$, each of which is even. But

$$T = E + O,$$

and therefore
$$O = T - E.$$

Hence O is a difference of two even integers, and so O is even.

By assumption, $\deg(v_i)$ is odd for all $i = 1, 2, \ldots, n$. Thus O, an even integer, is a sum of the n odd integers $\deg(v_1), \deg(v_2), \ldots, \deg(v_n)$. But if a sum of n odd integers is even, then n is even. (See exercise 32 at the end of this section.) Therefore, n is even *[as was to be shown]*.

Example 10.1.15 Applying the Fact That the Number of Vertices with Odd Degree Is Even

Is there a graph with ten vertices of degrees 1, 1, 2, 2, 2, 3, 4, 4, 4, and 6?

Solution   No. Such a graph would have three vertices of odd degree, which is impossible by Proposition 10.1.3.

Note that this same result could have been deduced directly from Corollary 10.1.2 by computing the total degree ($1 + 1 + 2 + 2 + 2 + 3 + 4 + 4 + 4 + 6 = 29$) and noting that it is odd. However, use of Proposition 10.1.3 gives the result without the need to perform this addition. ■

Test Yourself

Answers to Test Yourself questions are located at the end of each section.

1. A graph consists of two finite sets: _____ and _____, where each edge is associated with a set consisting of _____.

2. A loop in a graph is _____.

3. Two distinct edges in a graph are parallel if, and only if, _____.

4. Two vertices are called adjacent if, and only if, _____.

5. An edge is incident on _____.

6. Two edges incident on the same endpoint are _____.

7. A vertex on which no edges are incident is _____.

8. In a directed graph, each edge is associated with _____.

9. A simple graph is _____.

10. A complete graph on n vertices is a _____.

11. A complete bipartite graph on (m, n) vertices is a simple graph whose vertices can be partitioned into two disjoint sets

V_1 and V_2 in such a way that (1) each of the m vertices in V_1 is _____ to each of the n vertices in V_2, no vertex in V_1 is connected to _____, and no vertex in V_2 is connected to _____.

12. A graph H is a subgraph of a graph G if, and only if, (1) _____, (2) _____, and (3) _____.

13. The degree of a vertex in a graph is _____.

14. The total degree of a graph is defined as _____.

15. The handshake theorem says that the total degree of a graph is _____.

16. In any graph the number of vertices of odd degree is _____.

Exercise Set 10.1*

In 1 and 2, graphs are represented by drawings. Define each graph formally by specifying its vertex set, its edge set, and a table giving the edge-endpoint function.

1.

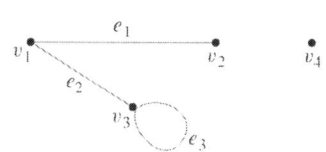

2.

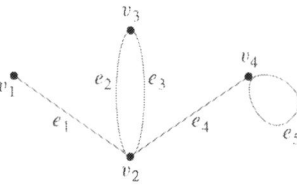

In 3 and 4, draw pictures of the specified graphs.

3. Graph G has vertex set $\{v_1, v_2, v_3, v_4, v_5\}$ and edge set $\{e_1, e_2, e_3, e_4\}$, with edge-endpoint function as follows:

Edge	Endpoints
e_1	$\{v_1, v_2\}$
e_2	$\{v_1, v_2\}$
e_3	$\{v_2, v_3\}$
e_4	$\{v_2\}$

4. Graph H has vertex set $\{v_1, v_2, v_3, v_4, v_5\}$ and edge set $\{e_1, e_2, e_3, e_4\}$ with edge-endpoint function as follows:

Edge	Endpoints
e_1	$\{v_1\}$
e_2	$\{v_2, v_3\}$
e_3	$\{v_2, v_3\}$
e_4	$\{v_1, v_5\}$

In 5–7, show that the two drawings represent the same graph by labeling the vertices and edges of the right-hand drawing to correspond to those of the left-hand drawing.

5.

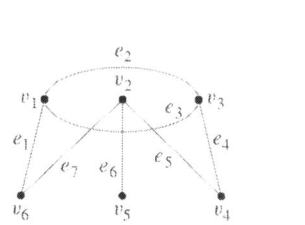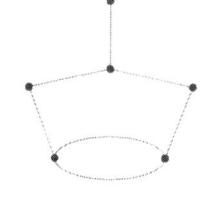

6.

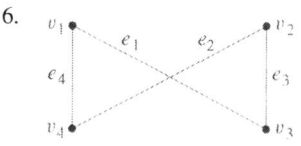

7.

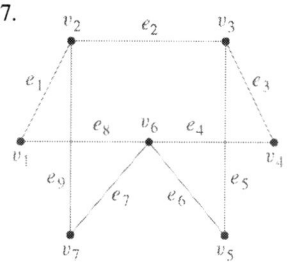

---

*For exercises with blue numbers or letters, solutions are given in Appendix B. The symbol H indicates that only a hint or a partial solution is given. The symbol ✳ signals that an exercise is more challenging than usual.

For each of the graphs in 8 and 9:
  (i) Find all edges that are incident on v_1.
  (ii) Find all vertices that are adjacent to v_3.
  (iii) Find all edges that are adjacent to e_1.
  (iv) Find all loops.
  (v) Find all parallel edges.
  (vi) Find all isolated vertices.
  (vii) Find the degree of v_3.
  (viii) Find the total degree of the graph.

8.

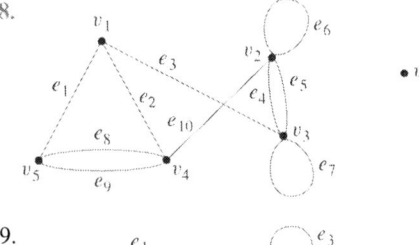

9.

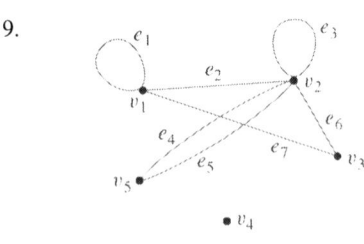

10. Use the graph of Example 10.1.6 to determine
  a. whether *Sports Illustrated* contains printed writing;
  b. whether *Poetry Magazine* contains long words.

11. Find three other winning sequences of moves for the vegetarians and the cannibals in Example 10.1.7.

12. Another famous puzzle used as an example in the study of artificial intelligence seems first to have appeared in a collection of problems, *Problems for the Quickening of the Mind*, which was compiled about A.D. 775. It involves a wolf, a goat, a bag of cabbage, and a ferryman. From an initial position on the left bank of a river, the ferryman is to transport the wolf, the goat, and the cabbage to the right bank. The difficulty is that the ferryman's boat is only big enough for him to transport one object at a time, other than himself. Yet, for obvious reasons, the wolf cannot be left alone with the goat, and the goat cannot be left alone with the cabbage. How should the ferryman proceed?

13. Solve the vegetarians-and-cannibals puzzle for the case where there are three vegetarians and three cannibals to be transported from one side of a river to the other.

H 14. Two jugs *A* and *B* have capacities of 3 quarts and 5 quarts, respectively. Can you use the jugs to measure out exactly 1 quart of water, while obeying the following restrictions? You may fill either jug to capacity from a water tap; you may empty the contents of either jug into a drain; and you may pour water from either jug into the other.

15. A graph has vertices of degrees 0, 2, 2, 3, and 9. How many edges does the graph have?

16. A graph has vertices of degrees 1, 1, 4, 4, and 6. How many edges does the graph have?

In each of 17–25, either draw a graph with the specified properties or explain why no such graph exists.

17. Graph with five vertices of degrees 1, 2, 3, 3, and 5.

18. Graph with four vertices of degrees 1, 2, 3, and 3.

19. Graph with four vertices of degrees 1, 2, 3, and 4.

20. Graph with four vertices of degrees 1, 1, 1, and 4.

21. Simple graph with four vertices of degrees 1, 2, 3, and 4.

22. Simple graph with nine edges and all vertices of degree 3.

23. Simple graph with five vertices of degrees 2, 3, 3, 3, and 5.

24. Simple graph with six edges and all vertices of degree 3.

25. Simple graph with five vertices of degrees 1, 1, 1, 2, and 3.

26. Find all subgraphs of each of the following graphs.

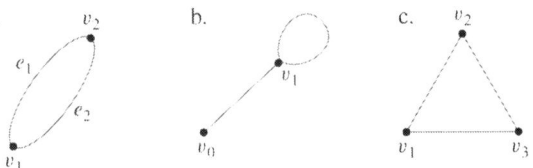

27. a. In a group of 15 people, is it possible for each person to have exactly 3 friends? Explain. (Assume that friendship is a symmetric relationship: If *x* is a friend of *y*, then *y* is a friend of *x*.)
  b. In a group of 4 people, is it possible for each person to have exactly 3 friends? Why?

28. In a group of 25 people, is it possible for each to shake hands with exactly 3 other people? Explain.

29. Is there a simple graph, each of whose vertices has even degree? Explain.

30. Suppose that *G* is a graph with *v* vertices and *e* edges and that the degree of each vertex is at least d_{min} and at most d_{max}. Show that

$$\frac{1}{2}d_{min} \cdot v \le e \le \frac{1}{2}d_{max} \cdot v.$$

31. Prove that any sum of an odd number of odd integers is odd.

H 32. Deduce from exercise 31 that for any positive integer *n*, if there is a sum of *n* odd integers that is even, then *n* is even.

33. Recall that K_n denotes a complete graph on *n* vertices.
  a. Draw K_6.
  H b. Show that for all integers $n \ge 1$, the number of edges of K_n is $\dfrac{n(n-1)}{2}$.

34. Use the result of exercise 33 to show that the number of edges of a simple graph with *n* vertices is less than or equal to $\dfrac{n(n-1)}{2}$.

35. Is there a simple graph with twice as many edges as vertices? Explain. (You may find it helpful to use the result of exercise 34.)

36. Recall that $K_{m,n}$ denotes a complete bipartite graph on (m, n) vertices.
    a. Draw $K_{4,2}$
    b. Draw $K_{1,3}$
    c. Draw $K_{3,4}$
    d. How many vertices of $K_{m,n}$ have degree m? degree n?
    e. What is the total degree of $K_{m,n}$?
    f. Find a formula in terms of m and n for the number of edges of $K_{m,n}$. Explain.

37. A **bipartite graph** G is a simple graph whose vertex set can be partitioned into two disjoint nonempty subsets V_1 and V_2 such that vertices in V_1 may be connected to vertices in V_2, but no vertices in V_1 are connected to other vertices in V_1 and no vertices in V_2 are connected to other vertices in V_2. For example, the graph G illustrated in (i) can be redrawn as shown in (ii). From the drawing in (ii), you can see that G is bipartite with mutually disjoint vertex sets $V_1 = \{v_1, v_3, v_5\}$ and $V_2 = \{v_2, v_4, v_6\}$.

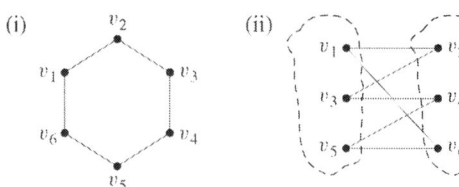

Find which of the following graphs are bipartite. Redraw the bipartite graphs so that their bipartite nature is evident.

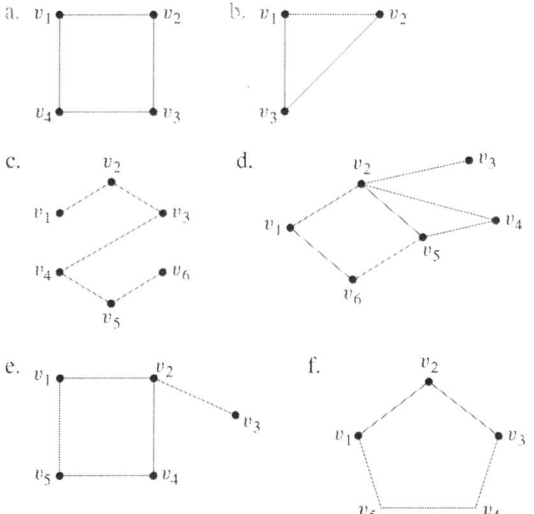

38. Suppose r and s are any positive integers. Does there exist a graph G with the property that G has vertices of degrees r and s and of no other degrees? Explain.

Definition: If G is a simple graph, the **complement of G,** denoted G', is obtained as follows: The vertex set of G' is identical to the vertex set of G. However, two distinct vertices v and w of G' are connected by an edge if, and only if, v and w are *not* connected by an edge in G. For example, if G is the graph

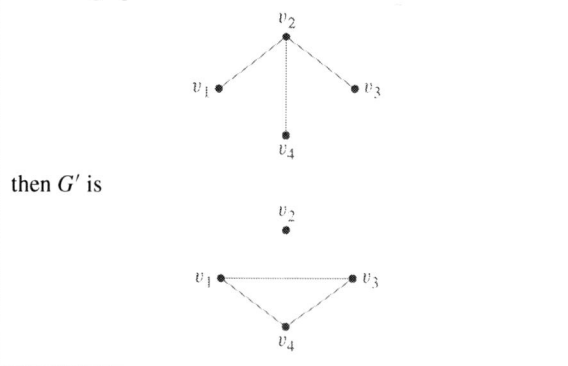

then G' is

39. Find the complement of each of the following graphs.

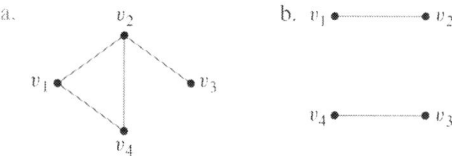

40. a. Find the complement of the graph K_4, the complete graph on four vertices. (See Example 10.1.9.)
    b. Find the complement of the graph $K_{3,2}$, the complete bipartite graph on $(3, 2)$ vertices. (See Example 10.1.10.)

41. Suppose that in a group of five people $A, B, C, D,$ and E the following pairs of people are acquainted with each other:
    A and C, A and D, B and C, C and D, C and E.
    a. Draw a graph to represent this situation.
    b. Draw a graph that illustrates who among these five people are *not* acquainted. That is, draw an edge between two people if, and only if, they are not acquainted.

H 42. Let G be a simple graph with n vertices. What is the relation between the number of edges of G and the number of edges of the complement G'?

43. Show that at a party with at least two people, there are at least two mutual acquaintances or at least two mutual strangers.

44. a. In a simple graph, must every vertex have degree that is less than the number of vertices in the graph? Why?
    b. Can there be a simple graph that has four vertices each of different degrees?
    H ✱ c. Can there be a simple graph that has n vertices all of different degrees?

H ✱ 45. In a group of two or more people, must there always be at least two people who are acquainted with the same number of people within the group? Why?

46. Imagine that the diagram shown below is a map with countries labeled *a–g*. Is it possible to color the map with only three colors so that no two adjacent countries have the same color? To answer this question, draw and analyze a graph in which each country is represented by a vertex and two vertices are connected by an edge if, and only if, the countries share a common border.

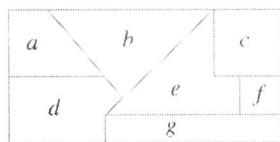

H 47. In this exercise a graph is used to help solve a scheduling problem. Twelve faculty members in a mathematics department serve on the following committees:

Undergraduate Education: Tenner, Peterson, Kashina, Cohen

Graduate Education: Gatto, Yang, Cohen, Catoiu

Colloquium: Sahin, McMurry, Ash

Library: Cortzen, Tenner, Sahin

Hiring: Gatto, McMurry, Yang, Peterson

Personnel: Yang, Wang, Cortzen

The committees must all meet during the first week of classes, but there are only three time slots available. Find a schedule that will allow all faculty members to attend the meetings of all committees on which they serve. To do this, represent each committee as the vertex of a graph, and draw an edge between two vertices if the two committees have a common member. Find a way to color the vertices using only three colors so that no two committees have the same color, and explain how to use the result to schedule the meetings.

48. A department wants to schedule final exams so that no student has more than one exam on any given day. The vertices of the graph below show the courses that are being taken by more than one student, with an edge connecting two vertices if there is a student in both courses. Find a way to color the vertices of the graph with only four colors so that no two adjacent vertices have the same color and explain how to use the result to schedule the final exams.

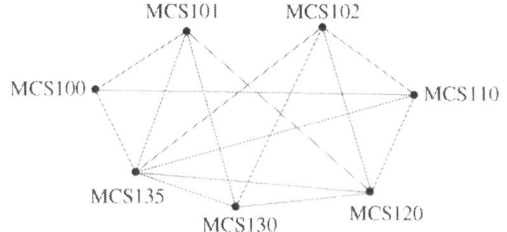

Answers for Test Yourself

1. a finite, nonempty set of vertices; a finite set of edges; one or two vertices called its endpoints   2. an edge with a single endpoint
3. they have the same set of endpoints   4. they are connected by an edge   5. each of its endpoints   6. adjacent   7. isolated   8. an ordered pair of vertices called its endpoints   9. a graph with no loops or parallel edges   10. simple graph with *n* vertices whose set of edges contains exactly one edge for each pair of vertices   11. connected by an edge; any other vertex in V_1; any other vertex in V_2 12. every vertex in *H* is also a vertex in *G*; every edge in *H* is also an edge in *G*; every edge in *H* has the same endpoints as it has in *G*   13. the number of edges that are incident on the vertex, with an edge that is a loop counted twice   14. the sum of the degrees of all the vertices of the graph   15. equal to twice the number of edges of the graph   16. an even number

10.2 Trails, Paths, and Circuits

One can begin to reason only when a clear picture has been formed in the imagination.
— W. W. Sawyer, *Mathematician's Delight*, 1943

The subject of graph theory began in the year 1736 when the great mathematician Leonhard Euler published a paper giving the solution to the following puzzle:

The town of Königsberg in Prussia (now Kaliningrad in Russia) was built at a point where two branches of the Pregel River came together. It consisted of an island and some land along the river banks. These were connected by seven bridges as shown in Figure 10.2.1.

The question is this: Is it possible for a person to take a walk around town, starting and ending at the same location and crossing each of the seven bridges exactly once?*

*In his original paper, Euler did not require the walk to start and end at the same point. The analysis of the problem is simplified, however, by adding this condition. Later in the section, we discuss walks that start and end at different points.

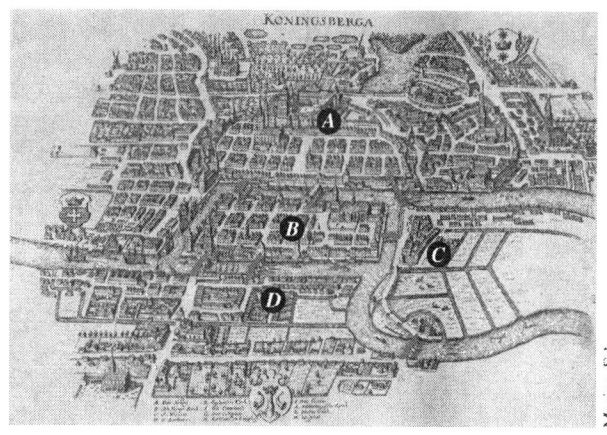

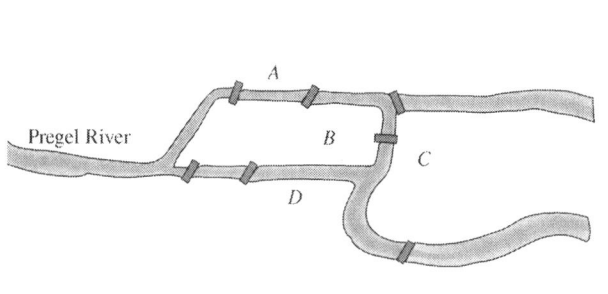

Pregel River

Merian-Erben

Figure 10.2.1 **The Seven Bridges of Königsberg**

Bettmann/CORBIS

Leonhard Euler
(1707–1783)

To solve this puzzle, Euler translated it into a graph theory problem. He noticed that all points of a given land mass can be identified with each other since a person can travel from any one point to any other point of the same land mass without crossing a bridge. Thus for the purpose of solving the puzzle, the map of Königsberg can be identified with the graph shown in Figure 10.2.2, in which the vertices A, B, C, and D represent land masses and the seven edges represent the seven bridges.

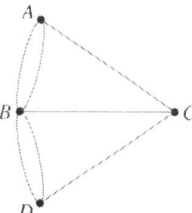

Figure 10.2.2 **Graph Version of Königsberg Map**

In terms of this graph, the question becomes the following:

> Is it possible to find a route through the graph that starts and ends at some vertex, one of A, B, C, or D, and traverses each edge exactly once?

Equivalently:

> Is it possible to trace this graph, starting and ending at the same point, without ever lifting your pencil from the paper?

Take a few minutes to think about the question yourself. Can you find a route that meets the requirements? Try it!

Looking for a route is frustrating because you continually find yourself at a vertex that does not have an unused edge on which to leave, while elsewhere there are unused edges that must still be traversed. If you start at vertex A, for example, each time you pass through vertex B, C, or D, you use up two edges because you arrive on one edge and depart on a different one. So, if it is possible to find a route that uses all the edges of the graph and starts and ends at A, then the total number of arrivals and departures from each vertex B, C, and D must be a multiple of 2. Or, in other words, the degrees of the vertices B, C, and D must be even. But they are not: $\deg(B) = 5$, $\deg(C) = 3$, and $\deg(D) = 3$. Hence there is no route that solves the puzzle by starting and ending at A. Similar reasoning can be used to show that there are no routes that solve the puzzle by starting and ending at B, C, or D. Therefore, it is impossible to travel all around the city crossing each bridge exactly once.

Definitions

Travel in a graph is accomplished by moving from one vertex to another along a sequence of adjacent edges. In the graph below, for instance, you can go from u_1 to u_4 by taking f_1 to u_2 and then f_7 to u_4. This is represented by writing

$$u_1 f_1 u_2 f_7 u_4.$$

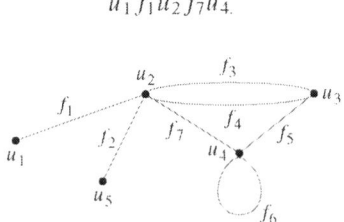

Or you could take the roundabout route

$$u_1 f_1 u_2 f_3 u_3 f_4 u_2 f_3 u_3 f_5 u_4 f_6 u_4 f_7 u_2 f_3 u_3 f_5 u_4.$$

Certain types of sequences of adjacent vertices and edges are of special importance in graph theory: those that do not have a repeated edge, those that do not have a repeated vertex, and those that start and end at the same vertex.

• Definition

Let G be a graph, and let v and w be vertices in G.

A **walk from v to w** is a finite alternating sequence of adjacent vertices and edges of G. Thus a walk has the form

$$v_0 e_1 v_1 e_2 \cdots v_{n-1} e_n v_n,$$

where the v's represent vertices, the e's represent edges, $v_0 = v$, $v_n = w$, and for all $i = 1, 2, \ldots n$, v_{i-1} and v_i are the endpoints of e_i. The **trivial walk from v to v** consists of the single vertex v.

A **trail from v to w** is a walk from v to w that does not contain a repeated edge.

A **path from v to w** is a trail that does not contain a repeated vertex.

A **closed walk** is a walk that starts and ends at the same vertex.

A **circuit** is a closed walk that contains at least one edge and does not contain a repeated edge.

A **simple circuit** is a circuit that does not have any other repeated vertex except the first and last.

For ease of reference, these definitions are summarized in the following table:

	Repeated Edge?	Repeated Vertex?	Starts and Ends at Same Point?	Must Contain at Least One Edge?
Walk	allowed	allowed	allowed	no
Trail	no	allowed	allowed	no
Path	no	no	no	no
Closed walk	allowed	allowed	yes	no
Circuit	no	allowed	yes	yes
Simple circuit	no	first and last only	yes	yes

Often a walk can be specified unambiguously by giving either a sequence of edges or a sequence of vertices. The next two examples show how this is done.

Example 10.2.1 Notation for Walks

a. In the graph below, the notation $e_1e_2e_4e_3$ refers unambiguously to the following walk: $v_1e_1v_2e_2v_3e_4v_3e_3v_2$. On the other hand, the notation e_1 is ambiguous if used to refer to a walk. It could mean either $v_1e_1v_2$ or $v_2e_1v_1$.

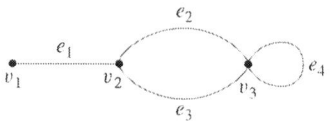

b. In the graph of part (a), the notation v_2v_3 is ambiguous if used to refer to a walk. It could mean $v_2e_2v_3$ or $v_2e_3v_3$. On the other hand, in the graph below, the notation $v_1v_2v_2v_3$ refers unambiguously to the walk $v_1e_1v_2e_2v_2e_3v_3$.

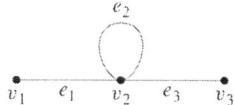

Note that if a graph G does not have any parallel edges, then any walk in G is uniquely determined by its sequence of vertices.

Example 10.2.2 Walks, Trails, Paths, and Circuits

In the graph below, determine which of the following walks are trails, paths, circuits, or simple circuits.

a. $v_1e_1v_2e_3v_3e_4v_3e_5v_4$ b. $e_1e_3e_5e_5e_6$ c. $v_2v_3v_4v_5v_3v_6v_2$

d. $v_2v_3v_4v_5v_6v_2$ e. $v_1e_1v_2e_1v_1$ f. v_1

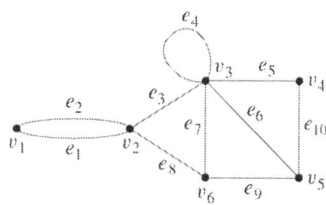

Solution

a. This walk has a repeated vertex but does not have a repeated edge, so it is a trail from v_1 to v_4 but not a path.

b. This is just a walk from v_1 to v_5. It is not a trail because it has a repeated edge.

c. This walk starts and ends at v_2, contains at least one edge, and does not have a repeated edge, so it is a circuit. Since the vertex v_3 is repeated in the middle, it is not a simple circuit.

d. This walk starts and ends at v_2, contains at least one edge, does not have a repeated edge, and does not have a repeated vertex. Thus it is a simple circuit.

e. This is just a closed walk starting and ending at v_1. It is not a circuit because edge e_1 is repeated.

f. The first vertex of this walk is the same as its last vertex, but it does not contain an edge, and so it is not a circuit. It is a closed walk from v_1 to v_1. (It is also a trail from v_1 to v_1.) ▪

Because most of the major developments in graph theory have happened relatively recently and in a variety of different contexts, the terms used in the subject have not been standardized. For example, what this book calls a *graph* is sometimes called a *multigraph*, what this book calls a *simple graph* is sometimes called a *graph*, what this book calls a *vertex* is sometimes called a *node*, and what this book calls an *edge* is sometimes called an *arc*. Similarly, instead of the word *trail*, the word *path* is sometimes used; instead of the word *path*, the words *simple path* are sometimes used; and instead of the words *simple circuit*, the word *cycle* is sometimes used. The terminology in this book is among the most common, but if you consult other sources, be sure to check their definitions.

Connectedness

It is easy to understand the concept of connectedness on an intuitive level. Roughly speaking, a graph is connected if it is possible to travel from any vertex to any other vertex along a sequence of adjacent edges of the graph. The formal definition of connectedness is stated in terms of walks.

> ● **Definition**
>
> Let G be a graph. Two **vertices v and w of G are connected** if, and only if, there is a walk from v to w. The **graph G is connected** if, and only if, given *any* two vertices v and w in G, there is a walk from v to w. Symbolically,
>
> $$G \text{ is connected} \quad \Leftrightarrow \quad \forall \text{ vertices } v, w \in V(G), \exists \text{ a walk from } v \text{ to } w.$$

If you take the negation of this definition, you will see that a graph G is *not connected* if, and only if, there are two vertices of G that are not connected by any walk.

Example 10.2.3 Connected and Disconnected Graphs

Which of the following graphs are connected?

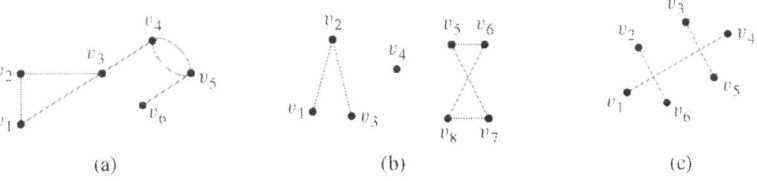

(a)　　　　(b)　　　　(c)

Solution The graph represented in (a) is connected, whereas those of (b) and (c) are not. To understand why (c) is not connected, recall that in a drawing of a graph, two edges may cross at a point that is not a vertex. Thus the graph in (c) can be redrawn as follows:

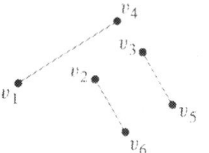

Some useful facts relating circuits and connectedness are collected in the following lemma. Proofs of (a) and (b) are left for the exercises. The proof of (c) is in Section 10.5.

Lemma 10.2.1

Let G be a graph.

a. If G is connected, then any two distinct vertices of G can be connected by a path.

b. If vertices v and w are part of a circuit in G and one edge is removed from the circuit, then there still exists a trail from v to w in G.

c. If G is connected and G contains a circuit, then an edge of the circuit can be removed without disconnecting G.

Look back at Example 10.2.3. The graphs in (b) and (c) are both made up of three pieces, each of which is itself a connected graph. A *connected component* of a graph is a connected subgraph of largest possible size.

• Definition

A graph H is a **connected component** of a graph G if, and only if,

1. H is subgraph of G;

2. H is connected; and

3. no connected subgraph of G has H as a subgraph and contains vertices or edges that are not in H.

The fact is that any graph is a kind of union of its connected components.

Example 10.2.4 Connected Components

Find all connected components of the following graph G.

Solution G has three connected components: H_1, H_2, and H_3 with vertex sets V_1, V_2, and V_3 and edge sets E_1, E_2, and E_3, where

$$V_1 = \{v_1, v_2, v_3\}, \qquad E_1 = \{e_1, e_2\},$$
$$V_2 = \{v_4\}, \qquad E_2 = \emptyset,$$
$$V_3 = \{v_5, v_6, v_7, v_8\}, \qquad E_3 = \{e_3, e_4, e_5\}.$$

Euler Circuits

Now we return to consider general problems similar to the puzzle of the Königsberg bridges. The following definition is made in honor of Euler.

• Definition

Let G be a graph. An **Euler circuit** for G is a circuit that contains every vertex and every edge of G. That is, an Euler circuit for G is a sequence of adjacent vertices and edges in G that has at least one edge, starts and ends at the same vertex, uses every vertex of G at least once, and uses every edge of G exactly once.

The analysis used earlier to solve the puzzle of the Königsberg bridges generalizes to prove the following theorem:

Theorem 10.2.2

If a graph has an Euler circuit, then every vertex of the graph has positive even degree.

Proof:

Suppose G is a graph that has an Euler circuit. *[We must show that given any vertex v of G, the degree of v is even.]* Let v be any particular but arbitrarily chosen vertex of G. Since the Euler circuit contains every edge of G, it contains all edges incident on v. Now imagine taking a journey that begins in the middle of one of the edges adjacent to the start of the Euler circuit and continues around the Euler circuit to end in the middle of the starting edge. (See Figure 10.2.3. There is such a starting edge because the Euler circuit has at least one edge.) Each time v is entered by traveling along one edge, it is immediately exited by traveling along another edge (since the journey ends in the *middle* of an edge).

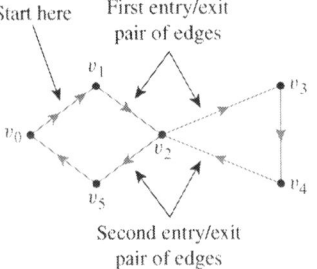

In this example, the Euler circuit is $v_0 v_1 v_2 v_3 v_4 v_2 v_5 v_0$, and v is v_2. Each time v_2 is entered by one edge, it is exited by another edge.

Figure 10.2.3 Example for the Proof of Theorem 10.2.2

Because the Euler circuit uses every edge of G exactly once, every edge incident on v is traversed exactly once in this process. Hence the edges incident on v occur in entry/exit pairs, and consequently the degree of v must be a positive multiple of 2. But that means that v has positive even degree *[as was to be shown]*.

Recall that the contrapositive of a statement is logically equivalent to the statement. The contrapositive of Theorem 10.2.2 is as follows:

Contrapositive Version of Theorem 10.2.2

If some vertex of a graph has odd degree, then the graph does not have an Euler circuit.

This version of Theorem 10.2.2 is useful for showing that a given graph does *not* have an Euler circuit.

Example 10.2.5 Showing That a Graph Does Not Have an Euler Circuit

Show that the graph below does not have an Euler circuit.

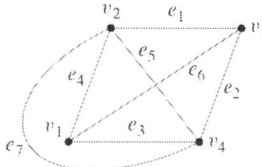

Solution   Vertices v_1 and v_3 both have degree 3, which is odd. Hence by (the contrapositive form of) Theorem 10.2.2, this graph does not have an Euler circuit. ▪

Now consider the converse of Theorem 10.2.2: If every vertex of a graph has even degree, then the graph has an Euler circuit. Is this true? The answer is no. There is a graph G such that every vertex of G has even degree but G does not have an Euler circuit. In fact, there are many such graphs. The illustration below shows one example.

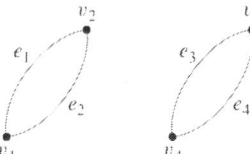

Every vertex has even degree, but the graph does not have an Euler circuit.

Note that the graph in the preceding drawing is not connected. It turns out that although the converse of Theorem 10.2.2 is false, a modified converse is true: If every vertex of a graph has positive even degree *and* if the graph is connected, then the graph has an Euler circuit. The proof of this fact is constructive: It contains an algorithm to find an Euler circuit for any connected graph in which every vertex has even degree.

> **Theorem 10.2.3**
>
> If a graph G is connected and the degree of every vertex of G is a positive even integer, then G has an Euler circuit.

Proof:

Suppose that G is any connected graph and suppose that every vertex of G is a positive even integer. *[We must find an Euler circuit for G.]* Construct a circuit C by the following algorithm:

Step 1: Pick any vertex v of G at which to start.
   [This step can be accomplished because the vertex set of G is nonempty by assumption.]

Step 2: Pick any sequence of adjacent vertices and edges, starting and ending at v and never repeating an edge. Call the resulting circuit C.
   [This step can be performed for the following reasons: Since the degree of each vertex of G is a positive even integer, as each vertex of G is entered by traveling on one edge, either the vertex is v itself and there is no other unused edge adjacent to v, or the vertex can be exited by traveling on another previously unused edge. Since the number of edges of the graph is finite (by definition of graph), the sequence of distinct edges cannot go on forever. The sequence can eventually return to v because the degree of v is a positive even integer, and so if an edge connects v to another vertex, there must be a different edge that connects back to v.]

Step 3: Check whether C contains every edge and vertex of G. If so, C is an Euler circuit, and we are finished. If not, perform the following steps.

   Step 3a: Remove all edges of C from G and also any vertices that become isolated when the edges of C are removed. Call the resulting subgraph G'.
   [Note that G' may not be connected (as illustrated in Figure 10.2.4), but every vertex of G' has positive, even degree (since removing the edges of C removes an even number of edges from each vertex, the difference of two even integers is even, and isolated vertices with degree 0 were removed.)]

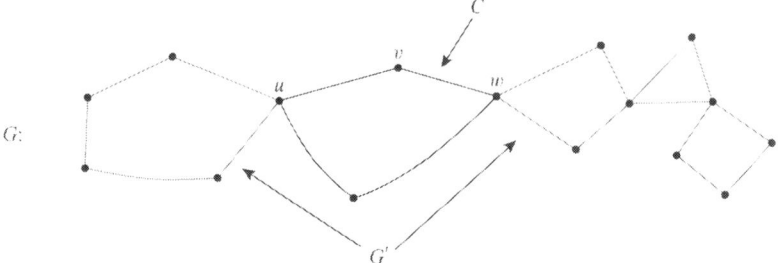

Figure 10.2.4

   Step 3b: Pick any vertex w common to both C and G'.
   [There must be at least one such vertex since G is connected. (See exercise 44.) (In Figure 10.2.4 there are two such vertices: u and w.)]

   Step 3c: Pick any sequence of adjacent vertices and edges of G', starting and ending at w and never repeating an edge. Call the resulting circuit C'.
   [This can be done since each vertex of G' has positive, even degree and G' is finite. See the justification for step 2.]

Step 3d: Patch C and C' together to create a new circuit C'' as follows: Start at v and follow C all the way to w. Then follow C' all the way back to w. After that, continue along the untraveled portion of C to return to v. [*The effect of executing steps 3c and 3d for the graph of Figure 10.2.4 is shown in Figure 10.2.5.*]

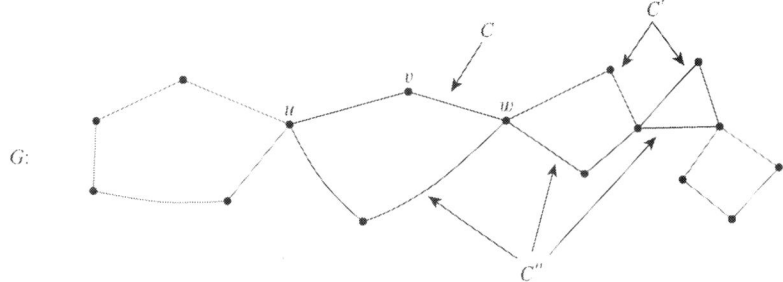

Figure 10.2.5

Step 3e: Let $C = C''$ and go back to step 3.

Since the graph G is finite, execution of the steps outlined in this algorithm must eventually terminate. At that point an Euler circuit for G will have been constructed. (Note that because of the element of choice in steps 1, 2, 3b, and 3c, a variety of different Euler circuits can be produced by using this algorithm.)

Example 10.2.6 Finding an Euler Circuit

Use Theorem 10.2.3 to check that the graph below has an Euler circuit. Then use the algorithm from the proof of the theorem to find an Euler circuit for the graph.

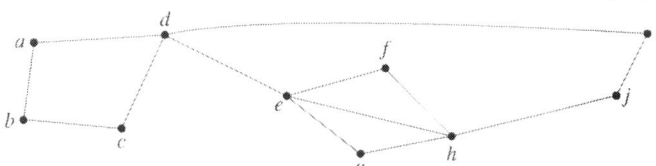

Solution Observe that

$$\deg(a) = \deg(b) = \deg(c) = \deg(f) = \deg(g) = \deg(i) = \deg(j) = 2$$

and that $\deg(d) = \deg(e) = \deg(h) = 4$. Hence all vertices have even degree. Also, the graph is connected. Thus, by Theorem 10.2.3, the graph has an Euler circuit.

To construct an Euler circuit using the algorithm of Theorem 10.2.3, let $v = a$ and let C be

$$C: abcda.$$

C is represented by the labeled edges shown below.

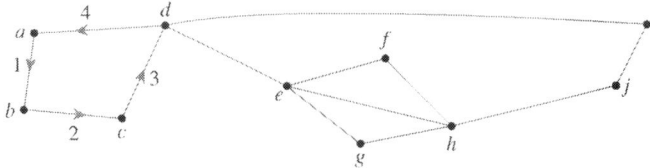

Observe that C is not an Euler circuit for the graph but that C intersects the rest of the graph at d. Let C' be

$$C': deghjid.$$

Patch C' into C to obtain

$$C'': abcdeghjida.$$

Set $C = C''$. Then C is represented by the labeled edges shown below.

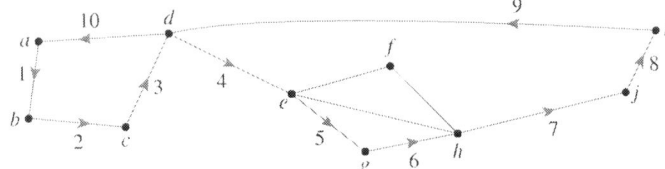

Observe that C is not an Euler circuit for the graph but that it intersects the rest of the graph at e. Let C' be

$$C': efhe.$$

Patch C' into C to obtain

$$C'': abcdefheghjida.$$

Set $C = C''$. Then C is represented by the labeled edges shown below.

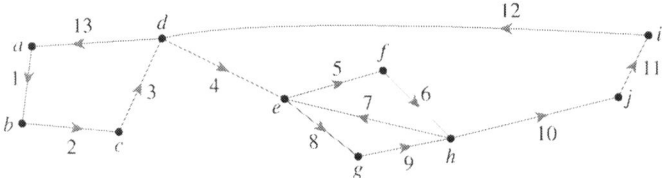

Since C includes every edge of the graph exactly once, C is an Euler circuit for the graph. ∎

In exercise 45 at the end of this section you are asked to show that any graph with an Euler circuit is connected. This result can be combined with Theorems 10.2.2 and 10.2.3 to give a complete characterization of graphs that have Euler circuits, as stated in Theorem 10.2.4.

> **Theorem 10.2.4**
>
> A graph G has an Euler circuit if, and only if, G is connected and every vertex of G has positive even degree.

A corollary to Theorem 10.2.4 gives a criterion for determining when it is possible to find a walk from one vertex of a graph to another, passing through every vertex of the graph at least once and every edge of the graph exactly once.

> **• Definition**
>
> Let G be a graph, and let v and w be two distinct vertices of G. An **Euler trail from v to w** is a sequence of adjacent edges and vertices that starts at v, ends at w, passes through every vertex of G at least once, and traverses every edge of G exactly once.

> **Corollary 10.2.5**
>
> Let G be a graph, and let v and w be two distinct vertices of G. There is an Euler trail from v to w if, and only if, G is connected, v and w have odd degree, and all other vertices of G have positive even degree.

The proof of this corollary is left as an exercise.

Example 10.2.7 Finding an Euler Trail

The floor plan shown below is for a house that is open for public viewing. Is it possible to find a trail that starts in room A, ends in room B, and passes through every interior doorway of the house exactly once? If so, find such a trail.

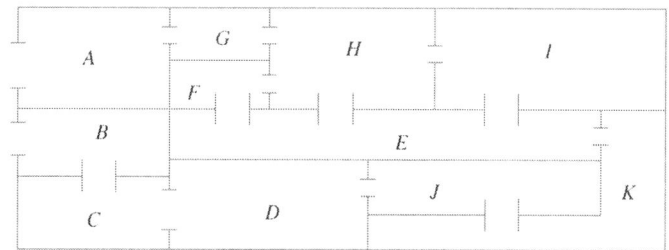

Solution   Let the floor plan of the house be represented by the graph below.

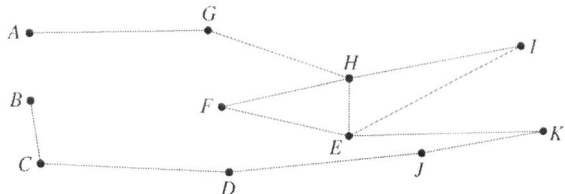

Each vertex of this graph has even degree except for A and B, each of which has degree 1. Hence by Corollary 10.2.5, there is an Euler path from A to B. One such trail is

$$AGHFEIHEKJDCB.$$

Hamiltonian Circuits

Theorem 10.2.4 completely answers the following question: Given a graph G, is it possible to find a circuit for G in which all the *edges* of G appear exactly once? A related question is this: Given a graph G, is it possible to find a circuit for G in which all the *vertices* of G (except the first and the last) appear exactly once?

In 1859 the Irish mathematician Sir William Rowan Hamilton introduced a puzzle in the shape of a dodecahedron (DOH-dek-a-HEE-dron). (Figure 10.2.6 contains a drawing of a dodecahedron, which is a solid figure with 12 identical pentagonal faces.)

Sir Wm. Hamilton
(1805–1865)

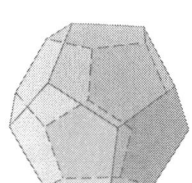

Figure 10.2.6 **Dodecahedron**

Each vertex was labeled with the name of a city—London, Paris, Hong Kong, New York, and so on. The problem Hamilton posed was to start at one city and tour the world by visiting each other city exactly once and returning to the starting city. One way to solve the puzzle is to imagine the surface of the dodecahedron stretched out and laid flat in the plane, as follows:

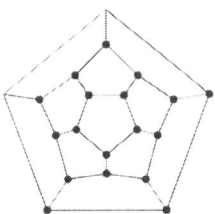

The circuit denoted with black lines is one solution. Note that although every city is visited, many edges are omitted from the circuit. (More difficult versions of the puzzle required that certain cities be visited in a certain order.)

The following definition is made in honor of Hamilton.

> ### • Definition
>
> Given a graph G, a **Hamiltonian circuit** for G is a simple circuit that includes every vertex of G. That is, a Hamiltonian circuit for G is a sequence of adjacent vertices and distinct edges in which every vertex of G appears exactly once, except for the first and the last, which are the same.

Note that although an Euler circuit for a graph G must include every vertex of G, it may visit some vertices more than once and hence may not be a Hamiltonian circuit. On the other hand, a Hamiltonian circuit for G does not need to include all the edges of G and hence may not be an Euler circuit.

Despite the analogous-sounding definitions of Euler and Hamiltonian circuits, the mathematics of the two are very different. Theorem 10.2.4 gives a simple criterion for determining whether a given graph has an Euler circuit. Unfortunately, there is no analogous criterion for determining whether a given graph has a Hamiltonian circuit, nor is there even an efficient algorithm for finding such a circuit. There is, however, a simple technique that can be used in many cases to show that a graph does *not* have a Hamiltonian circuit. This follows from the following considerations:

Suppose a graph G with at least two vertices has a Hamiltonian circuit C given concretely as

$$C: v_0 e_1 v_1 e_2 \cdots v_{n-1} e_n v_n.$$

Since C is a simple circuit, all the e_i are distinct and all the v_j are distinct except that $v_0 = v_n$. Let H be the subgraph of G that is formed using the vertices and edges of C. An example of such an H is shown below.

H is indicated by the black lines.

Note that H has the same number of edges as it has vertices since all its n edges are distinct and so are its n vertices $v_1, v_2, \ldots, v_n$. Also, by definition of Hamiltonian circuit, every vertex of G is a vertex of H, and H is connected since any two of its vertices lie on a circuit. In addition, every vertex of H has degree 2. The reason for this is that there are exactly two edges incident on any vertex. These are e_i and e_{i+1} for any vertex v_i except $v_0 = v_n$, and they are e_1 and e_n for $v_0 (= v_n)$. These observations have established the truth of the following proposition in all cases where G has at least two vertices.

Proposition 10.2.6

If a graph G has a Hamiltonian circuit, then G has a subgraph H with the following properties:

1. H contains every vertex of G.

2. H is connected.

3. H has the same number of edges as vertices.

4. Every vertex of H has degree 2.

Note that if G contains only one vertex and G has a Hamiltonian circuit, then the circuit has the form $v\, e\, v$, where v is the vertex of G and e is an edge incident on v. In this case, the subgraph H consisting of v and e satisfies conditions (1)–(4) of Proposition 10.2.6.

Recall that the contrapositive of a statement is logically equivalent to the statement. The contrapositive of Proposition 10.2.6 says that if a graph G does *not* have a subgraph H with properties (1)–(4), then G does *not* have a Hamiltonian circuit.

Example 10.2.8 Showing That a Graph Does Not Have a Hamiltonian Circuit

Prove that the graph G shown below does not have a Hamiltonian circuit.

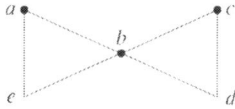

Solution   If G has a Hamiltonian circuit, then by Proposition 10.2.6, G has a subgraph H that (1) contains every vertex of G, (2) is connected, (3) has the same number of edges as vertices, and (4) is such that every vertex has degree 2. Suppose such a subgraph H exists. In other words, suppose there is a connected subgraph H of G such that H has five vertices (a, b, c, d, e) and five edges and such that every vertex of H has degree 2. Since the degree of b in G is 4 and every vertex of H has degree 2, two edges incident on b must be removed from G to create H. Edge $\{a, b\}$ cannot be removed because if it were, vertex a would have degree less than 2 in H. Similar reasoning shows that edges $\{e, b\}$, $\{b, a\}$, and $\{b, d\}$ cannot be removed either. It follows that the degree of b in H must be 4, which contradicts the condition that every vertex in H has degree 2 in H. Hence no such subgraph H exists, and so G does not have a Hamiltonian circuit. ■

The next example illustrates a type of problem known as a **traveling salesman problem.** It is a variation of the problem of finding a Hamiltonian circuit for a graph.

Example 10.2.9 A Traveling Salesman Problem

Imagine that the drawing below is a map showing four cities and the distances in kilometers between them. Suppose that a salesman must travel to each city exactly once, starting and ending in city A. Which route from city to city will minimize the total distance that must be traveled?

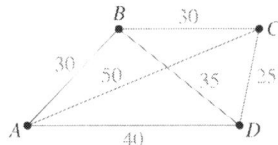

Solution This problem can be solved by writing all possible Hamiltonian circuits starting and ending at A and calculating the total distance traveled for each.

Route	Total Distance (In Kilometers)	
$ABCDA$	$30 + 30 + 25 + 40 = 125$	
$ABDCA$	$30 + 35 + 25 + 50 = 140$	
$ACBDA$	$50 + 30 + 35 + 40 = 155$	
$ACDBA$	140	[$ABDCA$ backwards]
$ADBCA$	155	[$ACBDA$ backwards]
$ADCBA$	125	[$ABCDA$ backwards]

Thus either route $ABCDA$ or $ADCBA$ gives a minimum total distance of 125 kilometers. ▪

The general traveling salesman problem involves finding a Hamiltonian circuit to minimize the total distance traveled for an arbitrary graph with n vertices in which each edge is marked with a distance. One way to solve the general problem is to use the method of Example 10.2.9: Write down all Hamiltonian circuits starting and ending at a particular vertex, compute the total distance for each, and pick one for which this total is minimal. However, even for medium-sized values of n this method is impractical. For a complete graph with 30 vertices, there would be $(29!)/2 \cong 4.42 \times 10^{30}$ Hamiltonian circuits starting and ending at a particular vertex to check. Even if each circuit could be found and its total distance computed in just one nanosecond, it would require approximately 1.4×10^{14} years to finish the computation. At present, there is no known algorithm for solving the general traveling salesman problem that is more efficient. However, there are efficient algorithms that find "pretty good" solutions—that is, circuits that, while not necessarily having the least possible total distances, have smaller total distances than most other Hamiltonian circuits.

Test Yourself

1. Let G be a graph and let v and w be vertices in G.

   (a) A walk from v to w is _____.

   (b) A trail from v to w is _____.

   (c) A path from v to w is _____.

   (d) A closed walk is _____.

   (e) A circuit is _____.

   (f) A simple circuit is _____.

   (g) A trivial walk is _____.

   (h) Vertices v and w are connected if, and only if, _____.

2. A graph is connected if, and only if, _____.

3. Removing an edge from a circuit in a graph does not _____.

4. An Euler circuit in a graph is _____.

5. A graph has an Euler circuit if, and only if, _____.

6. Given vertices v and w in a graph, there is an Euler path from v to w if, and only if, _____.

7. A Hamiltonian circuit in a graph is _____.

8. If a graph G has a Hamiltonian circuit, then G has a subgraph H with the following properties: _____, _____, _____, and _____.

9. A traveling salesman problem involves finding a _____ that minimizes the total distance traveled for a graph in which each edge is marked with a distance.

Exercise Set 10.2

1. In the graph below, determine whether the following walks are trails, paths, closed walks, circuits, simple circuits, or just walks.

    a. $v_0 e_1 v_1 e_{10} v_5 e_9 v_2 e_2 v_1$ b. $v_4 e_7 v_2 e_9 v_5 e_{10} v_1 e_3 v_2 e_9 v_5$

    c. v_2 d. $v_5 v_2 v_3 v_4 v_4 v_5$

    e. $v_2 v_3 v_4 v_5 v_2 v_4 v_3 v_2$ f. $e_5 e_8 e_{10} e_3$

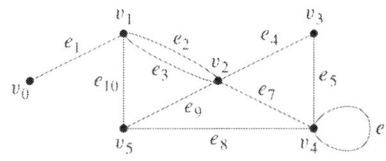

2. In the graph below, determine whether the following walks are trails, paths, closed walks, circuits, simple circuits, or just walks.

    a. $v_1 e_2 v_2 e_3 v_3 e_4 v_4 e_5 v_2 e_2 v_1 e_1 v_0$ b. $v_2 v_3 v_4 v_5 v_2$

    c. $v_4 v_2 v_3 v_4 v_5 v_2 v_4$ d. $v_2 v_1 v_5 v_2 v_3 v_4 v_2$

    e. $v_0 v_5 v_2 v_3 v_4 v_2 v_1$ f. $v_5 v_4 v_2 v_1$

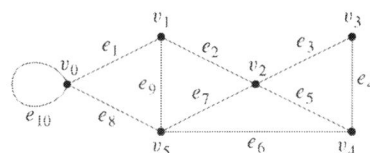

3. Let G be the graph

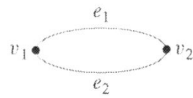

and consider the walk $v_1 e_1 v_2 e_2 v_1$.

   a. Can this walk be written unambiguously as $v_1 v_2 v_1$? Why?

   b. Can this walk be written unambiguously as $e_1 e_2$? Why?

4. Consider the following graph.

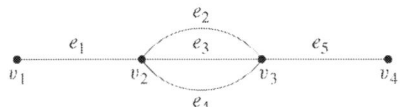

a. How many paths are there from v_1 to v_4?

b. How many trails are there from v_1 to v_4?

c. How many walks are there from v_1 to v_4?

5. Consider the following graph.

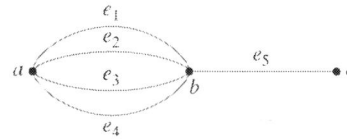

a. How many paths are there from a to c?

b. How many trails are there from a to c?

c. How many walks are there from a to c?

6. An edge whose removal disconnects the graph of which it is a part is called a **bridge.** Find all bridges for each of the following graphs.

   a. 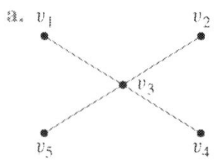   b.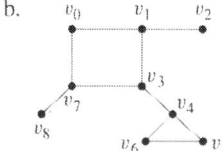

   c.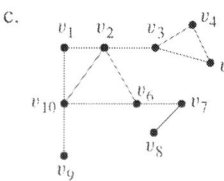

7. Given any positive integer n, (a) find a connected graph with n edges such that removal of just one edge disconnects the graph; (b) find a connected graph with n edges that cannot be disconnected by the removal of any single edge.

8. Find the number of connected components for each of the following graphs.

a.

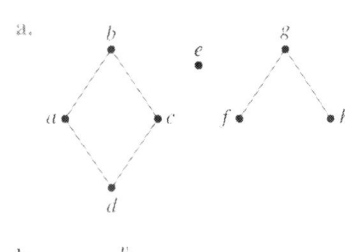

b.

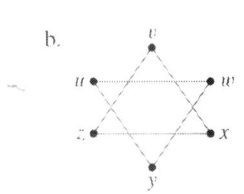

c.   d.

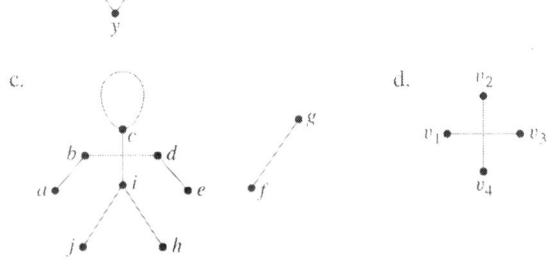

9. Each of (a)–(c) describes a graph. In each case answer *yes, no,* or *not necessarily* to this question: Does the graph have an Euler circuit? Justify your answers.
   a. G is a connected graph with five vertices of degrees 2, 2, 3, 3, and 4.
   b. G is a connected graph with five vertices of degrees 2, 2, 4, 4, and 6.
   c. G is a graph with five vertices of degrees 2, 2, 4, 4, and 6.

10. The solution for Example 10.2.5 shows a graph for which every vertex has even degree but which does not have an Euler circuit. Give another example of a graph satisfying these properties.

11. Is it possible for a citizen of Königsberg to make a tour of the city and cross each bridge exactly twice? (See Figure 10.2.1.) Why?

Determine which of the graphs in 12–17 have Euler circuits. If the graph does not have an Euler circuit, explain why not. If it does have an Euler circuit, describe one.

12.   13.

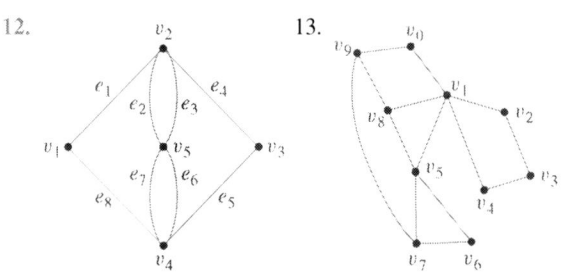

14.   15.

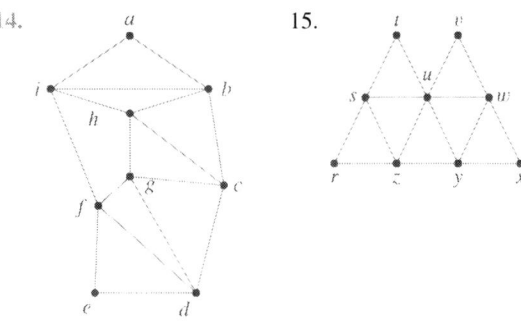

16.   17.

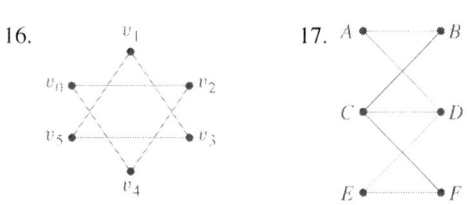

18. Is it possible to take a walk around the city whose map is shown below, starting and ending at the same point and crossing each bridge exactly once? If so, how can this be done?

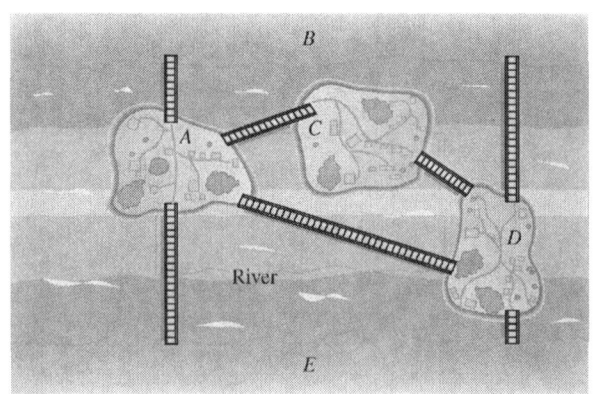

For each of the graphs in 19–21, determine whether there is an Euler path from u to w. If there is, find such a path.

19.   20.

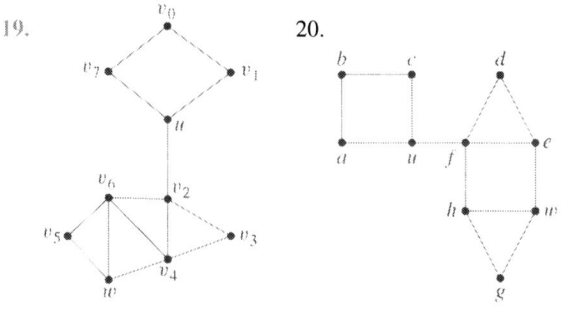

21.

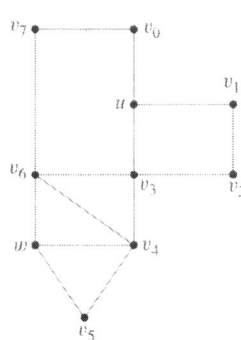

22. The following is a floor plan of a house. Is it possible to enter the house in room *A*, travel through every interior doorway of the house exactly once, and exit out of room *E*? If so, how can this be done?

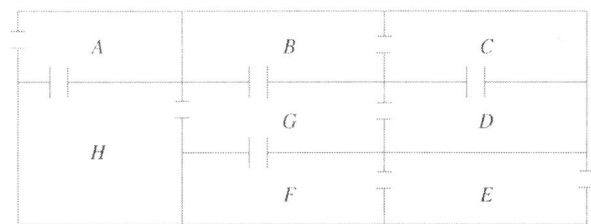

Find Hamiltonian circuits for each of the graphs in 23 and 24.

23.

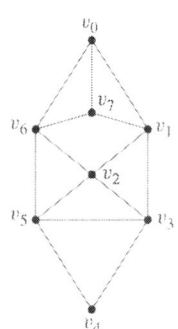

24.

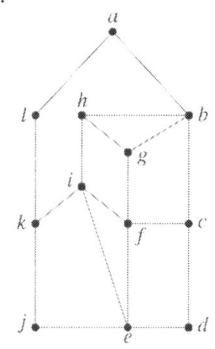

Show that none of the graphs in 25–27 has a Hamiltonian circuit.

H 25.

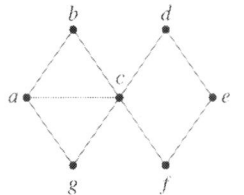

26.

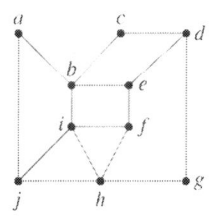

27.

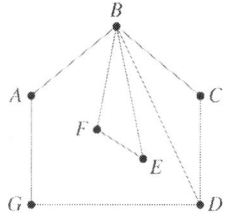

In 28–31 find Hamiltonian circuits for those graphs that have them. Explain why the other graphs do not.

H 28.

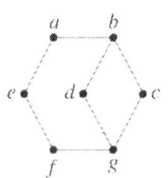

29.

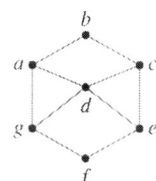

30.

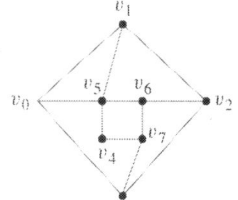

31.

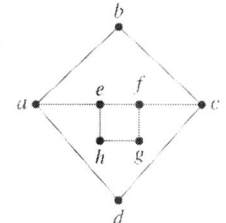

H 32. Give two examples of graphs that have Euler circuits but not Hamiltonian circuits.

H 33. Give two examples of graphs that have Hamiltonian circuits but not Euler circuits.

H 34. Give two examples of graphs that have circuits that are both Euler circuits and Hamiltonian circuits.

H 35. Give two examples of graphs that have Euler circuits and Hamiltonian circuits that are not the same.

36. A traveler in Europe wants to visit each of the cities shown on the map exactly once, starting and ending in Brussels. The distance (in kilometers) between each pair of cities is given in the table. Find a Hamiltonian circuit that minimizes the total distance traveled. (Use the map to narrow the possible circuits down to just a few. Then use the table to find the total distance for each of those.)

	Berlin	Brussels	Düsseldorf	Luxembourg	Munich
Brussels	783				
Düsseldorf	564	223			
Luxembourg	764	219	224		
Munich	585	771	613	517	
Paris	1,057	308	497	375	832

37. a. Prove that if a walk in a graph contains a repeated edge, then the walk contains a repeated vertex.
    b. Explain how it follows from part (a) that any walk with no repeated vertex has no repeated edge.

38. Prove Lemma 10.2.1(a): If G is a connected graph, then any two distinct vertices of G can be connected by a path.

39. Prove Lemma 10.2.1(b): If vertices v and w are part of a circuit in a graph G and one edge is removed from the circuit, then there still exists a trail from v to w in G.

40. Draw a picture to illustrate Lemma 10.2.1(c): If a graph G is connected and G contains a circuit, then an edge of the circuit can be removed without disconnecting G.

41. Prove that if there is a circuit in a graph that starts and ends at a vertex v and if w is another vertex in the circuit, then there is a circuit in the graph that starts and ends at w.

H 42. If a graph contains a circuit that starts and ends at a vertex v, does the graph contain a simple circuit that starts and ends at v? Why?

43. Prove that if there is a trail in a graph G from a vertex v to a vertex w, then there is a trail from w to v.

44. Let G be a connected graph, and let C be any circuit in G that does not contain every vertex of C. Let G' be the subgraph obtained by removing all the edges of C from G and also any vertices that become isolated when the edges of C are removed. Prove that there exists a vertex v such that v is in both C and G'.

45. Prove that any graph with an Euler circuit is connected.

46. Prove Corollary 10.2.5.

47. For what values of n does the complete graph K_n with n vertices have (a) an Euler circuit? (b) a Hamiltonian circuit? Justify your answers.

* 48. For what values of m and n does the complete bipartite graph on (m, n) vertices have (a) an Euler circuit? (b) a Hamiltonian circuit? Justify your answers.

* 49. What is the maximum number of edges a simple disconnected graph with n vertices can have? Prove your answer.

* 50. Show that a graph is bipartite if, and only if, it does not have a circuit with an odd number of edges. (See exercise 37 of Section 10.1 for the definition of bipartite graph.)

Answers for Test Yourself

1. (a) a finite alternating sequence of adjacent vertices and edges of G (b) a walk that does not contain a repeated edge (c) a trail that does not contain a repeated vertex (d) a walk that starts and ends at the same vertex (e) a closed walk that contains at least one edge and does not contain a repeated edge (f) a circuit that does not have any repeated vertex other than the first and the last (g) a walk consisting of a single vertex and no edge (h) there is a walk from v to w 2. given any two vertices in the graph, there is a walk from one to the other 3. disconnect the graph 4. a circuit that contains every vertex and every edge of the graph 5. the graph is connected, and every vertex has positive, even degree 6. the graph is connected, v and w have odd degree, and all other vertices have positive even degree 7. a simple circuit that includes every vertex of the graph 8. H contains every vertex of G; H is connected; H has the same number of edges as vertices; every vertex of H has degree 2 9. Hamiltonian circuit

10.3 Matrix Representations of Graphs

Order and simplification are the first steps toward the mastery of a subject.
— Thomas Mann, *The Magic Mountain*, 1924

How can graphs be represented inside a computer? It happens that all the information needed to specify a graph can be conveyed by a structure called a *matrix*, and matrices (*matrices* is the plural of *matrix*) are easy to represent inside computers. This section contains some basic definitions about matrices and matrix operations, a description of the relation between graphs and matrices, and some applications.

Matrices

Matrices are two-dimensional analogues of sequences. They are also called two-dimensional arrays.

• Definition

An **$m \times n$** (read "*m* by *n*") **matrix A over a set** S is a rectangular array of elements of S arranged into m rows and n columns:

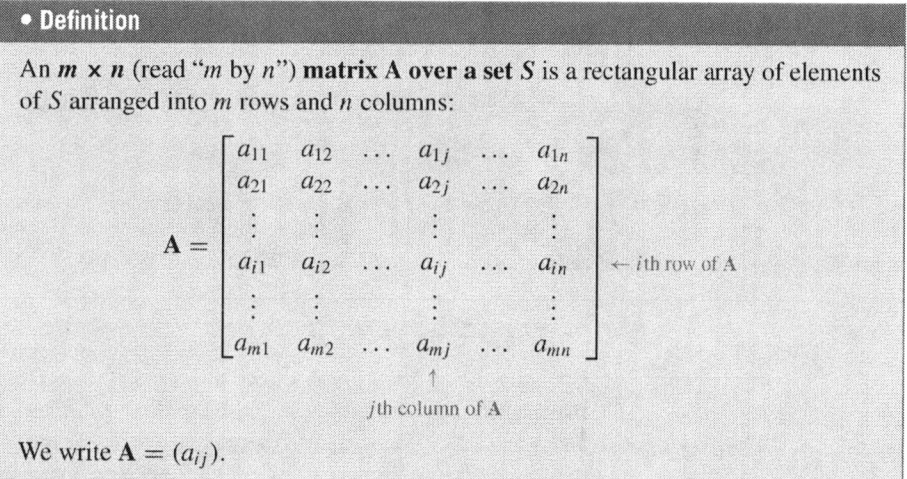

We write $\mathbf{A} = (a_{ij})$.

The **ith row of A** is

$$[a_{i1} \quad a_{i2} \quad \cdots \quad a_{in}]$$

and the **jth column of A** is

$$\begin{bmatrix} a_{1j} \\ a_{2j} \\ \vdots \\ a_{mj} \end{bmatrix}.$$

The entry a_{ij} in the ith row and jth column of $\mathbf{A}$ is called the **ijth entry of A.** An $m \times n$ matrix is said to have **size $m \times n$**. If $\mathbf{A}$ and $\mathbf{B}$ are matrices, then $\mathbf{A} = \mathbf{B}$ if, and only if, $\mathbf{A}$ and $\mathbf{B}$ have the same size and the corresponding entries of $\mathbf{A}$ and $\mathbf{B}$ are all equal; that is,

$$a_{ij} = b_{ij} \quad \text{for all } i = 1, 2, \ldots, m \text{ and } j = 1, 2 \ldots, n.$$

A matrix for which the numbers of rows and columns are equal is called a **square matrix.** If $\mathbf{A}$ is a square matrix of size $n \times n$, then the **main diagonal of A** consists of all the entries $a_{11}, a_{22}, \ldots, a_{nn}$:

$$\begin{bmatrix} a_{11} & a_{12} & \cdots & a_{1i} & \cdots & a_{1n} \\ a_{21} & a_{22} & \cdots & a_{2i} & \cdots & a_{2n} \\ \vdots & \vdots & & \vdots & & \vdots \\ a_{i1} & a_{i2} & \cdots & a_{ii} & \cdots & a_{in} \\ \vdots & \vdots & & \vdots & & \vdots \\ a_{n1} & a_{n2} & \cdots & a_{ni} & \cdots & a_{nn} \end{bmatrix}$$

main diagonal of A

Example 10.3.1 Matrix Terminology

The following is a 3×3 matrix over the set of integers.

$$\begin{bmatrix} 1 & 0 & -3 \\ 4 & -1 & 5 \\ -2 & 2 & 0 \end{bmatrix}$$

a. What is the entry in row 2, column 3?

b. What is the second column of A?

c. What are the entries in the main diagonal of A?

Solution

a. 5   b. $\begin{bmatrix} 0 \\ -1 \\ 2 \end{bmatrix}$ c. $1, -1$, and 0 ■

Matrices and Directed Graphs

Consider the directed graph shown in Figure 10.3.1. This graph can be represented by the matrix $A = (a_{ij})$ for which $a_{ij} =$ the number of arrows from v_i to v_j, for all $i = 1, 2, 3$ and $j = 1, 2, 3$. Thus $a_{11} = 1$ because there is one arrow from v_1 to v_1, $a_{12} = 0$ because there is no arrow from v_1 to v_2, $a_{23} = 2$ because there are two arrows from v_2 to v_3, and so forth. A is called the *adjacency matrix* of the directed graph. For convenient reference, the rows and columns of A are often labeled with the vertices of the graph G.

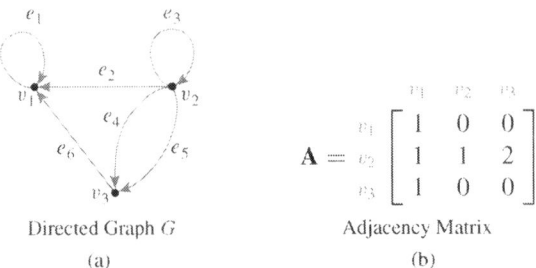

Directed Graph G

(a)

$$A = \begin{array}{c} v_1 \\ v_2 \\ v_3 \end{array}\begin{matrix} v_1 & v_2 & v_3 \\ \begin{bmatrix} 1 & 0 & 0 \\ 1 & 1 & 2 \\ 1 & 0 & 0 \end{bmatrix} \end{matrix}$$

Adjacency Matrix

(b)

Figure 10.3.1 A Directed Graph and Its Adjacency Matrix

• Definition

Let G be a directed graph with ordered vertices $v_1, v_2, \ldots, v_n$. The **adjacency matrix** of G is the $n \times n$ matrix $A = (a_{ij})$ over the set of nonnegative integers such that

$a_{ij} =$ the number of arrows from v_i to v_j for all $i, j = 1, 2, \ldots, n$.

Note that nonzero entries along the main diagonal of an adjacency matrix indicate the presence of loops, and entries larger than 1 correspond to parallel edges. Moreover, if the vertices of a directed graph are reordered, then the entries in the rows and columns of the corresponding adjacency matrix are moved around.

Example 10.3.2 The Adjacency Matrix of a Graph

The two directed graphs shown below differ only in the ordering of their vertices. Find their adjacency matrices.

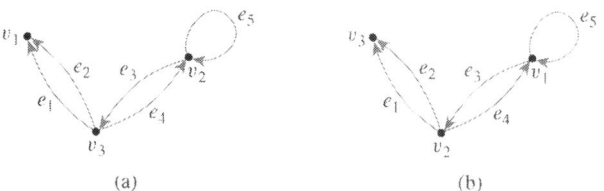

(a)   (b)

Solution   Since both graphs have three vertices, both adjacency matrices are 3×3 matrices. For (a), all entries in the first row are 0 since there are no arrows from v_1 to any other vertex. For (b), the first two entries in the first row are 1 and the third entry is 0 since from v_1 there are single arrows to v_1 and to v_2 and no arrows to v_3. Continuing the analysis in this way, you obtain the following two adjacency matrices:

$$
\begin{array}{c}
\begin{array}{ccc} v_1 & v_2 & v_3 \end{array} \\
\begin{array}{c} v_1 \\ v_2 \\ v_3 \end{array}
\begin{bmatrix} 0 & 0 & 0 \\ 0 & 1 & 1 \\ 2 & 1 & 0 \end{bmatrix}
\end{array}
\qquad
\begin{array}{c}
\begin{array}{ccc} v_1 & v_2 & v_3 \end{array} \\
\begin{array}{c} v_1 \\ v_2 \\ v_3 \end{array}
\begin{bmatrix} 1 & 1 & 0 \\ 1 & 0 & 2 \\ 0 & 0 & 0 \end{bmatrix}
\end{array}
$$

(a)   (b)

If you are given a square matrix with nonnegative integer entries, you can construct a directed graph with that matrix as its adjacency matrix. However, the matrix does not tell you how to label the edges, so the directed graph is not uniquely determined.

Example 10.3.3 Obtaining a Directed Graph from a Matrix

Let

$$
\mathbf{A} = \begin{bmatrix} 0 & 1 & 1 & 0 \\ 1 & 1 & 0 & 2 \\ 0 & 0 & 1 & 1 \\ 2 & 1 & 0 & 0 \end{bmatrix}.
$$

Draw a directed graph that has $\mathbf{A}$ as its adjacency matrix.

Solution   Let G be the graph corresponding to $\mathbf{A}$, and let v_1, v_2, v_3, v_4 be the vertices of G. Label $\mathbf{A}$ across the top and down the left side with these vertex names, as shown below.

$$
\mathbf{A} = \begin{array}{c}
\begin{array}{cccc} v_1 & v_2 & v_3 & v_4 \end{array} \\
\begin{array}{c} v_1 \\ v_2 \\ v_3 \\ v_4 \end{array}
\begin{bmatrix} 0 & 1 & 1 & 0 \\ 1 & 1 & 0 & 2 \\ 0 & 0 & 1 & 1 \\ 2 & 1 & 0 & 0 \end{bmatrix}
\end{array}
$$

Then, for instance, the 2 in the fourth row and the first column means that there are two arrows from v_4 to v_1. The 0 in the first row and the fourth column means that there is no arrow from v_1 to v_4. A corresponding directed graph is shown on the next page (without edge labels because the matrix does not determine those).

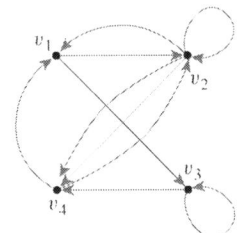

Matrices and Undirected Graphs

Once you know how to associate a matrix with a directed graph, the definition of the matrix corresponding to an undirected graph should seem natural to you. As before, you must order the vertices of the graph, but in this case you simply set the ijth entry of the adjacency matrix equal to the number of edges connecting the ith and jth vertices of the graph.

> **• Definition**
>
> Let G be an undirected graph with ordered vertices $v_1, v_2, \ldots, v_n$. The **adjacency matrix of G** is the $n \times n$ matrix $\mathbf{A} = (a_{ij})$ over the set of nonnegative integers such that
> $$a_{ij} = \text{the number of edges connecting } v_i \text{ and } v_j$$
> for all $i, j = 1, 2, \ldots, n$.

Example 10.3.4 Finding the Adjacency Matrix of a Graph

Find the adjacency matrix for the graph G shown below.

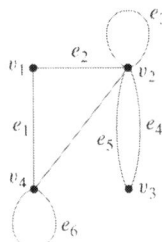

Solution

$$
\mathbf{A} = \begin{matrix} & \begin{matrix} v_1 & v_2 & v_3 & v_4 \end{matrix} \\ \begin{matrix} v_1 \\ v_2 \\ v_3 \\ v_4 \end{matrix} & \begin{bmatrix} 0 & 1 & 0 & 1 \\ 1 & 1 & 2 & 1 \\ 0 & 2 & 0 & 0 \\ 1 & 1 & 0 & 1 \end{bmatrix} \end{matrix}
$$

Note that if the matrix $\mathbf{A} = (a_{ij})$ in Example 10.3.4 is flipped across its main diagonal, it looks the same: $a_{ij} = a_{ji}$, for $i, j = 1, 2, \ldots, n$. Such a matrix is said to be *symmetric*.

> **• Definition**
>
> An $n \times n$ square matrix $\mathbf{A} = (a_{ij})$ is called **symmetric** if, and only if, for all $i, j = 1, 2, \ldots, n$,
> $$a_{ij} = a_{ji}.$$

Example 10.3.5 Symmetric Matrices

Which of the following matrices are symmetric?

a. $\begin{bmatrix} 1 & 0 \\ 1 & 2 \end{bmatrix}$
b. $\begin{bmatrix} 0 & 1 & 2 \\ 1 & 1 & 0 \\ 2 & 0 & 3 \end{bmatrix}$
c. $\begin{bmatrix} 2 & 0 & 0 \\ 0 & 1 & 0 \end{bmatrix}$

Solution   Only (b) is symmetric. In (a) the entry in the first row and the second column differs from the entry in the second row and the first column; the matrix in (c) is not even square. ■

It is easy to see that the matrix of *any* undirected graph is symmetric since it is always the case that the number of edges joining v_i and v_j equals the number of edges joining v_j and v_i for all $i, j = 1, 2, \ldots, n$.

Matrices and Connected Components

Consider a graph G, as shown below, that consists of several connected components.

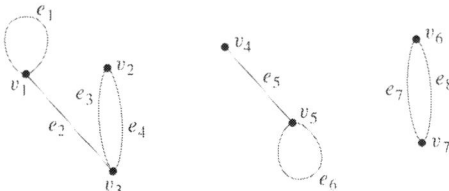

The adjacency matrix of G is

$$A = \begin{bmatrix} 1 & 0 & 1 & 0 & 0 & 0 & 0 \\ 0 & 0 & 2 & 0 & 0 & 0 & 0 \\ 1 & 2 & 0 & 0 & 0 & 0 & 0 \\ 0 & 0 & 0 & 0 & 1 & 0 & 0 \\ 0 & 0 & 0 & 1 & 1 & 0 & 0 \\ 0 & 0 & 0 & 0 & 0 & 0 & 2 \\ 0 & 0 & 0 & 0 & 0 & 2 & 0 \end{bmatrix}.$$

As you can see, A consists of square matrix blocks (of different sizes) down its diagonal and blocks of 0's everywhere else. The reason is that vertices in each connected component share no edges with vertices in other connected components. For instance, since v_1, v_2, and v_3 share no edges with v_4, v_5, v_6, or v_7, all entries in the top three rows to the right of the third column are 0 and all entries in the left three columns below the third row are also 0. Sometimes matrices whose entries are all 0's are themselves denoted 0. If this convention is followed here, A is written as

$$A = \begin{bmatrix} \begin{matrix} 1 & 0 & 1 \\ 0 & 0 & 2 \\ 1 & 2 & 0 \end{matrix} & 0 & 0 \\ 0 & \begin{matrix} 0 & 1 \\ 1 & 1 \end{matrix} & 0 \\ 0 & 0 & \begin{matrix} 0 & 2 \\ 2 & 0 \end{matrix} \end{bmatrix}$$

The previous reasoning can be generalized to prove the following theorem:

Theorem 10.3.1

Let G be a graph with connected components $G_1, G_2, \ldots, G_k$. If there are n_i vertices in each connected component G_i and these vertices are numbered consecutively, then the adjacency matrix of G has the form

$$
\begin{bmatrix}
A_1 & O & O & \cdots & O & O \\
O & A_2 & O & \cdots & O & O \\
O & O & A_3 & \cdots & O & O \\
\vdots & \vdots & \vdots & & \vdots & \vdots \\
O & O & O & \cdots & O & A_k
\end{bmatrix}
$$

where each A_i is the $n_i \times n_i$ adjacency matrix of G_i, for all $i = 1, 2, \ldots, k$, and the O's represent matrices whose entries are all 0.

Matrix Multiplication

Matrix multiplication is an enormously useful operation that arises in many contexts, including the investigation of walks in graphs. Although matrix multiplication can be defined in quite abstract settings, the definition for matrices whose entries are real numbers will be sufficient for our applications. The product of two matrices is built up of *scalar* or *dot* products of their individual rows and columns.

• Definition

Suppose that all entries in matrices **A** and **B** are real numbers. If the number of elements, n, in the ith row of **A** equals the number of elements in the jth column of **B**, then the **scalar product** or **dot product** of the ith row of **A** and the jth column of **B** is the real number obtained as follows:

$$
\begin{bmatrix} a_{i1} & a_{i2} & \cdots & a_{in} \end{bmatrix}
\begin{bmatrix} b_{1j} \\ b_{2j} \\ \vdots \\ b_{nj} \end{bmatrix}
= a_{i1}b_{1j} + a_{i2}b_{2j} + \cdots + a_{in}b_{nj}.
$$

Example 10.3.6 Multiplying a Row and a Column

$$
\begin{bmatrix} 3 & 0 & -1 & 2 \end{bmatrix}
\begin{bmatrix} -1 \\ 2 \\ 3 \\ 0 \end{bmatrix}
= 3 \cdot (-1) + 0 \cdot 2 + (-1) \cdot 3 + 2 \cdot 0
$$

$$
= -3 + 0 - 3 + 0 = -6 \qquad \blacksquare
$$

More generally, if **A** and **B** are matrices whose entries are real numbers and if **A** and **B** have *compatible sizes* in the sense that the number of columns of **A** equals the number of rows of **B**, then the product **AB** is defined. It is the matrix whose ijth entry is the scalar product of the ith row of **A** times the jth column of **B**, for all possible values of i and j.

• Definition

Let $\mathbf{A} = (a_{ij})$ be an $m \times k$ matrix and $\mathbf{B} = (b_{ij})$ a $k \times n$ matrix with real entries. The (matrix) product of **A** times **B**, denoted **AB**, is that matrix (c_{ij}) defined as follows:

$$
\begin{bmatrix}
a_{11} & a_{12} & \cdots & a_{1k} \\
a_{21} & a_{22} & \cdots & a_{2k} \\
\vdots & \vdots & & \vdots \\
a_{i1} & a_{i2} & \cdots & a_{ik} \\
\vdots & \vdots & & \vdots \\
a_{m1} & a_{m2} & \cdots & a_{mk}
\end{bmatrix}
\begin{bmatrix}
b_{11} & b_{12} & \cdots & b_{1j} & \cdots & b_{1n} \\
b_{21} & b_{22} & \cdots & b_{2j} & \cdots & b_{2n} \\
 & & & \cdot & & \cdot \\
 & & & \cdot & & \cdot \\
 & & & \cdot & & \cdot \\
b_{k1} & b_{k2} & \cdots & b_{kj} & \cdots & b_{kn}
\end{bmatrix}
$$

$$
=
\begin{bmatrix}
c_{11} & c_{12} & \cdots & c_{1j} & \cdots & c_{1n} \\
c_{21} & c_{22} & \cdots & c_{2j} & \cdots & c_{2n} \\
\vdots & \vdots & & \vdots & & \vdots \\
c_{i1} & c_{i2} & \cdots & c_{ij} & \cdots & c_{in} \\
\vdots & \vdots & & \vdots & & \vdots \\
c_{m1} & c_{m2} & \cdots & c_{mj} & \cdots & c_{mn}
\end{bmatrix}
$$

where

$$
c_{ij} = a_{i1}b_{1j} + a_{i2}b_{2j} + \cdots + a_{ik}b_{kj} = \sum_{r=1}^{k} a_{ir}b_{rj},
$$

for all $i = 1, 2, \ldots, m$ and $j = 1, 2, \ldots, n$.

Example 10.3.7 Computing a Matrix Product

Let $\mathbf{A} = \begin{bmatrix} 2 & 0 & 3 \\ -1 & 1 & 0 \end{bmatrix}$ and $\mathbf{B} = \begin{bmatrix} 4 & 3 \\ 2 & 2 \\ -2 & -1 \end{bmatrix}$. Compute **AB**.

Solution   **A** has size 2×3 and **B** has size 3×2, so the number of columns of **A** equals the number of rows of **B** and the matrix product of **A** and **B** can be computed. Then

$$
\begin{bmatrix} 2 & 0 & 3 \\ -1 & 1 & 0 \end{bmatrix}
\begin{bmatrix} 4 & 3 \\ 2 & 2 \\ -2 & -1 \end{bmatrix}
=
\begin{bmatrix} c_{11} & c_{12} \\ c_{21} & c_{22} \end{bmatrix},
$$

where

$$c_{11} = 2 \cdot 4 + 0 \cdot 2 + 3 \cdot (-2) = 2$$

$$\begin{bmatrix} 2 & 0 & 3 \\ -1 & 1 & 0 \end{bmatrix} \begin{bmatrix} 4 & 3 \\ 2 & 2 \\ -2 & -1 \end{bmatrix}$$

$$c_{12} = 2 \cdot 3 + 0 \cdot 2 + 3 \cdot (-1) = 3$$

$$\begin{bmatrix} 2 & 0 & 3 \\ -1 & 1 & 0 \end{bmatrix} \begin{bmatrix} 4 & 3 \\ 2 & 2 \\ -2 & -1 \end{bmatrix}$$

$$c_{21} = (-1) \cdot 4 + 1 \cdot 2 + 0 \cdot (-2) = 2$$

$$\begin{bmatrix} 2 & 0 & 3 \\ -1 & 1 & 0 \end{bmatrix} \begin{bmatrix} 4 & 3 \\ 2 & 2 \\ -2 & -1 \end{bmatrix}$$

$$c_{22} = (-1) \cdot 3 + 0 \cdot 2 + 3 \cdot (-1) = -1$$

$$\begin{bmatrix} 2 & 0 & 3 \\ -1 & 1 & 0 \end{bmatrix} \begin{bmatrix} 4 & 3 \\ 2 & 2 \\ -2 & -1 \end{bmatrix}.$$

Hence

$$\mathbf{AB} = \begin{bmatrix} 2 & 3 \\ -2 & -1 \end{bmatrix}.$$

Matrix multiplication is both similar to and different from multiplication of real numbers. One difference is that although the product of any two numbers can be formed, only matrices with compatible sizes can be multiplied. Also, multiplication of real numbers is commutative (for all real numbers a and b, $ab = ba$), whereas matrix multiplication is not. For instance,

$$\begin{bmatrix} 1 & 1 \\ 0 & 1 \end{bmatrix} \begin{bmatrix} 0 & 1 \\ 0 & 1 \end{bmatrix} = \begin{bmatrix} 0 & 2 \\ 0 & 1 \end{bmatrix}, \quad \text{but} \quad \begin{bmatrix} 0 & 1 \\ 0 & 1 \end{bmatrix} \begin{bmatrix} 1 & 1 \\ 0 & 1 \end{bmatrix} = \begin{bmatrix} 0 & 1 \\ 0 & 1 \end{bmatrix}.$$

On the other hand, both real number and matrix multiplications are associative $((ab)c = a(bc)$, for all elements a, b, and c for which the products are defined). This is proved in Example 10.3.8 for products of 2×2 matrices. Additional exploration of matrix multiplication is offered in the exercises.

Example 10.3.8 Associativity of Matrix Multiplication for 2×2 Matrices

Prove that if $\mathbf{A}$, $\mathbf{B}$, and $\mathbf{C}$ are 2×2 matrices over the set of real numbers, then $(\mathbf{AB})\mathbf{C} = \mathbf{A}(\mathbf{BC})$.

Solution   Suppose $\mathbf{A} = (a_{ij})$, $\mathbf{B} = (b_{ij})$, and $\mathbf{C} = (c_{ij})$ are particular but arbitrarily chosen 2×2 matrices with real entries. Since the numbers of rows and columns are all the same, $\mathbf{AB}$, $\mathbf{BC}$, $(\mathbf{AB})\mathbf{C}$, and $\mathbf{A}(\mathbf{BC})$ are defined. Let $\mathbf{AB} = (d_{ij})$ and $\mathbf{BC} = (e_{ij})$. Then for all integers $i = 1, 2$ and $j = 1, 2$,

$$\text{the } ij\text{th entry of } (\mathbf{AB})\mathbf{C} = \sum_{r=1}^{2} d_{ir} c_{rj} \qquad \text{by definition of the product of } \mathbf{AB} \text{ and } \mathbf{C}$$

$$= d_{i1} c_{1j} + d_{i2} c_{2j} \qquad \text{by definition of } \Sigma$$

$$= \left(\sum_{r=1}^{2} a_{ir} b_{r1} \right) c_{1j} + \left(\sum_{r=1}^{2} a_{ir} b_{r2} \right) c_{2j} \qquad \text{by definition of the product of } \mathbf{A} \text{ and } \mathbf{B}$$

$$= (a_{i1} b_{11} + a_{i2} b_{21}) c_{1j} \qquad \text{by definition of } \Sigma$$
$$\quad + (a_{i1} b_{12} + a_{i2} b_{22}) c_{2j}$$

$$= a_{i1} b_{11} c_{1j} + a_{i2} b_{21} c_{1j} + a_{i1} b_{12} c_{2j} + a_{i2} b_{22} c_{2j}.$$

Similarly, the ijth entry of $\mathbf{A(BC)}$ is

$$(\mathbf{A(BC)})_{ij} = \sum_{r=1}^{2} a_{ir}e_{rj}$$

$$= a_{i1}e_{1j} + a_{i2}e_{2j}$$

$$= a_{i1}\left(\sum_{r=1}^{2} b_{1r}c_{rj}\right) + a_{i2}\left(\sum_{r=1}^{2} b_{2r}c_{rj}\right)$$

$$= a_{i1}(b_{11}c_{1j} + b_{12}c_{2j}) + a_{i2}(b_{21}c_{1j} + b_{22}c_{2j})$$

$$= a_{i1}b_{11}c_{1j} + a_{i1}b_{12}c_{2j} + a_{i2}b_{21}c_{1j} + a_{i2}b_{22}c_{2j}$$

$$= a_{i1}b_{11}c_{1j} + a_{i2}b_{21}c_{1j} + a_{i1}b_{12}c_{2j} + a_{i2}b_{22}c_{2j}.$$

Comparing the results of the two computations shows that for all i and j,

the ijth entry of $(\mathbf{AB})\mathbf{C} =$ the ijth entry of $\mathbf{A(BC)}$.

Since all corresponding entries are equal, $(\mathbf{AB})\mathbf{C} = \mathbf{A(BC)}$, as was to be shown. ■

As far as multiplicative identities are concerned, there are both similarities and differences between real numbers and matrices. You know that the number 1 acts as a multiplicative identity for products of real numbers. It turns out that there are certain matrices, called *identity matrices,* that act as multiplicative identities for certain matrix products. For instance, mentally perform the following matrix multiplications to check that for any real numbers a, b, c, d, e, f, g, h and i,

$$\begin{bmatrix} 1 & 0 \\ 0 & 1 \end{bmatrix} \begin{bmatrix} a & b & c \\ d & e & f \end{bmatrix} = \begin{bmatrix} a & b & c \\ d & e & f \end{bmatrix}$$

and

$$\begin{bmatrix} a & b & c \\ d & e & f \\ g & h & i \end{bmatrix} \begin{bmatrix} 1 & 0 & 0 \\ 0 & 1 & 0 \\ 0 & 0 & 1 \end{bmatrix} \begin{bmatrix} a & b & c \\ d & e & f \\ g & h & i \end{bmatrix}.$$

These computations show that $\begin{bmatrix} 1 & 0 \\ 0 & 1 \end{bmatrix}$ acts as an identity on the left side for multiplication with 2×3 matrices and that $\begin{bmatrix} 1 & 0 & 0 \\ 0 & 1 & 0 \\ 0 & 0 & 1 \end{bmatrix}$ acts as an identity on the right side for multiplication with 3×3 matrices. Note that $\begin{bmatrix} 1 & 0 \\ 0 & 1 \end{bmatrix}$ cannot act as an identity on the right side for multiplication with 2×3 matrices because the sizes are not compatible.

● **Definition**

For each positive integer n, the **$n \times n$ identity matrix,** denoted $\mathbf{I}_n = (\delta_{ij})$ or just $\mathbf{I}$ (if the size of the matrix is obvious from context), is the $n \times n$ matrix in which all the entries in the main diagonal are 1's and all other entries are 0's. In other words,

$$\delta_{ij} = \begin{cases} 1 & \text{if } i = j \\ 0 & \text{if } i \neq j \end{cases}, \quad \text{for all } i, j = 1, 2, \dots, n.$$

The German mathematician Leopold Kronecker introduced the symbol δ_{ij} to make matrix computations more convenient. In his honor, this symbol is called the *Kronecker delta.*

Leopold Kronecker
(1823–1891)

Example 10.3.9 An Identity Matrix Acts as an Identity

Prove that if $\mathbf{A}$ is any $m \times n$ matrix and $\mathbf{I}$ is the $n \times n$ identity matrix, then $\mathbf{AI} = \mathbf{A}$. (In exercise 14 at the end of this section you are asked to show that if $\mathbf{I}$ is the $m \times m$ identity matrix, then $\mathbf{IA} = \mathbf{A}$.)

Proof:

Let $\mathbf{A}$ be any $n \times n$ matrix and let a_{ij} be the ijth entry of $\mathbf{A}$ for all integers $i = 1, 2, \ldots, m$ and $j = 1, 2, \ldots, n$. Consider the product $\mathbf{AI}$, where $\mathbf{I}$ is the $n \times n$ identity matrix. Observe that

$$
\begin{bmatrix}
a_{11} & a_{12} & \cdots & a_{1n} \\
a_{21} & a_{22} & \cdots & 2_{2n} \\
\vdots & \vdots & & \vdots \\
a_{m1} & a_{m2} & \cdots & a_{mn}
\end{bmatrix}
\begin{bmatrix}
1 & 0 & \cdots & 0 \\
0 & 1 & \cdots & 0 \\
\vdots & \vdots & & \vdots \\
0 & 0 & \cdots & 1
\end{bmatrix}
=
\begin{bmatrix}
a_{11} & a_{12} & \cdots & a_{1n} \\
a_{21} & a_{22} & \cdots & a_{2n} \\
\vdots & \vdots & & \vdots \\
a_{m1} & a_{m2} & \cdots & a_{mn}
\end{bmatrix}
$$

because

$$\text{the } ij\text{th entry of } \mathbf{AI} = \sum_{r=1}^{n} a_{ir}\delta_{rj} \qquad \text{by definition of I}$$

$$= a_{i1}\delta_{1j} + a_{i2}\delta_{2j} + \cdots \qquad \text{by definition of } \Sigma$$
$$\quad + a_{ij}\delta_{jj} + \cdots + a_{in}\delta_{nj}$$

$$= a_{ij}\delta_{jj} \qquad \text{since } \delta_{kj} = 0 \text{ whenever } k \neq j \text{ and } \delta_{jj} = 1$$

$$= a_{ij}$$

$$= \text{the } ij\text{th entry of } \mathbf{A}.$$

Thus $\mathbf{AI} = \mathbf{A}$, as was to be shown. ▪

There are also similarities and differences between real numbers and matrices with respect to the computation of powers. Any number can be raised to a nonnegative integer power, but a matrix can be multiplied by itself only if it has the same number of rows as columns. As for real numbers, however, the definition of matrix powers is recursive. Just as any number to the zero power is defined to be 1, so any $n \times n$ matrix to the zero power is defined to be the $n \times n$ identity matrix. The nth power of an $n \times n$ matrix $\mathbf{A}$ is defined to be the product of $\mathbf{A}$ with its $(n-1)$st power.

• Definition

For any $n \times n$ matrix $\mathbf{A}$, the **powers of A** are defined as follows:

$$\mathbf{A}^0 = \mathbf{I} \quad \text{where } \mathbf{I} \text{ is the } n \times n \text{ identity matrix}$$
$$\mathbf{A}^n = \mathbf{A}\mathbf{A}^{n-1} \quad \text{for all integers } n \geq 1$$

Example 10.3.10 Powers of a Matrix

Let $\mathbf{A} = \begin{bmatrix} 1 & 2 \\ 2 & 0 \end{bmatrix}$. Compute $\mathbf{A}^0, \mathbf{A}^1, \mathbf{A}^2,$ and $\mathbf{A}^3$.

Solution

$$\mathbf{A}^0 = \text{the } 2 \times 2 \text{ identity matrix} = \begin{bmatrix} 1 & 0 \\ 0 & 1 \end{bmatrix}$$

$$\mathbf{A}^1 = \mathbf{A}\mathbf{A}^0 = \mathbf{A}\mathbf{I} = \mathbf{A}$$

$$\mathbf{A}^2 = \mathbf{A}\mathbf{A}^1 = \mathbf{A}\mathbf{A} = \begin{bmatrix} 1 & 2 \\ 2 & 0 \end{bmatrix}\begin{bmatrix} 1 & 2 \\ 2 & 0 \end{bmatrix} = \begin{bmatrix} 5 & 2 \\ 2 & 4 \end{bmatrix}$$

$$\mathbf{A}^3 = \mathbf{A}\mathbf{A}^2 = \begin{bmatrix} 1 & 2 \\ 2 & 0 \end{bmatrix}\begin{bmatrix} 5 & 2 \\ 2 & 4 \end{bmatrix} = \begin{bmatrix} 9 & 10 \\ 10 & 4 \end{bmatrix}$$

Counting Walks of Length N

A walk in a graph consists of an alternating sequence of vertices and edges. If repeated edges are counted each time they occur, then the number of edges in the sequence is called the **length** of the walk. For instance, the walk $v_2e_3v_3e_4v_2e_2v_2e_3v_3$ has length 4 (counting e_3 twice). Consider the following graph G:

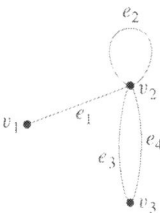

How many distinct walks of length 2 connect v_2 and v_2? Your can list the possibilities systematically as follows: From v_1, the first edge of the walk must go to *some* vertex of G: v_1, v_2, or v_3. There is one walk of length 2 from v_2 to v_2 that starts by going from v_2 to v_1:

$$v_2e_1v_1e_1v_2.$$

There is one walk of length 2 from v_2 to v_2 that starts by going from v_2 to v_2:

$$v_2e_2v_2e_2v_2.$$

And there are four walks of length 2 from v_2 to v_2 that start by going from v_2 to v_3:

$$v_2e_3v_3e_4v_2,$$
$$v_2e_4v_3e_3v_2,$$
$$v_2e_3v_3e_3v_2,$$
$$v_2e_4v_3e_4v_2.$$

Thus the answer is six.

The general question of finding the number of walks that have a given length and connect two particular vertices of a graph can easily be answered using matrix multiplication. Consider the adjacency matrix $\mathbf{A}$ of the graph G on the previous page:

$$\mathbf{A} = \begin{array}{c} \\ v_1 \\ v_2 \\ v_3 \end{array}\begin{array}{ccc} v_1 & v_2 & v_3 \end{array}\begin{bmatrix} 0 & 1 & 0 \\ 1 & 1 & 2 \\ 0 & 2 & 0 \end{bmatrix}.$$

Compute $\mathbf{A}^2$ as follows:

$$\begin{bmatrix} 0 & 1 & 0 \\ 1 & 1 & 2 \\ 0 & 2 & 0 \end{bmatrix}\begin{bmatrix} 0 & 1 & 0 \\ 1 & 1 & 2 \\ 0 & 2 & 0 \end{bmatrix} = \begin{bmatrix} 1 & 1 & 2 \\ 1 & 6 & 2 \\ 2 & 2 & 4 \end{bmatrix}.$$

Note that the entry in the second row and the second column is 6, which equals the number of walks of length 2 from v_2 to v_2. This is no accident! To compute a_{22}, you multiply the second row of A times the second column of A to obtain a sum of three terms:

$$\begin{bmatrix} 1 & 1 & 2 \end{bmatrix} \begin{bmatrix} 1 \\ 1 \\ 2 \end{bmatrix} = 1 \cdot 1 + 1 \cdot 1 + 2 \cdot 2.$$

Observe that

$$\begin{bmatrix} \text{the first term} \\ \text{of this sum} \end{bmatrix} = \begin{bmatrix} \text{number of} \\ \text{edges from} \\ v_2 \text{ to } v_1 \end{bmatrix} \cdot \begin{bmatrix} \text{number of} \\ \text{edges from} \\ v_1 \text{ to } v_2 \end{bmatrix} = \begin{bmatrix} \text{number of pairs} \\ \text{of edges from} \\ v_2 \text{ to } v_1 \text{ and } v_1 \text{ to } v_2 \end{bmatrix}.$$

Now consider the ith term of this sum, for each $i = 1, 2,$ and 3. It equals the number of edges from v_2 to v_i times the number of edges from v_i to v_2. By the multiplication rule this equals the number of pairs of edges from v_2 to v_i and from v_i back to v_2. But this equals the number of walks of length 2 that start and end at v_2 and pass through v_i. Since this analysis holds for each term of the sum for $i = 1, 2,$ and 3, the sum as a whole equals the total number of walks of length 2 that start and end at v_2:

$$1 \cdot 1 + 1 \cdot 1 + 2 \cdot 2 = 1 + 1 + 4 = 6.$$

More generally, if A is the adjacency matrix of a graph G, the ijth entry of A^2 equals the number of walks of length 2 connecting the ith vertex to the jth vertex of G. Even more generally, if n is any positive integer, the ijth entry of A^n equals the number of walks of length n connecting the ith and the jth vertices of G.

Theorem 10.3.2

If G is a graph with vertices $v_1, v_2, \ldots, v_m$ and A is the adjacency matrix of G, then for each positive integer n and for all integers $i, j = 1, 2, \ldots, m,$

the ijth entry of A^n = the number of walks of length n from v_i to v_j.

Proof:

Suppose G is a graph with vertices $v_1, v_2, \ldots, v_m$ and A is the adjacency matrix of G. Let $P(n)$ be the sentence

For all integers $i, j = 1, 2, \ldots, m,$ — $P(n)$
the ijth entry of A^n = the number of walks of length n from v_i to v_j.

We will use mathematical induction to show that $P(n)$ is true for all integers $n \geq 1$.

Show that $P(1)$ is true:

The ijth entry of A^1 = the ijth entry of A because $A^1 = A$

            = the number of edges   by definition of adjacency matrix
                connecting v_i to v_j

            = the number of walks of   because a walk of length 1
                length 1 from v_i to v_j contains a single edge.

Show that for all integers k with $k \geq 1$, if $P(k)$ is true then $P(k + 1)$ is true:

Let k be any integer with $k \geq 1$, and suppose that

For all integers $i, j = 1, 2, \ldots, m$,
the ijth entry of $\mathbf{A}^k$ = the number of walks of length k from v_i to v_j.   ← $P(k)$ inductive hypothesis

We must show that

For all integers $i, j = 1, 2, \ldots, m$,   ← $P(k+1)$
the ijth entry of $\mathbf{A}^{k+1}$ = the number of walks of length $k + 1$ from v_i to v_j.

Let $\mathbf{A} = (a_{ij})$ and $\mathbf{A}^k = (b_{ij})$. Since $\mathbf{A}^{k+1} = \mathbf{A}\mathbf{A}^k$, the ijth entry of $\mathbf{A}^{k+1}$ is obtained by multiplying the ith row of $\mathbf{A}$ by the jth column of $\mathbf{A}^k$:

$$\text{the } ij\text{th entry of } \mathbf{A}^{k+1} = a_{i1}b_{1j} + a_{i2}b_{2j} + \cdots + a_{im}b_{mj} \qquad 10.3.1$$

for all $i, j = 1, 2, \ldots, m$. Now consider the individual terms of this sum: a_{i1} is the number of edges from v_i to v_1; and, by inductive hypothesis, b_{1j} is the number of walks of length k from v_1 to v_j. But any edge from v_i to v_1 can be joined with any walk of length k from v_1 to v_j to create a walk of length $k + 1$ from v_i to v_j with v_1 as its second vertex. Thus, by the multiplication rule,

$$a_{i1}b_{1j} = \begin{bmatrix} \text{the number of walks of length } k + 1 \text{ from} \\ v_i \text{ to } v_j \text{ that have } v_1 \text{ as their second vertex} \end{bmatrix}.$$

More generally, for each integer $r = 1, 2, \ldots, m$,

$$a_{ir}b_{rj} = \begin{bmatrix} \text{the number of walks of length } k + 1 \text{ from} \\ v_i \text{ to } v_j \text{ that have } v_r \text{ as their second vertex} \end{bmatrix}.$$

Since any walk of length $k + 1$ from v_i to v_j must have *one* of the vertices $v_1, v_2, \ldots, v_m$ as its second vertex, the total number of walks of length $k + 1$ from v_i to v_j equals the sum in (10.3.1), which equals the ijth entry of $\mathbf{A}^{k+1}$. Hence

$$\text{the } ij\text{th entry of } \mathbf{A}^{k+1} = \text{the number of walks of length } k + 1 \text{ from } v_i \text{ to } v_j$$

[as was to be shown].
[Since both the basis step and the inductive step have been proved, the sentence $P(n)$ is true for all integers $n \geq 1$.]

Test Yourself

1. In the adjacency matrix for a directed graph, the entry in the ith row and jth column is _____.

2. In the adjacency matrix for an undirected graph, the entry in the ith row and jth column is _____.

3. An $n \times n$ square matrix is called symmetric if, and only if, for all integers i and j from 1 to n, the entry in row _____ and column _____ equals the entry in row _____ and column _____.

4. The ijth entry in the product of two matrices $\mathbf{A}$ and $\mathbf{B}$ is obtained by multiplying row _____ of $\mathbf{A}$ by row _____ of $\mathbf{B}$.

5. In an $n \times n$ identity matrix the entries on the main diagonal are all _____ and the off-diagonal entries are all _____.

6. If G is a graph with vertices $v_1, v_2, \ldots, v_m$ and $\mathbf{A}$ is the adjacency matrix of G, then for each positive integer n and for all integers i and j with $i, j = 1, 2, \ldots, m$, the ijth entry of $\mathbf{A}^n = $ _____.

Exercise Set 10.3

1. Find real numbers $a, b,$ and c such that the following are true.

a. $\begin{bmatrix} a+b & a-c \\ c & b-a \end{bmatrix} = \begin{bmatrix} 1 & 0 \\ -1 & 3 \end{bmatrix}$

b. $\begin{bmatrix} 2a & b+c \\ c-a & 2b-a \end{bmatrix} = \begin{bmatrix} 4 & 3 \\ 1 & -2 \end{bmatrix}$

2. Find the adjacency matrices for the following directed graphs.

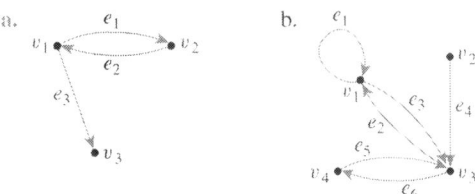

3. Find directed graphs that have the following adjacency matrices:

a. $\begin{bmatrix} 1 & 0 & 1 & 2 \\ 0 & 0 & 1 & 0 \\ 0 & 2 & 1 & 1 \\ 0 & 1 & 1 & 0 \end{bmatrix}$ b. $\begin{bmatrix} 0 & 1 & 0 & 0 \\ 2 & 0 & 1 & 0 \\ 1 & 2 & 1 & 0 \\ 0 & 0 & 1 & 0 \end{bmatrix}$

4. Find adjacency matrices for the following (undirected) graphs.

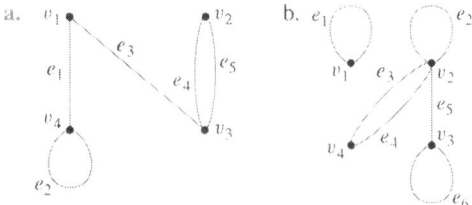

c. K_4, the complete graph on four vertices
d. $K_{2,3}$, the complete bipartite graph on $(2, 3)$ vertices

5. Find graphs that have the following adjacency matrices.

a. $\begin{bmatrix} 1 & 0 & 1 \\ 0 & 1 & 2 \\ 1 & 2 & 0 \end{bmatrix}$ b. $\begin{bmatrix} 0 & 2 & 0 \\ 2 & 1 & 0 \\ 0 & 0 & 1 \end{bmatrix}$

6. The following are adjacency matrices for graphs. In each case determine whether the graph is connected by analyzing the matrix without drawing the graph.

a. $\begin{bmatrix} 0 & 1 & 1 \\ 1 & 1 & 0 \\ 1 & 0 & 0 \end{bmatrix}$ b. $\begin{bmatrix} 0 & 2 & 0 & 0 \\ 2 & 0 & 0 & 0 \\ 0 & 0 & 1 & 1 \\ 0 & 0 & 1 & 1 \end{bmatrix}$

7. Suppose that for all positive integers i, all the entries in the ith row and ith column of the adjacency matrix of a graph are 0. What can you conclude about the graph?

8. Find each of the following products.

a. $\begin{bmatrix} 2 & -1 \end{bmatrix} \begin{bmatrix} 1 \\ 3 \end{bmatrix}$ b. $\begin{bmatrix} 4 & -1 & 7 \end{bmatrix} \begin{bmatrix} 1 \\ 2 \\ 0 \end{bmatrix}$

9. Find each of the following products.

a. $\begin{bmatrix} 3 & 0 \\ 1 & -2 \end{bmatrix} \begin{bmatrix} 1 & -1 & 4 \\ 0 & 2 & 1 \end{bmatrix}$

b. $\begin{bmatrix} 2 & 0 & 1 \\ 0 & -1 & 0 \end{bmatrix} \begin{bmatrix} 1 & 3 \\ 5 & -4 \\ -2 & 2 \end{bmatrix}$

c. $\begin{bmatrix} -1 \\ 2 \end{bmatrix} \begin{bmatrix} 2 & 3 \end{bmatrix}$

10. Let $\mathbf{A} = \begin{bmatrix} 1 & 1 & -1 \\ 0 & -2 & 1 \end{bmatrix}$, $\mathbf{B} = \begin{bmatrix} -2 & 0 \\ 1 & 3 \end{bmatrix}$, and

$$\mathbf{C} = \begin{bmatrix} 0 & -2 \\ 3 & 1 \\ 1 & 0 \end{bmatrix}.$$

For each of the following, determine whether the indicated product exists, and compute it if it does.

a. $\mathbf{AB}$ b. $\mathbf{BA}$ c. $\mathbf{A}^2$ d. $\mathbf{BC}$ e. $\mathbf{CB}$
f. $\mathbf{B}^2$ g. $\mathbf{B}^3$ h. $\mathbf{C}^2$ i. $\mathbf{AC}$ j. $\mathbf{CA}$

11. Give an example different from that in the text to show that matrix multiplication is not commutative. That is, find 2×2 matrices $\mathbf{A}$ and $\mathbf{B}$ such that $\mathbf{AB}$ and $\mathbf{BA}$ both exist but $\mathbf{AB} \neq \mathbf{BA}$.

12. Let O denote the matrix $\begin{bmatrix} 0 & 0 \\ 0 & 0 \end{bmatrix}$. Find 2×2 matrices $\mathbf{A}$ and $\mathbf{B}$ such that $\mathbf{A} \neq \mathbf{O}$ and $\mathbf{B} \neq \mathbf{O}$, but $\mathbf{AB} = \mathbf{O}$.

13. Let O denote the matrix $\begin{bmatrix} 0 & 0 \\ 0 & 0 \end{bmatrix}$. Find 2×2 matrices $\mathbf{A}$ and $\mathbf{B}$ such that $\mathbf{A} \neq \mathbf{B}$, $\mathbf{B} \neq \mathbf{O}$, and $\mathbf{AB} \neq \mathbf{O}$, but $\mathbf{BA} = \mathbf{O}$.

In 14–18 assume the entries of all matrices are real numbers.

H 14. Prove that if $\mathbf{I}$ is the $m \times m$ identity matrix and $\mathbf{A}$ is any $m \times n$ matrix, then $\mathbf{IA} = \mathbf{A}$.

15. Prove that if $\mathbf{A}$ is an $m \times m$ symmetric matrix, then $\mathbf{A}^2$ is symmetric.

16. Prove that matrix multiplication is associative: If $\mathbf{A}$, $\mathbf{B}$, and $\mathbf{C}$ are any $m \times k$, $k \times r$, and $r \times n$ matrices, respectively, then $(\mathbf{AB})\mathbf{C} = \mathbf{A}(\mathbf{BC})$.

17. Use mathematical induction and the result of exercise 16 to prove that if $\mathbf{A}$ is any $m \times m$ matrix, then $\mathbf{A}^n \mathbf{A} = \mathbf{A}\mathbf{A}^n$ for all integers $n \geq 1$.

18. Use mathematical induction to prove that if $\mathbf{A}$ is an $m \times m$ symmetric matrix, then for any integer $n \geq 1$, $\mathbf{A}^n$ is also symmetric.

19. a. Let $\mathbf{A} = \begin{bmatrix} 1 & 1 & 2 \\ 1 & 0 & 1 \\ 2 & 1 & 0 \end{bmatrix}$. Find $\mathbf{A}^2$ and $\mathbf{A}^3$.

b. Let G be the graph with vertices v_1, v_2, and v_3 and with $\mathbf{A}$ as its adjacency matrix. Use the answers to part (a) to find the number of walks of length 2 from v_1 to v_3 and the number of walks of length 3 from v_1 to v_3. Do not draw G to solve this problem.

c. Examine the calculations you performed in answering part (a) to find five walks of length 2 from v_3 to v_3. Then draw G and find the walks by visual inspection.

20. The following is an adjacency matrix for a graph:

$$\begin{array}{c c c c c} & v_1 & v_2 & v_3 & v_4 \\ \begin{matrix} v_1 \\ v_2 \\ v_3 \\ v_4 \end{matrix} & \begin{bmatrix} 0 & 1 & 1 & 0 \\ 1 & 0 & 2 & 1 \\ 1 & 2 & 0 & 1 \\ 0 & 1 & 1 & 1 \end{bmatrix} \end{array}$$

Answer the following questions by examining the matrix and its powers only, not by drawing the graph:
a. How many walks of length 2 are there from v_2 to v_3?
b. How many walks of length 2 are there from v_3 to v_4?
c. How many walks of length 3 are there from v_1 to v_4?
d. How many walks of length 3 are there from v_2 to v_3?

21. Let **A** be the adjacent matrix for K_3, the complete graph on three vertices. Use mathematical induction to prove that for each positive integer n, all the entries along the main diagonal of $\mathbf{A}^n$ are equal to each other and all the entries that do not lie along the main diagonal are equal to each other.

22. a. Draw a graph that has

$$\begin{bmatrix} 0 & 0 & 0 & 1 & 2 \\ 0 & 0 & 0 & 1 & 1 \\ 0 & 0 & 0 & 2 & 1 \\ 1 & 1 & 2 & 0 & 0 \\ 2 & 1 & 1 & 0 & 0 \end{bmatrix}$$

as its adjacency matrix. Is this graph bipartite? (For a definition of bipartite, see exercise 37 in Section 10.1.)

Definition: Given an $m \times n$ matrix **A** whose ijth entry is denoted a_{ij}, the **transpose of A** is the matrix $\mathbf{A}^t$ whose ijth entry is a_{ji}, for all $i = 1, 2, \ldots, m$ and $j = 1, 2, \ldots, n$.

Note that the first row of **A** becomes the first column of $\mathbf{A}^t$, the second row of **A** becomes the second column of $\mathbf{A}^t$, and so forth. For instance,

$$\text{if } \mathbf{A} = \begin{bmatrix} 0 & 2 & 1 \\ 1 & 2 & 3 \end{bmatrix}, \text{ then } \mathbf{A}^t = \begin{bmatrix} 0 & 1 \\ 2 & 2 \\ 1 & 3 \end{bmatrix}.$$

H b. Show that a graph with n vertices is bipartite if, and only if, for some labeling of its vertices, its adjacency matrix has the form

$$\begin{bmatrix} \mathbf{O} & \mathbf{A} \\ \mathbf{A}^t & \mathbf{O} \end{bmatrix}$$

where **A** is a $k \times (n-k)$ matrix for some integer k such that $0 < k < n$, the top left **O** represents a $k \times k$ matrix all of whose entries are 0, $\mathbf{A}^t$ is the transpose of **A**, and the bottom right **O** represents an $(n-k) \times (n-k)$ matrix all of whose entries are 0.

23. a. Let G be a graph with n vertices, and let v and w be distinct vertices of G. Prove that if there is a walk from v to w, then there is a walk from v to w that has length less than or equal to $n - 1$.

H b. If $\mathbf{A} = (a_{ij})$ and $\mathbf{B} = (b_{ij})$ are any $m \times n$ matrices, the matrix $\mathbf{A} + \mathbf{B}$ is the $m \times n$ matrix whose ijth entry is $a_{ij} + b_{ij}$ for all $i = 1, 2, \ldots, m$ and $j = 1, 2, \ldots, n$. Let G be a graph with n vertices where $n > 1$, and let **A** be the adjacency matrix of G. Prove that G is connected if, and only if, every entry of $\mathbf{A} + \mathbf{A}^2 + \cdots + \mathbf{A}^{n-1}$ is positive.

Answers for Test Yourself

1. the number of arrows from v_i (the ith vertex) to v_j (the jth vertex) 2. the number of edges connecting v_i (the ith vertex) and v_j (the jth vertex) 3. i; j; j; i 4. i; j 5. 1; 0 6. the number of walks of length n from v_i to v_j

10.4 Isomorphisms of Graphs

Thinking is a momentary dismissal of irrelevancies. — R. Buckminster Fuller, 1969

Recall from Example 10.1.3 that the two drawings shown in Figure 10.4.1 both represent the same graph: Their vertex and edge sets are identical, and their edge-endpoint functions are the same. Call this graph G.

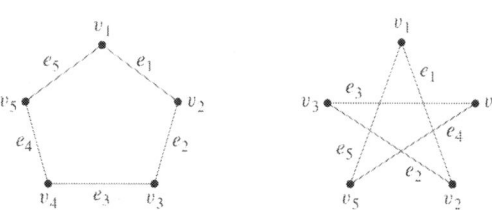

Figure 10.4.1

Now consider the graph G' represented in Figure 10.4.2.

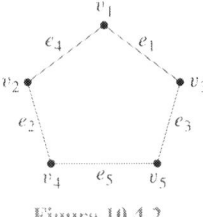

Figure 10.4.2

Observe that G' is a different graph from G (for instance, in G the endpoints of e_1 are v_1 and v_2, whereas in G' the endpoints of e_1 are v_1 and v_3). Yet G' is certainly very similar to G. In fact, if the vertices and edges of G' are relabeled by the functions shown in Figure 10.4.3, then G' becomes the same as G.

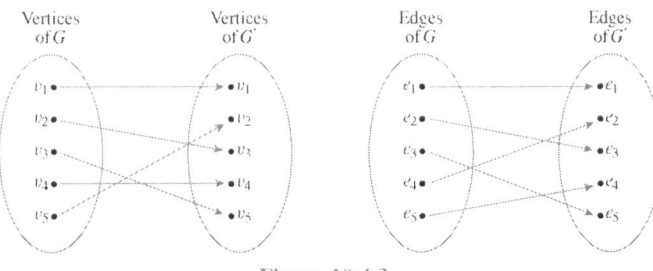

Figure 10.4.3

Note that these relabeling functions are one-to-one and onto.

Two graphs that are the same except for the labeling of their vertices and edges are called *isomorphic*. The word *isomorphism* comes from the Greek, meaning "same form." Isomorphic graphs are those that have essentially the same form.

• Definition

Let G and G' be graphs with vertex sets $V(G)$ and $V(G')$ and edge sets $E(G)$ and $E(G')$, respectively. **G is isomorphic to G'** if, and only if, there exist one-to-one correspondences $g: V(G) \to V(G')$ and $h: E(G) \to E(G')$ that preserve the edge-endpoint functions of G and G' in the sense that for all $v \in V(G)$ and $e \in E(G)$,

$$v \text{ is an endpoint of } e \quad \Leftrightarrow \quad g(v) \text{ is an endpoint of } h(e). \qquad \text{10.4.1}$$

In words, G is isomorphic to G' if, and only if, the vertices and edges of G and G' can be matched up by one-to-one, onto functions such that the edges between corresponding vertices correspond to each other.

It is common in mathematics to identify objects that are isomorphic. For instance, if we are given a graph G with five vertices such that each pair of vertices is connected by an edge, then we may identify G with K_5, saying that G is K_5 rather than that G is isomorphic to K_5.

Example 10.4.1 Showing That Two Graphs Are Isomorphic

Show that the following two graphs are isomorphic.

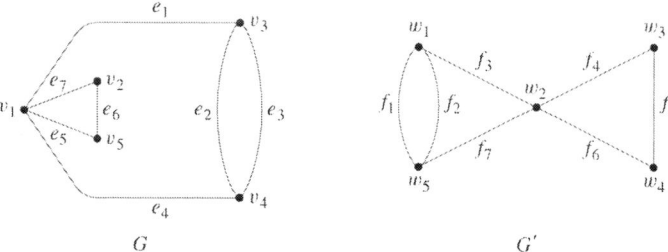

Solution   To solve this problem, you must find functions $g: V(G) \to V(G')$ and $h: E(G) \to E(G')$ such that for all $v \in V(G)$ and $e \in E(G)$, v is an endpoint of e if, and only if, $g(v)$ is an endpoint of $h(e)$. Setting up such functions is partly a matter of trial and error and partly a matter of deduction. For instance, since e_2 and e_3 are parallel (have the same endpoints), $h(e_2)$ and $h(e_3)$ must be parallel also. So $h(e_2) = f_1$ and $h(e_3) = f_2$ or $h(e_2) = f_2$ and $h(e_3) = f_1$. Also, the endpoints of e_2 and e_3 must correspond to the endpoints of f_1 and f_2, and so $g(v_3) = w_1$ and $g(v_4) = w_5$ or $g(v_3) = w_5$ and $g(v_4) = w_1$.

Similarly, since v_1 is the endpoint of four distinct edges (e_1, e_7, e_5, and e_4), $g(v_1)$ must also be the endpoint of four distinct edges (because every edge incident on $g(v_1)$ is the image under h of an edge incident on v_1 and h is one-to-one and onto). But the only vertex in G' that has four edges coming out of it is w_2, and so $g(v_1) = w_2$. Now if $g(v_3) = w_1$, then since v_1 and v_3 are endpoints of e_1 in G, $g(v_1) = w_2$ and $g(v_3) = w_1$ must be endpoints of $h(e_1)$ in G'. This implies that $h(e_1) = f_3$.

By continuing in this way, possibly making some arbitrary choices as you go, you eventually can find functions g and h to define the isomorphism between G and G'. One pair of functions (there are several) is the following:

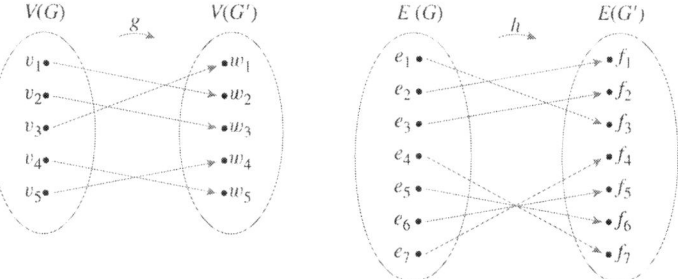

It is not hard to show that graph isomorphism is an equivalence relation on a set of graphs; in other words, it is reflexive, symmetric, and transitive.

Theorem 10.4.1 Graph Isomorphism is an Equivalence Relation

Let S be a set of graphs and let R be the the relation of graph isomorphism on S. Then R is an equivalence relation on S.

Proof:

R is reflexive: Given any graph G in S, define a graph isomorphism from G to G by using the identity functions on the set of vertices and on the set of edges of G.

R is symmetric: Given any graphs G and G' in S such that G is isomorphic to G', we must show that G' is isomorphic to G.

continued on page 678

But this is true because if g and h are vertex and edge correspondences from G to G' that preserve the edge-endpoint functions, then g^{-1} and h^{-1} are vertex and edge correspondences from G' to G that preserve the edge-endpoint functions.

R is transitive: Given any graphs G, G', and G'' in S such that G is isomorphic to G' and G' is isomorphic to G'', we must show that G is isomorphic to G''.

But this follows from the fact that if g_1 and h_1 are vertex and edge correspondences from G to G' that preserve the edge-endpoint functions of G and G' and g_2 and h_2 are vertex and edge correspondences from G' to G'' that preserve the edge-endpoint functions of G' and G'', then $g_2 \circ g_1$ and $h_2 \circ h_1$ are vertex and edge correspondences from G to G'' that preserve the edge-endpoint functions of G and G''.

Note As a consequence of the symmetry property, you can simply say "G and G' are isomorphic" instead of "G is isomorphic to G'" or "G' is isomorphic to G."

Example 10.4.2 Finding Representatives of Isomorphism Classes

Find all nonisomorphic graphs that have two vertices and two edges. In other words, find a collection of representative graphs with two vertices and two edges such that every such graph is isomorphic to one in the collection.

Solution There are four nonisomorphic graphs that have two vertices and two edges. These can be drawn without vertex and edge labels because any two labelings give isomorphic graphs.

(a)   (b)   (c)   (d)

To see that these four drawings show all the nonisomorphic graphs that have two vertices and two edges, first note whether one of the edges joins the two vertices or not. If it does, there are two possibilities: The other edge can also join the two vertices (as in (a)) or it can be a loop incident on one of them (as in (b)—it makes no difference *which* vertex is chosen to have the loop because interchanging the two vertex labels gives isomorphic graphs). If neither edge joins the two vertices, then both edges are loops. In this case, there are only two possibilities: Either both loops are incident on the same vertex (as in (c)) or the two loops are incident on separate vertices (as in (d)). There are no other possibilities for placing the edges, so the listing is complete. ■

Now consider the question, "Is there a general method to figure out whether graphs G and G' are isomorphic?" In other words, is there some algorithm that will accept graphs G and G' as input and produce a statement as to whether they are isomorphic? In fact, there is such an algorithm. It consists of generating all one-to-one, onto functions from the set of vertices of G to the set of vertices of G' and from the set of edges of G to the set of edges of G' and checking each pair to determine whether it preserves the edge-endpoint functions of G and G'. The problem with this algorithm is that it takes an unreasonably long time to perform, even on a high-speed computer. If G and G' each have n vertices and m edges, the number of one-to-one correspondences from vertices to vertices is $n!$ and the number of one-to-one correspondences from edges to edges is $m!$, so the total number of pairs of functions to check is $n! \cdot m!$. For instance, if $m = n = 20$, there would be $20! \cdot 20! \cong 5.9 \times 10^{36}$ pairs to check. Assuming that each check takes just 1 nanosecond, the total time would be approximately 1.9×10^{20} years!

Unfortunately, there is no more efficient general method known for checking whether two graphs are isomorphic. However, there are some simple tests that can be used to show that certain pairs of graphs are *not* isomorphic. For instance, if two graphs are isomorphic, then they have the same number of vertices (because there is a one-to-one correspondence from the vertex set of one graph to the vertex set of the other). It follows that if you are given two graphs, one with 16 vertices and the other with 17, you can immediately conclude that the two are not isomorphic. More generally, a property that is preserved by graph isomorphism is called an *isomorphic invariant*. For instance, "having 16 vertices" is an isomorphic invariant: If one graph has 16 vertices, then so does any graph that is isomorphic to it.

> **• Definition**
>
> A property P is called an **invariant for graph isomorphism** if, and only if, given any graphs G and G', if G has property P and G' is isomorphic to G, then G' has property P.

> **Theorem 10.4.2**
>
> Each of the following properties is an invariant for graph isomorphism, where $n, m,$ and k are all nonnegative integers:
>
> 1. has n vertices;
> 2. has m edges;
> 3. has a vertex of degree k;
> 4. has m vertices of degree k;
> 5. has a circuit of length k;
> 6. has a simple circuit of length k;
> 7. has m simple circuits of length k;
> 8. is connected;
> 9. has an Euler circuit;
> 10. has a Hamiltonian circuit.

Example 10.4.3 Showing That Two Graph Are Not Isomorphic

Show that the following pairs of graphs are not isomorphic by finding an isomorphic invariant that they do not share.

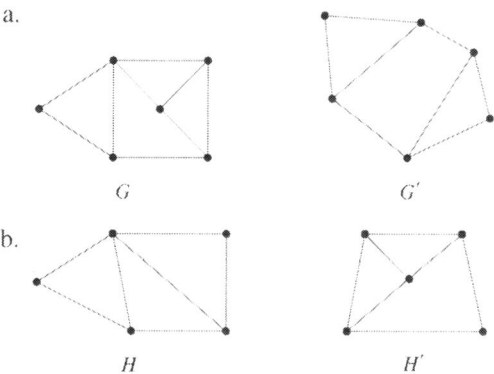

a.

G G'

b.

H H'

Solution

a. G has nine edges; G' has only eight.

b. H has a vertex of degree 4; H' does not.

We prove part (3) of Theorem 10.4.2 on the next page and leave the proofs of the other parts as exercises.

Example 10.4.4 Proof of Theorem 10.4.2, Part (3)

Prove that if G is a graph that has a vertex of degree k and G' is isomorphic to G, then G' has a vertex of degree k.

Proof:

Suppose G and G' are isomorphic graphs and G has a vertex v of degree k, where k is a nonnegative integer. *[We must show that G' has a vertex of degree k.]* Since G and G' are isomorphic, there are one-to-one, onto functions g and h from the vertices of G to the vertices of G' and from the edges of G to the edges of G' that preserve the edge-endpoint functions in the sense that for all edges e and all vertices u of G, u is an endpoint of e if, and only if, $g(u)$ is an endpoint of $h(e)$. An example for a particular vertex v is shown below.

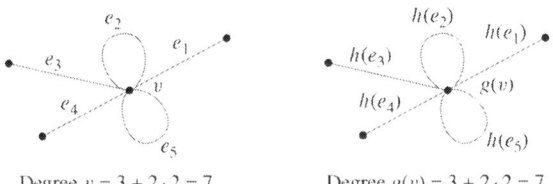

Degree $v = 3 + 2 \cdot 2 = 7$ Degree $g(v) = 3 + 2 \cdot 2 = 7$

Let $e_1, e_2, \ldots, e_m$ be the m distinct edges that are incident on a vertex v in G, where m is a nonnegative integer. Then $h(e_1), h(e_2), \ldots, h(e_m)$ are m distinct edges that are incident on $g(v)$ in G'. *[The reason why $h(e_1), h(e_2), \ldots, h(e_m)$ are distinct is that h is one-to-one and $e_1, e_2, \ldots, e_m$ are distinct. And the reason why $h(e_1), h(e_2), \ldots, h(e_m)$ are incident on $g(v)$ is that g and h preserve the edge-endpoint functions of G and G' and $e_1, e_2, \ldots, e_m$ are incident on v.]*

Also, there are no edges incident on $g(v)$ other than the ones that are images under g of edges incident on v *[because g is onto and g and h preserve the edge-endpoint functions of G and G']*. Thus the number of edges incident on v equals the number of edges incident on $g(v)$.

Finally, an edge e is a loop at v if, and only if, $h(e)$ is a loop at $g(v)$, so the number of loops incident on v equals the number of loops incident on $g(v)$. *[For since g and h preserve the edge-endpoint functions of G and G', a vertex w is an endpoint of e in G if, and only if, $g(w)$ is an endpoint of $h(e)$ in G'. It follows that v is the only endpoint of e in G if, and only if, $g(v)$ is the only endpoint of $h(e)$ in G'.]*

Now the degree of v, which is k, equals the number of edges incident on v plus the number of edges incident on v that are loops (since each loop contributes 2 to the degree of v). But we have already shown that the number of edges incident on v equals the number of edges incident on $g(v)$ and that the number of loops incident on v equals the number of loops incident on $g(v)$. Hence $g(v)$ also has degree k. ∎

Graph Isomorphism for Simple Graphs

When graphs G and G' are both simple, the definition of G being isomorphic to G' can be written without referring to the correspondence between the edges of G and the edges of G'.

> **• Definition**
>
> If G and G' are simple graphs, then **G is isomorphic to G'** if, and only if, there exists a one-to-one correspondence g from the vertex set $V(G)$ of G to the vertex set $V(G')$ of G' that preserves the edge-endpoint functions of G and G' in the sense that for all vertices u and v of G,
>
> $\{u, v\}$ is an edge in G $\Leftrightarrow$ $\{g(u), g(v)\}$ is an edge in G'. 10.4.2

Example 10.4.5 Isomorphism of Simple Graphs

Are the two graphs shown below isomorphic? If so, define an isomorphism.

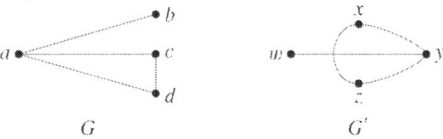

G G'

Solution   Yes. Define $f: V(G) \to V(G')$ by the arrow diagram shown below.

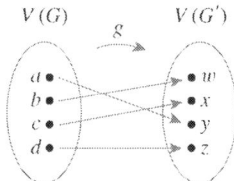

Then g is one-to-one and onto by inspection. The fact that g preserves the edge-endpoint functions of G and G' is shown by the following table:

Edges of G	Edges of G'
$\{a, b\}$	$\{y, w\} = \{g(a), g(b)\}$
$\{a, c\}$	$\{y, x\} = \{g(a), g(c)\}$
$\{a, d\}$	$\{y, z\} = \{g(a), g(d)\}$
$\{c, d\}$	$\{x, z\} = \{g(c), g(d)\}$

Test Yourself

1. If G and G' are graphs, then G is isomorphic to G' if, and only if, there exist a one-to-one correspondence g from the vertex set of G to the vertex set of G' and a one-to-one correspondence h from the edge set of G to the edge set of G' such that for all vertices v and edges e in G, v is an endpoint of e if, and only if, _____.

2. A property P is an invariant for graph isomorphism if, and only if, given any graphs G and G', if G has property P and G' is isomorphic to G then _____.

3. Some invariants for graph isomorphisms are _____, _____, _____, _____, _____, _____, _____, and _____.

Exercise Set 10.4

For each pair of graphs G and G' in 1–5, determine whether G and G' are isomorphic. If they are, give functions $g: V(G) \to V(G')$ and $h: E(G) \to E(G')$ that define the isomorphism. If they are not, give an invariant for graph isomorphism that they do not share.

1.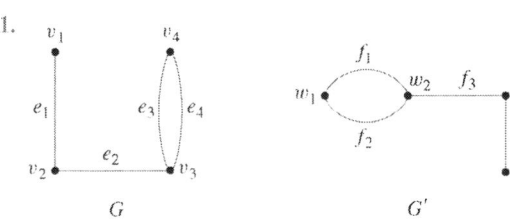

2.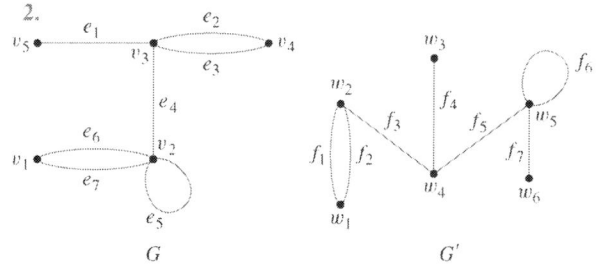

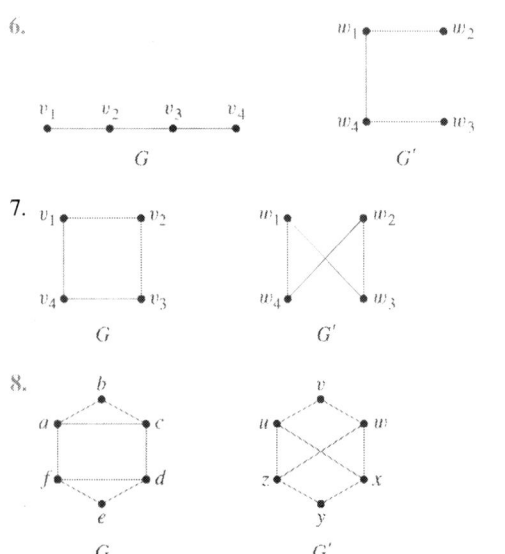

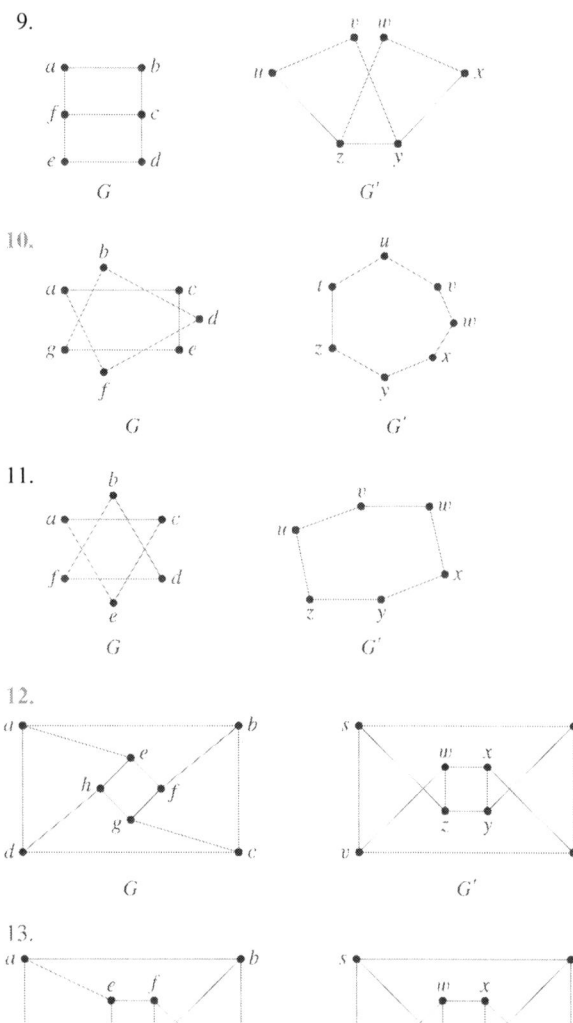

3.

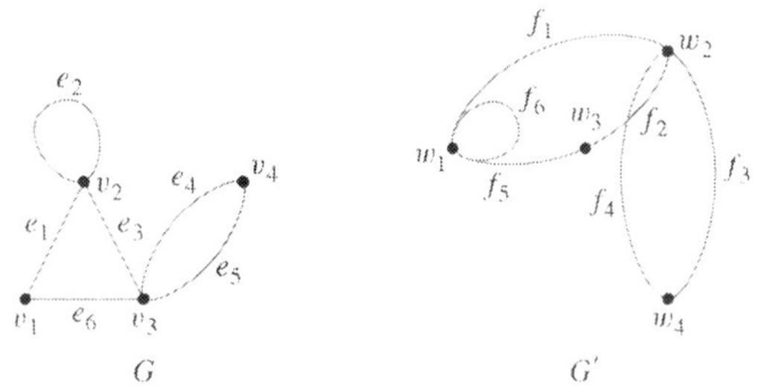

4.

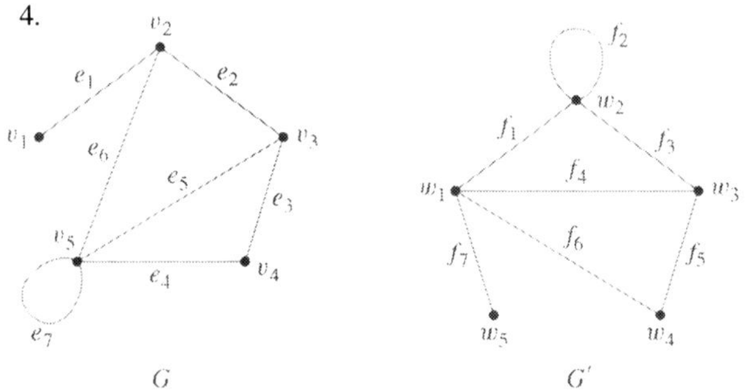

5.

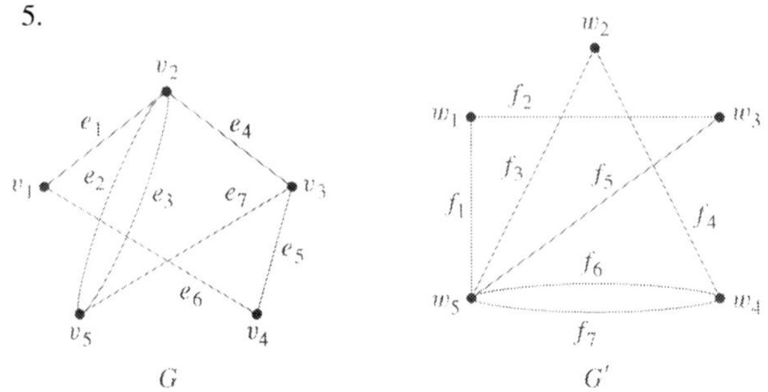

For each pair of simple graphs G and G' in 6–13, determine whether G and G' are isomorphic. If they are, give a function $g: V(G) \rightarrow V(G')$ that defines the isomorphism. If they are not, give an invariant for graph isomorphism that they do not share.

6.

7.

8.

9.

10.

11.

12.

13.

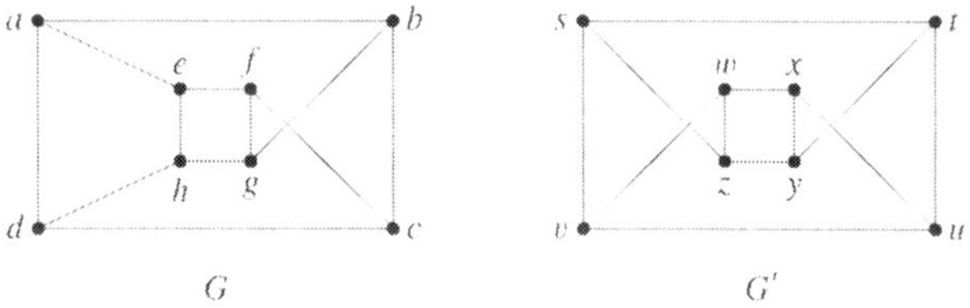

14. Draw all nonisomorphic simple graphs with three vertices.

15. Draw all nonisomorphic simple graphs with four vertices.

16. Draw all nonisomorphic graphs with three vertices and no more than two edges.

17. Draw all nonisomorphic graphs with four vertices and no more than two edges.

H 18. Draw all nonisomorphic graphs with four vertices and three edges.

19. Draw all nonisomorphic graphs with six vertices, all having degree 2.

20. Draw four nonisomorphic graphs with six vertices, two of degree 4 and four of degree 3.

Prove that each of the properties in 21–29 is an invariant for graph isomorphism. Assume that n, m, and k are all nonnegative integers.

21. Has n vertices

22. Has m edges

23. Has a circuit of length k

24. Has a simple circuit of length k

H 25. Has m vertices of degree k

26. Has m simple circuits of length k

H 27. Is connected

28. Has a Hamiltonian circuit

29. Has an Euler circuit

30. Show that the following two graphs are not isomorphic by supposing they are isomorphic and deriving a contradiction.

Answers for Test Yourself

1. $g(v)$ is an endpoint of $h(e)$ 2. G' has property P 3. has n vertices; has m edges; has a vertex of degree k; has m vertices of degree k; has a circuit of length k; has a simple circuit of length k; has m simple circuits of length k; is connected; has an Euler circuit; has a Hamiltonian circuit

10.5 Trees

We are not very pleased when we are forced to accept a mathematical truth by virtue of a complicated chain of formal conclusions and computations, which we traverse blindly, link by link, feeling our way by touch. We want first an overview of the aim and of the road; we want to understand the idea of the proof, the deeper context.
— Hermann Weyl, 1885–1955

If a friend asks what you are studying and you answer "trees," your friend is likely to infer you are taking a course in botany. But trees are also a subject for mathematical investigation. In mathematics, a tree is a connected graph that does not contain any circuits. Mathematical trees are similar in certain ways to their botanical namesakes.

> **• Definition**
>
> A graph is said to be **circuit-free** if, and only if, it has no circuits. A graph is called a **tree** if, and only if, it is circuit-free and connected. A **trivial tree** is a graph that consists of a single vertex. A graph is called a **forest** if, and only if, it is circuit-free and not connected.

Example 10.5.1 Trees and Non-Trees

All the graphs shown in Figure 10.5.1 are trees, whereas those in Figure 10.5.2 are not.

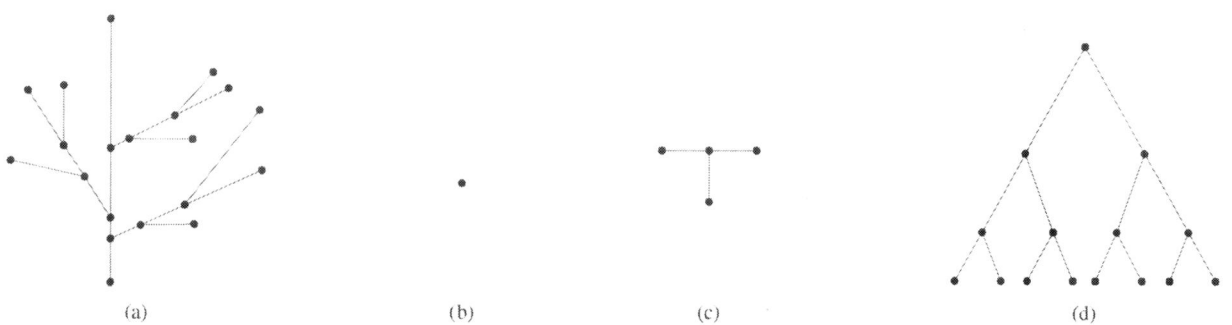

(a)   (b)   (c)   (d)

Figure 10.5.1 **Trees. All the graphs in (a)–(d) are connected and circuit-free.**

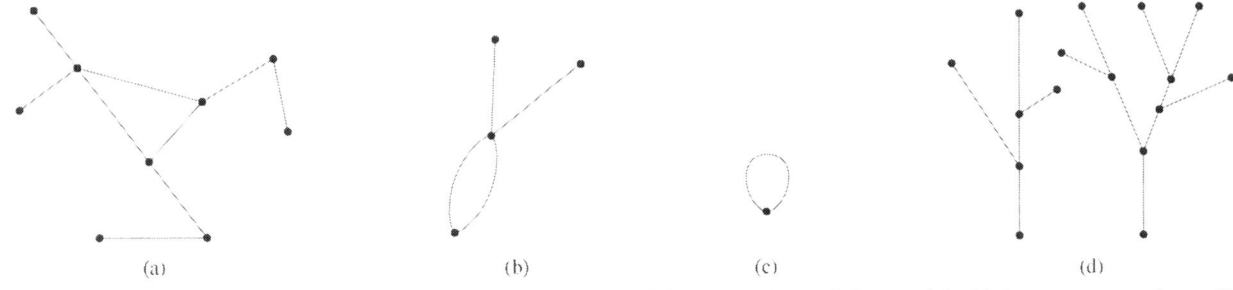

Figure 10.5.2 **Non-Trees. The graphs in (a), (b), and (c) all have circuits, and the graph in (d) is not connected.** ▪

Examples of Trees

The following examples illustrate just a few of the many and varied situations in which mathematical trees arise.

Example 10.5.2 A Decision Tree

During orientation week, a college administers an exam to all entering students to determine placement in the mathematics curriculum. The exam consists of two parts, and placement recommendations are made as indicated by the tree shown in Figure 10.5.3. Read the tree from left to right to decide what course should be recommended for a student who scored 9 on part I and 7 on part II.

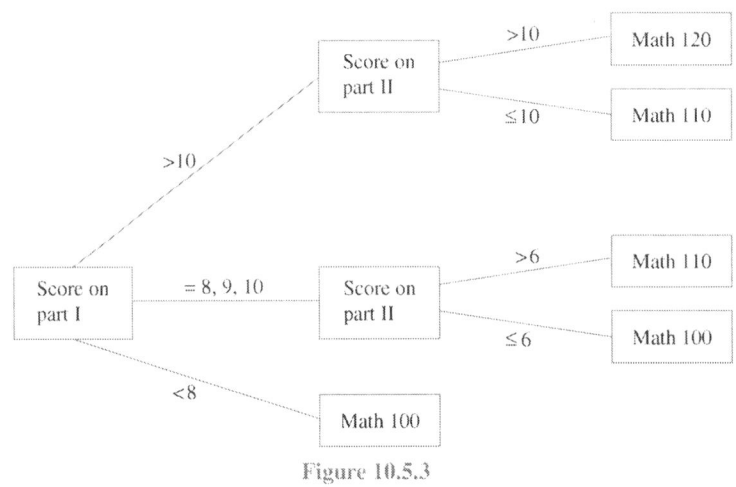

Figure 10.5.3

Solution   Since the student scored 9 on part I, the score on part II is checked. Since it is greater than 6, the student should be advised to take Math 110. ▪

Example 10.5.3 A Parse Tree

In the last 30 years, Noam Chomsky and others have developed new ways to describe the syntax (or grammatical structure) of natural languages such as English. As is discussed briefly in Chapter 12, this work has proved useful in constructing compilers for high-level computer languages. In the study of grammars, trees are often used to show the derivation of grammatically correct sentences from certain basic rules. Such trees are called **syntactic derivation trees** or **parse trees.**

A very small subset of English grammar, for example, specifies that

1. a sentence can be produced by writing first a noun phrase and then a verb phrase;

2. a noun phrase can be produced by writing an article and then a noun;

3. a noun phrase can also be produced by writing an article, then an adjective, and then a noun;

4. a verb phrase can be produced by writing a verb and then a noun phrase;

5. one article is "the";

6. one adjective is "young";

7. one verb is "caught";

8. one noun is "man";

9. one (other) noun is "ball."

The rules of a grammar are called **productions.** It is customary to express them using the shorthand notation illustrated below. This notation, introduced by John Backus in 1959 and modified by Peter Naur in 1960, was used to describe the computer language Algol and is called the **Backus-Naur notation.** In the notation, the symbol | represents the word *or,* and angle brackets ⟨ ⟩ are used to enclose terms to be defined (such as a sentence or noun phrase).

1. ⟨sentence⟩ → ⟨noun phrase⟩⟨verb phrase⟩

2., 3. ⟨noun phrase⟩ → ⟨article⟩⟨noun⟩ | ⟨article⟩⟨adjective⟩⟨noun⟩

4. ⟨verb phrase⟩ → ⟨verb⟩⟨noun phrase⟩

5. ⟨article⟩ → the

6. ⟨adjective⟩ → young

7, 8. ⟨noun⟩ → man | ball

9. ⟨verb⟩ → caught

The derivation of the sentence "The young man caught the ball" from the above rules is described by the tree shown below.

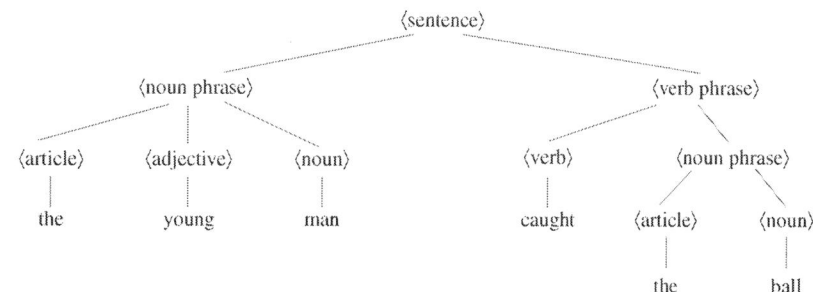

*John Backus
(1924–1998)*

*Peter Naur
(born 1928)*

In the study of linguistics, **syntax** refers to the grammatical structure of sentences, and **semantics** refers to the meanings of words and their interrelations. A sentence can be syntactically correct but semantically incorrect, as in the nonsensical sentence "The young ball caught the man," which can be derived from the rules given above. Or a sentence can contain syntactic errors but not semantic ones, as, for instance, when a two-year-old child says, "Me hungry!" ▨

Example 10.5.4 Structure of Hydrocarbon Molecules

The German physicist Gustav Kirchhoff (1824–1887) was the first to analyze the behavior of mathematical trees in connection with the investigation of electrical circuits. Soon after (and independently), the English mathematician Arthur Cayley used the mathematics of trees to enumerate all isomers for certain hydrocarbons. Hydrocarbon molecules are composed of carbon and hydrogen; each carbon atom can form up to four chemical bonds with other atoms, and each hydrogen atom can form one bond with another atom. Thus the structure of hydrocarbon molecules can be represented by graphs such as those shown following, in which the vertices represent atoms of hydrogen and carbon, denoted H and C, and the edges represent the chemical bonds between them.

Arthur Cayley
(1821–1895)

Butane   Isobutane

Note that each of these graphs has four carbon atoms and ten hydrogen atoms, but the two graphs show different configurations of atoms. When two molecules have the same chemical formulae (in this case C_4H_{10}) but different chemical bonds, they are called *isomers*.

Certain *saturated hydrocarbon* molecules contain the maximum number of hydrogen atoms for a given number of carbon atoms. Cayley showed that if such a saturated hydrocarbon molecule has k carbon atoms, then it has $2k + 2$ hydrogen atoms. The first step in doing so is to prove that the graph of such a saturated hydrocarbon molecule is a tree. Prove this using proof by contradiction. (You are asked to finish the derivation of Cayley's result in exercise 4 at the end of this section.)

Solution Suppose there is a hydrocarbon molecule that contains the maximum number of hydrogen atoms for the number of its carbon atoms and whose graph G is not a tree. *[We must derive a contradiction.]* Since G is not a tree, G is not connected or G has a circuit. But the graph of any molecule is connected (all the atoms in a molecule must be connected to each other), and so G must have a nontrivial circuit. Now the edges of the circuit can link only carbon atoms because every vertex of a circuit has degree at least 2 and a hydrogen atom vertex has degree 1. Delete one edge of the circuit and add two new edges to join each of the newly disconnected carbon atom vertices to a hydrogen atom vertex as shown below.

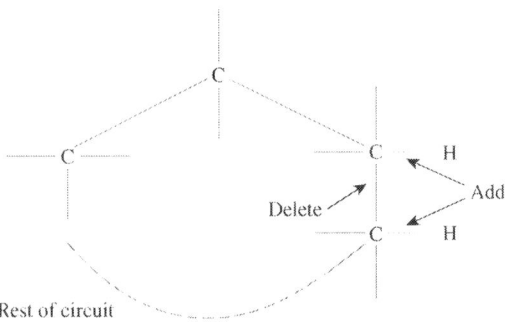

The resulting molecule has two more hydrogen atoms than the given molecule, but the number of carbon atoms is unchanged. This contradicts the supposition that the given molecule has the maximum number of hydrogen atoms for the given number of carbon atoms. Hence the supposition is false, and so G is a tree. ∎

Characterizing Trees

There is a somewhat surprising relation between the number of vertices and the number of edges of a tree. It turns out that if n is a positive integer, then any tree with n vertices (no matter what its shape) has $n - 1$ edges. Perhaps even more surprisingly, a partial converse to this fact is also true—namely, any *connected* graph with n vertices and $n - 1$ edges is a tree. It follows from these facts that if even one new edge (but no new vertex) is added to a tree, the resulting graph must contain a circuit. Also, from the fact that removing an edge from a circuit does not disconnect a graph, it can be shown that every connected graph has a subgraph that is a tree. It follows that if n is a positive integer, any graph with n vertices and *fewer* than $n - 1$ edges is not connected.

A small but very important fact necessary to derive the first main theorem about trees is that any nontrivial tree must have at least one vertex of degree 1.

Lemma 10.5.1

Any tree that has more than one vertex has at least one vertex of degree 1.

A constructive way to understand this lemma is to imagine being given a tree T with more than one vertex. You pick a vertex v at random and then search outward along a path from v looking for a vertex of degree 1. As you reach each new vertex, you check whether it has degree 1. If it does, you are finished. If it does not, you exit from the vertex along a different edge from the one you entered on. Because T is circuit-free, the vertices included in the path never repeat. And since the number of vertices of T is finite, the process of building a path must eventually terminate. When that happens, the final vertex v' of the path must have degree 1. This process is illustrated below.

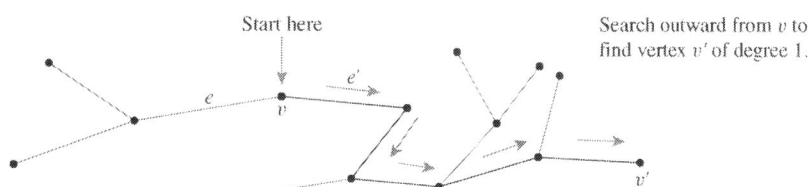

Start here | Search outward from v to find vertex v' of degree 1.

This discussion is made precise in the following proof.

Proof:

Let T be a particular but arbitrarily chosen tree that has more than one vertex, and consider the following algorithm:

Step 1: Pick a vertex v of T and let e be an edge incident on v.
    [If there were no edge incident on v, then v would be an isolated vertex. But this would contradict the assumption that T is connected (since it is a tree) and has at least two vertices.]

Step 2: While $\deg(v) > 1$, repeat steps 2a, 2b, and 2c:

---

continued on page 688

Step 2a: Choose e' to be an edge incident on v such that $e' \neq e$. *[Such an edge exists because* $\deg(v) > 1$ *and so there are at least two edges incident on* v.*]*

Step 2b: Let v' be the vertex at the other end of e' from v. *[Since T is a tree, e' cannot be a loop and therefore e' has two distinct endpoints.]*

Step 2c: Let $e = e'$ and $v = v'$. *[This is just a renaming process in preparation for a repetition of step 2.]*

The algorithm just described must eventually terminate because the set of vertices of the tree T is finite and T is circuit-free. When it does, a vertex v of degree 1 will have been found.

Using Lemma 10.5.1 it is not difficult to show that, in fact, any tree that has more than one vertex has at least *two* vertices of degree 1. This extension of Lemma 10.5.1 is left to the exercises at the end of this section.

• Definition

Let T be a tree. If T has only one or two vertices, then each is called a **terminal vertex**. If T has at least three vertices, then a vertex of degree 1 in T is called a **terminal vertex** (or a **leaf**), and a vertex of degree greater than 1 in T is called an **internal vertex** (or a **branch vertex**).

Example 10.5.5 Terminal and Internal Vertices

Find all terminal vertices and all internal vertices in the following tree:

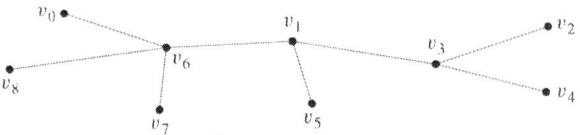

Solution   The terminal vertices are v_0, v_2, v_4, v_5, v_7, and v_8. The internal vertices are v_6, v_1, and v_3. ∎

The following is the first of the two main theorems about trees:

Theorem 10.5.2

For any positive integer n, any tree with n vertices has $n - 1$ edges.

The proof is by mathematical induction. To do the inductive step, you assume the theorem is true for a positive integer k and then show it is true for $k + 1$. Thus you assume you have a tree T with $k + 1$ vertices, and you must show that T has $(k + 1) - 1 = k$ edges. As you do this, you are free to use the inductive hypothesis that *any* tree with k vertices has $k - 1$ edges. To make use of the inductive hypothesis, you need to reduce the tree T with $k + 1$ vertices to a tree with just k vertices. But by Lemma 10.5.1, T has a vertex v of degree 1, and since T is connected, v is attached to the rest of T by a single edge e as sketched on the next page.

Rest of T

Now if e and v are removed from T, what remains is a tree T' with $(k+1) - 1 = k$ vertices. By inductive hypothesis, then, T' has $k-1$ edges. But the original tree T has one more vertex and one more edge than T'. Hence T must have $(k-1) + 1 = k$ edges, as was to be shown. A formal version of this argument is given below.

Proof (by mathematical induction):

Let the property $P(n)$ be the sentence

> Any tree with n vertices has $n - 1$ edges.   ← $P(n)$

We use mathematical induction to show that this property is true for all integers $n \geq 1$.

Show that $P(1)$ is true: Let T be any tree with one vertex. Then T has zero edges (since it contains no loops). But $0 = 1 - 1$, so $P(1)$ is true.

Show that for all integers $k \geq 1$, if $P(k)$ is true then $P(k+1)$ is true:
Suppose k is any positive integer for which $P(k)$ is true. In other words, suppose that

> Any tree with k vertices has k - 1 edges.   ← $P(k)$
> inductive hypothesis

We must show that $P(k+1)$ is true. In other words, we must show that

> Any tree with $k+1$ vertices has $(k+1) - 1 = k$ edges.   ← $P(k+1)$

Let T be a particular but arbitrarily chosen tree with $k+1$ vertices. *[We must show that T has k edges.]* Since k is a positive integer, $(k+1) \geq 2$, and so T has more than one vertex. Hence by Lemma 10.5.1, T has a vertex v of degree 1. Also, since T has more than one vertex, there is at least one other vertex in T besides v. Thus there is an edge e connecting v to the rest of T. Define a subgraph T' of T so that

$$V(T') = V(T) - \{v\}$$

Then

$$E(T') = E(T) - \{e\}.$$

1. The number of vertices of T' is $(k+1) - 1 = k$.

2. T' is circuit-free (since T is circuit-free, and removing an edge and a vertex cannot create a circuit).

3. T' is connected (see exercise 24 at the end of this section).

Hence, by the definition of tree, T' is a tree. Since T' has k vertices, by inductive hypothesis

$$\text{the number of edges of } T' = (\text{the number of vertices of } T') - 1$$
$$= k - 1.$$

continued on page 690

But then

$$\text{the number of edges of } T = (\text{the number of edges of } T') + 1$$
$$= (k - 1) + 1$$
$$= k.$$

[This is what was to be shown.]

Example 10.5.6 Determining Whether a Graph Is a Tree

A graph G has ten vertices and twelve edges. Is it a tree?

Solution   No. By Theorem 10.5.2, any tree with ten vertices has nine edges, not twelve. ∎

Example 10.5.7 Finding Trees Satisfying Given Conditions

Find all nonisomorphic trees with four vertices.

Solution   By Theorem 10.5.2, any tree with four vertices has three edges. Thus the total degree of a tree with four vertices must be 6. Also, every tree with more than one vertex has at least two vertices of degree 1 (see the comment following Lemma 10.5.1 and exercises 5 and 29 at the end of this section). Thus the following combinations of degrees for the vertices are the only ones possible:

$$1, 1, 1, 3 \quad \text{and} \quad 1, 1, 2, 2.$$

There are two nonisomorphic trees corresponding to both of these possibilities, as shown below.

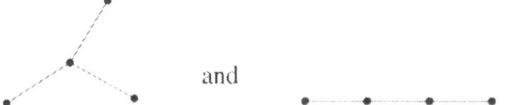

To prove the second major theorem about trees, we need another lemma.

> **Lemma 10.5.3**
>
> If G is any connected graph, C is any circuit in G, and any one of the edges of C is removed from G, then the graph that remains is connected.

Essentially, the reason why Lemma 10.5.3 is true is that any two vertices in a circuit are connected by two distinct paths. It is possible to draw the graph so that one of these goes "clockwise" and the other goes "counterclockwise" around the circuit. For example, in the circuit shown on the next page, the clockwise path from v_2 to v_3 is

$$v_2 e_3 v_3$$

and the counterclockwise path from v_2 to v_3 is

$$v_2 e_2 v_1 e_1 v_0 e_6 v_5 e_5 v_4 e_4 v_3.$$

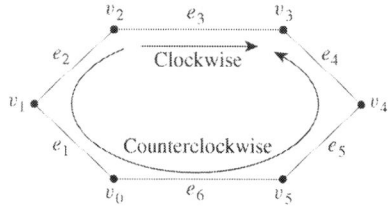

Proof:

Suppose G is a connected graph, C is a circuit in G, and e is an edge of C. Form a subgraph G' of G by removing e from G. Thus

$$V(G') = V(G)$$
$$E(G') = E(G) - \{e\}.$$

We must show that G' is connected. *[To show a graph is connected, we must show that if u and w are any vertices of the graph, then there exists a walk in G' from u to w.]* Suppose u and w are any two vertices of G'. *[We must find a walk from u to w.]* Since the vertex sets of G and G' are the same, u and w are both vertices of G, and since G is connected, there is a walk W in G from u to w.

Case 1 (e is not an edge of W): The only edge in G that is not in G' is e, so in this case W is also a walk in G'. Hence u is connected to w by a walk in G'.

Case 2 (e is an edge of W): In this case the walk W from u to w includes a section of the circuit C that contains e. Let C be denoted as follows:

$$C: v_0 e_1 v_1 e_2 v_2 \cdots e_n v_n \ (= v_0).$$

Now e is one of the edges of C, so, to be specific, let $e = e_k$. Then the walk W contains either the sequence

$$v_{k-1} e_k v_k \quad \text{or} \quad v_k e_k v_{k-1}.$$

If W contains $v_{k-1} e_k v_k$, connect v_{k-1} to v_k by taking the "counterclockwise" walk W' defined as follows:

$$W': v_{k-1} e_{k-1} v_{k-2} \cdots v_0 e_n v_{n-1} \cdots e_{k+1} v_k.$$

An example showing how to go from u to w while avoiding e_k is given in Figure 10.5.4.

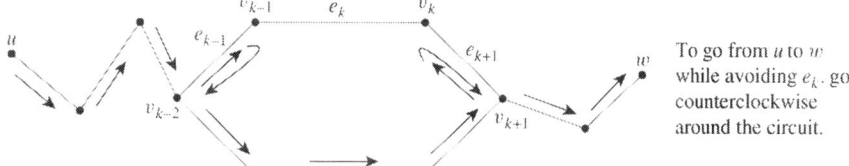

Figure 10.5.4 **An Example of a Walk from *u* to *w* That Does Not Include Edge e_k**

If W contains $v_k e_k v_{k-1}$, connect v_k to v_{k-1} by taking the "clockwise" walk W'' defined as follows:

$$W'': v_k e_{k+1} v_{k+1} \cdots v_n e_1 v_1 e_2 \cdots e_{k-1} v_{k-1}.$$

continued on page 692

Now patch either W' or W'' into W to form a new walk from u to w. For instance, to patch W' into W, start with the section of W from u to v_{k-1}, then take W' from v_{k-1} to v_k, and finally take the section of W from v_k to w. If this new walk still contains an occurrence of e, just repeat the process described previously until all occurrences are eliminated. *[This must happen eventually since the number of occurrences of e in C is finite.]* The result is a walk from u to w that does not contain e and hence is a walk in G'.

The previous arguments show that both in case 1 and in case 2 there is a walk in G' from u to w. Since the choice of u and w was arbitrary, G' is connected.

The second major theorem about trees is a modified converse to Theorem 10.5.2.

Theorem 10.5.4

For any positive integer n, if G is a connected graph with n vertices and $n-1$ edges, then G is a tree.

Proof:

Let n be a positive integer and suppose G is a particular but arbitrarily chosen graph that is connected and has n vertices and $n-1$ edges. *[We must show that G is a tree. Now a tree is a connected, circuit-free graph. Since we already know G is connected, it suffices to show that G is circuit-free.]* Suppose G is not circuit-free. That is, suppose G has a circuit C. *[We must derive a contradiction.]* By Lemma 10.5.3, an edge of C can be removed from G to obtain a graph G' that is connected. If G' has a circuit, then repeat this process: Remove an edge of the circuit from G' to form a new connected graph. Continue repeating the process of removing edges from circuits until eventually a graph G'' is obtained that is connected and is circuit-free. By definition, G'' is a tree. Since no vertices were removed from G to form G'', G'' has n vertices just as G does. Thus, by Theorem 10.5.2, G'' has $n-1$ edges. But the supposition that G has a circuit implies that at least one edge of G is removed to form G''. Hence G'' has no more than $(n-1)-1 = n-2$ edges, which contradicts its having $n-1$ edges. So the supposition is false. Hence G is circuit-free, and therefore G is a tree *[as was to be shown]*.

Theorem 10.5.4 is not a full converse of Theorem 10.5.2. Although it is true that every *connected* graph with n vertices and $n-1$ edges (where n is a positive integer) is a tree, it is not true that *every* graph with n vertices and $n-1$ edges is a tree.

Example 10.5.8 A Graph with n Vertices and $n-1$ Edges That Is Not a Tree

Give an example of a graph with five vertices and four edges that is not a tree.

Solution   By Theorem 10.5.4, such a graph cannot be connected. One example of such an unconnected graph is shown below.

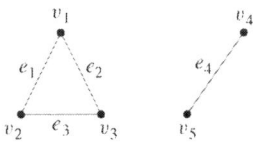

Test Yourself

1. A circuit-free graph is a graph with _____.

2. A forest is a graph that is _____, and a tree is a graph that is _____.

3. A trivial tree is a graph that consists of _____.

4. Any tree with at least two vertices has at least one vertex of degree _____.

5. If a tree T has at least two vertices, then a terminal vertex (or leaf) in T is a vertex of degree _____ and an internal vertex (or branch vertex) in T is a vertex of degree _____.

6. For any positive integer n, any tree with n vertices has _____.

7. For any positive integer n, if G is a connected graph with n vertices and $n - 1$ edges then _____.

Exercise Set 10.5

1. Read the tree in Example 10.5.2 from left to right to answer the following questions:
   a. What course should a student who scored 12 on part I and 4 on part II take?
   b. What course should a student who scored 8 on part I and 9 on part II take?

2. Draw trees to show the derivations of the following sentences from the rules given in Example 10.5.3.
   a. The young ball caught the man.
   b. The man caught the young ball.

H 3. What is the total degree of a tree with n vertices? Why?

4. Let G be the graph of a hydrocarbon molecule with the maximum number of hydrogen atoms for the number of its carbon atoms.
   a. Draw the graph of G if G has three carbon atoms and eight hydrogen atoms.
   b. Draw the graphs of three isomers of C_5H_{12}.
   c. Use Example 10.5.4 and exercise 3 to prove that if the vertices of G consist of k carbon atoms and m hydrogen atoms, then G has a total degree of $2k + 2m - 2$.
   H d. Prove that if the vertices of G consist of k carbon atoms and m hydrogen atoms, then G has a total degree of $4k + m$.
   e. Equate the results of (c) and (d) to prove Cayley's result that a saturated hydrocarbon molecule with k carbon atoms and a maximum number of hydrogen atoms has $2k + 2$ hydrogen atoms.

H 5. Extend the argument given in the proof of Lemma 10.5.1 to show that a tree with more than one vertex has at least two vertices of degree 1.

6. If graphs are allowed to have an infinite number of vertices and edges, then Lemma 10.5.1 is false. Give a counterexample that shows this. In other words, give an example of an "infinite tree" (a connected, circuit-free graph with an infinite number of vertices and edges) that has no vertex of degree 1.

7. Find all terminal vertices and all internal vertices for the following trees.

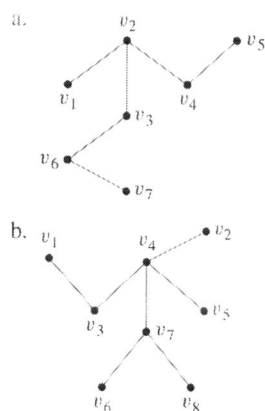

a.

b.

In each of 8–21, either draw a graph with the given specifications or explain why no such graph exists.

8. Tree, nine vertices, nine edges

9. Graph, connected, nine vertices, nine edges

10. Graph, circuit-free, nine vertices, six edges

11. Tree, six vertices, total degree 14

12. Tree, five vertices, total degree 8

13. Graph, connected, six vertices, five edges, has a circuit

14. Graph, two vertices, one edge, not a tree

15. Graph, circuit-free, seven vertices, four edges

16. Graph, six vertices, five edges, not a tree

17. Tree, twelve vertices, fifteen edges

18. Tree, five vertices, total degree 10

19. Simple graph, connected, six vertices, six edges

20. Graph, connected, ten vertices, nine edges, has a circuit

21. Tree, ten vertices, total degree 24

22. A connected graph has twelve vertices and eleven edges. Does it have a vertex of degree 1? Why?

23. A connected graph has nine vertices and twelve edges. Does it have a nontrivial circuit? Why?

24. Suppose that v is a vertex of degree 1 in a connected graph G and that e is the edge incident on v. Let G' be the subgraph of G obtained by removing v and e from G. Must G' be connected? Why?

25. A graph has eight vertices and six edges. Is it connected? Why?

H 26. If a graph has n vertices and $n - 2$ or fewer edges, can it be connected? Why?

27. A circuit-free graph has ten vertices and nine edges. Is it connected? Why?

H 28. Is a circuit-free graph with n vertices and at least $n - 1$ edges connected? Why?

29. Prove that every nontrivial tree has at least two vertices of degree 1 by filling in the details and completing the following argument: Let T be a nontrivial tree and let S be the set of all paths from one vertex to another of T. Among all the paths in S, choose a path P with the most edges. (Why is it possible to find such a P?) What can you say about the initial and final vertices of P? Why?

30. Find all nonisomorphic trees with five vertices.

31. a. Prove that the following is an invariant for graph isomorphism: A vertex of degree i is adjacent to a vertex of degree j.

    H b. Find all nonisomorphic trees with six vertices.

Answers for Test Yourself

1. no circuits   2. circuit-free and not connected; connected and circuit-free   3. a single vertex (and no edges)   4. 1   5. 1; greater than 1 (*Or*: at least 2)   6. $n - 1$ edges   7. G is a tree

10.6 Rooted Trees

Let us grant that the pursuit of mathematics is a divine madness of the human spirit, a refuge from the goading urgency of contingent happenings. — Alfred North Whitehead, 1861–1947

An outdoor tree is rooted and so is the kind of family tree that shows all the descendants of one particular person. The terminology and notation of rooted trees blends the language of botanical trees and that of family trees. In mathematics, a rooted tree is a tree in which one vertex has been distinguished from the others and is designated the *root*. Given any other vertex v in the tree, there is a unique path from the root to v. (After all, if there were two distinct paths, a circuit could be constructed.) The number of edges in such a path is called the *level* of v, and the *height* of the tree is the length of the longest such path. It is traditional in drawing rooted trees to place the root at the top (as is done in family trees) and show the branches descending from it.

> **• Definition**
>
> A **rooted tree** is a tree in which there is one vertex that is distinguished from the others and is called the **root**. The **level** of a vertex is the number of edges along the unique path between it and the root. The **height** of a rooted tree is the maximum level of any vertex of the tree. Given the root or any internal vertex v of a rooted tree, the **children** of v are all those vertices that are adjacent to v and are one level farther away from the root than v. If w is a child of v, then v is called the **parent** of w, and two distinct vertices that are both children of the same parent are called **siblings.** Given two distinct vertices v and w, if v lies on the unique path between w and the root, then v is an **ancestor** of w and w is a **descendant** of v.

These terms are illustrated in Figure 10.6.1.

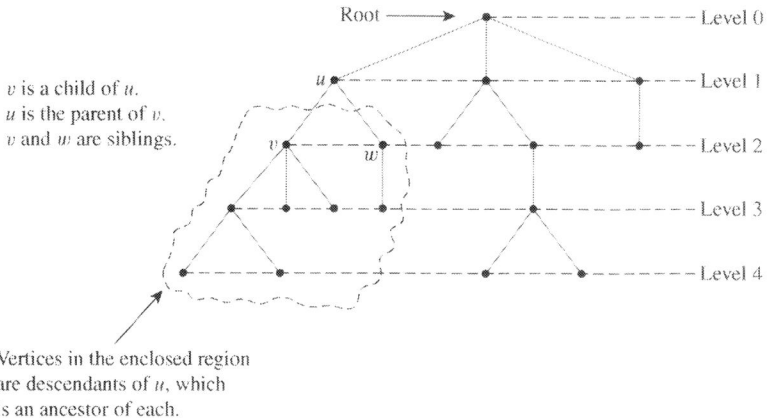

Figure 10.6.1 **A Rooted Tree**

Example 10.6.1 Rooted Trees

Consider the tree with root v_0 shown below.

a. What is the level of v_5?

b. What is the level of v_0?

c. What is the height of this rooted tree?

d. What are the children of v_3?

e. What is the parent of v_2?

f. What are the siblings of v_8?

g. What are the descendants of v_3?

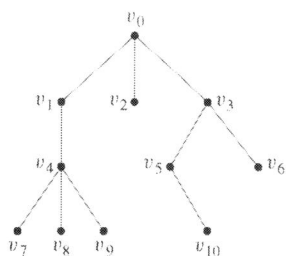

Solution

a. 2   b. 0   c. 3   d. v_5 and v_6 e. v_0 f. v_7 and v_9 g. v_5, v_6, v_{10}

Note that in the tree with root v_0 shown below, v_1 has level 1 and is the child of v_0, and both v_0 and v_1 are terminal vertices.

Binary Trees

When every vertex in a rooted tree has at most two children and each child is designated either the (unique) left child or the (unique) right child, the result is a *binary tree*.

● Definition

A **binary tree** is a rooted tree in which every parent has at most two children. Each child in a binary tree is designated either a **left child** or a **right child** (but not both), and every parent has at most one left child and one right child. A **full binary tree** is a binary tree in which each parent has exactly two children.

Given any parent v in a binary tree T, if v has a left child, then the **left subtree** of v is the binary tree whose root is the left child of v, whose vertices consist of the left child of v and all its descendants, and whose edges consist of all those edges of T that connect the vertices of the left subtree. The **right subtree** of v is defined analogously.

These terms are illustrated in Figure 10.6.2.

Root

v is the left child of u.

u

w

x is the right child of w.

v

Left subtree of w

Right subtree of w

Figure 10.6.2 **A Binary Tree**

Example 10.6.2 Representation of Algebraic Expressions

Binary trees are used in many ways in computer science. One use is to represent algebraic expressions with arbitrary nesting of balanced parentheses. For instance, the following (labeled) binary tree represents the expression a/b: The operator is at the root and acts on the left and right children of the root in left-right order.

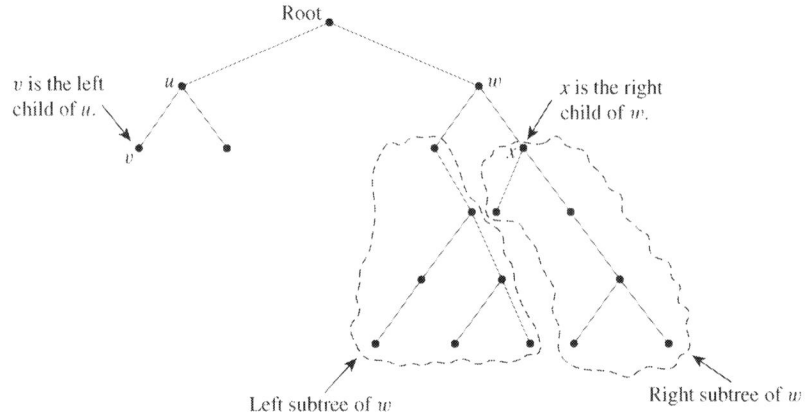

More generally, the binary tree shown below represents the expression $a/(c+d)$. In such a representation, the internal vertices are arithmetic operators, the terminal vertices are variables, and the operator at each vertex acts on its left and right subtrees in left-right order.

Draw a binary tree to represent the expression $((a-b)\cdot c)+(d/e)$.

Solution

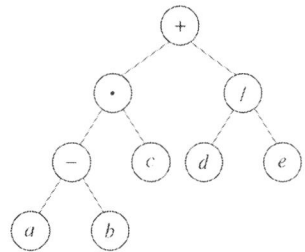

An interesting theorem about binary trees says that if you know the number of internal vertices of a full binary tree, then you can calculate both the total number of vertices and the number of terminal vertices, and conversely. More specifically, a full binary tree with k internal vertices has a total of $2k + 1$ vertices of which $k + 1$ are terminal vertices.

Theorem 10.6.1

If k is a positive integer and T is a full binary tree with k internal vertices, then T has a total of $2k + 1$ vertices and has $k + 1$ terminal vertices.

Proof:

Suppose k is a positive integer and T is a full binary tree with k internal vertices. Observe that the set of all vertices of T can be partitioned into two disjoint subsets: the set of all vertices that have a parent and the set of all vertices that do not have a parent. Now there is just one vertex that does not have a parent, namely the root. Also, since every internal vertex of a full binary tree has exactly two children, the number of vertices that have a parent is twice the number of parents, or $2k$, since each parent is an internal vertex. Hence

$$\begin{bmatrix} \text{the total number} \\ \text{of vertices of } T \end{bmatrix} = \begin{bmatrix} \text{the number of} \\ \text{vertices that} \\ \text{have a parent} \end{bmatrix} + \begin{bmatrix} \text{the number of} \\ \text{vertices that do} \\ \text{not have a parent} \end{bmatrix}$$

$$= \quad 2k \quad + \quad 1.$$

But it is also true that the total number of vertices of T equals the number of internal vertices plus the number of terminal vertices. Thus

$$\begin{bmatrix} \text{the total number} \\ \text{of vertices of } T \end{bmatrix} = \begin{bmatrix} \text{the number of} \\ \text{internal vertices} \end{bmatrix} + \begin{bmatrix} \text{the number of} \\ \text{terminal vertices} \end{bmatrix}$$

$$= \quad k \quad + \quad \begin{bmatrix} \text{the number of} \\ \text{terminal vertices} \end{bmatrix}$$

Now equate the two expressions for the total number of vertices of T:

$$2k + 1 = k + \begin{bmatrix} \text{the number of} \\ \text{terminal vertices} \end{bmatrix}$$

Solving this equation gives

$$\begin{bmatrix} \text{the number of} \\ \text{terminal vertices} \end{bmatrix} = (2k + 1) - k = k + 1.$$

Thus the total number of vertices is $2k + 1$ and the number of terminal vertices is $k + 1$ *[as was to be shown]*.

Example 10.6.3 Determining Whether a Certain Full Binary Tree Exists

Is there a full binary tree that has 10 internal vertices and 13 terminal vertices?

Solution No. By Theorem 10.6.1, a full binary tree with 10 internal vertices has $10 + 1 = 11$ terminal vertices, not 13. ∎

Another interesting theorem about binary trees specifies the maximum number of terminal vertices of a binary tree of a given height. Specifically, the maximum number of terminal vertices of a binary tree of height h is 2^h. Another way to say this is that a binary tree with t terminal vertices has height of at least $\log_2 t$.

Theorem 10.6.2

For all integers $h \geq 0$, if T is any binary tree with height h and t terminal vertices, then

$$t \leq 2^h.$$

Equivalently, $\qquad\qquad\qquad \log_2 t \leq h.$

Proof (by strong mathematical induction):

Let $P(h)$ be the sentence

> If T is any binary tree of height h, then the number of $P(h)$
> terminal vertices of T is at most 2^h.

Show that $P(0)$ is true: We must show that if T is any binary tree of height 0, then the number of terminal vertices of T is at most 2^0. Suppose T is a tree of height 0. Then T consists of a single vertex, the root. By definition this is a terminal vertex and so the number of terminal vertices is $t = 1 = 2^0 = 2^h$. Hence $t \leq 2^h$ [*as was to be shown*].

Show that for all integers $k \geq 0$, if $P(i)$ is true for all integers i from 0 through k, then it is true for $k + 1$:
Let k be any integer with $k \geq 0$, and suppose that

> For all integers i from 0 through k, if T is any
> binary tree of height i, then the number of   ← inductive hypothesis
> terminal vertices of T is at most 2^i.

We must show that

> If T is any binary tree of height $k + 1$, then the number of $P(k+1)$
> terminal vertices of T is 2^{k+1}.

Let T be a binary tree of height $k + 1$, root v, and t terminal vertices. Because $k \geq 0$, we have that $k + 1 \geq 1$ and so v has at least one child.

Case 1 (v has only one child): In this case we may assume without loss of generality that v's child is a left child and denote it by v_L. Let T_L be the left subtree of v. Then v_L is the root of T_L. (This situation is illustrated in Figure 10.6.3.) Because v has only one child, v is itself a terminal vertex, so the total number of terminal vertices in T equals the number of terminal vertices in T_L plus 1. Thus if t_L is the number of terminal vertices in T_L, then $t = t_L + 1$.

Now by inductive hypothesis, $t_L \leq 2^k$ because the height of T_L is k, one less than the height of T. Also, because v has a child, $k + 1 \geq 1$, and so $2^k \geq 2^0 = 1$. Therefore,

$$t = t_L + 1 \leq 2^k + 1 \leq 2^k + 2^k = 2 \cdot 2^k = 2^{(k+1)}.$$

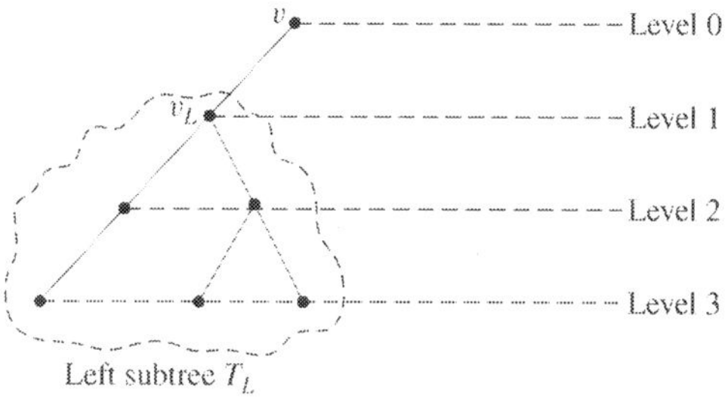

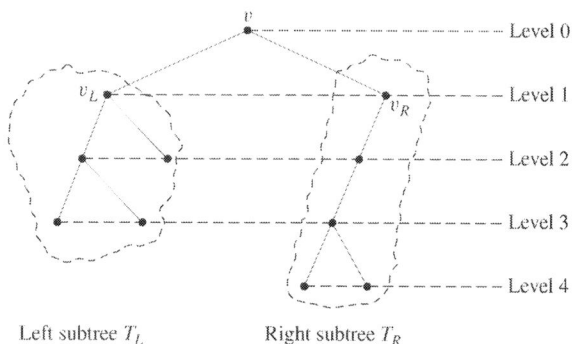

Figure 10.6.3 **A Binary Tree Whose Root Has One Child**

Case 2 (v has two children): In this case, v has both a left child, v_L, and a right child, v_R, and v_L and v_R are roots of a left subtree T_L and a right subtree T_R. Note that T_L and T_R are binary trees because T is a binary tree. (This situation is illustrated in Figure 10.6.4.)

Figure 10.6.4 **A Binary Tree Whose Root Has Two Children**

Now v_L and v_R are the roots of the left and right subtrees of v, denoted T_L and T_R, respectively. Note that T_L and T_R are binary trees because T is a binary tree. Let h_L and h_R be the heights of T_L and T_R, respectively. Then $h_L \leq k$ and $h_R \leq k$ since T is obtained by joining T_L and T_R and adding a level. Let t_L and t_R be the numbers of terminal vertices of T_L and T_R, respectively. Then, since both T_L and T_R have heights less than $k + 1$, by inductive hypothesis

$$t_L \leq 2^{h_L} \quad \text{and} \quad t_R \leq 2^{h_R}.$$

But the terminal vertices of T consist exactly of the terminal vertices of T_L together with the terminal vertices of T_R. Therefore,

$$t = t_L + t_R \leq 2^{h_L} + 2^{h_R} \qquad \text{by inductive hypothesis}$$
$$\text{since } h_L \leq k \text{ and } h_R \leq k$$

continued on page 700

Hence,

$$t \le 2^k + 2^k = 2 \cdot 2^k = 2^{k+1} \qquad \text{by basic algebra.}$$

Thus the number of terminal vertices is at most $2k + 1$ *[as was to be shown]*.

Since both the basis step and the inductive step have been proved, we conclude that for all integers $h \ge 0$, if T is any binary tree with height h and t terminal vertices, then $t \le 2^h$.

The equivalent inequality $\log_2 t \le h$ follows from the fact that the logarithmic function with base 2 is increasing. In other words, for all positive real numbers x and y,

$$\text{if } x < y \text{ then } \log_2 x < \log_2 y.$$

Thus if we apply the logarithmic function with base 2 to both sides of

$$t \le 2^h,$$

we obtain

$$\log_2 t \le \log_2(2^h).$$

Now by definition of logarithm, $\log_2(2^h) = h$ *[because $\log_2(2^h)$ is the exponent to which 2 must be raised to obtain 2^h]*. Hence

$$\log_2 t \le h$$

[as was to be shown].

Example 10.6.4 Determining Whether a Certain Binary Tree Exists

Is there a binary tree that has height 5 and 38 terminal vertices?

Solution No. By Theorem 10.6.2, any binary tree T with height 5 has at most $2^5 = 32$ terminal vertices, so such a tree cannot have 38 terminal vertices. ∎

Test Yourself

1. A rooted tree is a tree in which _____. The level of a vertex in a rooted tree is _____. The height of a rooted tree is _____.

2. A binary tree is a rooted tree in which _____.

3. A full binary tree is a rooted tree in which _____.

4. If k is a positive integer and T is a full binary tree with k internal vertices, then T has a total of _____ vertices and has _____ terminal vertices.

5. If T is a binary tree that has t terminal vertices and height h, then t and h are related by the inequality _____.

Exercise Set 10.6

1. Consider the tree shown at right with root a.
   a. What is the level of n?
   b. What is the level of a?
   c. What is the height of this rooted tree?
   d. What are the children of n?
   e. What is the parent of g?
   f. What are the siblings of j?
   g. What are the descendants of f?

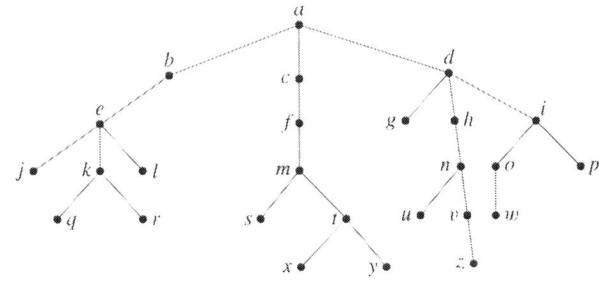

2. Consider the tree shown below with root v_0.
   a. What is the level of v_8?
   b. What is the level of v_0?
   c. What is the height of this rooted tree?
   d. What are the children of v_{10}?
   e. What is the parent of v_5?
   f. What are the siblings of v_1?
   g. What are the descendants of v_{12}?

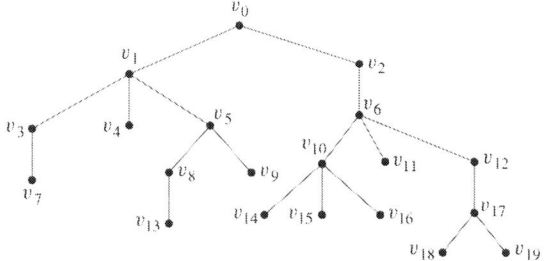

3. Draw binary trees to represent the following expressions:
   a. $a \cdot b - (c/(d + e))$ b. $a/(b - c \cdot d)$

In each of 4–20 either draw a graph with the given specifications or explain why no such graph exists.

4. Full binary tree, five internal vertices

5. Full binary tree, five internal vertices, seven terminal vertices

6. Full binary tree, seven vertices, of which four are internal vertices

7. Full binary tree, twelve vertices

8. Full binary tree, nine vertices

9. Binary tree, height 3, seven terminal vertices

10. Full binary tree, height 3, six terminal vertices

11. Binary tree, height 3, nine terminal vertices

12. Full binary tree, eight internal vertices, seven terminal vertices.

13. Full binary tree, seven vertices

14. Binary tree, height 4, eight terminal vertices

15. Full binary tree, nine vertices, five internal vertices

16. Full binary tree, height 3, seven terminal vertices

17. Full binary tree, four internal vertices

18. Full binary tree, sixteen vertices

19. Binary tree, height 4, eighteen terminal vertices

20. What can you deduce about the height of a binary tree if you know that it has the following properties?
    a. Twenty-five terminal vertices
    b. Forty terminal vertices
    c. Sixty terminal vertices

Answers for Test Yourself

1. one vertex is distinguished from the others and is called the root; the number of edges along the unique path between it and the root; the maximum level of any vertex of the tree   2. every parent has at most two children   3. every parent has exactly two children   4. $2k + 1$; $k + 1$ 5. $t \leq 2^h$, or, equivalently, $\log_2 t \leq h$

10.7 Spanning Trees and Shortest Paths

I contend that each science is a real science insofar as it is mathematics.
— Immanuel Kant, 1724–1804

An East Coast airline company wants to expand service to the Midwest and has received permission from the Federal Aviation Authority to fly any of the routes shown in Figure 10.7.1.

The company wishes to legitimately advertise service to all the cities shown but, for reasons of economy, wants to use the least possible number of individual routes to connect them. One possible route system is given in Figure 10.7.2.

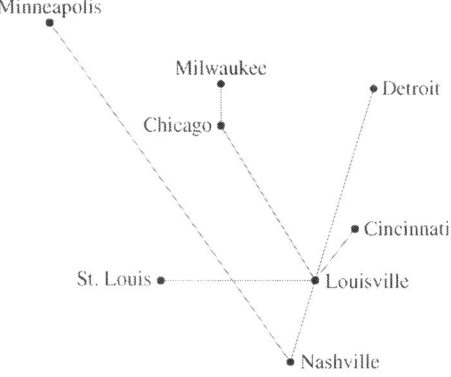

Figure 10.7.2

Clearly this system joins all the cities. Is the number of individual routes minimal? The answer is yes, and the reason may surprise you.

The fact is that the graph of any system of routes that satisfies the company's wishes is a tree, because if the graph were to contain a circuit, then one of the routes in the circuit could be removed without disconnecting the graph (by Lemma 10.5.3), and that would give a smaller total number of routes. But any tree with eight vertices has seven edges. Therefore, any system of routes that connects all eight vertices and yet minimizes the total number of routes consists of seven routes.

> **• Definition**
>
> A **spanning tree** for a graph G is a subgraph of G that contains every vertex of G and is a tree.

The preceding discussion contains the essence of the proof of the following proposition:

> **Proposition 10.7.1**
>
> 1. Every connected graph has a spanning tree.
>
> 2. Any two spanning trees for a graph have the same number of edges.

Proof of (1):

Suppose G is a connected graph. If G is circuit-free, then G is its own spanning tree and we are done. If not, then G has at least one circuit C_1. By Lemma 10.5.3, the subgraph of G obtained by removing an edge from C_1 is connected. If this subgraph is circuit-free, then it is a spanning tree and we are done. If not, then it has at least one circuit C_2, and, as above, an edge can be removed from C_2 to obtain a connected subgraph. Continuing in this way, we can remove successive edges from circuits, until eventually we obtain a connected, circuit-free subgraph T of G. *[This must happen at some point because the number of edges of G is finite, and at no stage does removal of an edge disconnect the subgraph.]* Also, T contains every vertex of G because no vertices of G were removed in constructing it. Thus T is a spanning tree for G.

The proof of part (2) is left as an exercise.

Example 10.7.1 Spanning Trees

Find all spanning trees for the graph G pictured below.

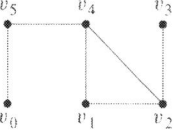

Solution The graph G has one circuit $v_2 v_1 v_4 v_2$, and removal of any edge of the circuit gives a tree. Thus, as shown below, there are three spanning trees for G.

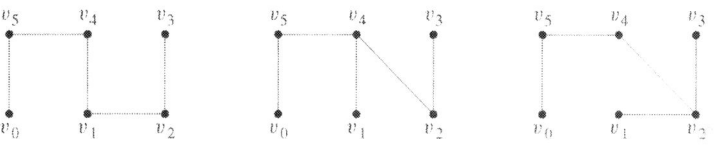

Minimum Spanning Trees

The graph of the routes allowed by the Federal Aviation Authority shown in Figure 10.7.1 can be annotated by adding the distances (in miles) between each pair of cities. This is done in Figure 10.7.3.

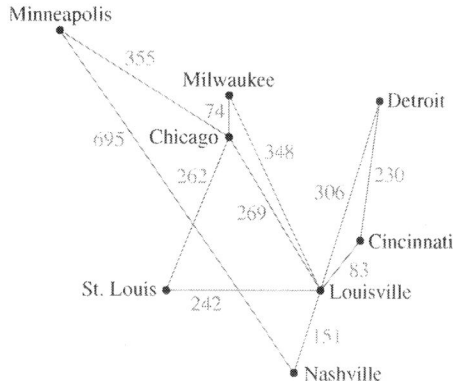

Figure 10.7.3

Now suppose the airline company wants to serve all the cities shown, but with a route system that minimizes the total mileage. Note that such a system is a tree, because if the system contained a circuit, removal of an edge from the circuit would not affect a person's ability to reach every city in the system from every other (again, by Lemma 10.5.3), but it would reduce the total mileage of the system.

More generally, a graph whose edges are labeled with numbers (known as *weights*) is called a *weighed graph*. A *minimum-weight spanning tree*, or simply a *minimum spanning tree,* is a spanning tree for which the sum of the weights of all the edges is as small as possible.

> **• Definition**
>
> A **weighted graph** is a graph for which each edge has an associated positive real number **weight.** The sum of the weights of all the edges is the **total weight** of the graph. A **minimum spanning tree** for a connected weighted graph is a spanning tree that has the least possible total weight compared to all other spanning trees for the graph.
>
> If G is a weighed graph and e is an edge of G, then $w(e)$ denotes the weight of e and $w(G)$ denotes the total weight of G.

The problem of finding a minimum spanning tree for a graph is certainly solvable. One solution is to list all spanning trees for the graph, compute the total weight of each, and choose one for which this total is a minimum. (Note that the well-ordering principle for the integers guarantees the existence of such a minimum total.) This solution, however, is inefficient in its use of computing time because the number of distinct spanning trees is so large. For instance, a complete graph with n vertices has n^{n-2} spanning trees. Even using the fastest computers available today, examining all such trees in a graph with approximately 100 vertices would require more time than is estimated to remain in the life of the universe.

In 1956 and 1957 Joseph B. Kruskal and Robert C. Prim each described much more efficient algorithms to construct minimum spanning trees. Even for large graphs, both algorithms can be implemented so as to take relatively short computing times.

Kruskal's Algorithm

Joseph Kruskal
(born 1928)

In Kruskal's algorithm, the edges of a connected weighted graph are examined one by one in order of increasing weight. At each stage the edge being examined is added to what will become the minimum spanning tree, provided that this addition does not create a circuit. After $n - 1$ edges have been added (where n is the number of vertices of the graph), these edges, together with the vertices of the graph, form a minimum spanning tree for the graph.

Algorithm 10.7.1 Kruskal

Input: G [*a connected weighted graph with n vertices, where n is a positive integer*]

Algorithm Body:
[*Build a subgraph T of G to consist of all the vertices of G with edges added in order of increasing weight. At each stage, let m be the number of edges of T.*]

1. Initialize T to have all the vertices of G and no edges.

2. Let E be the set of all edges of G, and let $m := 0$.

3. **while** $(m < n - 1)$

   3a. Find an edge e in E of least weight.
   3b. Delete e from E.
   3c. **if** addition of e to the edge set of T does not produce a circuit
        then add e to the edge set of T and set $m := m + 1$

   end while

Output: T [*T is a minimum spanning tree for G.*]

The following example shows how Kruskal's algorithm works for the graph of the airline route system.

Example 10.7.2 Action of Kruskal's Algorithm

Describe the action of Kruskal's algorithm on the graph shown in Figure 10.7.4, where $n = 8$.

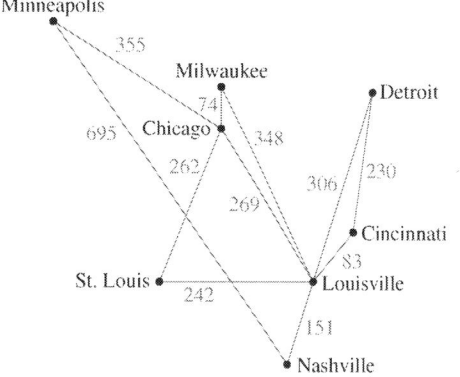

Figure 10.7.4

Solution

Iteration Number	Edge Considered	Weight	Action Taken
1	Chicago–Milwaukee	74	added
2	Louisville–Cincinnati	83	added
3	Louisville–Nashville	151	added
4	Cincinnati–Detroit	230	added
5	St. Louis–Louisville	242	added
6	St. Louis–Chicago	262	added
7	Chicago–Louisville	269	not added
8	Louisville–Detroit	306	not added
9	Louisville–Milwaukee	348	not added
10	Minneapolis–Chicago	355	added

The tree produced by Kruskal's algorithm is shown in Figure 10.7.5.

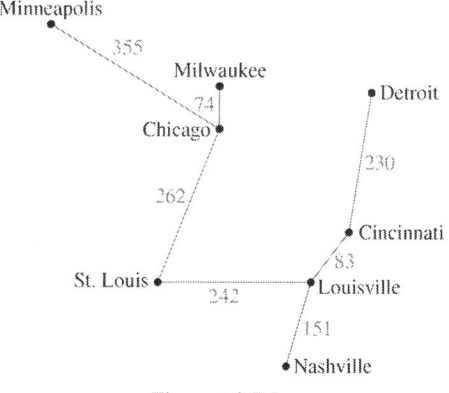

Figure 10.7.5

When Kruskal's algorithm is used on a graph in which some edges have the same weight as others, more than one minimum spanning tree can occur as output. To make the output unique, the edges of the graph can be placed in an array and edges having the same weight can be added in the order they appear in the array.

It is not obvious from the description of Kruskal's algorithm that it does what it is supposed to do. To be specific, what guarantees that it is possible at each stage to find an edge of least weight whose addition does not produce a circuit? And if such edges can be found, what guarantees that they will all eventually connect? And if they do connect, what guarantees that the resulting tree has minimum weight? Of course, the mere fact that Kruskal's algorithm is printed in this book may lead you to believe that everything works out. But the questions above are real, and they deserve serious answers.

Theorem 10.7.2 Correctness of Kruskal's Algorithm

When a connected, weighted graph is input to Kruskal's algorithm, the output is a minimum spanning tree.

Proof:

Suppose that G is a connected, weighted graph with n vertices and that T is a subgraph of G produced when G is input to Kruskal's algorithm. Clearly T is circuit-free *[since no edge that completes a circuit is ever added to T]*. Also T is connected. For as long as T has more than one connected component, the set of edges of G that can be added to T without creating a circuit is nonempty. *[The reason is that since G is connected, given any vertex v_1 in one connected component C_1 of T and any vertex v_2 in another connected component C_2, there is a path in G from v_1 to v_2. Since C_1 and C_2 are distinct, there is an edge e of this path that is not in T. Adding e to T does not create a circuit in T, because deletion of an edge from a circuit does not disconnect a graph and deletion of e would.]* The preceding arguments show that T is circuit-free and connected. Since by construction T contains every vertex of G, T is a spanning tree for G.

Next we show that T has minimum weight. Let T_1 be any minimum spanning tree for G such that the number of edges T_1 and T have in common is a maximum. Suppose that $T \neq T_1$. Then there is an edge e in T that is not an edge of T_1. *[Since trees T and T_1 both have the same vertex set, if they differ at all, they must have different, but same-size, edge sets.]* Now adding e to T_1 produces a graph with a unique circuit (see exercise 19 at the end of this section). Let e' be an edge of this circuit such that e' is not in T. *[Such an edge must exist because T is a tree and hence circuit-free.]* Let T_2 be the graph obtained from T_1 by removing e' and adding e. This situation is illustrated below.

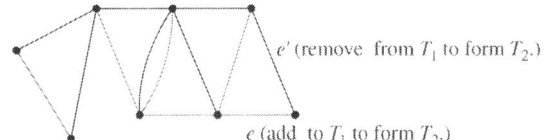

e' (remove from T_1 to form T_2.)

e (add to T_1 to form T_2.)

The entire graph is G. T_1 has black edges. e is in T but not T_1. e' is in T_1 but not T.

Note that T_2 has $n-1$ edges and n vertices and that T_2 is connected *[since by Lemma 10.5.3 the subgraph obtained by removing an edge from a circuit in a connected graph is connected]*. Consequently, T_2 is a spanning tree for G. In addition,

$$w(T_2) = w(T_1) - w(e') + w(e).$$

Now $w(e) \leq w(e')$ because at the stage in Kruskal's algorithm when e was added to T, e' was available to be added *[since it was not already in T, and at that stage its addition could not produce a circuit since e was not in T]*, and *e′ would* have been added had its weight been less than that of *e*. Thus

$$w(T_2) = w(T_1) - \underbrace{[w(e') - w(e)]}_{\geq 0}$$

$$\leq w(T_1).$$

But T_1 is a minimum spanning tree. Since T_2 is a spanning tree with weight less than or equal to the weight of T_1, T_2 is also a minimum spanning tree for G.

Finally, note that by construction, T_2 has one more edge in common with T than T_1 does, which contradicts the choice of T_1 as a minimum spanning tree for G with a maximum number of edges in common with T. Thus the supposition that $T \neq T_1$ is false, and hence T itself is a minimum spanning tree for G.

Prim's Algorithm

*Robert Prim
(born 1921)*

Courtesy of Alcatel-Lucent Technologies

Prim's algorithm works differently from Kruskal's. It builds a minimum spanning tree T by expanding outward in connected links from some vertex. One edge and one vertex are added at each stage. The edge added is the one of least weight that connects the vertices already in T with those not in T, and the vertex is the endpoint of this edge that is not already in T.

Algorithm 10.7.2

Input: *G [a connected weighted graph with n vertices where n is a positive integer]*

Algorithm Body:
[Build a subgraph T of G by starting with any vertex v of G and attaching edges (with their endpoints) one by one to an as-yet-unconnected vertex of G, each time choosing an edge of least weight that is adjacent to a vertex of T.]

1. Pick a vertex v of G and let T be the graph with one vertex, v, and no edges.

2. Let V be the set of all vertices of G except v.

3. **for** $i := 1$ **to** $n - 1$

    3a. Find an edge e of G such that (1) e connects T to one of the vertices in V, and (2) e has the least weight of all edges connecting T to a vertex in V. Let w be the endpoint of e that is in V.
    3b. Add e and w to the edge and vertex sets of T, and delete w from V.

    next i

Output: *T [T is a minimum spanning tree for G.]*

The following example shows how Prim's algorithm works for the graph of the airline route system.

Example 10.7.3 Action of Prim's Algorithm

Describe the action of Prim's algorithm for the graph in Figure 10.7.6 using the Minneapolis vertex as a starting point.

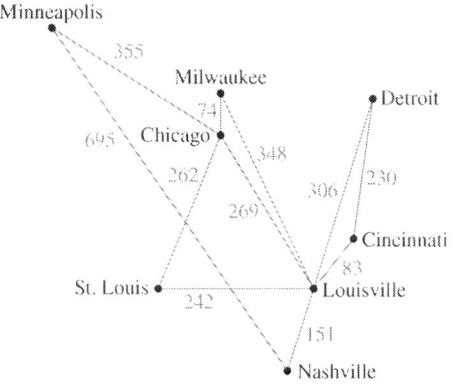

Figure 10.7.6

Solution

Iteration Number	Vertex Added	Edge Added	Weight
0	Minneapolis		
1	Chicago	Minneapolis–Chicago	355
2	Milwaukee	Chicago–Milwaukee	74
3	St. Louis	Chicago–St. Louis	262
4	Louisville	St. Louis–Louisville	242
5	Cincinnati	Louisville–Cincinnati	83
6	Nashville	Louisville–Nashville	151
7	Detroit	Cincinnati–Detroit	230

Note that the tree obtained is the same as that obtained by Kruskal's algorithm, but the edges are added in a different order.

As with Kruskal's algorithm, in order to ensure a unique output, the edges of the graph could be placed in an array and those with the same weight could be added in the order they appear in the array. It is not hard to see that when a connected graph is input to Prim's algorithm, the result is a spanning tree. What is not so clear is that this spanning tree is a minimum. The proof of the following theorem establishes that it is.

Theorem 10.7.3 Correctness of Prim's Algorithm

When a connected, weighted graph G is input to Prim's algorithm, the output is a minimum spanning tree for G.

Proof:

Let G be a connected, weighted graph, and suppose G is input to Prim's algorithm. At each stage of execution of the algorithm, an edge must be found that connects a vertex in a subgraph to a vertex outside the subgraph. As long as there are vertices outside the subgraph, the connectedness of G ensures that such an edge can always be found. *[For if one vertex in the subgraph and one vertex outside it are chosen, then by the connectedness of G there is a walk in G linking the two. As one travels along this walk, at some point one moves along an edge from a vertex inside the subgraph to a vertex outside the subgraph.]*

Now it is clear that the output T of Prim's algorithm is a tree because the edge and vertex added to T at each stage are connected to other edges and vertices of T

and because at no stage is a circuit created since each edge added connects vertices in two disconnected sets. *[Consequently, removal of a newly added edge produces a disconnected graph, whereas by Lemma 10.5.3, removal of an edge from a circuit produces a connected graph.]* Also, T includes every vertex of G because T, being a tree with $n - 1$ edges, has n vertices *[and that is all G has]*. Thus T is a spanning tree for G.

Next we show that T has minimum weight. Let T_1 be a minimum spanning tree for G such that the number of edges T_1 and T have in common is a maximum. Suppose that $T \neq T_1$. Then there is an edge e in T that is not an edge of T_1. *[Since trees T and T_1 both have the same vertex set if they differ at all, they must have different, same-size edge sets.]* Of all such edges, let e be the last that was added when T was constructed using Prim's algorithm. Let S be the set of vertices of T just before the addition of e. Then one endpoint, say v of e, is in S and the other, say w, is not. Since T_1 is a spanning tree, there is a path in T_1 joining v to w. And since $v \in S$ and $w \notin S$, as one travels along this path, one must encounter an edge e' that joins a vertex in S to one that is not in S and that therefore is not in T because e was the last edge added to T. Now at the stage when e was added to T, e' could also have been added and it *would* have been added instead of e had its weight been less than that of e. Since e' was not added at that stage, we conclude that

$$w(e') \geq w(e).$$

Let T_2 be the graph obtained from T_1 by removing e' and adding e. *[Thus T_2 has one more edge in common with T than T_1 does.]* Note that T_2 is a tree. The reason is that since e' is part of a path in T_1 from v to w, and e connects v and w, adding e to T_1 creates a circuit. When e' is removed from this circuit, the resulting subgraph remains connected. In fact, T_2 is a spanning tree for G since no vertices were removed in forming T_2 from T_1. The argument showing that $w(T_2) \leq w(T_1)$ is left as an exercise. *[It is virtually identical to part of the proof of Theorem 10.7.2.]* It follows that T_2 is a minimum spanning tree for G.

By construction, T_2 has one more edge in common with T than T_1, does which contradicts the choice of T_1 as a minimum spanning tree for G with a maximum number of edges in common with T. It follows that $T = T_1$, and hence T itself is a minimum spanning tree for G.

Example 10.7.4 Finding Minimum Spanning Trees

Find all minimum spanning trees for the following graph. Use Kruskal's algorithm and Prim's algorithm starting at vertex a. Indicate the order in which edges are added to form each tree.

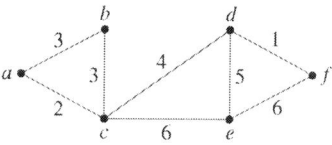

Solution   When Kruskal's algorithm is applied, edges are added in one of the following two orders:

1. $\{d, f\}, \{a, c\}, \{a, b\}, \{c, d\}, \{d, e\}$

2. $\{d, f\}, \{a, c\}, \{b, c\}, \{c, d\}, \{d, e\}$

When Prim's algorithm is applied starting at a, edges are added in one of the following two orders:

1. $\{a, c\}, \{a, b\}, \{c, d\}, \{d, f\}, \{d, e\}$

2. $\{a, c\}, \{b, c\}, \{c, d\}, \{d, f\}, \{d, e\}$

Thus, as shown below, there are two distinct minimum spanning trees for this graph.

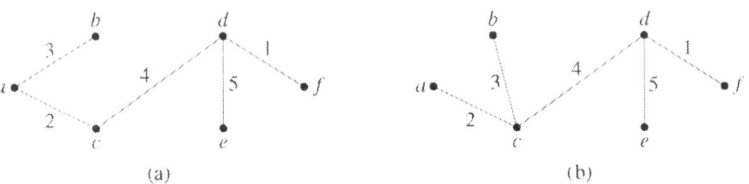

(a)   (b)

Dijkstra's Shortest Path Algorithm

Although the trees produced by Kruskal's and Prim's algorithms have the least possible total weight compared to all other spanning trees for the given graph, they do not always reveal the shortest distance between any two points on the graph. For instance, according to the complete route system shown in Figure 10.7.3, one can fly directly from Nashville to Minneapolis for a distance of 695 miles, whereas if you use the minimum spanning tree shown in Figure 10.7.5 the only way to fly from Nashville to Minneapolis is by going through Louisville, St. Louis, and Chicago, which gives a total distance of $151 + 242 + 262 + 355 = 1,010$ miles and the unpleasantness of three changes of plane.

In 1959 the computing pioneer, Edsgar Dijkstra (see Section 5.5), developed an algorithm to find the shortest path between a starting vertex and an ending vertex in a weighted graph in which all the weights are positive. It is somewhat similar to Prim's algorithm in that it works outward from a starting vertex a, adding vertices and edges one by one to construct a tree T. However, it differs from Prim's algorithm in the way it chooses the next vertex to add, ensuring that for each added vertex v, the length of the shortest path from a to v has been identified.

At the start of execution of the algorithm, each vertex u of G is given a label $L(u)$, which indicates the current best estimate of the length of the shortest path from a to u. $L(a)$ is initially set equal to 0 because the shortest path from a to a has length zero, but, because there is no previous information about the lengths of the shortest paths from a to any other vertices of G, the label $L(u)$ of each vertex u other than a is initially set equal to a number, denoted ∞, that is greater than the sum of the weights of all the edges of G. As execution of the algorithm progresses, the values of $L(u)$ are changed, eventually becoming the actual lengths of the shortest paths from a to u in G.

Because T is built up outward from a, at each stage of execution of the algorithm the only vertices that are candidates to join T are those that are adjacent to at least one vertex of T. Thus at each stage of Dijkstra's algorithm, the graph G can be thought of as divided into three parts: the tree T that is being built up, the set of "fringe" vertices that are adjacent to at least one vertex of the tree, and the rest of the vertices of G. Each fringe vertex is a candidate to be the next vertex added to T. The one that is chosen is the one for which the length of the shortest path to it from a through T is a minimum among all the vertices in the fringe.

An essential observation underlying Dijkstra's algorithm is that after each addition of a vertex v to T, the only fringe vertices for which a shorter path from a might be found are those that are adjacent to v *[because the length of the path from a to v was a minimum among all the paths from a to vertices in what was then the fringe]*. So after each addition of a vertex v to T, each fringe vertex u adjacent to v is examined and two numbers are compared: the current value of $L(u)$ and the value of $L(v) + w(v, u)$, where $L(v)$ is the length of the shortest path to v (in T) and $w(v, u)$ is the weight of the edge joining v and u. If $L(v) + w(v, u) < L(u)$, then the value of $L(u)$ is changed to $L(v) + w(v, u)$.

At the beginning of execution of the algorithm, the tree consists only of the vertex a, and $L(a) = 0$. When execution terminates, $L(z)$ is the length of a shortest path from a to z.

As with Kruskal's and Prim's algorithms for finding minimum spanning trees, there is a simple but dramatically inefficient way to find the shortest path from a to z: compute the lengths of all the paths and choose one that is shortest. The problem is that even for relatively small graphs using this method to find a shortest path could require billions of years, whereas Dijkstra's algorithm could do the job in a few seconds.

Algorithm 10.7.3 Dijkstra

Input: G *[a connected simple graph with a positive weight for every edge],* ∞ *[a number greater than the sum of the weights of all the edges in the graph],* $w(u, v)$ *[the weight of edge $\{u, v\}$],* a *[the starting vertex],* z *[the ending vertex]*

Algorithm Body:

1. Initialize T to be the graph with vertex a and no edges. Let $V(T)$ be the set of vertices of T, and let $E(T)$ be the set of edges of T.

2. Let $L(a) = 0$, and for all vertices in G except a, let $L(u) = \infty$.
   [The number $L(x)$ is called the label of x.]

3. Initialize v to equal a and F to be $\{a\}$.
   [The symbol v is used to denote the vertex most recently added to T.]

4. **while** ($z \notin V(T)$)

   4a. $F := (F - \{v\}) \cup \{$vertices that are adjacent to v and are not in $V(T)\}$
   [The set F is called the fringe. Each time a vertex is added to T, it is removed from the fringe and the vertices adjacent to it are added to the fringe if they are not already in the fringe or the tree T.]

   4b. For each vertex u that is adjacent to v and is not in $V(T)$,
   if $L(v) + w(v, u) < L(u)$ **then**

   $$L(u) := L(v) + w(v, u)$$

   $$D(u) := v$$

   [Note that adding v to T does not affect the labels of any vertices in the fringe F except those adjacent to v. Also, when $L(u)$ is changed to a smaller value, the notation $D(u)$ is introduced to keep track of which vertex in T gave rise to the smaller value.]

   Note The unique path in the tree T from a to z is the shortest path in G from a to z.

   4c. Find a vertex x in F with the smallest label
   Add vertex x to $V(T)$, and add edge $\{D(x), x\}$ to $E(T)$
   $v := x$ *[This statement sets up the notation for the next iteration of the loop.]*

   end while

Output: $L(z)$ *[$L(z)$, a nonnegative integer, is the length of the shortest path from a to z.]*

The action of Dijkstra's algorithm is illustrated by the flow of the drawings in Example 10.7.5.

Example 10.7.5 Action of Dijkstra's Algorithm

Show the steps in the execution of Dijkstra's shortest path algorithm for the graph shown below with starting vertex a and ending vertex z.

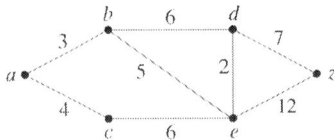

Solution

Step 1: Going into the **while** loop: $V(T) = \{a\}$, $E(T) = \emptyset$, and $F = \{a\}$

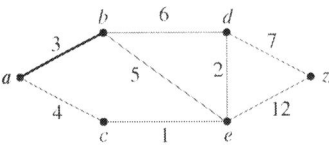

During iteration:
$F = \{b, c\}$, $L(b) = 3$, $L(c) = 4$.
Since $L(b) < L(c)$, b is added to
$V(T)$, $D(b) = a$, and $\{a, b\}$ is
added to $E(T)$.

Step 2: Going into the **while** loop: $V(T) = \{a, b\}$, $E(T) = \{\{a, b\}\}$

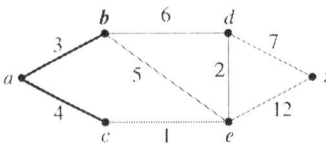

During iteration:
$F = \{c, d, e\}$, $L(c) = 4$, $L(d) = 9$,
$L(e) = 8$.
Since $L(c) < L(d)$ and $L(c) < L(e)$, c is
added to $V(T)$, $D(c) = a$, and $\{a, c\}$ is
added to $E(T)$.

Step 3: Going into the **while** loop: $V(T) = \{a, b, c\}$, $E(T) = \{\{a, b\}, \{a, c\}\}$

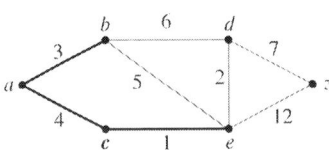

During iteration:
$F = \{d, e\}$, $L(d) = 9$, $L(e) = 5$
$L(e)$ becomes 5 because ace, which has
length 5, is a shorter path to e than abe,
which has length 8.
Since $L(e) < L(d)$, e is added to $V(T)$,
$D(e) = c$, and $\{c, e\}$ is added to $E(T)$.

Step 4: Going into the **while** loop: $V(T) = \{a, b, c, e\}$,
$E(T) = \{\{a, b\}, \{a, c\}, \{c, e\}\}$

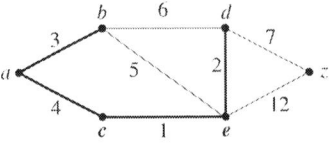

During iteration:
$F = \{d, z\}$, $L(d) = 7$, $L(z) = 17$
$L(d)$ becomes 7 because $aced$, which has
length 7, is a shorter path to d than abd,
which has length 9.
Since $L(d) < L(z)$, d is added to $V(T)$,
$D(d) = e$, and $\{e, d\}$ is added to $E(T)$.

Step 5: Going into the **while** loop: $V(T) = \{a, b, c, e, d\}$,
$E(T) = \{\{a, b\}, \{a, c\}, \{c, e\}, \{e, d\}\}$

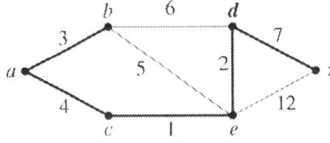

During iteration: $F = \{z\}$, $L(z) = 14$
$L(z)$ becomes 14 because $acedz$, which
has length 14, is a shorter path to d than
$abdz$, which has length 17.
Since z is the only vertex in F, its label is
a minimum, and so z is added to $V(T)$,
$D(z) = d$, and $\{d, z\}$ is added to $E(T)$.

Execution of the algorithm terminates at this point because $z \in V(T)$. The shortest path from a to z has length $L(z) = 14$. ■

Keeping track of the steps in a table is a convenient way to show the action of Dijkstra's algorithm. Table 10.7.1 does this for the graph in Example 10.7.5.

Table 10.7.1

Step	$V(T)$	$E(T)$	F	$L(a)$	$L(b)$	$L(c)$	$L(d)$	$L(e)$	$L(z)$
0	$\{a\}$	$\varnothing$	$\{a\}$	0	∞	∞	∞	∞	∞
1	$\{a\}$	$\varnothing$	$\{b, c\}$	0	3	4	∞	∞	∞
2	$\{a, b\}$	$\{\{a, b\}\}$	$\{c, d, e\}$	0	3	4	9	8	∞
3	$\{a, b, c\}$	$\{\{a, b\}, \{a, c\}\}$	$\{d, e\}$	0	3	4	9	5	∞
4	$\{a, b, c, e\}$	$\{\{a, b\}, \{a, c\}, \{c, e\}\}$	$\{d, z\}$	0	3	4	7	5	17
5	$\{a, b, c, e, d\}$	$\{\{a, b\}, \{a, c\}, \{c, e\}, \{e, d\}\}$	$\{z\}$	0	3	4	7	5	14
6	$\{a, b, c, e, d, z\}$	$\{\{a, b\}, \{a, c\}, \{c, e\}, \{e, d\}, \{e, z\}\}$							

It is clear that Dijkstra's algorithm keeps adding vertices to I until it has added z. The proof of the following theorem shows that when the algorithm terminates, the label z goes the length of the shortest path to it from a.

Theorem 10.7.4 Correctness of Dijkstra's Algorithm

When a connected, simple graph with a positive weight for every edge is input to Dijkstra's algorithm with starting vertex a and ending vertex z, the output is the length of a shortest path from a to z.

Proof:

Let G be a connected, weighted graph with no loops or parallel edges and with a positive weight for every edge. Let T be the graph built up by Dijkstra's algorithm, and for each vertex u in G, let $L(u)$ be the label given by the algorithm to vertex u. For each integer $n \geq 0$, let the property $P(n)$ be the sentence

> After the nth iteration of the while loop in Dijkstra's algorithm,
> (1) T is a tree, and (2) for every vertex v in T, $L(v)$ is the length of a shortest path in G from a to v. ← $P(n)$

We will show by mathematical induction that $P(n)$ is true for all integers n from 0 through the termination of the algorithm.

Show that P(0) is true: When $n = 0$, the graph T is a tree because it is defined to consist only of the vertex a and no edges. In addition, $L(a)$ is the length of the shortest path from a to a because the initial value of $L(a)$ is 0.

Show that for all integers k ≥ 0, if P(k) is true then P(k + 1) is also true: Let k be any integer with $k \geq 0$ and suppose that

> After the kth iteration of the while loop in Dijkstra's algorithm, (1) T ← $P(k)$
> is a tree, and (2) for every vertex v in T, $L(v)$ is the length of a   inductive
> shortest path in G from a to v.   hypothesis

We must show that

> After the $(k + 1)$st iteration of the **while** loop in Dijkstra's
> algorithm, (1) T is a tree, and (2) for every vertex v in T,   ← $P(k + 1)$
> $L(v)$ is the length of a shortest path in G from a to v.

continued on page 714

So suppose that after the $(k + 1)$st iteration of the **while** loop in Dikjstra's algorithm, the vertex v and edge $\{x, v\}$ have been added to T, where x is in $V(T)$. Clearly the new value of T is a tree because adding a new vertex and edge to a tree does not create a circuit and does not disconnect the tree. By inductive hypothesis for each vertex y in the tree before the addition of v, $L(y)$ is the length of a shortest path from a to y. So it remains only to show that $L(v)$ is the length of a shortest path from a to v.

Now, according to the algorithm, the final value of $L(v) = L(x) + w(x, v)$. Consider *any* shortest path from a to v, and let $\{s, t\}$ be the first edge in this path to leave T, where $s \in V(T)$ and $t \notin V(T)$. This situation is illustrated below.

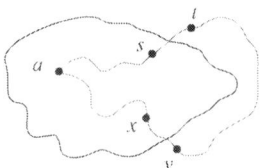

Let $LSP(a, v)$ be the length of a shortest path from a to v, and let $LSP(a, s)$ be the length of a shortest path from a to s. Observe that

$$LSP(a, v) \geq LSP(a, s) + w(s, t) \qquad \text{because the path from } t \text{ to } v \text{ has length} \geq 0$$

$$\geq L(s) + w(s, t) \qquad \text{by inductive hypothesis because } s \text{ is a vertex in } T$$

$$\geq L(x) + w(x, v) \qquad \begin{array}{l} t \text{ is in the fringe of the tree, and so if } L(s) + w(s, t) \\ \text{were less than } L(x) + w(x, v), \text{ then } t \text{ would have} \\ \text{been added to } T \text{ instead of } v. \end{array}$$

On the other hand

$$L(x) + w(x, v) \geq LSP(a, v) \qquad \begin{array}{l} \text{because } L(x) + w(x, v) \text{ is the length of a path from} \\ a \text{ to } v \text{ and so it is greater than or equal to the length} \\ \text{of the shortest path from } a \text{ to } v. \end{array}$$

It follows that $\qquad\qquad LSP(a, v) = L(x) + w(x, v),$

and, since $\qquad\qquad\qquad L(v) = L(x) + w(x, v),$

$L(v)$ is the length of a shortest path from a to v. This completes the proof by mathematical induction.

The algorithm terminates as soon as z is in T, and, since we have proved that the label of every vertex in the tree gives the length of the shortest path to it from a, then, in particular, $L(z)$ is the length of a shortest path from a to z.

Test Yourself

1. A spanning tree for a graph G is _____.

2. A weighted graph is a graph for which _____, and the total weight of the graph is _____.

3. A minimum spanning tree for a connected, weighted graph is _____.

4. In Kruskal's algorithm, the edges of a connected, weighted graph are examined one by one in order of _____ starting with _____.

5. In Prim's algorithm, a minimum spanning tree is built by expanding outward from an _____ in a sequence of _____.

6. In Dijkstra's algorithm, a vertex is in the fringe if it is _____ vertex in the tree that is being built up.

7. At each stage of Dijkstra's algorithm, the vertex that is added to the tree is a vertex in the fringe whose label is a _____.

Exercise Set 10.7

Find all possible spanning trees for each of the graphs in 1 and 2.

1.
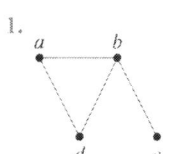

2.
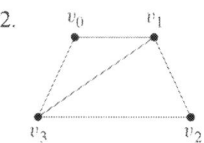

Find a spanning tree for each of the graphs in 3 and 4.

3.
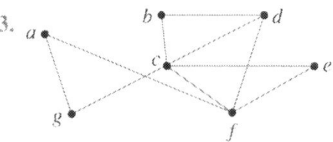

4.
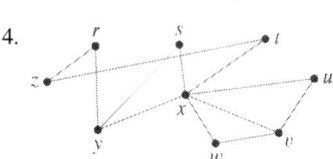

Use Kruskal's algorithm to find a minimum spanning tree for each of the graphs in 5 and 6. Indicate the order in which edges are added to form each tree.

5.
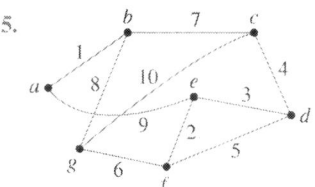

6.
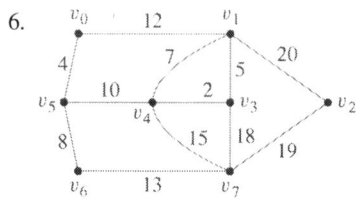

Use Prim's algorithm starting with vertex a or v_0 to find a minimum spanning tree for each of the graphs in 7 and 8. Indicate the order in which edges are added to form each tree.

7. The graph of exercise 5.   8. The graph of exercise 6.

For each of the graphs in 9 and 10, find all minimum spanning trees that can be obtained using (a) Kruskal's algorithm and (b) Prim's algorithm starting with vertex a or t. Indicate the order in which edges are added to form each tree.

9.
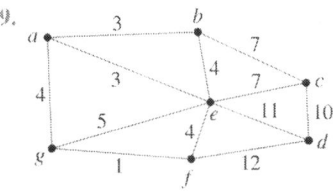

10.
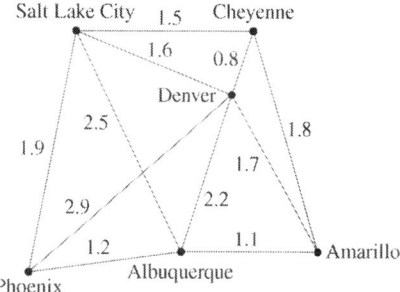

11. A pipeline is to be built that will link six cities. The cost (in hundreds of millions of dollars) of constructing each potential link depends on distance and terrain and is shown in the weighted graph below. Find a system of pipelines to connect all the cities and yet minimize the total cost.

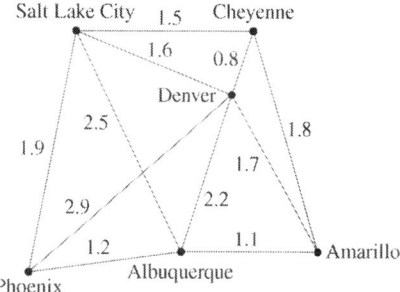

12. Use Dijkstra's algorithm for the airline route system of Figure 10.7.3 to find the shortest distance from Nashville to Minneapolis. Make a table similar to Table 10.7.1 to show the action of the algorithm.

Use Dijkstra's algorithm to find the shortest path from a to z for each of the graphs in 13–16. In each case make tables similar to Table 10.7.1 to show the action of the algorithm.

13.
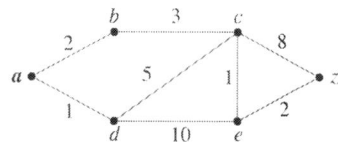

14.
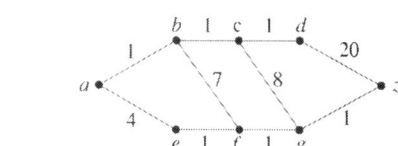

15. The graph of exercise 9 with $a = a$ and $z = f$

16. The graph of exercise 10 with $a = u$ and $z = w$

17. Prove part (2) of Proposition 10.7.1: Any two spanning trees for a graph have the same number of edges.

18. Given any two distinct vertices of a tree, there exists a unique path from one to the other.
    a. Give an informal justification for the above statement.
    ✳ b. Write a formal proof of the above statement.

19. Prove that if G is a graph with spanning tree T and e is an edge of G that is not in T, then the graph obtained by adding e to T contains one and only one set of edges that forms a circuit.

20. Suppose G is a connected graph and T is a circuit-free subgraph of G. Suppose also that if any edge e of G not in T is added to T, the resulting graph contains a circuit. Prove that T is a spanning tree for G.

21. a. Suppose T_1 and T_2 are two different spanning trees for a graph G. Must T_1 and T_2 have an edge in common? Prove or give a counterexample.
    b. Suppose that the graph G in part (a) is simple. Must T_1 and T_2 have an edge in common? Prove or give a counterexample.

H 22. Prove that an edge e is contained in every spanning tree for a connected graph G if, and only if, removal of e disconnects G.

23. Consider the spanning trees T_1 and T_2 in the proof of Theorem 10.7.3. Prove that $w(T_2) \leq w(T_1)$.

24. Suppose that T is a minimum spanning tree for a connected, weighted graph G and that G contains an edge e (not a loop) that is not in T. Let v and w be the endpoints of e. By exercise 18 there is a unique path in T from v to w. Let e' be any edge of this path. Prove that $w(e') \leq w(e)$.

H 25. Prove that if G is a connected, weighted graph and e is an edge of G (not a loop) that has smaller weight than any other edge of G, then e is in every minimum spanning tree for G.

✳ 26. If G is a connected, weighted graph and no two edges of G have the same weight, does there exist a unique minimum spanning tree for G? Use the result of exercise 19 to help justify your answer.

✳ 27. Prove that if G is a connected, weighted graph and e is an edge of G that (1) has greater weight than any other edge of G and (2) is in a circuit of G, then there is no minimum spanning tree T for G such that e is in T.

28. Suppose a disconnected graph is input to Kruskal's algorithm. What will be the output?

29. Suppose a disconnected graph is input to Prim's algorithm. What will be the output?

30. Prove that if a connected, weighted graph G is input to Algorithm 10.7.4 (shown below), the output is a minimum spanning tree for G.

Algorithm 10.7.4

Input: G [a connected graph]

Algorithm Body:

1. $T := G$.

2. $E :=$ the set of all edges of G, $m :=$ the number of edges of G.

3. while $(m > 0)$

    3a. Find an edge e in E that has maximal weight.
    3b. Remove e from E and set $m := m - 1$.
    3c. if the subgraph obtained when e is removed from the edge set of T is connected **then** remove e from the edge set of T

    end while

Output: T [a minimum spanning tree for G]

---

31. Modify Algorithm 10.7.3 so that the output consists of the sequence of edges in the shortest path from a to z.

Answers for Test Yourself

1. a subgraph of G that contains every vertex of G and is a tree.   2. each edge has an associated positive real number weight; the sum of the weights of all the edges of the graph   3. a spanning tree that has the least possible total weight compared to all other spanning trees for the graph   4. weight; an edge of least weight   5. initial vertex; adjacent vertices and edges   6. adjacent to a 7. minimum among all those in the fringe

CHAPTER 11

ANALYSIS OF ALGORITHM EFFICIENCY

René Descartes
(1596–1650)

In 1637 the French mathematician and philosopher René Descartes published his great philosophical work *Discourse on Method*. An appendix to this work, called "Geometry," laid the foundation for the subject of analytic geometry, in which geometric methods are applied to the study of algebraic objects, such as functions, equations, and inequalities, and algebraic methods are used to study geometric objects, such as straight lines, circles, and half-planes.

The analytic geometry of Descartes provides the foundation for the main topic of this chapter: the big-*O*, big-Omega, and big-Theta notations and their application to the analysis of algorithms. In Section 11.1 we briefly discuss certain properties of graphs of real-valued functions of a real variable that are needed to understand these notations. In Section 11.2 we define the notations and apply them to power and polynomial functions, and in Section 11.3 we show how the notations are used to study the efficiency of algorithms. Because the analysis of algorithms often involves logarithmic and exponential functions, we develop the needed properties of these functions in Section 11.4 and use them to analyze several algorithms in Section 11.5.

11.1 Real-Valued Functions of a Real Variable and Their Graphs

The first precept was never to accept a thing as true until I knew it as such without a single doubt — René Descartes, 1637

A **Cartesian plane** or **two-dimensional Cartesian coordinate system** is a pictorial representation of **R** × **R** obtained by setting up a one-to-one correspondence between ordered pairs of real numbers and points in a Euclidean plane. To obtain it, two perpendicular lines, called the **horizontal** and **vertical axes,** are drawn in the plane. Their point of intersection is called the **origin,** and a unit of distance is chosen for each axis. An ordered pair (x, y) of real numbers corresponds to the point P that lies $|x|$ units to the right or left of the vertical axis and $|y|$ units above or below the horizontal axis. On each axis the positive direction is marked with an arrow.

A **real-valued function of a real variable** is a function from one set of real numbers to another. If f is such a function, then for each real number x in the domain of f, there is a unique corresponding real number $f(x)$. Thus it is possible to define the *graph of f* as follows:

• Definition

Let f be a real-valued function of a real variable. The **graph of** f is the set of all points (x, y) in the Cartesian coordinate plane with the property that x is in the domain of f and $y = f(x)$.

The definition of graph (see Figure 11.1.1) means that for all x in the domain of f:

$$y = f(x) \quad \Leftrightarrow \quad \text{the point } (x, y) \text{ lies on the graph of } f.$$

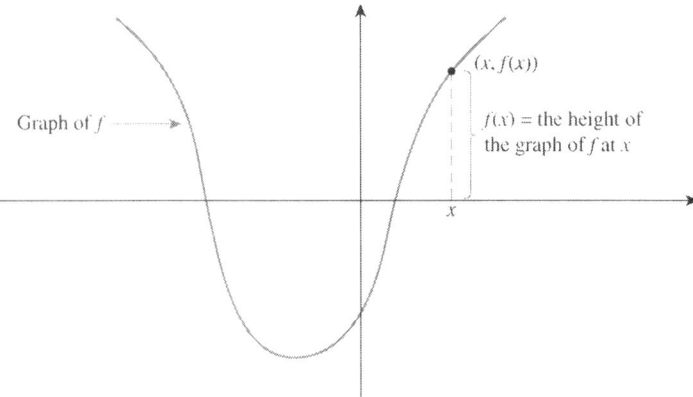

Figure 11.1.1 **Graph of a Function f**

Note that if $f(x)$ can be written as an algebraic expression in x, the graph of the function f is the same as the graph of the equation $y = f(x)$ where x is restricted to lie in the domain of f.

Power Functions

A function that sends a real number x to a particular power, x^a, is called a *power function*. For applications in computer science, we are almost invariably concerned with situations where x and a are nonnegative, and so we restrict our definition to these cases.

> **• Definition**
>
> Let a be any nonnegative real number. Define p_a, the **power function with exponent a**, as follows:
>
> $$p_a(x) = x^a \quad \text{for each nonnegative real number } x.$$

Example 11.1.1 Graphs of Power Functions

Plot the graphs of the power functions p_0, $p_{1/2}$, p_1, and p_2 on the same coordinate axes.

Solution   Because the power function with exponent zero satisfies $p_0(x) = x^0 = 1$ for all nonnegative numbers x,* all points of the form $(x, 1)$ lie on the graph of p_0 for all such x. So the graph is just a horizontal half-line of height 1 lying above the horizontal axis. Similarly, $p_1(x) = x$ for all nonnegative numbers x, and so the graph of p_1 consists of all points of the form (x, x) where x is nonnegative. The graph is therefore the half-line of slope 1 that emanates from $(0, 0)$.

Since for each nonnegative number x, $p_{1/2}(x) = x^{1/2} = \sqrt{x}$, any point with coordinates $(x, \sqrt{x})$, where x is nonnegative, is on the graph of $p_{1/2}$. For instance, the graph of

---

*As in Section 9.7 (see page 598), for simplicity we define $0^0 = 1$.

$p_{1/2}$ contains the points $(0, 0)$, $(1, 1)$, $(4, 2)$, and $(9, 3)$. Similarly, since $p_2(x) = x^2$, any point with coordinates (x, x^2) lies on the graph of p_2. Thus, for instance, the graph of p_2 contains the points $(0, 0)$, $(1, 1)$, $(2, 4)$, and $(3, 9)$.

The graphs of all four functions are shown in Figure 11.1.2.

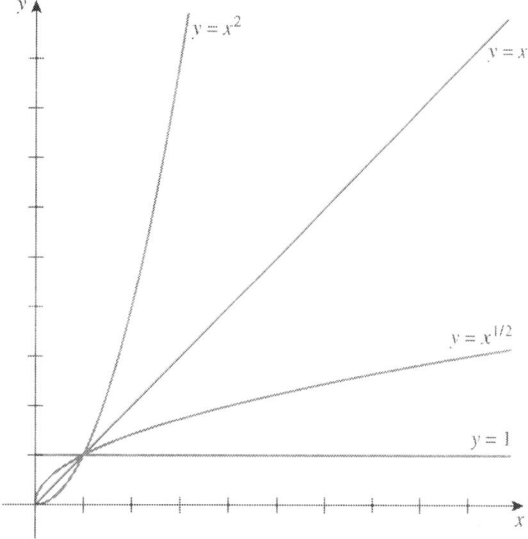

Figure 11.1.2 **Graphs of Some Power Functions**

The Floor Function

The floor and ceiling functions arise in many computer science contexts. Example 11.1.2 illustrates the graph of the floor function. In exercise 6 at the end of this section you are asked to draw the graph of the ceiling function.

Example 11.1.2 Graph of the Floor Function

Recall that each real number either is an integer itself or sits between two consecutive integers: For each real number x, there exists a unique integer n such that $n \leq x < n + 1$. The floor of a number is the integer immediately to its left on the number line. More formally, the floor function F is defined by the rule

For each real number x,

$$F(x) = \lfloor x \rfloor$$
$$= \text{the greatest integer that is less than or equal to } x$$
$$= \text{the unique integer } n \text{ such that } n \leq x < n + 1.$$

Graph the floor function.

Solution   If n is any integer, then for each real number x in the interval $n \leq x < n + 1$, the floor of x, $\lfloor x \rfloor$, equals n. Thus on each such interval, the graph of the floor function is horizontal; for each x in the interval, the height of the graph is n.

It follows that the graph of the floor function consists of horizontal line segments, like a staircase, as shown in Figure 11.1.3. The open circles at the right-hand edge of each step are used to show that those points are *not* on the graph.

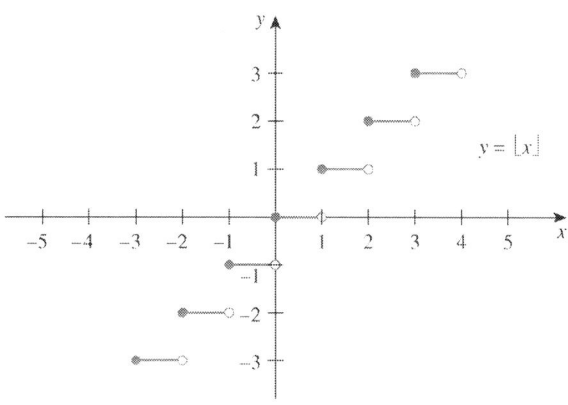

Figure 11.1.3 **Graph of the Floor Function**

Graphing Functions Defined on Sets of Integers

Many real-valued functions used in computer science are defined on sets of integers and not on intervals of real numbers. Suppose you know what the graph of a function looks like when it is given by a certain formula on an interval of real numbers. You can obtain the graph of the function defined by the same formula on the integers in the interval by selecting out only those points on the known graph with integers as their first coordinates. For instance, if f is the function defined by the same formula as the power function p_1 but having as its domain the set of nonnegative integers, then $f(n) = n$ for all nonnegative integers n. The graphs of p_1, reproduced from Example 11.1.2, and f are shown side-by-side below.

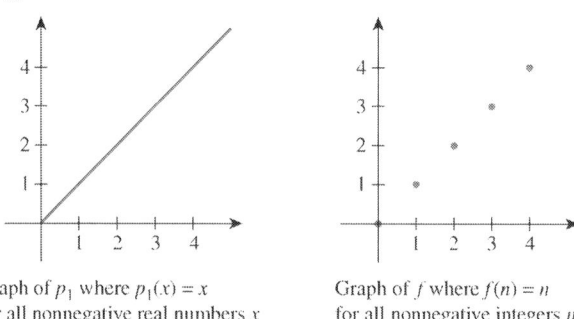

Graph of p_1 where $p_1(x) = x$
for all nonnegative real numbers x

Graph of f where $f(n) = n$
for all nonnegative integers n

Example 11.1.3 Graph of a Function Defined on a Set of Integers

Consider an integer version of the power function $p_{1/2}$. In other words, define a function g by the formula $g(n) = n^{1/2}$ for all nonnegative integers n. Draw the graph of g.

Solution   Look back at the graph of $p_{1/2}$ in Figure 11.1.2. Draw the graph of g by reproducing only those points on the graph of $p_{1/2}$ with integer first coordinates. Thus for each nonnegative integer n, the point $(n, n^{1/2})$ is on the graph of g.

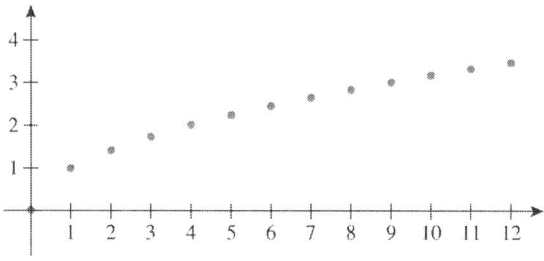

Graph of g where $g(n) = n^{1/2}$ for all nonnegative integers n

Graph of a Multiple of a Function

A *multiple* of a function is obtained by multiplying every value of the function by a fixed number. To understand the concept of O-notation, it is helpful to understand the relation between the graph of a function and the graph of a multiple of the function.

> **• Definition**
>
> Let f be a real-valued function of a real variable and let M be any real number. The function Mf, called the **multiple of f by M or M times f**, is the real-valued function with the same domain as f that is defined by the rule
>
> $$(Mf)(x) = M \cdot (f(x)) \quad \text{for all } x \in \text{domain of } f.$$

If the graph of a function is known, the graph of any multiple can easily be deduced. Specifically, if f is a function and M is a real number, the height of the graph of Mf at any real number x is M times the quantity $f(x)$. To sketch the graph of Mf from the graph of f, you plot the heights $M \cdot (f(x))$ on the basis of knowledge of M and visual inspection of the heights $f(x)$.

Example 11.1.4 Graph of a Multiple of a Function

Let f be the function whose graph is shown below. Sketch the graph of $2f$.

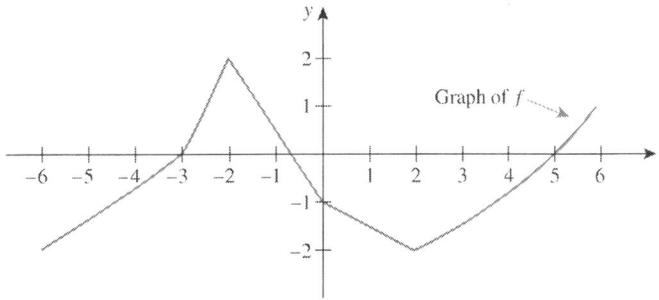

Solution   At each real number x, you obtain the height of the graph of $2f$ by measuring the height of the graph of f at x and multiplying that number by 2. The result is the following graph. Note that the general shapes of f and $2f$ are very similar, but the graph of $2f$ is "stretched out": the "highs" are twice as high and the "lows" are twice as low.

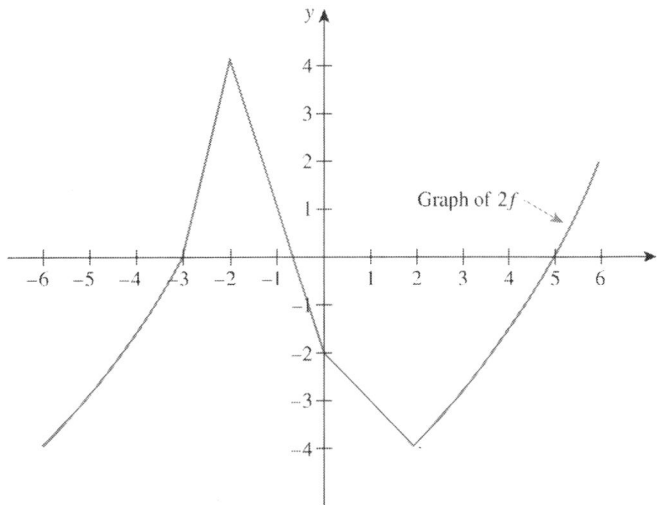

Increasing and Decreasing Functions

Consider the *absolute value function, A,* which is defined as follows:

$$A(x) = |x| = \begin{cases} x & \text{if } x \geq 0 \\ -x & \text{if } x < 0 \end{cases} \quad \text{for all real numbers } x.$$

When $x \geq 0$, the graph of A is the same as the graph of $y = x$, the straight line with slope 1 that passes through the origin $(0, 0)$. For $x < 0$, the graph of A is the same as the graph of $y = -x$, which is the straight line with slope -1 that passes through $(0, 0)$. (See Figure 11.1.4.)

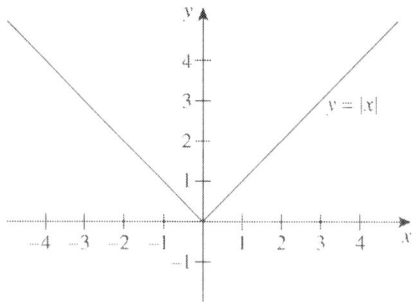

Figure 11.1.4 **Graph of the Absolute Value Function**

Note that as you trace from left to right along the graph to the left of the origin, the height of the graph continually *decreases*. For this reason, the absolute value function is said to be *decreasing* on the set of real numbers less than 0. On the other hand, as you trace from left to right along the graph to the right of the origin, the height of the graph continually *increases*. Consequently, the absolute value function is said to be *increasing* on the set of real numbers greater than 0.

Since the height of the graph of a function f at a point x is $f(x)$, these geometric concepts translate to the following analytic definition.

• **Definition**

Let f be a real-valued function defined on a set of real numbers, and suppose the domain of f contains a set S. We say that f is **increasing on the set S** if, and only if,

for all real numbers x_1 and x_2 in S, if $x_1 < x_2$ then $f(x_1) < f(x_2)$.

We say that f is **decreasing on the set S** if, and only if,

for all real numbers x_1 and x_2 in S, if $x_1 < x_2$ then $f(x_1) > f(x_2)$.

We say that f is an **increasing** (or **decreasing**) **function** if, and only if, f is increasing (or decreasing) on its entire domain.

Figure 11.1.5 illustrates the analytic definitions of increasing and decreasing.

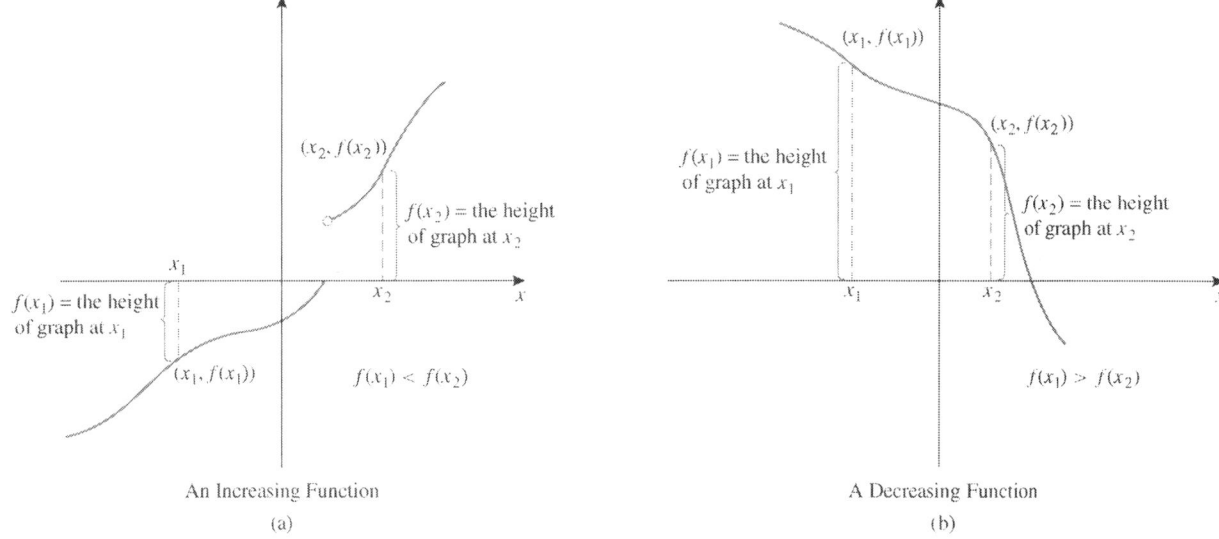

Figure 11.1.5

It follows almost immediately from the definitions that both increasing functions and decreasing functions are one-to-one. You are asked to show this in the exercises.

Example 11.1.5 A Positive Multiple of an Increasing Function Is Increasing

Suppose that f is a real-valued function of a real variable that is increasing on a set S of real numbers, and suppose M is any positive real number. Show that Mf is also increasing on S.

Solution Suppose x_1 and x_2 are particular but arbitrarily chosen elements of S such that

$$x_1 < x_2.$$

[We must show that $(Mf)(x_1) < (Mf)(x_2)$.] From the facts that $x_1 < x_2$ and f is increasing, it follows that

$$f(x_1) < f(x_2).$$

Then

$$Mf(x_1) < Mf(x_2),$$

since multiplying both sides of the inequality by a positive number does not change the direction of the inequality. Hence, by definition of Mf,

$$(Mf)(x_1) < (Mf)(x_2),$$

and, consequently, Mf is increasing on S. ■

It is also true that a positive multiple of a decreasing function is decreasing, that a negative multiple of a increasing function is decreasing, and that a negative multiple of a decreasing function is increasing. The proofs of these facts are left to the exercises.

Test Yourself

Answers to Test Yourself questions are located at the end of each section.

1. If f is a real-valued function of a real variable, then the domain and co-domain of f are both _____.

2. A point (x, y) lies on the graph of a real-valued function of a real variable f if, and only if, _____.

3. If a is any nonnegative real number, then the power function with exponent a, p_a, is defined by _____.

4. Given a function $f : \mathbf{R} \to \mathbf{R}$ and a real number M, the function Mf is defined by _____.

Exercise Set 11.1*

1. The graph of a function f is shown below.
   a. Is $f(0)$ positive or negative?
   b. For what values of x does $f(x) = 0$?
   c. Find approximate values for x_1 and x_2 so that $f(x_1) = f(x_2) = 1$ but $x_1 \neq x_2$.
   d. Find an approximate value for x such that $f(x) = 1.5$.
   e. As x increases from -3 to -1, do the values of f increase or decrease?
   f. As x increases from 0 to 4, do the values of f increase or decrease?

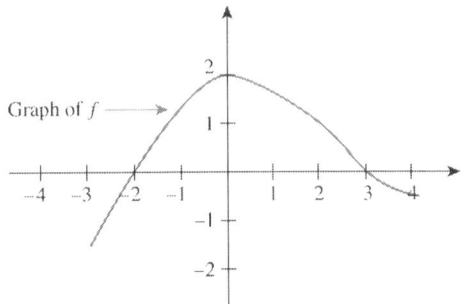

2. The graph of a function g is shown below.
   a. Is $g(0)$ positive or negative?
   b. Find an approximate value of x so that $g(x) = 0$.
   c. Find approximate values for x_1 and x_2 so that $g(x_1) = g(x_2) = 1$ but $x_1 \neq x_2$.
   d. Find an approximate value for x such that $g(x) = -2$.
   e. As x increases from -2 to 1, do the values of g increase or decrease?
   f. As x increases from 1 to 3, do the values of g increase or decrease?

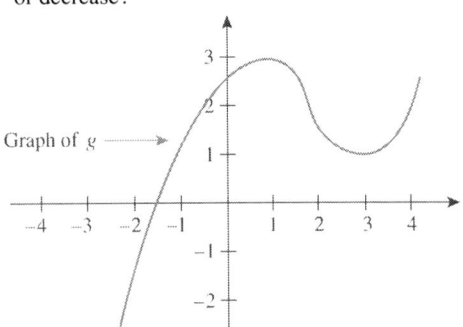

3. Draw the graphs of the power functions $p_{1/3}$ and $p_{1/4}$ on the same set of axes. When $0 < x < 1$, which is greater: $x^{1/3}$ or $x^{1/4}$? When $x > 1$, which is greater: $x^{1/3}$ or $x^{1/4}$?

4. Draw the graphs of the power functions p_3 and p_4 on the same set of axes. When $0 < x < 1$, which is greater: x^3 or x^4? When $x > 1$, which is greater: x^3 or x^4?

5. Draw the graphs of $y = 2\lfloor x \rfloor$ and $y = \lfloor 2x \rfloor$ for all real numbers x. What can you conclude from these graphs?

Graph each of the functions defined in 6–9 below.

6. $g(x) = \lceil x \rceil$ for all real numbers x (Recall that the ceiling of x, $\lceil x \rceil$, is the least integer that is greater than or equal to x. That is, $\lceil x \rceil$ = the unique integer n such that $n - 1 < x \leq n$.)

7. $h(x) = \lceil x \rceil - \lfloor x \rfloor$ for all real numbers x

8. $F(x) = \lfloor x^{1/2} \rfloor$ for all real numbers x

9. $G(x) = x - \lfloor x \rfloor$ for all real numbers x

In each of 10–13 a function is defined on a set of integers. Graph each function.

10. $f(n) = |n|$ for each integer n

11. $g(n) = (n/2) + 1$ for each integer n

12. $h(n) = \lfloor n/2 \rfloor$ for each integer $n \geq 0$

13. $k(n) = \lfloor n^{1/2} \rfloor$ for each integer $n \geq 0$

14. The graph of a function f is shown below. Find the intervals on which f is increasing and the intervals on which f is decreasing.

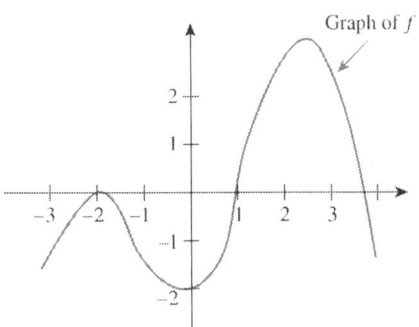

15. Show that the function $f : \mathbf{R} \to \mathbf{R}$ defined by the formula $f(x) = 2x - 3$ is increasing on the set of all real numbers.

16. Show that the function $g : \mathbf{R} \to \mathbf{R}$ defined by the formula $g(x) = -(x/3) + 1$ is decreasing on the set of all real numbers.

5. Given a function $f : \mathbf{R} \to \mathbf{R}$, to prove that f is increasing, you suppose that _____ and then you show that _____.

6. Given a function $f : \mathbf{R} \to \mathbf{R}$, to prove that f is decreasing, you suppose that _____ and then you show that _____.

---

*For exercises with blue numbers or letters, solutions are given in Appendix B. The symbol H indicates that only a hint or a partial solution is given. The symbol $*$ signals that an exercise is more challenging than usual.

17. Let *h* be the function from **R** to **R** defined by the formula $h(x) = x^2$ for all real numbers *x*.
    a. Show that *h* is decreasing on the set of all real numbers less than zero.
    b. Show that *h* is increasing on the set of all real numbers greater than zero.

18. Let $k: \mathbf{R} \to \mathbf{R}$ be the function defined by the formula $k(x) = (x - 1)/x$ for all real numbers $x \neq 0$.
    a. Show that *k* is increasing for all real numbers $x > 0$.
    b. Is *k* increasing or decreasing for $x < 0$? Prove your answer.

19. Show that if a function $f: \mathbf{R} \to \mathbf{R}$ is increasing, then *f* is one-to-one.

20. Given real-valued functions *f* and *g* with the same domain *D*, the sum of *f* and *g*, denoted $f + g$, is defined as follows:

    For all real numbers x, $(f + g)(x) = f(x) + g(x)$.

    Show that if *f* and *g* are both increasing on a set *S*, then $f + g$ is also increasing on *S*.

21. a. Let *m* be any positive integer, and define $f(x) = x^m$ for all nonnegative real numbers *x*. Use the binomial theorem to show that *f* is an increasing function.
    b. Let *m* and *n* be any positive integers, and let $g(x) = x^{m/n}$ for all nonnegative real numbers *x*. Prove that *g* is an increasing function.
    The results of this exercise are used in the exercises for Sections 11.2 and 11.4.

22. Let *f* be the function whose graph is shown below. Draw the graph of $3f$.

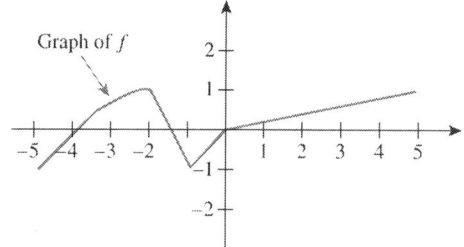

23. Let *h* be the function whose graph is shown below. Draw the graph of $2h$.

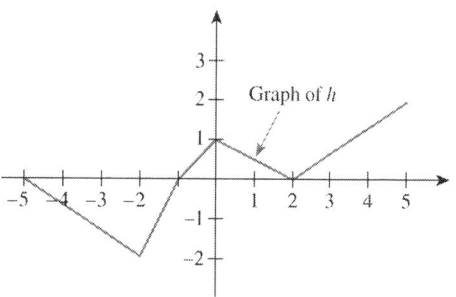

24. Let *f* be a real-valued function of a real variable. Show that if *f* is decreasing on a set *S* and if *M* is any positive real number, then *Mf* is decreasing on *S*.

25. Let *f* be a real-valued function of a real variable. Show that if *f* is decreasing on a set *S* and if *M* is any negative real number, then *Mf* is increasing on *S*.

26. Let *f* be a real-valued function of a real variable. Show that if *f* is increasing on a set *S* and if *M* is any negative real number, then *Mf* is decreasing on *S*.

In 27 and 28, functions *f* and *g* are defined. In each case draw the graphs of *f* and 2*g* on the same set of axes and find a number x_0 so that $f(x) \leq 2g(x)$ for all $x > x_0$. You can find an exact value for x_0 by solving a quadratic equation, or you can find an approximate value for x_0 by using a graphing calculator.

27. $f(x) = x^2 + 10x + 11$ and $g(x) = x^2$ for all real numbers $x \geq 0$

28. $f(x) = x^2 + 125x + 254$ and $g(x) = x^2$ for all real numbers $x \geq 0$

Answers for Test Yourself

1. sets of real numbers   2. $y = f(x)$ 3. $p_a(x) = x^a$ for all real numbers x 4. $(Mf)(x) = M \cdot f(x)$ for $x \in \mathbf{R}$ 5. x_1 and x_2 are any real numbers such that $x_1 < x_2$; $f(x_1) < f(x_2)$ 6. x_1 and x_2 are any real numbers such that $x_1 < x_2$; $f(x_1) > f(x_2)$

11.2 *O*-, Ω-, and Θ-Notations

Although this may seem a paradox, all exact science is dominated by the idea of approximation. — Bertrand Russell, 1872–1970

It often happens that any one of several algorithms could be used to do a certain job but the time or memory space they require varies dramatically. The *O*-, Ω-, and Θ-notations provide approximations that make it easy to evaluate large-scale differences in algorithm efficiency, while ignoring differences of a constant factor and differences that occur only for small sets of input data.

The oldest of the notations, O-notation (read "big-O notation"), was introduced by the German mathematician Paul Bachmann in 1894 in a book on analytic number theory. Both the Ω- (read "big-Omega") and Θ- (read "big-Theta") notations were developed by Donald Knuth, one of the pioneers of the science of computer programming.

The idea of the notations is this. Suppose f and g are real-valued functions of a real variable x.

1. If, for sufficiently large values of x, the values of $|f|$ are less than those of a multiple of $|g|$, then f is of order *at most g*, or $f(x)$ is $O(g(x))$.

2. If, for sufficiently large values of x, the values of $|f|$ are greater than those of a multiple of $|g|$, then f is of order *at least g*, or $f(x)$ is $\Omega(g(x))$.

3. If, for sufficiently large values of x, the values of $|f|$ are bounded both above and below by those of multiples of $|g|$, then f is of order g, or $f(x)$ is $\Theta(g(x))$.

These relationships are illustrated in Figure 11.2.1.

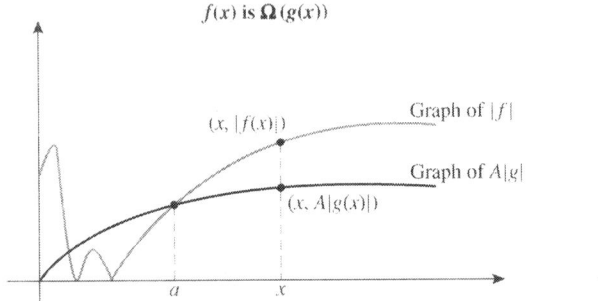

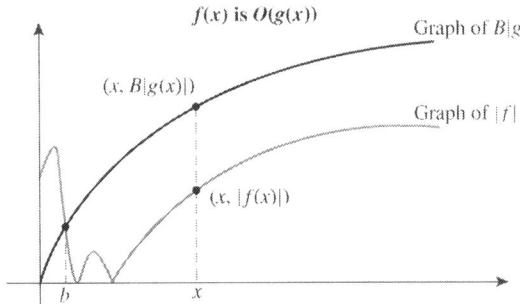

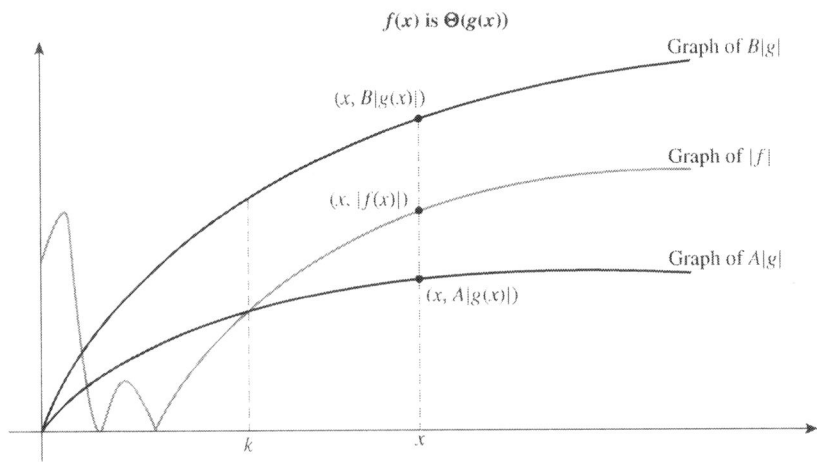

Figure 11.2.1

> ● **Definition**
>
> Let f and g be real-valued functions defined on the same set of non
> numbers. Then
>
> 1. **f is of order at least g,** written $f(x)$ is $\Omega(g(x))$, if, and only if, there exist a positive real number A and a nonnegative real number a such that
> $$A|g(x)| \le |f(x)| \quad \text{for all real numbers } x > a.$$
>
> 2. **f is of order at most g,** written $f(x)$ is $O(g(x))$, if, and only if, there exist a positive real number B and a nonnegative real number b such that
> $$|f(x)| \le B|g(x)| \quad \text{for all real numbers } x > b.$$
>
> 3. **f is of order g,** written $f(x)$ is $\Theta(g(x))$, if, and only if, there exist a positive real number A, B, and a nonnegative real number k such that
> $$A|g(x)| \le |f(x)| \le B|g(x)| \quad \text{for all real numbers } x > k.$$

Remark on Notation: In Section 7.1 we stated that we would generally make a careful distinction between a function f and its value $f(x)$. The traditional use of the order notation violates this general rule. For instance, in the statement "$f(x)$ is $\Theta(g(x))$," the symbols $f(x)$ and $g(x)$ are understood to refer to the functions f and g defined by the expressions $f(x)$ and $g(x)$, respectively. Thus the statement

$$3\sqrt{x} + 4 \text{ is } \Theta(x^{1/2})$$

means that f is of order g where f and g are defined by $f(x) = 3\sqrt{x} + 4$ and $g(x) = x^{1/2}$ with some common domain (usually the largest set of nonnegative real numbers for which both function formulas are defined).

Example 11.2.1 Translating to Θ-Notation

Use Θ-notation to express the statement

$$10|x^6| \le |17x^6 - 45x^3 + 2x + 8| \le 30|x^6| \quad \text{for all real numbers } x > 2.$$

Solution   Let $A = 10$, $B = 30$, and $k = 2$. Then the statement translates to

$$A|x^6| \le |17x^6 - 45x^3 + 2x + 8| \le B|x^6| \quad \text{for all real numbers } x > k.$$

So, by definition of Θ-notation,

$$17x^6 - 45x^3 + 2x + 8 \text{ is } \Theta(x^6). \quad \blacksquare$$

Example 11.2.2 Translating to O- and Ω-Notations

a. Use Ω and O notations to express the statements

(i) $15|\sqrt{x}| \le \left| \dfrac{15\sqrt{x}(2x+9)}{x+1} \right| \quad \text{for all real numbers } x > 0.$

(ii) $\left| \dfrac{15\sqrt{x}(2x+9)}{x+1} \right| \le 45|\sqrt{x}| \quad \text{for all real numbers } x > 7.$

b. Justify the statement: $\dfrac{15\sqrt{x}(2x+9)}{x+1}$ is $\Theta\left(\sqrt{x}\right).$

Solution

a. (i) Let $A = 15$ and $a = 0$. The given statement translates to

$$A|\sqrt{x}| \leq \left| \frac{15\sqrt{x}(2x+9)}{x+1} \right| \quad \text{for all real numbers } x > a.$$

So by definition of Ω-notation,

$$\frac{15\sqrt{x}(2x+9)}{x+1} \quad \text{is } \Omega(\sqrt{x}).$$

(ii) Let $B = 45$ and $b = 7$. The given statement translates to

$$\left| \frac{15\sqrt{x}(2x+9)}{x+1} \right| \leq B|\sqrt{x}| \quad \text{for all real numbers } x > b$$

So by definition of O-notation,

$$\frac{15\sqrt{x}(2x+9)}{x+1} \quad \text{is } O(\sqrt{x}).$$

b. Let $A = 15$, $B = 45$, and let k be the larger of 0 and 7. Then when $x > k$, both inequalities in a(i) and a(ii) are satisfied, and so

$$A|\sqrt{x}| \leq \left| \frac{15\sqrt{x}(2x+9)}{x+1} \right| \leq B|\sqrt{x}| \quad \text{for all real numbers } x > k.$$

Hence by definition of Θ-notation, $\dfrac{15\sqrt{x}(2x+9)}{x+1}$ is $\Theta(\sqrt{x})$. ■

Part (b) of Example 11.2.2 illustrates the fact that if you know both that f is of order at most g and that f is of order at least g, then you may take k to be the larger of the numbers a and b promised in the definitions for big-Omega and big-O and conclude that f is of order g. Conversely, if f is of order g, then both a and b may be taken to be the number k promised in the definition for big-Theta to show that f is of order at most g and f is of order at least g. These results, and a transitive property of order, are stated formally in the following theorem. Additional useful properties of the notations are included in the exercises at the end of the section.

Theorem 11.2.1 Properties of O-, Ω-, and Θ-Notations

Let f and g be real-valued functions defined on the same set of nonnegative real numbers.

1. $f(x)$ is $\Omega(g(x))$ and $f(x)$ is $O(g(x))$ if, and only if $f(x)$ is $\Theta(g(x))$.

2. $f(x)$ is $\Omega(g(x))$ if, and only if, $g(x)$ is $O(f(x))$.

3. If $f(x)$ is $O(g(x))$ and $g(x)$ is $O(h(x))$, then $f(x)$ is $O(h(x))$.

Proof:

1. The proof of this property was given before the statement of the theorem.

2. We first show that if $f(x)$ is $\Omega(g(x))$, then $g(x)$ is $O(f(x))$. Thus, suppose $f(x)$ is $\Omega(g(x))$. By definition of Ω-notation, there exist a positive real number A and a nonnegative real number a such that

$$A|g(x)| \leq |f(x)| \quad \text{for all real numbers } x > a.$$

Divide both sides by A to obtain

$$|g(x)| \leq \frac{1}{A}|f(x)| \quad \text{for all real numbers } x > a$$

Let $B = 1/A$ and $b = a$. Then B is a positive real number and b is a nonnegative real number, and

$$|g(x)| \leq B|f(x)| \quad \text{for all real numbers } x > b,$$

and so $g(x)$ is $O(f(x))$ by definition of O-notation.

The proof that if $g(x)$ is $O(f(x))$ then $f(x)$ is $\Omega(g(x))$ is left as exercise 10 at the end of the section.

3. Suppose $f(x)$ is $O(g(x))$ and $g(x)$ is $O(h(x))$. By definition of O-notation, there exist positive real numbers B_1 and B_2, and nonnegative real numbers b_1 and b_2 such that

$$|f(x)| \leq B_1|g(x)| \quad \text{for all real numbers } x > b_1,$$

and

$$|g(x)| \leq B_2|h(x)| \quad \text{for all real numbers } x > b_2.$$

Let $B = B_1 B_2$, and let b be the greater of b_1 and b_2. Then if $x > b$,

$$|f(x)| \leq B_1|g(x)| \leq B_1(B_2|h(x)|) \leq B|h(x)|.$$

Thus, by definition of O-notation, $f(x)$ is $O(h(x))$.

Orders of Power Functions

Observe that if $\qquad 1 < x,$

then $\qquad x < x^2 \quad$ multiplying both sides by x (which is positive)

and so $\qquad x^2 < x^3 \quad$ multiplying again by x.

Thus if $1 < x$, then $\qquad 1 < x < x^2 < x^3.$

The following generalization of this result is developed in exercises 15 and 50 at the end of this section.

For any rational numbers r and s,

$$\text{if } x > 1 \text{ and } r < s, \text{ then } x^r < x^s. \qquad (11.2.1)$$

Property (11.2.1) has the following consequence for orders.

For any rational numbers r and s,

$$\text{if } r < s, \text{ then } x^r \text{ is } O(x^s). \qquad (11.2.2)$$

The relation among the graphs of various positive power functions of x for $x \geq 1$ is shown graphically in Figure 11.2.2 on the next page.

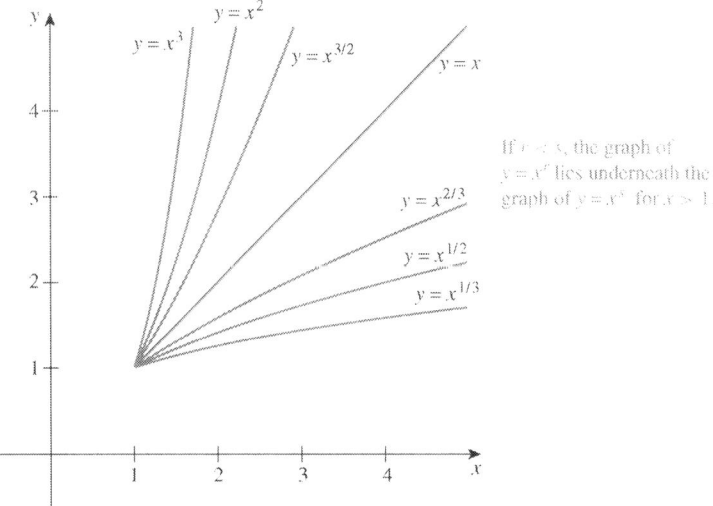

Figure 11.2.2 **Graphs of Powers of x for $x \geq 1$**

Orders of Polynomial Functions

The following example shows how to use property (11.2.1) to derive a polynomial inequality.

Example 11.2.3 A Polynomial Inequality

Show that for any real number x,

$$\text{if } x > 1, \quad \text{then} \quad 3x^3 + 2x + 7 \leq 12x^3.$$

Solution   Suppose x is a real number and $x > 1$. Then by property (11.2.1),

$$x < x^3 \quad \text{and} \quad 1 < x^3.$$

Multiply the left-hand inequality by 2 and the right-hand inequality by 7 to get

$$2x < 2x^3 \quad \text{and} \quad 7 < 7x^3.$$

Now add $3x^3 \leq 3x^3$, $2x < 2x^3$, and $7 < 7x^3$ to obtain

$$3x^3 + 2x + 7 \leq 3x^3 + 2x^3 + 7x^3 = 12x^3. \qquad \blacksquare$$

The method of Example 11.2.3 is used in the next example (more compactly) to show that a polynomial function has a certain order.

Example 11.2.4 Using the Definitions to Show That a Polynomial Function with Positive Coefficients Has a Certain Order

Use the definitions of big-Omega, big-O, and big-Theta to show that $2x^4 + 3x^3 + 5$ is $\Theta(x^4)$.

Solution   Define functions f and g as follows. For all nonnegative real numbers x,

$$f(x) = 2x^4 + 3x^3 + 5, \text{ and}$$
$$g(x) = x^4.$$

Observe that for all real numbers $x > 0$,

$$2x^4 \leq 2x^4 + 3x^3 + 5 \qquad \text{because } 3x^3 + 5 > 0 \text{ for } x > 0,$$

and so

$$2|x^4| \leq |2x^4 + 3x^3 + 5|$$

because all terms on both sides of the inequality are positive.

Let $A = 2$ and $a = 0$. Then

$$A|x^4| \leq |2x^4 + 3x^3 + 5| \quad \text{for all } x > a,$$

and so by definition of Ω-notation, $2x^4 + 3x^3 + 5$ is $Ω(x^4)$.
 Also for $x > 1$,

$$2x^4 + 3x^3 + 5 \ \leq \ 2x^4 + 3x^4 + 5x^4$$

because by (11.2.1), $x^3 < x^4$ and $1 < x^4$, and so $3x^3 < 3x^4$ and $5 < 5x^4$

$$\Rightarrow \quad 2x^4 + 3x^3 + 5 \ \leq \ 10x^4$$

because $2 + 3 + 5 = 10$

$$\Rightarrow \quad |2x^4 + 3x^3 + 5| \ \leq \ 10|x^4|$$

because all terms on both sides of the inequality are positive

Note   When the implication arrow, ⇒, is placed at the beginning of a line, it means that every number x that makes the inequality in the line above true also makes the inequality in the given line true.

Let $B = 10$ and $b = 1$. Then

$$|2x^4 + 3x^3 + 5| \leq B|x^4| \quad \text{for all } x > b,$$

and so, by definition of O-notation, $2x^4 + 3x^3 + 5$ is $O(x^4)$.
 Since $2x^4 + 3x^3 + 5$ is both $Ω(x^4)$ and $O(x^4)$, by Theorem 11.2.1, it is $Θ(x^4)$. ■

The technique used in Example 11.2.4 can be generalized to show that any polynomial with nonnegative coefficients is big-Theta of its highest-power term. Taken together, the next two examples show that such a result can hold for a polynomial with negative as well as positive coefficients.

Example 11.2.5 A Big-*O* Approximation for a Polynomial with Some Negative Coefficients

a. Use the definition of O-notation to show that $3x^3 - 1000x - 200$ is $O(x^3)$.

b. Show that $3x^3 - 1000x - 200$ is $O(x^s)$ for all integers $s > 3$.

Solution

a. According to the triangle inequality for absolute value (Theorem 4.4.6),

$$|a + b| \ \leq \ |a| + |b| \quad \text{for all real numbers } a \text{ and } b.$$

triangle inequality

If $-b$ is substituted in place of b, the result is

$$|a - b| \ = \ |a + (-b)| \ \leq \ |a| + |-b| \ = \ |a| + |b|, \quad \text{or}$$
$$|a - b| \ \leq \ |a| + |b|.$$

It follows that for all real numbers $x > 1$,

$$|3x^3 - 1000x - 200| \ \leq \ |3x^3| + |1000x| + |200|$$

$$\Rightarrow \quad |3x^3 - 1000x - 200| \ \leq \ 3x^3 + 1000x + 200$$

because all terms on the right side of the inequality are positive when x > 1

$$\Rightarrow \quad |3x^3 - 1000x - 200| \ \leq \ 3x^3 + 1000x^3 + 200x^3$$

because by (11.2.1), $x < x^3$ and $1 < x^3$, and so $1000x < 1000x^3$ and $200 < 200x^3$

$$\Rightarrow \quad |3x^3 - 1000x - 200| \ \leq \ 1203x^3$$

because $3 + 1000 + 200 = 1203$

$$\Rightarrow \quad |3x^3 - 1000x - 200| \ \leq \ 1203|x^3|$$

because x^3 is positive.

Let $b = 1$ and $B = 1203$. Then

$$|3x^3 - 1000x - 200| \leq B|x^3| \quad \text{for all real numbers } x > b.$$

So, by definition of O-notation, $3x^3 - 1000x - 200$ is $O(x^3)$.

b. Suppose s is an integer with $s > 3$. By property (11.2.1), $x^3 < x^s$ for all real numbers $x > 1$. So $B|x^3| < B|x^s|$ for all real numbers $x > b$ (because $b = 1$), and thus by part (a),

$$|3x^3 - 1000x - 200| \leq B|x^s| \quad \text{for all real numbers } x > b.$$

Hence, by definition of O-notation, $3x^3 - 1000x - 200$ is $O(x^s)$ for all integers $s > 3$.

∎

Example 11.2.6 A Big-Omega Approximation for a Polynomial with Some Negative Coefficients

a. Use the definition of Ω-notation to show that $3x^3 - 1000x - 200$ is $\Omega(x^3)$.

b. Show that $3x^3 - 1000x - 200$ is $\Omega(x^r)$ for all integers $r < 3$.

Solution

a. To show that $3x^3 - 1000x - 200$ is $\Omega(x^3)$, you need to find numbers a and A so that $A|x^3| \leq |3x^3 - 1000x - 200|$ for all real numbers $x > a$. Exercise 27 at the end of the section shows that the following procedure for choosing a will always produce an A that will give the desired result.

Choose a as follows: Add up the absolute values of the coefficients of the lower-order terms of $3x^3 - 1000x - 200$, divide by the absolute value of the highest-power term, and multiply the result by 2. The result is $a = 2(1000 + 200)/3$, which equals 800. If you follow the steps below, you will see that when a is chosen in this way, A can be taken to be one-half of the absolute value of the highest power of the polynomial. Accordingly, assume that $x > a$. Then

$$x > 800$$

$$\Rightarrow \qquad x > 2\left(\frac{1000 + 200}{3}\right) \qquad \text{because} \atop 2(1000 + 200)/3 = 800$$

$$\Rightarrow \qquad x > \frac{2 \cdot 1000}{3} + \frac{2 \cdot 200}{3} \qquad \text{by the rules for adding} \atop \text{fractions}$$

$$\Rightarrow \qquad x > \frac{2 \cdot 1000}{3} \cdot \frac{1}{x} + \frac{2 \cdot 200}{3} \cdot \frac{1}{x^2} \qquad \text{because } x > 800 \text{ and so by} \atop (11.2.1), 1 > \frac{1}{x} \text{ and } 1 > \frac{1}{x^2}$$

$$\Rightarrow \qquad \frac{3}{2}x^3 > 1000x + 200 \qquad \text{by multiplying both sides} \atop \text{by } \frac{3}{2}x^2$$

$$\Rightarrow \qquad 3x^3 - \frac{3}{2}x^3 > 1000x + 200 \qquad \text{because } \frac{3}{2} = 3 - \frac{3}{2}$$

$$\Rightarrow \quad 3x^3 - 1000x - 200 > \frac{3}{2}x^3 \qquad \text{by adding} \atop \frac{3}{2}x^3 - 1000x - 200 \atop \text{to both sides}$$

$$\Rightarrow \quad |3x^3 - 1000x - 200| > \frac{3}{2}|x^3| \qquad \text{because the expressions on} \atop \text{both sides of the inequality} \atop \text{are positive when } x > 800.$$

Let $A = \frac{3}{2}$ and let $a = 800$. Then

$$A|x^3| \leq |3x^3 - 1000x - 200| \quad \text{for all real numbers } x > a.$$

So, by definition of Ω-notation, $3x^3 - 1000x - 200$ is $\Omega(x^3)$.

b. Suppose r is an integer with $r < 3$. By property (11.2.1), $x^r < x^3$ for all real numbers $x > 1$. So, since $a = 800 > 1$, $A|x^r| < A|x^3|$ for all real numbers $x > a$. Thus, by part (a),

$$A|x^r| \leq |3x^3 - 1000x - 200| \quad \text{for all real numbers } x > a.$$

Hence, by definition of Ω-notation, $3x^3 - 1000x - 200$ is $\Omega(x^r)$ for all integers $r < 3$.
∎

By Theorem 11.2.1, it follows immediately from Examples 11.2.5(a) and 11.2.6(a) that $3x^3 - 1000x - 200$ is big-Theta of x^3, and the techniques used in the examples can be generalized to show that every polynomial is big-Theta of the power function of its highest power. Moreover, the findings in parts (b) of the examples—that $3x^3 - 1000x - 200$ is also big-*O* of x^s for every integer s greater than 3 and is big-Omega of x^r for every integer r less than 3—can also be generalized to all polynomials. These facts are summarized in the next theorem.

Theorem 11.2.2 On Polynomial Orders

Suppose $a_0, a_1, a_2, \ldots, a_n$ are real numbers and $a_n \neq 0$.

1. $a_n x^n + a_{n-1} x^{n-1} + \cdots + a_1 x + a_0$ is $O(x^s)$ for all integers $s \geq n$.

2. $a_n x^n + a_{n-1} x^{n-1} + \cdots + a_1 x + a_0$ is $\Omega(x^r)$ for all integers $r \leq n$.

3. $a_n x^n + a_{n-1} x^{n-1} + \cdots + a_1 x + a_0$ is $\Theta(x^n)$.

Theorem 11.2.2 can easily be proved using calculus. As suggested by Examples 11.2.5 and 11.2.6, however, it can also be derived without calculus. (See exercises 26, 27, and 49 at the end of this section.)

Example 11.2.7 Calculating Polynomial Orders Using the Theorem on Polynomial Orders

Use the theorem on polynomial orders to find orders for the functions given by the following formulas.

a. $f(x) = 7x^5 + 5x^3 - x + 4$, for all real numbers x.

b. $g(x) = \dfrac{(x-1)(x+1)}{4}$, for all real numbers x.

Solution

a. By direct application of the theorem on polynomial orders, $7x^5 + 5x^3 - x + 4$ is $\Theta(x^5)$

b. $g(x) = \dfrac{(x-1)(x+1)}{4}$

$= \dfrac{1}{4}(x^2 - 1)$

$= \dfrac{1}{4}x^2 - \dfrac{1}{4}$ by algebra

Thus $g(x)$ is $\Theta(x^2)$ by the theorem on polynomial orders.
∎

Example 11.2.8 Showing That Two Power Functions Have Different Orders

Show that x^2 is not $O(x)$, and deduce that x^2 is not $\Theta(x)$.

Solution   *[Argue by contradiction.]* Suppose that x^2 is $O(x)$. *[Derive a contradiction.]* By the supposition that x^2 is $O(x)$, there exist a positive real number B and a nonnegative real number b such that

$$|x^2| \le B|x| \quad \text{for all real numbers } x > b. \qquad (*)$$

Let x be a positive real number that is greater than both B and b. Then

$$x \cdot x > B \cdot x \qquad \text{by multiplying both sides of}$$
$$x > B \text{ by } x \text{ which is positive}$$

$$\Rightarrow \quad |x^2| > B|x| \qquad \text{because } b \text{ is positive.}$$

Thus there is a real number $x > b$ such that

$$|x^2| > B|x|.$$

This contradicts $(*)$. Hence the supposition is false, and so x^2 is not $O(x)$.

By Theorem 11.2.1, if x^2 is $\Theta(x)$, then x^2 is $O(x)$. But x^2 is not $O(x)$, and thus x^2 is not $\Theta(x)$. ■

The technique used in Example 11.2.8 can be extended and generalized to prove that any polynomial function in x of degree n is *not* big-O (or big-Theta) of the mth power function x^m for any $m < n$. (See exercise 53 at the end of this section.)

Theorem 11.2.3 Limitation on Orders of Polynomial Functions

Let n be a positive integer, and let $a_0, a_1, a_2, \ldots, a_n$ be real numbers with $a_n \ne 0$. If m is any integer with $m < n$, then

$$a_n x^n + a_{n-1} x^{n-1} + \cdots + a_1 x + a_0 \quad \text{is not} \quad O(x^m)$$

and

$$a_n x^n + a_{n-1} x^{n-1} + \cdots + a_1 x + a_0 \quad \text{is not} \quad \Theta(x^m).$$

It follows from Theorems 11.2.2 and 11.2.3 that integral power functions are convenient benchmarks for comparisons among general polynomial functions because every polynomial function has the same order as some integral power function, and no power function has the same order as any other.

Orders for Functions of Integer Variables

It is traditional to use the symbol x to denote a real number variable, whereas n is used to represent an integer variable. Thus, given a statement of the form

$$f(n) \quad \text{is} \quad \Theta(g(n)),$$

we assume that f and g are functions defined on sets of *integers*. If it is true that

$$f(x) \quad \text{is} \quad \Theta(g(x)),$$

where f and g are functions defined for *real numbers*, then it is certainly true that $f(n)$ is $\Theta(g(n))$. The reason is that if $f(x)$ is $\Theta(g(x))$, then an inequality

$$A|g(x)| \le |f(x)| \le B|g(x)|$$

holds for all real numbers $x > k$. Hence, in particular, the inequality

$$A|g(n)| \leq |f(n)| \leq B|g(n)|$$

holds for all integers $n > k$.

Example 11.2.9 An Order for the Sum of the First *n* Integers

Sums of the form $1 + 2 + 3 + \cdots + n$ arise in the analysis of computer algorithms such as selection sort. Show that for a positive integer variable n,

$$1 + 2 + 3 + \cdots + n \text{ is } \Theta(n^2).$$

Solution   By the formula for the sum of the first n integers (see Theorem 5.2.2), for all positive integers n,

$$1 + 2 + 3 + \cdots + n = \frac{n(n+1)}{2}.$$

But

$$\frac{n(n+1)}{2} = \frac{1}{2}n^2 + \frac{1}{2}n \qquad \text{by basic algebra}$$

And, by the theorem on polynomial orders,

$$\frac{1}{2}n^2 + \frac{1}{2}n \text{ is } \Theta(n^2).$$

Hence

$$1 + 2 + 3 + \cdots + n \text{ is } \Theta(n^2). \qquad \blacksquare$$

Extension to Functions Composed of Rational Power Functions

Consider a function of the form

$$\frac{(x^{3/2} + 3)(x - 2)^2}{x^{1/2}(2x^{1/2} + 1)} = \frac{x^{7/2} - 4x^{5/2} + 4x^{3/2} + 3x^2 - 12x + 12}{2x + x^{1/2}}.$$

When the numerator and denominator are expanded, each is a sum of terms of the form ax^r, where a is a real number and r is a positive rational number. The degree of such a sum can be taken to be the largest exponent of x that occurs in one of its terms. If the difference between the degree of the numerator and that of the denominator is called the degree of the function and denoted d, then it can be shown that $f(x)$ is $\Theta(x^d)$, that $f(x)$ is $O(x^c)$ for all real numbers $c > d$, and that $f(x)$ is not $O(x^c)$ for any real number $c < d$. For the example given above, this means that $d = 7/2 - 1 = 5/2$ and that

$$\frac{(x^{3/2} + 3)(x - 2)^2}{x^{1/2}(2x^{1/2} + 1)} \text{ is } \Theta(x^{5/2}),$$

$$\frac{(x^{3/2} + 3)(x - 2)^2}{x^{1/2}(2x^{1/2} + 1)} \text{ is } O(x^c) \quad \text{for all real numbers } c > 5/2,$$

and

$$\frac{(x^{3/2} + 3)(x - 2)^2}{x^{1/2}(2x^{1/2} + 1)} \text{ is not } O(x^c) \quad \text{for any real number } c < 5/2.$$

We state the general result as Theorem 11.2.4.

Theorem 11.2.4 Orders of Functions Composed of Rational Power Functions

Let m and n be positive integers, and let $r_0, r_1, r_2, \ldots, r_n$ and $s_0, s_1, s_2, \ldots, s_m$ be nonnegative rational numbers with $r_0 < r_1 < r_2 < \cdots < r_n$ and $s_0 < s_1 < s_2 < \cdots < s_m$. Let $a_0, a_1, a_2, \ldots, a_n$ and $b_0, b_1, b_2, \ldots, b_m$ be real numbers with $a_n \neq 0$ and $b_m \neq 0$. Then

$$\frac{a_n x^{r_n} + a_{n-1} x^{r_{n-1}} + \cdots + a_1 x^{r_1} + a_0 x^{r_0}}{b_m x^{s_m} + b_{m-1} x^{s_{m-1}} + \cdots + b_1 x^{s_1} + b_0 x^{s_0}} \quad \text{is } \Theta(x^{r_n - s_m}).$$

$$\frac{a_n x^{r_n} + a_{n-1} x^{r_{n-1}} + \cdots + a_1 x^{r_1} + a_0 x^{r_0}}{b_m x^{s_m} + b_{m-1} x^{s_{m-1}} + \cdots + b_1 x^{s_1} + b_0 x^{s_0}} \quad \text{is } O(x^c) \quad \text{for all real numbers } c > r_n - s_m.$$

$$\frac{a_n x^{r_n} + a_{n-1} x^{r_{n-1}} + \cdots + a_1 x^{r_1} + a_0 x^{r_0}}{b_m x^{s_m} + b_{m-1} x^{s_{m-1}} + \cdots + b_1 x^{s_1} + b_0 x^{s_0}} \quad \text{is not } O(x^c) \quad \text{for any real number } c < r_n - s_m.$$

Test Yourself

1. A sentence of the form "$A|g(x)| \leq |f(x)|$ for all $x > a$" translates into Ω-notation as _____.

2. A sentence of the form "$|f(x)| \leq B|g(x)|$ for all $x > b$" translates into O-notation as _____.

3. A sentence of the form "$A|g(x)| \leq |f(x)| \leq B|g(x)|$ for all $x > k$" translates into Θ-notation as _____.

4. When $x > 1$, x^2 _____ x and x^5 _____ x^2.

5. According to the theorem on polynomial orders, if $p(x)$ is a polynomial in x, then $p(x)$ is $\Theta(x^n)$, where n is _____.

6. If n is a positive integer, then $1 + 2 + 3 + \cdots + n$ has order _____.

Exercise Set 11.2

1. The following is a formal definition for Ω-notation, written using quantifiers and variables: $f(x)$ is $\Omega(g(x))$ if, and only if, $\exists$ positive real numbers a and A such that $\forall x > a$,

$$A|g(x)| \leq |f(x)|.$$

   a. Write the formal negation for the definition using the symbols $\forall$ and $\exists$.
   b. Restate the negation less formally without using the symbols $\forall$ and $\exists$.

2. The following is a formal definition for O-notation, written using quantifiers and variables: $f(x)$ is $O(g(x))$ if, and only if, $\exists$ positive real numbers b and B such that $\forall x > b$,

$$|f(x)| \leq B|g(x)|.$$

   a. Write the formal negation for the definition using the symbols $\forall$ and $\exists$.
   b. Restate the negation less formally without using the symbols $\forall$ and $\exists$.

3. The following is a formal definition for Θ-notation, written using quantifiers and variables: $f(x)$ is $\Theta(g(x))$ if, and only if, $\exists$ positive real numbers k, A, and B such that $\forall x > k$,

$$A|g(x)| \leq |f(x)| \leq B|g(x)|.$$

   a. Write the formal negation for the definition using the symbols $\forall$ and $\exists$.
   b. Restate the negation less formally without using the symbols $\forall$ and $\exists$.

In 4–9, express each statement using Ω-, O-, or Θ-notation.

4. $|5x^8 - 9x^7 + 2x^5 + 3x - 1| \leq 6|x^8|$ for all real numbers $x > 3$. (Use O-notation.)

5. $|x| \leq \left| \dfrac{(x^2 - 1)(12x + 25)}{3x^2 + 4} \right| \leq 6|x|$ for all real numbers $x > 2$.

6. $|x^{7/2}| \leq \left| \dfrac{(x^2 - 7)^2(10x^{1/2} + 3)}{x + 1} \right|$ for all real numbers $x > 4$. (Use Ω-notation.)

7. $\dfrac{1}{2} x^4 \leq |x^4 - 50x^3 + 1|$ for all real numbers $x > 101$. (Use Ω-notation.)

8. $|3x^6 + 5x^4 - x^3| \leq 9|x^6|$ for all real numbers $x > 1$. (Use O-notation.)

9. $\dfrac{1}{2} x^2 \leq |3x^2 - 80x + 7| \leq 3|x^2|$ for all real numbers $x > 33$.

In each of 10–14 assume f and g are real-valued functions defined on the same set of nonnegative real numbers.

10. Prove that if $g(x)$ is $O(f(x))$, then $f(x)$ is $\Omega(g(x))$.

11. Prove that $f(x)$ is $\Theta(f(x))$.

12. Prove that if $f(x)$ is $O(h(x))$ and $g(x)$ is $O(k(x))$, then $f(x) + g(x)$ is $O(G(x))$, where, for each x in the domain, $G(x) = \max(|h(x)|, |k(x)|)$.

13. Prove that if $f(x)$ is $O(g(x))$ and c is any nonzero real number, then $cf(x)$ is $O(g(x))$.

14. Prove that if $f(x)$ is $O(h(x))$ and $g(x)$ is $O(k(x))$, then $f(x)g(x)$ is $O(h(x)k(x))$.

15. a. Use mathematical induction to prove that if x is any real number with $x > 1$, then $x^n > 1$ for all integers $n \geq 1$.
    H b. Prove that if x is any real number with $x > 1$, then $x^m < x^n$ for any integers m and n with $m < n$.

16. a. Show that for any real number x,
$$\text{if } x > 1 \text{ then } |x^2| \leq |2x^2 + 15x + 4|.$$
    b. Show that for any real number x,
$$\text{if } x > 1 \text{ then } |2x^2 + 15x + 4| \leq 21|x^2|.$$
    c. Use the Ω- and O-notations to express the results of parts (a) and (b).
    d. What can you deduce about the order of $2x^2 + 15x + 4$?

17. a. Show that for any real number x,
$$\text{if } x > 1 \text{ then } |x^4| \leq |23x^4 + 8x^2 + 4x|.$$
    b. Show that for any real number x,
$$\text{if } x > 1 \text{ then } |23x^4 + 8x^2 + 4x| \leq 35|x^4|.$$
    c. Use the Ω- and O-notations to express the results of parts (a) and (b).
    d. What can you deduce about the order of $23x^4 + 8x^2 + 4x$?

18. Use the definition of Θ-notation to show that
$$5x^3 + 65x + 30 \text{ is } \Theta(x^3).$$

19. Use the definition of Θ-notation to show that
$$x^2 + 100x + 88 \text{ is } \Theta(x^2).$$

20. a. Show that for any real number x, if $x > 1$ then
$$|x^2| \leq |\lceil x^2 \rceil|.$$
    b. Show that for any real number x, if $x > 1$ then
$$\tfrac{1}{2}|\lceil x^2 \rceil| \leq |x^2|.$$
    c. Use the Ω- and O-notations to express the results of parts (a) and (b).
    d. What can you deduce about the order of $\lceil x^2 \rceil$?

21. a. Show that for any real number x, if $x > 1$ then
$$|\lfloor \sqrt{x} \rfloor| \leq |\sqrt{x}|.$$
    b. Show that for any real number x, if $x > 1$ then
$$\tfrac{1}{2}|\sqrt{x}| \leq |\lfloor x \rfloor|.$$
    c. Use the Ω- and O-notation to express the results of parts (a) and (b).
    d. What can you deduce about the order of $\lfloor \sqrt{x} \rfloor$?

22. a. Show that for any real number x, if $x > 1$ then
$$|7x^4 - 95x^3 + 3| \leq 105|x^4|.$$
    b. Use O-notation to express the result of part (a).

23. a. Show that for any real number x, if $x > 1$ then
$$|\tfrac{1}{5}x^2 - 42x - 8| \leq 51|x^2|.$$
    b. Use O-notation to express the result of part (a).

24. a. Show that for any real number x, if $x > 1$ then
$$|\tfrac{1}{4}x^5 - 50x^3 + 3x + 12| \leq 66|x^5|.$$
    b. Use O-notation to express the result of part (a).

H 25. Show that x^5 is not $O(x^2)$.

26. Suppose $a_0, a_1, a_2, \ldots, a_n$ are real numbers and $a_n \neq 0$. Use the generalization of the triangle inequality to n integers (exercise 43, Section 5.5) to show that
$$a_n x^n + a_{n-1}x^{n-1} + \cdots + a_1 x + a_0 \text{ is } O(x^n).$$

27. Suppose $a_0, a_1, a_2, \ldots, a_n$ are real numbers and $a_n \neq 0$. Show that $a_n x^n + a_{n-1}x^{n-1} + \cdots + a_1 x + a_0$ is $\Omega(x^n)$ by letting
$$d = 2\left(\frac{|a_0| + |a_1| + |a_2| + \cdots + |a_{n-1}|}{|a_n|}\right).$$
and letting $a = \max(d, 1)$.

In 28–30: (a) Let d be the number obtained by adding up the absolute values of the coefficients of the lower-order terms of the given polynomial, dividing by the absolute value of the highest-order term, and multiplying the result by 2. Let a be the maximum number of d and 1, and let A be half the coefficient of the absolute value of the highest-order term of the polynomial. (b) Show that if $x > a$, the absolute value of the polynomial will be greater than the product of A and the absolute value of x^4, where n is the degree of the polynomial. (c) Deduce the result given in the exercise.

28. $7x^4 - 95x^3 + 3$ is $\Omega(x^4)$.

29. $\tfrac{1}{5}x^2 - 42x - 8$ is $\Omega(x^2)$.

30. $\tfrac{1}{4}x^5 - 50x^3 + 3x + 12$ is $\Omega(x^5)$.

31. Refer to the results of exercises 22 and 28 to find an order for $7x^4 - 95x^3 + 3$ from among the set of power functions.

32. Refer to the results of exercises 23 and 29 to find an order for $\tfrac{1}{5}x^2 - 42x - 8$ from among the set of power functions.

33. Refer to the results of exercises 24 and 30 to find an order for $\tfrac{1}{4}x^5 - 50x^3 + 3x + 12$ from among the set of power functions.

Use the theorem on polynomial orders to prove each of the statements in 34–39.

34. $\dfrac{(x+1)(x-2)}{4}$ is $\Theta(x^2)$.

35. $\dfrac{x}{3}(4x^2 - 1)$ is $\Theta(x^3)$.

36. $\dfrac{x(x-1)}{2} + 3x$ is $\Theta(x^2)$.

37. $\dfrac{n(n+1)(2n+1)}{6}$ is $\Theta(n^3)$.

38. $\left[\dfrac{n(n+1)}{2}\right]^2$ is $\Theta(n^4)$.

39. $2(n-1)+\dfrac{n(n+1)}{2}+4\left(\dfrac{n(n-1)}{2}\right)$ is $\Theta(n^2)$.

Prove each of the statements in 40–47, assuming n is a variable that takes positive integer values. (Use formulas from the exercise set of Section 5.2 and the theorem on polynomial orders as appropriate.)

40. $1^2+2^2+3^2+\cdots+n^2$ is $\Theta(n^3)$.

41. $1^3+2^3+3^3+\cdots+n^3$ is $\Theta(n^4)$.

42. $2+4+6+\cdots+2n$ is $\Theta(n^2)$.

43. $5+10+15+20+25+\cdots+5n$ is $\Theta(n^2)$.

44. $\displaystyle\sum_{i=1}^{n}(4i-9)$ is $\Theta(n^2)$.   45. $\displaystyle\sum_{k=1}^{n}(k+3)$ is $\Theta(n^2)$.

H 46. $\displaystyle\sum_{i=1}^{n}i(i+1)$ is $\Theta(n^3)$.   47. $\displaystyle\sum_{k=3}^{n}(k^2-2k)$ is $\Theta(n^3)$.

H 48. (Requires the concept of limit from calculus)
   a. Let $a_0, a_1, a_2, \ldots, a_n$ be real numbers with $a_n \neq 0$. Prove that
   $$\lim_{x\to\infty}\left|\frac{a_nx^n+a_{n-1}x^{n-1}+\cdots+a_1x+a_0}{a_nx^n}\right|=1.$$
   b. Use the result of part (a) and the definition of limit to prove that
   $$a_nx^n+a_{n-1}x^{n-1}+\cdots+a_1x+a_0 \text{ is } \Theta(x^n).$$

49. Another approach to proving part of the theorem on polynomial orders uses properties of O-notation.
   a. Show that if f, g, and h are functions from **R** to **R** and $f(x)$ is $O(h(x))$ and $g(x)$ is $O(h(x))$, then $f(x)+g(x)$ is $O(h(x))$.
   b. How does it follow from part (a) and Theorem 11.2.1(3) that x^4+x^2 is $O(x^4)$?
   c. The result of exercise 11 states that if f is a function from **R** to **R**, $f(x)$ is $O(g(x))$, and c is any nonzero real number, then $cf(x)$ is $O(g(x))$. How does it follow from this result and part (a) that $12x^5-34x^2+7$ is $O(x^5)$?
   d. Use the results of part (a) and exercise 11 to show that if n is any positive integer and $a_1, a_2, \ldots, a_n$ are real numbers with $a_n \neq 0$, then
   $$a_nx^n+a_{n-1}x^{n-1}+\cdots+a_1x+a_0 \text{ is } O(x^n).$$

50. a. Let x be any positive real number. Use mathematical induction to prove that for all integers $n \geq 1$, if $x \leq 1$ then $x^n \leq 1$.
   b. Explain how it follows from part (a) that if x is any positive real number, then for all integers $n \geq 1$, if $x^n > 1$ then $x > 1$.
   c. Explain how it follows from part (b) that if x is any positive real number, then for all integers $n \geq 1$, if $x > 1$ then $x^{1/n} > 1$.

H d. Let p, q, and s be positive integers, let r be a nonnegative integer, and suppose $p/q > r/s$. Use part (c) and the result of exercise 15 to prove property (11.2.1). In other words show that for any real number x, if $x > 1$ then $x^{p/q} > x^{r/s}$.

Explain how each statement in 51 and 52 follows from exercise 50, exercise 13, and parts (a) and (c) of exercise 49.

51. $4x^{4/3}-15x+7$ is $O(x^{4/3})$.

52. $\sqrt{x}(38x^5+9)$ is $O(x^{11/2})$.

H 53. Prove that if r and s are rational numbers with $r > s$, then x^r is not $O(x^s)$.

In 54–56, use Theorem 11.2.4 to find an order for each of the given functions from among the set of rational power functions.

54. $f(x)=\dfrac{\sqrt{x}(3x+5)}{2x+1}$

55. $f(x)=\dfrac{(5x^2+1)\left(\sqrt{x}-1\right)}{4x^{3/2}-2x}$

56. $f(x)=\dfrac{(2x^{7/2}+1)(x-1)}{(x^{1/2}+1)(x+1)}$

* 57. a. Use mathematical induction to prove that
   $$\sqrt{1}+\sqrt{2}+\sqrt{3}+\cdots+\sqrt{n}\leq n^{3/2}$$
   for all integers $n \geq 1$.
   H h. Use mathematical induction to prove that
   $$\frac{1}{2}n^{3/2}\leq\sqrt{1}+\sqrt{2}+\sqrt{3}+\cdots+\sqrt{n}.$$
   c. What can you conclude from parts (a) and (b) about an order of $\sqrt{1}+\sqrt{2}+\sqrt{3}+\cdots+\sqrt{n}$?

* 58. a. Use mathematical induction to prove that
   $$1^{1/3}+2^{1/3}+\cdots+n^{1/3}\leq n^{4/3}, \text{ for all integers } n \geq 1.$$
   b. Use mathematical induction to prove that
   $$\frac{1}{2}n^{4/3}\leq 1^{1/3}+2^{1/3}+3^{1/3}+\cdots+n^{1/3}.$$
   c. What can you conclude from parts (a) and (b) about an order for $1^{1/3}+2^{1/3}+3^{1/3}+\cdots+n^{1/3}$?

Exercises 59–61 use the following definition, which requires the concept of limit from calculus.

> **Definition:** If f and g are real-valued functions of a real variable and $\lim_{x\to\infty}g(x)\neq 0$, then
> $$f(x) \text{ is } o(g(x)) \quad\Leftrightarrow\quad \lim_{x\to\infty}\frac{f(x)}{g(x)}=0.$$
> The notation $f(x)$ is $o(g(x))$ is read "$f(x)$ is little-oh of $g(x)$."

59. Prove that if $f(x)$ is $o(g(x))$, then $f(x)$ is $O(g(x))$.

60. Prove that if $f(x)$ and $g(x)$ are both $o(h(x))$, then for all real numbers a and b, $af(x) + bg(x)$ is $o(h(x))$.

61. Prove that for any positive real numbers a and b, if $a < b$ then x^a is $o(x^b)$.

Answers for Test Yourself

1. $f(x)$ is $\Omega(g(x))$ 2. $f(x)$ is $O(g(x))$ 3. $f(x)$ is $\Theta(g(x))$ 4. $>$; $>$ 5. the degree of $p(x)$ 6. n^2

11.3 Application: Analysis of Algorithm Efficiency I

As soon as an Analytical Engine exists, it will necessarily guide the future course of the science. Whenever any result is sought by its aid, the question will then arise—by what course of calculation can these results be arrived at by the machine in the shortest time?
— Charles Babbage, 1864

Charles Babbage (1792–1871)

Bettmann/CORBIS

Charles Babbage's Analytical Engine was similar in concept to a modern computer, and the quotation shown above suggests that well over a hundred years ago he anticipated the importance of analyzing the efficiencies of computer algorithms. Starting in the late 1940s, a number of mathematicians and computer scientists contributed to the development of algorithm analysis. Alan Turing may have been the first to suggest a concrete way for doing this. In a 1948 paper he wrote: "It is convenient to have a measure of the amount of work involved in a computing process, even though it be a very crude one. . . . We might, for instance, count the number of additions, subtractions, multiplications, divisions, recording of numbers . . ."[*] In the early 1960s, Donald Knuth started writing *The Art of Computer Programming*, a multivolume work, which provides a solid and extensive foundation for the subject that is both elegant and mathematically rigorous.[†]

The Sequential Search Algorithm

Note For more about the work of Alan Turing, see Sections 6.4 and 12.2.

The object of a search algorithm is to hunt through an array of data in an attempt to find a particular item x. In a sequential search, x is compared to the first item in the array, then to the second, then to the third, and so on. The search is stopped if a match is found at any stage. On the other hand, if the entire array is processed without finding a match, then x is not in the array. An example of a sequential search is shown diagrammatically in Figure 11.3.1.

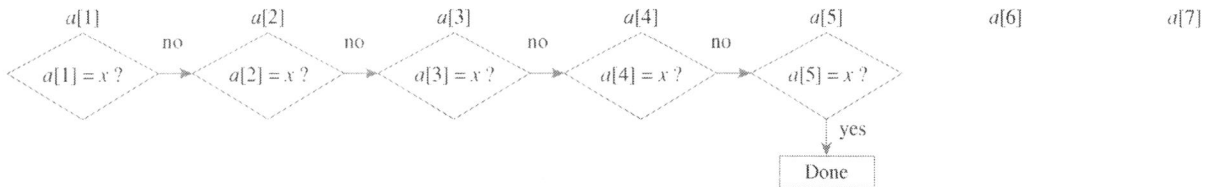

Figure 11.3.1 Sequential Search of $a[1], a[2], \ldots, a[7]$ for x where $x = a[5]$

[*]*Quarterly Journal of Mechanics and Applied Mathematics*, vol. 1 (1948), pp. 287–308.

[†]Donald E. Knuth, *The Art of Computer Programming*, vol. 1: *Fundamental Algorithms*, 3rd ed. (1997); vol. 2: *Seminumerical Algorithms*, 3rd ed., (1997); vol. 3: *Searching and Sorting*, 2nd ed. (1998) (Reading, MA: Addison-Wesley).

Example 11.3.1 Best- and Worst-Case Orders for Sequential Search

Find best- and worst-case orders for the sequential search algorithm from among the set of power functions.

Solution   Suppose the sequential search algorithm is applied to an input array $a[1], a[2],$ $\ldots, a[n]$ to find an item x. In the best case, the algorithm requires only one comparison between x and the items in $a[1], a[2], \ldots, a[n]$. This occurs when x is the first item in the array. Thus in the best case, the sequential search algorithm is $\Theta(1)$. (Note that $\Theta(1) = \Theta(n^0)$.) In the worst case, however, the algorithm requires n comparisons. This occurs when $x = a[n]$ or when x does not appear in the array at all. Thus in the worst case, the sequential search algorithm is $\Theta(n)$. ∎

The Insertion Sort Algorithm

Insertion sort is an algorithm for arranging the items in an array into ascending order. Initially, the second item is compared to the first. If the second item is less than the first, their values are interchanged, and as a result the first two array items are in ascending order. The idea of the algorithm is gradually to lengthen the section of the array that is known to be in ascending order by inserting each subsequent array item into its correct position relative to the preceding ones. When the last item has been placed, the entire array is in ascending order.

Figure 11.3.2 illustrates the action of step k of insertion sort on an array $a[1], a[2],$ $a[3], \ldots, a[n]$.

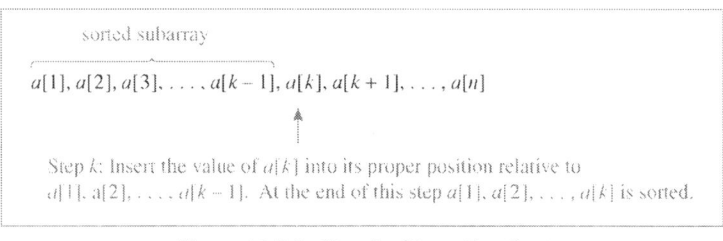

sorted subarray

$$a[1], a[2], a[3], \ldots, a[k-1], a[k], a[k+1], \ldots, a[n]$$

Step k: Insert the value of $a[k]$ into its proper position relative to $a[1], a[2], \ldots, a[k-1]$. At the end of this step $a[1], a[2], \ldots, a[k]$ is sorted.

Figure 11.3.2 **Step k of Insertion Sort**

Courtesy of Donald Knuth

Donald Knuth
(born 1938)

Understanding the relative efficiencies of algorithms designed to do the same job is of much more than academic interest. In industrial and scientific settings, the choice of an efficient over an inefficient program may result in the saving of many thousands of dollars or may make the difference between being able or not being able to do a project at all.

Two aspects of algorithm efficiency are important: the amount of time required to execute the algorithm and the amount of memory space needed when it is run. In this chapter we introduce basic techniques for calculating time efficiency. Similar techniques exist for calculating space efficiency. Occasionally, one algorithm may make more efficient use of time but less efficient use of memory space than another, forcing a trade-off based on the resources available to the user.

Time Efficiency of an Algorithm

How can the time efficiency of an algorithm be calculated? The answer depends on several factors. One is the size of the set of data that is input to the algorithm; for example, it takes longer for a sort algorithm to process 1,000,000 items than 100 items. Consequently, the execution time of an algorithm is generally expressed as a function of its input size.

Another factor that may affect the run time of an algorithm is the nature of the input data. For instance, a program that searches sequentially through a list of length n to find a data item requires only one step if the item is first on the list, but it uses n steps i is last on the list. Thus algorithms are frequently analyzed in terms of their "best case, "worst case," and "average case" performances for an input of size n.

Roughly speaking, the analysis of an algorithm for time efficiency begins by trying to count the number of elementary operations that must be performed when the algorithm is executed with an input of size n (in the best case, worst case, or average case). What is classified as an "elementary operation" may vary depending on the nature of the problem the algorithms being compared are designed to solve. For instance, to compare two algorithms for evaluating a polynomial, the crucial issue is the number of additions and multiplications that are needed, whereas to compare two algorithms for searching a list to find a particular element, the important distinction is the number of comparisons that are required. As is common, we will classify the following as **elementary operations**: addition, subtraction, multiplication, division, and comparisons that are indicated explicitly in an if-statement using one of the relational symbols $<, \leq, >, \geq,$ $=,$ or $\neq$.

When algorithms are implemented in a particular programming language and run on a particular computer, some operations are executed faster than others, and, of course, there are differences in execution times from one machine to another. In certain practical situations these factors are taken into account when we decide which algorithm or which machine to use to solve a particular problem. In other cases, however, the machine is fixed, and rough estimates are all that we need to determine the clear superiority of one algorithm over another. Since each elementary operation is executed in time no longer than the slowest, the time efficiency of an algorithm is approximately proportional to the number of elementary operations required to execute the algorithm.

Consider the example of two algorithms, A and B, designed to do a certain job. Suppose that for an input of size n, the number of elementary operations needed to perform algorithm A is between $10n$ and $20n$ (at least for large n) and the number of elementary operations needed to perform algorithm B is between $2n^2$ and $4n^2$. Note that $20n < 2n^2$ whenever $n > 10$, which means that the maximum number of operations required to execute A is less than the *minimum* number of operations required to execute B whenever $n > 10$. In fact, $20n$ is very much less than $2n^2$ when n is large. For instance, if $n = 1000$, then $20n = 20{,}000$, whereas $2n^2 = 2{,}000{,}000$. We say that in the worst case, algorithm A is $\Theta(n)$ (or has worst-case order n) and that in the worst case, algorithm B is $\Theta(n^2)$ (or has worst-case order n^2).

• Definition

Let A be an algorithm.

1. Suppose the number of elementary operations performed when A is executed for an input of size n depends on n alone and not on the nature of the input data; say it equals $f(n)$. If $f(n)$ is $\Theta(g(n))$, we say that **A is $\Theta(g(n))$** or **A is of order $g(n)$**.

2. Suppose the number of elementary operations performed when A is executed for an input of size n depends on the nature of the input data as well as on n.

   a. Let $b(n)$ be the *minimum* number of elementary operations required to execute A for all possible input sets of size n. If $b(n)$ is $\Theta(g(n))$, we say that **in the best case, A is $\Theta(g(n))$** or **A has a best-case order of $g(n)$**.

   b. Let $w(n)$ be the *maximum* number of elementary operations required to execute A for all possible input sets of size n. If $w(n)$ is $\Theta(g(n))$, we say that **in the worst case, A is $\Theta(g(n))$** or **A has a worst-case order of $g(n)$**.

Some of the orders most commonly used to describe algorithm efficiencies are shown in Table 11.3.1. As you see from the table, differences between the orders of various types of algorithms are more than astronomical. The time required for an algorithm of order 2^n to operate on a data set of size 100,000 is approximately $10^{30,076}$ times the estimated 15 billion years since the universe began (according to one theory of cosmology). On the other hand, an algorithm of order $\log_2 n$ needs at most a fraction of a second to process the same data set.

Table 11.3.1 **Time Comparisons of Some Algorithm Orders**

Approximate Time to Execute $f(n)$ Operations Assuming One Operation per Nanosecond*				
$f(n)$	$n = 10$	$n = 1{,}000$	$n = 100{,}000$	$n = 10{,}000{,}000$
$\log_2 n$	3.3×10^{-9} sec	10^{-8} sec	1.7×10^{-8} sec	2.3×10^{-8} sec
n	10^{-8} sec	10^{-6} sec	0.0001 sec	0.01 sec
$n \log_2 n$	3.3×10^{-8} sec	10^{-5} sec	0.0017 sec	0.23 sec
n^2	10^{-7} sec	0.001 sec	10 sec	27.8 hr
n^3	10^{-6} sec	1 sec	11.6 days	31,688 yr
2^n	10^{-6} sec	3.4×10^{284} yr	3.1×10^{30086} yr	2.9×10^{3010283} yr

*one nanosecond $= 10^{-9}$ second

Example 11.3.2 Computing an Order of an Algorithm Segment

Assume n is a positive integer and consider the following algorithm segment:

$$p := 0, x := 2$$
for $i := 2$ **to** n
$$p := (p + i) \cdot x$$
next i

a. Compute the actual number of additions and multiplications that must be performed when this algorithm segment is executed.

b. Use the theorem on polynomial orders to find an order for this algorithm segment.

Solution

a. There are one multiplication and one addition for each iteration of the loop, so there are twice as many multiplications and additions as there are iterations of the loop. Now the number of iterations of the **for-next** loop equals the top index of the loop minus the bottom index plus 1; that is, $n - 2 + 1 = n - 1$. Hence there are $2(n - 1) = 2n - 2$ multiplications and additions.

b. By the theorem on polynomial orders,

$$2n - 2 \text{ is } \Theta(n),$$

and so this algorithm segment is $\Theta(n)$.

The next example looks at an algorithm segment that contains a nested loop.

Example 11.3.3 An Order for an Algorithm with a Nested Loop

Assume n is a positive integer and consider the following algorithm segment:

$$s := 0$$
$$\textbf{for } i := 1 \textbf{ to } n$$
$$\qquad \textbf{for } j := 1 \textbf{ to } i$$
$$\qquad\qquad s := s + j \cdot (i - j + 1)$$
$$\qquad \textbf{next } j$$
$$\textbf{next } i$$

a. Compute the actual number of additions, subtractions, and multiplications that must be performed when this algorithm segment is executed.

b. Use the theorem on polynomial orders to find an order for this algorithm segment.

Solution

a. There are two additions, one multiplication, and one subtraction for each iteration of the inner loop, so the total number of additions, multiplications, and subtractions is four times the number of iterations of the inner loop. Now the inner loop is iterated

$$\text{one time when } i = 1,$$
$$\text{two times when } i = 2,$$
$$\text{three times when } i = 3,$$
$$\vdots$$
$$n \text{ times when } i = n.$$

You can see this easily if you construct a table that shows the values of i and j for which the statements in the inner loop are executed. There is one iteration for each column in the table.

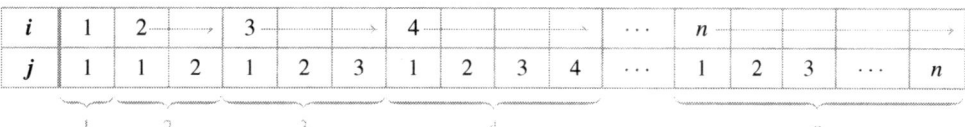

Hence the total number of iterations of the inner loop is

$$1 + 2 + 3 + \cdots + n = \frac{n(n+1)}{2} \quad \text{by Theorem 5.2.2,}$$

and so the number of additions, subtractions, and multiplications is

$$4 \cdot \frac{n(n+1)}{2} = 2n(n+1).$$

An alternative method for computing the number of columns of the table uses an approach discussed in Example 9.6.3. Observe that the number of columns in the table is the same as the number of ways to place two $\times$'s in n categories, $1, 2, \ldots, n$, where the location of the $\times$'s indicates the values of i and j with $j \leq i$. By Theorem 9.6.1, this number is

$$\binom{n-1+2}{2} = \binom{n+1}{2} = \frac{(n+1)!}{2!((n+1)-2)!} = \frac{(n+1)n(n-1)!}{2(n-1)!} = \frac{n(n+1)}{2}.$$

Although, for this example, the alternative method is more complicated than the one preceding it, it is simpler when the number of loop nestings exceeds two. (See exercise 19.)

b. By the theorem on polynomial orders, $2n(n+1) = 2n^2 + 2n$ is $\Theta(n^2)$, and so this algorithm segment is $\Theta(n^2)$. ◼

Example 11.3.4 When the Number of Iterations Depends on the Floor Function

Assume n is a positive integer and consider the following algorithm segment:

$$\textbf{for } i := \lfloor n/2 \rfloor \textbf{ to } n$$
$$a := n - i$$
$$\textbf{next } i$$

a. Compute the actual number of subtractions that must be performed when this algorithm segment is executed.

b. Use the theorem on polynomial orders to find an order for this algorithm segment.

Solution

a. There is one subtraction for each iteration of the loop, and the loop is iterated $n - \left\lfloor \dfrac{n}{2} \right\rfloor + 1$ times. If n is even, then $\left\lfloor \dfrac{n}{2} \right\rfloor = \dfrac{n}{2}$, and so the number of subtractions is

$$n - \left\lfloor \frac{n}{2} \right\rfloor + 1 = n - \frac{n}{2} + 1 = \frac{n+2}{2}.$$

If n is odd, then $\left\lfloor \dfrac{n}{2} \right\rfloor = \dfrac{n-1}{2}$, and so the number of subtractions is

$$n - \left\lfloor \frac{n}{2} \right\rfloor + 1 = n - \frac{n-1}{2} + 1 = \frac{2n - (n-1) + 2}{2} = \frac{n+3}{2}.$$

b. By the theorem on polynomial orders,

$$\frac{n+2}{2} \text{ is } \Theta(n) \quad \text{and} \quad \frac{n+3}{2} \text{ is } \Theta(n)$$

also. Hence, regardless of whether n is even or odd, this algorithm segment is $\Theta(n)$. ◼

The following is a formal algorithm for insertion sort.

Algorithm 11.3.1 Insertion Sort

[The aim of this algorithm is to take an array $a[1], a[2], a[3], \ldots, a[n]$, where $n \geq 1$, and reorder it. The output array is also denoted $a[1], a[2], a[3], \ldots, a[n]$. It has the same values as the input array, but they are in ascending order. In the kth step, $a[1], a[2], a[3], \ldots, a[k-1]$ is in ascending order, and $a[k]$ is inserted into the correct position with respect to it.]

Input: n *[a positive integer]*, $a[1], a[2], a[3], \ldots, a[n]$ *[an array of data items capable of being ordered]*

Algorithm Body:

$\textbf{for } k := 2 \textbf{ to } n$

[Compare $a[k]$ to previous items in the array $a[1], a[2], a[3], \ldots, a[k-1]$, starting from the largest and moving downward. Whenever $a[k]$ is less than a preceding array

item, increment the index of the preceding item to move it one position to the right. As soon as a[k] is greater than or equal to an array item, insert the value of a[k] to the right of that item. If a[k] is greater than or equal to a[k − 1], then leave the value of a[k] unchanged.]

$x := a[k]$

$j := k − 1$

while ($j \neq 0$)

    if $x < a[j]$ **then**

        $a[j + 1] := a[j]$

        $a[j] := x$

        $j := j − 1$

        else $j := 0$

    end if

    end while

next k

Output: $a[1], a[2], a[3], \ldots, a[n]$ *[in ascending order]*

Figure 11.3.3 shows the result of each step when insertion sort is applied to the particular array

$$a[1] = 6, \quad a[2] = 3, \quad a[3] = 5, \quad a[4] = 7, \quad a[5] = 2.$$

	$a[1]$	$a[2]$	$a[3]$	$a[4]$	$a[5]$
Initial	6	3	5	7	2
Result of step 1	3	6	5	7	2
Result of step 2	3	5	6	7	2
Result of step 3	3	5	6	7	2
Result of step 4	2	3	5	6	7

The top row of the table shows the initial values of the array, and the bottom row shows the final values. The result of each step is shown in a separate row. For each step, the sorted section of the array is shaded.

Figure 11.3.3 **Action of Insertion Sort on an Array**

Example 11.3.5 develops a trace table for the action of insertion sort on a particular array.

Example 11.3.5 A Trace Table for Insertion Sort

Construct a trace table showing the action of insertion sort on the array

$$a[1] = 6, a[2] = 3, a[3] = 5, a[4] = 7, a[5] = 2.$$

Solution

The first column on the next page shows the state of the variables before the first iteration of the **for-next** loop. When the **for-next** loop is first iterated, k is assigned the value 2; x the value of $a[2]$, which is 3; and j the value of $k − 1$, which is 1. Because $j \neq 0$, the **while** loop is entered and the condition for the **if-then-else** statement is tested. Because $a[1] > x$, then $a[2]$ is assigned the value of $a[1]$, which is 6, j is assigned the value of $j − 1$, which is 0, and $a[1]$ is assigned the value of x, which is 3. The condition governing the **while** loop is tested again, but since $j = 0$, it is not satisfied, and so the **while** loop is not entered. Thus the value of k is incremented by 1 (so that it equals 3), and the **for-next** loop is entered a second time. This process continues until the value of

k has been incremented to 6. Because 6 is greater than the top value in the **for-next** loop, execution of the algorithm ceases, and the array items are seen to be in ascending order.

n	5												
$a[1]$	6	3									2		
$a[2]$	3	6		5							2	3	
$a[3]$	5		6							2	5		
$a[4]$	7									2	6		
$a[5]$	2									7			
k	2		3			4	5						6
x	3		5			7	2						
j	1	0	2	1	0	3	0	4	3	2	1	0	

Example 11.3.6 Finding a Worst-Case Order for Insertion Sort

a. When the comparisons in the for-next and while loops are counted along with those in the if-then-else statement, what is the maximum number of comparisons that are performed when insertion sort is applied to the array $a[1], a[2], a[3], \ldots, a[n]$?

b. Use the theorem on polynomial orders to find a worst-case order for insertion sort.

Solution

a. In each iteration of the **while** loop, two explicit comparisons are made: one to test whether $j \neq 0$ and the other to test whether $a[j] > x$. During the time that $a[k]$ is put into position relative to $a[1], a[2], \ldots, a[k-1]$, the maximum number of attempted iterations of the **while** loop is k. This happens when $a[k]$ is less than every $a[1]$, $a[2], \ldots, a[k-1]$; on the kth attempted iteration, another comparison yields the result that the condition of the **while** loop is not satisfied because $j = 0$. In addition, each increment in k is tested to see whether the result is greater than n. Thus the maximum number of comparisons for a given value of k is $2(k-1) + 1 + 1 = 2k$. Because k goes from 2 to n, it follows that the maximum total number of comparisons occurs when the items in the array are in reverse order, and it equals

$$
\begin{aligned}
2 \cdot 2 + 2 \cdot 3 + \cdots + 2 \cdot n &= 2(2 + 3 + \cdots + n) && \text{by factoring out the 2} \\
&= 2[(1 + 2 + 3 + \cdots + n) - 1] && \text{by adding and subtracting 1} \\
&= 2\left(\frac{n(n+1)}{2} - 1\right) && \text{by Theorem 5.2.2} \\
&= n(n+1) - 2 \\
&= n^2 + n - 2 && \text{by algebra.}
\end{aligned}
$$

b. By the theorem on polynomial orders, $n^2 + n - 2$ is $\Theta(n^2)$, and so the insertion sort algorithm has worst-case order $\Theta(n^2)$.

The definition of expected value that was introduced in Section 9.8 can be used to find an average-case order for insertion sort.

Example 11.3.7 Finding an Average-Case Order for Insertion Sort

a. What is the average number of comparisons that are performed when insertion sort is applied to the array $a[1], a[2], a[3], \ldots, a[n]$?

b. Use the theorem on polynomial orders to find an average-case order for insertion sort.

Solution

a. Let E_n be the average, or expected, number of comparisons used to sort $a[1], a[2], \ldots,$ $a[n]$ with insertion sort. Note that for each integer $k = 2, 3, \ldots, n,$

$$
\begin{bmatrix}
\text{the expected number of} \\
\text{comparisons used to} \\
\text{sort } a[1], a[2], \ldots, a[k]
\end{bmatrix}
$$
$$
=
\begin{bmatrix}
\text{the expected number of} \\
\text{comparisons used to} \\
\text{sort } a[1], a[2], \ldots, a[k-1]
\end{bmatrix}
+
\begin{bmatrix}
\text{the expected number of comparisons} \\
\text{used to place } a[k] \text{ into position} \\
\text{relative to } a[1], a[2], \ldots, a[k-1]
\end{bmatrix}.
$$

Thus

$$
E_k = E_{k-1} +
\begin{bmatrix}
\text{the expected number of comparisons} \\
\text{used to place } a[k] \text{ into position} \\
\text{relative to } a[1], a[2], \ldots, a[k-1]
\end{bmatrix}.
$$

Also, $E_1 = 0$ because when there is just one item in the array, $n = 1$ and no iterations of the outer loop are performed.

Now at the time $a[k]$ is placed relative to $a[1], a[2], \ldots, a[k-1]$, a reasonable assumption is that it is equally likely to belong in any one of the first k positions. Thus the probability of its belonging in any particular position is $1/k$. If it actually belongs in position j, then $2(k - j + 1)$ comparisons will be used in moving it, because there will be $k - j + 1$ attempted iterations of the **while** loop and there are 2 comparisons per attempted iteration.

According to the definition of expected value given in Section 9.8, the expected number of comparisons used to place $a[k]$ relative to $a[1], a[2], \ldots, a[k-1]$ is therefore

$$
\sum_{j=1}^{k} \frac{1}{k} 2(k - j + 1) = \frac{2}{k}[k + (k - 1) + \cdots + 3 + 2 + 1] \qquad \text{by writing the summation in expanded form}
$$
$$
= \frac{2}{k}\left(\frac{k(k + 1)}{2}\right) \qquad \text{by Theorem 5.2.2}
$$
$$
= k + 1 \qquad \text{by algebra.}
$$

Hence

$$
E_k = E_{k-1} + k + 1 \quad \text{for all integers } k \geq 2, \quad \text{and}
$$
$$
E_1 = 0.
$$

Exercise 27 at the end of the section asks you to solve this recurrence relation to show that

$$
E_n = \frac{n^2 + 3n - 4}{2} \qquad \text{for each integer } n \geq 1.
$$

b. By the theorem on polynomial orders, $\dfrac{n^2 + 3n - 4}{2} = \dfrac{1}{2}n^2 + \dfrac{3}{2}n - 2$ is $\Theta(n^2)$, and so the average-case order of insertion sort is also $\Theta(n^2)$. ∎

Test Yourself

1. When an algorithm segment contains a nested **for-next** loop, you can find the number of times the loop will iterate by constructing a table in which each column represents _____.

2. In the worst case for an input array of length n, the sequential search algorithm has to look through _____ elements of the array before it terminates.

3. The worst-case order of the insertion sort algorithm is _____, and its average-case order is _____.

Exercise Set 11.3

1. Suppose a computer takes 1 nanosecond ($= 10^{-9}$ second) to execute each operation. Approximately how long will it take for the computer to execute the following numbers of operations? Convert your answers into seconds, minutes, hours, days, weeks, or years, as appropriate. For example, instead of 2^{50} nanoseconds, write 13 days.
   a. $\log_2 200$ b. 200 c. $200 \log_2 200$
   d. 200^2 e. 200^8 f. 2^{200}

2. Suppose an algorithm requires cn^2 operations when performed with an input of size n (where c is a constant).
   a. How many operations will be required when the input size is increased from m to $2m$ (where m is a positive integer)?
   b. By what factor will the number of operations increase when the input size is doubled?
   c. By what factor will the number of operations increase when the input size is increased by a factor of ten?

3. Suppose an algorithm requires cn^3 operations when performed with an input of size n (where c is a constant).
   a. How many operations will be required when the input size is increased from m to $2m$ (where m is a positive integer)?
   b. By what factor will the number of operations increase when the input size is doubled?
   c. By what factor will the number of operations increase when the input size is increased by a factor of ten?

Exercises 4–5 explore the fact that for relatively small values of n, algorithms with larger orders can be more efficient than algorithms with smaller orders.

4. Suppose that when run with an input of size n, algorithm A requires $2n^2$ operations and algorithm B requires $80n^{3/2}$ operations.
   a. What are orders for algorithms A and B from among the set of power functions?
   b. For what values of n is algorithm A more efficient than algorithm B?
   c. For what values of n is algorithm B at least 100 times more efficient than algorithm A?

5. Suppose that when run with an input of size n, algorithm A requires $10^6 n^2$ operations and algorithm B requires n^3 operations.
   a. What are orders for algorithms A and B from among the set of power functions?
   b. For what values of n is algorithm A more efficient than algorithm B?
   c. For what values of n is algorithm B at least 100 times more efficient than algorithm A?

For each of the algorithm segments in 6–19, assume that n is a positive integer. (a) Compute the actual number of additions, subtractions, multiplications, divisions, and comparisons that must be performed when the algorithm segment is executed. For simplicity, however, count only comparisons that occur within if-then statements; ignore those implied by for-next loops. (b) Use the theorem on polynomial orders to find an order for the algorithm segment.

6. **for** $i := 3$ **to** $n - 1$
   $\quad a := 3 \cdot n + 2 \cdot i - 1$
   next i

7. $max := a[1]$
   for $i := 2$ **to** n
   $\quad$ **if** $max < a[i]$ **then** $max := a[i]$
   next i

8. **for** $i := 1$ **to** $\lfloor n/2 \rfloor$
   $\quad a := n - i$
   next i

9. **for** $i := 1$ **to** n
   $\quad$ **for** $j := 1$ **to** $2n$
   $\quad\quad a := 2 \cdot n + i \cdot j$
   $\quad$ **next** j
   next i

10. **for** $k := 2$ **to** n
    $\quad$ **for** $j := 1$ **to** $3n$
    $\quad\quad x := a[k] - b[j]$
    $\quad$ **next** j
    next k

11. **for** $k := 1$ **to** $n - 1$
    $\quad$ **for** $j := 1$ **to** $k + 1$
    $\quad\quad x := a[k] + b[j]$
    $\quad$ **next** j
    next k

12. **for** $k := 1$ **to** $n - 1$
    $\quad max := a[k]$
    $\quad$ **for** $i := k + 1$ **to** n
    $\quad\quad$ **if** $max < a[i]$ **then** $max := a[i]$
    $\quad$ **next** i
    $a[k] := max$
    next k

13. **for** $i := 1$ **to** $n - 1$
    $\quad$ **for** $j := i$ **to** n
    $\quad\quad$ **if** $a[j] > a[i]$ **then do**
    $\quad\quad\quad temp := a[i]$
    $\quad\quad\quad a[i] := a[j]$
    $\quad\quad\quad a[j] := temp$
    $\quad\quad$ **end do**
    $\quad$ **next** j
    next i

14. $t := 0$
 for $i := 1$ **to** n
   $s := 0$
   for $j := 1$ **to** i
     $s := s + a[j]$
   next j
   $t := t + s^2$
 next i

15. $r := 0$
 for $i := 1$ **to** $n - 1$
   $p := 1$
   $q := 1$
   for $j := i + 1$ **to** n
     $p := p \cdot c[j]$
     $q := q \cdot (c[j])^2$
   next j
   $r := p + q$
 next i

16. $t := 0$
 for $i := 1$ **to** n
   $s := 0$
   for $j := 1$ **to** $i - 1$
     $s := s + j \cdot (i - j + 1)$
   next j
   $r := s^2$
 next i

17. **for** $i := 1$ **to** n
   for $j := 1$ **to** $\lfloor (i + 1)/2 \rfloor$
     $a := (n - i) \cdot (n - j)$
   next j
 next i

18. **for** $i := 1$ **to** n
   for $j := \lfloor (i + 1)/2 \rfloor$ **to** n
     $x := i \cdot j$
   next j
 next i

✳ 19. **for** $i := 1$ **to** n
   for $j := 1$ **to** i
     for $k := 1$ **to** j
       $x := i \cdot j \cdot k$
     next k
   next j
 next i

20. Construct a table showing the result of each step when insertion sort is applied to the array $a[1] = 6$, $a[2] = 2$, $a[3] = 1$, $a[4] = 8$, and $a[5] = 4$.

21. Construct a table showing the result of each step when insertion sort is applied to the array $a[1] = 7$, $a[2] = 3$, $a[3] = 6$, $a[4] = 9$, and $a[5] = 5$.

22. Construct a trace table showing the action of insertion sort on the array of exercise 20.

23. Construct a trace table showing the action of insertion sort on the array of exercise 21.

24. How many comparisons between values of $a[j]$ and x actually occur when insertion sort is applied to the array of exercise 20?

25. How many comparisons between values of $a[j]$ and x actually occur when insertion sort is applied to the array of exercise 21?

26. According to Example 11.3.6, the maximum number of comparisons needed to perform insertion sort on an array of length five is $5^2 + 5 - 2 = 28$. Find an array of length five that requires the maximum number of comparisons when insertion sort is applied to it.

H 27. Consider the recurrence relation that arose in Example 11.3.7: $E_1 = 0$ and $E_k = E_{k-1} + k + 1$, for all integers $k \geq 2$.
  a. Use iteration to find an explicit formula for the sequence.
  b. Use mathematical induction to verify the correctness of the formula.

Exercises 28–35 refer to *selection sort*, which is another algorithm to arrange the items in an array in ascending order.

Algorithm 11.3.2 Selection Sort

[Starting with an array $a[1]$, $a[2]$, $a[3]$, $\ldots$, $a[n]$, this algorithm sorts the array by selecting the correct item to place in each position by moving sequentially through the elements of the array. In general, for each $k = 1$ to $n - 1$, the kth step of the algorithm finds the index of the array item with minimum value from among $a[k + 1]$, $a[k + 2]$, $a[k + 3]$, $\ldots$, $a[n]$. Once this index is found, the value of the corresponding array item is interchanged with the value of $a[k]$ if it is less than $a[k]$. At the end of execution the array elements are in order.]

Input: n *[a positive integer]*, $a[1]$, $a[2]$, $a[3]$, $\ldots$, $a[n]$ *[an array of data items capable of being ordered]*

Algorithm Body:

for $k := 1$ **to** $n - 1$
  IndexOfMin $:= k$
  for $i := k + 1$ **to** n
    if $(a[i] < a[IndexOfMin])$
    then *IndexOfMin* $:= i$
  next i
  if IndexOfMin $\neq k$ **then**
    Temp $:= a[k]$
    $a[k] := a[IndexOfMin]$
    $a[IndexOfMin] := Temp$
next k

Output: $a[1]$, $a[2]$, $a[3]$, $\ldots$, $a[n]$ *[in ascending order]*

The action of selection sort can be represented pictorially as follows:

$$a[1] | a[2] | \cdots | \boxed{a[k]} | a[k+1] | \cdots a[n]$$

If the value of this array element is less than the value of $a[k]$, then its value and the value of $a[k]$ are interchanged.

28. Construct a table showing the interchanges that occur when selection sort is applied to the array $a[1] = 5, a[2] = 3, a[3] = 4, a[4] = 6$, and $a[5] = 2$.

29. Construct a table showing the interchanges that occur when selection sort is applied to the array $a[1] = 6, a[2] = 4, a[3] = 5, a[4] = 8$, and $a[5] = 1$.

30. Construct a trace table showing the action of selection sort on the array of exercise 28.

31. Construct a trace table showing the action of selection sort on the array of exercise 29.

32. When selection sort is applied to the array of exercise 28, how many times is the comparison in the **if-then** statement performed?

33. When selection sort is applied to the array of exercise 29, how many times is the comparison in the **if-then** statement performed?

34. When selection sort is applied to an array $a[1], a[2], a[3], a[4]$, how many times is the comparison in the **if-then** statement performed?

35. Consider applying selection sort to an array $a[1], a[2], a[3], \ldots, a[n]$.
    a. How many times is the comparison in the **if-then** statement performed when $a[1]$ is compared to each of $a[2], a[3], \ldots, a[n]$?
    b. How many times is the comparison in the **if-then** statement performed when $a[2]$ is compared to each of $a[3], a[4], \ldots, a[n]$?
    c. How many times is the comparison in the **if-then** statement performed when $a[k]$ is compared to each of $a[k-1], a[k+2], \ldots, a[n]$?
    H d. Using the number of times the comparison in the **if-then** statement is performed as a measure of the time efficiency of selection sort, find a worst case order for selection sort. Use the theorem on polynomial orders.

Exercises 36–39 refer to the following algorithm to compute the value of a real polynomial.

Algorithm 11.3.3 Term-by-Term Polynomial Evaluation

[This algorithm computes the value of the real polynomial $a[n]x^n + a[n-1]x^{n-1} + \cdots + a[2]x^2 + a[1]x + a[0]$ by computing each term separately, starting with $a[0]$, and adding it on to an accumulating sum.]

Input: n *[a nonnegative integer]* $a[0], a[1], a[2], \ldots, a[n]$ *[an array of real numbers], x [a real number]*

Algorithm Body:
    $polyval := a[0]$
    for $i := 1$ **to** n
        $term := a[i]$
        for $j := 1$ **to** i
            $term := term \cdot x$
        next j
        $polyval := polyval + term$
    next i
    [At this point
    $polyval = a[n]x^n + a[n-1]x^{n-1}$
                $+ \cdots + a[2]x^2 + a[1]x + a[0].]$

Output: $polyval$ *[a real number]*

---

36. Trace Algorithm 11.3.3 for the input $n = 3, a[0] = 2, a[1] = 1, a[2] = -1, a[3] = 3$, and $x = 2$.

37. Trace Algorithm 11.3.3 for the input $n = 2, a[0] = 5, a[1] = -1, a[2] = 2$, and $x = 3$.

38. Let s_n = the number of additions and multiplications that must be performed when Algorithm 11.3.3 is executed for a polynomial of degree n. Express s_n as a function of n.

39. Use the theorem on on polynomial orders to find an order for Algorithm 11.3.3.

Exercises 40–43 refer to another algorithm, known as Horner's rule, for finding the value of a real polynomial.

Algorithm 11.3.4 Horner's Rule

[This algorithm computes the value of the real polynomial $a[n]x^n + a[n-1]x^{n-1} + \cdots + a[2]x^2 + a[1]x + a[0]$ by nesting successive additions and multiplications as indicated in the following parenthesization:

$$((\cdots((a[n]x + a[n-1])x + a[n-2])x$$
$$+ \cdots + a[2])x + a[1])x + a[0].$$

At each stage, starting with $a[n]$, the current value of polyval is multiplied by x and the next lower coefficient of the polynomial is added on.]

Input: n *[a nonnegative integer]* $a[0], a[1], a[2], \ldots, a[n]$ *[an array of real numbers], x [a real number]*

Algorithm Body:
    $polyval := a[n]$
    for $i := 1$ **to** n
        $polyval := polyval \cdot x + a[n-i]$
    next i
    [At this point
    $polyval = a[n]x^n + a[n-1]x^{n-1}$
                $+ \cdots + a[2]x^2 + a[1]x + a[0].]$

Output: $polyval$ *[a real number]*

40. Trace Algorithm 11.3.4 for the input $n = 3, a[0] = 2, a[1] = 1, a[2] = -1, a[3] = 3$, and $x = 2$.

41. Trace Algorithm 11.3.4 for the input $n = 2, a[0] = 5, a[1] = -1, a[2] = 2$, and $x = 3$.

H 42. Let t_n = the number of additions and multiplications that

must be performed when Algorithm 11.3.4 is e: a polynomial of degree n. Express t_n as a functi

43. Use the theorem on polynomial orders to find an order for Algorithm 11.3.4. How does this order compare with that of Algorithm 11.3.3?

Answers for Test Yourself

1. one iteration of the innermost loop   2. n   3. n^2; n^2

11.4 Exponential and Logarithmic Functions: Graphs and Orders

We ought never to allow ourselves to be persuaded of the truth of anything unless on the evidence of our own reason. — René Descartes, 1596–1650

Exponential and logarithmic functions are of great importance in mathematics in general and in computer science in particular. Several important computer algorithms have execution times that involve logarithmic functions of the size of the input data (which means they are relatively efficient for large data sets), and some have execution times that are exponential functions of the size of the input data (which means they are quite inefficient for large data sets). In addition, since exponential and logarithmic functions arise naturally in the descriptions of many growth and decay processes and in the computation of many kinds of probabilities, these functions are used in the analysis of computer operating systems, in queuing theory, and in the theory of information.

Graphs of Exponential Functions

As defined in Section 7.2, the exponential function with base $b > 0$ is the function that sends each real number x to b^x. The graph of the exponential function with base 2 (together with a partial table of its values) is shown in Figure 11.4.1. Note that the values of this function increase with extraordinary rapidity. If we tried to continue drawing the graph using the scale shown in Figure 11.4.1, we would have to plot the point $(10, 2^{10})$ more than 21 feet above the horizontal axis. And the point $(30, 2^{30})$ would be located more than 610,080 miles above the axis—well beyond the moon!

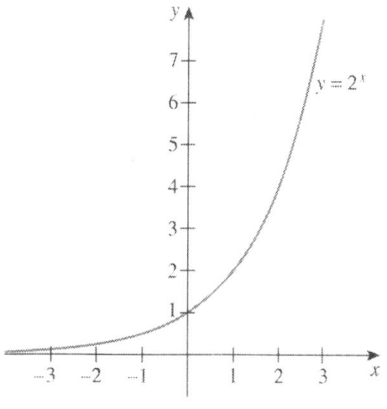

x	2^x
0	$2^0 = 1$
1	$2^1 = 2$
2	$2^2 = 4$
3	$2^3 = 8$
-1	$2^{-1} = 0.5$
-2	$2^{-2} = 0.25$
-3	$2^{-3} = 0.125$
0.5	$2^{0.5} \cong 1.414$
-0.5	$2^{-0.5} \cong 0.707$

Figure 11.4.1 The Exponential Function with Base 2

The graph of any exponential function with base $b > 1$ has a shape that is similar to the graph of the exponential function with base 2. If $0 < b < 1$, then $1/b > 0$ and the graph of the exponential function with base b is the reflection across the vertical axis of the exponential function with base $1/b$. These facts are illustrated in Figure 11.4.2.

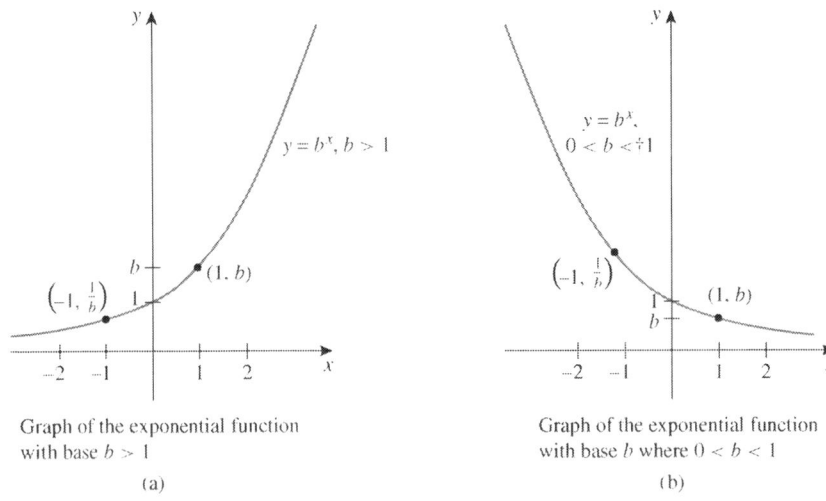

Graph of the exponential function with base $b > 1$

(a)

Graph of the exponential function with base b where $0 < b < 1$

(b)

Figure 11.4.2 **Graphs of Exponential Functions**

Graphs of Logarithmic Functions

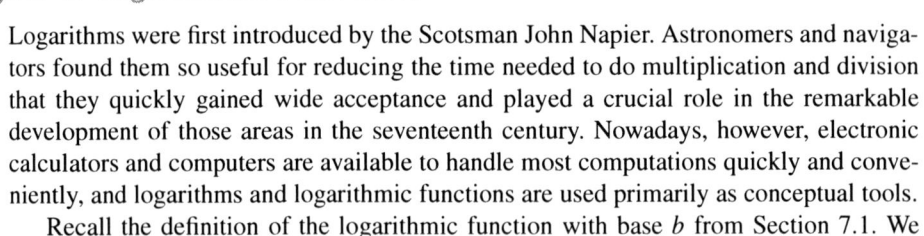

John Napier (1550–1617)

Bettmann/CORBIS

Logarithms were first introduced by the Scotsman John Napier. Astronomers and navigators found them so useful for reducing the time needed to do multiplication and division that they quickly gained wide acceptance and played a crucial role in the remarkable development of those areas in the seventeenth century. Nowadays, however, electronic calculators and computers are available to handle most computations quickly and conveniently, and logarithms and logarithmic functions are used primarily as conceptual tools.

Recall the definition of the logarithmic function with base b from Section 7.1. We state it formally below.

• Definition

If b is a positive real number not equal to 1, then the **logarithmic function with base b, $\log_b$: $\mathbf{R}^+ \to \mathbf{R}$**, is the function that sends each positive real number x to the number $\log_b x$, which is the exponent to which b must be raised to obtain x.

The logarithmic function with base b is, in fact, the inverse of the exponential function with base b. (See exercise 10 at the end of this section.) It follows that the graphs of the two functions are symmetric with respect to the line $y = x$. The graph of the logarithmic function with base $b > 1$ is shown in Figure 11.4.3 on the next page.

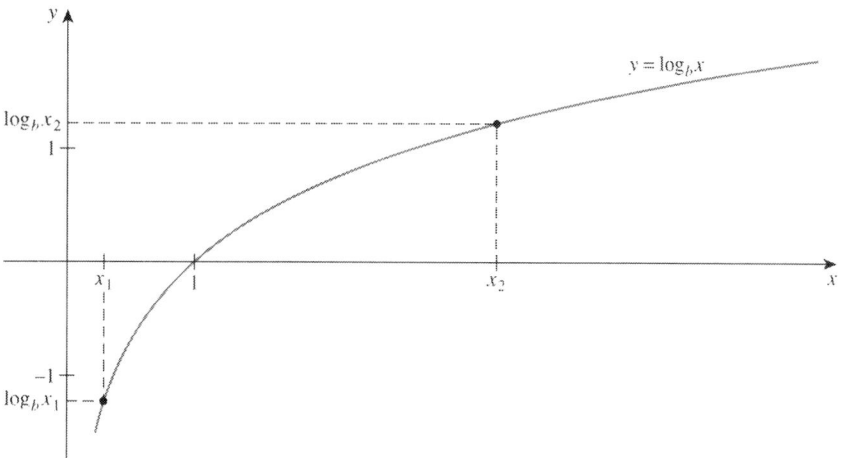

Figure 11.4.3 **The Graph of the Logarithmic Function with Base $b > 1$**

If its base b is greater than 1, the logarithmic function is increasing. Analytically, this means that

---

if $b > 1$, then for all positive numbers x_1 and x_2,

$$\text{if } x_1 < x_2, \text{ then } \log_b(x_1) < \log_b(x_2).$$ 11.4.1

Note   As examples, $\log_2(1,024)$ is only 10 and $\log_2(1,048,576)$ is just 20.

Corresponding to the rapid growth of the exponential function, however, is the very slow growth of the logarithmic function. Thus you must go very far out on the horizontal axis to find points whose logarithms are large numbers.

The following example shows how to make use of the increasing nature of the logarithmic function with base 2 to derive a remarkably useful property.

Example 11.4.1   Base 2 Logarithms of Numbers between Two Consecutive Powers of 2

Prove the following property:

a.

If k is an integer and x is a real number with

$$2^k \leq x < 2^{k+1}, \text{ then } \lfloor \log_2 x \rfloor = k.$$ 11.4.2

---

b. Describe property (11.4.2) in words and give a graphical interpretation of the property for $x > 1$.

Solution

a. Suppose that k is an integer and x is a real number with

$$2^k \leq x < 2^{k+1}.$$

Because the logarithmic function with base 2 is increasing, this implies that

$$\log_2(2^k) \leq \log_2 x < \log_2(2^{k+1}).$$

But $\log_2(2^k) = k$ *[the exponent to which you must raise 2 to get 2^k is k]* and $\log_2(2^{k+1}) = k + 1$ *[for a similar reason]*. Hence

$$k \leq \log_2 x < k + 1.$$

By definition of the floor function, then,

$$\lfloor \log_2 x \rfloor = k.$$

b. Recall that the floor of a positive number is its integer part. For instance, $\lfloor 2.82 \rfloor = 2$. Hence property (11.4.2) can be described in words as follows:

> If x is a positive number that lies between two consecutive integer powers of 2, the floor of the logarithm with base 2 of x is the exponent of the smaller power of 2.

A graphical interpretation follows:

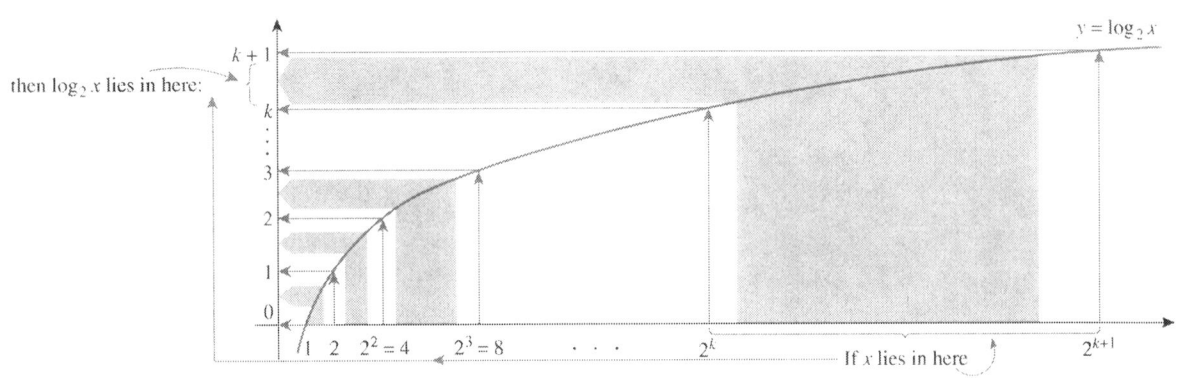

One consequence of property (11.4.2) does not appear particularly interesting in its own right but is frequently needed as a step in the analysis of algorithm efficiency.

Example 11.4.2 When $\lfloor \log_2(n-1) \rfloor = \lfloor \log_2 n \rfloor$

Prove the following property:

> For any odd integer $n > 1$, $\lfloor \log_2(n-1) \rfloor = \lfloor \log_2 n \rfloor$. 11.4.3

Solution   If n is an odd integer that is greater than 1, then n lies strictly between two successive powers of 2:

$$2^k < n < 2^{k+1} \quad \text{for some integer } k > 0. \qquad 11.4.4$$

It follows that $2^k \leq n - 1$ because $2^k < n$ and both 2^k and n are integers. Consequently,

$$2^k \leq n - 1 < 2^{k+1}. \qquad 11.4.5$$

Applying property (11.4.2) to both (11.4.4) and (11.4.5) gives

$$\lfloor \log_2 n \rfloor = k \quad \text{and also} \quad \lfloor \log_2(n-1) \rfloor = k.$$

Hence $\lfloor \log_2 n \rfloor = \lfloor \log_2(n-1) \rfloor$.

Application: Number of Bits Needed to Represent an Integer in Binary Notation

Given a positive integer n, how many binary digits are needed to represent n? To answer this question, recall from Section 5.4 that any positive integer n can be written in a unique way as

$$n = 2^k + c_{k-1} \cdot 2^{k-1} + \cdots + c_2 \cdot 2^2 + c_1 \cdot 2 + c_0,$$

where k is a nonnegative integer and each $c_0, c_1, c_2, \ldots c_{k-1}$ is either 0 or 1. Then the binary representation of n is

$$1 c_{k-1} c_{k-2} \cdots c_2 c_1 c_0,$$

and so the number of binary digits needed to represent n is $k + 1$.

What is $k + 1$ as a function of n? Observe that since each $c_i \leq 1$,

$$n = 2^k + c_{k-1} \cdot 2^{k-1} + \cdots + c_2 \cdot 2^2 + c_1 \cdot 2 + c_0 \leq 2^k + 2^{k-1} + \cdots + 2^2 + 2 + 1.$$

But by the formula for the sum of a geometric sequence (Theorem 5.2.3),

$$2^k + 2^{k-1} + \cdots + 2^2 + 2 + 1 = \frac{2^{k+1} - 1}{2 - 1} = 2^{k+1} - 1.$$

Hence, by transitivity of order,

$$n \leq 2^{k+1} - 1 < 2^{k+1} \qquad\qquad 11.4.6$$

In addition, because each $c_i \geq 0$,

$$2^k \leq 2^k + c_{k-1} \cdot 2^{k-1} + \cdots + c_2 \cdot 2^2 + c_1 \cdot 2 + c_0 = n. \qquad\qquad 11.4.7$$

Putting inequalities (11.4.6) and (11.4.7) together gives the double inequality

$$2^k \leq n < 2^{k+1}.$$

But then, by property (11.4.2),

$$k = \lfloor \log_2 n \rfloor.$$

Thus the number of binary digits needed to represent n is $\lfloor \log_2 n \rfloor + 1$.

Example 11.4.3 Number of Bits in a Binary Representation

How many binary digits are needed to represent 52,837 in binary notation?

Solution   If you compute the logarithm with base 2 using the formula in part (a) of Theorem 7.2.1 and a calculator that gives you approximate values of logarithms with base 10, you find that

$$\log_2(52,837) \cong \frac{\log_{10}(52,837)}{\log_{10}(2)} \cong \frac{4.722938151}{0.3010299957} \cong 15.7.$$

Thus the binary representation of 52,837 has $\lfloor 15.7 \rfloor + 1 = 15 + 1 = 16$ binary digits. ∎

Application: Using Logarithms to Solve Recurrence Relations

In Chapter 5 we discussed methods for solving recurrence relations. One class of recurrence relations that is very important in computer science has solutions that can be expressed in terms of logarithms. One such recurrence relation is discussed in the next example.

Example 11.4.4 A Recurrence Relation with a Logarithmic Solution

Define a sequence $a_1, a_2, a_3, \ldots$ recursively as follows:

$$a_1 = 1,$$
$$a_k = 2a_{\lfloor k/2 \rfloor} \quad \text{for all integers } k \geq 2.$$

a. Use iteration to guess an explicit formula for this sequence.

b. Use strong mathematical induction to confirm the correctness of the formula obtained in part (a).

Solution

a. Begin by iterating to find the values of the first few terms of the sequence.

$$a_1 = 1 \qquad\qquad 1 = 2^0$$

$$\left.\begin{array}{l} a_2 = 2a_{\lfloor 2/2 \rfloor} = 2a_1 = 2 \cdot 1 = 2 \\ a_3 = 2a_{\lfloor 3/2 \rfloor} = 2a_1 = 2 \cdot 1 = 2 \end{array}\right\} \qquad 2 = 2^1$$

$$\left.\begin{array}{l} a_4 = 2a_{\lfloor 4/2 \rfloor} = 2a_2 = 2 \cdot 2 = 4 \\ a_5 = 2a_{\lfloor 5/2 \rfloor} = 2a_2 = 2 \cdot 2 = 4 \\ a_6 = 2a_{\lfloor 6/2 \rfloor} = 2a_3 = 2 \cdot 2 = 4 \\ a_7 = 2a_{\lfloor 7/2 \rfloor} = 2a_3 = 2 \cdot 2 = 4 \end{array}\right\} \qquad 4 = 2^2$$

$$\left.\begin{array}{l} a_8 = 2a_{\lfloor 8/2 \rfloor} = 2a_4 = 2 \cdot 4 = 8 \\ a_9 = 2a_{\lfloor 9/2 \rfloor} = 2a_4 = 2 \cdot 4 = 8 \\ \qquad \vdots \qquad\qquad\qquad \vdots \\ a_{15} = 2a_{\lfloor 15/2 \rfloor} = 2a_7 = 2 \cdot 4 = 8 \end{array}\right\} \qquad 8 = 2^3$$

$$\left.\begin{array}{l} a_{16} = 2a_{\lfloor 16/2 \rfloor} = 2a_8 = 2 \cdot 8 = 16 \\ \qquad \vdots \end{array}\right\} \qquad 16 = 2^4$$

Note that in each case when the subscript n is between two powers of 2, a_n equals the smaller power of 2. More precisely:

$$\text{If } 2^i \leq n < 2^{i+1}, \text{ then } a_n = 2^i. \tag{11.4.8}$$

But since n satisfies the inequality

$$2^i \leq n < 2^{i+1},$$

then (by property 11.4.2)

$$i = \lfloor \log_2 n \rfloor.$$

Substituting into statement (11.4.8) gives

$$a_n = 2^{\lfloor \log_2 n \rfloor}.$$

b. The following proof shows that if $a_1, a_2, a_3, \ldots$ is a sequence of numbers that satisfies

$$a_1 = 1, \quad \text{and} \quad a_k = 2a_{\lfloor k/2 \rfloor} \quad \text{for all integers } k \geq 2,$$

then the sequence satisfies the formula

$$a_n = 2^{\lfloor \log_2 n \rfloor} \quad \text{for all integers } n \geq 1.$$

Proof:

Let $a_1, a_2, a_3, \ldots$ be the sequence defined by specifying that $a_1 = 1$ and $a_k = 2_{\lfloor a_{k/2} \rfloor}$ for all integers $k \geq 2$, and let the property $P(n)$ be the equation

$$a_n = 2^{\lfloor \log_2 n \rfloor}. \qquad \leftarrow P(n)$$

We will use strong mathematical induction to prove that for all integers $n \geq 1$, $P(n)$ is true.

Show that P (1) is true: By definition of $a_1, a_2, a_3, \ldots$, we have that $a_1 = 1$. But it is also the case that $2^{\lfloor \log_2 1 \rfloor} = 2^0 = 1$. Thus $a_1 = 2^{\lfloor \log_2 1 \rfloor}$ and $P(1)$ is true.

Show that for all integers $k \geq 1$, if $P(i)$ is true for all integers i from 1 through k, then $P(k + 1)$ is also true: Let k be any integer with $k \geq 1$, and suppose that

$$a_i = 2^{\lfloor \log_2 i \rfloor} \text{ for all integers } i \text{ with } 1 \leq i \leq k. \qquad \leftarrow \text{inductive hypothesis}$$

We must show that

$$a_{k+1} = 2^{\lfloor \log_2 (k+1) \rfloor} \qquad \leftarrow P(k+1)$$

Consider the two cases: k is even and k is odd.

Case 1 (k is even): In this case, $k + 1$ is odd, and

$$
\begin{aligned}
a_{k+1} &= 2a_{\lfloor (k+1)/2 \rfloor} && \text{by definition of } a_1, a_2, a_3, \ldots \\
&= 2a_{k/2} && \text{because } \lfloor (k+1)/2 \rfloor = k/2 \text{ since } k+1 \text{ is odd} \\
&= 2 \cdot 2^{\lfloor \log_2 (k/2) \rfloor} && \text{by inductive hypothesis because, since } k \text{ is even,} \\
& && k \geq 2, \text{ and so } k/2 \geq 1 \\
&= 2^{\lfloor \log_2 (k/2) \rfloor + 1} && \text{by the laws of exponents from algebra (7.2.1)} \\
&= 2^{\lfloor \log_2 k - \log_2 2 \rfloor + 1} && \text{by the identity } \log_b(x/y) = \log_b x - \log_b y \\
& && \text{from Theorem 7.2.1} \\
&= 2^{\lfloor \log_2 k - 1 \rfloor + 1} && \text{since } \log_2 2 = 1 \\
&= 2^{\lfloor \log_2 k \rfloor - 1 + 1} && \text{by substituting } x = \log_2 k \text{ into the identity} \\
& && \lfloor x - 1 \rfloor = \lfloor x \rfloor - 1 \text{ derived in exercise 15 of Section 4.5} \\
&= 2^{\lfloor \log_2 k \rfloor} \\
&= 2^{\lfloor \log_2 (k+1) \rfloor} && \text{by property (11.4.3)}
\end{aligned}
$$

Case 2 (k is odd): The analysis of this case is very similar to that of case 1 and is left as exercise 56 at the end of the section.

Thus in either case, $a_n = 2^{\lfloor \log_2 (k+1) \rfloor}$, as was to be shown. ■

Exponential and Logarithmic Orders

Now consider the question "How do graphs of logarithmic and exponential functions compare with graphs of power functions?" It turns out that for large enough values of x, the graph of the logarithmic function with any base $b > 1$ lies *below* the graph of any positive power function, and the graph of the exponential function with any base $b > 1$ lies *above* the graph of any positive power function. In analytic terms, this says the following:

For all real numbers b and r with $b > 1$ and $r > 0$,

$$\log_b x \leq x^r \quad \text{for all sufficiently large real numbers } x. \qquad 11.4.9$$

and $\qquad x^r \leq b^x \qquad$ for all sufficiently large real numbers x. $\qquad 11.4.10$

These statements have the following implications for O-notation.

For all real numbers b and r with $b > 1$ and $r > 0$,

$$\log_b x \quad \text{is} \quad O(x^r) \qquad\qquad 11.4.11$$

and

$$x^r \quad \text{is} \quad O(b^x) \qquad\qquad 11.4.12$$

Another important function in the analysis of algorithms is the function f defined by the formula

$$f(x) = x \log_b x \quad \text{for all real numbers } x > 0.$$

For large values of x, the graph of this function fits in between the graph of the identity function and the graph of the squaring function. More precisely:

For all real numbers b with $b > 1$ and for all sufficiently large real numbers x,

$$x \le x \log_b x \le x^2. \qquad\qquad 11.4.13$$

The O-notation versions of these facts are as follows:

For all real numbers $b > 1$,

$$x \quad \text{is} \quad O(x \log_b x) \quad \text{and} \quad x \log_b x \quad \text{is} \quad O(x^2). \qquad\qquad 11.4.14$$

Although proofs of some of these facts require calculus, proofs of some cases can be obtained using the algebra of inequalities. (See the exercises at the end of this section.) Figure 11.4.4 illustrates the relationships among some power functions, the logarithmic function with base 2, the exponential function with base 2, and the function defined by the formula $x \to x \log_2 x$. Note that different scales are used on the horizontal and vertical axes.

Example 11.4.5 shows how to use inequalities such as (11.4.9), (11.4.10), and (11.4.13) to derive additional orders involving the logarithmic function.

Example 11.4.5 Deriving an Order from Logarithmic Inequalities

Show that $x + x \log_2 x$ is $\Theta(x \log_2 x)$.

Solution First observe that $x + x \log_2 x$ is $\Omega(x \log_2 x)$ because for all real numbers $x > 1$,

$$x \log_2 x \le x + x \log_2 x,$$

and since all quantities are positive,

$$|x \log_2 x| \le |x + x \log_2 x|.$$

Let $A = 1$ and $a = 1$. Then

$$A|x \log_2 x| \le |x + x \log_2 x| \quad \text{for all } x > a.$$

Hence, by definition of Ω-notation,

$$x + x \log_2 x \quad \text{is} \quad \Omega(x \log_2 x).$$

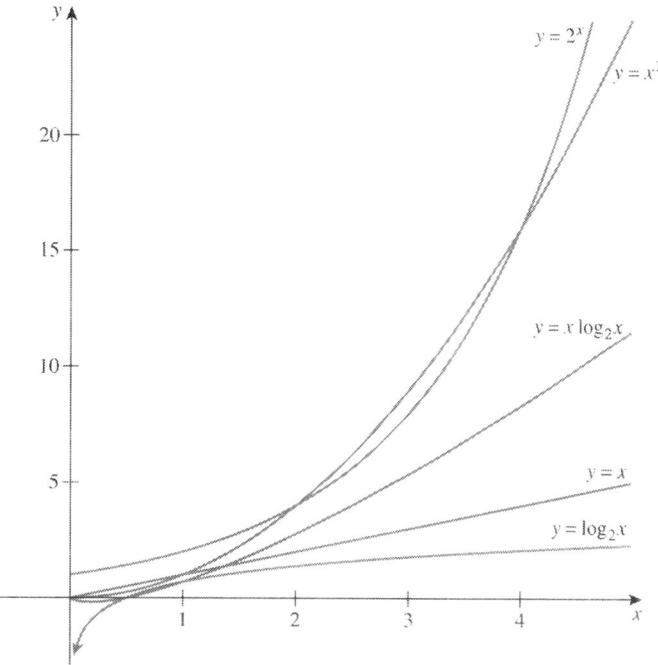

Figure 11.4.4 Graphs of Some Logarithmic, Exponential, and Power Functions

To show that $x + x \log_2 x$ is $O(x \log_2 x)$, note that according to property (11.4.13) with $b = 2$, there is a number b such that for all $x > b$,

$$x < x \log_2 x$$
$$\Rightarrow \quad x + x \log_2 x < 2x \log_2 x \qquad \text{by adding } x \log_2 x \text{ to both sides}$$

Thus, if b is taken to be greater than 2, then

$$|x + x \log_2 x| \; < \; 2|x \log_2 x| \qquad \begin{array}{l}\text{because when } x > 2, x \log_2 x > 0, \text{ and so} \\ |x + x \log_2 x| = x + x \log_2 x \text{ and} \\ \log_2 x = |x \log_2 x|.\end{array}$$

Let $B = 2$. Then

$$|x + x \log_2 x| \le B|x \log_2 x| \quad \text{for all } x > b.$$

Hence, by definition of O-notation

$$x + x \log_2 x \quad \text{is} \quad O(x \log_2 x).$$

Therefore, since $x + x \log_2 x$ is $\Omega(x \log_2 x)$ and $x + x \log_2 x$ is $O(x \log_2 x)$, by Theorem 11.2.1,

$$x + x \log_2 x \quad \text{is} \quad \Theta(x \log_2 x). \qquad\qquad\qquad ▧$$

Example 11.4.5 illustrates a special case of a useful general fact about O-notation: *If one function "dominates" another (in the sense of being larger for large values of the variable), then the sum of the two is big-O of the dominating function.* (See exercise 49a in Section 11.2.)

Example 11.4.6 shows that any two logarithmic functions with bases greater than 1 have the same order.

Example 11.4.6 Logarithm with Base b Is Big-Theta of Logarithm with Base c

Show that if b and c are real numbers such that $b > 1$ and $c > 1$, then $\log_b x$ is $\Theta(\log_c x)$.

Solution Suppose b and c are real numbers and $b > 1$ and $c > 1$. To show that $\log_b x$ is $\Theta(\log_c x)$, positive real numbers A, B, and k must be found such that

$$A|\log_c x| \le |\log_b x| \le B|\log_c x| \quad \text{for all real numbers } x > k.$$

By part (d) of Theorem 7.2.1,

$$\log_b x = \frac{\log_c x}{\log_c b} = \left(\frac{1}{\log_c b}\right)\log_c x. \tag{$*$}$$

Since $b > 1$ and the logarithmic function with base c is strictly increasing, then $\log_c b > \log_c 1 = 0$, and so $\dfrac{1}{\log_c b} > 0$ also. Furthermore, if $x > 1$, then $\log_b x > 0$ and $\log_c x > 0$. It follows from equation $(*)$, therefore, that

$$\left(\frac{1}{\log_c b}\right)\log_c x \le \log_b x \le \left(\frac{1}{\log_c b}\right)\log_c x \tag{$**$}$$

for all real numbers $x > 1$. Accordingly, let $A = \dfrac{1}{\log_c b}$, $B = \dfrac{1}{\log_c b}$, and $k = 1$. Then, since all quantities in $(**)$ are positive,

$$A|\log_c x| \le |\log_b x| \le B|\log_c x| \quad \text{for all real numbers } x > k.$$

Hence, by definition of Θ-notation,

$$\log_b x \quad \text{is} \quad \Theta(\log_c x).$$ ■

Example 11.4.7 shows how a logarithmic order can arise from the computation of a certain kind of sum. It requires the following fact from calculus:

The area underneath the graph of $y = 1/x$ between $x = 1$ and $x = n$ equals $\ln n$, where $\ln n = \log_e n$. This fact is illustrated in Figure 11.4.5.

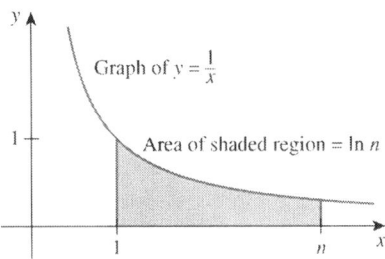

Graph of $y = \dfrac{1}{x}$

Area of shaded region $= \ln n$

Figure 11.4.5 **Area Under Graph of** $y = \dfrac{1}{x}$ **Between** $x = 1$ **and** $x = n$

Example 11.4.7 Order of a Harmonic Sum

Sums of the form $1 + \dfrac{1}{2} + \cdots + \dfrac{1}{n}$ are called *harmonic sums*. They occur in the analysis of various computer algorithms such as quick sort. Show that $1 + \dfrac{1}{2} + \dfrac{1}{3} + \cdots + \dfrac{1}{n}$ is $\Omega(\ln n)$ by performing the steps on the next page:

a. Interpret Figure 11.4.6 to show that

$$\frac{1}{2} + \frac{1}{3} + \cdots + \frac{1}{n} \le \ln n.$$

and

$$\ln n \le 1 + \frac{1}{2} + \frac{1}{3} + \cdots + \frac{1}{n}.$$

b. Show that if n is an integer that is at least 3, then $1 \le \ln n$.

c. Deduce from (a) and (b) that if the integer n is greater than or equal to 3, then

$$\ln n \le 1 + \frac{1}{2} + \frac{1}{3} + \cdots + \frac{1}{n} \le 2 \ln n.$$

d. Deduce from (c) that

$$1 + \frac{1}{2} + \frac{1}{3} + \cdots + \frac{1}{n} \text{ is } \Theta(\ln n).$$

Solution

a. Figure 11.4.6(a) shows rectangles whose bases are the intervals between each pair of integers from 1 to n and whose heights are the heights of the graph of $y = 1/x$ above the right-hand endpoints of the intervals. Figure 11.4.6(b) shows rectangles with the same bases but whose heights are the heights of the graph above the left-hand endpoints of the intervals.

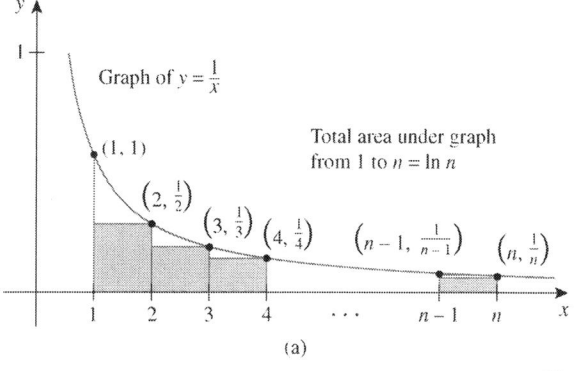

(a)

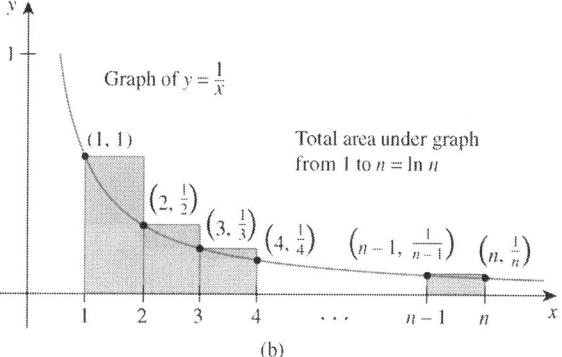

(b)

Figure 11.4.6

Now the area of each rectangle is its base times its height. Since all the rectangles have base 1, the area of each rectangle equals its height. Thus in Figure 11.4.6(a),

the area of the rectangle from 1 to 2 is $\frac{1}{2}$;

the area of the rectangle from 2 to 3 is $\frac{1}{3}$;

$$\vdots$$

the area of the rectangle from $n - 1$ to n is $\frac{1}{n}$.

So the sum of the areas of all the rectangles is $\frac{1}{2} + \frac{1}{3} + \cdots + \frac{1}{n}$. From the picture it is clear that this sum is less than the area underneath the graph of f between $x = 1$ and $x = n$, which is known to equal $\ln n$. Hence

$$\frac{1}{2} + \frac{1}{3} + \cdots + \frac{1}{n} \leq \ln n.$$

A similar analysis of the areas of the combined blue and gray rectangles in Figure 11.4.6(b) shows that

$$\ln n \leq 1 + \frac{1}{2} + \frac{1}{3} + \cdots + \frac{1}{n}.$$

b. Suppose n is an integer and $n \geq 3$. Since $e \cong 2.718$, then $n \geq e$. Now the logarithmic function with base e is strictly increasing. Thus since $e \leq n$, then $1 = \ln e \leq \ln n$.

c. By part (a),

$$\frac{1}{2} + \frac{1}{3} + \cdots + \frac{1}{n} \leq \ln n,$$

and by part (b),

$$1 \leq \ln n.$$

Adding these two inequalities together gives

$$1 + \frac{1}{2} + \frac{1}{3} + \cdots + \frac{1}{n} \leq 2 \ln n \quad \text{for any integer } n \geq 3.$$

d. Putting together the results of parts (a) and (c) leads to the conclusion that for all integers $n \geq 3$,

$$\ln n \leq 1 + \frac{1}{2} + \frac{1}{3} + \cdots + \frac{1}{n} \leq 2 \ln n.$$

And because all the quantities are positive for $n \geq 3$,

$$|\ln n| \leq \left| 1 + \frac{1}{2} + \frac{1}{3} + \cdots + \frac{1}{n} \right| \leq 2|\ln n|.$$

Let $A = 1$, $B = 2$, and $k = 3$. Then

$$A|\ln n| \leq \left| 1 + \frac{1}{2} + \frac{1}{3} + \cdots + \frac{1}{n} \right| \leq B|\ln n| \quad \text{for all } n > k.$$

Hence by definition of Θ-notation,

$$1 + \frac{1}{2} + \frac{1}{3} + \cdots + \frac{1}{n} \text{ is } \Theta(\ln n). \qquad \blacksquare$$

Test Yourself

1. The domain of any exponential function is _____, and its range is _____.

2. The domain of any logarithmic function is _____, and its range is _____.

3. If k is an integer and $2^k \leq x < 2^{k+1}$, then $\lfloor \log_2 x \rfloor = $ _____.

4. If b is a real number with $b > 1$ and if x is a sufficiently large real number, then when the quantities x, x^2, $\log_b x$, and $x \log_b x$ are arranged in order of increasing size, the result is _____.

5. If n is a positive integer, then $1 + \frac{1}{2} + \frac{1}{3} + \cdots + \frac{1}{n}$ has order _____.

Exercise Set 11.4

Graph each function defined in 1–8.

1. $f(x) = 3^x$ for all real numbers x

2. $g(x) = \left(\frac{1}{3}\right)^x$ for all real numbers x

3. $h(x) = \log_{10} x$ for all positive real numbers x

4. $k(x) = \log_2 x$ for all positive real numbers x

5. $F(x) = \lfloor \log_2 x \rfloor$ for all positive real numbers x

6. $G(x) = \lceil \log_2 x \rceil$ for all positive real numbers x

7. $H(x) = x \log_2 x$ for all positive real numbers x

8. $K(x) = x \log_{10} x$ for all positive real numbers x

9. The scale of the graph shown in Figure 11.4.1 is one-fourth inch to each unit. If the point $(2, 2^{64})$ is plotted on the graph of $y = 2^x$, how many miles will it lie above the horizontal axis? What is the ratio of the height of the point to the distance of the earth from the sun? (There are 12 inches per foot and 5,280 feet per mile. The earth is approximately 93,000,000 miles from the sun on average.) ($\frac{1}{4}$ inch $\cong 0.635$ cm, 1 mile $\cong 0.62$ km)

10. a. Use the definition of logarithm to show that $\log_b b^x = x$ for all real numbers x.
    b. Use the definition of logarithm to show that $b^{\log_b x} = x$ for all positive real numbers x.
    c. By the result of exercise 25 in Section 7.3, if $f: X \to Y$ and $g: Y \to X$ are functions and $g \circ f = I_X$ and $f \circ g = I_Y$, then f and g are inverse functions. Use this result to show that $\log_b$ and $\exp_b$ (the exponential function with base b) are inverse functions.

11. Let $b > 1$.
    a. Use the fact that $u = \log_b v \Leftrightarrow v = b^u$ to show that a point (u, v) lies on the graph of the logarithmic function with base b if, and only if, (v, u) lies on the graph of the exponential function with base b.
    b. Plot several pairs of points of the form (u, v) and (v, u) on a coordinate system. Describe the geometric relationship between the locations of the points in each pair.
    c. Draw the graphs of $y = \log_2 x$ and $y = 2^x$. Describe the geometric relationship between these graphs.

12. Give a graphical interpretation for property (11.4.2) in Example 11.4.1(a) for $0 < x < 1$.

13. Suppose a positive real number x satisfies the inequality $10^m \le x < 10^{m+1}$ where m is an integer. What can be inferred about $\lfloor \log_{10} x \rfloor$? Justify your answer.

14. a. Prove that if x is a positive real number and k is a nonnegative integer such that $2^{k-1} < x \le 2^k$, then $\lceil \log_2 x \rceil = k$.
    b. Describe in words the statement proved in part (a).

15. If n is an odd integer and $n > 1$, is $\lceil \log_2(n - 1) \rceil = \lceil \log_2(n) \rceil$? Justify your answer.

16. If n is an odd integer and $n > 1$, is $\lceil \log_2(n + 1) \rceil = \lceil \log_2(n) \rceil$? Justify your answer.

17. If n is an odd integer and $n > 1$, is $\lfloor \log_2(n + 1) \rfloor = \lfloor \log_2(n) \rfloor$? Justify your answer.

In 18 and 19, indicate how many binary digits are needed to represent the numbers in binary notation. Use the method shown in Example 11.4.3.

18. 148,206

19. 5,067,329

20. It was shown in the text that the number of binary digits needed to represent a positive integer n is $\lfloor \log_2 n \rfloor + 1$. Can this also be given as $\lceil \log_2 n \rceil$? Why or why not?

In each of 21 and 22, a sequence is specified by a recurrence relation and initial conditions. In each case, (a) use iteration to guess an explicit formula for the sequence; (b) use strong mathematical induction to confirm the correctness of the formula you obtained in part (a).

21. $a_k = a_{\lfloor k/2 \rfloor} + 2$, for all integers $k \ge 2$
    $a_1 = 1$

22. $b_k = b_{\lceil k/2 \rceil} + 1$, for all integers $k \ge 2$
    $b_1 = 1$.

H 23. Define a sequence $c_1, c_2, c_3, \ldots,$ recursively as follows:

$$c_1 = 0,$$
$$c_k = 2c_{\lfloor k/2 \rfloor} + k, \quad \text{for all integers } k \ge 2.$$

Use strong mathematical induction to show that $c_n \le n^2$ for all integers $n \ge 1$.

* H 24. Use strong mathematical induction to show that for the sequence of exercise 23, $c_n \le n \log_2 n$, for all integers $n \ge 4$.

Exercises 25–28 refer to properties 11.4.9 and 11.4.10. To solve them, think big!

25. Find a real number $x > 3$ such that $\log_2 x < x^{1/10}$.

26. Find a real number $x > 1$ such that $x^{50} < 2^x$.

27. Find a real number $x > 2$ such that $x < 1.0001^x$.

28. Use a graphing calculator or computer graphing program to find two distinct approximate values of x such that $x = 1.0001^x$. On what approximate intervals is $x > 1.0001^x$? On what approximate intervals is $x < 1.0001^x$?

29. Use Θ-notation to express the following statement:

$$|x^2| \le |7x^2 + 3x \log_2 x| \le 10|x^2|,$$

for all real numbers $x > 2$.

Derive each statement in 30–33.

30. $2x + \log_2 x$ is $\Theta(x)$.

31. $x^2 + 5x \log_2 x$ is $\Theta(x^2)$.

32. $n^2 + 2^n$ is $\Theta(2^n)$.

H 33. 2^{n+1} is $\Theta(2^n)$.

H 34. Show that 4^n is not $O(2^n)$.

Prove each of the statements in 35–40, assuming n is an integer variable that takes positive integer values. Use identities from Section 5.2 as needed.

35. $1 + 2 + 2^2 + 2^3 + \cdots + 2^n$ is $\Theta(2^n)$.

H 36. $4 + 4^2 + 4^3 + \cdots + 4^n$ is $\Theta(4^n)$.

37. $\dfrac{1}{5} + \dfrac{4}{5^2} + \dfrac{4^2}{5^3} + \cdots + \dfrac{4^n}{5^{n+1}}$ is $\Theta(1)$.

38. $2 + 2 \cdot 3^2 + 2 \cdot 3^4 + \cdots + 2 \cdot 3^{2n}$ is $\Theta(3^{2n})$.

39. $n + \dfrac{n}{2} + \dfrac{n}{4} + \cdots + \dfrac{n}{2^n}$ is $\Theta(n)$.

40. $\dfrac{2n}{3} + \dfrac{2n}{3^2} + \dfrac{2n}{3^3} + \cdots + \dfrac{2n}{3^n}$ is $\Theta(n)$.

41. Quantities of the form

$$k_1 n + k_2\, n \log n \quad \text{for positive integers } k_1, k_2, \text{ and } n$$

arise in the analysis of the merge sort algorithm in computer science. Show that for any positive integer k,

$$k_1 n + k_2 n \log_2 n \ \text{ is } \ \Theta(n \log_2 n).$$

42. Calculate the values of the harmonic sums

$$1 + \dfrac{1}{2} + \dfrac{1}{3} + \cdots + \dfrac{1}{n} \quad \text{for } n = 2, 3, 4, \text{ and } 5.$$

43. Use part (d) of Example 11.4.7 to show that

$$n + \dfrac{n}{2} + \dfrac{n}{3} + \cdots + \dfrac{n}{n} \ \text{ is } \ \Theta(n \ln n).$$

44. Use the fact that $\log_2 x = \left(\dfrac{1}{\log_e 2}\right) \log_e x$ and $\log_e x = \ln x$, for all positive numbers x, and part (c) of Example 11.4.7 to show that

$$1 + \dfrac{1}{2} + \dfrac{1}{3} + \cdots + \dfrac{1}{n} \ \text{ is } \ \Theta(\log_2 n).$$

45. a. Show that $\lfloor \log_2 n \rfloor$ is $\Theta(\log_2 n)$.
    b. Show that $\lfloor \log_2 n \rfloor + 1$ is $\Theta(\log_2 n)$.

46. Prove by mathematical induction that $n \leq 10^n$ for all integers $n \geq 1$.

H 47. Prove by mathematical induction that $\log_2 n \leq n$ for all integers $n \geq 1$.

H 48. Show that if n is a variable that takes positive integer values, then 2^n is $O(n!)$.

49. Let n be a variable that takes positive integer values.
    a. Show that $n!$ is $O(n^n)$.

b. Use part (a) to show that $\log_2(n!)$ is $O(n \log_2 n)$.

H c. Show that $n^n \leq (n!)^2$ for all integers $n \geq 1$.

d. Use part (c) to show that $\log_2(n!)$ is $\Omega(n \log_2 n)$.

e. Use parts (b) and (d) to find an order for $\log_2(n!)$.

* 50. a. For all positive real numbers u, $\log_2 u < u$. Use this fact to show that for any positive integer n, $\log_2 x < nx^{1/n}$ for all real numbers $x > 0$.
     b. Interpret the statement of part (a) using O-notation.

51. a. For all real numbers x, $x < 2^x$. Use this fact to show that for any positive integer n, $x^n < n^n 2^x$ for all real numbers $x > 0$.
    b. Interpret the statement of part (a) using O-notation.

* 52. For all positive real numbers u, $\log_2 u < u$. Use this fact and the result of exercise 21 in Section 11.1 to prove the following: For all integers $n \geq 1$, $\log_2 x < x^{1/n}$ for all real numbers $x > (2n)^{2n}$.

53. Use the result of exercise 52 above to prove the following: For all integers $n \geq 1$, $x^n < 2^x$ for all real numbers $x > (2n)^{2n}$.

Exercises 54 and 55 use L'Hôpital's rule from calculus.

54. a. Let b be any real number greater than 1. Use L'Hôpital's rule and mathematical induction to prove that for all integers $n \geq 1$,

$$\lim_{x \to \infty} \frac{x^n}{b^x} = 0.$$

b. Use the result of part (a) and the definitions of limit and of O-notation to prove that x^n is $O(b^x)$ for any integer $n \geq 1$.

55. a. Let b be any real number greater than 1. Use L'Hôpital's rule to prove that for all integers $n \geq 1$,

$$\lim_{x \to \infty} \frac{\log_b x}{x^{1/n}} = 0.$$

b. Use the result of part (a) and the definitions of limit and of O-notation to prove that $\log_b x$ is $O(x^{1/n})$ for any integer $n \geq 1$.

56. Complete the proof in Example 11.4.4.

Answers for Test Yourself

1. the set of all real numbers; the set of all positive real numbers   2. the set of all positive real numbers; the set of all real numbers
3. k 4. $\log_b x < x < x \log_b x < x^2$ 5. $\ln x$ (or, equivalently, $\log_2 x$)

11.5 Application: Analysis of Algorithm Efficiency II

Pick a Number, Any Number — Donal O'Shea, 2007

Have you ever played the "guess my number" game? A person thinks of a number between two other numbers, say 1 and 10 or 1 and 100 for example, and you try to figure out what it is, using the least possible number of guesses. Each time you guess a number, the person tells you whether you are correct, too low, or too high.

If you have played this game, you have probably already hit upon the most efficient strategy: Begin by guessing a number as close to the middle of the two given numbers as possible. If your guess is too high, then the number is between the lower of the two given numbers and the one you first chose. If your guess is too low, then the number is between the number you first chose and the higher of the two given numbers. In either case, you take as your next guess a number as close as possible to the middle of the new range in which you now know the number lies. You repeat this process as many times as necessary until you have found the person's number.

The technique described previously is an example of a general strategy called **divide and conquer,** which works as follows: To solve a problem, reduce it to a fixed number of smaller problems of the same kind, which can themselves be reduced to the same fixed number of smaller problems of the same kind, and so forth until easily resolved problems are obtained. In this case, the problem of finding a particular number in a given range of numbers is reduced at each stage to finding a particular number in a range of numbers approximately half as long.

It turns out that algorithms using a divide-and-conquer strategy are generally quite efficient and nearly always have orders involving logarithmic functions. In this section we define the *binary search* algorithm, which is the formalization of the "guess my number" game described previously, and we compare the efficiency of binary search to the sequential search discussed in Section 11.3. Then we develop a divide-and-conquer algorithm for sorting, *merge sort,* and compare its efficiency with that of insertion sort and selection sort, which were also discussed in Section 11.3.

Binary Search

Whereas a sequential search can be performed on an array whose elements are in any order, a binary search can be performed only on an array whose elements are arranged in ascending (or descending) order. Given an array $a[1], a[2], \ldots, a[n]$ of distinct elements arranged in ascending order, consider the problem of trying to find a particular element x in the array.

To use binary search, first compare x to the "middle element" of the array. If the two are equal, the search is successful. If the two are not equal, then because the array elements are in ascending order, comparing the values of x and the middle array element narrows the search either to the lower subarray (consisting of all the array elements below the middle element) or to the upper subarray (consisting of all array elements above the middle element).

The search continues by repeating this basic process over and over on successively smaller subarrays. It terminates either when a match occurs or when the subarray to which the search has been narrowed contains no elements. The efficiency of the algorithm is a result of the fact that at each step, the length of the subarray to be searched is roughly half the length of the array of the previous step. This process is illustrated in Figure 11.5.1.

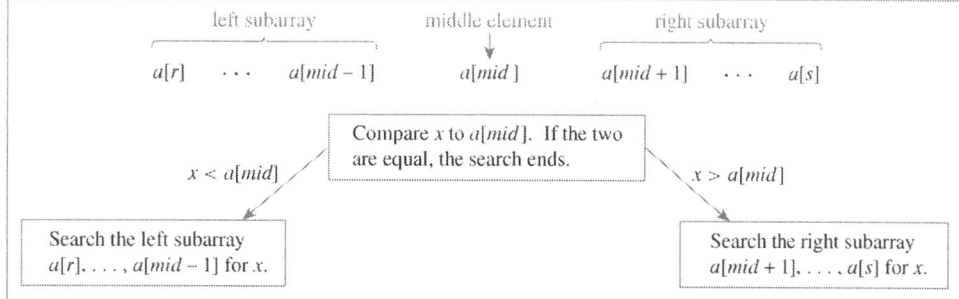

Figure 11.5.1 **One Iteration of the Binary Search Process**

To write down a formal algorithm for binary search, we introduce a variable *index* whose final value will tell us whether or not x is in the array and, if so, will indicate the location of x. Since the array goes from $a[1]$ to $a[n]$, we intialize *index* to be 0. If and when x is found, the value of *index* is changed to the subscript of the array element equaling x. If index still has the value 0 when the algorithm is complete, then x is not one of the elements in the array. Figure 11.5.2 shows the action of a particular binary search.

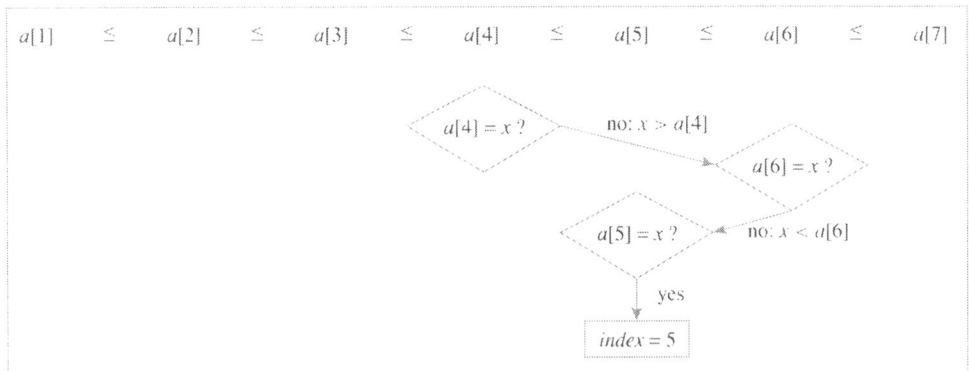

Figure 11.5.2 Binary Search of $a[1]$, $a[2]$, ..., $a[7]$ for x where $x = a[5]$

Formalizing a binary search algorithm also requires that we be more precise about the meaning of the "middle element" of an array. (This issue was side-stepped by careful choice of n in Figure 11.5.2.) If the array consists of an even number of elements, there are two elements in the middle. For instance, both $a[6]$ and $a[7]$ are equally in the middle of the following array.

$$a[3] \quad \underbrace{a[4] \quad a[5]}_{\text{three elements}} \quad \underbrace{a[6] \quad a[7]}_{\substack{\text{two middle} \\ \text{elements}}} \quad \underbrace{a[8] \quad a[9] \quad a[10]}_{\text{three elements}}$$

In a case such as this, the algorithm must choose which of the two middle elements to take, the smaller or the larger. The choice is arbitrary—either would do. We will write the algorithm to choose the smaller. The index of the smaller of the two middle elements is the floor of the average of the top and bottom indices of the array. That is, if

$$bot = \text{the bottom index of the array,}$$
$$top = \text{the top index of the array,} \quad \text{and}$$
$$mid = \text{the lower of the two middle indices of the array,}$$

then

$$mid = \left\lfloor \frac{bot + top}{2} \right\rfloor.$$

In this case, $bot = 3$ and $top = 10$, so the index of the "middle element" is

$$mid = \left\lfloor \frac{3 + 10}{2} \right\rfloor = \left\lfloor \frac{13}{2} \right\rfloor = \lfloor 6.5 \rfloor = 6.$$

The following is a formal algorithm for a binary search.

Algorithm 11.5.1 Binary Search

[The aim of this algorithm is to search for an element x in an ascending array of elements a[1], a[2], ..., a[n]. If x is found, the variable index is set equal to the index of the array element where x is located. If x is not found, index is not changed from its initial value, which is 0. The variables bot and top denote the bottom and top indices of the array currently being examined.]

Input: *n [a positive integer], a[1], a[2], ..., a[n] [an array of data items given in ascending order], x [a data item of the same data type as the elements of the array]*

Algorithm Body:

    index := 0, *bot* := 1, *top* := *n*

    [Compute the middle index of the array, mid. Compare x to a[mid]. If the two are equal, the search is successful. If not, repeat the process either for the lower or for the upper subarray, either giving top the new value mid − 1 or giving bot the new value mid + 1. Each iteration of the loop either decreases the value of top or increases the value of bot. Thus, if the looping is not stopped by success in the search process, eventually the value of top will become less than the value of bot. This occurrence stops the looping process and indicates that x is not an element of the array.]

    while *(top ≥ bot and index = 0)*

$$mid := \left\lfloor \frac{bot + top}{2} \right\rfloor$$

        if *a[mid] = x* **then** *index := mid*

        if *a[mid] > x*

            then *top := mid − 1*

            else *bot := mid + 1*

    end while

    [If index has the value 0 at this point, then x is not in the array. Otherwise, index gives the index of the array where x is located.]

Output: *index [a nonnegative integer]*

Example 11.5.1 Tracing the Binary Search Algorithm

Trace the action of Algorithm 11.5.1 on the variables *index, bot, top, mid,* and the values of *x* given in (a) and (b) below for the input array

$$a[1] = \text{Ann}, a[2] = \text{Dawn}, a[3] = \text{Erik}, a[4] = \text{Gail}, a[5] = \text{Juan},$$
$$a[6] = \text{Matt}, a[7] = \text{Max}, a[8] = \text{Rita}, a[9] = \text{Tsuji}, a[10] = \text{Yuen}$$

where alphabetical ordering is used to compare elements of the array.

a. *x* = Max   b. *x* = Sara

Solution

a.

index	0				7
bot	1	6		7	
top	10		7		
mid		5	8	6	7

b.

index	0			
bot	1	6	9	
top	10			8
mid		5	8	9

The Efficiency of the Binary Search Algorithm

The idea of the derivation of the efficiency of the binary search algorithm is not difficult. Here it is in brief. At each stage of the binary search process, the length of the new subarray to be searched is approximately half that of the previous one, and in the worst case, every subarray down to a subarray with a single element must be searched. Consequently, in the worst case, the maximum number of iterations of the **while** loop in the binary search algorithm is 1 more than the number of times the original input array can be cut approximately in half. If the length n of this array is a power of 2 ($n = 2^k$ for some integer k), then n can be halved exactly $k = \log_2 n = \lfloor \log_2 n \rfloor$ times before an array of length 1 is reached. If n is not a power of 2, then $n = 2^k + m$ for some integer k (where $m < 2^k$), and so n can be split approximately in half k times also. So in this case, $k = \lfloor \log_2 n \rfloor$ also. Thus in the worst case, the number of iterations of the **while** loop in the binary search algorithm, which is proportional to the number of comparisons required to execute it, is $\lfloor \log_2 n \rfloor + 1$. The derivation is concluded by noting that $\lfloor \log_2 n \rfloor + 1$ is $O(\log_2 n)$.

The details of the derivation are developed in Examples 11.5.2–11.5.6. Throughout the derivation, for each integer $n \geq 1$, let

$w_n = $ the number of iterations of the **while** loop
in a *worst-case* execution of the binary search
algorithm for an input array of length n.

The first issue to consider is this. If the length of the input array for one iteration of the **while** loop is known, what is the greatest possible length of the array input to the next iteration?

Example 11.5.2 The Length of the Input Array to the Next Iteration of the Loop

Prove that if an array of length k is input to the **while** loop of the binary search algorithm, then after one unsuccessful iteration of the loop, the input to the next iteration is an array of length at most $\lfloor k/2 \rfloor$.

Solution Consider what occurs when an array of length k is input to the **while** loop in the case where $x \neq a[mid]$:

$$\underbrace{a[\text{bot}], a[\text{bot}+1], \ldots, a[\text{mid}-1]}_{\substack{\text{new input to the while} \\ \text{loop if } x < a[\text{mid}]}}, \underbrace{a[\text{mid}]}_{\substack{\text{"middle} \\ \text{element"}}}, \underbrace{a[\text{mid}+1], \ldots, a[\text{top}-1], a[\text{top}]}_{\substack{\text{new input to the while} \\ \text{loop if } x > a[\text{mid}]}}.$$

Since the input array has length k, the value of *mid* depends on whether k is odd or even. In both cases we match up the array elements with the integers from 1 to k and analyze the lengths of the left and right subarrays. In case k is odd, both the left and the right subarrays have length $\lfloor k/2 \rfloor$. In case k is even, the left subarray has length $\lfloor k/2 \rfloor - 1$ and the right subarray has length $\lfloor k/2 \rfloor$. The reasoning behind these results is shown in Figure 11.5.3.

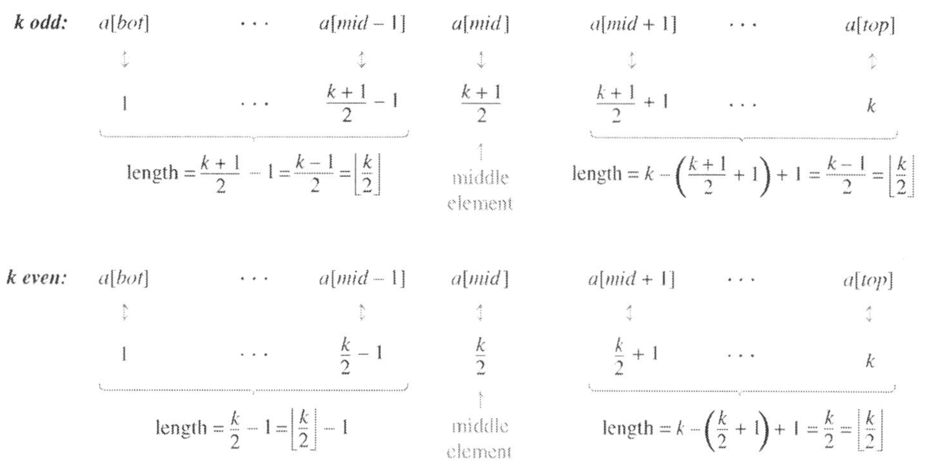

Figure 11.5.3 Lengths of the Left and Right Subarrays

Because the maximum of the numbers $\lfloor k/2 \rfloor$ and $\lfloor k/2 \rfloor - 1$ is $\lfloor k/2 \rfloor$, in the worst case this will be the length of the array input to the next iteration of the loop.

To find the order of the algorithm, a formula for $w_1, w_2, w_3, \ldots$ is needed. The next example derives a recurrence relation for the sequence.

Example 11.5.3 A Recurrence Relation for $w_1, w_2, w_3, \ldots$

Prove that the sequence $w_1, w_2, \ldots, w_n, \ldots$ satisfies the recurrence relation and initial condition

$$w_1 = 1,$$
$$w_k = 1 + w_{\lfloor k/2 \rfloor} \quad \text{for all integers } k > 1.$$

Solution   Example 11.5.2 showed that given an input array of length k to the **while** loop, the worst that can happen is that the next iteration of the loop will have to search an array of length $\lfloor k/2 \rfloor$. Hence the maximum number of iterations of the loop is 1 more than the maximum number necessary to execute it for an input array of length $\lfloor k/2 \rfloor$. In symbols,

$$w_k = 1 + w_{\lfloor k/2 \rfloor}.$$

Also
$$w_1 = 1$$

because for an input array of length 1 ($bot = top$), the **while** loop iterates only one time.

Now that a recurrence relation for $w_1, w_2, w_3, \ldots$ has been found, iteration can be used to come up with a good guess for an explicit formula.

Example 11.5.4 An Explicit Formula for $w_1, w_2, w_3, \ldots$

Apply iteration to the recurrence relation found in Example 11.5.3 to conjecture an explicit formula for $w_1, w_2, w_3, \ldots$.

Solution   Begin by iterating to find the values of the first few terms of the sequence.

$$w_1 = 1 \qquad\qquad\qquad 1 = 2^0; 1 = 0 + 1$$

$$\left.\begin{aligned} w_2 &= 1 + w_{\lfloor 2/2 \rfloor} = 1 + w_1 = 1 + 1 = 2 \\ w_3 &= 1 + w_{\lfloor 3/2 \rfloor} = 1 + w_1 = 1 + 1 = 2 \end{aligned}\right\} \quad 2 = 2^1; 2 = 1 + 1$$

$$\left.\begin{aligned} w_4 &= 1 + w_{\lfloor 4/2 \rfloor} = 1 + w_2 = 1 + 2 = 3 \\ w_5 &= 1 + w_{\lfloor 5/2 \rfloor} = 1 + w_2 = 1 + 2 = 3 \\ w_6 &= 1 + w_{\lfloor 6/2 \rfloor} = 1 + w_3 = 1 + 2 = 3 \\ w_7 &= 1 + w_{\lfloor 7/2 \rfloor} = 1 + w_3 = 1 + 2 = 3 \end{aligned}\right\} \quad 4 = 2^2; 3 = 2 + 1$$

$$\left.\begin{aligned} w_8 &= 1 + w_{\lfloor 8/2 \rfloor} = 1 + w_4 = 1 + 3 = 4 \\ w_9 &= 1 + w_{\lfloor 9/2 \rfloor} = 1 + w_4 = 1 + 3 = 4 \\ &\quad\vdots \qquad\qquad\qquad\qquad\qquad\qquad \vdots \\ w_{15} &= 1 + w_{\lfloor 15/2 \rfloor} = 1 + w_7 = 1 + 3 = 4 \end{aligned}\right\} \quad 8 = 2^3; 4 = 3 + 1$$

$$\left.\begin{aligned} w_{16} &= 1 + w_{\lfloor 16/2 \rfloor} = 1 + w_8 = 1 + 4 = 5 \\ &\quad\vdots \qquad\qquad\qquad\qquad\qquad\qquad \vdots \end{aligned}\right\} \quad 16 = 2^4; 5 = 4 + 1$$

Note that in each case when the subscript n is between two powers of 2, w_n is 1 more than the exponent of the lower power of 2. In other words:

$$\text{If } 2^i \le n < 2^{i+1}, \text{ then } w_n = i + 1. \tag{11.5.1}$$

But if $\qquad\qquad\qquad\qquad 2^i \le n < 2^{i+1}$,

then *[by property (11.4.2) of Example 11.4.1]*

$$i = \lfloor \log_2 n \rfloor.$$

Substitution into statement (11.5.1) gives the conjecture that

$$w_n = \lfloor \log_2 n \rfloor + 1.$$ ▪

Now mathematical induction can be used to verify the correctness of the formula found in Example 11.5.4.

Example 11.5.5 Verifying the Correctness of the Formula

Use strong mathematical induction to show that if $w_1, w_2, w_3, \ldots$ is a sequence of numbers that satisfies the recurrence relation and initial condition

$$w_1 = 1 \qquad \text{and} \qquad w_k = 1 + w_{\lfloor k/2 \rfloor} \quad \text{for all integers } k > 1,$$

then $w_1, w_2, w_3, \ldots$ satisfies the formula

$$w_n = \lfloor \log_2 n \rfloor + 1 \quad \text{for all integers } n \ge 1.$$

Solution   Let $w_1, w_2, w_3, \ldots$ be the sequence defined by specifying that $w_1 = 1$ and $w_k = 1 + w_{\lfloor k/2 \rfloor}$ for all integers $k \ge 2$, and let the property $P(n)$ be the equation

$$w_n = \lfloor \log_2 n \rfloor + 1. \qquad \leftarrow P(n)$$

We will use mathematical induction to prove that for all integers $n \ge 1$, $P(n)$ is true.

Show that P(1) is true: By definition of $w_1, w_2, w_3, \ldots$, we have that $w_1 = 1$. But it is also the case that $\lfloor \log_2 1 \rfloor + 1 = 0 + 1 = 1$. Thus $w_1 = \lfloor \log_2 1 \rfloor + 1$ and $P(1)$ is true.

Show that for all integers $k \geq 1$, if $P(i)$ is true for all integers i from 1 through k, then $P(k + 1)$ is also true: Let k be any integer with $k \geq 1$, and suppose that

$$w_i = \lfloor \log_2 i \rfloor + 1 \quad \text{for all integers } i \text{ with } 1 \leq i \leq k. \quad \leftarrow \text{ inductive hypothesis}$$

We must show that

$$w_{k+1} = \lfloor \log_2(k + 1) \rfloor + 1 \qquad \leftarrow P(k+1)$$

Consider the two cases: k is even and k is odd.

Case 1 (k is even): In this case, $k + 1$ is odd, and

$$
\begin{aligned}
w_{k+1} &= 1 + w_{\lfloor (k+1)/2 \rfloor} &&\text{by definition of } w_1, w_2, w_3, \ldots \\
&= 1 + w_{\lfloor k/2 \rfloor} &&\text{because } \lfloor (k+1)/2 \rfloor = k/2 \text{ since } k+1 \text{ is odd} \\
&= 1 + \left(\lfloor \log_2(k/2) \rfloor + 1 \right) &&\text{by inductive hypothesis because, since } k \text{ is even,} \\
& &&k \geq 2, \text{ and so } 1 \leq \lfloor k/2 \rfloor \leq k/2 < k \\
&= \lfloor \log_2(k) - \log_2 2 \rfloor + 2 &&\text{by substituting into the identity} \\
& &&\log_b(x/y) = \log_b x - \log_b y \text{ from} \\
& &&\text{Theorem 7.2.1} \\
&= \lfloor \log_2(k) - 1 \rfloor + 2 &&\text{since } \log_2 2 = 1 \\
&= (\lfloor \log_2(k) \rfloor - 1) + 2 &&\text{by substituting } x = \log_2(k) \text{ into the identity} \\
& &&\lfloor x - 1 \rfloor = \lfloor x \rfloor - 1 \text{ derived in exercise 15 of Section 4.5} \\
&= \lfloor \log_2(k + 1) \rfloor + 1 &&\text{by property (11.4.3) in Example 11.4.2}
\end{aligned}
$$

Case 2 (k is odd): In this case, it can also be shown that $w_k = \lfloor \log_2 k \rfloor + 1$. The analysis is very similar to that of case 1 and is left as exercise 16 at the end of the section.

Hence regardless of whether k is even or k is odd,

$$w_{k+1} = \lfloor \log_2(k + 1) \rfloor + 1,$$

as was to be shown. *[Since both the basis and the inductive steps have been demonstrated, the proof by strong mathematical induction is complete.]*   ∎

The final example shows how to use the formula for $w_1, w_2, w_3, \ldots$ to find a worst-case order for the algorithm.

Example 11.5.6   The Binary Search Algorithm Is Logarithmic

Given that by Example 11.5.5, for all positive integers n,

$$w_n = \lfloor \log_2 n \rfloor + 1,$$

show that in the worst case, the binary search algorithm is $\Theta(\log_2 n)$.

Solution   For any integer $n > 2$,

$$
\begin{aligned}
& w_n = \lfloor \log_2 n \rfloor + 1 &&\text{by Example 11.5.5} \\
\Rightarrow \quad & \log_2 n \leq w_n \leq \log_2 n + 1 &&\text{because } x < \lfloor x \rfloor + 1 \text{ and } \lfloor x \rfloor \leq x \\
& &&\text{for all real numbers } x \\
\Rightarrow \quad & \log_2 n \leq w_n \leq \log_2 n + \log_2 n &&\text{since the logarithm with base 2 is increas-} \\
& &&\text{ing, if } 2 < n, \text{ then } 1 = \log_2 2 < \log_2 n \\
\Rightarrow \quad & \log_2 n \leq w_n \leq 2 \log_2 n.
\end{aligned}
$$

Both w_n and $\log_2 n$ are positive for $n > 2$. Therefore,

$$|\log_2 n| \le |w_n| \le 2|\log_2 n| \quad \text{for all integers } n > 2.$$

Let $A = 1$, $B = 2$, and $k = 2$. Then

$$A|\log_2 n| \le |w_n| \le B|\log_2 n| \quad \text{for all integers } n > k.$$

Hence by definition of Θ-notation,

$$w_n \text{ is } \Theta(\log_2 n).$$

But w_n, the number of iterations of the **while** loop, is proportional to the number of comparisons performed when the binary search algorithm is executed. Thus the binary search algorithm is $\Theta(\log_2 n)$. ▪

Examples 11.5.2–11.5.6 show that in the worst case, the binary search algorithm has order $\log_2 n$. As noted in Section 11.3, in the worst case the sequential search algorithm has order n. This difference in efficiency becomes increasingly more important as n gets larger and larger. Assuming one loop iteration is performed each nanosecond, then performing n iterations for $n = 100,000,000$ requires 0.1 second, whereas performing $\log_2 n$ iterations requires 0.000000027 second. For $n = 100,000,000,000$ the times are 1.67 minutes and 0.000000037 second, respectively. And for $n = 100,000,000,000,000$ the respective times are 27.78 hours and 0.000000047 second.

Merge Sort

Note that it is much easier to write a detailed algorithm for sequential search than for binary search. Yet binary search is much more efficient than sequential search. Such trade-offs often occur in computer science. Frequently, the straightforward "obvious" solution to a problem is less efficient than a clever solution that is more complicated to describe.

In the text and exercises for Section 11.3, we gave two methods for sorting, insertion sort and selection sort, both of which are formalizations of methods human beings often use in ordinary situations. Can a divide-and-conquer approach be used to find a sorting method more efficient than these? It turns out that the answer is an emphatic "yes." In fact, over the past few decades, computer scientists have developed several divide-and-conquer sorting methods all of which are somewhat more complex to describe but are significantly more efficient than either insertion sort or selection sort.

One of these methods, **merge sort,** is obtained by thinking recursively. Imagine that an efficient way for sorting arrays of length less than k is already known. How can such knowledge be used to sort an array of length k? One way is to suppose the array of length k is split into two roughly equal parts and each part is sorted using the known method. Is there an efficient way to combine the parts into a sorted array? Sure. Just "merge" them.

Figure 11.5.4 illustrates how a merge works. Imagine that the elements of two ordered subarrays, 2, 5, 6, 8 and 3, 6, 7, 9, are written on slips of paper (to make them easy to move around). Place the slips for each subarray in two columns on a tabletop, one at the left and one at the right. Along the bottom of the tabletop, set up eight positions into which the slips will be moved. Then, one-by-one, bring down the slips from the bottoms of the columns. At each stage compare the numbers on the slips currently at the column bottoms, and move the slip containing the smaller number down into the next position in the array as a whole. If at any stage the two numbers are equal, take, say, the slip on the left to move into the next position. And if one of the columns is empty at any stage, just move the slips from the other column into position one-by-one in order.

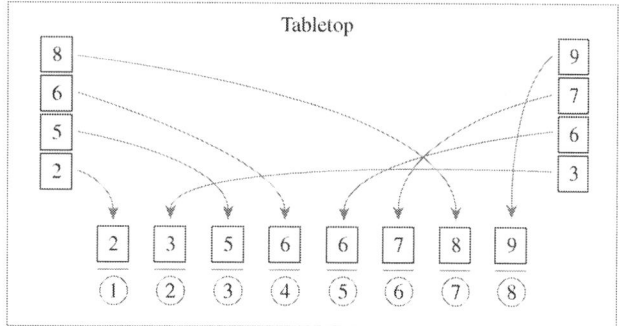

Figure 11.5.4 **Merging Two Sorted Subarrays to Obtain a Sorted Array**

One important observation about the merging algorithm described previously: It requires memory space to move the array elements around. A second set of array positions as long as the original one is needed into which to place the elements of the two subarrays in order. In Figure 11.5.4 this second set of array positions is represented by the positions set up at the bottom of the tabletop. Of course, once the elements of the original array have been placed into this new array, they can be moved back in order into the original array positions.

In terms of time, however, merging is efficient because the total number of comparisons needed to merge two subarrays into an array of length k is just $k - 1$. You can see why by analyzing Figure 11.5.4. Observe that at each stage, the decision about which slip to move is made by comparing the numbers on the slips currently at the bottoms of the two columns—execpt when one of the columns is empty, in which case no comparisons are made at all. Thus in the worst case there will be one comparison for each of the k positions in the final array except the very last one (because when the last slip is placed into position, the other column is sure to be empty), or a total of $k - 1$ comparisons in all.

The merge sort algorithm is recursive: Its defining statements include references to itself. The algorithm is well defined, however, because at each stage the length of the array that is input to the algorithm is shorter than at the previous stage, so that, ultimately, the algorithm has to deal only with arrays of length 1, which are already sorted. Specifically, merge sort works as follows.

Given an array of elements that can be put into order, if the array consists of a single element, leave it as it is. It is already sorted. Otherwise:

1. Divide the array into two subarrays of as nearly equal length as possible.

2. Use merge sort to sort each subarray.

3. Merge the two subarrays together.

Figure 11.5.5 illustrates a merge sort in a particular case.

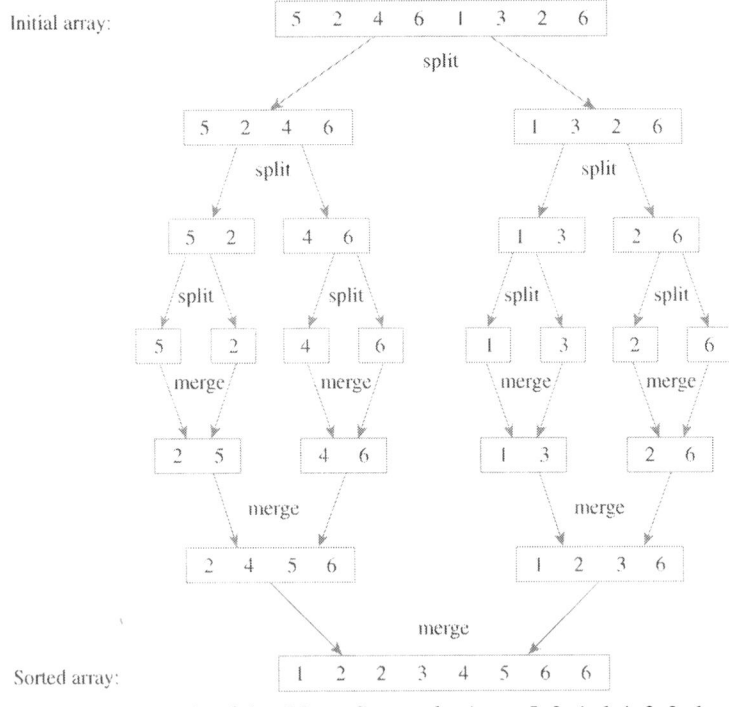

Figure 11.5.5 **Applying Merge Sort to the Array 5, 2, 4, 6, 1, 3, 2, 6**

As in the case of the binary search algorithm, in order to formalize merge sort we must decide at exactly what point to split each array. Given an array denoted by $a[bot]$, $a[bot + 1], \ldots, a[top]$, let $mid = \lfloor (bot + top)/2 \rfloor$. Take the left subarray to be $a[bot]$, $a[bot + 1], \ldots, a[mid]$ and the right subarray to be $a[mid + 1], a[mid + 2], \ldots, a[top]$. The following is a formal version of merge sort.

Algorithm 11.5.2 Merge Sort

[The aim of this algorithm is to take an array of elements $a[r], a[r + 1], \ldots, a[s]$ (where $r \leq s$) and to order it. The output array is denoted $a[r], a[r + 1], \ldots, a[s]$ also. It has the same values as the input array, but they are in ascending order. The input array is split into two nearly equal-length subarrays, each of which is ordered using merge sort. Then the two subarrays are merged together.]

Input: r and s, *[positive integers with $r < s$]* $a[r], a[r + 1], \ldots, a[s]$ *[an array of data items that can be ordered]*

Algorithm Body:

$bot := r, top := s$

while $(bot < top)$

$$mid := \left\lfloor \frac{bot + top}{2} \right\rfloor$$

call **merge sort** with input bot, mid, and

$a[bot], a[bot + 1], \ldots, a[mid]$

call **merge sort** with input $mid + 1$, top and

$a[mid + 1], a[mid + 2], \ldots, a[top]$

*[After these steps are completed, the arrays $a[bot], a[bot + 1], ..$
$a[mid + 1], a[mid + 2], ..., a[top]$ are both in order.]*

merge $a[bot], a[bot + 1], ..., a[mid]$ and
$\quad a[mid + 1], a[mid + 2], ..., a[top]$

[This step can be done with a call to a merge algorithm. To put the final array in ascending order, the merge algorithm must be written so as to take two arrays in ascending order and merge them into an array in ascending order.]

end while

Output: $a[r], a[r + 1], ..., a[s]$ *[an array with the same elements as the input array but in ascending order]*

To derive the efficiency of merge sort, let

$m_n = $ the maximum number of comparisons used
$\qquad$ when merge sort is applied to an array of length n.

Then $m_1 = 0$ because no comparisons are used when merge sort is applied to an array of length 1. Also for any integer $k > 1$, consider an array $a[bot], a[bot + 1], ..., a[top]$ of length k that is split into two subarrays, $a[bot], a[bot + 1], ..., a[mid]$ and $a[mid + 1], a[mid + 2], ..., a[top]$, where $mid = \lfloor (bot + top)/2 \rfloor$. In exercise 24 you are asked to show that the right subarray has length $\lfloor k/2 \rfloor$ and the left subarray has length $\lceil k/2 \rceil$. From the previous discussion of the merge process, it is known that to merge two subarrays into an array of length k, at most $k - 1$ comparisons are needed.

Consequently,

$$\begin{bmatrix} \text{the number of comparisons} \\ \text{when merge sort is applied} \\ \text{to an array of length } k \end{bmatrix} = \begin{bmatrix} \text{the number of comparisons} \\ \text{when merge sort is applied} \\ \text{to an array of length } \lfloor k/2 \rfloor \end{bmatrix}$$

$$+ \begin{bmatrix} \text{the number of comparisons} \\ \text{when merge sort is applied} \\ \text{to an array of length } \lceil k/2 \rceil \end{bmatrix} + \begin{bmatrix} \text{the number of comparisons} \\ \text{used to merge two subarrays} \\ \text{into an array of length } k \end{bmatrix}.$$

Or, in other words,

$$m_k = m_{\lfloor k/2 \rfloor} + m_{\lceil k/2 \rceil} + (k - 1) \quad \text{for all integers } k > 1.$$

In exercise 25 you are asked to use this recurrence relation to show that

$$\frac{1}{2}n \log_2 n \leq m_n \leq 2n \log_2 n \quad \text{for all integers } n \geq 1.$$

It follows that merge sort is $\Theta(n \log_2 n)$.

In the text and exercises for Section 11.3, we showed that insertion sort and selection sort are both $\Theta(n^2)$. How much difference can it make that merge sort is $\Theta(n \log_2 n)$? If $n = 100,000,000$ and a computer is used that performs one operation each nanosecond, the time needed to perform $n \log_2 n$ operations is about 2.7 seconds, whereas the time needed to perform n^2 operations is over 115 days.

Tractable and Intractable Problems

At an opposite extreme from an algorithm such as binary search, which has logarithmic order, is an algorithm with exponential order. For example, consider an algorithm to direct the movement of each of the 64 disks in the Tower of Hanoi puzzle as they are transferred one by one from one pole to another. In Section 5.7 we showed that such a transfer requires $2^{64} - 1$ steps. If a computer took a nanosecond to calculate each transfer step, the total time to calculate all the steps would be

$$(2^{64} - 1) \cdot \left(\frac{1}{10^9}\right) \cdot \left(\frac{1}{60}\right) \cdot \left(\frac{1}{60}\right) \cdot \left(\frac{1}{24}\right) \cdot \left(\frac{1}{365.25}\right) \cong 584 \text{ years.}$$

number of   moves   seconds   minutes   hours   days
moves   per   per   per   per   per
             second   minute   hour   day   year

Problems whose solutions can be found with algorithms whose worst-case order with respect to time is a polynomial are said to belong to **class P.** They are called **polynomial-time algorithms** and are said to be **tractable.** Problems that cannot be solved in polynomial time are called **intractable.** For certain problems, it is possible to check the correctness of a proposed solution with a polynomial-time algorithm, but it may not be possible to find a solution in polynomial time. Such problems are said to belong to **class NP.**[*] The biggest open question in theoretical computer science is whether every problem in class NP belongs to class P. This is known as the **P vs. NP** problem. The Clay Institute, in Cambridge, Massachusetts, has offered a prize of $1,000,000 to anyone who can either prove or disprove that $P = NP$.

In recent years, computer scientists have identified a fairly large set of problems, called **NP-complete,** that all belong to class NP but are widely believed not to belong to class P. What is known for sure is that if any one of these problems is solvable in polynomial time, then so are all the others. One of the NP-complete problems, commonly known as the *traveling salesman problem,* was discussed in Section 10.2.

A Final Remark on Algorithm Efficiency

This section and the previous one on algorithm efficiency have offered only a partial view of what is involved in analyzing a computer algorithm. For one thing, it is assumed that searches and sorts take place in the memory of the computer. Searches and sorts on disk-based files require different algorithms, though the methods for their analysis are similar. For another thing, as mentioned at the beginning of Section 11.3, time efficiency is not the only factor that matters in the decision about which algorithm to choose. The amount of memory space required is also important, and there are mathematical techniques to estimate space efficiency very similar to those used to estimate time efficiency. Furthermore, as parallel processing of data becomes increasingly prevalent, current methods of algorithm analysis are being modified and extended to apply to algorithms designed for this new technology.

Test Yourself

1. To solve a problem using a divide-and-conquer algorithm, you reduce it to a fixed number of smaller problems of the same kind, which can themselves be _____, and so forth until _____.

2. To search an array using the binary search algorithm in each step, you compare a middle element of the array to _____. If the middle element is less than _____, you _____, and if the middle element is greater than _____, you _____.

3. The worst case order of the binary search algorithm is _____.

4. To sort an array using the merge sort algorithm, in each step until the last one you split the array into approximately two equal sections and sort each section using _____. Then you _____ the two sorted sections.

5. The worst case order of the merge sort algorithm is _____.

[*]Technically speaking, a problem whose solution can be verified on an ordinary computer (or *deterministic sequential machine*) with a polynomial-time algorithm can be solved on a *nondeterministic sequential machine* with a polynomial-time algorithm. Such problems are called NP, which stands for *nondeterministic polynomial-time algorithm.*

Exercise Set 11.5

1. Use the facts that $\log_2 10 \cong 3.32$ and that for all real numbers a, $\log_2(10^a) = a \log_2 10$ to find $\log_2(1,000)$, $\log_2(1,000,000)$, and $\log_2(1,000,000,000,000)$.

2. Suppose an algorithm requires $c\lfloor \log_2 n \rfloor$ operations when performed with an input of size n (where c is a constant).
   a. By what factor will the number of operations increase when the input size is increased from m to m^2 (where m is a positive integer power of 2)?
   b. By what factor will the number of operations increase when the input size is increased from m to m^{10} (where m is a positive integer power of 2)?
   c. When n increases from $128 (= 2^7)$ to $268,435,456$ $(= 2^{28})$, by what factor is $c\lfloor \log_2 n \rfloor$ increased?

Exercises 3 and 4 illustrate that for relatively small values of n, algorithms with larger orders can be more efficient than algorithms with smaller orders. Use a graphing calculator or computer to answer these questions.

3. For what values of n is an algorithm that requires n operations more efficient than an algorithm that requires $\lfloor 50 \log_2 n \rfloor$ operations?

4. For what values of n is an algorithm that requires $\lfloor n^2/10 \rfloor$ operations more efficient than an algorithm that requires $\lfloor n \log_2 n \rfloor$ operations?

In 5 and 6, trace the action of the binary search algorithm (Algorithm 11.5.1) on the variables *index*, *bot*, *top*, *mid*, and the given values of x for the input array $a[1] = $ Chia, $a[2] = $ Doug, $a[3] = $ Jan, $a[4] = $ Jim, $a[5] = $ José, $a[6] = $ Mary, $a[7] = $ Rob, $a[8] = $ Roy, $a[9] = $ Sue, $a[10] = $ Usha, where alphabetical ordering is used to compare elements of the array.

5. a. $x = $ Chia   b. $x = $ Max

6. a. $x = $ Amanda   b. $x = $ Roy

7. Suppose *bot* and *top* are positive integers with $bot \leq top$. Consider the array
$$a[bot], a[bot + 1], \ldots, a[top].$$
   a. How many elements are in this array?
   b. Show that if the number of elements in the array is odd, then the quantity $bot + top$ is even.
   c. Show that if the number of elements in the array is even, then the quantity $bot + top$ is odd.

Exercises 8–11 refer to the following algorithm segment, each positive integer n, let a_n be the number of iterations of a while loop.

> while $(n > 0)$
> $\quad n := n \ div \ 2$
> end while

8. Trace the action of this algorithm segment on n when the initial value of n is 27.

9. Find a recurrence relation for a_n.

10. Find an explicit formula for a_n.

11. Find an order for this algorithm segment.

Exercises 12–15 refer to the following algorithm segment. For each positive integer n, let b_n be the number of iterations of the while loop.

> while $(n > 0)$
> $\quad n := n \ div \ 3$
> end while

12. Trace the action of this algorithm segment on n when the initial value of n is 424.

13. Find a recurrence relation for b_n.

H 14. a. Use iteration to guess an explicit formula for b_n.
   b. Prove that if k is an integer and x is a real number with $3^k \leq x < 3^k$, then $\lfloor \log_3 x \rfloor = k$.
   c. Prove that for all integers $m \geq 1$,
   $$\lfloor \log_3(3m) \rfloor = \lfloor \log_3(3m + 1) \rfloor = \lfloor \log_3(3m + 2) \rfloor.$$
   d. Prove the correctness of the formula you found in part (a).

15. Find an order for the algorithm segment.

16. Complete the proof of case 2 of the strong induction argument in Example 11.5.5. In other words, show that if k is an odd integer and $w_i = \lfloor \log_2 i \rfloor + 1$ for all integers i with $1 \leq i \leq k$, then $w_{k+1} = \lfloor \log_2 k + 1 \rfloor + 1$.

For 17–19, modify the binary search algorithm (Algorithm 11.5.1) to take the upper of the two middle array elements in case the input array has even length. In other words, in Algorithm 11.5.1 replace
$$mid := \left\lfloor \frac{bot + top}{2} \right\rfloor \text{ with } mid := \left\lceil \frac{bot + top}{2} \right\rceil.$$

17. Trace the modified binary search algorithm for the same input as was used in Example 11.5.1.

· of length k is input to the **while** loop of
ry search algorithm. Show that after one
op, if $a[mid] \neq x$, the input to the next
· of length at most $\lfloor k/2 \rfloor$.

.. ine number of iterations of the **while** loop in a
worst-case execution of the modified binary search algorithm for an input array of length n. Show that $w_k = 1 +$
$w_{\lfloor k/2 \rfloor}$ for $k \geq 2$.

In 20 and 21, draw a diagram like Figure 11.5.4 to show how to
merge the given subarrays into a single array in ascending order.

20. 3, 5, 6, 9, 12 and 2, 4, 7, 9, 11

21. F, K, L, R, U and C, E, L, P, W (alphabetical order)

In 22 and 23, draw a diagram like Figure 11.5.5 to show how
merge sort works for the given input arrays.

22. R, G, B, U, C, F, H, G (alphabetical order)

23. 5, 2, 3, 9, 7, 4, 3, 2

24. Show that given an array $a[bot], a[bot + 1], \ldots, a[top]$ of
length k, if mid $= \lfloor (bot + top)/2 \rfloor$ then
a. the subarray $a[mid + 1], a[mid + 2], \ldots, a[top]$ has
length $\lfloor k/2 \rfloor$.
b. the subarray $a[bot], a[bot + 1], \ldots, a[mid]$ has length
$\lceil k/2 \rceil$.

H 25. The recurrence relation for $m_1, m_2, m_3, \ldots$, which arises in
the calculation of the efficiency of merge sort, is

$$m_1 = 0$$
$$m_k = m_{\lfloor k/2 \rfloor} + m_{\lceil k/2 \rceil} + k - 1.$$

Show that for all integers $n \geq 1$,
a. $\frac{1}{2} n \log_2 n \leq m_n$ b. $m_n \leq 2n \log_2 n$

26. You might think that $n - 1$ multiplications are needed to
compute x^n, since

$$x^n = \underbrace{x \cdot x \cdots x}_{n-1 \text{ multiplications}}.$$

But observe that, for instance, since $6 = 4 + 2$,

$$x^6 = x^4 x^2 = (x^2)^2 x^2.$$

Thus x^6 can be computed using three multiplications: one
to compute x^2, one to compute $(x^2)^2$, and one to multiply
$(x^2)^2$ times x^2. Similarly, since $11 = 8 + 2 + 1$,

$$x^{11} = x^8 x^2 x^1 = ((x^2)^2)^2 x^2 x$$

and so x^{11} can be computed using five multiplications:
one to compute x^2, one to compute $(x^2)^2$, one to compute
$((x^2)^2)^2$, one to multiply $((x^2)^2)^2$ times x^2, and one to multiply that product by x.

a. Write an algorithm to take a real number x and a positive
integer n and compute x^n by
(i) calling Algorithm 5.1.1 to find the binary representation of n:

$$(r[k]\, r[k-1] \cdots r[0])_2,$$

where each $r[i]$ is 0 or 1;
(ii) computing $x^2, x^{2^2}, x^{2^3}, \ldots, x^{2^k}$ by squaring, then
squaring again, and so forth,
(iii) computing x^n using the fact that

$$x^n = x^{r[k]2^k + \cdots + r[2]2^2 + r[1]2^1 + r[0]2^0}$$
$$= x^{r[k]2^k} \cdots x^{r[2]2^2} \cdot x^{r[1]2^1} \cdot x^{r[0]2^0}$$

b. Show that the number of multiplications performed by
the algorithm of part (a) is less than or equal to
$2\lfloor \log_2 n \rfloor$.

Answers for Test Yourself

1. reduced to the same finite number of smaller problems of the same kind; easily resolved problems are obtained   2. the element you
are looking for; the element you are looking for; apply the binary search algorithm to the lower half of the array; the element you are
looking for; apply the binary search algorithm to the upper half of the array   3. $\log_2 n$, where n is the length of the array   4. merge
sort; merge   5. $n \log_2 n$

INDEX

Contents

Appendix J

Updates to Chapman

J.1   legend, pp. 66–67 of Chapman

The syntax of specifying legends on MatLab plots has changed. The example line of page 67 should read

`legend(string1,string2,...,'Location',pos)`

Hence the penultimate line of the code below should read, instead of `'tl'` (meaning the "Top Left" corner), `'Location','NorthWest'`. Chapman's Table 2.11 should be replaced by Table J.1 (see below), and Figure 2.10 is obsolete. It is worth noting that you can use a string matrix, or a cell array of strings, rather than specifying each string as a separate argument.

It is also possible to specify

`legend(string1,string2,...,'Orientation',,dir)`

where `dir` can be one of `'vertical'` (the default) and `'horizontal'`.

J.2   eps, p. 42 of Chapman

This is described by Chapman in Table 2.2 as

> This variable name is short for "epsilon" It is the smallest difference between two numbers that can be represented on the computer.

In fact, `eps` is a *function*, which *may* have no arguments, and therefore be called as `eps` rather than `eps()`. A more accurate definition of `eps(x)`, for $x > 0$ (`eps(-x)=eps(x)`), would be

> it is the smallest number that can be added to x such that, as represented on the computer, $x+$`eps(x)` is different from x. The default value of x is 1.0.

Table J.1: Replacement for Table 2.11

`'North'`	inside plot box near top
`'South'`	inside bottom
`'East'`	inside right
`'West'`	inside left
`'NorthEast'`	inside top right (default for 2-D plots)
`'NorthWest'`	inside top left
`'SouthEast'`	inside bottom right
`'SouthWest'`	inside bottom left
`'NorthOutside'`	outside plot box near top
`'SouthOutside'`	outside bottom
`'EastOutside'`	outside right
`'WestOutside'`	outside left
`'NorthEastOutside'`	outside top right (default for 3-D plots)
`'NorthWestOutside'`	outside top left
`'SouthEastOutside'`	outside bottom right
`'SouthWestOutside'`	outside bottom left
`'Best'`	least conflict with data in plot
`'BestOutside'`	least used space outside plot

(Taken from the source code for `legend`, except that the description of `'BestOutside'` has been rectified.) Note that `'Best'` and `'BestOutside'` have no equivalent in the old table.

Figure J.1: Simplistic version of `eps`

```
function [ out ] = JHDeps( x )
% JHDeps mimics the (simple) functionality of MatLab's eps
% JHD 9 July 2012 based on 2010 version
if (nargin ==0)
    x=1.0;
else
    x=abs(x);
end
out=x;
while (x+(out/2)~=x) % we're on a binary computer!
    out=out/2;
end
% Only one bit of out matters now
out=(out+x)-x; %necessary to trim this to smallest possible value
end
```

A simplistic version of `eps` (which doesn't handle all the options of the real one, or non-default precisions) is given in Figure J.1. Note that it uses the `nargin` feature of MatLab (Chapman section 6.3) to have a default input value.

To understand how it works, we need to know more about how MatLab (and indeed the underlying computer) actually *stores* the data items of type `double`. Note that there is one underlying storage format for these, irrespective of how we ask MatLab to *display* them, with `format`, `disp` or `fprintf` (Chapman section 2.6). This representation is closely linked to the standard, or "scientific", means of storing floating point numbers, where x is represented as

$$x = \pm M \cdot 10^E, \tag{J.1}$$

where M, the *mantissa*, is a number in the range $1 \le M < 10$, and E, the *exponent* is a positive or negative integer. Computers do the same, generally in a standard format known as IEEE 754[1], but using the base 2 rather than 10, i.e.

$$x = \pm M \cdot 2^E \tag{J.2}$$

where M, the *mantissa*, is a number in the range $1 \le M < 2$, and E, the *exponent* is a positive or negative integer. In fact, what is stored in the machine is a triple $(S, M' = M - 1, E' = E + 1023)$, where S is 0 for positive and 1 for negative, M' is the fractional part of M, stored with 52 bits of precision, and E' is a non-negative number stored in 11 bits, so $0 \le E' \le 2047$. The extreme values of E' have special meanings.

---

[1] IEEE Standard 754 for Binary Floating-Point Arithmetic. IEEE, 1985. Reprinted in SIGPLAN Notices **22**(1987) pp. 9–25. Now updated to 754-2008 (http://ieeexplore.ieee.org/servlet/opac?punumber=4610933).

4

$E' = 0$, $M' = 0$ The number represents 0. Note that there are therefore two potential zeros, $+0$ and -0, depending on S (see next item but one).

$E' = 0$, $M' \neq 0$ This is a number so small that, if it were represented according to (J.2), it would actually have to be stored as zero. This is a concept known as "gradual underflow", and such numbers are known as *denormalized numbers*. In this case, we store M rather than M' in this 52-bit field.

$E' = 2047$, $M' = 0$ The number represents ∞. Note that there are therefore two infinities, $+\infty$ and $-\infty$. MatLab represents these as Inf and -Inf. It may seem more natural to have two infinities than two zeros, but $1/+0 = +\infty$ and $1/-0 = -\infty$, so the two actually go together.

$E' = 2047$, $M' \neq 0$ This is a way of encoding "I am meant to be a number, but am really not a describable one", known as "Not-a-number" or NaN. They can be created in a variety of ways, such as 0/0 or Inf+(-Inf).

Hence the number 1.0 is represented according to (J.2) with $M = 1$ and $E = 0$, i.e. $M' = 0$ and $E' = 1023$, hence in binary

$$\underbrace{0}_{\text{Sign}} \underbrace{01111111111}_{\text{Exponent}} \underbrace{0000000000000000000000000000000000000000000000000000}_{\text{Mantissa}}. \quad \text{(J.3)}$$

What of

$$\underbrace{0}_{\text{Sign}} \underbrace{01111111111}_{\text{Exponent}} \underbrace{0000000000000000000000000000000000000000000000000001}_{\text{Mantissa}}? \quad \text{(J.4)}$$

In terms of (J.2), this is the "next" number to 1.0. Their difference, 2^{-52}, is the number eps(1.0).

It is possible to see the mantissa/exponent representation of a number in matLab by using the *two argument form* of log2, which returns the signed mantissa and the (true) exponent, as in

```
>> [SM,E]=log2(pi)
```

```
SM =
    0.785398163397448
```

```
E =
    2
```

We can also see denormalised numbers, as in

```
>> [SM,E]=log2(10^-320)

SM =

    0.988281250000000


E =

       -1063
```

where the give-away is that the exponent is less than -1022. Note also that the mantissa is suspiciously round. Compare

```
>> [SM,E]=log2(10^-322)

SM =

    0.625000000000000


E =

       -1069
```

(where the mantissa is even rounder) and the extreme case

```
>> [SM,E]=log2(10^-323)

SM =

    0.500000000000000


E =

       -1072
```

J.3   The Symbolic Toolbox

One optional extra to MatLab is the "symbolic toolbox". This addition to MatLab allows it to come much closer to "pen and paper" mathematics, or at least "pen and paper algebra". Such symbolic values can be recognised in the workspace window by being described as objects of type **sym**, as a, x and y are in Figure J.3. In general, a symbolic object is created by means of a call to the function **sym**, which interprets its argument, generally a string, as a **symbolic object**, i.e. an object to be manipulated in accordance with the usual rules of mathematics.

So, in Figure J.2, a is the symbolic object 2, whereas b is the usual MatLab 2. The two can be distinguished by their type in Figure J.3, or by the difference in indentation in Figure J.2. They also behave differently — see Figure J.4.

We said above that the argument to **sym** is generally a string. In fact it can be any MatLab object, but this can be dangerous: compare c and d in Figure J.5. c was created from a string, whereas d was created by first forming the number 12345678901234567890

6

```
>> syms x y
>> a=sym('2')
a =
2
>> b=2
b =
    2
```

in MatLab arithmetic (see section J.2) and then creating a symbolic object from it. At the first step an approximation is made because Matlab's standard arithmetic cannot handle this large number exactly.

The command `syms x y` declares that we wish `x` and `y` to be treated as *mathematical indeterminates*, rather than as programming variables. In fact that declaration is equivalent to the commands

```
x=sym('x');
y=sym('y');
```

which say that the values of the programming variables should be the corresponding[2] mathematical indeterminates.

While the Symbolic Toolbox will perform "obvious" cancellations and collections automatically, more sophisticated ones have to be asked for, as in Figure J.6. Various useful commands are listed below.

`expand` applies the distributive law, writing the expression as a sum of simple products.

`factor` will try to factorise the expressions as a product of factors.

`simplify` tries various simplification rules.

`simple` returns the shortest result given by various simplification rules. Note that if this is called with no return output, e.g. as `simple(s)` rather than `r=simple(s)`, it will display all the simplifications it tried, with the command used, before returning the shortest.

`pretty` will print the result in an approximation to the two-dimensional layout of "pen and paper" mathematics, as in Figure J.7.

---

[2]Note the scope for confusion if one wrote x=sym('y')! This is why the `syms` command is **strongly** recommended for this purpose.

Figure J.3: The Matlab Workspace Window corresponding to Figure J.2

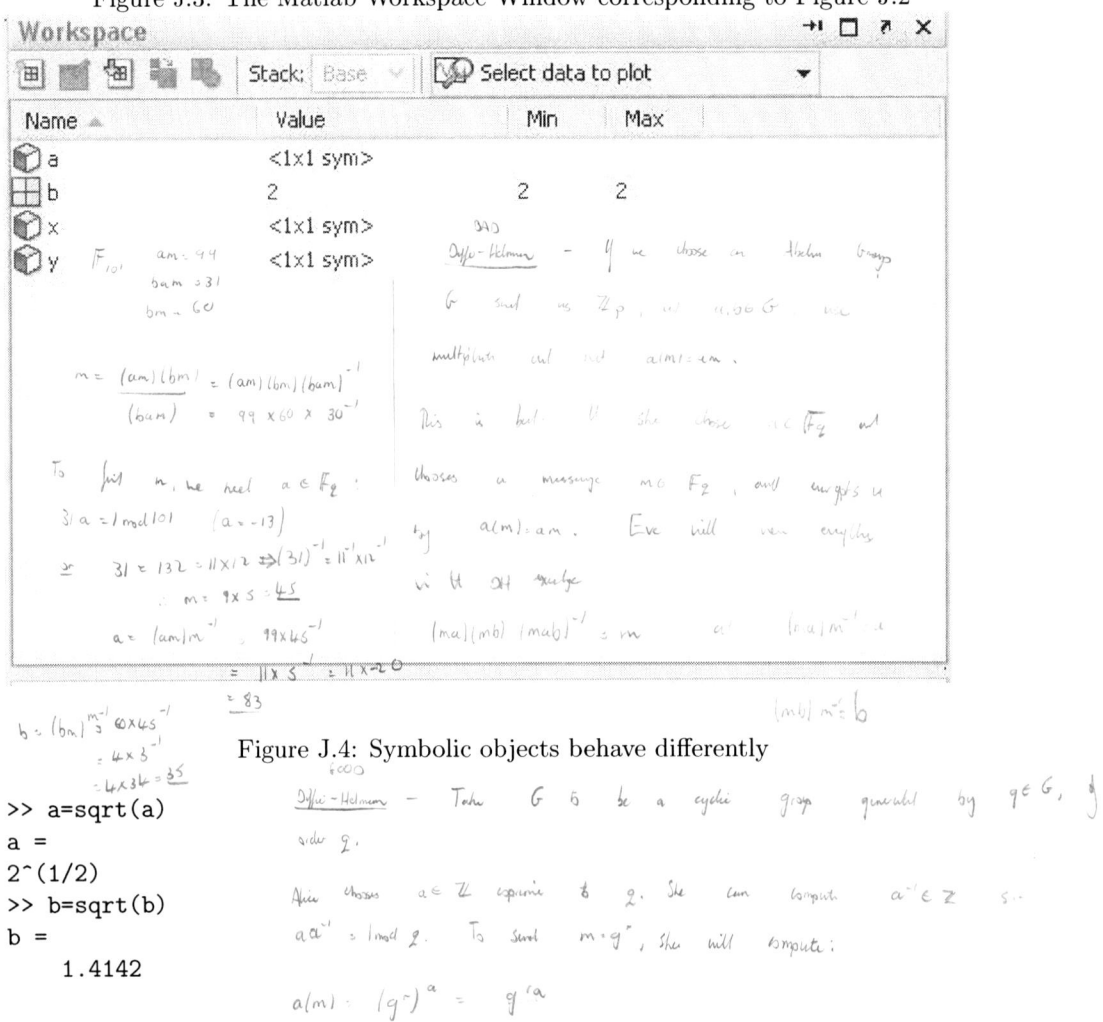

Figure J.4: Symbolic objects behave differently

```
>> a=sqrt(a)
a =
2^(1/2)
>> b=sqrt(b)
b =
    1.4142
```

Figure J.5: sym should be called with string arguments

```
>> c=sym('12345678901234567890')
c =
12345678901234567890
>> d=sym(12345678901234567890)
d =
12345678901234567168
```

8

Figure J.6: Use of MatLab **expand**

```
>> z=(x+y)*(x-y)-x^2+y^2
z =
(x + y)*(x - y) - x^2 + y^2
>> expand(z)
ans =
0
```

Figure J.7: Use of MatLab **pretty**

```
>> sqrt(sym('2'))
ans =
2^(1/2)
>> pretty(ans)
   1/2
  2
>>
```

Appendix K

Additional Definitions

K.1 Coding Theory

We assume communication of symbols from an alphabet K along a channel which is noisy, i.e. sometimes makes mistakes. We also assume:

1. The alphabet is a field (hence the name K). Usually $K = \mathbf{F}_2$.

2. The channel is assumed to make random independent symmetric errors. In the binary (i.e. $\mathbf{F}_2$) case, this means that, with (small, unchanging) probability p, it transmits 1 instead of 0, or 0 instead of 1.

3. We wish to transmit units of m symbols, i.e. elements of K^m, which is a vector space.

Definition 1 *A* **linear code** *C is an m-dimensional subspace of an n-dimensional vector space V (normally K^n).*

This section only deals with linear codes.

Definition 2 *C is called an (m, n)-**code** if C is m-dimensional and V is n-dimensional. We often write r for $n - m$, i.e. the amount of redundancy in the code.*

K.1.1 Examples

Here are two examples, both with $K = \mathbf{F}_2$. The first is very commonly used in computing, the second is a useful theoretical illustraion.

Parity bit Transmit in addition an $m + 1$th bit, generally known as the *parity bit*, which is the sum (modulo 2) of the m bits of the message. Hence 1001001 is sent as 10010011, and 0001100 is sent as 00011000. So the receiver can check that the

$m+1$th bit is correct, in which case we delete it and believe the rest of the emssage: otherwise we *know* that an error has occurred. Note that this will detect 1 mistake, but not 2. Alternatively, the received message should have an *even* number of 1 bits. So $C = \{(a_i) : \sum a_i = 0\}$. The parity code is therefore an $(m, m+1)$ code.

A richer code Transmit the data and all pairwise sums: so (x_1, x_2, x_3) becomes $(x_1, x_2, x_3, x_1+x_2, x_1+x_3, x_2+x_3)$. 110 becomes 110011. $V = \mathbf{F}_2^6$ and $C = \{(x_1, \ldots, x_6) | x_1 + x_2 + x_4 = 0, x_1 + x_3 + x_5 = 0, x_2 + x_3 + x_6 = 0\}$. This code is a (3,6) code, and if we had m data items rather than three would be an $(m, m(m+1)/2)$ code.

K.1.2 Useful notation

Definition 3 *Define $d(x, y)$ to be the number of places in which x and y differ, i.e. $|\{i : x_i \neq y_i\}|$. Define $d(C) = \min_{x,y \in C, x \neq y}\{d(x, y)\}$, normally called the* **Hamming distance**.

If $d(C) \geq s+1$ we can, at least in principle, detect up to s errors, since s errors can't move us from one valid element of C to another. If $d(C) \geq 2k+1$ we can correct up to k errors, since there is a unique "nearest" element. For the parity example above, $d(C) = 2$ (if we change one data bit, we have to change the parity bit).

Definition 4 *The* **rate** *of an (m, n)-code (one which transmits m symbols as an n-symbol encoding) is m/n.*

So we want a high rate (as close to 1 as possible) but also a high d.

Definition 5 *The* **weight** *of a codeword $(x_1, \ldots, x_n)$ over $\mathbf{F}_2$ is the number of 1s in the word: e.g. the weight of (1100100) is 3.*

For a linear code, the Hamming distance is the minimal non-zero weight of a valid codeword.

Encoding is done by applying a linear map $\phi : K^m \to K^n$, with $\phi(K^m) = C$. Such a ϕ is given by a generator matrix G.

Definition 6 *A* **generator matrix** *for C is an $n \times m$ matrix whose columns, thought of as vectors in $K^n = V$, span the linear subspace C.*

Parity bit With $m = 5$, we have the generator matrix

$$G = \begin{pmatrix} 1 & 0 & 0 & 0 & 0 \\ 0 & 1 & 0 & 0 & 0 \\ 0 & 0 & 1 & 0 & 0 \\ 0 & 0 & 0 & 1 & 0 \\ 0 & 0 & 0 & 0 & 1 \\ 1 & 1 & 1 & 1 & 1 \end{pmatrix},$$

where the first five rows correspond to the transmission unchanged of the bits, and the last row computes the parity bit.

11

A richer code
$$\begin{pmatrix} 1 & 0 & 0 \\ 0 & 1 & 0 \\ 0 & 0 & 1 \\ 1 & 1 & 0 \\ 1 & 0 & 1 \\ 0 & 1 & 1 \end{pmatrix}.$$

Definition 7 *A* **decoder matrix** *is an* $m \times n$ *matrix* D *such that* $DG = I_m$.

Parity bit With $m = 5$, we have the decoder matrix

$$D = \begin{pmatrix} 1 & 0 & 0 & 0 & 0 & 0 \\ 0 & 1 & 0 & 0 & 0 & 0 \\ 0 & 0 & 1 & 0 & 0 & 0 \\ 0 & 0 & 0 & 1 & 0 & 0 \\ 0 & 0 & 0 & 0 & 1 & 0 \end{pmatrix}.$$

A richer code
$$\begin{pmatrix} 1 & 0 & 0 & 0 & 0 & 0 \\ 0 & 1 & 0 & 0 & 0 & 0 \\ 0 & 0 & 1 & 0 & 0 & 0 \end{pmatrix}.$$

Definition 8 *A* **check matrix** *is a* $r \times n$ *matrix* H *whose kernel (i.e. null space) is precisely* C. *In other words* $H^T v = 0$ *if and only if* $v \in C$. *The rows of* H *are the coefficients of equations for* C.

Parity bit $\begin{pmatrix} 1 & 1 & 1 & 1 & 1 & 1 \end{pmatrix}$.

A richer code
$$\begin{pmatrix} 1 & 1 & 0 & 1 & 0 & 0 \\ 1 & 0 & 1 & 0 & 1 & 0 \\ 0 & 1 & 1 & 0 & 0 & 1 \end{pmatrix}.$$

Observation 1 *We therefore have three ways of describing a code:* C, G *and* H.

K.2 Fast Fourier Transforms

Assumption 1 *In this section only, we will adopt zero-based indexing for our vectors and arrays, so that an n-vector will be* $(x_0, x_1, \ldots, x_{n-1})$, *and an* $n \times n$ *matrix will be*

$$M = \begin{pmatrix} m_{0,0} & m_{0,1} & \cdots & m_{0,n-1} \\ m_{1,0} & m_{1,1} & \cdots & m_{1,n-1} \\ \vdots & \vdots & \ddots & \vdots \\ m_{n-1,0} & m_{n-1,1} & \cdots & m_{n-1,n-1} \end{pmatrix}$$

K.2.1 Background: Fourier series

Assumption 2 *Let $f : \mathbf{R} \to \mathbf{R}$ be a continuous function that is periodic with period 2π i.e. $f(x) = f(x + 2\pi) = f(x + 4\pi) = \cdots$ for $x \in \mathbf{R}$.*

Example 1 $\cos x$, $\sin x$ *and indeed* $\cos nx$ *and* $\sin nx$ *where* $n \in \mathbf{Z}$ *are periodic.*

Observation 2 *These are, in some sense, the only ones, i.e. any such f can be written as*

$$f(x) = \sum_{n=0}^{\infty} a_n \cos nx + b_n \sin nx. \tag{K.1}$$

This expression does raise all the usual questions of continuity, convergence etc., but under reasonable assumptions on f, this can be done.

Example 2 *The sound produced by a musical instrument consists of the fundamental frequency ($n = 1$) plus overtones, which are in fact the higher terms in this series.*

When we move to the complex numbers, we can in fact write

$$f(x) = \sum_{n=0}^{\infty} c_n e^{inx} \tag{K.2}$$

Either (K.1) or (K.2) will be called **Fourier series**.

To do this on a finite machine we will truncate the sum, and the numbers, and trig/exponential functions, will be approximations. Also, all we can do is *sample* the input. This leads us to consider the *Discrete Fourier process*.

K.2.2 Fourier Series

In the discrete case it is convenient to change notation, and make the period 1, rather than 2π, so the Fourier series becomes

$$f(x) = \sum_{n=0}^{\infty} c_n e^{2\pi i n x} \tag{K.3}$$

We will sample f at m equally-spaced points $x_r = r/m$ (N.B. $0 \le r < m$, so we are indexing from 0 throughout: see Assumption 1). Let

$$y_r = f(x_r) = \sum_{n=0}^{m-1} c_r e^{2\pi i n r/m}. \tag{K.4}$$

Let $\zeta = e^{2\pi i/m}$ — a primitive mth root of unity. Therefore the solutions of $z^m - 1 = 0$ (other than $z = 1$) are $\zeta, \zeta^2, \ldots, \zeta^{m-1} = 1/\zeta$. Then

$$y_r = f(x_r) = \sum_{n=0}^{m-1} c_r \zeta^{nr}. \tag{K.5}$$

13

K.2.3   Fourier Matrix

Definition 9 *The m-th* **Fourier matrix** *F_m is the matrix with $(F_m)_{r,n} = \zeta^{nr}$. This is*

$$F_m = \begin{pmatrix} 1 & 1 & 1 & \cdots & 1 \\ 1 & \zeta & \zeta^2 & \cdots & \zeta^{n-1} \\ 1 & \zeta^2 & \zeta^4 & \cdots & \zeta^{2(n-1)} \\ \vdots & \vdots & \vdots & \ddots & \\ 1 & \zeta^{n-1} & \zeta^{2(n-1)} & \cdots & \zeta^{(n-1)^2} = \zeta \end{pmatrix}. \tag{K.6}$$

This matrix is symmetric, since $\zeta^{nr} = \zeta^{rn}$.

Theorem 1 *The* **inverse of the Fourier matrix**, *F_m^{-1}, is the symmetric matrix*

$$G_m = \frac{1}{m} \begin{pmatrix} 1 & 1 & 1 & \cdots \\ 1 & \zeta^{-1} & \zeta^{-2} & \cdots \\ 1 & \zeta^{-2} & \zeta^{-4} & \cdots \\ \vdots & \vdots & \vdots & \ddots \\ 1 & \zeta^{-(n-1)} & \zeta^{-2(n-1)} & \cdots & \zeta^{-(n-1)^2} = \zeta^{-1} \end{pmatrix}. \tag{K.7}$$

Note that some writers put a factor of $\frac{1}{\sqrt{m}}$ in both F_m and G_m, rather than our 1 in F_m and $\frac{1}{m}$ in G_m.

K.2.4   The Fast Fourier Transform — A

We wish to multiply by F_m (K.6) or, similarly, G_m (K.7). If $m = 2n$, we can express the computation of $y = F_m{}^T c$ as

$$y_r = \sum_{k=0}^{2n-1} (F_{2n})_{r,k} c_k \tag{K.8}$$

$$= \sum_{k=0}^{2n-1} \zeta^{kr} c_k \tag{K.9}$$

$$= \underbrace{\sum_{k=0}^{m-1} \zeta^{2kr} c_{2k}}_{\substack{\text{even terms: new} \\ k \text{ is old } 2k}} + \zeta^r \underbrace{\sum_{k=0}^{m-1} \zeta^{2kr} c_{2k+1}}_{\substack{\text{odd terms: new} \\ k \text{ is old } 2k+1}} \tag{K.10}$$

14

Write c^+ as the even part of c, so $c_k^+ = c_{2k}$, and c^- as the odd part of c, so $c_k^- = c_{2k+1}$. Note that $\zeta^{2kr} = (F_n)_{k,r}$. Hence

$$y_r = \left(F_n^T c^+\right)_r + \left(\zeta^r F_n^T c^-\right)_r \qquad \text{(K.11)}$$

where the *sub*script r on the right-hand side are read modulo n, as they are indexing into n-vectors, but *not* the superscript r.

In MatLab, remembering that we have to number vectors etc. starting at 1, not 0, this looks as follows (after [Mol04a, Mol04b, p. 250]):

```
m=length(c);
omega=exp(2*pi*i/m);
k=(0:m/2-1)';
w=omega .^ k;        % appropriate powers of omega
u=fft(c(1:2:m-1));   % that's the c+ vector
v=w.*fft(c(2:2:m));  % and the c- vector
answer=[u+v;u-v];
```

K.2.5   The Fast Fourier Transform — B

An alternative formulation is the following.

$$F_m = \begin{pmatrix} I & \Delta_n \\ I & -\Delta_n \end{pmatrix} \begin{pmatrix} F_n & 0 \\ 0 & F_n \end{pmatrix} \mathcal{P} \qquad \text{(K.12)}$$

where $\mathcal{P}$ is the permutation matrix that splits the even elements from the odd elements, i.e. the rewriting of c as c^+ and c^- in (K.11) or the :2: in the MatLab code. The MatLab code above takes a slightly different rewriting: we can express (K.12) as

$$F_m = \begin{pmatrix} I & I \\ I & -I \end{pmatrix} \begin{pmatrix} F_n & 0 \\ 0 & \Delta_n F_n \end{pmatrix} \mathcal{P} \qquad \text{(K.13)}$$

Note that we compute $\Delta_n(F_n^T c^-)$, not $(\Delta_n F_n)^T c^-$, since the first takes $O(n)$ operations and the second $O(n^2)$!

There's a complete Fast Fourier Transform described at [Mol04a, Mol04b, Section 8.7].

15

Appendix L

Extra Material — JHD

L.1 Merge Sort

Epp section 11.5 introduces merge sort, and states (p. 775) that the complexity (actually the number of comparisons, but everything else is proportional to this) is $\Theta(n \log n)$.

Theorem 2 *Any algorithm for sorting n objects which is based purely on comparing objects with each other must, on average, make at least $\log_2 n!$ such comparisons.*

Proof. To rearrange the objects into the correct order may require applying any one of the $n!$ possible permutations of n objects, since they may initally have been in any order. A single choice can distinguish two possibilities, two consective choices 4 possibilities, and in general c choices can distinguish 2^c possibilities. Hence $2^c \geq n!$, i.e. $c \geq \log_2 n!$.

    It is also true, though we shall not prove it here, that $\log n! = \Theta(n \log n)$ (note that the base of the logarithms does not matter, since any such factor can be absorbed in the constants implied by Θ). This shows that merge sort is optimal (in terms of the Θ notation). So why look further? There are several reasons.

1. With $C(n)$ denoting the complexity of merge sort, there exist constants A and B such that for all n sufficiently large,

$$An \log n \ \leq \ C(n) \ \leq \ Bn \log n. \tag{L.1}$$

   On the other hand the complexity $C'(n)$ of insertion sort is $\Theta(n^2)$, so that

$$A'n^2 \ \leq \ C'(n) \ \leq \ B'n^2, \tag{L.2}$$

   for n large enough, for some other constants A', B'. However neither statement tells us anything about the values of the constants A, B, A', B'. In fact computational experiments with MatLab[1] show that insertion sort is in fact faster than merge sort

---

[1] This number is critically dependent on the programming language used. MatLab is good at loops and comparatively bad at recursion, for example.

for n up to about 200. So the values of the constants do become important in the running times for any given n and so there is great interest in looking for other algorithms which may still be $\Theta(n \log n)$ but for which the constants in estimates like (L.1) may be better. This is a motivation for the next section, which looks at the constants for small n, and for QuickSort.

2. Merge sort requires at least as much space again as that required for the input, as we create the sorted data in a new array. The recursive nature of merge sort actually means that a great deal of intermediate storage is used in the course of the algorithm.

3. These sorting algorithms assume that we have *all* the data available before we sort, whereas in practice we may want to maintain a sorted list as new items arrive (or even are deleted).

L.2 Sorting a small number of objects

We note that the obvious way of sorting two objects is to compare them, and this is clearly as well as we can do. To compare three objects we need three comparisons in the worst case (a_1 with a_2, and if necessary a_3 with both of them). For four objects, merge sort will take one comparison for each of the two subsets of two elements, and three more for the merging: five in all. Again, this is optimal, since $2^4 < 4! < 2^5$.

For five objects, merge sort would split into a pair and a triple, take $1+3$ comparisons to sort them, and then take 4 more for the merge, totalling 8. However, $2^7 > 5!$ (albeit by a small margin), so we might hope to be able to do it in seven comparisons.

Lemma 1 *It is possible to sort 5 objects in 7 comparisons.*

1. Sort, i.e. swap if necessary, two pairs, so that $b_1 \leq a_1$, $b_2 \leq a_2$, and call the extra element e. **2 comparisons**.

2. Sort a_1, a_2. **1 comparisons**.

3. we now have

$$
\begin{array}{ccccc}
 & & a_1 & \to & a_2 \\
 & \nearrow & & \nearrow & \\
b_1 & & b_2 & &
\end{array}
$$

4. Insert e into the chain b_1, a_1, a_2, using, by binary search (Epp p. 765), **2 comparisons**.

5. This gives us either

$$
\begin{array}{ccccccc}
 & & a_1 & \to & a_2 & \to & e \\
 & \nearrow & & \nearrow & & & \\
b_1 & & b_2 & & & &
\end{array}
$$

17

or

$$c_1 \;\to\; c_2 \quad b_2 \quad \nearrow \quad c_3 \;\to\; a_2 \quad \nearrow$$

where $\{c_1, c_2, c_3\} = \{b_1, a_1, e\}$.

6. We can now insert b_2 into a chain, either $b_1 < a_1$ ($< a_2$, but we already know that $b_2 < a_2$) or $c_1 < c_2 < c_3$ ($< a_2$, but we already know that $b_2 < a_2$) of length at most three, using, by binary search, **2 comparisons**.

Note that the number of possibilities we have to distinguish, 5!, is 120 and the number of possibilities we *can* distinguish with seven comparisons, 2^7, is 128, so we are sailing pretty close to the limits here.

Lemma 2 *It is possible to sort 6 objects in 10 comparisons.*

Proof: sort 5 (by Lemma 1) then insert by binary search.

Lemma 3 *It is possible to sort 7 objects in 13 comparisons.*

Proof: sort 6 (by Lemma 2) then insert by binary search.

In fact we are going to stop here. Our results, and others, can be summarised as the following table. The algorithm marked "ingenious" is due to [FJ59]. Note that, even for 8 objects, we can do better than merge sort. We also observe that, although $2^{29} > 12!$,

Table L.1: Cost of sorting n objects

n	Best way	Number of comparisons Best=k	Merge	Insert	Efficiency $\frac{1}{k}\log_2 n!$
2	Direct	1	1	1	1.0000
3	Direct	3	3	3	0.8617
4	Merge	5	5	6	0.9170
5	Lemma 8.1	7	8	10	0.9867
6	Lemma 8.2	10	11	15	0.9492
7	Lemma 8.3	13	14	21	0.9461
8	Lemma 8.4	16	17	28	0.9562
9	Ingenious*	19	21	36	0.9721
10	Ingenious	22	25	45	0.9905
11	10+Insert	26	29	55	0.9712
12	11+Insert	30	33	66	0.9612
13	Ingenious	34	37	78	0.9569
14	Ingenious	38	41	91	0.9564

*Note that the methods of 8.1–4 would give 20 here.

the efficiency ratio of a 29-comparison sort on 12 elements would be $\frac{1}{29}\log_2 12! \approx 0.9943$,

Figure L.1: Splitting an array about pivot p

Input: Array a of n elements; element p (neither the greatest nor the least)
Output: Integer t, and a rearranged such that $a_1, \ldots, a_t \leq p$ and $a_{t+1}, \ldots, a_n > p$.

$l := 1$;
$h := n$
while $l \leq h$
      while $a(l) \leq p$
          $l := l + 1$;
      end while
      while $a(h) > p$
          $h := h - 1$;
      end while
      [If $l < h$ swap $a(l)$ and $a(h)$ since they're in the wrong place]
      if $l < h$
          $z := a(l); a(l) := a(h); a(h) := z$;
          $l := l + 1$;   *[The new $a(l) \leq p$]*
          $h := h - 1$;   *[The new $a(h) > p$]*
      end if
$t := l$

and it has been demonstrated [Wel65] that no such procedure *can* exist. We should note that the true result for $n = 12$, 30, is still substantially better than merge sort. This loss of the apparently 'best possible' carries over to 13 and more elements [Pec04], and in fact the next time we can achieve $\lceil \log_2 n! \rceil$ is with $n = 20$, and 62 comparisons.

L.3   Quick sort

Quicksort was invented by Sir Antony Hoare (Epp p. 282), as one of the first applications of recursion in general-purpose algorithmics. The outline is very similar to merge sort (Epp p. 773).

0. Choose an element, hopefully in the middle, known as the *pivot p*.

1. Split the array into two — those elements $\leq p$ and those $> p$. This is done according to the algorithm in Figure L.1, which takes precisely n comparisons, since each element is compared with the pivot element exactly once (this is the reason for the $l := l + 1$ and $h := h - 1$ lines: the algorithm would be correct without them, but this assertion would not be).

2. Use quick sort to sort each subarray.

19

3. Place the two halves together to form the sorted array.

Note that, unlike merge sort, step 3 does not require merging, because, by construction, all elements in the first array are less than all those in the second array. By analogy with Epp p. 775, if we assume that the pivot splits the original array of k elements into one with l elements and one with $k - l$ elements,

$$\begin{bmatrix} \text{The number of comparisons when} \\ \text{quick sort is applied to } k \text{ objects} \end{bmatrix} = \begin{bmatrix} \text{The number of comparisons to split} \\ \text{an array of } k \text{ objects about the pivot} \end{bmatrix} +$$

$$\begin{bmatrix} \text{The number of comparisons when} \\ \text{quick sort is applied to } l \text{ objects} \end{bmatrix} + \begin{bmatrix} \text{The number of comparisons when} \\ \text{quick sort is applied to } k - l \text{ objects} \end{bmatrix},$$

which can be written as

$$q_k = k + q_l + q_{k-l},$$

where q_l is the number of comparisons needed for quicksort on l objects.

Lemma 4 *If this pivot, and all the pivots in the recursive calls, are perfect, i.e. split the input array into two equal-sized sub-arrays, then*

$$n \log_2 n \leq q_n \leq 2n \log_2 n.$$

Proof: As in Epp exercise 25 (p. 778).

However, if the pivot is pessimal, i.e. always splits the array into one sub-array of length 1 and another of length $n - 1$, then quicksort is essentially analogous to insertion sort, and the time is $O(n^2)$.

We note that an optimal pivot would have half the elements less than it and half more, which a statistician would call the *median* of the set of elements. We note that we don't actually need a perfect median: it is possible to show that if we get least a guaranteed fraction of the way through the array for our split, the time is still $\Theta(n \log n)$, where the implied constant depends on the guaranteed fraction.

Picking the first element as the pivot is not recommended, as in the case of an already sorted array, this is in fact pessimal, and gives us $O(n^2)$ cost. A common strategy is to pick the median of the first, middle and last element, i.e. $\text{median}(a_1, a_{\lceil n/2 \rceil}, a_n)$. This has the advantage of being the precise median if the array is already sorted, and needs a fairly perverse initial distribution to be be pessimal. Can we do better?

L.4 Guaranteed Medians

It might seem as if we *had* to sort an array a to find its median, thereby needing time $\Theta(n \log n)$ but in fact that is not the case. It turns out to be possible to find the median of n objects in time $O(n)$, by the procedure of figure L.2. The basic idea is relatively simple:

20

1. Split the array into blocks of length 7;

2. Find the median of each block of 7 (by direct sorting);

3. Find the median of these medians (by recursion) — call this p;

4. Use p to partition the array, and find the appropriate element of the correct component.

However, the last step is quite challenging. Say $n = 101$, and we have found p, and split the array a so that 40 are less than p (call this subset $a_<$), and 61 greater (call this $a_>$). Then the median of the orignal array, that is element 51 after we have sorted, will be the 11th element of $a_>$ after we have sorted that. Hence we actually need to solve a more general problem, and find the t-th element of a set of n, not necessarily the $\lceil (n+1)/2 \rceil$-th, which would be the median.

Further complications are the following:

- The algorithm is quite heavy-weight for a small number of objects, and this will cause problems in the recursion and the complexity proof (hence the initial check for whether we have more than 1023 elements);

- What to do if we don't have an exact multiple of 7 objects (and in fact it turns out we need an odd multiple of 7).

The full algorithm is given in Figure L.2.

Theorem 3 *The number of comparisons needed by the algorithm of Figure L.2, for any t, is at most $15n - 163$, for $n > 32$.*

Proof: by (strong) induction.

Let $P(n)$ be the statement "for any t, the number of comparisons needed by this algorithm is at most $15n - 163$"

Base $P(k)$ is true for any $32 < k < 1024$ since we are using merge sort, which takes $k\lceil \log_2 k \rceil \leq 10k < 15k - 163$

Induction Assume $P(33), \ldots P(k)$ and try to prove $P(k+1)$.

Sorting the groups of 7 By Lemma 3, this takes $13(2q+1)$ comparisons.

Finding the median By induction (noting that if $n > 1023$, $q > 32$) this takes at most $15(2q+1) - 163 = 30q - 148$ comparisons.

Working out relationship to m $4q$ comparisons.

Recursion There are at least $4q + 3$ elements at each side of m, so at most $10q + 3$ to the other. Hence this cost is at most $15(10q + 3) - 163 = 150q - 118$.

21

Figure L.2: Finding the t-th

Input: Array a of n elements; integer t $(1 \le t \le n)$

Output: What would be a_t, the t-th element, **if** we had sorted a in increasing order

if $(n < 1024)$

   then   [*It's not worth recursing*]

        sort a

        return a_t

end if

[*We now have $n \ge 1024$ to sort.*]

$q := \lceil \frac{n-7}{14} \rceil$

$n' := 7(2q + 1)$ % The least odd multiple of $7 \ge n$

Pad a to have n' elements, by adding up to 6 ∞, and if necessary

        a dummy block of 7 further ∞.

Sort $a_{7k-6}, \ldots, a_{7k}$ for $k = 1$ to $2q + 1$

[*Note that a_4, a_{11}, $a_{18} \ldots$ are each the median of their group of 7.*]

Recursively, find the median m of these $2q + 1$ elements S

[*We now have $4q + 3$ elements **known** to be greater than m (the three in its group of 7,*

        and there are q elements of S greater than m, and they and the three greater

        than them are all greater than m)

Similarly, we have $4q + 3$ less than m

There are $2q$ group of 3 undecided (those greater than $s_i < m$,

        or less than some $s_i > m$).]

For each group $\{c_1 \le c_2 \le c_3\}$

        if $c_2 < m$

          then [*obviously $c_1 < m$, so*] check c_3 against m

          else [*obviously $c_3 > m$, so*] check c_1 against m

[*We now know there are r elements $\le m$ and $n' - r \ge m$*]

if $t < r$

        then find the t-th in the first set

        elseif $t = r$ we have found it!

        else find the $(n' - t)$-th in the second set

Total

$$\text{sort+median+separate+recurse}$$

$$
\begin{aligned}
&= (26q + 13) + (30q - 148) + 4q + (150q - 118) \\
&= 210q - 253 \\
&= 15(14q - 6) - 163 \\
&\leq 15n - 163.
\end{aligned}
$$

Notice that there has been a great deal of information (the sorting of the groups of 7) that is thrown away when we recurse, and deeper study has produced algorithms which are $3n + O((n \log n)^{3/4})$.

Corollary 1 *We can find an element which is between 2/7 and 5/7 of the way along (the "median" from the above) in at most $26q - 135 < 4n$ comparisons.*

Theorem 4 *The number of comparisons needed by quicksort, when using the algorithm of Figure L.2 for the pivot, but insertion sort of ≤ 32 elements (as in* `myHsort`*), is at most $16n\lceil \log_2 n \rceil$.*

Proof: by (strong) induction.

Let $P(n)$ be the statement "the number of comparisons, as above, is at most $16n\lceil \log_2 n \rceil$".

base For $n \leq 32$, we use insertion sort, whose number of comparisons is at most $n^2 \leq 16n \log_2 n$.

Induction Assume $P(1), \ldots, P(k)$ for $k \geq 32$, and try to prove $P(k+1)$. By Theorem 3, the pivoting process takes at most $15(k+1)$ comparisons to choose the pivot, and $k+1$ to do the splitting. The two recursive sorts take, respectively,

$$
16\lfloor \frac{k+1}{2} \rfloor \left\lceil \log_2 \lfloor \frac{k+1}{2} \rfloor \right\rceil \quad \text{and} \quad 16\lceil \frac{k+1}{2} \rceil \left\lceil \log_2 \lceil \frac{k+1}{2} \rceil \right\rceil
$$

comparisons. As in the proof of merge sort, we can write

$$
16(k+1) = 16\lfloor \frac{k+1}{2} \rfloor + \lceil \frac{k+1}{2} \rceil,
$$

so the total cost becomes

$$
16\lfloor \frac{k+1}{2} \rfloor \left\lceil 1 + \log_2 \lfloor \frac{k+1}{2} \rfloor \right\rceil + 16\lceil \frac{k+1}{2} \rceil \left\lceil 1 + \log_2 \lceil \frac{k+1}{2} \rceil \right\rceil
$$

and, as before, when $k-1$ is even, all the interior $\lfloor \ldots \rfloor$ constructs collape, and when $k+1$ is odd, so $2\lceil \frac{k+1}{2} \rceil = k+2$ rather than $k+1$, the ceiling on the log term saves us.

23

Bibliography

[FJ59]   L. Ford and S. Johnson. A Tournament Problem. *Amer. Math. Monthly*, 66:387–389, 1959.

[Mol04a] C.B. Moler. Numerical Computing with MATLAB. *SIAM*, 2004.

[Mol04b] C.B. Moler. Numerical Computing with MATLAB. `http://www.mathworks.com/moler`, 2004.

[Pec04] M. Peczarski. New Results in Minimum-Comparison Sorting. *Algorithmica*, 40:133–145, 2004.

[Wel65] M. Wells. Applications of a language for computing in combinatorics. *In Proc. IFIP Congress 1965 volume 2*, pages 497–498, 1965.